T0201578

ENERGY-EFFICIENT DISTRIBUTED COMPUTING SYSTEMS

**WILEY SERIES ON PARALLEL
AND DISTRIBUTED COMPUTING**

Editor: Albert Y. Zomaya

A complete list of titles in this series appears at the end of this volume.

ENERGY-EFFICIENT DISTRIBUTED COMPUTING SYSTEMS

Edited by

Albert Y. Zomaya
Young Choon Lee

A JOHN WILEY & SONS, INC., PUBLICATION

Cover Image: Baris Simsek/iStockphoto

Published by John Wiley & Sons, Inc., Hoboken, New Jersey
Published simultaneously in Canada

For general information on our other products and services or for technical support, please contact our Customer Care Department within the United States at (800) 762-2974, outside the United States at (317) 572-3993 or fax (317) 572-4002.

Wiley also publishes its books in a variety of electronic formats. Some content that appears in print may not be available in electronic formats. For more information about Wiley products, visit our web site at www.wiley.com.

Library of Congress Cataloging-in-Publication Data:

Zomaya, Albert Y.
   Energy-efficient distributed computing systems / Albert Y. Zomaya, Young Choon Lee.
    p. cm.
     ISBN 978-0-470-90875-4 (hardback)
  1. Computer networks–Energy efficiency. 2. Electronic data processing–Distributed processing–Energy conservation. 3. Green technology. I. Lee, Young Choon, 1973– II. Title.
   TK5105.5.Z66 2012
   004'.36–dc23

                                                                        2011042246

Printed in the United States of America

ISBN: 9780470908754

10 9 8 7 6 5 4 3 2 1

To our families for their help, support, and patience.

CONTENTS

**7 COMPARISON AND ANALYSIS OF GREEDY
ENERGY-EFFICIENT SCHEDULING ALGORITHMS
FOR COMPUTATIONAL GRIDS**

*Peder Lindberg, James Leingang, Daniel Lysaker, Kashif Bilal,
Samee Ullah Khan, Pascal Bouvry, Nasir Ghani, Nasro Min-Allah,
and Juan Li*

8   TOWARD ENERGY-AWARE SCHEDULING USING MACHINE LEARNING   215

Josep LL. Berral, Iñigo Goiri, Ramon Nou, Ferran Julià, Josep O. Fitó, Jordi Guitart, Ricard Gavaldá, and Jordi Torres

16 EMBRACING THE MEMORY AND I/O WALLS FOR ENERGY-EFFICIENT SCIENTIFIC COMPUTING   417

Chung-Hsing Hsu and Wu-Chun Feng

17 MULTIPLE FREQUENCY SELECTION IN DVFS-ENABLED PROCESSORS TO MINIMIZE ENERGY CONSUMPTION   443

Nikzad Babaii Rizvandi, Albert Y. Zomaya, Young Choon Lee, Ali Javadzadeh Boloori, and Javid Taheri

PREFACE

The scope of energy-efficient computing is not limited to main computing components (e.g., processors, storage devices, and visualization facilities), but it can expand to a much larger range of resources associated with computing facilities, including auxiliary equipment, water used for cooling, and even physical and floor space that these resources occupy. Energy consumption in computing facilities raises various monetary, environmental, and system performance concerns.

Recent advances in hardware technologies have improved the energy consumption issue to a certain degree. However, it still remains a serious concern for energy-efficient computing because the amount of energy consumed by computing and auxiliary hardware resources is affected substantially by their usage patterns. In other words, resource underutilization or overloading incurs a higher volume of energy consumption when compared with efficiently utilized resources. This calls for the development of various software energy-saving techniques and new algorithms that are more energy efficient.

This book, *Energy-Efficient Distributed Computing Systems*, seeks to provide an opportunity for researchers to explore different energy consumption issues and their impact on the design of new computing systems. The book is quite timely since the field of distributed computing as a whole is undergoing many changes. Vast literature exists today on such energy consumption paradigms and frameworks and their implications for a wide range of distributed platforms.

The book is intended to be a virtual roundtable of several outstanding researchers, which one might invite to attend a conference on energy-efficient computing systems. Of course, the list of topics that is explored here is by no means exhaustive, but most of the conclusions provided here should be extended to other computing platforms that are not covered here. There was a decision to limit the number of chapters while providing more pages for contributing authors to express their ideas, so that the book remains manageable within a single volume.

We also hope that the topics covered in this book will get the readers to think of the implications of such new ideas on the developments in their own fields. The book endeavors to strike a balance between theoretical and practical coverage of innovative problem-solving techniques for a range of distributed platforms. The book is intended to be a repository of paradigms, technologies, and applications that target the different facets of energy consumption in computing systems.

The 26 chapters were carefully selected to provide a wide scope with minimal overlap between the chapters to reduce duplications. Each contributor was asked that his/her chapter should cover review material as well as current developments. In addition, the choice of authors was made so as to select authors who are leaders in their respective disciplines.

ALBERT Y. ZOMAYA
YOUNG CHOON LEE

ACKNOWLEDGMENTS

First and foremost, we would like to thank and acknowledge the contributors to this volume for their support and patience, and the reviewers for their useful comments and suggestions that helped in improving the earlier outline of the book and presentation of the material. Also, I should extend my deepest thanks to Simone Taylor and Diana Gialo from Wiley (USA) for their collaboration, guidance, and most importantly, patience in finalizing this handbook. Finally, I would like to acknowledge the efforts of the team from Wiley's production department for their extensive efforts during the many phases of this project and the timely manner in which the book was produced.

ALBERT Y. ZOMAYA
YOUNG CHOON LEE

CONTRIBUTORS

PRITI, AGHERA, University of California, San Diego, CA, USA.

AL-NASHIF, YOUSSIF, NSF Center for Autonomic Computing, The University of Arizona, USA.

AYOUB, RAID, University of California, San Diego, CA, USA.

BERRAL, JOSEP LL., Computer Architecture Dept. and Department of Software, UPC-Barcelona Tech., Catalonia, Spain.

BILAL, KASHIF, Department of Computer Science, North Dakota State University, Fargo, ND, USA.

BOLOORI, ALI JAVADZADEH, Centre for Distributed and High Performance Computing, School of Information Technologies, University of Sydney, NSW, Australia.

BORGETTO, DAMIEN, University Paul Sabatier, Toulouse, France.

BOUVRY, PASCAL, Faculty of Sciences, Technology, and Communications, University of Luxembourg, Luxembourg.

CAMERON, KIRK W., Virginia Tech, VA, USA.

CASANOVA, HENRI, University of Hawai'i at Manoa, Hawai'i, USA.

COMITO, CARMELA, DEIS, University of Calabria, Rende (CS), Italy.

DA COSTA, GEORGES, University Paul Sabatier, Toulouse, France.

DELICATO, FLAVIA C., Computer Science Department, Federal University of Rio de Janeiro—RN, Brazil.

DHIMAN, GAURAV, University of California, San Diego, CA, USA.

FENG, WU-CHUN, Virginia Tech, Blacksburg, Virginia, USA.

JOSEPH. O. FITO, Computer Architecture Dept. and Barcelona Supercomputing Center, UPC-Barcelona Tech., Catalonia, Spain.

GAVALDA, RICARD, Department of Software, UPC-Barcelona Tech., Catalonia, Spain.

GE, RONG, The Department of Mathematics, Statistics, and Computer Science, Marquette University, WI, USA.

GHANI, NASIR, Department of Electrical and Computer Engineering, University of New Mexico, Albuquerque, NM, USA.

GOIRI, INIGO, Computer Architecture Dept. and Barcelona Supercomputing Center, UPC-Barcelona Tech., Catalonia, Spain.

GONG, JIAYU, Department of Electrical and Computer Engineering, Wayne State University, MI, USA.

DE GROOT, MARTIN, CSIRO ICT Center, Epping, NSW, Australia.

GUITART, JORDI, Computer Architecture Dept. and Barcelona Supercomputing Center, UPC-Barcelona Tech., Catalonia, Spain.

GURUMURTHI, SUDHANVA, Dept. of Computer Science, University of Virginia, Charlottesville, VA, USA.

HARIRI, SALIM, NSF Center for Autonomic Computing, The University of Arizona, USA.

HARTENSTEIN, REINER, Department of Computer Science, Kaiserslautern University of Technology, Kaiserslautern, Germany.

HSU, CHUNG-HSING, Oak Ridge National Laboratory, Oak Ridge, TN, USA.

JIANG, WEIRONG, Juniper Networks, Inc., Sunnyvale, CA, USA.

JULIA, FERRAN, Computer Architecture Dept., UPC-Barcelona Tech., Catalonia, Spain.

KANDEMIR, MAHMUT, Pennsylvania State University, PA, USA.

KHAN, SAMEE ULLAH, Department of Electrical and Computer Engineering, North Dakota State University, Fargo, ND, USA.

KHARGHARIA, BITHIKA, Cisco Systems, Inc., Durham, NC, USA.

KIM, JONG-KOOK, School of Electrical Engineering, Korea University, Korea.

LEE, YOUNG CHOON, Centre for Distributed and High Performance Computing, School of Information Technologies, University of Sydney, NSW, Australia.

LEFEVRE, LAURENT, INRIA, Ecole Normale Superieure de Lyon, University of Lyon, France.

LEINGANG, JAMES, Department of Electrical and Computer Engineering, North Dakota State University, Fargo, ND, USA.

LI, JUAN, Department of Computer Science, North Dakota State University, Fargo, ND, USA.

LI, KEQIN, State University of New York, New Paltz, NY, USA.

LINDBERG, PEDER, Department of Electrical and Computer Engineering, North Dakota State University, Fargo, ND, USA.

LUO, HAOTING, NSF Center for Autonomic Computing, The University of Arizona, AZ, USA.

LYSAKER, DANIEL, Department of Electrical and Computer Engineering, North Dakota State University, Fargo, ND, USA.

MANZANARES, ADAM, Los Alamos National Laboratory, Los Alamos, NM, USA.

MIN-ALLAH, NASRO, Department of Computer Science, COMSATS Institute of Information Technology, Pakistan.

NARAYANAN, SRI HARI KRISHNA, Argonne National Laboratory, IL, USA.

NIKZAD, NIMA, University of California, San Diego, CA, USA.

NOU, RAMON, Computer Architecture Dept. and Barcelona Supercomputing Center, UPC-Barcelona Tech., Catalonia, Spain.

ORGERIE, ANNE-CECILE, Ecole Normale Superieure de Lyon, Lyon, France.

OZTURK, OZCAN, Bilkent University, Turkey.

PARASHAR, MANISH, NSF Cloud and Autonomic Computing Center and Rutgers Discovery Informatics Institute, Rutgers University, NJ, USA.

PEDRAM, MASSOUD, University of Southern California, Los Angeles, CA, USA.

PIERSON, JEAN-MARC, University Paul Sabatier, Toulouse, France.

PIRES, PAULO F., Computer Science Department, Federal University of Rio de Janeiro - RN, Brazil.

PRASANNA, VIKTOR K., University of Southern California, Los Angeles, CA, USA.

QIN, XIAO, Auburn University, Auburn, AL, USA.

RIZVANDI, NIKZAD BABAII, Centre for Distributed and High Performance Computing, School of Information Technologies, University of Sydney, NSW, Australia.

RODERO, IVAN, NSF Cloud and Autonomic Computing Center and Rutgers Discovery Informatics Institute, Rutgers University, NJ, USA.

RONG, PENG, Brocade Communications Systems, San Jose, CA, USA.

ROSING, TAJANA SIMUNIC, University of California, San Diego, CA, USA.

RUAN, XIAOJUN, Auburn University, Auburn, AL, USA.

SIVASUBRAMANIAM, ANAND, Dept. of Computer Science and Engineering, The Pennsylvania State University, PA, USA.

TAHERI, JAVID, Centre for Distributed and High Performance Computing, School of Information Technologies, University of Sydney, NSW, Australia.

TALIA, DOMENICO, DEIS, University of Calabria, Rende (CS), Italy.

TORRES, JORDI, Computer Architecture Dept. and Barcelona Supercomputing Center, UPC-Barcelona Tech., Catalonia, Spain.

TRUNFIO, PAOLO, DEIS, University of Calabria, Rende (CS), Italy.

WANG, CHEN, CSIRO ICT Center, Epping, NSW, Australia.

XU, CHENG-ZHONG, Department of Electrical and Computer Engineering, Wayne State University, MI, USA.

YIN, SHU, Auburn University, Auburn, AL, USA.

YOUSIF, MAZIN, T-Systems International, Inc., Portland, OR, USA.

ZAPPI, PIERO, University of California, San Diego, CA, USA.

ZOMAYA, ALBERT Y., Centre for Distributed and High Performance Computing, School of Information Technologies, University of Sydney, NSW, Australia.

CHAPTER 1

POWER ALLOCATION AND TASK SCHEDULING ON MULTIPROCESSOR COMPUTERS WITH ENERGY AND TIME CONSTRAINTS

KEQIN LI

1.1 INTRODUCTION

1.1.1 Energy Consumption

Performance-driven computer development has lasted for over six decades. Computers have been developed to achieve higher performance. As of June 2010, three supercomputers have achieved petaflops speed: Cray Jaguar (224,162 processors, 1.759 petaflops), Dawning Nebulae (120,640 processors, 1.271 petaflops), and IBM Roadrunner (122,400 processors, 1.042 petaflops) [1]. According to Moore's law of computing hardware, the following quantities increase (decrease) exponentially, doubling (halving) approximately every 2 years: the number of transistors per integrated circuit (cost per transistor), processing speed, memory/storage capacity (cost per unit of information), and network capacity [2].

While performance/cost has increased dramatically, power consumption in computer systems has also increased according to Moore's law. To achieve higher computing performance per processor, microprocessor manufacturers have doubled the power density at an exponential speed over decades, which will soon reach that of a nuclear reactor [3]. Such increased energy consumption causes severe economic, ecological, and technical problems.

- *Economic Impact.* Computer systems consume tremendous amount of energy and natural resources. It has been reported that desktop computers in the United States account for over 10% of commercial electricity

Energy-Efficient Distributed Computing Systems, First Edition.
Edited by Albert Y. Zomaya and Young Choon Lee.
© 2012 John Wiley & Sons, Inc. Published 2012 by John Wiley & Sons, Inc.

consumption [4]. A large-scale multiprocessor computing system consumes millions of dollars of electricity and natural resources every year, equivalent to the amount of energy used by tens of thousands US households [5]. A large data center such as Google can consume as much electricity as does a city. Furthermore, the cooling bill for heat dissipation can be as high as 70% of the above cost [6]. Supercomputers are making less efficient use of space, which often results in the design and construction of new machine rooms or even entirely new buildings.

- *Ecological Impact*. Desktop computers produce as much carbon dioxide (CO_2) as millions of cars. A recent report reveals that the global information technology industry generates as much greenhouse gas as the world's airlines, about 2% of global CO_2 emissions [7]. The heat dissipation problem gets increasingly worse because of higher computing speeds, shrinking packages, and growing energy-hungry applications such as multimedia and communications.

- *Technical Impact*. Large-scale multiprocessor computers require expensive packaging and cooling technologies, and demand for sophisticated fault-tolerant mechanisms that deal with decreased reliability due to heat dissipation caused by increased energy consumption. Despite sophisticated cooling facilities constructed to ensure proper operation, the reliability of large-scale multiprocessor computing systems is measured in hours, and the main source of outage is hardware failure caused by excessive heat. It is conceivable that a supercomputing system with 10^5 processors would spend most of its time in checkpointing and restarting [8].

It is clear that there are compelling economic, environmental, and technical reasons for emphasis on energy efficiency.

1.1.2 Power Reduction

Power conservation is critical in many computation and communication environments and has attracted extensive research activities. For high performance supercomputers, energy-aware design has significance impact on system performance. It is noticed that performance per rack equals to performance per watt times watt per rack, where watt per rack is determined by thermal cooling capabilities and can be considered as a constant of order 20 kW for an air-cooled rack. Therefore, it is the performance per watt term that determines the rack performance. It is found that in terms of performance per watt, the low frequency and low power embedded IBM PowerPC consistently outperforms high frequency and high power microprocessors by a factor of 2–10. This is one of the main reasons why IBM chose the low power design for the Blue Gene/L supercomputer that was developed around a processor with moderate frequency. In mobile computing and communication environments, efficient processor power management increases the lifetime of battery operated devices such as hand-held mobile computers and portable embedded systems. Energy efficiency is a major design constraint in these portable devices, since battery technology has not been developed in the same pace as semiconductor industry.

Reducing processor energy consumption has been an important and pressing research issue in recent years. There has been increasing interest and importance in developing high performance and energy-efficient computing systems. There exists a large body of literature on power-aware computing and communication. The reader is referred to References [3, 9–11] for comprehensive surveys.

There are two approaches to reducing power consumption in computing systems. The first approach is the method of thermal-aware hardware design, which can be carried out at various levels, including device level power reduction, circuit and logic level techniques, and architecture level power reduction (low power processor architecture adaptations, low power memories and memory hierarchies, and low power interconnects). Low power consumption and high system reliability, availability, and usability are main concerns of modern high performance computing system development. In addition to the traditional performance measure using FLOPS, the Green500 list uses FLOPS per watt to rank the performance of computing systems, so that the awareness of other performance metrics such as energy efficiency and system reliability can be raised [12]. All the current systems that can achieve at least 400 MFLOPS/W are clusters of low power processors, aiming to achieve high performance/power and performance/space. For instance, the Dawning Nebulae, currently the world's second fastest computer, which achieves peak performance of 2.984 PFLOPS, is also the fourth most energy-efficient supercomputer in the world with an operational rate of 492.64 MFLOPS/W [12]. Intel's Tera-scale research project has developed the world's first programmable processor that delivers supercomputer-like performance from a single 80-core chip, which uses less electricity than most of today's home appliances and achieves over 16.29 GFLOPS/W [13].

The second approach to reducing energy consumption in computing systems is the method of power-aware software design at various levels, including operating system level power management, compiler level power management, application level power management, and cross-layer (from transistors to applications) adaptations. The power reduction technique discussed in this chapter belongs to the operating system level, which we elaborate in the next section.

1.1.3 Dynamic Power Management

Software techniques for power reduction are supported by a mechanism called *dynamic voltage scaling* (equivalently, dynamic frequency scaling, dynamic speed scaling, and dynamic power scaling). Many modern components allow voltage regulation to be controlled through software, for example, the BIOS or applications such as PowerStrip. It is usually possible to control the voltages supplied to the CPUs, main memories, local buses, and expansion cards [14]. Processor power consumption is proportional to frequency and the square of supply voltage. A power-aware algorithm can change supply voltage and frequency at appropriate times to optimize a combined consideration of performance and energy consumption. There are many existing technologies and commercial processors that support dynamic voltage (frequency, speed, power) scaling. SpeedStep is a series of dynamic frequency scaling technologies built into some Intel microprocessors that allow the clock speed of a processor to be dynamically changed by software [15]. LongHaul is a technology developed by VIA Technologies, which supports dynamic frequency scaling and dynamic voltage scaling. By executing specialized operating system instructions, a processor driver can exercise fine control on the bus-to-core frequency ratio and core voltage according to how much load is put on the processor [16]. LongRun and LongRun2 are power management technologies introduced by Transmeta. LongRun2 has been licensed to Fujitsu, NEC, Sony, Toshiba, and NVIDIA [17].

Dynamic power management at the operating system level refers to supply voltage and clock frequency adjustment schemes implemented while tasks are running. These energy conservation techniques explore the opportunities for tuning the energy-delay tradeoff [18]. Power-aware task scheduling on processors with variable voltages and speeds has been extensively studied since the mid-1990s. In a pioneering paper [19], the authors first proposed an approach to energy saving by using fine grain control of CPU speed by an operating system scheduler. The main idea is to monitor CPU idle time and to reduce energy consumption by reducing clock speed and idle time to a minimum. In a subsequent work [20], the authors analyzed offline and online algorithms for scheduling tasks with arrival times and deadlines on a uniprocessor computer with minimum energy consumption. These research have been extended in References [21–27] and inspired substantial further investigation, much of which focus on real-time applications, namely, adjusting the supply voltage and clock frequency to minimize CPU energy consumption while still meeting the deadlines for task execution. In References [28–42] and many other related work, the authors addressed the problem of scheduling independent or precedence constrained tasks on uniprocessor or multiprocessor computers where the actual execution time of a task may be less than the estimated worst-case execution time. The main issue is energy reduction by slack time reclamation.

1.1.4   Task Scheduling with Energy and Time Constraints

There are two considerations in dealing with the energy-delay tradeoff. On the one hand, in high performance computing systems, power-aware design techniques and algorithms attempt to maximize performance under certain energy consumption constraints. On the other hand, low power and energy-efficient design techniques and algorithms aim to minimize energy consumption while still meeting certain performance requirements. In Reference 43, the author studied the problems of minimizing the expected execution time given a hard energy budget and minimizing the expected energy expenditure given a hard execution deadline for a single task with randomized execution requirement. In Reference 44, the author considered scheduling jobs with equal requirements on multiprocessors. In Reference 45, the authors studied the relationship among parallelization, performance, and energy consumption, and the problem of minimizing energy-delay product. In References 46, 47, the authors attempted joint minimization of energy consumption and task execution time. In Reference 48, the authors investigated the problem of system value maximization subject to both time and energy constraints.

In this chapter, we address energy and time constrained power allocation and task scheduling on multiprocessor computers with dynamically variable voltage, frequency, speed, and power as combinatorial optimization problems. In particular, we define the problem of minimizing schedule length with energy consumption constraint and the problem of minimizing energy consumption with schedule length constraint on multiprocessor computers [49]. The first problem has applications in general multiprocessor and multicore processor computing systems, where energy consumption is an important concern, and in mobile computers, where energy conservation is a main concern. The second problem has applications in real-time multiprocessing systems and environments such as parallel signal processing, automated target recognition, and real-time MPEG encoding, where timing constraint is a major requirement. Our scheduling problems are defined such that the energy-delay product is optimized by fixing one factor and minimizing the other.

1.1.5 Chapter Outline

The rest of the chapter is organized as follows: In Section 1.2, we present the power consumption model; define our power allocation and task scheduling problems on multiprocessor computers with energy and time constraints; describe various task models, processor models, and scheduling models; discuss problem decomposition and subproblems; and mention different types of algorithms. In Section 1.3, we develop optimal solution to our problems on uniprocessor computers and multiprocessor computers with given partitions of tasks, prove the strong NP-hardness of our problems, derive lower bounds for optimal solutions, and the energy-delay tradeoff theorem. In Section 1.4, we present and analyze the performance of pre-power-determination algorithms, including equal-time algorithms, equal-energy algorithms, and equal-speed algorithms. We show both numerical data and simulation results of our performance bounds. In Section 1.5, we present and analyze the performance of post-power-determination algorithms. We demonstrate both numerical data and simulation results of our performance bounds. In Section 1.6, we summarize the chapter and point out several further research directions.

1.2 PRELIMINARIES

1.2.1 Power Consumption Model

Power dissipation and circuit delay in digital CMOS circuits can be accurately modeled by simple equations, even for complex microprocessor circuits. CMOS circuits have dynamic, static, and short-circuit power dissipation; however, the dominant component in a well-designed circuit is dynamic power consumption p (i.e., the switching component of power), which is approximately $p = aCV^2f$, where a is an activity factor, C is the loading capacitance, V is the supply voltage, and f is the clock frequency [50]. Since $s \propto f$, where s is the processor speed, and $f \propto V^{\phi}$ with $0 < \phi \le 1$ [51], which implies that $V \propto f^{1/\phi}$, we know that the power consumption is $p \propto f^{\alpha}$ and $p \propto s^{\alpha}$, where $\alpha = 1 + 2/\phi \ge 3$.

Assume that we are given n independent sequential tasks to be executed on m identical processors. Let r_i represent the execution requirement (i.e., the number of CPU cycles or the number of instructions) of task i, where $1 \le i \le n$. We use p_i (V_i, f_i, respectively) to represent the power (supply voltage, clock frequency, respectively) allocated to execute task i. For ease of discussion, we will assume that p_i is simply s_i^{α}, where $s_i = p_i^{1/\alpha}$ is the execution speed of task i. The execution time of task i is $t_i = r_i/s_i = r_i/p_i^{1/\alpha}$. The energy consumed to execute task i is $e_i = p_i t_i = r_i p_i^{1-1/\alpha} = r_i s_i^{\alpha-1}$.

We would like to mention the following number of basic and important observations: (i) $f_i \propto V_i^{\phi}$ and $s_i \propto V_i^{\phi}$: Linear change in supply voltage results in up to linear change in clock frequency and processor speed; (ii) $p_i \propto V_i^{\phi+2}$ and $p_i \propto f_i^{\alpha}$ and $p_i \propto s_i^{\alpha}$: Linear change in supply voltage results in at least quadratic change in power supply and linear change in clock frequency and processor speed results in at least cubic change in power supply; (iii) $s_i/p_i \propto V_i^{-2}$ and $s_i/p_i \propto s_i^{-(\alpha-1)}$: The processor energy performance, measured by speed per watt [12], is at least quadratically proportional to the supply voltage and speed reduction; (iv) $r_i/e_i \propto V_i^{-2}$ and $r_i/e_i \propto s_i^{-(\alpha-1)}$, where r_i is the amount of work to be performed for task i: The processor energy performance, measured by work per Joule [19], is at least quadratically proportional to the supply voltage and speed reduction; (v) $e_i \propto p_i^{1-1/\alpha} \propto V_i^{(\phi+2)(1-1/\alpha)} = V_i^2$: Linear change in supply voltage results in quadratic change in energy consumption; (vi) $e_i = r_i s_i^{\alpha-1}$: Linear change in processor speed results in at least quadratic change in energy consumption; (vii) $e_i = r_i p_i^{1-1/\alpha}$: Energy consumption reduces at a sublinear speed, as power supply reduces; (viii) $e_i t_i^{\alpha-1} = r_i^{\alpha}$ and $p_i t_i^{\alpha} = r_i^{\alpha}$: For a given task, there exist energy-delay and power-delay tradeoffs. (Later, we will extend such tradeoff to a set of tasks, i.e., the energy-delay tradeoff theorem.)

1.2.2 Problem Definitions

The power allocation and task scheduling problems on multiprocessor computers with energy and time constraints addressed in this chapter are defined as the following optimization problems.

Problem 1.1 (Minimizing Schedule Length with Energy Consumption Constraint)

Input: A set of n independent sequential tasks, a multiprocessor computer with m identical processors, and energy constraint E.

Output: *Power supplies* p_1, p_2, ..., p_n to the n tasks and a schedule of the n tasks on the m processors such that the schedule length is minimized and the total energy consumption does not exceed E.

Problem 1.2 (Minimizing Energy Consumption with Schedule Length Constraint)

Input: A set of n independent sequential tasks, a multiprocessor computer with m identical processors, and time constraint T.

Output: Power supplies p_1, p_2, ..., p_n to the n tasks and a schedule of the n tasks on the m processors such that the total energy consumption is minimized and the schedule length does not exceed T.

The framework of investigation can be established based on the product of three spaces, namely, the task models, the processors models, and the scheduling models. The above research problems have many variations and extensions, depending on the task models, processors models, and scheduling models. These power allocation and task scheduling problems can be investigated in a variety of ways to consider sophisticated application environments, realistic processor technologies, and practical scheduling algorithms.

1.2.3 Task Models

Our independent sequential tasks can be extended to precedence constrained tasks, parallel tasks, and dynamic tasks, which arise in various application environments.

- *Independent and Precedence Constrained Tasks*. A set of independent tasks can be scheduled in any order. A set of n precedence constrained tasks can be represented by a partial order $\prec$ on the tasks, that is, for two tasks i and j, if $i \prec j$, then task j cannot start its execution until task i finishes. It is clear that the n tasks and the partial order $\prec$ can be represented by a directed task graph, in which, there are n vertices for the n tasks and (i, j) is an arc if and only if $i \prec j$. Furthermore, such a task graph must be a directed acyclic graph (dag).

- *Sequential and Parallel Tasks*. A sequential task requires one processor to execute. A parallel task requires several processors to execute. Assume that task i requires π_i processors to execute and any π_i of the m processors can be allocated to task i. We call π_i the *size* of task i. It is possible that in executing task i, the π_i processors may have different execution requirements. Let r_i represent the maximum execution requirement on the π_i processors executing task i. The execution time of task i is $t_i = r_i/s_i = r_i/p_i^{1/\alpha}$. Note that all the π_i processors allocated to task i have the same speed s_i for duration t_i, although some of the π_i processors may be idle for some time. The energy consumed to execute task i is $e_i = \pi_i p_i t_i = \pi_i r_i p_i^{1-1/\alpha} = \pi_i r_i s_i^{\alpha-1}$.

- *Static and Dynamic Tasks*. A set of tasks are static if they are all available for scheduling at the same time. A schedule can be determined before the execution of any task. A set of tasks are dynamic if each task has its own arrival time. A scheduling algorithm should be able to schedule currently available tasks without knowing the arrival of future tasks.

1.2.4 Processor Models

The following processor technologies can be incorporated into our power allocation and task scheduling problems.

- *Continuous and Discrete Voltage/Frequency/Speed/Power Levels*. Most existing research assume that tasks can be supplied with any power and processors can be set at any speed, that is, voltage/frequency/speed/power can be changed continuously. However, the currently available processors have only discrete voltage/frequency/speed/power settings [40, 52, 53]. Such discrete settings certainly make our optimization problems more difficult to solve.

- *Bounded and Unbounded Voltage/Frequency/Speed/Power Levels*. Much existing research also assumes that voltage/frequency/speed/power can be changed in any range. However, the currently available processors can only change voltage/frequency/speed/power in certain bounded range. Power-aware task scheduling algorithms developed with such constraints, though more complicated, will be more practically useful.

- *Regular and Irregular Voltage/Frequency/Speed/Power Levels*. Much existing research also assume that voltage/frequency/speed/power can be changed according to certain analytical and mathematical relation. However, real processors hardly follow such regular models and exhibit irregular relation among voltage, frequency, speed, and power. Such irregularity makes analytical study of algorithms very hard.

- *Homogeneous and Heterogeneous Processors*. A multiprocessor computer is homogeneous if all the processors have the same power–speed relationship. A multiprocessor computer is heterogeneous with α_1, α_2, ..., α_m, if each processor k has its own α_k, such that power dissipation on processor k is $\propto s_k^{\alpha_k}$, where $1 \leq k \leq m$. Heterogeneity makes the scheduling of sequential tasks more difficult and the specification of parallel tasks more sophisticated.

- *Overheads for Voltage/Frequency/Speed/Power Adjustment and Idle Processors*. In reality, it takes time and consumes energy to change voltage, frequency, speed, and power. A processor also consumes energy when it is idle [40]. Although these overheads are ignored in most existing research, it would be interesting to take these overheads into consideration to produce more realistic solutions.

- *Single and Multiple Systems*. Processors can reside on a single computing system or across multiple computing systems.

1.2.5 Scheduling Models

As in traditional scheduling theory, different types of scheduling algorithms can be considered for power-aware task scheduling problems.

- *Preemptive and Nonpreemptive Scheduling*. In a nonpreemptive schedule, the execution of a task cannot be interrupted. Once a task is scheduled on a processor, the task runs with the same power supply until it is completed. In a preemptive schedule, the execution of a task can be interrupted at any time and resumed later. When the execution of a task is resumed, the task may be assigned to a different processor, supplied with different power, and executed at different speed. Depending on the processor model, such resumption may be performed with no cost or with overheads for relocation and/or voltage/frequency/speed/power adjustment.
- *Online and Offline Scheduling*. An offline scheduling algorithm knows all the information (execution requirements, precedence constraints, sizes, arrival times, deadlines, etc.) of the tasks to be scheduled. An online algorithm schedules the tasks in certain given order. When task j is scheduled, an online algorithm only knows the information of tasks $1, 2, \ldots, j$ but does not know the information of tasks $j + 1, j + 2, \ldots$ Current tasks should be scheduled without any knowledge of future tasks.
- *Clairvoyant and Non-Clairvoyant Scheduling*. Virtually all research in scheduling theory has been concerned with clairvoyant scheduling, where it is assumed that the execution requirements of the tasks are known a priori. However, in many applications, the execution requirement of a task is not available until the task is executed and completed. A non-clairvoyant scheduling algorithm only knows the precedence constraints, sizes, arrival times, and deadlines of the tasks and has no access to information about the execution requirements of the tasks it is to schedule. The execution requirement of a task is known only when it is completed.

1.2.6 Problem Decomposition

Our power allocation and task scheduling problems contain four nontrivial subproblems, namely, system partitioning, precedence constraining, task scheduling, and power supplying. Each subproblem should be solved efficiently, so that heuristic algorithms with overall good performance can be developed.

- *System Partitioning*. Since each parallel task requests for multiple processors, a multiprocessor computer should be partitioned into clusters of processors to be assigned to the tasks.
- *Precedence Constraining*. Precedence constraints make design and analysis of heuristic algorithms more difficult.
- *Task Scheduling*. Precedence constrained parallel tasks are scheduled together with system partitioning and precedence constraining, and is NP-hard even when scheduling independent sequential tasks w. system partitioning and precedence constraint.

- *Power Supplying*. Tasks should be supplied with appropriate powers and execution speeds, such that the schedule length is minimized by consuming given amount of energy or the energy consumed is minimized without missing a given deadline.

The above decomposition of our optimization problems into several subproblems makes design and analysis of heuristic algorithms tractable. Our approach is significantly different from most existing studies. A unique feature of our work is to compare the performance of our algorithms with optimal solutions analytically and validate our results experimentally, and not to compare the performance of heuristic algorithms among themselves only experimentally. Such an approach is consistent with traditional scheduling theory.

1.2.7 Types of Algorithms

There are naturally three types of power-aware task scheduling algorithms, depending on the order of power supplying and task scheduling.

- *Pre-Power-Determination Algorithms*. In this type of algorithms, we first determine power supplies and then schedule the tasks.
- *Post-Power-Determination Algorithms*. In this type of algorithms, we first schedule the tasks and then determine power supplies.
- *Hybrid Algorithms*. In this type of algorithms, scheduling tasks and determining power supplies are interleaved among different stages of an algorithm.

1.3 PROBLEM ANALYSIS

Our study in this chapter assumes the following models, namely, task model: independent, sequential, static tasks; processor model: a single system of homogeneous processors with continuous and unbounded and regular voltage/frequency/speed/power levels and without overheads for voltage/frequency/speed/power adjustment and idle processors; scheduling model: nonpreemptive, offline, clairvoyant scheduling. The above combination of task model, processor model, and scheduling model yields the easiest version of our power allocation and task scheduling problems.

1.3.1 Schedule Length Minimization

1.3.1.1 Uniprocessor computers. It is clear that on a uniprocessor computer with energy constraint E, the problem of minimizing schedule length with energy consumption constraint is simply to find the power supplies $p_1, p_2, \ldots, p_n$, such that the schedule length

$$T(p_1, p_2, \ldots, p_n) = \frac{r_1}{p_1^{1/\alpha}} + \frac{r_2}{p_2^{1/\alpha}} + \cdots + \frac{r_n}{p_n^{1/\alpha}}$$

is minimized and the total energy consumed $e_1 + e_2 + \cdots + e_n$ does not exceed E, that is,

$$F(p_1, p_2, \ldots, p_n) = r_1 p_1^{1-1/\alpha} + r_2 p_2^{1-1/\alpha} + \cdots + r_n p_n^{1-1/\alpha} \leq E.$$

Notice that both the schedule length $T(p_1, p_2, \ldots, p_n)$ and the energy consumption $F(p_1, p_2, \ldots, p_n)$ are viewed as functions of $p_1, p_2, \ldots, p_n$.

We can minimize $T(p_1, p_2, \ldots, p_n)$ subject to the constraint $F(p_1, p_2, \ldots, p_n) = E$ by using the Lagrange multiplier system:

$$\nabla T(p_1, p_2, \ldots, p_n) = \lambda \nabla F(p_1, p_2, \ldots, p_n),$$

where λ is a Lagrange multiplier. Since

$$\frac{\partial T(p_1, p_2, \ldots, p_n)}{\partial p_i} = \lambda \cdot \frac{\partial F(p_1, p_2, \ldots, p_n)}{\partial p_i},$$

that is,

$$r_i \left(-\frac{1}{\alpha} \right) \frac{1}{p_i^{1+1/\alpha}} = \lambda r_i \left(1 - \frac{1}{\alpha} \right) \frac{1}{p_i^{1/\alpha}},$$

where $1 \leq i \leq n$, we have $p_i = 1/\lambda(1 - \alpha)$, for all $1 \leq i \leq n$. Substituting the above p_i into the constraint $F(p_1, p_2, \ldots, p_n) = E$, we get $R(1/\lambda(1 - \alpha))^{1-1/\alpha} = E$, where $R = r_1 + r_2 + \cdots + r_n$ is the total execution requirement of the n tasks. Therefore, we obtain $p_i = 1/\lambda(1 - \alpha) = (E/R)^{\alpha/(\alpha-1)}$, for all $1 \leq i \leq n$.

The above discussion is summarized in the following theorem, which gives the optimal power supplies and the optimal schedule length.

Theorem 1.1 *On a uniprocessor computer, the schedule length is minimized when all tasks are supplied with the same power $p_i = (E/R)^{\alpha/(\alpha-1)}$, where $1 \leq i \leq n$. The optimal schedule length is $T_{\text{OPT}} = R^{\alpha/(\alpha-1)}/E^{1/(\alpha-1)}$.*

1.3.1.2 *Multiprocessor computers.*

Let us consider a multiprocessor computer with m processors. Assume that a set of n tasks is partitioned into m groups, such that all the tasks in group k are executed on processor k, where $1 \leq k \leq m$. Let R_k denote group k and the total execution requirement of the tasks in group k. For a given partition of the n tasks into m groups $R_1, R_2, \ldots, R_m$, we are seeking power supplies that minimize the schedule length.

Let E_k be the energy consumed by all the tasks in group k. We observe that by fixing E_k and adjusting the power supplies for the tasks in group k to the same power $(E_k/R_k)^{\alpha/(\alpha-1)}$ according to Theorem 1.1, the total execution time of the tasks in group k can be minimized to $T_k = R_k^{\alpha/(\alpha-1)}/E_k^{1/(\alpha-1)}$. Therefore, the problem of finding power supplies $p_1, p_2, \ldots, p_n$, which minimize the schedule length is equivalent to finding $E_1, E_2, \ldots, E_m$, which minimize the schedule length. It is clear that the schedule length is minimized when all the m processors complete their execution of the m groups of tasks at the same time T, that is, $T_1 = T_2 = \cdots = T_m = T$, which implies that $E_k = R_k^\alpha / T^{\alpha-1}$. Since $E_1 + E_2 + \cdots + E_m = E$, we have

$$\frac{R_1^\alpha + R_2^\alpha + \cdots + R_m^\alpha}{T^{\alpha-1}} = E,$$

that is,

$$T = \left(\frac{R_1^\alpha + R_2^\alpha + \cdots + R_m^\alpha}{E} \right)^{1/(\alpha-1)}$$

and

$$E_k = \left(\frac{R_k^\alpha}{R_1^\alpha + R_2^\alpha + \cdots + R_m^\alpha} \right) E.$$

Thus, we have proved the following theorem.

Theorem 1.2 *For a given partition R_1, R_2, ..., R_m of n tasks into m groups on a multiprocessor computer, the schedule length is minimized when all the tasks in group k are supplied with the same power $(E_k/R_k)^{\alpha/(\alpha-1)}$, where*

$$E_k = \left(\frac{R_k^\alpha}{R_1^\alpha + R_2^\alpha + \cdots + R_m^\alpha} \right) E$$

for all $1 \le k \le m$. The optimal schedule length is

$$T_{\text{OPT}} = \left(\frac{R_1^\alpha + R_2^\alpha + \cdots + R_m^\alpha}{E} \right)^{1/(\alpha-1)}$$

for the above power supplies.

1.3.2 Energy Consumption Minimization

1.3.2.1 Uniprocessor computers. It is clear that on a uniprocessor computer with time constraint T, the problem of minimizing energy consumption with schedule length constraint is simply to find the power supplies p_1, p_2, ..., p_n, such that the total energy consumption

$$E(p_1, p_2, \ldots, p_n) = r_1 p_1^{1-1/\alpha} + r_2 p_2^{1-1/\alpha} + \cdots + r_n p_n^{1-1/\alpha}.$$

is minimized and the schedule length $t_1 + t_2 + \cdots + t_n$ does not exceed T, that is,

$$F(p_1, p_2, \ldots, p_n) = \frac{r_1}{p_1^{1/\alpha}} + \frac{r_2}{p_2^{1/\alpha}} + \cdots + \frac{r_n}{p_n^{1/\alpha}} \le T.$$

The energy consumption $E(p_1, p_2, \ldots, p_n)$ and the schedule length $F(p_1, p_2, \ldots, p_n)$ are viewed as functions of $p_1, p_2, \ldots, p_n$.

We can minimize $E(p_1, p_2, \ldots, p_n)$ subject to the constraint $F(p_1, p_2, \ldots, p_n) = T$ by using the Lagrange multiplier system:

$$\nabla E(p_1, p_2, \ldots, p_n) = \lambda \nabla F(p_1, p_2, \ldots, p_n),$$

where λ is a Lagrange multiplier. Since

$$\frac{\partial E(p_1, p_2, \ldots, p_n)}{\partial p_i} = \lambda \cdot \frac{\partial F(p_1, p_2, \ldots, p_n)}{\partial p_i},$$

that is,

$$r_i \left(1 - \frac{1}{\alpha}\right) \frac{1}{p_i^{1/\alpha}} = \lambda r_i \left(-\frac{1}{\alpha}\right) \frac{1}{p_i^{1+1/\alpha}},$$

where $1 \le i \le n$, we have $p_i = \lambda/(1 - \alpha)$, for all $1 \le i \le n$. Substituting the above p_i into the constraint $F(p_1, p_2, \ldots, p_n) = T$, we get $R((1 - \alpha)/\lambda)^{1/\alpha} = T$ and $p_i = \lambda/(1 - \alpha) = (R/T)^\alpha$, for all $1 \le i \le n$.

The above discussion gives rise to the following theorem, which gives the optimal power supplies and the minimum energy consumption.

Theorem 1.3   *On a uniprocessor computer, the total energy consumption is minimized when all tasks are supplied with the same power $p_i = (R/T)^\alpha$, where $1 \le i \le n$. The minimum energy consumption is $E_{\mathrm{OPT}} = R^\alpha/T^{\alpha-1}$.*

1.3.2.2   *Multiprocessor computers.*   By Theorem 1.3, the energy consumed by tasks in group k is minimized as $E_k = R_k^\alpha/T^{\alpha-1}$ by allocating the same power $(R_k/T)^\alpha$ to all the tasks in group k without missing the time deadline T. The minimum energy consumption is simply

$$E_1 + E_2 + \cdots + E_m = \frac{R_1^\alpha + R_2^\alpha + \cdots + R_m^\alpha}{T^{\alpha-1}}.$$

The following result gives the optimal power supplies that minimize energy consumption for a given partition of n tasks into m groups on a multiprocessor computer.

Theorem 1.4   *For a given partition $R_1, R_2, \ldots, R_m$ of n tasks into m groups on a multiprocessor computer, the total energy consumption is minimized when all the tasks in group k are supplied with the same power $(R_k/T)^\alpha$, where $1 \le k \le m$. The minimum energy consumption is*

$$E_{\mathrm{OPT}} = \frac{R_1^\alpha + R_2^\alpha + \cdots + R_m^\alpha}{T^{\alpha-1}}$$

for the above power supplies.

1.3.3 Strong NP-Hardness

The *sum of powers* problem is defined as follows:

Problem 1.3 (Sum of Powers)

Input: A set of integers $\{r_1, r_2, \ldots, r_n\}$ and an integer $m \geq 2$.

Output: A partition of the set into m disjoint subsets, where the sum of integers in subset k is R_k, $1 \leq k \leq m$, such that $R_1^{\alpha} + R_2^{\alpha} + \cdots + R_m^{\alpha}$ is minimized.

Theorems 1.2 and 1.4 imply that on a multiprocessor computer, the problem of minimizing schedule length with energy consumption constraint and the problem of minimizing energy consumption with schedule length constraint are equivalent to finding a partition R_1, R_2, $\ldots$, R_m of the n tasks into m groups such that $R_1^{\alpha} + R_2^{\alpha} + \cdots + R_m^{\alpha}$ is minimized. This is exactly the same problem as the sum of powers problem. Hence, we have reached the following theorem.

Theorem 1.5 *On a multiprocessor computer with $m \geq 2$ processors, the problem of minimizing schedule length with energy consumption constraint and the problem of minimizing energy consumption with schedule length constraint are equivalent to the sum of powers problem.*

We can easily prove that the sum of powers problem is NP-hard even when $m = 2$ and $\alpha = 2$. We use a reduction from the well-known *partition problem* [54], that is, to decide whether there is a partition of a set of integers $\{r_1, r_2, \ldots, r_n\}$ into two disjoint subsets, such that $R_1 = R_2$, where R_1 and R_2 are the sums of integers in the two subsets. Let $R = R_1 + R_2$ be the sum of all integers. Since $R_1^2 + R_2^2 = R_1^2 + (R - R_1)^2 = 2(R_1 - R/2)^2 + R^2/2$, we know that $R_1^2 + R_2^2$ is minimized as $R^2/2$ if and only if $R_1 = R/2$, that is, there is a partition. Actually, the following result is known in Reference 54 (p. 225).

Theorem 1.6 *The sum of powers problem is NP-hard in the strong sense for all rational $\alpha > 1$. Consequently, on a multiprocessor computer with $m \geq 2$ processors, the problem of minimizing schedule length with energy consumption constraint and the problem of minimizing energy consumption with schedule length constraint are NP-hard in the strong sense.*

1.3.4 Lower Bounds

Assume that R_1, R_2, $\ldots$, R_m are continuous variables. By using a Lagrange multiplier system, it is easy to show that the multivariable function

$$f(R_1, R_2, \ldots, R_m) = R_1^{\alpha} + R_2^{\alpha} + \cdots + R_m^{\alpha}$$

subject to the constraint $R_1 + R_2 + \cdots + R_m = R$ is minimized when $R_1 = R_2 = \cdots = R_m = R/m$. If there exists such a partition, we have the optimal schedule length $T_{OPT} = ((m/E)(R/m)^\alpha)^{1/(\alpha-1)}$, by Theorem 1.2. Of course, in general, there may not exist such a partition and the above quantity can only serve as a lower bound for the optimal schedule length. The following theorem gives a lower bound for the optimal schedule length T_{OPT} for the problem of minimizing schedule length with energy consumption constraint.

Theorem 1.7 *For the problem of minimizing schedule length with energy consumption constraint on a multiprocessor computer, we have the following lower bound:*

$$T_{OPT} \geq \left(\frac{m}{E} \left(\frac{R}{m} \right)^\alpha \right)^{1/(\alpha-1)}$$

for the optimal schedule length.

Similarly, we know that if there exists a partition that results in $R_1 = R_2 = \cdots = R_m = R/m$, the minimum total energy consumption could be $E_{OPT} = m(R/m)^\alpha / T^{\alpha-1}$ by Theorem 1.4. The following theorem gives a lower bound for the minimum energy consumption E_{OPT} for the problem of minimizing energy consumption with schedule length constraint.

Theorem 1.8 *For the problem of minimizing energy consumption with schedule length constraint on a multiprocessor computer, we have the following lower bound:*

$$E_{OPT} \geq m \left(\frac{R}{m} \right)^\alpha \frac{1}{T^{\alpha-1}}$$

for the minimum energy consumption.

Since it is infeasible to compute optimal solutions in reasonable amount of time, the lower bounds in Theorems 1.7 and 1.8 can be used to evaluate the performance of heuristic algorithms when they are compared with optimal solutions.

1.3.5 Energy-Delay Trade-off

The lower bounds in Theorems 1.7 and 1.8 essentially state the following important theorem.

$ET^{\alpha-1}$ Lower Bound Theorem (Energy-Delay Trade-off Theorem). *For any execution of a set of tasks with total execution requirement* R *on* m *processors with schedule length* T *and energy consumption* E, *we must have the following tradeoff:*

$$ET^{\alpha-1} \geq m \left(\frac{R}{m} \right)^\alpha$$

by using any scheduling algorithm.

The above energy-delay tradeoff theorem implies that our power allocation and task scheduling problems are defined such that the energy-delay product is optimized by fixing one factor and minimizing the other.

Notice that the lower bounds in Theorems 1.7 and 1.8 and the energy-delay tradeoff theorem are applicable to various sequential task models (independent or precedence constrained, static or dynamic tasks), various processor models (regular homogeneous processors with continuous or discrete voltage/frequency/speed/power levels, bounded or unbounded voltage/frequency/speed/power levels, with/without overheads for voltage/frequency/speed/power adjustment, and idle processors), and all scheduling models (preemptive or nonpreemptive, online or offline, clairvoyant, or non-clairvoyant scheduling). These lower bounds have also been extended to parallel tasks [55].

1.4 PRE-POWER-DETERMINATION ALGORITHMS

1.4.1 Overview

We observe that for independent sequential tasks considered in this chapter, we only need to deal with two subproblems, namely, scheduling tasks and determining power supplies. Depending on which subproblem is solved first, we have two types of power-aware task scheduling algorithm, namely, pre-power-determination algorithms and post-power-determination algorithms.

In pre-power-determination algorithms, we first determine power supplies and then schedule the tasks. Let A_1-A_2 denote a pre-power-determination algorithm, where A_1 is an algorithm for power allocation and A_2 is an algorithm for task scheduling. Algorithm A_1-A_2 works as follows: First, algorithm A_1 is used to assign powers to the n tasks. Second, algorithm A_2 is used to produce a schedule of the n tasks (whose execution times are known) on the m processors.

In this section, we consider the following pre-power-determination algorithms:

- *Equal-Time Algorithms* (ET-A). The power supplies $p_1, p_2, \ldots, p_n$ are determined in such a way that all the n tasks have the identical execution time, that is, $t_1 = t_2 = \cdots = t_n$.
- *Equal-Energy Algorithms* (EE-A). The power supplies $p_1, p_2, \ldots, p_n$ are determined in such a way that all the n tasks consume the same amount of energy, that is, $e_1 = e_2 = \cdots = e_n$.
- *Equal-Speed Algorithms* (ES-A). All the n tasks are supplied with the same power and executed at the same speed, that is, $p_1 = p_2 = \cdots = p_n$ and $s_1 = s_2 = \cdots = s_n$.

In all the above algorithms, A is any task scheduling algorithm.

We propose to use the classic list scheduling algorithm [56] and its variations to solve the task scheduling problem.

- *List Scheduling* (LS). The algorithm works as follows to schedule a list of tasks 1, 2, $\ldots$, n. Initially, task k is scheduled on processor k, where

$1 \leq k \leq m$, and tasks 1, 2, $\ldots$, m are removed from the list simultaneously. On the completion of a task k, the first unscheduled task in the list, that is, task $m + 1$, is removed from the list and scheduled to be executed on processor k. This process repeats until all tasks in the list are finished.

Algorithm LS has many variations depending on the strategy used in the initial ordering of the tasks. We mention two of them here.

- *Largest Requirement First* (LRF). This algorithm is the same as the LS algorithm, except that the tasks are arranged such that $r_1 \geq r_2 \geq \cdots \geq r_n$.
- *Smallest Requirement First* (SRF). This algorithm is the same as the LS algorithm, except that the tasks are arranged such that $r_1 \leq r_2 \leq \cdots \leq r_n$.

We call algorithm LS and its variations simply as *list scheduling algorithms*.

Notice that for equal-time algorithms ET-*A*, since all tasks have the same execution time, all list scheduling algorithms generate the same schedule. Hence, we basically have one algorithm ET-LS. However, for equal-energy algorithms, EE-*A*, and equal-speed algorithms, ES-*A*, different list scheduling algorithms generate different schedules and have different performance. Therefore, we will distinguish algorithms EE-SRF, EE-LS, EE-LRF, and ES-SRF, ES-LS, ES-LRF.

1.4.2 Performance Measures

Let T_A denote the length of the schedule produced by algorithm A and E_A denote the total amount of energy consumed by algorithm A. The following performance measures are used to analyze and evaluate the performance of our power allocation and task scheduling algorithms.

Definition 1.1   The *performance ratio* of an algorithm A that solves the problem of minimizing schedule length with energy consumption constraint is defined as $\beta_A = T_A / T_{\text{OPT}}$. If $\beta_A \leq B$, we call B a *performance bound* of algorithm A. The *asymptotic performance ratio* of algorithm A is defined as $\beta_A^{\infty} = \lim_{R/r^* \to \infty} \beta_A$ (by fixing m), where $r^* = \max\{r_1, r_2, \ldots, r_n\}$ is the maximum task execution requirement. If $\beta_A^{\infty} \leq B$, we call B an *asymptotic performance bound* of algorithm A. Algorithm A is called *asymptotically optimal* if $\beta_A^{\infty} = 1$.

Definition 1.2   The *performance ratio* of an algorithm A that solves the problem of minimizing energy consumption with schedule length constraint is defined as $\gamma_A = E_A / E_{\text{OPT}}$. If $\gamma_A \leq C$, we call C a *performance bound* of algorithm A. The *asymptotic performance ratio* of algorithm A is defined as $\gamma_A^{\infty} = \lim_{R/r^* \to \infty} \gamma_A$ (by fixing m), where $r^* = \max\{r_1, r_2, \ldots, r_n\}$ is the maximum task execution requirement. If $\gamma_A^{\infty} \leq C$, we call C an *asymptotic performance bound* of algorithm A. Algorithm A is called *asymptotically optimal* if $\gamma_A^{\infty} = 1$.

When tasks have random execution requirements, T_A, T_{OPT}, β_A, β_A^{∞}, B, E_A, E_{OPT}, γ_A, γ_A^{∞}, and C are all random variables. Let $\bar{x}$ be the expectation of a random variable x.

Definition 1.3   If $\beta_A \leq B$, then $\overline{B}$ is an *expected performance bound* of algorithm A. If $\beta_A^\infty \leq B$ then $\overline{B}$ is an *expected asymptotic performance bound* of algorithm A.

Definition 1.4   If $\gamma_A \leq C$ then $\overline{C}$ is an *expected performance bound* of algorithm A. If $\gamma_A^\infty \leq C$ then $\overline{C}$ is an *expected asymptotic performance bound* of algorithm A.

1.4.3 Equal-Time Algorithms and Analysis

1.4.3.1 Schedule length minimization. To solve the problem of minimizing schedule length with energy consumption constraint E by using the equal-time algorithm ET-LS, we notice that $t_1 = t_2 = \cdots = t_n = t$, that is, $t_i = r_i / p_i^{1/\alpha} = t$, for all $1 \leq i \leq n$, where t is the identical task execution time. The above equation gives $p_i = (r_i/t)^\alpha$, where $1 \leq i \leq n$. Since the total energy consumption is

$$r_1 p_1^{1-1/\alpha} + r_2 p_2^{1-1/\alpha} + \cdots + r_n p_n^{1-1/\alpha} = E,$$

namely,

$$\frac{r_1^\alpha + r_2^\alpha + \cdots + r_n^\alpha}{t^{\alpha-1}} = E,$$

we get

$$t = \left(\frac{r_1^\alpha + r_2^\alpha + \cdots + r_n^\alpha}{E} \right)^{1/(\alpha-1)}.$$

Therefore, the schedule length of algorithm ET-LS is

$$T_{\text{ET-LS}} = \left\lceil \frac{n}{m} \right\rceil t = \left\lceil \frac{n}{m} \right\rceil \left(\frac{r_1^\alpha + r_2^\alpha + \cdots + r_n^\alpha}{E} \right)^{1/(\alpha-1)}.$$

By Theorem 1.7, the performance ratio of algorithm ET-LS is

$$\beta_{\text{ET-LS}} = \frac{T_{\text{ET-LS}}}{T_{\text{OPT}}} \leq m \left\lceil \frac{n}{m} \right\rceil \left(\frac{r_1^\alpha + r_2^\alpha + \cdots + r_n^\alpha}{R^\alpha} \right)^{1/(\alpha-1)}.$$

The above discussion is summarized in the following theorem.

Theorem 1.9   *By using the equal-time algorithm ET-LS to solve the problem of minimizing schedule length with energy consumption constraint on a multiprocessor computer, the schedule length is*

$$T_{\text{ET-LS}} = \left\lceil \frac{n}{m} \right\rceil \left(\frac{r_1^\alpha + r_2^\alpha + \cdots + r_n^\alpha}{E} \right)^{1/(\alpha-1)}.$$

The performance ratio is $\beta_{\text{ET-LS}} \leq B_{\text{ET-LS}}$, where the performance bound is

$$B_{\text{ET-LS}} = m \left\lceil \frac{n}{m} \right\rceil \left(\frac{r_1^\alpha + r_2^\alpha + \cdots + r_n^\alpha}{(r_1 + r_2 + \cdots + r_n)^\alpha} \right)^{1/(\alpha-1)}.$$

1.4.3.2 *Energy consumption minimization.*

To solve the problem of minimizing energy consumption with schedule length constraint T by using the equal-time algorithm ET-LS, we notice that enough energy $E_{\text{ET-LS}}$ should be given such that $T_{\text{ET-LS}} = T$, that is,

$$\left\lceil \frac{n}{m} \right\rceil \left(\frac{r_1^\alpha + r_2^\alpha + \cdots + r_n^\alpha}{E_{\text{ET-LS}}} \right)^{1/(\alpha-1)} = T.$$

The above equation implies that the energy consumed by algorithm ET-LS is

$$E_{\text{ET-LS}} = \left(\left\lceil \frac{n}{m} \right\rceil \frac{1}{T} \right)^{\alpha-1} \left(r_1^\alpha + r_2^\alpha + \cdots + r_n^\alpha \right).$$

By Theorem 1.8, the performance ratio of algorithm ET-LS is

$$\gamma_{\text{ET-LS}} = \frac{E_{\text{ET-LS}}}{E_{\text{OPT}}} \leq \left(m \left\lceil \frac{n}{m} \right\rceil \right)^{\alpha-1} \left(\frac{r_1^\alpha + r_2^\alpha + \cdots + r_n^\alpha}{R^\alpha} \right).$$

The above discussion is summarized in the following theorem.

Theorem 1.10   *By using the equal-time algorithm ET-LS to solve the problem of minimizing energy consumption with schedule length constraint on a multiprocessor computer, the energy consumed is*

$$E_{\text{ET-LS}} = \left(\left\lceil \frac{n}{m} \right\rceil \frac{1}{T} \right)^{\alpha-1} \left(r_1^\alpha + r_2^\alpha + \cdots + r_n^\alpha \right).$$

The performance ratio is $\gamma_{\text{ET-LS}} \leq C_{\text{ET-LS}}$, where the performance bound is

$$C_{\text{ET-LS}} = \left(m \left\lceil \frac{n}{m} \right\rceil \right)^{\alpha-1} \left(\frac{r_1^\alpha + r_2^\alpha + \cdots + r_n^\alpha}{(r_1 + r_2 + \cdots + r_n)^\alpha} \right).$$

1.4.4   Equal-Energy Algorithms and Analysis

1.4.4.1 *Schedule length minimization.*

To solve the problem of minimizing schedule length with energy consumption constraint E by using an equal-energy algorithm EE-A, where A is a list scheduling algorithm, we notice that $e_1 = e_2 = \cdots = e_n = E/n$, that is, $e_i = r_i p_i^{1-1/\alpha} = E/n$, for all

$1 \leq i \leq n$, where E/n is the identical energy consumption of the n tasks. The above equation gives $p_i = (E/nr_i)^{\alpha/(\alpha-1)}$, $s_i = p_i^{1/\alpha} = (E/nr_i)^{1/(\alpha-1)}$, and $t_i = r_i/s_i = r_i^{\alpha/(\alpha-1)} (n/E)^{1/(\alpha-1)}$, where $1 \leq i \leq n$.

Let $A(t_1, t_2, \ldots, t_n)$ represent the length of the schedule produced by algorithm A for n tasks with execution times $t_1, t_2, \ldots, t_n$, where A is a list scheduling algorithm. We notice that for all $x \geq 0$, we have $A(t_1, t_2, \ldots, t_n) = xA(t_1', t_2', \ldots, t_n')$, if $t_i = xt_i'$ for all $1 \leq i \leq n$. That is, the schedule length is scaled by a factor of x if all the task execution times are scaled by a factor of x. Therefore, we get the schedule length of algorithm EE-A as

$$T_{\text{EE-}A} = A(t_1, t_2, \ldots, t_n) = A(r_1^{\alpha/(\alpha-1)}, r_2^{\alpha/(\alpha-1)}, \ldots, r_n^{\alpha/(\alpha-1)}) \left(\frac{n}{E}\right)^{1/(\alpha-1)}.$$

By Theorem 1.7, the performance ratio of algorithm EE-A is

$$\beta_{\text{EE-}A} = \frac{T_{\text{EE-}A}}{T_{\text{OPT}}} \leq \frac{mn^{1/(\alpha-1)} A(r_1^{\alpha/(\alpha-1)}, r_2^{\alpha/(\alpha-1)}, \ldots, r_n^{\alpha/(\alpha-1)})}{R^{\alpha/(\alpha-1)}}.$$

By using any list scheduling algorithm A, we get

$$A(t_1, t_2, \ldots, t_n) \leq \frac{t_1 + t_2 + \cdots + t_n}{m} + t^*,$$

where $t^* = \max\{t_1, t_2, \ldots, t_n\}$ is the longest task execution time. Hence, we obtain

$$\beta_{\text{EE-}A} \leq \frac{n^{1/(\alpha-1)} \left((r_1^{\alpha/(\alpha-1)} + r_2^{\alpha/(\alpha-1)} + \cdots + r_n^{\alpha/(\alpha-1)}) + m(r^*)^{\alpha/(\alpha-1)}\right)}{R^{\alpha/(\alpha-1)}}$$

$$= n^{1/(\alpha-1)} \left(\frac{r_1^{\alpha/(\alpha-1)} + r_2^{\alpha/(\alpha-1)} + \cdots + r_n^{\alpha/(\alpha-1)}}{R^{\alpha/(\alpha-1)}} + m\left(\frac{r^*}{R}\right)^{\alpha/(\alpha-1)}\right),$$

where $r^* = \max\{r_1, r_2, \ldots, r_n\}$ is the maximum task execution requirement. The asymptotic performance ratio of algorithm EE-A is

$$\beta_{\text{EE-}A}^{\infty} = \lim_{R/r^* \to \infty} \beta_{\text{EE-}A} \leq \frac{n^{1/(\alpha-1)}(r_1^{\alpha/(\alpha-1)} + r_2^{\alpha/(\alpha-1)} + \cdots + r_n^{\alpha/(\alpha-1)})}{R^{\alpha/(\alpha-1)}}.$$

The above discussion is summarized in the following theorem.

Theorem 1.11   *By using an equal-energy algorithm EE-*A *to solve the problem of minimizing schedule length with energy consumption constraint on a multiprocessor computer, the schedule length is*

$$T_{\text{EE-}A} = A(r_1^{\alpha/(\alpha-1)}, r_2^{\alpha/(\alpha-1)}, \ldots, r_n^{\alpha/(\alpha-1)}) \left(\frac{n}{E}\right)^{1/(\alpha-1)}.$$

The performance ratio is

$$\beta_{\text{EE-}A} \leq n^{1/(\alpha-1)} \left(\frac{r_1^{\alpha/(\alpha-1)} + r_2^{\alpha/(\alpha-1)} + \cdots + r_n^{\alpha/(\alpha-1)}}{R^{\alpha/(\alpha-1)}} + m \left(\frac{r^*}{R} \right)^{\alpha/(\alpha-1)} \right).$$

As $R/r^* \to \infty$, the asymptotic performance ratio is $\beta_{\text{EE-}A}^{\infty} \leq B_{\text{EE-}A}$, where the asymptotic performance bound is

$$B_{\text{EE-}A} = \frac{n^{1/(\alpha-1)} (r_1^{\alpha/(\alpha-1)} + r_2^{\alpha/(\alpha-1)} + \cdots + r_n^{\alpha/(\alpha-1)})}{(r_1 + r_2 + \cdots + r_n)^{\alpha/(\alpha-1)}}.$$

1.4.4.2 Energy consumption minimization. To solve the problem of minimizing energy consumption with schedule length constraint T by using an equal-energy algorithm EE-A, we notice that enough energy $E_{\text{EE-}A}$ should be given such that $T_{\text{EE-}A} = T$, that is,

$$A(r_1^{\alpha/(\alpha-1)}, r_2^{\alpha/(\alpha-1)}, \ldots, r_n^{\alpha/(\alpha-1)}) \left(\frac{n}{E_{\text{EE-}A}} \right)^{1/(\alpha-1)} = T.$$

The above equation implies that the energy consumed by algorithm EE-A is

$$E_{\text{EE-}A} = \frac{n}{T^{\alpha-1}} \left(A(r_1^{\alpha/(\alpha-1)}, r_2^{\alpha/(\alpha-1)}, \ldots, r_n^{\alpha/(\alpha-1)}) \right)^{\alpha-1}.$$

By Theorem 1.8, the performance ratio of algorithm EE-A is

$$\gamma_{\text{EE-}A} = \frac{E_{\text{EE-}A}}{E_{\text{OPT}}}$$

$$\leq n \left(\frac{m A(r_1^{\alpha/(\alpha-1)}, r_2^{\alpha/(\alpha-1)}, \ldots, r_n^{\alpha/(\alpha-1)})}{R^{\alpha/(\alpha-1)}} \right)^{\alpha-1}$$

$$\leq n \left(\frac{r_1^{\alpha/(\alpha-1)} + r_2^{\alpha/(\alpha-1)} + \cdots + r_n^{\alpha/(\alpha-1)}}{R^{\alpha/(\alpha-1)}} + m \left(\frac{r^*}{R} \right)^{\alpha/(\alpha-1)} \right)^{\alpha-1}.$$

The asymptotic performance ratio of algorithm EE-A is

$$\gamma_{\text{EE-}A}^{\infty} = \lim_{R/r^* \to \infty} \gamma_{\text{EE-}A} \leq \frac{n (r_1^{\alpha/(\alpha-1)} + r_2^{\alpha/(\alpha-1)} + \cdots + r_n^{\alpha/(\alpha-1)})^{\alpha-1}}{R^{\alpha}}.$$

The above discussion is summarized in the following theorem.

Theorem 1.12   *By using an equal-energy algorithm EE-A to solve the problem of minimizing energy consumption with schedule length constraint on a multiprocessor computer, the energy consumed is*

$$E_{EE-A} = \frac{n}{T^{\alpha-1}} \left(A(r_1^{\alpha/(\alpha-1)}, r_2^{\alpha/(\alpha-1)}, \dots, r_n^{\alpha/(\alpha-1)}) \right)^{\alpha-1}.$$

The performance ratio is

$$\gamma_{EE-A} \le n \left(\frac{r_1^{\alpha/(\alpha-1)} + r_2^{\alpha/(\alpha-1)} + \cdots + r_n^{\alpha/(\alpha-1)}}{R^{\alpha/(\alpha-1)}} + m \left(\frac{r^*}{R} \right)^{\alpha/(\alpha-1)} \right)^{\alpha-1}.$$

As $R/r^* \to \infty$, the asymptotic performance ratio is $\gamma_{EE-A}^{\infty} \le C_{EE-A}$, where the asymptotic performance bound is

$$C_{EE-A} = \frac{n(r_1^{\alpha/(\alpha-1)} + r_2^{\alpha/(\alpha-1)} + \cdots + r_n^{\alpha/(\alpha-1)})^{\alpha-1}}{(r_1 + r_2 + \cdots + r_n)^{\alpha}},$$

1.4.5   Equal-Speed Algorithms and Analysis

1.4.5.1   Schedule length minimization.   To solve the problem of minimizing schedule length with energy consumption constraint E by using an equal-speed algorithm ES-A, we notice that $p_1 = p_2 = \cdots = p_n = p$, that is,

$$E = r_1 p^{1-1/\alpha} + r_2 p^{1-1/\alpha} + \cdots + r_n p^{1-1/\alpha} = R p^{1-1/\alpha},$$

which gives $p = (E/R)^{\alpha/(\alpha-1)}$. Since $s_1 = s_2 = \cdots = s_n = s$, we get $s = p^{1/\alpha} = (E/R)^{1/(\alpha-1)}$ and $t_i = r_i/s = r_i (R/E)^{1/(\alpha-1)}$. Hence, we get the schedule length of algorithm ES-A as

$$T_{ES-A} = A(t_1, t_2, \dots, t_n) = A(r_1, r_2, \dots, r_n) \left(\frac{R}{E} \right)^{1/(\alpha-1)}.$$

By Theorem 1.7, the performance ratio of algorithm ES-A is

$$\beta_{ES-A} = \frac{T_{ES-A}}{T_{OPT}} \le \frac{A(r_1, r_2, \dots, r_n)}{R/m}.$$

By using any list scheduling algorithm A, we get

$$A(r_1, r_2, \dots, r_n) \le \frac{R}{m} + r^*,$$

which implies that

$$\beta_{ES-A} \le 1 + \frac{mr^*}{R}.$$

It is clear that for a fixed m, $\beta_{\text{ES-}A}$ can be arbitrarily close to 1 as R/r^* becomes large.

The above discussion yields the following theorem.

Theorem 1.13 *By using an equal-speed algorithm ES-A to solve the problem of minimizing schedule length with energy consumption constraint on a multiprocessor computer, the schedule length is*

$$T_{\text{ES-}A} = A(r_1, r_2, \ldots, r_n) \left(\frac{R}{E} \right)^{1/(\alpha-1)}.$$

The performance ratio is

$$\beta_{\text{ES-}A} \leq 1 + \frac{mr}{R}.$$

As $R/r^* \to \infty$, the asymptotic performance ratio is $\beta_{\text{ES-}A}^{\infty} = 1$.

1.4.5.2 *Energy consumption minimization.* To solve the problem of minimizing energy consumption with schedule length constraint T by using an equal-speed algorithm ES-A, we notice that enough energy $E_{\text{ES-}A}$ should be given such that $T_{\text{ES-}A} = T$, that is,

$$A(r_1, r_2, \ldots, r_n) \left(\frac{R}{E_{\text{ES-}A}} \right)^{1/(\alpha-1)} = T.$$

The above equation implies that the energy consumed by algorithm ES-A is

$$E_{\text{ES-}A} = \left(\frac{A(r_1, r_2, \ldots, r_n)}{T} \right)^{\alpha-1} R.$$

By Theorem 1.8, the performance ratio of algorithm ES-A is

$$\gamma_{\text{ES-}A} = \frac{E_{\text{ES-}A}}{E_{\text{OPT}}} \leq \left(\frac{A(r_1, r_2, \ldots, r_n)}{R/m} \right)^{\alpha-1} \leq \left(1 + \frac{mr^*}{R} \right)^{\alpha-1}.$$

As R/r^* becomes large, $\gamma_{\text{ES-}A}$ can be arbitrarily close to 1.

Theorem 1.14 *By using an equal-speed algorithm ES-A to solve the problem of minimizing energy consumption with schedule length constraint on a multiprocessor computer, the energy consumed is*

$$E_{\text{ES-}A} = \left(\frac{A(r_1, r_2, \ldots, r_n)}{T} \right)^{\alpha-1} R.$$

The performance ratio is

$$\gamma_{\text{ES-}A} \leq \left(1 + \frac{mr^*}{R}\right)^{\alpha-1}.$$

As $R/r^* \to \infty$, the asymptotic performance ratio is $\gamma_{\text{ES-}A}^{\infty} = 1$.

1.4.6 Numerical Data

In Table 1.1, we demonstrate numerical data for the expectation of the performance bound $B_{\text{ET-LS}}$ given in Theorem 1.9 and the expectation of the performance bound $C_{\text{ET-LS}}$ given in Theorem 1.10, where $n = 1, 2, 3, \ldots, 15$ and $\alpha = 3.0, 4.0, 5.0$. For each combination of n and α, we generate 20,000 sets of n random execution requests. In each set, the n execution requests are independent and identically distributed (i.i.d.) random variables uniformly distributed in $[0, 1]$. For each set of n random execution requests $r_1, r_2, \ldots, r_n$, we calculate $B_{\text{ET-LS}}$. The average of the 20,000 values of $B_{\text{ET-LS}}$ is reported as the expected performance bound $\overline{B}_{\text{ET-LS}}$. A similar process is performed to get the expected performance bound $\overline{C}_{\text{ET-LS}}$. The maximum 99% confidence interval of all the data in the table is also given. We observe that as n increases, $\overline{B}_{\text{ET-LS}}$ ($\overline{C}_{\text{ET-LS}}$, respectively) quickly approaches its stable value, that is, the limit $\lim_{n\to\infty} \overline{B}_{\text{ET-LS}}$ ($\lim_{n\to\infty} \overline{C}_{\text{ET-LS}}$, respectively). Both $\overline{B}_{\text{ET-LS}}$ and $\overline{C}_{\text{ET-LS}}$ increase as α increases.

TABLE 1.1   Numerical Data for the Expected Performance Bounds $\overline{B}_{\text{ET-LS}}$ and $\overline{C}_{\text{ET-LS}}$ [a]

	$\alpha = 3$		$\alpha = 4$		$\alpha = 5$	
n	$\overline{B}_{\text{ET-LS}}$	$\overline{C}_{\text{ET-LS}}$	$\overline{B}_{\text{ET-LS}}$	$\overline{C}_{\text{ET-LS}}$	$\overline{B}_{\text{ET-LS}}$	$\overline{C}_{\text{ET-LS}}$
1	1.0000000	1.0000000	1.0000000	1.0000000	1.0000000	1.0000000
2	1.2640340	1.6907929	1.2880188	2.4780966	1.3061883	3.8923041
3	1.3532375	1.9228341	1.3904990	3.2061946	1.4189932	5.8662235
4	1.3867956	1.9966842	1.4310920	3.4847355	1.4713283	6.5784617
5	1.3982354	2.0269460	1.4521804	3.5441669	1.4888736	6.6706692
6	1.4057998	2.0470706	1.4584030	3.5018100	1.5022930	6.5576159
7	1.4104677	2.0506264	1.4637247	3.4949204	1.5088842	6.5677028
8	1.4134329	2.0410096	1.4678481	3.4582288	1.5122321	6.3209251
9	1.4156317	2.0348810	1.4711866	3.4471772	1.5159571	6.2137416
10	1.4151582	2.0379807	1.4698276	3.4048056	1.5154895	6.1304240
11	1.4160890	2.0323743	1.4719247	3.3859182	1.5156527	6.0539296
12	1.4139975	2.0254020	1.4739329	3.3727408	1.5190419	6.0878647
13	1.4138615	2.0243764	1.4748107	3.3570116	1.5200183	6.0082183
14	1.4145436	2.0204771	1.4754312	3.3439681	1.5226907	5.8638511
15	1.4136195	2.0204157	1.4739066	3.3324817	1.5193218	5.8842350

[a]99% confidence interval, ±2.718%.

TABLE 1.2   Numerical Data for the Expected Asymptotic Performance Bounds $\overline{B}_{EE-A}$ **and** $\overline{C}_{EE-A}{}^{a}$

n	$\alpha = 3$		$\alpha = 4$		$\alpha = 5$	
	$\overline{B}_{EE-A}$	$\overline{C}_{EE-A}$	$\overline{B}_{EE-A}$	$\overline{C}_{EE-A}$	$\overline{B}_{EE-A}$	$\overline{C}_{EE-A}$
1	1.0000000	1.0000000	1.0000000	1.0000000	1.0000000	1.0000000
2	1.0883879	1.1970545	1.0545042	1.1854814	1.0386468	1.1819932
3	1.1108389	1.2494676	1.0674159	1.2306497	1.0479554	1.2207771
4	1.1195349	1.2633028	1.0725624	1.2440485	1.0515081	1.2326371
5	1.1232283	1.2708740	1.0749250	1.2505880	1.0531375	1.2394887
6	1.1256815	1.2736246	1.0763288	1.2524318	1.0541672	1.2428750
7	1.1263593	1.2759891	1.0768743	1.2565030	1.0544601	1.2447639
8	1.1286415	1.2738426	1.0771574	1.2545767	1.0551808	1.2436191
9	1.1289966	1.2757221	1.0774763	1.2568825	1.0552782	1.2447769
10	1.1292004	1.2766495	1.0776918	1.2572239	1.0555105	1.2442652
11	1.1291663	1.2781207	1.0783142	1.2570462	1.0556260	1.2471731
12	1.1293388	1.2786435	1.0784883	1.2569814	1.0559882	1.2457928
13	1.1294392	1.2786065	1.0786491	1.2577500	1.0560901	1.2458283
14	1.1291546	1.2797332	1.0786508	1.2576963	1.0561657	1.2480804
15	1.1294269	1.2792081	1.0787218	1.2584264	1.0561504	1.2476369

[a] 99% confidence interval, $\pm 0.375\%$.

In Table 1.2, we demonstrate numerical data for the expectation of the performance bound B_{EE-A} given in Theorem 1.11 and the expectation of the performance bound C_{EE-A} given in Theorem 1.12. The data are obtained using a method similar to that of Table 1.1. It is observed that as n increases, $\overline{B}_{EE-A}$ ($\overline{C}_{EE-A}$, respectively) quickly approaches its stable value. Surprisingly, both $\overline{B}_{EE-A}$ and $\overline{C}_{EE-A}$ decrease as α increases. It is clear that the asymptotic performance of equal-energy algorithms is better than the performance of equal-time algorithms, especially for large α.

1.4.7   Simulation Results

In this section, we demonstrate some experimental data. Our experimental performance evaluation is based on two performance measures, namely, normalized schedule length and normalized energy consumption.

Definition 1.5   The *normalized schedule length* NSL_A of an algorithm A that solves the problem of minimizing schedule length with energy consumption constraint is defined as

$$\mathrm{NSL}_A = \frac{T_A}{((m/E)(R/m)^{\alpha})^{1/(\alpha-1)}}.$$

According the the above definition, the normalized schedule length of the equal-time algorithm ET-LS is

$$\text{NSL}_{\text{ET-LS}} = m \left\lceil \frac{n}{m} \right\rceil \left(\frac{r_1^\alpha + r_2^\alpha + \cdots + r_n^\alpha}{R^\alpha} \right)^{1/(\alpha-1)}.$$

For an equal-energy algorithm EE-A, the normalized schedule length is

$$\text{NSL}_{\text{EE-}A} = \frac{mn^{1/(\alpha-1)} A(r_1^{\alpha/(\alpha-1)}, r_2^{\alpha/(\alpha-1)}, \ldots, r_n^{\alpha/(\alpha-1)})}{R^{\alpha/(\alpha-1)}}.$$

For an equal-speed algorithm ES-A, the normalized schedule length is

$$\text{NSL}_{\text{ES-}A} = \frac{A(r_1, r_2, \ldots, r_n)}{R/m}.$$

We notice that NSL_A serves as a performance bound for the performance ratio $\beta_A = T_A/T_{\text{OPT}}$ of any algorithm A that solves the problem of minimizing schedule length with energy consumption constraint on a multiprocessor computer. When the r_i's are random variables, T_A, T_{OPT}, β_A, and NSL_A all become random variables. It is clear that for the problem of minimizing schedule length with energy consumption constraint, we have $\overline{\beta}_A \leq \overline{\text{NSL}}_A$, that is, the expected performance ratio is no greater than the expected normalized schedule length. (Recall that we use $\overline{x}$ to represent the expectation of a random variable x.)

Definition 1.6 The *normalized energy consumption* NEC_A of an algorithm A that solves the problem of minimizing energy consumption with schedule length constraint is defined as

$$\text{NEC}_A = \frac{E_A}{R^\alpha/(mT)^{\alpha-1}}.$$

According the the above definition, the normalized energy consumption of the equal-time algorithm ET-LS is

$$\text{NEC}_{\text{ET-LS}} = \left(m \left\lceil \frac{n}{m} \right\rceil \right)^{\alpha-1} \left(\frac{r_1^\alpha + r_2^\alpha + \cdots + r_n^\alpha}{R^\alpha} \right).$$

For an equal-energy algorithm EE-A, the normalized energy consumption is

$$\text{NEC}_{\text{EE-}A} = \frac{n(mA(r_1^{\alpha/(\alpha-1)}, r_2^{\alpha/(\alpha-1)}, \ldots, r_n^{\alpha/(\alpha-1)}))^{\alpha-1}}{R^\alpha}.$$

For an equal-speed algorithm ES-A, the normalized energy consumption is

$$\text{NEC}_{\text{ES-}A} = \left(\frac{A(r_1, r_2, \ldots, r_n)}{R/m} \right)^{\alpha-1}.$$

TABLE 1.3   Simulation Results for the Expected NSL[a]

n	ET-LS	EE-SRF	EE-LS	EE-LRF	ES-SRF	ES-LS	ES-LRF
30	1.4160086	1.5788606	1.5358982	1.1830203	1.2950870	1.2777859	1.0570897
40	1.4162681	1.4614432	1.4275593	1.1598898	1.2209157	1.2095402	1.0326068
50	1.4160963	1.3939270	1.3671321	1.1476734	1.1778906	1.1681927	1.0210129
60	1.4142811	1.3501833	1.3289118	1.1419086	1.1484774	1.1398580	1.0147939
70	1.4145643	1.3183999	1.2995623	1.1387841	1.1277784	1.1188316	1.0106644
80	1.4137537	1.2940370	1.2787042	1.1364289	1.1116303	1.1047328	1.0081871
90	1.4141781	1.2760247	1.2622851	1.1350882	1.0990160	1.0933288	1.0065092

[a]99% confidence interval, ±0.355%.

TABLE 1.4   Simulation Results for the Expected NEC[a]

n	ET-LS	EE-SRF	EE-LS	EE-LRF	ES-SRF	ES-LS	ES-LRF
30	2.0166361	2.4942799	2.3687384	1.3987777	1.6795807	1.6387186	1.1184317
40	2.0141396	2.1375327	2.0427624	1.3452555	1.4955667	1.4714876	1.0671827
50	2.0101674	1.9436148	1.8768266	1.3208927	1.3900636	1.3667759	1.0421333
60	2.0079074	1.8256473	1.7667130	1.3062980	1.3195213	1.2992718	1.0294409
70	2.0065212	1.7388610	1.6960039	1.2976417	1.2720398	1.2538434	1.0214559
80	2.0112500	1.6743670	1.6388005	1.2911207	1.2366120	1.2199077	1.0165503
90	2.0061604	1.6282674	1.5961585	1.2881397	1.2087291	1.1947753	1.0129208

[a]99% confidence interval, ±0.720%.

It is noticed that NEC_A is a performance bound for the performance ratio $\gamma_A = E_A/E_{OPT}$ of any algorithm A that solves the problem of minimizing energy consumption with schedule length constraint on a multiprocessor computer. It is also clear that for the problem of minimizing energy consumption with schedule length constraint, we have $\overline{\gamma}_A \leq \overline{NEC}_A$, that is, the expected performance ratio is no greater than the expected normalized schedule length.

Notice that for a given power allocation and task scheduling algorithm A, the expected normalized schedule length $\overline{NSL}_A$ and the expected normalized energy consumption $\overline{NEC}_A$ are determined by m, n, α, and the probability distribution of the r_i's. In our simulations, the number of processors is set as $m = 10$. The number of tasks is in the range $n = 30, 40, \ldots, 90$. The parameter α is set as 3. The r_i's are i.i.d. random variables with a uniform distribution in $[0, 1]$.

In Tables 1.3 and 1.4, we show our simulation results. For each combination of n and algorithm $A \in$ {ET-LS, EE-SRF, EE-LS, EE-LRF, ES-SRF, ES-LS, ES-LRF}, we generate 5000 sets of n tasks, produce their schedules by using algorithm A, calculate their NSL_A (or NEC_A), and report the average of NSL_A (or NEC_A), which is the experimental value of $\overline{NSL}_A$ (or $\overline{NEC}_A$). The 99% confidence interval of all the data is also given in the same table. We observe the following facts:

- The equal-time algorithm ET-LS exhibits quite stable performance. The expected normalized schedule length $\overline{NSL}_{\text{ET-LS}}$ (the expected normalized energy consumption $\overline{NEC}_{\text{ET-LS}}$, respectively) is almost identical to the expected performance bound $\overline{B}_{\text{ET-LS}}$ ($\overline{C}_{\text{ET-LS}}$, respectively) given in Table 1.1.

- The performance of equal-energy algorithms improves as n increases. The expected normalized schedule length $\overline{NSL}_{\text{EE-}A}$ (the expected normalized energy consumption $\overline{NEC}_{\text{EE-}A}$, respectively) decreases as n increases, that is, R/r^* increases, and eventually approaches the expected performance bound $\overline{B}_{\text{EE-}A}$ ($\overline{C}_{\text{EE-}A}$, respectively) given in Table 1.2. The speed of convergence depends on algorithm A. It is clear that algorithm LRF leads to faster speed of convergence than LS and SRF.

- The performance of equal-speed algorithms improves as n increases. The expected normalized schedule length $\overline{NSL}_{\text{ES-}A}$ and the expected normalized energy consumption $\overline{NEC}_{\text{ES-}A}$ decrease as n increases, that is, R/r^* increases, and eventually approaches 1, as claimed in Theorems 1.13 and 1.14. Again, algorithm LRF leads to faster speed of convergence than LS and SRF.

- The performance of the three list scheduling algorithms are ranked as SRF, LS, LRF, from the worst to the best. Algorithm EE-LRF performs noticeably better than EE-SRF and EE-LS. Similarly, Algorithm ES-LRF performs noticeably better than ES-SRF and ES-LS. This is not surprising since LRF schedules tasks with long execution times earlier and cause less imbalance of task distribution among the processors. On the other hand, SRF schedules tasks with short execution times earlier, and tasks with long execution times scheduled later cause more imbalance of task distribution among the processors. It is known that LRF exhibits better performance in other scheduling environments.

- The equal-time algorithm ET-LS performs better than equal-energy algorithms EE-SRF and EE-LS for small n. As n gets larger, ET-LS performs worse than EE-A and ES-A for all A. The equal-speed algorithm ES-A performs better than the equal-energy algorithm EE-A for all A. For large n, the performance of the seven pre-power-determination algorithms are ranked as ET-LS, EE-SRF, EE-LS, EE-LRF, ES-SRF, ES-LS, ES-LRF, from the worst to the best.

1.5 POST-POWER-DETERMINATION ALGORITHMS

1.5.1 Overview

As mentioned earlier, both the problem of minimizing schedule length with energy consumption constraint and the problem of minimizing energy consumption with schedule length constraint on a multiprocessor computer are equivalent to the sum of powers problem in the sense that they can be solved by finding a partition R_1, R_2, ..., R_m of the n tasks into m groups such that the sum of powers $R_1^\alpha + R_2^\alpha + \cdots + R_m^\alpha$ is minimized. Such a partition is essentially a schedule of the n tasks on m processors. Once a partition (i.e., a schedule) is determined, Theorems 1.2 and 1.4 can be used to decide actual power supplies, which minimize either schedule length or energy consumption. This is exactly the idea of post-power-determination algorithms, where we first schedule the tasks and then determine power supplies, that is, power supplies p_1, p_2, ..., p_n are determined after a schedule of the n tasks on the m processors is decided, and a schedule is produced without knowing the actual task execution times but based only on task execution requirements.

Again, we can decompose our optimization problems into two subproblems, namely, scheduling tasks and determining power supplies. We use the notation A_1-A_2 to represent a post-power-determination algorithm, where A_1 is an algorithm for task scheduling and A_2 is an algorithm for power allocation. Algorithm A_1-A_2 works as follows: First, algorithm A_1 is used to produce a schedule of the n tasks (whose execution times are unknown) by using $r_1, r_2, \ldots, r_n$ as task execution times. Second, algorithm A_2 is used to assign powers to the n tasks on the m processors. We propose to use the list scheduling algorithm and its variations to solve the scheduling problem (i.e., the sum of powers problem). Since our power allocation algorithms based on Theorems 1.2 and 1.4 yields optimal solutions, we have post-power-determination algorithm LS-OPT, SRF-OPT, and LRF-OPT.

1.5.2 Analysis of List Scheduling Algorithms

1.5.2.1 Analysis of algorithm LS. Let P_{LS} be the sum of powers of the partition of a list of tasks into m groups produced by algorithm LS, and P_{OPT} be the minimum sum of powers of an optimal partition of the list of tasks. The following theorem characterizes the performance of algorithm LS in solving the sum of powers problem.

Theorem 1.15 *By using algorithm LS to solve the sum of powers problem for a list of tasks, we have $P_{LS}/P_{OPT} \leq B_{LS}$, where the performance bound is*

$$
B_{LS} = \max_{\substack{1 \leq m' \leq m-1 \\ 0 \leq r \leq 1/m'}} \left\{ \frac{(m - m')\left(\dfrac{1 - m'r}{m}\right)^\alpha + m'\left(\dfrac{1 - m'r}{m} + r\right)^\alpha}{\left(r \leq \dfrac{1}{m}\right) ? \dfrac{1}{m^{\alpha-1}} : r^\alpha + (m - 1)\left(\dfrac{1 - r}{m - 1}\right)^\alpha} \right\}.
$$

(Note: An expression in the form (c) ? u : v means that if a boolean condition c is true, the value of the expression is u; *otherwise, the value of the expression is* v.)

The proof of the above theorem is lengthy and sophisticated. The interested reader is referred to Reference 49 for the proof.

1.5.2.2 *Analysis of algorithm LRF.* Let P_{LRF} be the sum of powers of the partition of a list of tasks into m groups produced by algorithm LRF. The following theorem characterizes the performance of algorithm LRF in solving the sum of powers problem.

Theorem 1.16 *By using algorithm LRF to solve the sum of powers problem for a list of tasks, we have $P_{\text{LRF}}/P_{\text{OPT}} \leq B_{\text{LRF}}$, where the performance bound is*

$$B_{\text{LRF}} = m^{\alpha-1} \left(\max_{1 \leq m' \leq m-1} \left\{ (m-m') \left(\frac{m+1-m'}{m(m+1)} \right)^{\alpha} + m' \left(\frac{2m+1-m'}{m(m+1)} \right)^{\alpha} \right\} \right).$$

The above theorem can be proved by following the same reasoning in the proof of Theorem 1.15. Again, the interested reader is referred to Reference 49 for the proof.

1.5.3 Application to Schedule Length Minimization

Theorem 1.15 can be used to analyze the performance of algorithm LS-OPT, which solves the problem of minimizing schedule length with energy consumption constraint on a multiprocessor computer. By Theorem 1.2, the schedule length produced by algorithm LS-OPT is $T_{\text{LS-OPT}} = \left(P_{\text{LS}}/E \right)^{1/(\alpha-1)}$, where P_{LS} is the sum of powers of the partition produced by algorithm LS. Also, the optimal schedule length is $T_{\text{OPT}} = \left(P_{\text{OPT}}/E \right)^{1/(\alpha-1)}$, where P_{OPT} is the minimum sum of powers of an optimal partition. Hence, we get

$$\beta_{\text{LS-OPT}} = \frac{T_{\text{LS-OPT}}}{T_{\text{OPT}}} = \left(\frac{P_{\text{LS}}}{P_{\text{OPT}}} \right)^{1/(\alpha-1)} \leq B_{\text{LS}}^{1/(\alpha-1)}.$$

Notice that the condition $R/r^* \to \infty$ is equivalent to $r \to 0$ in Theorem 1.15, and it is easy to see that $\lim_{r \to 0} B_{\text{LS}} = 1$. Thus, we have $\beta_{\text{LS-OPT}}^{\infty} = \lim_{R/r^* \to \infty} \beta_{\text{LS-OPT}} \leq \lim_{r \to 0} B_{\text{LS}}^{1/(\alpha-1)} = 1$.

Theorem 1.17 *By using algorithm LS-OPT to solve the problem of minimizing schedule length with energy consumption constraint on a multiprocessor computer, the schedule length is*

$$T_{\text{LS-OPT}} = \left(\frac{P_{\text{LS}}}{E} \right)^{1/(\alpha-1)}.$$

The performance ratio is $\beta_{\text{LS-OPT}} \leq B_{\text{LS-OPT}} = B_{\text{LS}}^{1/(\alpha-1)}$, where B_{LS} is given by Theorem 1.15. As $R/r^* \to \infty$, the asymptotic performance ratio is $\beta_{\text{LS-OPT}}^{\infty} = 1$.

The following theorem can be obtained in a way similar to that of Theorem 1.17.

Theorem 1.18 *By using algorithm LRF-OPT to solve the problem of minimizing schedule length with energy consumption constraint on a multiprocessor computer, the schedule length is*

$$T_{\text{LRF}-\text{OPT}} = \left(\frac{P_{\text{LRF}}}{E} \right)^{1/(\alpha-1)}.$$

The performance ratio is $\beta_{\text{LRF}-\text{OPT}} \leq B_{\text{LRF}-\text{OPT}} = B_{\text{LRF}}^{1/(\alpha-1)}$, *where* B_{LRF} *is given by Theorem 1.16. As* $R/r^* \to \infty$, *the asymptotic performance ratio is* $\beta_{\text{LRF}-\text{OPT}}^{\infty} = 1$.

1.5.4 Application to Energy Consumption Minimization

Theorem 1.15 can be used to analyze the performance of algorithm LS-OPT, which solves the problem of minimizing energy consumption with schedule length constraint on a multiprocessor computer. By Theorem 1.4, the energy consumption of the schedule produced by algorithm LS-OPT is $E_{\text{LS}-\text{OPT}} = P_{\text{LS}}/T^{\alpha-1}$, where P_{LS} is the sum of powers of the partition produced by algorithm LS. Also, the minimum energy consumption of an optimal schedule is $E_{\text{OPT}} = P_{\text{OPT}}/T^{\alpha-1}$, where P_{OPT} is the minimum sum of powers of an optimal partition. Hence, we get $\gamma_{\text{LS}-\text{OPT}} = E_{\text{LS}-\text{OPT}}/E_{\text{OPT}} = P_{\text{LS}}/P_{\text{OPT}} \leq B_{\text{LS}}$. The asymptotic performance ratio $\gamma_{\text{LS}-\text{OPT}}^{\infty}$ can be obtained in a way similar to that of Theorem 1.17.

Theorem 1.19 *By using algorithm LS-OPT to solve the problem of minimizing energy consumption with schedule length constraint on a multiprocessor computer, the energy consumed is*

$$E_{\text{LS}-\text{OPT}} = \frac{P_{\text{LS}}}{T^{\alpha-1}}.$$

The performance ratio is $\gamma_{\text{LS}-\text{OPT}} \leq C_{\text{LS}-\text{OPT}} = B_{\text{LS}}$, *where* B_{LS} *is given by Theorem 1.15. As* $R/r^* \to \infty$, *the asymptotic performance ratio is* $\gamma_{\text{LS}-\text{OPT}}^{\infty} = 1$.

The following theorem can be obtained in a way similar to that of Theorem 1.19.

Theorem 1.20 *By using algorithm LRF-OPT to solve the problem of minimizing energy consumption with schedule length constraint on a multiprocessor computer, the energy consumed is*

$$E_{\text{LRF}-\text{OPT}} = \frac{P_{\text{LRF}}}{T^{\alpha-1}}.$$

The performance ratio is $\gamma_{\text{LRF}-\text{OPT}} \leq C_{\text{LRF}-\text{OPT}} = B_{\text{LRF}}$, *where* B_{LRF} *is given by Theorem 1.16. As* $R/r^* \to \infty$, *the asymptotic performance ratio is* $\gamma_{\text{LRF}-\text{OPT}}^{\infty} = 1$.

TABLE 1.5   Numerical Data for the Performance Bounds $B_{\text{LS-OPT}}$ and $C_{\text{LS-OPT}}$

	$\alpha = 3$		$\alpha = 4$		$\alpha = 5$	
m	$B_{\text{LS-OPT}}$	$C_{\text{LS-OPT}}$	$B_{\text{LS-OPT}}$	$C_{\text{LS-OPT}}$	$B_{\text{LS-OPT}}$	$C_{\text{LS-OPT}}$
2	1.3660254	1.8660254	1.3999105	2.7434735	1.4212571	4.0802858
3	1.4168919	2.0075827	1.4721932	3.1907619	1.5098182	5.1963533
4	1.4517046	2.1074462	1.4886206	3.2987700	1.5361359	5.5682478
5	1.5235253	2.3211293	1.5274255	3.5635275	1.5430156	5.6686715
6	1.5653646	2.4503664	1.5695451	3.8665303	1.5814389	6.2547465
7	1.6075236	2.5841321	1.5955042	4.0615694	1.6094683	6.7101114
8	1.6621450	2.7627259	1.6149005	4.2115046	1.6277417	7.0200781
9	1.7031903	2.9008574	1.6495521	4.4884680	1.6399180	7.2325010
10	1.7406107	3.0297256	1.6757104	4.7054035	1.6627810	7.6443430

TABLE 1.6   Numerical Data for the Performance Bounds $B_{\text{LRF-OPT}}$ and $C_{\text{LRF-OPT}}$

	$\alpha = 3$		$\alpha = 4$		$\alpha = 5$	
m	$B_{\text{LRF-OPT}}$	$C_{\text{LRF-OPT}}$	$B_{\text{LRF-OPT}}$	$C_{\text{LRF-OPT}}$	$B_{\text{LRF-OPT}}$	$C_{\text{LRF-OPT}}$
2	1.1547005	1.3333333	1.1885514	1.6790123	1.2141069	2.1728395
3	1.1858541	1.4062500	1.2382227	1.8984375	1.2806074	2.6894531
4	1.2165525	1.4800000	1.2568900	1.9856000	1.3012612	2.8672000
5	1.2360331	1.5277778	1.2893646	2.1435185	1.3286703	3.1165123
6	1.2453997	1.5510204	1.3018050	2.2061641	1.3496519	3.3180818
7	1.2593401	1.5859375	1.3116964	2.2568359	1.3585966	3.4069214
8	1.2636090	1.5967078	1.3236611	2.3191587	1.3675714	3.4978408
9	1.2727922	1.6200000	1.3284838	2.3446000	1.3781471	3.6073000
10	1.2771470	1.6311044	1.3351801	2.3802336	1.3833651	3.6622436

1.5.5   Numerical Data

In Table 1.5, we demonstrate numerical data for the performance bounds in Theorems 1.17 and 19. For each combination of $\alpha = 3, 4, 5$ and $m = 2, 3, \ldots,$ 10, we show $B_{\text{LS-OPT}}$ and $C_{\text{LS-OPT}}$.

In Table 1.6, we demonstrate numerical data for the performance bounds in Theorems 1.18 and 20. For each combination of $\alpha = 3, 4, 5$ and $m = 2, 3, \ldots, 10$, we show $B_{\text{LRF-OPT}}$ and $C_{\text{LRF-OPT}}$.

It is clear that algorithm LRF leads to improved performance compared with algorithm LS. Tighter performance bounds can be obtained by more involved analysis.

1.5.6   Simulation Results

In this section, we demonstrate some experimental data.

TABLE 1.7   Simulation Results for the Expected NSL^a

n	SRF-OPT	LS-OPT	LRF-OPT
30	1.0535521	1.0374620	1.0024673
40	1.0303964	1.0214030	1.0008078
50	1.0195906	1.0134978	1.0003326
60	1.0136363	1.0092786	1.0001669
70	1.0100516	1.0068138	1.0000894
80	1.0076977	1.0052356	1.0000527
90	1.0060781	1.0041218	1.0000335

^{a}99% confidence interval, $\pm0.058\%$.

For a post-power-determination algorithm A-OPT, where A is a list scheduling algorithm, the normalized schedule length is

$$\text{NSL}_{A-\text{OPT}} = \left(\frac{R_1^\alpha + R_2^\alpha + \cdots + R_m^\alpha}{m(R/m)^\alpha} \right)^{1/(\alpha-1)},$$

where $R_1, R_2, \ldots, R_n$ is a partition into m groups produced by algorithm A for n tasks. The normalized energy consumption is

$$\text{NEC}_{A-\text{OPT}} = \frac{R_1^\alpha + R_2^\alpha + \cdots + R_m^\alpha}{m(R/m)^\alpha}.$$

In Tables 1.7 and 1.8, we show our simulation results. For each combination of n and algorithm $A \in \{$ SRF-OPT, LS-OPT, LRF-OPT $\}$, we generate 5000 sets of n tasks, produce their schedules by using algorithm A, calculate their NSL_A (or NEC_A), and report the average of NSL_A (or NEC_A), which is the experimental value of $\overline{\text{NSL}_A}$ (or $\overline{\text{NEC}_A}$). The 99% confidence interval of all the data in the same table is also given. We observe the following facts:

- The performance of the three post-power-determination algorithms are ranked as SRF-OPT, LS-OPT, LRF-OPT, from the worst to the best.
- The post-power-determination algorithms perform better (as measured by $\overline{\text{NSL}_A}$ and $\overline{\text{NEC}_A}$) than the pre-power-determination algorithms, although there is no direct comparison among the performance bounds given in Theorems 1.9, 1.11, 1.13, 1.17, and 1.18, and the performance bounds given in Theorems 1.10, 1.12, 1.14, 1.19, and 1.20.

1.6   SUMMARY AND FURTHER RESEARCH

We have investigated nonpreemptive offline non-clairvoyant scheduling of independent sequential static tasks on a single computing system of homogeneous processors with continuous and unbounded and regular voltage/frequency/speed/power levels and without overheads for voltage/frequency/speed/power

TABLE 1.8   Simulation Results for the Expected NEC^a

n	SRF-OPT	LS-OPT	LRF-OPT
30	1.1102206	1.0765611	1.0051583
40	1.0619973	1.0427680	1.0016418
50	1.0395262	1.0268312	1.0006819
60	1.0274261	1.0187010	1.0003373
70	1.0201289	1.0136876	1.0001829
80	1.0154632	1.0104982	1.0001088
90	1.0122283	1.0082873	1.0000684

^{a}99% confidence interval, $\pm 0.117\%$.

adjustment and idle processors. We have developed and analyzed pre-power-determination and post-power-determination algorithms, which solve the problems of minimizing schedule length with energy consumption constraint and minimizing energy consumption with schedule length constraint. The performance of all our algorithms is compared with optimal solutions. It is found that the best algorithm among all our algorithms in this chapter is LRF-OPT, whose performance ratio is very close to optimal.

Possible further research can be directed toward precedence constrained tasks, parallel tasks, discrete and/or bounded voltage/frequency/speed/power levels, heterogeneous processors, and online scheduling. These extensions to our study in this chapter are likely to yield analytically tractable algorithms.

ACKNOWLEDGMENT

The materials presented in Sections 1.3 and 1.5 are based in part on the author's work in Reference 49.

REFERENCES

1. Available at http://www.top500.org/.
2. Available at http://en.wikipedia.org/wiki/Moore's_law.
3. Venkatachalam V, Franz M. Power reduction techniques for microprocessor systems. ACM Comput Surv 2005;37(3):195–237.
4. Srivastava MB, Chandrakasan AP, Rroderson RW. Predictive system shutdown and other architectural techniquesfor energy efficient programmable computation. IEEE Trans Very Large Scale Integr (VLSI) Syst 1996;4(1):42–55.
5. Gara MA, Blumrich D, Chen GL.-T, Chiu P, Coteus ME, et al. Overview of the Blue Gene/L system architecture. IBM J Res Dev 2005;49(2/3):195–212.
6. Feng W-C. The importance of being low power in high performance computing. CTWatch Quarterly; 2005;1(3), Los Alamos National Laboratory.
7. Available at http://www.foxnews.com/story/0,2933,479127,00.html.

8. Graham SL, Snir M, Patterson CA, editors. Getting up to speed: the future of super-computing. *Committee on the Future of Supercomputing*. National Research Council, National Academies Press; Washington, D.C. 2005.

9. Albers S. Energy-efficient algorithms. Commun ACM 2010;53(5):86–96.

10. Benini L, Bogliolo A, De Micheli G. A survey of design techniques for system-level dynamic power management. IEEE Trans Very Large Scale Integrat (VLSI) Syst 2000;8(3):299–316.

11. Unsal OS, Koren I. System-level power-aware design techniques in real-time systems. Proc IEEE 2003;91(7):1055–1069.

12. Available at http://www.green500.org/.

13. Available at http://techresearch.intel.com/articles/Tera-Scale/1449.htm.

14. Available at http://en.wikipedia.org/wiki/Dynamic/voltage/scaling.

15. Available at http://en.wikipedia.org/wiki/SpeedStep.

16. Available at http://en.wikipedia.org/wiki/LongHaul.

17. Available at http://en.wikipedia.org/wiki/LongRun.

18. Stan MR, Skadron K. Guest editors' introduction: power-aware computing. IEEE Comput 2003;36(12):35–38.

19. Weiser M, Welch B, Demers A, Shenker S. Scheduling for reduced CPU energy. In: Proceedings of the 1st USENIXSymposium on Operating Systems Design and Implementation; 1994. pp. 13–23, Monterey, California.

20. Yao F, Demers A, Shenker S. A scheduling model for reduced CPU energy. In: Proceedings of the 36thIEEE Symposium on Foundations of Computer Science; 1995. pp. 374–382, Milwaukee, Wisconsin.

21. Bansal N, Kimbrel T, Pruhs K. Dynamic speed scaling to manage energy and temperature. In: Proceedings of the 45th IEEE Symposium on Foundation of Computer Science; 2004. pp. 520–529, Rome, Italy.

22. Chan H-L, Chan W-T, Lam T-W, Lee L-K, Mak K-S, Wong PWH. Energy efficient online deadline scheduling. In: Proceedings of the 18th ACM-SIAM Symposium on Discrete Algorithms; 2007. pp. 795–804, New Orleans, Louisiana.

23. Kwon W-C, Kim T. Optimal voltage allocation techniques for dynamically variable voltage processors. ACM Trans Embedded Comput Syst 2005;4(1):211–230.

24. Li M, Liu BJ, Yao FF. Min-energy voltage allocation for tree-structured tasks. J Comb Optim 2006;11:305–319.

25. Li M, Yao AC, Yao FF. Discrete and continuous min-energy schedules for variable voltage processors. Proc Natl Acad Sci U S A 2006;103(11):3983–3987.

26. Li M, Yao FF. An efficient algorithm for computing optimal discrete voltage schedules. SIAM J Comput 2006;35(3):658–671.

27. Yun H-S, Kim J. On energy-optimal voltage scheduling for fixed-priority hard real-time systems. ACM Trans Embedded Comput Syst 2003;2(3):393–430.

28. Aydin H, Melhem R, Mossé D, Mejía-Alvarez P. Power-aware scheduling for periodic real-time tasks. IEEE Trans Comput 2004;53(5):584–600.

29. Hong I, Kirovski D, Qu G, Potkonjak M, Srivastava MB. Power optimization of variable-voltage core-based systems. IEEE Trans Comput Aided Des Integr Circ Syst 1999;18(12):1702–1714.

30. Im C, Ha S, Kim H. Dynamic voltage scheduling with buffers in low-power multimedia applications. ACM Trans Embedded Comput Syst 2004;3(4):686–705.

31. Krishna CM, Lee Y-H. Voltage-clock-scaling adaptive scheduling techniquesfor low power in hard real-time systems. IEEE Trans Comput 2003;52(12):1586–1593.

32. Lee Y-H, Krishna CM. Voltage-clock scaling for low energy consumption infixed-priority real-time systems. Real-Time Syst 2003;24(3):303–317.

33. Lorch JR, Smith AJ. PACE: a new approach to dynamic voltage scaling. IEEE Trans Comput 2004;53(7):856–869.

34. Mahapatra RN, Zhao W. An energy-efficient slack distribution techniquefor multimode distributed real-time embedded systems. IEEE Trans Parallel Distrib Syst 2005;16(7):650–662.

35. Quan G, Hu XS. Energy efficient DVS schedule for fixed-priority real-time systems. ACM Trans Embedded Comput Syst 2007;6(4):Article No. 29.

36. Shin D, Kim J. Power-aware scheduling of conditional task graphs in real-time multiprocessor systems. In: Proceedings of the International Symposium on Low Power Electronics and Design; Seoul, Korea; 2003. pp. 408–413.

37. Shin D, Kim J, Lee S. Intra-task voltage scheduling for low-energy hard real-time applications. IEEE Des Test Comput 2001;18(2):20–30.

38. Yang P, Wong C, Marchal P, Catthoor F, Desmet D, Verkest D, Lauwereins R. Energy-aware runtime scheduling for embedded-multiprocessor SOCs. IEEE Des Test Comput 2001;18(5):46–58.

39. Zhong X, Xu C-Z. Energy-aware modeling and scheduling for dynamic voltage scaling with statistical real-time guarantee. IEEE Trans Comput 2007;56(3):358–372.

40. Zhu D, Melhem R, Childers BR. Scheduling with dynamic voltage/speed adjustmentusing slack reclamation in multiprocessor real-time systems. IEEE Trans Parallel Distrib Syst 2003;14(7):686–700.

41. Zhu D, Mossé D, Melhem R. Power-aware scheduling for AND/OR graphs in real-time systems. IEEE Trans Parallel Distrib Syst 2004;15(9):849–864.

42. Zhuo J, Chakrabarti C. Energy-efficient dynamic task scheduling algorithms for DVS systems. ACM Trans Embedded Comput Syst 2008;7(2):Article No. 17.

43. Barnett JA. Dynamic task-level voltage scheduling optimizations. IEEE Trans Comput 2005;54(5):508–520.

44. Bunde DP. Power-aware scheduling for makespan and flow. In: Proceedings of the 18th ACM Symposium on Parallelism in Algorithms and Architectures; 2006. pp. 190–196, Cambridge, Massachusetts

45. Cho S, Melhem RG. On the interplay of parallelization, program performance, and energy consumption. IEEE Trans Parallel Distrib Syst 2010;21(3):342–353.

46. Khan SU, Ahmad I. A cooperative game theoretical technique for joint optimization of energy consumption and response time in computational grids. IEEE Trans Parallel Distrib Syst 2009;20(3):346–360.

47. Lee YC, Zomaya AY. Energy conscious scheduling for distributed computing systemsunder different operating conditions. IEEE Trans Parallel Distrib Syst. 2011;22(8):1374–1381

48. Rusu C, Melhem R, Mossé D. Maximizing the system value while satisfying time and energy constraints. In: Proceedings of the 23rd IEEE Real-Time Systems Symposium; 2002. pp. 256–265, Austin, Texas

49. Li K. Performance analysis of power-aware task scheduling algorithmson multiprocessor computers with dynamic voltage and speed. IEEE Trans Parallel Distrib Syst 2008;19(11):1484–1497.

50. Chandrakasan AP, Sheng S, Brodersen RW. Low-power CMOS digital design. IEEE J Solid-State Circ 1992;27(4):473–484.

51. Zhai B, Blaauw D, Sylvester D, Flautner K. Theoretical and practical limits of dynamic voltage scaling. In: Proceedings of the 41st Design Automation Conference; California, USA; 2004. pp. 868–873.

52. Intel, *Enhanced Intel SpeedStep Technology for the Intel Pentium M Processor—White Paper*, March 2004.

53. Qu G. What is the limit of energy saving by dynamic voltage scaling. In: Proceedings of the International Conference on Computer-Aided Design; 2001. pp. 560–563, San Jose, California

54. Garey MR, Johnson DS. *Computers and Intractability—A Guide to the Theory of NP-Completeness*. New York: W. H. Freeman; 1979.

55. Li K. Energy efficient scheduling of parallel tasks on multiprocessor computers. J Supercomput. 2012;60(2):223–247

56. Graham RL. Bounds on multiprocessing timing anomalies. SIAM J Appl Math 1969;2:416–429.

CHAPTER 2

POWER-AWARE HIGH PERFORMANCE COMPUTING

RONG GE and KIRK W. CAMERON

2.1 INTRODUCTION

High performance computing (HPC) is indispensable for scientific discovery and technological revolution. Today's HPC computers are able to perform peta (10^{15}) floating-point operations per second by using hundreds of thousands of processing units. Such unprecedented computational capability enables scientists to solve complex problems previously deemed intractable. With the aid of HPC systems, scientists are able to make breakthroughs in a wide spectrum of fields such as nanoscience, fusion, climate modeling, and astrophysics [1, 2].

Computational capability, albeit growing at a relatively healthy rate, still remains a bottleneck to the advances of many national and global priority grand challenge problems. Understanding and mitigating the effects of global warming require finer resolution simulation with regional details in more complex models. Facilitating regional adaption to climate variability and change needs 1000-fold increase to exaflop-scale (10^{18}) [3] in computing power. Nuclear energy science and engineering simulations also require similar computing power to create robust, predictive simulations that have quantifiable uncertainties for reactors over 40–60 year lifetime [4]. Ten exaflop-scale of computing power is necessary for computational simulations of highly efficient combustion design for transportation. To meet the demand of these applications, petascale computers will continue to increase in performance and exascale computers are expected to debut around 2018.

Power and energy are key challenges in future HPC systems, and they must be efficiently used for HPC to be affordable, scalable, and available. Large-scale computer systems have to use massive numbers of processing units for designed peak performance. Consequently, the power and energy consumption is huge.

Energy-Efficient Distributed Computing Systems, First Edition.
Edited by Albert Y. Zomaya and Young Choon Lee.
© 2012 John Wiley & Sons, Inc. Published 2012 by John Wiley & Sons, Inc.

For example, the Jaguar system at Oak Ridge Nation Laboratory that is ranked as the #1 supercomputer in the top 500 list in November 2009 contains 26,520 compute nodes and 224,162 cores, and delivers 1.76 petaflops at the expense of 7 MW of electrical power [5]. As a rule of thumb, 1 MW of power incurs $1 million energy bill and requires additional 1 MW of power in cooling. Powering and cooling Jaguar and another petascale system to be built by 2012 will cost Oakridge National Lab and University of Tennessee $33 million annually. An exascale computer could consist of ∼100 million of processor cores [6]. Even using today's *most* energy-efficient design such as PowerXCell architecture, the exascale computer will consume 1.3 GW of power. Such power consumption is unacceptable. *The practical power is limited around 20 MW*. At present, about 90% of the data center failures and unavailability are due to power outages. The larger power requirement for the future systems is certain to exacerbate data center failures and unavailability.

Energy-efficient HPC requires not only efficient hardware and system design but also aggressive runtime power management to adapt the power use to application demand. Without adaptive power allocation, the exascale systems with the most power-efficient design technology will be around 67 MW [6]. Runtime adaptive power allocation must be applied in order to reduce the system power to acceptable levels *with 20 MW*. With the adaptive power allocation, an application segment that demands very high floating-point operations and operates entirely out of registers can throttle/shut down memory or communication, and a different application segment that demands high DRAM bandwidth and relatively little floating-point operations can throttle down floating-point units.

Adaptive power allocation is challenging because it is employed at component level and on application segments. It requires fine-grain, detailed power and energy profiles of every system component, particularly the processing units, the memory and storage subsystems, and networking. Meanwhile, adaptive power allocation must not sacrifice performance for HPC applications, which in turn require in-depth understanding of the detailed interrelation between application performance and power consumption. Segment level performance quantification for the variety of HPC applications will be challenging, especially provided that their execution patterns vary with the underlying architecture and system scale.

We are in dire need of techniques for obtaining fine-grain, detailed power profiles of system components to identify best adaptive power allocations for energy efficiency. Most existing power profiling research is focused on a specific single computer component at microarchitecture level such as processor [7, 8], disk [9], memory [8], and networking interface [10] using simulation, direct measurement, and analytical estimation. Neither of these techniques can be adapted to all the components on the system nor can they be integrated easily to reveal the power profile of the entire system. Some have studied the power efficiency of parallel and distributed systems at the system or building level [11–13]. However, coarse grained power profiling is not particularly useful for determining exactly where and how power is consumed by an application and the individual components in a distributed system.

We are also in dire need of analytical models for quantifying and predicting the performance impact of adaptive power allocations. Most existing scalability models focus on the performance speedup from parallel processing. They are unable to capture the combined performance scalability at multiple dimensions, including system size, power modes of components, and affinity of processing units.

In this chapter, we introduce the models and techniques that are designed to meet these needs and enable adaptive power allocation for HPC systems and applications. Specifically, the models and techniques include the following:

- *PowerPack hardware/software toolkit* for fine-grain, detailed power profiling of multiple system components, synchronized with application segments in HPC systems.
- *Practical power and performance models* for quantifying the interrelation between application performance and power consumption on HPC systems capable of power adaptation.
- *Model-directed adaptive power allocation* for performance-constrained energy-efficient computing.

The rest of the chapter is organized as follows. Some background about current technology and power consumption are introduced in the next section. Section 2.4 presents the PowerPack tool for fine-grain power and energy profiling for HPC applications and systems. Section 2.5 presents the Power-Aware Speedup model for quantifying the performance impact of dynamic processor power allocation. Section 2.6 describe a model-directed design of adaptive power allocation. Section 2.7 concludes our work.

2.2 BACKGROUND

2.2.1 Current Hardware Technology and Power Consumption

2.2.1.1 Processor power. Complementary metal oxide semiconductor (CMOS) is a technology for constructing integrated circuits for computer components, including microprocessors, microcontrollers, and static RAM. The power consumption of silicon CMOS logic circuits [14] is approximated by

$$P = ACV^2f + P_{\text{short}} + P_{\text{leak}}. \tag{2.1}$$

The power consumption of CMOS logic consists of three components: dynamic power $P_{\text{d}} = ACV^2f$, which is caused by the charging and discharging of the capacitive load on each gate's output; short circuit power P_{short}, which is caused by the short-circuit current momentarily flowing within the cell; and leak power P_{leak}, which is caused by leakage current regardless of the gate's state. Here f is the operating frequency, A is the activity of the gates in the system (reduced activity corresponds to smaller A value), C is the total capacitance seen by the gate outputs, and V is the supply voltage. Dynamic power P_d dominates total power P, accounting for 70% or more on today's CMOS devices, P_{short} typically accounts for 10–30% and P_{leak} accounts for about 1% [15] of total P.[1]

The dominant dynamic power suggests three key strategies for power reduction on today's microprocessors and caches.

1. Using two processing units with a frequency f consumes less power compared with using a single processing unit with doubled frequency $2f$ for the same computational capacity. Multicore architecture follows this strategy. Multicore technology uses multiple slower, low power cores instead of faster single cores. At present, quad-core and hexa-core processors are commonplace on production high performance computing systems, and processors with tens to hundreds of cores have merged [19].

2. Reducing voltage and frequency can exponentially reduce power. Both low power design and power-aware dynamic voltage and frequency scaling (DVFS) technology follow this strategy. Low power processors such as PowerPC used in BlueGene systems run at low frequency. In contrast, high performance processors such as Intel Xeon and AMD Opteron run at high frequency with higher power consumption. A DVFS processor can be switched among several performance states, each determined by a pair of voltage and frequency. Normally, the frequency is proportional to the voltage, and scaling a processor to low frequency results in cubic power reduction on DVFS processors. DVFS technology is available on most commodity server processors. The performance states are normally controlled by operating systems or users.

3. Low activity consumes less power compared to high activity.

2.2.1.2 Memory subsystem power. DRAM is the mainstream memory technology used in HPC systems. Commodity DRAM devices have only recently begun to address power concerns as low power DRAM devices have become standard for applications in mobile phones and portable electronics [6].

To understand the DRAM device power consumption, it is necessary to understand the basic functionality of DRAM devices. DRAM devices have several operating states, including idle, refresh, precharge, active, read, and write. During the idle state the DRAM clock and input buffers are turned off. Refresh is periodically performed on the cells to keep information. In order to activate a bank with a row for reading or writing, the bank must first be charged. The charge is carried out by the precharge operation. The charge allows the chip to sense a particular row and amplify the signal from that row. The active operation presents bank and row addresses and causes a read of the wordline into a sense amplifier. Activating the row is also known as *opening* the row. Once the row has been activated or "opened", Read command is possible to that row by steering

---

[1]In the future, leakage power (P_{leak}) will grow in significance with continuing decreases in feature size and increases in processor frequency and reducing leakage power will also be important [16–18].

the data from the sense amplifiers, through registers and pipelines to the output. A write operation is similar to a read operation. It begins with precharge and then activate. The data to be written is driven into the cells by the sense amplifiers.

The power consumption of the memory subsystem varies with the states. The power consumption can be classified into three levels: background power, activation power, and read/write power. Background power is the base power consumed by the memory cells for storing data, and it is aggregated over idle, refresh, and precharging states. Activation power is the extra power consumed by addressing the row and copying the data to the sensor amplifier. Read/write power are the power consumption for steering the actual data from the sensor amplifier. The activation power and read/write power are normally larger than the background power.[2] Figure 2.1 shows the power consumption of a DDR3 [20].

The power breakdown on the commodity DRAM device suggests the following:

- Reducing the number of memory rows that are opened reduces power consumption of memory subsystem.
- Reducing the number of reads/writes *and* thus reducing power consumption.

Good memory locality reduces both activation and read/write power consumption.

2.2.2 Performance

Execution time T (or delay D for the same meaning) is the ultimate measure of performance for an application on a given system [21]. The execution time

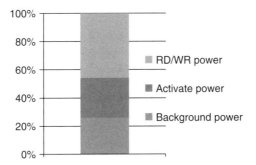

Figure 2.1 The memory subsystem power consumption of a commodity DRAM device. The power consumed by opening a row is a little more than background power. The read/write power dominates the power consumption of the memory subsystem.

---

[2]The numbers are extracted from Reference 20.

of an application is affected by CPU speed, memory hierarchy, and application execution pattern.

The sequential execution time $T(1)$ for a program on a single processor consists of two parts: the time that the processor is busy executing instructions T_{comp} and the time that the processor waits for data from the local memory system T_{mem} [22], that is,

$$T(1) = T_{comp}(1) + T_{mem}(1). \tag{2.2}$$

Memory access is expensive: the latency for a single memory access is equivalent to the time for the CPU to execute hundreds of instructions. Memory time T_{mem} can account for up to 50% of execution time for an application that hits the closest cache for 99% of the data accesses.

The parallel execution time on n processors $T(n)$ consists of additional items that are denoted as parallel overhead. Synchronization time, $T_{sync}(n)$, is due to load imbalance and serialization. Communication time, $T_{comm}(n)$, occurs when the processor is stalled waiting for a data transfer from or to a remote processing node. The time that the processor is busy executing extra work, $T_{extra}(n)$, is due to parallel data decomposition and task assignment. The parallel execution time is formalized as

$$T(n) = T_{comp}(n) + T_{mem}(n) + T_{sync}(n) + T_{comm}(n) + T_{extra}(n). \tag{2.3}$$

Parallel overhead, the sum of $T_{sync}(n)$, $T_{comm}(n)$, and $T_{extra}(n)$), is quite expensive. For example, the network communication time for a single piece of data can be as large as the computation time for thousands of instructions. Moreover, parallel overhead tends to increase with the number of processing nodes.

The ratio of sequential execution time to parallel execution time on n processors is the parallel speedup, that is,

$$\text{speedup}(n) = \frac{T(1)}{T(n)}. \tag{2.4}$$

Ideally, the speedup grows linearly with the number of processors for a fixed-size problem and is equal or close to n when n processors are used. However, the achieved speedup for real applications is typically sublinear due to parallel overhead.

2.2.3 Energy Efficiency

The energy (E) consumed by an application is the aggregated power over its execution time. Energy can be calculated as the product of the average power during its execution and the time interval between the starting time t_1 and finishing time $t_2 = t_1 + D$, where D is the delay:

$$E = \int_{t_1}^{t_2} P \, dt = P_{avg} \times (t_2 - t_1) = P_{avg} \times T. \tag{2.5}$$

Equation 2.5 suggests that energy reduction requires less execution time, smaller average power, or both.

Energy efficiency is measured by energy-delay product (e.g., $E \cdot D$ or $E \cdot D^2$) [23]. Lower numbers represent "better" efficiency.

2.3 RELATED WORK

We focus our discussion in three close related subareas: power profiling on large-scale systems, performance scalability on power-aware parallel systems, and adaptive power allocation for energy-efficient computing. Owing to the space limit, we limit our discussions in embedded systems [24] and mobile systems [25], even though these systems can share same techniques for energy efficiency.

2.3.1 Power Profiling

There are three primary approaches used to profile power of systems and components such as simulators, direct measurements, and performance-counter-based models.

2.3.1.1 *Simulator-based power estimation.* The power simulators are normally built on or used in conjunction with performance simulators. The performance simulators provide resource usage counts, while the power simulators estimate energy consumption using power models for the resources. Most of the power simulators are at architecture level and for single computer components such as processor, memory, disk, or interconnect. Few of them are at system level and estimate power consumption of software and applications.

Component Power Simulators. Several processor power simulators are available. These simulators are usually built on instruction-level performance simulators and add extra modules to performance simulator to estimate power consumption. Wattch [7] and SimplePower [8, 26] model the total processor power as the dominant dynamic power CMOS chips without considering leakage power and short-circuit power. These two simulators are based on SimpleScalar [27] performance simulator. PowerTimer [28] is a simplified version of Wattch for PowerPC processors. TEM2P2EST [29] and the Cai-Lim model [30] are also built on SimpleScalar [27] but models both dynamic and leakage power. Power simulators for other major computer components are also available. For example, DRAMSim [31] simulates the power consumption of DRAM system. Orion [10] simulates interconnection network power at the architectural level based on the performance simulator LSE [32]. Dempsey [33] simulates the power consumption of hard disk drives.

System Power Simulators. The system power simulators simulate the power consumption of applications or software. Softwatt [34] quantifies the power behavior of both the application and operating system based on SimOS [35]. Powerscope [36] samples system activity by periodically recording the program counter (PC) and process identifier (PID) of the currently executing process, collects and stores current, and then maps the energy to specific processes and procedures.

2.3.1.2   Direct measurements. Power can be directly measured both intrusively [37, 38] and nonintrusively. The intrusive measurements require inserting precision resistors into the power supply lines to components under study and use power meters to measure the voltage drop on the resistor. The current through the component is calculated by the voltage drop over the resistor divided by its resistance. The nonintrusive approach [39, 40] uses ammeters to measure the current flow of the power supply lines directly.

Tiwari et al. [40] use ammeters to measure the current drawn by a processor while running programs on an embedded system and develope a power model to estimate power cost. Isci and Martonosi [39] use ammeters to measure the power for P4 processors to derive their event-count-based power model. Bellosa et al. [37] derive CPU power by measuring current on a precision resistor inserted between the power line and supply for a Pentium II CPU; they use this power to validate their event-count-based power model and save energy. Joseph et al. [38] use precision resistor to measure power for a Pentium Pro processor. These approaches can be extended to measure single processor system power. Flinn et al. [41] use a multimeter to sample the current being drawn by a laptop from its external power source.

2.3.1.3   Event-based estimation. Most high-end CPUs have a set of hardware counters to count performance events such as cache hit/miss, and memory load. If power is mainly dissipated by these performance events, power can be estimated based on performance counters. Isci and Martonosi [39] develop a runtime power monitoring model that correlates performance event counts with CPU subunit power dissipation on real machines. CASTLE [38] does similar work on performance simulators (SimpleScalar) instead of real machines. Joule Watcher [37] also correlates power with performance events, the difference is that it measures the energy consumption for a single event, such as a floating-point operation and L2 cache access, and uses this energy consumption for energy-aware scheduling.

2.3.2   Performance Scalability on Power-Aware Systems

Parallel speedup models analytically describe how application performance scales with the number of concurrent computing processors. Such models often also indicate performance bound and limiting factors. Several models have been proposed [42–49], each focusing on a unique limiting factor. The first parallel speedup model is Amdahl's law [42]. Amdahl's Law states that speedup is limited by the fraction of the workload that cannot be computed in parallel. Amdahl's law is also known as *strong scaling*, as problem sizes under study will not change with the number of computing units. Later, Gustafson [45] argues that one tends to scale problem size, instead of keeping it constant, for accuracy when more computing units available, and thus proposes a fixed-time speedup model. It quantifies the ability to scale up workload with the number of computational nodes while maintaining the same execution time. As memory wall emerges as a limiting factor of performance, Sun and Ni [47] argue that the problem size can be scaled further in large memory systems to gain more speedup and increase simulation accuracy. They accordingly present a memory-bounded speedup model, where speedup is constrained by main memory size. While fixed-time speedup and memory-bounded speedup models study how to scale workload to gain parallel speedup and simulation accuracy, whereas isoefficiency metric proposed by Grama et al. [44] studies how to scale workload to obtain same parallel computing efficiency. These models are powerful in analyzing parallel performance and scalability in parallel computing but limited to conventional systems. They are problematic when used to analyze the performance effects of power mode on the emerging power-scalable systems. The analytical model proposed by Cho and Melhem [50] studies the interaction between parallelism and energy consumption. This model assumes that frequency scaling unanimously affects executions of any workload and thus cannot guide the design of adaptive power allocation.

2.3.3 Adaptive Power Allocation for Energy-Efficient Computing

Adaptive power allocation in HPC is premised by energy savings without performance impact for applications. Adaptive power allocation can be deployed at node level by consolidating the application to a few servers and shutting down unused nodes [51, 52]. Adaptive power allocation can also be deployed at the component level. At present, major computer components such as processor, disk, memory [53], and monitor accommodate Advanced Configuration and Power Interface (ACPI) components. These components have one or more active modes and several sleep modes. Usually the deeper sleep modes consume less power but require longer time to transit to active modes. These components can be put to sleep states to reduce power consumption when there are no user and no system accesses. Only processor has more than one active mode in production systems, while other components such as multiple-speed disks [54, 55] are studied in simulations. If the processor is designed with high performance, it is normally capable of DVFS and can be switched among several active performance states, each determined by a pair of frequency and voltage. If the processor is designed with low power, it is normally capable of clock gating. Clock gating does not change processor frequency. However, it prevents clock from propagating to portions of the circuitry, so that the flip-flops in the portion do not change state and their dynamic power consumption is zero.

Adaptive power allocation using DVFS is studied most on high performance systems for scientific computation. Experiments on real systems show that energy is more efficiently utilized by scaling processor to low power modes during its slack times, that is, communication [56–59], memory access [60, 61], load imbalance [62, 63], and their combinations [64, 65]. One difficulty in adapting processor power/performance is the identification of CPU slackness. One approach to address this difficulty is to profile the code execution and find out code regions with low processor utilization offline [56, 57, 66].

This static approach can provide optimal power reduction but requires pre-execution profiling and instrumentation. Another approach is to predict applications' CPU slack times based on history execution and schedule processor power modes at run time [64, 65, 67]. This approach is more desirable as it is transparent to applications. However, it requires characterizing the power requirements of code segments and execution patterns.

The other difficulty in adapting processor power is the identification of the target CPU frequency to guarantee performance. To solve this, we must know how exactly CPU frequency would affect performances of typical execution patterns and applications. Owing to the unavailability of such knowledge, previous work use assumptions and simplifications. For example, [59] assumes that the execution times of communication function calls do not vary with processor frequency. On the basis of this assumption, the target frequency during communication would be the lowest available processor frequency. Nevertheless, the execution times of communication function calls *do* vary with processor frequency [59], since there are still some computation involved, and consequently the designated target frequency results in underestimated performance loss.

To maximally save energy and minimally impact performance, we need models and techniques to understand power consumption and the interaction with performance. The following sections present the models and techniques for these purposes.

2.4 POWERPACK: FINE-GRAIN ENERGY PROFILING OF HPC APPLICATIONS

2.4.1 Design and Implementation of PowerPack

2.4.1.1 Overview. PowerPack is designed to address the need for fine-grained power/energy profiling on typical parallel and distributed systems (i.e., computer clusters). PowerPack comprises both hardware and software components. The hardware components include sensors, meters, circuits, and data acquisition devices that enable direct power measurement and instrumentation. The software components include drivers for various meters and sensors, and user-level APIs (application programming interfaces) for controlling power profiling and code synchronization. Together, these hardware and software components enable two unique features: (i) fine-grained component-level power measurement and (ii) automatic synchronization between power profiles and application code segments. At present, PowerPack is portable to any commodity-based cluster with a standard power supply (e.g., ATX, BTX), and any number or types of processors, disks, memory, and NICs (network interface cards). We are working on extending PowerPack to high density blade systems and accelerated blade systems.

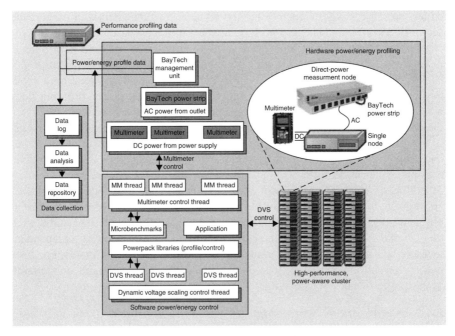

Figure 2.2   PowerPack overview.

Figure 2.2 shows a typical PowerPack deployment for power profiling on a high performance commodity-based cluster. PowerPack simultaneously measures power consumption of the entire system and constituent components. To obtain isolated component power, we tap a precision sensing resistor into each individual DC power line (explained in detail later in this section) and then measure the voltage difference at two ends of the resistor using a digital meter. All system DC power lines are measured simultaneously and used to derive component power according to a derived mapping between lines and components. To obtain total system power including AC/DC conversion, AC power is measured via an inline sensor device between the system power cable and the wall outlet. PowerPack supports various types of power sensors (or meters): (i) National Instruments data acquisition system such as Analog Input Module NI 9205NI and cDAQ chassis NI cDAQ9172 for DC power measurement; (ii) Watt's Up Pro power meter for AC power measurement; and (iii) ACPI-enabled power supply. The combination of DC and AC measurements allows us to capture and isolate total power usage, including inefficiencies in AC to DC conversion. This redundant set of measurements allows us to verify the accuracy of each technique.

The software contained in PowerPack serves two purposes: online data recording and postmortem data analysis. The online data recording components record meter readings and synchronize power profiling with code segments. PowerPack supports two types of synchronization methods. The first type uses client-server structures to synchronize power profiling with code segments, that is, the data collection servers poll the meters and record data; then the client API triggers the server to record data. The second type uses a timestamp-based approach to synchronize multiple data streams from various meters, sensors, and performance instruments. We note that the gathering of power profiling data is purposely "out-of-band," meaning the data is collected, collated, and analyzed on a separate computer (Fig. 2.1). Such measurement ensures that power profiling does not impact the system under test. Postmortem data analysis software processes the data and creates the power profiles of applications, systems, and components.

PowerPack directly measures one node at a time. To obtain in-depth power consumption of an entire cluster, we use a node remapping approach. Node remapping works as follows. Suppose we are running a parallel application on M nodes, we fix the measurement equipment to one physical node (e.g., node 1) and repeatedly run the same workload M times. Each time we map the tested physical node to a different virtual node. Since all slave nodes are identical (as they should be and we experimentally confirmed), we use the M independent measurements on one node to emulate one measurement on M nodes. For fine-grain analysis of a heterogeneous environment, we can instrument one version of each type of node for coverage.

2.4.1.2 Fine-grain systematic power measurement. PowerPack uses direct or derived measurements to isolate components within nodal power profiles. Specifically, we isolate CPU, memory, disk, motherboard, CPU fans, and system fans. Using combined AC and DC measurements, we can also isolate the power supply. The remaining components are treated as "others," which includes onboard video card, keyboard, onboard network adapter, etc. Our measurement approach is as follows: if a component is powered through individual pins, we measure power consumption through every pin and use the sum as the component power; if two or more components are powered through shared pins, we observe the changes on all pins while adding/removing components and running different micro-benchmarks to infer the mapping between components and pins.

In the following discussion, we use a 9-node cluster as the exemplar platform to detail the fine-grain power measurement for each component. Each node of the cluster is equipped with two dual-core AMD Opteron processors running at 1.8 GHz, six 1-GB SDRAM modules, one Western Digital WD800 SATA hard drive, one Tyan Thunder S2882 motherboard, two CPU fans, and two system fans. The dual-core dual-processor system was selected to further demonstrate the effectiveness of PowerPack for profiling dominant multicore architecture in HPC [28]. Unless explicitly stated, the measurement results in the succeeding sections are obtained at this system.

CPU Power. According to our experiments confirmed by the ATX power supply design guide, the four cores are powered through four +12 VDC pins. Thus, we can profile CPU power consumption by measuring all +12 VDC pins directly.

Disk Power. The disk is connected to a peripheral power connection independently and powered by one +12 VDC pin and one +5 VDC pin. By directly measuring both +12 VDC and +5 VDC pins, we can profile disk power consumption directly.

Memory Power. Memory modules are powered through four +5 VDC pins. The power consumption for memory is directly measured from these four pins. In previous work, we relied on a linear extrapolation technique to deduce memory power consumption. For systems where memory is not powered through dedicated pins, we recommend using our previous linear extrapolation techniques [25] to isolate memory power consumption.

Motherboard Power. NIC and other onboard components are powered through +3.3 VDA pins. It is challenging to separate NIC power consumption from other onboard components directly. However, our measurements indicate that the onboard NIC only consumes a minimal amount of power under maximum load. We have verified this by monitoring the total system power consumption changes under saturated network card bandwidth, and by consulting the documentation of the NIC. Thus, based on our empirical measurements, NIC power can be approximated with a constant value. For simplicity, the power consumption of other onboard components can be treated as constant too. This simplification can be further justified by the fact that compute nodes typically do not access onboard components such as the video card. In addition, dynamic power usage from the memory and processors far exceeds NIC and motherboard power consumption. At present, PowerPack isolates the energy use for CPU, memory, NIC, and disk. Profiling and analysis of other components, including PCI devices is left to future work.

CPU and System Fans. Integrating multiple cores into a single computing node demands more powerful cooling. In the system under test, there are two CPU fans, with one for each processor, and two system fans on each node of our dual-core dual-processor cluster. Each fan is powered by a +12 VDC pin and a +5 VDC pin.

2.4.1.3 *Automatic power profiling and code synchronization.* Once the manual instrumentation setup is complete, the process of obtaining and controlling power profiling is fully automated by software. In fact, the PowerPack software includes all the micro-benchmarks necessary to isolate power lines in the instrumented node. Additionally, all the experimental data gathered herein are obtained remotely via local intranet. In this section, we describe the software components of PowerPack that automate the entire profiling process and correlate the power profiles with application source code. PowerPack provides a suite of API calls for the application to control and communicate with a meter control process.

The structure of the profiling software is shown in Figure 2.3, in which the data collection computer executes a meter control thread and a group of meters read threads where each meter read thread corresponds to one digital meter. The meter read threads collect readings from the meters and send them to the meter control thread. The meter control thread monitors messages from applications running on the cluster and modifies shared variables of the meter read threads according to the messages received.

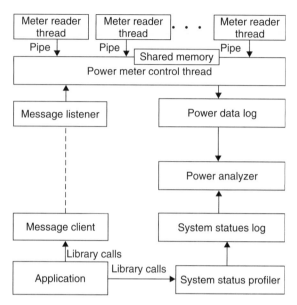

Figure 2.3 Software architecture for automatic power and energy profiling. Our software automates the process of profiling power data and correlating the results to source code in a distributed system. Through modular design, the system software is portable to different systems, meters, etc.

To synchronize the live power profiling process with the running application, profiled applications trigger message operations through a set of user-level APIs or library calls informing the meter control thread to take corresponding actions to annotate the power profile. Thus, by inserting the power profile API pmeter_ start_session and pmeter_end_session before and after the code region of interest, we are able to map the power profile to the source code. In Figure 2.4, we list a commonly used subset of the power profile API in PowerPack.

```
//connect to meter control thread
pmeter_init ( char *ip_address, int *port);

//set power profile log file and options
pmeter_log (char *log_file, int *option );

//start a new profile session and label it
pmeter_start_session ( char *session_label );

//stop current profile session
pmeter_end_seesion ( );

//disconnect from the meter control thread
pmeter_finalize( );
```

Figure 2.4   The commonly used PowerPack power meter profile API.

PowerPack also supports commercial data acquisition software such as the NI LabView system that only has GUI (graphic user interface) and is triggered by human input. Instead of implementing drivers for this meter, we record time-stamped data samples coming from the NI cDAQ9172 chassis with user configured LabView modules, then align and merge these samples with other data sources using time information.

2.4.2   Power Profiles of HPC Applications and Systems

2.4.2.1   *Power distribution over components.* We begin our analysis with
system-wide power distribution for sequential applications on a single compute node. Figure 2.5 shows the snapshots of power distribution under two kinds of scenarios—case 1: no user application is running on the system; and case 2: the system is running one of the three applications from the SPEC CPU 2000 benchmark suite cite (164.gzip and 171.swim) and the Linux standard file copy command (cp) programs. These three benchmarks are computation intensive (164.gzip), memory access intensive (171.swim), and disk access intensive (cp), respectively. Compared against idle system, their power profiles reveal how components' power changes when one computing component is stressed. For case 2, the system is running four instances of the same program such that each

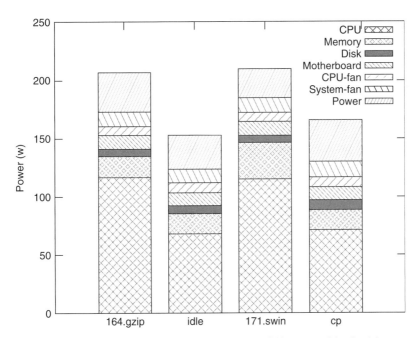

Figure 2.5   Power distribution for a single node under different workloads: (a) zero user workload or idle; (b) CPU bounded workload 164.zip; (c) memory-bounded workload 171.swim; and (d) disk bounded workload cp.

of the four cores simultaneously executes one copy of the application and the load is symmetric. We obtain the following observations from Figure 2.5:

1. Since different workloads stress different components, both system power and individual component power vary with workload. Component usage is also reflected in the power profile.
2. The system power under zero user workload (152.2 W) is more than 72.9% of the total system power under load. Reducing power consumption of the power supply and fans could save significant energy. We note that cheap, inefficient power supplies are typical in clusters that use commodity parts. Power supplies traditionally account for less than 2% of the acquisition budget of a server node. Improving power supply and fan efficiencies is important but well beyond the scope of our work.
3. When the system is under load, CPU power dominates (e.g., for 164.gzip, CPU power is 56% of system power). However, depending on the workload characteristics, disk and memory may also be significant consumers of the total power budget. The components that dominate the power budget in a system should be the first targets of optimizations for power and energy reduction.

2.4.2.2 *Power dynamics of applications.*

As a case study and proof of concept, we profile the power and energy consumption of the NAS FT benchmark on our cluster using the PowerPack framework. We measured CPU, memory, disk, CPU fan, and motherboard power consumption over time for different benchmarks running on different numbers of compute nodes. The FT benchmark exhibits obvious alternating computation phase, memory phase, and communication phase. Therefore, its power profile reveals how components' power change with execution phases for a single application. In particular, the FT benchmark begins with a warm up phase and an initialization phase followed by a certain number of iterations. Each iteration consists of computation (fft), memory access (matrix transpose), all-to-all communication, memory access, computation, and a reduced communication. In Figure 2.6, we plot the power profiles of the NPB FT benchmark with problem size B during 1 iteration when running on 16 cores of 4 nodes. The illustrated power profiles of a parallel application are for one of the computing nodes unless explicitly stated otherwise.

The CPU power consumption varies from 119 W in the computation function (cffts-1) to 72 W in all-to-all communication intensive function (mpi_all-to-all). The memory power consumption varies from 28 W in the memory-intensive function (transpose_local) to 18 W in communication functions. The power profiles of CPU and memory are interrelated: when memory power increases, CPU power typically decreases and vice versa. We also observe fairly constant power consumption for the disk since the FT benchmark requires few disk accesses. The power consumed by the motherboard (NIC + other chipset components) and fans (CPU and system fans) is constant. For simplification, we will not discuss the

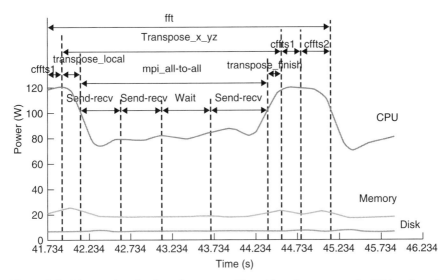

Figure 2.6 The synchronization of power profiles with code segments for FT benchmark with Class B, 16 processes on 4 nodes. The synchronization allows us to perform detailed power-efficiency analysis on selected code segments and identify application segments and components for power-performance optimization.

disk, motherboard, and fans power consumption in succeeding discussions since none of the benchmarks under study task the disk extensively, and we observe motherboard and fan power consumption varies little across applications.

The fine-grain power profiles are useful for identifying application segments and corresponding components for power reduction. For example, the CPU still consumes almost 41% of its peak power during sending and receiving communications. This is likely due to spin locks running on the processor while blocked waiting for a data transmission.

2.4.2.3 Power bounds on HPC systems. The HPC Challenge (HPCC) benchmark [6] is a benchmark suite that aims to evaluate the performance of HPC architectures from multiple aspects and to explore the performance boundaries of current systems. HPCC organizes the benchmarks into four categories; each category represents a type of memory access pattern characterized by the benchmark's memory access spatial and temporal locality. Currently, HPCC consists of seven benchmarks: HPL, STREAM, RandomAccess, PTRANS, FFTE, DGEMM, and b_eff Latency/Bandwidth. In this work, we use PowerPack to explore the critical power aspects of a system corresponding to HPCC performance bounds.

A single HPCC run tests eight benchmark tests in a sequence as follows: (i) Global PTRANS, (ii) Global HPL, (iii) Star DGEMM + Local DGEMM, (iv) Star STREAM, (v) Global MPI RandomAccess, (vi) Star RandomAccess, (vii) Local RandomAccess, and (viii) Global MPI FFT, Star FFT, Local FFT,

and Latency/Bandwidth. Figure 2.7 shows one power profile of the HPCC benchmarks with a problem size where HPL achieves its maximum performance on two
nodes. Power consumption is tracked for major computing components including CPU, memory, disk, and motherboard. The power profile is unique of each
application. These four components capture nearly all the dynamic power usage
of the system that is dependent on the application. From the data, we observe
the following:

1. Each test in the benchmark suite stresses processor and memory power
   relative to their use. For example, as Global HPL and Star DGEMM have
   high temporal and spatial locality, they spend little time waiting on data
   and stress the processor's floating-point execution units intensively and
   consume more processor power than other tests. In contrast, Global MPI
   RandomAccess has low temporal and spatial memory access locality, thus
   this test consumes less processor power because of more memory access
   delay, and more memory power because of cache misses.

2. Changes in processor and memory power profiles correspond to communication to computation ratios. Power variation patterns are similar for global
   tests such as PTRAN, HPL, and MPI_FFT because of similarities in their

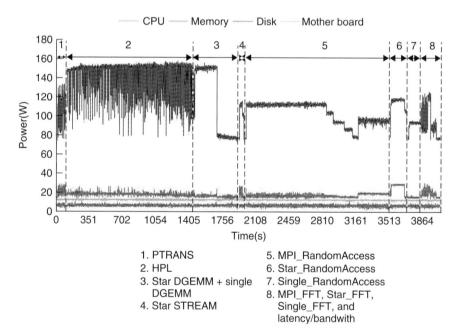

Figure 2.7   A snapshot of the HPCC power profile when running a full HPCC benchmark
suite using eight cores. The single run of HPCC consists of seven micro-benchmark tests
in order as follows: (1) PTRANS, (2) HPL, (3) Star DGEMM + single DGEMM, (4) Star
STREAM, (5) MPI_RandomAccess, (6) Star_RandomAccess, (7) Single_RandomAccess,
and (8) MPI_FFT, Star_FFT, single FFT, and latency/bandwidth.

computation and communication phases. For example, HPL computation phases run 50 W higher than its communication phases. Processor power does not vary as much during STAR (embarrassingly parallel) and LOCAL (sequential) tests because of limited processing variability in the code running on each core. In GLOBAL modes, memory power varies but total power doesn't change much since memory power is substantially less than processor power on the system under test.

3. Disk power and motherboard power are relatively stable over all tests in the benchmarks. None of the HPCC benchmarks stresses local disks heavily. Thus, power variations due to disk accesses are not substantial. On this system, the NIC, and thus its power consumption, is integrated in the motherboard. Nonetheless, communication using the gigabit Ethernet card does not result in significant power use under even the most intensive communication phases.

4. Processors consume more power during GLOBAL and STAR tests since they use all processor cores in the computation. LOCAL tests use only one core per node and thus consume less energy.

2.4.2.4 *Power versus dynamic voltage and frequency scaling.*

At present, many distributed systems have various power modes available to conserve energy. For example, typical AMD Opteron and Intel Xeon processors can scale power through changing a frequency and voltage pair; this technique is referred as *dynamic voltage and frequency scaling* (DVFS). The power consumption on such processors typically changes significantly with frequency [22].

DVFS has been used for power reduction and energy conservation in high performance distributed systems [7, 15, 16, 18, 19, 23] by scaling down processor frequency during processor slackness, or when slower processor speed does not impact performance significantly. Our intention in this work is to demonstrate the insight that PowerPack provides to quantitatively explain the power-performance efficiency and energy conservation of applications using DVFS. The AMD Opteron processors on our experimental cluster have two publicly available (i.e., exposed) frequencies 1000 and 1800 MHz.

Figure 2.8 shows the profiles of FT with two different processor frequencies. The impact of voltage and frequency scaling varies with computation, memory, and communication phases. When scaling down processor frequency from 1800 to 1000 MHz, the CPU power drops about 40 W from 124 W to 84 W during computation phases, and drops about 22 W from around 82 W to 60 W during communication phases. Although not shown, processor power consumption with a fixed frequency is larger during communications than during idle time (no user applications running), indicating there are some computations involved during communications. CPU frequency scaling also impacts the memory access pattern and memory power consumption for FT; the memory power profile of FT fluctuates more at 1000 MHz than at 1800 MHz. Meanwhile, scaling down processor

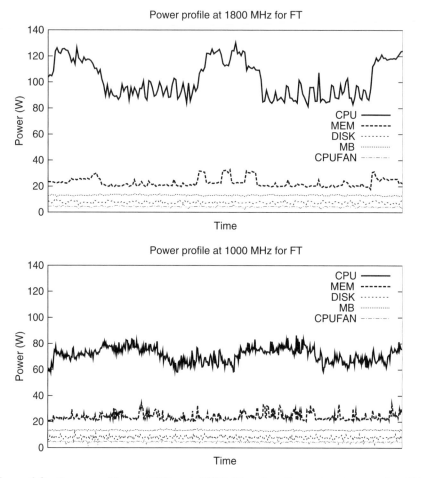

Figure 2.8 Power profiles at 1800 and 1000 MHz when the system is executing FT. When CPU frequency decreases from 1800 MHz to 1000 Hz, CPU power consumption decreases from about 110 W to about 69 W, and power consumption of other components is unchanged.

frequency slightly increases the execution time of FT because of a large portion of communication, which execution time nearly changes with frequency. Despite the overall execution time increases, scaling down CPU frequency conserves energy for FT.

The power profiles under various voltages and frequencies indicate that adapting the CPU frequency to meet the different computation needs during various execution phases for an application such as FT would achieve the best combination of energy and performance. Specifically, if we scale up CPU frequency to its maximum during computation and scale down CPU frequency during memory and communication, we can potentially save energy with negligible impact on execution time. Figure 2.9 shows the resulting power profiling of an intelligent scheduling following this idea. In this scheduling, the CPU frequency is set to 1800 MHz during computation- and memory-intensive phases, and 1200 MHz during communication phases. As we can see, the power consumption during communications with intelligent scheduling is about 30 W lower than that with fixed 1800 MHz, and the execution times are similar. Overall, this scheduling achieves 12.1% energy savings with 1.2% performance impact.

2.5   POWER-AWARE SPEEDUP MODEL

In this section, we introduce an analytical model to formalize the interacting performance effects of parallel computing and frequency scaling on power-aware parallel systems. We will also demonstrate the model usage in predicting application performance and scalability and guiding the design of adaptive processor power allocation for energy efficiency.

2.5.1   Power-Aware Speedup

We propose *power-aware speedup* and denote it as

$$S_N(w, f) = \frac{T_1(w, f_0)}{T_N(w, f)}, \tag{2.6}$$

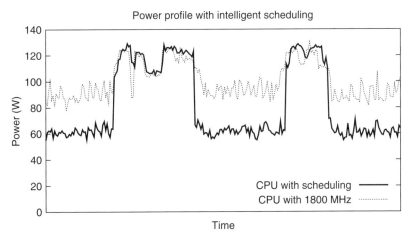

Figure 2.9 Profiles of FT when intelligent DVFS scheduling is employed. Compared to the profiles when CPU is fixed at 1800 MHz, the power consumption during communication drops about 30 W with minimal increase in execution time.

where

> S, the *speedup* gained from scaling of processor count N and frequency f for an application execution on power-aware parallel systems;
>
> w, the *workload* or total amount of work (in instructions or computations);
>
> f, the clock *frequency* in clock cycles per second, and f_0 is the base frequency;
>
> $T_1(w, f)$, the *sequential execution time* or the amount of time to complete workload w on 1 processor with frequency f; and
>
> $T_N(w, f)$, the *parallel execution time* or the amount of time to complete workload w on N processors with frequency f.

Power-aware speedup is the ratio of sequential execution time for a workload w and base frequency f_0 on 1 processor to the parallel execution time for the workload and frequency f on N processors.

Given this definition, next we detail the additional equations necessary to quantify the execution times of Equation 2.6. We will use the terms defined by Equation 2.6 and introduce definitions as needed to understand each derivation step and then use the defined terms to express equations that build on one another. By the end, the equations will be quite large, but our hope is that the fundamental concepts remain straightforward.

2.5.1.1 Sequential execution time for a single workload $T_1(w, f)$.

CPI: the average number of clock *cycles per workload*.

Using this definition and others from Equation 2.6, we define sequential execution time as

$$T_1(w, f) = w \frac{\text{CPI}}{f}. \tag{2.7}$$

This is a variant of the CPU performance equation [22]. The time to execute a program on 1 processor is the product of the workload w and the rate at which workloads execute CPI/f or seconds per workload. For now, we assume that f is a fixed value, noting that $T_1(w, f)$ depends on the processor frequency.

2.5.1.2 Sequential execution time for an ON-chip/OFF-chip workload.

$T_1(w^{\text{ON}}, f^{\text{ON}})$, $T_1(w^{\text{OFF}}, f^{\text{OFF}})$

> w^{ON}, ON-chip *workload*, or all workloads that do not require data residing OFF-chip at the time of execution,
>
> w^{OFF}, OFF-chip *workload*, or all workloads that require OFF-chip data accesses at the time of execution,

f^{ON}, ON-chip *clock frequency* in clock cycles per second. Affected by processor DVFS,

f^{OFF}, OFF-chip *clock frequency* in clock cycles per second. Not affected by processor DVFS, and

CPI^{ON}, CPI^{OFF}, the average number of clock cycles per ON-chip (CPI^{ON}) or OFF-chip (CPI^{OFF}) workload.

Other work [60, 68] has shown that a given workload w can be divided into ON-chip w^{ON} workload and OFF-chip w^{OFF} workload. Under these constraints, the total amount of work (in instructions or computations) is given as $w = w^{\text{ON}} + w^{\text{OFF}}$. We can modify our simple representation of sequential execution time[3] as

$$T_1(w, f) = T_1(w^{\text{ON}}, f^{\text{ON}}) + T_1(w^{\text{OFF}}, f^{\text{OFF}}) = w^{\text{ON}}\frac{\text{CPI}^{\text{ON}}}{f^{\text{ON}}} + w^{\text{OFF}}\frac{\text{CPI}^{\text{OFF}}}{f^{\text{OFF}}}.$$
$$(2.8)$$

Assuming that ON-chip and OFF-chip frequencies are equal ($f^{\text{ON}} = f^{\text{OFF}}$) and $\text{CPI} = \frac{(\text{CPI}^{\text{ON}}+\text{CPI}^{\text{OFF}})}{2}$, this equation reduces to Equation 2.7. We observe that generally for ON-chip and OFF-chip workloads $f^{\text{ON}} \neq f^{\text{OFF}}$, meaning CPU and memory bus frequencies differ, and $\text{CPI}^{\text{OFF}} \neq \text{CPI}^{\text{OFF}}$, meaning the workload throughput is different for ON- and OFF-chip workloads.

2.5.1.3 Parallel execution time on N processors for an ON-/OFF-chip workload with DOP = i. $T_N(w_i{}^{\text{ON}})$, $T_N(w_i{}^{\text{OFF}})$

where

i, the *degree of parallelism* or DOP defined as the maximum number of processors that can be busy computing a workload for an observation period given an unbounded number of processors;

m, the *maximum DOP* for a given workload;

w_i, the amount of work (in instructions or computations) with DOP $= i$;

$w_i{}^{\text{ON}}$, the number of ON-chip workloads with DOP $= i$;

$w_i{}^{\text{OFF}}$, the number of OFF-chip workloads with $DOP = i$;

N, the *number of homogeneous processors* available for computing the workloads;

w_{PO}, the *parallel overhead workload* due to extra work for communication, synchronization, etc.;

$T(w_{\text{PO}}, f)$: the *execution time* for parallel overhead w_{PO} for frequency f;

---

[3]This does not account for out-of-order execution and overlap between memory access and computation, simplifying the discussion for now.

$T_N(w, f)$: the *parallel execution time* or the amount of time to complete workload w on N processors for frequency f.

The total amount of work (in instructions or computations) is given as $w = \sum_{1 \le i \le m}(w_i^{\text{ON}} + w_i^{\text{OFF}})$, where $1 \le i \le m$. Thus,

$$T_N(w_i, f) = T_N(w_i^{\text{ON}}, f^{\text{ON}}) + T_N(w_i^{\text{OFF}}, f^{\text{OFF}})$$
$$= \frac{w_i^{\text{ON}}}{i} \cdot \frac{\text{CPI}^{\text{ON}}}{f^{\text{ON}}} + \frac{w_i^{\text{OFF}}}{i} \cdot \frac{\text{CPI}^{\text{OFF}}}{f^{\text{OFF}}}, \qquad (2.9)$$

where $(m \le N)$.[4] Next, we include the additional execution time $T(w_{\text{PO}}, f)$ for parallel overhead. We assume parallel overhead workload cannot be parallelized, but that it is divisible into ON-chip ($w_{\text{PO}}^{\text{ON}}$) and OFF-chip ($w_{\text{PO}}^{\text{OFF}}$) workloads. Thus,

$$T_N(w, f) = \sum_{i=1}^{m}\left(T_N(w_i^{\text{ON}}, f^{\text{ON}}) + T_N(w_i^{\text{OFF}}, f^{\text{OFF}})\right) + T(w_{\text{PO}}, f) \qquad (2.10)$$

and

$$T_N(w, f) = \sum_{i=1}^{m}\left(\frac{w_i^{\text{ON}}}{i} \cdot \frac{\text{CPI}^{\text{ON}}}{f^{\text{ON}}} + \frac{w_i^{\text{OFF}}}{i} \cdot \frac{\text{CPI}^{\text{OFF}}}{f^{\text{OFF}}}\right)$$
$$+ \left(T_N(w_{\text{PO}}^{\text{ON}}, f^{\text{ON}}) + T_N(w_{\text{PO}}^{\text{OFF}}, f^{\text{OFF}})\right). \qquad (2.11)$$

2.5.1.4 *Power-aware speedup for DOP and ON-/OFF-chip workloads.* $S_N(w, f)$.

f_0^{ON}: the lowest available ON-chip frequency.

$S_N(w, f)$: the ratio of sequential execution time $T_1(w, f_0)$ to parallel execution time $T_N(w, f)$.

On power-aware parallel systems, ON-chip frequency f^{ON} may change because of DVFS scheduling of the processor. As a consequence, power-aware speedup has two key variables: ON-chip clock frequency (f^{ON}) and the number of available processors (N) computing workload w. Speedup is computed relative to the sequential execution time to complete workload w on 1 processor

---

[4]Strictly speaking, this limitation is not required. For $M > N$, we can add an $\lceil i/N \rceil$ term to Equation 2.9 and succeeding equations to limit achievable speedup to the number of available processors, N. We omit this term to simplify the discussion and resulting formulae.

at the lowest available ON-chip frequency, f_0^{ON}. Power-aware speedup is defined using Equations 2.8 and 2.11 as

$$S_N(w, f) = \frac{T_1(w, f_0)}{T_N(w, f)} = \left[w^{ON} \frac{CPI^{ON}}{f_0^{ON}} + w^{OFF} \frac{CPI^{OFF}}{f^{OFF}} \right] \Bigg/$$

$$\left[\sum_{i=1}^{m} \left(\frac{w_i^{ON}}{i} \cdot \frac{CPI^{ON}}{f^{ON}} + \frac{w_i^{OFF}}{i} \cdot \frac{CPI^{OFF}}{f^{OFF}} \right) \right.$$

$$\left. + (T_N(w_{PO}^{ON}, f^{ON}) + T_N(w_{PO}^{OFF}, f^{OFF})) \right]. \qquad (2.12)$$

Equation 2.12 illustrates how to calculate power-aware speedup. For a more intuitive description, assume the workload is broken into a serial portion w_1 and a perfect parallelizable portion w_N such that $w = w_1 + w_N$, $N = m$, and $w_i = 0$ for $i \neq 1$, $i \neq m$. Then, allowing for flexibility in our execution time notation, we can express the power-aware speedup under these conditions as

$$S_N(w, f) = \left[T_1(w^{ON}, f_0^{ON}) + T_1(w^{OFF}, f^{OFF}) \right] \Bigg/$$

$$\left[\left[T_N(w_1^{ON}, f^{ON}) + T_N(w_1^{OFF}, f^{OFF}) \right] + \left[T_N(w_N^{ON}, f^{ON}) + T_N(w_N^{OFF}, f^{OFF}) \right] \right.$$

$$\left. + \left[T_N(w_{PO}^{ON}, f^{ON}) + T_N(w_{PO}^{OFF}, f^{OFF}) \right] \right].$$

$$(2.13)$$

Here, $T_1(w^{ON}, f_0^{ON}) + T_1(w^{OFF}, f^{OFF})$ is the base line sequential execution time when neither of parallel computing and frequency scaling is applied. $T_N(w_1^{ON}, f^{ON})$ is the sequential portion of the workload affected by CPU frequency scaling but not affected by parallelism. $T_N(w_1^{OFF}, f^{OFF})$ is the sequential portion of the workload not affected by CPU frequency scaling or parallelism. $T_N(w_N^{ON}, f^{ON})$ is the parallelizable portion of the workload, also affected by CPU frequency. $T_N(w_N^{OFF}, f^{OFF})$ is the parallelizable portion of the workload not affected by CPU frequency. $T_N(w_{PO}^{ON}, f^{ON})$ is the parallel overhead affected by CPU frequency. $T_N(w_{PO}^{OFF}, f^{OFF})$ is the parallel overhead not affected by CPU frequency.

2.5.2 Model Parametrization and Validation

In the previous section, we have focussed on analytical modeling of simultaneous speedup of parallelism and frequency scaling. In this section, we present methodologies to derive model parameters and apply the model to real applications on power-scalable clusters to examine its correctness and accuracy. We first present a coarse-grain parametrization method that estimates simultaneous speedup of frequency scaling and parallelism using their individual speedups, and then present a fine-grain parametrization that estimates speedup using detailed application and system profiles.

2.5.2.1   Coarse-grain parametrization and validation.

Parametrization. The idea of this coarse-grain parametrization is using speedups from each individual enhancement for an application to estimate their interactions and the overall speedup. Specifically, we first obtain the speedups solely from frequency scaling while processor count is fixed at 1. Second, we obtain the speedups solely from parallel computing while the processor frequency is fixed at base frequency, and further use this information to derive parallel overhead. Third, we estimate the effects of frequency scaling on parallel overhead. Finally, we use the obtained information to estimate the performances and speedups if both enhancements are applied. For this parametrization method, we make two assumptions.

Assumption 2.1   A majority of the workload can be completely parallelized, such that $w = \sum_{i=1}^{m} w_i = w_N$, where $N = m$ and $w_i = 0$ for $i \neq m$. Under this assumption,[5] sequential execution time $T_1(w, f)$ in Equation 2.8 is simplified as

$$T_1(w, f) = \left[T_1(w_N^{ON}, f^{ON}) + T_1(w_N^{OFF}, f^{OFF}) \right]$$

$$= w_N^{ON} \cdot \frac{CPI^{ON}}{f^{ON}} + w_N^{OFF} \cdot \frac{CPI^{OFF}}{f^{OFF}}. \qquad (2.14)$$

Parallel execution time $T_N(w, f)$ in Equation 2.11 is simplified as

$$T_N(w, f) = \left[T_N(w_N^{ON}, f^{ON}) + T_N(w_N^{OFF}, f^{OFF}) \right]$$
$$+ \left[T(w_{PO}^{ON}, f^{ON}) + T(w_{PO}^{OFF}, f^{OFF}) \right]$$
$$= \frac{T_1(w, f)}{N} + \left[T_N(w_{PO}^{ON}, f^{ON}) + T_N(w_{PO}^{OFF}, f^{OFF}) \right]. \qquad (2.15)$$

Assumption 2.2   Parallel overhead is not affected by ON-chip frequency [48], that is, $w_{PO}^{ON} = 0$. Under Assumption 2, Equation 2.15 reduces to

$$T_N(w, f) = \frac{T_1(w, f)}{N} + T_N(w_{PO}^{OFF}, f^{OFF}). \qquad (2.16)$$

Equation 2.16 holds for all the available processor frequencies. Our coarse-grain parametrization method focuses on this equation and uses several steps to derive its parameters for performance prediction.

---

[5]Most speedup models are calculated only analytically. Thus, it is common to make the assumption that $w = w_1 + w_N$. In practice, speedup analysis focuses solely on the parallelizable portion of the code and w_1 is considered negligible. We follow this common practice, though we are exploring ways to measure w_1 directly.

Step 1. Measure the sequential execution time at base frequency $T_1(w, f_0)$ and parallel execution time at ON-chip base frequency $T_N(w, f_0^{ON})$ for each available processor count.

Step 2. Derive the parallel overhead time using the measured times from Step 1 and Equation 2.16 such that the parallel overhead $T(w_{PO}^{OFF}, f^{OFF})$ for a processor count N is

$$T(w_{PO}^{OFF}, f^{OFF}) = T_N(w, f_0^{ON}) - \frac{T_1(w, f_0^{ON})}{N}. \tag{2.17}$$

Step 3. Measure the workload sequential execution time $T_1(w, f)$ for each available frequency f when processor count is fixed at 1.

Step 4. Use the derived parallel overhead in Step 2 and measured sequential execution time from Step 3 to predict the parallel execution time $T_N(w, f)$ for any given combination of processor count $N > 1$ and frequency $f > f_0^{ON}$.

$$T_N(w, f) = \frac{T_1(w, f)}{N} + T_N(w_{PO}^{OFF}, f^{OFF}) = \frac{T_1(w, f)}{N}$$
$$+ \left[T_N(w, f_0^{ON}) - \frac{T_1(w, f_0^{ON})}{N} \right]. \tag{2.18}$$

Validation. We apply the proposed power-aware speedup model and coarse-gain parametrization method to predict the overall speedup for FT from simultaneous scaling of processor count and frequency. The power-aware cluster is the same one for evaluating extended Amdahl's law. The cluster consists of 16 computer nodes, where the processor on each node can be scheduled among five frequencies from 600 to 1400 MHz with 200 MHz increment. Table 2.1 shows that prediction errors for FT are less than 3% using our model, compared to as large as 72% using extended Amdahl's Law. With these results, our assumptions

TABLE 2.1 Performance Prediction Using Power-Aware Speedup Model and Coarse-Grain Parametrization on a Power-Scalable Cluster

N	Frequency, MHz				
	600, %	800, %	1000, %	1200, %	1400, %
1	0	0	0	0	0
2	0	0.2	0.2	0.2	0.3
4	0	0	0.1	0.1	0.2
8	0	0.4	2.0	1.2	0.7
16	0	2.1	2.2	2.3	1.4

Each table entry is the prediction error of speedup from a combination of processor frequency and processor count using coarse-grain parametrization against the measured speedup. A processor frequency 600 MHz and processor count 1 are used as the basis for comparison. Their values show no error since they are measured values exemplifying individual speedups from parallelism and frequency scaling.

appear reasonable. In fact, this is a very practical means of predicting application performance and power-aware speedup. Nonetheless, there are drawbacks to this approach. First, this technique requires several measurements of the sequential $T_1(w, f)$ and parallel $T_N(w, f_0^{ON})$ execution times. Second, this technique does not quantitatively separate ON-chip and OFF-chip workloads. Thus, the effects of frequency scaling are accounted for but inseparable from the execution time. Third, the assumptions are the root cause of observable error: assuming that perfect parallelizable workload overestimates the returns of parallel computing; and assuming that frequency-independent parallel overhead underestimates the returns of frequency scaling.

2.5.2.2   *Fine-grain parametrization and validation.*

Parametrization. The drawbacks in coarse-grain parametrization can be partly resolved by a fine-grain parametrization method presented here. The key idea of this fine-grain parametrization method is evaluating every and each single item on the right-hand side of Equation 2.11 and using these items to estimate execution time. The evaluation is conducted with the aid of application and system profiling tools, including hardware counters [69], mpptest [70], and LMbenchmark [71]. While the coarse-grain parametrization method depends on several preruns of an application to collect the execution times, this method requires only one prerun to profile application. This method can be used to design and implement frequency scheduler for energy conservation, as shown in Section 2.6.

This fine-grain parametrization technique consists of three steps: workload profiling, unit workload execution time estimation, and overall execution time estimation.

Step 1: Workload profiling (w^{ON}, w^{OFF})

The goal of this step is to obtain the distribution of the ON-/OFF-chip workloads for an application. Typically, ON-chip workloads consist of computations with data residing in on-chip devices such as registers, L1 or L2 cache; OFF-chip workloads consist of computations with data from off-chip devices such as main memory or disk. These workloads can be profiled using hardware performance counters, some special registers that accurately track low level operations and events such as the number of executed instructions, and cache hits and cache misses with minimum overhead. An API PAPI [69] is available to read the event counts from hardware counters.

The limited number of counters requires us to select a few important low level events to monitor. In this work, we focus on executed instructions and cache accesses and use these events to estimate ON-/OFF-chip workloads. Specifically, we count the following PAPI events: total instructions (PAPI_TOT_INS), L1 data cache accesses (PAPI_L1_DCA), L1 data cache misses (PAPI_L1_DCM), L2 cache accesses (PAPI_L2_TCA), and L2 cache misses (PAPI_L2_TCM). Table 2.2 shows the mapping of these events[6] to ON-/OFF-chip workload for

---

[6]We use data cache access to approximate total cache access, as the latter is not available from performance counter.

TABLE 2.2 Workload Measurement and Decomposition

Workload	Memory Level	Derivation from PAPI events
ON-chip	CPU/Register	PAPI_TOT_INS-PAPI_L1_DCA
	L1 Cache	PAPI_L1_DCA-PAPI_L1_DCM
	L2 Cache	PAPI_L2_TCA-PAPI_L2_TCM
OFF-chip	Main memory	PAPI_L2_TCM

an application on a system with a on-chip L2 cache. The total on-chip work-load is then estimated using the sum of instructions, L1 cache accesses, and L2 cache accesses, and the total off-chip workload is estimated using the number of main memory accesses (or L2 cache misses). We assume that hardware event counts are similar across different processors for the same workload and obtain measurements on one of the processors.[7]

Step 2: Unit workload execution time $\mathrm{CPI}^{\mathrm{ON}}/f^{\mathrm{ON}}$, $\mathrm{CPI}^{\mathrm{OFF}}/f^{\mathrm{OFF}}$, *and* $T_N(w_{\mathrm{PO}}, f)$

Next, we measure the average event time CPI_j/f where $j = [1, 2, 3, 4]$ for CPU/Register, L1 cache, L2 cache, main memory, respectively. Essentially, each event time is determined by system characteristics such as memory and I/O bandwidths and latencies. In our work, we use LMBENCH [71] benchmarks to evaluate event time of access to L1 cache, L2 cache, and main memory with each available frequency. Some of the event times such as cache access times are inversely proportional to processor frequency, and some such as main memory access time are independent of processor frequency. The weighted sum of register, L1 cache, and L2 cache event times is the unit on-chip workload time, where the weight of each event is the percentage of this event count toward the entire on-chip event count. The measured average main memory event time is the unit off-chip workload time. Parallel overhead $T_N(w_{\mathrm{PO}}, f)$ is measured using MPPTEST [70] toolset. We figure out the communication types and their message sizes that are involved in the application, and then use MPPTEST to measure the communication times. The total time to finish all the communication given a frequency is then the parallel overhead under this frequency. Theoretically, the time does not change with processor frequency and we observe this in our results.

Step 3. Overall execution time and speedup estimation

After we profiled workload and obtained system characteristics from Steps 1 and 2, we use them to estimate the execution time of an application using Equations 2.8 and 2.11. We substitute the parameters into Equation 2.8 to predict sequential execution time, $T_1(w, f)$, and its variations with processor frequency. This means we rely on Assumption 1 that the total workload is parallelizable. We substitute the obtained parameters into Equation 2.11 to predict parallel execution time for any given processor count and frequency.

---

[7]This technique is commonly used for regular SPMD codes. We observe the performance event counts are within 2% from sequential execution to parallel execution. For non-SPMD codes, we could obtain results from individual processors and perform similar (albeit more cumbersome) analyses.

Validation. We have applied power-aware speedup model and this fine-grain parametrization technique to FT on the same power-scalable cluster introduced before and obtained error rates similar to those in Table 2.1. Here, we use the lower–upper diagonal (LU) benchmark from the NAS Parallel Benchmark suite as a case study. LU uses a symmetric, successive overrelaxation numerical scheme to solve a regular-sparse, block lower, and upper triangular system. LU is an iterative solver with a limited amount of parallelism and a memory footprint comparable to FFT. LU exhibits a regular communication pattern and fairly intensive memory accesses.

Our workload profiling shows ON-chip workloads w^{ON} account for 98.8% and OFF-chip workload or memory instructions account for 1.2% of application LU. Despite of LU's significant memory footprint, most data (97.4%) are hit on L1 cache. The distribution of ON-chip workload is 44.6% CPU/Register instructions, 53.8% L1 cache instructions, and 1.4% L2 cache instructions. Given this ON-chip workload distribution, we can calculate the weighted average CPI/f for ON-chip workloads, $CPI^{ON}/f = 0.446 \cdot (CPI_1/f) + 0.538 \cdot (CPI_2/f) + 0.014 \cdot (CPI_3/f)$, where f is any of the available frequencies.[8] Similarly, the weighted average CPI/f for OFF-chip workloads is $CPI^{OFF}/f = CPI_4/f$.

Table 2.3 presents the seconds per ON-/OFF-chip workload for each available processor frequency on the system. Our premise is that ON-chip workload time is affected by frequency while OFF-chip workload time is not. The results basically comply with this premise. The discrepancy on OFF-chip workload execution time is due to a hardware-driven decrease in the bus speed f^{OFF} for lower CPU clock frequencies. This is system-specific behavior captured by our parameter measurements. So, the effects are included in our predictions. Nonetheless, we are investigating this further to determine if it is common across platforms.

LU transmits 310 doubles per message when running on two nodes and 155 doubles per message when running on four nodes. Table 2.3 shows the

TABLE 2.3 Unit ON-/OFF-Chip Workload Time and Parallel Overhead Time in Seconds

	600 MHz	800 MHz	1000 MHz	1200 MHz	1400 MHz
$CPI^{ON}/f^{ON}(10^{-9})$	3.65	2.74	2.19	1.83	1.56
$CPI^{OFF}/f^{OFF}(10^{-9})$	140	140	110	110	110
Communication cost for 155 doubles (10^{-6})	25	25	25	25	25
Communication cost for 310 doubles (10^{-6})	200	167	167	167	167

---

[8]This assumes one floating-point double (FPD) computation per memory operation. For the actual predictions, we adjust to account for instruction-level parallelism that enables about 2.42 FPD computations per memory operation.

communication times for each of these cases. The trend is similar as the number of nodes increases. Basically, processor frequency has no noticeable effects on communication cost. The only exception is message size (310 doubles) on the slowest frequency where communication cost is influenced by the processor (f^{ON}). We use the product of number of messages and communication time to compute $T_N(w_{\text{PO}}, f)$.

Table 2.4 presents the prediction error using power-aware speedup model and the fine-grain parametrization on LU and a comparison with coarse-grain parametrization. We observe that errors using coarse-grain parametrization increase steadily when processor count and frequency increase. Errors using fine-grain parametrization increase with processor count but appear to be leveling off with frequency scaling. Our assumptions explain these observations. Assuming the workload is completely parallelizable in both techniques increases the error rates. We are presently working to obtain better estimates of DOP to help reduce these errors—though all speedup models suffer this problem. We separate the ON- and OFF-chip workloads in fine-grain parametrization, which leads to better accuracy. The trade-off is a more detailed application and system profiling.

2.6 MODEL USAGES

This section demonstrates the practical usages of power-aware speedup model in improving power-performance efficiency of parallel applications on power-scalable systems. In this work, we choose $E \cdot D$ to evaluate power-performance efficiency.

We will first show a model usage in identifying system configuration in processor count and frequency for an application execution that delivers optimal power-performance efficiency. Then we will show another usage in designing runtime scheduler that adapts processor power/performance modes to save energy while maintaining application performance. Fine-grain parametrization method is used in both usages.

TABLE 2.4 Power-Aware Speedup Errors in percent for LU

					Frequency, MHz					
	600		800		1000		1200		1400	
N	FP	SP	FP	SP	FP	SP	FP	SP	FP	SP
1	5	0	7	0	3	0	4	0	1	0
2	6	0	6	2	5	4	6	3	8	6
4	2	0	6	3	8	4	10	7	7	7
8	3	0	1	4	8	8	11	10	7	13

FP uses fine-grain parameterizations to perform predictions. CP uses course-grain parameterizations to perform predictions.

2.6.1 Identification of Optimal System Configurations

This usage focuses on identifying system configuration, that is, a pair of processor count and processor frequency, which will deliver the best power-performance efficiency for an application ahead of its actual execution.

It takes three steps to identify the optimal system configurations for an given application. First, use power-aware speedup model, application profile, and system profile to predict application performance for any combination of processor count and frequency on the system. Second, estimate system power consumption for the same combinations of processor count and processor frequency in step 1. Third, calculate and evaluate energy-performance efficiencies in $E \cdot D$ and identify the configuration with optimal efficiency.

Performance prediction is performed using methodology introduced in Section 2.5.2.2. We use system and application profiling tools to collect system and application characteristics and derive model parameters. These parameters are then plugged into Equation 2.11 to predict application performances at various system configurations. Power estimation is conducted using the methodology presented in Reference 59. We assume that there are two levels of power consumption of a computer node: one is when the system is dedicated to computation and the other is when the system is dedicated to communication. The former further varies with CPU frequency, while the latter does not. Both do not change with processor count for application execution.

Figure 2.10 shows the projected power-performance efficiencies in EDP (Energy-Delay Product) values for LU benchmark class B if the cluster introduced earlier can scale up to 1024 nodes. Executing LU on more processors before reaching 128 leads to power-performance efficiency improvement. However, further increasing processor count causes efficiency degradation. This is explained by the fact that when processor count increases, performance gain from parallel computing diminishes because of parallel overhead; while energy consumption steadily increases. The effect of frequency scaling on power-performance efficiency is dependent on processor count, as indicated by our power-aware speedup model. Scaling up processor frequency leads to efficiency improvement when processor count is small. Nevertheless, when processor count is equal to or larger than 256, increasing frequency beyond a certain point would degrade efficiency. Using power-performance efficiency metric prevents us from giving unwarranted preference to configurations that deliver relative faster execution but with much higher energy consumption. Our power-aware speedup model recommends allocating 256 processors each running at 1200 MHz to execute application LU class B for best power-performance efficiency.

Further increasing either processor frequency or count incurs worse power-performance efficiency. Although we do not show here, we would like to note that our model can easily identify for users the maximum speedup achievable on the system as well as system configurations that meet a user-specified energy budget for an application.

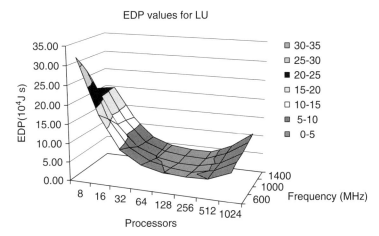

Figure 2.10   Power-performance efficiencies with EDP under various system configurations. *X* axis is number of processors, *Y* axis is processor frequency, and *Z* axis is the power-performance efficiency in EDP. Optimal System Configuration is 256 processors with 1200 MHz CPU Frequency.

   High performance computing systems normally use batch systems for job and resource scheduling. In a batch system, each job uses a batch script file for users to specify job information and request resources. One of the items in resource request is processor count. It only requires a simple extension for a batch system to incorporate optimal system configuration for power-performance efficiency on a power-scalable system. That is, add an item *processor frequency* to the script file. The processor count and frequency will be fixed throughout the application execution. It is shown that such scheduling minimizes energy consumption [72] for an application in which CPU utilization is uniform during its execution.

2.6.2   PAS-Directed Energy-Driven Runtime Frequency Scaling

Previous section presents an approach to improving efficiency by identifying and allocating optimal system configuration for an application. This approach is most energy efficient for applications where CPU utilization is consistent during their executions [72]. Nevertheless, this approach may miss opportunities of further energy saving for other applications where CPU utilization varies dramatically over time. For example, application FFT repeatedly executes a computation-intensive code segment followed by a communication code segment. For applications such as FFT, dynamically adapting processor frequency to computation demand saves more energy without adversely degrading application performance [73]. This section presents the design of such a dynamic frequency scheduling using power-aware speedup model.

   The challenges of the design lie in online identifying (i) phases when processor is not fully utilized and (ii) the proper frequencies for these phases that

TABLE 2.5 Power/Performance Modes Available on Dual-Core Dual Processor Cluster

Frequency, MHz	Voltage, V
1000	1.10
1800	1.15
2000	1.15
2200	1.20
2400	1.25
2600	1.30

maintain performance and save energy. To address these challenges, we discretize an application execution to a series of time intervals, and for each interval use our power-aware speedup model to predict performance and identify a minimum frequency that meets the performance constraint. The performance constraint is represented as a performance loss, such as 5%, compared to performance at maximum frequency. Specifically, we first instrument and profile workload for an interval using methodology presented in Section 2.5.2.2. We monitor on-chip cache accesses and off-chip memory accesses, and derive communication time during this interval. These information will tell whether the current interval is appropriate to scale down frequency for power reduction. Second, we use history-based prediction schemes to predict the workload at next interval [64]. The simplest prediction scheme is PAST, which uses the very recent history and assumes that the workload at the next interval would remain the same. PAST is able to provide good prediction for steady workloads but not for alternating workloads. In this work, we adopt exponential moving average (EMA) that uses all the workload in the history but gives more weight to the latest. Third, we substitute the predicted workload to Equation 2.11 to calculate the execution time at each available frequency and identify the target frequency, which is the minimal frequency that meets the performance constraint.

We use NPB FT benchmark as a case study and show the efficiency improvement through model-oriented dynamic frequency scheduling. The results are obtained from a dual-core dual-processor cluster. Each core has six power/performance modes available, as shown in Table 2.5. One iteration of this three-dimensional FFT implementation involves a collective all-to-all communication where each process exchanges a large amount of data with all the other processes. A realization of one-dimensional FFT and a local transposition precedes this communication and a transposition close-up and two other one-dimensional FFTs follow this communication. The iteration ends with a collective all-reduce communication.

Figure 2.11 shows the workload profile captured on one process when FT is running with 16 processes on 16 cores: (a) the retired instructions, (b) and (c) the on-chip L1 and l2 cache accesses, and (d) the off-chip main memory accesses. We observe that (i) there is an evident alternation between high plateau and low

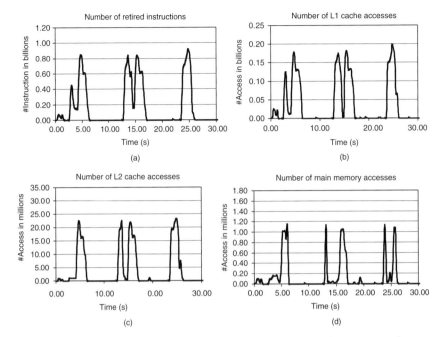

Figure 2.11 The workload characteristics of NPB FT benchmark on 1 core when executing with 16 parallel processes on 16 cores. (a) shows the number of retired instructions over the time, (b) and (c) show the on-chip cache accesses, and (d) shows the off-chip main memory accesses.

plateau for all the events. The high plateau represents the computation memory phase and the low plateau represents the communication phase; (ii) cache accesses are intensive during computation phases; (iii) most of the data are hit in the L1 cache for FFT computation; and (iv) main memory access spikes during local transposition.

Figure 2.12 is the resulting dynamic frequency settings by the model-oriented scheduler. The settings meet our expectations: the frequency is scaled down during communication phases and scaled up during computation phases. In addition, the scheduler recognizes the memory-intensive phases (local transposition) and scales down frequency according. Overall, this model-oriented scheduler achieves 14% energy savings with 3% performance degradation (5% allowable specified by the user) and improves power-performance efficiency by 11%.

2.7 CONCLUSION

Improving power-performance efficiency is critical for future high-end computing systems. Although innovative computer architectures and revolutionary computing approaches may provide partial solutions to break efficiency barriers,

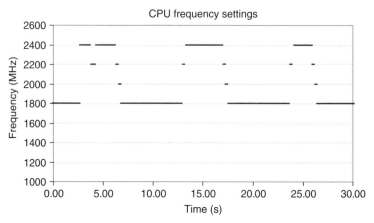

Figure 2.12 The dynamic frequency scaling for FT directed by power-aware speedup model. The time interval is 250 ms.

exploiting adaptive power allocation during application execution is needed to bring the energy consumption to practical level.

This chapter presents theories, techniques, and toolkits for analyzing, controlling, and improving the energy efficiency of high-end computing systems. Specifically, our contributions and findings presented in this work include the following:

1. *Power and Energy Profiling for Distributed Scientific Applications.* As a measurement infrastructure for efficient high-end computing, we present a software and hardware toolkit named *PowerPack* for profiling, evaluating, and characterizing power and energy consumption of distributed parallel systems and applications. PowerPack provides fast and accurate power-performance evaluation of large-scale systems at component level and at function granularity. Typical applications of PowerPack include but are not limited to (i) quantifying the power, energy, and power-performance efficiency of given distributed systems and applications; (ii) understanding the interactions between power and performance at a fine granularity; (iii) validating the effectiveness of candidate technology for efficiency improvement. In our work, we apply PowerPack to several case studies and obtain numerous insights on improving power-performance efficiencies of distributed scientific computing.

2. *Predictive Models of Performance Scaling on Power-Scalable Clusters.* Adaptive power allocation for energy-efficient computing requires accurate prediction of the impacts of different system configurations on application performance. We present a new power-aware speedup model that quantifies the performance effects of parallelism, power/performance modes, and their combinations. Coupled with metrics for efficiency evaluation,

this new speedup model can predict system configurations that result in power-performance efficiency.

We show that the model is practical for using on power-scalable parallel systems. The model-directed power management can automatically and transparently improve energy efficiency for applications on large-scale power-aware clusters.

We expect that other components such as memory, disk, networking, and cooling systems will support power-aware features. In the future, we would like to explore holistic performance and power management and exploit all available power-aware components to improve the system's overall energy efficiency. We will also study how to adapt our work to innovative architectures such as heterogenous multicore and accelerator-based systems.

REFERENCES

1. HECRTF. Federal plan for high-end computing: Report of the high-end computing revitalization task force. Technical report; 2004.

2. NERSC. Doe greenbook-needs and directions in high-performance computing for the office of science. Technical report; 2005.

3. Kothe DB. Science prospects and benefits with exascale computing; 2007.

4. SciDAC. The role of exascale computing in energy security. Availabe at http://www.scidacreview.org/1001/html/energy.html.

5. Top500 supercomputers. 2008. Available at http://top500.org.

6. Bergman K, Borkar S, Campbell D, Carlson W, Dally W, Denneau M, Franzon P, Harrod W, Hiller J, Karp S, Keckler S, Klein D, Lucas R, Richards M, Scarpelli A, Scott S, Snavely A, Sterling T, Williams RS, Yelick K, Bergman K, Borkar S, Campbell D, Carlson W, Dally W, Denneau M, Franzon P, Harrod W, Hiller J, Keckler S, Klein D, Kogge P, Williams RS, Yelick K. Exascale computing study: technology challenges in achieving exascale systems; 2008.

7. Brooks D, Tiwari V, Martonosi M. Wattch: A framework for architectural-level power analysis and optimizations. In: 27th International Symposium on Computer Architecture; Vancouver (BC); 2000. pp. 83–94.

8. Ye W, Vijaykrishnan N, Kandemir MT, Irwin MJ. The design and use of simplepower: a cycle-accurate energy estimation tool. In: Design Automation Conference. Los Angeles (CA) 2000. pp. 340–345.

9. Zedlewski J, Sobti S, Garg N, Zheng F, Krishnamurthy A, Wang R. Modeling hard-disk power consumption. In: *FAST '03: Proceedings of the 2nd USENIX Conference on File and Storage Technologies*. Berkeley (CA): USENIX Association; 2003. pp. 217–230.

10. Wang T-Y, Chen CC-P. 3-d thermal-adi: a linear-time chip level transient thermal simulator. IEEE Trans Comput Aided Des Integr Circ Syst 2002;21(12):1434–1445.

11. Powerexecutive. Available at http://www-03.ibm.com/systems/management/director/about/director52/extensions/powerexec.html.

12. Kamil S, Shalf J, Strohmaier E. Power efficiency in high performance computing. In: IPDPS. IEEE; 2008. pp. 1–8.

13. Xu T. Data center energy benchmarking: Part 5 case studies on a corporate data center; 2007. Available at http://escholarship.org/uc/item/4r6711d7.

14. Mudge Trevor. Power: a first class design constraint for future architectures. Computer 2001;34(4):52–57.

15. Borkar S. Low power design challenges for the decade. In: *Proceedings of the 2001 Conference on Asia South Pacific Design Automation*. Yokohama, Japan: ACM Press; 2001. pp. 293–296.

16. Halter J, Najm F. A gate-level leakage power reduction method for ultra-low-power cmos circuits. In: Proceedings of IEEE Custom Integrated Circuits Conference. Santa Clara (CA) 1997. pp. 475–478.

17. Chen Z, Johnson M, Wei L, Roy K. Estimation of standby leakage power in cmos circuits considering accurate modeling of transistor stacks. In: *ISLPED '98: Proceedings of the 1998 International Symposium on Low Power Electronics and Design*. New York: ACM Press; 1998. pp. 239–244.

18. Naidu SR, Jacobs ETAF. Minimizing stand-by leakage power in static CMOS circuits. In: Proceedings of Design, Automation, and Test in Europe (DATE '01). Munich, Germany 2001. p. 0370.

19. Held J, Bautista J, Koehl S. White paper from a few cores to many: a tera-scale computing research review. Intel; 2006.

20. Micron. Calculating memory system power for ddr3. Micron Technology, Inc; 2007.

21. Cpufreq. Available at http://www.kernel.org/pub/linux/utils/kernel/cpufreq/cpufreq.html.

22. Patterson DA, Hennessy JL. *Computer Architecture: A Quantitative Approach*. 3rd ed. San Fancisco (CA): Morgan Kaufmann Publishers; 2003. CPI formulas found in pages pp. 35–38.

23. Brooks D, Martonosi M, Wellman J-D, Bose P. Power-performance modeling and tradeoff analysis for a high end microprocessor. In: Workshop on Power-Aware Computer Systems (PACS2000, held in conjuction with ASPLOS-IX); Cambridge (MA); 2000.

24. Pisharath J, Jiang J, Choudhary A. Evaluation of application-aware heterogeneous embedded systems for performance and energy consumption. In: The 38th IEEE/ACM International Symposium on Microarchitecture (MICRO-38); Marcelona, Spain; 2005.

25. Lorch JR, Smith AJ. Pace: a new approach to dynamic voltage scaling. IEEE Trans Comput 2004;53(7):856–869.

26. Vijaykrishnan N, Kandemir M, Irwin M, Kim H, Ye W. Energy-driven integrated hardware-software optimizations using simplepower. In: 27th International Symposium on Computer Architecture; Vancouver, British Columbia; 2000.

27. Burger DC, M Todd. Austin. The simplescalar toolset, version 2.0. Comput Arch News 1997;25(3):13–25.

28. Brooks D, Bose P, Srinivasan V, Gschwind MK. New methodology for early-stage, microarchitecture-level power-performance analysis of microprocessors. IBM J Res Dev 2003;47(5.6):653–670.

29. Dhodapkar A, Lim CH, Cai G, Daasch WR. Tem2p2est: a thermal enabled multi-model power/performance estimator. In: *The 1st International Workshop on Power-Aware Computer Systems*. London: Springer-Verlag; 2000.

30. Cai G, Lim C. Architectural level power/performance optimization and dynamic power optimization. In: Cool Chips Tutorial at 32nd ISCA; Haifa, Israel; 1999.

31. Wang D, Ganesh B, Tuaycharoen N, Baynes K, Jaleel A, Jacob B. Dramsim: a memory system simulator. SIGARCH Comput Arch News 2005;33(4):100–107.

32. Vachharajani M, Vachharajani N, Penry DA, Blome JA, August DI. Microarchitectural exploration with liberty. In: 35th International Symposium on Microarchitecture (Micro-35); Istanbul, Turkey; 2002.

33. Zedlewski J, Sobti S, Garg N, Zheng F, Krishnamurthy A, Wang R. Modeling hard-disk power consumption. In: *Proceedings of the 2nd USENIX Conference on File and Storage Technologies*. USENIX Association; 2003. pp. 230.

34. Gurumurthi S, Sivasubramaniam A, Irwin MJ, Vijaykrishnan N, Kandemir M. Using complete machine simulation for software power estimation: the softwatt approach. In: 8th International Symposium on High-Performance Computer Architecture (HECA'02); Boston (MA); 2002. p. 0141.

35. Rosenblum M, Herrod SA, Witchel E, Gupta A. Complete computer simulation: the SimOS approach. In: IEEE Parallel and Distributed Technology; Fall; 1995.

36. Flinn J, Satyanarayanan M. Powerscope: a tool for profiling the energy usage of mobile applications. In: The 2nd IEEE Workshop on Mobile Computer Systems and Applications; New Orleans, LA; 1999.

37. Bellosa F. The benefits of event-driven energy accounting in power-sensitive systems. In: Proceedings of 9th ACM SIGOPS European Workshop; Kolding, Denmark; 2000.

38. Joseph R, Brooks D, Martonosi M. Live, runtime power measurements as a foundation for evaluating power/performance tradeoffs. In: Workshop on Complexity-effective Design; Goteborg, Sweden; 2001.

39. Isci C, Martonosi M. Runtime power monitoring in high-end processors: methodology and empirical data. In: The 36th annual IEEE/ACM International Symposium on Microarchitecture; San Diego, CA; 2003. p. 93.

40. Tiwari V, Singh D, Rajgopal S, Mehta G, Patel R, Baez F. Reducing power in high-performance microprocessors. In: *Proceedings of the 35th Conference on Design Automation*. San Francico (CA); ACM Press; 1998. pp. 732–737.

41. Flinn J, Satyanarayanan M. Energy-aware adaptation for mobile applications. In: 17th ACM Symposium on Operating Systems Principles, Kiawah Island Resort, SC; 1999.

42. Amdahl GM. Validity of the single processor approach to achieving large-scale computing capabilities. In: AFIPS Spring Joint Computer Conference; Reston (VA); 1967. pp. 483–485.

43. Eager DL, Zahorjan J, Lazowska ED. Speedup versus efficiency in parallel systems. IEEE Trans Comput 1989;38(3):408–423.

44. Grama AY, Gupta A, Kumar V. Isoefficiency: Measuring the scalability of parallel algorithms and architectures. IEEE Concurrency 1993;1(3):12–21.

45. Gustafson J. Reevaluating amdahl's law. Commun ACM 1988;31:532–533.

46. Karp AH, Flatt HP. Measuring parallel processor performance. Commun ACM 1990;33(5):539–543.

47. Sun X-H, Ni L. Scalable problems and memory-bounded speedup. J Parallel Distrib Comput 1993;19:27–37.

48. Sun X-H, Ni LM. Another view on parallel speedup. In: Proceedings of Supercomputing '90; 1990. pp. 324–333.

49. Worley PH. The effect of time constraints on scaled speedup. SIAM J Sci Stat Comput 1990;11(5):838–858.

50. Cho S, Melhem R. Corollaries to amdahl's law for energy. Comput Arch Lett 2008;7(1):25–28.

51. Pinheiro E, Bianchini R, Carrera EV, Heath T. Load balancing and unbalancing for power and performance in cluster-based systems. Technical Report DCS-TR-440; Rutgers University; 2001.

52. Lefurgy C, Tesauro G, Levine DW, Das R, Kephart JO, Chan H. Autonomic multi-agent management of power and performance in data centers. In: The 7th International Conference on Autonomous Agents and Multiagent Systems (AAMAS); Estoril, Portugal; 2008.

53. Fan X, Ellis CS, Lebeck AR. Memory controller policies for dram power management. In: International Symposium on Low Power Electronics and Design (ISLPED); Huntington Beach, CA; 2001. pp. 129–134.

54. Carrera EV, Pinheiro E, Bianchini R. Conserving disk energy in network servers. In: The 17th International Conference on Supercomputing; San Francisco, CA; 2003.

55. Gurumurthi S, Sivasubramaniam A, Kandemir M, Franke H. Drpm: Dynamic speed control for power management in server class disks. In: The 30th Annual International Symposium on Computer Architecture; San Diego (CA); 2003. p. 169.

56. Ge R, Feng X, Cameron KW. Improvement of power-performance efficiency for high-end computing. In: The 1st HPPAC workshop in conjection with 19th IEEE/ACM International Parallel and Distributed Processing Symposium (IPDPS); Denver (CO); 2005.

57. Freeh VW, Lowenthal DK, Pan F, Kappiah N. Using multiple energy gears in MPI programs on a power-scalable cluster. In: 10th ACM Symposium on Principles and Practice of Parallel Programming (PPoPP); Chicago, Illinois; 2005.

58. Freeh VW, Lowenthal DK, Springer R, Pan F, Kappiah N. Exploring the energy-time tradeoff in MPI programs. In: 19th IEEE/ACM International Parallel and Distributed Processing Symposium (IPDPS); Denver (CO); 2005.

59. Springer R, Lowenthal DK, Rountree B, Freeh VW. Minimizing execution time in mpi programs on an energy-constrained, power-scalable cluster. In: 11th ACM Symposium on Principles and Practice of Parallel Programming (PPOPP); 2006.

60. Wu Q, Reddi VJ, Wu Y, Lee J, Connors D, Brooks D, Martonosi M, Clark DW. A dynamic compilation framework for controlling microprocessor energy and performance. In: The 38th IEEE/ACM International Symposium on Microarchitecture; Barcelona, Spain; 2005. pp. 271–282.

61. Hsu C-H, Kremer U. The design, implementation, and evaluation of a compiler algorithm for cpu energy reduction. In: ACM SIGPLAN Conference on Programming Languages, Design, and Implementation (PLDI'03); San Diego (CA); 2003.

62. Chen G, Malkowski K, Kandemir M, Raghavan P. Reducing power with performance contraints for parallel sparse applications. In: The 1st Workshop on High-Performance, Power-Aware Computing; Denver (CO); 2005.

63. Kappiah N, Freeh VW, Lowenthal DK. Just in time dynamic voltage scaling: exploiting inter-node slack to save energy in MPI programs. In: IEEE/ACM Supercomputing 2005 (SC '05); Seattle, WA; 2005.

64. Ge R, Feng X, Feng W-C, Cameron KW. Cpu miser: a performance-directed, run-time system for power-aware clusters. In: International Conference in Parallel Processing (ICPP) 2007; Xian, China; 2007.

65. Hsu C-H, Feng W-C. Towards efficient supercomputing: choosing the right efficiency metric. In: The 1st Workshop on High-Performance, Power-Aware Computing; Denver (CO); 2005.

66. Hsu C-H. Compiler-directed dynamic voltage and frequency scaling for Cpu power and energy reduction [PhD thesis]. Director-Ulrich Kremer; 2003.

67. Lim MY, Freeh VW, Lowenthal DK. MPI and communication-adaptive, transparent frequency and voltage scaling of communication phases in MPI programs. In: Proceedings of the ACM/IEEE Supercomputing 2006 (SC'06); Tampa, FL; 2006.

68. Choi K, Soma R, Pedram M. Fine-grained dynamic voltage and frequency scaling for precise energy and performance trade-off based on the ratio of off-chip access to on-chip computation times. In: DATE '04: Proceedings of the conference on Design, automation and test in Europe; Paris, France; 2004.

69. PTOOLS. Performance API home page; May 1999.

70. Gropp W, Lusk E. Reproducible measurements of MPI performance. In: PVM/MPI '99 User's Group Meeting; Barcelona, Spain; 1999. pp. 11–18.

71. McVoy L, Staelin C. lmbench: Portable tools for performance analysis. In: USENIX 1996 Annual Technical Conference; San Diego (CA); 1996.

72. Ishihara T, Yasuura H. Voltage scheduling problem for dynamically variable voltage processors; 1998. pp. 197–202.

73. Ge R, Feng X, Cameron K. Performance-constrained, distributed dvs scheduling for scientific applications on power-aware clusters. In: 2005 ACM/IEEE conference on Supercomputing (SC 2005); Seattle (WA); 2005.

CHAPTER 3

ENERGY EFFICIENCY IN HPC SYSTEMS

IVAN RODERO and MANISH PARASHAR

3.1 INTRODUCTION

Power consumption in high performance computing (HPC) platforms is becoming a major concern for a number of reasons including cost, reliability, energy conservation, and environmental impact. At present, high-end HPC systems consume several megawatts of power, enough to power small towns, and are in fact, soon approaching the limits of the power available to them. For example, the Cray XT_5 Jaugar supercomputer at Oak Ridge National Laboratory (ORNL) with 182,000 processing cores consumes about 7 MW. The cost of power for this and similar HPC systems runs into millions per year.

To further add to the concerns, because of power and cooling requirements and associated costs, empirical data show that every $10°C$ increase in temperature results in a doubling of the system failure rate, which reduces the reliability of these expensive system. As supercomputers, large-scale data centers are meant to be clusters composed by hundreds of thousands or even millions processing cores [1] with similar power consumption concerns.

Existing and ongoing research in power efficiency and power management has addressed the problem at different levels, including data center design, resource allocation, workload layer strategies, cooling techniques, etc. At the platform level (individual node or server), current power management research broadly falls into the following categories—processor and other subsystems (e.g., memory, disk, etc.) level, operating system (OS) level, and application level.

Although the processor is the most power consuming component, other subsystems have incorporated energy management functionalities such as memory, storage, and network interfaces (NICs). Within the OS, there are fewer power

Energy-Efficient Distributed Computing Systems, First Edition.
Edited by Albert Y. Zomaya and Young Choon Lee.
© 2012 John Wiley & Sons, Inc. Published 2012 by John Wiley & Sons, Inc.

management techniques available and include OS control of processor C-states, P-states, and device power states or sleep states.

At the application level, several approaches have also been proposed such as those based on exploiting communication bottlenecks in MPI (Message Passing Interface) programs.

In this chapter, we study the potential of proactive application-centric aggressive power management of data center's resources for HPC workloads. Specifically, we consider power management mechanisms and controls (currently or soon to be) available at different levels and for different subsystems, and leverage several innovative approaches that have been taken to tackle this problem in the last few years, that can be effectively used in a cross-layer application-aware manner for HPC workloads.

To do this, we first profile standard HPC benchmarks with respect to behaviors, resource usage, and power dissipation. Specifically, we profile the HPC benchmarks in terms of processor, memory, storage subsystem, and NIC usage. From the profiles, we observe that across different workloads the utilization of these subsystems varies significantly, and there are significant periods of time in which one or more of these subsystems are idle but still require a large amount of power.

On the basis of the empirical power characterization and quantification of the HPC benchmarks, we investigate using simulations the potential energy saving of proactive, application-aware, power management strategies. We use traces from different systems and focus on performance and energy consumption metrics.

The obtained results show that by using proactive, component-based power management, we can reduce the average energy consumption. The results also show that proactive configuration of subsystems works better with a higher number of nodes and with workloads composed of bursts of job requests with similar requirements, which is common in scientific HPC workflows.

The main contributions of this work are summarized as follows:

(i) We argue that different existing techniques for energy management can be combined to improve energy efficiency of data center's servers by configuring them dynamically depending on the workloads' resource requirements,

(ii) We profile HPC benchmarks with respect to behaviors, resource usage, and power impact on individual computing nodes and determine empirically (rather than with estimations) possible ways to save energy,

(iii) We propose different algorithms for proactive, component-based power management, attempting to improve energy efficiency with little or no performance loss, and

(iv) We quantify possible energy savings of the proposed power management strategies at both server and datacenter levels.

The rest of this chapter is organized as follows:

- Discussion of background and related work (Section 3.2),
- Description of proactive, component-based power management (Section 3.3),

- Quantification of possible power savings through component-based power management (Section 3.4),
- Experimental evaluation and discussion of obtained results (Section 3.5),
- Concluding remarks (Section 3.7).

3.2   BACKGROUND AND RELATED WORK

HPC is the application of parallel processing for running advanced application programs (that are either too large for standard computers or would take too long) efficiently, reliably, and quickly. A HPC system is essentially a network of nodes, each of which contains one or more processing units, as well as its own memory. These systems are ranked by the Top 500 list[1] that lists the fastest supercomputers worldwide based on the highest score measured using the Linpack benchmark suite in terms of TFlops (trillions of floating point operations per second).

As demand for processing power and speed grows, issues related to power consumption, air conditioning, and cooling infrastructures are critical concerns in terms of operating costs. Furthermore, power and cooling rates are increasing eight-fold every year [2] and are becoming a dominant part of IT budgets. Addressing these issues is thus an important and immediate task for HPC systems.

While Top 500 focuses on performance, the Green500 list[2] provides rankings of the most energy-efficient supercomputers in the world based on the "Flops-per-Watt" metric [3].

In the following, we review the most significant power management techniques using different approaches, among the vast literature in the area of power management and energy efficiency for HPC.

3.2.1   CPU Power Management

In their recent work, Liu and Zhu [4] survey power management approaches for HPC systems. As they discuss, since processors dominate the system power consumption in HPC systems, processor level power management is the most addressed aspect at server level. The most commonly used technique for CPU power management is dynamic voltage and frequency scaling (DVFS), which is a technique to reduce power dissipation by lowering processor clock speed and supply voltage [5, 6].

3.2.1.1   OS-level CPU power management.   OS-level CPU power management involves controlling the sleep states or the C-states [7] and the P-states of the processor when the processor is idle [8]. C-state is the capability of the processor to be in various low power idle states with varying wake-up latency. P-state is the capability of running the processor at different voltage and frequency levels [9].

---

[1]Top 500 Supercomputers site: http://www.top500.org/.
[2]Top 500 Most Energy-Efficient Supercomputer Site. http://www.green500.org.

The advanced configuration and power interface (ACPI) specification provides the policies and mechanisms to control the C-states and P-states of the processor when they are idle. Modern OSs (e.g., Linux kernel) implement ACPI-based policies to reduce the processor performance and power when it is less active or in idle state [10].

3.2.1.2 *Workload-level CPU power management.* Several approaches to enforce power management based on the workload characteristics have already been developed. Some of the most successful approaches were based on overlapping computation with communication in MPI programs and using historical data and heuristics.

Kappiah et al. [11] developed a system called *Jitter* that exploits internode bottleneck in MPI programs (i.e., executed blocked processes due to synchronization points in lower P-sates). Lim et al. [12] developed an MPI runtime system that dynamically reduces CPU performance during communication regions assuming that in these regions the processor is not on the critical path.

Other approaches have also studied the bound on the energy saving for an application without incurring in significant delay [13].

Freeh et al. proposed a model to predict execution time and energy consumed of an application running at lower P-states [14] and techniques based on phase characterization of the applications, assigning different P-states to phases according the previous measurements and heuristics [15].

Cameron et al. [16] proposed power management strategies based on application profiles, but they concentrate only on power management of the CPU using DVFS and does not implement any power control of the peripheral devices.

Researchers have developed different scheduling algorithms and mechanisms to save energy to provide resources under deadline restrictions. Chen et al. [17] address resource provisioning proposing power management strategies with SLA constraints based on steady state queuing analysis and feedback control theory. They use server turn on/off and DVFS for enhancing power savings.

3.2.1.3 *Cluster-level CPU power management.* Ranganathan et al. [18] designed cluster-level power management controller and employed a management agent running on each server and the server that exceeded the power budget according to the SLA (Service Level Agreement) was throttled down to an appropriate level.

Horvath and Skadron [19] exploited DVFS for use with dynamic reconfiguration for multitier server clusters, which is a typical architecture of current server clusters.

Wang and Chen [20] proposed a control algorithm to manage power consumption of multiple servers simultaneously. The controller monitors the power value and CPU utilization of each server, computes a new CPU frequency for each processor, and directs each processor to change frequency in a coordinated way.

Leveraging DVFS mechanism, Hsu and Feng [6] propose automatically adapting, power-aware algorithm that is transparent to end-user applications and deliver considerable energy savings with tight control over DVFS-induced performance slowdown.

Rountree et al. [21] developed a system called *Adagio* to collect statistical data on task execution slacks, compute the desired frequency, and represent the result in a hash table. When task is executed again, an appropriate frequency can be found in the hash table.

Raghavendra et al. [22] propose a framework that coordinates and unifies five individual power management solutions (consisting of HW/SW mechanisms). Their work leverages feedback mechanisms to federate multiple power management solutions and builds an approach to unify solutions with minimum interference across controllers. Moreover, their coordination solution gives higher power savings than individual methods.

3.2.2 Component-Based Power Management

Although the CPU is the component that requires most power of the server, the relative power demand by other components is increasing very quickly, specially for multi- and many-core architectures, where different cores and an important amount of memory are included in the same chip die.

Figure 3.1 illustrates a possible decomposition of the power requirements of a server by components for a state of the art multicore server. We can appreciate that the aggregation of power requirements of memory, disk, and network are comparable to the power dissipated by the CPU. However, the power required by each component depend on the workload characteristics [23]. Other components include the motherboard, chipset, fans, power supplies, etc., but we do not consider them in our approach.

In the following sections, we discuss existing power management approaches at the component level.

3.2.2.1 Memory subsystem. Substantial work has also been done for adapting the RAM memory subsystem for saving energy. Delaluz et al. [24, 25]

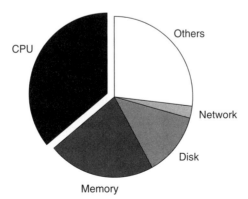

Figure 3.1 Possible distribution of power requirements per component.

studied compiler-directed techniques and OS-based approaches [26, 27] to reduce the energy consumed by the memory subsystem. Huang et al. [28] proposed power-aware virtual memory implementation in OS to reduce memory energy consumption.

Fradj et al. [29, 30] propose multibanking techniques that consist of individually setting banks in lower-power modes when they are not accessed.

Diniz et al. [31] study dynamic approaches for limiting the power consumption of main memories by limiting consumption by adjusting the power states of the memory devices as a function of the memory load.

Hur and Lin [32] propose using the memory controller (thus, at chip level) to improve RAM energy efficiency. They exploit low power modes of modern RAMs extending the idea of adaptive history-based memory schedulers.

3.2.2.2 *Storage subsystem.*

Existing research work also addresses the storage subsystem management to improve energy efficiency of servers. Rotem et al. [33] focus on the energy consumed by the storage devices such as hard disks in standby mode. They suggest file allocation strategies to save energy with a minimal effect on the system performance, that is, the file retrieval time, while reducing the I/O activity when there is no data transfer.

Pinheiro and Bianchini [34] study energy conservation techniques for disk array-based network servers and propose a technique that leverages the redundancy in storage systems to conserve disk energy [35]. Colarelli and Grunwald [36] analyze an alternative design using massive arrays of idle disks (spin-down/up disks).

Other approaches have addressed energy efficiency of storage systems by spinning-down/up disk [36] and the reliability of such techniques [37].

Solid state drive (SSD) disks have also been taken into account toward saving energy consumption for the storage subsystem [38, 39].

The research work discussed earlier addresses energy efficiency by managing different subsystems individually (e.g., CPU via DVFS). However, recent approaches have proposed energy efficiency techniques for processor and memory adaptations [40, 41].

Li et al. [42] combine memory and disk management techniques to provide performance guarantees for control algorithms.

Ranganathan et al. [18] highlight the current issue of underutilization and over provisioning of the servers. They present a solution of peak power budget management across a server ensemble to avoid excessive over provisioning considering DVS (Dynamic Voltage Scaling) and memory/disk scaling.

In contrast to all these approaches, we consider dynamic configuration of multiple subsystems within a single server. Thus, we propose using different mechanisms and techniques that have been already developed in different domains. Our approach is then complimentary to existing and ongoing solutions for energy management for HPC data centers.

3.2.3   Thermal-Conscious Power Management

Several approaches have been proposed for energy efficiency in datacenters, including factors such as cooling and thermal considerations. More et al. [43] propose a method to infer a model of thermal behavior to automatically reconfigure the thermal load management systems, thereby improving cooling efficiency and power consumption. In Reference 44, they also propose thermal management solutions focusing on scheduling workloads considering temperature-aware workload placement. Bash and Forman [45] propose a policy to place the workload in areas of a data center that are easier to cool resulting in cooling power savings. Tang et al. [46] formulate and solve a mathematical problem that maximizes the cooling efficiency of a data center. This is focused on task assignment that maximizes the cooling efficiency.

Bianchini et al. [47] propose emulation tools for investigating the thermal implications of power management. In Reference 48, they present C-Oracle, a software prediction infrastructure that makes online predictions for data center thermal management based on load redistribution and DVFS.

3.2.4   Power Management in Virtualized Datacenters

With the increase of cloud computing, virtualized datacenters are being increasingly considered for traditional HPC applications.

In the context of virtualized datacenters, Nathuji and Schwan [49] investigate the integration of power management and virtualization technologies. In particular, they propose VirtualPower to support the isolated and independent operation of virtual machine (VM) and control the coordination among VMs to reduce the power consumption. Rusu et al. [50] propose a cluster-wide on/off policy based on dynamic reconfiguration and DVS. They focus on power, execution time, and server capacity characterization to provide energy management. Kephart et al. [51, 52] address the coordination of multiple autonomic managers for power/performance trade-offs by using a utility function approach in a nonvirtualized environment.

A large body of work in data center energy management addresses the problem of the request distribution at the VM management level in such a way that the performance goals are met and the energy consumption is minimized. Song et al. [53] propose an adaptive and dynamic scheme for adjusting resources (specifically, CPU and memory) between VMs on a single server to share the physical resources efficiently. Kumar et al. [54] present vManage, a practical coordination approach that loosely couples platform and virtualization management toward improving energy savings and QoS and reducing VM migrations. Soror et al. [55] address the problem of optimizing the performance of database management systems by controlling the configurations of the VMs in which they run. Laszewski et al. [56] present a scheduling algorithm for VMs in a cluster to reduce power consumption using DVFS.

3.3 PROACTIVE, COMPONENT-BASED POWER MANAGEMENT

Our approach is based on power management of the different components at the physical server layer in a proactive manner. We assume that the application's profiles (in terms of resource usage) are known in advance. Therefore, we can power down subsystems or use low power modes of a host system that are not required by the jobs mapped to it based on the application's profiles. We also map jobs to physical servers attempting to optimize energy efficiency with minimum penalty in performance.

In contrast to other typical approaches that allocate jobs with nonconflicting, that is, dissimilar, resource requirements together on the same physical server in order to optimize the performance, our policy is to allocate jobs with similar resource requirements together on the same physical server. This allows us to downgrade the subsystems of the server that are not required to run the requested jobs in order to save energy. To do this, we consider specific configurations of the physical servers' subsystems to reduce their energy demand. Specifically, it follows an energy model that leverages previous research on energy-efficient hardware configurations (e.g., low power modes) in the following four different dimensions:

- *CPU Speed using Dynamic Voltage and Frequency Scaling (DVFS).* We are able to reduce the energy consumed by those applications that are, for example, memory bound [57].
- *Memory Usage.* For those applications that do not require high memory bandwidth, we consider the possibility of slightly reducing the memory frequency or possibly shutting down some banks or channels of memory in order to save power [58].
- *High Performance Storage.* It may be possible to power down unneeded disks (e.g., using flash memory devices that require less power) or by spinning-down disks [59].
- *High Performance Network Interfaces.* It may be possible to power down some network subsystems (e.g., Myrinet interfaces) or using idle/sleep modes.

3.3.1 Job Allocation Policies

We have implemented two different job allocation policies: a static approach where physical servers maintain their initial subsystem configuration and a dynamic one that allows the physical servers to be reconfigured dynamically. The algorithm followed by the static resource provisioning approach for a given job is shown in Equation 3.1. For readability, we have simplified the algorithm assuming that each job can be allocated in a single server. The complete approach returns a set of servers. Given the resource requirements of a job request $(req_{cpu}, req_{mem}, req_{disk}, req_{nic})$, the available physical servers $(s_1, \ldots, s_n)$, it returns the most appropriate server to run the requested job. The resource requirements of the job request are the CPU, memory, storage, and network demand, respectively:

$$\underline{job\_mapping}(req : job\ request, \hspace{3cm} (3.1)$$

$$(req_{cpu}, req_{mem}, req_{disk}, req_{nic}) : resource\ requirements,$$

$$S = (s_1, \ldots, s_n) : physical\ servers) = s_k \ :$$

$$s_k \in S \ \wedge \ S' = \underline{match\_reqs}(req, S) \ \wedge$$

$$s_k \in S' \ \wedge \ s_k \in \underline{less\_reqs}(S') \ ).$$

First, the algorithm discards the servers that do not match the resource requirements of the job request. To do this, it uses the $\underline{match\_reqs}$ function, which is defined in Equation 3.2:

$$\underline{match\_reqs}(req, S) = S' \Leftrightarrow S' \subseteq S \ \wedge \ \forall s_i \in S' : \hspace{1.5cm} (3.2)$$

$$(\ s_{i_{cpu}} \geq req_{cpu} \wedge s_{i_{mem}} \geq req_{mem} \ \wedge$$

$$s_{i_{disk}} \geq req_{disk} \wedge s_{i_{nic}} \geq req_{nic} \ ).$$

If a server that matches the job requirements is not available, the job request cannot be served. If we follow a first come first serve (FCFS) scheduling policy with the static approach, a request may remain queued (thus blocking all following queued jobs) until a server with the required configuration becomes available. However, the scheduling policy may decide selecting another job from the queue (e.g., backfilling jobs).

Otherwise, we select the server with lowest power requirements (i.e., with the most subsystems disabled or in low power mode) and hosting the fewest jobs from the set of matching servers. It allows us to balance the load among the servers and avoid possible contention of resources. To select the server that best matches the conditions described earlier, the $less\_reqs$ function is used.

In our dynamic approach, when required physical resources are unavailable, we reconfigure an available physical server to provide the appropriate characteristics and then provision it. Specifically, we can reconfigure servers if they are idle, but if there are no idle servers available, we can reconfigure only those servers that are configured to use fewer subsystems than those that are requested (if a server is configured to deliver high memory bandwidth, we cannot reconfigure it to reduce its memory frequency, since that would negatively impact jobs already running on it. However, if a server is configured with reduced memory frequency, we can reconfigure it to deliver full memory bandwidth without negatively impacting running jobs). Moreover, we try to fill servers with requests of similar types. Not only does this efficiently load servers it also allows more servers to remain fully idle, which allows them to be configured to host new jobs.

3.3.2 Workload Profiling

In order to define the application's profiles, we characterize the workload behavior into I/O intensive, memory intensive, communication intensive, and compute intensive regions with respect to time. Most of the standard profiling utilities are designed for comparing computation efficiency of the workloads and systems on which they are running, hence their outputs are not very useful from the subsystem usage point of view. On the basis of the workload characterization, we can perform an efficient job allocation as described in Section 3.3.1.

We profiled standard HPC benchmarks with respect to behaviors and subsystem usage on individual servers. It allows us to estimate the possibilities of component-based power management in HPC workloads (Section 3.4). To collect runtime OS-level metrics for CPU utilization, hard disk I/O, and network I/O we used different mechanisms such as "mpstat", "iostat", "netstat", or "PowerTOP" from Intel. We also patched the Linux kernel 2.6.18 with the "perfctr" patch so that we can read hardware performance counters online with relatively small overhead. We instrumented the applications with PAPI (Performance Application Programming Interface) and, since the server architecture does not support total memory LD/ST counter, we counted the number of L2 cache misses, which indicates (approximately) the activity of memory.

A comprehensive set of HPC benchmark workloads has been chosen. Each stresses a variety of subsystems—compute power, memory, disk (storage), and network communication. They can be classified in three different classes as follows:

- *Standard*. **HPL** Linpack that solves a (random) dense linear system in double precision arithmetic, and **FFTW** that computes the discrete Fourier transform.
- *CPU Intensive*. **TauBench**, which is an unstructured grid benchmark of Navier Stokes solver kernels.
- *I/O Intensive*. **b_eff_io**, which is an MPI-I/O application, and **bonnie++** that focus on hard drive and file system performance. We ran two distributed instances of bonnie++ using a script and ssh.

Figure 3.2 shows the obtained profiles for three representative benchmarks with different behaviors and trends.

Axes of the plots have time as the X-axis, and on the Y-axis we show from the top to the bottom CPU utilization, memory utilization (L2 cache misses), disk utilization (number of blocks accessed), network utilization (traffic of packets on the NIC), and the average P-state residency of the CPU's cores. The plots show the measurements and the bezier curves (dashed lines) to better identify their trends, except the plots of P-state residency that only show the bezier curves, for readability.

The application's profiles show different usage level of the subsystems over time. However, subsystem's usage can be discretized into CPU-, memory-, disk-, and network bound based on the potential impact of using low power modes on the application execution's performance.

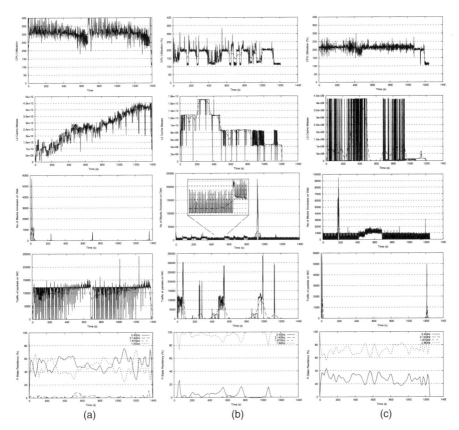

Figure 3.2   Application profiles for (a) HPL, (b) b_eff_io, and (c) bonnie++ benchmarks.

For example, in Figure 3.2, we can appreciate that HPL shows low disk usage, b_eff_io shows low CPU usage, and bonnie++ shows low CPU and NIC usages. However, there are other subsystems that have low usage only during some intervals of time, such as memory in bonnie++.

In Section 3.4, we discuss the trends and quantify the power saving opportunities based on the application profiles such as those shown in Figure 3.2.

3.4   QUANTIFYING ENERGY SAVING POSSIBILITIES

The fundamental requirement to study the potential energy saving with the approach suggested in this chapter is to gather reliable usage data for processor, memory, storage subsystem, and the NIC, and their associated power requirements for a set of representative and standard HPC workloads.

It allows us to quantify the potentials of component-level power management and to define an upper bound for possible energy savings. Along with the potential energy savings of using component-based power management, we also study the possible overheads of using these low power modes and switching between the different modes.

To do this, we characterize and analyze the power dissipation of the different subsystems and quantify the possible saving using existing techniques based on using low power modes to reduce the energy consumption.

Although we first focus on single servers, using the profiling information we will be able to proactively map job requests to servers configured with the appropriate low power modes at the datacenter level.

3.4.1   Methodology

We conducted experiments with two Dell servers, each with a Intel quad-core Xeon X3220 processors, 4 GB of memory, two SATA (Serial Advanced Technology Attachment) hard disks, and two 1 Gb ethernet interfaces. We also used a 160 GB Intel X25-M Mainstream SATA SSD disk. The processors operate at four frequencies ranging from 1.6 to 2.4 GHz. This is intended to represent a general-purpose rack server configuration widely used in large data centers.

To empirically measure the "instantaneous" power consumption of the servers, we used a *"Watts Up?"*.NET power meter that was attached between the wall power and the server. This power meter has an accuracy of $\pm 1.5\%$ of the measured power with sampling rate of 1 Hz. We estimate that the consumed energy integrating the actual power measures over time.

3.4.2   Component-Level Power Requirements

In order to quantify the possible power savings of using component-based power management in a server, we have studied empirically the power characteristics of different subsystems individually. Specifically, we have studied CPU, RAM memory, disk storage, and NIC.

Equation 3.3 shows the simplified dynamic power dissipation model that we consider for CPU, where C is the capacitance of the processor (that we consider fixed), α is an activity factor (also known as *switching activity*), and V and f are the operational voltage and frequency, respectively:

$$P_{\mathrm{cpu}} \sim C \times V^2 \times \alpha \times f. \tag{3.3}$$

Table 3.1 summarizes the server's power savings and the associated delays for the different subsystem. For the CPU, the workload was generated with lookbusy (a synthetic load generator). During CPU activity, the power demand differs up to around 82 W (i.e., 39% of total server power) depending of the frequency used, but without any load, the difference is only up to around 8 W (i.e., 3.78% of total server power). However, although CPU power is the more power demanding subsystem of the server, we rely on the CPU frequency management performed within the OS with "cpufreq" using the "ondemand" governor. For disk storage,

TABLE 3.1   Server's Power Savings and Associated Delays

Subsystem	Savings	Delay
CPU frequency (idle)	8 W	"Instantaneous"
CPU frequency (loaded)	82 W	"Instantaneous"
RAM memory	8 W	"Instantaneous"
Hard disk	10 W	5–7 s
Solid state disk	14 W	"instantaneous"
NIC	3 W	0.15 s (on) 3–4 s (off)

we consider two different possibilities, on the one hand, using spin-down/up techniques with traditional disks, and, on the other hand, using an SSD disk. With a traditional disk, we can save almost 10 W of power (i.e., around 7.5%). However, there is an overhead for spinning-down/up the disk. For spinning down the disk the delay is around 0.05 s and for spinning up the delay is around 5–6 s. There is also an overhead of energy due to the peak power required to spin up the disk's motor (around 60 J of energy, according to our experiments). We also consider using an SSD drive, which can save around 14 W of power when it is idle (i.e., 3% less power with respect to a disk in low power mode), according to our experiments. The SSD drive also has a much faster access time and does not require spinning-down techniques to reduce its power consumption.

We use low power mode for the network subsystem switching on/off the NIC dynamically. We made the assumption that data centers' servers have usually two different NICs (a faster one for actual computations and a slower one for control/administration purposes). Disabling the NIC, we can save around 3 W (i.e., 2.47%) and the overheads for switching on and switching off the NIC are around 0.15 and 3–4 s, respectively.

Memory power dissipation can be classified as being dynamic power dissipation that occurs only during reads and writes, or static power dissipation due to transistor leakage. Equation 3.4 shows a simple model for memory static power dissipation, where Vcc is the supply voltage, N is the number of transistors, k_{design} is a design-dependent parameter, and I_{leak} is a technology-dependent parameter. We will consider k_{design} and I_{leak} as fixed parameters:

$$P_{\text{static}} = Vcc \times N \times k_{\text{design}} \times \hat{I}_{\text{leak}}. \tag{3.4}$$

Since the increasing contribution of static power is clearly evident even in today's design, we can reduce the static power dissipation, reducing either Vcc or N. Some existing approaches based on multibanking techniques try to set banks of memory in lower-power modes when they are not accessed, thus reducing N. Other approaches may dynamically reduce the voltage when memory is not in the critical path of the running workload. Since these techniques are not standardly available in widely used systems (such as ours), we estimate the potential savings from memory removing physically two of the four banks of memory that are available in the server. Using the same subsystems configurations, but with only 2 GB of RAM memory installed, we were able to save around 8 W of power (i.e., 5.78%), on an average. We estimate short delay for switching to low power mode.

3.4.3 Energy Savings

In this section, we first present the estimated energy savings for a single server using a power model based on the empirical measurements shown in Table 3.1 and assuming an accurate use of low power modes ("Simulation" in Figure 3.3). Thereby, we assume that the workload profile is known in advance. The simulations were conducted using MATLAB. We used the benchmarks presented in Section 3.3.2, which, as we discussed previously, have different requirements and behaviors in terms of subsystems utilization.

We also present the energy saving obtained from actual experiments on real hardware ("Validation" in Fig. 3.3). We applied low power modes based on the application profiles with minimal penalty in performance. In addition, we performed experiments using SSD technology for storage ("With SSD" in Fig. 3.3). Although we present the saving for a single server, the results were obtained using the testbed described in Section 3.4.1.

Figure 3.3 shows the relative energy savings with respect to the energy used without component-level power management techniques, for each of five different benchmarks.

We can appreciate that CPU- and network-intensive benchmarks provide more opportunities of energy savings from disk optimization (e.g., FFTW), while I-/O-intensive benchmarks provide more opportunities of energy savings from other subsystems (e.g., NIC). Furthermore, benchmarks with higher utilization of the different subsystems (i.e., HPL) obtain less energy savings.

The average energy saving with actual executions is lower than the energy saving estimated through simulations due to the lack of memory power management in the real hardware and the lesser accuracy in switching between power modes.

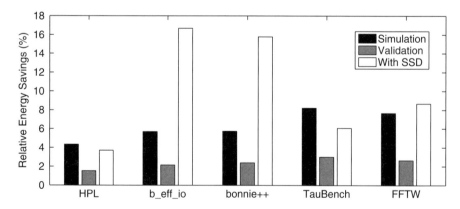

Figure 3.3 Relative energy savings per benchmark.

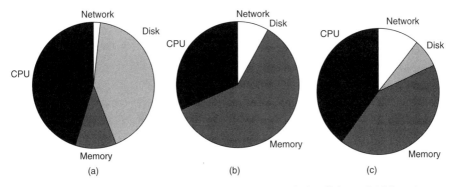

Figure 3.4   Energy savings per component for (a) HPL, (b) b_eff_io, and (c) bonnie++.

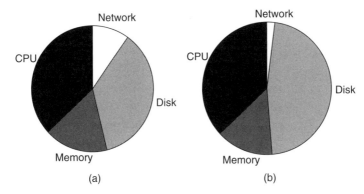

Figure 3.5   Energy savings per component for (a) TauBench and (b) FFTW.

Using SSD, technology reduces the energy consumption significantly. For nondisk intensive benchmarks (e.g., HPL) the savings are moderate, while the energy savings are much higher for I-/O-intensive benchmarks.

Figures 3.4 and 3.5 show the distribution of energy savings per component for the different benchmarks using simulation.

We do not observe any clear correlation between the distribution of energy savings per component and the total energy savings because, among other things, the total savings may depend on the amount of time for which the subsystems are used in low power mode during the benchmark's execution.

3.5   EVALUATION OF THE PROPOSED STRATEGIES

In this section, we evaluate the possible energy savings that can be achieved at the datacenter level using proactive, component-based power management with a deterministic approach. To do this, we use simulation with traces of parallel workloads. Along with traces, we also use the profiling of workloads and energy savings at server level shown previously.

3.5.1 Methodology

To evaluate the performance and energy efficiency of the proposed approach, we used real HPC workload traces from widely distributed production systems. Since not all of the required information is obtainable from these traces, some data manipulation was needed.

For our experiments, we have used the kento–perf simulator (formerly called *Alvio* [60]), which is a C++ event-driven simulator that was designed to study scheduling and allocation policies in HPC systems.

We have simulated a homogeneous cluster system based on servers with four CPUs and 8 GB of RAM each, which is a state of the art server configuration.

We also have considered the number of nodes that conformed the original systems of the workloads described in Section 3.5.2.

Using our measurements and existing research [61, 62] (e.g., to obtain the power required by a subsystem scaling from the total server power), we configured the simulations with the power required for the different subsystems and the switch latencies shown in Table 3.1. The model has some simplifications, such as using a coarse grain level for switch latencies (we use longer latencies) due to the accuracy of the simulator is by the order of seconds.

Specifically, for the CPU, we consider three different states: running mode, that is, C0 C-state and highest P-state (no savings), low power mode, that is, C0 C-state and the deepest P-state, and idle state, that is, C-state different to C0 (saving shown in Table 3.1). For the memory and storage subsystems, we consider two states (regular and low power mode) based on Table 3.1 assuming the use of newer technology for memory power management.

Since we assume that modern systems use power management techniques within the OS, we consider low power mode in our simulations when the servers are idle because low power modes may be significantly lower in the idle state than when they are in a running state [63]. We also assume that when an application is running on a server with one of its required subsystems in idle mode, the OS will switch the required subsystems to running mode.

Also taking into account the power required by the previous subsystems, we also include the power required by other components such as motherboard and fans in our model. Therefore, some fixed amount of power is always required, independent of the specific physical server configuration used. However, we do not consider the power required for cooling and to manage external elements.

Although this model is not completely accurate with respect to applications' execution behaviors, it gives us a base framework to evaluate the possibilities of proactive, component-based power management.

3.5.2 Workloads

In the present work, we have used traces from the Grid Observatory,[3] which collects, publishes, and analyzes logs on the behavior of the EGEE Grid,[4] and

---

[3]Grid Observatory Site: http://www.grid-observatory.org/.
[4]Enabling Grid for E-sciencE Site, http://www.eu-egee.org/

traces of the Intel Paragon system located at the San Diego Supercomputer Center (SDSC) from the parallel workload archive. While SDSC is a traditional HPC system composed by 416 homogeneous nodes, the EGEE Grid is a large-scale heterogeneous and distributed system composed of more than 4200 nodes.

Since the traces are in different formats and include data that is not used, they are preprocessed before being given as input to the simulation framework. First, we convert the input traces to standard workload format (SWF).[5] We also combine the multiple files of which they are composed into a single file. Then, we clean the trace in SWF format in order to eliminate failed jobs, cancelled jobs, and anomalies.

As the traces found from different systems do not provide all the information needed for our analysis, we needed to complete them using a model based on the benchmarking of HPC applications (Section 3.3.2).

After calculating the average percentage of CPU, memory, storage, and network usage for each benchmark, we randomly assign one of the possible benchmark profiles to each request in the input trace, following a uniform distribution.

We also generate two variants of each trace randomly assigning benchmark profiles by bursts. The bursts of job requests are sized (randomly) from 1 to 5 job requests and from 1 to 10 job requests. These traces are intended to illustrate the submission of scientific HPC workflows that are composed of sets of jobs with the same resource requirements.

3.5.3 Metrics

We evaluate the impact of our approach on the following metrics: makespan (workload execution time, which is the difference between the earliest time of submission of any of the workload tasks and the latest time of completion of any of its tasks), average-bounded slowdown (BSLD), energy consumption (based on both static and dynamic energy consumption), and energy delay product (EDP).

We define BSLD for a given job:

$$\text{BSLD}_{\text{job}} = \max\left(1, \frac{\text{runtime}_{\text{job}} + \text{waittime}_{\text{job}}}{\max(\text{runtime}_{\text{job}}, \ \text{threshold})}\right),$$

We consider a threshold of 60 s, which is commonly used in HPC systems to avoid the influence of unrepresentative (very short) jobs.

3.6 RESULTS

We have conducted our simulations using the proposed strategies, workloads, and system models described in the previous sections with respect to a reference approach, which represents the most commonly used configuration in HPC datacenters. Specifically, we have evaluated the following strategies:

---

[5]Parallel Workload Archive Site: http://www.cs.huji.ac.il/labs/parallel/workload/.

- *REFERENCE (REF)*. It implements the typical reactive power management at the OS level (i.e., DVFS when the CPU is not loaded). It follows the First-Fit resource selection policy to allocate job requests to servers. This means that it maps a given job to the first available physical servers that match the request requirements.
- *STATIC*. It implements our proactive approach with the proposed static allocation policy. It means that the servers' configurations remain constant; therefore a physical server can host only applications that match its specific characteristics. Specifically, we consider eight classes of configurations (one for each possible combination of their subsystems configuration) and we model the same amount of servers with each one.
- *DYNAMIC*. It implements our proposed approach similarly to the STATIC strategy, but implementing dynamic resource reconfigurations when they are necessary. This means that when there are not available resources configured with the requested configuration, it reconfigures servers reactively in order to service new application requests.
- *DYNAMIC-2*. It implements the same policy of the DYNAMIC strategy, but it allows to reconfigure the subsystems of a server only when it is idle.

We have used three different variants of the workloads described in Section 3.5.2 as follows:

- *NO-BURSTS*. It follows the original distribution of the workloads described in the previous section.
- *BURSTS-5* and **series BURSTS-10**. The job requests are by bursts sized randomly from 1 to 5 and from 1 to 10, respectively.

Figures 3.6–3.8, and 3.9 show the relative makespan, average BSLD, energy consumption, and EDP results, respectively. In each of these figures, we show the results obtained from both EGEE and SDSC traces in the same Y-axis scale. For readability, the results are normalized to the results obtained with the REFERENCE configuration and the NO-BURSTS workload variant.

Figures 3.6 and 3.7 show that both makespan and BSLD results follow similar patterns. With the REFERENCE strategy, the delays are shorter than those obtained with the STATIC strategy. However, the delays obtained with the REFERENCE and the DYNAMIC strategy are very similar. This is explained by the fact that using STATIC strategy with available resources matching the request requirements is harder because the number of resources with the same subsystem configuration is fixed. This is specially significant with the SDSC because it has less number of nodes and, therefore, a small number of nodes of each subsystem configuration.

In fact, the obtained results from EGEE are, in general, better than those obtained from SDSC because with EGEE there are a much higher number of nodes of each configuration, which results in higher probability to find resources that matches the job's requirements.

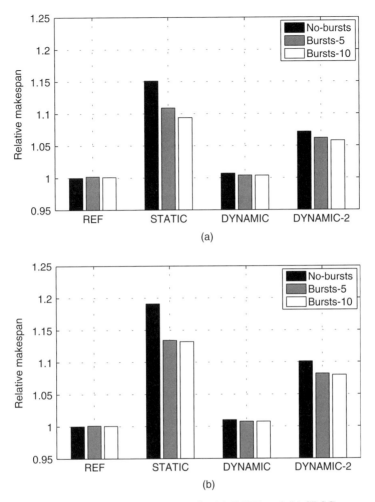

Figure 3.6   Relative makespan for (a) EGEE and (b) SDSC.

As with the STATIC strategy, the makespan obtained from the DYNAMIC-2 policy is longer than that obtained from the REFERENCE strategy. In both cases, the makespan is longer because of scheduling issues (resource limitations cause job blocking in the queue) and not because of the use of low power modes.

The BSLD is higher with the STATIC and DYNAMIC-2 strategies. It means that with both of these policies the job waiting times are much longer than the job waiting times with STATIC and DYNAMIC.

The impact of the size of the workload bursts on the different metrics is significant with the STATIC and DYNAMIC-2 strategies. This is explained because of the fact that it is easier to allocate jobs in nodes with the same configuration when they are submitted together (filling servers with jobs with same requirements).

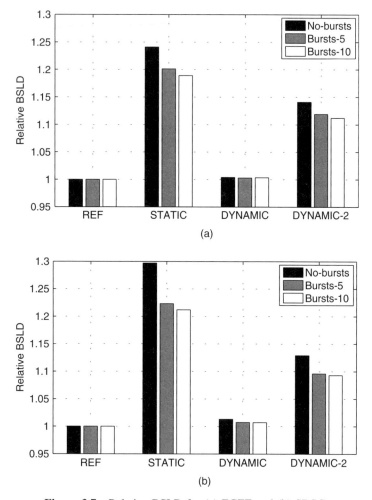

Figure 3.7 Relative BSLD for (a) EGEE and (b) SDSC.

However, using the SDSC workload, there is not much difference between bursts of up to 5 and bursts up to 10 because in SDSC the number of nodes is smaller.

Although the makespan is shorter with the REFERENCE approach, the energy consumption is lower with our proposed strategies than that obtained with REF-ERENCE. Specifically, both STATIC and DYNAMIC approaches obtain between 6% and 12% of energy savings with respect to the REFERENCE approach.

The EDP obtained with the DYNAMIC strategy is around 5% lower (on average) than the that obtained with the REFERENCE approach. However, the DYNAMIC-2 strategy presents a higher EDP. In both cases, the energy efficiency is better for those workloads composed by bursts of jobs with similar requirements. It allows us to perform a more efficient mapping because the probabilities to reconfigure a server are lower. It also results in lower over provisioning of the

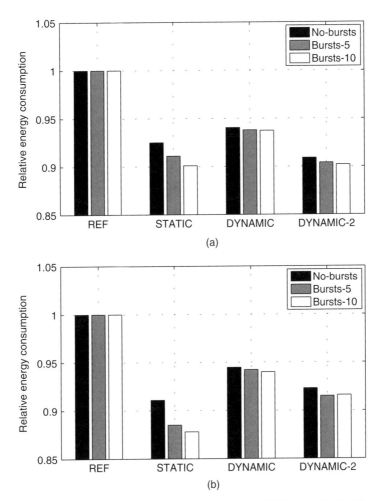

Figure 3.8 Relative energy consumption for (a) EGEE and (b) SDSC.

server's subsystems, which is the difference between the subsystems that are in active mode and the subsystems required by the applications.

Although the energy consumption is lower in STATIC approach with respect to the REFERENCE approach, the EDP is much higher. This is explained by the fact that the limitations in the subsystems availability results in lower resource utilization and, therefore, even though the energy consumption of the resources is lower, the resources are used during longer time.

Therefore, we can conclude that STATIC and DYNAMIC-2 strategies do not provide significant improvements with respect to the REFERENCE approach, but DYNAMIC presents better energy efficiency (more than 5%, on average) with very little penalty on the performance (makespan). Moreover, we have stated that a higher number of nodes facilitates the proactive configuration of subsystems

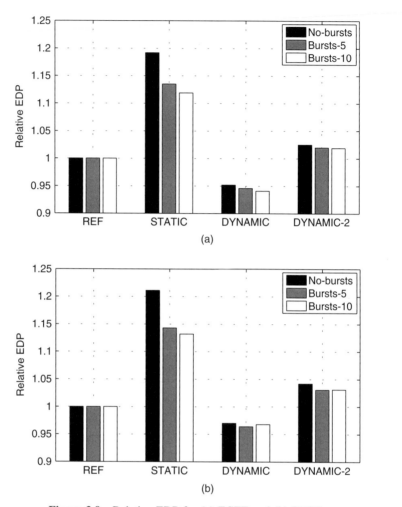

Figure 3.9 Relative EDP for (a) EGEE and (b) SDSC.

in scenarios with restrictions (STATIC and DYNAMIC-2), provides more energy savings, and reduces the over provisioning (in terms of subsystems).

3.7 CONCLUDING REMARKS

In this chapter, we studied the potential impact of deterministic application-centric power control at the device level on the overall energy efficiency of a system. Specifically, we analyzed the energy consumption of a node according to the usage of its processor, memory, storage subsystem, and the NIC. Moreover, we evaluated the possible energy savings at a datacenter level through the use of proactive power management.

Our simulations showed that proactive, component-based power management can be effective to save energy if the systems have sufficient mechanisms to provide an accurate dynamic management of the subsystems based on the characteristics of the workload. The results stated that using application-aware subsystem, power control can save additional energy, so it is fundamental to characterize the workload appropriately.

We conclude that power management at the subsystem level cannot be neglected because of the increasing requirements of energy efficiency optimization in large-scale data centers. We believe that our proposed predictive application-aware power management approach has sufficient potential to tackle this problem at the datacenter level. Moreover, we stated that the potential of proactive power management techniques is higher when the number of nodes available is higher. We also can conclude that current and ongoing technologies such as memory that allow DVS must be adopted and supported in large-scale data centers to enhance global energy optimizations. Finally, the findings of this work showed that there are opportunities to improve the job scheduling and resource allocation strategies in HPC systems considering proactive, component-level power management.

3.8 SUMMARY

Energy efficiency of large-scale data centers is becoming a major concern not only for reasons of energy conservation, failures, and cost reduction but also because such systems are soon reaching the limits of power available to them. HPC systems may consume power in megawatts, and of all the power consumed by such a system only a fraction is used for actual computations.

In this chapter, we studied the potential of application-centric proactive power management of data center's resources for HPC workloads. Specifically, we considered power management mechanisms and controls (currently or soon to be) available at different levels and for different subsystems, and leverage several innovative approaches that have been taken to tackle this problem in the last few years, can be effectively used in a application-aware manner for HPC workloads.

To do this, we first profiled standard HPC benchmarks with respect to behaviors, resource usage, and power impact on individual computing nodes. On the basis of the findings at the server level, we proposed proactive, component-based power management techniques with the purpose of improving energy efficiency with little or no performance loss. We then evaluated our proposed algorithm through simulations using empirical power characterization and quantification.

The obtained results showed that by using proactive, component-level power management, we can reduce the average energy consumption without significant penalty in performance if the systems have sufficient mechanisms to provide an accurate dynamic management of the subsystems based on the characteristics of the workload.

The results also stated that the potential of proactive power management techniques is higher when the number of nodes available is higher.

Our findings motivate the development of autonomic components responsible for component-based power management and the implementation of power-aware scheduling and resource allocation strategies in HPC systems.

ACKNOWLEDGMENTS

The research presented in this work is supported in part by National Science Foundation (NSF) via grants numbers IIP 0758566 and DMS-0835436, by the Department of Energy ExaCT Combustion Co-Design Center via subcontract number 4000110839 from UT Battelle and via the grant numbers DE-SC0007455 and DE-FG02-06ER54857, and by an IBM Faculty Award, and was conducted as part of the NSF Cloud and Autonomic Computing (CAC) Center at Rutgers University. The authors would like to thank Sharat Chandra, Rajeev Muralidhar, Harinarayanan Seshadri, Andres Quiroz, Francesc Guim, and Steve Poole for their contributions and the Grid Observatory, which is part of the EGEE-III EU project INFSO-RI-222667.

REFERENCES

1. Dean J. Large-scale distributed systems at google: Current systems and future directions. In: 3rd ACM SIGOPS International Workshop on Large Scale Distributed Systems and Middleware; Big Sky (MT); 2009 Oct.

2. Brown R, Masanet E, Nordman B, Tschudi B, Shehabi A, Stanley J, et al., Report to Congress on Server and Data Center Energy Efficiency: Public Law 109–431. Lawrence Berkeley National Laboratory, Berkeley (CA), 2008.

3. Sharma S, Hsu C-H, Feng W. Making a case for a green500 list. In: Workshop on High-Performance, Power-Aware Computing (HPPAC) in conjunction with IPDPS; 2006. p. 8.

4. Liu Y, Zhu H. A survey of the research on power management techniques for high-performance systems. Softw Pract Exp 2010;40(11):943–964.

5. Hsu C, Feng W. A feasibility analysis of power awareness in commodity-based high-performance clusters. In: IEEE International Conference on Cluster Computing; Boston (MA); 2005. pp. 1–10.

6. Hsu C-H, Feng W. A power-aware run-time system for high-performance computing. In: ACM/IEEE Conference on High Performance Networking and Computing (SC'05); Seattle (WA); 2005. p. 1.

7. Naveh A, Rotem E, Mendelson A, Gochman S, Chabukswar R, Krishnan K, Kumar A. Power and Thermal Management in the Intel Core Duo Processor. Technical report, Intel Technology Journal; 2006 May.

8. Pallipadi V, Li S, Belay A. Cpuidle-do nothing efficiently... In: Ottawa Linux Symposium (OLS'07); 2007 Jun; Ottawa,Ontario, Canada.

9. Pallipadi V, Siddha SB. Processor power management features and process scheduler: do we need to tie them together? LinuxConf Europe; 2007 Sep.

10. Siddha S, Pallipadi V, Van De Ven A. Getting maximum mileage out of tickless. In: Ottawa Linux Symposium (OLS'07); 2007 Jun; Ottawa, Ontario, Canada. pp. 201–208.

11. Kappiah N, Freeh VW, Lowenthal DK. Just in time dynamic voltage scaling: exploiting inter-node slack to save energy in MPI programs. In: SC '05: Proceedings of the 2005 ACM/IEEE conference on Supercomputing; Seattle (WA); 2005. p. 33.

12. Lim MY, Freeh VW, Lowenthal DK. Adaptive, transparent frequency and voltage scaling of communication phases in MPI programs. In: SC '06: Proceedings of the 2006 ACM/IEEE conference on Supercomputing; Tampa (FL); 2006. p. 107.

13. Rountree B, Lowenthal DK, Funk S, Freeh VW, de Supinski BR, Schulz M. Bounding energy consumption in large-scale MPI programs. In: SC '07: Proceedings of the 2007 ACM/IEEE conference on Supercomputing; New York; 2007. pp. 1–9.

14. Freeh VW, Pan F, Kappiah N, Lowenthal DK, Springer R. Exploring the energy-time tradeoff in MPI programs on a power-scalable cluster. In: IPDPS '05: Proceedings of the 19th IEEE International Parallel and Distributed Processing Symposium (IPDPS'05) - Papers; Washington (DC); 2005. p. 4.1.

15. Freeh VW, Lowenthal DK. Using multiple energy gears in MPI programs on a power-scalable cluster. In: PPoPP '05: Proceedings of the 10th ACM SIGPLAN Symposium on Principles and Practice of Parallel Programming; Chicago (IL); 2005. pp. 164–173.

16. Cameron KW, Ge R, Feng X. High-performance, power-aware distributed computing for scientific applications. Computer 2005;38(11):40–47.

17. Chen Y, Das A, Qin W, Sivasubramaniam A, Wang Q, Gautam N. Managing server energy and operational costs in hosting centers. In: ACM SIGMETRICS International Conference on Measurement and Modeling of Computer Systems; Banff, Alberta, Canada; 2005. pp. 303–314.

18. Ranganathan P, Leech P, Irwin D, Chase J. Ensemble-level power management for dense blade servers. SIGARCH Comput Arch News 2006;34(2):66–77.

19. Horvath T, Skadron K. Multi-mode energy management for multi-tier server clusters. In: International Conference on Parallel Architectures and Compilation Techniques (PACT'08); Toronto, Canada 2008. pp. 270–279.

20. Wang X, Chen M. Cluster level feedback power control for power optimization. In: International Symposium on High Performance Computer Architecture (HPCA'08); Knoxville (TN) 2008. pp. 101–110.

21. Rountree B, Lownenthal DK, Supinski BR, Schulz M, Freeh VW, Bletsch T. Adagio: making DVS practical for complex HPC applications. In: ICS '09 Proceedings of the 23rd International Conference on Supercomputing; Portland (OR) 2009. pp. 460–469.

22. Raghavendra R, Ranganathan P, Talwar V, Wang Z, Zhu X. No "power" struggles: coordinated multi-level power management for the data center. SIGOPS Oper Syst Rev 2008;42(2):48–59.

23. Feng X, Ge R, Cameron KW. Power and energy profiling of scientific applications on distributed systems. In: IPDPS '05: Proceedings of the 19th IEEE International Parallel and Distributed Processing Symposium (IPDPS'05) - Papers; Denver (CO); 2005. p. 34.

24. Delaluz V, Kandemir MT, Vijaykrishnan N, Irwin MJ. Energy-oriented compiler optimizations for partitioned memory architectures. In: CASES '00: Proceedings of the 2000 International Conference on Compilers, Architecture, and Synthesis for Embedded Systems; San Jose (CA); 2000. pp. 138–147.

25. Delaluz V, Kandemir M, Vijaykrishnan N, Sivasubramaniam A, Irwin MJ. Hardware and software techniques for controlling dram power modes. IEEE Trans Comput 2001;50(11):1154–1173.

26. Delaluz V, Kandemir MT, Kolcu I. Automatic data migration for reducing energy consumption in multi-bank memory systems. In: DAC '02: Proceedings of the 39th Annual Design Automation Conference; New Orleans (LA); 2002. pp. 213–218.

27. Delaluz V, Sivasubramaniam A, Kandemir MT, Vijaykrishnan N, Irwin MJ. Scheduler-based dram energy management. In: DAC '02: Proceedings of the 39th annual Design Automation Conference; New Orleans (LA) 2002. pp. 697–702.

28. Huang MC, Renau J, Torrellas J. Positional adaptation of processors: application to energy reduction. In: ISCA '03: Proceedings of the 30th Annual International Symposium on Computer Architecture; 2003. pp. 157–168.

29. Fradj HB, Belleudy C, Auguin M. System level multi-bank main memory configuration for energy reduction. In: PATMOS; 2006. pp. 84–94.

30. Fradj HB, Belleudy C, Auguin M. Multi-bank main memory architecture with dynamic voltage frequency scaling for system energy optimization. In: DSD; Dubrovnik, Croatia; 2006. pp. 89–96.

31. Diniz B, Guedes D, Meira W Jr., Bianchini R. Limiting the power consumption of main memory. In: ISCA '07: Proceedings of the 34th Annual International Symposium on Computer Architecture; San Diego (CA); 2007. pp. 290–301.

32. Hur I, Lin C. A comprehensive approach to dram power management. In: 14th International Conference on High-Performance Computer Architecture (HPCA); Salt Lake Citi, UT, USA; 2008. pp. 305–316.

33. Rotem D, Otoo E, Tsao S-C. Analysis of trade-off between power saving and response time in disk StorageSystems. In: 5th Workshop on High-Performance Power-Aware Computing (HPPAC'09) with IPDPS'09; Rome, Italy; 2009 May.

34. Pinheiro E, Bianchini R. Energy conservation techniques for disk array-based servers. In: ICS '04: Proceedings of the 18th Annual International Conference on Supercomputing; Saint-Malo, France; 2004. pp. 68–78.

35. Pinheiro E, Bianchini R, Dubnicki C. Exploiting redundancy to conserve energy in storage systems. SIGMETRICS Perform Eval Rev 2006;34(1):15–26.

36. Colarelli D, Grunwald D. Massive arrays of idle disks for storage archives. In: Supercomputing '02: Proceedings of the 2002 ACM/IEEE conference on Supercomputing; 2002. pp. 1–11.

37. Yin S, Ruan X, Manzanares A, Qin X. How reliable are parallel disk systems when energy-saving schemes are involved? In: IEEE International Conference on Cluster Computing and Workshops; New Orleans (LA); 2009. pp. 1–9.

38. Seo E, Park SY, Urgaonkar B. Empirical analysis on energy efficiency of flash-based SSDS. In: 1st Workshop on Power Aware Computing and Systems (HotPower'08), Co-located with OSDI 2008, San Diego (CA); 2008.

39. Lee HJ, Lee KH, Noh SH. Augmenting raid with an ssd for energy relief. In: 1st Workshop on Power Aware Computing and Systems (HotPower'08), Co-located with OSDI 2008; San Diego (CA); 2008.

40. Li X, Gupta R, Adve SV, Zhou Y. Cross-component energy management: joint adaptation of processor and memory. ACM Trans Arch Code Optim 2007;4(3):14.

41. Cho Y, Chang N. Memory-aware energy-optimal frequency assignment for dynamic supply voltage scaling. In: ISLPED '04: Proceedings of the 2004 International Symposium on Low Power Electronics and Design; Newport (CA) 2004. pp. 387–392.

42. Li X, Li Z, Zhou Y, Adve S. Performance directed energy management for main memory and disks. ACM Trans Storage 2005;1(3):346–380.

43. Moore JD, Chase JS, Ranganathan P. Weatherman: automated, online and predictive thermal mapping and management for data centers. In: International Conference on Autonomic Computing; Dublin, Ireland; 2006. pp. 155–164.

44. Moore J, Chase J, Ranganathan P, Sharma R. Making scheduling "cool": temperature-aware workload placement in data centers. In: Annual Conference on USENIX Annual Technical Conference; Anaheim (CA); 2005. pp. 5–5.

45. Bash C, Forman G. Cool job allocation: measuring the power savings of placing jobs at cooling-efficient locations in the data center. In: USENIX Annual Technical Conference; Santa Clara (CA); 2007. pp. 363–368.

46. Tang Q, Gupta SKS, Varsamopoulos G. Energy-efficient thermal-aware task scheduling for homogeneous high-performance computing data centers: a cyber-physical approach. IEEE Trans Parallel Distrib Syst 2008;19(11):1458–1472.

47. Heath T, Centeno AP, George P, Ramos L, Jaluria Y, Bianchini R. Mercury and freon: temperature emulation and management for server systems. In: International Conference on Architectural Support for Programming Languages and Operating Systems; San Jose (CA) 2006. pp. 106–116.

48. Ramos L, Bianchini R. C-oracle: predictive thermal management for data centers. In: International Symposium on High-Performance Computer Architecture; Salt Lake City (UT) 2008. pp. 111–122.

49. Nathuji R, Schwan K. Virtualpower: coordinated power management in virtualized enterprise systems. In: ACM SIGOPS Symposium on Operating Systems Principles; Stevenson (WA) 2007. pp. 265–278.

50. Rusu C, Ferreira A, Scordino C, Watson A. Energy-efficient real-time heterogeneous server clusters. In: IEEE Real-Time and Embedded Technology and Applications Symposium; San Jose (CA); 2006. pp. 418–428.

51. Kephart JO, Chan H, Das R, Levine DW, Tesauro G, Rawson F, Lefurgy C. Coordinating multiple autonomic managers to achieve specified power-performance tradeoffs. In: International Conference on Autonomic Computing; Jacksonville (FL); 2007. p. 24.

52. Das R, Kephart JO, Lefurgy C, Tesauro G, Levine DW, Chan H. Autonomic multi-agent management of power and performance in data centers. In: International Joint Conference on Autonomous Agents and Multiagent Systems; Estoril, Portugal; 2008. pp. 107–114.

53. Song Y, Sun Y, Wang H, Song X. An adaptive resource flowing scheme amongst vms in a vm-based utility computing. In: IEEE International Conference on Computer and Information Technology; Aizu-Wakamatsu City, Fukushima, Japan; 2007. pp. 1053–1058.

54. Kumar S, Talwar V, Kumar V, Ranganathan P, Schwan K. vmanage: loosely coupled platform and virtualization management in data centers. In: International Conference on Autonomic Computing; Barcelona, Spain; 2009. pp. 127–136.

55. Soror AA, Minhas UF, Aboulnaga A, Salem K, Kokosielis P, Kamath Sunil. Automatic virtual machine configuration for database workloads. In: ACM SIGMOD International Conference on Management of Data; Vancouver, BC, Canada; 2008. pp. 953–966.

56. Laszewski G, Wang L, Younge AJ, He X. Power-aware scheduling of virtual machines in DVFS-enabled clusters. In: IEEE International Conference on Cluster Computing; New Orleans (LA) 2009. pp. 1–10.

57. Isci C, Contreras G, Martonosi M. Live, runtime phase monitoring and prediction on real systems with application to dynamic power management. In: IEEE/ACM International Symposium on Microarchitecture; Orlando (FL); 2006. pp. 359–370.

58. Fradj HB, Belleudy C, Auguin Michel. Multi-bank main memory architecture with dynamic voltage frequency scaling for system energy optimization. In: EUROMICRO Conference on Digital System Design; Dubrovnik, Croatia; 2006. pp. 89–96.

59. Bisson T, Brandt SA, Long DDE. A hybrid disk-aware spin-down algorithm with i/o subsystem support. In: IEEE International Performance, Computing, and Communications Conference; New Orleans (LA); 2007. pp. 236–245.

60. Guim F, Labarta J, Corbalan J. Modeling the impact of resource sharing in backfilling policies using the alvio simulator. In: IEEE International Symposium on Modeling, Analysis and Simulation of Computer and Telecommunication Systems. Istanbul, Turkey; 2007. pp. 145–150.

61. Minas L, Ellison B. *Energy Efficiency for Information Technology: How to Reduce Power Consumption in Servers and Data Centers*. Intel Press; Hillsboro (OR); 2009.

62. Pfluenger J, Hanson S. Data center efficiency in the scalable enterprise. Dell Power Solutions; 2007 Feb.

63. Cai Q, González J, Rakvic R, Magklis G, Chaparro P, González Antonio. Meeting points: using thread criticality to adapt multicore hardware to parallel regions. In: International Conference on Parallel Architectures and Compilation Techniques; Toronto, Canada; 2008. pp. 240–249.

CHAPTER 4

A STOCHASTIC FRAMEWORK FOR HIERARCHICAL SYSTEM-LEVEL POWER MANAGEMENT

PENG RONG and MASSOUD PEDRAM

4.1 INTRODUCTION

Dynamic power management (DPM), which refers to a selective shut off or slow down of components that are idle or underutilized, has proven to be a particularly effective way of reducing power dissipation in such systems. In the literature, various DPM techniques have been proposed, from heuristic methods presented in early works [1, 2] to stochastic optimization approaches [3, 4]. Among the heuristic DPM methods, the time-out policy is the most widely used approach and has been implemented in many operating systems. The time-out policy is simple and easy to implement, but it has many shortcomings, such as not making use of the statistical information about the service request (SR) rates and having a limited ability to trade off performance and energy dissipation. Stochastic approaches are mathematically rigorous approaches that are based on stochastic models of SRs and are thus able to derive provably optimal DPM policies.

Reference 5 considered job scheduling as part of a power management policy and proposed an on-line scheme that groups jobs based on their device usage requirements and then checks every possible execution sequence of the job groups to find out the one with minimal power consumption. This work is quite valuable because it demonstrates the potential for additional power saving by doing job scheduling. However, this work also has a few shortcomings. First, each time a new job is generated, the search procedure to find the minimal-power execution sequence has to be repeated. Second, this scheme does not explore the possibility of reducing the system energy by changing the working state of devices that have

Energy-Efficient Distributed Computing Systems, First Edition.
Edited by Albert Y. Zomaya and Young Choon Lee.
© 2012 John Wiley & Sons, Inc. Published 2012 by John Wiley & Sons, Inc.

multiple functional states. Third, exact knowledge of the device usage of a job is required before the job can be scheduled. It is also assumed that this device usage profile does not change during the lifetime of a job. It is not clear how this scheme can capture the dependence between two parts of the same job, if the two parts exhibit very different device usage behavior. Finally, this scheme does not make use of any prediction or expectation of the future behavior of the system and thus can only make a greedy on-line decision.

To capture dependencies between different system components, a power manager must have a global view of the system architecture, connection among components, system resources that are shared among these components, and any possible functional dependency between the components. In addition, application-level scheduling requires the power manager to work closely with the operating system scheduler. Both these tasks are beyond the capabilities of the existing component-level power management solutions.

A number of power saving mechanisms have been already incorporated into various standards and protocols. Examples are the power management function defined in USB bus standard and the power saving mode in the IEEE 802.11 protocol. An USB device will automatically enter a suspended state if there is no bus activity for 3 ms. A wireless local area network (WLAN) card operating in the power saving mode needs to wake up periodically at the beginning of a beacon interval and listen for traffic identification message.

In most cases, these built-in power management solutions cannot be changed because they ensure the correct functionality of a device running the related protocol. In this sense, we consider such a device as an uncontrollable or self-power-managed component. Even beyond protocol considerations, vendors have already begun to develop power management software specifically designed for their products. An example is the enhanced adaptive battery life extender (EABLE) for Hitachi (IBM Storage Systems, originally) disk drive, which is self-managed and is incorporated into the device driver [6]. EABLE dynamically determines the appropriate mode based on the actual disk access pattern and the internal level of drive activity. Finally, implementation of the device power manager by the designers and manufacturers of the device itself may relieve the system integrators of the burden of mastering detailed hardware and device driver expertise and thus facilitates power awareness in system integration with multiple components.

The component designer does not know the global characteristics and performance requirements of the system in which the component will be incorporated. Therefore, the best the designer can do is to provide a generic local power management policy for the component but make some tuning parameters of the local policy controllable by the system designer and the system-level power manager. On the other hand, a system engineer, who devises the architecture of an EMC system and takes care of interfacing and synchronization issues among the selected components, can devise a global power management policy that may help the local power manager (LPM) to improve power efficiency of the component.

On the basis of the above considerations, we define the problem of hierarchical power management (HPM) for an EMC system with self-power-managed components. More specifically, this chapter targets a uniprocessor computer system that consists of multiple I/O devices. It is possible to extend the proposed approach and apply it to a multiprocessor system or a computer cluster, a task which is beyond the scope of this chapter. The problem is then formulated as a mathematical program with the aid of continuous-time Markovian decision process (CTMDP) models and solved accordingly.

The key contributions of this chapter may be summarized as follows.

1. A hierarchical DPM architecture is proposed, where the power management function is decomposed into system and component levels. This division facilitates the integration of various power management techniques into a two-tiered organization and enhances system-level power awareness. At the system level, flow control on the SR traffic is used to improve the effectiveness of built-in component-level power management solutions. Note that the proposed power management architecture can easily handle service providers (SPs) with or without built-in LPMs.

2. CTMDP-based application-level scheduling is incorporated into system-level power management to achieve further power reduction. This scheduling is stochastically optimized by using the CTMDP model. Applications are scheduled based on the global system state comprising the states of the individual components, the number of waiting tasks, and application stochastic characteristics. In this way, our proposed solution is very different from that in Reference 5.

3. The proposed system-level power management handles component state dependencies, where the state of a SP is affected by states of the other SPs.

The remainder of this chapter is organized as follows. In Section 4.2, related works are discussed. The background of CTMDP is introduced in Section 4.3. Details of the proposed hierarchical DPM framework are described in Section 4.4. In Section 4.5, stochastic model of the system-level power management is provided. The energy optimization problem is formulated and solved as a mathematical program in Section 4.6. Experimental results and conclusions are provided in Sections 4.7 and 4.8, respectively.

4.2 RELATED WORK

The CTMDP-based DPM approach was first proposed in Reference 4. CTMDP-based approach makes policy changes in an asynchronous and event-driven manner and thus surmounts the shortcoming of an earlier work based on discrete-time Markovian decision processes [3], which relied on periodical policy evaluation. Therefore, CTMDP-based DPM approach is more suitable for implementation as part of a real-time operating system environment because of its event-driven nature. Owing to space limitation, the background for CTMDP models is not provided here. Interested readers may refer to Reference 7.

The literature also proposes other stochastic DMP approaches. Reference 8 improved on the modeling technique in Reference 3 using time-indexed semi-Markovian decision processes. Recently, Theocharous et al. [9] discussed several promising DPM techniques including partially observable Markovian decision processes based approach; however, no results are published so far.

In the literature, some works related to HPM have been reported. Reference 10 proposes a DPM methodology for networks-on-chips, which combines node- and network-centric DPM decisions. More specifically, the node-centric DPM uses time-indexed semi-Markovian decision processes, whereas the network-centric DPM allows a source node to use network sleep/wake-up requests to force sink nodes to enter specified states. Our proposed work differs from this approach by providing a more general and mathematically rigorous framework for defining and solving hierarchical DPM problems in an EMC system. In particular, application-level scheduling is exploited and component state dependency is considered by the system-level power manager. In addition, by using a globally controlled SR flow regulation process, our framework can handle self-power-managed SPs and dynamically adjust their local power management policies. Reference 11 proposes a hierarchical scheme for adaptive DPM under nonstationary SRs, where the term *hierarchical* refers to the manner by which the authors construct a DPM policy. This is different from what is proposed in this chapter. More precisely, in their work, the authors formulate policy optimization as a problem of seeking an optimal rule that switches policies among a set of precomputed ones. However, this chapter assumes that the SPs are fully controllable and have no built-in power management policy. This work differentiates SR generation between "modes" (applications), but application-level scheduling is not considered. In addition, it focuses on developing power management policies for a single device.

Another kind of HPM schemes incorporate into one platform multiple hardware components with identical or exchangeable functionality but different levels of power and performance. Reference 12 proposes a scheme that equips each mobile node two complementary radios (long-distance high power vs. short-distance low power) and uses both radios to participate in contact discovery. This scheme controls the wake-up interval of each radio to trade between energy savings and the performance of message delivery. Reference 13 presents a HPM architecture that focuses on providing high levels of consistency in a laptop by integrating two additional low power processors: StrongARM and ATmega. In this chapter, a dedicated distribution of each application over the processors is predesigned to evaluate power saving.

4.3   A HIERARCHICAL DPM ARCHITECTURE

In this chapter, we consider a uniprocessor computer system that consists of multiple I/O devices, for example, hard disk, WLAN card, or USB devices. Batches of applications keep running on the system. When an application is running on the CPU, it may send requests to one or more devices for services. A performance constraint is imposed on the average throughput of the computer system. The constraint is defined as a minimum amount of completed application workloads over a fixed period of time. It is also required that each application gets a proportional (fair) amount of CPU execution time over a long period. Our objective is to minimize the energy consumption of the computer system. More precisely, this chapter focuses on reducing energy consumption of the I/O devices. Saving processor and memory energy is out of the scope of this chapter. Readers interested in these power components can refer to References 14 and 15.

The architecture of our proposed hierarchical DPM framework that contains two SPs, that is, two I/O devices, is presented in Figure 4.1. This architecture has two levels of PM: the component level and the system level. In the former, each SP is controlled by a LPM. The LPM performs a conventional PM function, that is, it monitors the number of SRs that are waiting in the component queue (CQ) and consequently adjusts the state of the SP. In the latter level, the global power manager (GPM) acts as the central controller that attempts to meet a global performance constraint while reducing the system power consumption. In particular, GPM performs three separate functions.

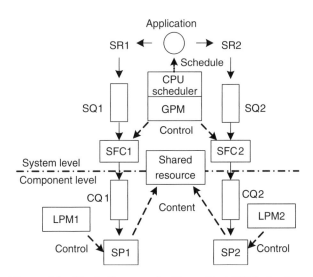

Figure 4.1   Block diagram of a hierarchical DPM structure.

1. It determines the state of the service flow controller (SFC) and regulates the SR traffic that is subsequently fed into the CQs. Note that in this architecture, the GPM cannot overwrite the LPM policy or directly control the state transition of an SP. Thus, regulating SR flow is the method used by GPM to guide the local PM policy and improve the power efficiency of the SPs.

2. It works with the CPU scheduler to select the right applications to run so as to reduce the system power dissipation. This decision is in turn made on the basis of the current state of the PM system, including the states of the SPs and the number of SRs waiting in a service queue (SQ).

3. It resolves the contention for shared resources between different SPs and dynamically assigns the resources so as to increase the system power efficiency. As the side note, the SFC performs three functions, namely, SR transfer, SR blocking, and fake SR generation, to adjust the statistics of the SR flow that reaches the SP. The SRs that are blocked by the SFC are kept in a SQ.

4.4 MODELING

We represent the hierarchical DPM structure by a CTMDP model as shown in Figure 4.2. This model, which is constructed from the point of view of the GPM, is utilized to derive a system-level PM policy. The CTMDP model contains the following components: an application model (APPL), the SQ, the SFC, and a simulated service provider (SSP).

The SSP is a CTMDP model of the LPM-controlled SP as seen by the GPM. More precisely, it is a composition of the state-transition diagram of the SP and the corresponding LPM policy. Notice that the CQ model is not needed because from the viewpoint of the GPM, the CQ and SQ are identical. In the following subsections, the APPL, SFC, and SSP models are described in detail followed by modeling of the dependencies between the SPs. An example transition diagram for the SSP is provided in Figure 4.2.

4.4.1 Model of the Application Pool

It is assumed that the applications running on the computer system can be classified into different types based on their *workload characteristics*, that is, their SR generation rates and the target SPs (i.e., service destinations.) In Reference 11, the authors report that the pattern of SRs generated by an application and sent to a hard disk may be modeled by a Poisson process. Here, we use a more general model, that is, a CTMDP model, to describe the complex nature of SR generation of an application. When an application that is running on the CPU moves from one internal state to next, it generates various types of SRs with different rates. For example, as illustrated in Figure 4.3, in state r_{1a}, application type 1 generates SR1 with a rate of $\lambda_{1a}^{(1)}$ and SR2 with a rate of $\lambda_{1a}^{(2)}$. Similarly, in state r_{1b}, the

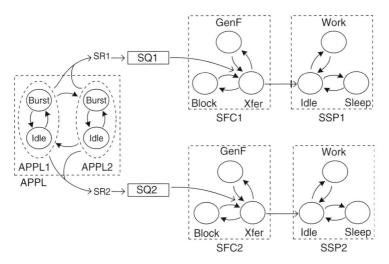

Figure 4.2 CTMDP model of the hierarchical DPM structure.

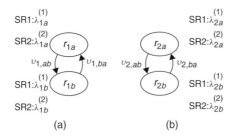

Figure 4.3 CTMDP models of application types (a) 1 and (b) 2.

generation rates for these two SRs become $\lambda_{1b}^{(1)}$ and $\lambda_{1b}^{(2)}$, respectively. In state r_{1a}, application type 1 transits to state r_{1b} with a rate of $\upsilon_{1,ab}$, which also implies that the average time for application type 1 to stay in state r_{1a} is $1/\upsilon_{1,ab}$.

Using the CTMDP model for each application type, we can set up the CTMDP model of an *application pool*, S_{APPL}. A state of S_{APPL} is a tuple comprising the corresponding state for every application type and information about the application currently running on the CPU. The CTMDP model of the example S_{APPL}, as depicted in Figure 4.4, has eight global states, $(r_{1x}, r_{2y}, flag)$, where r_{1x} denotes the service generation state x for application 1 and r_{2y} denotes state y for application type 2. $flag = 1$ (2) meaning the first (second) application is running. For example, $(r_{1a}, r_{2a}, 1)$ means that application type 1 is running and it is in state r_{1a}. Furthermore, the state of application type 2 was r_{2a} just before it was swapped out. The CTMDP model has a set of autonomous transitions between state pairs with the same activation flag value. The transition rates are denoted by $\upsilon_{i,xy}$, where x and y denote the service generation states of application type i. For

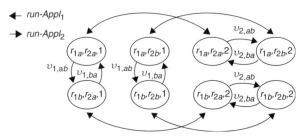

Figure 4.4   CTMDP model of an application pool.

example, the transition between $(r_{1a}, r_{2a}, 1)$ and $(r_{1b}, r_{2a}, 1)$ is autonomous. Notice that a transition from $(r_{1a}, r_{2a}, 1)$ to $(r_{1b}, r_{2b}, 1)$ is disallowed because application 2 is not running; therefore, it cannot possibly change its service generation state. The model also has a set of action-controlled transitions between global states with the same r_{1x}, r_{2y} values.

The action set is $A_{APPL} = \{run\_Appl_i\}$, where $Appl_i$ denotes application type i. For example, if the global state of the S_{APPL} is $(r_{1x}, r_{2y}, 1)$ and the action run_Appl_2 is issued then the new global state of the system will be $(r_{1x}, r_{2y}, 2)$. A transition between $(r_{1a}, r_{2b}, 1)$ and $(r_{1a}, r_{2a}, 2)$ is not allowed because it implies that during context switch from application type 1 to type 2, the service generation state of application 2 changed, an impossibility in our model.

The number of states grows exponentially with the number of application types. Thus, to mitigate scalability issue, one must group all interesting applications into a relatively small number of application types. According to our experimental results and observations, although the number of different applications may be large, the number of different application classes is rather small.

The reason why application scheduling based on the global system state can reduce the total system power consumption can be explained by a simple example. Let us consider a system with only one SP. There are two application types A1 and A2. A1 generates SRs at a rate of one request per unit time, while A2 generates three requests per unit time. The SP wakes up as soon as a request is generated and sleeps when all requests have been serviced. Two execution sequences are considered. In the first sequence, there is no application scheduling. Each application is alternately executed for exactly one unit of time. In the second sequence, we perform application scheduling based on the number of waiting requests in the SQ. More precisely, during the running period of A1, as soon as a request is generated, the scheduler switches to A2. After A2 is run for one unit of time, A1 will be brought back to continue its execution. This policy ensures that all SRs that are targeted to the SP are bundled together and that the SP sleep time is maximized. Assuming that the wake-up and sleep transition times and energy dissipation values are fixed, the total energy consumption of the SP under these two execution sequences is depicted in Figure 4.5. It is seen that application scheduling can maximize the SP sleep time.

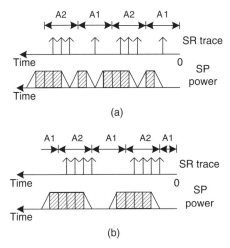

Figure 4.5 An example of the effectiveness of application scheduling: (a) without application scheduling and (b) with application scheduling.

We must convert the performance constraint for individual applications to those for the individual SPs. The total execution time of an application is the sum of the CPU time, the memory stall time, and the I/O device access time. The throughput of a computer system may then be defined as the ratio of the completed computational workload to the total execution time of the application. Although in a multiprogramming system, the calculation of stall time due to I/O devices can be very complicated, it is straightforward to bound the total I/O stall time by constraining the average delay experienced by each I/O operation. This is because the total I/O stall time is never more than the total I/O operation delay.[1] On the basis of this observation, we impose constraints on the average service delay of every request sent to each SP to capture the performance constraint on each application.

It is also important to allocate a fair share of the CPU time to each application. In a Linux system, the GPM-based application scheduling algorithm can be implemented using multiple run queues, each associated with a different application type. On the basis of the decision made by the power manager, at the context switch time, some run queue will be selected and the scheduler will pick one task from this queue to run on the CPU. Inside a run queue, the original priority-based scheduling algorithm of the Linux kernel is used for task selection. Thus,

---

[1]This is because the I/O operation delay of a request is the waiting time plus the service operation time. The I/O stall time refers to the delay that is encountered during application execution due to I/O operations. If there is only one running thread that is stalled after generating each I/O request, the I/O stall time will be equal to the I/O operation delay. However, in a multithreaded parallel execution environment, the total I/O stall time for the entire batch of executing programs has to be considered. Therefore, the total I/O stall time tends to be less than the total I/O operation delay because some portion of the I/O stall time may be effectively utilized by running other ready applications.

it is clearly seen that the GPM does not intervene in the scheduling of applications that have the same workload characteristics. The existing fair scheduling schemes [16] such as the FCFS or round-robin can be used for these applications. For applications that exhibit different workload characteristics, we must impose a *fairness constraint* as follows. Let $f_r^{a_r}$ denote the frequency that APPL state r is entered and action a_r is chosen in that state, $r \in S_{APPL}$ and $a_r \in A_{APPL}$. Let $\tau_r^{a_r}$ denote the expected duration of time that APPL will stay in state r when action a_r is chosen. Let $flag(r)$ denote the flag value component of state r. A fairness constraint states that application type i cannot, on average, occupy more than c_i percentage of the CPU time. This can be written as

$$\sum_{r:flag(r)=i} f_r^{a_{r,i}} \tau_r^{a_{r,i}} \le c_i \times 100\%, \quad \text{where } a_{r,i} = run\_Appl_i \qquad (4.1)$$

where $f_r^{a_{r,i}} \tau_r^{a_{r,i}}$ is the probability that APPL stays in state r and chooses action $a_{r,i}$. One way to determine the value of c_i is to make it proportional to the computation workload of application type i. The calculation of $f_r^{a_r}$ and $\tau_r^{a_r}$ actually involves variables and states of other component models in the system, and therefore, it is not convenient to present here. The actual form of this constraint is given in Section 4.5.

4.4.2 Model of the Service Flow Control

As illustrated in Figure 4.2, the SFC is modeled as a stationary, CTMDP with a state set $S_{SFC} = \{Block, Xfer, GenF\}$ and an action set $A_{SFC} = \{Goto\_Block, Goto\_Xfer, Goto\_GenF\}$. The detailed states and transitions of the SFC are explained as follows:

> *GenF.* In this state, the SFC generates a fake service request (FSR). An FSR is treated in the same way as a regular SR by the SP but requires no service from the SP. FSRs are used to wake up the SP when the GPM decides it is the right time to do so. The purpose of FSR is mainly to improve the response time of SP and prevent it from entering a wrong (deep sleep or off) state when the GPM expects a lot of activity in the near future. Delay and energy consumption associated with the transition from Xfer to GenF account for the overhead of generating an FSR. The action *Goto_Xfer* takes place autonomously when the SFC is in GenF.
>
> *Block.* In this state, the SFC blocks all incoming SRs from entering the CQ of the SP. This state may be entered from the Xfer state only when all generated SRs have been serviced by the SP. Therefore, when the SFC remains in the Block state, the SSP sees that there are no pending SRs. The purpose of blocking SRs is to reduce the wake-up times of the SP and extend the SP sleep time.
>
> *Xfer.* In this state, the SFC continuously moves SRs from the SQ to the CQ, and therefore, the SP will wake up to provide the requested services. As

noted earlier, the CQ is not included in the system-level DPM model, so the function of SFC at the Xfer state is different from its real function, which is described as follows. In this model, when the SFC is in the Xfer state, the SSP knows the status of SQ and acts the same way that the SP does when the real SRs arrive in the CQ. The time and energy consumption associated with the transition from the Block to the Xfer state accounts for the overhead of moving about the SRs. The action *Goto_Block* works autonomously when and only when the SFC is in the Xfer state and SQ is empty.

All other state transitions, which have not been mentioned above, take effect immediately and consume no energy.

4.4.3 Model of the Simulated Service Provider

The SSP is a CTMDP model that simulates the behavior of the SP under the control of the LPM. Since in the proposed hierarchical DPM architecture, the GPM cannot directly control the state transition of the SP, the SSP is modeled as an independent automaton. If the LPM employs a CTMDP-based PM policy then the modeling of SSP will be easy; that is, the CTMDP model of SP with the LPM policy can be used directly, except that the SRs waiting in the SQ must be considered together when the SSP is making a decision. However, if the LPM uses another PM algorithm, a question will arise as to how accurately a CTMDP SSP model can simulate the behavior of the power-managed SP.

Let us consider an SP with fixed time-out policy, for example, a typical hard disk drive, which has two power states: active at 2.1 W and low power idle at 0.65 W. The transition power and time between the two states are 1.4 W and 0.4 s, respectively. The LPM adopts a two-competitive time-out policy, where the time-out value is set to 0.8 s.

The CTMDP model of the corresponding SSP is depicted in Figure 4.6.

Sleep. This is a low power state. The SSP goes to the idle state when the SFC is in Xfer or GenF state, and the SQ is not empty.

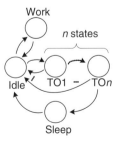

Figure 4.6 CTMDP SSP model of HDD with fixed time-out policy.

Work. A functional state, where the SSP provides service to the SR that is waiting in the SQ.

Idle. This is a nonfunctional state. If the SFC is in either Xfer or GenF state and the SQ is not empty, the SSP goes to the work state; otherwise, it goes to TO_1 state.

TO_i. $i = 1, 2, \ldots, n$. This is one of the n full-power but nonfunctional time-out states. These states are used to simulate the time-out policy. When the SFC is in Xfer or GenF state and the SQ is not empty, the SSP goes back to the idle state; otherwise, the SSP goes to the TO_{i+1} state or sleep state if the SSP is in the TO_n state. Since the time for the SSP to transfer from the idle to the TO_n state is a random variable, whereas in the time-out policy, the time-out value is fixed, multiple TO states are used to improve the simulation accuracy.

The reason for using multiple TO_i states (instead of just one) is explained as follows. Assume a chain with n TO states is used to approximate a time-out policy whose time-out value is set to t. Let τ denote the time for the SSP to transfer from the idle to the TO_n state. Let τ_0 and $\tau_1, \ldots, \tau_{n-1}$, respectively, denote the period for which the SSP stays in the idle and the $TO_1, \ldots, TO_{n-1}$ states when there are no incoming SRs. As required by the CTMDP model, τ_0 and $\tau_1, \ldots, \tau_{n-1}$ are independent random variables, each following an exponential distribution with mean $1/\lambda$ and variance $1/\lambda^2$. To make the expected value of τ equal to the desired time-out value t, it is required that $E(\tau) = n/\lambda = t$, where $\tau = \sum_{i=0}^{n-1} \tau_i$. Thus, variance of τ is $D(\tau) = \sum_{i=0}^{n-1} D(\tau_i) = n/\lambda^2 = t^2/n$. From this equation, we can see that for a given t, as n increases, $D(\tau)$ is reduced. In other words, the accuracy of the CTMDP model of a fixed time-out policy increases.

We performed a simulation study to evaluate how the approximation accuracy is related to the number of TO states in the SSP model in terms of energy and service delay for the above-mentioned hard disk example. Results are presented in Figure 4.7. The average power and delay of the SP under a fixed time-out policy is compared with three SSPs, which each use one, two, and three TO states to simulate the same time-out policy. It is demonstrated that with three TO states, behavior of the SSP becomes indistinguishable from that of the hard disk with a fixed time-out policy.

4.4.4 Modeling Dependencies between SPs

There are different types of dependencies between SPs. The first type is mutual exclusion that arises, for example, when two SPs contend for the same non-sharable resource, such as a low speed I/O bus. Consequently, at any time, only one SP can be in its working state. When constructing the CTMDP model of the system, one can account for this type of hard dependency constraint by marking any system state that violates mutual exclusion as invalid and by forbidding all

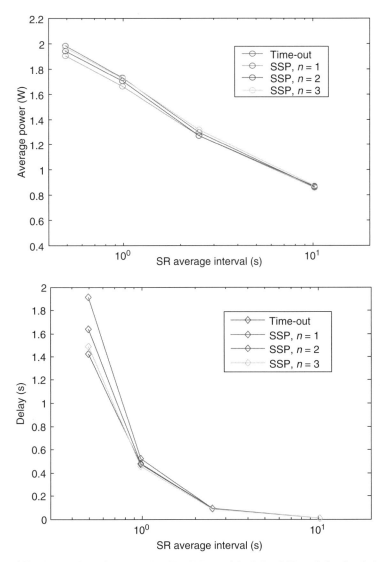

Figure 4.7   Comparison between the CTMDP model of the SSP and the fixed time-out policy for the hard disk.

state-action pairs that cause the system to transit to an invalid state. The second type is shared resource constraint, where two SPs indirectly influence one another's behavior because of their utilization of a shared resource. For example, SPs may want to buffer their SRs in a shared buffering area of a finite size. So when the number of SRs for one SP goes up, the probability that SRs for the other SP will be blocked increases. In this case, the first SP may have to work harder to ensure that it is not overutilizing the shared buffer area. This type of soft dependency constraint is handled by adding appropriate constraints to the system-level power optimization problem formulation.

4.5   POLICY OPTIMIZATION

4.5.1   Mathematical Formulation

Let I denote the number of SPs in the power-managed system. Let x represent the global state of this system, which is a vector whose elements are the states of the APPL, SQ_i, SFC_i, and SSP_i models, where $i = 1, 2, \ldots I$. Let a_x denote an action enabled in state x, which is a tuple composed of the actions of the APPL and SFC_i models. The constrained energy optimization problem is formulated as a linear program as follows:

$$\text{Minimize}_{\{f_x^{a_x}\}} \left(\sum_x \sum_{a_x} f_x^{a_x} \gamma_x^{a_x} \right), \tag{4.2}$$

where $f_x^{a_x}$ is the frequency that global state x is entered in and action a_x is chosen in that state. $\gamma_x^{a_x}$ is the expected cost, which represents the expected energy consumed when the system is in state x and action a_x is chosen, and is calculated as

$$\gamma_x^{a_x} = \tau_x^{a_x} pow(x, a_x) + \sum_{x' \neq x} p_{x,x'}^{a_x} ene(x, x'), \tag{4.3}$$

where $\tau_x^{a_x} = 1 / \sum_{x' \neq x} \sigma_{x,x'}^{a_x}$ denotes the expected duration of time that the system will stay in state x when action a_x is chosen, and $\sigma_{x,x'}^{a_x}$ is the rate of the transition from state x to state x' when action a_x is chosen. In addition, $p_{x,x'}^{a_x} = \sigma_{x,x'}^{a_x} / \sum_{x'' \neq x} \sigma_{x,x''}^{a_x}$ denotes the probability that the system will next come to state x' if it is in state x and action a_x is chosen. This linear program is solved for variables $f_x^{a_x}$ while satisfying the following constraints:

$$\sum_{a_x} f_x^{a_x} = \sum_{x' \neq x} \sum_{a_x'} f_{x'}^{a_x'} p_{x',x}^{a_x'} \qquad \forall x \in X \tag{4.4}$$

$$\sum_x \sum_{a_x} f_x^{a_x} \tau_x^{a_x} = 1 \tag{4.5}$$

$$f_x^{a_x} \geq 0 \tag{4.6}$$

$$\sum_x \sum_{a_x} f_x^{a_x} \tau_x^{a_x} (q_{i,x} - D_i \lambda_{i,x}) \leq 0, \quad i = 1, 2, \ldots, I \tag{4.7}$$

$$\sum_{x: flag(r_x) = i} \sum_{a_{r,j} \in a_x} f_x^{a_x} \tau_x^{a_x} \leq c_j \times 100\%, \quad j = 1, 2, \ldots, J \tag{4.8}$$

where r_x denotes the state of APPL in global state x and $a_{r,j} = run\_Appl_j$.

$$\sum_x \sum_{a_x} f_x^{a_x} \tau_x^{a_x} \delta(q_{i,x}, Q_i) \leq P_{i,b} \quad i = 1, 2, \dots, I \tag{4.9}$$

or

$$\sum_x \sum_{a_x} f_x^{a_x} \tau_x^{a_x} \delta\left(\sum_i q_{i,x}, Q\right) \leq P_b \quad \text{with a shared } Q. \tag{4.10}$$

where

$$\delta(x, y) = \begin{cases} 1, & \text{if } x = y; \\ 0, & \text{otherwise.} \end{cases}$$

Equations 4.4–4.6 capture properties of a CTMDP. Inequalities (Eq. 4.7), based on the Little theorem [17], impose constraints on the expected task delay of SP_i, where $q_{i,x}$ represents the number of waiting tasks in the queue SQ_i when the system is in state x, D_i is the expected service delay experienced by SR_i, and $\lambda_{i,x}$ is the generation rate of the SR_i at system state x. Inequalities 4.8 are the same as 4.1 and state that on average, application type j should not use more than c_j percent of the CPU time. J is the number of application types in APPL. Constraints 4.9 and 4.10) ensure that the probability that SQ becomes full is less than a preset threshold. Constraint 4.9 is imposed when each type of SR utilizes its own nonsharable SQ, while constraint 4.10 is applied when a shared SQ is used for all types of SRs. This linear program is solved by using a standard solver, that is, MOSEK [18].

4.5.2 Optimal Time-Out Policy for Local Power Manager

The DPM optimization discussed up to now assumes that the time-out policy used for LPM has been given and is unable to change. However, in many real cases, the embedded power management solutions provide mechanisms for the user to tune the local policy parameters. For example, Windows power manager provides multiple optional schemes and allows users to change the length of idle duration that triggers to enter low power mode. Also, some latest WLAN cards can be configured to wake up every so many multiples of the beacon intervals and the length of a beacon interval is negotiable. In terms of this observation, we define an optimization problem that simultaneously optimizes the system-level power management policy and the time-out policy of the LPM.

The optimization of time-out values cannot be directly incorporated into CTMDP-based DPM optimization framework. A perturbation-analysis-based time-out optimization technique was proposed in Reference 19. Here, we are proposing an indirect approach to obtain a near-optimal solution for time-out values. For this purpose, the CTMDP SSP model that was presented in

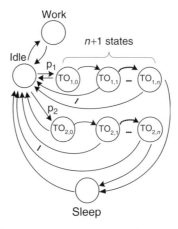

Figure 4.8   CTMDP SSP model of HDD for time-out optimization.

Figure 4.6 has been modified as shown in Figure 4.8. In this model, there are two TO state chains starting from a low power nonfunctional state, for example, the idle state. The two chains correspond to different time-out values, denoted as t_1 and t_2. Apart from the SSP model in Figure 4.6, a $TO_{,0}$ state is added to each TO chain, representing the start of an idle period. Once the model enters the idle state, if no task is queuing, it immediately transfers to the $TO_{2,0}$ state with probability p_1 or to the $TO_{1,0}$ state with probability $p_2 = 1 - p_1$ and takes no time. This models the behavior that during each idle period, time-out value t_1 is taken with probability p_1 and time-out t_2 with probability p_2. Here, p_1 and p_2 are the controlling parameters to be optimized with the system-level DPM policy. Once they are solved, the optimal time-out value t_{opt} can be approximated by

$$t_{\mathrm{opt}} \approx p_1 t_1 + p_2 t_2. \tag{4.11}$$

To combine the optimization of local time-outs with system-level DPM policy and use the linear programming approach, we need to define an action set for the SSP model, as $A_{SSP} = \{Goto\_TO_{1,0}, Goto\_TO_{2,0}\}$. Now, the system action a_x should be a tuple composed of the actions of the APPL, SFC, and SSP models. Thus, after updating the linear program 4.2–4.10 accordingly and solving the optimization problem, we can obtain the values of p_1 and p_2 as

$$p_1 = \sum_{\substack{q=0,s=\mathrm{Idle} \\ a_x=Goto\_TO_{1,0}}} f_x^{a_x} \Bigg/ \sum_{q=0,s=\mathrm{Idle}} f_x^{a_x}, \quad p_2 = 1 - p_1, \tag{4.12}$$

where q and s denote the states of the SQ and SSP when the system is in state x, respectively. Equation 4.11 is next used to determine the optimal time-out values of the local policy. It is worth noting that to achieve a good approximation of the optimal value, the t_1 and t_2 values should be selected carefully to ensure that t_{opt} is between t_1 and t_2. This can be achieved using an iterative approach. In case that either p_1 or p_2 is close to 1, we choose a new set of time-out values and redo the optimization. Assuming $p_1 = 1$ and $t_1 < t_2$, the new time-outs are

$$t_1' = \max(0, t_1 - t_2'), \quad t_2' = \frac{t_1 + t_2}{2}. \tag{4.13}$$

Further, we can simply use more than two TO state chains for a low power physical state to improve the accuracy.

Notice that the SSP model presented in Figure 4.8 is for a device that has only one low power nonfunctional state, that is, a "Sleep" state as marked in the figure. The two time-out values t_1 and t_2, which are approximated by the two TO state branches in the SSP model in Figure 4.8, are predetermined values used to calculate the t_{opt} value that will be used by the LPM to control the state transition from idle to sleep. For a device with two low power states, that is, a shallow sleep (drowsy) state and a deep sleep state, this simple model may be extended in a straightforward manner by adding a pair of TO states between every two neighboring system states to capture the time-out state transition between the corresponding system states.

4.6 EXPERIMENTAL RESULTS

For this experiment, we recorded a real trace of device requests generated by four concurrently running applications on a Linux PC. The applications were of two types. Three of the applications were file manipulation programs, which read some data file, edit it, and write back to the disk. The fourth application was a program that periodically reads data from another machine through a WLAN card, searches for relevant information, and saves this information onto the disk. The request generation pattern of the first type of application was modeled with a Poisson process with an average rate of 0.208 requests per second. The request generation statistics of the second program type can be best characterized by a two-state CTMDP model. The state transition rate and generation rates of SR to hard disk λ_{hd} and to WLAN card λ_{wlan} are

$$\begin{bmatrix} 0 & 0.0415 \\ 0.0063 & 0 \end{bmatrix} (s^{-1}), \quad \begin{matrix} \lambda_{hd} = [0.0826, 0.0187] \\ \lambda_{wlan} = [0.1124, 0.1124] \end{matrix} (s^{-1}).$$

The CPU usage ratio for these two groups of applications (i.e., two application types) is 53:47. For our experiments, we used the hard disk drives Hitachi Travelstar 7K60 and Orinoco WLAN card as SPs. Power dissipation and start-up energy and latency of the disk drive and the WLAN card are reported in Table 4.1.

For the first set of simulations, we only consider the hard disk driver. The average service time for a disk request is 67 ms. In this case, with the help

TABLE 4.1   Energy/Transition Data of Hard Disk Driver and WLAN Card

	State	Power (W)	Start-Up Energy (J)	Wake-Up Time (s)
Hitachi 7K60	Active	2.5	—	—
	Performance idle	2.0	0	0
	Low power idle	0.85	1.86	0.4
	Stand-by	0.25	10.5	2
Orinoco WLAN	Transfer	1.4	—	—
	Receive	0.9	—	—
	Sleep	0.05	0.15	0.12

of the operating system, FSR can be designed as a disk read operation that accesses the latest data read from the hard disk. Since this data must have been stored in the data cache of the hard disk, it does not have to be read out from the disk, so the service time of an FSR is only the sum of the disk controller's overhead and the data transfer time, which is about 3 ms.

We used the lower envelope algorithm [20], which is a two-competitive policy extended for a device with multiple low power states, as the time-out policy for the LPM. The LPM policy has two time-out values, 1.7 and 14.4 s, each corresponding to one low power state. Under this policy (named TO1), the SP starts in the highest power state ("Active" = "Performance idle"). If there are no new requests, after 1.7 s, it enters the "Low-power-idle" state. If no requests arrive, after 14.4 s, it enters into the "Stand-by" state. We also experimented with a different set of time-out values, that is, 0.34 and 14.4 s. This version is denoted by TO2. The results are presented in Table 4.2.

In Table 4.2, the first column gives the CPU usage ratio between the two types of applications. The type of the built-in LPM policy is reported in the

TABLE 4.2   Hierarchal PM Simulation Results for Single SP

CPU Usage	LPM Policy	Performance Constraints	1PM-TO (W)	1PM-CTMDP (W)	HPM (W)	HPM-S (W)
0.53:0.47	TO1	0.0765	1.2728	1.0467	1.2591	0.9505
		0.5	1.2728	0.9309	1.0443	0.788
	TO2	0.0882	1.1582	1.0414	1.1436	0.8651
		0.5	1.1582	0.9309	1.0106	0.7274
0.7:0.3	TO1	0.078	1.3805	1.1152	1.342	0.9951
		0.5	1.3805	0.9956	1.1047	0.8302
	TO2	0.0903	1.2559	1.1107	1.2032	1.0594
		0.5	1.2559	0.9956	1.0966	0.8734
0.3:0.7	TO1	0.0685	1.19	0.9647	1.1058	0.957
		0.5	1.19	0.7922	0.9276	0.788
	TO2	0.076	1.0162	0.9451	1.012	0.7373
		0.5	1.0162	0.7922	0.8422	0.6015

second column. For each LPM policy, we simulate twice for different performance constraints in terms of the bound on the average number of waiting SRs in the SQ. This bound is reported in the third column. In each case, the smaller bound corresponds to the actual SR delay in the time-out policy simulation. The second one is a looser constraint given for the purpose of examining the ability of our proposed hierarchical DPM approach to trade off latency for lower energy consumption.

Four policies are compared in Table 4.2, they are one-level time-out policy (1PM-TO), one-level CTMDP policy (1PM-CTMDP), HPM, and HPM with application scheduling (HPM-S). For the stochastic policies, the SR generation statistics is assumed to be known. The average power consumptions of the SP under different policies are reported in the last four columns of the table. Comparing HPM with local power management policy 1PM-TO, it can be seen that HPM improves the energy efficiency of LPM-controlled SPs, especially when there is a large positive slack, in which case up to 22% energy saving is achieved. This saving is made possible because of the system-level service flow control policy incorporated in HPM, which monitors the state of LPM and subsequently adjusts the rate of SRs sent to the SP in order to make the SP run more power efficiently and increase the chance that it stays in its lower power states. HPM-S even outperforms the optimal component-level CTMDP policy by as much as 24% in terms of saving energy consumption.

To better understand how the energy saving is achieved by HPM policies, the break down of the total power consumptions of the SP under different policies is presented in Figure 4.9, where TO1 is used as the local policy with the CPU usage ratio 0.53:0.47 and the performance constraint set to 0.5. As compared to the time-out policy, HPM and HPM-S significantly reduced the SP energy consumed at

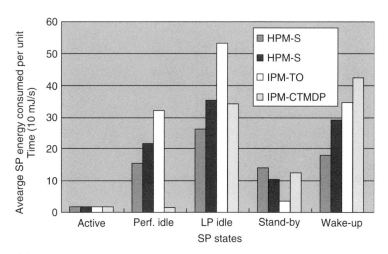

Figure 4.9 Breakdown of the power consumption of the service provider. Perf. Idle., performance-idle; LP Idle, low-power-idle.

high power idle states and dissipated for wake-ups by a total amount of 33.9 and 60.3 mJ/s, respectively, with a small increase in average standby power by 6.9 and 10.8 mW, respectively, because of the SP staying longer in the standby mode. From this figure, it is demonstrated that HPM approaches allow the SP to spend more time at the lowest power state while reducing wake-up overhead simultaneously. When compared to 1PM-CTMDP, HPM and HPM-S reduce the wake-up energy dissipation at the cost of extra energy consumed in high power idle states. This difference lies in the fact that 1PM-CTMDP makes a decision to transit to a low power state as soon as it becomes idle, whereas HPM and HPM-S must wait until a local time-out counter expires.

The application-level scheduling incorporated into HPM selects applications to run based on the global system state, that is, states of the SP and the SQ, and dynamically adjusts the SR generation rate to help reduce the SP state-transition times and increase the duration that the SP stays in low power states, while meeting the given timing and fairness constraints. To emphasize on the effect of application scheduling on power management, the CPU usage of each application type is divided into bins corresponding to the SSP states and compared in Figure 4.10 between the HPM and HPM-S policies, where the simulation setup is the same as that used to generate Figure 4.9. The labels on the x-axis, TOHn and TOLn, $n = 1, 2$, respectively, represent the time-out states while the SP is in Hitachi performance-idle and low-power-idle states. Note that in Figure 4.9, energies consumed in the TOH and TOL states are added to those consumed in performance-idle and low-power-idle states, respectively.

In Figure 4.10, each bar represents the CPU usage of an application type with respect to an SSP state, which equals to the time when the application is running while the SSP is in the associated state divided by the overall running time of

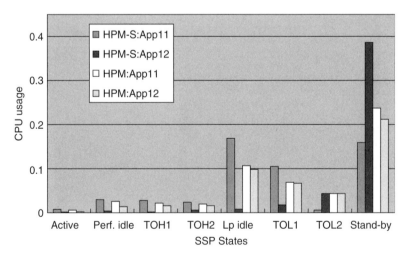

Figure 4.10 Breakdown of CPU usage of applications under HPM policies.

TABLE 4.3 Hierarchal PM Simulation Results for Single SP with Optimal Local Time-Out Policy

CPU Usage Ratio	Performance Constraints	Optimal TOH (s)	Optimal TOL (s)	HPM (W)	Optimal TOH (s)	Optimal TOL (s)	HPM-S (W)
0.53 :	0.088	0.035	50.0	1.057	0.024	22.3	0.868
0.47	0.5	0.019	15.7	0.887	0.020	13.1	0.697
0.7 :	0.090	0.028	63.1	1.125	0.027	43.4	1.000
0.3	0.5	0.023	30.2	0.996	0.022	21.8	0.838
0.3 :	0.076	0.021	41.0	0.978	0.017	10.6	0.709
0.7	0.5	0.016	10.0	0.731	0.015	10.0	0.563

all application types. As shown in the figure, without application scheduling, the two application types Appl1 and Appl2 have very close CPU usages on all SSP states. However, under the HPM-S policy, at highest power SSP states, the CPU usages of Appl1 are much higher than those of Appl2, while the reverse exists at the lowest power state, standby. Appl1 has a higher SR generation rate than Appl2. Executing Appl1 rather than Appl2 at high power state will make more likely that a new SR is generated while the SP is still in a high power state. In this case, the SP will be easier to transit back to the work state with less energy dissipated for state transition and faster response time. On the other hand, performing Appl2 at a state closer to the lowest power state is likely to increase the interval before the next SR and thus creates more idle duration for the SP to stay in the lowest power state and reduce the energy consumption.

In the second set of simulations, we still considered a single SP but exploited the technique presented in Section 4.5.2 to determine the optimal time-out values for the LPM. The results are presented in Table 4.3. In this table, the obtained optimal time-out values are listed before the corresponding HPM policy. As compared to the results in Table 4.2, it is observed that for the HPM-S policy, using optimal local time-outs does not incur much energy saving. The main reason is that the incorporated application scheduling technique is able to counteract the impairment introduced by an imperfect local time-out policy. However, the HPM policy did benefit from an optimal local time-out and improve the energy saving by 8.7% on average.

In the third set of simulations, we considered two SPs: a hard disk and a WLAN card. The average service time for a wireless request is 830 ms. In this simulation, policy TO2 is used for the LPM of the hard disk driver and a two-competitive policy with a time-out value of 200 ms is used for the WLAN card. The WLAN card also wakes up every second to listen for traffic identification message. We used the SR trace with a CPU usage ratio 53:47 in this simulation. The results of the power consumption of each component are presented in Table 4.4. The experimental results demonstrate that the HPM-S algorithm can jointly schedule applications for different SPs to achieve minimal total system energy consumption.

TABLE 4.4   Hierarchal PM Simulation Results for Two SPs

	Performance Constraints for Different SPs	1PM-TO2 (W)	1PM-CTMDP (W)	HPM (W)	HPM-S (W)
Sim1	HD	0.09	1.157	1.045	1.142	0.881
	WLAN	0.05	0.384	0.343	0.378	0.310
Sim2	HD	0.2	1.157	1.01	1.066	0.788
	WLAN	0.2	0.384	0.322	0.331	0.282

4.7   CONCLUSION

This chapter presented an HPM architecture that aims to facilitate power awareness in an EMC system with multiple components. Given a performance constraint, this architecture improves both component-level and system-wide power savings using information about SR rates by tuning the PM policies of components. The technique to obtain an optimal time-out for LPM is also presented. Experimental results demonstrate that the system-level PM approach can result in significant extra energy savings.

An interesting direction for future work is to extend the HPM approach to handle nonstationary SR generation. One possible solution is to construct off-line a policy tree where each leaf node represents an optimal policy for a given set of system parameters, for example, delay constraint, request generation rates, and the CPU share of different application types. At run time, system parameters will be dynamically detected and used as an index in the policy tree. The policy table that matches the current settings will be exploited.

REFERENCES

1. Srivastava M, Chandrakasan A, Brodersen R. Predictive system shutdown and other architectural techniques for energy efficient programmable computation. IEEE Trans VLSI Syst 1996;4(3):42–55.
2. Hwang C-H, Wu A. A predictive system shutdown method for energy saving of event-driven computation. In: Proceedings International Conference on Computer-Aided Design; San Jose, California; 1997. pp. 28–32.
3. Benini L, Paleologo G, Bogliolo A, De Micheli G. Policy optimization for dynamic power management. IEEE Trans Comput Aided Des 1999;18(1):813–33.
4. Qiu Q, Wu Q, Pedram M. Stochastic modeling of a power-managed system-construction and optimization. IEEE Trans Comput Aided Des 2001;20(10):1200–1217.
5. Lu Y-H, Benini L, De Micheli G. Power-aware operating systems for interactive systems. IEEE Trans VLSI Syst 2002;10(4):119–134.
6. Storage Systems Division, IBM Corp., APM for Mobile Hard Disks; 1999. Available at www.almaden.ibm.com/almaden/mobile_hard_drives.html.

7. Bhat UN. *Elements of Applied Stochastic Processes*. Wiley-Interscience, 2002.

8. Simunic T, Benini L, Glynn P, De Micheli G. Event-driven power management. IEEE Trans Comput Aided Des 2001;20(7):840–857.

9. Theocharous G, Mannor S, Shah N, Gandhi P, Kveton B, Siddiqi, Yu CH. Machine learning for adaptive power management. Intel Technol J 2006;10(4):299–312.

10. Simunic T, Boyd S, Glynn P. Managing power in networks on chips. IEEE Trans VLSI Syst 2004;12(1):96–107.

11. Ren Z, Krogh BH, Marculescu R. Hierarchical adaptive dynamic power management. IEEE Trans Comput 2005;54(4):409–420.

12. Jun H, Ammar M, Corner M, Zegura E. Hierarchical power management in disruption tolerant networks with traffic-aware optimization. In: Proceedings SIGCOMM Workshop on CHANTS; Paris, France; 2006 Sept. pp. 245–252.

13. Sorber J, Banerjee N, Corner M, Rollins S. Turducken: hierarchical power management for mobile devices. Proceedings MobiSystems; 2005 Jun; Seattle (WA). pp. 261–274.

14. Choi K, Soma K, Pedram M. Fine-grained DVFS for precise energy and performance trade-off based on the ratio of off-chip access to on-chip computation times. In: Proceedings Design and Test in Europe; New Orleans, Louisiana; 2004 Feb. pp. 4–9.

15. Delaluz V, Sivasubramaniam A, Andemir M, Vijaykrishnan N, Irwin MJ. Scheduler-based DRAM energy management. In: Proceedings of Design Automation Conference; Munich, Germany; 2002 Jun. pp. 697–702.

16. Silberschatz A, Galvin PB, Gagne G. *Operating System Concepts*. John Wiley and Sons; 2004.

17. Feinberg EA, Shwartz A. *Handbook of Markov Decision Processes: Methods and Applications*. Kluwer Academic; 2002.

18. Andersen ED, Andersen KD. The MOSEK interior point optimizer for linear programming: an implementation of the homogeneous algorithm. *High Performance Optimization*. Kluwer Academic; 2000. pp. 197–232.

19. Rong P, Pedram M. Determining the optimal timeout values for a power-managed system based on the theory of Markovian processes: Offline and online algorithms. In: Proceedings Design and Test in Europe; Paris, France; 2006 Mar. pp. 1128–1133.

20. Irani S, Shukla S, Gupta R. Competitive analysis of dynamic power management strategies for systems with multiple power saving states. Proceedings Design and Test in Europe; 2002 Feb. pp. 117–123.

CHAPTER 5

ENERGY-EFFICIENT RESERVATION INFRASTRUCTURE FOR GRIDS, CLOUDS, AND NETWORKS

ANNE-CÉCILE ORGERIE and LAURENT LEFÈVRE

5.1 INTRODUCTION

In the age of petascale machines, cloud computing and peer-to-peer systems, large-scale distributed systems need an ever-increasing amount of energy. These systems urgently require effective and scalable solutions to manage and limit their electrical consumption. As of now, most efforts are focused on energy-efficient hardware designs. Thus, the challenge is to coordinate all these low level improvements at the middleware level to improve the energy efficiency of the overall systems. Resource management solutions can indeed benefit from a broader view to pool the resources and to share them according to the needs of each user.

Large-scale distributed systems consist in collections of multiple computing and storage resources that communicate through a communication system that can either be shared with other infrastructures or not. The overall energy consumption of such systems is huge and can be split into the following two parts:

- the fixed part, which depends on the system's size and type of each equipment (computing, storing, and networking equipment);
- the variable part, which depends on the usage of computing and storage facilities and on the networking traffic.

To reduce the fixed energy costs, equipments can be put into sleep modes when they are not in use; for example, computers and cores can be turned off. Likewise, to reduce the variable costs, some slowdown techniques can be used,

Energy-Efficient Distributed Computing Systems, First Edition.
Edited by Albert Y. Zomaya and Young Choon Lee.
© 2012 John Wiley & Sons, Inc. Published 2012 by John Wiley & Sons, Inc.

such as dynamic voltage frequency scaling (DVFS) [1] for processors or adaptive link rate (ALR) [2] for network interface cards (NICs). These techniques adjust the processor speed or the transmission rate with respect to load when the full resource capacity is not required, thus saving energy with only a minor impact on performance. Improvements on the design of hardware components are also desirable to enhance the energy efficiency of each equipment. These techniques can be combined at the system management level to coordinate the local energy-aware decisions and to tightly couple energy consumption and workload. The goal is to achieve a consumption–workload relation as proportional as possible in a consume-as-you-use manner [3]. Thus, the fixed part of the energy costs will be suppressed, and so will be the wastage due to idle consuming resources.

In-advance reservation mechanisms are widely used in large-scale distributed systems [4–6] since they guarantee users a certain quality of service, including with respect to deadlines and specific hardware and software constraints, in an infrastructure-as-a-service way. Indeed, users can specify a deadline (when the job should be completed), a start time, and some hardware and software constraints, for example. In-advance reservations also allow a more flexible and predictable resource management: the length of each reservation is known at its submission, thus making the task of scheduling algorithms easier.

We propose an *e*nergy-efficient *r*eservation *i*nfrastructure for large-scale *di*stributed *s*ystems (ERIDIS) in order to optimize the energy used by such systems. This infrastructure acts at the resource manager level and includes the following:

- energy sensors that collect, in real time, the energy consumption of resources and directly measure the impact of the taken decisions;
- allocating and scheduling algorithms to optimize the reservation placement;
- on/off facilities to put resources into sleep mode when they are not used;
- prediction algorithms to anticipate the workload;
- workload aggregation policies to avoid frequent on/off cycles for the resources.

Section 5.2 deals with the related works. ERIDIS is presented in Section 5.3. Then, we propose three applications of this infrastructure: in a grid and data center context in Section 5.4, in a cloud context in Section 5.5, and finally in a network context in Section 5.6. Section 5.7 concludes and presents our perspectives.

5.2 RELATED WORKS

Although energy has been a matter of concern for sensor networks and battery-constrained systems since their creation, energy issues are recent for plugged systems. We present some related works in the domain of energy efficiency that can be used in data centers, grids, clouds, and wired networks.

5.2.1 Server and Data Center Power Management

A huge waste of energy can be observed for various computing and networking equipment: PCs, switches, routers, servers, etc. because they remain fully powered on during idle periods. In a data center context, different policies can be applied on different levels: the node level, the cluster level, or the network level.

Data centers are made up of a large number of servers with high power requirements concentrated in a small area. They need huge power capacities and the first difficulty is to find out the consumption of all their components (network equipment, nodes, cooling system). In Reference 7, the authors make a model of energy consumption that uses the CPU's activity. A different approach consists in deducing it by using event-monitoring counters [8], for example.

Naturally, the first idea to save energy is to be able to shut down idle nodes [9]. This leads to a problem: how to wake them up when required? Wake-On-LAN is a mechanism implemented on Ethernet cards to allow a distant user to wake up a PC by sending it some packets via the network [10]. However, such a mechanism requires the Ethernet card to be powered at all times.

Another issue is to have an energy-aware scheduling algorithm to attribute nodes to the tasks, which can either be divisible or not [9, 11], requiring synchronization [12], etc. In Reference 13, the authors discuss minimization of consumed energy by minimizing the number of joules per operation. The resource manager gets a set of awake nodes and should minimize its size as much as possible. When a task ends on a node, it tries to move the other tasks on this node to the other running nodes. And if a new task arrives, it tries to put it on the awake nodes. The other nodes remain off. This algorithm includes no load-balancing mechanisms, so it seems that some nodes will be worn prematurely, while others will stay unused.

Other energy-aware resource management algorithms include load balancing [8] and thermal management concerns [14, 15]. As presented for all the algorithms, the unnecessary wake-ups waste energy twice: by the wake-up power spike and during the idle state on time before going to sleep again. Such algorithms should thus be carefully designed in order not to shut down nodes unnecessarily.

5.2.2 Node Optimizations

Energy savings at the node level can also lead to great energy savings with the scale effects. To reduce the wake-up power spike and the booting time, "suspend to disk" techniques can be used. When a node switches to that state, all the content of the main memory is saved to the hard drive in an hibernate file, preserving the state of the operating system (all the open applications, documents, etc.). All of the node's components are turned off and, at the next state switch, the node will load the hibernate file, restoring the previous state.

Other hardware improvements could be done into the CPU. Some algorithms include DVFS techniques [1, 7, 11, 12]. The CPU reduces its frequency and voltage when it is under use [1]. These techniques have already been standards

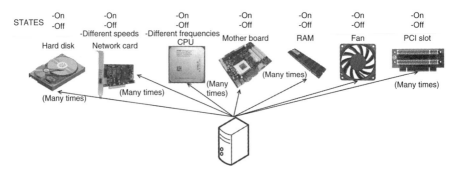

Figure 5.1 Possible states per node component.

on laptops since few years. This increases the range of possible energy savings a lot since they allow to save energy when the nodes are not idle, and not fully used either.

Actually, each computing node is made up of an assembly of several components, as shown in Figure 5.1, and each component can be optimized to save energy. The node components are summarized in Figure 5.1. This figure shows which node components can be switched off or put in lower modes. Each component indeed benefits from different states from fully on to fully off, which correspond to different energy consumptions. For example, a CPU has one off-state and several on-states, which correspond to each possible frequency and scaling on this CPU [1]. Most of the components are the subject of specific studies: NICs [10], disks [16], and CPUs [17], for example. However, the motherboard remains the component consuming the most energy, and it can only be turned off when the entire node can. Thus, IPMI (Intelligent Platform Management Interface) techniques are really useful to remotely and quickly switch nodes on and off [18].

5.2.3 Virtualization to Improve Energy Efficiency

Virtualization is now widely used to provide a large number of computing resources, and the energy consumption of cloud infrastructures is as problematic as in data centers and grids [19–21]. Yet, even if virtualization adds a software layer that consumes energy [22], it actually allows finer load consolidation on each node [23] and offers the possibility to use live migration techniques [24] to strengthen load aggregation. Still, these techniques have a cost [25] and should be carefully studied in order to reduce the overall consumption of clouds.

5.2.4 Energy Awareness in Wired Networking Equipment

The consumption of wired networking devices has been considered for about 10 years by two research teams, mainly, one in Portland [26–29] and the other in Florida [10, 30]. In Reference 26, the authors present an interesting approach [26]: they want to switch off network interfaces, routers, and switch components.

They first analyze traces and check whether there really are periods of inactivity [26, 27]. Then, they design algorithms to shut down resources based on periodic protocol behavior and traffic estimation [27]. They analyze that a lot of energy can be saved this way, by running their algorithm onto utilization traces. Then, they propose to save energy even on underutilization periods. Therefore, they use the low power modes available on most Ethernet interfaces [28] (that means using Gigabit Ethernet cards at 10 MBps, 100 MBps, or 1 GBps). Their results show that their algorithm does not affect the communication performance in terms of both delay and packet loss.

Their algorithms are based on predictions to take sleeping decisions. They use buffer occupancy, the behavior of previous packet (arrival times), and a maximum bounded delay [29]. They assume that the routers are able to store packets in their buffer even if they are asleep. When the buffer occupancy reaches a certain size, they wake up the whole router.

The real problem of shutting down networking devices is how to ensure network presence. Indeed, when a switch is asleep, it cannot answer to the requests (ARP requests or PING, for example). Moreover, normally when a link is re-established, an auto-negotiation protocol is run (to synchronize clocks, to determine link type, and to determine link rate, etc.) and this takes about few hundreds of milliseconds, which is too long on high capacity links. To address this, they modify the auto-negotiation protocol for their algorithms [29]: the auto negotiation is not run after sleeping periods because those are really short and the link has not changed state during the process.

Another solution is to use proxying techniques: the Ethernet card or the switch filter packets that require no response (such broadcasts), replies to packets that require minimal response (such as ping), and only wakes up the system for packets requiring a nontrivial response [10]. In Reference 10, the authors give a complete analysis of the traffic received by an idle PC, and they explain that most of this traffic would be filtered out or trivially responded to by a proxy.

These authors have also proposed an algorithm called *ALR*, which changes the link's data rate based on an output buffer threshold policy [30]. This algorithm does not affect the mean packet delay.

5.2.5 Synthesis

Lots of computing and networking equipment are concerned by these overall observations on the waste of energy: PCs, switches, routers, servers, etc. In a context of large-scale distributed systems, different policies can be applied depending on where users want to make savings: at the node level, the data center level, or the network level.

At the node level, you can use direct voltage-scaling techniques and frequency-scaling techniques to reduce the energy consumption of the CPU. But one can also imagine putting into sleep cores, memory benches, or disks, for example. Indeed, computers are increasingly multicore and multibank. So it should be possible to turn on and shut down one core or one bank on request.

At the data center level, different solutions are also possible to reduce energy consumption, such as energy-efficient task scheduling, proxying techniques to ensure network presence, or resource virtualization. With the scale effect, the potential savings are huge.

At the network level, we can consider the possibility to shut down entire redundant routes with all their components. But we can also shut down, one by one, the interfaces of the routers, switches, and computers or just scale their speed.

5.3 ERIDIS: ENERGY-EFFICIENT RESERVATION INFRASTRUCTURE FOR LARGE-SCALE DISTRIBUTED SYSTEMS

Different techniques are available to improve the energy efficiency in large-scale distributed systems, but they require a unified framework to associate them. In order to reach this goal, we propose an ERIDIS.

5.3.1 ERIDIS Architecture

With the growing number of deadline-driven applications such as meteorological disaster or earthquake forecast, or important large data transfers (e.g., for daily news), reservation infrastructures for large-scale distributed systems are increasingly important.

Our ERIDIS strives to optimize energy consumption in such systems. This infrastructure acts at the resource manager level and includes the following:

- energy sensors that collect, in real time, the energy consumption of resources and directly measure the impact of the taken decisions;
- allocating and scheduling algorithms to optimize the reservation placement;
- on/off facilities to put resources into sleep mode when they are not used;
- prediction algorithms to anticipate the workload;
- workload aggregation policies to avoid frequent on/off cycles for the resources.

The premise behind ERIDIS is that parts of the computing and networking resources can be put into sleep state when not needed to execute user tasks in order to consume less energy. Through coordinated resource management, both the opportunity to allow resources to go to sleep and the duration of these sleeping events can be increased. Depending on whether they have a computation or a data transfer to be done, users make reservation requests that consist of, at least, the following:

- an earliest possible start time, a deadline, a number of computing resource required, and a duration in the case of a computing job, or

- an earliest possible start time, a deadline, a data volume to be transferred (in GB, for example), a source node, and a destination node in the case of a networking job.

Other precisions can be included as a particular computing environment or a particular geographic location to use for a computing job, or a bit-rate transmission profile (maximum possible bit-rate over time) for a networking job. These particular additional options are detailed in the following sections.

Figure 5.2 presents the logical architecture of ERIDIS: users are connected to a reservation portal, which is the ERIDIS gateway for them. Each portal is directly connected to an ERIDIS manager, which is a local resource manager and is in charge of the management of a whole cluster of resources (computing, cloud, or networking resources). For example, for a grid infrastructure, each cluster (e.g., grid site) has its own *ERIDIS resource manager* to keep the overall architecture scalable, fast, and robust. So, users send their requests to their local gateway, which is a part of the resource manager, and this latter is in charge of dealing with the other resource managers, if required.

Each resource managed by ERIDIS is monitored by energy sensors (wattmeter), which provides accurate and periodical measurements to the manager. Thus, at the end of each reservation, ERIDIS is able to compute

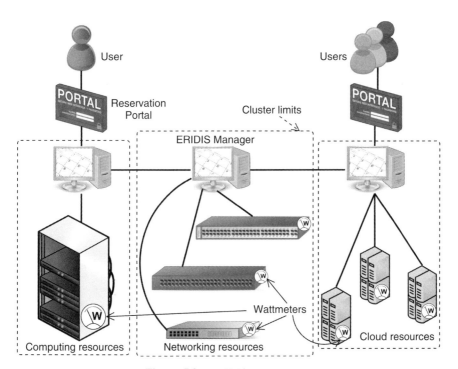

Figure 5.2 ERIDIS components.

the energy consumption of this particular reservation, and can provide this information to the user in order to increase energy awareness.

The structure of an ERIDIS manager is presented in Figure 5.3. Administrators and system designers can specify the green policies they want to use: on/off techniques, DVFS techniques, etc. These choices are taken into account in the reservation scheduler and in the resource management modules. The reservation scheduler is in charge of scheduling the incoming reservation requests and allocating resources to them. The resource management module is responsible for putting resources into sleep state or waking them up if required. All the components of this manager are described in detail in parallel with the explanation of the working of ERIDIS.

Each ERIDIS manager maintains an *agenda* for each resource that it is in charge of (resource agendas shown in Fig. 5.3). An agenda stores all the future reservations concerning the resource. So, it may contain different *resource states*: powered on but idle, turned off, booting, switching off, or partially or fully reserved, with the duration spent in each state. The resource management module is responsible for updating the agendas if some resources are down.

An example of such a resource agenda is shown in Figure 5.4. This agenda contains two reservations and the resource is switched off between these two reservations and again after the second reservation. The date of a change in resource state is called an *event*.

This model uses a continuous time model in order to have the storage of the agendas be more flexible and less space using. The storage of the agendas is structured in *time–capacity list*, which is made of $(t[i], c[i])$ tuples, where $t[i]$ represents an event (time) and $c[i]$ is the percentage of the resource that is used from that event to the next one. For example, for a bandwidth reservation, the capacity is the reserved bandwidth portion; and for a computing job, the capacity represents the percentage of CPU that has been reserved for this job. Thus, at each time, a resource knows which percentage of its overall capacity is used. Some particular values are used for the capacity to represent the power-on and shut-down periods.

These tuples are sorted in increasing order of $t[i]$. If $(t[n], c[n])$ is the last tuple then it means that the resource is unused from $t[n]$ to ∞. The ERIDIS

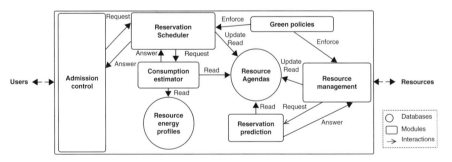

Figure 5.3   Structure of an ERIDIS manager.

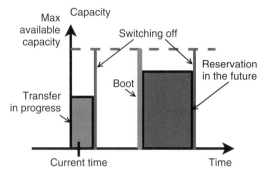

Figure 5.4 Example of an agenda of a given resource.

manager is in charge of updating the agendas of the resources it is managing. Yet, each resource stores each own agenda to know when it should go to sleep and when it should wake up.

As a matter of fact, the architecture of ERIDIS is semidecentralized since each local manager gets full control of the resources it manages. Moreover, local managers discuss among themselves in a point-to-point manner without a global supervisor on top of them. For example, in a cloud context, if a user requires more resources than its local manager can offer him, then the local manager will contact another manager to request the number of resources that it lacks. If the number of available resources is still insufficient, the local manager will ask another manager in addition, and so on, until it depletes the whole list of resource managers. This is why each ERIDIS manager is not necessarily directly linked to a user portal.

This semidecentralized feature ensures that the architecture is scalable, fast, and robust since any ERIDIS manager is in charge of a limited number of resource and has a privileged access to the other ERIDIS managers.

5.3.2   Management of the Resource Reservations

A reservation is like a lease contract between the resource provider and the resource user: the user can use the reserved resources during a limited time interval that has been fixed during the negotiation process between the user and the provider. The negotiation takes place in a three-step handshake process (Fig. 5.5).

First, the user sends a *request* that contains its resource and time constraints, that is, at least the type of resources, the required number, the reservation duration, and a deadline. Second, the reservation manager proposes a solution, which can either fulfill the user's requirements if it is possible or propose the earliest possible reservation start time if the deadline constraint cannot be respected (due to system load). If the request is not acceptable because it asks for too many resources or it does not respect the system's admission rules, the request is rejected and is notified to the user.

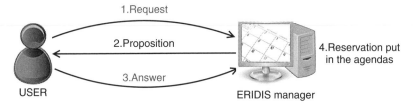

Figure 5.5 Reservation negotiation between the user and an ERIDIS manager.

Finally, if the reservation manager has made a proposition, the user has a fixed amount of time to answer it and express his agreement or disagreement. Otherwise, the request is rejected. If the user accepts the manager's proposition, the manager updates all the concerned agendas by adding this new reservation. Algorithm 5.1 details the algorithm used to process the request. The scheduling algorithm will be detailed later (Algorithm 5.2).

The reservation management system should guarantee that the negotiated reservation terms are well respected. It also has to dynamically schedule in time the reservations and allocate them the most appropriate resources.

Algorithm 5.1

```
Request Processing:
if the request is not acceptable
  reject it
else
  launch the scheduling algorithm
  if the request cannot be satisfied
    propose the earliest possible start time
              (given by the scheduling)
  else
      send the offer to the user (given by the scheduling)
      wait for the answer
  if there is no answer or the answer is no
    discard the request
  else
      place the reservation on each concerned agenda
```

Figure 5.6 presents the different reservation states. First, the user sends a requests that is either rejected or accepted, and in that case, the manager makes a proposition. Then, this proposition is either accepted or rejected by the user. If it is accepted, the reservation is scheduled. This reservation can be rescheduled before its start time if the manager needs to move this reservation to accept a new one. This rescheduling is still bound by the resource and time constraints negotiated between the user and the ERIDIS manager. No renegotiation is allowed in our model. During the reservation, the user has access to the reserved resources until the reservation's end time.

Algorithm 5.2

Scheduling-Algorithm:
find d the earliest possible start time with a satisfying set r of
          free resources
$List = [d]$
for each agenda event between d and (deadline-reservation duration)
    if the reservation can be placed before this event
        find the set of the least consuming free resources at that time
        add the possible start time to $List$ with the resource set
    else if the reservation can be placed after this event
        find the set of the least consuming free resources at that time
        add this event to $List$ with the set of resources
    if $List$ contains only d
        return d and r
    else
        for each date in$List$
         estimate the reservation energy consumption if it starts at
         this date
          with the corresponding set of resources
         propose the less energy consuming date and set of resources to
          the user

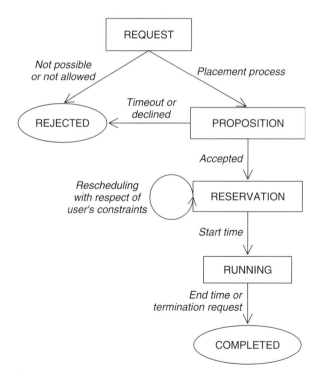

Figure 5.6   Management of a reservation: the different states.

The scheduling algorithm should provide either the most energy-efficient possibility in terms of both time placement and resource allocation or the earliest possible start time if the deadline constraint cannot be satisfied. This algorithm is executed after the admission control process, that is, to say that it is executed on requests that respect the system's rules and can be accepted depending on the system's load.

If the reservation is possible, the scheduling algorithm provides a reservation start time and a set of resources to be used during the reservation. Algorithm 5.2 details the scheduling method. The first step is to find the earliest possible start time. As the request has passed the admission control, it is acceptable and thus, the user constraints in terms of resources can be satisfied at one time or another. So, this first step will determine if the deadline constraint can be satisfied or not. Indeed, if the earliest possible start time does not allow the reservation to end before the deadline because of the system load, this start time is directly proposed to the user, which can either accept or decline this proposition.

The earliest possible start time is found by looking linearly at each event from the current time to see if a reservation satisfying the user's constraints can be placed before or after this event. Only the feasible solutions are examined, the algorithm does not put a reservation start time before the current time, for example. This restriction of the solution space to certain dates (i.e., the events) ensures that the algorithm is fast and scalable and that the found solution is energy efficient, since the reservation has been aggregated with at least another one (by definition of the events).

When the earliest possible d has been found, the scheduling algorithm looks linearly at all the resources that can accept a reservation starting at d, and it picks the N least consuming resources at that time (taking into account the necessary switching on and off), where N is the number of resources required by the user. The energy-consumption estimation of a reservation is detailed in Section 5.3.4 (consumption estimator module in Fig. 5.3). This set of N resources should satisfy the user's constraints (e.g., if he or she specified some particular hardware or software constraints), and should be the least consuming set of resources among all the possible sets at d.

When the earliest possible solution (d and r) has been found, the algorithm (Algorithm 5.2) searches if there is a better solution, in terms of energy consumption, after d but still before the deadline. So, the algorithm examines each event in the time interval between d and the deadline minus the reservation duration requested by the user. The process is similar to the one used to find d and r. However, each event of the time interval is considered, and for each event, the set of the N least consuming resources is determined. At the end, all these solutions are compared in terms of energy consumption and the best one is chosen. This solution is optimal, since the algorithm tests all the possibilities that can be the less consuming ones because of the energy-saving properties of reservation aggregation.

5.3.3 Resource Management and On/Off Algorithms

The scheduling algorithm aims at aggregating as much as possible the reservations in order to save energy, and especially the energy used to switch the resources on and off. However, switching the resources on and off can be difficult and requires time and energy. Thus, when a resource is switched off, it should stay off for a certain period of time to save more energy than is being used when switching it off then on again. Switched-off resources consume energy but less energy than when they are idle (powered on but not in use) [25]. Thus, a subtle balance needs to be adopted to ensure energy savings by switching resources off. That is why, at the end of each reservation, the resource manager determines if the freed resources should remain on or switched off.

First, for each resource, the manager examines the resource agenda to see whether another reservation has been put just after it. If this is the case, the resource stays on. Otherwise, the manager uses a prediction algorithm (detailed in Section 5.3.5) to estimate whether the resource is going to be used soon (reservation prediction module in Figure 5.3). If this is the case, it stays on; otherwise, the resource is switched off. This process is described by Algorithm 5.3.

Algorithm 5.3

Reservation End:
Provide the energy consumed by the overall reservation to the user
for each reserved resource
    if this resource has an imminent reservation
      let it on
    else
    launch the prediction algorithm
    if the resource is going to be used soon
      let it on
    else
      turn it off

The problem here is to have a reliable and fast solution to remotely switch the resources on and off when necessary. This requires some hardware facilities on the resources and a dedicated infrastructure to access them. For example, in a grid or cloud context, IPMI facilities can be used [18].

Moreover, each resource has a copy of its own agenda, and thus, when it goes into sleep state, it uses a timer to know when it should wake up again. So, the previous mechanism to remotely switch on and off the resources is used only when a reservation, which was not planned when the resource went to sleep, occurs. Yet, switching operations on and off should be fast enough to avoid impacting the reactivity of the whole system.

5.3.4   Energy-Consumption Estimates

As seen in the architecture, ERIDIS embeds energy sensors to monitor in real time the energy consumption of the resources it manages. So, at the end of each reservation, the ERIDIS manager reports the energy consumption of the overall reservation to the user to increase his energy awareness (Algorithm 5.3).

As seen previously, estimations of the energy consumption of some reservations are needed to take best scheduling decisions. To make these estimations, the ERIDIS manager requires an energy profile for each resource it is managing. This energy profile contains information about the following:

- the energy and time required to switch the resource off;
- the energy and time required to switch the resource on;
- the mean power used by the resource when it is off (i.e., sleep state);
- the mean power used by the resource when it is idle (i.e., powered on but not used);
- the relation between the capacity usage (in percentage) and the mean power usage of the resource (function giving the power consumption as a function of the percentage utilization of the resource).

The ERIDIS manager is responsible for drawing up these energy profiles by using benchmarks and energy sensors (resource energy profiles illustrated in Fig. 5.3). These profiles are periodically updated (e.g., each month) because hardware usage ("wear and tear"), heat, or humidity conditions, among others, can impact the energy consumption of the resources.

By exploiting these energy profiles, it becomes easy for the resource manager to estimate the energy consumption of a reservation. This estimation includes the energy cost to wake up and to switch off resources if it is necessary. Thus, if, for example, the reservation is aggregated after another one, the energy cost to wake up the resources is saved. Similarly, if a reservation shares some resources with another one, because it does not require the full resource, the working energy cost of the resources is split between the two reservations according to the percentage of the resource that each of them is using.

5.3.5   Prediction Algorithms

As explained earlier, prediction algorithms are used to ensure a good planning of the off–on cycles. Our prediction algorithms rely on the recent history (the past part of the agenda). They are based on average values of past inactivity period durations and feedbacks, which are average values of differences between the past predictions and the past corresponding real events in the agenda.

For example, with computing resources, when a node is freed the average value of the last few free intervals of time (when the node is not used) is computed, and it is assumed to be the value of the next free interval of time. This prediction algorithm has been tested in Reference 31 with usage traces of a cluster belonging to French experimental grid, Grid'5000. In about 70% of the cases, the algorithm takes a good decision between switching off the resource and leaving it on. More generally, the energy gain is significant.

To illustrate how ERIDIS works, three use cases will be presented: grid management (Section 5.4), cloud management (Section 5.5), and data transfer in a network overlay (Section 5.6).

5.4 EARI: ENERGY-AWARE RESERVATION INFRASTRUCTURE FOR DATA CENTERS AND GRIDS

The energy consumption of data centers worldwide has doubled between 2000 and 2006 [32]. The incremental US demand for data center energy between 2008 and 2010 is the equivalent of 10 new power plants [32]. These alarming figures lead to thinking about new technologies and infrastructures in order to increase the energy efficiency of large-scale distributed systems such as data centers, grids, and clouds.

The main leverage to make large-scale distributed infrastructures more energy-efficient is to reduce energy wastage. Indeed, resources are always fully powered on even when they are not in use. So, grids require energy-aware frameworks capable of switching unused resources off without impacting user applications in terms of both performance and usage. This is why, we propose the energy-aware reservation infrastructure (EARI) [31, 33, 34] based on the ERIDIS model.

EARI is devoted to grid infrastructures that support in-advance reservations: users submit reservation requests. They specify the duration, the number of resources, and the start time they want. When a reservation is accepted, the scheduler puts it in its agenda and cannot move it afterwards.

5.4.1 EARI's Architecture

Figure 5.7 presents the architecture of EARI for a cluster. It is composed of a traditional data center infrastructure: users, a portal, a scheduler and resource manager, and the grid resources. However, it is also composed of energy-aware components: a set of energy sensors plugged to the resources and an energy-aware manager that is responsible for applying the green policies of EARI.

All the resources managers are linked and communicate between them in order to satisfy user requests. The global EARI is evaluated in Reference 33 by simulating a replay of 1 year of logs of Grid'5000. On the Lyon site of Grid'5000 (150 nodes), we have deployed energy sensors that fully monitor the site [35]. This provides an experimental test bed where we can test our frameworks with real energy measurements.

5.4.2 Validation of EARI on Experimental Grid Traces

To evaluate EARI, we conducted experiments based on a replay of the 2007 traces of the Grid'5000 platform (these traces have been studied in Reference 31).

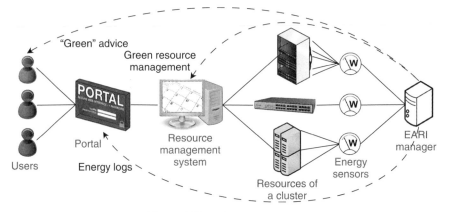

Figure 5.7 EARI components.

We moved the reservations on a time scale by respecting several policies. Our replay mechanism worked as follows: each reservation was treated when its submission time came, so no arrival law was needed for the reservations. A timer simulated the running time of the experiment, and at each second, the manager looked into the log database to see if there was a new event, and the scheduling algorithm was launched when required.

We designed the following six policies to conduct our experiments:

- *User*. We always selected the solution that fitted the most with the user's demand (the date asked by the user or the nearest possible date);
- *Fully Green*. We always selected the solution that saved the most energy (where we need to switch on and off the smallest number of resources);
- *25% Green*. We processed 25% of the submission, taken at random, with the previous *fully green* policy and the remaining ones with the *user* policy;
- *50% Green*. We processed 50% of the submission, taken at random, with the *fully green* policy and the others with the *user* policy;
- *75% Green*. We processed 75% of the submission, taken at random, with the *fully green* policy and the others with the *user* policy;
- *Deadlined*. We used the *fully green* policy if it did not delay the reservation from the initial user's demand for more than 24 h, otherwise we used the *user* policy.

These policies simulate the behavior of real users: there is a percentage of "green" users who follow the advice given by EARI. Maybe they do not want to delay their reservation for too long, as in the *deadlined* policy. Some users do not want to move their reservation even if they can save energy by following this; this is the *user* policy. The *fully green* policy can illustrate the case of an administrator decision: the administrator always chooses the most energy-efficient option.

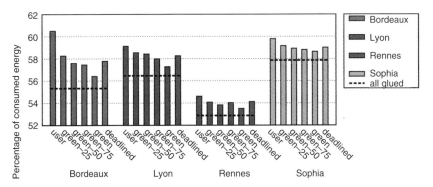

Figure 5.8 Energy consumption of EARI for four Grid'5000 sites.

These replay experiments have been conducted on four site traces: Bordeaux, Lyon, Rennes, and Sophia (Fig. 5.8). These four scenarios represent four different workloads over a 1-year period. The graphs represent the results for the six different policies in order to compare their energy savings. A percentage of 100 represents the actual consumption of the platform when no energy saving is used and so, all the resources are always fully powered on even when they are not used. We also represent the ideal lowest bound that we called *all glued*. It is an unreachable ideal case where we could glue all the reservations: they are all put one after the other, and the resources are switched off the rest of the time. In that case, we do not need any prediction, and thus we cannot make prediction errors. This ideal case is not reachable because it assumes that we know all the reservations in advance, yet the future is never known!

Aside from that, we see that sometimes our *75%-green* policy consumes more than that of the *50%-green* one. This is due to the random factor: we can move a small reservation that will prevent us from moving a big one at this place or that will block several others. This behavior is not energy efficient. Therefore, adding randomness does not necessarily lead to decreasing the energy consumption.

In all the cases, our *fully green* policy is the best one. As we can see, using EARI can lead to energy gains up to 46% depending on the cluster's load. In all the cases, this value is close to the unreachable optimal value ("all glued").

5.5 GOC: GREEN OPEN CLOUD

The cloud's most well-known features are virtualization, accounting, scalability, reliability, and security. The *r*esources-as-a-*s*ervice (RaaS) philosophy leads to a more flexible management of the physical nodes: clouds provide a strong isolation that allows users to share the same physical resources. Thus, this strong virtual machine (VM) isolation can also lead to energy savings. Indeed, physical resources can be exploited more using workload consolidation.

For this reason, we adapt ERIDIS to cloud environments in order to benefit from the cloud's features. Still, some of the following differences between grids and clouds have to be taken into account:

- agenda (no advance reservation in current cloud infrastructures);
- virtualization and possibility to use live migration;
- usage and thus predictions;
- resource management.

cloud computing seems to be a promising solution to the increasing demand of computing power needed by more and more complex applications. However, the studies often lack real values o_1 for the electric consumption of virtualized infrastructures. That is why, as a preliminary step, we have studied the energy consumption of VMs completing basic operations: boot, shut down, doing a CPU-burn task, and migrating [36, 37].

These analyses led us to propose the green open cloud (GOC) framework to manage cloud resources in an energy-efficient way. Among the components of a cloud architecture, we have decided to focus on virtualization, which appears as the main technology used in these architectures. We also use migration to dynamically unbalance the load between the cloud nodes in order to shut down some nodes, and thus to save energy.

As EARI, GOC supports the "do the same for less" approach and deals with energy-efficient on/off models combined with prediction solutions [36, 37].

The main features of GOC are the following:

- to switch unused resources off;
- to predict usage;
- to aggregate reservations;
- to use green policies for the users.

In addition, when a user frees some VMs, a consolidation algorithm is used to aggregate the remaining VMs on the smaller number of nodes. This consolidation process is launched in coordination with predictions algorithms in order to avoid switching off physical resources that will be required right afterwards. GOC also provides green advice to users such as EARI, in order to aggregate the reservations in time. This double aggregation in time and space is the core functionality of GOC. GOC's manager architecture is presented in Figure 5.9.

5.5.1 GOC's Resource Manager Architecture

The resource manager is a key component in a cloud infrastructure. To be compatible with the broadest possible range of resource management systems, GOC's resource manager is built as an overlay of existing cloud resource manager. The components of GOC's resource manager are the green boxes shown in Figure 5.9.

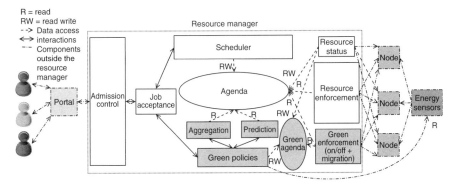

Figure 5.9   Architecture of GOC's resource manager.

The user's access portal is directly linked with the admission control module that is responsible for security. Then, the job acceptance module determines if the user's submission is acceptable according to management policies (for example, the system administrator can put a limit on the resources for a single user). If the submission is accepted, it is sent to the scheduler and the green policies module. The scheduler looks at the agenda to see if the submission can be put into this agenda (enough resources at the date wished by the user). According to the green policies defined by the admin and by using aggregation, the green policies module computes other possible slots for this job that are more energy efficient (the job will consume less energy because it will be aggregated with others).

The answers of the scheduler and the green policies module are sent back to the user who picks out one solution between the one he has submitted and the energy-efficient solutions proposed by the green policies module. Afterward, the solution chosen by the user is returned to the scheduler, which puts it into the agenda.

At the end of each reservation, if there is totally or partially free nodes (with few VMs), the green policies use prediction to anticipate the next use of the freed resources. If they will be used in a short time, we do not switch them off or migrate their remaining VMs. We switch them off if they are totally free. If they are partially free and if their jobs will not end in a short time, we try to migrate their VMs on other nodes to minimize the number of nodes that are powered on. Otherwise, if they are partially free and if their jobs will end in a short time, we do not change anything. It will indeed cost more energy to migrate the VMs for such a short time.

The green policies module is in charge of taking the on/off and migration decisions, then it inscribes it in the green agenda, which is read by the green enforcement module. The latter module is in charge of switching the resources on an off and migrating the VMs. This part is totally transparent for the nongreen modules. Indeed, they have no access to the green agenda and the presence proxy is informed when a node is switched off and so can answer in its place. The green enforcement module has access to the agenda in order to switch on the resources at the beginning of a job.

The resource enforcement module launches the jobs and creates and installs the VMs of the users. It reads the agenda to know the reservations features (e.g., start time, VM configuration). It ensures that the user will not take more resources than he is allowed to.

The resource status module checks whether the nodes are dead (not working properly). If the node has been switched off by the green enforcement module, the presence proxy answers instead. If a node is dead, the module writes it in the agenda.

5.5.2 Validation of the GOC Framework

In order to validate GOC, we have made real experiments on a small Cloud test bed in our lab. Our Cloud platform consists of HP Proliant 85 G2 servers (2.2 GHz, 2 dual-core CPUs per node). XenServer 5.0 is installed on each node. The resource manager is on another machine plugged on the same network switch.

We have tested two different scheduling, round-robin and unbalanced, to show the adaptability of GOC to any kind of cloud resource manager. The following four scenarios are used to compare GOC with other traditional resource management systems:

- *Basic*: nothing is changed;
- *Balancing*: migration is used to balance the load between the cloud nodes;
- *On/off*: the unused nodes are switched off;
- *Green* the unused nodes are switched off and migration is used to unbalance the load between cloud nodes. This allows aggregating the load on some nodes and switching the other ones off. This is the scenario that corresponds to GOC.

Each scenario is launched on a cloud job arrival example for each scheduling. All the results are provided in Reference 37. Figure 5.10 presents the average consumption for these eight experiments. As expected, the green scenario is the less consuming one. With the unbalanced scheduling, energy consumption is 25% less than the basic scenario.

5.6 HERMES: HIGH LEVEL ENERGY-AWARE MODEL FOR BANDWIDTH RESERVATION IN END-TO-END NETWORKS

Scientists increasingly rely on the network for high speed data transfers, dissemination of results, and collaborations. Networks are thus becoming the critical component. In 2007, to distribute the entire collection of data from the Hubble telescope (about 120 TB) to various research institutions, scientists chose to

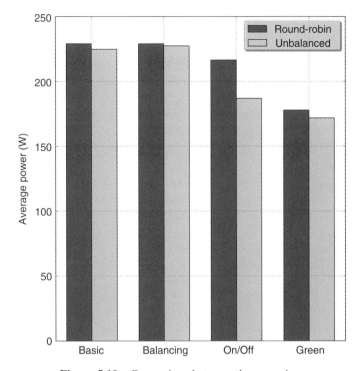

Figure 5.10   Comparison between the scenarios.

copy this data on hard disks and send these hard disks via mail. It was faster than using the network [38]. To solve this issue, dedicated networks were built to transfer large amounts of scientific data, for example, for the LHC (Large Hadron Collider), which produces 15 million GB of data every year [39].

Bandwidth provisioning is feasible for network operators for several years thanks to protocols such as *m*ulti*p*rotocol *l*abel *s*witching (MPLS) [40] and reservation protocol (RSVP) [41]. However, for end users with no knowledge of network traffic, this task is impossible without collaboration with the other nodes.

On the other hand, as networks become increasingly essential, their electric consumption reaches unprecedented peaks [42]. Up to now, the main concern to design network equipment and protocols was performance only; energy consumption was not taken into account. With the costly growth in network electricity demand, it is high time to consider energy as a main priority for network design.

To this end, we propose a new complete and energy-efficient bulk data transfer (BDT) framework, including scheduling algorithms, which provide an adaptive and predictive management of the advance bandwidth reservations (ABR). This model is called *HERMES*: *h*igh level *e*nergy-awa*r*e *m*odel for bandwidth reservation in *e*nd-to-end network*s* [43]. It is adapted from ERIDIS to this particular dedicated network case with BDTs.

To achieve energy efficiency, HERMES combines several techniques as follows:

- unused network components are put into sleep mode;
- energy optimization of the reservation scheduling through reservation aggregation;
- minimization of the control messages required by the infrastructure;
- usage of DTN (disruption-tolerant networking) to manage the infrastructure;
- network usage prediction to avoid too frequent on/off cycles.

When a user (end host) has data to transfer, he or she submits a data transfer reservation that corresponds to a data volume (e.g., 10 GB), a deadline (e.g., "in 2 h"), and a destination (receiver end host). These basic information requirements are the only ones required for simple data transfer requests. These transfers are *malleable*, they are flexible enough to use any transmission rate, to have variable transmission rates over time, or to be split in several parts.

Additional features can be specified, such as maximal and minimal bandwidths (e.g., for video streaming or if the receiver is limited by its storage capacities) and transfer profiles (step functions that express variable bandwidth requirement over time). These transfers are called *rigid* in contrast with malleable transfers.

Each network equipment (routers, switches, bridges, repeaters, hubs, transmitters) has two agendas per port (per outgoing link) for both ways (in and out). An agenda stores all the future reservations concerning its one-way link. This information is sometimes called the *book-ahead interval* [44].

Furthermore, each network equipment has also an agenda stating the on and off periods and the switching stages between on and off. This global agenda is in fact the combination of all the per-port agendas of the equipment: when no port is used for a certain amount of time (not too small), the network equipment can be switched off. Usage prediction algorithms are used to avoid switching the equipment off if it is going to be useful in a near future.

5.6.1 HERMES' Architecture

Wired networks are usually not organized as clusters of resources such as grids and clouds naturally are. However, this kind of self-organization is used since a long time in ad hoc networks for routing and energy management purposes [45]. Network nodes are divided into virtual clusters with a cluster head managing each cluster. In our case, the cluster head is the HERMES manager. This manager is responsible for the agendas of the nodes belonging to its cluster.

The architecture of HERMES is shown in Figure 5.11. Here, the user portal to access the reservation system is called a *gateway*. The network case is particular because it requires the coordinated reservation of several resources at the same time, but for a particular request, this number of resources is not known in advance. Indeed, for a data transfer job, several network paths may be possible, and they may not have the same length.

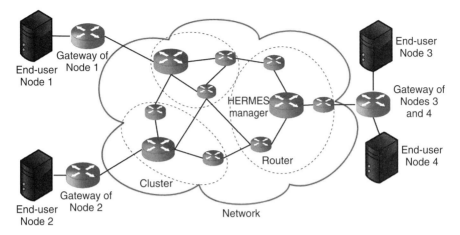

Figure 5.11   Organization in clusters with HERMES.

5.6.2   The Reservation Process of HERMES

When a gateway receives a reservation request, the first operation to execute is admission control. The validity of the request is checked. Then, each request requires to collect the agendas of all the equipment (ports and routers) along the network paths between the source and the destination.

In order to do this agenda collection, all the agendas of the possible paths will be sent to the gateway of the receiver. The sender gateway will send a particular management message. The first node to receive it will transmit it to its HERMES manager. The manager needs to compute the availability agenda of the possible subpaths that can be used for this requested reservation. A *subpath* of a cluster is a path between two nodes of the cluster that both have a link going outside of the cluster to another cluster. The *availability agenda* of a path is obtained by merging all the agendas of the network components actually on this path. It contains all the residual bandwidths (unused portions) of the whole path. Each cluster has a fixed number of subpaths and can maintain an availability agenda for each of them, and it can update these availability agendas when it updates the regular resources agendas. So, all the availability agendas are precomputed and stored using the same format as regular agendas (tuple list).

The manager transmits these subpaths agendas to the next HERMES manager toward the requested destination with a list for each subpath end node of all the nodes outside the cluster connected to this particular end node. This allows building up a path from the source to the destination when all these agendas are gathered by the receiving gateway. The next HERMES manager does the same process: it transmits its subpaths and corresponding node lists with the ones it received from the first manager to the next HERMES manager toward the requested destination. This algorithm limits the number of clusters that are involved in the reservation since each manager only transmits the request to the next manager toward the requested destination and not to all of its neighbors.

This limitation does not compromise the energy efficiency of HERMES because one expects that long paths (using numerous nodes) will be more energy consuming than short ones. Moreover, this limitation considerably reduces the computing time since it does not consider all the paths of the network.

Thus, the receiver gateway ends up with all the required agendas. The gateway then makes the link between all the possible subpaths to constitute *end-to-end paths* between the source and the destination, and it merges the corresponding availability agenda of the subpaths to obtain one availability agenda per end-to-end path. Once they are computed, the end-to-end paths can be put into cache in order to avoid doing this computation too often.

Each end-to-end availability agenda is scanned using the ERIDIS scheduling algorithm (Algorithm 5.2) to find the solution consuming the least energy. At each time, the solution tries to use as much bandwidth as it can to reduce the reservation's duration, and thus its cost. Then, the solutions of all the end-to-end paths are compared and the least consuming one is sent back to the sender gateway and proposed to the user. A global view of this reservation process is presented in Figure 5.12.

However, this process works only if the necessary ports and routers are on when the agenda collection is done. Indeed, when they are not used, the network equipment (individual ports or entire routers) are put into sleep mode. To solve this issue, DTN [46] technologies are used. Indeed, DTN is perfectly adapted to this type of scenario where parts of the network are not always available without any guarantee of end-to-end connectivity at any time.

The idea is to add a kind of TTL (time-to-live) in seconds to each end-user request: when the TTL expires, if the request has not reached the receiver gateway and has not come back, then all the sleeping nodes of the path are awaken and the agenda collection is performed. While the TTL is not expired, the agenda collection message moves forward along the path until meeting a sleeping node. Then, as long as the TTL has not expired, the message waits in the previous node for the sleeping node to wake up, and when it wakes up (wake-up detection managed by the DTN protocol), the message is sent to it and continues its way.

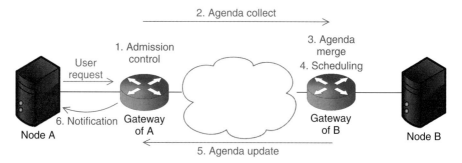

Figure 5.12 Reservation process.

Thus, hop by hop, the agenda collection message moves toward the receiver gateway.

HERMES gateways and managers are always fully powered on to ensure high availability and reactivity for the overall system. The gateways are able to wake up the nodes they are linked to and the managers are able to wake up the nodes of their clusters. So, each sleeping node need just one awake component (or two if it is connected to a gateway) linked to its manager to be remotely awaken and not one component per link.

5.6.3 Discussion

The proposed network management optimizes the energy consumption of the overall architecture at any time. However, we have not yet studied the energy optimization of transfers themselves.

Indeed, we have assumed that at any time, the most energy-efficient behavior is to use as much bandwidth as possible (from source to destination). However, we have not proved that this algorithm leads to the minimum energy consumption.

Let us consider this example: node A wants to send 200 MB of data to node B and nodes A and B are directly linked by a 1 GB/s link. Our algorithm will schedule the transfer and set the bandwidth at 1 GB/s (minus the free bandwidth portion). If we assume that the free bandwidth portion is negligible, it takes 0.2 s to transmit 200 MB of data at 1 GB/s. Thus, this transfer will consume $E_{transfer}$ with $P_{EthernetCard}(NodeA, 1GB/s)$, which denotes the power consumed by node A when it transmits data at 1 GB/s:

$$E_{transfer} = E_{EthernetCard}(NodeA, 1 \text{ GB/s}, 0.2 \text{ s})$$
$$+ E_{EthernetCard}(NodeB, 1 \text{ GB/s}, 0.2 \text{ s})$$
$$= P_{EthernetCard}(NodeA, 1 \text{ GB/s}) \times 0.2$$
$$+ P_{EthernetCard}(NodeB, 1 \text{ GB/s}) \times 0.2.$$

However, another solution could be to adjust the Ethernet card to work at 100 MB/s, and thus, it does not use the full capacity and takes more time. In that case, the transfer consumes

$$E'_{transfer} = E_{EthernetCard}(NodeA, 100 \text{ MB/s}, 2 \text{ s})$$
$$+ E_{EthernetCard}(NodeB, 100 \text{ MB/s}, 2 \text{ s})$$
$$= P_{EthernetCard}(NodeA, 100 \text{ MB/s}) \times 2$$
$$+ P_{EthernetCard}(NodeB, 100 \text{ MB/s}) \times 2.$$

If we assume that the NICs are identical and thus have the same power consumption $P_{EthernetCard}(100 \text{ MB/s})$ and $P_{EthernetCard}(1 \text{ GB/s})$ depending on the rate, then the second solution uses less energy to transfer the data if and only if

$$P_{EthernetCard}(1 \text{ GB/s}) > 10 \times P_{EthernetCard}(100 \text{ MB/s}).$$

If we use the figures provided in Reference 47, we have $P_{\text{EthernetCard}}$ $(100 \text{ MB/s}) = 0.4$ W and $P_{\text{EthernetCard}}(1 \text{ GB/s}) = 3.6$ W for an NIC. In that case, our scenario is the most energy efficient with a consumption equal to 0.72 J (and 0.8 J for the second scenario). However, here, we only considered the energy used to transfer data and not the overall energy of the infrastructure during a certain period of time. These two energy consumptions thus do not represent the same period of time (0.2 and 2 s). To compare them over an identical time period, we should add to E_{transfer} the cost of staying off during 1.8s.

We have not taken into account the energy required to switch the NICs on at the beginning and to switch them off at the end of the transfer since these energy costs are identical in both scenarios.

This remark shows that our algorithm should be compared with other solutions and that the optimal solution is hard to find, even in scenarios with fixed routing. This situation is the result of the nonproportionality between energy and usage: cost functions are linear by steps and not just linear.

5.7 SUMMARY

Owing to their size and heterogeneity, large-scale distributed systems require scalable, robust, fault-tolerant, and energy-efficient resource management infrastructures. This chapter presented ERIDIS: an Energy-efficient Reservation Infrastructure for large-scale DIstributed Systems. ERIDIS is empowered to optimize the energy consumption of the computing and networking resources and to have a flexible and adaptive reservation management that satisfies user requirements through strict reservation policies.

We have adapted ERIDIS to the following three different application fields to demonstrate its capabilities:

- data center and grid management with the EARI;
- virtualized environments and cloud management with the GOC;
- dedicated network with large data transfers with the (HERMES).

Our next step is to refine the ERIDIS model to take advantage of divisible tasks that can be suspended and resumed as required if some more urgent tasks need to be executed. These tasks allow a higher level of flexibility in the reservation management.

REFERENCES

1. Hotta Y, Sato M, Kimura H, Matsuoka S, Boku T, Takahashi D. Profile-based optimization of power performance by using dynamic voltage scaling on a PC cluster. In: Parallel and Distributed Processing Symposium (IPDPS); Rhodes Island, Greece; 2006.

2. Bennett M, Christensen K, Nordman B. Improving the energy efficiency of ethernet: adaptive link rate proposal. Ethernet Alliance White Paper; 2006.

3. Barroso LA, Holzle U. The case for energy-proportional computing. Computer 2007;40(12):33–37.

4. Sotomayor B, Montero RS, Llorente IM, Foster I. Resource leasing and the art of suspending virtual machines. In: Conference on High Performance Computing and Communications (HPCC); Seoul, Korea; 2009. pp. 59–68.

5. Castillo C, Rouskas GN, Harfoush K. Efficient resource management using advance reservations for heterogeneous Grids. In: International Symposium on Parallel and Distributed Processing (IPDPS); Miami, Florida, USA; 2008. pp. 1–12.

6. Palansuriya C, Buchli M, Kavoussanakis K, Patil A, Tziouvaras C, Trew A, Simpson A, Baxter R. End-to-end bandwidth allocation and reservation for grid applications. In: Conference on Broadband Communications, Networks and Systems (BROADNETS); California, USA; 2006. pp. 1–9.

7. Fan X, Weber W-D, Barroso LA. Power provisioning for a warehouse-sized computer. In: ISCA '07: Proceedings of the 34th Annual International Symposium on Computer Architecture; California, USA; 2007. pp. 13–23.

8. Merkel A, Bellosa F. Balancing power consumption in multiprocessor systems. SIGOPS Oper Syst Rev 2006;40(4):403–414.

9. Chase J, Anderson D, Thakar P, Vahdat A, Doyle R. Managing energy and server resources in hosting centers. In: SOSP '01: Proceedings of the 18th ACM Symposium on Operating Systems Principles; Banff, Canada; 2001. pp. 103–116.

10. Gunaratne C, Christensen K, Nordman B. Managing energy consumption costs in desktop PCs and LAN switches with proxying, split TCP connections, and scaling of link speed. Int J Netw Manage 2005;15:(5):297–310.

11. Wang L, von Laszewski G, Dayal J, Wang F. Towards energy aware scheduling for precedence constrained parallel tasks in a cluster with DVFS. In: Conference on Cluster, Cloud and Grid Computing (CCGrid); Melbourne, Australia; 2010. pp. 368–377.

12. Jejurikar R, Gupta R. Energy aware task scheduling with task synchronization for embedded real-time systems. In: IEEE Transactions on Computer-Aided Design of Integrated Circuits and Systems; 2006. pp. 1024–1037.

13. Chase J, Doyle R. Balance of power: energy management for server clusters. In: Proceedings of the 8th Workshop on Hot Topics in Operating Systems (HotOS'01); Oberbayern, Germany; 2001.

14. Patel C, Sharma R, Bash C, Graupner S. Energy aware grid: global workload placement based on energy efficiency. Technical report, HP Laboratories; 2002.

15. Sharma R, Bash C, Patel C, Friedrich R, Chase J. Balance of power: dynamic thermal management for internet data centers. IEEE Internet Comput 2005;9(1):42–49.

16. Allalouf M, Arbitman Y, Factor M, Kat R, Meth K, Naor D. Storage modeling for power estimation. In: SYSTOR 2009: The Israeli Experimental Systems Conference; Haifa, Israel; 2009. pp. 1–10.

17. Dietz HG, Dieter WR. Compiler and runtime support for predictive control of power and cooling. In: Parallel and Distributed Processing Symposium (IPDPS); Rhodes Island, Greece; 2006.

18. Leangsuksun C, Rao T, Tikotekar A, Scott S, Libby R, Vetter J, Fang Y, Ong H IPMI-based efficient notification framework for large scale cluster computing. In: International Symposium on Cluster Computing and the Grid Workshops (CCGrid), Volume 2; Singapore; 2006.

19. Nathuji R, Schwan K. VirtualPower: coordinated power management in virtualized enterprise systems. In: Symposium on Operating Systems Principles (SOPS); Stevenson, USA; 2007. pp. 265–278.

20. Stoess J, Lang C, Bellosa F. Energy management for hypervisor-based virtual machines. In: USENIX Annual Technical Conference (ATC); 2007. pp. 1–14.

21. Talaber R, Brey T, Lamers L. Using virtualization to improve data center efficiency. Technical report, The Green Grid; 2009.

22. Torres J, Carrera D, Hogan K, Gavalda R, Beltran V, Poggi N. Reducing wasted resources to help achieve green data centers. In: IEEE International Symposium on Parallel and Distributed Processing (IPDPS); Miami, Florida, USA; 2008. pp. 1–8.

23. Srikantaiah S, Kansal A, Zhao F. Energy aware consolidation for cloud computing. In: Conference on Power aware computing and systems (HotPower). USENIX Association; California, USA; 2008.

24. Travostino F, Daspit P, Gommans L, Jog C, de Laat C, Mambretti J, Monga I, van Oudenaarde B, Raghunath S, Wang P. Seamless live migration of virtual machines over the MAN/WAN. Future Gener Comput Syst 2006;22(8):901–907.

25. Orgerie A-C, Lefèvre L, Gelas J-P. Demystifying energy consumption in grids and clouds. In: Work in Progress in Green Computing, IGCC Workshop; Chicago, USA; 2010.

26. Gupta M, Singh S. Greening of the Internet. In: SIGCOMM '03: Proceedings of the 2003 Conference on Applications, Technologies, Architectures, and Protocols for Computer Communications; Karlsruhe, Germany; 2003. pp. 19–26.

27. Gupta M, Grover S, Singh S. A feasibility study for power management in LAN switches. In: ICNP '04: Proceedings of the Network Protocols, 12th IEEE International Conference; Berlin, Germany; 2004. pp. 361–371.

28. Gupta M, Singh S. Using low-power modes for energy conservation in ethernet LANs. In: INFOCOM 2007. 26th IEEE International Conference on Computer Communications. IEEE; Alaska, USA; 2007. pp. 2451–2455.

29. Gupta M, Singh S. Dynamic ethernet link shutdown for energy conservation on ethernet links. In: IEEE International Conference on Communications (ICC'07); Glasgow, Scotland; 2007. pp. 6156–6161.

30. Gunaratne C, Suen S. Ethernet adaptive link rate (ALR): analysis of a buffer threshold policy. Global Telecommunications Conference, 2006. GLOBECOM '06; San Francisco, USA; 2006.

31. Orgerie A-C, Lefèvre L, Gelas J-P. Chasing gaps between bursts: towards energy efficient large scale experimental grids. In: PDCAT: International Conference on Parallel and Distributed Computing, Applications and Technologies; Dunedin, New Zealand; 2008. pp. 381–389.

32. McKinsey & Company. Revolutionizing Data Center Efficiency. Technical report; 2009.

33. Orgerie A-C, Lefèvre L, Gelas J-P. Save watts in your grid: green strategies for energy-aware framework in large-scale distributed systems. In: ICPADS: IEEE International Conference on Parallel and Distributed Systems; Melbourne, Australia; 2008. pp. 171–178.

34. Lefèvre L, Orgerie A-C. Towards energy aware reservation infrastructure for large-scale experimental distributed systems. Parallel Process Lett 2009;19(3):419–433.

35. Dias de Assuncao M, Gelas J-P, Lefèvre L, Orgerie A-C. The green grid'5000: instrumenting a grid with energy sensors. In: International Workshop on Distributed Cooperative Laboratories: Instrumenting the Grid (INGRID); Poznan, Poland; 2010.

36. Orgerie A-C, Lefèvre L. When clouds become green: the green open cloud architecture. In: Parco: International Conference on Parallel Computing; Lyon, France; 2009.

37. Lefèvre L, Orgerie A-C. Designing and evaluating an energy efficient cloud. J Super-Comput 2010;51(3):352–373.

38. Farivar C. Google's Next-Gen of Sneakernet; 2007. newline[online]. Available at http://www.wired.com/science/discoveries/news/2007/03/73007. access year: 2012.

39. Available at http://lcg.web.cern.ch/lcg/public/default.htm. Website of the Worldwide LHC Computing Grid (WLCG) project, access year: 2012.

40. Rosen E, Viswanathan A, Callon R. Multiprotocol label switching architecture. RFC 3031; 2001. Available at http://www.ietf.org/rfc/rfc3031.txt. access year: 2012.

41. Zhang L, Deering S, Estrin D, Shenker S, Zappala D. RSVP: a new resource reservation protocol. IEEE Netw 1993;7:8–18.

42. Baldi M, Ofek Y. Time for a "Greener" internet. In: GreenCom: International Workshop On Green Communications (in conjunction with the IEEE ICC); Dresden, Germany; 2009.

43. Orgerie A-C, Lefèvre L., Guérin-Lassous I. Energy-efficient bandwidth reservation for bulk data transfers in dedicated wired networks. J Supercomput Spec Issue Green Netw 2011. published online.

44. Burchard L-O. Networks with advance reservations: applications, architecture, and performance. J Netw Syst Manage 2005;13(4):429–449.

45. Anastasi G, Conti M, Di Francesco M, Passarella A. Energy conservation in wireless sensor networks: A survey. Ad Hoc Netw 2009.;7(3):537–568.

46. Farrell S, Cahill V, Geraghty D, Humphreys I, McDonald P. When TCP breaks: delay- and disruption- tolerant networking. IEEE Internet Comput 2006;10(4):72–78.

47. Zhang B, Sabhanatarajan K, Gordon-Ross A, George A. Real-time performance analysis of adaptive link rate. In: IEEE Conference on Local Computer Networks (LCN); 2008. pp. 282–288.

CHAPTER 6

ENERGY-EFFICIENT JOB PLACEMENT ON CLUSTERS, GRIDS, AND CLOUDS

DAMIEN BORGETTO, HENRI CASANOVA, GEORGES DA COSTA, and JEAN-MARC PIERSON

6.1 PROBLEM AND MOTIVATION

Since the advent of large-scale systems such as clusters with thousands of cores and grids with thousands of nodes, the job placement problem, due to its crucial importance, has been studied by many researchers. Job placement algorithms, often implemented as part of usable software infrastructures, have been developed, which attempt to optimize job placement with respect to different criteria. These criteria are typically related to notions of time (e.g., response time, wait time, slowdown), throughput (e.g., number of jobs processed per unit time), and fairness (e.g., variance of job slowdowns, maximum wait time). Many proposed approaches tackle job placement as a multiobjective problem so as to address two or more criteria simultaneously.

This chapter discusses energy consumption as a new criterion for job placement. Energy has long been ignored in the theory and practice of job placement, but it has now become a crucial issue for the deployment of large-scale computing platforms. In recent years, energy has been considered as yet another metric (to minimize) or even as the main optimization goal for job placement. This chapter highlights and discusses some of the current trends in this context.

In the rest of the sections, we define our context more precisely and provide a roadmap of the chapter, identifying content that we have left out of our scope.

6.1.1 Context

In this chapter, we focus on the placement of independent jobs, where a job is an instance of an application that must be executed on behalf of a user. We assume

Energy-Efficient Distributed Computing Systems, First Edition.
Edited by Albert Y. Zomaya and Young Choon Lee.
© 2012 John Wiley & Sons, Inc. Published 2012 by John Wiley & Sons, Inc.

that each job has its own characteristics, that is, its own CPU and memory requirements, without any data or control dependency with other jobs. Consequently, a job can be placed on resources independently from other jobs already placed and other jobs yet to be placed, provided sufficient resources are available. In real applications such as scientific workflows [1], jobs exhibit dependencies with each other, for example, represented as a directed acyclic graph (DAG). In this chapter, we do not consider job dependencies. In other words, if data/control dependencies exist between jobs, they are not taken into account by the job placement algorithm. Instead, we assume that the application execution is managed via an application scheduler. This application scheduler invokes job placement each time a new job is available for execution (because its dependencies are cleared). Issues of job synchronization and data movements are thus handled in an application-specific manner and decoupled from job placement decisions.

We assume that a job's memory requirement is a hard requirement and that the job cannot be executed with less memory than required. However, a job can be executed with a various amount of CPU resource, achieving only a fraction of peak performance if only a fraction of its CPU requirement is met.

We assume that several jobs may run together on a time-shared host. The placement algorithm can allocate a fraction of the host (i.e., a fraction of the CPU resources and a fraction of the memory) to each job. This has become eminently feasible with virtualization technology. But we also discuss solutions that do not take advantage of this capability.

The computing infrastructure that hosts the jobs (once they have been placed) comprises a set of heterogeneous hosts, linked together with an interconnection network. We assume that the placement algorithm can place each job directly on any host(s) in the infrastructure. Host heterogeneity encompasses CPU power, amount of memory, and energy consumption characteristics.

6.1.2 Chapter Roadmap

The rest of the chapter is organized as follows. Section 6.2 highlights techniques for designing energy-aware infrastructures and defining energy metrics that characterize these infrastructures. Section 6.3 gives an overview of the state of the art of job placement in production clusters, grids, and clouds. Section 6.4 outlines a set of scientific and technical challenges that arise when energy is taken into account for job placement. Section 6.5 reviews recent energy-aware job placement algorithms proposed in the literature and present details about one particular approach. Section 6.6 discusses remaining roadblocks and opportunities. Finally, Section 6.7 concludes with a brief summary.

6.2 ENERGY-AWARE INFRASTRUCTURES

Although this chapter focuses on energy-aware job placement issues, this section first provides a brief description of the infrastructures that will host jobs and the current techniques used to reduce the energy consumption of these infrastructures.

6.2.1 Buildings

As environmental concerns become increasingly prevalent, new buildings are designed with energy management as a priority. For instance, the EnergyStar program was established to evaluate energy efficiency of products and practices, including that of buildings.[1] The energy efficiency of a building is quantified via a score between 0 and 100, and buildings that achieve a score of 75 or above receive the EnergyStar label. There are several comparable efforts in the industry. For instance, IBM provides tools to evaluate thenergy efficiency of IT infrastructure.[2]

More specifically, to evaluate the energy efficiency of a data center, several of the following metrics are used:

- *Perf/Watt*. This metric is mainly used, for instance, by Green500[3] to rank the most powerful supercomputers, the vast majority of which are clusters. It does not encompass the whole energy consumption of the room (such as air conditioning) but only the consumption of the compute nodes.
- *PUE (Power Usage Effectiveness)*. This metric is complementary to perf/watt. It quantifies the ratio between the total energy consumed by the data center and the energy provided to the computing elements.[4] In 2006, a common PUE (power usage effectiveness) value was about 2.0 [2, 3], meaning that half of the energy consumed was not for computing but was in fact mostly dedicated to cooling. State-of-the-art data centers today have a PUE value of 1.5. Yahoo has recently constructed a data center near Niagara Falls that uses circulating exterior air to cool the servers and is able to achieve a PUE value around 1.1.[5]

Even if not directly connected to job placement at the cluster level, these metrics could be used to inform job placement in a grid or cloud when choosing among various data centers.

6.2.2 Context-Aware Buildings

A commonly held belief is that a data center in Greenland would consume less than a data center in the Sahara, since the external average temperature is lower. But it has been shown (for instance, in the Energy Star study[6]) that external temperature has little impact on the overall electricity consumption of data centers.

---

[1] http://www.energystar.gov/

[2] http://ibmgreen.bathwick.com/

[3] http://www.green500.org

[4] http://www.google.com/corporate/green/datacenters/measuring.html

[5] http://green.yahoo.com/blog/ecogeek/1125/yahoo-data-center-will-be-powered-by-niagara-falls.html

[6] http://www.thegreengrid.org/media/TechForumPresentations2010/ENERGYSTARforDataCenters.ashx?lang=en

However, this study does not account for the specifics of the building's infrastructure and of the server room cooling mechanism. In fact, with air circulation coming from outside, the difference can be be significant, as seen in the Yahoo data center at Niagara Falls. If instead traditional air conditioning is used then outside temperature has little influence. Some studies take such infrastructure aspects into account for deciding on job placement [4].

More and more data centers are built to exploit renewable energy sources. Solar panels (AISO,[7] Phoenix,[8] Intel,[9] Sun,[10] Google,[11] etc.) and wind mills (Google,[12] OWC,[13] Green House Data,[14] Baryonyx[15]) produce today a part of the electricity needed by data centers, and at least in one case all the electricity needed.[16] Most of these deployments are small and experimental, mostly because of the fact that the consumer price of energy from these renewable source is still higher than standard electricity in many cases.

Solutions are also developed to consume renewable electricity in data centers in cases in which the price of standard electricity is higher than that of renewable electricity (typically during daytime), sometimes using chillers to conserve the cold produced using cheaper standard electricity during nighttime. The chillers are then put to contribution along with cheaper renewable electricity during daytime.[17] This difference in electricity generation and usage can also reflect on the data centers usage itself, that is, offloading some work to other data centers during daytime (e.g., if only standard electricity sources are available locally or if most of the locally available energy is renewable but from solar panels).

The placement of jobs could take advantage of information about the sources of electricity used to power clusters. Indeed, an energy-efficient placement should not only consider electrical concerns (watts) but could also encompass ecological concerns. Unfortunately, only few works include these concerns for job scheduling and placement [5, 6].

6.2.3 Cooling

An important part of the data centers' energy consumption is due to the need to cool running components. As explained earlier, the typical PUE of a data center

---

[7]http://www.aiso.net/technology-network-sun.html
[8]http://www.datacenterknowledge.com/archives/2009/06/16/solar-power-at-data-center-scale/
[9]http://www.datacenterknowledge.com/archives/2009/01/19/intel-testing-solar-power-for-data-centers/
[10]http://www.datacenterknowledge.com/archives/2008/05/22/the-solar-powered-blackbox/
[11]http://www.google.com/corporate/green/clean-energy.html
[12]http://www.datacenterknowledge.com/archives/2007/11/29/googles-data-center-windmill-farm/
[13]http://www.datacenterknowledge.com/archives/2009/12/21/data-center-powered-entirely-by-the-wind/
[14]http://www.datacenterknowledge.com/archives/2007/11/29/wind-powered-data-center-in-wyoming/
[15]http://www.datacenterknowledge.com/archives/2009/07/20/wind-powered-data-center-planned/
[16]http://www.datacenterknowledge.com/archives/2009/06/16/solar-power-at-data-center-scale/
[17]http://www.datacenterknowledge.com/archives/2009/06/16/solar-power-at-data-center-scale/

was about 2.0 in 2006, meaning that 1 W for the infrastructure is wasted for each watt used to compute. A large fraction of this waste accounts for cooling.

Several techniques exist and often coexist to cooldown server rooms. Traditionally, air conditioning has been used, but problems arise when the air circulation between the racks in the rooms has not been optimized. In this case, some hot spots can exist, and a full investigation, taking into account CFD models and cold and hot aisle locations, must be conducted. Some vendors (HP with Dynamic Smart Cooling,[18] DegreeC with AdaptivCool[19]) offer tools for monitoring and adjusting cooling according to heat dispersion and air circulation. Some researchers [7–9] have proposed placing jobs in a cluster room according to current hot spots, in order to balance the heat and reduce the use of air conditioning.

6.3 CURRENT RESOURCE MANAGEMENT PRACTICES

6.3.1 Widely Used Resource Management Systems

A job's life cycle proceeds through the following steps when submitted through to a resource manager:

1. The job is submitted via an interface to the resource manager.
2. The resource manager component uses a job placement algorithm to choose a resource or a resource set on which the job will be executed and to decide at which time the job will begin executing.
3. Once the time at which the job is supposed to execute has arrived, the job is launched on the selected resources by a launcher component.
4. When the job finishes executing, the user who submitted the job is notified (and results may be sent back to that user).

Depending on the structure of the system, the decision regarding the resources on which the job is executed may happen either in step 2 or 3, or may happen in step 2 but refined between step 2 and 3 and/or at step 3.

The vast majority of clusters used for high performance computing (HPC) are controlled by a batch scheduler that serves as a gateway to the cluster nodes. This scheduler maintains several queues, corresponding to different priorities, to which users can submit job requests. Each job request specifies a number of nodes or processors, as well as a duration. The batch scheduler decides when each job request can be fulfilled and on which cluster nodes and enforces quotas (or charges) based on the CPU hours utilized by each user. A job that runs longer than its specified duration is terminated, often leading users to specify conservative durations. While a simple approach is for job requests to make

---

[18]http://www.hp.com/hpinfo/newsroom/press/2006/061129xa.html
[19]http://www.adaptivcool.com/

progress in a queue according to a first come first serve (FCFS) strategy, most production batch schedulers enable backfilling. Backfilling allows a job request to jump ahead in a queue. In conservative backfilling, this is allowed provided that no other job request is postponed [10]. In practice, the only constraint is that the request at the top of the queue is not postponed [11]. In essence, backfilling allows small and/or short jobs to jump ahead to fill holes in the schedule. These holes are due not only to imperfect bin packing of jobs onto cluster nodes but also to the fact that jobs often get finished before their specified duration. Since queue waiting times are nondeterministic, most production batch schedulers allow users to reserve cluster nodes for a specified duration starting at a specified date. Popular batch schedulers used in production today, many of them are open source, part of larger software suites, and interoperable, include SGE,[20] OAR, [12] TORQUE,/Moab/Maui[21] PBS,[22] and LSF.[23]

Batch scheduling is used routinely for workloads that consist of parallel jobs, that is, jobs that run concurrently on multiple cluster nodes. However, many relevant applications fall in the high throughput (HT) category: they consist of large numbers of sequential tasks. Most batch schedulers are not well suited to such workloads. A popular resource management solution for HT applications is provided by Condor.[24] [13] Condor can actually be used as a standard batch scheduler for parallel workloads. However, because it does not require a shared file system and because it can exploit idle CPU cycles of nondedicated resources, it is particularly attractive for running HT applications. Its "glide-in" feature allows it to interact with and acquire resources from batch-scheduled clusters. Finally, because it can integrate more diverse resources, Condor provides a richer way for jobs to express resource requirements (beyond number of nodes and time) and for resources to advertise their capabilities.

The above-mentioned schedulers provide control over resources at a site, but multiple sites can be aggregated to form a grid. Schedulers have been developed, who provide access to grid resources based on the Globus toolkit,[25] one example of which is the integration of Condor and Globus. Furthermore, frameworks to manage application execution on such grids, including data movements and task synchronizations, are available. A well-known example is Pegasus[26] (which builds on top of the DAGMan metascheduler for Condor). Commercial solutions have also been developed. For instance, Synfiniway[27] provides a framework that interfaces with batch schedulers at multiple sites and manages data movements and task synchronizations on behalf of grid users.

---

[20]http://gridengine.sunsource.net/
[21]http://www.clusterresources.com/products.php
[22]http://www.pbsworks.com/Default.aspx
[23]http://www.platform.com/workload-management/high-performance-computing
[24]http://www.cs.wisc.edu/condor/
[25]http://www.globus.org
[26]http://pegasus.isi.edu/
[27]http://www.synfiniway.com

In recent years, the cloud computing vision has emerged as a new way to share computer resources: the computing, networking, and storage needs of applications can be outsourced to clusters made available as part of a "cloud." This outsourcing alleviates management overhead of clients, relies on strong expertise of cloud providers, and promises to afford unprecedented levels of transparency, control, and customization. Cloud computing has been embraced both in proprietary solutions (Amazon's EC2,[28] IBM's Smart Business,[29] Microsoft's WindowAzure,[30] Google's AppEngine,[31] Platform's ISF,[32] etc.) and in the open-source community (Opennebula,[33] Eucalyptus,[34] Nimbus[35]). In these systems, clustered resources are managed using virtual machine (VM) technology. Users are allocated VM instances that are customizable and decoupled from underlying physical resources. VM technology thus enables consolidation of physical resources and enforces performance isolation among instances. In most systems, users can lease instances at an hourly rate, picking desirable instance hardware configurations among several provided options (e.g., a high RAM instance, a high CPU instance). Furthermore, with current technology, there is negligible overhead involved when running an application within a VM instance when compared to running it on the bare metal.

6.3.2   Job Requirement Description

A job submitted for execution typically comes with resource requirements. The job placement decision should thus account for these requirements to ensure that selected resources can meet them.

As mentioned earlier, in traditional HPC settings, jobs are submitted directly to a cluster and require a given number of cluster nodes for a certain duration. In a more general grid setting, since there are typically many possible sites that can accommodate the same job, a job can specify a variety of additional requirements. Examples of such requirements include the fact that a particular library must be installed, that a certain amount of scratch disk space is available, or a certain type of processor architecture is required. In spite of the added expressive power of requirements beyond the number of nodes and duration, several studies [14–16] have found that in real-world grid systems such requirements are typically not provided, or specify only a simple processor architecture requirement.

An evolved, and commercially popular, way to describe job requirements is the use of SLAs (Service Level Agreement) [17]. SLAs are especially relevant for emerging cloud platforms, as they allow interactions between a resource

---

[28]http://aws.amazon.com/ec2

[29]http://www.ibm.com/ibm/cloud

[30]http://www.microsoft.com/windowsazure

[31]http://code.google.com/appengine/

[32]http://www.platform.com/private-cloud-computing/private-clo ud-platform-isf

[33]https://help.ubuntu.com/community/OpenNebula

[34]http://open.eucalyptus.com/

[35]http://www.nimbusproject.org/

provider and a resource user. At a high level, an SLA is a contract stating that the provider will provide resources with certain performance guarantees and/or flexibility. Using SLAs, it is possible to change the requirements of a job as part of a resource negotiation (e.g., changing the number of required nodes could be done at a price discount). The use of SLAs has been proposed for grids [18], but adoption has not been as widespread as for clouds.

6.4 SCIENTIFIC AND TECHNICAL CHALLENGES

6.4.1 Theoretical Difficulties

Most previous job placement approaches are formulated with a clear goal in mind. Two common such goals are minimizing job turnaround time (i.e., ensuring that jobs complete quickly, which is correlated with user satisfaction) or maximizing job throughput (i.e., ensure that many jobs are processed per time unit, which is correlated with resource provider needs to keep their resources utilized). Such seemingly straightforward objectives turn out to render the job placement problem NP-complete, and no polynomial-time job placement algorithm is known that can lead to an optimal solution. As a result, many practical job scheduling solution do not attempt the explicit optimization of a particular metric but rather provide many mechanisms by which an administrator can implement custom job placement strategies.

For many decades, energy was rarely considered as a possible optimization metric for distributed computing systems since energy was thought to be more or less free (or at least not a roadblock). Performance was thus the overriding concern, quantified by different but related metrics. One area in which energy was always a prime concern is embedded systems. For these systems, the optimization objective is often dual, encompassing both energy and performance. The same duality is now pertinent for large-scale wired systems such as clusters, grids, and clouds, due to rising energy prices and increasing environmental awareness.

6.4.2 Technical Difficulties

To be optimized, a metric must be measurable with reasonable accuracy. One factor contributing to the relatively slow adoption of energy as an optimization is the challenge faced by energy measurement techniques. A known technical limitation here is the accuracy of fine-grain spatiotemporal measures. The ACPI 4.0 standard is not fully implemented in all components. Furthermore, the available sampling rate of energy measurements may not be sufficient for desired accuracy levels. Finally, components have different functions that are interdependent (e.g., communication between memory and processors, communication between machines of a distributed platform). Consequently, it is difficult to derive the energy consumption due to the execution of an application based on energy measurements of individual components.

Even with techniques that provide accurate measures of energy consumption, several technical limitations remain. For instance, energy consumption is not necessarily linearly related to workload. For instance, a component running at 20% capacity may consume 80% of its maximum power. For such a component, reducing the workload may not have a large impact on energy efficiency.

A more general difficulty comes from the fact that the means to adjust energy consumption to achieve a precise trade-off with levels of performance are limited. This is due to the small number of necessary actuators or the difficulties to access them on current computers. While dynamically changing the clock rate of a CPU is now a commonplace feature, it is still difficult to switch off memory banks completely or to change the rotation speed of a hard drive at runtime.

The field of embedded systems has provided some answers regarding energy optimization. But while measuring accurate data at small scale on a limited and controlled set of components is feasible, it is typically impractical at large scale with heterogeneous components.

6.4.3 Controlling and Tuning Jobs

Controlling the hardware is not the only way to influence energy consumption, and energy actuators can be applied on the software, that is, the jobs themselves. For instance, it is possible to simply stop a job (e.g., suspend, checkpointing, and termination) so that another job can be executed. While this idea was used in gang scheduling [19], it can be used for the purpose of controlling energy consumption. For the same purpose, it is possible to migrate jobs among computers, especially since live migration [20] can be used at the expense of minimal performance overheads.

Beyond generic mechanisms for controlling the execution of jobs, the jobs themselves can be implemented to provide ways for the resource manager to influence their execution. For instance, in the HPC context, jobs can be implemented so that they are "malleable," meaning that the number of nodes on which they execute can be modified at runtime. During their execution, it is thus possible to tune the trade-off between performance and energy consumption. Similarly, some jobs can be implemented so that part of their execution can be carried out on several types of devices (e.g., CPU or GPU), selecting the target device(s) at runtime. These devices typically lead to different ratios of performance to energy consumption, thus making it possible to tune the trade-off between the two during job execution. Alternately, users can specify that once a job begins execution, it is possible to slow down or power off some cluster components, for example, power off the hard drive and reduce clock rate via dynamic voltage frequency scaling (DVFS) [21]. In the context of parallel applications, both Rong et al. [22] and Etinski et al. [23] use DVFS for exploiting load imbalance and communication delays inherent to an application for the purpose of energy reduction. The key idea is to deliberately slow down nodes executing shorter tasks to match the task with the longest execution time. While in Reference 22, this capability is provided by enhancing the job's implementation itself; in Reference 23, it is part of a runtime job execution environment. An additional possibility, used in Reference 23, is to use overclocking to reduce critical task execution times. The additional energy cost due to overclocking could be offset by the savings in execution time.

The more tunable jobs are, the more it is possible to control overall energy consumption while maintaining a particular trade-off with performance. While job tuning affords tremendous opportunity, the challenge is that most jobs today do not allow tuning by the runtime system; for example, many applications are often static as opposed to autonomic, workflow structures are often statically implemented instead of being adaptable. Even with jobs that support tuning, it is crucial that the resource management system be made aware of the tuning options for each job so as to inform job placement decisions, which is not possible with most production resource management systems today.

6.5   ENERGY-AWARE JOB PLACEMENT ALGORITHMS

As seen in Section 6.3.1, several resource managers are currently used in production clusters. In the vast majority of the cases, energy concerns are not taken into account explicitly by these resource managers. The resulting job placement may leave some nodes unutilized, in which case they can be powered off to conserve energy.

At any rate, in all the above, job placement decisions are made without explicitly accounting for energy consumption. In this section, we review selected research works that have proposed strategies and algorithms for energy-aware job placement. We present one such approach in detail.

6.5.1   State of the Art

The two commonly available mechanisms for reducing power consumption are (i) to power off cluster nodes and (ii) to slow down cluster nodes via DVFS. Several works have studied the job placement problem using one or both of these mechanisms.

Several authors have proposed extensions to standard batch scheduling algorithms to make them energy aware. Nodes are powered off when not used, and job placement decisions attempt to power a node back on only when absolutely necessary [24]. When placing jobs on cluster nodes that support DVFS, for instance, during a backfilling step, nodes are slowed down as much as possible while still respecting constraints on job duration [25].

Beyond extending extant schedulers, many researchers have proposed new scheduling and job placement algorithms that attempt to optimize energy-related metrics directly. All these algorithms attempt to provide a sensible trade-off between performance and energy. Note that a popular mechanism for implementing the produced job placement, used in many of the works cited hereafter, is VM technology. If job tasks are encapsulated in VM instances, then it is easier to control their resource usage and to possibly migrate them among cluster nodes to better consolidate workload.

Kamitsos et al. [26] attempt to find an optimal policy for powering nodes on and off using a Markov decision process. Solving the Markov decision process makes it possible to find a Pareto optimal trade-off between performance and energy. A similar approach is proposed in Reference 27, in which three metrics are considered: queue waiting time, power consumption, and job blocking probability.

Benoit et al. [28] propose to optimize performance and energy for the mapping of concurrent pipelined streaming applications on a multiprocessor platform. Such optimizations are achieved using the optimal solution obtained via the resolution of an integer linear program. They develop polynomial-time heuristics that reduce energy consumption while maintaining the application's latency below a fixed threshold. Petrucci et al. [29] also formulate the job placement problem as a linear program, which is solved periodically in a control loop manner. They consider a heterogeneous cluster with DVFS-enabled nodes and minimize energy consumption under a set of constraints while allowing task migration. Another approach that uses a linear program formulation is that in Borgetto et al. [30], which is detailed in Section 6.5.2.

Hoyer et al. [31] propose statistical allocation planning using two different approaches for resource allocation. The first approach is pessimistic and allocates to each job the maximum resource fraction it could need, using vector packing to perform the allocation. Their second approach is optimistic and tries to overbook each node while maintaining each job over a certain threshold on performance reduction. Interestingly, their approach entails dynamic monitoring of VM instances.

Rodero et al. [32] attempt to reduce energy consumption by powering off subsystems when they are not needed as well as carefully managing VM provisioning.

Entropy [33] is a resource manager for homogeneous clusters, which performs dynamic consolidation of resources based on constraint programming, using migration and accounting for migration overhead.

Berral et al. [34] achieve significant power consumption reduction via resource consolidation using machine learning to make resource allocation decisions. Essentially, their approach favors the allocation of new jobs to already powered up nodes, possibly using migration.

Power consumption reductions via intelligent resource allocation is not only studied at the cluster scale but also at a global scale. For instance, in Reference 4, Le et al. propose a framework to reduce costs in geographically distributed system. The goal is to exploit the differences and variability between the energy costs of data centers, the different time zone where these data centers are located, and their proximity to "green" power sources. The optimization problem is to minimize cost while meeting SLAs. A similar approach is followed by Garg et al. [5].

6.5.2 Detailing One Approach

The approach we have chosen to detail here for the energy-aware job placement problem can be partly found in Reference 35, with some extensions in the problem modeling and formulation.

We chose to investigate the placement of infinite or very long jobs in a virtualized homogeneous cluster, with a static or periodic placement system.

Each host is characterized by its idle power consumption and its loaded power consumption (both can vary even for homogeneous clusters [36] depending on the spatial location of the server). We model the dynamic power consumption as linearly dependent to the CPU usage of the server. As we place ourselves in a virtualized environment, we are able to assign jobs to each individual shares of the server capabilities. That way, we will allocate to a job, for example, 50% of the CPU and 70% of the memory. We also assume that the jobs all require a certain amount of computation capability to execute themselves, and that this amount is known.

We derive constraints that form the basis for a linear program formulation of the resource allocation problem. This program extends that in Reference 37 to account for power consumption. We first define the following variables. e_{ih} is a binary variable that takes value 1 if job i is allocated to host h, and takes value 0 otherwise. α_{ih} is a rational variable that denotes the CPU fraction allocated to job i on host h. Finally, p_h is a binary variable that is set to 1 if host h is powered on. Our constraints for these variables are as follows:

$$\forall i, h \quad e_{ih} \in \{0, 1\} \tag{6.1}$$

$$\forall i, h \quad \alpha_{ih} \in Q \tag{6.2}$$

$$\forall h \quad p_h \in \{0, 1\} \tag{6.3}$$

$$\forall i \quad \sum_h e_{ih} = 1 \tag{6.4}$$

$$\forall i, h \quad 0 \leq \alpha_{ih} \leq e_{ih} \tag{6.5}$$

$$\forall i, h \quad p_h \geq \alpha_{ih} \tag{6.6}$$

$$\forall h \quad p_h \leq \sum_i e_{ih} \tag{6.7}$$

$$\forall h \quad \sum_i \alpha_{ih} \leq p_h \tag{6.8}$$

$$\forall h \quad \sum_i e_{ih} m_i \leq p_h \tag{6.9}$$

$$\forall i \quad \sum_h \alpha_{ih} \leq \alpha_i \tag{6.10}$$

Constraints 6.1–6.3 define the range of the variables. Constraint 6.4 states that job is allocated to a single host, meaning that for a given i only one e_{ih} value is nonzero. Constraint 6.5 states that a job can consume CPU resources only on the host to which it is allocated, meaning that for a given i only one α_{ih} value is nonzero. Constraint 6.6 states that if a job consumes CPU resources on a host then that host must be powered on. Constraint 6.7 states that if no job is allocated to a host then that host is powered off. Constraint 6.8 states that the CPU resources of a host that is powered on are not to be exceeded, and that no CPU resources are consumed on a host that is powered off. Constraint 6.9 states that the RAM resources of a host that is powered on are not to be exceeded, and that no RAM resources are consumed on a host that is powered off. Finally, Constraint 6.10 states that a job never receives a CPU share that is larger than its CPU need.

We use as a metric for the job performance what is called the *yield* (defined by Eq. 6.12), which is the ratio between what was required by the job and what job is effectively allocated to it. The energy consumption metric will be the instant power consumption of the whole system (defined by Eq. 6.11), $C^{\min}$ being the idle consumption of a server and $C^{\max}$ the power consumption when fully loaded.

$$E = \sum_h C_h^{\min} P_h + \sum_h (C_h^{\max} - C_h^{\min}) \sum_i \alpha_{ih} \qquad (6.11)$$

$$\forall i, \quad \sum_h \frac{\alpha_{ih}}{\alpha_i} \geq Y \qquad (6.12)$$

We then model the different objective functions in order to define three distinct problems. First, we define the BOUNDEDYIELD problem, which models when we want to optimize the energy consumption of our system and are willing to lose a certain percentage of performance. The objective here will be to minimize the energy consumption E while matching the additional constraint of the service deterioration bound that we fixed ($Y \geq$ bound).

Second, we define the BOUNDEDPOWER problem, which models the case where our system cannot exceed a certain bound of power consumption for electric supply reasons, or simply cost concerns. In this case, the objective will be to maximize the minimum yield (meaning making the worst allocated job of the system as happy as possible) while matching the additional constraint of the total system power consumption that should not be exceeded ($E \leq$ bound).

Those methods have the advantage to allow us to bound one objective while optimizing the other, making solutions to the problem easier to compare with each other.

Finally, we define the MIXEDOBJECTIVE problem, which models the fact that we want to reduce the energy consumption of our system, without compromising too much the performance of the jobs, and without having any particular need on either the energy consumption or the yield. This problem, as its name states, is a dual objective problem, with often antagonist objective. The value we will seek to optimize is a linear combination of both the aforementioned problems. As Y and E are not in the same order of magnitude, we had to normalize it so it could be between 0 and 1, in order to make Z between those values as well. This normalized value is $X = \min(1, E/E^{\max})$, with $E^{\max}$ being the smallest upper bound to E for which the theoretical bound on the optimal yield is no lower than that obtained assuming the highest possible power consumption.

The metric is defined as follows:

$$Z = \lambda Y + (1 - \lambda)(1 - X) \tag{6.13}$$

with λ between 0 and 1.

The problem being defined, we can now solve it. To this purpose, we have at our disposition a tool to find the optimal solution of a linear program called *GLPK*.[36] This will allow us to find the optimal solution, therefore being able to compare ourselves to this optimal. However, finding the solution of this NP-hard problem [37] cannot be done in reasonable computation time. We will only be able to compute the optimal solution for small problems (denoted MILP is the following). To cope with this issue, one solution is to relax the mixed integer linear program formulation, making the integer variables rational. This way, we can compute in polynomial time a rational bound on the optimal solution, thus obtaining a point of comparison for our heuristics (denoted LPBOUND in the following).

We defined several algorithms in order to solve the energy-aware job placement problem. We used greedy algorithms for each different problem and modified our algorithm EA-ResAlloc described in Reference 35 in order to match the constraints of each problem.

Four Greedy algorithms were defined by deriving well-known vector packing algorithm. Two Greedy algorithms were variants of the first fit, the other variant of the best fit algorithm. The difference between each pair is the order of jobs to be packed, here decreasing CPU and decreasing memory demand. Here, we will only plot the best performing greedy algorithm.

To solve the BOUNDEDYIELD problem, the algorithms will place the jobs at a yield equal to the yield bound, on the smallest $C^{\max}$ that can accommodate the job's resource need.

To solve the BOUNDEDPOWER problem, the algorithms will place the jobs at a yield of 1, and then iteratively decrease each job's allocated resource by small steps in a round robin manner.

To solve the MIXEDOBJECTIVE problem, the algorithms are built on the above BOUNDEDPOWER algorithm. They first calculate $H_Z = max(1, \lceil (1 - \lambda) \times (\sum_i \alpha_i) \rceil)$, which gives the theoretical number of hosts that is needed to achieve a resource allocation with a given λ value. The energy bound is then calculated using the H_Z first hosts in the host list (the hosts are sorted by increasing $C^{\max}$). This energy bound is then used to solve the problem using the BOUNDEDPOWER algorithms.

In Reference 35, we proposed a resource allocation heuristic based on the work in Reference 37 that aims at addressing two antagonist objectives: maximizing the job yield and minimizing power consumption. This heuristic relies on the

---

[36]http://www.gnu.org/software/glpk/

"energy-aware yield" of a job that is used by the heuristic to conciliate the following three different goals:

- maximizing job yield;
- placing jobs on energy-efficient hosts; and
- aggregating jobs on a reduced number of hosts in order to power off as many hosts as possible.

This metric is used in a task allocation heuristic using vector packing. In our work, we have built on this heuristic so that it can be applied to solve the BOUNDEDYIELD, BOUNDEDPOWER and MIXEDOBJECTIVE problems.

As we have in the energy-aware yield, a parameter that allows one to favor the energy savings at the expense of the performance or the opposite, the transposition of the algorithm to each different problem is rather direct. The BOUNDEDPOWER problem will be solved by doing a binary search on the aforementioned parameter. For the BOUNDEDYIELD problem, we allocate the jobs with an objective yield equal to the bound, and set the trade-off parameter to favor only the performance. Finally, for the MIXEDOBJECTIVE problem, we use the energy-aware yield as it is, as it was designed especially for the bicriteria problem.

We then defined a set of different problems to be solved by each algorithm. Only for the small problems the mixed integer linear program formulation is solved; for all the other problems, we compare the different algorithms' rational formulation of the linear program. We ran simulations from 4 hosts and 4 jobs to 64 hosts and 192 jobs, randomly generating both host characteristics and job CPU and memory needs. For each combination of host and job number, 100 simulations were computed. The graphs were generated by averaging the results of the corresponding simulation.

Figure 6.1 plots the average minimum yield for each algorithm of the BOUND-EDPOWER problem, grouped by number of hosts. As expected, the best results are for MILP and LPBOUND. For the other algorithms, we can see that the EA-RESALLOC_BOUND_E outperforms the other algorithms on average.

Figure 6.2 plots the average energy consumed by each algorithm of the BOUND-EDYIELD problem, grouped by number of hosts in the instance. We only have MILP results for the instances with four hosts, since computing it, for instances, with six hosts and above takes prohibitive amounts of time. As expected, LPBOUND and MILP achieve the smallest average energy consumption. For small number of hosts (4, 6, and 8), our heuristics lead to comparable results. The EA-RESALLOC_BOUND_Y algorithm begins to behave differently from the greedy algorithms, for instances, with over 16 hosts. For the largest instances, it achieves the best results, giving allocation of an average of 5900 W. For these instances, EA-RESALLOC_BOUND_Y is approximately 6% away from LPBOUND, while the GREEDY_BOUNDEDYIELD_4, which is the best of the greedy algorithms for these instances, is +10% away from the bound.

For the MIXEDOBJECTIVE, Figures 6.3 and 6.4 plot, respectively, the average energy consumption and the average minimum yield for each algorithm, grouped

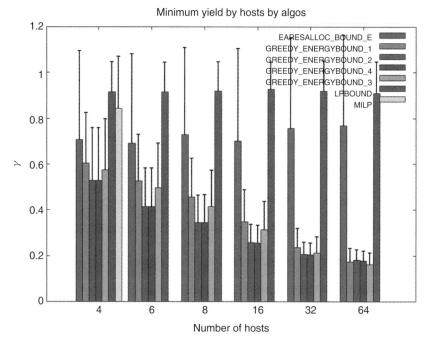

Figure 6.1   Minimum yield by algorithms by number of hosts.

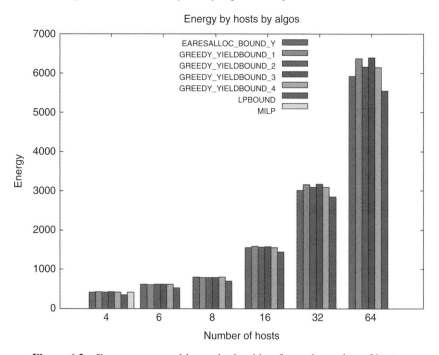

Figure 6.2   Energy consumed by each algorithm for each number of hosts.

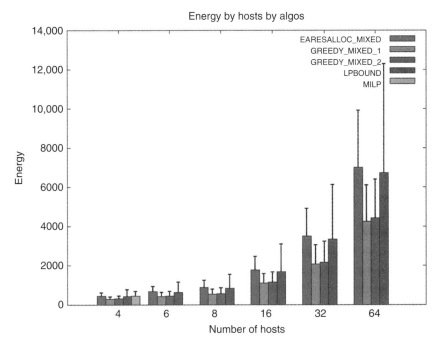

Figure 6.3 Energy consumed by each algorithm for each number of hosts.

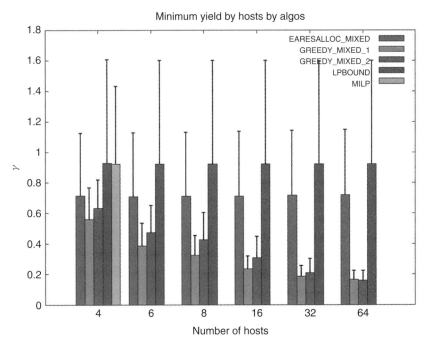

Figure 6.4 Minimum yield by each algorithm for each number of hosts.

by number of hosts in the instances. The best energy consumption is achieved by the GREEDY_MIXED_1 algorithm, as it focuses on the energy reduction. However, this algorithm also has the smallest minimum yield of all the algorithms. The opposite goes for the EA-RESALLOC_MIXED algorithm, which achieves the highest energy consumption and also the highest minimum yield. This demonstrates the fact that bicriterion optimization is difficult.

We also ran other types of evaluation of the algorithms. Time spent in solving the problem is one of them. We have seen that the optimal, given by solving the problem using the MILP formulation, took unreasonable time to solve once six hosts and six jobs were past. That is why we chose to use heuristics, here with the EA-RESALLOC algorithm, which takes really reasonable time to compute a solution, even for large systems. For an instance of 500 hosts and 1500 jobs, EA-RESALLOC_BOUND_Y produces a solution in 1 s, which is highly acceptable. The same goes for all the Greedy algorithms that are fast to compute but lack performance in the solutions.

Good performance is achieved by EA-RESALLOC in both the BOUNDEDYIELD and BOUNDEDPOWER problems. It outperforms the greedy algorithms in those problems. For the MIXEDOBJECTIVE problem, we can see that it does not perform well in terms of energy savings but perform well regarding the job performance.

6.6 DISCUSSION

6.6.1 Open Issues and Opportunities

We have seen that, in spite of the diversity of proposed approaches for solving the energy-aware job placement problem, many solutions share the same foundations: (i) powering nodes on and off; (ii) migrating jobs for better workload consolidation; (iii) exploiting techniques to influence CPU energy consumption; (iv) developing sensible job placement algorithms given the above capabilities; and (v) providing to these algorithms accurate estimates of energy consumption. Hereafter, we discuss technical challenges and opportunities for each of these five foundations.

The approach consisting in powering hosts on and off is simple and effective. Not only is energy saved due to the node being powered off but also there is a saving in energy because of reduced cooling needs [38]. One issue, however, is that the time for suspending and restarting (i.e., rebooting) a node can be significant. Suspending a node to RAM or using Powernap reduces this time dramatically with negligible energy cost [39] but is not always available. Furthermore, powering a node on or off leads to a brief peak in energy consumption. In general, powering off a node should only be done based on a reasonable prediction that the node will not have to be powered up again in the short term. Such predictions are feasible in some cases [40] but are difficult to obtain in environments that experience highly dynamic workloads. Given the above, powering nodes off and on in a near-optimal manner is a difficult problem. As a result, in production data centers, the decision to power off nodes is often taken only in "obvious" cluster underutilization cases.

Powering off and on cluster nodes is more effective if used in conjunction with techniques to consolidate the workload on those nodes that remain powered on. A mentioned earlier, a now common approach to perform such consolidation is to encapsulate jobs (or job tasks) within VM instances and migrate these instances across cluster nodes. Migration has a performance overhead that can impact an application negatively, even though live migration techniques can be used to migrate a VM instance with little overhead [41–43]. However, the energy overhead of migration is often overlooked. In particular, when migrating a VM instance between two nodes, both nodes must be powered on until completion of the migration operation [29, 36]. It is therefore crucial to account for both the time and the energy overhead of migration, which is done only rarely in the literature in the context of job placement [33, 44].

A commonplace technique for energy saving is DVFS, and we have seen that previous research work has advocated the use of DVFS while making job placement decisions. While DVFS allows significant saving in terms of CPU energy consumption, the share of the energy consumption due to the CPU is actually decreasing [45]. In this sense, the use of DVFS for energy saving is thus likely to become increasingly less effective. To make matters worse, the energy savings because of DVFS are also limited by the advent of multicore systems. As explained in Reference 46, significant energy saving requires voltage scaling and frequency scaling. Unfortunately, even when the core frequencies can be scaled independently, there is only one voltage rail to the cores from the motherboard and the voltage is constrained by the highest frequency of any core. On the basis of advances made in the area of mobile computing and devices, modern CPUs change their power requirements dynamically based on resource demands.[37] We conclude that, given current technology and trends, job placement algorithms must go beyond simply enacting DVFS if the goal is near-optimal energy saving. This raises the interesting question of the interface between the resource manager in charge of job placement and the hardware. One option is for the resource manager to consider cluster nodes such as "black boxes" that perform their own power management. Another is for the resource manager to actively influence power consumption at the node level (e.g., DVFS, powering off cores, overclocking cores, switching off memory banks). This latter option might lead to increased power saving. However, it complexifies job placement algorithms especially for managing a node that hosts multiple jobs that share hardware resources.

The job placement problem is algorithmically difficult in most relevant scenarios. In fact, it is not only difficult to solve but, before even attempting to solve it, also difficult to define. Examining the literature, it is quickly apparent that the authors propose diverse formulations of the problem for different optimization objectives. A crucial issue is thus to identify appropriate metrics in a

---

[37]http://www.acpi.info/

view to defining a family of relevant job placement problems as optimizations of these metrics. Standard problem definitions are, for instance, widely accepted in the theoretical scheduling literature [47] and following the same approach for energy-aware job placement would be a useful development. Those problem definitions that have been proposed to date all boil down to solving NP-complete resource allocation problems (finding optimal solutions are constrained to small size problem [29]), thus motivating the development of polynomial-time heuristics. However, only few authors develop heuristics that are compared to (bounds on) the optimal, thus making it possible to quantify their efficacy in an absolute sense [28, 30, 48]. However, given that there is no consensus on the definition of the energy-aware job placement problem, it is not possible to compare these heuristics to each other. One overriding challenge is that the energy-aware job placement problem is inherently multicriteria since typically several notions of performance and energy are optimization goals. Multicriteria optimization is notoriously difficult. The technique that consists in optimizing a weighted linear (or other) combination of the optimization criteria only provides ad hoc solutions that may not translate to sensible trade-offs between the criteria. The technique that consists in bounding all but one criterion and optimizing this criterion may still be far from a Pareto-optimal solution. Consequently, in spite of results in the literature thus far, many algorithmic challenges remain.

Investing effort in addressing the aforementioned algorithmic challenges is worthwhile only if a job placement algorithm has the ability to precisely quantify the energy saving or cost brought about by job placement and resource management decisions (e.g., adding a job, suspending a job, modifying the resource fraction allocated to a job, powering on a node, slowing down a node). A crucial issue is thus the development and validation of analytical models of energy consumption [49–51]. These models must be based on accurate observations of energy consumption under a wide spectrum of hardware resource utilizations. These observations must be compiled into analytical models to inform job placement decisions, either off-line using representative benchmarks or at runtime. One difficulty is that accurate models must be obtained via fine-grain energy measurements at a resolution that may not be achievable today for all hardware components. Another is that these models can be instantiated and used effectively for job placement only if the resource utilization of jobs in the workload at hand can be discovered and characterized at runtime. Such discovery can be done by monitoring running jobs, for example, using VM instance monitoring techniques [43, 52–55], which may be intrusive and lead to both performance and energy penalties.

6.6.2 Obstacles for Adoption in Production

In this chapter, we have seen that many algorithms have been proposed for solving the job placement problem in an energy-aware manner. However, these algorithms are developed and evaluated with models that make several simplifying assumptions (e.g., homogeneous platform, simple linear models of energy consumptions, perfect information regarding the workload). Adoption of these novel energy-aware algorithms in production resource managers, which are to be used for complex systems is thus not immediate. However, such adoption is required for research in this area to lead to any practical impact. For instance, adoption of new resource management technology is notoriously difficult in production HPC installations that have relied on standard batch schedulers for decades. In spite of countless advances in the job scheduling literature showing promises of improved job performance and/or platform utilization, a surprisingly small number of these advances have made their way into production batch schedulers. Similarly, one can expect that adoption of newly proposed energy-aware job placement algorithms in production will be challenging at best. If adoption is to be reached, it must be achieved via incremental enhancements to existing production batch schedulers.

The above disconnect between research and production is commonplace and definitely not unique to the area of energy-aware job placement. We note that the obtained results show that naïve job placement solutions can lead to vastly suboptimal energy consumption. By contrast, proposed novel algorithms can instead be relatively close to optimal, which should provide compelling motivation for adopting these algorithms in production systems. Beyond the need for incremental adoption, identified earlier, another obstacle to adoption is that most efforts in production systems today are focused on reducing the energy consumption of the infrastructure itself. For instance, given the large amount of energy spent for cooling, there is still a large energy payoff for enhancing the infrastructure (e.g., building, hardware) rather than focusing on software and algorithms. We are, however, reaching a point of diminishing return in terms of infrastructure enhancements. The PUE of state-of-the-art production data centers has globally decreased over the past 5 years from around 2 [2, 3] to below 6.5 today. It is thus reasonable to expect that software and algorithmic issues, including job placement algorithms, will play a crucial role in reducing energy consumption in production data centers in the near future.

6.7 CONCLUSION

In this chapter, we have motivated the development of energy-aware job placement in clusters, grids, and clouds. After describing current computing infrastructures, state-of-the-art techniques for making these infrastructures energy efficient, and current resource management approaches, we have identified the challenges underlying the energy-aware job placement problem. We have reviewed relevant works in the literature that attempt to tackle some of these challenges, and detailed one particular approach. Finally, we have discussed remaining limits and outstanding opportunities. Beyond the need to address remaining scientific and technical challenges, we have demonstrated that there are today strong incentives for energy-aware job placement algorithms to be integrated in production systems.

REFERENCES

1. Fox G, Gannon D. Workflow in grid systems. Concurr Comput Pract Exp 2006;2006:1009–1019.
2. Malone C, Belady C. Metrics to characterize data center & it equipment energy use. In: Digital Power Forum; Richardson (TX); 2006.
3. Greenberg S, Mills E, Tschudi B, Rumsey P, Myatt B. Best practices for data centers: Lessons learned from benchmarking 22 data centers. In: Proceedings of the ACEEE Summer Study on Energy Efficiency in Buildings in Asilomar, CA. ACEEE; 2006 August; 2006. pp. 3: 76–87.
4. Le K, Bianchini R, Martonosi M, Nguyen TD. Cost- and energy-aware load distribution across data centers. In: HotPower'09: Workshop on Power Aware Computing and Systems; Big Sky, MT; 2009.
5. Garg SK, Yeo CS, Anandasivam A, Buyya R. Energy-efficient scheduling of HPC applications in cloud computing environments. CoRR 2009. abs/0909.1146.
6. Pierson J-M. Allocating resources greenly: reducing energy consumption or reducing ecological impact? In: Meer H, Singh S, Braun T, editors. *e-Energy*. ACM; 2010. pp. 127–130.
7. Bash Cullen, Forman George. Cool job allocation: measuring the power savings of placing jobs at cooling-efficient locations in the data center. In: 2007 USENIX Annual Technical Conference on Proceedings of the USENIX Annual Technical Conference. Berkeley (CA); USENIX Association. 2007. pp. 29-1–29-6.
8. Shi B, Srivastava A. Thermal and power-aware task scheduling for hadoop based storage centric datacenters. In: International Green Computing Conference, IGCC 2010; Chicago, IL; 2010.
9. Banerjee A, Mukherjee T, Varsamopoulos G, Gupta S. Cooling-aware and thermal-aware workload placement for green HPC data centers. In: International Green Computing Conference, IGCC 2010; Passau, Germany; 2010.
10. Mu'alem AW, Feitelson DG. Utilization, Predictability, Workloads, and User Runtime Estimates in Scheduling the IBM SP2 with Backfilling. IEEE Trans Parallel Distrib Comput 2001;12:529–543.
11. Lifka D. The ANL/IBM SP scheduling system. In: Proceedings of the 1st Workshop on Job Scheduling Strategies for Parallel Processing, LCNS, Volume 949; California, USA; 1995. pp. 295–303.
12. Capit N, Da Costa D, Georgiou Y, Huard G, Martin C, Mounié G, Neyron P, Richard O. A batch scheduler with high level components. In: Proceedings of the CCGrid; Cardiff, UK; 2005.
13. Thain D, Tannenbaum T, Livny M. Distributed computing in practice: the Condor experience. Concurr Pract Exp 2005;17(2–4):323–356.
14. Iosup A, Dumitrescu C, Epema D, Li H, Wolters L. How are real grids used? the analysis of four grid traces and its implications. In: GRID '06: Proceedings of the 7th IEEE/ACM International Conference on Grid Computing; Dubna, Russia; 2006.
15. Da Costa G, Dikaiakos MD, Orlando S. Nine months in the life of egee: a look from the south. In: MASCOTS '07: Proceedings of the 2007 15th International Symposium on Modeling, Analysis, and Simulation of Computer and Telecommunication Systems; Istanbul, Turkey; 2007.

16. Medernach E. Workload analysis of a cluster in a grid environment. In: Job Scheduling Strategies for Parallel Processing, 11th International Workshop (JSSPP 05); Massachusetts, USA; 2005.

17. Hathaway J. Service level agreements: keeping a rein on expectations. In: SIGUCCS '95: Proceedings of the 23rd Annual ACM SIGUCCS Conference on User Services; Missouri, USA; 1995.

18. Balakrishnan P, Thamarai Selvi S, Rajesh Britto G. Service level agreement based grid scheduling. In: ICWS '08: Proceedings of the 2008 IEEE International Conference on Web Services. Washington (DC): IEEE Computer Society; 2008. pp. 203–210.

19. Ousterhout JK. Scheduling Techniques for Concurrent Systems. In: Proceedings of the 3rd International Conference on Distributed Computing Systems; Florida, USA; 1982. pp. 22–30.

20. Clark C, Fraser K, Hand S, Hansen JG, Jul E, Limpach C, Pratt I, Warfield A. Live migration of virtual machines. In: Proceedings of the 2nd Symposium on Networked Systems Design and Implementation; Massachusetts, USA; 2005. pp. 273–286.

21. Costa GD, Assuncao MDD, Gelas J-P, Georgiou Y, LefÈvre L, Orgerie A-CE, Pierson J-M, Richard O, Sayah A. Multi-facet approach to reduce energy consumption in clouds and grids: the GREEN-NET framework. In: ACM/IEEE International Conference on Energy-Efficient Computing and Networking (e-Energy); Passau, Germany, 13/04/2010-15/04/2010. ACM; 2010. pp. 95–104.

22. Ge R, Feng X, Cameron KW. Performance-constrained distributed dvs scheduling for scientific applications on power-aware clusters. In: SC '05: Proceedings of the 2005 ACM/IEEE Conference on Supercomputing. Washington (DC): IEEE Computer Society; 2005. p. 34.

23. Etinski M, Corbalan J, Labarta J, Valero M, Veidenbaum A. Power-aware load balancing of large scale mpi applications. In: IPDPS '09: Proceedings of the 2009 IEEE International Symposium on Parallel &Distributed Processing. Washington (DC); IEEE Computer Society; 2009. pp. 1–8.

24. Lawson B, Smirni E. Power-aware resource allocation in high-end systems via online simulation. In: Proceedings of the 19th Annual International Conference on Supercomputing, ICS '05. New York: ACM; 2005. pp. 229–238.

25. Etinski M, Corbalan J, Labarta J, Valero M. Utilization driven power-aware parallel job scheduling. Comput Sci Res Dev 2010;25:207–216. DOI.: 10.1007/s00450-010-0129-x.

26. Kamitsos Y, Andrew LLH, Kim H, Chiang Mung. Optimal sleep patterns for serving delay tolerant jobs. In: ACM eEnergy, University of Passau; 2010 April 13–15; Germany.

27. Niyato D, Chaisiri S, Sung LB. Optimal power management for server farm to support green computing. In: CCGRID '09: Proceedings of the 2009 9th IEEE/ACM International Symposium on Cluster Computing and the Grid. Washington (DC): IEEE Computer Society; 2009. pp. 84–91.

28. Benoit A, Goud PR, Robert Y. Sharing resources for performance and energy optimization of concurrent streaming applications. RR-LIP-2010-05.

29. Petrucci V, Loques O, Mossé D. A dynamic optimization model for power and performance management of virtualized clusters. In: ACM eEnergy, University of Passau; April 13–15; Germany; 2010.

30. Borgetto D, Casanova H, Costa GD, Pierson J-M. Energy-aware service allocation. Technical Report IRIT/RT-2010-7-FR. IRIT; 2010.

31. Hoyer M, Schröder K, Nebel W. Statistical static capacity management in virtualized data centers supporting fine grained QoS specification. In: ACM eEnergy, University of Passau; 2010 April 13–15; Germany.

32. Rodero I, Jamarillo J, Quiroz A, Parashar M, Guim F, Poole S. Energy-efficient application-aware online provisioning for virtualized clouds and data centers. In: 1st IEEE sponsored International Green Computing Conference; Illinois, USA; 2010.

33. Hermenier F, Lorca X, Menaud J-M, Muller G, Lawall J. Entropy: a consolidation manager for clusters. Research Report RR-6639. INRIA; 2008.

34. Berral JL, Goiri l, Nou R, Julià F, Guitart J, Gavaldà R, Torres J. Towards energy-aware scheduling in data centers using machine learning. In: ACM eEnergy, University of Passau; 2010 April 13–15; Germany.

35. Borgetto D, Costa GD, Pierson J-M, Sayah A. Energy-aware resource allocation. In: Proceedings of the Energy Efficient Grids, Clouds and Clusters Workshop (E2GC2), page (electronic medium). IEEE; 2009 Oct.

36. Orgerie A-CE, LefËvre L, Gelas J-P. Demystifying energy consumption in grids and clouds. In: The Work in Progress in Green Computing (WIPGC) Workshop, in conjunction with the 1st IEEE sponsored International Green Computing Conference; 2010 Aug; Chicago, USA.

37. Stillwell M, Schanzenbach D, Vivien F, Casanova H. Resource allocation algorithms for virtualized service hosting platforms. J Parallel Distrib Comput 2010;70(9):962–974.

38. Liu J, Zhao F, O'Reilly J, Souarez A, Manos M, Liang C-JM, Tersiz A. Project genome: wireless sensor network for data center cooling. Arch J Microsoft 2008; 44:205–216.

39. Meisner D, Gold BT, Wenisch TF. Powernap: eliminating server idle power. SIGPLAN Not 2009;44:205–216.

40. Orgerie A-C, Lefevre L, Gelas J-P. Chasing Gaps between Bursts: towards Energy Efficient Large Scale Experimental Grids. In: Proceedings of 9th International Conference on Parallel and Distributed Computing, Applications and Technologies; Dunedin, New Zealand; 2008. pp. 381–389.

41. Zhao M, Figueiredo RJ. Experimental study of virtual machine migration in support of reservation of cluster resources. In: Proceedings of the 2nd International Workshop on Virtualization Technology in Distributed Computing, VTDC '07. New York: ACM; 2007. pp. 5–1–5–8.

42. Keir CC, Clark C, Fraser K, Jacob SH, Hansen G, Jul E, Limpach C, Pratt I, Warfield A. Live migration of virtual machines. In: Proceedings of the 2nd ACM/USENIX Symposium on Networked Systems Design and Implementation (NSDI); Massachusetts, USA; 2005. pp. 273–286.

43. Liu L, Wang H, Liu X, Jin X, He WB, Wang QB, Chen Ying. Greencloud: a new architecture for green data center. In: Proceedings of the 6th International Conference Industry Session on Autonomic Computing and Communications Industry Session, ICAC-INDST '09. New York: ACM; 2009. pp. 29–38.

44. Verma A, Ahuja P, Neogi A. pmapper: power and migration cost aware application placement in virtualized systems. In: Issarny V, Schantz RE, editors. Volume 5346, *Middleware*, Lecture Notes in Computer Science. Springer; 2008. pp. 243–264.

45. Barroso LA, Hölzle U. The case for energy-proportional computing. IEEE Comput 2007;40(12):33–37.

46. Nathuji R, Schwan K. Virtualpower: coordinated power management in virtualized enterprise systems. In: Bressoud TC, Kaashoek MF, editors. *SOSP*. ACM; 2007. pp. 265–278.

47. Bender MA, Chakrabarti S, Muthukrishnan S. Flow and stretch metrics for scheduling continuous job streams. In: Proceedings of the 9th Annual ACM-SIAM Symposium on Discrete Algorithms; California, USA; 2008. pp. 270–279.

48. Cardosa M, Korupolu MR, Singh A. Shares and utilities based power consolidation in virtualized server environments. In: Integrated Network Management. IEEE; New York, USA; 2009. pp. 327–334.

49. Pelley S, Meisner D, Wenisch TF, VanGilder JW. Understanding and abstracting total data center power. In: Proceedings of the 2009 Workshop on Energy Efficient Design (WEED); Texas, USA; 2009.

50. Bertran R, Becerra Y, Carrera D, Beltran V, Gonzalez M, Martorell X, Torres J, Ayguade E. Accurate energy accounting for shared virtualized environments using PMC-based power modeling techniques. In: The 11th IEEE/ACM International Conference on Grid Computing (GRID-2010); Brussels, Belgium; 2010 Oct.

51. Costa GD, Hlavacs H. Methodology of measurement for energy consumption of applications. In: Energy Efficient Grids, Clouds and Clusters Workshop (co-located with Grid) (E2GC2 2010). Brussels: IEEE; 2010 Oct.

52. Gupta D, Gardner R, Cherkasova L. XenMon: QoS monitoring and performance profiling tool. Technical Report HPL-2005-187. Hewlett-Packard Labs; 2005.

53. Grit L, Irwin D, Marupadi V, Shivam P, Yumerefendi A, Chase JS, Albrecht J. Harnessing virtual machine resource control for job management. In: Proceedings of the 1st Workshop on System-level Virtualization for High Performance Computing; Lisbon, Portugal; 2007.

54. Jones ST, Arpaci-Dusseau AC, Arpaci-Dusseau RH. Antfarm: tracking processes in a virtual machine environment. In: Proceedings of the 2006 USENIX Annual Technical Conference; Massachusetts, USA; 2006. pp. 1–14.

55. Jones ST, Arpaci-Dusseau AC, Arpaci-Dusseau RH. Geiger: monitoring the buffer cache in a virtual machine environment. In: Proceedings of the 12th international conference on Architectural Support for Programming Languages and Operating Systems; California, USA; 2006. pp. 14–24.

CHAPTER 7

COMPARISON AND ANALYSIS OF GREEDY ENERGY-EFFICIENT SCHEDULING ALGORITHMS FOR COMPUTATIONAL GRIDS

PEDER LINDBERG, JAMES LEINGANG, DANIEL LYSAKER, KASHIF BILAL, SAMEE ULLAH KHAN, PASCAL BOUVRY, NASIR GHANI, NASRO MIN-ALLAH, and JUAN LI

A computational grid is a distributed computational network enabled with software that allows cooperation and sharing of resources. The energy consumption of these large-scale distributed systems is an important problem. As our society becomes more technologically advanced, the size of these computational grids and energy consumption continue to increase. In this chapter, we study the problem of optimizing energy consumption and makespan by focusing on different techniques to schedule the tasks to the computational grid. A computational grid is simulated using a wide range of task heterogeneity and size variety. The heuristics are used with the simulated computational grid and the results are compared extensively against each other.

7.1 INTRODUCTION

A computational grid is a distributed computational network enabled with software that allows cooperation and sharing of resources. The energy consumption of these large-scale distributed systems is an important problem in today's society. As our society becomes more technologically dependent, the size of these computational grids and amount of energy consumed continues to increase [1].

Energy is the amount of power used over a specific time interval. Power and time are the two major factors analyzed to reduce energy consumption in a

Energy-Efficient Distributed Computing Systems, First Edition.
Edited by Albert Y. Zomaya and Young Choon Lee.
© 2012 John Wiley & Sons, Inc. Published 2012 by John Wiley & Sons, Inc.

computational grid. Power is defined as *the rate the distributed system consumes electrical energy during operation*. There are a few common ways (listed below) to help minimize the energy consumption of these large-scale distributed systems. One method is dynamic voltage scaling (DVS) [2]. DVS is used to reduce power by scaling down each processing element's (PE) supply voltage (V_{dd}) to one of a few discrete (V_{dd}) levels. Reducing power consumption will increase the execution time of a task on a PE; however, the overall energy consumption will decrease because less power is consumed.

Another method is dynamic frequency scaling (DFS). DFS can be used either for energy conservation or for lowering the heat produced by a processor by lowering the frequency at which the processor can issue instructions. Lowering the frequency will increase the amount of time a PE needs to complete a task, but this leads to energy conservation. Energy is conserved with DFS because the PE consumes less power when running at lower frequencies.

A third technique commonly used to conserve energy on the PE level is clock gating. Clock gating adds additional logic to the PE, which disables certain portions of the switching activity from changing states. This method reduces the power by preventing the PE from constantly switching, which accounts for a large fraction of the PE's energy consumption.

We chose to use the DVS approach because the approach: (i) accurately simulates real-world problems, (ii) has no switching, and (iii) has a closed form relationship among voltage, power, energy, and makespan.

In this chapter, we study and analyze seven greedy heuristics-based algorithms. The greedy heuristics are used to find solutions for the energy-aware task allocation (EATA) problem of assigning a group of tasks to a set of PEs. Each greedy heuristic is given the same conditions and parameters to maintain a fair comparison. The proposed heuristics are Greedy-Min, Greedy-Max, Greedy-Deadline, MaxMin, MinMin StdDev, MinMax StdDev, and ObFun.

Each PE in a large-scale computational grid is composed of many hardware devices (hard drives, memory, communication links, etc.) that contribute to the total energy consumption. The presented heuristics provide enough accuracy to give a good estimate of the total energy consumption while still allowing one to simulate a large-scale data center [3].

Initially, Greedy-Min, Greedy-Max, Greedy-Deadline, MaxMin, MinMin StdDev, and MinMax StdDev *rearrange* the tasks so that they are in the order, and they will be distributed to PEs. Greedy-Min schedules the tasks with the shortest completion times first. Greedy-Max schedules the tasks with the longest completion times first. Greedy-Deadline schedules the tasks with the most urgent deadlines first. MaxMin initially schedules the tasks to the least efficient PEs to allow easier scheduling of the subsequent tasks. MinMin StdDev first schedules the tasks in ascending order and then *rearranges* the tasks in ascending order based on their standard deviation. MinMax StdDev is similar except that the tasks are *rearranged* in descending order after the standard deviation of each task is determined. After a task is assigned to a PE, the PE is set to the minimum DVS level that keeps the task from overshooting the deadline constraint.

ObFun is a greedy heuristic that uses two objective functions to assign tasks to appropriate PEs. The first objective function decides which task will be assigned to a PE during each iteration by examining the runtime and power consumption of each task on every PE. The second objective function determines the most appropriate PE for the task.

We will compare and analyze the above techniques by examining the results of numerous simulations. To incorporate variance in our simulations, we vary the task and PE heterogeneity. The number of tasks also varied from 1000 to 100,000. A detailed explanation of our simulation test bed is given in Section 7.5.

The remainder of this chapter is organized as follows. The problem formulation is introduced in Section 7.2. Next, the task scheduling heuristics is discussed in Section 7.3. The simulation results are reviewed in Section 7.4. In Section 7.5, we present related research. Finally, we present a conclusion in Section 7.6.

7.2 PROBLEM FORMULATION

7.2.1 The System Model

Consider a large-scale distributed system, which is a set of tasks (referred to as a *metatask*) and a collection of PEs.

7.2.1.1 PEs. Let the set of PEs be denoted as $\mathcal{PE} = \{PE_1, PE_2, \ldots, PE_m\}$. Each PE is assumed to be equipped with a DVS module, which we will describe in the subsequent sections. A PE is characterized by the following:

- The instantaneous power consumption of the PE, p_j. Depending on the PE's DVS level, p_j may vary between p_j^{min} and p_j^{max}, where $0 < p_j^{min} < p_j^{max}$.
- The available memory of PE, m_{PE_j}.

7.2.1.2 DVS. DVS is a method that can be used to conserve energy in a data center [2]. With the DVS technique, each PE's supply voltage (V_{dd}) can be scaled to a discrete number of V_{dd} levels. By decreasing the operational frequency (f) and V_{dd}, the amount of energy conserved may be increased. A PE will complete fewer computational cycles while operating at a lower frequency; therefore, decreasing the frequency increases the makespan. The makespan is defined as the amount of time taken to complete all the tasks given to the data center. The following equations give the relationship between f, power consumption, and energy consumption over the period $[0, T]$:

$$f = \frac{k \cdot (V_{dd} - V_t)^2}{V_{dd}}, \tag{7.1}$$

$$P = C_L \cdot N_{0 \to 1} \cdot f \cdot V_{dd}^2, \tag{7.2}$$

$$E = \int_0^T P(t)dt, \tag{7.3}$$

where C_L is the switching capacitance, $N_{0 \to 1}$ is the switching activity, k is a constant that is dependent on the circuit, T is the total time, and V_t is the circuit threshold voltage.

7.2.1.3 *Tasks.* A metatask, $T = \{t_1, t_2, \dots, t_n\}$, is a set of tasks where t_i is a task. Each task is characterized by the following:

- The number of computational cycles, c_i, that need to be completed.
- The memory requirement of a task, m_{t_i}.
- The deadline, d_i, which is the time by which a task must be finished.

7.2.1.4 *Preliminaries.* Suppose that we are given a set of PEs and a metatask, T. Each $t_i \in T$ must be mapped to a PE such that the deadline constraint of t_i is fulfilled. That is, the runtime of PE_j must be less than d_i. Let the runtime of PE_j be denoted by m_j. A feasible task to PE mapping occurs when each task in the metatask can be mapped to at least one PE_j while satisfying all of the associated task constraints. If $m_{\text{PE}_j} < m_{t_i}$, then t_i cannot be executed on PE_j.

7.2.2 Formulating the Energy-Makespan Minimization Problem

Given is a set of PEs and a metatask, T. *The problem can be stated as follows:*

- The total energy consumed by the PEs is minimized.
- The *makespan*, M, of the metatask, t, is minimized.

We can say mathematically,

$$\text{minimize} \sum_{i=1}^{n} \sum_{j=1}^{m} p_{ij} x_{ij} \text{ and minimize max } \sum_{i=1}^{n} t_{ij} x_{ij}$$

subject to the following constraints:

$$x_{ij} \in 0, 1, i = 1, 2, \dots, n; j = 1, 2, \dots, m \tag{7.4}$$

$$t_i \to m_j, \forall i, \forall j; \text{ if } m_{\text{PE}_j} > m_{t_i}; \text{ then } x_{ij} = 1 \tag{7.5}$$

$$t_{ij} x_{ij} \le d_i, \forall i, \forall j, x_{ij} = 1 \tag{7.6}$$

$$(t_{ij} x_{ij} \le d_i) \in 0, 1 \tag{7.7}$$

$$\prod_{i=1}^{n} (t_{ij} x_{ij} \le d_i) = 1, \forall i, \forall j, x_{ij} = 1 \tag{7.8}$$

Constraint 7. is the mapping constraint. t_i is assigned to PE_j when $x_{ij} = 1$. Constraint 7.5 elaborates on this mapping in conjunction to the memory requirements and states that a mapping can exist only if PE_j has enough memory to execute t_i. Constraint 7.6 relates to the fulfillment of the deadline of each task. Constraint 7.7 shows that there is a Boolean relationship between the deadline and the actual execution time of the tasks. Constraint 7.8 relates to the deadline constraints of the metatask that will hold if and only if the deadline, d_i, for each $t_i \in T$ is satisfied.

The EATA problem formulation is a multiconstrained, multiobjective optimization problem. The preference must be given to one objective over the other because the optimization of energy and M oppose each other. The formulation is in the same form as the generalized assignment problem (GAP) except for Constraints 7.6–7.8. The major difference between GAP and EATA is that the capacity of resources in GAP, in terms of the utilization of instantaneous power, is defined individually, whereas in EATA the capacity of resources is defined in groups [4].

7.3 PROPOSED ALGORITHMS

In this section, we describe the inner workings of our seven proposed heuristics.

All of the task execution times are obtained from an estimated time of completion (ETC) matrix [5]. An ETC matrix is a two-dimensional array with $|T|$ rows and $|\mathcal{PE}_p|$ columns. Each element in the ETC matrix corresponds to an execution time of t_i on PE_j, where i is the row and j is the column. To generate the ETC matrix, we use a coefficient-of-variation-based (CVB) ETC matrix generation method [6]. There are three major parameters that determine the heterogeneity of the ETC matrix as follows:

1. the average execution time of each $t_i \in T$, μ_{task};
2. the variance in the task execution time, V_{task};
3. the variance in the PE heterogeneity, V_{PE}.

Because CVB uses a γ distribution [7], the characteristic shape parameter, α, and scale parameter, β, must be defined. The gamma distribution's parameters, α_{task}, α_{PE}, β_{task}, and β_{PE} can be interpreted in terms of μ_{task}, V_{task}, and V_{PE}. For a gamma distribution, $\mu = \beta\alpha$ and $V = 1/\sqrt{\alpha}$. Then

$$\alpha_{\text{task}} = \frac{1}{V_{\text{task}}^2}, \tag{7.9}$$

$$\alpha_{\text{PE}} = \frac{1}{V_{\text{PE}}^2}, \tag{7.10}$$

$$\beta_{\text{task}} = \frac{\mu_{\text{task}}}{\alpha_{\text{task}}}, \tag{7.11}$$

$$\beta_{\text{PE}} = \frac{G(\alpha_{\text{task}}, \beta_{\text{task}})}{\alpha_{\text{PE}}}, \tag{7.12}$$

where $G(\alpha_{\text{task}}, \beta_{\text{task}})$ is a number sampled from a gamma distribution.

The d_i for each t_i is derived from the ETC matrix and can be represented by

$$d_i = \frac{|t_i|}{|\mathcal{PE}|} \cdot \arg_j \max(t_{ij}) \cdot k_d, \tag{7.13}$$

where k_d is a parameter that can tighten d_i [8, 9].

7.3.1 Greedy Heuristics

The resource allocation for the following six greedy heuristics is achieved by CRAH. Algorithm 7.1 shows the pseudocode for CRAH. The CRAH algorithm takes as inputs an ETC matrix, $\mathcal{PE}_p$, and d_i for all $t_i \in T$. The output of CRAH is the T to $\mathcal{PE}$ mapping, the energy consumption of the best solution, $\mathcal{E}_{\min}$, and M.

Algorithm 7.1: Constructive Resource Allocation Heuristic (CRAH)

```
Input: ETC, PEₚ, dᵢ ∀tᵢ ∈ T
Output T to PE mapping, ℰₘᵢₙ, M
INVOKE Greedy Heuristic to rearrange ETC and generate EEC;
While k < kₘₐₓ do
    Generate Random PE;
    CALCULATE Eₛₒₗ;
    Eₘᵢₙ ← Eₛₒₗ
    Repeat
        Eₘᵢₙ ≥ E'ₘᵢₙ;
        ForEach PEⱼ ∈ PEₚ do
            Add PEⱼ to PE;
            CALCULATE Eₛₒₗ;
            If Eₛₒₗ < Eₘᵢₙ then Eₘᵢₙ ← Eₛₒₗ Remove PEⱼ from PE;
        end
        ForEach PEⱼ ∈ PE do
            Remove PEⱼ from PE;
            CALCULATE Eₛₒₗ;
            If Eₛₒₗ < Eₘᵢₙ then Eₘᵢₙ ← Eₛₒₗ Add PEⱼ to PE;
        end
        If Eₘᵢₙ ≥ ℰₘᵢₙ then
            INCREMENT k
        else
            k ← 0
            ℰₘᵢₙ ← Eₘᵢₙ
        end
    until Eₘᵢₙ ≥ Eₘᵢₙ
end
```

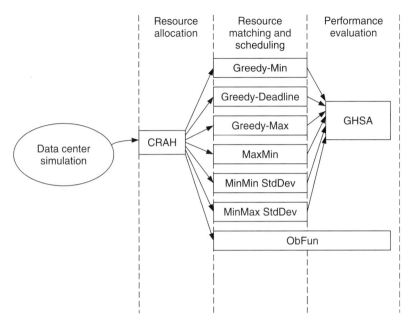

Figure 7.1 Simulation flow chart.

At Line 1, one of the six greedy heuristics is invoked to *rearrange* the ETC matrix in the order the tasks will be scheduled. This step is different for each heuristic. Figure 7.2 illustrates one method of *rearranging* the ETC matrix. Figure 7.2a shows the original ETC matrix. The rows are sorted in ascending order (Fig. 7.2b). Next, the rows of the ETC matrix are swapped such that the execution times in the first column are arranged in ascending order (Fig. 7.2c). Because one must maintain indexing for a given ETC matrix, under each operation we maintain the associated index with each element of the matrix. For the above mentioned matrix *rearranging* procedures, the corresponding index matrices (*I-ETC*'s) are shown in Figures 7.2d–f. Next, an EEC matrix is generated by multiplying the PE's instantaneous power consumption by the task's estimated completion time.

The outer **while** loop (Line 3) repeats until there is no significant improvement in solution quality. Let k be the number of loops with no improvement. The solution is considered sufficient when $k \geq k_{\max}$. An initial resource allocation,

$$
\begin{vmatrix} 8 & 7 & 10 \\ 10 & 9 & 5 \\ 6 & 12 & 7 \end{vmatrix}
\begin{vmatrix} 7 & 8 & 10 \\ 5 & 9 & 10 \\ 6 & 7 & 12 \end{vmatrix}
\begin{vmatrix} 5 & 9 & 10 \\ 6 & 7 & 12 \\ 7 & 8 & 10 \end{vmatrix}
$$

$$
\begin{vmatrix} 1 & 2 & 3 \\ 1 & 2 & 3 \\ 1 & 2 & 3 \end{vmatrix}
\begin{vmatrix} 2 & 1 & 3 \\ 3 & 2 & 1 \\ 1 & 3 & 2 \end{vmatrix}
\begin{vmatrix} 3 & 2 & 1 \\ 1 & 3 & 2 \\ 2 & 1 & 3 \end{vmatrix}
$$

Figure 7.2 ETC matrix *rearranged* for Greedy-Min. (a–c) ETC matrices; (d–f) index matrices.

$\mathcal{PE}$, is generated by randomly adding PEs until D is violated. Next, one of the six greedy heuristics is invoked to schedule the tasks, calculate M, and determine the energy consumption of this solution, E_{sol}.

Inside the **repeat-until** loop (Line 6), $\mathcal{PE}$ is modified (every $\text{PE}_j \in \mathcal{PE}_p$ is added and removed from $\mathcal{PE}$) until a locally optimal solution has been found. In Line 7, note that E'_{min} is the energy minima found in the previous iteration. In Line 10 and 15, the solution is evaluated. The change to $\mathcal{PE}$ that results in the largest decrease in E_{sol} is recorded as $\mathcal{PE}$. When a local energy minima is reached, E_{min} (i.e., CRAH can no longer add or remove a PE to decrease the energy consumption), the **repeat-until** loop terminates. If E_{min} is less than the global energy minimum, $\mathcal{E}_{\text{min}}$, then $\mathcal{E}_{\text{min}}$ is set to E_{min}. A new random $\mathcal{PE}$ is generated and the outer **while** loop repeats.

Algorithm 7.2: Greedy Heuristic Scheduling Algorithm (GHSA)

Input ETC, $\mathcal{PE}_p$, $d_i \forall t_i \in T$, and $\mathcal{PE}$
Output T to $\mathcal{PE}$ mapping, E_{sol}, M
ForEach $t_i \in T$ **do**
  ForEach $\text{PE}_j \in \mathcal{PE}$ **do**
    For $DVS_k = 1$ to 4 **do**
      If $t_{ijk} + m_j \leq d_i$ **then**
        Assign t_i to PE_j at DVS_k
        $m_j \leftarrow m_j + \text{ETC}(ij)$
        $E_{\text{sol}} \leftarrow E_{\text{sol}} + EEC(ij)$
      end
    end
    If t_i not assigned **then**
      $d_{\text{flag}} \leftarrow 1$
      EXIT
    end
  end
end
ForEach $\text{PE}_j \in \mathcal{PE}$ **do**
  $E_{\text{sol}} \leftarrow E_{\text{sol}} + E_{\text{idle}}$
end

7.3.1.1 Greedy heuristic scheduling algorithm. The greedy heuristic scheduling algorithm (GHSA) performs the task scheduling for Greedy-Min, Greedy-Deadline, Greedy-Max, MaxMin, MinMin Std Dev, and MinMax StdDev (Fig. 7.1). The major difference among the six greedy heuristics is how these heuristics schedule T to $\mathcal{PE}$. Algorithm 7.1 shows the pseudocode for GHSA. GHSA takes as input an ETC matrix, $\mathcal{PE}_p$, $d_i \tilde{} \forall t_i \in T$, and $\mathcal{PE}$. The output of GHSA is the T to $\mathcal{PE}$ mapping, E_{sol}, and M. GHSA starts at the first element of the ETC matrix and assigns the task to the most suitable PE. Because a t_i to PE_j mapping must adhere to the d_i constraint, at Line 5, the GHSA heuristic must set PE_j to the minimum DVS level, DVS_1 (Table 7.1). The DVS_k is incrementally increased until d_i is met. If the task does not meet

TABLE 7.1   **Power Scalars for Each DVS Level**

DVS Level	Speed, %	Power Scalar
1	70	0.3430
2	80	0.5120
3	90	0.7290
4	100	1

the deadline when running at the highest DVS level (DVS$_4$)then GHSA attempts to assign t_i to the next PE in the ETC matrix. If GHSA fails to schedule t_i to any of the PEs then the deadline constraint cannot be satisfied and a flag, d_{flag}, is set (Line 9) to indicate that there does not exist any feasible solution. When t_i is successfully assigned to a PE, we must take into account the runtime of t_i and the energy consumed by PE$_j$. In Line 6, ETC(ij) is added to m_j and in Line 7, EEC(ij) is added to E_{sol}. If a feasible solution is obtained, we must calculate the energy consumed, E_{sol}, to process the t_i to $\mathcal{PE}$ mapping. Note that the energy consumed during idle time is accounted for at Line 15. That is,

$$E_{\text{idle}} = p_j \cdot t_{\text{idle}} \cdot k_{\text{idle}}, \tag{7.14}$$

where t_{idle} is the difference between M and m_j. k_{idle} is a scalar relating the instantaneous power of a PE under load to an idle PE.

7.3.1.2 *Greedy-min.* The Greedy-Min heuristic (Algorithm 7.3) schedules the tasks with the shortest execution times first. The motivation behind scheduling the shortest tasks first is to induce slack in the schedule. This slack allows the subsequent tasks with longer execution times to be scheduled without violating the deadline constraints. Greedy-Min receives an ETC matrix as inputs and outputs the *rearranged* ETC matrix, EEC matrix, and *I-ETC*. Let R be a row in the ETC matrix and C_i be the ith column in the ETC matrix. Note that Greedy-Min, Greedy-Deadline, Greedy-Max, and MaxMin all have the same inputs and outputs. Figure 7.2 illustrates the process of *rearranging* the ETC matrix. Greedy-Min *rearranges* the ETC matrix.

Algorithm 7.3: Greedy-Min

Input *ETC* **Output** *ETC*, *EEC*, *I-ETC*
ForEach $R \in$ ETC   **do**
  Sort *R* in ascending order
  Sort corresponding row in *I-ETC*
end
$\forall R \in ETC$, swap *R* such that C_1 is in ascending order
Apply same changes to *I-ETC*

7.3.1.3 Greedy-deadline. One of the major differences between Greedy-Deadline and Greedy-Min is in the task scheduling. In Greedy-Deadline (Algorithm 7.4), the tasks with the most urgent deadlines are scheduled first. Because tasks are scheduled based on urgency, the tasks that are scheduled later would have a better chance of being scheduled. Figure 7.3 shows how the ETC matrix is *rearranged*. As seen in Figure 7.3c, the rows are sorted in ascending order. In Figure 7.3d, the rows are swapped such that the execution times in the first column in the ETC matrix are arranged in ascending order based on the task's deadline. After Greedy-Deadline *rearranges* the ETC matrix, GHSA is invoked.

Algorithm 7.4: Greedy-Deadline

Input *ETC* **Output** *ETC, EEC, I-ETC*
ForEach $R \in$ ETC **do**
  Sort R in ascending order according to each t_i's d_i;
  Sort corresponding row in *I-ETC*
end
$\forall R \in ETC$, swap R such that C_1 is in ascending order;
Apply same changes to *I-ETC*;
INVOKE GHSA;

7.3.1.4 Greedy-max. In Greedy-Max (Algorithm 7.5), the tasks with the longest execution times are scheduled first. When the tasks with the longest execution times are scheduled first, only the tasks with the shortest execution times remain. Because these tasks have the shortest execution times, GHSA can more easily schedule these tasks without violating the deadline constraints. Figure 7.4 demonstrates the process of *rearranging* the ETC matrix for Greedy-Max. In Figure 7.4b, the rows of the ETC matrix are sorted in ascending order. In Figure 7.4c, the rows are swapped so that the execution times in the first column are arranged in descending order.

Algorithm 7.5: Greedy-Max

Input *ETC*
Output *ETC, EEC, I-ETC*
ForEach $R \in$ ETC **do**
  Sort R in ascending order;
  Sort corresponding row in *I-ETC*;
end
$\forall R \in$ ETC, swap R such that C_1 is in descending order;
Apply same changes to *I-ETC*;
INVOKE GHSA;

$$
\begin{vmatrix} \text{Deadlines} & \\ t_1 & 13 \\ t_2 & 15 \\ t_3 & 10 \end{vmatrix}
$$

$$
\begin{vmatrix} 8 & 7 & 10 \\ 10 & 9 & 5 \\ 6 & 12 & 7 \end{vmatrix} \begin{vmatrix} 7 & 8 & 10 \\ 5 & 9 & 10 \\ 6 & 7 & 12 \end{vmatrix} \begin{vmatrix} 6 & 7 & 12 \\ 7 & 8 & 10 \\ 5 & 9 & 10 \end{vmatrix}
$$

Figure 7.3 ETC matrix *rearranged* for Greedy-Deadline. (a) Deadline; (b–d) ETC matrix.

$$
\begin{vmatrix} 8 & 7 & 10 \\ 10 & 9 & 5 \\ 6 & 12 & 7 \end{vmatrix} \begin{vmatrix} 7 & 8 & 10 \\ 5 & 9 & 10 \\ 6 & 7 & 12 \end{vmatrix} \begin{vmatrix} 7 & 8 & 10 \\ 6 & 7 & 12 \\ 5 & 9 & 10 \end{vmatrix}
$$

Figure 7.4   ETC matrix *rearranged* for Greedy-Max. (a–c) ETC matrix.

7.3.1.5 *MaxMin.*

During the initial phase of MaxMin (Algorithm 7.6), tasks are scheduled to the least efficient PEs. The major motivation behind MaxMin is to allow a slack in the schedules of the most efficient PEs late in the scheduling process. The subsequent tasks can be executed on the most efficient PEs. Figure 7.5 shows the process of *rearranging* the ETC matrix. In Figure 7.5b, the rows of the ETC matrix are sorted in descending order. In Figure 7.5c, the rows are swapped so that the execution times in the first column are arranged in descending order.

Algorithm 7.6: MaxMin

```
Input ETC
Output ETC, EEC, I-ETC
ForEach R ∈ ETC do
  Sort R in descending order
  Sort corresponding row in I-ETC
end
∀R ∈ ETC, swap R such that C₁ is in ascending order
Apply same changes to I-ETC
INVOKE GHSA
```

7.3.1.6 *ObFun.*

ObFun is a greedy heuristic that uses two objective functions to determine task to PE mappings. The pseudocode for ObFun is presented in Algorithm 7.7. ObFun takes as input an ETC matrix, $\mathcal{PE}_p$, $d_i \: \forall t_i \in T$, and $\mathcal{PE}$. The output of ObFun is T to $\mathcal{PE}$ mapping, the energy consumed by this solution, E_{sol}, and M.

$$\begin{vmatrix} 8 & 7 & 11 \\ 10 & 9 & 5 \\ 6 & 12 & 7 \end{vmatrix} \begin{vmatrix} 11 & 8 & 7 \\ 10 & 9 & 5 \\ 12 & 7 & 6 \end{vmatrix} \begin{vmatrix} 10 & 9 & 5 \\ 11 & 8 & 7 \\ 12 & 7 & 6 \end{vmatrix}$$

Figure 7.5   ETC matrix *rearranged* for MaxMin. (a–c) ETC matrix.

Algorithm 7.7: ObFun

Input ETC, $\mathcal{PE}_p$, $d_i \forall t_i \in T$, and $\mathcal{PE}$
Output T to $\mathcal{PE}$ mapping, E_{sol}, M
ForEach $t_i \in T$ **do**
  Calculate TS_i
end
Sort TS in descending order
ForEach $t_i \in TS$ **do**
  ForEach PE$_j \in \mathcal{PE}$
    Calculate PS$_{ij}$
  end
  $j \leftarrow arg_j min(PS_{ij})$
  For $DVS_k = 1$ to 4
    If $t_{ijk} + m_j \le d_i$
      Assign t_i to PE$_j$ at DVS_k
      $m_j \leftarrow m_j + ETC(ij)$
      $E_{sol} \leftarrow E_{sol} + EEC(ij)$
    end
  end
  If t_i not assigned **then**
    $d_{flag} \leftarrow 1$
    EXIT
  end
end
ForEach PE$_j \in \mathcal{PE}$
  $E_j \leftarrow E_j + E_{idle}$
end

In Line 2, ObFun generates the *TaskSelect* array (*TS*). Every t_i has an entry in *TS* that is based on the following:

$$TS_i = \alpha_1(T_{2,i} - T_{1,i}) + \alpha_2(P_{2,j} - P_{1,j})$$
$$+ \alpha_3 \frac{T_{1,i} + T_{2,i}}{\sum\limits_{k=1}^{tasks}(T_{1,k} + T_{2,k})} + \alpha_4 + \alpha_5 + \alpha_6, \tag{7.15}$$

where $T_{1,i}$ denotes the minimum estimated completion time of t_i. $T_{2,i}$ represents the second shortest estimated completion time of t_i. $P_{1,j}$ and $P_{2,j}$ are the first and second most power-efficient PEs for task t_i, respectively. α_{1-3} are weight parameters and α_{4-6} are values added to TS if the following conditions are met:

- α_4 is added if the PE with the shortest execution time for t_i is also the most power efficient.
- α_5 is added if the PE with the shortest execution time for t_i and the PE that is the second most power efficient are the same, or *vice versa*.
- α_6 is added if the PE with the second shortest execution time for t_i and the PE that is second most power efficient are the same.

The values of these parameters are recorded in Table 7.2.

In Line 4, TS is sorted in descending order to allow ObFun to schedule the most appropriate task (according to the objective function) first. In Line 7, the most suitable PE for each task is determined and placed in the *PE Select* array, PS. Each PE is given a value for every task from the following objective function:

$$PS = \beta_1 T_{1,\text{PE}_j,t_i} + \beta_2 P_{1,\text{PE}_j,t_i} + \beta_3 \text{load}(\text{PE}_j), \qquad (7.16)$$

where T_{1,PE_j,t_i} is the execution time of t_i on processor PE_j, P_{1,PE_j,t_i} is the instantaneous power consumption of processor PE_j when executing task t_i, and $\text{load}(\text{PE}_j)$ is a value added when certain conditions are met. The value of $\text{load}(\text{PE}_j)$ is zero if t_i satisfies d_i when assigned to PE_j. If t_i does not satisfy d_i then $\text{load}(\text{PE}_j)$ equals $m_j - d_i$. Following the above, t_i is assigned to the PE with the lowest PS value. In Line 12, ObFun determines the lowest DVS_k that PE_j can be set before scheduling t_i to PE_j. After t_i is scheduled, the executing time of t_i and the energy consumed by PE_j must be recorded. In Line 13, $\text{ETC}(ij)$ is added to m_j; and in Line 14, $\text{EEC}(ij)$ is added to E_{sol}. If t_i cannot meet d_i when PE_j is running at the highest DVS level (DVS_4), then a flag is set (Line 16) to indicate a feasible solution does not exist. If a feasible solution is found, then the total energy consumption of the solution is calculated in a manner analogous to GHSA.

TABLE 7.2 Parameters Used in TaskSelect and PE Select

Parameters	
α_1	0.520656
α_2	0.381958
α_3	0.0431519
α_4	0.160583
α_5	0.522339
α_6	0.696564
β_1	0.0970764
β_2	0.400818
β_3	0.773407

7.3.1.7 *MinMin StdDev.* The MinMin StdDev heuristic (Algorithm 7.8) schedules tasks with the shortest execution times first, then the rows are *rearranged* in ascending order based on each row's standard deviation. The motivation behind this algorithm is to schedule the tasks with the most consistent execution run first. Such a method will provide consistent results each time the algorithm is run and also will induce slack at the end of the algorithm to schedule the tasks with more inconsistent runtimes. Figure 7.6 shows how the ETC matrix is *rearranged*. In Figure 7.6b, the rows are sorted in ascending order. The standard deviation function is then run to find the standard deviation of each row, then the rows are *rearranged* based on these values as seen in Figure 7.6c. The first row of Figure 7.6c has a standard deviation of 0.67, the second row has a standard deviation of 1.82, and the third row has a standard deviation of 2.78.

Algorithm 7.8: MinMin StdDev

```
Input ETC Output ETC, EEC, I-ETC
ForEach R ∈ ETC do
    Find standard deviation of each tᵢ ∈ Rᵢ
    Sort R in ascending order according to each tᵢ's
        standard deviation
    Sort corresponding row in I-ETC
end
∀R ∈ ETC, swap R such that C₁ is in ascending order
Apply same changes to I-ETC
INVOKE GHSA
```

Input ETC Output ETC, EEC, I-ETC

ForEach $R \in$ ETC do

Find standard deviation of each $t_i \in R_i$

Sort R in ascending order according to each t_i's standard deviation

Sort corresponding row in I-ETC

end

$\forall R \in ETC$, swap R such that C_1 is in ascending order

Apply same changes to I-ETC

INVOKE GHSA

7.3.1.8 *MinMax StdDev.* MinMax StdDev (Algorithm 7.9) runs very similarly to MinMin StdDev. One major difference is that the rows are *rearranged* in descending order based on the standard deviation of each row. There are two advantages that come from *rearranging* the rows in this manner. Because the rows are arranged in ascending order and the row with the highest standard deviation is scheduled first, the first task will be scheduled on a PE where it has the shortest projected runtime. It follows that the subsequent tasks will be more consistent in runtime over the span of PE's due to the low standard deviation of the row. Such an algorithm is able to perform well in the case where many of the PEs are at full capacity and the algorithm must search to find an available PE. Figure 7.7c shows how the rows are *rearranged* in descending order based on their standard deviation.

$$\begin{vmatrix} 5 & 13 & 7 \\ 10 & 9 & 8 \\ 6 & 12 & 7 \end{vmatrix} \begin{vmatrix} 5 & 7 & 13 \\ 8 & 9 & 10 \\ 6 & 7 & 12 \end{vmatrix} \begin{vmatrix} 8 & 9 & 10 \\ 6 & 7 & 12 \\ 5 & 7 & 13 \end{vmatrix}$$

Figure 7.6 ETC matrix *rearranged* for MinMin StdDev. (a–c) ETC matrix.

Algorithm 7.9: MinMax StdDev

```
Input ETC Output ETC, EEC, I-ETC
ForEach R ∈ ETC do
   Find standard deviation of each tᵢ ∈ Rᵢ
   Sort R in descending order according to each tᵢ's
     standard deviation
   Sort corresponding row in I-ETC
end
∀R ∈ ETC, swap  R such that C₁ is in ascending order
Apply same changes to I-ETC
INVOKE GHSA
```

7.4 SIMULATIONS, RESULTS, AND DISCUSSION

All of the heuristics introduced in this chapter were implemented in Matlab. Matlab can efficiently perform operations on large matrices [10]. Because our simulations make use of large matrices, using Matlab appeared to be the best choose. The dimensions of the ETC matrix used in our simulation were as large as 100,000 tasks by 16 PEs. Our results were obtained on a 2.4 GHz Core 2 Duo system with 2 GB of main memory running the Windows 7 operating system.

The set of tasks used in this simulation study were obtained from an ETC matrix (explained in the subsequent text). There were two major goals for our simulation study as follows:

1. To compare and analyze the performance of the seven introduced scheduling heuristics.
2. To measure the impact of system parameter variation.

7.4.1 Workload

For the workload, we obtained task characteristics from an ETC matrix. An explanation of the generation of our CVB ETC matrix was detailed in Section 7.3. The mean task execution time, μ_{task}, was fixed at 10, while the variance in the tasks, V_{task}, and the variance in the PEs, V_{PE}, varied between 0.1 and 0.35. These values were chosen to incorporate variance in our task execution times and are supported in previous studies [6, 11, 12]. The deadline, d_i, of each t_i is based on the ETC matrix and given by Equation 7.13. To vary the heterogeneity of d_i, the

$$\begin{vmatrix} 5 & 13 & 7 \\ 10 & 9 & 8 \\ 6 & 12 & 7 \end{vmatrix} \begin{vmatrix} 5 & 7 & 13 \\ 8 & 9 & 10 \\ 6 & 7 & 12 \end{vmatrix} \begin{vmatrix} 5 & 7 & 13 \\ 6 & 7 & 12 \\ 8 & 9 & 10 \end{vmatrix}$$

Figure 7.7 ETC matrix *rearranged* for MinMax StdDev. (a–c) ETC matrix.

k_d parameter in Equation 7.13 is varied from 1 to 1.8. For small-size problems, the number of tasks is varied from 1000 to 1000 and the number of PEs is set to 16 [13]. One can choose a large number of PEs; however, studies show that in essence, the number of PEs proportionally relates to the number of tasks [14]. Therefore, if one must have 256 PEs to choose from, then they must have at least 500,000 tasks to solve. The number of DVS levels was set to 4. We admit that having larger numbers of DVS levels can produce refined solutions. However, the general characteristics of the algorithms will have no bearing on larger or smaller numbers of DVS levels [3,15–17]. For large-size problems, the number of tasks varied from 10,000 to 100,000. The rest of the parameters were kept the same as those for the small-size problems. To facilitate readability, all of the above system parameters are summarized in Table 7.3.

7.4.2 Comparative Results

7.4.2.1 Small-size problems.
The simulation results for the small-size problems are shown in Figure 7.8a and 7.8b. These figures show the average energy consumption and *makespan* of the seven proposed heuristics. To thoroughly benchmark our heuristics, we varied the simulation system parameters considerably in order to compile a wide range of data. The V_{task}, V_{PE}, and k_d parameters each have three possible values as observed in Table 7.3. That means that there will be 3^3 combinations, which gives us a total of 27 sets of parameters. This represents every combination of the system parameters listed in Table 7.3. To gain confidence in our results, the simulations were run 10 times for each set of parameters, that is, a total of 270 simulations per heuristic.

There is a great deal of information that can be gathered from the plots. The gray box is the range that represents ±1 times the standard deviation. The mean is represented by a black box in the middle of the gray box. The whiskers extend to ±1.5 times the standard deviation. The bold line that spans the entire plot is the grand mean. The outliers and extremes are denoted by circles and asterisks, respectively. Outliers and extremes mark results that fall outside of ±1.5 times the standard deviation. In the subsequent text, we discuss the results for 1000, 10,000, and 100,000 tasks.

TABLE 7.3 Summary of System Parameters

	System Parameters
μ_{task}	10
V_{task}	{0.1, 0.15, 0.35}
V_{PE}	{0.1, 0.15, 0.35}
k_d	{1, 1.3, 1.8}
$|\mathcal{PE}|$	16
$|T|$	{1,000, 10,000, 100,000}
DVS levels	4

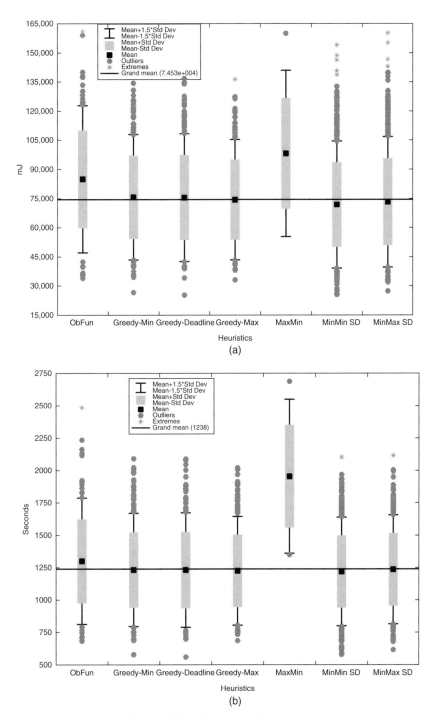

Figure 7.8 1000 task problem size.

Tasks. Figure 7.8(a) shows the energy consumption for 1000 task problems. We can notice that Greedy-Max no longer has the lowest mean energy. MinMin StdDev now has the lowest mean energy consumption (3.39% lower than Greedy-Max.) Observe that the two standard deviation heuristics are the only heuristics that are clearly better than the grand mean. Greedy-Max is the only other Heuristic that consumes less energy than the Grand Mean. MinMin StdDev and MinMax StdDev also display the widest range of results observed. This range can be seen in Figure 7.8(a).

Figure 7.8(b) depicts the *makespan* of the seven heuristics. Greedy-Min, Greedy-Deadline, Greedy-Max, MinMin StdDev, and MinMax StdDev all had a mean *makespan* within 0.89% of each other, so there is not one heuristics that is significantly better than others. MaxMin again performed poorly compared to the rest. ObFun continues to improve as the number of tasks increase, but still has a higher *makespan* than the grand mean. If we look at values from individual sets of parameters then there may be some situations where a certain heuristic performs better than others. When k_d was set to 1.8, and there was high heterogeneity in the ETC matrix ($V_{task} = V_{PE} = 0.35$). MinMin StdDev performed 21% better than Greedy-Max and 7.9% better than MinMax StdDev, which was the heuristic that had the closest *makespan* in this case. These results are depicted in Figure 7.9(a). When there is a high degree of heterogeneity in the ETC matrix, there are more tasks with longer execution times. In such a circumstance, Min-Min StdDev is designed to perform consistently better than the rest. Observe that almost the entire range of MinMin StdDev falls below the grand mean for a case with a high degree of heterogeneity.

7.4.2.2 Large-size problems.
10,000 task problem size. Figure 7.10(a) shows that there are six heuristics with highly comparable results, namely, Greedy-Min, Greedy-Deadline, Greedy-Max, ObFun, MinMin StdDev, and MinMax StdDev. MinMin StdDev obtained a mean energy consumption only 3.96% greater than the Greedy-Min. We also can observe that as the problem size increases, ObFun performs better. In certain cases, ObFun obtained the lowest mean energy consumption compared to the other heuristics by up to 20% of the mean. Figure 7.9(b) illustrates the mean energy consumption when V_{PE} is set to 0.1, V_{task} is set to 0.1, and k_d is set to 1.3. In the above case, ObFun had a mean energy consumption 23.4% higher than any other heuristic. When there is low task heterogeneity, the objective function used in ObFun (Eq. 7.15) is especially ineffective. In the case of high heterogeneity, ObFun usually outperforms the other six heuristics. Equation 7.15 considers the tasks with the first and second shortest execution times. When the heterogeneity of the tasks is high, it is important to inspect more than one task during the task scheduling process. Because ObFun considers multiple tasks with its objective function, ObFun produces better results in the case of high heterogeneity and worse results in the case of low heterogeneity.

The plot in Figure 7.10(b) shows that for a 10,000 task problem, ObFun identifies the lowest mean *makespan*. The *TaskSelect* and *PE Select* objective

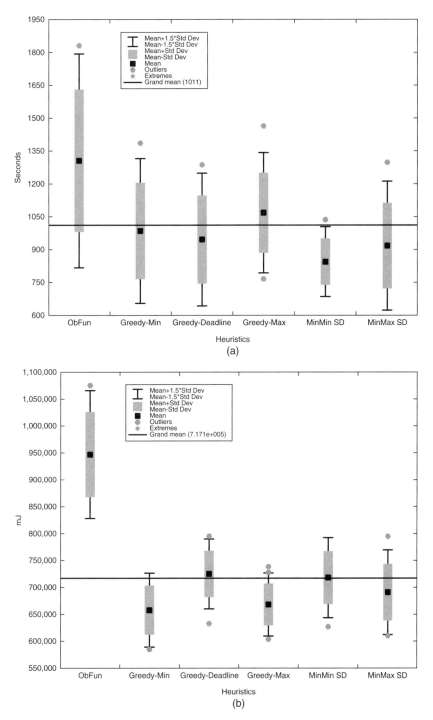

Figure 7.9 1000 and 10,000 case examples.

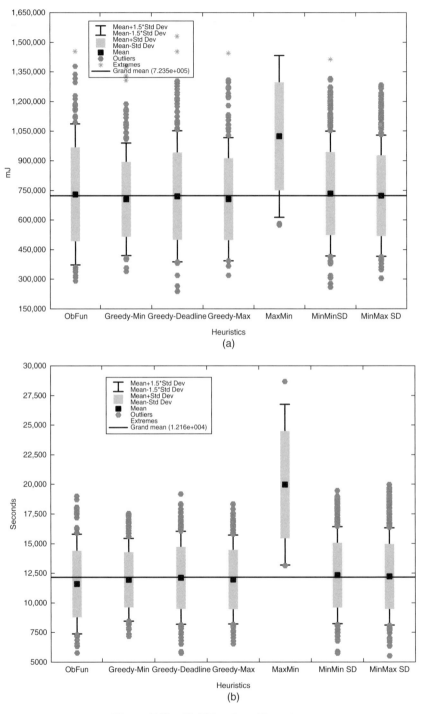

Figure 7.10 10,000 task problem size.

functions are introduced in ObFun factor in the loads of each PE when scheduling tasks. This prevents ObFun from scheduling a majority of the tasks to a few (most efficient) PEs. This induces a scheduling slack for the later tasks. When there are more tasks in the problem, it becomes critical that tasks are more evenly distributed among the PEs. Our results show that heuristics that initially assign tasks to the most efficient PEs exhibit better results.

100,000 tasks. Figures 7.11(a) and 7.11(b) details the energy consumption and *makespan* of the seven heuristics with a 100,000 task problem. ObFun had the lowest mean energy consumption and was 55.18% smaller than the next lowest solution. The lowest mean *makespan* was also achieved by ObFun (41.56% lower than any other heuristic). Because the objective functions implemented in ObFun examine the effects of multiple tasks and multiple PEs before selecting a task-PE pair, ObFun performs extremely well in large-sized problems. We can see that MaxMin had the largest mean energy consumption and largest mean *makespan*. MaxMin continues to demonstrate the same weaknesses observed in all of the other simulations. On the basis of mean energy consumption and mean *makespan*, Greedy-Deadline had the second best solution. Greedy-Deadline schedules tasks with the most urgent deadline first. If the tasks with the most urgent deadlines are not scheduled first, then these tasks may need to be scheduled to an inefficient PE to meet its deadline constraint. Because of the dominance of ObFun, Greedy-Min, Greedy-Max, MinMin StdDev, MinMax StdDev, and MaxMin all had mean energy consumptions and a mean *makespan* higher than the grand mean. In rare cases, the outliers of Greedy-Max, MinMin StdDev, and MinMax StdDev can compete with the mean of ObFun with Greedy-Max coming the closest. Even in the best case scenario for Greedy-Max (low heterogeneity) does not compete with ObFun.

The runtimes of the seven proposed heuristics can be seen in Table 7.4. For small-sized scenarios, the Heuristics have very similar runtimes with the exception of MaxMin, which was much higher. The complexity of ObFun cannot be seen in the average runtimes for small-scale problems, but for the large scale (10,000 and 100,000 tasks) it can be observed that ObFun takes considerably longer to execute than the rest of the Heuristics. The runtime of ObFun at 100,000 tasks is many times longer than the other heuristics. It is this extended runtime that allows the objective function in ObFun to work and produce the dominating results seen in a 100,000 task problem.

To summarize, when solving problems with 1000 tasks, Greedy-Min, Greedy-Deadline, Greedy-Max, MinMin StdDev, and MinMax StdDev obtained solutions with the lowest energy consumption and the shortest *makespan*. For 10,000 task problems, ObFun, Greedy-Min, Greedy-Deadline, Greedy-Max, MinMin Std-Dev, and MinMax StdDev demonstrated the highest solution quality. Finally, for the 100,000 task problems, ObFun vastly outperformed all other heuristics. Overall, we may conclude that ObFun is the best heuristic for large-sized problems. Greedy-Min, Greedy-Deadline, Greedy-Max, MinMin StdDev, and MinMax StdDev can each outperform the rest depending on the heterogeneity of tasks and machines in the distributed system. Some examples were shown

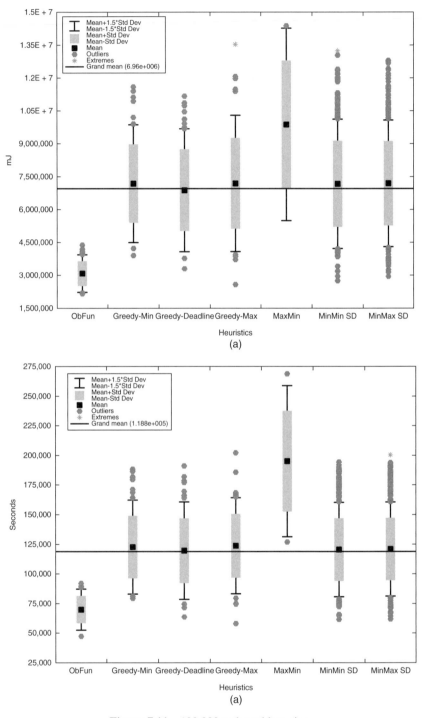

Figure 7.11   100,000 task problem size.

TABLE 7.4 Average Runtime in Seconds

Number of tasks	1,000	10,000	100,000
ObFun	$2.89E^{-2}$	0.439	21.16
Greedy-Min	$2.43E^{-2}$	0.233	2.38
Greedy-Deadline	$2.38E^{-2}$	0.228	2.34
Greedy-Max	$2.50E^{-2}$	0.235	2.47
MaxMin	$4.12E^{-2}$	0.404	4.04
MinMin StdDev	$2.42E^{-2}$	0.262	2.49
MinMax StdDev	$2.42E^{-2}$	0.252	2.45

above to detail when a Heuristic will outperform the rest. Task and machine heterogeneity should be taken into account when choosing a heuristic to model a distributed system.

7.5 RELATED WORKS

In this section, we discuss the related works to the proposed research. To keep the discussion short and relevant, only a subset of the related works is discussed. This is due to the fact that a bulk of the related work has already been disseminated in surveys, such as [18–20].

Most DPM techniques utilize instantaneous power management features supported by hardware. For example, in Reference 21, the operating system's power manager is extended by an adaptive power manager. This adaptive power manager uses the processor's DVS capabilities to reduce or increase the CPU frequency, thereby minimizing the total energy consumption [22]. The DVS technique combined with a turn on/off technique is used to achieve high power savings while maintaining all deadlines in Reference 23. In Reference 24, a scheme to concentrate the workload on a limited number of processors is introduced. This technique allows the rest of the processors to remain switched off for a longer time.

There are a wide variety of power management techniques such as heuristic-based approaches [1,25–28], genetic algorithms [29–32], and constructive algorithms [33]. Most of these techniques have been studied using relatively small sets of tasks. The techniques introduced in this chapter were given large sets of tasks allowing one to compare and analyze some traditional power management techniques when applied to large-scale distributed systems.

7.6 CONCLUSION

This chapter introduced an energy-minimizing task scheduling strategy in distributed systems. The problem was formulated as an extension of the generalized assignment problem. Seven heuristics were proposed to solve this problem. All seven of these heuristics were greedy heuristics, namely, ObFun, Greedy-Min, Greedy-Deadline, Greedy-Max, MaxMin, MinMin StdDev, and MinMax Std-Dev. The seven heuristics were compared against each other with both small and large problem sizes. The simulation results showed that for small-sized problems, Greedy-Min, Greedy-Deadline, Greedy-Max, MinMin StdDev, and MinMax StdDev performed the best. For large-sized problems, ObFun had superior performance in terms of mean energy consumption and mean *makespan* against all of the other proposed heuristics.

REFERENCES

1. Heath T, Diniz B, Carrera EV, Meira W Jr., Bianchini R. Energy conservation in heterogeneous server clusters. In: PPoPP '05: Proceedings of the Tenth ACM SIGPLAN Symposium on Principles and Practice of Parallel Programming. New York: ACM; 2005. pp. 186–195.

2. Weiser M, Welch B, Demers A, Shenker S. Scheduling for reduced CPU energy. In: OSDI '94: Proceedings of the 1st USENIX Conference on Operating Systems Design and Implementation. Berkeley (CA): USENIX Association; 1994. pp. 13–23.

3. Khan SU, Ahmad Ishfaq. A cooperative game theoretical technique for joint optimization of energy consumption and response time in computational grids. IEEE Trans Parallel Distrib Syst 2009;21(4):346–360.

4. Luenberger DG. *Linear and Nonlinear Programming*. 2nd ed. Reading (MA): Addison-Wesley; 1984.

5. Li YA, Antonio JK, Siegel HJ, Tan M, Watson DW. Determining the execution time distribution for a data parallel program in a heterogeneous computing environment. J Parallel Distrib Comput 1997;44(1):35–52.

6. Ali S, Siegel HJ, Maheswaran M, Ali S, Hensgen D. Task execution time modeling for heterogeneous computing systems. In: HCW '00: Proceedings of the 9th Heterogeneous Computing Workshop. Washington (DC): IEEE Computer Society; 2000. p. 185.

7. Papoulis A. *Probability, Random Variables, and Stochastic Processes*. McGraw-Hill; New York, USA; 1984.

8. Yu Y, Prasanna VK. Power-aware resource allocation for independent tasks in heterogeneous real-time systems. In: ICPADS '02: Proceedings of the 9th International Conference on Parallel and Distributed Systems. Washington (DC): IEEE Computer Society; 2002. pp. 341–348.

9. Khan SU, Ardil C. Energy efficient resource allocation in distributed computing systems. In: International Conference on Distributed, High-Performance and Grid Computing. Singapore; 2009. pp. 667–673.

10. Moler CB. *Numerical Computing with Matlab*. Philadelphia (PA): Society for Industrial Mathematics; 2004.

11. Khan SU, Ardil C. On the joint optimization of performance and power consumption in data centers. In: International Conference on Distributed, High-Performance and Grid Computing. Singapore; 2009. pp. 660–660.

12. Ahmad I, Ranka S, Khan SU. Using game theory for scheduling tasks on multi-core processors for simultaneous optimization of performance and energy. In: 22nd IEEE International Parallel and Distributed Processing Symposium; Florida, USA; 2008. pp. 1–6.

13. Siegel HJ, Ali S. Techniques for mapping tasks to machines in heterogeneous computing systems. J Syst Arch 2000;46(8):627–639.

14. Ali S, Siegel HJ, Maheswaran M, Hensgen D, Ali S. Representing task and machine heterogeneities for heterogeneous computing systems. Tamkang J Sci Eng 2000;3(3):195–207.

15. Khan SU, Ahmad I. Comparison and analysis of ten static heuristics-based internet data replication techniques. J Parallel Distrib Comput 2008;68(2):113–136.

16. Khan SU, Ahmad I. A cooperative game theoretical replica placement technique. In: 2007 International Conference on Parallel and Distributed Systems; Hsinchu, Taiwan; 2007.

17. Khan SU. A self-adaptive weighted sum technique for the joint optimization of performance and power consumption in data centers. In: 22nd International Conference on Parallel and Distributed Computing and Communication Systems; Kentucky, USA; 2009.

18. Chedid W, Yu C. Survey on power management techniques for energy efficient computer systems; 2002.

19. Unsal OS, Koren I. System-level power-aware design techniques in real-time systems. Proceedings of the IEEE 2003;91(7): pp. 1055–1069.

20. Venkatachalam V, Franz M. Power reduction techniques for microprocessor systems. ACM Comput Surv 2005;37(3):195–237.

21. Abdelzaher TF, Lu C. Schedulability analysis and utilization bounds for highly scalable real-time services. In: IEEE Real-Time Technology and Applications Symposium; Taipei, Taiwan; 2001. pp. 15–25.

22. Bianchini R, Rajamony R. Power and energy management for server systems. IEEE Comput 2004;37(11):68–74.

23. Elnozahy ENM, Kistler M, Rajamony R. Energy-efficient server clusters. In: Proceedings of the 2nd Workshop on Power-Aware Computing Systems; Massachusetts, USA; 2002. pp. 179–196.

24. Pinheiro E, Bianchini R, Carrera EV, Heath T. Load balancing and unbalancing for power and performance in cluster-based systems. In: Workshop on Compilers and Operating Systems for Low Power; Barcelona, Spain; 2001.

25. Nathuji R, Isci C, Gorbatov E. Exploiting platform heterogeneity for power efficient data centers. In: ICAC '07: Proceedings of the 4th International Conference on Autonomic Computing; Florida, USA; 2007.

26. Hsu CH, Kremer U. The design, implementation, and evaluation of a compiler algorithm for cpu energy reduction. In: Proceedings of ACM SIGPLAN Conference on Programming Language Design and Implementation, California, USA; 2003. pp. 38–48.

27. Hwang C-H, Wu AC-H. A predictive system shutdown method for energy saving of event-driven computation. In: Proceedings of the 34th Conference on Design Automation. Anaheim (CA); 1997. pp. 28–32.

28. Kirovski D, Potkonjak M. System-level synthesis of low-power hard real-time systems. In: DAC '97: Proceedings of the 34th annual Design Automation Conference. New York: ACM; 1997. pp. 697–702.

29. Dick RP, Jha NK. Mogac: a multiobjective genetic algorithm for the co-synthesis of hardware-software embedded systems. IEEE Trans Comput Aided Des Integr Circ Syst 1997;17:920–935.

30. Schmitz MT, Al-Hashimi BM. Considering power variations of dvs processing elements for energy minimisation in distributed systems. In: Proceedings 14th International Symposium on System Synthesis. Montreal, Canada; 2001. pp. 250–255.

31. Dick RP, Jha NK. Cowls: Hardware-software cosynthesis of wireless low-power distributed embedded client-server systems. IEEE Trans Comput Aided Des Integr Circ Syst 2004;23(1):2–16.

32. Hassani MM, Berangi R. Improving the COWLS algorithm for hardware sofware cosynthesis of wireless client-server systems using preference vectors and peak power information. In: Proceedings of the International Conference on Computer Systems and Technologies. Bulgaria; 2007. pp. 1–5.

33. Dave BP, Lakshminarayana G, Jha NK. Cosyn: hardware-software co-synthesis of embedded systems. In: DAC '97: Proceedings of the 34th annual Design Automation Conference. New York: ACM; 1997. pp. 703–708.

CHAPTER 8

TOWARD ENERGY-AWARE SCHEDULING USING MACHINE LEARNING

JOSEP LL. BERRAL, IÑIGO GOIRI, RAMON NOU, FERRAN JULIÀ, JOSEP O. FITÓ, JORDI GUITART, RICARD GAVALDÁ, and JORDI TORRES

8.1 INTRODUCTION

The cloud and the Web 2.0 have contributed to *democratize* the Internet, allowing everybody to share information, services, and IT resources around the network. With the arrival of digital social networks and the introduction of new IT infrastructures in the business world, the Internet population has grown enough to make the need for computing resources an important matter to be handled. While few years ago enterprises had all their IT infrastructures in privately owned data centers, nowadays the big IT corporations have started a *data-center race*, offering computing and storage resources at low prices, looking for outside companies to trust them for their data or IT needs.

A single web application in the cloud can be easily used by people from around the world, so data and computation need to be available from everywhere, having in mind things such as the quality of service (QoS) and the service-level agreements (SLAs) between users and servers. Services offered by Google and YouTube, for example, must be replicated around the globe or just be efficient enough to move data, jobs, or applications among the *data-center farms* spread along the planet. Given the amount of applications running now on the cloud and the amount that will come, coordinating all its applications, resources, and services becomes by itself a hard optimization problem.

Energy-Efficient Distributed Computing Systems, First Edition.
Edited by Albert Y. Zomaya and Young Choon Lee.
© 2012 John Wiley & Sons, Inc. Published 2012 by John Wiley & Sons, Inc.

8.1.1 Energetic Impact of the Cloud

Having powerful enough data-centers to server applications or computation time is not the only thing to keep in mind when building the Cloud. As energy-related costs have become a major cost factor for IT infrastructures and data centers, power consumption has become an important element to keep in mind when designing and managing them. This energetic cost is reflected in the electric consumption, which is sometimes nonlinear with the capacity of that data centers. It also has direct environmental impact and is conditioned by social pressure for efficiency. Companies dedicated to cloud-based services, and the research community are being challenged to find better and more efficient power-aware resource management strategies.

Until now technological improvement sufficed to cover the increasing IT demand, bringing faster processors, bigger storage devices, and faster connections between resources. The energetic factor was not relevant enough to be focused on. Now the demand is growing faster than technological improvement, so each time we need bigger data centers to be cooled down in colder places, having enough power supply [1].

Reaching an optimal performance of cloud services and resource management requires an *intelligent management*, conscious of the importance of each resource used, each service given, the way power is consumed, and the relation between power consumed and work done. This intelligent management complements the technological improvement, allowing better resource use, borrowing and lending resources when it is convenient to do so, and improving the QoS without scaling up the data centers unnecessarily.

8.1.2 An Intelligent Way to Manage Data Centers

This intelligent management would be easy if the manager knew in detail the structure and elements in the cloud, if system administrators could keep constantly watching the system, and if experts could advise what to do in each situation. Unfortunately this is often not possible. Unfortunately, this is not often possible. The cloud, as its name suggests, becomes an abstract cloud of resources. Each domain of resources has its own resource broker and interface for dealing with resource borrowers and lenders, so a part of the cloud cannot manage or get all the information from other parts of it.

Also, systems running on the cloud are hard to model, as well as predict. There are no experts in some applications of the cloud, and some predictive variables are hidden to the naked eye, so it is very difficult to predict the behavior of the whole (or just a part of) system when lots of variables are involved. Furthermore, keeping a human operator watching over all events and resources of the system; reacting to each change when changes happen so fast; and executing the best solution each time is not possible. Intelligent management must be automated, must "understand" what is happening in the system, and must "learn" about actions to be taken.

8.1.3 Current Autonomic Computing Techniques

Current data centers and large-scale distributed computing systems are increasingly implementing the techniques of autonomic computing. Automation on large-scale systems has become a hot spot on system improvements, letting the systems manage themselves (self-healing, self-protection, self-optimization, and self-configuring) from expert systems, statistic models, and ad hoc rules.

The intermediary software (also known as *middleware*) in charge of performing these autonomic computing techniques requires models that capture the most important factors of the systems while allowing abstract reasoning. The models must allow formalizing behaviors and interactions that help the use of optimization techniques (from simple heuristics to complex techniques) based on, that is, what-if predicting techniques or expectation formulas for action results. It is important to remark that optimizations at different system levels interfere between them. This makes the behavior of the current systems unmanageable at execution time, requiring novel optimization techniques that implement self-properties at runtime. These autonomic techniques must be developed to manage workload fluctuations and to determine optimal trade-offs between performance and energy costs.

All these solutions can also be improved if the system learns from itself, becoming itself an expert, modeling from statistics, and writing and improving its rules or management policies. ML (and the closely related field, data mining) brings a set of methods and ideas to, given a set of observations from the system, infer and induce the behavior of the system. Also, these methods are often easy to update in front of changes, or just or general enough to accept changes. This ability to learn for improving the performance of large-scale systems opens a new wide research area combining the self-capabilities of autonomic computing and the capabilities of discovering knowledge from systems.

8.1.4 Power-Aware Autonomic Computing

Middleware requires new advanced management mechanisms to provide the necessary control actuators to successfully manage the resources in order to add energy efficiency as an operating parameter. Nowadays, the most common techniques used in the research literature of the area can be summarized as virtualization, turning on/off servers, DVFS (Dynamic Voltage and Frequency Scaling), and hybrid nodes/hybrid data centers.

- Virtualization is key to reducing power consumption. With virtualization, multiple virtual servers can be hosted on a smaller number of more powerful physical servers, using less electricity. Virtualization mechanisms are currently used for consolidation.
- Turning on/off servers reduces the overall consumption through consolidation. As reduction of needed resources is the goal of consolidation, shutting down of these resources when possible is where actual energy saving is achieved.

- DVFS is the reduction of voltage and frequency, providing substantial saving in power at the cost of slower program execution. Current microprocessors allow power management by DVFS.
- In hybrid data centers, it is possible to choose among a variety of resources, depending on the system load and requirements taking into account energy consumption. Even more, we would like to have the system (not a human supervisor) choose and learn to choose among different resources with the same final functionality but with different characteristics.

Usually, all these techniques can also be combined, improving the level of consolidation and effectiveness. By deciding to turn the physical machines on and off when virtualized machines are consolidated or specializing the physical machines where virtual machines (VMs) are going to be consolidated, power saving can be improved.

8.1.5   State of the Art and Case Study

In this chapter, a brief survey of the state of the art of "intelligent management" and power-aware techniques is shown in Sections 8.2 and 8.3, focusing on the works that are introducing machine learning and other artificial intelligence techniques. Also, a case study summarizing our experiences, applying some of these techniques is introduced in Section 8.4, explaining some practical applications of each technique and showing results and conclusions on the application of the learning mechanisms on a self-management system.

8.2   INTELLIGENT SELF-MANAGEMENT

Adaptive and updatable mechanisms have been developed in order to optimize the management of the cloud and improve the resource usage and the QoS. But the cloud is becoming more complex and application requirements are increasing and knowledge-based and data mining techniques are starting to be applied. Once information about the execution, resources, and requirements is available, artificial intelligence (AI) and machine learning (ML) can be applied to improve prediction and information retrieval, letting the system make some decisions with more autonomy and with more accuracy.

In *intelligent management*, there are different techniques that are beginning to be researched and applied. The first ones are the standard AI-based techniques. These techniques use prediction and heuristic algorithms in order to anticipate system performance and act in consequence. Fuzzy logic, genetic algorithms, and other AI methods are used in order to improve QoS, resource allocation, and execution of applications. The second ones are the ML-based applications. These techniques use the recorded information from past behaviors to create a model that best fits the usual behavior and lets the system detect anomalies and make decisions over the system.

8.2.1 Classical AI Approaches

AI methods have been historically defined as *a machine thinking like human* methods, but nowadays, AI is more like *finding a suitable/intelligent solution with limited time/space*. The classical AI methods are about searching a good solution to a problem on a representation space, or representing knowledge using ontologies and expert systems, and all of these as optimal as possible. Exhaustive searches on a representation space are often NP-hard or exponential problems, and the same happens with many ontology systems or huge expert systems, so searching methods using heuristics, genetic algorithms, and fuzzy knowledge techniques are used to perform these searches in a viable way, not finding always the best solution but having a suboptimal solution in the available space and time. The solution is intelligent in the sense that it does not examine the whole space of solutions.

8.2.1.1 Heuristic algorithms. With the capability of using knowledge and heuristic algorithms, it is possible to predict some situations with good accuracy. This prediction can be applied to detect unwanted situations or behaviors or to view the near future situations such as imminent changes in the workload, changes in the resource demand, or limit situations of resource offers. In approaches such as those presented by Vraalsen [2] and Fahringer [3], some prediction models for parallel programs and grid-based applications are presented, where a method based on heuristics for predicting application performance is presented. With these methods, the system looks for detecting unexpected behaviors, usually caused by unanticipated load on shared grid resources. Once the heuristics detect these unexpected execution behaviors, a fuzzy logic-based algorithm is used to check and decide how to maintain the QoS of each execution. The fuzzy logic algorithm uses the information monitored from the application execution sensors and the performance contracts for the application based on an application signature model to decide what action must be taken.

8.2.1.2 AI planning. Furthermore, we can find AI techniques not only predicting behaviors or situations but also managing workflows among machines of a distributed system. These methods are basically AI planning, methods for planning, and scheduling events using as guide a set of operators and a set of observations. Some works done by Deelman et al. [4] and Gil et al. [5] show methods for scheduling jobs on a grid environment generating, for each job, resource requirements and available resource workflows. These workflows are searched and used by AI planning methods to schedule the application execution matching resource requirements with resource availability.

8.2.1.3 Semantic techniques. Another AI approach to improve the management and adaption of applications is to use semantics. On the basis of the principles of the semantic representation systems, there are some ideas presented about ordering grids and clouds toward an architecture in which information and services are given a well-defined meaning, thus better allowing computers and people to work in cooperation. Acting above syntactic or static valuable rules, by relating systems, resources, and applications, some approaches look for ordering the cloud using logical and coherent matchings between user, resource, and application. These approaches are no more than ideas and research challenges yet, and there are some skeptics about the viability of semantic processes in high performance computing (HPC). Although some works and outlines can be found in the overview done by De Roure et al. [6] and Ejarque et al. [7], exposing the current research on the ontology-based resource management is shown in this chapter.

8.2.1.4 *Expert systems and genetic algorithms.* There are a lot of approaches dedicated to use expert systems and genetic algorithms for self-configuring systems. All these approaches are not directly oriented to the management of clouds or distributed systems, but they give the idea of AI methods for automatically configuring and optimizing a tasks system, such as the ones by Wolpert et al. [8], Sirlantzis et al. [9], and Rahman et al. [10]. These methods, combining classifiers with AI methods, can be used as reference for the management and planning of autonomic systems and clouds.

But AI approaches usually have to be built and validated by experts, or once a model is found, it is very difficult to renew it, and the search process must be repeated. Machine learning techniques supply a new vision of the modeling process, letting us to find these system models without the explicit requirement of experts and the ability of being able to update the model in a more easy way.

8.2.2 Machine Learning Approaches

Although some AI planning and other AI methods have been created to self-optimize or self-configure grid and cloud executions, some problems are related to lack of adaptation, uncertainty of the model, or extreme complexity of the system to build a model by experts or single patterns. To solve these problems, one very relevant solution is machine learning, which allows the creation of decision and classification models of very complex systems from the examples of the same system, in an easy way to update that models, or being possible to make a model that is general or specific enough, extracting the knowledge directly from the system execution and its environment.

Machine learning mines for data, obtaining the relevant information and attributes from it, creating the model that explains the system, and finally using the model to make decisions. The machine learning techniques consist, generally, on collecting a *training data set* from the system with data composed of system values and response attributes and creating a model through induction, able to explain these examples, expecting that new data will fit in.

The machine learning techniques are divided into supervised learning (such as classification and regression), unsupervised learning (discover the relationship between the input data), clustering (find similarities on data), and reinforcement learning (select the best decision from the past experiences and feedback). Here, we discuss briefly about instance-based learning techniques as part of the supervised learning and reinforcement learning (RL) as the two most applied group of techniques in grid and cloud management. Also, feature and example selection are techniques important in the learning process and also important to understand how the examined system works.

8.2.2.1 *Instance-based learning.*

Instance-based machine learning, as part of the supervised learning techniques, allows to predict from a system and its set of resources and elements information that is often not clear at simple sight, often fuzzy, and also inaccurate, uncertain, or incomplete. After obtaining this information, we can use it to create a classifier model or regression model, and obtain from that information the one required to improve the decision making process. Then, the model is able to predict or estimate this useful information, also showing what kind of relation exists between observed data and system behavior, letting us to understand the system better.

For this prediction process, we need to choose suitable prediction algorithms, computationally light but able to obtain good results once trained with data from various workloads. Also, we need to obtain a good training set (a set of data containing labeled instances from representative executions) and another test (or validation) set. If, after training, the predictor guesses are close to the correct values on the test set, we expect that they will also be correct on future data sets. Figure 8.1 shows the basic schema of a supervised machine learning process.

Before the cloud, when all the research was based on the grid model, some methods and solutions were created for grid self-management and adaption of the system to the applications running on it. For example, some works like [11] presented a comparison of different machine learning algorithms such nearest-neighbor, weighted-average, and locally-weighted polynomial regression, upon the resource managing PUNCH framework, to model and predict application performances in order to be able to allocate or schedule the application in a grid

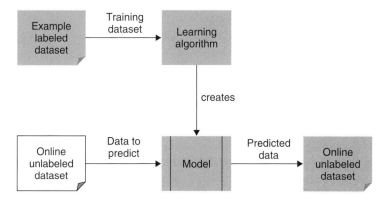

Figure 8.1   Supervised machine learning schema.

environment. Job and resource scheduling is a problem when expert systems and policy-based algorithms become expensive or too complex, so we need another cheaper and more simple system for doing it.

Other works use machine learning on self-management, focusing specifically on self-healing and fault diagnosis. Detecting failures in resources and applications, and also the root of failures, has become a very interesting area where inductive learning methods are also applied. Approaches such the one presented by Hofer and Fahringer [12] shows an application-specific fault diagnosis based on indicators, symptoms, and rules. For this approach, two techniques have been used: a supervised classification to find the reason of the failure and clustering techniques to find what failures are the result of the same cause. Other works such as those presented by Zhang et al. [13] focus explicitly on regression functions to find memory leaks. Also, works by Alonso et al. [14–16] presented a framework for monitoring a complex web application server and estimate, through learning and regression techniques, the time until fault of the server caused by resource leaking, such as memory or CPU. It also proposes a technique for detecting the root cause component of the fault. All these supervised learning techniques are usually combined with macropolicies and utility functions, where, depending on the results, a set of specific decisions are taken in order to adjust the system according to the prediction. Example given, Poggi et al. [17–19] presented a framework where, depending on user modeling predictions, machines are set up or shut down, saving energy by closing as many web servers as possible, keeping the users predicted as "customers" in the on-line machines.

Thanks to the appearance of the Weka Toolkit [20], several autonomic computing researchers have been able to introduce machine learning into their work as well as improve them. Wildstrom et al. [21–23] presented an approach for online hardware reconfiguration using algorithms for rules and decision making. Currently, researchers who wish to introduce some ML techniques into their approaches have the possibility of using that toolkit. With a better research on machine learning applications, the autonomic computing approaches will be improved in a better way.

8.2.2.2 *Reinforcement learning.*
Reinforcement learning is the problem faced by an agent that must learn behavior through trial-and-error interactions in a dynamic environment [24]. As Kaelbling states, there are two main strategies for solving reinforcement learning problems: first, to search the space of behaviors in order to find one that performs well in the environment, by work in genetic algorithms and genetic programming and second, to use statistical techniques and dynamic programming methods to estimate the utility of taking actions in states of the world. While supervised learning involves learning from labeled examples provided by an external supervisor, in reinforcement learning, an agent must be able to learn from its own experience.

Current self-management approaches tend to apply the second kind of reinforcement techniques, as it is easier to be applied to handle system drifts and changes. This kind of reinforcement basically consists on defining a function, representing the system goal to be maximized. This goal usually is the benefit obtained by the system expressing all the revenues and costs of it; the resources or power consumption to be reduced; or any random variable representing weighted factors from the system expressing the interests of the system manager.

The learning process consists on learning what policies or actions must be applied given the system status, observing the results of applying them, and modifying the decision maker depending on the observed results. Policies and actions are basically operations or sets of operations done to elements from the system. These policies and actions are ranked for each situation or status by their maximum expected return for the goal function in a determined number of steps, so the decision maker selects the best ranked action given a specific status, and depending on the result, the ranking is modified. At long term, the ranks may converge to an optimal ⟨status,action⟩, whether the system does not change dramatically its configuration (Fig 8.2).

The implementation of learning algorithms is based on dynamic programming, showing the ranking function as a recursive formula, looking for the maximum return of a function at infinite steps forward. So the evaluation of each ⟨status, action⟩ pair could be defined as

$$Q(s, a) = \Sigma_{s'} E[R|s', \pi] P(s'|s, a),$$

where s is the status, π is the policy being followed, a is the action being evaluated, R is the return for the goal function, and s' is the each possible status

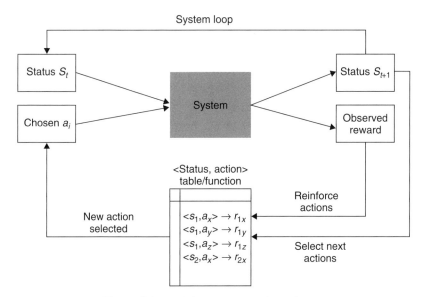

Figure 8.2 Reinforcement-learning schema.

resulting after applying a to s. The probabilities and expectations are trained by running examples and modified online with each resolution after applying the selected actions for each state. Specifically, the expectation is trained as a recursive Bellman equation

$$E[R|s_t] = r_t + \gamma E[R|s_{t+1}],$$

where the direct reward r_t and the future expected reward are weighted depending on the importance of the immediate results.

In the simplest case, the set of states and actions are discrete, and we can have a map with each estimation for each state. But as seen in the previous definition, the ⟨status, action⟩ space can be incredibly large depending on the system, as large as the amount of states and actions that can be reached and performed. This makes the problem of action selection expensive in space and in time. Thus, it is often interesting to learn the $Q(s, a)$ function using induction learning techniques, complementing the reinforcement. The expectations can be replaced by estimations, so $\hat{Q}(s, a)$ function can be trained, acting as a reward function for each action.

As a simple practical example, let us imagine a system where several actions can be chosen to be applied given a status, and from scratch, all actions are equally scored in order to obtain a good result for this status. By choosing the first random action, the system can check after if the result has been good or bad, so the score of this action will be modified by raising or degrading it. By repeating this for some iterations, the scores for each action/status will indicate what actions have been better rewarded or penalized for each status. At this point, the system can continue by choosing the most scored actions given a specific status, as well as continue evaluating them. At long term, the scorings in a stable system may converge to a stable ranking action/status. More about the mathematics and basics on reinforcement learning can be found in the works and tutorials of Kaelbling et al. [24], Sutton and Barto [25], and Bertsekas and Tsitsiklis [26].

The reinforcement-based algorithms have become recently trendy because of the potential and promising results on autonomic computing self-management, as explained by Tesauro et al. [27]. In reinforcement learning based algorithms, rules and policies can be prioritized and applied depending on the success in previous executions. As the autonomic computing control loop adjusts all the systems, the reinforcement learning modules can evaluate applied policies and decide which ones must be used or avoided in the next iteration. Approaches such as those proposed by Vienne and Sourrouille [28] use reinforcement learning to select the rules to be applied for each decision to be taken, having goals such as a performance level for resources. Other works such as those presented by Vengerov and Iakovlev [29, 30] and Perez et al. [31] show frameworks for scheduling resources using reinforcement learning, using as objective function the optimization of the utility of resources. There are also other works such as the one presented by Fenson and Howard [32] that show approaches for self-rejuvenation and self-management functions using these reinforcement learning techniques.

8.2.2.3 Feature and example selection. Feature selection is the process of, given a huge set of observed data, finding those variables and data that are really useful from those that only bring noise or are irrelevant. Usually, we can obtain several data from observing a grid or cloud system. But in order to predict or estimate a specific interesting value, not all the collected data is useful, and including this data in the learning process makes it harder in space or in time, or makes it inaccurate due to noise.

It also happens when applying knowledge to the self-methods, as all the self-management aspects must use the correct information to work: self-healing systems must have the correct signals to detect anomalies and predict the causes and consequences for failures. Self-protection systems must be able to see the indicators about attacks when attackers are cloaked or use evasion techniques. And the self-optimization and self-configuring systems must know about the execution and requirements of applications, as well as utility of the resources in order to find the best configuration and best performance. The feature selection methods are in charge of discovering the relevant attributes from all the data obtained.

Also, there is the example selection process. When finding or training a model, the examples must be "good" examples that cause minimum noise and are less redundant as possible. This example selection process is not trivial, as you want to keep enough examples for your data set to be general enough, or to give enough support to cases hard to be learned. Blum and Langley [33] described in their survey the basics of feature and example selection.

Furthermore, some works on self-management used to perform a principal component analysis (PCA) [34, 35] in order to find the attributes that can differentiate better our examples. PCA is a feature selection technique by itself, but it can also find the combination of features that are most relevant, and is able to treat high dimensional data, reducing the complexity without losing much information. Zheng et al. [36, 37] proposed the utilization of PCA for detecting and locating anomalies in large-scale clusters. In their approaches, after collecting data and finding the combination of attributes that better differentiate the collected examples, an outlier detection is done using the cell-based detection algorithm. Other works such as those by Lakhina et al. [38, 39] use the PCA method to detect anomalies in network traffic, also using classification techniques (supervised learning) to identify network anomalies.

8.3 INTRODUCING POWER-AWARE APPROACHES

At this moment, green computing is being introduced into self-management middleware, adding to these frameworks new advanced management mechanisms to successfully optimize the resource usage to add energy efficiency as one of the fundamental parameters in its management. The current main power-saving techniques applied in the cloud and grid environments are related with virtualization technology, the turning on/off policies, the DVFS, and the hybrid architecture on data centers.

These four technical areas are being covered by approaches that include ad hoc methods, heuristic algorithms, and determined policies, taking into account that this requires experts in the whole system and changes in the system make these approaches to require updates. In order to introduce the *intelligent management*, letting the system to configure and adapt to changes easily, machine learning techniques are starting to be used to improve the previous methods.

8.3.1   Use of Virtualization

Virtualization is one of the key technologies in the cloud that has enabled cost reduction and easier resource management for service providers. As virtualization allows to run several processes, jobs, guest operating system (OS), and also VMs in one or several physical machines or platforms, it makes possible the consolidation of applications, multiplexing them onto physical resources, and supporting isolation from other applications sharing the same physical resource. Tasks can be run everywhere and migrated without many handicaps on the base systems, but VMs can also perform optimizations over the host OS and physical machine. The cloud and grid infrastructure take advantage from this technology, decoupling them from the system software of the underlying resource, and letting the movement and migration of VMs in order to place them in the most convenient place.

The main goals of virtualization are to provide a confined environment where applications can be run, limit hardware resource access and usage or expand it transparently for the applications, adapt the runtime environment to the application, use dedicated or optimized OS mechanisms for each application, and manage the whole applications and processes running within VMs. Primet et al. [40] provided a survey on current OS and network virtualization solutions for grids. The summarized basic aspects are listed in the following.

- *OS-Level Approaches*. These approaches allow to virtualize a physical server enabling multiple isolated and secure virtualized servers to run on a single physical server. No guest OS is used, and applications are run in a specific view of the only one OS as if they were running alone on the OS. Some of these approaches are VServer [41], a kernel patch based on partitioning, using a "security context" inside a UNIX OS, FreeBSD Jail [42], and also Solaris Containers, OpenVZ, etc.
- *Emulators*. VMs simulate the complete hardware used by a guest OS. VMware [43] is a virtualization software for machines based on x86 architecture, where virtualization works at the processor level, the VM privileged instructions are trapped and virtualized by the VMware process, and other instructions are directly executed by the host processor. All hardware resources of the machine are also virtualized. Other solutions are Microsoft VirtualPC, VirtualBox, QEMU [44], etc.
- *OS in User Space*. These approaches provide virtualization through the execution of guest OSs directly in user space. Some approaches are User Mode

Linux [45], which allows launching Linux OS as applications of a host machine running Linux, as well as coLinux, Adeos, L4Ka-based projects, etc.

- *Paravirtualization*. The paravirtualization technique does not necessarily simulate the hardware but instead offers a special API requiring modifications to the guest OS. The hardware resources are abstract resources not necessarily similar to the actual hardware resources of the host machine. Xen [46] is a VM monitor for x86 architecture, allowing the concurrent executions of multiple OS while providing resource isolation and execution confinement between them. Other projects using this paravirtualization approach are Denali and Trango.

- *Hardware-Assisted Virtualization*. This virtualization allows to run unmodified guest OS, giving to the VM its own hardware. This is possible thanks to an increased set of processor instructions provided by Intel VT (IVT [47]), AMD (AMD Pacifica x86 virtualization [48]), IBM (IBM Advanced POWER virtualization [49]), and Sun (Sun UltraSPARC T1 hypervisor [50]).

This virtualization technology has become a hot research topic for maximizing benefits, but it has added another layer of abstraction to the management systems, preventing or making more complex the conventional energy management for performing efficiently or correctly in virtual environments. During the past years, works such as the ones presented by Vogels [51] studied the consolidation advantages using virtualization while other works such as the ones from Nathuji et al. [52] have widely explored its advantages from a power efficiency point of view.

Recent work by Petrucci et al. [53] proposed a dynamic configuration approach for power optimization in virtualized server clusters and outlined an algorithm to dynamically manage it. All these techniques, applying consolidation policies, are mainly focused on a power efficiency strategy, taking into account the cost of turning on or off the resources, as it is explained in Section 8.3.2. Also, VM migration and VM placement optimization are studied in the work of Liu et al. [54] to improve the VM placement and consolidate in a better way. On the basis of these works, Goiri et al. [55, 56] introduced the SLA-factor into the self-managing virtualized resource policies. The SLA-driven policies look for facilitating resource management in service providers, allowing cost reduction and at the same time the SLA agreed QoS fulfillment.

So virtualization technology has opened a wide research area to explore in order to optimize cloud and grid management. The capability to isolate jobs inside VMs, and migrate the VMs along physical machines, permits optimizing task placement and dynamic scheduling without much overhead. Recently, machine learning techniques are being applied to help manage virtualized platforms to decide what VMs must be started and how to schedule them, complementing information about the system or predicting useful information a priori. Also, these techniques are able to look for patterns in the behavior of the VMs and host systems to predict their imminent and long-term behavior, making long-term policies more accurate. These approaches are often applied within turning on and off machines or DVFS, as described in the following section.

8.3.2   Turning On and Off Machines

Another energy-saving technique is to determine when a node should be turned off to save power consumption or when to turn it on to bring service to the cloud. These actions can be driven by fixed policies or heuristics, depending on the load being received at each moment or the load expected in a short-term window time. For example, first approaches such as the ones presented by Pinheiro et al. [57], Chase et al. [58], and Elnozahy et al. [59] applied turning on and off mechanisms for power management, as well as by Chen et al. [60] that includes predictive techniques in a proactive and also reactive automated control.

Goiri et al. [56, 61] showed that a decrease in the number of online machines obviously assures a decrease in the consumed power and also the system is often unable to bring service given an increase in load, so a compromise between online machines and energy saving must be found. In their works, this decision is driven by means of two thresholds: the minimum *working nodes* threshold λ_{min}, which determines when the provider can start to turn off nodes, and the maximum *working nodes* threshold λ_{max}, which determines when the provider must turn on new nodes. After modeling specific loads and machine consumptions, using different kinds of scheduling and consolidation techniques, the influence of the turning on/off thresholds by showing the SLA and the power consumption can be evaluated. Adequate thresholds can be obtained (this time empirically) in order to decide how many physical machines are needed online, and the rest can be shut down.

On the basis of the same works, Berral et al. [62] proposed a framework that provides an *intelligent* consolidation methodology using different techniques such as the turning on/off machines, power-aware consolidation algorithms, and machine learning techniques to deal with uncertain information while maximizing performance. Using the information from system behaviors, the machine learning approach used a learned model to predict power consumption levels, CPU loads, and SLA timings and to improve scheduling decisions. The experiments performed using grid workloads and a cloud environment demonstrate how consolidation-aware policies give a better energy efficiency than nonconsolidating ones, and also, the machine learning model responses are much better with respect to power consumption when the information obtained from users and tasks is not uniformly accurate.

This turn-on and off technique is also applied by the approach of Kamitsos et al. [63], which sets unused hosts in a low consumption state to save energy. In their approach a Bellman's function based on dynamic programming and recursive methodology, is used to decide when to set into sleeping status those hosts that are not needed, maintaining the other submitted jobs in the online hosts.

But turning on and off is not limited to machines. Components and resources can also be started up and shut down. Policies can decide whether to set on or off the full machine or a specific component, and Tan et al. [64] showed a framework for controlling the system power manager using reinforcement learning algorithms. In this case, the learner uses a Q-learning algorithm, a popular algorithm originally designed to find policies in Markovian decision processes.

Summarizing, the main point in the strategy of turning on and off devices, machines, or resources is to determine at each time what to switch on and off in order to optimize our goals. Optimal policies select at the best time those elements that are necessary for the good performance of the system and maintain the rest in a shutdown or low consumption status. These selection policies can be improved or optimized by reinforcement learning techniques by adjusting the number of elements that are not necessary in the system at each time, and inductive learning techniques can be used to expect the amount of resources to be used a priori in order to plan on/off device schedulers.

8.3.3 Dynamic Voltage and Frequency Scaling

Another currently applied technique to obtain power efficiency is the Dynamic Voltage and Frequency Scaling (DVFS). The DVFS techniques allow the reduction of voltage and frequency, providing substantial saving in power at the cost of slower program execution. Current microprocessors and other kind of resources allow the power management by DVFS, reducing the voltage and frequency of the given devices and allowing the application of policies in order to provide saving in power at the cost of not offering the full capabilities of the resource when not needed. As Chen [60] stated in his work, new power-saving policies, such as DVFS or turning off idle servers, can increase hardware problems and the problem of meeting SLAs in reduced environments. This can be solved by adding a smarter scheduling policy to dynamically turn off idle machines to reduce the overall consumption.

Earlier works on DVFS were mainly focused on power saving on mobile devices while preserving QoS and performance. The first approaches on power management used turning server machines on and off, one of the firsts to combine turning on and off with dynamic voltage scaling in data centers and was studied by Elnozahy et al. [59], exploring the use of DVFS to respond to changes in server demands. This work and the work of Sharma et al. [65] have referred to applying these techniques for server applications, and from here on, other works have developed this idea toward refining and detailing the scheduling procedure in order to decide when and how much voltage and frequency scaling should be applied at each moment.

Reinforcement learning is also used to drive DVFS policies as shown in the works of Tesauro and Kephart et al. [66, 67]. Their goal was to let the system learn the actions to be performed with a trial-and-error method, making decisions by selecting the expected best action and checking the results, allowing to adjust the ranking for the action. In this case, actions control the CPU frequency, adjusting it to the optimal trade-off between electric consumption and response time for transactional jobs running on the given data center.

So tuning the processor voltage and frequency has become an effective method to reduce the power consumption while tasks can be delayed in time, or the required performance is under the system capabilities. The main challenge here is to know when it is possible to scale up and down voltage/frequency, what policies are optimal to decide when and how much to do so, and what trade-off must be permitted between power consumption and QoS. Current techniques using heuristics and fixed policies are being improved using reinforcement learning methods, finding the optimal policies that assure the lowest power consumption without compromising the performance and service requirements.

8.3.4   Hybrid Nodes and Data Centers

Finally, another power-saving technique is to design data centers and machines as a hybrid architecture, combining high performance and energy-efficient elements, to switch between one another in the order of the load requirements. Turning on and off resources or modifying their consumption, by switching resource usage between the ones designed for energy saving or high performance, could be a good option depending on the situation or requirement of the load. Combining low power designed processors with high performance processors or devices in the same data center provides the system a new degree of freedom, so that there is no need to modify the elements in the system but to use those elements that are more prepared to our energy or performance needs.

This combination of different kind of resources has been tackled in local hosts in some approaches such as the ones presented by Chun et al. [68], who proposed a hybrid architecture that combines the selective usage of processors with different power consumptions and performances in a single host in order to apply local energy-saving policies only when allowed by performance. Also, approaches presented by Nathuji et al. [69] state that a good approach for saving energy is mixing low power systems and high performance ones in the same data center.

Machine learning techniques applied to the utilization of hybrid data centers are still in process, as the current state-of-the-art research applies the knowledge of induction learning works for improving autonomic computing approaches. Again, the works of Goiri et al. [70, 71] have included learned functions [62] as management parameters. Also the techniques presented in Section 8.2, referring to search policies applying reinforcement learning [27, 66], can be applied in order to decide whether to use a determined kind of resource or another. In conclusion, the use of hybrid systems is giving new elements to *intelligent* decision makers, so new solutions are able to optimize, thus regulating the properties of individual elements in order to adapt them to loads and scenarios or instead to decide to select specific elements to fit the specific scenario.

8.4   EXPERIENCES OF APPLYING ML ON POWER-AWARE SELF-MANAGEMENT

After looking at all the works and publications referring to the new techniques improving power-aware self-managed systems using data mining and machine learning, some experiences on applying them to specific cases of study are shown here. These cases of study refer to the conclusions obtained from some works mentioned before [56, 62], where a cloud is scheduled and managed in a power-aware way, using learning techniques over some of the previously explained power-saving techniques.

8.4.1 Case Study Approach

The techniques proposed for this case study are consolidation techniques, reducing power consumption by scheduling virtualized environments, all without degrading their SLAs in excess. This scheduling policy must consolidate workloads preserving the QoS of the tasks inside a virtual machine (VM) each one, agreed on the SLA and taking into account virtualization overheads such as VM creation, checkpointing, and migration. All of this can be achieved by unifying different provider requirements in addition to power consumption, namely, reliability and dynamic SLA enforcement (be able to recover from an SLA violation during the execution).

This is done by deciding the best location for executing a new job depending on the resources it requires in order to fulfill its SLA, derived from the information of the system, including job execution and node status. The proposed policy periodically calculates whether to move jobs in order to improve global system utility. This approach decides when and where to create VMs containing jobs, migrate them, and start up or shut down physical machines, also being aware that machines in a cluster can have different properties so the data center can be heterogeneous.

In this section, the whole proposed policy is summarized and evaluation and improvements obtained in a first implementation, including virtualization overheads and power consumption, are shown. It is compared against common policies in a simulated environment that models a virtualized data center, mainly focusing in this occasion on CPU and memory as a resource. This first proof of concept is based on HPC jobs and uses deadlines as QoS metric in order to define the SLA constraints. After evaluating the different power-aware techniques, the concept of ML is introduced in order to improve the consolidation mechanisms by predicting information about SLAs before applying the selected schedule.

8.4.2 Scheduling and Power Trade-Off

The scheduling policy consists on finding, on each system status change the optimal combination of <host,VM> to use as input information: the hardware and software requirements of the VM, the amount of resources required, the resources offered by the host machine (i.e., those that are available), the energy consumption of the physical machine, the user SLA constraints, and the reliability of the host. It gives to each machine a dynamic score depending on these parameters and solves the allocation of each VM on the best machine, taking into account all those different factors.

A scheduling round is started when a new VM enters the system, a VM finishes its execution, a violation in the SLA is detected, or the reliability of a machine changes. Then, the best <host,VM> combination is found by mapping all the tentative VM allocations in a scoring matrix filled with the benefit of each VM temptatively hold in each host machine. Each score indicates the utility (or benefit) of holding a VM in a host by aggregating all the penalties related to migration, leaving a machine empty or violating the SLA or any other needed constraint. At this point, a hill-climbing search algorithm [72] finds the set of movements optimizing the <host,VM> matrix. And finally, the system performs the set of operations decided by the new schedule (creation, migration, etc.). Each value in this scoring matrix represents the score (penalization) of hosting a VM in a specific host, including the costs involved due to virtualization, power consumption, reliability, and dynamic SLA enforcement. For example, those hosts that cannot hold a VM, due to insufficient free resources or hardware/software constraints, have an ∞ value; those hosts that have jobs that can be consolidated are penalized in order to force the scheduler to empty it; and the opposite happens with the nearly full hosts that can allocate jobs from nearly empty hosts. In this case, those hosts that have the lowest value for a VM are supposed to be the most suitable.

As it has been already presented, consolidation is applied in order to turn off unneeded machines (also referred as nodes). Nevertheless, a too aggressive node-turning-off policy will result in not offering enough resources to execute tasks, while a passive one will have bigger power consumption. This trade-off depends on the λ_{min} and λ_{max} thresholds. The effect of these two thresholds has been tested by executing the grid workload on top of the simulated data center using the score-based (SB) policy, which is the one that makes a more aggressive consolidation. This allows evaluating the influence of the turning on/off thresholds by showing the client satisfaction and the power consumption, respectively.

Figure 8.3 shows that waiting for the nodes to reach a high utilization before adding new nodes (high λ_{max}) makes the power consumption smaller. In the same manner, the earlier the system shut downs a machine (high λ_{min}), the smaller the power consumption is. It demonstrates how turning on and off machines in a dynamic way can be used to dramatically increase the energy efficiency in a consolidated data center. On the other hand, as shown in Figure 8.4, client satisfaction decreases when the turn on/off mechanism is more aggressive and it shuts down more machines (in order to increase energy efficiency). Therefore, this is a trade-off between the fulfillment of the SLAs and the reduction of the power consumption, whose resolution will eventually depend on the provider interests. For instance, if the provider is having a high client satisfaction, the provider could decide to reduce it slightly while keeping the client between the limits of satisfaction, allowing a greater power reduction by letting resources unused and shutting down them.

Fortunately, average threshold values give a balanced trade-off between energy and QoS. Experimentally, we found that our environment's best values are $\lambda_{min} = 30\%$ and $\lambda_{max} = 90\%$ to ensure almost complete fulfillment of the SLAs while

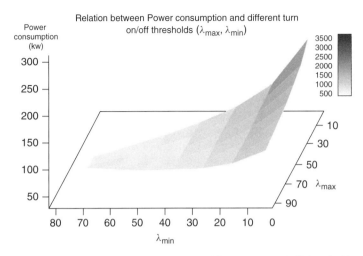

Figure 8.3   Power consumption using different turn on/off thresholds.

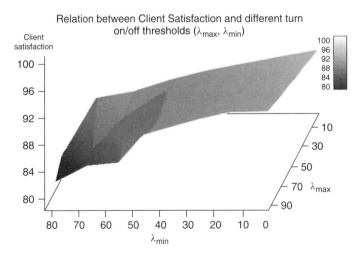

Figure 8.4   Client satisfaction using different turn on/off thresholds.

getting substantial power reduction. A next step would be to dynamically adjust these thresholds, which is part of our current and future work.

8.4.3   Experimenting with Power-Aware Techniques

The experimental environment set for this case study consists of the simulation of a whole virtualized data center with 100 nodes using the EEFSIM, a cloud simulator designed following the procedure in [73] but focused on the energy consumption and on the CPU power scheduling among VMs. The simulator loads a workload trace, simulates the execution on several machines with different a configuration for each one, and generates the output results using different global scheduling policies. In addition, these machines can be dynamically turned on/off. The simulation takes into account both the physical machine boot time and power consumption and the VM creation and migration power consumption.

The data center is configured to have different types of nodes according to their virtualization overheads, basically different times for creating and migrating VMs. The presented approach intends to take benefit of consolidation in large virtualized data centers executing HPC jobs. For this reason, the evaluation of this case study has been performed using a grid workload, which has been obtained from Grid5000 [74] on the week that starts on Monday, October 1, 2007. The set of policies is evaluated according to different metrics including number of used nodes, CPU usage, power consumption, and SLA fulfillment. The consolidation of the system is reflected in the average number of working nodes (those that are executing a VM), online nodes (those that are turned on) and the power consumption.

Once the parameters to turn nodes on/off have been set up, according to the number of loaded nodes, a first basic experimentation is run. The energy efficiency and SLA fulfillment is compared with four static scheduling algorithms that do not use migration: a random scheduler (RD), which assigns the tasks Random; a Round-Robin scheduler (RR), which assigns a task to each available node; a backfilling strategy (BF), which tries to fill the nodes as much as possible; and a basic version of the presented SB policy (SB0), which just takes into account hardware and software requirements (this time, without migrations).

The results presented in Table 8.1 show the power consumption (Pwr) and different metrics such as the average number of nodes that are actually working (Work), the average number of nodes running (ON), the client satisfaction (S), and the delay. It shows that nonconsolidating policies such as *Random* and *RR* give poor energy efficiency while violating a significant amount of SLAs: they give the worst results on both criteria. *BF* gets better SLA fulfillment with substantially lower cost, as it uses fewer nodes. Finally, the SB policy, which works with no penalties on virtualization overheads, behaves very similar to the *BF* policy.

Using the nonmigrative approach, the SB policy is tested with different configurations (SB1 = SB0 + P_{virt}, SB2 = SB1 + P_{conc}) to test the impact of considering virtualization overheads (creation and concurrency). Table 8.2 shows that SB1, which adds VM creation overheads, makes a better use of the resources

TABLE 8.1   Scheduling Results of Policies Without Migration

	Work/ON	CPU, h	Pwr, kW	S, %	Delay, %
RD	24.3 / 41.7	14597.2	1952.1	33.2	474.5
RR	23.5 / 51.9	11844.2	2321.0	60.4	338.4
BF	10.1 / 22.2	6055.3	1007.3	98.0	10.4
SB0	9.9 / 22.4	6055.3	1016.3	98.2	10.4

TABLE 8.2 Scheduling Results of Score-Based Policies Without Migration

	λ	Work/ON	CPU	Pwr	S	Delay
SB0	30–90	9.85/22.4	6055.3	1016.3	98.2	10.4
SB1	30–90	10.2/22.2	6055.3	1006.7	97.9	10.7
SB2	30–90	10.2/23.0	6068.5	1038.5	99.2	8.8
SB2	40–90	10.4/19.0	6055.1	880.5	98.1	10.2

TABLE 8.3 Scheduling Results of Policies With Migration

	λ	Work/ON	CPU	Pwr	S	Delay	Mig
DBF	30–90	9.7/21.3	6056.0	970.6	98.1	12.9	124
SB	30–90	9.7/21.0	6055.8	956.4	99.1	9.0	87
SB	40–90	9.7/18.3	6055.8	850.2	98.4	9.9	87

because it takes into account the time to create VMs and selects better nodes to perform the same. In addition, it gets worse by SLA fulfillment than solving it using the SB2, taking care of concurrency overheads, which also causes a small increment on the power consumption. This is because considering the cost of concurrent creation of VMs reduces the consolidation ratio but gets better SLA fulfillment since it produces faster VM creation.

Even though it implies a power consumption increment regarding the basic configuration, the client satisfaction has been increased and allows the provider to make a more aggressive turn on/off policy resulting in higher consolidation and lower power consumption.

Table 8.3 shows the results of the SB scheduler when introducing the capability to migrate VMs in order to get a better consolidation, applying a *dynamic backfilling* (DBF) policy. This applies *BF* and migrates VMs between nodes in order to provide a higher consolidation level and the SB proposal using all the penalties, including the migration capability.

Results for DBF showed a small improvement in power efficiency with respect to nonmigration variation while getting much better consolidation, caused by the overheads introduced by migrating VMs, and the SLA fulfillment is maintained at a medium level as in the nonmigration approach. On the other hand, the SB policy takes virtualization overheads such as creation and migration into account, which makes it to get more client satisfaction. And as in the previous experiment, to give a measure of the improvement in client satisfaction terms, a similar SLA fulfillment target for DBF and the best of the SB configurations are set, getting more aggressive turn on/off parameters of $\lambda_{min} = 40\%$ and $\lambda_{max} = 90\%$. Using this configuration, a reduction in the data-center power consumption of 15% with regard to *BF* is obtained and of 12% when compared with the dynamic variant. These experiments demonstrate how the SB proposal gets the best power consumption and SLA fulfillment, as it takes into account the migration overheads.

TABLE 8.4 **Score-Based Scheduling Results With Different Costs**

C_e	C_f	Work/ON	CPU	Pwr	S	Delay	Mig
0	40	10.4/22.9	6055.2	1036.4	99.3	8.6	0
20	40	9.7/21.0	6055.8	956.4	99.1	9.0	87
60	100	9.3/22.0	6057.8	998.8	97.7	11.2	432

One of the advantages of the power-aware SB policy is that it can be easily configured according to the provider's requirements. In this experiment, some variants of the policy are shown: without penalizing empty hosts, using typical parameters penalizing empty hosts and rewarding near full host, and using more aggressive parameters for consolidation.

Table 8.4 shows the results of tweaking this parameter. The first variant does not penalize empty hosts, which implies lower consolidation and worst power performance, and also does not migrate any VMs since the fillable reward is not worthwhile. The second variant uses the values used in the previous experiments, which include the empty host penalization and gets better consolidation while maintaining similar client satisfaction as it performs an accurate number of migrations. Finally, the third variant has been set up with aggressive parameters, getting the best consolidation in terms of working nodes, but getting poor energy efficiency and lower SLA fulfillment, which is mainly because it rewards the occupation and penalties too much empty hosts, which implies a big amount of migrations.

8.4.4 Applying Machine Learning

Applying consolidation mechanisms such as the dynamic backfilling described earlier helps to improve power consumption, but often this can be improved or easily done by applying knowledge-based techniques such as machine learning. A first approach focused on learning about the behavior of a job being placed in a specific target physical machine is discussed here.

The machine learning-aided policy implements a dynamic BF scheduler, using the information provided directly by the user and using as decision maker the results of performance and power consumption estimators. When having a pair <host,VM> in the schedule, the impact the job will cause in the potential host machine is predicted using context information. So the scheduler has better confidence on the fact that the selected jobs schedule will not degrade their performance violating SLAs.

When a new job arrives, the system will try to allocate it, so the candidate moves will be like "move VM v from its initial temporary host to host h". Performing a sample run the scheduler can obtain for each combination of VMs and hosts the performance result of this combination, joint with the information of the VM (size, requirements, resources used) and the information of the host (capacity, resources available, information about the other jobs running on it).

From here on, using machine learning algorithms, a model can be set up, learning the relation of these elements with the response variable (the resulting performance of the job). This model will help the decision maker in predicting values of expected performance for a given combination before the schedule is applied.

Running some experimentation over the presented scheduling problem the behavior and performance of different scheduling policies are evaluated using three different workloads (an HPC, a transactional workload, and an heterogeneous one) and using the turn on/off thresholds $\lambda_{min} = 30\%$ and $\lambda_{max} = 60\%$. Also, some scheduling algorithms are evaluated for comparing them with the power-aware one: Random and RR do not use any user-provided information about the VMs and do not consolidate. For BF and DBF, the user provides for each VM a figure indicating which percentage of a CPU capacity should suffice to satisfy the VM SLAs. The algorithms trust this figure as totally reliable and therefore will make decisions that may fit the SLAs very tightly, thus saving power. The algorithm applying machine learning does not use the user-provided information but only uses information about the online requirements of the VM in order to expect the SLA future performance. The results are presented in Table 8.5.

The results obtained using the grid workload show that nonconsolidating policies such as Random and RR give a poor energy efficiency while violating some SLAs. BF and DBF fulfill all SLAs with substantially lower cost, and machine learning performs almost perfectly with respect to SLAs (as we have seen that

TABLE 8.5   Scheduling Results

	Work	ON	CPU usage, h	Power, kW	SLA, %
		Grid workload			
RD	16.51	40.76	6017.85	1671.16	88.38
RR	16.11	41.37	5954.91	1696.66	85.99
BF	10.18	27.10	6022.34	1141.65	100.00
DBF	9.91	26.46	6104.33	1118.86	100.00
Machine learning DBF	15.04	37.92	6022.27	1574.78	99.69
		Service workload			
RD	218.46	400.00	75336.88	19784.38	100.00
RR	290.99	400.00	78419.97	19761.54	100.00
BF	108.79	352.88	59792.09	16257.26	100.00
DBF	108.79	352.88	59748.10	16229.22	100.00
Machine learning DBF	99.61	270.50	61379.38	13673.71	100.00
		Heterogeneous workload			
RD	224.08	400.00	82137.27	19763.63	88.53
RR	260.66	400.00	84432.96	19713.72	94.20
BF	110.85	330.19	65894.46	16304.38	99.50
DBF	111.03	329.07	66020.58	16214.49	99.59
Machine learning DBF	124.20	307.89	68554.01	15110.33	98.63

predictions for SLA fulfillment are very accurate). The reason is that the user-provided figures for the tasks are very close to the real ones (and the load quite steady), so the BF algorithms will take many decisions that will not violate any SLA but that look too risky to machine learning, which pays a high price in consumption for its caution.

On the service workload, the machine learning scheduler is much better with respect to energy consumption. Note that in this workload, all the schedulers executed all the tasks, so all SLAs were fulfilled. The workload has a very variable CPU usage. This means that the user-provided estimation about the CPU to be used for the given jobs will be a large overestimation for large periods (while it was very tight on the grid workload), and power will be unnecessarily wasted. The machine learning scheduler, as being more conservative, estimates better the SLA fulfillment, and so it is able to reduce the power consumption just to the required.

Finally, the results obtained using the heterogeneous workload are, as expected, a mix of the two previous workloads. In this case, the overall SLA fulfillment by the ML is worse by about 1%, but its overall power consumption is better by about 10%.

8.4.5 Conclusions from the Experiments

These works and experimentations applying power-aware mechanisms introducing machine learning are looking to provide a vertical and intelligent consolidation methodology to deal with uncertain information, keeping in mind performance and power consumption. And the results obtained indicated that significant improvements can be achieved using machine learning models to predict schedules a priori and decide the movements and operations to be done within scheduling functions.

The experiments using the grid workload demonstrate how non-consolidation policies result in poor energy efficiency compared to consolidation-aware policies such as the BF and scoring policies. Also, the machine learning method is close enough to these models that use external information with respect to SLA fulfillment (performance) and much better with respect to power consumption when the information provided by the users is not uniformly accurate, or the information is more variable.

8.5 CONCLUSIONS ON INTELLIGENT POWER-AWARE SELF-MANAGEMENT

As discussed in this chapter, data-center power-aware management techniques are mainly focused on the autonomic computing field, so power optimization is done automatically by middleware software in order to deal with the big growth of the IT infrastructure and the cloud. Furthermore, this automated control is not just having refined policies, as the systems usually change, requiring the need of self-adaption. While autonomic computing properties have several techniques to update their status, the most useful and currently applied techniques are data mining and machine learning. These learning methods not only can model the system with good accuracy from examples but also let adapt the model to changes easily.

From the four power-saving strategies presented in this chapter (virtualization, turning on/off machines, DVFS, and hybrid architecture), recent approaches have started to apply knowledge-based systems, improving the techniques or allowing to apply them all together. Instance-based learning can help to complement inexistent or uncertain data when dealing with observed data, and also, it can find new data or discover hidden variables from the system that can be relevant for determining the behavior of the resources, the clients, or any other element of the cloud or data center. Furthermore, reinforcement learning techniques are being applied to decide changes in the system policies, so at each step in the system loop the learner can observe how good was the previously applied action and then prioritize again the actions and modify its policies. Also feature and example selection, with techniques such as PCA, are being applied to identify which information obtained from the system is useful, erase outliers and not correct examples, and find the important attributes that influence most of the system.

In the case of virtualization, most machine learning techniques are dedicated to predict the system status before and after each creation, migration, or modification of VMs. Estimating a priori the benefit of realizing a VM operation can reduce the number of useless operations or drawbacks after operating. Consolidation is applied as the principal technique when virtualizing, so estimating and predicting the correct level of consolidation helps to find the optimal power-saving schedule in the system.

The policies based on turning machines on and off tend to apply reinforcement learning and dynamic programming formulas, mainly because deciding when to turn needed or unused machines on or off is an *easy* policy to learn from executions. The same happens with DVFS, where resources and devices are regulated using reinforcement learning too, so finding good policies in order to adjust levels of power or processor frequency in an optimal way can be achieved by trial and error during executions and is also a very adaptive technique.

Finally, the construction and usage of hybrid architecture allow the manager to decide what kind of resources to use in each moment. If self-adaptive management is applied using techniques such as load prediction, RL learned policies and a priori data obtainment, the decision maker has some help to find the most suitable resource scheduling, evaluating not only the load but also the kind of resources to be used, always using power consumption as one of the most important parameters.

To conclude this chapter, there are many works applying knowledge and learning techniques in self-management, but there is more to do so that traditional decision makers can evolve into new ones that are able to detect the relevant information to describe a system, adapt the decision rules when the system changes or when new elements enter into it, or use the experience and learn to predict future states of the system and act in consequence. There are several useful works on machine learning and data mining awaiting to be applied in cloud and data-center management situations, and there are many works in self-management awaiting to be improved and upgraded using new knowledge and learning methods.

REFERENCES

1. Koomey J. Estimating regional power consumption by servers: A technical note; 2007.
2. Vraalsen F. Performance contracts: Predicting and monitoring grid application behavior; 2001.
3. Fahringer T. Automatic performance prediction of parallel programs; 1996.
4. Deelman E, Blythe J, Gil Y, Kesselman C. Mapping abstract complex workflows onto grid environments; 2004.
5. Gil Y, Deelman E, Blythe J, Kesselman C, Tangmunarunkit H. Artificial intelligence and grids: workflow planning and beyond; 2004.
6. Shadbolt NR De Roure D, Jennings NR. The semantic grid: past, present, and future; 2005.
7. Ejarque J, de Palol M, Goiri I, Juliã F, Guitart J, Badia R, Torres J. Exploiting semantics and virtualization for sla-driven resource allocation in service providers; 2010.
8. Wolpert DH, Wheeler KR, Tumer K. Collective intelligence for control of distributed dynamical systems; 1999.
9. Sirlantzis K, Fairhurst MC, Hoque S. Genetic algorithms for multi-classifier system configuration: A case study in character recognition. In: MCS '01: Proceedings of the 2nd International Workshop on Multiple Classifier Systems. London: Springer-Verlag; 2001. pp. 99–108.
10. Rahman AFR, Fairhurst MC, Hoque S. Novel approaches to optimized self-configuration in high performance multiple-expert classifiers. In: IWFHR '02: Proceedings of the 8th International Workshop on Frontiers in Handwriting Recognition (IWFHR'02). Washington (DC): IEEE Computer Society; 2002. p. 189.
11. Kapadia NH, Fortes JAB, Brodley CE. Predictive application-performance modeling in a computational grid environment; 1999.
12. Hofer J, Fahringer T. Grid application fault diagnosis using wrapper services and machine learning. In: ICSOC '07: Proceedings of the 5th International Conference on Service-Oriented Computing. Berlin, Heidelberg: Springer-Verlag; 2007. pp. 233–244.
13. Zhang Q, Cherkasova L, Mi N, Smirni E. A regression-based analytic model for capacity planning of multi-tier applications. Cluster Comput 2008;11(3):197–211.
14. Alonso J, Torres J, Silva LM, Griffith R, Kaiser G. Towards self-adaptable monitoring framework for self-healing. Technical Report TR-0150, Institute on Architectural issues: scalability, dependability, adaptability, CoreGRID - Network of Excellence; 2008 July.
15. Alonso J, Berral JL, Gavaldà R, Torres J. Predicting web application crashes using machine learning. In: Submitted to ACM/IFIP/USENIX 10th International Middleware Conference; 2009 Nov; Urbana Champaign (IL).

16. Alonso J, Torres J, Gavalda R. Predicting web server crashes: A case study in comparing prediction algorithms. In: ICAS 2009: Proceedings of the International Conference on Autonomous Systems; April 20–25, 2009. Valencia, Spain.

17. Poggi N, Moreno T, Berral JL, Gavaldà R, Torres J. Web customer modeling for automated session prioritization on high traffic sites. In: UM '07: Proceedings of the 11th International Conference on User Modeling. Berlin, Heidelberg: Springer-Verlag; 2007. pp. 450–454.

18. Moreno T, Poggi N, Berral JL, Gavaldà R, Torres J. Policy-based autonomous bidding for overload management in ecommerce websites. In: Proceedings of the Group Decision and Negotiation 2007. Springer-Verlag; Montreal, Canada; 14-1 of May, 2007; pp. 162–166.

19. Poggi N, Moreno T, Berral JL, Gavaldí R, Torres J. Self-adaptive utility-based web session management. Comput Netw 2009;53(10):1712–1721.

20. Witten Ian H., Frank E., Hall Mark A.: Data Mining: Practical Machine Learning Tools and Techniques (Third Edition). Morgan Kaufmann; January 2011; 629 pages; ISBN 978-0-12-374856-0.

21. Wildstrom J, Witchel E, Mooney RJ. Towards self-configuring hardware for distributed computer systems. In: ICAC '05: Proceedings of the 2nd International Conference on Automatic Computing. Washington (DC): IEEE Computer Society; 2005. pp. 241–249.

22. Wildstrom J, Stone P, Witchel E, Dahlin M. Machine learning for on-line hardware reconfiguration. In: Proceedings of the 20th International Joint Conference on Artificial Intelligence; Hyderabad, India; 2007. pp. 1113–1118.

23. Wildstrom J, Stone P, Witchel E. Autonomous return on investment analysis of additional processing resources. In: ICAC '07: Proceedings of the 4th International Conference on Autonomic Computing. Jacksonville, Florida, USA; June 11–15, 2007; IEEE Computer Society; 2007. p. 15.

24. Kaelbling LP, Littman ML, Moore AW. Reinforcement learning: A survey. J Artif Intell Res 1996;4:237–285.

25. Sutton RS, Barto AG. Reinforcement learning: an introduction (Adaptive Computation and Machine Learning). The MIT Press; Massachusetts, USA; 1998.

26. Bertsekas DP, Tsitsiklis JN. Neuro-Dynamic Programming (Optimization and Neural Computation Series, 3). Athena Scientific; 1996 May.

27. Tesauro G, Jong NK, Das R, Bennani MN. On the use of hybrid reinforcement learning for autonomic resource allocation. Cluster Comput 2007;10(3):287–299.

28. Vienne P, Sourrouille J-L. A middleware for autonomic qos management based on learning; 2005.

29. Vengerov D, Iakovlev N. A reinforcement learning framework for dynamic resource allocation: First results. In: ICAC '05: Proceedings of the 2nd International Conference on Automatic Computing. Washington (DC): IEEE Computer Society; 2005. pp. 339–340.

30. Vengerov D. A reinforcement learning framework for online data migration in hierarchical storage systems. J Supercomput 2008;43(1):1–19.

31. Perez J, Germain-Renaud C, Kégl B, Loomis C. Utility-based reinforcement learning for reactive grids. In: ICAC '08: Proceedings of the 2008 International Conference on Autonomic Computing. Washington (DC): IEEE Computer Society; 2008. pp. 205–206.

32. Fenson E, Howard R. Reinforcement learning for autonomic network repair. In: ICAC '04: Proceedings of the 1st International Conference on Autonomic Computing. Washington (DC): IEEE Computer Society; 2004. pp. 284–285.

33. Blum AL, Langley P. Selection of relevant features and examples in machine learning. Artif Intell 1997;97(1–2):245–271.

34. Duda RO, Hart PE, Stork DG. *Pattern Classification*. 2nd ed. Wiley-Interscience; New York, USA; 2000.

35. Smith LI. A tutorial on principal components analysis; 2002.

36. Zheng AX, Lloyd J, Brewer E. Failure diagnosis using decision trees. In: ICAC '04: Proceedings of the 1st International Conference on Autonomic Computing. Washington (DC): IEEE Computer Society; 2004. pp. 36–43.

37. Zheng Z, Li Y, Lan Z. Anomaly localization in large-scale clusters. In: 2007 IEEE International Conference on Cluster Computing; Texas, USA; 2007 Sept. pp. 322–330.

38. Lakhina A, Crovella M, Diot C. Mining anomalies using traffic feature distributions. SIGCOMM Comput Commun Rev 2005;35(4):217–228.

39. Lakhina A, Crovella M, Diot C. Diagnosing network-wide traffic anomalies; 2004.

40. Vicat-Blanc Primet P, Gelas J-P, Mornard O, Mon Divakaran D, Bozonnet P, Jan M, Roca V, Giraud L. State of the art of os and network virtualization solutions for grids. Technical report, INRIA, September 2007. "Delivrable #1: HIPCAL ANR-06-CIS-005".

41. Linux Vserver. Linux vserver. Available at http://linux-vserver.org/Paper; April 2012.

42. The FreeBSD Project. The freebsd documentation project; 2007.

43. VMware Inc. Vmware. Available at http://www.vmware.com/; April 2012.

44. Bellard F. Qemu, a fast and portable dynamic translator. In: ATEC '05: Proceedings of the Annual Conference on USENIX Annual Technical Conference. Berkeley (CA): USENIX Association; 2005. pp. 41–41.

45. Hoxer H, Buchacker K, Sieh V. Implementing a user mode linux with minimal changes from original kernel. In: Proceedings of the 2002 International Linux System Technology Conference; Cologne, Germany; 2002. pp. 72–82.

46. Barham P, Dragovic B, Fraser K, Hand S, Harris T, Ho A, Neugebauer R, Pratt I, Warfield A. Xen and the art of virtualization. In: SOSP '03: Proceedings of the 19th ACM Symposium on Operating Systems Principles. New York: ACM; 2003. pp. 164–177.

47. Intel. Intel virtualization technologies. Available at http://www.intel.com/technology/virtualization/; April 2012.

48. AMD. Pacifica x86 virtualization. Available at http://enterprise.amd.com/us-en/AMD-Business/Business-Solutions/Consolidation/Virtualization.aspx; April 2012.

49. IBM. IBM advanced power virtualization. Available at http://www-03.ibm.com/systems/p/apv/f; April 2012.

50. Sun Microsystems. Sun ultrasparc t1 hypervisor. Available at http://opensparc-t1.sunsource.net/specs/Hypervisor-api-current-draft.pdf; April 2012.

51. Vogels W. Beyond server consolidation. Queue 2008;6(1):20–26.

52. Nathuji R, Schwan K, Somani A, Joshi Y. Vpm tokens: virtual machine-aware power budgeting in datacenters. Cluster Comput 2009;12(2):189–203.

53. Petrucci V, Loques O, Mossé D. A dynamic configuration model for power-efficient virtualized server clusters. In: 11th Brazillian Workshop on Real-Time and Embedded Systems (WTR); 2009 May 25; Recife, Brazil.

54. Liu L, Wang H, Liu X, Jin X, He WB, Wang QB, Chen Y. GreenCloud: a new architecture for green data center. In: 6th International Conference on Autonomic Computing and Communications, Industry Session; 2009 June 15–19. Barcelona, Spain: ACM; 2009. pp. 29–38.

55. Goiri I, Julià F, Ejarque J, De Palol M, Badia RM, Guitart J, Torres J. Introducing virtual execution environments for application lifecycle management and SLA-driven resource distribution within service providers. In: Proceedings of the 8th IEEE International Symposium on Network Computing and Applications (NCA'09); 2009 July 9–11; Cambridge (MA). pp. 211–218.

56. Goiri I, Julià F, Nou R, Berral J, Guitart J, Torres J. Energy-aware scheduling in virtualized datacenters. In: Proceedings of the 12th IEEE International Conference on Cluster Computing (Cluster 2010); 2010 Sept 20–24; Heraklion, Crete, Greece.

57. Pinheiro E, Bianchini R, Carrera EV, Heath T. Load balancing and unbalancing for power and performance in cluster-based systems. In: Workshop on Compilers and Operating Systems for Low Power, Volume 180. Citeseer; 2001. pp. 182–195.

58. Chase JS, Anderson DC, Thakar PN, Vahdat AM, Doyle RP. Managing energy and server resources in hosting centers. SIGOPS Oper Syst Rev 2001;35(5):103–116.

59. Elnozahy E, Kistler M, Rajamony R. Energy-efficient server clusters. In: Falsafi B, Vijaykumar T, editors. Volume 2325, Power-Aware Computer Systems, Lecture Notes in Computer Science. Berlin, Heidelberg: Springer; 2003. pp. 179–197.

60. Chen Y, Das A, Qin W, Sivasubramaniam A, Wang Q, Gautam N. Managing server energy and operational costs in hosting centers. ACM SIGMETRICS Perform Eval Rev 2005;33(1):303–314.

61. Fitó JO, Goiri I, Guitart J. SLA-driven elastic cloud hosting provider. In: Proceedings of the 18th Euromicro Conference on Parallel, Distributed and Network-based Processing (PDP'10); 2010 Feb 17–19; Pisa, Italy. pp. 111–118.

62. Berral J, Goiri I, Nou R, Julià F, Guitart J, Gavalda R, Torres J. Towards energy-aware scheduling in data centers using machine learning. In: 1st International Conference on Energy-Efficient Computing and Networking (eEnergy'10), University of Passau; 2010 Apr 13–15 Germany; 2010. pp. 215–224.

63. Kamitsos I, Andrew L, Kim H, Chiang M. Optimal sleep patterns for serving delay-tolerant jobs. In: 1st International Conference on Energy-Efficient Computing and Networking (eEnergy'10), University of Passau; 2010 Apr 13–15; Germany.

64. Tan Y, Liu W, Qiu Q. Adaptive power management using reinforcement learning. In: ICCAD '09: Proceedings of the 2009 International Conference on Computer-Aided Design. New York: ACM; 2009. pp. 461–467.

65. Sharma V, Thomas A, Abdelzaher T, Skadron K, Lu Z. Power-aware qos management in web servers. In: RTSS '03: Proceedings of the 24th IEEE International Real-Time Systems Symposium. Washington (DC): IEEE Computer Society; 2003. p. 63.

66. Tesauro G, Das R, Chan H, Kephart JO, Lefurgy C, Levine DW, Rawson F. Managing power consumption and performance of computing systems using reinforcement learning. In: Advances in Neural Information Processing Systems 20; Vancouver, Canada; 2008.

67. Kephart JO, Chan H, Das R, Levine DW, Tesauro G, Rawson F, Lefurgy C. Coordinating multiple autonomic managers to achieve specified power-performance tradeoffs. In: ICAC '07: Proceedings of the 4th International Conference on Autonomic Computing. Washington (DC): IEEE Computer Society; 2007. p. 24.

68. Chun B, Iannaccone G, Iannaccone G, Katz R, Gunho L, Niccolini L. An energy case for hybrid datacenters. In: Workshop on Power Aware Computing and Systems (HotPower'09); 2009 Oct 10; Big Sky (MT).

69. Nathuji R, Isci C, Gorbatov E. Exploiting platform heterogeneity for power efficient data centers. In: Proceedings of the IEEE International Conference on Autonomic Computing (ICAC'07); 2007 Jun 11–15; Jacksonville (FL).

70. Goiri I, Fitó O, Julià F, Nou R, Berral J, Guitart J, Torres J. Multifaceted Resource Management for Dealing with Heterogeneous Workloads in Virtualized Data Centers. In: Proceedings of the 11th ACM/IEEE International Conference on Grid Computing (Grid 2010); 2010 Oct 25–29; Brussels, Belgium.

71. Goiri I, Guitart J, Torres J. Characterizing cloud federation for enhancing Providers' profit. In: Proceedings of the 3rd International conference on Cloud Computing (CLOUD 2010); 2010 Jul 5–10; Miami (FL). pp. 123–130.

72. Russell S, Norvig P. Artificial intelligence: a modern approach. Pearson Education; 2003.

73. Nou R, Kounev S, Julià F, Torres J. Autonomic QoS Control in Enterprise Grid Environments using Online Simulation. J Syst Softw 2009;82(3):486–502.

74. The Grid Workloads Archive. 2009. Available at http://gwa.ewi.tudelft.nl; April 2012.

CHAPTER 9

ENERGY EFFICIENCY METRICS FOR DATA CENTERS

JAVID TAHERI and ALBERT Y. ZOMAYA

9.1 INTRODUCTION

Over the last few decades, computers have become more integral to our lifestyles, from exchanging simple e-mails to complex discoveries and breakthroughs in science, engineering, and medicine. Increasing computational power combined with advances in data storage and global networking are major components of such shift in our quality of life [1]. Despite such countless benefits, computers and more specifically data centers—buildings that accommodate a large number of networked computer servers—have come under scrutiny because of their consumption of massive amounts of energy [2]. For example, the energy used by US servers and data centers has doubled for the period from 2000 to 2006. Because these capital-intensive facilities are essential to our current digital economy, rapid increase in data centers' energy consumption and interest in opportunities to create efficiencies in the use of such facilities have became a major concern in recent years.

9.1.1 Background

In general, a data center is composed of the following components: (i) computer servers to process data, (ii) storage elements to store data, and (iii) network equipment to communicate, that is, send/receive, data. Data centers also contain non-IT equipment such as (i) power conversions to provide electricity, (ii) backup facilities to maintain data reliability, and (iii) environmental control units to maintain proper temperature and humidity of IT equipment.

Energy-Efficient Distributed Computing Systems, First Edition.
Edited by Albert Y. Zomaya and Young Choon Lee.
© 2012 John Wiley & Sons, Inc. Published 2012 by John Wiley & Sons, Inc.

As our economy and society shifts from paper to digital management systems, data centers invade all sectors of our economy and play a major role in communication, business, academic, and governmental systems. Small companies usually house their data centers within their commercial buildings. Large companies with higher needs, however, usually construct special buildings (thousands of square feet sometimes) to host their large number of servers. Such data centers are used by many other third party organizations (i.e., universities, municipalities, and government institutions) to perform information management and communication functions.

9.1.2 Data Center Energy Use

Regardless of their use and configuration, data centers are usually more energy hungry than other buildings, mainly because of high power requirements by IT equipment as well as their corresponding cooling infrastructures. In fact, data centers can use as much as 40 times more energy than conventional office buildings [1]. Thus, large data centers resemble industrial facilities more than commercial buildings in many cases. For example, data centers in the United States consumed about 1.5% of national electricity in 2006. Power density of data centers is also increasing every year as the number of servers is expected to continually grow to expand current data center capabilities. In such a trend, squeezing more computing power into less space can easily result in more than 20 kW for a single rack of servers. According to AFCOM's Data Centre Institute [3], future power failures/availability can interrupt more than 90% of data centers in the next 5 years if appropriate actions are not foreseen. As a result, energy-intensive data centers will consume a significant portion of our future energy and produce massive greenhouse gas emissions.

9.1.3 Data Center Characteristics

Data centers are housed in specially designed buildings, either new or retrofitted, without windows and circulation of fresh air to host only computers (not people). They may range from small rooms (server closets) within conventional buildings to dedicated large buildings (enterprise-class data centers) to house servers, storage devices, and network equipment. Data center rooms are filled with racks of servers, storage devices, and network equipment. Data centers also include power delivery systems to provide backup power, regulated voltage, and AC/DC convertors. Before reaching IT equipment racks, electricity is first supplied to an uninterruptible power supply (UPS) unit to prevent experiencing power disruptions that can cause serious business disruptions as well as data losses. UPS prevents such interruptions as it uses the AC power to keep its batteries (DC) fully charged at all times. Power from these batteries is then reconverted from DC to AC before leaving the UPS and enters the power distribution unit (PDU) that directly feeds IT equipment racks. Each server, in turn, receives AC power from PDU and converts it to low voltage DC to be used by its many internal components, including the central processing unit (CPU), memory, disk drives, chipset,

TABLE 9.1   Sample Component Peak Power Consumption for a Server. Reproduced with permission from [4].

Component	Peak Power (kW)
CPU	80
Memory	36
Disks	12
Peripheral slots	50
Motherboard	25
Fan	10
PSU losses	38
Total	251

fans. The DC voltage serving the CPU is further adjusted by load-specific voltage regulators (VRs) before reaching the CPU. Table 9.1 shows typical power levels for various server components [4]. Electricity is also routed to storage devices and network equipment to facilitate storage and transmission of data. As a result, the continuous operation of IT equipment and power delivery systems generates a significant amount of heat that must be removed from the data center so that its equipment can operate properly. Cooling in data centers is usually provided by computer room air-conditioning (CRAC) units, while the entire air handling unit (AHU) is usually situated on the floor. The AHU is responsible for conditioning and distributing air throughout the data center using its fans, filters, and cooling coils. In a typical cooling procedure, air enters the top of the CRAC unit and is conditioned as it passes across coils containing chilled water, which is pumped from a chiller located outside the room. The conditioned air is then supplied to IT equipment (primarily servers) through a raised floor plenum, for example, fans within servers pull in this cold air to reduce their heat. The warmed air, in this case, stratifies toward the ceiling and reaches CRAC intake.

Because most air circulation in data centers is limited to internal zones, majority of data centers are designed to allow entering only a small amount of outside air. Therefore, many data centers provide no ductwork for outside air to directly enter their internal zones—outside air is only provided to adjacent zones such as office space in such designs. Others admit only a relatively small percentage of outside air to pressurize their zones.

Data centers use a significant amount of energy to supply three key components: IT equipment, cooling, and power delivery. Heat removal procedures cannot be efficiently designed without careful examination of these components.

9.1.3.1   Electric power. Figure 9.1 symbolically shows how energy is consumed within a typical data center [4, 5]; this also includes equipment that continuously work to ensure uninterrupted execution of primary IT functions. Because IT equipment performs the most critical operations, UPS equipment is designed to maintain their electricity supplies even during major utility disruptions. Data

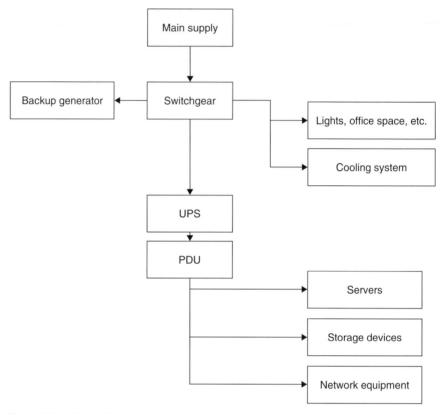

Figure 9.1 Symbolic energy consumption flow of a data center. Reproduced with permission from [4] and [5].

center equipment usually exhibits high power intensities while all electric powers are converted to heat during their processes. For example, a recent survey of power usage in 22 data centers found that a data center's IT equipment alone can use almost between 10 and 100 W/sq ft of raised floor area [6, 7]. Since that report, power intensities have even been increasing over time, largely because of the increasing heat density of data-processing equipment. As a result, power and cooling overheads needed to support IT equipment are almost twice the actual power needs of IT equipment. Overheads are mainly used for power conversions, backup power, and cooling facilities.

Peak power usage for data centers range from tens of kilowatts to tens of megawatts for small to large centers, respectively. Increasing power density is even further worsened when companies are forced to build new data centers. New buildings are necessary in this case not because of the floor space shortage, but for their limited capacity in producing extra power and cooling for new equipment. In fact, this situation has motivated most of the recent works to improve energy efficiency for data centers. Here, reducing power consumption will have a direct impact on reducing the resulting heat. Therefore, existing infrastructure might still be capable of providing power and cooling needs for new expansions to defer many costly investments in future data centers.

9.1.3.2 Heat removal. Maintaining temperature/humidity within specific ranges is the main objective of air-conditioning systems in data centers. Because electronic equipment in confined spaces generate a significant amount of heat, equipment reliability can be seriously jeopardized if it is not adequately/properly cooled. Similarly, high and low relative humidity levels in data centers can significantly increase failure rates of IT equipment. To further explain the importance of a proper cooling infrastructure, consider a fully populated rack of blade servers that require up to 20–25 kW of power to operate [1]. This amount of power is equivalent to the peak electricity demand of about 15 typical California homes [1], but in a much concentrated space (i.e., $2' \times 3.5' \times 6'$). As all this electric power is roughly converted to heat, each rack is expected to further require 20–25 kW of power to support its associated cooling and power conversion equipment. To overcome such cooling/power challenges, many configurations are designed to organize IT equipment inside a data center. Because smaller data centers rarely face such problem, they sometimes arbitrarily place their IT equipment throughout the room. Large data centers, however, use specific configurations to facilitate the cooling process. Figure 9.2 shows a common best practice in which racks are in alternating hot and cold aisles so that the resulting hot air is removed from the overhead. IT equipment, in this case, are mounted in racks that are positioned together in long rows. These racks are then placed on a raised floor that delivers conditioned air. As a standard terminology, the computer room's floor area is always called the *raised floor area*, even though some rooms do not have actual raised floors.

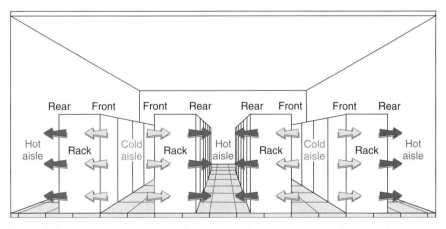

Figure 9.2 A common best arranging practice for cooling servers inside a data center. Reproduced with permission from [1].

9.1.4 Energy Efficiency

Data reliability used to be the only concern of data center designers/operators, with little or almost no focus on energy efficiency. Because of the exponential growth of energy consumption in current data centers, this traditional perspective has recently shifted toward considering energy efficiency as well. As a result, there is a growing interest in energy efficiency as a potential solution to power and cooling limitations of current designs.

9.2 FUNDAMENTALS OF METRICS

Despite the hard work of many agencies around the world, reliable information regarding the total size, power consumption, or efficiency of the data center market is still unavailable [8]. In the absence of such vital information, it is very difficult to predict the growth of the data center industry or even set effective metrics and targets for the industry. To deal with these issues, proper understanding of the scale of the problem to deliver improvements is the first essential step. This can be followed by agreeing on an initial set of measurements and metrics so that data collection can be commenced on a large scale.

9.2.1 Demand and Constraints on Data Center Operators

Incompatible demands and constraints between many organizations—commercial, political, or industrial—and data centers have significantly influenced operation of such centers in recent years. The energy use and environmental impact of data centers also added another dimension of complexity for both operators and policy makers. For example, recent public perception of climate changes substantially influenced our current environmental policies and social responsibilities. Among many IT industries, data centers were also targeted, as they demand very high level of energy consumption—policy makers have identified IT and specifically data center energy consumption as one of the fastest rising sectors—and it is much easier to measure their performance in comparison with other IT sectors. This issue became even more serious as the commodity price of energy has risen sharply in recent years. As a result, data center operators have substantially changed their commercial/business models to match the current high rising cost of energy. Energy security and availability also add to this complexity as the combined pressures of fossil fuel availability, generation, and distribution; infrastructure capacity; and environmental energy policy make the prediction of energy availability and its associated cost almost impossible in the future.

Despite all these constraints, the underlying growth in demand for IT services in business is growing every day. This puts more pressure on IT services and requires better designs to satisfy such exponentially growing requirements. Besides all these complexities, misunderstanding the proper relationship between the falling capital cost of IT equipment and the rising costs of housing and powering of data center creates massive capacity and financial challenges to this very particular sector.

9.2.2 Metrics

As the general concept of energy efficiency and its environmental impact, direct or indirect, become the main concern of many recent developments, data center operators are also expected to measure the efficiency of their facilities. On the basis of this motivation, many agencies worldwide have started working to develop and apply several metrics to measure efficiency of current and future data centers. The EU Data Centre Code of Conduct [9] is a major step in this direction. The scope of metrics in this attempt is only restricted to the data center's mechanical and electrical infrastructure. Thus, these metrics do not reflect the efficiency of IT services (the end product) delivered to users.

9.2.2.1 *Criteria for good metrics.* Appropriate metrics for evaluating energy and power efficiency of data centers are essential, as they can significantly manipulate both organizational profits and environmental goals. These metrics must also be defined very clear and as productive as possible so that data center stakeholders can discuss and make decisions on them. The following criteria are believed to be essential for such metrics [10]:

1. *Intuitive*. Their meaning should be as clear as possible so that just by stating the term one can judge if it should be increased or decreased. Such terms (or terminology) must not be too simple or must not ignore important details, however.
2. *Scientifically Accurate*. The definitions of the metrics must be accurate enough so that they can be precisely deployed.
3. *Granular*. They must be designed so that individual aspects of data centers can be analyzed in manageable chunks.
4. *Nest Together Elegantly*. They must be designed so that they can cover the overall energy efficiency of data centers and nicely complement each other.
5. *Easy to Calculate*. They must be fairly easy to measure/calculate so that data centers can use them to determine the amount of their wasted power and/or energy in any arbitrary practice, process, or configuration.
6. *Easy to Extend*. They must be deployable to both current and future IT hardware products, that is, servers, storage, networking.
7. *Sufficiently Flexible*. They must be flexible to respond to new technologic developments; that is, they must not need to be rewritten on arrival of every new industrial development to increase efficiency in future.
8. *Distinguish between Power and Energy*. These terms are technically and semantically distinct and affect different aspects of data centers; they must be distinguishable in the metrics too.

9. *Precise*. They must avoid ambiguous terms that might be seen similar however very different in semantics; for example, "full load" can be referred
to as both *full compute load* and *full power load*.

9.2.2.2 Methodology. Measurement methodologies must also be designed
along with the metrics so that reasonable approximations of the total environmental and financial cost of services for data centers can be obtained. Many industrial
bodies agree on the following phases for providing better IT energy efficiency for
data centers: (i) determining how efficiently energy is delivered from the power
source to the IT equipment in the facility; (ii) determining how many units of
computing, storage, or networking each IT device can deliver on receiving one
unit of energy; and (iii) determining how many units of useful, end-user work,
each IT service can deliver per benchmark unit of computing. Although the first
phase is more challenging and efficiency metrics are trying to target this part
of the overall holistic energy consumption of data centers, the other two phases
have received more attention from both governmental and industrial agencies.

9.2.2.3 Stability of metrics. To support effective decision making and planning, metrics must be as stable as possible, at the same time as independent as
possible, so that efficiency in varying IT workloads and equipment within a facility can be properly reflected. This goes against the general conception of having
sensitive measures to obtain systems performance in different time frames. This
is mainly because local measures are inherently sensitive to changes with volatile
values.

9.3 DATA CENTER ENERGY EFFICIENCY

There are many opportunities to improve energy efficiency of data centers by
proper analysis of metrics and tools that assist operators in understanding their
facilities and the impact of their choices. However, using a sole metric cannot
provide a valid benchmark for making decisions or build business cases in many
occasions. For example, some metrics only have a very limited scope to measure
efficiency of either mechanical or electrical equipment housed within a data
center. It is also unwise to compare delivery efficiency of two operators solely
based on their local infrastructure measurement, as it is only one component
of the delivery chain and cannot properly reflect the efficiency of the whole IT
equipment, software packages, or system architectures.

9.3.1 Holistic IT Efficiency Metrics

IT efficiency metrics should be able to report both energy and financial costs of
delivering IT services. In fact, both business cost modeling and internal/external
carbon markets require at least this level of capability so that effective
management information about IT services can be delivered and used for future

predictions. As a result, data center infrastructure analysis metrics must be reversible and independent of IT equipment to determine the total energy use of an IT device within a data center.

To provide such holistic measurements, a number of individual, single value measures and metrics have been already proposed to indicate efficiency of various layers of the IT delivery chain, that is, software efficiency, IT hardware utilization, IT hardware efficiency, and data center efficiency. Although the product of component metrics seems to be descriptive enough to reflect the overall efficiency of data centers, operators should also avoid such flawed approaches with misleading results. In fact, such metrics are particularly weak in all forms of economic analysis and should not be used to determine marginal costs.

To better demonstrate why simple and sole energy metrics can mislead management decisions, an analogy is made between electrical efficiency of a data center and the fuel efficiency of a vehicle. Table 9.2 shows sample characteristics of three vehicles for this purpose. On the basis of this table, the 38-ton articulated lorry with 240 ton miles per gallon should be chosen for ordinary shopping! An obvious wrong decision would be one based on the simple metric of getting the maximum ton-mileage per each gallon of petrol. In fact, such inappropriate decision is made simply because the vital information of their suitability to our use (shopping) is naively discarded; thus, the metric led to a wrong conclusion.

Table 9.3 shows how similarly weak designed metrics for IT equipment consolidation in data centers can result in a wrong decision as well. In this example, an operator spends significant capital, operational expense and tolerates migration risk to reduce its power use to another service platform. Assume the old platform is several years old and the IT equipment draws 200 kW at the power supply unit (PSU), while the new more efficient platform draws only 50 kW at the PSU. As shown in this table, the facility has a fixed overhead of 100 kW, a rated IT electrical load of 500 kW and would draw 850 kW from the utility feed at full rated IT load. Here, a simple metric is used to measure how much percentage of the input power is actually delivered to the IT equipment: the old and new platforms would have the efficiency of $200/400 = 50\%$ and $50/175 = 29\%$, respectively. As a result, the old platform is favored to the new platform despite its obvious advantages. Such wrong decision could have also been avoided if more sophisticated metrics that consider fixed and proportional consumption ratios were used instead.

TABLE 9.2   Sample Vehicles for Shopping. Reproduced with permission from [8].

	38-Ton Articulated	4-Ton Van	Family Hatchback
Fuel economy (miles per gallon)	8	30	36
Load weight (tons)	30	3	0.5
Load economy (ton miles per gallon)	240	90	30

TABLE 9.3 **Sample Characteristics of Two Platforms. Reproduced with permission from [8].**

	Old Platform	New Platform
Fixed utility load of facility (kW)	100	100
Related IT load of facility (kW)	500	500
IT electrical load (kW)	200	50
Proportional electrical load (kW)	300	75
Total utility load (kW)	400	175
Achieved performance	200/400 = 50%	50/175 = 29%

9.3.1.1 *Fixed versus proportional overheads.*

Fixed and proportional overhead scalars provide a more intuitive understanding of the overall facility efficiency to operators of data centers. Determining such overheads is particularly very useful when modular provisioning is used.

Fixed overheads provide a deep understanding of the unchangeable committed power to a facility. Facilities with high fixed overheads should be upgraded, decommissioned, or filled to their best practice to minimize the impact of such fixed losses. Proportional overheads, on the other hand, provide information to discover the usual complex relationship between the energy consumption of a center and its IT load. Such analysis can also help to predict the level of energy reduction as the IT load is reduced.

9.3.1.2 *Power versus energy.*

Power and energy are different. In fact, distinguishing between these terms is extremely helpful to highlight the benefits that would be achieved by improving the metrics. Several improvements only save power, others only save energy, and most save both. In a data center, peak power demand determines the size of UPS, cooling system, and other utility feeders. Therefore, saving power tends to reduce the capital expenditure (CapEx) for new data centers and to defer expensive capacity expansions for existing ones. As a result, it will have much greater economical impacts on data centers than does the utility bills, also referred to as *operating expenditure (OpEx)*. Thus, the majority of data center operators are more interested in saving power to reduce or defer CapEx. Despite this, policy makers and corporate level enterprise sustainability initiatives are more interested in energy, as it determines the quantity of fuel that must be burned at power plants with its requisite emissions of carbon dioxide and other pollutants.

The following points highlight major differences between these two terms: (i) power is a spot measurement at a particular point in time, while energy is consumption over a period of time; (ii) power is measured in kilowatts (kW), while energy is measured in kilowatt hours (kW h); and (iii) the peak or highest power drawn at any point of time is the major concern for power-based designs, while the summation of energy consumption over a period of time is the major concern for energy-based designs.

These distinctions are also important because these terms are completely independent design entities; a system may draw a large amount of power without using

TABLE 9.4   Power versus Energy. Reproduced with permission from [10].

Power	Energy
Kilowatts	Kilowatt hours
Capacity constraints	Electricity bill
Demand charge/utility feeders	Kilowatt hour charge
No pollution	CO_2 emission
Spot measurement, at a peak time	Sum, over a period of time
Full load efficiency	Part load efficiency

much energy, and vice versa. For example, a 1500-W hair dryer that is used only 5 min a day consumes 15 times more instantaneous power than a 100-W light bulb does in a whole year. In this case, however, the hair dryer uses only about one-twentieth as much energy as the light bulb. For data centers, although an IT manager can save energy by hibernating its idle servers at night, the peak power demand cannot be reduced. This is because the site's physical infrastructure must still be able to support peak computing demands when all servers are fully deployed.

Despite their fundamental differences, because many analysts and even a very few energy experts still inaccurately use the terms power and energy interchangeably, future discussions of data center energy/power efficiency must be technically precise to avoid ambiguities. Table 9.4 compares power and energy in terms relevant to data center operators.

9.3.1.3   Performance versus productivity. Data centers must simultaneously consider computational needs, network availability needs, and environmental goals in their designs. Although some of these goals may look conflicting, decision makers still need to critically think to find better ways to implement such systems. For example, data center cooling system design engineers are already accustomed to search for chillers that use the fewest possible kilowatt per ton to produce chilled water. Although improving cooling efficiency will have a positive impact on the overall energy efficiency of the whole system, these facility experts may still need to think why chilled water needs to be at the 42°F (6°C), which is commonly specified for an office building, instead of 49°F (9°C) that is more appropriate for computer rooms. In fact, compared with chillers working at 42°F (6°C), those working at 49°F (9°C) would deliver more cooling efficiency, as they do not need dehumidification anymore.

Analogous examples exist on the IT hardware side of servers and storage as well. For example, rather than using the most efficient 7200 rpm storage drives, storage managers can use lower speed drivers to store less frequently used data because power consumption by such devices is almost cubically related to their spindle speed. As a result, 7200-rpm drives consume eight times more power than 3600-rpm drives. Thus, by storing rarely used data on slower drives or tapes, both power and energy consumption can be significantly reduced; this kind of changes may be economically implemented without necessarily buying new or more hardware. Business-line application managers might similarly choose to consolidate few servers via virtualization rather than replacing them with new more efficient ones during the next IT hardware refresh cycle. In this case, virtualization can immediately cut power and/or energy by 90%, whereas implementing more efficient power supplies for all hardware devices may only save 5–10% of the total power and/or energy. Therefore, although energy efficiency initiatives should not jeopardize IT availability as well as its associated quality of service in any condition, data center decision makers can still find efficiency opportunities by considering new configurations that better serve their firms' business needs.

9.3.2 Code of Conduct

The Code of Conduct (CoC) [9] is a voluntary initiative aimed to bring interested stakeholders, manufacturers, vendors, consultants, and utilities together to follow and abide a set of agreed commitments. The CoC has been created in response to the current increasing energy consumption in data centers as well as the current demands to reduce its related environmental, economic, and energy supply security impacts. The CoC also aims to inform and stimulate data center operators/owners to reduce their energy consumptions without hampering their critical functions as data centers. This mission can be achieved by better understanding the energy demands within data centers and raising their awareness so that best energy-efficient practices become natural solutions in many cases.

9.3.2.1 Environmental statement. Electricity consumed in data centers, including enterprise servers, Information and Communication Technology (ICT) equipment, cooling and power equipment, is expected to substantially contribute to electricity consumption in the EU commercial sector 1 in the near future. Western European electricity consumption of 56 TW h per year is estimated to increase to 104 TW h per year by 2020 [9]. Such an increase in projected energy consumption poses serious problems for the EU energy and environmental policies if they are not dealt with properly. As a natural solution, energy efficiency of data centers should be maximized so that negative impacts of such developments, such as the carbon emissions, and strain on infrastructure associated with increases in energy consumption are efficiently mitigated.

9.3.2.2 Problem statement. Data centers have traditionally been designed with large tolerances for operational and capacity changes as well as possible future expansions. These factors led to power consumption inefficiencies, as many today use design practices that have been outdated. As a result, for many data centers, only a small fraction of the input power is consumed by its IT systems. Furthermore, most enterprise data centers are even equipped with redundant power and cooling systems to provide higher levels of reliability, while IT systems are frequently utilized at lower averages. Ensuring availability and its associated costs was usually ignored as risks to business performance when energy costs used to be relatively small in comparison to the IT budget. Environmental responsibilities were also not applicable to IT departments in many cases. With rise of energy prices, energy consumption of individual data centers became increasingly important where the operational energy expenditures of its associated ecological impacts play one of the most important roles in determining the overall ownership cost of a data center. Increasing willingness of manufacturers and vendors toward energy efficiency of data centers also led to many techniques (e.g., simply using existing power management technologies) to reduce the total cost of ownership (TCO) without prohibiting its initial costs. Despite many businesses that are already aware of their environmental impacts and ways to reduce them, many data center operators are still unaware of the financial, environmental, and infrastructural benefits they can make by improving the energy efficiency of their facilities.

To make data centers more energy efficient, a multidimensional challenge to optimize power distribution, cooling infrastructure, IT equipment, and IT output must be simultaneously dealt with. Although many activities have been initiated within the industry with numerous vendor-specific products and services, there are still the risks of confusion, mixed messages, and uncoordinated activities. For example, independent assessment and coordination tailored to European conditions, such as climate and energy markets regulation, are required to recognize different energy-saving opportunities.

9.3.2.3 *Scope of the CoC.*

Definition of "data center" in CoC includes all buildings, facilities, and rooms, containing enterprise servers, server communication equipment, cooling equipment, and power equipment. CoC covers two main areas: IT and facility loads. IT load relates to all IT equipment consumption efficiencies and can be described as the IT work capacity available for a given IT power consumption; facility load relates to all mechanical and electrical systems such as cooling systems (chiller plant, fans, and pumps), air-conditioning units, UPS, PDU that support IT electrical loads.

Although it is very important to consider utilization as a part of efficiency in data centers, CoC considers each center as a complete system and tries to optimize the whole system (IT systems and infrastructures) to efficiently deliver all sorts of desired services. Similar to other industrial bodies, CoC will also initially use the ratio of IT to facility load as a key metric in assessing infrastructure efficiency; this metric will be known as *facility efficiency*. The CoC also targets the efficiency of IT equipment on receiving their delivered power; this will be known as *asset efficiency*. The CoC will adopt more comprehensive metrics to cover IT system designs, IT hardware asset utilizations, and IT hardware efficiencies once these preliminary metrics are developed and agreed.

The CoC deals with both equipment and system-level issues. At the equipment level, CoC covers typical deployment of all required sort of equipment within a data center to provide data, internet, and communication services. Rack-optimized and non-rack-optimized enterprise servers, blade servers, storage and networking equipment, CRAC units, UPSs, PDUs, and other miscellaneous equipment such as lighting are all included in this level. At system level, CoC proposes actions to minimize overall energy consumption related to equipment interactions and system designs for both existing and new data centers. Improved cooling designs, correct sizing of cooling, correct air management and temperature settings, and correct selection of power distribution are sample examples for such actions.

9.3.2.4 Aims and objectives of CoC. To minimize energy consumption of data centers, CoC involves different stakeholders, especially data center owner/operators, to improve efficiency in their own areas of competence. More specifically, CoC aims to

1. develop and promote a set of easily understood metrics to measure current efficiencies and improvement in conjunction with other industrial partners;
2. provide an open process/forum to represent/discuss European stakeholder requirements;
3. produce a common set of principles in coordination with other international initiatives to be referred to;
4. create awareness among managers, owners, and investors about opportunities to improve efficiency of energy suppliers, services, and equipment;
5. create and provide an enabling tool to implement cost-effective energy-saving opportunities;
6. develop practical voluntary commitments where methods for energy efficiency of data centers can be implemented and improved so that the TCO can be minimized;
7. determine and accelerate application of energy-efficient technologies;
8. foster development of tools to promote energy-efficient practices;
9. support criteria to measure equipment efficiency, similar to or based on the ENERGY STAR program specifications, and recommend a set of best practices;
10. monitor and assess actions to properly determine both progress and areas of improvement;
11. set energy efficiency targets for public and corporate data center owners and operators. Targets are differentiated according to the size and status of existing data centers, their geographical locations, their return on investments, etc.;
12. provide reference for other participants who might not have initially signed and committed themselves to CoC or principles that do not want to make public commitments.

The CoC should be primarily addressed by data center owners and operators who may become a participant and then by service providers who may become endorsers. CoC is also

13. flexible and open so that it can be applied to a great variety of data center situations;

14. sufficiently precise to ensure that committed companies will achieve a significant part of transparently reported potential energy savings;

15. adaptable to a large variety of national efficiency programs, climates, and energy infrastructures.

9.3.3   Power Use in Data Centers

As mentioned earlier, a key part of the national Market Transformation Programs and the EU CoC is to create effective incentives and reporting measures for efficient use of energy in data centers. It has also been identified that proper measurement of a data center as well as its IT equipment energy efficiency are key factors changing the behavior of future IT operators.

Utility power entering a data center needs to pass through a number of stages of voltage transformation, distribution, and cleaning before being delivered to IT equipment. In fact, as most of the power consumed within a center is converted to heat, one way or another, an efficient high capacity cooling system to draw such additional heat/load is required. Additional power is also needed for a number of auxiliary support systems (such as lighting, generator preheaters, fire suppression systems, and human occupied areas) within each center. Figure 9.3 shows a simplified representation of power delivery and its associated losses for a typical data center. In this figure, the utility power enters the building on the left and passes through the power delivery chain to the IT equipment on the right; each stage in such delivery chain has inherent losses as shown.

9.3.3.1 Data center IT power to utility power relationship. To better understand, measure, and model the overall energy efficiency of a data center, the relationship between electrical load of the housed equipment and the utility

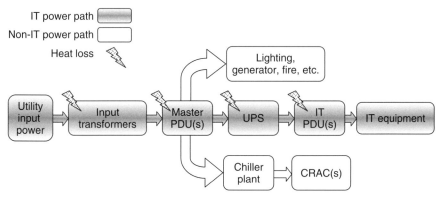

Figure 9.3 IT/non-IT power delivery in a data center. Reproduced with permission from [8].

TABLE 9.5   Sample Loss Parameters for a Typical Data Center. Reproduced with permission from [8].

Devices	Rated Power (watts)	Fixed Losses, %	Proportional Losses, %	Square Law Losses, %
Cabling and switchgear	1,000,000	0.0	0.0	1.5
Power distribution units	1,600,000	0.5	0.0	0.5
UPS	1,100,000	2.0	2.5	5.0
Computer room air conditioners	1,200,000	10.0	1.5	0.0
Chiller plant	1,500,000	5.0	30.0	0.0
Transformers	2,100,000	0.5	0.0	2.5

power drawn to power and cool such housed equipment must be investigated first. The power consumed by IT equipment within a data center is passed through a series of inefficient power conditioning and distribution devices. As a result, in addition to IT equipment, these auxiliary devices also produce heat. In a relatively simple model, inefficiency loss for each component is composed of three factors: fixed, proportional, and square law losses. Fixed losses are for devices that have a fixed load component every time they are switched on, even before IT equipment are powered, for example, battery charge maintenance power of UPS devices. Proportional losses are proportional to the load drawn through the device, for example, the ratio of compressor pumps inside chillers being switched on and off is greatly dependent on the cooling load. Square law losses are electrical losses that are proportional to the square of the carried currents, for example, electrical losses in transformers and cabling. Table 9.5 shows sample loss parameters for a typical data center.

In data centers, it is not only the fixed load overheads that affect the fixed load power draw for zero IT electrical load. In fact, fixed load overheads in power and cooling chains create extra electrical loads on their parent devices to generate more heat. This results in further proportional and square law losses in power and cooling systems, beyond that of the individual fixed losses.

9.3.3.2   Chiller efficiency and external temperature. As most data centers' Heating, Ventilation, and Air Conditioning (HVAC) systems are influenced by both internal and external air temperatures, efficiency of their chillers' pumps improves when the external temperature falls. This phenomenon is particularly more significant where fresh air-cooling systems and/or waterside economizers are used.

9.4   AVAILABLE METRICS

To address all issues mentioned in the previous sections, several metrics are proposed. The most influential metrics proposed by The Green Grid, McKinsey, and Uptime Institute are presented in the following sections.

9.4.1 The Green Grid

The Green Grid [11] is a nonprofit trade organization of IT professionals that addresses power and cooling requirements for data centers as well as its entire information service delivery ecosystem. The Green Grid does not endorse any vendor-specific products or solutions but instead provides recommendations on best practices, metrics, and technologies designed to improve the overall data center efficiency. The Green Grid believes that several metrics can help data centers to better understand and improve their energy efficiency; such metrics can help to make smarter decisions on new data center deployments. Furthermore, these metrics provide a dependable way to measure their results against comparable IT organizations. The Green Grid has already designed three metrics (power usage effectiveness (PUE), data center efficiency (DCE), and data center infrastructure efficiency (DCiE)), and is already working toward its fourth metric (data center productivity (DCP)) [12, 13].

9.4.1.1 Power usage effectiveness (PUE). This metric is designed to measure the amount of extra power needed to perform effective computation in a data center; it is defined as follows:

$$PUE = \frac{\text{Total facility power}}{\text{IT equipment power}}.$$

Figure 9.4 shows the overall power flowchart The Green Grid assumes in designing its metrics. Here, its equipment power includes the load associated with all IT equipment, such as computer, storage, and network equipment, along with supplemental equipment such as KVM switches, monitors, and workstations/laptops used to monitor or otherwise control the data center. Total facility

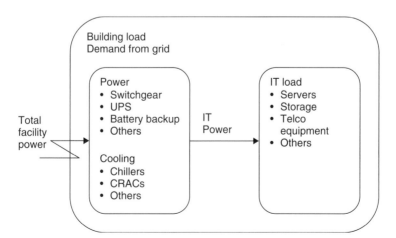

Figure 9.4 The Green Grid's overall power flowchart. Reproduced with permission from [11].

power includes everything that supports IT equipment load such as power delivery components (e.g., UPS, switchgear, generators, PDUs, batteries, and distribution losses external to the IT equipment); cooling system components (e.g., chillers, CRAC units, direct expansion air handler (DX) units, pumps, and cooling towers); computer, network, and storage nodes; and other miscellaneous component loads (e.g., data center lighting).

9.4.1.2 Data center efficiency (DCE). This metric is designed to measure the percentage of power actually consumed for computing inside a data center and is defined as follows:

$$DCE = \frac{1}{PUE} = \frac{IT\ equipment\ power}{Total\ facility\ power}.$$

9.4.1.3 Data center infrastructure efficiency (DCiE). Because DCE was rather confusing, The Green Grid decided to rename it to DCiE.

$$DCiE = DCE = \frac{1}{PUE} = \frac{IT\ equipment\ power}{Total\ facility\ power}.$$

Both PUE and DCiE provide ways to determine (i) opportunities to improve a data center's operational efficiency, (ii) how a given data center compares with competitive data centers, (iii) if data center operators are improving the designs and processes over time, and (iv) opportunities to repurpose energy for additional IT equipment.

Because both these metrics are essentially the same, they can be equally used to illustrate the energy allocation in a data center. For example, PUE equal to 3.0 means that a data center demands three times more energy than what it actually needs to power its IT equipment and DCiE equal to 33% (equivalent to a PUE of 3.0) suggests that IT equipment consume 33% of the data center's total power.

The Green Grid will also consider the development of metrics that provide more granularities for the PUE and DCiE metrics by breaking it down into the following components:

$$PUE = \frac{1}{DCiE} = Cooling\ load\ factor\ (CLF) + power\ load\ factor\ (PLF) + 1.0,$$

where, cooling load factor (CLF) is the total power consumed by chillers, cooling towers, CRAC units, pumps, etc. divided by the IT load; power load factor (PLF) is the total power dissipated by switchgears, UPSs, PDUs, etc. divided by the IT load; and 1.0 represents the normalized IT load. These metrics will be designed to address the blurring of the lines between the IT equipment and facility infrastructure as discussed above.

9.4.1.4 Data center productivity (DCP).

For the long term, The Green Grid is working on a metric to define DCP. DCP is envisioned to naturally evolve from PUE and DCiE and could be defined as follows:

$$DCP = \frac{\text{Useful work}}{\text{Total facility power}}.$$

Although DCP is much more difficult to determine, members of The Green Grid predict that it will be a key strategic focus for the industry. In effect, this calculation defines data centers as black boxes—power and data enter, heat and data exist—where a net amount of useful work is performed.

9.4.2 McKinsey

McKinsey proposes a new Corporate Average Datacenter Efficiency (CADE) metric to measure the individual and combined energy efficiency of corporate and public sector and third-party-hosted data centers [14]. Similar to the automotive style CAFE standards, CADE measures DCE across the entire corporate footprint. Compared to other industry metrics, CADE is the first standard to offer the much needed double lens by combining facilities with IT. To measure how effectively a data center uses energy coming into the facility, CADE takes the amount of power consumed by IT, or the IT load, and divides it by the total power consumed by the data center. To determine how fully the physical equipment installed at the facility level is being used, the CADE formula divides the IT load by the facility's total capacity. This facility efficiency measure is then multiplied by the average CPU server utilization and yields the organization's CADE rating. Figures 9.5 and 9.6 show individual components of CADE with an example of how the calculations are performed.

Each data center is measured independently with a weighted average value based on the installed facility capacity. Since data centers may draw upon different sources of energy, CADE can be used to determine the relative "cleanliness" of the company's greenhouse gas emissions.

CADE confers a number of advantages. In contrast to other industry metrics, the CIOs, CEOs and Boards now have a single, integrated metric that combines facility and IT energy efficiency levels to evaluate the total performance of their information factories. Just as the automotive industry can point to the miles per gallon their vehicles achieve, the senior leadership can use CADE to reveal just how much efficiency their capital-intensive data centers are driving. Most importantly, CADE is a metric that can propel tangible action. To set targets for improvement, McKinsey has established five CADE tiers as illustrated in exhibit (X). Data centers operating at level 1 have a CADE rating of 0–5% and are weakest from the efficiency point of view. Centers operating at level 5 are maximally efficient and have CADE ratings greater than 40%. While most organizations are likely to fall within the lower bounds initially, the leadership can use CADE tiering to establish performance goals. The ranges themselves will vary as more organizations seek to standardize them. However, since the results

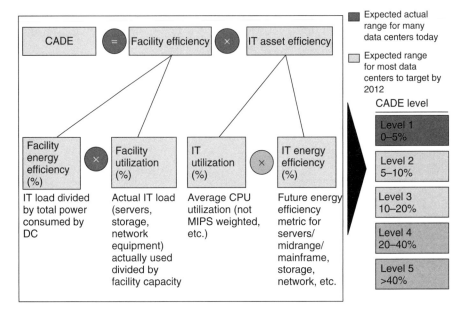

Figure 9.5   Components of CADE. Reproduced with permission from [14].

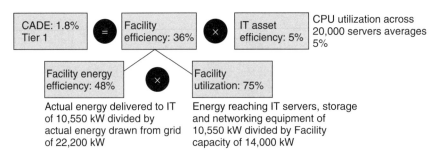

Figure 9.6   CADE calculation example. Reproduced with permission from [14].

are measurable, performance becomes easier to gauge across the organization as well as among individual data centers. CADE has the potential to make a significant contribution to the data center community.

9.4.3   Uptime Institute

The Uptime Institute assumes a data center electricity flow to be as in Figure 9.7. It proposed three vital measuring points to collect efficiency data as (i) data center consumption at the meter, (ii) hardware load at the plug, and (iii) hardware compute load. On the basis of these measurements, four metrics are designed to gauge efficiency of different aspects of a data center [10].

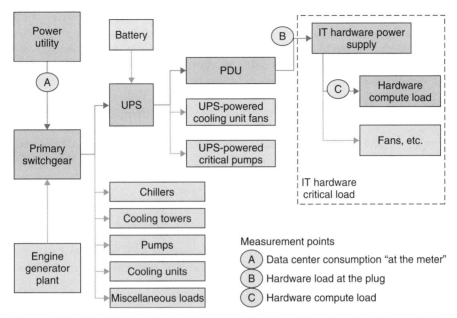

Figure 9.7 The Uptime Institute's power flowchart. Reproduced with permission from [10].

9.4.3.1 Site infrastructure power overhead multiplier (SI-POM).

The Site Infrastructure Power Overhead Multiplier (SI-POM) is a dimensionless ratio to determine the amount of overhead a data center consumes to power up its critical IT equipment and is defined as follows:

$$\text{SI-POM} = \frac{\text{Data center consumption at utility meter}}{\substack{\text{Total hardware AC power consumption at the plug} \\ \text{for all IT equipment}}}.$$

SI-POM thus captures all the conversion losses in transformers, UPS, PDU, and critical power distribution losses, as well as cooling systems, lights, and other minor building loads. Determining SI-POM is important for two reasons. First, it can be reduced by improving the energy efficiency of the cooling, UPS, and PDU system components. Second, its value is significantly influenced by operator skill in the running of the mechanical plant. Although these opportunities occur either when a data center is first built or during major upgrading, because physical site infrastructure lasts for a long time, component and system choices (good or bad) regarding SI-POM last a long time as well.

It is important to note that many design and operational features that save energy will not necessarily affect SI-POM. For instance, free cooling strategies using outside air are unlikely to improve SI-POM because a data center must still size cooling, UPS, and PDU systems large enough to handle peak cooling demands when free cooling is not available. The only way for free cooling to affect SI-POM is for it to somehow reliably contribute to cooling year-round. This is unlikely to the extent that peak cooling demands probably occur when a data center is running a high compute load on a hot, humid summer day, while free cooling is mostly available on cool winter nights or in low humidity environments.

9.4.3.2   IT hardware power overhead multiplier (H-POM).

The Hardware Power Overhead Multiplier (H-POM) is a dimensionless ratio to determine the amount of power wasted in power supply conversion losses or diverted to internal fans, rather than being in useful computing. For a single device, H-POM is defined as follows:

$$\text{H-POM} = \frac{\text{AC hardware load at the plug}}{\text{DC hardware computer load}}.$$

For an entire data center, H-POM is the ratio of the total hardware load at the plug for the entire data center to the total hardware compute load for the entire data center.

9.4.3.3   DC hardware compute load per unit of computing work done.

This quantitative metric determines how power hungry a particular platform is, despite the fact that H-POM excludes differences in power supply and fan losses and focuses on how effectively a piece of equipment utilizes its internal DC watts. For example, different server architectures consume different levels of DC power to perform the same amount of computing work or different spindle speeds of disk storage consume different amounts of power per terabyte of storage provided. Although it is extremely difficult, from a technical point of view, to create a single quantitative metric for this measurement, it is important to inform vendors who wish to reduce their at-the-plug hardware power uses through this factor in addition to their overall H-POM.

9.4.3.4   Deployed hardware utilization ratio (DH-UR).

This metric is a dimensionless ratio and determines a power fraction in which IT equipment are not running any application or handling important data. This metric is designed because most IT equipment are always switched on—unless specifically intended not to—as it is often impossible to check if a given box is doing something important or not. As a result, such dormant equipment can waste significant amount of power during their lifetime. Deployed Hardware Utilization Ratio (DH-UR) can be defined for both servers and storage elements as follows:

$$\text{DH-UR}_{\text{(Servers)}} = \frac{\text{Number of servers running live applications}}{\text{Total number of deployed servers}},$$

$$\text{DH-UR}_{\text{(Storage)}} = \frac{\text{Number of terabytes of storage holding important frequently accessed data}}{\text{Total terabytes of deployed storage}}.$$

Although accurately measuring these metrics is almost impossible—if dormant equipment could be easily identified, they would have already been turned off and removed—managers can still estimate these values or utilize industry average numbers to estimate the amount of power/energy being wasted within an organization.

9.4.3.5 *Deployed hardware utilization efficiency (DH-UE).* Deployed Hardware Utilization Efficiency (DH-UE) is a dimensionless ratio to determine the number of servers and storage units that can increase their utilization through virtualization. This metric is designed because many servers run only a single application with maximum 25% of their computing load. Since servers running at low compute loads often draw nearly as much power as those running at high loads, a large number of such partly loaded servers can quickly consume valuable UPS and HVAC capacity and raise the electricity bill. DH-UE for servers is defined as follows:

$$\text{DH-UE}_{\text{(Servers)}} = \frac{\text{Minimum number of servers necessary to handle peak computing load}}{\text{Total number of deployed servers}}.$$

The minimum number of servers necessary to handle peak computational load is defined as the sum of the highest percentage of compute load each server experiences, plus any overhead incurred in virtualization, expressed as a percentage of the maximum compute load of a single server. This calculation uses peak percentage of compute load, not the average percentage. A similar definition can be developed for storage.

9.5 HARMONIZING GLOBAL METRICS FOR DATA CENTER ENERGY EFFICIENCY

As business demands and energy costs for data centers rise, owners and operators have focused on the energy efficiency of the data center as a whole, frequently using energy efficiency metrics. However, the metrics are not always applied clearly and consistently. To address these inconsistencies, a group of leaders from across the industry met on January 13, 2010, to agree on data center energy efficiency measurements, metrics, and reporting conventions [15]. Organizations represented were the 7×24 Exchange [16], ASHRAE [17], The Green Grid [11], Silicon Valley Leadership Group [18], US Department of Energy's Save Energy Now and Federal Energy Management Programs [19], US Environmental Protection Agency's ENERGY STAR program [20], US Green Building Council [21], and Uptime Institute [21].

These organizations aimed to share global lessons and practices with an objective of arriving at a set of metrics, indices, and measurement protocols to be formally endorsed or adopted by each participant organization. The following specific goals were highlighted:

1. identify an initial set of metrics;
2. define each metric;
3. define the process for measurement of each metric;
4. establish ongoing dialog for development of additional metrics.

During this meeting, the following guiding principles were agreed on:

1. PUE using source energy consumption is the preferred energy efficiency metric for data centers.
2. When calculating PUE, IT energy consumption should, at a minimum, be measured at the output of the UPS. However, the industry should progressively improve measurement capabilities over time so that measurement of IT energy consumption directly at the IT load (i.e., servers) becomes the common practice.
3. For a dedicated data center, the total energy in the PUE formula will include all energy sources at the point of utility handoff to the data center owner or operator. For a data center in a mixed-use building, the total energy will be all the energy required to operate the data center, similar to a dedicated data center, and should include IT energy, cooling, lighting, and support infrastructure for the data center operations.

These principles are meant to help the industry have a common understanding of energy efficiency metrics that can generate dialog to improve data center efficiencies and reduce energy consumption. Member organizations are committed to apply and promote these guidelines to their programs. A task force has also been created to further refine these metrics and identify a road map for the future. The group also aspires to address IT productivity and carbon accounting in the future.

REFERENCES

1. Brown R, Eric M, Bruce N, Bill T, Arman S, John S, Jonathan K, Dale S, Peter C, Joe L, Steve C, Bruce H, Rebecca D, Evan H, Danielle S, Andrew F. 2007. *Report to Congress on Server and Data Center Energy Efficiency: Public Law 109–431*. Berkeley, CA: Lawrence Berkeley National Laboratory. LBNL-363E. August 2.
2. Loper J, Parr S. *Energy Efficiency in Data Centers: A New Policy Frontier*. Washington (DC): Alliance to Save Energy; 2007.
3. AFCOM. 2006. Five bold predictions for the data center industry that will change your future [Keynote Slides]. Available at http://www.afcom.com/files/PDF/DCI_Keynote_Final.pdf. Accessed 2010 July.
4. Fan X, Weber W-D, Barroso LA. Power provisioning for a warehouse-sized computer. In: Proceedings of the 34th International Symposium on Computer Architecture in San Diego, CA. Association for Computing Machinery, ISCA '07; 2007.

5. Turner WP, Seader JH, Brill KG. *Industry Standard Tier Classifications Define Site Infrastructure Performance*. Santa Fe (NM): Uptime Institute; 2005.

6. Greenberg S, Mills E, Tschudi B, Rumsey P, Myatt B. Best practices for data centers: lessons learned from benchmarking 22 data centers. In: Proceedings of the ACEEE Summer Study on Energy Efficiency in Buildings in Asilomar, CA. ACEEE; 2006. pp. 76–87.

7. LBNL. *High-Performance Buildings for High-Tech Industries, Data Centers*. Lawrence Berkeley National Laboratory; 2006.

8. Newcombe L. Data centre energy efficiency metrics. Data Centre Specialist Group: BCS; 2008.

9. European Commission, Code of Conduct on Data Centres Energy Efficiency (Version 2): Endorser Guidelines and Registration forms. European Commission, Directorate-General Joint Research Centre; 2009.

10. Stanley JR, Brill KG, Koomey J. *Four Metrics Define Data Center "Greenness": Enabling Users to Quantify Energy Consumption Initiatives for Environmental Sustainability and "Bottom Line" Profitability*. Santa Fe (NM): The Uptime Institute; 2007. Available at www.uptimeinstitute.org/. (visited 2012).

11. The Green Grid: gdcmetrics@ lists.thegreengrid.org.

12. Rawson A, Pfleuger J, Cader T. Green grid data center power efficiency metrics: PUE and DCiE. In: Belady C, editor. White Paper #6; 2008 www.eni.com/green-data-center/it_IT/static/.../Green_Grid_DC.pdf, visited 2012.

13. Dan Azevedo, Nick Gruendler, Hugh Barrass, Bob Macarthur, Stephen Berard, Phil Morris, Mark Bramfitt, Andy Rawson, Tahir Cader, Jim Simonelli, Tommy Darby, Harkeeret Singh, John Wallerich, Christine Long. The Green Grid Metrics: Data Center Infrastructure Efficiency (DCiE) Detailed Analysis. In: Verdun G, editor. White Paper #14; 2008, www.rittal.it/mod_cert_dc_eu.pdf, (visited 2012).

14. Kaplan JM, Forrest W, Kindler N. *Revolutionizing Data Center Energy Efficiency*. McKinsey & Company; Technical Report, 2008.

15. Harmonizing Global Metrics for Data Centre Energy Efficiency. http://www.thegreengrid.org/en/Global/Content/Reports/HarmonizingGlobalMetricsForDataCenterEnergyEfficiency, visited 2012.

16. 7x24 Exchange. Available at http://www.7x24exchange.org/eemetrics.html, visited 2012.

17. ASHRAE. Avauilable at http://tc99.ashraetcs.org/, visited 2012.

18. Silicon Valley Leadership Group. Available at http://svlg.org/, visited 2012.

19. U.S. Department of Energy Save Energy Now Program. Available at http://www1.eere.energy.gov/industry/datacenters/contacts.html, visited 2012.

20. U.S. Environmental Protection Agency's ENERGY STAR Program. Available at http://www.energystar.gov/, visited 2012.

21. U.S. Green Building Council. Available at http://www.usgbc.org/, visited 2012.

CHAPTER 10

AUTONOMIC GREEN COMPUTING IN LARGE-SCALE DATA CENTERS

HAOTING LUO, BITHIKA KHARGHARIA, SALIM HARIRI, and YOUSSIF AL-NASHIF

10.1 INTRODUCTION

The need for energy-efficient large-scale computing systems such as data centers has increased because of the rise in business demands and energy costs. The US Environmental Protection Agency (EPA) [1] has recently been devoting efforts with the IT industry to reach consensus on the measurement and improvement of data center energy efficiency [2]. The overall efficiency of data centers relies on power usage efficiency (PUE), server power usage efficiency (SPUE), and server energy efficiency (SEE). Careful floor planning and IT equipment energy saving can help reduce PUE and SPUE. Dynamic power within the equipment provides a more flexible and swift solution without changing the organization and alignment of the high performance servers.

Today's data centers are meant to scale up in a rapid manner to match the increasing service request workload, thus bringing enormous expected issues and research opportunities. The capability to do energy-aware studies in real time will not only provide more information for heterogeneous resource configuration for improved systems but also allow us to study events that cannot be repeated or that change the entire environment.

Over the past several years, there has been an increasing interest in autonomic computing methods because of their ability to achieve active control and management of heterogeneous and dynamic behaviors of large-scale data centers. These methods could be applied to a wide range of environments such as cybersecurity systems [3], wireless communications [1], and on-demand applications [1]. Clients such as medical institutions [3], military bases [3], and web service

Energy-Efficient Distributed Computing Systems, First Edition.
Edited by Albert Y. Zomaya and Young Choon Lee.
© 2012 John Wiley & Sons, Inc. Published 2012 by John Wiley & Sons, Inc.

providers [4], would benefit in terms of real-time robustness, easier management schemes, and better resource utilization. It has been validated in real applications that the overhead for building autonomic computing for self-management is tolerable compared with respect to the baseline performance and power standards.

Autonomic computing [5–7] can be implemented as a closed-loop-controlled system that can periodically detect the anomalies and restore the system to its normal state. Dynamic power management is achieved by configuring the system into one of the several power states such that the system operation is confined within the normal operating region.

In this chapter, we are particularly interested in the dynamic power manageability of large-scale and massively distributed computing systems, for example, data centers and clouds [8]. There are several challenges that must be addressed to achieve autonomic control and management of large-scale data centers.

- Given the state-of-the-art architecture and application-specific heterogeneous floor planning of data center resources, how do we organize and orchestrate the distributed system so that it could be accessed fairly and efficiently?
- Given the variable incoming workload and stationary data center composition, how do we dynamically identify the workload requirements and allocate available resources that meet the performance requirements with minimal energy consumption?
- What kinds of features are necessary and sufficient for any data center resource that can accurately characterize the current operational state and whether or not it is operating normally?
- What data-center-specific power management approaches are applicable in this research in order to configure the resources to deliver service within a tight power budget and temperature threshold while meeting the demand for a maximum possible performance level?
- What are the cost, runtime complexity, and start-up/reconfiguration overhead associated with real-time management techniques, and how can they be minimized?

The objective is twofold, besides the energy-efficient goal; we also take into account the optimization in performance while searching for dynamic configurations that lead to power savings.

10.2 RELATED TECHNOLOGIES AND TECHNIQUES

10.2.1 Power Optimization Techniques in Data Centers

Although data center architecture differ from one another, most data centers are collections of host servers, storage units, and networking fabrics. Defining a data center involves confirming the issues such as design model, network, and storage topology.

10.2.2 Design Model

The differences in data center design models lie in the dominant types of applications, the kinds of host servers that compose the data center, and how those hosts are different from each other. There are two mainstream design models: the multitier data center model and the server cluster design [9]. The multitier approach includes web, application, and database tiers of servers, which may or may not occupy the same physical server. Today, most web-based applications are built as multitier applications. They are favored by those applications for their resiliency and high security. The server cluster design model is similar to a tight collection of homogeneous cores that share a common OS or software for high performance computing purposes—military applications or high performance scientific computing usually benefit from this design model. Commercial applications are also introducing this cost-benefit model in their clusters for better manageability, higher bandwidth, and lower latency. A high speed interconnect network is typically associated with this design model to maximize the performance values as part of a service-level agreement (SLA). In this research, we mainly focus on the server cluster design model.

Figure 10.1 demonstrates a commonly structured data center hierarchy. Groups of servers are piled up within the server rack/blades, which are interconnected with each other using Ethernet switches to form the server clusters. Data centers are thus composed of several clusters or even whole rooms of clusters. In order to maintain reliability, data centers usually include redundant components or detailed a backup plan.

According to the complexity and robustness of the design, data centers are classified into four tiers. Following the basic guidance for installing a data center room, tier I data centers can be built in a very straightforward manner. In tier II, availability and throughput can be improved by adding redundant components

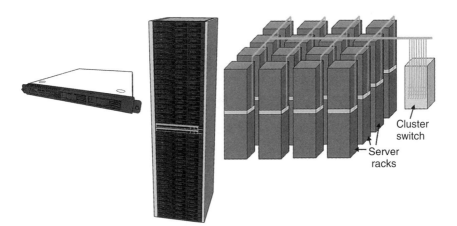

Figure 10.1 Typical data center element and hierarchy. Reproduced from [10] with permission from Morgan and Claypool Publishers © 2009.

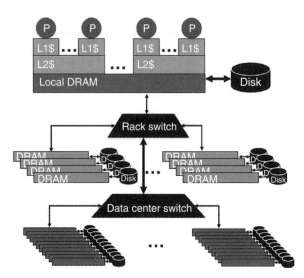

Figure 10.2   Data center hardware hierarchy. Reproduced from [10] and [11] with permission.

to the design. Tier III data centers have multiple power and cooling distribution paths but only one active path. They also have redundant components and are concurrently maintainable. Tier IV data centers have two active power and cooling distribution paths, with redundant components in each path, and are supposed to tolerate any single equipment failure without affecting the load. Most commercial data centers are tier III or IV, and our research focuses on applying autonomic computing techniques to develop self-management high performance platforms that are commonly used in such systems. As seen by programers, the hardware organization of a typical server is shown in Figure 10.2.

Multicore CPUs are usually favored by data center designers for their performance and per-unit cost advantages. The model of a single processor with its associated L1 cache represents the finest granularity in a data center. The next hierarchy would be the CPU cluster shared by the L2 cache, local DRAM, and local disk on the server. As the storage unit, DRAM slices and disks are shared within the whole data center resources. Those resources are interconnected by the rack switch or even the higher data switches/cluster switches. So we can think of the whole data center resource as a collection of cores and memory chips. We also divide the memory into slices that we call *ranks*. In this research, we consider a single core and single memory rank as the finest grain for processing and storing data, respectively.

10.2.3   Networks

Network fabrics comprise several important features such as the manageability of distributed systems, response time of the accessing request, and load balancing of networked entities. High connectivity for these fabrics helps offset the accessing

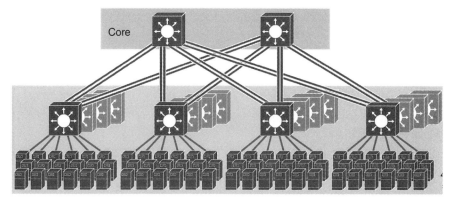

Figure 10.3 Data center networking fabric. Reproduced from [7] with permission from the CISCO Data Center Infrastructure 2.5 © 2010.

overhead when complexity is increased. Therefore, the choice of networking topology for data centers involves trade-offs among cost, power, and performance.

Figure 10.3 is an example of data center networking architecture: a four-way ECMP (equal cost multiple path) tree topology with two core nodes. In this architecture, two core nodes are connected to the intermediate switches on the sublayer using 10-gigabit Ethernet and the intermediate nodes are linked with low end servers by gigabit Ethernet.

Clearly, networking is one of the predominant factors in large-scale distributed systems and it requires careful consideration. Our focus in this work is not only on how to improve the performance of the networking system but rather on techniques that would improve power efficiency in these systems.

10.2.4 Data Center Power Distribution

As shown in Figure 10.4, in addition to the racks and switches with servers running and connected, a typical data center is composed of several critical power system parts [4]. The uninterruptible power supply (UPS) module takes care of the whole room's power provision, which is delivered through the power distribution units (PDUs) to other places in the room. Fuel storage tanks and backup diesel generators are on hand in case of utility-supplied power fails. Cooling units and a computer air handling unit (namely, computer room air conditioner (CRAC)) are essential for controlling the temperature. Other facilities such as the switchgear, collocation units, and pump room for supplying the chilled water used by the CRAC should also be included.

From the power dissipation point of view, the cooling systems and the PDUs use up a considerable portion of the delivered power, so there is not really much remaining power that could be actually used by the IT equipment for operational use, thus making the power optimization within computing resources the utmost issue that needs to be solved. In this chapter, we introduce techniques that can be used to maximize the server power utilization while maintaining their optimal performance.

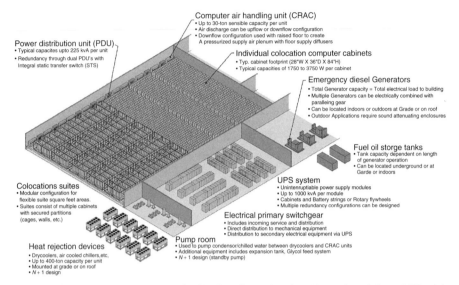

Figure 10.4 Data center power distribution floor planning. Reproduced from [10] with permission from Morgan and Claypool Publishers; © 2009.

10.2.5 Data Center Power-Efficient Metrics

As discussed in Reference 10, an agreement has been established by industry leaders on the metrics for data center power efficiency (DCPE). The traditional way of defining DCPE (PUE), as the total energy of the data center divided by the IT energy consumption, is favored for measuring the efficiency ratio.

In this particular work, as we try to minimize the power consumption while considering the optimal performance metric, we find it useful to count the computation factor as well. A good way to take both factors into account is to use the energy proportional efficiency (EPE), as opposed to Reference 4. EPE has three factorized components:

$$
\begin{aligned}
\text{EPE} &= \frac{\text{Computation}}{\text{Total energy supply}} \\
&= \left(\frac{\text{IT energy supply}}{\text{Total energy supply}} \right) \times \left(\frac{\text{Server energy}}{\text{IT energy supply}} \right) \times \left(\frac{\text{Computation}}{\text{Server energy}} \right) \\
&= \left(\frac{1}{\text{PUE}} \right) \times \left(\frac{1}{\text{SPUE}} \right) \times \left(\frac{1}{\text{SEPE}} \right),
\end{aligned}
$$

where SEPE refers to the server energy proportion efficiency.

In this metric, we can see that different techniques can be contributed to optimize the EPE for data centers. PUE and SPUE values are related to the initial design, floor planning of the data center, and the architecture of the server's non-processing components; this should be mainly handled by data center designers and server product engineers and is beyond the capability of the research scope of this chapter. What could be really taken seriously is the SEPE factor, which is basically manipulating the computing process and analyzing the power statistics within the servers' functionality. In this research, we focus on developing an effective performance-per-watt algorithm for improving the SEPE, which is discussed later.

10.2.6   Modeling Prototype and Testbed

An actual testbed would be useful to represent the data Cloud and center architecture and thus validate our approach. At the UA NSF Center for Autonomic Computing, we have used the IBM blade system to build 168 cores data center. We use it as a modeling prototype for our autonomic power efficiency research. The IBM BladeCenter (Fig. 10.5) has 14 HS22 blades each with two Xeon® (6-core) 2.66-GHz processors with 12-MB L2 cache, 12 8-GB VLP-DRIMM DRAM chips, and 160-GB SATA disk. Considering the software aspect of this system, each individual blade, including the head node, has CentOS installed. A virtualization tool, Xen, regards the whole blade center platform as one machine. Eucalyptus also functions as a controller which creates virtual machines (VMs) and allocates the required physical resources for each application. The Blade-Center is a good testbed to experiment and evaluate our optimization algorithms and techniques. Emerging technologies and techniques have promoted modularity and autonomy for data center power management. The dynamic voltage and frequency scaling (DVFS) technology has been used to achieve energy saving [8, 12, 13]. Virtualization has been adopted in the design of large-scale data centers and cloud computing testbeds and is considered a promising approach to implement massive data orchestration and migration. Virtualization technology reduces the energy demands of data centers through server consolidation and dynamic management of computer assets across a pool of servers. The virtualized infrastructure uses middleware to allocate the resources. Customers can dramatically reduce energy consumption without sacrificing reliability or service levels [13, 14].

Figure 10.5   IBM BladeCenter HS22.

Theoretical works have provided possible solutions from different perspectives such as game theory [16, 17], dynamic analysis [18], and gradient-based methods [16]. Many systems such as Smart Power Management [8], PSALM [8], and Consil [8] have provided a blueprint for power-aware data center architecture. Wang and Kandasamy [19] proposed a large-scale power controller that shifts power among servers based on their performance needs, while controlling the total power of the system within a constraint. Koller et al. [20] proposed an application-driven power meter that can estimate and predict the power consumption with low computing complexity for various real applications, thus addressing the challenge of energy overuse.

Some researchers have placed a more holistic view for real-application scenarios. Barroso states the conflict between CPU utilization and delivered amount of power in mainstream power management techniques. As proposed in Reference 20, he provides a straightforward solution of "energy proportional computing" based on sorted efficiency levels. The core principle behind energy proportionality is that computing equipment should consume power in proportion to its utilization level. By combining the load factor with efficiency, the energy usage profile would be largely improved for various computing systems and would achieve large energy savings.

Fan et al. [21] showed that there is a huge potential for improvement in energy saving by power management and reducing peak power for large-scale power provisioning. According to Zheng et al. [19], managing data center resources for real experiment scenarios with the given knowledge on the virtualized level can help reduce overhead and complete on-line reconfiguration. Many other methods are proposed in References 3, 6, 22 to provide solutions that allow energy-efficient large-scale computing systems. However, none of these techniques consider the use of an autonomic management to holistically solve the most urgent issues of today's data centers.

10.2.7 Green Computing

A green computer/server is one that has the following features: it is built from eco-friendly materials, features low power consumption, and has computer power management (CPM) capabilities; it has fewer and smaller component parts and generates less heat than previous models; and it is ultimately responsible for the emission of less CO_2 into the atmosphere. A wholly green product will be packaged in recyclable materials and, at the end of its useful life cycle, will be traded to the manufacturer or to another organization that will reuse and recycle the equipment, rather than dumping it into a landfill [23].

There is no common agreement on the definition of "green computing"; however, the idea can be applied in hardware implementations, algorithms, tools, services, applications, or whatever can make computing systems more environmentally friendly, for example, by reducing power consumption or CO_2 emissions. The computing systems considered here include chips; hard disks; desktops/laptops; servers; network switches/routers; SAN (storage area network),

RAID (redundant array of inexpensive disks), and other storage systems; clusters; racks; data centers; and grids and clouds.

Green computing is receiving a lot of interests these days not only because of the rising energy costs and the potential savings but also because of the impact on the environment. Energy to manufacture, store, operate, and cool computing systems has grown significantly in recent years, primarily because of the exponential growth in the number of these systems and their computing power.

Promoting green, or energy-efficient, computing is critically important for many reasons. First and foremost, conclusive research shows that CO_2 and other emissions are causing global climate warming and environmental damage. Preserving the planet is a moral goal because it aims at preserving life in Earth. Planets like ours, which support life, are very rare. None of the planets in our solar system, or in the nearby star systems, have M-class planets as we know them.

There has been a huge increase in energy use by industries and in everyday life. In August 2007, an EPA report [6] anticipated a dramatic growth in energy costs ($4.5 billion in 2006, $7.4 billion projected by 2011) and power consumption (61 billion kW h in 2006, 100 billion projected by 2011) for IT systems. As reported by the EPA, total electrical demand growth is predicted to increase 30% to 5021 billion kW h in 2035. The largest percentage increase is in the commercial sector (42%), with the service industries continuing to lead the growth. However, the dominant share of energy supply lies in coal-fired power plants, which deplete limited resources. Although the share in other energy resources such as natural gas, solar energy, and other renewable sources is projected to rise, the total growth in electricity demand will still run ahead of the supply side by a substantial amount.

Computing power consumption by large data centers has reached a critical point. For example, an e-commerce business with 100,000 servers can easily spend up to $20 million a year on server power. Add another $10 million for cooling and it tops $30 million a year in power alone. Clearly there is a huge potential for savings in their infrastructure.

The climate initiative aims to reduce the IT carbon dioxide emissions from computer operations by 50% between 2007 and 2010. A group, led by PC manufacturers such as Dell, Hewlett-Packard, Lenovo, presented energy-efficient IT products in a special "green village," with central information that will point visitors to other companies with environmentally friendly products. Despite the huge surge in computing power demands, there are many existing technologies and methods by which significant savings can be made. There is clear evidence that a typical organization can reduce their energy footprint while maintaining the required levels of computing performance. Green computing can lead to appreciable cost savings over time. Reductions in energy costs from servers, cooling, and lighting are generating substantial savings and considerable increase in the return of capital in the long run for many corporations. As energy demands in the world go up, energy supply is flat or declining. Energy-efficient systems help ensure healthy power systems and the reliability of appliances in case of unexpected outage. Also, more companies are generating more of their own electricity, which further motivates them to keep power consumption low.

Corporate data centers face limitations and constraints in space, power consumption, and the rising costs associated with energy and physical plant leasing or rentals. The mismatch between expanded demand and restricted usage affects corporate growth, which calls for reaching a solution that maximizes profits but minimizes costs (the Pareto solution). The identification of certain enabling techniques and hardware design is required to implement the resource reconfigurations and exercise the required power management features to deliver the power savings.

Data centers are beginning to exceed usable power and cooling supply due to high densities, raising issues for green computing studies. The following lists the main capabilities or requirements for green computing data centers.

- *Manageability*. The expansion of system scale adds to the complexity of managing a massively distributed data center. Hence, an efficient tracking method should be developed to position the targeting node with the least amount of effort and overhead.
- *Overhead*. The frequency of configuration changes to a single node directly influences the dynamism of power management. Adequate node access ensures fast response but requires low overhead techniques for sensing and controlling.
- *Autonomy*. For a data center as large as a room, manual management is unrealistic. In order to dynamically manage large-scale data center resources, autonomic management techniques and tools are critically important.

10.2.8 Energy Proportional Computing

Traditional energy-efficient computing focuses on single-objective optimization, without considering other factors such as the quality of service (QoS), reliability. Today's computing systems cannot endure too much degradation of the system performance when energy-saving schemes are applied. Energy proportional computing introduces a balanced solution and a holistic view of the green system problem.

The basic idea of energy proportional computing relates the consumed energy and computation in one metric. This method attempts to devote energy in proportion to the work that has to be performed, that is, utilization. As a single value that conveys two parameters, this method aims to develop machines that can optimize the energy according to computing behavior, which is very similar to our goal in this work. As claimed in Reference 20, energy proportional machines would barely consume any power if the system is in the idle state, require very little power with a light workload, and gradually add more power as the activity level increases, until reaching full energy budget when the system is heavily loaded.

This chapter later discusses how to use the idea of energy proportional computing to achieve more efficient computing resource utilization. We use the power proportional efficiency to measure the power performance optimal level for a data center. We also use this concept in our performance-per-watt power management algorithm for autonomic controllers.

10.2.9 Hardware Virtualization Technology

In a data center that contains thousands and even millions of server hosts, a substantial number of applications are processed by those host nodes. A mismatch between server capability and an application requesting resource volume results in imperfect utilization of the host machines. This brings up the problem of data center collective underutilization and leaves a huge space for improvement of wasted computation power. If there is a scheme that can help bring together the unused resources, a tremendous amount of resources and computation power could be saved.

Virtualization technology [24] has been proposed to address this problem. In a virtualization technique, there are two kinds of resources, the physical resources and virtual resources that act as the provisioning task (Fig. 10.6). Physical resources are the actual host hardware on which applications run. They have a fixed hardware such as processors, memory, I/O whose capacity and computation capability cannot be varied. On the other hand, the virtual resources are the abstracted hardware interface for the "guest applications." With the virtualized system, applications are run on the VMs if they are seen by the service end. The VM still has hardware resources such as processors, memories for services to run; however, it has no idea which physical machine the process is running on. Each VM delivers a distinct service to its customers using (virtual) resources provided by its dedicated VM. In this sense, the physical machine can be seen as a pool of resources that has the total privilege to allocate, provide, and alter resources on demand.

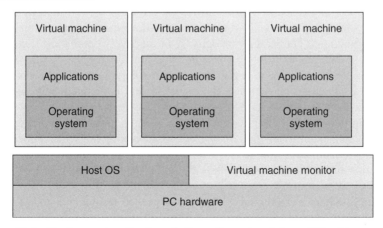

Figure 10.6 Hardware virtualization platform. Reproduced from [24] with permission from the Intel Press © 2006.

A global resource allocator is responsible for mapping virtual resources onto physical resources. Multiple VMs can be placed on a single host machine without interaction and interference between them, and also multiplex physical hardware can hold across VMs. The allocator should manage the contention based on administration policies, guarantee predictable service rates, and exploit under-committed resources for efficient utilization.

Clearly, virtualization technology provides flexible and dynamic partitioning, meets absolute SLAs, and arbitrates VMs by controlled relative importance. Furthermore, this technology is a key feature for our approach to implement autonomic management of a data center's power and performance.

10.2.10   Autonomic Computing

The concept of autonomic computing is being developed in order to overcome the growing complexity of data center management. Inspired by the human autonomic neural system, an autonomic computing system can be viewed as a closed-loop control system. Variation of its essential variables (e.g., power, performance, fault, security) can generate a reconfiguration process that will drive the system toward a target state that meets the required multiobjective function of the system.

The target state could be an equilibrium point, a constrained region, or a preset boundary. In all, configuring variables and the states set are the necessary conditions for the autonomic management. In cybersecurity, the target states are usually referred to as the characteristic of "survivability," that is, the system intends to protect itself and recover from attacks and/or faults. Autonomic performance management maintains the system at a desired performance level regardless of the dynamic changes in the environment. In power-efficient systems, the focus is on how to satisfy a given power budget constraint without any performance degradation.

In typical autonomic managed systems, an MAPE (monitor, analysis, predict, and execute) loop is usually involved. An MAPE loop is controlled by an autonomic manager (AM), which implements real-time monitoring, analyzing, and actuator functions. The monitor proactively or reactively obtains the system state information and passes it to the analyzer for characterizing the current state and predicting the next states, so it can determine the appropriate actions that can be executed by the actuator. In cases where the system is hierarchically structured, each subsystem will have its AM as shown in Figure 10.7.

The autonomic computing research in this work is based on hierarchical autonomic management. The global controller makes decisions and allocates the resources to competing requests so that violations of resource SLAs between application providers and data centers can be avoided. Meanwhile, a local loop controller takes care of further improvements of the performance values for the computing systems, estimating the resources needed by the application's workloads on each specific subsystem or low level device.

This multilevel resource control system is ideal for largely distributed computing systems, which require hierarchical management. In such an environment, a

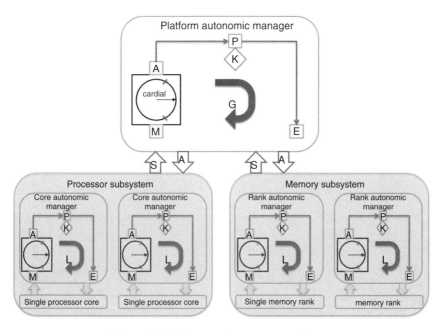

Figure 10.7   Autonomic management loops.

local controller adapts to the dynamic changes in workloads of its assigned set of resources. Furthermore, the separation of functionalities between local controllers is also suitable for heterogeneous system floor plans. As the responsibility for internal control functions has been overtaken by local controllers and transformed into straightforward local resource requests, the complexities of global controllers reduce significantly and hence improve the overall efficiency of the autonomic management of the system. This scheme provides a framework for local sub-systems to carry out different self-management operations without affecting the global controller.

10.3   AUTONOMIC GREEN COMPUTING: A CASE STUDY

Inspired by the autonomic computing techniques and green computing techniques, we present in this section our approach to develop autonomic green distributed computing systems that exploit the technologies discussed previously. In this scheme, autonomic resource provisioning is continuously performed for certain applications such that their performance requirements are maintained while minimizing the energy consumption. The AM takes the responsibility of dynamically mapping sufficient physical resources to each VM assigned to run the data center applications. Power-aware management tools such as DVFS and use system proportions for idle elements

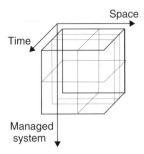

Figure 10.8 Application Flow (AppFlow).

provide the required power management mechanisms for large-scale distributed data centers. The autonomic power managers are embedded in each level and they cooperate with upper-level managers to achieve the overall system objectives in terms of performance and energy consumption. This requires the information across all levels to be exchanged in a hierarchical manner.

A successful management scheme for large distributed systems such as data centers requires identification of the appropriate features that can accurately characterize the behavior and current state of the management component or element (e.g., server, memory rank, or core in a multicore system). To effectively manage the resources of the system, the AM must determine whether the system operational state meets all the runtime system requirements. We have developed an Application Flow (AppFlow) data structure that will be used by the AM to characterize the behavior of the changing "environment" and use that as a predictor for how it can prepare itself better to manage those changes, as shown in Figure 10.8. *AppFlow* is a three-dimensional array of *features* where the x-dimension captures spatial variability and the z-dimension captures temporal variability of these *features* for each Managed System (MS) (plotted along the y-dimension) as the workload changes dynamically. These set of necessary and sufficient *features* are categorized into two distinct classes: capacity spatial features (CSFs) and operating region spatial features (ORSFs). CSFs can be further broken down into static capacity spatial features (SCSFs) and dynamic capacity spatial features (DCSFs). As the names suggest, SCSF indicates the maximum possible capacity of the *MS* and DCSF indicates the current dynamic capacity (configuration) of the *MS* that is changed by the *AM* based on the requirements of the application at runtime. The ORSF is the set of *features* that the *AM* manages and maintains in order to ensure the "survivability" of the *MS*. It is to be noted that CSFs are a set of *absolute features* and ORSFs are a set of *dependent features* that can be derived from CSFs. Along the y-axis of *AppFlow*, the "time" vector captures the behavior of the *MS* over a period of time. In essence, it captures the temporal variability of the CSFs and ORSFs during workload execution that help identify trends and predict workload dynamic resource requirements.

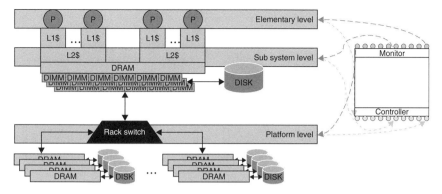

Figure 10.9   Hierarchical autonomic management platform.

10.3.1   Autonomic Management Platform

10.3.1.1   Platform architecture. In this section, we focus on a virtualized platform that is modeled as a collection of networked devices, namely, the multicore processors and the multirank memory subsystems. They constitute the managed system that is continuously controlled by the platform autonomic manager (PAM). An autonomic power efficiency management is accomplished by allocating the platform resources to match the requirements of the platform workloads.

Figure 10.9 shows a platform architecture from the programer's viewpoint, with autonomic management modules shown on the right side. There are three levels: the elementary level, the subsystem level, and the platform level. The elementary level mainly refers to atomic models such as processor cores, L1 cache associated with it, and memory ranks. Elements at this level are modeled as "atomic models" and are scalable in terms of power efficiency as determined by the DVFS mechanisms. Each atomic model is managed by a job queue for scheduling incoming jobs and power manager for sensing or affecting the model state.

In the subsystem level, the processor and memory subsystem collects the power states and performance states of the job queues from the atomic models and controls the configuration within the subsystem. In this level, the subsystems are scalable due to the variable number of atomic models assigned by the scheduler. The platform level, which consists of the subsystems, further adjusts the lower level components according to the application requirements as abstracted in the current state of its AppFlow.

10.3.1.2   DEVS-based modeling and simulation platform. We use the DEVS (discrete event system)-based modeling and simulation to model the behavior of the platform architecture shown in Figure 10.9. The DEVS modeling framework of the platform is shown in Figure 10.10 where each component (core, rank, etc.) is modeled as a DEVS atomic model. These *DEVS* models

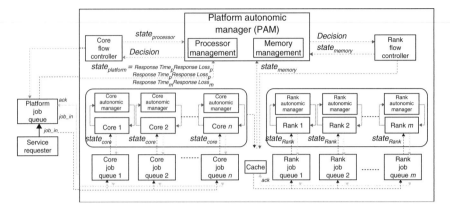

Figure 10.10 Block schematic of autonomic management platform.

enable us to accurately model the behavior of the system components and their interactions and how they impact the overall system behavior for a wide range of power and performance optimization strategies at each level of the hierarchy.

A DEVS atomic model is a finite state machine and is defined as [5, 25]

$$M_{\text{Atomic}} = \langle X, S, Y, \delta_{\text{int}}, \delta_{\text{ext}}, \lambda, t_a \rangle,$$

where

X = the set of inputs accepted by the model;

S = the set of states of the model;

Y = the output set generated by the model;

$\delta_{\text{int}} : S \rightarrow S$ = the function that captures the internal state transitions for the model;

$\delta_{\text{ext}} : S \times X \rightarrow S$ = the function that captures the state transitions for the model in response to external inputs;

$\lambda : S \rightarrow Y$ = the output function that maps a state to an output from the output set;

t_a = the time advance function for remaining in a state before an internal state transition occurs.

We have implemented the PAM simulation that is running on the DEVS-Java environment to evaluate different kinds of optimization and management algorithms. The implementation of the PAM closely models the platform architecture discussed previously that can be viewed as a collection of cores and memory chips, and the CPUs and DRAMs are the most power-consuming IT components in today's data centers. What is unique about our approach is that we manage the platform in a hierarchical scheme with observers and controllers at each level—platform, subsystem, and elementary levels—in order to implement the required self-management functions with minimal overhead.

The core operating features are recorded by the monitors of the core power manager (CPM), which collects features such as the average job wait time, average job response time that define the current operational state of the core subsystem. With such information, the CPM can accurately characterize the current core's state and consequently send the control information required to change the core configuration if it is required to maintain the performance and energy consumption requirements. At the same time, a similar procedure is applied to the memory subsystem.

At the subsystem level, each subsystem (core and memory) interacts with the flow controller. A core flow controller (CFC) tracks the subsystem behavior based on AppFlow features such as request loss rate or average response time across all cores. CFC then analyzes if there is any change in the workload and makes a decision whether to scale the core's configuration up or down. Similarly, on the memory side, a memory flow controller (MFC) also acts as the autonomic power manager that controls the configuration of the whole memory in each VM using the appropriate AppFlow memory features such as memory loss, average memory access time, or memory reference rate.

The PAM applies a further power proportional efficiency algorithm to the whole system. Serving as an observer and controller of the platform, PAM collects AppFlow information associated with its subsystems to determine the current operating states of its components, such as the number of active cores/memory ranks, current power consumption, or other statistics, to characterize the workload patterns. PAM then analyzes those dynamic features to determine whether or not an optimal configuration has been reached with respect to both power and performance. In case, it does not meet the application requirements, PAM will determine the right scale for the VM's execution environment (we refer to as *VM template*) and then passes that decision to the platform job queue (PJQ) or flow controllers. The PJQ operates as an actuator that sends the job or the instructions to reconfigure platform subsystems. For example, the PJQ in the memory subsystem directs memory-accessed jobs to available memory ranks or processes an incoming job if it requests a cache access.

In the following sections, we discuss the various aspects of this platform simulator, such as the effects of different workloads on the systems behavior, how the platform parameters would be evaluated, its scalability as a multicore multimemory system, and how the PAM uses the AppFlow features to manage platform energy consumption.

10.3.1.3 Workload generator. In order to evaluate our autonomic management algorithms, we need to generate a wide range of workload scenarios. The service requester is responsible for generating jobs that will be queued at the PJQ. Different job-injecting patterns will lead to different workloads and consequently different platform operations. In our analysis, we divide the workloads into two categories: CPU intensive and memory intensive. CPU-intensive workloads are modeled as programs having high ratios of logic or arithmetic operations when compared to memory access operations. The opposite behavior characterizes the memory-intensive workloads where most of the operations are memory load/save operations.

When a workload is generated, it is broken down into PC instructions, jobs that require core access, cache access, or memory access. CPU-intensive workloads lead to intensive access to the cores, and memory-intensive workloads would burden the memory with instructions after shortly visiting the core and cache. It is possible that certain cache access or memory access would have misses. Parameters such as cache/memory reference/hit ratio can be used to characterize the type of the current workload. We assign to each generated job its own cache/memory access features based on a Gaussian distribution. By varying the miss ratio and cache referencing rate, a specific type of workload behavior can be generated.

In the service requester model, we also assume a Poisson distribution for the intervals between successive job generations. Changing the λ value of the interval function defines heavy or light application workloads. Likewise, the processing time of an instruction is modeled as a Gaussian distribution, and the parameters associated with this distribution are the average (μ) and variation (σ^2) of the job processing time.

10.3.2 Model Parameter Evaluation

10.3.2.1 State transitioning overhead. We assume that the platform can operate in several states, where each state will deliver different performance and energy consumption. The goal of the autonomic management algorithm is to determine for each workload type the ideal platform state that meets this workload performance and energy consumption. In identifying the optimal operational state for the platform, we need to take into consideration the transition overhead that will be incurred by moving the platform from the current state to the desired target state.

We use Intel® Xeon 5650 processor as an example in our platform simulation [26]. The 6-core processors are based on a low power microarchitecture that supports operation within various C-states. C0 is the normal operating state in which the processor operates with full voltage and frequency. C1, C3, and C6 are low power states for different levels of power-saving targets. Transitions from core-active states to sleep states are also supported for long-time idle operations or no operations. This processor also enables the Intel Turbo Boost Technology, which allows the processors to run opportunistically faster than the normal frequency, here the frequency can upscale to 3.06 GHz instead of 2.66 GHz. The transition overheads between states, even to the turbo and sleep states, are very short, and in the order of microseconds. The power consumption and performance values for the core to transition from one state to another are shown in Figure 10.11.

Another case study for the memory rank model was also conducted (Fig. 10.12). The actual design for this modeling is the Micron VLP RDIMM modules, as part of the IBM BladeCenter machine. Associated with the memory rank model are active states and two energy-effective states, which support a

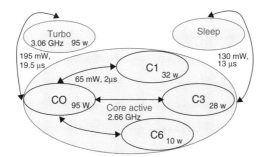

Figure 10.11   Core state and transition graph.

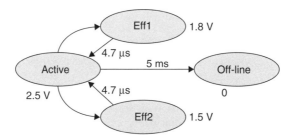

Figure 10.12   Memory rank state and transition graph.

lower operation voltage. The switching time between low power states and the active state is very short (4.7 µs), and it takes a quite long time for the memory rank to hibernate (5 ms).

The platform state is defined by the number of processor cores in the turbo state and active state, the number of memory ranks in the active state, and their physical location within the memory hierarchy. Hence, the power consumed by a platform state is the sum of the power consumed by its constituent parts (cores and memory ranks). The performance of the platform state depends on the physical configuration of the platform (number of cores, number of ranks, physical location of ranks) in that state and the rate of arrival and the type of the incoming workload (CPU intensive, memory intensive) as shown in Figure 10.13. For example, the performance and power consumption by a platform state with two active cores running would be different from those of a platform operating with four active cores. Furthermore, two states with the same number of active cores operate differently because they might use different memory states.

10.3.2.2 VM template evaluation. In this task, we need to determine the optimal configuration in terms of platform state as a function of job request rate. One metric to determine the appropriate state (template) for a given workload is the saturation rate. The platform reaches a saturation state when its performance does not improve as we add more active cores and/or bring memory ranks to

Platform state 0:
Core job queue 1, Core job queue 2
Rank job queue 1, Rank job queue 2

Platform state 2:
Core job queue 1, Core job queue 2,
Core job queue 3, Core job queue 4,
Rank job queue 1, Rank job queue 2

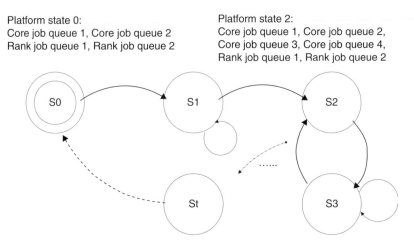

Figure 10.13   Platform state and transition graph.

a high performance state. Using the saturation requesting rate, we can determine if the current platform state is too powerful for the current workload (too
much wasted computing and memory resources) or too small so that the platform cannot handle efficiently the assigned workload. This mismatch between
the platform current state and workload will cause either excessive job losses
due to insufficient resources or enormous wait time for each job, which would
affect either the QoS or the average performance and consumed energy. The
saturation job request rate can be used to measure whether or not the current job
requesting rate can be handled by the current platform state (VM template). For
each platform state (number of active cores and their states, number of memory ranks and their states), we define the maximum job request rate that can be

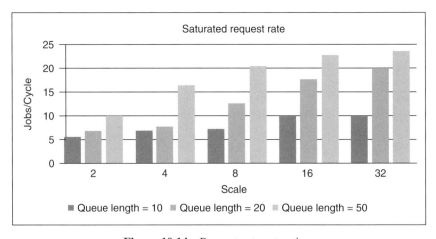

Figure 10.14   Request rate saturation.

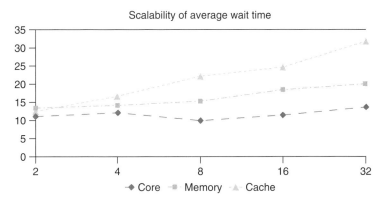

Figure 10.15   Scalability of average wait time.

handled by that state (saturation state), and any increase beyond that saturation rate would require changing the platform state to another template, as shown in Figure 10.14. Similarly, if the job request rate decreases, the ideal template or platform state (e.g., less active cores, low power states) will be selected and the PAM will reconfigure the platform to operate in that state, and so on. In the simulation, we also consider the impact of queue length on the saturation rate and consequently its impact on the ideal platform template for a given job request rate. We also study the impact on performance as the platform size scales up and whether or not the degradation in the saturated request rate is within tolerated limits.

10.3.2.3   Scalability analysis.   Resource scalability is also an important factor to be analyzed. We need to make sure that the communication and arbitration overhead does not cause considerable impact on the system performance while saving energy. As can be seen in Figure 10.15, the average wait time remains tens of cycles per job per core/rank as the platform size enlarges. However, for cache jobs, it keeps the jobs waiting more than expected. Overall, the job-sending overhead does not exceed 35 instruction cycles, which is tolerable in this platform. Limited scheduling and communication overhead have been included as the system scales up in order to ensure better job processing capacity and more opportunity for energy savings.

10.3.3   Autonomic Power Efficiency Management Algorithm (Performance Per Watt)

In this section, we present several autonomic power management algorithms. The search for the optimal platform state as executed by the PAM is formulated as a performance-per-watt maximization problem as shown below.

Problem Formulation: Energy Proportional Computing

$$\underset{t}{\text{Max }} \eta_t = \prod_{i=1}^{N} \frac{nJPQ_{i,t}}{E_{i,t}}$$

which is equal to

$$\underset{t}{\text{Max }} L = \ln\left(\eta_t\right) = \sum_{i=1}^{N} \ln\ nJPQ_{i,t} - \sum_{i=1}^{N} \ln E_{i,t}$$

Such that

1. $rTime_{min} \leq rTime_i \leq rTime_{max}$
2. $rLoss_{min} \leq rLoss_i \leq rLoss_{max}$
3. $d_{min} \leq d_i \leq d_{max}$
4. $\sum_{i=1}^{N_s} x_{ij} = 1$
5. $\vee\ x_{ij} = 0|1$

where

η_t = the power proportional efficiency for the instance i during interval t;

$rTime_i$ = the platform responseTime expressed as a sum of the wait-Time and procTime;

E_i = the platform energy consumed in target state

p_i, and E_i is given by $E_i = \sum_{i=1}^{N_s} \left(c_{ij} * \tau_{trans_{ij}} + p_r * n_r * t_p + p_c * n_c * t_p\right) * x_{ij}$,

= the sum of the transition energy consumed ($c_{ij} * \tau_{trans_{jk}}$), the energy consumed by the processor subsystem in the target state ($p_r * n_r * t_p$), and the energy consumed by the memory subsystem in the target state ($p_c * n_c * t_p$);

p_r = the power consumed by a memory rank in the active state;

p_c = the power consumed by a processor core in turbo state;

n_r = the number of memory ranks in active state;

n_c = the number of processor cores in turbo state;

N_s = the total number of platform states;

c_{ij} = the power consumed in state transition;

$\tau_{trans_{ij}}$ = the time taken for state transition;

$rLoss_k$ = the platform requestLoss in target state Si;

$[rTime_{min}, rTime_{max}]$ and $[rLoss_{min}, rLoss_{max}]$ = the threshold response-Time and threshold requestLoss range for the platform, respectively;

$[d_{min}, d_{max}]$ = the threshold delay range for the memory subsystem;

x_{ij} = the decision variable for transition from state p_j to p_k.

Constraints 1 and 2 of the optimization equation state that in the target state, the responseTime and the requestLoss must stay within the required threshold ranges. Constraint 3 states that in the target state, the end-to-end memory access delay should stay within the threshold range. Constraint 4 states that the optimization problem leads to only one decision. The decision variable corresponding to that is 1 and the rest of the decision variables are set to 0, meaning the decision variable is binary. Constraint 5 states that the decision variable is a $0-1$ integer. Following is the platform autonomic management algorithm (Algorithm 10.1).

Algorithm 10.1: APP for EPC

```
Initialization;
While (reqRate == getReqRate()) or (t mod interval == 0)
     [#core, #rank] = Template[reqRate];
        reqLoss = getReqLoss(); rspTime = getRspTime();dLay
        = getDelay();
     updateStates();
     if boundaries are violated, Template-; else do EPC;
end
```

10.3.4   Simulation Results and Evaluation

Case 1: Memory-intensive workload.   As shown in Figure 10.16, the average wait time experienced by a platform job is nearly negligible at the core and cache level compared to that at the memory level; the average wait time at the memory level follows the arrival rate of incoming jobs. We have noticed that at around 2000 simulation cycles, the wait time increases even when the arrival rate drops. This is because the platform memory was initially overprovisioned to handle the incoming traffic. At around 2000 simulation cycles, the platform memory configuration has been increased from one to two ranks, resulting in bringing down the average wait time. Our scheme gives an average energy savings of 56.25%.

Case 2: CPU-intensive workload.   Initially, the platform is configured with two processor cores and two memory ranks. As it can be seen from Figure 10.17, the job arrival rate starts increasing from around 4000 simulation cycles, and this increases the average wait time experienced by the jobs. It is clear that the average wait time experienced by the jobs is significantly higher in the processor subsystem than in the cache or the memory subsystem. In order to avert this increase in the average wait time, the PAM scales up the processor subsystem from one core at 5000 simulation cycles to two cores at 6000 simulation cycles and then to three cores at 7000 simulation cycles, bringing it down to one core again at 9000 simulation cycles when the rate of arrival drops again. Note that the configuration of the memory subsystem remains more or less static when

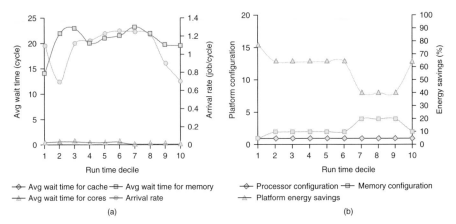

Figure 10.16   Platform operating features and energy savings for memory-intensive traffic patterns. (a) Performance parameters for memory-intensive workload. (b) Platform configurations for memory-intensive workload.

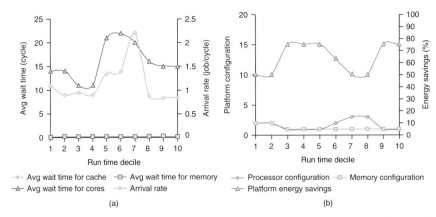

Figure 10.17   Platform operating features and energy savings for CPU-intensive traffic patterns. (a) Performance parameters for CPU-intensive workload. (b) Platform configurations for CPU-intensive workload.

the number of ranks is reduced from two to one around 3000 simulation cycles and remains there once the PAM establishes that the memory subsystem does not contribute to the increase in the average wait time as seen by platform jobs. This leads to a platform energy savings of up to 63.75%. Note that there is a distinctive phase lag between the monitored average wait time core and the core configuration.

This phase lag occurs because the PAM has room for improvement in terms of predicting the arrival rate of the incoming workload. If the PAM accurately predicts the arrival rate, it could configure the processor subsystem proactively even before it starts seeing a real increase in the arrival rate. However, in this actual case, we notice that the PAM is almost one observation cycle behind in terms of predicting and appropriately configuring the processor subsystem. We are investigating this issue further.

Case 3: Mixed workloads. Figure 10.18 shows a mixed workload that consists of both processor-intensive and memory-intensive phases. As expected, the workload impacts the average wait time experienced by jobs at the processor subsystem different than the average wait time experienced by the jobs at the memory subsystem. The request arrival rate increases at around 3000 simulation cycles, but the average wait time—memory increases at around 2000 simulation cycles and the average wait time—processor increases at around 5000 simulation cycles. This is because the memory was initially configured at one rank and the processor was configured with two cores. The initial memory configuration was too small to handle the incoming traffic and this causes the PAM to scale out the size of the memory subsystem to two ranks and eventually to four ranks at around 7000 simulation cycles. At that time, the memory subsystem was configured to its maximum capacity leading to zero savings in memory energy. This reconfiguration in the memory subsystem resulted in reducing the average wait time experienced by jobs in the memory subsystem.

For the processor subsystem, however, the average wait time starts increasing only around 5000 simulation cycles. It is around this time that the workload changes phase into becoming more processor intensive and the processor subsystem needs to scale out to a bigger capacity to handle the workload. Hence, the PAM reconfigures the processor subsystem from one core to two cores and then to three cores in the subsequent cycle. This brings down the average wait time experienced by jobs in the processor subsystem. In this manner, the PAM reconfigures the platform to an optimal configuration that has a direct impact on

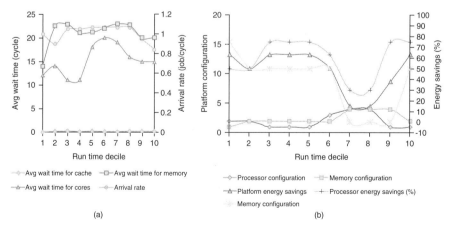

Figure 10.18   Platform operating features and energy savings for hybrid traffic patterns. (a) Performance parameters for hybrid workload. (b) Platform configurations for hybrid workload.

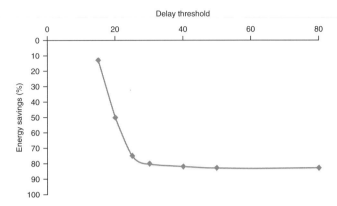

Figure 10.19 Energy-savings comparison and QoS trade-offs for energy savings.

the overall platform response time, thereby saving platform energy and maintaining platform performance. Note that there is zero energy savings in the memory subsystem for simulation cycles 7000–9000 because the memory subsystem is operating at its maximum capacity during this phase.

Our technique gives an overall average platform energy savings of 47.5% while always maintaining the platform response time within the acceptable threshold level. Next, we study the impact of changing the threshold values on the platform performance and energy savings.

10.3.4.1 Analysis of energy and performance trade-offs. We varied the threshold value of the end-to-end delay for the memory subsystem and measured the impact of that change on the memory energy savings for the same workload. As expected, for a more stringent threshold value, the opportunity for energy savings is very little (Fig. 10.19). For example, an increase in the threshold value from 15 to 20 will increase the savings by around 40%, and an increase in threshold to 25 will result in an increase that can reach up to 80% in energy savings. The convergent energy saving will be around 80% for best cases. This demonstrates the opportunity of increasing power savings when it is acceptable to degrade performance within threshold values.

We compare our algorithm with five other algorithms as shown in Figure 10.20—the single-objective optimization algorithms that focus on minimizing energy or delay only, the previous AppFlow management without Energy Proportional Computing (EPC), and multiobjective algorithm with or without the GGA algorithm. For the platform resource utilization aspect, our approach ranks the highest with around 93% since it targets to have the least wasted resources throughout the whole process. Also, we achieved best proportional energy efficiency among all other methods. The energy savings and

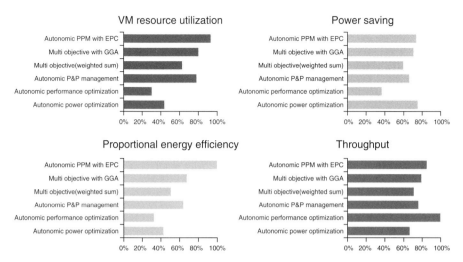

Figure 10.20 Multiobjective evaluation in the algorithm aspect.

performance that have been achieved are quite comparable with the best cases and better than the other ones.

10.4 CONCLUSION AND FUTURE DIRECTIONS

The dynamic and heterogeneous resources and workloads in large-scale data centers require self-management services. We presented an architecture for platform autonomic management that performs power and performance management of high performance server platforms with multicore processors and multirank memory subsystems. We also presented a power proportional computing algorithm and evaluated its performance using DEVS simulation environment. In the simulation, we model the platform as an IBM blade system. Our experimental results show that considerable energy savings can be achieved for both memory-intensive and the CPU-intensive workloads.

In future research, our goal is to validate the simulation results on our IBM Blade Data Center. In addition, we will evaluate the performance of the PAM self-management algorithms when applied to a wide range of scientific and engineering applications.

ACKNOWLEDGMENT

This work is partially supported by National Science Foundation research projects NSF IIP-0758579, NCS-0855087 and IIP-1127873.

REFERENCES

1. EPA. Epa report to congress on server and data center energy efficiency. U.S. Environmental Protection Agency, Tech. Rep. 2007.

2. Energy Star Data Center Energy Efficiency Initiatives. http://www.energystar.gov/index.cfm?c=prod_development.server_efficiency.

3. Felter W, Rajamani K, Keller T, Rusu C. A performance-conserving approach for reducing peak power consumption in server systems. In: Proceedings of the 19th Annual international Conference on Supercomputing; 2005 Jun 20–22; Cambridge (MA), ICS '05. New York: ACM; 2005. pp. 293–302.

4. Hasson J. Top data center issues: social networks, energy costs, Free CIO Newletter; 2009. Available at http://www.fiercecio.com/story/top-data-center-issues-social-networks-energy-costs/2009-12-02#ixzz0tsuhVj00. Access year: 2009.

5. Zeigler BP, Praehofer H, Kim TG. *Theory of Modeling and Simulation*. 2nd ed. Academic Press; 2000. Available at http://www.amazon.com/exec/obidos/redirect?tag=citeulike07-20&path=ASIN/0127784551. Access year: 2000.

6. Zheng W, Bianchini R, Janakiraman GJ, Santos JR, Turner Y. JustRunIt: experiment-based management of virtualized data centers. In: Proceedings of the USENIX Annual Technical Conference; 2009 Jun. Washington (DC): Computer Society; 2009. pp. 68–75. Data Center Industry Leaders Reach Agreement on Guiding Principles for Energy Efficiency Metrics; 2010.

7. CISCO Data Center Infrastructure 2.5, Design Guide, CISCO Validation Design 1, December 2010.

8. Kimura H, Sato M, Imada T, Hotta Y. Runtime DVFS control with instrumented code in power-scalable cluster system. In: Proceedings of the 10th IEEE International Conference on Cluster Computing (CLUSTER 2008), Japan. pp. 354–359.

9. Gurumurthi US, Sivasubramaniam A, Natarajan VK. Disk drive roadmap from the thermal perspective: A case for dynamic thermal management. SIGARCH Comput Archit News 2005;33(2):38–49.

10. Hoelzle U, Barroso LA. *The Datacenter as a Computer: An Introduction to the Design of Warehouse-Scale Machines*. Morgan and Claypool Publishers; 2009.

11. Heath T, Centeno AP, George P, Ramos L, Jaluria Y, Bianchini R. Mercury and freon: temperature emulation and management for server systems. In: Proceedings of the 12th international Conference on Architectural Support For Programming Languages and Operating Systems; 2006 Oct 21–25; San Jose (CA). New York: ACMASPLOS-XII; 2006. pp. 106–116.

12. Xia F, Liu L, Ma L, Sun Y, Dong J. Performance-aware power management in embedded controllers with multiple-voltage processors. Inf Technol J 2008;7(6):942–947.

13. Hsu C, Feng W. Effective dynamic voltage scaling through CPU-boundedness detection. Lecture Notes in Computer Science; Portland, Oregon; 2005. LA-UR 04–7195.

14. Lee H, Baek J, Chung T, Oh S. Thermal management of high power memory module. In: 2006 IEEE Twenty-Second Annual Semiconductor Thermal Measurement and Management Symposium; Texas, USA; 2006 Mar 14–16. pp. 216–221.

15. Available at http://magazine40.blogspot.com/2010/03/ibm-bladecenter-hs22.html.

16. Goh LK, Veeravalli B, Viswanathan S. Design of fast and efficient energy-aware gradient-based scheduling algorithms heterogeneous embedded multiprocessor systems. IEEE Trans Parallel Distrib Syst 2009;20(1):1–12.

17. Ramos RL, Bianchini R. C-Oracle: Predictive thermal management for data centers. In: 2008. IEEE 14th International Symposium on High Performance Computer Architecture(HPCA); Utah, USA; 2008 Feb. pp. 111–122, 16–20.

18. Ge R, Feng X, Song S, Chang HC, Li D, Cameron KW. PowerPack: energy profiling and analysis of high-performance systems and applications. IEEE Trans Parallel Distrib Syst 2010;21(5):658–671.

19. Wang R, Kandasamy N. A distributed control framework for performance management of virtualized computing environments: some preliminary results. In: Proceedings of the 1st Workshop on Automated Control For Datacenters and Clouds; 2009 Jun 19–19; Barcelona, Spain. New York: ACDC '09. ACM; 2009. pp. 7–12.

20. Barroso LA, Hölzle U. The case for energy-proportional computing. Computer 2007;40(12):33–37.

21. Fan SX, Weber W, Barroso LA. Power provisioning for a warehouse-sized computer. In: Proceedings of the 34th ACM International Symposium on Computer Architecture; 2007 Jun; San Diego (CA).

22. Chen G, He W, Liu J, Nath S, Rigas L, Xiao L, Zhao F. Energy-aware server provisioning and load dispatching for connection-intensive internet services. In: Crowcroft J, Dahlin M, editors. In: Proceedings of the 5th USENIX Symposium on Networked Systems Design and Implementation; 2008 16–18 Apr; San Francisco (CA). Berkeley (CA): USENIX Association; 2008. pp. 337–350.

23. Green PCs for a Smarter Future, Intel Green Computing White Paper. Available at www.lenovo.com/green.

24. Campbell S, Jeronimo M. *Applied Virtualization Technology: Usage Models for IT Professionals and Software Developers*. Intel Press; 2006.

25. Huang S, Feng W. Energy-efficient cluster computing via accurate workload characterization. In: Proceedings of the 2009 9th IEEE/ACM international Symposium on Cluster Computing and the Grid; 2009 May 18–21; CCGRID. IEEE S.

26. Intel Xeon Processor 5600 Series, Datasheet, Volume 1, March 2010, http://www.intel.com/content/www/us/en/processors/xeon/xeon-5600-vol-1-datasheet.html.

CHAPTER 11

ENERGY AND THERMAL AWARE SCHEDULING IN DATA CENTERS

GAURAV DHIMAN, RAID AYOUB, and TAJANA S. ROSING

11.1 INTRODUCTION

Power consumption is a critical design parameter in modern data center and enterprise environments, since it directly impacts both the deployment (peak power delivery capacity) and operational costs (power supply, cooling). The energy consumption of the compute equipment and the associated cooling infrastructure is a major component of these costs. The state-of-the-art servers that populate the data centers are commonly equipped with multiple CPU sockets to meet the ever-increasing computation demands. However, this enormous level of integration coupled with high performance does not only lead to higher energy consumption but also to high power density [1]. The direct consequence of such high power density is the increase in thermal stress that requires a large and energy-hungry cooling system to deal with. Hence, modern data centers not only grapple with the problem of high energy consumption due to computation but also energy costs due to the cooling subsystem.

The electricity consumption for powering and cooling the data centers in the United States is projected to cross $7 billions by the end of 2010 [2, 3]. This provides strong motivation for developing mechanisms to efficiently manage computation in data centers to reduce both the energy consumption and power density.

Modern data centers and cloud computing providers (such as Amazon EC2 [4]) use virtualization (e.g., Xen [5] and VMware [6]) to get better fault isolation, improved system manageability, and reduced infrastructure cost through resource consolidation and live migration [7]. Consolidating multiple servers running in different virtual machines (VMs) on a single physical machine (PM) increases the

Energy-Efficient Distributed Computing Systems, First Edition.
Edited by Albert Y. Zomaya and Young Choon Lee.
© 2012 John Wiley & Sons, Inc. Published 2012 by John Wiley & Sons, Inc.

overall utilization and efficiency of the equipment across the whole deployment. However, naive consolidation can lead to higher temperatures and resource bottlenecks, which can dramatically deteriorate the performance and increase cooling costs. In this chapter, we show that based on the characteristics of the different VMs, the scheduler can highly optimize energy efficiency of the whole cluster. The scheduler employs multilevel hierarchical optimizations, one at the cluster level and the other at the PM level. A brief description of these two levels is given as follows:

- *Intermachine Scheduling*. The objective is to generate the most energy-efficient combination of VMs across the PMs. This can be done by exploiting the characteristics of the VMs to generate a VM combination that is resource efficient. We show how resource efficiency directly results in high energy efficiency in the following sections.
- *Intramachine Scheduling*. The objective is to manage computation within a PM in order to minimize the energy consumption of that PM. This can be achieved through exploiting the characteristics of computation to generate a schedule, which results in an improved thermal profile in a PM. This, as we show in the subsequent sections, results in energy savings because of reduction in the cooling requirements.

Thus, we have a hierarchical solution, where at the intermachine level, the scheduler optimizes energy consumption of the computation based on detecting the most energy-efficient combination, whereas at the intramachine level, the scheduler optimizes the cooling energy by eliminating power hotspots. The major benefit of such an approach is that it nicely decouples cluster- and machine-level scheduling, resulting in a low overhead and scalable solution. We describe both the scheduling techniques in detail in forthcoming sections.

11.2   RELATED WORK

A lot of research work has been done in the area of workload (VMs), power management, and thermal management in data centers. Most of the work largely ignores the basic architectural characteristics of the VMs. They treat the overall CPU utilization of the PM and its VMs as an indicator of their respective power consumption and resource utilization, and use it for guiding the VM management policy decisions (VM migration, scheduling, dynamic voltage frequency scaling/DVFS, etc.). However, our work shows that for energy-efficient intermachine and intramachine scheduling, VM workload characterization is very critical, and just CPU utilization can mislead the scheduling policies into making decisions that can create hotspots of activity, and degrade overall performance and increase cooling energy costs.

Systems for management of VMs across a cluster of PMs have been proposed in the past. Eucalyptus [8], OpenNebula [9], and Usher [10] are open source systems, which include support for managing VM creation and allocation across a

PM cluster. For management of VMs on larger scale, for instance, across multiple data center sites, systems such as Grid Virtualization Engine (GVE) [11] have been proposed. However, these solutions do not have VM scheduling policies to dynamically consolidate or redistribute VMs. VM scheduling policies for this purpose have also been investigated in the past. In Reference 12, the authors propose a VM scheduling system, which dynamically schedules the VMs across the PMs based on their CPU, memory, and network utilization to avoid hotspots of activity on PMs for better overall performance. The distributed resource scheduler (DRS) from VMware [13] also uses VM scheduling to perform automated load balancing in response to CPU and memory pressure. Similarly, in Reference 14, the authors propose VM scheduling algorithms for dynamic consolidation and redistribution of VMs for managing performance and SLA (service-level agreement) violations. In Reference 15, the authors model application performance across VMs to dynamically control the CPU allocation to each VM with the objective of maximizing the profits. The authors in Reference 16 propose Entropy, which uses constraint programming to determine a globally optimal solution for VM scheduling in contrast to the first fit decreasing heuristic used by Wood et al. [12] and Bobroff et al. [14], which can result in globally suboptimal placement of VMs. However, none of these VM scheduling algorithms take into account the impact of the policy decisions on the energy consumption in the system.

Power management in data center like environments has been an active area of research. In Reference 17, the data center power consumption is managed by turning servers off depending on demand. Reducing operational costs by performing temperature-aware workload placement has also been explored [18].

In Reference 19, DVFS is performed based on the memory intensiveness of workloads on the server clusters to reduce energy costs. Similarly, Ranganathan et al. and Fan et al. [20, 21] use DVFS to reduce average power consumption in blade servers with the objective of performing power budgeting. Recent studies [2, 22] have shown that in modern server systems, the effectiveness of DVFS for energy management has diminished significantly because of its impact on the performance of the workloads. In the earlier sections, we had confirmed this observation and shown how intelligent VM colocation outperforms state-of-the-art DVFS policies [23, 24] in terms of energy savings.

The problem of power management in virtualized environments has also been investigated. In Reference 25, the authors propose VirtualPower that uses the power management decisions of the guest OS (operating system) on virtual power states as hints to run local and global policies across the PMs. It relies on efficient power management policies in the guest OS and does no VM characterization at the hypervisor level. This makes it difficult to port some of the state-of-the-art power management policies such as [23, 24] in guest OS because of lack of exclusive access to privileged resources such as CPU performance counters. This problem has led to adoption of power management frameworks such as *cpufreq* and *cpuidle* in recent virtualization solutions (such as Xen [5]). In Reference 26, the authors develop a power and performance model of a transaction-based application running within the VMs and use it to drive cluster-level energy management through DVFS. However, they assume that the application characteristics to be known. In Reference 27, a coordinated multilevel solution for power management in data centers is proposed. Their solution is based on a model that uses power estimation (using CPU utilization) and overall utilization levels to drive VM placement and power management. The model and results are based on off-line trace driven analysis and simulations. In Reference 28, the authors present GreenCloud, an infrastructure to dynamically consolidate VMs based on CPU utilization to produce idle machines, which could be turned off to generate energy savings. None of these solutions [25–28] take the architectural characteristics of the VM into account, which, as we show in Section 11.3.1, directly determine the VM performance and power profile. In Reference 29, the authors use VM characteristics such as cache footprint and working set to drive power aware placement of VMs. But their study assumes an HPC application environment, where the VM characteristics are known in advance. Besides, their evaluation is based on simulations. In contrast, vGreen assumes a general purpose workload setup with no a priori knowledge on their characteristics.

The concept of dynamic architectural characterization of workloads using CPU performance counters for power management [23, 24], performance management [30], and thermal management [31] on nonvirtualized systems has been explored before. For a standalone virtualized PM, the authors in Reference 32 use performance counters to enforce power budgets across VMs on that PM. In Reference 33, the authors identify resource contention as a problem for energy efficiency but primarily focus on scheduling and power management on a single PM. In some recent literature, performance counters have been used in virtualized clusters to perform power metering [34–36], QoS management [37], and power budgeting [38] to aid efficient power provisioning. However, using architectural characterization to drive cluster-level VM management from the perspective of energy efficiency and balanced power consumption has been largely unexplored.

At a PM level, power management techniques are not sufficient to solve the thermal problems. This is because temperature is a function of power density rather than the average power. Hence, to optimize energy further, thermal optimizations must be considered. A number of processor-level dynamic thermal techniques have been suggested in the recent years. They can be broadly classified into reactive and proactive categories. Reactive techniques include clock gating [39], DVFS [40], activity migration [41], etc. Recently introduced proactive techniques manage overheating by predicting the temperature and rescheduling the workload appropriately [42]. The authors in Reference 43 suggest a fan control algorithm that manages temperature based on input from thermal sensors only. A class of techniques have been suggested to improve cooling efficiency at the data center level [44, 45]. The research in these techniques suggest the use of workload scheduling to help with the air circulation problem in the data center; hence, better cooling efficiency. However, these techniques cannot be reused at the socket level since their air flow is highly contained. The authors in Reference 46 propose a methodology for modeling the convection thermal resistance between the heat sink and ambient temperature as a function of the air flow rate, which is leveraged in our work.

In the subsequent sections, we explain our technique for workload management at both the intermachine and intramachine levels. We show how, through architectural characterization, the system can gain invaluable insights into the performance and power profile of the workloads, which allows our policies to outperform the existing state-of-the-art techniques.

11.3 INTERMACHINE SCHEDULING

In this section, we introduce vGreen, a multitiered software system to manage VM scheduling across different PMs with the objective of managing the overall energy efficiency and performance. The basic premise behind vGreen is to understand and exploit the relationship between the architectural characteristics of a VM (e.g., instructions per cycle, memory accesses, etc.) and its performance and power consumption. vGreen is based on a client-server model, where a central server (referred to as *vgserv*) performs the management (scheduling, DVFS, etc.) of VMs across the PMs (referred to as *vgnodes*). The *vgnodes* perform online characterization of the VMs running on them and regularly update the *vgserv* with this information. These updates allow *vgserv* to understand the performance and power profile of the different VMs and aids it to intelligently place them across the *vgnodes* to improve overall performance and energy efficiency.

11.3.1 Performance and Power Profile of VMs

In this discussion, we assume Xen as the underlying virtualization hypervisor. It is a standard open-source virtualization solution, which also forms the baseline technology for commercial products such as XenSource, Oracle VM, etc. However, the ideas presented in this section are independent of Xen and can be applied to other virtualization solutions such as kernel-based virtual machines (KVM), etc. as well. In Xen, a VM is an instance of an OS, which is configured with virtual CPUs (VCPUs) and a memory size. The number of VCPUs and memory size is configured at the time of VM creation. Xen virtualizes the real hardware to the VM making the OS running within it believe that it is running on a real machine. A PM can have multiple VMs active on it at any point in time, and Xen multiplexes them across the real physical CPUs (PCPUs) and memory. The entity that Xen schedules over the PCPU is the VCPU, making it the fundamental unit of execution. Thus, a VCPU is analogous to a thread, and a VM is analogous to a process in a system running a single OS such as Linux. In addition, Xen provides a control VM, referred to as Domain-0 (or Dom-0), which is what the machine running Xen boots into. It acts as an administrative interface for the user and provides access to privileged operations such as creating, destroying, or migrating VMs.

The nature of workload executed in each VM determines the power profile and performance of the VM, and hence its energy consumption. As discussed before, VMs with different or same characteristics could be colocated on the same PM. In this section, we show that colocation of VMs with heterogeneous characteristics on PMs is beneficial for overall performance and energy efficiency across the PM cluster. For understanding this, we performed some experiments and analysis on two benchmarks from SPEC-CPU 2000 suite, namely, *eon* and *mcf*. These two benchmarks have contrasting characteristics in terms of their CPU and memory utilization. While *mcf* has high memory per cycle (MPC) accesses and low instructions committed per cycle (IPC), *eon* has low MPC and high IPC. We use a test bed of two dual Intel quad core Xeon- (hyperthreading equipped) based PMs (16 CPUs each) running Xen. On each of these PMs, we create two VMs with eight virtual CPUs (VCPUs) each (total of four VMs). Inside each VM, we execute either *eon* or *mcf* as the workload. We use multiple instances/threads of the benchmarks to generate higher utilization levels. For our PM (16 CPUs), this implies 4 instances for 25% utilization, 8 instances for 50%, and 16 instances for 100% utilization. Each PM is equipped with power sensors, which are interfaced to the Dom-0 OS in a standardized manner using intelligent platform management interface (IPMI) [47]. We periodically (every 2 s) query the IPMI interface to log the power consumption of the whole PM for all our experiments.

In our first set of experiments, we run homogeneous VMs on each PM, that is, the two VMs with *mcf* on one PM and two with *eon* on the other. We refer to this VM placement schedule as "same" indicating homogeneity. During the execution, we record the execution time of all the benchmark instances. Figure 11.1a shows the normalized execution time results for different number of instances of the benchmarks, where the execution times are normalized against the execution time with two instances (one instance per VM). We can observe that for *mcf* in the "same" schedule (shown as "mcf-same"), as the CPU utilization increases, the execution time almost increases linearly. For 100% utilization *mcf*, the execution time is almost 8.5 × compared to the baseline execution time. The primary reason for such an observation is the high MPC of *mcf*. The high MPC results in higher cache conflict rate and pressure on the memory bandwidth when multiple threads execute, which decreases the effective IPC per thread and hence increases its execution time. This is illustrated by the plot of aggregate IPC and MPC of all *mcf* threads in Figure 11.1c. We can see how the MPC increases by around 7 × as CPU utilization goes from 12% to 100%. However, the aggregate IPC almost remains constant, which implies that IPC per thread goes down significantly, resulting in increased execution time observed in Figure 11.1a. In contrast, for *eon* ("eon-same"), the execution time is fairly independent of the CPU utilization because of its much lower MPC. We can observe that the execution time shows an increase beyond 50% utilization. This happens since our machine has 8 cores and 16 CPUs (due to hyperthreading), with two CPUs per core. When we reach 50% utilization that corresponds to eight threads of the benchmark, and beyond that the threads start sharing the pipeline, which reduces the individual IPC of threads sharing the pipeline. This phenomena is illustrated in Figure 11.1c, where the IPC slope of *eon* drops off a little beyond 50% CPU utilization. However,

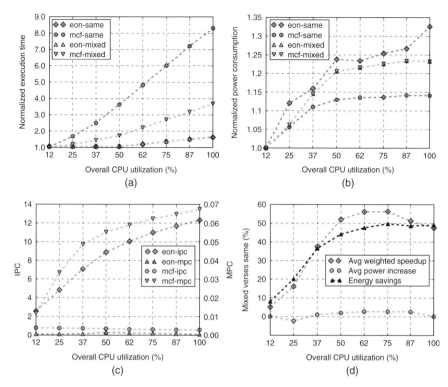

Figure 11.1 Comparison of *eon* and *mcf*. (a) Normalized execution time, (b) normalized power consumption, (c) comparison of aggregate IPC and MPC, and (d) comparison of "mixed" versus "same" VM placement schedules.

this increase in execution time is trivial compared to that of *mcf* as seen in Figure 11.1a and c. In summary, this analysis indicates that the performance of a VM has a strong negative corelation to utilization rate of the memory subsystem.

Similarly, Figure 11.1b shows the system-level power consumption of the PMs normalized against the power consumption with just two threads. We can observe that for *eon* ("eon-same"), the power consumption increases almost linearly to the increase in utilization. This happens since it has high IPC, which implies higher CPU resource utilization and power consumption. We can observe that the slope of increase in power changes at 50% utilization. This is again due to pipeline sharing between threads beyond 50% utilization, which lowers the contribution of new threads to power consumption (Fig. 11.1c). In contrast, for *mcf*, the power consumption increases initially, but then it saturates. This primarily happens because of the lower IPC of threads at higher utilization levels as discussed earlier. As a consequence of this, the difference in power consumption between the two PMs is almost 20% (~45 W in our measurements). This analysis indicates that the power consumption of a VM has direct correlation to IPC of the workload running inside it.

These results indicate that coscheduling VMs with similar characteristics is not beneficial from energy efficiency point of view at the cluster level. The PM running *mcf* contributes to higher system energy consumption, since it runs for a significantly longer period of time. To understand the benefits of coscheduling heterogeneous workloads in this context, we swapped two VMs on the PMs, hence running VMs with *mcf* and *eon* on both the PMs. We refer to this VM placement schedule as "mixed," indicating the heterogeneity. Figure 11.1 shows the results (indicated as "mixed") achieved for this configuration in terms of normalized execution time and power consumption. We can observe that *eon* execution time almost stays the same, whereas *mcf* execution time goes down significantly at higher utilization rates (around 450% reduction at 100% utilization). This happens because we now get rid of the hot spot of intense activity in the memory subsystem on one PM (running just the *mcf* VMs in the "same" schedule) and share the overall system resources in a much more efficient manner. The average power consumption of the two PMs becomes similar and roughly lies between that of the two PMs in the "same" schedule, as the overall IPC is also much better balanced across the cluster.

Figure 11.1d illustrates the comparison of the "mixed" and "same" VM schedules and highlights the benefits of the "mixed" schedule. It plots the following three key metrics to capture this:

1. *Energy Savings.* We estimate the energy reduction in executing each combination of VMs using "mixed" over "same" schedule. This is calculated by measuring the total energy consumption for a VM combination with two schedules, and then taking their difference. We can observe that across all utilization levels, the "mixed" schedule is clearly more energy efficient compared to the "same" schedule. At higher utilization rates (50% and beyond), it achieves as high as 50% energy savings. This primarily happens because of the high speedup achieved by it compared to "same" schedule, as discussed earlier, while keeping the average power consumption almost similar. The next two metrics provides details on these.

2. *Average Weighted Speedup (AWS).* This metric captures how fast the workload runs on the "mixed" schedule compared to "same" schedule. The AWS is based on a similar metric defined in Reference 48. It is defined as

$$\text{AWS} = \frac{\sum_{\text{VM}_i} \frac{T_{\text{same}_i}}{T_{\text{alone}_i}}}{\sum_{\text{VM}_i} \frac{T_{\text{mixed}_i}}{T_{\text{alone}_i}}} - 1, \tag{11.1}$$

where T_{alone_i} is the execution time of VM_i when it runs alone on a PM, and T_{same_i} and T_{mixed_i} are its execution time as part of a VM combination with "same" and "mixed" schedules, respectively. To calculate AWS, we normalize T_{same_i} and T_{mixed_i} against T_{alone_i} for each VM, and then take ratio of the sum of these normalized times across all the VMs in the combination as shown in Equation 11.1. AWS > 0 implies that the VM combination runs faster with "mixed" schedule and vice versa. Figure 11.1d clearly shows that the "mixed" schedule is able to achieve significant speedup. The AWS reaches as high as 57% because of efficient resource sharing and contributes significantly to the energy savings discussed earlier.

3. *Increase in Power Consumption*. This metric captures the difference between the average power consumption of the PMs under the "mixed" and "same" schedule. This is important since we need to make sure that the speedup achieved does not result in much higher average power consumption across the cluster. Figure 11.1d shows that the increase in system power consumption is trivial ($<3\%$) across all the utilization levels. Thus, high speedups at almost similar average power consumption results in significant energy savings illustrated in Figure 11.1d.

In summary, this discussion provides us key insights into the VM management problem. (i) VM characteristics provide invaluable information on both the power and performance profile of VMs. (ii) VM scheduling policies should try to coschedule VMs with heterogeneous characteristics on the same PM. This results in efficient sharing of resources across the cluster and as a consequence is beneficial from both energy efficiency and performance point of view. This is achievable in virtualized environments, since VMs can be dynamically migrated at runtime across PMs at low overhead using *live migration* [7].

This provides strong motivation to use online characterization of VMs for systemwide VM management. In the next section, we describe the overall architecture of vGreen and present details on how it constructs VM characteristics dynamically at runtime using a novel hierarchical approach.

11.3.2   Architecture

Figure 11.2 illustrates the overall architecture of vGreen, which is based on a client-server model. Each PM in the cluster is referred to as a *vGreen client/node* (*vgnode*). There is one central vGreen server (*vgserv*), which manages VM scheduling across the *vgnodes* based on a policy (*vgpolicy*) running on the *vgserv*. The *vgpolicy* decisions are based on the value of different metrics, which capture MPC, IPC, and utilization of different VMs, that it receives as updates from the *vgnodes* running those VMs. The metrics are evaluated and updated dynamically by the vGreen modules in Xen (*vgxen*) and Dom-0 (*vgdom*) on each *vgnode*. Regular updates from the *vgnodes* on the metrics allow the *vgpolicy* to balance both the power consumption and overall performance across the PMs. We now describe the vGreen components and the metrics employed in detail.

11.3.2.1   vgnode. A *vgnode* refers to an individual PM in the cluster. A *vgnode* might have multiple VMs running on it at any given point in time as shown in Figure 11.2. Each *vgnode* has vGreen modules (*vgxen* and *vgdom*) installed on them.

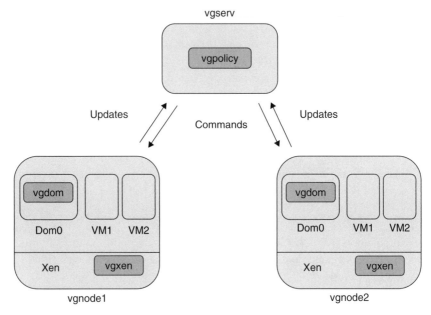

Figure 11.2 Overall vGreen design.

11.3.2.2 vgxen. The *vgxen* is a module compiled into Xen (Fig. 11.2) and is responsible for characterizing the CPU and memory behavior (specifically IPC and MPC) of running VMs. Since multiple VMs with possibly multiple VCPUs might be active concurrently, it is important to cleanly isolate the characteristics of each of these different entities. vGreen adopts a hierarchical approach for this purpose as illustrated in Figure 11.3. The lowest level of the hierarchy is the VCPU level, which is the fundamental unit of execution and scheduling in Xen. When a VCPU is scheduled on a PCPU by the Xen scheduler, *vgxen* starts the CPU performance counters of that PCPU to count the events: (i) instructions retired (INST), (ii) clock cycles (CLK), and (iii) memory accesses (MEM).

When that VCPU consumes its time slice (or blocks) and is removed from the PCPU, *vgxen* reads the performance counter values and estimates its MPC (MEM/CLK) and IPC (INST/CLK) for the period it executed. This process is performed for every VCPU executing in the system across all the PCPUs. To effectively estimate the impact of these metrics on the VCPU power consumption and performance, *vgxen* also keeps track of the CPU utilization (*util*) of each VCPU, that is, how much time it actually spends executing on a PCPU over a period of time. This is important, since even a high IPC benchmark will cause high power consumption only if it is executing continuously on the PCPU. Hence,

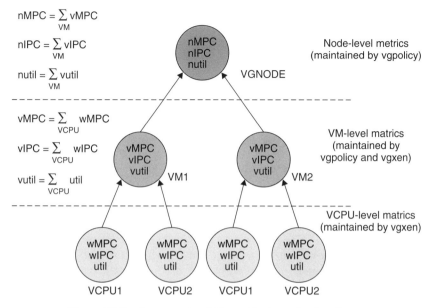

Figure 11.3 An example of hierarchical metrics in vGreen.

the metric derived for each VCPU is weighted by its *util* and is referred to as the *current weighted MPC* and *IPC* (wMPC$_{cur}$ and wIPC$_{cur}$) shown as follows:

$$wMPC_{cur} = MPC \cdot util,$$
$$wIPC_{cur} = IPC \cdot util. \tag{11.2}$$

They are referred to as current, since they are estimated based on the IPC/MPC values from the latest run of a VCPU. To also take into account the previous value of these metrics, we maintain them as running exponential averages. The following equation shows how weighted MPC is estimated:

$$wMPC = \alpha \cdot wMPC_{cur} + (1 - \alpha) \cdot wMPC_{prev}, \tag{11.3}$$

where the new value of weighted MPC (wMPC) is calculated as an exponential average of wMPC$_{prev}$, the previous value of wMPC, and wMPC$_{cur}$ (Eq. 11.2). The factor α determines the weight of current value (wMPC$_{cur}$) and history (wMPC$_{prev}$). In our implementation, we use $\alpha = 0.5$, thus giving equal weight to both. The IPC metric is computed in a similar manner as discussed earlier. We store these averaged metrics in the Xen VCPU structure to preserve them faithfully across VCPU context switches. This constitutes the metric estimation at the lowest level of the hierarchy as shown in Figure 11.3.

At the next level, *vgxen* estimates the aggregate metrics (vMPC, vIPC, vutil) for each VM by adding up the corresponding metrics of its constituent VCPUs, as shown in the middle level of Figure 11.3. This information is stored in VM structure of Xen to personalize metrics at per VM level and is exported to Dom-0 through a shared page, which is allocated by *vgxen* at the boot-up time.

11.3.2.3   vgdom. The second vGreen module of *vgnode* is the *vgdom* (Fig. 11.2). Its main role is to periodically (T_{up_period}) read the shared page exported by *vgxen* to get the latest characteristics metrics for all the VMs running on the vgnode and update the *vgserv* with it. In addition, *vgdom* also acts as an interface for the *vgnode* to the *vgserv*. It is responsible for registering the *vgnode* with the *vgserv* and also for receiving and executing the commands sent by the *vgserv* as shown in Figure 11.2.

11.3.2.4   vgserv. The *vgserv* acts as the cluster controller and is responsible for managing VM scheduling and power management across the *vgnode* cluster. The *vgpolicy* is the core of *vgserv*, which makes the scheduling and power management decisions based on periodic updates on the VM metrics from the *vgnodes*. The metrics of each VM are aggregated by the *vgpolicy* to construct the top-level or node-level metrics (nMPC, nIPC, nutil) as shown in Figure 11.3. Thus, the knowledge of both the node-level and VM-level metrics allow the *vgpolicy* to understand not only the overall power and performance profile of the whole *vgnode* but also fine grained knowhow of the breakdown at VM level.

On the basis of these metrics, the *vgpolicy* runs its balancing and power management algorithm periodically (T_{p_period}). The basic algorithm is motivated by the fact that VMs with heterogeneous characteristics should be coscheduled on the same *vgnode* (Section 11.3.1). The problem of consolidation of VMs in minimum possible PMs has been explored in previous work [12, 16] and is similar to bin-packing problem, which is computationally NP-hard. As discussed in Section 11.2, the existing solutions perform the consolidation based on just CPU utilization. Our balancing algorithms build on top of these existing algorithms to perform balancing based on MPC and IPC as well. The overall algorithm runs in the following four steps:

Algorithm 11.1: MPC Balance Algorithm

Input: *vgnode* n1
1: **If** $nMPC_{n1} < nMPC_{th}$ **then**
2:     **return**
3: **end if**
4: *pm_min* $\leftarrow NULL$
5: **for** all vgnodes n_i except n1 **do**
6:     **If** $(nMPC_{n_i} < nMPC_{th})$ and $(nMPC_{n1} - nMPC_{th}) < (nMPC_{th} - nMPC_{n_i})$ **then**
7:         **If** !*pm_min* or $nMPC_{pm\_min} > nMPC_{n_i}$ **then**
8:             *pm_min* $\leftarrow n_i$

```
 9:        end if
10:     end if
11:  end for
12:  vm_mig ← NULL
13:  for all vm_i in n1 do
14:      if (nMPC_th − nMPC_pm_min) > vMPC_vm_i  and  vMPC_vm_i > vMPC_vm_mig  then
15:          vMPC_vm_mig ← vMPC_vm_i
16:      end if
17:  end for
18:  if pm_min and vm_mig then
19:      do_migrate(vm_mig, n1, pm_min)
20:  end if
```

1. *MPC Balance*. This step ensures that nMPC is balanced across all the *vgnodes* in the system for better overall performance and energy efficiency across the cluster. Algorithm 11.1 gives an overview of how the MPC balance algorithm works for a *vgnode* $n1$.

   The algorithm first of all checks if the nMPC of $n1$ is greater than a threshold $nMPC_{th}$ (step 1 in Algorithm 11.1). This threshold is representative of whether high MPC is affecting the performance of the VMs in that *vgnode*. This is based on the observation in Section 11.3.1, that for lower MPC workloads (such as *eon*), the memory subsystem is lightly loaded and has little impact on the performance of the workload. Hence, if nMPC is smaller, the function returns, since there is no MPC balancing required for $n1$ (step 2 in Algorithm 11.1). If it is higher, then in steps 4–11, the algorithm tries to find the target *vgnode* with the minimum nMPC (*pm_min*) to which a VM from $n1$ could be migrated to resolve the MPC imbalance, subject to the condition in step 6. The condition states that the target *vgnode* (n_i) nMPC ($nMPC_{n_i}$) must be below $nMPC_{th}$ by atleast ($nMPC_{n1} − nMPC_{th}$). This is required, since otherwise migration of a VM from $n1$ to n_i cannot bring $n1$ below the MPC threshold or might make n_i go above the MPC threshold. In steps 7 and 8, it stores the node n_i as target minimum nMPC *vgnode* (*pm_min*), if its nMPC ($nMPC_{n_i}$) is lower than the nMPC of the *vgnode* currently stored as *pm_min*. This way, once the loop in step 5 completes, it is able to locate the *vgnode* in the system with the least nMPC (*pm_min*).

   Once the *pm_min* is found, the algorithm finds the VM (vm_{mig}), which could be migrated to *pm_min* for resolving the MPC imbalance (steps 12–17). For this purpose, it scans the list of VMs on $n1$ to find the VM with the maximum vMPC, which if migrated, does not reverse the imbalance by making nMPC of *pm_min* more than $nMPC_{th}$ (steps 14–15). If such a VM is found, the algorithm invokes the *do_migrate* function to live migrate vm_{mig} from $n1$ to *pm_min* [7] in step 19. The decisions taken by the *vgpolicy* (updates, migration) are communicated to the *vgnodes* in the form of commands as shown in Figure 11.2, while the *vgdom* component on the *vgnode* actually accomplishes the migration.

The complexity of the MPC balance algorithm (Algorithm 11.1) is linear $(O(n)$, where n is the number of *vgnodes* in steps 5–11, and number of VMs on $n1$ in steps 13–17) for resolving an MPC bottleneck, since it requires a single scan of vgnodes and VMs to detect and resolve it. Hence, in terms of implementation and performance the algorithm is simple and scalable.

2. *IPC Balance*. This step ensures nIPC is balanced across the *vgnodes* for better balance of power consumption across the PMs. The algorithm is similar to MPC balance but uses nIPC instead of nMPC.

3. *Util Balance*. This step balances the CPU utilization of *vgnodes* to ensure that there are no overcommitted nodes in the system, if there are other underutilized *vgnodes*. The algorithm is again similar to MPC balance but uses *nutil* instead of nMPC.

4. *Dynamic Voltage Frequency Scaling (DVFS)*. The *vgpolicy* may issue a command to scale the voltage–frequency setting (v–f setting) of a *vgnode*, if it deems that it is more energy efficient than VM migration. This may happen, if there are no enough heterogeneous VMs across the cluster to be able to balance the resource utilization evenly. The DVFS policy is itself based on state-of-the-art DVFS policies [23, 24], which exploit the characteristics of the workload to determine the best suited v–f setting for it. Specifically, it aggressively downscales the v–f setting if the overall MPC is high ($> \text{nMPC}_{\text{th}}$), otherwise keeps the system at the highest v–f setting.

Figure 11.4 gives the intuition behind the policy using an example of two benchmarks, *mcf* and *eon*, running at 90% CPU utilization level. It plots the execution time (Fig. 11.4a) and energy consumption (Fig. 11.4b) at five different v–f settings. The execution time, energy consumption, and the v–f settings are normalized against the values at the highest v–f setting. We can observe that as the frequency is decreased, the execution time of *eon* almost increases in proportion to the drop in frequency. For instance, at normalized frequency of 0.54, the increase in execution time is more than 80% ($\sim \frac{1}{0.54}$). This happens since *eon* has high IPC and uses the pipeline of the processor intensively, which makes its execution time a function of the clock rate of the pipeline or the CPU frequency. This huge performance degradation has a direct impact on the energy consumption of eon at lower v–f settings as shown in Figure 11.4b. We can observe that at all the frequencies the system consumes more energy compared to the highest v–f setting, reaching as high as 40% more. This implies that for high IPC workloads, DVFS is actually energy inefficient.

In contrast, for *mcf*, which has high MPC, we observe that the execution time (Fig. 11.4a) is actually fairly independent of the CPU frequency. This is a consequence of the high degree of CPU stalls that occur during its execution due to frequent memory accesses, which makes its execution time insensitive to actual CPU frequency. The low performance degradation translates into system-level energy savings (Fig. 11.4b), which reaches 10% at the lowest frequency.

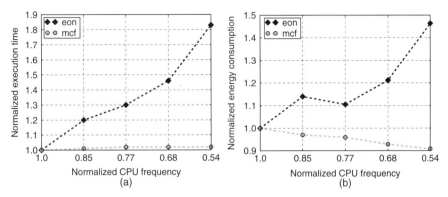

Figure 11.4 Comparison of execution time and energy consumption of *mcf* and *eon* at different frequency levels. (a) Normalized execution time and (b) normalized energy consumption.

This example also illustrates the fact, that the effectiveness of DVFS for energy savings is not very significant in modern server class systems. This has also been observed in previous researches [2, 22] and the reasons for such a trend include lower contribution of CPU in total system power consumption, finer voltage settings in modern CPUs due to shrinking process technology, etc. These observations also motivate our approach to focus more on efficient VM scheduling to achieve higher energy savings rather than on aggressive DVFS. Rather, the system resorts to DVFS only when no further benefits are achievable through scheduling and the MPC is high enough to achieve energy savings. As we show in Section 11.5, such an approach enables energy savings under both heterogeneous and homogeneous workload scenarios through VM scheduling and aggressive DVFS, respectively.

The four steps described earlier in the overall algorithm have relative priorities to resolve conflicts, if they occur. MPC balance is given the highest priority, since memory bottleneck severely impacts overall performance and energy efficiency as identified in Section 11.3.1 (Fig. 11.1a). IPC balance results in a more balanced power consumption profile, which helps create an even thermal profile across the cluster and hence reduces cooling costs [49], and is next in the priority order. Finally, Utilization balance results in a fairly loaded system, and is representative of the prior state-of-the-art scheduling algorithms. DVFS step (step 4), as explained earlier, is invoked only if the system is already balanced from the perspective of MPC, IPC, and CPU utilization, and no further savings are possible through VM scheduling.

11.4 INTRAMACHINE SCHEDULING

Traditional workload scheduling algorithms, for example, dynamic load balancing, implemented in OS do not consider either thermal/cooling characteristics of the processors they run on or the inherent power characteristics of the threads running in the system. Not considering thermal/cooling issues has a big drawback since the heat being dissipated by these running threads actually contributes to the thermal profile of the system at any given point in time. In this section, we discuss scheduling algorithm called *Cool and Save*, which performs thread scheduling based on the dynamic characterization of the thermal profile of the active threads. The algorithm incorporates an air-forced convective model to understand the interaction between thermal characteristics and the fans. It uses performance counters to predict workload induced power density, and therefore the likely temperature on the die with associated cooling costs. Such a model helps the algorithm to estimate the new thermal state and the cooling cost associated with any scheduling event. On the basis of this understanding, it is able to dynamically consolidate or spread the running threads, hence achieving an overall balanced thermal profile that results in higher energy savings due to lower fan speeds. This algorithm is evaluated using benchmarks with varying runtime power character-istics and show that *Cool and Save* is able to achieve up to 85% reduction in cooling-related energy consumption compared to traditional scheduling policies.

11.4.1 Air-Forced Thermal Modeling and Cost

To provide sufficient cooling to the sockets, each socket is normally associated with fans. For example, the Sunfire x4270 server has two sockets, where each has two sets of fans [50]. Figure 11.5 shows a thermal model of two CPU sockets. The modeling of the individual sockets can be done using an RC network similar to what is done in HotSpot [1]. To simplify the modeling, the heat path between the two sockets can be safely neglected since there is no effective conductive or convective heat path between them, as they are typically placed apart in the motherboard. The convective resistance, R_{conv}, between the top of the heat sink and the ambient temperature, which can be computed as follows:

$$R_{\text{conv}} = \frac{1}{hA}, \tag{11.4}$$

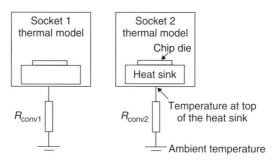

Figure 11.5 Multisocket thermal modeling.

where A is the effective heat sink area and h is the convective heat transfer. The heat transfer h can be modeled as a function of air flow rate as shown in the following equation [46]:

$$h(V) \propto V^{\alpha}, \tag{11.5}$$

where α is a factor with a range of $(0.9–1.0)$ for high-end servers heat sinks. For the estimation of the cooling costs, the results from Reference 46 are used, which relate the fan speed, F, with the air flow rate, as $V \propto F$. As a result, the cooling costs for changing the air flow rate from V_1 to V_2 can be computed as

$$\frac{FP_2}{FP_1} = \left(\frac{V_2}{V_1}\right)^3, \tag{11.6}$$

where FP_1 and FP_1 represent the fan power dissipation at V_1 and V_2, respectively. This formula shows that optimizing the fan speed is crucial for power savings since reducing the temperature requires an increase in the fan power in the order of $3/\alpha$.

11.4.2   Cooling Aware Dynamic Workload Scheduling

Energy of cooling subsystems could be reduced by intelligently distributing the workload across the machine's sockets to reduce fans' speeds [49, 51]. To illustrate this, two machines are used, each with two quad core sockets, where each socket has its own fan. Two types of jobs are executed, one highly active that consumes 14 W and the other moderately active consuming 9.5 W. Temperature threshold is set to $85°C$ and ambient temperature is set to $42°C$. For thermal simulation, an extended version of HotSpot simulator [1] is used, which includes the cooling model as described earlier in this chapter. Figure 11.6 shows the impact of workload assignment on cooling cost savings at the socket level. The left part of the figure shows the thread assignments by state-of-the-art schedulers, while the right part shows their assignments using cooling aware scheduling algorithm. The top part of this figure shows how to save the cooling cost when there is a

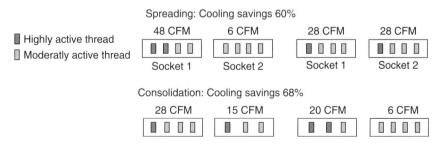

Figure 11.6   Cooling aware scheduling at the socket level.

big imbalance in the total power across the sockets. For such cases, the efficient solution is to balance power across the sockets. The savings are substantial and reach 60%. This class of scheduling is called *spreading*. In the second scenario, the air flow rate of socket 1 in the original assignment is about twice of that of socket 2. To minimize the cooling costs, the scheduler migrates the hot thread from socket 2 to 1 and migrate the two moderate threads from socket 1 to 2. The new assignment lowers the heat in socket 1 since the total socket power is reduced by 5 W while maintaining the maximum core power at the same level. The savings are significant and reach 67%. This class of assignment is called *consolidation*. In summary, scheduling the workload is an effective way to minimize the cooling energy.

To leverage the benefits of controlling both cooling and workload scheduling, we implement our technique at the OS level. Figure 11.7 depicts the operational framework of our approach. The input to the scheduler consists of thermal sensors at each socket, runtime workload characterization, and the incoming workload. On the basis of this set of inputs, the OS scheduler decides whether to redistribute or consolidate the current workload through migrating some of the threads across the sockets. The rescheduling period is large (order of seconds) since the heat sink has a large thermal time constant. This implies that the overhead of rescheduling the workload is negligible since it is in the range of microseconds. The rescheduling overhead primarily comes from the OS, transferring the state of the threads across the cores and any L2 cache misses. Incoming workload is always assigned to the sockets with lower fan speeds.

11.4.3 Scheduling Mechanism

The cooling cost of the individual servers is equal to the sum of the cubes of their fans speeds. The fan speed of a socket depends on both the total socket power and the maximum power consumed by a core, as it will be explained shortly. Therefore, to lower the heat, we can minimize the maximum power, reduce the total power, or both. To minimize cooling energy, it is desirable to keep the fan speed as low as possible. In order to do so, first the threads are *spread* across different sockets in order to balance the power density and reduce the socket

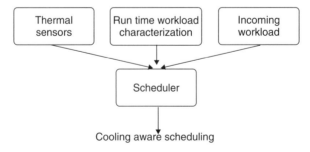

Figure 11.7 Cooling aware scheduling framework.

temperatures and their fan speeds. At this point, consolidation is performed to further reduce the fans speed. The consolidation phase lowers the cooling cost by focusing the workload on a smaller set of the fans (higher speed ones) while keeping their speed in a similar range. This is achieved by consolidating more hot workload into the sockets that are associated with those fans and unloading from them multiple moderately active workload to maintain similar total power.

The evaluation of potential cooling savings is performed by a predictor whose inputs are the power characteristics of the workload and the ambient temperature of the server. The information required for predictions is periodically collected and sent to the scheduler. The following thread scheduling algorithm illustrates workload spreading phase. The consolidation algorithm can be developed in a similar manner. The period for scheduling is in the order of seconds, which incur minimal overhead.

Algorithm 11.2: Workload Spreading

```
 1: while not all threads are marked do
 2:   srcSocket ⇐ pick the socket with the highest CoolingCost
 3:   destSocket ⇐ pick the socket with the lowest CoolingCost
 4:   while (not all threads of srcSocket are marked) do
 5:     Thread₁ ⇐ the highest power unmarked thread of srcSocket
 6:     Thread₂ ⇐ the highest power unmarked thread of
             destSocket
 7:     Thread₃ ⇐ the second highest power unmarked thread of
             destSocket
 8:     evaluate the CoolingCosts when these migrations are
           done:
 9:       migrating Thread₁ to destSocket
10:       migrating Thread₁ to destSocket and Thread₂ to
             srcSocket
11:       migrating Thread₁ to destSocket and {Thread₂ + Thread₃} to
             srcSocket
12:     If (any new CoolingCost is lower than current
           CoolingCost) then
13:         do the migration resulting in the lowest CoolingCost
14:         mark the migrated Threads
15:     end if
16:   end while
17: end while
```

11.4.4   Cooling Costs Predictor

Figure 11.8 shows the thermal model of a single socket incorporating both the ambient temperature, T_{amb}, and the convective resistance, R_{conv}. The lateral thermal flow between the socket's cores is ignored because of the high ratio of the core area to the die thickness [41]. R_v is the die component's vertical thermal

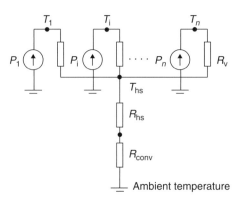

Figure 11.8   Steady-state single socket thermal modeling.

resistance, including the thermal interface resistance. R_{hs} represents the sum of heat spreader and the heat sink thermal resistances. The thermal resistance R_{conv} corresponds to the convective resistance.

To design a low cost runtime predictor, we can utilize the fact that the heat sink represents a low pass filter with a narrow bandwidth (range of 0.01 Hz since the heat sink time constant is in the order of tens of seconds), which allows only the average power to pass that is typically highly stable over a period of seconds. As a result, steady-state analysis can be used to predict the heat sink temperature ahead of time while not compromising accuracy. The predicted value of the convective resistance, R_{conv}^{new}, that is required to calculate the new air flow can be computed as follows:

$$R_{conv}^{new} = \frac{T_c - T_{amb} - P_{max} R_{core}}{\sum_{j=1}^{m} P_j} - R_{hs}, \tag{11.7}$$

where T_c is the critical temperature threshold and P is the power dissipation of the individual components. The core power can be estimated based on the temperature readings of their thermal sensors. The temperature is a good metric since it reflects the density of both dynamic and leakage power. The power of the individual cores, P_i, can be estimated as

$$P_i = \frac{\beta_i T_i + \left(\sum_{j=1}^{N} \frac{\Delta_{ij}}{R_{core}} \left(R_{hs} + R_{conv}^{cur}\right)\right) - \Theta}{R_{core} + N(R_{hs} + R_{conv}^{cur})}, \tag{11.8}$$

where T_i' is the average core thermal sensor reading, where the temperature is averaged over the socket rescheduling period. $\Delta_{ij} = (\beta_i T_i - \beta_j T_j)$, R_{conv}^{cur} is the current convective resistance, β is a factor to convert the thermal sensor readings of the core to its average temperature (can be estimated at the design time), and N is the number of cores in the die. The value of $\Theta = P_{extra}(R_{hs} + R_{conv}^{cur})$ corresponds to the contribution of L2 cache and the interconnect between the cores to the heat sink temperature. The power of these components, P_{extra}, can be estimated using the access frequency (estimated using processor performance counters) multiplied by the power of each access since they are highly regular. The power of each access can be estimated during the design time. The predicted cooling power, P_{cp}^{new}, can be estimated as

$$P_{cp}^{new} = \left(\frac{R_{conv}^{cur}}{R_{conv}^{new}} \right)^{\frac{3}{\alpha}} P_{cp}^{cur}, \tag{11.9}$$

where P_{cp}^{cur} is the current cooling power. The average prediction accuracy across the set of the benchmarks used in Section 11.5.3.1 is in the range of 5%, which is good enough for our approach.

11.5 EVALUATION

In this section, we perform a comprehensive evaluation of our multitier energy management scheduler. We start with evaluating the top-level scheduler that optimizes energy through efficient VM scheduling across the PMs in the deployment. We show that this can result in average weighted speedup and energy savings of 40% across diverse workload combinations. Following that, we evaluate the energy savings of the scheduler at the PM level that focuses on reducing the cooling energy through intelligent job assignment between the CPU packages. We show that our intramachine scheduler can reduce the cooling costs by as much as 72%.

11.5.1 Intermachine Scheduler (vGreen)

The test bed for evaluating vGreen includes two state-of-the-art 45 nm Dual Intel Quad Core Xeon X5570 (Intel Nehalem architecture with 16 PCPUs each) based server machines with 24 GB of memory, which act as the *vgnodes*, and a Core2Duo-based desktop machine that acts as the *vgserv*. The *vgnodes* run Xen3.3.1 and use Linux 2.6.30 for Dom-0.

For workloads, we use benchmarks with varying characteristics from the SPEC-CPU 2000 benchmark suite. The used benchmarks and their characteristics are illustrated in Table 11.1. We run each of these benchmarks inside a VM, which is initialized with eight VCPUs and 4 GB of memory. We generate experimental workloads by running multiple VMs together, each running one of the benchmarks. For each combination run, we sample the system power consumption of both the vgnodes every 2 s using the power sensors in the PM, which we query through the IPMI interface [47].

We compare vGreen to a VM scheduler that mimics the Eucalyptus VM scheduler [8] for our evaluation. Eucalyptus is an open source cloud computing system that can manage VM creation and allocation across a cluster of

TABLE 11.1   Benchmarks Used

Benchmark	Characteristics
eon	High IPC/Low MPC
applu	Medium IPC/High MPC
perl	High IPC/Low MPC
bzip2	Medium IPC/Low MPC
equake	Low IPC/High MPC
gcc	High IPC/Low MPC
swim	Low IPC/High MPC
mesa	High IPC/Low MPC
art	Medium IPC/High MPC
mcf	Low IPC/High MPC

PMs. The default Eucalyptus VM scheduler assigns VMs using a greedy policy, that is, it allocates VMs to a PM until its resources (number of CPUs and memory) are full. However, this assignment is static, and it does not perform any dynamic VM migration based on actual PM utilization at runtime. For fair comparison, we augment the Eucalyptus scheduler with the CPU utilization metrics and algorithm proposed in the previous section, which allow it to redistribute/consolidate VMs dynamically at runtime. This enhancement is representative of the metrics employed by the existing state-of-the-art policies, which use CPU utilization for balancing (Section 11.2). We refer to this enhanced scheduler as E+. For further fairness in comparison, we use the same initial assignment of VMs to PMs as done by the default Eucalyptus scheduler for both E+ and vGreen.

We report the comparative results of vGreen and E+ for the following two primary parameters:

1. *System-Level Energy Savings*. We estimate the energy reduction in executing each combination of VMs using vGreen over E+. This is calculated by measuring the total system-level energy consumption for a VM combination with E+ and vGreen, and then taking their difference. Note that the combinations may execute for different times with E+ and vGreen, and since we do not know the state of the system after the execution (could be active if there are more jobs, or be in sleep state if nothing to do), we only compare the energy consumed during active execution of each combination.

2. *Average Weighted Speedup*. We also estimate the average speedup of each VM combination with vGreen. For this, we use the weighted speedup (AWS) based on a similar metric defined earlier in Section 11.3.1 (refer to

Equation 11.1). It is defined as

$$\text{AWS} = \frac{\sum_{\text{VM}_i} \frac{T_{e+_i}}{T_{\text{alone}_i}}}{\sum_{\text{VM}_i} \frac{T_{\text{vgreen}_i}}{T_{\text{alone}_i}}} - 1, \quad (11.10)$$

where T_{alone_i} is the execution time of VM_i when it runs alone on a PM, and T_{e+_i} and T_{vgreen_i} are its execution time as part of a VM combination with E+ and vGreen, respectively. AWS > 0 implies that the VM combination runs faster with vGreen and vice versa.

For all our experiments, we use P_{p_period} and P_{up_period} as 5s.

On the basis of our experiments across different benchmarks, we choose nMPC$_{\text{th}}$ as 0.02 and nIPC$_{\text{th}}$ as 8. These threshold values allowed us to cleanly separate memory- and CPU-intensive VMs from each other.

11.5.2 Heterogeneous Workloads

In the first set of experiments, we use combinations of VMs running benchmarks with heterogeneous characteristics. Each VM consists of multiple instances of the benchmark to generate different CPU utilization levels. In total we run four VMs, varying the overall CPU utilization of *vgnodes* between 50% and 100%. We choose this range of CPU utilization, since it is representative of a consolidated environment, where multiple VMs are consolidated to get higher overall resource utilization across the cluster [12]. We run CPU-intensive benchmarks in two VMs and memory intensive benchmarks in the other two. We did experiments across all possible heterogeneous VM combinations, but for the sake of clarity and brevity, have included results for 19 workloads in the following discussion. The excluded results lead to similar average metrics and conclusions as reported below.

Figure 11.9 shows the results across different utilization levels for the vGreen system normalized to that with E+. The *x*-axis on the graphs shows the initial distribution of VMs on the PMs by the default Eucalyptus scheduler. For instance, *2gcc/2art* means that two VMs running *gcc* are on the first PM, while the two VMs running *art* are on the second. We can observe in Figure 11.9a that vGreen achieves an average of between 30 and 40% system-level energy savings across all the utilization levels, reaching as high as 60%. The high energy savings are a result of the fact that vGreen schedules the VMs in a much more efficient manner resulting in higher speedups while maintaining similar average power consumption. This results in energy savings, since now the benchmarks run and consume active power for a smaller duration.

Figure 11.9b shows that vGreen achieves an average of around 30–40% weighted speedup over E+ across all the combinations at all utilization levels,

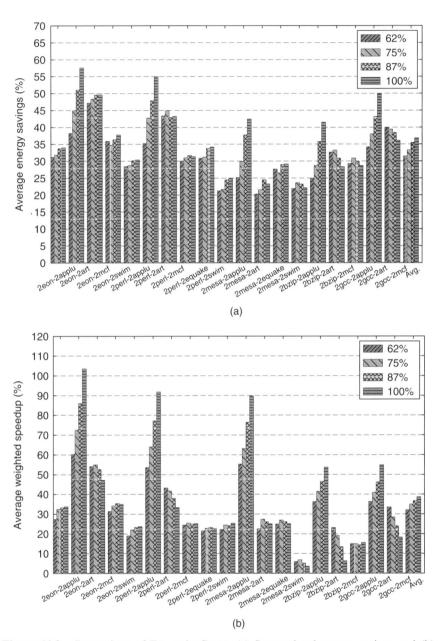

Figure 11.9 Comparison of E+ and vGreen. (a) System-level energy savings and (b) average weighted speedup.

reaching as high as 100%. The reason for this is that E+ colocates the high IPC VMs on one *vgnode* and the high MPC ones on the second one. Thereafter, since the CPU utilization of both the *vgnodes* is balanced, no dynamic relocation of VMs is done. With vGreen, although the initial assignment of the VMs is same as with E+, the dynamic characterization of VMs allows the *vgserv* to detect a heavy MPC imbalance. This initiates migration of a high MPC VM to the second *vgnode* running the high IPC VMs. This results in an IPC and utilization imbalance between the two *vgnodes*, since the second *vgnode* now runs a total of three high utilization VMs. This is detected by *vgserv*, and it responds by migrating a high IPC VM to the first *vgnode*. This creates a perfect balance in terms of MPC, IPC, and utilization across both the *vgnodes*. This results in significant speedup as observed in Figure 11.9b. We can see in Figure 11.9b that some combinations achieve higher weighted speedup compared to others. For instance, for *2eon/2applu* combination, it is around 30%, while for *2eon/2art* it is over 100%. This difference is due to the fact that colocation of *art* and *eon* VMs significantly benefits *art* from the point of view of larger cache and memory bandwidth availability, since it has very high MPC. In contrast, *applu* benefits lesser because of its lower overall MPC compared to *art*, which results in relatively smaller weighted speedup.

Another disadvantage of not taking the characteristics of the workload into account for scheduling is that there could be significant imbalance in power consumption across the nodes in a cluster. For instance, the node running high IPC workloads might have much higher power consumption compared to the node running high MPC workloads (as observed in Section 11.3.1). This can create power hot spots on certain nodes in the cluster and be detrimental to the overall cooling energy costs [49]. Figure 11.10 illustrates the imbalance in power consumption across the two *vgnodes* under the E+ system. We can see that the average imbalance in power consumption could be as high as 30 W, with the highest imbalance close to 45 W. With vGreen system, this imbalance is almost negligible because of the better balance of IPC and utilization across the machines. This results in a better overall thermal and power profile and reduces power hotspots in the cluster.

11.5.2.1 *Comparison with DVFS policies.* A possible way for saving energy with the E+ system is to augment it with a DVFS policy. For comparison, we consider the following two policies for the E+ system:

1. *The "naive" policy.* This policy simply resorts to throttling the CPU in order to reduce the energy consumption in the system. We refer to the system with the "naive" policy as E+nDVFS.
2. *The "smart" policy.* This policy is the same as incorporated into the vGreen system (Section 11.3.2). The policy throttles the CPU only if it deems that it would result in lower performance impact and higher energy savings. We refer to the system with the "smart" policy as E+sDVFS.

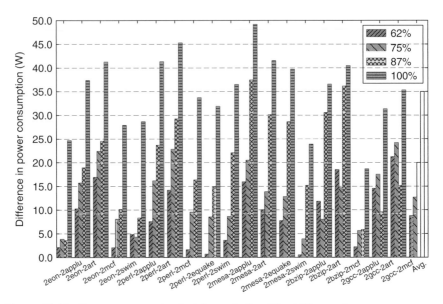

Figure 11.10 Power consumption imbalance in E+: The difference in power consumption between the two PMs under the E+ scheduling algorithm.

Figure 11.11 shows the average weighted speedup and energy consumption results for the E+sDVFS, E+nDVFS, and the vGreen system normalized against the results for the E+ system. Figure 11.11a illustrates the average weighted speedup results across all the combinations at 100% CPU utilization. The vGreen results are the same as those plotted in Figure 11.9b but have been included for the sake of comparison. We can observe that across all the combinations, both the DVFS policies perform slower than the baseline E+ system. This is intuitive, since the DVFS policies run the system at a lower frequency. However, the E+sDVFS clearly outperforms the E+nDVFS system across all the workload combinations. While the E+sDVFS system is on an average always within 2% of the E+ system, and E+nDVFS system is on an average 22% slower than the E+ system. This happens since the E+sDVFS system exploits the characteristics of the VMs and performs aggressive throttling only on the nodes running VMs with high MPC. As discussed in Section 11.3.2, this results in minimal performance degradation, since such high MPC workloads are highly stall intensive and have little dependence on CPU frequency. In contrast, the E+nDVFS system naively throttles even the nodes running high IPC VMs, resulting in the high performance slowdown as observed in Figure 11.11a.

The average weighted speedups have a direct impact on the energy savings as illustrated in Figure 11.11b. The E+nDVFS system gets an average of just 1% energy savings across all the combinations. For some workloads, such as *2mesa/2art*, it infact consumes more energy than the baseline system. This indicates that the power reduction due to E+nDVFS system is outweighed by the

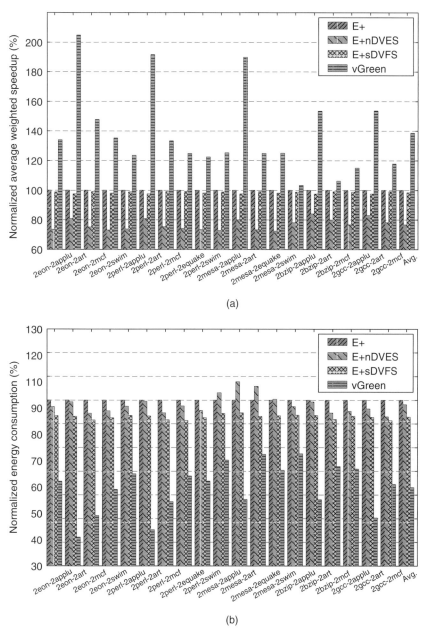

Figure 11.11 Comparison of E+, E+nDVFS, E+sDVFS, and vGreen. (a) Normalized average weighted speedup and (b) normalized energy consumption.

huge performance slowdown. The E+sDVFS system does better by achieving around 9% energy savings due to the small performance slowdown. However, both are clearly outperformed by the vGreen system, which achieves close to 35% energy savings. This shows that efficient resource utilization across a cluster is a key to energy efficient computing in virtualized environments.

11.5.2.2 Homogeneous workloads. We also experimented with combination of VMs running homogeneous benchmarks to evaluate the performance of our system under cases, where there is no heterogeneity across VMs. We conducted experiments for all the benchmarks in Table 11.1, where all the four VMs ran the same benchmark. We observed that in all the experiments, there was no possibility of rebalancing based on characteristics, since the MPC and IPC of the VMs were already balanced. However, for the case of high MPC workloads, the vGreen system effectively applies DVFS to get energy savings. Figure 11.12 illustrates the average weighted speedup and energy savings achieved across the homogeneous set of high MPC workloads. We can observe that vGreen achieves average system-level energy savings of between 6% and 9% across all the utilization levels. The slowdown due to DVFS is between 2% and 5% as indicated in Figure 11.12a. For high IPC workloads, the results were identical to E+ system, since vGreen neither does any VM migration nor DVFS.

11.5.3 Intramachine Scheduler (Cool and Save)

The intramachine scheduler called *Cool and Save*, adds another level of optimization on top of the interlevel by reducing the cooling energy within the individual PMs. For the experimental evaluation, we focus on reducing the cooling energy of a server that has two sockets with four cores each. Simulation is used instead of the real measurements because the fan algorithm implemented in the servers change the whole set of fans at once and cannot be modified by the user to have individual control over the fans. Table 11.2 gives the parameters that have been

TABLE 11.2 Simulation Parameters

Parameter	Value
Issue width	4
ROB	128
Functional units	4 IntALU, 1 IntMult/Div
	1 FPALU, 1 FPMult/Div
Branch predictor	Tournament 2048 local predictor
	8192 global predictor
BTB	2K entries, 1 way
LSQ	32
L1 I-cache	32 kB, 4 ways, 32 B blocks, 1 cycle
L1 D-cache	32 kB, 4 ways, 32 B blocks, 1 cycle
L2	4 MB, 8 ways, 64 B blocks, 12 cycles
Memory latency	200 cycles

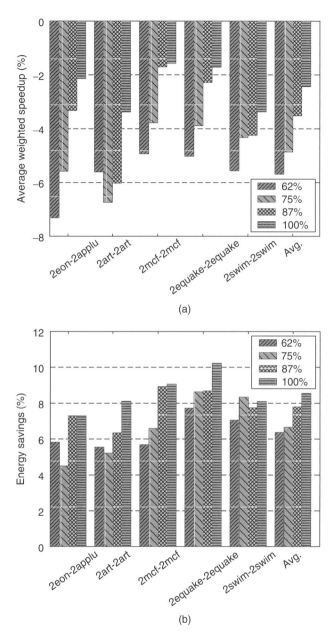

Figure 11.12 Comparison of E+ and vGreen with homogeneous workloads. (a) Average weighted speedup and (b) system-level energy savings.

used in the simulations. Three simulators are used to perform the evaluation, M5 [52], Wattch [53], and HotSpot-4.0 [1]. The M5 simulator is used to obtain the architectural-level performance simulation. The M5 traces are fed into Wattch to obtain the power values of the processor functional units. The power values are then used to estimate the temperature through the HotSpot simulator. The OS initiates cooling aware scheduling, CAS, every 4 s, which is sufficient since the heat sink thermal time constant is in the range of 10 s of seconds. The CAS algorithm is evaluated against traditional OS scheduling, and *dynamic load balancing (DLB)* estimates the level of benefit. The *DLB* enhances the utilization of the system resources by scheduling the workload in a way that minimizes the difference in task queue length across the individual sockets and the individual cores. The fan control algorithm is assumed to be the industry standard closed loop feedback controller that adjusts the fan speed based on the thermal sensors readings. When the temperature is below the threshold, the fan speed is set to baseline speed. In case of overheating, the fan algorithm adjusts the fan speed accordingly to ensure that the cores temperatures do not exceed the thermal threshold.

Figure 11.13 shows the floorplan obtained by scaling ALPHA 21264 processor into 65 nm technology. In these simulations the processor clock speed is set to 2 GHz. L2 cache area is estimated based on Cacti simulation tool [54]. In these experiments, a die thickness of 0.2 mm is used. To account for CPU cores leakage power temperature dependency, the second-order polynomial model that is proposed in Reference 55 is used. The leakage model coefficients are extracted empirically based on the given normalized leakage values. To estimate the leakage values for 65 nm technology, the reported value of leakage power density (0.5 W/mm^2 at 383 K [56]) are incorporated in the second-order polynomial model. For the crossbar bus power consumption, the active power is scaled depending on the activity in the cores and L2 cache. To obtain accurate results, the warm-up is also considered since the heat sink has a longer time constant than the die. The core critical temperature is set to 85°C, which is common to such designs [42]. For the socket package, a convection thermal resistance equal to 0.18°C/W at air flow of 23 CFM is used, which is in the range to what is being deployed in the state-of-the-art quad core Xeon processor used in server platforms [57].

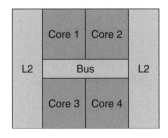

Figure 11.13 Socket floorplan.

TABLE 11.3   Benchmarks Characteristics

Benchmark	Average Dynamic Power, W	Power Standard Deviation
gcc	4.12	1.8
gzip	5.51	1.65
swim	6.35	1.77
bzip2	7.9	2.25
crafty	9.11	0.66

TABLE 11.4   Workload List

Workload #	Benchmarks (Socket 1/Socket 2)
1	{crafty+gzip+gcc}/{crafty+gzip+gcc}
2	{bzip2+gzip+swim+swim}/{crafty+gzip+gcc}
3	{bzip2+swim+gcc+gcc}/{bzip2+swim+gzip+gzip}
4	{crafty+crafty+swim}/{gzip+swim+swim}
5	{bzip2+bzip2+bzip2+bzip2}/{gcc+gcc+gcc+gcc}

The workload is set of SPEC2000 suite shown in Table 11.3, which belongs to the same class of workload that is used to evaluate vGreen. The selected set of benchmarks exhibit various levels of power intensity to represent real life applications. Each benchmark is executed for a representative interval of 5 s and then repeated the bench execution to obtain a total execution time of 300 s, which is sufficient to evaluate the given policies. To better evaluate the given policies under various workload conditions, the selected benchmark combinations (Table 11.4) have different average power intensity and variance.

11.5.3.1   *Results.* The reported results show that our policy, CAS, outperforms the state-of-the-art DLB drastically in energy savings and minimizing air flow rate that reaches as high as *85%* and *53%*, respectively. Minimizing these metrics has a big advantage on lowering the overall cooling costs and acoustic noise.

Figure 11.14 shows the air flow rate breakdown across two sockets when using the DLB and CAS polices for all the workload given in Table 11.4. The results are reported using air flow rate metric instead of absolute fan speed since this is a standard metric for characterizing the fans. The air flow rate is proportional to fan speed. The first observation is that CAS is able to reduce the maximum air flow rate by as high as *53%*. This figure shows cases for two sources of air flow improvements, hot cores *consolidation* (workloads 1, 2, 3), and *spreading* (workloads 4, 5). For the consolidation case, we can observe that CAS is able to maintain cooling with half of the fans only running at similar speed to the case of DLB. To explain this, let us take the case of workload

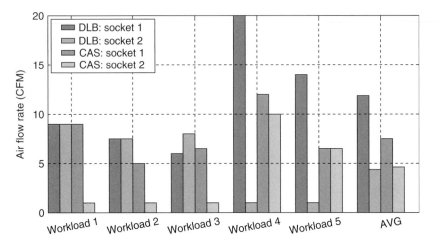

Figure 11.14   Air flow rate in the multisocket system.

1:{*crafty*+*gzip*+*gcc*}/{*crafty*+*gzip*+*gcc*}. Before applying CAS, the power is balanced across the two sockets where each is required an air flow rate of 9 CFM. To improve cooling efficiency, CAS migrates the hot thread, *crafty*, from socket 2 to 1 and the two cold threads, gzip and gcc, from socket 1 to 2 to maintain power balancing. As a result, socket 1 will be executing {2 *crafty*} while socket 2 runs {*gcc*+*gzip*+*gcc*+*gzip*}. Although socket 1 is running two hot threads, its fan speed stays almost the same since the socket total power is maintained at the same level. This indicates that thread consolidation is an effective way to improve cooling efficiency.

The CAS algorithm performs hot threads spreading when there is a strong imbalance in the socket power as the case in workload 5. Before applying CAS, the workload is assigned to the two sockets as {*bzip2*+*bzip2*+*bzip2*+*bzip2*}/{*gcc*+*gcc*+*gcc*+*gcc*}. In this case, socket 2 fan is in idle state (*gcc* threads are cold) while the air flow in socket 1 is at a high rate. In this case, the power dissipation in socket 1 is about double of what is in socket 2. Such power imbalance between them leads to cooling inefficiency due to nonlinear relation between power cost and temperature reduction. To lower the cooling costs, CAS algorithm balances the power across the two cores by migrating two instances of *bzip2* to socket 2 and two instances of *gcc* to socket 1. From the results, it can be seen that the air flow is lowered from one fan running at 20 CFM to two fans running at range close to 10 CFM, which leads to drastic power savings.

Figure 11.15 shows the cooling energy savings of applying CAS over the DLB. The cooling savings is calculated by applying Equation 11.6 to the results of Figure 11.14. It is clear from the results that applying CAS results in significant energy savings; the improvement as high as 85%. The appreciable improvement comes from applying our consolidating or spreading the hot threads as required. For the consolidating cases, the savings come from running one of the sockets

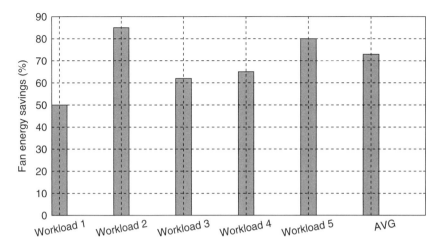

Figure 11.15   Fan energy savings over DLB.

fans in idle mode while not increasing the speed of the running fan. The savings in case of workload 2:{*bzip2+gzip+swim+swim*}/{*crafty+gzip+gcc*} is the highest, 85%, which is attained by migrating *crafty* to socket 1 and the two instances of *swim* to socket 2. The improvement is high in this case, since it reduces the total power dissipation in socket 1 while allowing socket 2 to run its fan in idle mode since its temperature becomes below the threshold. When CAS performs hot threads spreading, the energy savings come from exploiting the nonlinearity between cooling cost and temperature reduction. This can be seen in the case of workload 5, where the savings is 80%. The overhead of migrating the thread and running CAS is expected to be negligible since it is infrequent (order of seconds). As a result, one can conclude that employing CAS algorithm is a highly effective approach for reducing the cooling costs.

11.5.3.2   Overhead of CAS.   In these experiments, the CAS algorithm runs every 4 s to reschedule the workload as required. The total overhead of each run including the migration overhead is less than 5 ms on average. Consequently, the overall overhead is below 1%, which is negligible.

11.6   CONCLUSION

In this chapter, we discussed a novel approach to managing workload within and across the machine with the objective of reducing overall energy consumption. We first introduced vGreen, a system for energy efficient VM management across a cluster of machines. The key idea behind vGreen is linking workload characterization of VMs to VM scheduling and power management decisions to achieve better performance, energy efficiency, and power balance in the system.

Novel hierarchical metrics to capture VM characteristics as well as scheduling and DVFS policies to achieve the earlier mentioned benefits were explained. We then showed how "Cool and Save," a cooling and thermal aware scheduling algorithm within a server, can significantly reduce the energy costs and improve the life and reliability of the fans. Thus, a combination of "vGreen" and "Cool and Save" can work together to greatly reduce the operational costs in a data center.

REFERENCES

1. Skadron K, Stan M, Sankaranarayanan K, Huang W, Velusamy S, Tarjan D. Temperature-aware microarchitecture: modeling and implementation. ACM Trans Archit Code Optim 2004;1(1):94–125.
2. Meisner D, Gold B, Thomas W. Powernap: eliminating server idle power. In: Proceedings of the 14th International Conference on Architectural Support for Programming Languages and Operating Systems; 2009.
3. Pakbaznia E, Pedram M. Minimizing data center cooling and server power costs. In: ISLPED '09. ACM; 2009. pp. 145–150.
4. Amazon. *Amazon Elastic Compute Cloud (Amazon EC2)*. Amazon Inc.; 2008. Available at http://aws.amazon.com/ec2/.
5. Barham P, Dragovic B, Fraser K, Hand S, Harris T, Ho A, Neugebauer R, Pratt I, Warfield A. Xen and the art of virtualization. In: SOSP '03: Proceedings of the nineteenth ACM symposium on Operating systems principles. New York: ACM; 2003. pp. 164–177.
6. Haletky EL. VMware ESX Server in the Enterprise: Planning and Securing Virtualization Servers; 2008.
7. Clark C, Fraser K, Hand S, Hansen JG, Jul E, Limpach C, Pratt I, Warfield A. Live migration of virtual machines. In: NSDI'05: Proceedings of the 2nd conference on Symposium on Networked Systems Design & Implementation. Berkeley (CA): USENIX Association; 2005. pp. 273–286.
8. Nurmi D, Wolski R, Grzegorczyk C, Obertelli G, Soman S, Youseff L, Zagorodnov D. The eucalyptus open-source cloud-computing system. In: Proceedings of Cloud Computing and Its Applications; 2008.
9. OpenNebula. Opennebula homepage.
10. McNett M, Gupta D, Vahdat A, Voelker GM. Usher: an extensible framework for managing custers of virtual machines. In: LISA'07: Proceedings of the 21st Conference on Large Installation System Administration Conference. Berkeley (CA); USENIX Association; 2007. pp. 1–15.
11. Wang L, Laszewski G, Tao J, Kunze M. Grid virtualization engine: design, implementation and evaluation. IEEE Syst J 12/2009 2009;3(4):477–488.
12. Wood T, Shenoy P, Venkataramani A. Black-box and gray-box strategies for virtual machine migration. In: NSDI'07; 2007. pp. 229–242.
13. VMware. Vmware distributed resource scheduler; 2009.

14. Bobroff N, Kochut A, Beaty K. Dynamic placement of virtual machines for managing SLA violations. In: Integrated Network Management. IEEE; 2007. pp. 119–128.

15. Wang R, Kandasamy N. A distributed control framework for performance management of virtualized computing environments: some preliminary results. In: ACDC '09: Proceedings of the 1st Workshop on Automated Control for Datacenters and Clouds. New York: ACM; 2009. pp. 7–12.

16. Hermenier F, Lorca X, Menaud J-M, Muller G, Lawall J. Entropy: a consolidation manager for clusters. In: VEE '09: Proceedings of the 2009 ACM SIGPLAN/SIGOPS International Conference on Virtual Execution Environments. New York: ACM; 2009. pp. 41–50.

17. Chase JS, Anderson DC, Thakar PN, Vahdat AM, Doyle RP. Managing energy and server resources in hosting centers. In: SOSP '01: Proceedings of the 18th ACM Symposium on Operating Systems Principles. New York: ACM; 2001. pp. 103–116.

18. Moore J, Chase J, Ranganathan P, Sharma R. Making scheduling "cool": temperature-aware workload placement in data centers. In: ATEC '05: Proceedings of the Annual Conference on USENIX Annual Technical Conference. Berkeley (CA): USENIX Association; 2005. pp. 5–5.

19. Ge R, Feng X, Feng W-C, Cameron KW. Cpu miser: a performance-directed, run-time system for power-aware clusters. In: ICPP '07: Proceedings of the 2007 International Conference on Parallel Processing. Washington (DC): IEEE Computer Society; 2007. p. 18.

20. Ranganathan P, Leech P, Irwin D, Chase J. Ensemble-level power management for dense blade servers. In: ISCA '06: Proceedings of the 33rd Annual International Symposium on Computer Architecture. Washington (DC): IEEE Computer Society; 2006. pp. 66–77.

21. Fan X, Weber W-D, Barroso LA. Power provisioning for a warehouse-sized computer. In: ISCA '07: Proceedings of the 34th Annual International Symposium on Computer Architecture. New York: ACM; 2007. pp. 13–23.

22. Dhiman G, Pusukuri K, Rosing TS. Analysis of dynamic voltage scaling for system level energy management. In: HotPower '08: Workshop on Power Aware Computing and Systems; 2008.

23. Dhiman G, Rosing TS. Dynamic voltage frequency scaling for multi-tasking systems using online learning. In: ISLPED '07: Proceedings of the 2007 International Symposium on Low Power Electronics and Design. New York: ACM; 2007. pp. 207–212.

24. Isci C, Contreras G, Martonosi M. Live, runtime phase monitoring and prediction on real systems with application to dynamic power management. In: MICRO 39: Proceedings of the 39th Annual IEEE/ACM International Symposium on Microarchitecture. Washington (DC): IEEE Computer Society; 2006. pp. 359–370.

25. Nathuji R, Schwan K. Virtualpower: coordinated power management in virtualized enterprise systems. In: SOSP '07: Proceedings of 21st ACM SIGOPS Symposium on Operating Systems Principles. New York: ACM; 2007. pp. 265–278.

26. Abdelsalam HS, Maly K, Mukkamala R, Zubair M, Kaminsky D. Analysis of energy efficiency in clouds. Future Computing, Service Computation, Cognitive, Adaptive, Content, Patterns, Computation World; 2009. pp. 416–421.

27. Raghavendra R, Ranganathan P, Talwar V, Wang Z, Zhu X. No "power" struggles: coordinated multi-level power management for the data center. In: ASPLOS XIII: Proceedings of the 13th International Conference on Architectural Support for Programming Languages and Operating Systems. New York: ACM; 2008. pp. 48–59.

28. Liu L, Wang H, Liu X, Jin X, He WB, Wang QB, Chen Y. Greencloud: a new architecture for green data center. In: ICAC-INDST '09: Proceedings of the 6th International Conference Industry Session on Autonomic Computing and Communications Industry Session. New York: ACM; 2009. pp. 29–38.

29. Verma A, Ahuja P, Neogi A. Power-aware dynamic placement of HPC applications. In: ICS '08: Proceedings of the 22nd Annual International Conference on Supercomputing. New York: ACM; 2008. pp. 175–184.

30. Knauerhase RC, Brett P, Hohlt B, Li T, Hahn S. Using os observations to improve performance in multicore systems. IEEE Micro 2008;28(3):54–66.

31. Merkel A, Bellosa F. Balancing power consumption in multiprocessor systems. SIGOPS Oper Syst Rev 2006;40(4):403–414.

32. Stoess J, Lang C, Bellosa F. Energy management for hypervisor-based virtual machines. In: ATC'07: Proceedings of the USENIX Annual Technical Conference. Berkeley (CA): USENIX Association; 2007. pp. 1–14.

33. Merkel A, Stoess J, Bellosa F. Resource-conscious scheduling for energy efficiency on multicore processors. In: EuroSys '10: Proceedings of the 5th European Conference on Computer Systems. New York: ACM; 2010. pp. 153–166.

34. Kansal A, Zhao F, Liu J, Kothari N, Bhattacharya AA. Virtual machine power metering and provisioning. In: SoCC '10: Proceedings of the 1st ACM Symposium on Cloud Computing. New York: ACM; 2010. pp. 39–50.

35. Koller R, Verma A, Neogi A. Wattapp: an application aware power meter for shared data centers. In: ICAC '10: Proceeding of the 7th International Conference on Autonomic Computing. New York: ACM; 2010. pp. 31–40.

36. Dhiman G, Mihic K, Rosing T. A system for online power prediction in virtualized environments using Gaussian mixture models. In: DAC '10: Proceedings of the 47th Design Automation Conference. New York: ACM; 2010. pp. 807–812.

37. Nathuji R, Kansal A, Ghaffarkhah A. Q-clouds: managing performance interference effects for qos-aware clouds. In: EuroSys '10: Proceedings of the 5th European Conference on Computer Systems. New York: ACM; 2010. pp. 237–250.

38. Nathuji R, England P, Sharma P, Singh A. Feedback driven qos-aware power budgeting for virtualized servers. In: FeBID '09: 4th International Workshop on Feedback Control Implementation and Design in Computing Systems and Networks; 2009.

39. Hinton G, Sagar D, Upton M, Boggs D, Carmean D, Roussel P. The microarchitecture of the pentium 4 processor. Intel Technol J 2001;5(1):1–12.

40. Brooks D, Martonosi M. Dynamic thermal management for high-performance microprocessors. In: HPCA; 2001. pp. 171–182.

41. Heo S, Barr K, Asanovic K. Reducing power density through activity migration. In: ISLPED; 2003. pp. 217–222.

42. Coskun A, Rosing T, Gross K. Proactive temperature management in MPSOC. In: ISLPED; 2008. pp. 165–170.

43. Chiueh H, Luh L, Draper J, Choma J. A novel fully integrated fan controller for advanced computer systems. In: SSMSD; 2000. pp. 191–194.

44. Moore J, Chase J, Ranganathan P, Sharma R. Making scheduling "cool": temperature-aware workload placement in data centers. In: USENIX; 2005. pp. 61–75.

45. Tang Q, Gupta S, Varsamopoulos G. Thermal-aware task scheduling for data centers through minimizing heat recirculation. In: ICCC; 2007. 129–138.

46. Patterson M. The effect of data center temperature on energy efficiency. In: ITHERM; 2008. pp. 1167–1174.

47. IPMI. Intelligent platform management interface v2.0 specification; 2004.

48. Snavely A, Tullsen DM. Symbiotic jobscheduling for a simultaneous multithreading processor. SIGPLAN Not 2000;35(11):234–244.

49. Ayoub R, Sharifi S, Rosing T. Gentlecool: cooling aware proactive workload scheduling in multi-machine systems. In: IEEE Design, Automation Test in Europe; 2010. DATE '10.

50. Available at www.sun.com/servers/x64/x4270/.

51. Ayoub R, Rosing T. Cool and save: cooling aware dynamic workload scheduling in multi-socket CPU systems. In: ASP-DAC; 2010. pp. 891–896.

52. Binkert N, Dreslinski R, Hsu L, Lim K, Saidi A, Reinhardt S. The m5 simulator: modeling networked systems. IEEE Micro 2006;26(4):52–60.

53. Brooks D, Tiwari V, Martonosi M. Wattch: a framework for architectural-level power analysis and optimizations. In: ISCA; 2000. pp. 83–94.

54. Tarjan D, Thoziyoor S, Jouppi N. Cacti 4.0. Technical report, HP Laboratories; 2006. pp. 1–15.

55. Su H, Liu F, Devgan A, Acar E, Nassif S. Full chip leakage estimation considering power supply and temperature variations. 2003. pp. 78–83.

56. Bose P. Power-efcient microarchitectural choices at the early design stage. In: Workshop on Power-Aware Computer Systems; 2003.

57. Quad-Core Intel Xeon Processor 5300 Series: Thermal/Mechanical Design Guidelines.

CHAPTER 12

QOS-AWARE POWER MANAGEMENT IN DATA CENTERS

JIAYU GONG and CHENG-ZHONG XU

12.1 INTRODUCTION

Power and cooling are emerging to be the key challenges in data-center environments. An IDC report of 2007 showed that the cost on power and cooling reached $25 billion in 2005 and was expected to continue to raise to $40 billion in 2010. The cost of power and cooling has increased at four times the growth rate for new server spending. In 2005, the cost of power and cooling was around half of that on new server spending. It was estimated to be 75% of the cost on new server spending in 2010. It is likely to even surpass spending on new server hardware. On one hand, the increasing power consumption leads to increased spending on cooling and power delivery equipment. For example, a data center consisting of 30,000 ft^2 and consuming 10 MW requires an accompanying cooling system that costs from $2 to $5 million [1] with annual running cost of $4–$8 million [2]; the nearly 60 A per rack currently provisioned in data centers could become a bottleneck for high density configuration [3]. On the other hand, the increased power indicates the increased costs on electricity bill. In 2006, servers and data centers in United States consumed around 61 billion kilowatt hours (kWh) at a cost of about $4.5 billion [4]. By 2011, US data centers will consume 100 billion kWh at a cost of $7.4 billion per year [4].

High power consumption in a data center can lead to tremendous environment pollutions. According to the US Environmental Protection Agency (EPA), each 1000 kWh of energy consumption generates 0.72 tons of CO_2 emission. The CO_2 emission due to US data centers in 2006 was estimated to be 44 million tons, which is equivalent to the output of 8 million passenger vehicles [4]. In addition, power consumption can impact reliability and availability of the system as well.

Energy-Efficient Distributed Computing Systems, First Edition.
Edited by Albert Y. Zomaya and Young Choon Lee.
© 2012 John Wiley & Sons, Inc. Published 2012 by John Wiley & Sons, Inc.

At present, power consumption becomes a major area of concern for researchers and leading IT vendors. Power management attracting research interest since the 1990s in different context of mobile or embedded systems emphasized on extending battery life. It has since expanded to include reducing peak power because thermal constraints can limit further CPU performance improvement. There are a number of previous energy-saving techniques developed for mobile or embedded systems that can be adapted for power management in data centers. However, data centers are quite different from the mobile or embedded devices in the sense of power supplies, workloads, scale, etc. A large body of recent work on power management in servers and data centers has been proposed. In this chapter, we investigate the relevant work in this space. We start this investigation from the definition and classification criteria of this power management problem.

12.2   PROBLEM CLASSIFICATION

The power management techniques in servers and data centers are focusing on different dimensions [5]. There are four main categorization criteria: (i) objective and constraint, (ii) scope and time granularity, (iii) methodology, and (iv) power management mechanism.

12.2.1   Objective and Constraint

In general, there are two types of objectives in power management. One focuses on average power optimization by minimizing the power needed to achieve the performance target. This can be translated to a tracking problem, which means that the consumed power should track the resource demands of the applications. The other category emphasizes on peak power in order to optimize the power provisioning delivery and cooling in data centers. This is essentially a capping problem that ensures that the power consumption of a system will not violate the power budget. The power budget is usually required because of power supply capacity or the heat extraction capacity of the air and cooling infrastructure. High temperature due to over heat dissipation can compromise the reliability of the affected components, leading to misbehaviors and failures. Thermal management is thus necessary in data centers. It can be translated into a capping problem as well. We categorize thermal management as a branch of power capping problem.

Controlling power will inevitably affect the performance in most systems. When performance is added as a constraint, the power management problem can be converted to a constrained optimization problem that minimizes performance degradation and maximizes power saving.

12.2.2   Scope and Time Granularities

Power management can take place at different scopes, ranging from a component, a platform, a cluster, to an entire data center. There are many solutions focusing on individual component, such as CPU, disk, and memory. Because the execution of an application tends to involve more than one component, an optimal solution at component level is not necessarily optimal for power management of system level. Server virtualization, which proliferates in today's data centers, adds one more level of complexity in power management due to the resource sharing among the virtual machines colocating in the same physical server [6, 7]. We distinguish the work on power management in virtualized environments from that for nonvirtualized environments. In data centers, a cluster of servers that cooperate to process jobs requires to extend power management from server to cluster level. The server cluster can be either homogeneous or heterogeneous. Most of existing power management solutions at cluster level focuses on the homogeneous clusters. And only a few are available for heterogeneous clusters [8–10]. Ultimately, the power consumption of the entire data center, including cooling infrastructures and power supplies, should be taken into account. The power management schemes with respect to cooling infrastructures and power supplies is beyond the focus in this chapter.

Power management can take place in different scopes. With regard to time, it can be operated at a granularity from milliseconds to seconds, even to hours. Software solutions to power management relying on application-level information tend to operate at a relatively coarse granularity (seconds to hours). In contrast, hardware and firmware solutions can operate at a finer granularity, from milliseconds to seconds, since they have access to more low level hardware information.

12.2.3 Methodology

We categorized the underlying power management methodologies into indirect and direct methods.

An indirect method assumes an explicit model to capture the behaviors of a target system. This method is model based. It relies on a system identification procedure to build analytical models of the controlled system and determine the control rule from the model. Such models can abstract the power consumption and performance as analytic functions on a set of system and application parameters. These models can even be used for prediction. On the basis of the models, both optimization and control approaches can be applied for power management. The most widely used indirect method is the control-theoretic approach.

Control theory provides a powerful mechanism to handle disturbances, uncertainties, and unpredictable changes in systems using feedback [11]. There are a number of key benefits of the control-theoretic approaches [11]. First, the quantitative input–output model, such as first-order model, is extremely useful in feedback control design. Second, the properties of controller, such as stability and accuracy, based on this quantitative model can be validated formally thus theoretical guarantee is provided. Third, control theory provides methods to estimate dynamic models as well. For example, auto-regressive-moving-average (ARMA) models can autocorrelate time series data to capture short-term, transient behaviors. Using control theory, we can develop multiple-input-multiple-output (MIMO) models to capture the correlations between different inputs and outputs. Finally, control theory provides a large variety of well-studied control algorithms to use in practice.

There are also a number of challenges when applying control theory to power management. Modeling is difficult because most interrelationships in the system are nonlinear. Modeling itself requires system identification, which may not cover all relevant correlations. Classical control theory only deals with continuous inputs, while the input variables for power management can only take on discrete values. Although adaptive control can deal with dynamic models, a limitation still exists on how fast the workloads or system behaviors can change. In addition, using dynamic models may not provide theoretic guarantee on the properties of controllers.

In contrast, direct methods determine control rules without needs for an explicit model of a system. One representative example is reinforcement learning (RL), which learns the impact on system behaviors, such as performance and power consumption, because of the action taken on the system, such as power state change. Compared with control theory, RL is model free. It does not require an explicit model of either the computing system being managed or the external process that generates workload or traffic. RL is fundamentally a sequential decision theory that properly treats dynamics in the system. It can improve decision making policy over time, similar to adaptive control [12]. However, there are also a few challenges in RL. One is the trade-off between exploitation, which is to select from what it already knows, and exploration, which is to make better action selection from unknowns in the future. Performance of the initialization phase that explores without any knowledge during live online training may be unacceptably poor. The convergence is hard to prove and the convergence rate is low. In addition, RL can suffer from poor scalability in large state spaces.

12.2.4 Power Management Mechanism

Essentially, power management is done by transitioning hardware components back and forth between high- and low-power states or modes. The components are fully active and operational in high power mode, while the functionality associated with the low power modes depends on the particular component. Switching between power modes may introduce non-negligible overhead in terms of both energy and performance [13].

Multiple classes of execution states are supported in today's server processors for the purpose of power management. These states include the frequency and voltage (P-state) in active mode, sleep states (C-states) in idle time, and throttle state (T-state).

Dynamic voltage and frequency scaling (DVFS) is used to switch among different P-states. DVFS relies on the fact that the dynamic power consumed by microprocessor is a cubic function of its operating voltage. Thus, reducing the operating voltage/frequency provides substantial saving in power at the cost of slower execution [14]. Most of today's processors have well-documented interfaces for DVFS, such as AMD's Cool'n'Quiet technology [15] and Intel's Enhanced SpeedStep technology [16]. However, the number of voltage or frequency stages is very limited. In multicore processors, it is not flexible to manipulate P-states because of the dependencies among the cores residing in the same die. T-states can further throttle down a CPU by inserting stop clock signals and thus omitting duty cycles. The mechanism to enter different T-states is to manipulate the processor clock modulation setting (throttling) by modulating the duty cycle of the processor clock, which changes the effective frequency of the processors [17].

Sleeping states (C-state) can be utilized when the CPU is idle. In ACPI standard, C0 is the active state and the sleep states are called C1, C2, ..., Cn [13]. The deeper the C-state is the more power the processor can save. C-states can relatively cause large switch overhead and might not be effective when the system is not idle but in a low utilization state.

Current disks also enable power management by deactivation. In active mode, the disk is being actively used and consumes more power. In idle mode, the disk can still spin at its regular speed and accesses can be performed without delay. In low power mode, relatively high transition overhead will be involved, such as turning the spindle motor off (standby) and turning the disk interface off (sleep) [18, 19]. Multispeed disk [20] can also be employed to manage power consumption of disk subsystems.

Power dissipated by a memory subsystem largely depends on its capacity and bus frequency. In practice, the power consumed by periodic refresh is very small. Most of the power is consumed by row and column decoders, sense amplifiers, and external bus drivers because of large arrays with very long and high capacitance internal bus lines. To reduce power consumption, one or more of these subcomponents can be disabled by switching a device to one of several predefined low power states when it is not being actively accessed. Memory controllers and chipsets can switch the subcomponents to low power states [21] or switch a memory rank's power on and off [22]. The non-negligible performance penalty, called *resynchronization cost*, is incurred to transition from current low power state to an active state before access. In addition, multifrequency memory can dynamically scale the working frequency and consequently the data rate [23].

At system-level, the entire computer can be managed as active, sleep (suspended, hibernated), and power-off states with time and energy overhead for the transitions between these states [13].

In virtualized environments, although P-states are still useful to regulate power consumption when they are enabled, problems might occur when manipulating P-states. Since multiple virtual machines may share a single core, tuning P-states of a core could threaten desired performance isolation. T-states can further throttle down a CPU by inserting stop clock signals and thus omitting duty cycles. However, T-states are not always well documented; access to the T-states may need modification of the clock modulation register. In contrast, C-states can be utilized when the CPU is idle. However, it incurs relatively large switch overhead and might not be effective when the system is less utilized. Instead, in virtualized environments, reallocating CPU resources, by limiting processing time, to virtual machines can both regulate power consumption and meanwhile retain performance isolation brought by virtualization. This functionality is provided by a hypervisor scheduler such as Credit Scheduler [24] in Xen [25]. One more important power management mechanism introduced by virtualization is virtual machine migration. Virtual machine migration lead to power consumption migration. Consolidation enabled by migration can idle servers so that the idle servers can enter low power states for more power saving.

These four dimensions, objective and constraint, scope and time granularity, methodology, and power management mechanism, form a large combinatorial space. We present the power management techniques in data centers along the dimension of objective in the following sections. Details of the techniques along other dimensions are elaborated as well.

12.3   ENERGY EFFICIENCY

In this section, we first introduce the metrics used to measure energy efficiency in clusters and data centers. Then, we investigate the representative techniques to improve energy efficiency or achieve the goal of energy-proportional computing.

12.3.1   Energy-Efficiency Metrics

There are a variety of metrics proposed and used in power management. In Reference 26, the authors categorized them into three types: metrics for solo equipment and devices, metrics for parallel systems, and metrics for cluster systems and data centers. The most common metric for power efficiency is the formula ED^n, where E is the energy consumed when running an application, D is the execution time to complete the application, and n is a nonnegative integer parameter to characterize the trade-off between E and D. The reciprocal variant of ED^n means performance^n/power or flops^n/W, which can be used to measure the power efficiency of parallel systems, such as supercomputers. Here, we only focus on the metrics for cluster systems and data centers.

The performance of commercial servers and data centers is usually measured by service output, which is a complex mix of computational processing, data storage, and network communication [4]. In data centers, energy efficiency is broadly defined as the amount of work processed (performance), mostly computational work, divided by the total energy consumed in this process, denoted as Green Grid's data-center performance efficiency (DCPE) [27]. Standard performance evaluation corporation (SPEC) set up an industry-standard power-performance benchmark, SPECpower_ssj2008 [28]. However, there is no actual metric of DCPE that has been defined yet [29]. Although it is feasible to run a standard data center workload and measure the total power consumption, the level of DCPE is still too high and DCPE cannot be used as a practical metric in power management.

Thus, it is suggested to factor DCPE into three components that can be independently measured and optimized [29], as shown in the following equation:

$$\text{Energy Efficiency} = \frac{\text{Computation}}{\text{Total energy}}$$

$$= \left(\frac{1}{\text{PUE}}\right) \times \left(\frac{1}{\text{SPUE}}\right) \times \left(\frac{\text{Computation}}{\text{Total energy to electronic component}}\right), \quad (12.1)$$

where PUE and SPUE stand for power usage efficiency and server power usage efficiency, respectively. We explain these two terms in the following text.

In data centers, the power consumption includes not only the power consumed by the servers but also that by cooling, power supplying, and all other facilities. Thus, Green Grid [27] proposed two metrics, power usage efficiency and its reciprocal, data-center infrastructure efficiency (DCiE), to measure the energy efficiency of data centers. PUE is defined as follows:

$$\text{PUE} = \frac{\text{Total facility power}}{\text{IT equipment power}}, \quad (12.2)$$

where total facility power is the total power provisioned to the whole data center, which consists of IT equipment power and support system power. IT equipment power is to support all IT equipment in a data center, including both the functional equipment for computing, storage, and networking, and the supplemental equipment such as monitors. PUE reflects the quality of the data center itself. PUE ranges from 1.0 to ∞. A PUE value approaching 1.0 indicates 100% efficiency. It was estimated that 85% of current data centers have a PUE value greater than 3.0 and only 5% have a PUE value of 2.0 [30]. This can be improved to 1.6 or better with proper design. For example, the data center at Lawrence Berkley National Labs (LBNL) has a PUE value of 1.3 [27]. A survey [31] shows a better result of an average PUE of around 2.0 for a set of 22 data center surveyed. A recent update to Reference 31 shows that the PUE value is 1.83 in an average and the minimum can be around 1.35 for 24 data center surveyed.

The cause of high PUE values is multiple sources of power overhead. Emerson Network Power [32] modeled energy consumption for a typical 5000-ft^2 data center and analyzed how energy is used within facility. Cooling infrastructure is the largest fraction of power overhead, which is around 30–50%. The AC–DC–AC conversion losses in UPS usually consumes 7–12% of power and it may be even reach 18% [29]. Other facility elements, including PDU and lighting, further contribute to more power waste. On the basis of these observations, the most possible opportunities for efficiency improvements rely on the use of evaporative cooling towers, more efficient air movement, and the elimination of unnecessary power conversion losses [29].

Analogous to PUE, SPUE is defined to reflect the efficiency of a server as follows:

$$SPUE = \frac{\text{Total server input power}}{\text{Useful power}}, \qquad (12.3)$$

where useful power only includes the power consumed by the electronic components directly involved in computation, such as CPU, disk, memory, and motherboard. Total server input power include useful power and all power losses in power supplies, fans, and voltage regulator modules (VRM). SPUE ratios of 1.6–1.8 is common in current servers.

In addition to PUE, there are two other metrics used for data centers [33]. One is IT productivity per embedded watt (IT-PEW). The other is data-center energy efficiency and productivity (DC-EEP) index. Their definitions are shown as follows:

$$IT\text{-}PEW = \frac{\text{IT productivity}}{\text{Embedded watt}}, \qquad (12.4)$$

$$DC\text{-}EEP\ index = \frac{IT\text{-}PEW}{PUE} = \frac{\text{IT productivity}}{\text{Total facility power}}, \qquad (12.5)$$

where IT Productivity is the IT service output of the data center, which can be regarded as performance, and embedded watt equals to IT equipment power in Equation 12.2. IT-PEW indicated the power efficiency of IT equipment. DC-EEP index indicates that of the whole data center.

12.3.2 Improving Energy Efficiency

It is desirable to improve PUE by careful design of data centers so that the energy efficiency can be improved. These design issues may touch upon careful air flow handling, use of free cooling, per server 12-V DC UPS [29]. In this chapter, our focus is on power management techniques for IT equipment itself in data centers. We do not emphasize on issues of data centers to improve PUE. This kind of discussion can be found in References 27 and 29.

Power management for improving energy efficiency can be conducted for different objectives: minimizing energy consumption with performance guarantee, maximizing performance under power budget, and making trade-off between power and performance.

12.3.2.1 Energy minimization with performance guarantee. To improve energy efficiency of a data center, a popular design methodology is to minimize the energy consumption for processing applications. From data-center administrators' perspective, the primary concern is application performance, which can be represented as quality of service (QoS), service-level agreement (SLA), etc. It is required to meet performance target and meanwhile minimize energy consumption.

Early power management study focused on power-on/off scheme. Pinheiro et al. [34] proposed a load concentration strategy to manage clusterwide power consumption, in which the nodes in a cluster are turned on or off to ensure the expected performance is just about acceptable according to the workload. They presented a heuristic approach based on a simplified throughput estimation model. When the number of nodes in a cluster is changed, it is needed to redistribute the incoming requests for load balancing.

Recently, DVFS became widely employed because it could provide significant energy saving while avoiding the comparatively large switching overhead between power-on and power-off states. Sharma et al. [35] investigated adaptive algorithms for DVS in QoS-enabled web servers to minimize energy consumption subject to service delay constraints, which can be represented by different deadlines for different client classes. The authors employed synthetic utilization bounds as control set points for DVS. The control is done on the granularity of sessions rather than individual requests. Further, for multitier server clusters, for example, a three-tier web server, Horvath et al. [36] presented a coordinated DVFS strategy. Each tier has a varying number of servers. All the servers in one tier run the same application and a request goes through all tiers. The decisions on frequency adjustments are made on each tier locally according to a simple stage delay model.

Horvath et al. extended the work [36] to combine both DVFS and power-on/off mechanism in a cluster with dynamic configuration [37]. They made performance and power trade-off decisions using end-to-end delay as a simple SLA metric, and they took into account the overheads for each transition between multiple sleep modes and standby power levels. Their periodic energy optimization consists of both active and inactive portions. The active portion has two phases: finding the minimum number of servers so that the SLA can be met using the highest frequency of the machines and scaling frequency. The inactive portion deals with sleep energy optimization by making a trade-off between system wake-up time overhead and sleep energy conservation.

It is observed that the portion of power due to processors is small in comparison with total system power in some recent clusters. There are still a number of work using power-on/off mechanism only due to the nontrivial power consumption for active idle servers. Chen et al. [38] proposed a dynamic provisioning technique to turn on a minimum number of servers required to satisfy application-specific SLA with consideration of time taken for turning on/off a server and load dispatching algorithms. The authors established a power model with respect to CPU utilization and a performance model with respect to number of connections and login rate. In addition, load can be predicted using a sparse periodic autoregression (SPAR) model. On the basis of these models, the provisioning techniques are developed.

In virtualization environments, the resource allocation, such as CPU, memory, and disk I/O, to each virtual machine should be taken into account as well in order to achieve performance guarantee. Wang et al. [39] proposed a two-layer control architecture to provide response time guarantees for virtualized enterprise servers. The primary control loop uses a MIMO control over CPU resources to balance load among virtual machines so that they can achieve roughly the same normalized response time. The secondary loop controls the normalized response time of all virtual machines to a desired level by DVFS for power efficiency.

We note that the key issue of minimization clusterwide energy consumption is modeling. The models may include power model, performance model, and workload prediction model. On the basis of these models, control theory or optimization approach can be applied. From the perspective of methodology, indirect methods can be applied to this kind of problems.

There are few works done in an attempt to solve this problem using direct methods such as RL. For example, Tan et al. [40] proposed an approach to learn the power management policy to minimize power consumption for a given performance constraint by RL in a model-free manner. We still believe that the indirect methods should be more efficient for this kind of problems.

12.3.2.2 Performance maximization under power budget. In addition to reducing energy consumption, another energy-efficient design objective is to control power consumption to adapt to a given power budget so as to reduce the power (then the performance) of the components when actual power consumption of the server or cluster exceeds the budget [41]. As a result of controlling power consumption, the performance should be maximized without using power more than the budget.

For example, given a budget of power, Gandhi et al. [42] studied the problem of how to allocate power among a server farm so that the performance can be optimized. A queuing theoretic model is developed to predict the optimal power allocation in a variety of scenarios. The optimal power allocation scheme depends on many factors such as power-to-frequency relationship and the arrival rate of jobs.

Most of the work of performance maximization under power budget have overlap with the solutions to power capping. We present more techniques related to this topic in Section 12.4.

12.3.2.3 Trade-off between power and performance. In data centers, it is required to enable resource provisioning in accordance with flexible SLAs that specify dynamic trade-off between performance and cost that can be translated as power consumption. Indirect methods are mostly employed toward this purpose.

The work by Chase et al. [43] is one of the earliest focusing on energy-conscious clusterwide resource management. It is based on an economic model in which the amount of resource is a function of service quality. SLA is used to make trade-off between service quality and energy consumption. On the basis of this model, an appropriate amount of resource is allocated to each request. The number of active servers is determined with the objective of maximizing the resource efficiency and meanwhile minimizing unproductive cost. The idles servers can enter to lower-power states for more energy saving.

Chen et al. [44] used SLA to direct trade-off between energy and performance as well. Unlike Jeffrey et al. [43], they considered power-on/off and DVFS. They proposed three online strategies based on steady state queuing analysis, feedback control theory, and a hybrid mechanism of both. Time and energy overhead of turning on/off is considered as well.

Kephart et al. [45] proposed an approach to address trade-off between power and performance, which designed an agent to deal with each aspect of system behavior, such as power, performance, and availability.

The ultimate goal is to optimize multiple aspects of data-center behavior.

Such a multiagent approach employs a utility function defined as a joint of power and performance for trade-off decision.

By conveying the utility function between power and performance manager, a management action can be taken on according to the utility-optimizing power management policy, which is done by power manager. Meanwhile, performance manager will get feedback of relevant information. In addition, the authors employed an RL technique to adaptively learn models of the dependence of performance and power consumption on workload intensity and the power cap.

Kusic et al. [46] further considered power and performance trade-off in virtualization environments. They presented an online resource provisioning framework for combined power and performance management with consideration of switching costs incurred when provisioning virtual machines. The authors formulated this management problem as one of sequential optimization under uncertainty. They suggested a limited lookahead control approach to solve this optimization problem. This work relies on the workload-specific performance models and the power model is coarse grained without consideration of system usage.

The workload information may not always be available a priori in practice. In light of this, Gong and Xu [47] suggested that the management of power and performance should be adaptive. They developed a feedback-control-based coordination system to provide guarantees on an SLA with respect to performance and a power budget for virtualized servers. Two self-tuning prediction models are proposed for power and performance. A utility function can be defined to represent different levels of trade-off between power and performance. The optimal solution to this utility function directs the resource allocation among virtual machines. In contrast to Reference 46, the power model in this work is fine grained considering the system usage.

On another track, virtual machine migration provides an alternative way to save energy by consolidation, which reduces the number of hosts.

Verma et al. [48–50] investigated static/semistatic/dynamic job placement to achieve different goals in power and performance, such as power minimization and performance maximization, enabled by virtual machine migration.

There are a few works done using RL to achieve trade-off of power and performance as well. Tesauro et al. [51] presented an RL approach to developing effective control policies for real-time power management in application servers. A trade-off between power and performance is conveyed by a utility function. This utility function can be used as a reward signal in RL. A hybrid RL approach is employed. Hybrid RL combines the advantage of both explicit model-based methods and RL. Instead of training an RL module online, hybrid RL uses off-line training on data collected while an externally supplied initial policy is running. Then, a standard RL approximator can be applied. This approach refers to the fact that expert domain knowledge can be engineered into initial policy without needing explicit engineering or interfacing into the RL module.

Tan et al. [40] proposed an online power management technique using RL to minimize power consumption for a given performance constraint or achieve different levels of trade-off between power and performance. The best power management policy can be learned without knowing the workload information a priori. This approach is model free since it learns the policy directly instead of selecting from the existing set. However, the experiments were conducted for hard disk only without deployment at server- or cluster level.

In general, a utility function can be defined to represent different levels of trade-off between power and performance. Thus the problem can be formulated as optimization of the defined function. The solution to this category of problems are mostly model based, which means that the power and performance models, even the workload prediction model, are needed to solve this optimization problem. If this kind of models are not available, the indirect method, such as RL, can treat this utility function as a reward to optimize. To improve the poor performance of indirect methods during live online training, the initial policy is usually provided.

12.3.3 Energy-Proportional Computing

The concept of energy-proportional computing was first proposed by Barroso and Holzle in Reference 52. It was based on the observation that the lowest energy-efficiency region corresponds to the most common operating mode in today's servers. In Reference 52, the authors analyzed average CPU utilization of a sample of 5000 Google servers over a period of 6 months. Although the distribution of CPU utilization may vary across different clusters and workloads, a common trend is that servers spend most of time within the 10–50% CPU utilization range and relatively little aggregate time at high utilization levels.

Server power consumption increases with system utilization. In Reference 52, the authors studied the power consumption and energy efficiency of a typical energy-efficient server at different utilization levels. This study shows that even an energy-efficient server can still consume almost half of its peak power when it is idle. One more important result from this study is that the energy efficiency drops quickly as utilization decreases. In the typical operating range, the energy efficiency is much lower than that at peak performance. For example, the energy efficiency in 20–30% utilization range is only half of that at peak usage [52]. Obviously, such a profile is not acceptable.

The mismatch between server workload profile and server energy-efficiency behavior must be addressed largely at hardware level [52]. For example, Fan et al. evaluated the potential benefit of proportional energy efficiency. They used traced of activity levels of thousands of machines over 6 months to simulate the energy saving gained from more energy-proportional servers. If the servers only consume 10% power of the peak instead of 50%, the energy usage can be decreased by 50% by increased energy proportionality alone.

Software alone may not be efficient unless the servers are in inactive idle modes or running at full speed. Using low power states with low activation or deactivation and power-friendly task scheduling schemes can enhance energy proportionality. Meisner et al. [53] designed the entire system to transition rapidly between a high performance active state and a minimal-power nap state in response to instantaneous load. By applying this technique, the energy-proportional behavior can be achieved. The power-friendly task scheduling enabled by consolidation can concentrate the loads to a few active servers and let other idle servers enter low power state. But it can lead to availability degradation caused by spikes in data centers. Further, in data centers, servers are unlikely to be fully idle even during periods of lower service demand. It is because the load will be distributed to a large number of servers instead of concentrating in fewer servers. Another reason is the need for resilient distributed storage. GFS [54], the Google File System, spreads data across the entire cluster to improve availability, reliability, and resiliency. Thus, all servers must be available even during low load periods. As a result, the software approach might not be feasible.

The poor energy proportionality can be attributed to the poor energy proportionality of each subsystem of a server. The CPU no long dominates platform power at peak usage in modern servers. It only takes less than 60%. According to Reference 29, server-class CPUs have a dynamic power range greater than 3.0×. By comparison, the dynamic range of memory, disk, and networking equipment is much lower: around 2.0 × for memory, 1.3 × for disk, and 1.2 × for networking switches. As a result, to improve energy proportionality at system level should take into account all the components.

We note that energy-proportional behavior should target the entire data center, including the power distribution and cooling infrastructure. The efficiency of power supply units (PSUs) are often 90% efficient at their optimal point, usually 75% load, but it can drop off rapidly below 40% load, sometimes dropping below 50% efficiency [55]. This indicates lack of energy proportionality. Since PSUs are designed to have much greater peak capacity than the corresponding computing systems, they are apt to operate at a low load zone. Thus, poor efficiency occurs.

12.4 POWER CAPPING

Traditionally, servers are designed to provide for the worst-case scenario by over-provisioning, which adds costs with only few benefits for the real environments. In contrast, a "better-than-worst-case" design approach has been adopted by limiting power consumption (power capping) [56]. Power determines overall facility cost in data centers because much of the construction cost is directly related to the maximum power draw supported. Energy usage determines the electricity bill. Although today's servers rarely reach the maximum power draws in practice, it is still a must to control power to avoid overloading the facility's power delivery system. Enforcement of power limits can be physical, which means that overloading of electrical circuits will cause outage, or contractual, which considers the economic penalties for exceeding the negotiated load [57]. Power capping is a promising technique to manage the power of a single server or the aggregate power of a cluster of servers. It is effective for data centers, especially at the cluster level, by monitoring the power usage of an actual data center as well [58].

There are a few works that have proposed control-theoretic approaches for power capping at system level [41, 59]. Wang and Chen [60] extended the work [41] from single server to multiple servers. They claimed that the management of the servers in a cluster should be coordinated since they are coupled because of the same running application or shared power supply. A MIMO control algorithm is developed to control multiple servers simultaneously. In each control period, the controller collects the power measurement and CPU utilization of each server, computing a new CPU frequency for each server, and directs the servers to scale CPU frequencies in a coordinated manner.

At cluster level, Femal et al. [58] noticed the uneven distribution of workload among nodes. Thus, they allocated power nonuniformly according to demands. A cluster-level manager collects information of all nodes and allocates power to each node while satisfying total power budget. A node-level manager allocates power to each device at a fine level of granularity.

Further, the long-term data from real-world servers have been studied in Reference 2. Two trends were summarized: (i) low resource utilization with infrequent and short-lived bursts; (ii) the probability of synchronized spikes on all servers at the same time is rather low. On the basis of these observations, Ranganathan et al. [2] proposed a power budgeting approach across an ensemble of servers by leveraging statistical properties of concurrent resource usage.

A enclosure-level controller chooses power budget for each blade, monitors the blades, and sets servers to throttle or unthrottle. A local agent provides local power monitoring and control per server. The benefit of this approach is to provision the power budget of the ensemble to a value much lower than the sum of the worst-case power for each of the individual servers.

In virtualized environments, the power capping problem is also addressed. Multilayer control approach is widely used in this scenario. Nathuji et al. [61] developed a two-layer feedback controller for power budgeting with QoS management in virtualized servers. One loop monitors power consumption and determines a platform-level CPU allocation to meet power budget. The other loop is distributed across virtual machines to bid resource based on shadow price for each virtual machine. In Reference 62, both power budget and performance are guaranteed. The power consumption is constrained in a cluster-level power control loop by scaling CPU frequency. The performance guarantee is achieved by allocating CPU resources among virtual machines in a performance control loop.

Thermal management techniques are similar to power capping in that they also consist of heat sensing and heat throttling subsystems [26]. There are two ways to monitor heat: one is to use direct thermal profiling; the other is to correlate power and temperature so that the temperature can be inferred indirectly. Heat can be throttled by either power management or strengthened cooling, which will increase the cooling cost. Here, we focus on using power management techniques for thermal management. Skadron et al. [63] employed a proportional-integral-differential (PID) controller for dynamic thermal management. This technique was proposed for a single server. At clusterwide, Heath et al. [64] proposed a thermal management system. Three temperature thresholds are defined for different actions: no action, load adjustment, and turning off. They further developed an approach combining both energy saving and thermal management. This strategy turns off as many servers as possible without degrading performance based on usage prediction. Moore et al. [1] investigated the use of temperature-aware workload placement as a manner to reducing cooling cost. The thermodynamics is studied in data centers and this information is used to prioritize the servers according to cooling costs. The scheduling algorithm is directed by the cooling costs in order to minimize the total cooling cost. The computer room air conditioning (CRAC) supply temperature is adjusted as well in addition to dynamic turning on/off mechanism.

To address power capping problem, the power model is essential. Thus, only indirect methods can be applied. Control-based approach using power models is the mostly a common technique toward this goal.

12.5 CONCLUSION

Power conservation has become a key challenge in data centers. There are a large variety of power management techniques developed. We summarized representative work in Table 12.1, with respect to the dimensions of objective, mechanism, methodology, and scope.

Energy efficiency is a key cost driver for data centers. The average real-world data centers and servers remains inefficient. They waste two-thirds or more of their energy because of energy overhead of support systems, including cooling, UPS, PDU, etc. Although the energy efficiency at data-center level can be improved by applying best practices to data center and server designs, challenges still exist as the inherent complex problems and unfavorable technology trends are difficult to tackle. In this chapter, our focus is not the energy-efficiency enhancement due to improvement on support system, but the power management techniques on IT equipment itself.

Power management techniques for data centers can be divided into two groups: energy-efficiency improvement and power capping. Energy usage determines the electricity bill. Power determines overall facility cost in data centers because much of the construction cost is directly related to the maximum power draw supported. Energy efficiency can be improved by either reducing energy expenditures while maintaining required performance target or increasing performance gain while satisfying the power budget. In addition, performance and power are often coordinated to achieve a flexible SLAs specifying dynamic trade-off. Although today's servers rarely reach the maximum power draws in practice, it is still a must to control power to avoid overloading the facility's power delivery system. Power capping is a promising technique to manage the power of a single

TABLE 12.1   Summary of Representative Power Management Techniques in Data Centers

Technique (Taken from References)	Objective	Mechanism	Methodology	Scope
[34]	Energy saving acceptable performance	Node on/off	Heuristic analytical model	Clusters
[35]	Energy minimization with delay constraints	DVFS	Analytical model	Clusters
[36, 37]	Energy optimization with end-to-end delay control	Node on/off, DVFS, multiple sleep states	Optimization, feedback control, analytical model	Multitier clusters
[39]	Response time guarantee with power efficiency	DVFS, CPU resource	Two-layer control, MIMO	Virtualized servers
[38]	Power saving SLA	Node on/off	Analytical model	Clusters data centers
[43]	Trade-off	Low power, states	Optimization, analytical model	Clusters
[44]	Trade-off	Node on/off, DVFS	Feedback control, queuing, hybrid	Clusters
[45]	Trade-off	Workload intensity	Optimization	Clusters
[46]	Trade-off	CPU resource	LLC	Virtualized clusters
[47]	Trade-off	CPU resource	Adaptive control	Virtualized servers
[51]	Trade-off	Workload intensity	RL	Clusters
[58]	Power budget, throughput	DVFS, device on/off	Analytical model	Clusters
[2]	Power budget, SLA	DVFS	Heuristic	Clusters
[60]	Power budget	DVFS	MPC, MIMO	Clusters
[61]	Power budget	CPU resource	Two-layer feedback control	Virtualized clusters

TABLE 12.1 (*Continued*)

Technique (Taken from References)	Objective	Mechanism	Methodology	Scope
[62]	Power budget, performance	DVFS, CPU resource	Two-layer feedback control	Virtualized clusters
[1]	Cooling cost, temperature threshold	Node on/off CRAC temperature	Analytic model, optimization	Data centers
[64]	Temperature threshold utilization threshold	Node on/off	Analytical model heuristic	Data centers
[48–50]	Performance, power budget, trade-off	Node on/off	Analytical model, optimization	Virtualized heterogeneous clusters
[8]	Power/throughput ratio	Node on/off	Analytical model	Heterogeneous clusters
[9]	Energy saving, QoS-aware	Node on/off, DVFS	Analytical model	Heterogeneous clusters
[10]	Power efficiency	Workload allocation	Analytic model	Heterogeneous clusters

server or the aggregate power of a cluster of servers. High temperature due to over heat dissipation can compromise the reliability of the affected components, leading to misbehaviors and failures. Thermal management is thus necessary in data centers.

We note that most of the work in this field rely on analytical models. These models may cover power model, performance model, and workload prediction model. Guaranteeing correctness and effectiveness is a challenge. Control-theoretic techniques provide a meaningful hint for the development in power management in data centers. The limitations of model-based approaches include the difficulty in modeling, adaptation to system dynamics, etc. In contrast, there are a few other direct approaches that determine the control rules without explicit system models. One representative example is RL. It suffers from poor performance due to exploration without any knowledge during live online training. The scalability might be poor in large state spaces.

The power management mechanisms are closely related to the scope where they are applied. The systemwide power consumption was regulated by control on CPU in previous work since CPU used to be the dominant power consumption component and multiple low power states are enabled. When the power consumption on other subsystems, such as memory and disk, keeps increasing, more power management mechanisms on these subsystems are required and provided. The entire server can be managed as active, sleep, and power-off states to further save power in a cluster.

Virtualization has been widely employed in data centers and brings a number of benefits, such as performance isolation, server consolidation, and system manageability. It also shed a new light on power management mechanisms by enabling virtual CPU resource allocation and virtual machine migration. Meanwhile, new challenges introduced by virtualization have been imposed on traditional power management techniques mainly because of resource sharing among cohosted virtual machines. The work on power management in virtualization environments focuses on resource allocation among virtual machines and virtual machine placement across a cluster to meet power and performance requirements.

We also notice that today's hardware cannot gracefully adapt its power usage to load change. Low energy efficiency under light load leads to energy inefficiency in data centers since most of time is spent at low load level in data centers. Energy proportionality was proposed to be a promising approach to address this problem. However, the challenge still remains in the hardware of subsystems. Consolidation can create energy-proportional behavior in clusters built with non-energy-proportional components by turning off idle servers. But this strategy can lead to availability degradation due to spikes. In addition, high performance and high availability system tends to spread the data and computation across the entire cluster, thus all servers should be available even during low load periods. Software alone may not reach energy proportionality. To achieve energy proportionality, both hardware and software aspects should be considered.

REFERENCES

1. Moore J, Chase J, Ranganathan P, Sharma R. Making scheduling "cool": temperature-aware workload placement in data centers. In: ATEC '05: Proceedings of the Annual Conference on USENIX Annual Technical Conference. Berkeley (CA): USENIX Association; 2005. pp. 5–5.

2. Ranganathan P, Leech P, Irwin D, Chase J, Packard H. Ensemble-level power management for dense blade servers. In: The International Symposium on Computer Architecture (ISCA); 2006. pp. 66–77.

3. Patel C, Ranganathan P. Enterprise power and cooling. ASPLOS Tutorial; 2006.

4. EPA. Epa report to congress on server and data center energy efficiency. Technical report. U.S. Environmental Protection Agency; 2007. Available at http://www.energystar.gov/ia/partners/prod_development/downloads/EPA_Datacenter_Report_Congress_Final1.pdf.

5. Raghavendra R, Ranganathan P, Talwar V, Wang Z, Zhu X. No "power" struggles: coordinated multi-level power management for the data center. In: ASPLOS; 2008. pp. 48–59.

6. Nathuji R, Schwan K. Virtualpower: coordinated power management in virtualized enterprise systems. In: SOSP '07: Proceedings of 21st ACM SIGOPS Symposium on Operating Systems Principles. ACM; 2007. 265–278.

7. Stoess J, Lang C, Bellosa F. Energy management for hypervisor-based virtual machines. In: ATC'07: 2007 USENIX Annual Technical Conference on Proceedings of the USENIX Annual Technical Conference. USENIX Association; 2007. pp. 1–14.

8. Heath T, Diniz B, Carrera EV, Meira W Jr., Bianchini R. Energy conservation in heterogeneous server clusters. In: PPoPP '05: Proceedings of the 10th ACM SIGPLAN Symposium on Principles and Practice of Parallel Programming. New York: ACM; 2005. pp. 186–195.

9. Rusu C, Ferreira A, Scordino C, Watson A. Energy-efficient real-time heterogeneous server clusters. In: RTAS '06: Proceedings of the 12th IEEE Real-Time and Embedded Technology and Applications Symposium. IEEE Computer Society; 2006. pp. 418–428.

10. Nathuji R, Isci C, Gorbatov E. Exploiting platform heterogeneity for power efficient data centers. In: ICAC '07: Proceedings of the 4th International Conference on Autonomic Computing. IEEE Computer Society; 2007. pp. 5.

11. Zhu X, Uysal M, Wang Z, Singhal S, Merchant A, Padala P, Shin K. What does control theory bring to systems research? SIGOPS Oper Syst Rev 2009;43(1):62–69.

12. Sutton RS, Barto AG, Williams RJ. Reinforcement learning is direct adaptive optimal control. In: The American Control Conference; 1991. pp. 2143–2146.

13. Hoelzle Hewlett-Packard, Intel Microsoft, Pheonix and Toshiba. Advanced configuration and power interface specification revision 4.0; 2009.

14. Venkatachalam V, Franz M. Power reduction techniques for microprocessor systems. ACM Comput Surv 2005;37(3):195–237.

15. AMD. White paper publication 26094: Bios and kernel developer's guide for ame athlon 64 and amd opteron processors; 2006.

16. Intel. White paper publication 301170: Enhanced intel speedstep technology for the intel pentium m processor; 2004.

17. Intel Corporation. Intel 64 and IA-32 architectures software developer's Manual-Volume 3A: system programming guide Part 1; 2009.

18. Colarelli D, Grunwald D. Massive arrays of idle disks for storage archives. In: Supercomputing '02: Proceedings of the 2002 ACM/IEEE Conference on Supercomputing. IEEE Computer Society Press; 2002. pp. 1–11.

19. Pinheiro E, Bianchini R, Dubnicki C. Exploiting redundancy to conserve energy in storage systems. SIGMETRICS Perform Eval Rev 2006;34(1):15–26.

20. Carrera EV, Pinheiro E, Bianchini R. Conserving disk energy in network servers. In: ICS '03: Proceedings of the 17th Annual International Conference on Supercomputing. ACM; 2003. pp. 86–97.

21. Joo Y, Choi Y, Shim H, Lee HG, Kim K, Chang N. Energy exploration and reduction of sdram memory systems. In: DAC '02: Proceedings of the 39th Annual Design Automation Conference. ACM; 2002. pp. 892–897.

22. Pandey V, Jiang W, Zhou Y, Bianchini R. Dma-aware memory energy management. In: HPCA '06: Proceedings of the 12th International Symposium on High-Performance Computer Architecture; 2006.

23. Micron Technology Inc. Calculating memory system power for ddr3; 2007.

24. credit scheduler. Available at http://wiki.xensource.com/xenwiki/CreditScheduler.

25. Barham P, Dragovic B, Fraser K, Hand S, Harris T, Ho A, Neugebauer R, Pratt I, Warfield A. Xen and the art of virtualization. In: SOSP '03: Proceedings of the 19th ACM Symposium on Operating Systems Principles. ACM; 2003. pp. 164–177.

26. Liu Y, Hong Z. A survey of the research on power management techniques for high-performance systems. Software: Practice and Experience; 2010.

27. Urs Hoelzle, Luiz Andre Barroso. *The Datacenter as a Computer: An Introduction to the Design of Warehouse-Scale Machines*. Morgan and Claypool Publishers; 2009.

28. Standard Performance Evaluation Corporation. Specpower _ssj2008; 2009. Available at http://www.spec.org/power_ssj2008/.

29. Barroso LA, Hölzle U. *The Datacenter as a Computer: An Introduction to the Design of Warehouse-Scale Machines*. Morgan and Claypool Publishers; 2009.

30. Lim K, Ranganathan P, Chang J, Patel C, Mudge T, Reinhardt S. Understanding and designing new server architectures for emerging warehouse-computing environments. In: ISCA '08: Proceedings of the 35th Annual International Symposium on Computer Architecture. Washington (DC): IEEE Computer Society; 2008. pp. 315–326.

31. Greenberg S, Mills E, Tschudi B, Rumsey P, Myatt B. Best practices for data centers: Lessons learned from benchmarking 22 data centers; 2006. Available at http://evanmills.lbl.gov/pubs/pdf/aceee-datacenters.pdf.

32. Emerson Network Power. Energy logic: Reducing data center energy consumption by creating savings that cascade across systems; 2007.

33. Brill KG. Data center energy efficiency and productivity; 2007. Available at http://www.uptimeinstitute.org/symp_pdf/(TUI3004C)DataCenterEnergy Efficiency.pdf.

34. Pinheiro E, Bianchini R, Carrera EV, Heath T. Load balancing and unbalancing for power and performance in cluster-based systems. In: Workshop on Compilers and Operating Systems for Low Power (COLP); 2001.

35. Sharma V, Thomas A, Abdelzaher T, Skadron K, Lu Z. Power-aware qos management in web servers. In: RTSS '03: Proceedings of the 24th IEEE International Real-Time Systems Symposium. IEEE Computer Society; 2003. pp. 63.

36. Horvath T, Abdelzaher T, Skadron K, Liu X. Dynamic voltage scaling in multitier web servers with end-to-end delay control. IEEE Trans Comput 2007;56(4).

37. Horvath T, Skadron K. Multi-mode energy management for multi-tier server clusters. In: PACT '08: Proceedings of the 17th International Conference on Parallel Architectures and Compilation Techniques. ACM; 2008.

38. Chen G, He W, Liu J, Nath S, Rigas L, Xiao L, Zhao F. Energy-aware server provisioning and load dispatching for connection-intensive internet services. In: NSDI'08: Proceedings of the 5th USENIX Symposium on Networked Systems Design and Implementation. USENIX Association; 2008. pp. 337–350.

39. Wang Y, Wang X, Chen M, Zhu X. Power-efficient response time guarantees for virtualized enterprise servers. In: RTSS '08: Proceedings of the 2008 Real-Time Systems Symposium. Washington (DC): IEEE Computer Society; 2008. pp. 303–312.

40. Tan Y, Liu W, Qiu Q. Adaptive power management using reinforcement learning. In: ICCAD '09: Proceedings of the 2009 International Conference on Computer-Aided Design. ACM; 2009. pp. 461–467.

41. Lefurgy C, Wang X, Ware Malcolm. Server-level power control. In: ICAC '07: Proceedings of the 4th International Conference on Autonomic Computing. Washington (DC): IEEE Computer Society; 2007. p. 4.

42. Gandhi A, Harchol-Balter M, Das R, Lefurgy C. Optimal power allocation in server farms. In: SIGMETRICS '09: Proceedings of the 11th International Joint Conference on Measurement and Modeling of Computer Systems. ACM; 2009. pp. 157–168.

43. Chase JS, Anderson DC, Thakar PN, Vahdat AM, Doyle RP. Managing energy and server resources in hosting centers. In: SOSP '01: Proceedings of the 18th ACM Symposium on Operating Systems Principles. ACM; 2001. pp. 103–116.

44. Chen Y, Das A, Qin W, Sivasubramaniam A, Wang Q, Gautam N. Managing server energy and operational costs in hosting centers. SIGMETRICS Perform Eval Rev 2005.

45. Kephart JO, Chan H, Das R, Levine DW, Tesauro G, Rawson F, Lefurgy C. Coordinating multiple autonomic managers to achieve specified power-performance tradeoffs. In: ICAC '07: Proceedings of the 4th International Conference on Autonomic Computing. IEEE Computer Society; 2007. p. 24.

46. Kusic D, Kephart JO, Hanson JE, Kandasamy N, Jiang G. Power and performance management of virtualized computing environments via lookahead control. In: ICAC '08: Proceedings of the 2008 International Conference on Autonomic Computing. IEEE Computer Society; 2008. pp. 3–12.

47. Gong J, Xu C-Z. vpnp: automated coordination of power and performance in virtualized datacenters. In: IWQoS '10; 2010.

48. Verma A, Ahuja P, Neogi A. pmapper: power and migration cost aware application placement in virtualized systems. In: Middleware '08: Proceedings of the 9th ACM/IFIP/USENIX International Conference on Middleware. New York: Springer-Verlag; 2008. pp. 243–264.

49. Verma A, Ahuja P, Neogi A. Power-aware dynamic placement of hpc applications. In: ICS '08: Proceedings of the 22nd Annual International Conference on Supercomputing. ACM; 2008. pp. 175–184.

50. Verma A, Dasgupta G, Nayak TK, De P, Kothari R. Server workload analysis for power minimization using consolidation. In: USENIX'09: Proceedings of the 2009 conference on USENIX Annual Technical Conference. USENIX Association; 2009. pp. 28–28.

51. Tesauro G, Das R, Chan H, Kephart JO, Levine D, Rawson FL III, Lefurgy C. Managing power consumption and performance of computing systems using reinforcement learning. In: Advances in Neural Information Processing Systems (NIPS). MIT Press; 2007.

52. Barroso LA, Hölzle U. The case for energy-proportional computing. Computer 2007;40(12):33–37.

53. Meisner D, Gold BT, Wenisch TF. Powernap: eliminating server idle power. In: ASPLOS '09: Proceeding of the 14th International Conference on Architectural Support for Programming Languages and Operating Systems. ACM; 2009. pp. 205–216.

54. Ghemawat S, Gobioff H, Leung S-T. The google file system. SIGOPS Oper Syst Rev 2003;37(5):29–43.

55. ECOS and ERPI. Efficient power supplies for data center and enterprise servers; 2008.

56. Colwell B. We may need a new box. Computer 2004.

57. Fan X, Weber W-D, Barroso LA. Power provisioning for a warehouse-sized computer. In: ISCA '07: Proceedings of the 34th Annual International Symposium on Computer Architecture. ACM; 2007. pp. 13–23.

58. Femal ME, Freeh VW. Boosting data center performance through non-uniform power allocation. In: ICAC '05: Proceedings of the 2nd International Conference on Automatic Computing. IEEE Computer Society; 2005. pp. 250–261.

59. Gong J, Xu C-Z. A gray-box feedback control approach for system-level peak power management. In: ICPP'10: Proceedings of the 2010 International Conference on Parallel Processing. IEEE Computer Society; 2010. pp. 555–564.

60. Wang X, Chen M. Cluster-level feedback power control for performance optimization. In: HPCA '08: Proceedings of the 14th International Symposium on High-Performance Computer Architecture. IEEE Computer Society; 2008.

61. Nathuji R, England P, Sharma P, Singh A. Feedback driven qos-aware power budgeting for virtualized servers. In: FeBID '09; 2009.

62. Wang X, Wang Y. Co-con: Coordinated control of power and application performance for virtualized server clusters. In: IWQoS '09; 2009.

63. Skadron K, Abdelzaher T, Stan MR. Control-theoretic techniques and thermal-RC modeling for accurate and localized dynamic thermal management. In: HPCA '02: Proceedings of the 8th International Symposium on High-Performance Computer Architecture. Washington (DC): IEEE Computer Society; 2002. pp. 17.

64. Heath T, Centeno AP, George P, Ramos L, Jaluria Y, Bianchini R. Mercury and freon: temperature emulation and management for server systems. In: ASPLOS-XII: Proceedings of the 12th International Conference on Architectural Support for Programming Languages and Operating Systems. New York: ACM; 2006. pp. 106–116.

CHAPTER 13

ENERGY-EFFICIENT STORAGE SYSTEMS FOR DATA CENTERS

SUDHANVA GURUMURTHI and ANAND SIVASUBRAMANIAM

13.1 INTRODUCTION

Data centers play a central role in today's computing infrastructure. Ubiquitous connectivity to the Internet (often through high speed broadband and 3G/4G networks), the proliferation of network-enabled mobile devices such as smartphones, and the commoditization of processor and storage hardware have given rise to a plethora of Internet-based data-centric applications. These range from classic Internet applications, such as search engines, e-mail, and transaction processing, to newer ones, such as social networking and on-line photo and video sharing. In addition, enterprises are getting increasingly data centric, collecting and storing voluminous data for information processing, driving enterprise-scale optimizations through analytics, enhancing user/customer experience, and meeting regulatory requirements. Furthermore, there is a push toward "cloud"-based computing and storage, where user applications and data reside in data centers and are accessed through a thin client via a network.

A key aspect shared by many of these applications is that they store and process enormous amounts of data. An estimate of the scale and pace of this data growth was provided in a 2008 report from the International Data Corporation (IDC) [1]. According to the IDC, the amount of data generated worldwide by the year 2011 would have reached a staggering *1800 EB* (18×10^{20} B). This report also highlights that while most of this data is expected to be generated by individuals (e.g., taking photos on their mobile phones), a substantial portion of the data will be stored and managed centrally in data centers. In order to meet current and future storage requirements, data centers accommodate these storage needs typically on large arrays/farms of hard disk drives (HDDs).

Energy-Efficient Distributed Computing Systems, First Edition.
Edited by Albert Y. Zomaya and Young Choon Lee.
© 2012 John Wiley & Sons, Inc. Published 2012 by John Wiley & Sons, Inc.

In addition to storage capacity, disk arrays/farms can enhance I/O throughput. There already exists a significant latency gap between processors and disks, which can create severe performance bottlenecks for I/O-intensive applications.

The shift from single-core to multicore processors widens the gap even further [2]. Therefore, as more cores are added to the die, using such processors to run I/O-intensive applications will require a large number of disks.

The compounding consequence of using a large number of HDDs for capacity and performance exacerbates their power consumption [3–5]. In fact, storage equipment constitutes nearly 10% of the total data center equipment, and as much as 5% of the data center power goes into powering the storage [6]. This chapter provides an overview of various techniques to reduce the energy usage of storage systems in servers and data centers.

We first begin with a tutorial on disk drives, the sources of power consumption within disks, and the abstraction of disk power in the form of power states (Section 13.2). We then proceed to discuss various hardware and software approaches to disk power reduction in Section 13.3. In Section 13.4, we discuss the relevance of alternate technologies such as nonvolatile memories (NVMs) and solid-state disks (SSDs) to reduce storage power and present ways of incorporating them in the server storage stack. Section 13.5 concludes this chapter.

13.2   DISK DRIVE OPERATION AND DISK POWER

This section provides an overview of the basic operation of a disk drive, the low level disk operations that consume power, and how disk power consumption can be abstracted at a higher level as a state machine consisting of power states. The state machine abstraction of disk power serves as the basis to understand the rationale behind various approaches to reducing disk power described in the next section.

13.2.1   An Overview of Disk Drives

An HDD is an electromechanical magnetic storage device. The internal organization of an HDD is shown in Figure 13.1. An HDD consists of a stack of circular platters that are coated with magnetic material on both surfaces. The magnetic medium is used to store the data bits. The recording area on each platter surface is divided into circular or serpentine *tracks* and each track is further divided into *sectors*. The platters are mounted on a central spindle that is rotated at a constant speed (expressed in rotations per minute or RPM) by a DC brushless motor called the *spindle motor* (*SPM*). Reading and writing of data from and to a platter is achieved via a read/write head that is mounted on a slider and floats over the platter surface in an extremely thin cushion of air. Each slider is connected to an arm and the arms are connected to a central assembly known as the *actuator*. Each platter surface has one read/write head and arm. All the arms

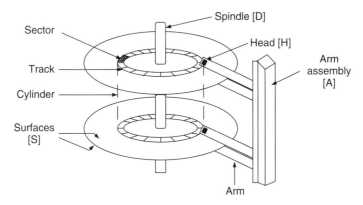

Figure 13.1   Internal structure of a hard disk drive. Reproduced with permission from [7].

move in unison over the surface of the platters, and this movement is effected by a *voice coil motor* (*VCM*). The disk arms of modern HDDs also contain piezoelectric microactuators for fine-grained positioning of the heads. In addition to these electromechanical components, modern HDDs also have a considerable amount of electronics, such as disk controllers, interface controllers, SPM and VCM drivers, a large DRAM-based disk cache, error correction code (ECC) chips, and the data channel. A detailed description of HDD design is given in References 8 and 9.

13.2.2   Sources of Disk Power Consumption

There are three sources of power consumption within an HDD: the SPM, the VCM, and the electronics. The power consumed by the electronic components can be reduced using low power design techniques such as voltage and frequency scaling, clock gating, and power gating. Since this chapter specifically focuses on storage-related issues and the power consumption and optimization of electronic devices have come under extensive scrutiny in the past decade, we primarily concentrate on the power consumption of the electromechanical components in the HDD.

Of the two electromechanical components, the SPM consumes the most power. The power consumed by the SPM can be expressed as [10]

$$\text{SPM Power} \propto n \cdot \omega_{\text{SPM}}^{2.8} \cdot (2r)^{4.6}, \tag{13.1}$$

where n is the number of platters, ω_{SPM} is the angular velocity of the SPM (i.e., the RPM of the disk), and r is the radius of the platters. Since the platters are always rotating when the disk is powered, Equation 13.1 represents the "static" power consumed by the disk, whether it is merely idling or actively performing I/O operations. As the equation indicates, the size of the disk platter has the largest impact on SPM power, followed by the rotational speed of the spindle and then the number of platters in the drive.

The VCM power, on the other hand, is more "dynamic." The VCM consumes power only when a disk seek needs to be performed and that too only during specific phases of a seek operation, depending on the distance that the arms have to travel across the platter surface.

A seek operation consists of four phases:

- An acceleration phase, during which the VCM consumes power.
- A coast phase of constant velocity, during which the VCM does not consume power.
- A deceleration phase to stop the arms near the desired track. In order to accomplish this, the VCM is again powered but the current is reversed to generate the braking effect.
- A head settling phase.

Figure 13.2 illustrates these four phases for three different seek distances. The physical behavior of disk seeks can be modeled using the Bang-Bang Triangular model [11]. In this model, the acceleration and deceleration times are assumed to be equal. V_{max} is the maximum velocity of the arm, and D_{avg} is the average seek distance. The energy consumed by the VCM is the highest when performing seeks of distance D_{avg}, since the arms accelerate to the maximum velocity and subsequently decelerate without coasting, as shown in Figure 13.2b, and the VCM remains powered during this entire time period.

The energy consumed by the VCM for one seek operation is given by [12]

$$E_{VCM} = \frac{n \cdot J_{VCM} \cdot \omega_{VCM}^2}{2} + \frac{n \cdot b_{VCM} \cdot \omega_{VCM}}{3}, \qquad (13.2)$$

where J_{VCM} is the inertia of the arm actuator, ω_{VCM} is the maximum angular velocity of the VCM, and b_{VCM} is the friction coefficient of the arm actuator. As we can see from Equation 13.2, slowing the speed of disk seeks and/or using fewer platters in the spindle can reduce VCM power.

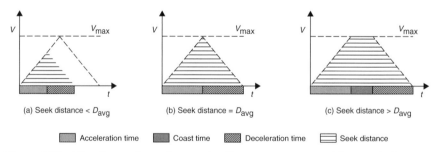

(a) Seek distance < D_{avg} (b) Seek distance = D_{avg} (c) Seek distance > D_{avg}

▓ Acceleration time   ▓ Coast time   ▓ Deceleration time   ▭ Seek distance

Figure 13.2   The phases of a seek operation for short, average, and long seek distances. Reproduced with permission from [13].

13.2.3   Disk Activity and Power Consumption

Although HDD power consumption is governed by low level issues such as the physical design of the drive and the dynamic behavior of the electromechanical components, as shown in Equations 13.1 and 13.2, most storage power reduction techniques view disk power at a higher level of abstraction. This abstraction is provided in the form of HDD *power states*, where each state corresponds to a certain type of high level disk activity and has an associated power cost. In addition, transitioning between the different states may also entail power costs and extra latencies. Therefore, the power consumption of an HDD can be represented as a state machine, where the nodes correspond to the power states and the edges denote the state transitions. A typical HDD power state machine is shown in Figure 13.3. This state machine corresponds to a Seagate Barracuda disk drive [14].

When the disk is spinning and not servicing any requests, it is said to be in the IDLE power state. Most of the power consumed in the idle state is due to the SPM. When a request comes to the disk and a physical seek (i.e., movement of the arms) is required, the VCM is activated and the disk transitions out of IDLE. Although not treated as a power state per se in Figure 13.3, this time period during which a seek is performed (SEEK) also consumes power. The transfer of bits between the platters and the data buffers within the drive occurs when the disk is in the ACTIVE state, during which the data channel is also active and hence consumes power. Regardless of whether the disk is in IDLE, SEEK, or ACTIVE state, the SPM always consumes power. In order to reduce SPM power, most disks have a low power STANDBY state in which the SPM is turned off and the platters are spun down till they are stationary. The disk cannot perform any I/O when in the STANDBY state. Therefore, when an I/O request arrives at the disk when it is in STANDBY, it needs to be spun back to service the request. Transitioning into

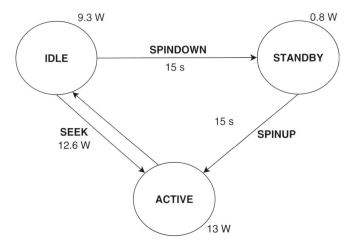

Figure 13.3   Power state machine of a 750-GB Seagate Barracuda 7200.10 disk drive.

and out of STANDBY typically incurs significant latency overheads (as indicated in Figure 13.3).

13.3   DISK AND STORAGE POWER REDUCTION TECHNIQUES

Since a substantial fraction of the power consumed by the disk is due to the electromechanical parts, techniques to reduce disk power have targeted these components. While there is a large body of research on reducing disk power, the majority of the techniques can be classified based on a few basic principles. Therefore, before we delve into the details of the specific techniques, we first discuss these principles. The principles can be understood by examining the power state machine in Figure 13.3.

Principle 1: Spin Down the Platters

As we can see in the figure, the difference in power consumption between the IDLE, SEEK, and ACTIVE states is much smaller than the difference between them and the STANDBY state. Therefore, turning off the spindle provides the largest power reduction. However, since the transition latencies into and out of STANDBY are large, one has to be careful about when to initiate a disk spin-down decision in order to reduce the performance impact.

Principle 2: Reduce Seek Activity

Among the powered states of the HDD, we can see that there is a small but nonnegligible difference in the power consumed when the disk is idle versus when it is seeking. Therefore, although the VCM is a less effective knob for managing disk power than the SPM, reducing overall seek activity, by reducing the number of seeks, the seek distances, and/or the speed of individual seek operations, can reduce disk power.

Principle 3: Provide for Energy Proportionality

When a disk is not in the STANDBY state, its power consumption varies between IDLE and its peak power (which is either ACTIVE or SEEK, based on the disk configuration). This variation in the power is based on the I/O load on the disk (i.e., the number of I/O requests to the disk in a given interval of time). As we have seen previously, the difference in power between these states is relatively small compared to putting the disk in STANDBY. Therefore, there is a large gap in the power consumption between when the disk is in STANDBY and when it is powered, but the power variation based on the I/O load is small. This scenario is qualitatively illustrated in Figure 13.4.

The x-axis of the graph indicates the I/O load; the y-axis, the resulting power consumption. Let us first look at the solid line, which corresponds to a conventional HDD. When the disk is in STANDBY, denoted as an I/O load value of zero in

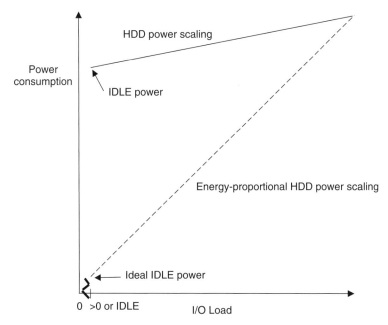

Figure 13.4 Energy proportionality of hard disk drives. The jagged line on the x-axis shows the transition from a no I/O load condition when the HDD is in STANDBY to a nonzero I/O load condition or when the disk is in IDLE.

the graph, the power consumption is negligible. However, if the disk is in IDLE or has a very low but nonzero number of requests to service, the incremental power needed is significantly higher. Beyond this point, the power consumed by the disk varies over a small range based on the I/O load. (Although the exact amount of power consumed during seek operations depends on the seek distance, an increased I/O load typically leads to higher seek activity and the upward power trend shown in the figure is a reasonable approximation of the disk power in such a scenario.)

Ideally, an HDD should consume little to no power when there are no I/O requests and it may consume its peak power when the I/O load is very high. However, in between these two extremes, the power consumption should vary in proportion to the I/O load. This scenario is shown by the dashed line in Figure 13.4. This desirable property is known as *energy proportionality* [15]. While processors provide energy proportionality to some extent through dynamic voltage and frequency scaling, HDDs exhibit poor energy proportionality. Although the eventual goal of storage power management is to achieve *energy efficiency* and not just energy proportionality (i.e., the amount of power consumed to perform a certain task should be as low as possible), it is important to provide the latter in order to achieve the former, especially in modern data centers, where long-duration idle periods are less likely and therefore the disk power needs to be controlled based on variations in the I/O load.

Using these three principles, storage power techniques can be implemented through software-only approaches, by redesigning the HDD hardware, or via a combination of both. We now provide an overview of these techniques. Note that while we discuss specific techniques, the following discussion is not meant to be an exhaustive survey of all the proposed techniques in the literature.

13.3.1 Exploiting the STANDBY State

Disk power management by leveraging the STANDBY state involves two steps: (i) detecting suitable idle periods and (ii) spinning down the platters when it is predicted that this action would save energy. The first step usually involves tracking the history of previous idle period characteristics and predicting the duration of the next idle period based on this history. If this period is determined to be sufficiently long to outweigh the spin-down and the subsequent spin-up penalties, the disk is transitioned to STANDBY.

Several idleness predictors use a time threshold to estimate the duration of the next idle period and to decide whether to spin down the disk. Li et al. [16] used a fixed threshold for predicting idleness, wherein if the idle period lasts over 2 s, the disk is spun down. However, this work was performed in the context of a laptop-style HDD, which can transition to and from STANDBY in 1–2 s. The spin-down threshold could be varied adaptively over the execution of the program [17, 18]. Golding et al. [19] carried out a detailed study on the effectiveness of various idle-time predictors for disk power management. Gurumurthi et al. [20] studied the idleness characteristics of storage systems of servers running transaction processing workloads. Their study indicated that the bulk of the power consumed by the storage system is when the disks are in the IDLE state, but the idleness is in the form of a large number of very short periods that are difficult to leverage to use the STANDBY power state without paying large performance penalties. Carrera et al. [21] carried out a similar study for network servers and arrived at similar conclusions.

Several techniques have been proposed to extend the idle periods of server disks in order to increase opportunities to spin them down. Papathanasiou and Scott [22] proposed to cluster disk operations through a combination of delaying certain disk requests and using aggressive prefetching to increase disk burstiness. Colarelli and Grunwald [23] proposed a system called *massive array of idle disks* (MAID) for archival storage, where a small number of disks are used as a cache for a larger number of disks that are put in STANDBY. Narayanan et al. [24] proposed a technique similar to MAID called *write offloading*, where write data bound to disks that are spun down are written to disks that are currently not in the STANDBY state and then moved to their home disks later. Pinheiro and Bianchini [25] proposed Popular Data Concentration (PDC), in which hot/popular data is moved to a subset of the disks in the storage system while the remaining ones are spun down. In a later work, Pinheiro et al. [26] proposed diverted access techniques for storage systems that employ redundancy (which is typical of most data center storage). Here, the original and redundant data are stored on separate disks and the data accesses are concentrated on the original disks, while the disks that house the redundant data are kept in STANDBY for long intervals of time.

In addition to using a subset of the disks within the storage system as a cache, which is the approach followed by MAID, PDC, and write offloading, disk idleness can also be increased by introducing a caching layer above the disks. Many server storage systems use large caches to improve performance, and there are several papers in the literature on effectively leveraging disk and storage caches to boost performance [27–29]. This performance boost can indirectly help reduce power consumption by reducing disk seek activity and also extend idle times to increase opportunities to spin down the platters. However, effective leveraging of such storage caches to reduce power requires careful tuning of the various aspects of the caching strategy, such as the replacement policy [30].

13.3.2 Reducing Seek Activity

Since disk seeks are one the biggest limiters of HDD performance, there has been extensive research into reducing their occurrence. Prior research in this area attempted to either reduce head movements to access data placed on disk or optimize the data placement to reduce seek activity [31–35]. In addition to these performance-centric approaches for reducing seek activity, there have been a few attempts to develop seek reduction strategies to reduce disk power consumption. Huang et al. [36] proposed a "Free Space File System" (FS2) that dynamically creates copies of data blocks in unoccupied disk blocks to reduce mechanical positioning delays and power consumption. Gurumurthi et al. [37] analyzed the use of VCM control to manage the operating temperature of disk drives. Such VCM control can be performed by leveraging the multiple seek speeds provided in certain disks [38].

13.3.3 Achieving Energy Proportionality

Techniques to provide energy proportionality for storage fall into two categories: (i) those that change the HDD hardware and (ii) software-only approaches that provide energy proportionality at the storage system level.

13.3.3.1 Hardware approaches. As Equation 13.1 indicates, there are three parameters that affect the power consumed by the spindle. While the number of platters and the size of the platter are fixed when the disk is manufactured, the RPM of the disk could potentially be varied at runtime. Given the nearly cubic exponent on the RPM, varying the speed of the spindle can allow the disk power consumption to vary along a large dynamic range and hence pave the way for a power characteristic similar to that shown in Figure 13.4. However, changing the rotational speed of the disk will affect rotational latency and transfer time and hence will also have a performance impact. Gurumurthi et al. [39] proposed such a dynamic RPM (DRPM) HDD, which has multiple RPM states and can perform disk I/O in each of these states, and proposed a control policy for managing power and performance in server storage systems. Carrera et al. [21] proposed a simpler two-speed variant of DRPM and highlighted its benefit for network servers. There have been several studies on the use of DRPM disks to design energy-efficient server storage systems [3, 30, 40, 41]. Disks with DRPM-like features have been commercialized (e.g., Hitachi Deskstar 7K400 [42]). Although this particular drive has only two RPM levels and it cannot perform I/O at the lower RPM, it can still provide energy savings by transitioning to the lower RPM state when in the IDLE state with significantly lower latency than the time it takes for a conventional HDD go to STANDBY.

Sankar et al. [7] proposed an alternative approach to energy-proportional HDD design called *intradisk parallelism* (IDP). IDP extends the architecture of conventional HDDs to exploit parallelism in the I/O request stream. IDP provides energy proportionality by exploiting the fact that the VCM consumes significantly lower power than the SPM. One way to exploit this property is to design an IDP drive to operate at a lower RPM, but provision multiple actuators to do parallel I/O within the drive to enhance performance. A two-actuator IDP drive is illustrated in Figure 13.5. The power-performance point at which the drive operates depends on the number of actuators that are enabled at a given instant.

13.3.3.2 *Software approaches.* Guerra et al. [43] provided an overview of the potential benefits of software-based approaches to energy proportionality in server storage systems with commonly available storage hardware. They considered a few disk-level knobs, such as the STANDBY state and variable seek speeds, as well as several techniques that control data placement and migration across several disks, such as consolidation, write offloading, and MAID. In general, software approaches to energy proportionality attempt to manage the ensemble

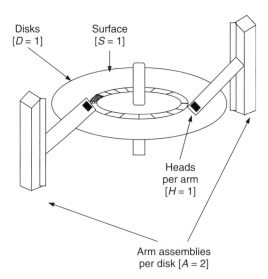

Figure 13.5   A two-actuator IDP Drive. Reproduced with permission from [7].

of storage devices to provide power-performance trade-offs over a wide dynamic range.

Weddle et al. [44] proposed a storage array design called *PARAID* that provides energy proportionality. PARAID uses a striping technique that allows data to be accessed from fewer or more number of disks based on the I/O load. When the load is light, several disks can be put into the STANDBY state and data can be served off a small set of disks. However, when the load is heavy, all the disks in the array may be necessary to provide acceptable performance. This "gear-shifting" capability facilitates energy-proportional behavior at the storage system level.

Verma et al. [45] proposed a storage consolidation layer called *SRCMap* that provides energy proportionality. SRCMap creates partial replicas of data volumes that contain the active data sets within these volumes on multiple disks and chooses the number of disks that need to be powered up (i.e., number of replicas) based on the I/O load at coarse time granularities. SRCMap also uses write offloading [24] to keep disks in STANDBY as long as possible.

13.4 USING NONVOLATILE MEMORY AND SOLID-STATE DISKS

The preceding discussions have centered around reducing the power consumption of HDD-based storage and addressing some of the limitations imposed by the electromechanical nature of disk drives. While HDDs remain the bedrock of data center storage, an effective way of reducing disk power is to use disks that use some form of solid-state NVM as the storage medium. Such disks, which are known as *SSDs*, currently use NAND Flash as the NVM to store data. In the future, SSDs may employ emerging NVM technologies such as phase change memory (PCM) or spin transfer torque RAM (STT-RAM).

Flash has traditionally been used in mobile devices and consumer electronic products, and the commoditization of this memory technology in recent years has made it cost-effective for complementing, supplementing, and/or even replacing HDDs. However, this memory technology is not without its limitations. There can be performance bottlenecks due to the erase-before-write requirement, the inability to perform in-place updates, and the lifetime constraint of having an upper bound on program and erase cycles. Some of these issues can be resolved through the use of nonvolatile write logging [46] and nonvolatile merge caching [47], using higher endurance, byte-addressable NVMs such as PCM or STT-RAM, and more sophisticated flash translation layer (FTL) designs [48].

Most commercially available SSDs have standard storage interfaces (e.g., SATA) and can therefore be used as drop-in replacements for HDDs.

The power efficiency of SSDs for sequential and random writes is shown in Figure 13.6. The three sets of bars on the left correspond to SSDs, whereas the ones on the right correspond to enterprise-class HDDs. The performance data was obtained from Polte et al. [49]. The average power was estimated from datasheets and on-line reviews. As the graph indicates, SSDs provide significant power efficiency benefits for both sequential and random I/O.

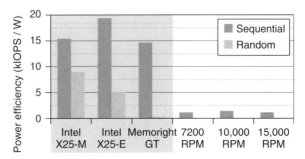

Figure 13.6   Power efficiency of writes for various storage devices. Reproduced with permission from [47].

Given the benefits of SSDs, it may appear tempting to replace all HDDs in a data center with SSDs. However, there is still a cost differential between the two storage media that make SSDs prohibitively expensive as the only storage medium in a data center. While the cost per megabyte of HDD storage and NAND Flash has narrowed considerably in recent years, Flash memory is still more expensive than disk-based storage at present. Moreover, until the density of Flash memory becomes competitive with magnetic media, replacing large storage volumes with SSDs will not provide large power gains either [50]. Instead, the more likely option would be to use Flash and SSDs as a caching tier (albeit a large one) above the HDDs [50–52]. However, Flash memory can serve as a storage building block for energy-efficient servers, such as FAWN [53].

13.5   CONCLUSIONS

The explosion in data volumes and our increasing reliance on data-centric applications continue to stress the storage needs of a data center. One well-exploited approach to addressing the storage capacity and bandwidth needs is to exploit the space and parallelism offered by large disk arrays/farms. The number and size of these disk farms is likely to continue to grow in the future, making their power consumption a serious concern in the goal toward building cost-effective green data centers. The thermal stress of placing several drives within a small footprint is also likely to significantly increase operating costs. While semiconductor components have received significant attention for power reduction over the past couple of decades, the electromechanical components of disk drives pose several key challenges. In this chapter, we have discussed these power-consuming components and broad solution strategies that have been developed to optimize these components at the hardware and software levels.

Newer NVM technologies offer the promise of significant performance and power savings, but their price points are still significantly higher than those of their disk counterparts. Consequently, in the foreseeable future, they can at best serve as a layer in the storage stack rather than as a complete replacement for disk drives. In this layer, they can also play a key role in alleviating the power consumption of the disk drives, providing a wider continuum of energy-proportional operation in the storage hierarchy.

REFERENCES

1. Gantz JF, et al. The Diverse and Exploding Digital Universe: An Updated Forecast of Worldwide Information Growth Throughout 2011, IDC Whitepaper; 2008 Mar.
2. Gurumurthi S. Architecting storage for the cloud computing Era. IEEE Micro 2009;29(6):68–71.
3. Zhu Q, Chen Z, Tan L, Zhou Y, Keeton K, Wilkes J. Hibernator: helping disk arrays sleep through the winter. In: Proceedings of the Symposium on Operating Systems Principles (SOSP); Brighton, UK; 2005. pp. 177–190.
4. Freitas RF, Wilcke WW. Storage-class memory: the next storage system technology. IBM J Res Dev 2008;52(4):439–447.
5. Barroso LA, Hölzle U. *The Datacenter as a Computer: An Introduction to the Design of Warehouse-Scale Machines*. Morgan and Claypool Publishers; 2009.
6. Koomey J, Brill K, Turner P, Stanley J, Taylor B. A simple model for determining true total cost of ownership for data centers. Technical report. Uptime Institute; 2007 Nov.
7. Sankar S, Gurumurthi S, Stan MR. Intra-disk parallelism: an idea whose time has come. In: Proceedings of the International Symposium on Computer Architecture (ISCA); Beijing, China; 2008 Jun. pp. 303–314.
8. Ashar KG. *Magnetic Disk Drive Technology: Heads, Media, Channel, Interfaces, and Integration*. IEEE Press; 1997.
9. Jacob B, Ng SW, Wang DT. *Memory Systems: Cache, DRAM, Disk*. Morgan Kaufmann Publishers; 2007.
10. Sato I, Otani K, Mizukami M, Oguchi S, Hoshiya K, Shimokura K-I. Characteristics of heat transfer in small disk enclosures at high rotation speeds. IEEE Trans Compon Packag Manuf Technol 1990;13(4):1006–1011.
11. Ho H. Fast servo bang-bang seek control. IEEE Trans Magn 1997;33(6):4522–4527.
12. Sankar S, Zhang Y, Gurumurthi S, Stan MR. Sensitivity-based optimization of disk architecture. IEEE Trans Comput 2009;58(1):69–81.
13. Kim Y, Gurumurthi S, Sivasubramaniam A. Understanding the performance-temperature interactions in disk I/O of server workloads. In: Proceedings of the International Symposium on High Performance Computer Architecture (HPCA); Texas, USA; 2006 Feb. pp. 179–189.
14. Seagate Barracuda 7200.10 PATA Product Manual. Available at http://www.seagate.com/staticfiles/support/disc/manuals/desktop/Barracuda207200.10/100402369f.pdf.
15. Barroso LA, Hölzle U. The case for energy-proportional computing. IEEE Comput 2007;40(12):33–37.
16. Li K, Kumpf R, Horton P, Anderson TE. Quantitative analysis of disk drive power management in portable computers. In: Proceedings of the USENIX Winter Conference; California, USA; 1994. pp. 279–291.

17. Douglis F, Krishnan P. Adaptive disk spin-down policies for mobile computers. Comput Syst 1995;8(4):381–413.

18. Helmbold D, Long D, Sconyers T, Sherrod B. Adaptive disk spin-down for mobile computers. ACM/Baltzer Mobile Netw Appl (MONET) J 2000;5(4):285–297.

19. Golding R, Bosch P, Wilkes J. Idleness is not sloth. Technical Report HPL-96-140. HP Laboratories; 1996 Oct.

20. Gurumurthi S, Zhang J, Sivasubramaniam A, Kandemir M, Franke H, Vijaykrishnan N, Irwin MJ. Interplay of energy and performance for disk arrays running transaction processing workloads. In: Proceedings of the International Symposium on Performance Analysis of Systems and Software (ISPASS); Texas, USA; 2003 Mar. pp. 123–132.

21. Carrera EV, Pinheiro E, Bianchini R. Conserving disk energy in network servers. In: Proceedings of the International Conference on Supercomputing (ICS); California, USA; 2003 Jun.

22. Papathanasiou AE, Scott ML. Increasing disk burstiness for energy efficiency. Technical Report 792. University of Rochester; 2002.

23. Colarelli D, Grunwald D. Massive arrays of idle disks for storage archives. In: Proceedings of Supercomputing; Maryland, USA; 2002 Nov.

24. Narayanan D, Donnelly A, Rowstron A. Write off-loading: practical power management for enterprise storage. In: Proceedings of the USENIX Conference on File and Storage Technologies (FAST); California, USA; 2008 Feb. pp. 253–267.

25. Pinheiro E, Bianchini R. Energy conservation techniques for disk array-based servers. In: Proceedings of the International Conference on Supercomputing (ICS); Saint Malo, France; 2004 Jun.

26. Pinheiro E, Bianchini R, Dubnicki C. Exploiting redundancy to conserve energy in storage systems. SIGMETRICS Perform Eval Rev 2006;34(1):15–26.

27. Smith A. Disk cache - miss ratio analysis and design considerations. ACM Trans Comput Syst (TOCS) 1985;3(3):161–203.

28. Hu Y, Yang Q. DCD—disk caching disk: a new approach for boosting I/O performance. In: Proceedings of the International Symposium on Computer Architecture (ISCA); Pennsylvania, USA; 1996 May. pp. 169–178.

29. Chen Z, Zhou Y, Li K. Eviction based cache placement for storage caches. In: Proceedings of the USENIX Annual Technical Conference (ATC); Texas, USA; 2003 Jun. pp. 269–282.

30. Zhu Q, David FM, Devraj C, Li Z, Zhou Y, Cao P. Reducing energy consumption of disk storage using power-aware cache management. In: Proceedings of the International Symposium on High-Performance Computer Architecture (HPCA); Madrid, Spain 2004 Feb.

31. Ruemmler C, Wilkes J. Disk shuffling. Technical Report HPL-91-156. HP Laboratories; 1991 Oct.

32. Worthington BL, Ganger GR, Patt YN. Scheduling algorithms for modern disk drives. In: Proceedings of the ACM SIGMETRICS Conference on Measurement and Modeling of Computer Systems; Tennessee, USA; 1994 May. pp. 241–251.

33. Akyürek S, Salem K. Adaptive block rearrangement. ACM Trans Comput Syst (TOCS) 1995;13(2):89–121.

34. Lumb C, Schindler J, Ganger G, Nagle D, Riedel E. Towards higher disk head utilization: extracting free bandwidth from busy disk drives. In: Proceedings of the USENIX Symposium on Operating Systems Design and Implementation (OSDI); California, USA; 2000 Oct.

35. Hsu W, Smith A, Young H. The automatic improvement of locality in storage systems. ACM Trans Comput Syst (TOCS) 2005;23(4):424–473.

36. Huang H, Hung W, Shin KG. FS2: dynamic data replication in free disk space for improving disk performance and energy consumption. In: Proceedings of the Symposium on Operating Systems Principles (SOSP); Brighton, UK; 2005 Oct. pp. 263–276.

37. Gurumurthi S, Sivasubramaniam A, Natarajan V. Disk drive roadmap from the thermal perspective: a case for dynamic thermal management. In: Proceedings of the International Symposium on Computer Architecture (ISCA); Wisconsin, USA; 2005 Jun. pp. 38–49.

38. Seagate's Sound Barrier Technology (SBT). 2000 Nov. Available at http://www.seagate.com/docs/pdf/whitepaper/sound_barrier.pdf.

39. Gurumurthi S, Sivasubramaniam A, Kandemir M, Franke H. DRPM: dynamic speed control for power management in server class disks. In: Proceedings of the International Symposium on Computer Architecture (ISCA). California, USA; 2003 Jun. pp. 169–179.

40. Li X, Li Z, David F, Zhou P, Zhou Y, Adve S. Performance directed energy management for main memory and disks. In: Proceedings of the International Conference on Architectural Support for Programming Languages and Operating Systems (ASPLOS); Massachusetts, USA; 2004 Oct. pp. 271–283.

41. Sankar S, Gurumurthi S, Stan MR. Sensitivity based power management of enterprise storage systems. In: International Symposium on Modeling, Analysis, and Simulation of Computer and Telecommunication Systems (MASCOTS); Maryland, USA; 2008 Sep.

42. Hitachi Power and Acoustic Management - Quietly Cool. 2004 Mar. Available at http://www.hitachigst.com/tech/techlib.nsf/productfamilies/White_Papers.

43. Guerra J, Belluomini W, Glider J, Gupta K, Pucha H. Energy proportionality for storage: impact and feasibility. In: Proceedings of the Workshop on Hot Topics in Storage and File Systems (HotStorage); Montana, USA; 2009 Oct.

44. Weddle C, Oldham M, Qian J, Wang A, Reiher P, Kuenning G. PARAID: a gear-shifting power-aware RAID. In: Proceedings of the USENIX Conference on File and Storage Technologies (FAST); California, USA; 2007 Feb. pp. 245–260.

45. Verma A, Koller R, Useche L, Rangaswami R. SRCMap: energy proportional storage using dynamic consolidation. In: Proceedings of the USENIX Conference on File and Storage Technologies (FAST); California, USA; 2010 Feb.

46. Sun G, Joo Y, Chen Y, Xie Y, Li H. A hybrid solid-state storage architecture for the performance, energy consumption, and lifetime improvement. In: Proceedings of the International Symposium on High Performance Computer Architecture (HPCA); Bangalore, India; 2010 Jan.

47. Smullen C, Coffman J, Gurumurthi S. Accelerating enterprise solid-state disks with non-volatile merge caching. In: Proceedings of the International Green Computing Conference (IGCC); Illinois, USA; 2010 Aug.

48. Gupta A, Kim Y, Urgaonkar B. DFTL: a flash translation layer employing demand-based selective caching of page-level address mappings. In: Proceedings of the International Conference on Architectural Support for Programming Languages and Operating Systems (ASPLOS); Washington, USA; 2009 Mar. pp. 229–240.

49. Polte M, Simsa J, Gibson G. Comparing performance of solid state devices and mechanical disks. In: Proceedings of the Petascale Data Storage Workshop; Texas, USA; 2008 Nov.

50. Narayanan D, Thereska E, Donnelly A, Elnikety S, Rowstron A. Migrating server storage to SSDs: analysis of tradeoffs. In: Proceedings of the European Conference on Computer Systems (EUROSYS); Nuremberg, Germany; 2009 Apr. pp. 145–158.

51. Kgil T, Roberts D, Mudge T. Improving NAND flash based disk caches. In: Proceedings of the International Symposium on Computer Architecture (ISCA); Beijing, China 2008 Jun. pp. 327–338.

52. Pritchett T, Thottethodi M. SieveStore: a highly-selective, ensemble-level disk cache for cost-performance. In: Proceedings of the International Symposium on Computer Architecture (ISCA); Saint Malo, France; 2010 Jun. pp. 163–174.

53. Andersen D, Franklin J, Kaminsky M, Phanishayee A, Tan L, Vasudevan V. FAWN: a fast array of wimpy nodes. In: Proceedings of the Symposium on Operating Systems Principles (SOSP); 2009 Oct. pp. 1–14.

CHAPTER 14

AUTONOMIC ENERGY/PERFORMANCE OPTIMIZATIONS FOR MEMORY IN SERVERS

BITHIKA KHARGHARIA and MAZIN YOUSIF

With the increased computing demand coupled with server sprawl in data centers, power consumption is reaching unsustainable limits. With over a decade of laser focus on server processor power management, both from industry and academia, today's processors have an energy consumption that is reasonably proportional to their actual workload [1]. However, the same cannot be said about the other components on the platform, such as main memory and disks. Consequently, these components waste a large percentage of the server's energy consumption when they are idling during periods of inactivity. Given that these components contribute to an increasing percentage of the data center server's energy usage [1], it becomes highly imperative that we not only capitalize on opportunities to save energy during periods of inactivity but also proactively create opportunities to extend these periods of inactivity and thereby save more energy. In this chapter, we focus on the servers' memory subsystem that has been reported to consume a major part of the total data center power consumption [2].

This chapter is organized as follows. In Section 14.1, we chart the territory of power management techniques that exist in the domain of computing systems. In Section 14.2, we investigate different classes of dynamic power management (DPM), which is the most popular software power management technique. In Section 14.3, we discuss different applications of DPM techniques for energy conservation in platform components (CPU, memory, etc.), in whole systems (servers, laptops etc.), and in system-of-systems such as today's data centers. In Section 14.4, we discuss a DPM-based research technique for power and performance management of system memory in data center server platforms, which delivers as much as 89.7% improvement in *performance per watt* compared to the

Energy-Efficient Distributed Computing Systems, First Edition.
Edited by Albert Y. Zomaya and Young Choon Lee.
© 2012 John Wiley & Sons, Inc. Published 2012 by John Wiley & Sons, Inc.

best performing traditional technique [3]. We then discuss the counterpart memory power and performance management techniques that exist in the industry landscape today. We then conclude with Section 14.5.

14.1 INTRODUCTION

As shown in Figure 14.1, power management techniques can be broadly classified into software techniques and hardware techniques.[1] Hardware techniques deal with hardware design of power-efficient systems such as low leakage power supplies, power-efficient components such as transistors and DRAMs, and so on. Software techniques, on the other hand, deal with power management of hardware components (processor, memory, hard disk, network card, display, etc.) within a system, such as a server, laptop, PDA, or system-of-systems such as e-commerce data centers, by transitioning the hardware components into one of the several different low power states when they are idle for a long period of time. This technique is also known as *dynamic power management* (DPM). DPM is by far the most popular software power management technique and can be grouped into three most discernable subclasses, as shown in Figure 14.1: predictive techniques, heuristic techniques, and QoS and energy trade-offs. The main distinction between these techniques is in the manner in which they determine when to trigger power state transitions for a hardware component from a high power state to a low power state or vice versa. Heuristic techniques are more ad hoc and static in their approach, whereas predictive techniques employ simple to sophisticated predictive mechanisms to determine how long into the future the hardware component is expected to stay idle and use that knowledge

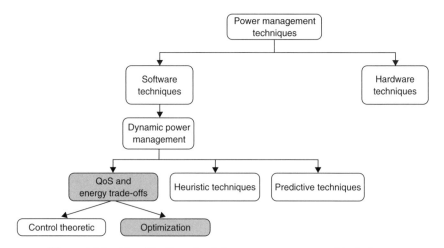

Figure 14.1 Classification of existing power management techniques.

---

[1]This is an excerpt from Reference 3.

to determine when to reactivate the component into a high power state so that it can service jobs again. Recently, researchers have started looking into QoS and energy trade-offs as a DPM technique to determine how long a hardware component can be put to "sleep" such that it does not hurt the performance of the applications. This is a more aggressive power management technique that takes advantage of the fact that "acceptable performance degradations" can be used to let the hardware components sleep longer and hence save more power. This is specifically true for power-hungry domains such as huge data centers that have service-level agreement (SLA) contracts with their customers that clearly define the "acceptable performance degradations" such as 97% response time, 0.05% MTBF (mean time between failures), and so on. This concept is depicted in Figure 14.2, where the data center size (and hence the power consumed) is always configured a little below than what is required by the incoming traffic, such that at that configuration, the perceivable degradation in performance is still acceptable.

As shown in Figure 14.1, QoS and energy trade-off DPM techniques can be either control-theoretic or optimization-based techniques. Control-theoretic techniques use feedback mechanisms to refine and adjust power management decisions based on runtime system behavior. Optimization-based techniques, on the other hand, employ rigorous mathematical modeling of the problem formulated with a necessary and sufficient set of constraints. Solving these constraints would yield theoretical maximum power savings while maintaining performance constraints.

Software power management techniques can also be subdivided based on where they reside within the system. This is shown in Figure 14.3. They could be power-aware applications, power-aware compilers that perform optimizations on the code for power efficiency, and power-aware operating systems (OSs) that employ the DPM techniques mentioned earlier. Then we have the hardware design optimizations for power efficiency at the very bottom. Note that, it is possible for a high level technique to build on top of low level techniques or share borders across techniques as shown by the dotted boxes in Figure 14.3. For

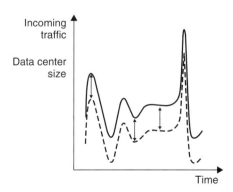

Figure 14.2 Amplitude lag between data center capacity and incoming traffic.

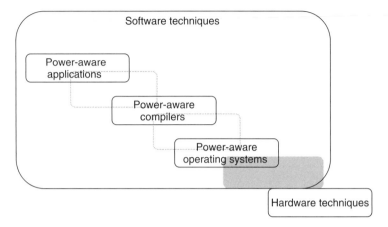

Figure 14.3 Location-based classification of software power management techniques.

example, power-aware compilers can perform code transformations for power efficiency such that the targeted hardware component can sleep longer. At runtime, the power-aware OS then triggers the transition of the hardware component into the low power sleep state and reactivates it back when required.

Now let us look into some of the research in this field classified based on the type of DPM technique that they employ.

14.2   CLASSIFICATIONS OF DYNAMIC POWER MANAGEMENT TECHNIQUES

DPM techniques can be predictive, can be heuristic, or may involve QoS trade-offs for energy savings.[2]

14.2.1   Heuristic and Predictive Techniques

Heuristic approaches [5–8] employ simple heuristics to transition a system component to a low power mode after it is observed to have remained idle for a predetermined period of time. Reference 9 proposes various threshold predictors to determine the maximum amount of time that a memory module must remain idle before it is transitioned back to a low power state. Reference 10 investigates memory controller (MC) policies in cache-based systems and concluded that the simple policy of immediately transitioning the DRAM chip to a lower power state when it becomes idle is superior compared to more sophisticated policies that try to predict the idle time of the DRAM chip.

Researchers have also looked at cooperative hardware–software schemes for DPM. Reference 2 studies page allocation techniques to cluster an application's

---

[2]This is an excerpt from Reference 4.

pages onto a minimum number of memory modules, thereby increasing the idleness for the other modules. Reference 11 uses such page allocation schemes combined with the page miss ratio curve metric to determine the optimal memory size that would give the maximum possible *hit ratio* for the application. Reference 12 proposes a scheduler-based policy that uses prior knowledge of memory modules used by a specific process to allocate the same memory modules the next time the process is scheduled. Reference 13 builds on this idea to develop power-aware virtual memory (PAVM), where the OS and the MC communicate to enhance memory energy savings through leveraging NUMA memory infrastructure to reduce energy consumption on a per-process basis. Reference 14 uses a similar idea to actively reshape memory traffic to aggregate idle periods. Reference 15 demonstrates how adaptive history-based memory schedulers can be naturally extended to manage DRAM power and energy.

14.2.2 QoS and Energy Trade-Offs

While heuristic and predictive DPM techniques take into consideration the performance attribute in their energy-saving schemes, research that has focused on QoS trade-offs for energy savings has specifically studied the impact of power savings on performance. For example, Reference 15 demonstrates that for aggressive DRAM power management, a throttling approach can be used that arbitrarily reduces DRAM activity by delaying the issuance of memory commands. Clearly, this may have an impact on memory performance, but it has to take that performance hit while trying to stay within its power budget. The philosophy here is to maximize the performance for a given power budget, the constraint being the power budget. The same problem can also be expressed in the reverse way where the constraint is the performance. In this case, DPM techniques are used to reduce power as aggressively as possible as long as it does not hurt the performance.

Most techniques that manage both power and performance often bind the power and performance problems in more mathematically rigorous formulations providing statistical guarantees of performance for their power management schemes. They investigate and generate power-saving opportunities that can be obtained at the cost of QoS trade-offs within acceptable limits.

This has given rise to the application of proactive mathematically rigorous optimization techniques as well as reactive control-theoretic techniques being applied for power management while maintaining performance. For example, References 16–19 have developed a myriad of stochastic optimization techniques for portable devices. In the server domain, Reference 20 presents three on-line approaches for server provisioning and dynamic voltage scaling (DVS) control for multiple applications, namely, a predictive stochastic queuing technique, reactive feedback control technique, and another hybrid technique where they use predictive information for server provisioning and feedback control for DVS. Reference 21 studies the impact of reducing power consumption of large server installations subject to QoS constraints. They develop algorithms for DVS in QoS-enabled web servers to minimize energy consumption subject to service delay constraints. They use a utilization bound for schedulability of aperiodic tasks [22] to maintain the timeliness of processed jobs while conserving power. Reference 23 investigates autonomic power control policies for Internet servers and data centers. They use both the system load and thermal status to vary the utilized processing resources to achieve acceptable delay and power performance. They use dynamic programing to solve their optimization problem. Reference 24 presents a technique that controls the peak power consumption of a high density server by implementing a feedback controller that performs precise system-level power measurements to periodically select the highest performance state while keeping the system within a fixed power constraint. Reference 25 proposes a *performance-directed dynamic* (PD) algorithm that dynamically adjusts the thresholds for transitioning devices to low power states, based on available slack and recent workload characteristics. A departure to this approach is provided by the work of Diniz et al. [26], which shows that limiting power is as effective an energy conservation approach as techniques explicitly designed for performance-aware energy conservation.

These DPM techniques have been applied for energy conservation of a wide range of platforms, devices, and system components. Let us now look at some of these use cases.

14.3 APPLICATIONS OF DYNAMIC POWER MANAGEMENT (DPM)

Most software power management techniques exploit the overprovisioning of components, devices, or platforms for power savings. This technique, also known as *dynamic power management (DPM)*, is extensively used for reducing power dissipation in systems by slowing or shutting down components when they are idle or underutilized. DPM techniques can be used for power management of a single system component such as the processor, system memory, or the NIC (network interface card). They can also be used for joint power management of multiple system components or power management of the whole system.

14.3.1 Power Management of System Components in Isolation

Most DPM techniques utilize power management features supported by the hardware. For example, frequency scaling, clock throttling, and DVS are three processor power management techniques [27] extensively utilized by DPM. Reference 28, for example, extends the OS's power manager by an *adaptive power manager* that uses the processor's DVS capabilities to reduce or increase the CPU frequency, thereby minimizing the overall energy consumption. Reference 29 combines the DVS technique at the processor level together with a server turn on/turn off technique at the cluster level to achieve high power savings while maintaining the response time for server clusters. Reference 30 introduces a scheme to concentrate the workload on a limited number of servers in a cluster such that the rest of the servers can remain switched off for a longer time. Reference 21 proposes power-aware QoS management in web servers where the algorithms reduce processor voltage and frequency as much as possible but not enough to cause per-class response time constraint violations. Other techniques use a utilization bound for schedulability of aperiodic tasks [22, 31] to maintain the timeliness of processed jobs while conserving power. Similarly, for dynamic memory power management, Reference 2 uses multiple power modes of Rambus DRAM (RDRAM) memory and dynamically turns off memory chips with power-aware page allocation in OS. Reference 15 uses intelligent memory scheduling using the MC to improve DRAM energy efficiency and manage DRAM power by exploiting low power modes of modern DRAMs. Hard disk DPM also requires hard disks supporting multiple disk rotation speeds, a technique that did not remain hugely popular mainly because of performance issues. For example, disk time-out determines how long a hard disk must be idle before it spins down [32]. Reference 33 uses periods of inactivity between disk accesses to determine if the disk can be transitioned to a low power state.

14.3.2   Joint Power Management of System Components

Researchers have also explored joint power management techniques that involve techniques to jointly maintain power consumption of multiple system components such as the memory and the hard disk. The synergy between system components (processor and memory) has been clearly presented in the work of Douglis et al. [33]. Reference 34 has used the relationship between memory and disk (smaller the memory size, the higher the page misses and the higher the disk accesses) to achieve power savings by proactively changing disk I/O by expanding or contracting the size of the memory depending on the workload. They minimize power consumption by computing the optimal values for disk time-out and memory size dynamically at runtime under varying workloads. However, they do not consider the impact of their scheme on performance. Reference 35 addresses base power consumption for web servers using a *power-shifting* technique that dynamically distributes power among components using workload-sensitive policies. They use the processor and memory power-budget redistribution to achieve that objective.

14.3.3   Holistic System-Level Power Management

Most techniques for DPM justify the need to consider components in isolation. For example, Reference 36 makes the case that processor is the major power-consuming component in servers. Following this thread, Reference 37 presents a request-batching scheme where jobs are forwarded to the processor in a batch after certain time such that the response time constraint is met for all classes of customers. This lets the processor be in a lower power state for a longer period of time and process the jobs in the batch at a later time. Reference 38, on the other hand, states that data center storage devices can consume over 25% power. Instructions invoking memory operations have a relatively high power cost, both within the processor and in the memory system [39]. This has spawned research in memory power management. However, there has not been much effort to exploit these existing techniques for different classes of resources (processor, memory, cache, disk, network card, etc.) in a unified framework from a whole system/platform perspective. While the closest to combining device power models to build a whole system has been presented in References 1 and 40 aims at building a general framework for autonomic power and performance management, where they bring together and exploit existing device power management techniques from a whole system's perspective. They extend it for power and performance management of a high performance server platform within a data center. They introduce a hierarchical framework for power management that starts at individual devices within a server to server clusters and cluster of clusters, enabling power management at every level of the hierarchy of a data center with the solutions being more and more refined as we travel down the hierarchy from cluster of heterogeneous servers to independent devices. The closest to this approach is the work done by Rong and Pedram [41], which solves the problem of hierarchical power management for an energy-managed computer (EMC) system with self-power-managed components while exploiting application-level scheduling.

14.4   AUTONOMIC POWER AND PERFORMANCE OPTIMIZATION OF MEMORY SUBSYSTEMS IN SERVER PLATFORMS

In this section, we first discuss a DPM-based research technique [1] for autonomic power and performance management of memory subsystems in server platforms. We then discuss some of the counterpart technique(s) that exist in industry today.

14.4.1   Adaptive Memory Interleaving Technique for Power and Performance Management

This technique (depicted in shaded boxes in Figure 14.1) employs optimization-based power and performance (QoS) management of server memory. They formulate the power and performance management problem as an optimization problem, where they constantly maintain the hardware components in a power state such that they consume minimal possible power while maintaining the performance within the acceptable threshold bounds. This technique, as depicted by the shaded box in Figure 14.1, resides under the cover of the OS very close to the hardware while sharing some borders with it. They also employ DPM for power management from a whole system perspective by power managing multiple system components in a cooperative manner.

   This technique leverages the wide range of variations observed in the data center server workloads' dynamic memory requirements. It uses multipower state memory technologies such as RDRAM [2] and fully buffered dual in-line memory module (FBDIMM) [42] to save energy and maintain performance by allocating just the required amount of memory to applications at runtime and transitioning any additional memory capacity to low power states.

   However, given that server platforms in data center are often configured at peak performance, the memory subsystem is most often configured at the maximum degree of interleaving. This introduces a challenge for the memory power management problem. Owing to symmetrical distribution of memory accesses across all memory modules, interleaving does not offer much opportunity for energy saving and thus provides less opportunity for idleness of the memory modules. For example, an experimental study to measure the idleness of memory modules when executing the SPECjbb2005 [43] benchmark on a server platform (two Dual-Core Intel™ Xeon processors, 5000P Memory Controller Hub, 8-GB DDR2 FBDIMM memory) with fully interleaved (16-way) memory showed that memory modules were idle for less than 5% of the total application runtime. Applying existing power management techniques [10, 11] to this memory subsystem would yield only approximately 4.5% total saving. However, conducting the same experiment with a smaller degree of interleaving (12-way) created an imbalance in idleness, making some modules more idle and others busier. By power managing the idle memory modules, they gained an energy saving of 25% (14.7 kJ) with negligible impact on SPECjbb2005 performance. This demonstrates an opportunity to maximize the memory *performance per watt* by dynamically scaling down the degree of interleaving (16-way to 12-way) to adapt to the application's memory requirements at runtime. With this objective in mind, they design an autonomic memory subsystem that addresses the following research challenges related to memory power and performance management.

1. How to exploit an application's memory reference behavior to guide the choice of an appropriate degree of interleaving for the memory subsystem? This depends on how physical allocation of application's *working set pages* on memory modules impacts the power consumed by the memory subsystem and the application-level performance.

2. How to dynamically predict the impact of a specific degree of interleaving on the *performance-per-watt* metric for the platform?

3. How to design smart interleaving techniques that effectively exploit the platform's memory hierarchy architecture to maximize its *performance per watt?*

4. What enabling techniques and hardware design changes are required to implement this paradigm shift from static (boot time) interleaving to dynamically reconfigurable memory interleaving?

5. How to design a dynamic interleaving technique that leverages existing fine-grained power management techniques to maximize *performance per watt* for platforms with interleaved memory?

6. What are the cost, runtime complexity, and reconfiguration overhead associated with this technique, and how they can be reduced to attain a greater return-on-investment?

7. What is the ideal *mean time between reconfigurations(MTBRs)* for the technique such that it maintains adaptation to incoming workload without significantly increasing the overhead of reconfiguration?

They apply the autonomic computing paradigm to architect an intelligent MC that continuously reconfigures and scales the memory subsystem for maintaining power and performance. The objective of the MC is to always maintain the size and configuration of the memory subsystem in a *state* where power consumed is minimal and the system still meets the threshold values for the performance parameters. Scaling the memory size to a minimum would give huge savings in power but may impact performance by increasing the *miss* ratio as well as the delay experienced by a single memory *access time*. Hence, the task of the MC is to allocate as much memory as is required by the application, and the unused amount of memory can then be transitioned to one of the low power *states* as supported by an FBDIMM (Fig. 14.2). We can estimate the application's memory requirement at runtime by measuring the application's current *heap usage* and the total number of memory accesses going to each rank. On the basis of the monitored values, at the end of each time epoch, the MC maintains the system at the *maximum performance per watt* by determining (i) what is the minimum number of memory ranks to be maintained in an *active state*? and (ii) which ranks should be selected to be active?

We formulate the MC decision-making process as an optimization problem where we index time into equidistant epochs of value t_{obs}. The MC searches for an optimal solution at the beginning of each epoch. Let us consider a *state* transition from *state* S_j to *state* S_k, where S_j has n_j ranks ($Rank_0$ to $Rank_j$) and S_k has n_k ranks ($Rank_0$ to $Rank_k$), as shown in Figure 14.3. The data migration process during this *state* transition involves a rank pair, one from the source pool of ranks in the *state* S_j and the other from the destination pool of ranks in the *state* S_k. In what follows, we discuss how to determine the target *state* S_k among all possible *states*. Data is then dynamically migrated from a source rank to a destination rank.

14.4.1.1 *Formulating the optimization problem.*

At the beginning of time epoch i, the MC searches for the *state* where the sum of the transition energy consumed ($c^*_{jk} t_{trans_{jk}}$) and the energy consumed in the target *state* ($p^* n^*_k t_{obs}$) by the memory subsystem is the smallest, given that in the target *state* S_k, the system can meet all the constraints. The objective function is given by the following.

Minimize energy for interval i

$$e_i = \sum_{k=0}^{N} (c^*_{jk} t_{trans_{jk}} + p^* n^*_k t_{obs})^* x_{jk},$$

such that

$$n^*_k Size \ / \ Rank >= N^*_{opt} \ pageSize$$

$$\text{Max}(\vee_{ch:A,C} chBW_{ch}) <= threshold\_chBW$$

$$\text{Min}(\vee_{rank:0}^{n_n/2} arrTime_{rank}) >= threshold\_arrTime_{rank}$$

$$\sum_{k=0}^{n} x_{jk} = 1$$

$$\vee \ x_{jk} = 0|1,$$

where

$N =$ maximum ranks in the system;

$n_k =$ total ranks in state S_k;

$p =$ power consumed per rank;

$t_{obs} =$ unit of time epoch;

$c_{jk} =$ power consumed in transition;

$t_{trans\,jk} =$ time taken to transition;

$x_{jk} =$ decision variable for transition from S_j to S_k;

$chBW_{ch}, arrTime_{Rank} =$ channel BW and interarrival time in state S_k;

$threshold\_chBW, threshold\_arrTime_{Rank} =$ threshold channel BW and request interarrival time;

$pageSize =$ size of a single page (4 kB for our system);

N_{opt} optimal number of pages for maximum hit ratio [11];

$Size/Rank$ 512 MB for our system.

The first constraint states that the target *state* should have enough memory to hold all the N_{opt} *pages*. The second constraint *states* that in the target *state*, the maximum of the *percent channel BW* on a channel should be smaller than the threshold value set for the channel BW. Ideally, it can be the theoretical upper limit. The third constraint states that in the target *state*, the minimum *request interarrival* among all the active ranks should be larger than the threshold value set for the rank where the threshold value is a percentage of the *access time*. This is to be experimentally determined. The fourth constraint states that the optimization problem leads to one and only one solution. The decision variable corresponding to that is 1, the rest are 0. The fifth constraint states that the decision variable is a 0–1 integer.

Evaluation of Migration Time $t_{trans_{jk}}$ and Energy c_{jk}. This technique assumes a simplistic migration mechanism that is performed under the cover of the OS and requires minimal changes in hardware itself. During migration, the MC stalls all memory access requests, and consequently, the time for data migration is a sum of the data migration time (read time, transfer time, and write time) and the time needed to make power transition. Given that, fraction of a page per rank is given by

$$\text{ppr} = \frac{[n_k/2]}{[pageSize/CLSize]}.$$

The migration time per rank (MTR) pair ($Rank_j$, $Rank_k$) is given by

$$\text{MTR} = \frac{\text{ppr}^* N_{\text{opt}}{}^* pgSize}{CLSize_{Rank_j}/2^* tRead^* 1024} + \frac{\text{ppr}^* N_{\text{opt}}{}^* pgSize}{CLSize_{Rank_k}/2^* tWrite^* 1024}$$

$$+ \frac{\text{ppr}^* N_{\text{opt}}{}^* pg\,Size}{\text{MaxThPut}_{Ch_{Rank_j}}} + t_{act_{jk}}.$$

Power state transition overhead is the time taken to transition from one power *state* to another. Figure 14.4 gives the power *state* transition overhead per DIMM. The energy consumed in migration is the sum of the power consumed by two sources,

$$c_{jk} = n_k{}^* P_{\text{trans}} t_{\text{trans}\,jk}^* P_{\text{MC}},$$

where p_{trans} is the transition power consumed by a DIMM rank and p_{MC} is the power consumed in buffers during data migration (Fig. 14.5).

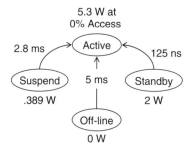

Figure 14.4   FBDIMM power states. Reproduced with permission from [42].

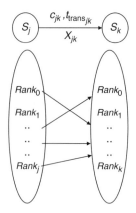

Figure 14.5   State transition.

14.4.1.2 Memory appflow. At runtime, the MC monitors a set of application and memory features to compute the application memory requirements ($N_{opt}^* pageSize$), the energy consumed by the memory subsystem, and the application end-to-end *delay* (depends on channel bandwidth utilization *chBW* and request arrival rate *arrTime*). As shown in Figure 14.6, at runtime, they constitute the memory subsystem *operating point* in a three-dimensional space. The *operating point* changes in response to the incoming workload. The MC triggers a *state* transition whenever the *operating point* goes outside the safe operating zone. This is depicted by the *decision, d_Z*, in Figure 14.6. The *decision* is computed using the *optimization* approach discussed earlier. Note that the safe operating zone is defined by threshold bounds along the *delay* (x) axis, *energy* (z) axis, and along the application memory requirements (y) axis. For this work, the threshold *delay* bounds were predetermined and kept set at that value, the threshold *energy* bounds is defined by [$e_{min} = 0, e_{max} = N^*p_a$], where e_{max} represents the maximum power that is consumed by the memory subsystem when it is configured at its maximum capacity. However, the third threshold bound defined by the application memory requirements varies as the application behavior changes.

As long as the MC maintains the memory subsystem in the safe operating zone, it ensures that the subsystem consumes minimal power and maintains application performance at all workload activity levels.

14.4.2 Industry Techniques

To reduce the power consumption of server memory subsystems, industry solutions have primarily targeted hardware techniques such as

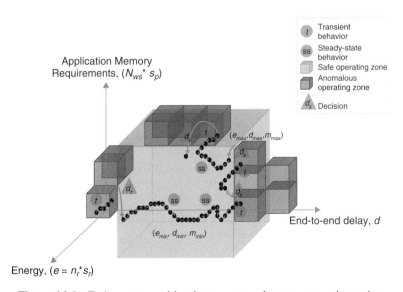

Figure 14.6 Trajectory traced by the memory subsystem operating point.

1. memory design enhancements to consume less active and idle power;
2. memory power management hooks such as multiple active and low power operating states for use by software for more granular and aggressive power management.

Some of these techniques are listed below.

14.4.2.1   Enhancements in memory hardware design.

1. "Samsung's 1.35V, 2 Gb DDR3 is an ultra-low-power memory technology, with more than a 76% power savings over traditional DDR2 at 2 times the bandwidth" [44].
2. "Micron's 1-Gb DDR3 modules operate at 1.35-volts giving 21 percent less power in comparison to standard 1.5-volt, 1-Gb DDR3 memory modules. In addition, its 2 Gb DDR2 modules operate at 1.5-volts giving 58 percent power reduction over standard 1 Gb-based 8 Gb 1.8-volt DDR2 memory modules" [45].

14.4.2.2   Adding more operating states.

1. "Intel is experimenting with three Memory power states - Memory Self Refresh, Memory Standby, and Memory Offline, all of which use ACPI (advanced configuration and power interface) to set a server's memory into one of the three states depending upon its needs. Memory in self-refresh mode requires about half the amount of power of memory in the standard "active idle" mode. Memory in the standby mode would use only about a third of active-idle power, and memory that's placed offline requires no power whatsoever" [4, 46, 47].

14.4.2.3   Faster transition to and from low power states.

1. Intel Nehalem EX claims five times faster transitions to and from low power states [4, 47]. This makes power management techniques very attractive because it reduces the risk of any impact on performance owing to sleeping memory ranks taking too long to wake up and start processing traffic as they arrive.

14.4.2.4   Memory consolidation.

1. VMware is working with Intel to experiment with another technology that can swap memory pages around such that most frequently used memory

pages by VMs or hypervisors could be consolidated onto some riser cards, allowing other riser cards to be taken off-line entirely [46]. The philosophy of this technique is close to that discussed in Section 14.4.1 with the major differences being this technique is closer to the hardware working with memory accesses directly rather than application pages and solves an optimization problem to determine the theoretical maximum energy savings with FBDIMM-based server memory subsystems.

It can be argued that the design of more power-efficient memory subsystems would contribute significantly to reduce server energy consumption by automatically transitioning themselves to low power operating modes whenever they are idle. However, the parallelization of memory accesses would provide little opportunity for relative idleness between memory ranks as discussed in Section 14.4.1. Hence, both software and hardware techniques would have to work hand in glove at best in order to make significant savings without sacrificing performance.

14.5 CONCLUSION

In summary, this chapter discusses power and performance management techniques for memory subsystems in data center servers. We have looked at a technique that adaptively changes the degree of interleaving in order to consolidate memory accesses on a smaller subset of memory ranks such that the other ranks are idle and can be transitioned to low power states. This technique is demonstrated to have given a *performance per watt* (performance per watt of power consumed by the platform) improvement of 89.7% compared to the best performing traditional technique. In addition, we also looked at equivalent techniques prevalent in industry today and identified how software and hardware techniques would complement each other to give the maximum energy savings and make the memory subsystem energy consumption as proportional to its level of activity as we see it in today's energy-aware processors [1].

REFERENCES

1. Barroso LA, Holzle U. The case for energy-proportional computing. IEEE Comput 2007;40(12):3–37.

2. Lebeck AR, Fan X, Zeng H, Ellis C. Power aware page allocation. In: ASPLOS; 2000. pp. 105–116.

3. Khargharia B. Adaptive power and performance management of computing systems [PhD Dissertation]. 2008.

4. Intel shows Nehalem EX handling memory errors and cutting power consumption. Available at http://blogs.techrepublic.com.com/itdojo/?p=987.

5. Srivastava M, Chandrakasan A, Brodersen R. Predictive system shutdown and other architectural techniques for energy efficient programmable computation. IEEE Trans VLSI Syst 1996;4:42–55.

6. Hwang CH, Wu A. A predictive system shutdown method for energy saving of event-driven computation. In: Proceedings of the International Conference on Computer Aided Design. San Francisco (CA): Morgan Kaufmann; 1997. pp. 28–32.

7. Hsu C, Kremer U. The design, implementation, and evaluation of a compiler algorithm for CPU energy reduction. In: Proceedings of PLDI; 2003 Jun; San Diego (CA).

8. Weiser M, Welch B, Demers A, Shenker S. Scheduling for reduced CPU energy. In: 1st Symposium on Operating Systems Design and Implementation; 1994; Monterey (CA). pp. 13–23.

9. Delaluz V, Kandemir M, Vijaykrishnan N, Sivasubramaniam A, Irwin MJ. Hardware and software techniques for controlling DRAM power modes. IEEE Trans Comput 2001;50(11):1154–1173.

10. Fan X, Ellis C, Lebeck AR. Memory controller policies for dram power management. In: Proceedings of the International Symposium on Low Power Electronics and Design; 2011 Aug; Huntington Beach (CA). pp. 129–134.

11. Zhou P, Pandey V, Sundaresan J, Raghuraman A, Zhou Y, Kumar S. Dynamic tracking of page miss ratio curve for memory management. Proceedings of the 11th International Conference on Architectural Support for Programming Languages and Operating Systems; 2004 Oct; Boston (MA). pp. 177–188.

12. De La Luz V, Sivasubramaniam A, Kandemir M, Vijaykrishnan N, Irwin MJ. Scheduler-based DRAM energy management. In: Proceedings of the 39th Design Automation Conference; 2002 Jun; New Orleans (LA). pp. 697.

13. Huang H, Pillai P, Shin KG. Design and implementation of power-aware virtual memory. In: Proceedings of the USENIX Technical Conference; 2003 Jun; San Antonio (TX). pp. 57–70.

14. Huang H, Lefurgy C, Keller T, Shin KG. Memory traffic reshaping for energy-efficient memory. Proceedings of the International Symposium on Low Power Electronics and Design; 2005 Aug; San Diego (CA). pp. 393–398.

15. Hur I, Lin C. A comprehensive approach to dram power management. In: Proceedings of the 13th International Symposium on High-Performance Computer Architecture; Utah, USA; 2008 Aug.

16. Paleologo G, Benini L, Bogliolo A, De Micheli G. Policy optimization for dynamic power management. IEEE Trans Comput Aided Des 1999;18(6):813–33.

17. Qiu Q, Wu Q, Pedram M. Stochastic modeling of a power-managed system-construction and optimization. IEEE Trans Comput Aided Des 2001;20:1200–1217.

18. Chung E, Benini L, Bogliolo A, Micheli G. Dynamic Power Management for non-stationary service requests. IEEE Trans Comput 2002;51(11):1345–1361.

19. Simunic T. Dynamic management of power consumption. In: Graybill R, Mehlem R, editor. *Power Aware Computing*. Kluwer Academic Publishers; 2002. pp. 101–125, 2002, ISBN: 0-306-46786-0.

20. Chen Y, Das A, Qin W, Sivasubramaniam A, Wang Q, Gautam N. Managing server energy and operational costs in hosting centers. In: Proceedings of the 2005 ACM SIGMETRICS International Conference on Measurement and Modeling of Computer Systems (SIGMETRICS); Alberta, Canada; 2005.

21. Sharma V, Thomas A, Abdelzaher T, Skadron K, Lu Z. Power-aware QoS Management in Web Servers. In: Proceedings of the 24th IEEE International Real-Time Systems Symposium; 2003 Dec 03–05. p. 63.

22. Abdelzaher T, Sharma V. A synthetic utilization bound for a-periodic tasks with resource requirements. In: Euromicro Conference on Real Time Systems; 2003 July; Porto, Portugal.

23. Mastroleon L, Bambos N, Kozyrakis C, Economou D. Autonomic power management schemes for internet servers and data centers. In: Proceedings of the IEEE Global Telecommunications Conference (GLOBECOM); St. Louis, USA; 2005 Nov.

24. Lefurgy C, Wang X, Ware M. Server-level power control. International Conference on Autonomic Computing (ICAC); 2007; Jacksonville (FL).

25. Li X, Li Z, David F, Zhou P, Zhou Y, Adve S, Kumar S. Performance-directed energy management for main memory and disks. In: Proceedings of the 11th International Conference on Architectural Support for Programming Languages and Operating Systems; 2004 Oct; Boston (MA).

26. Diniz B, Guedes D, Meira W Jr., Bianchini R. Limiting the power consumption of main memory. In: Proceedings of the 34th Annual International Symposium on Computer Architecture; 2007 Jun; San Diego (CA).

27. Miyoshi A, Lefurgy C, Van Hensbergen E, Rajamony R, Rajkumar R. Critical power slope: understanding the runtime effects of frequency scaling. In: Proceedings of the 16th International Conference on Supercomputing; 2002 June 22–26; New York.

28. Shin H, Lee J. Application specific and automatic power management based on whole program analysis. Final Report; 2004 Aug 20. Available at http://cslab.snu.ac.kr/~egger/apm/final-report.pdf.

29. Elnozahy EN, Kistler M, Rajamony R. Energy-efficient server clusters. In: Proceedings of the 2nd Workshop on Power-Aware Computing Systems; Massachusetts, USA; 2002 Feb.

30. Pinheiro E, Bianchini R, Carrera EV, Heath T. Load balancing and unbalancing for power and performance in cluster-based systems. In: Proceedings of the Workshop on Compilers and Operating Systems for Low Power; Barcelona, Spain; 2001 Sept.

31. Abdelzaher TF, Lu C. Schedulability analysis and utilization bounds for highly scalable real-time services. In: IEEE Real-Time Technology and Applications Symposium; 2001 Jun; Taipei, Taiwan.

32. The PC Guide 2001. Hard disk power down timeout. 2001. Available at http://www.pcguide.com/ref/mbsys/bios/set/pmDisk-c.html. Retrieved 2005.

33. Douglis F, Krishnan P, Marsh B. Thwarting the power hungry disk. In: Proceedings of the 1994 Winter USENIX Conference; 1994 Jan; San Francisco (CA).

34. Cai L, Yung L. Joint power management of memory and disk. In: Proceedings of the Conference on Design, Automation and Test in Europe; Munich, Germany; 2005 March 07–11. pp. 86–91.

35. Felter W, Rajamani K, Keller T, Rusu C. A performance-conserving approach for reducing peak power consumption in server systems. ACM International Conference on Supercomputing (ICS); 2005 June; Cambridge (MA).

36. Bohrer P, Elnozahy E, Keller T, Kistler M, Lefurgy C, McDowell C, Rajamony R. The case for power management in web servers. In: Graybill R, Melhem R, editors. *Power Aware Computing*. Klewer Academic Publishers; 2002.

37. Elnozahy M, Kistler M, Rajamony R. Energy conservation policies for web servers. In: Proceedings of the 4th USENIX Symposium on Internet Technologies and Systems; Texas, USA; 2003 Mar.

38. Zhu Q, David FM, Devaraj C, Li Z, Zhou Y, Cao P. Reducing energy consumption of disk storage using power-aware cache management. In: Proceedings of the International Symposium on High Performance Computer Architecture; Madrid, Spain; 2004. pp. 118–129.

39. Tiwari V, Malik S, Wolfe A. Power analysis of embedded software: a first step towards software minimization. IEEE Trans Very Large Scale Integr 1994;2(4):437–445.

40. Gurumurthi S, Sivasubramaniam A, Irwin MJ, Vijaykrishnan N, Kandemir M, Li T, John LK. Using complete machine simulation for software power estimation: the SoftWatt approach. In: Proceedings of the International Symposium on High Performance Computer Architecture (HPCA-8); 2002 Feb 2–6; Cambridge (MA). pp. 141–150.

41. Rong P, Pedram M. Hierarchical power management with application to scheduling. In: ISLPED (International Symposium on Low Power Electronics and Design); California, USA; 2005.

42. DDR2 FBDIMM Technical Product Specifications. Available at http://www.samsung.com/Products/Semiconductor/DDR_DDR2/DDR2SDRAM/Module/FBDIMM/M395T2953CZ4/ds_512mb_c_die_based_fbdimm_rev13.pdf.

43. SPEC JBB. 2005. Available at http://www.spec.org/jbb2005/docs/WhitePaper.html.

44. Green DDR3. Less Energy More Memory. Available at http://www.samsung.com/global/business/semiconductor/Greenmemory/Products/DDR3/DDR3_Overview.html.

45. Micron Expands Green DRAM Line. Available at http://www.eetimes.com/electronics-news/4076805/ Micron-expands-green-DRAM-line.

46. Intel and VMware get their RAS on: Server memory futures. Available at http://www.theregister.co.uk/2009/09/25/memory_ras_and_power_management/.

47. Top Ten for Intel® Nehalem-based Xeon® Processor Platforms and Emulex® LightPulse® and OneConnectTM Adapters, Tech Brief.

CHAPTER 15

ROD: A PRACTICAL APPROACH TO IMPROVING RELIABILITY OF ENERGY-EFFICIENT PARALLEL DISK SYSTEMS

SHU YIN, XIAOJUN RUAN, ADAM MANZANARES, and XIAO QIN

15.1 INTRODUCTION

Parallel disk systems, providing high performance data-processing capacity, are of great value to large-scale parallel computers [1]. A parallel disk system comprising of an array of independent disks can be built from low cost commodity hardware components. In the past few decades, parallel disk systems have become increasingly popular for data-intensive applications running on massively parallel computing platforms [2].

Existing energy conservation techniques can yield significant energy savings in disks. While several energy conservation schemes such as cache-based energy saving approaches normally have marginal impact on disk reliability, many energy saving schemes (e.g., dynamic power management (DPM) and workload-skew techniques) inevitably have noticeable adverse impacts on storage systems [3, 4]. For example, DPM techniques save energy by using frequent disk spin-downs and spin-ups, which in turn can shorten disk lifetime [5–7], redundancy techniques [8–11], workload skew [12–14], and multispeed settings [15, 16]. Unlike DPM, workload-skew techniques such as MAID [17] and PDC [18] move popular data sets to a subset of disks arrays acting as workhorses, which are kept busy in a way that other disks can be turned into the standby mode to save energy. Compared with disks storing cold data, disks archiving hot data inherently have higher risk of breaking down.

Unfortunately, it is often difficult for storage researchers to improve reliability of energy-efficient disk systems. One of the main reasons lies in the challenge

Energy-Efficient Distributed Computing Systems, First Edition.
Edited by Albert Y. Zomaya and Young Choon Lee.
© 2012 John Wiley & Sons, Inc. Published 2012 by John Wiley & Sons, Inc.

that every disk energy saving research faces today: how to evaluate reliability impacts of power management strategies on disk systems. Although reliability of disk systems can be estimated by simulating the behaviors of energy saving algorithms, there is lack of fast and accurate methodology to evaluate reliability of modern storage systems with high energy efficiency. To address this problem, we developed a mathematical reliability model called *MINT* to estimate the reliability of a parallel disk system that employs a variety of reliability-affecting energy conservation techniques [19].

In this chapter, we first study the reliability of a parallel disk system equipped with a well-known energy saving scheme—the MAID [17] technique. I/O load skewing techniques such as MAID inherently affect reliability of parallel disks because of two reasons: First, disks storing popular data tend to have high I/O utilization than disks storing cold data. Second, disks with higher utilization are likely to have higher risk of breaking down. To address the adverse impact of load skewing techniques on disk reliability, a disk-swapping strategy was proposed to improve disk reliability in MAID by switching the roles of data disks and cache disks. We evaluate impacts of the disk swapping scheme on the reliability of MAID-based parallel disk systems.

We summarize our contributions as follows:

1. We developed a model for MAID based on mathematical reliability models for energy-efficient parallel disk system (MINT) [19].
2. We built single disk swapping and multiple disk swapping mechanisms to improve reliability of various load skewing techniques.
3. We studied the impacts of the disk swapping schemes on the reliability of MAID.

The remainder of this chapter is organized as follows. Section 15.2 presents the framework of the MINT model and MAID system. Section 15.3 studies single disk swapping and multiple disk swapping strategies on MAID. Section 15.4 presents experimental results and performance evaluation. In Section 15.5, the related work is discussed. Finally, Section 15.6 concludes the chapter with discussions.

15.2 MODELING RELIABILITY OF ENERGY-EFFICIENT PARALLEL DISKS

15.2.1 The MINT Model

MINT is a framework developed to model reliability of parallel disk systems employing energy conservation techniques [19]. In the MINT framework, we studied the reliability impacts of a well-known energy saving technique—the MAID. One critical module in MINT is to model how MAID affects the utilization and power-state transition frequency of each disk in a parallel disk system.

A second important module developed in MINT is to calculate the annual failure rate (AFR) of each disk as a function of the disk's utilization, power-state transition frequency, and as operating temperature. Given the AFR of each disk in the parallel disk system, MINT is able to derive the reliability of an energy-efficient parallel disk system. As such, we used MINT to study the reliability of a parallel disk system equipped with the MAID technique.

Figure 15.1 outlines the MINT reliability modeling framework. MINT is composed of a single disk reliability model, a system-level reliability model, and three reliability-affecting factors—temperature, power-state transition frequency (hereinafter referred to as *transition frequency* or *frequency*), and utilization. Many

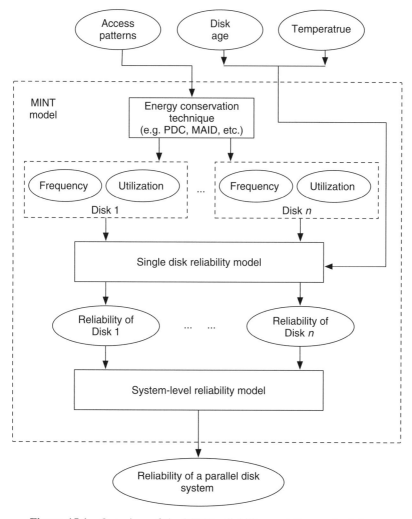

Figure 15.1   Overview of the MINT reliability modeling methodology.

energy saving schemes (e.g., MAID [17]) inherently affect reliability-related factors such as disk utilization and transition frequency. Given an energy optimization mechanism, MINT first transfers data access patterns into the two reliability-affecting factors—frequency and utilization. The single disk reliability model can derive individual disk's AFR from utilization, power-state transition frequency, age, and temperature because these parameters are the key reliability-affecting factors. Each disk's reliability is used as input to the system-level reliability model that estimates the AFR of parallel disk systems. For simplicity without losing generality, we considered in MINT four reliability-related factors, namely, disk utilization, age, temperature, and power-state transitions. This assumption does not necessarily indicate by any means that there are only four parameters affecting disk reliability. Other factors having impacts on reliability include handling, humidity, voltage variation, vintage, duty cycle, and altitude [20]. That means if a new factor has to be taken into account, one can extend the single reliability model (Section 15.2.1.4) by integrating the new factor with other reliability-affecting factors in MINT. Since the infant mortality phenomenon is out of the scope of this study, we pay attention to disks that are more than 1 year old.

15.2.1.1 Disk utilization. Disk utilization, a reliability-related factor, can be characterized as the fraction of active time of a disk drive out of its total powered-on-time [21]. In our single disk reliability model, the impacts of disk utilization on reliability is a good way of providing a baseline characterization of disk AFR. Pinheiro et al. studied the impact of utilization on AFR across different disk age groups [21]. They categorized disk utilization in three levels—low, medium, and high. Since the single disk reliability model needs a baseline AFR derived from a numerical value of utilization, we applied the polynomial curve-fitting technique to model the baseline value of a single disk's AFR as a function of utilization. Thus, the baseline value (i.e., Base Value in Equation 15.1) of AFR for a disk can be calculated from the disk's utilization.

15.2.1.2 Temperature. Temperature is often considered as the most important environmental factor affecting disk reliability. For example, results from Google show that at very high temperatures, higher failure rates are associated with higher temperatures. In the low and middle temperature ranges, failure rate decreases when temperature increases [21].

In the MINT model, the temperature factor is a multiplier to base failure rates, which reflect reliability at base environmental conditions [20]. The temperature factor (i.e., Temperature Factor in Equation 15.1) is set to 1 when temperature is $25°C$ because room temperatures of many data centers are kept to $25°C$ by cooling systems. Suppose T is the average temperature, we define the temperature factor in case of T as $T/25$ if T is larger than $25°C$. When T exceeds $45°C$, the temperature factor becomes a constant (i.e., $1.8 = 45/25$) because the cooling systems would not let the room temperature higher than that.

15.2.1.3 *Power-state transition frequency.* To conserve energy, power management policies turn idle disks from the active state into standby. The disk power-state transition frequency (or frequency for short) is often measured as the number of power-state transitions (i.e., from active to standby or vice versa) per month. The reliability of an individual disk is affected by power-state transitions and, therefore, the increase in failure rate as a function of power-state transition frequency has to be added to a baseline failure rate (Eq. 15.1).

15.2.1.4 *Single disk reliability model.* Single disk reliability cannot be accurately described by one-valued parameter because the disk drive reliability is affected by multiple factors (Sections 15.2.1.1–15.2.1.3). We first compute a baseline failure rate as a function of disk utilization. Second, the temperature factor is used as a multiplier to the baseline failure rate. Finally, we add frequency to the baseline value of the AFR. Hence, the failure rate R of an individual disk can be expressed as

$$R = \alpha \times \text{Base Value} \times \text{Temperature Factor}$$
$$+ \beta \times \text{Frequency Adder,} \qquad (15.1)$$

where Base Value is the baseline failure rate derived from disk utilization (Section 15.2.1.1), Temperature Factor is the temperature multiplier (Section 15.2.1.2), Frequency Adder is the power-state transition frequency adder to the baseline failure rate (Section 15.2.1.3), and α and β are two coefficients to reliability R. If reliability R is more sensitive to frequency than to utilization and temperature, then β must be greater than α. Otherwise, β is smaller than α. In either cases, α and β can be set in accordance with R's sensitivities to utilization, temperature, and frequency. In our experiments, we assume that all the three reliability-related factors are equally important (i.e., $\alpha = \beta = 1$).

Ideally, extensive field tests allow us to analyze and test the two coefficients. Although α and β are not fully evaluated by field testing, reliability results are valid because of two reasons: (i) we have used the same values of α and β to evaluate impacts of the two energy saving schemes on disk reliability (Section 15.2.2); (ii) the failure rate trend of a disk when α and β are set to 1 are very similar to those of the same disk when the values of α and β do not equal to 1.

With Equation 15.1 in place, we can analyze a disk's reliability in turns of AFR. Figure 15.2 shows AFR of a 3-year-old disk when its utilization is in the range between 20% and 80%.

We observe from Figure 15.2 that increasing the temperature from 35 to 40°C gives rise to a significant increase in AFR. Unlike temperature, power-state transition frequency in the range of a few hundreds per month has marginal impact on AFR. It is expected that when transition frequency is extremely high, AFR becomes more sensitive to frequency than to temperature.

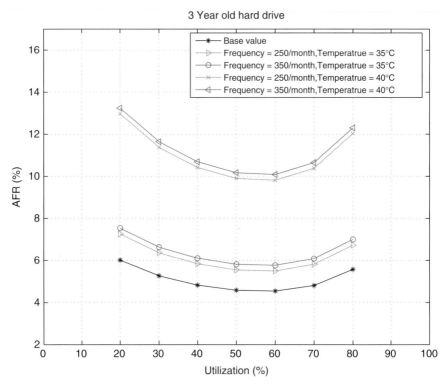

Figure 15.2 Impacts of combined factors on the annual failure rate of a 3-year-old HDD (single disk reliability model).

15.2.2 MAID, Massive Arrays of Idle Disks

The MAID technique—developed by Colarelli and Grunwald—aims to reduce energy consumption of large disk arrays while maintaining acceptable I/O performance [17]. MAID relies on data temporal locality to place replicas of active files on a subset of cache disks, thereby allowing other disks to spin-down.

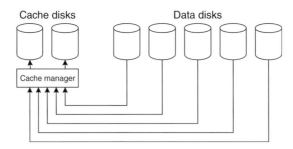

Figure 15.3 The MAID system structure.

Figure 15.3 shows that MAID maintains two types of disks—cache disks and data disks. Frequently accessed files are copied from data disks into cache disks, where the LRU policy is implemented to manage data replacement in cache disks. Replaced data is discarded by a cache disk if the data is clean; dirty data has to be written back to the corresponding data disk. To prevent cache disk from being overloaded, MAID can avoid copying data to cache disks that have reached their maximum bandwidth. The following three parameters will be used in systems:

1. power management policy, by using which drives that have not seen any requests for a specified period are spun down to sleep, or an adaptive spin-down to active;
2. data layout, which is either linear, with successive blocks being placed on the same drive, or striped across multiple drives;
3. cache, which indicates the number of drives of the array that will be used for cache [17].

15.3 IMPROVING RELIABILITY OF MAID VIA DISK SWAPPING

15.3.1 Improving Reliability of Cache Disks in MAID

Cache disks in MAID are more likely to fail than data disks because of the two reasons. First, cache disks are always kept active to maintain short I/O response times. Second, the utilization of cache disks is expected to be much higher than that of data disks. From the aspect of data loss, the reliability of MAID relies on the failure rate of data disks rather than that of cache disks. However, cache disks tend to be a single point of failure in MAID, which if the cache disks fail, will stop MAID from conserving energy. In addition, frequently replacing failed cache disks can increase hardware and management costs in MAID. To address this single point of failure issue and make MAID cost-effective, we designed a disk swapping strategy for enhancing the reliability of cache disks in MAID.

Figure 15.4 shows the basic idea of the disk swapping mechanism, according to which disks rotate to perform the cache-disk functionality. In other words, the roles of cache disks and data disks will be periodically switched in a way that all the disks in MAID have equal chance to perform the role of caching popular data. For example, the two cache disks on the left-hand side in Figure 15.4 are swapped with the two data disks on the right-hand side after a certain period of time (see Section 15.4.3 for circumstances under which disks should be swapped). For simplicity without losing generality, we assume that all the data disks in MAID initially are identical in terms of reliability. This assumption is reasonable because when a MAID system is built, all the new disks with the same model come from the same vendor. Initially, the two cache disks in Figure 15.4 can be swapped with any data disk. After the initial phase of disk swapping, the cache disks switched their role of storing replica data with the data disks with the lowest AFR. In doing so, we ensure that cache disks are the most reliable

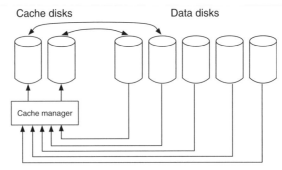

Cache disks   Data disks

Cache manager

Figure 15.4 Disk swapping in MAID: The two cache disks on the left-hand side are swapped with the two data disks on the right-hand side.

ones among all the disks in MAID after each disk swapping process. It is worth noting that the goal of disk swapping is not to increase mean time to data loss but to boost mean time to cache-disk failure by balancing failure rates across all disks in MAID.

Figure 15.5 is the logic diagram of the single disk swapping mechanism, which demonstrates more details about the swapping. When the access rate reaches the threshold, which is set beforehand, a data disk's capacity will be checked. If the data disk has enough free space to hold all the replicas that are hold by a cache disk, it will be paired with the cache disk for swapping later. Otherwise, other data disks' capacity will be checked until a disk that meets the requirement. If there is no disk that meets the requirement, the disk swapping would not be executed. This step needs to be executed first to prevent the original data from misdeleting on the data disk. In our research, we assumed that the data disk's capacity is large enough to hold all the cache data and to keep the original data. The capacity of the cache disk will be examined when it is paired with a data disk.

If the cache disk has enough free space to hold all the data that are held by the data disk, the data disk will duplicate all the cache data from the cache disk while holding all the original data. Then the cache disk will copy the data from the data disk and keeps all replicas of its own. On the other hand, if the cache disk does not have enough free space to hold all the data from the data disk, all replicas it holds will be deleted after they are duplicated to the destination releasing the space for the data copied from the data disk. At this step, irrespective of whether or not the cache disk has available capacity, the data needs to be transferred from cache disk first to prevent original data from either miss-deleting or losing.

Algorithm 15.1 is the single disk swapping algorithm that switches the roles of cache disks and data disks to improve the reliability of cache disks. The algorithm is called *single disk swapping* because the disk swapping occurs only once in MAID.

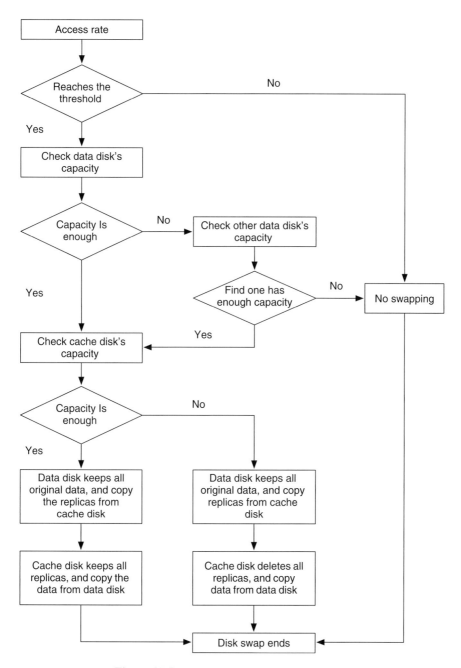

Figure 15.5   Logic diagram of disk swapping.

Algorithm 15.1: Single Disk Swapping Algorithm

```
1.  Input The Access Rate of The System;
2.  if The Access Rate Reaches The Threshold then
3.    Check the Available Capacity of Data Disk;
4.    if The Available Capacity of Data Disk Is Enough then
5.      Check the Available Capacity of Cache Disk;
6.      if The Available Capacity of Cache Disk Is Enough then
7.          Data Disk Keeps All Original Data and Duplicates
               Cache Data From Cache Disk;
            Cache Disk Keeps All Replicas and Copies Data From
               Data Disk;
8.      else
9.        if The Available Capacity of Cache Disk Is NOT
               Enough then
10.           Data Disk Keeps All Original Data and Duplicates
                 Cache Data From Cache Disk;
              Cache Disk Deletes All Replicas and Copies Data
                 From Data Disk;
11.       end if
12.     end if
13. else
14.   if The Available Capacity of Data Disk Is NOT Enough then
15.       while There Is A Data Disk That Has Enough
               Available Capacity
            do
16.           Check the Available Capacity of Cache Disk;
17.       end while
18.     end if
19.   end if
10.   else
21.     Don't Do Swap;
22.   end if
23.   Disk Swap Ends;
```

Disk swapping is very beneficial to MAID for two reasons. First, disk swapping further improves the energy efficiency of MAID because any failed cache disk can prevent MAID from effectively saving energy. Second, disk swapping reduces maintenance cost of MAID by making cache disks less likely to fail.

15.3.2 Swapping Disks Multiple Times

Now we consider the case where disk swapping is invoked multiple times in MAID. As described in Section 15.3.1, the single disk swapping mechanism improves the reliability of the MAID system by making all disks have equal chance to perform the role of cache disks that have high I/O workload and high utilization. The single disk swapping algorithm has a major limitation because disks are swapped only once throughout their lifetimes. That means single disk swapping only affects the reliability for a very short period of time. After each disk swapping, the utilization of those disks with low AFRs are likely to be kept at a high level, which in turn leads to an increasing AFR of the entire disk system. In order to improve the reliability of the MAID system for a long time period (e.g., 1,000,000 h or over 100 years [22]), we address the issue of swapping disks multiple times (see multiple disk swapping shown in Algorithm 15.2).

In the multiple disk swapping algorithm, the number of disk swapping per month is an important parameter affecting both reliability and performance of MAID. This parameter can either be manually set as a constraint or be configured dynamically according to changing workload conditions. In the static approach, the disk swapping mechanism is triggered after MAID has been operating for a certain number of days regardless I/O workload. For example, if the frequency is set as three times per month, disks will be swapped once every 10 days.

In the dynamic approach, the disk swapping function is invoked once workload conditions (i.e., access rate) meet the configured value regardless of the time intervals between two swaps. For instance, if the access rate is set as $2 * 10^5$ numbers per month, the disks will be swapped every time the access rate reaches $2 * 10^5$ numbers per month. The dynamic multiple disk swapping scheme ensures that disk swaps occur only when it is necessary.

Algorithm 15.2: Algorithm for Multiple Disk Swapping

```
1. while The Frequency of Disk Swapping Is No More Than
        The Given Ones do
2.    Run Algorithm 15.1
3. end while
4. Disk Swap Ends;
```

15.4 EXPERIMENTAL RESULTS AND EVALUATION

15.4.1 Experimental Setup

We developed a simulator to validate the reliability model for MAID. It might be unfair to compare the reliability of MAID with any non-energy-efficient parallel disks, since MAID trades extra cache disks for high energy efficiency. To make fair comparisons, we considered a MAID system with two configurations. The first configuration referred to as *MAID-1* employs existing disks in a parallel disk system as cache disks to store frequently accessed data. Thus, the first configuration of MAID improves energy efficiency of the parallel disk system at the cost of capacity. In contrast, the second configuration—called *MAID-2*—needs extra disks to be added to the disk system to serve as cache disks.

Our experiments were started by evaluating the reliability of the original MAID system without disk swapping. Then, we studied the reliability impacts of the single disk swapping strategy on MAID. Finally, we assessed the reliability impacts

TABLE 15.1   The Characteristics of the Simulated Parallel Disk System Used to Evaluate the Reliability of MAID-1 and MAID-2

Energy Efficiency Scheme	Number of Disks	File Access Rate, Numbers per Month	File Size, kB
NONE[a]	20 data (20 in total)	$0-10^6$	300
MAID-1	15 data + 5 cache (20 in total)	$0-10^6$	300
MAID-2	20 data + 5 cache (25 in total)	$0-10^6$	300

[a]Original disk system without any energy efficiency scheme.

of the multiple disk swapping scheme. We simulated MAID-1 and MAID-2 coupled with the disk swapping strategies in two parallel disk systems as described in Table 15.1. For the MAID-1 configuration, there are 5 cache disks and 15 data disks. In the disk system for the MAID-2 configuration, there are 5 cache disks and 20 data disks. As for the case of non-energy-efficient scheme, we fixed the number of disks to 20. Thus, we studied MAID-2 and PDC using a parallel disk system with 20 disks; we used a similar disk system with totally 25 disks to investigate MAID-1. We varied the file access rate in the range between 0 and 10^6 times per month. The average file size considered in our experiments is 300 kB. The base operating temperature is set to 35°C. In this study, we focused on read-only workload. Nevertheless, the MINT model should be readily extended to capture the characteristics of read/write workloads.

15.4.2   Disk Utilization

Figure 15.6 shows that when the average file access rate increases, the utilizations of MAID-1 and MAID-2 increase accordingly. Compared with the utilization of MAID-2, the utilization of MAID-1 is more sensitive to the file access rate. Under low I/O load, the utilizations of MAID-1 and MAID-2 are very close to each other. When I/O load becomes relatively high, the utilization of MAID-1 is slightly higher than that of MAID-2. This is mainly because the capacity of MAID-2 is larger than that of MAID-1.

15.4.3   The Single Disk Swapping Strategy

A key issue of the disk swapping strategies is to determine circumstances under which the disks should be swapped in order to improve disk system reliability. One straightforward way to address this issue is to periodically initiate the disk swapping process. For example, we can swap disks in MAID once every month. Periodically swapping disks, however, might not always enhance the reliability of parallel disk systems. For instance, swapping disks under very light workloads cannot substantially improve disk system reliability. In some extreme cases, swapping disks under light workload may worsen disk reliability due to overhead of swapping. As such, our disk swapping strategies do not periodically swap disks. Rather, the disk swapping process is initiated when the average I/O

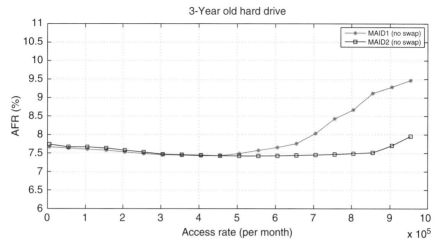

Figure 15.6   Utilization comparison of the MAID access rate impacts on AFR (no swapping).

access rates exceed a threshold. In our experiments, we evaluated the impact of this access rate threshold on the reliability of a parallel disk system. More specifically, the threshold is set to $2 * 10^5, 5 * 10^5$, and $8 * 10^5$ times per month. These three values are representative values for the threshold because when the access rate hits $5 * 10^5$, the disk utilization lies in the range between 80% and 90% [21], which in turn ensures that AFR increases with the increasing value of utilization (Fig. 15.2).

Figures 15.7–15.9 reveal the AFRs of MAID-1 and MAID-2 with and without using the proposed disk swapping strategy. The results plotted in

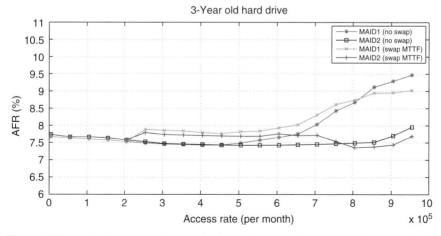

Figure 15.7   Utilization comparison of the MAID access rate impacts on AFR (threshold $= 2 * 10^5$).

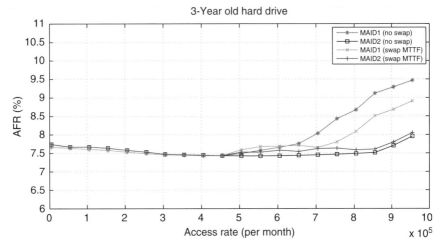

Figure 15.8   Utilization comparison of the MAID access rate impacts on AFR (threshold $= 5 * 10^5$).

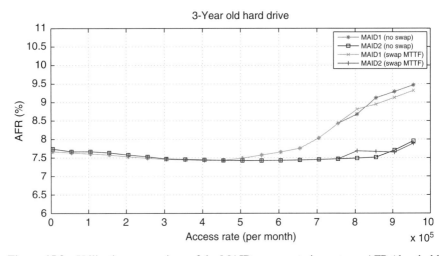

Figure 15.9   Utilization comparison of the MAID access rate impacts on AFR (threshold $= 8 * 10^5$).

Figures 15.7–15.9 show that for both MAID-1 and MAID-2, the disk swapping process reduces the reliability of data disks in the disk system. We attribute the reliability degradation to the following reasons. MAID-1 and MAID-2 only store replicas of popular data; the reliability of the entire disk system is not affected by failures of cache disks. The disk swapping processes increase the average utilization of data disks, thereby increasing the AFR values of data disks. Nevertheless, the disk swapping strategy has its own unique advantage. Disk swapping is intended to reduce hardware maintenance cost by increasing the lifetime of cache disks. In other words, disk swapping is capable of extending the mean time to failure or MTTF [21] of the cache disks.

We observed from Figures 15.7–15.9 that for the MAID-based disk system with the disk swapping strategy, a small threshold leads to a low AFR. Compared with the other two thresholds, the $2 * 10^5$ threshold showed in Figure 15.7 results in the lower AFR. The reason is that when the access rate is $2 * 10^5$ numbers per month, the disk utilization is around 35% [21], which lies in the monotone decreasing area of the curve shown in Figure 15.2. Thus, disk swapping reduces AFR for a while until the disk utilization reaches 60%.

15.4.4   The Multiple Disk Swapping Strategy

Section 15.4.3 shows that single disk swapping strategy can improve the reliability of the MAID system. However, the single disk swapping has minimal reliability impact in a long period of time. For example, Figure 15.7 indicates that after swapping cache and data disks, the failure rate of the disk system continues going up as the access rate keeps increasing. We observed that after the first disk swap without any consecutive disk swaps, the failure rate of disk-swapping-enabled MAID will become close to that of non-disk-swapping MAID. Thus, disk swapping must be repeatedly conducted under the condition that the failure rate of MAID increases.

To evaluate the multiple disk swapping scheme, we configured the access rate threshold to $2 * 10^5, 2.5 * 10^5$, and $4 * 10^5$ numbers per month. For example, if the threshold is set to $2 * 10^5$, the total access rate can be as high as $8 * 10^5$, which is one of the thresholds chosen for the single disk swapping strategy.

Figures 15.10–15.12 reveal the AFRs of MAID-1 and MAID-2 with both a single disk swap and multiple disk swaps. The results show that the multiple

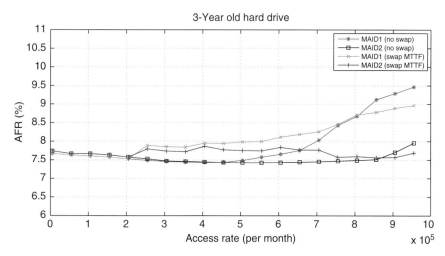

Figure 15.10   Utilization comparison of the MAID access rate impacts on AFR (multiple threshold $= 2 * 10^5$).

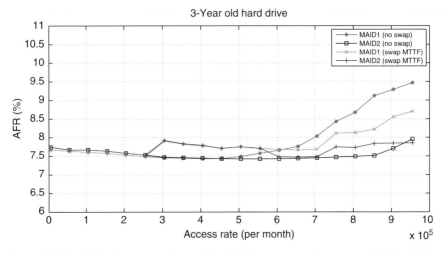

Figure 15.11   Utilization comparison of the MAID access rate impacts on AFR (multiple threshold $= 2.5 * 10^5$).

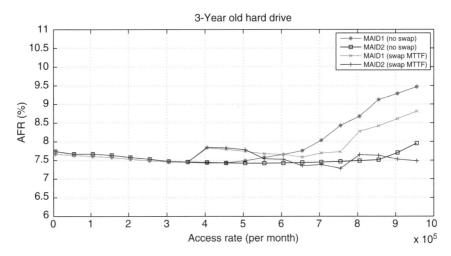

Figure 15.12   Utilization comparison of the MAID access rate impacts on AFR (multiple threshold $= 4 * 10^5$).

disk swapping process further reduces the failure rate of data disks in the MAID system. Comparing the AFR values plotted in Figures 15.7–15.9, we noticed that the failure rate of MAID with multiple disk swaps is lower than that of the same with a single disk swap at access rate $10 * 10^5$. As the access rate increases, the reliability improvement achieved by the multiple disk swapping scheme becomes more pronounced. The major reason behind the improvement is that swapping disks multiple times can continue balancing I/O workload of each disk in the

MAID system in the long run. After each disk swap, if the failure rate of MAID increases to a certain point (Fig. 15.6), a subsequent disk swap will be initiated.

Figures 15.10–15.12 demonstrate that the failure rate of the multiswapping MADI system changes periodically. For example, Figure 15.10 shows that immediately after each disk swapping process, the failure rate of MAID increases 5% because of the overhead caused by copying data among cache disks and data disks. Then, the failure rate stays stable for a while until the next disk swapping occurs. We observe that at the second disk swap, the cumulative access rate is $4 * 10^5$, which is the same as the first swapping threshold shown in Figure 15.12. The forth disk swapping point in Figure 15.10 is the same as that of single disk swapping threshold shown in Figure 15.9. Comparing Figures 15.12 and 15.9, we conclude that when access rate reaches $10 * 10^5$, the failure rate of the multiple disk swapping scheme is lower than that of the single disk swapping scheme. This reliability improvement is made possible by multiple disk swaps, because cache disks and data disks are switched after the failure rates of the cache disks become higher than those of the data disks. Repeatedly swapping cache and data disks can well balance the failure rates of all the disks in the MAID system.

15.5 RELATED WORK

A hard disk drive (HDD) is a complex dynamic system made up of various electrical, electronic, and mechanical components [23]. An array of techniques were developed to save energy in single HDDs. Energy dissipation in disk drives can be reduced at the I/O level (e.g., dynamic power management [5, 7] and multispeed disks [6]), the operating system level (e.g., power-aware caching/prefetching [9, 16]), and the application level (e.g., software DMP [24] and cooperative I/O [25]). Existing energy saving techniques for parallel disk systems often rely on one of the two basic ideas—power management and workload skew. Power management schemes conserve energy by turning disks into standby after a period of idle time. Although multispeed disks are not widely adopted in storage systems, power management has been successfully extended to address the energy saving issues in multispeed disks [6, 15, 26]. The basic idea of workload skew is to concentrate I/O workloads from a large number of parallel disks into a small subset of disks allowing other disks to be placed in the standby mode [17, 18, 27, 28].

Recent studies show that both power management and workload skew schemes inherently impose adverse impacts on disk systems [3, 4]. For example, the power management schemes are likely to result in a huge number of disk spin-downs and spin-ups that can significantly reduce hard disk lifetime. The workload skew techniques dynamically migrates frequently accessed data to a subset of disks [29, 30], which inherently have higher risk of breaking down than other disks usually being kept on standby. Disks that store popular data tend to have high failure rates due to extremely unbalanced workload. Thus, the popular data disks have a strong likelihood to become reliability bottleneck. The design of our

MINT is orthogonal to the aforementioned energy saving studies, because MINT is focused on reliability impacts of the power management and workload skew schemes in parallel disks.

A malfunction of any component in a hard disk drive could lead to a failure of the disk. Reliability—one of the key characteristics of disks—can be measured in terms of mean-time-between-failure (MTBF). Disk manufacturers usually investigate MTBFs of disks either by laboratory testing or mathematical modeling. Although disk drive manufacturers claim that MTBF of most disks is more than 1 million hours [22], users have experienced a much lower MTBF from their field data [20]. More importantly, it is challenging to measure MTBF because of a wide range of contributing factors including disk age, utilization, temperature, and power-state transition frequency [20].

A handful of reliability models have been successfully developed for storage systems. For example, Pâris et al. [31] investigated an approach to computing both average failure rate and mean time to failure in distributed storage systems; Elerath and Pecht [32] proposed a flexible model for estimating reliability of RAID storage; and Xin et al. [33] developed a model to study disk infant mortality. Unlike these reliability models tailored for conventional parallel and distributed disk systems, our MINT model pays special attention to reliability of parallel disk systems coupled with energy saving mechanisms.

Very recently, Xie and Sun developed an empirical reliability model called *PRESS* (predictor of reliability for energy saving schemes) [4]. The PRESS model can be used to estimate reliability of an entire disk array [4]. To fully leverage PRESS to study the reliability of disk arrays, one has to properly simulate the disk arrays. Our MINT approach differs itself from PRESS in the sense that the goal of MINT is to evaluate reliability of disk systems by modeling the behavior of parallel disks where energy conservation mechanisms are integrated.

Swapping mechanisms have been thoroughly studied in the arena of memory and file systems. For example, Paul et al. [34] developed an efficient virtual memory swapping system—called *LocalSwap*—to improve performance of clusters; Plank [35] addressed the issue of checkpoint placement and its impact on the performance of the PVM platform; Pei and Edward [36] investigated the performance of a file system based on the LRU-SP (least recently used with swapping) policy. Our disk swapping approaches are fundamentally different from the aforementioned swapping mechanisms in the sense that the goal of disk swapping is to improve the reliability of energy-efficient parallel disk systems by balancing the failure rates of parallel disks.

15.6 CONCLUSIONS

This chapter presents a reliability model to quantitatively study the reliability of energy-efficient parallel disk systems equipped with the MAID technique. Note that MAID is a well-known effective energy saving schemes for parallel disk systems. It aims to skew I/O load toward a few disks so that the other disks can be transitioned to low power states to conserve energy. I/O load skewing techniques such as MAID inherently affect reliability of parallel disks because disks storing popular data tend to have high failure rates than disks storing cold data. To address the reliability issue in MAID, we developed single disk swapping strategies to improve disk reliability by alternating disks storing hot data with disks holding cold data. In addition, we introduced multiple disk swapping scheme to further improve reliability of MAID. Then, we quantitatively evaluated the impacts of the disk swapping strategies on reliability of MAID-based disk systems. We demonstrated that the disk swapping strategies can not only increase the lifetime of cache disks in MAID-based parallel disk systems but can also improve its reliability in the long period of time by balancing the workload of cache disks and data disks and then balancing the their utilization correspondingly.

Future directions of this research can be performed in the following order. First, we will extend the MINT model to investigate mixed read/write work-loads in the future. Second, we will investigate a fundamental trade-off between reliability and energy efficiency in the context of energy-efficient disk arrays. A trade-off curve will be used as a unified framework to justify whether or not it is worth trading reliability for high energy efficiency. Finally, we will study the most appropriate conditions under which disk swapping processes should be initiated.

ACKNOWLEDGMENT

The work reported in this chapter was supported by the US National Science Foundation under Grants CCF-0845257 (CAREER), CNS-0757778 (CSR), CCF-0742187 (CPA), CNS-0917137 (CSR), CNS-0831502 (CyberTrust), CNS-0855251 (CRI), OCI-0753305 (CI-TEAM), DUE-0837341 (CCLI), and DUE-0830831 (SFS), as well as Auburn University under a startup grant and a gift (Number 2005-04-070) from the Intel Corporation.

REFERENCES

1. Laboratory L. B. N. The distributed-parallel storage system (DPSS) home pages. 2004 June Available at http://www-didc.lbl.gov/DPSS/.

2. Varman P, Verma R. Tight bounds for prefetching and buffer management algorithms for parallel I/O systems. IEEE Trans Parallel Distrib Syst 1999; 10(12): 1262–1275.

3. Bellam K, Manzanares A, Ruan X, Qin X, Yang Y.-M. Improving reliability and energy efficiency of disk systems via utilization control. In: Proceedings IEEE Symposium Computers and Communications; Marrakech, Morocco; 2008.

4. Xie T, Sun Y. Sacrificing reliability for energy saving: is it worthwhile for disk arrays? In: Proceedings IEEE Symposium Parallel and Distributed Processing; Miami, USA; 2008 Apr, pp. 1–12.

5. Douglis F, Krishnan P, Marsh B. Thwarting the power-hungry disk. In: Proceedings USENIX Winter 1994 Technical Conference; 1994, pp. 23–23.

6. Helmbold D, Long D, Sconyers T, Sherrod B. Adaptive disk spin–down for mobile computers. Mob Netw Appl 2000;5(4):285–297.

7. Li K, Kumpf R, Horton P, Anderson T. A quantitative analysis of disk drive power management in portable computers. In: Proceedings USENIX Winter Technical Conference; California, USA; 1994, pp. 22–22.

8. Pinheiro E, Bianchini R, Dubnicki C. Exploiting redundancy to conserve energy in storage systems. In: Proceedings Joint International Conference Measurement and Modeling of Computer Systems; St. Malo, France; 2006.

9. Zhu Q.-B, David F, Devaraj C, Li Z.-M, Zhou Y.-Y, Cao P. Reducing energy consumption of disk storage using power-aware cache management. In: Proceedings International Symposium High Performance Computer Architecture; 2004; Washington (DC). p. 118.

10. Wang J, Zhu H.-J, Li D. eraid: Conserving energy in conventional disk-based raid system. IEEE Trans Comput 2008;57(3):359–374.

11. Xie T. Sea: a striping-based energy-aware strategy for data placement in raid-structured storage systems. IEEE Trans Comput 2008;57(6):748–761.

12. Papathanasiou A. E, Scott M. L. Power-efficient server-class performance from arrays of laptop disks. 2004. [Online]. Available at http://hdl.handle.net/1802/314, Access year -2004.

13. Jin S, Bestavros A. Gismo: a generator of internet streaming media objects and workloads. ACM SIGMETRICS Perform Eval Rev 2001.

14. Yang Q, Hu Y.-M. DCD - Disk Caching Disk: a new approach for boosting I/O performance. In: Proceedings International Symposium Computer Architecture; Philadelphia, USA; 1996 May. pp. 169–169.

15. Gurumurthi S, Sivasubramaniam A, Kandemir M, Franke H. Drpm: dynamic speed control for power management in server class disks. In: Proceedings International Symposium Computer Architecture; California, USA; 2003 June. pp. 169–179.

16. Son S, Kandemir M. Energy-aware data prefetching for multi-speed disks. In: Proceedings International Conference Computing Frontiers; Italy; 2006.

17. Colarelli D, Grunwald D. Massive arrays of idle disks for storage archives. In: Proceedings ACM/IEEE Conference Supercomputing; Baltimore, USA; 2002. pp. 1–11.

18. Pinheiro E, Bianchini R. Energy conservation techniques for disk array-based servers. In: Proceedings 18th International Conference Supercomputing; France; 2004.

19. Yin S, Ruan X, Manzanares A, Qin X. How reliable are parallel disk systems when energy-saving schemes are involved? In: Proceedings IEEE International Conference on Cluster Computing (CLUSTER); New Orleans, USA; 2009.

20. Elerath J. Specifying reliability in the disk drive industry: No more mtbf's; 2000. pp. 194–199.

21. Pinheiro E, Weber W.-D, Barroso L. Failure trends in a large disk drive population. In: Proceedings USENIX Conference on File and Storage Technologies; California, USA; 2007 Feb.

22. Schroeder B, Gibson G. Disk failures in the real world: what does an mttf of 1,000,000 hours mean to you? In: Proceedings USENIX Conference File and Storage Technologies; California, USA; 2007. p. 1.

23. Yang J, Sun F.-B. A comprehensive review of hard-disk drive reliability. In: Proceedings Annual Reliability and Maintainability Symposium; Philadelphia, USA; 1999.

24. Son S. W, Kandemir M, Choudhary A. Software-directed disk power management for scientific applications. In: Proceedings IEEE Internatinal Parallel and Distributed Processing Symposium; California, USA; 2005.

25. Weissel A, Beutel B, Bellosa F. Cooperative I/O: a novel I/O semantics for energy-aware applications. In: Proceedings the 5th Symposium Operating Systems Design and Implementation. New York: ACM; 2002. pp. 117–129.

26. Krishnan P, Long M. P, Vitter S. J. Adaptive disk spindown via optimal rent-to-buy in probabilistic environments. Tech Rep Durham (NC); 1995.

27. Run X.-J. R, Manzanares A, Yin S, Zong Z.-L, Qin X. Performance evaluation of energy-efficient parallel I/O systems with write buffer disks. In: Proceedings 38th International Conference Parallel Processing; Vienna, Austria; 2009 Sept.

28. Pinheiro E, Bianchini R, Carrera E, Heath T. Load balancing and unbalancing for power and performance in cluster-based systems. Proceedings of the Workshop Compilers and Operating Systems for Low Power; 2001 Sept.

29. Ruan X. J, Manzanares A, Bellam K, Zong Z. L, Qin X. Daraw: a new write buffer to improve parallel I/O energy-efficiency. In: Proceedings of the ACM Symposium Applied Computing; Honolulu, USA; 2009.

30. Manzanares A, Ruan X, Yin S, Nijim M. Energy-aware prefetching for parallel disk systems: algorithms, models, and evaluation. In: IEEE International Symposium on Network Computing and Applications; 2009.

31. Pâris J.-F, Schwarz T, Long D. Evaluating the reliability of storage systems. In: Proceedings of IEEE International Symposium on Reliable and Distributed System; Leeds, UK; 2006.

32. Elerath J, Pecht M. Enhanced reliability modeling of raid storage systems. In: Proceedings IEEE/IFIP International Conference Dependable System and Networks; Edinburgh, UK; 2007.

33. Xin Q, Thomas J, Schwarz S, Miller E. Disk infant mortality in large storage systems. In: Proceedings IEEE International Symposium Modeling, Analysis, and Simulation of Computer and Telecommunication Systems; Atlanta USA; 2005.

34. Werstein P, Jia X, Huang Z. A remote memory swapping system for cluster computers. In: PDCAT '07: Proceedings of the 8th International Conference on Parallel and Distributed Computing, Applications and Technologies. Washington (DC): IEEE Computer Society; 2007. pp. 75–81.

35. Plank J. S. Improving the performance of coordinated checkpointers on networks of workstations using raid techniques. In: SRDS '96: Proceedings of the 15th Symposium on Reliable Distributed Systems. Washington (DC): IEEE Computer Society; 1996. p. 76.

36. Cao P, Felten E. W, Karlin A. R, Li K. Implementation and performance of integrated application-controlled file caching, prefetching, and disk scheduling. ACM Trans Comput Syst 1996;14(4):311–343.

CHAPTER 16

EMBRACING THE MEMORY AND I/O WALLS FOR ENERGY-EFFICIENT SCIENTIFIC COMPUTING

CHUNG-HSING HSU and WU-CHUN FENG

16.1 INTRODUCTION

Scientific computing helps computers to analyze and solve scientific problems. It generally demands the highest level of computational power. The *memory wall* and the *power wall* present two technical obstacles toward realizing high performance from a computer. The memory wall refers to the growing disparity between processor speed and main memory speed. In other words, the data retrieving rate lags behind the data processing rate, which oftentimes leaves the processor in a computer stalled. The power wall refers to the inability to significantly increase the clock frequency of a processor (CPU) without heroic cooling measures. While the high performance computing (HPC) community is actively addressing both problems, no satisfactory solutions have been found. The introduction of the multicore architecture only exacerbates the problems [1, 2]. In this chapter, we take a rather different approach—*we embrace the memory wall in order to address the power wall*. The converse is also possible, but its discussion is beyond the scope of this chapter.

The underlying idea is quite simple. If a program runs into a period of intensive off-chip memory accesses, its performance during this period will largely be limited by the speed of the memory rather than the CPU, that is, the memory wall [3]. As a result, decreasing the CPU speed will have little negative effect on performance, yet it will allow the CPU to run at a lower-power state (via dynamic voltage and frequency scaling or DVFS,) and thus reduce the power consumption. Similarly, if the period consists of intensive I/O accesses—the "I/O wall"—we can apply the same optimization strategy to reduce power consumption.

Energy-Efficient Distributed Computing Systems, First Edition.
Edited by Albert Y. Zomaya and Young Choon Lee.
© 2012 John Wiley & Sons, Inc. Published 2012 by John Wiley & Sons, Inc.

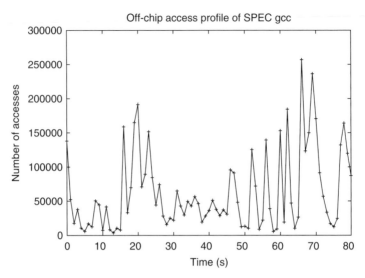

Figure 16.1   The off-chip access pattern of SPEC gcc.

While being seemingly simple, the implementation of the idea is nontrivial. There are at least two challenges that need to be tackled. The first challenge is the varying intensity of memory accesses over time. For scientific computing, the intensity level of memory accesses is different from one time interval to another, making it difficult to predict the intensity at any given time interval correctly.

Figure 16.1 demonstrates such difficulty by plotting the number of off-chip accesses for every second of the execution of the SPEC gcc benchmark. Ideally, when the interval size is as large as 1 s, fluctuations that occur at the interval size of a millisecond should be smoothed out. However, Figure 16.1 still shows a significant amount of fluctuation. This means that correctly predicting the number of off-chip accesses over any given time interval is not easy. To put it quantitatively, if we use the number of off-chip accesses in the previous interval to predict the intensity level of the upcoming interval, we will overestimate accesses 55% of the time by 157% on an average and underestimate accesses the rest of the time by 53% on an average.

The second challenge is to relate the memory-access intensity to the performance impact on the program precisely. Even if we have perfect knowledge of the off-chip access pattern such as in Figure 16.1, this knowledge is still insufficient for us to determine which performance state the CPU should use, that is, to produce an effective DVFS schedule. Choosing the wrong state may result in either undesirable performance slowdown or missed opportunities to maximize energy savings.

For example, one might think that a high cache-miss rate indicates that program execution is in a memory-intensive phase. But for a DVFS-enabled CPU with five performance states, how do we determine which range of cache-miss rates is appropriate for each state? Unless we can predict fairly accurately to what degree the execution time will be lengthened by putting the CPU in each performance state, knowing the high cache-miss rate will *not* help in the selection of the appropriate state while simultaneously ensuring the tight control of DVFS-induced performance slowdown. Therefore, we need a model that can associate the memory-access intensity with the impact on program performance.

The approach presented in this chapter provides a way to address the earlier mentioned challenges. It is also unique in two other respects. First, it is a type of *active-state* power management, that is, it manages power while the processor is active. In contrast, idle-state power management, typically found on laptops, manages power while the processor is idle; specifically, it reduces the power consumption of the processor when the system is idle.

For scientific computing, however, idle-state power management is infeasible given that the processor is active when executing a program. Hence, idle-state power management is best used in enterprise environments, where the CPU load varies at different times of a day. As a result, approaches such as multiple sleep modes and demand-based switching (DBS) [4] are not appropriate for scientific computing. Figure 16.2 shows the power-usage pattern induced by DBS for the SPEC gcc benchmark. We can see that DBS does not affect the power-consumption behavior when the system is in the active state.

Second, our approach is a *software-based* one rather than a hardware-based one. Hardware-based approaches rely on the invention of novel low power hardware [5], whereas software-based approaches exploit the different levels of impact that each execution pattern has on energy and performance, and it alters the execution pattern or operating hardware in order to achieve energy-efficient computing. In many cases, the hardware that supports software-based optimization

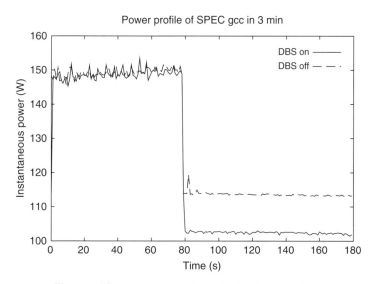

Figure 16.2   The energy effect of a DBS mechanism.

implements the DVFS technology to provide various power-performance trade-offs for the software to choose from and change on the fly in pseudo-real-time.

The rest of the chapter is organized as follows. Section 16.2 characterizes current DVFS algorithms that embrace the memory wall to address the power wall. The section also lists the main issues that these algorithms have. With this characterization in hand, we then present a new DVFS algorithm in Section 16.3 that addressed the identified issues above. Section 16.4 describes our evaluation of the new algorithm through a series of physical measurements on real systems. To enhance our understanding of what constitutes a good DVFS algorithm, we discuss in-depth two features of the new algorithm that make it effective. Finally, Section 16.5 concludes and presents some future directions.

16.2 BACKGROUND AND RELATED WORK

In Section 16.1, we mention that DVFS can be used for software-based, active-state power management. In this section, we present the related work that uses the DVFS technology to address the power wall. We refer the readers to Reference 6 for other types of power-reduction techniques.

16.2.1 DVFS-Enabled Processors

The idea of a DVFS-enabled processor (i.e., CPU) can be traced back as early as 1994 [7], when the focus was on how to lower the CPU supply voltage until the desired clock frequency was reached. The advantage in lowering the CPU supply voltage because of a reduced frequency lies in the fact that a CPU's *power draw* is proportional to its frequency and to the square of its supply voltage. Moreover, a CPU's *energy usage* is proportional to the square of voltage [8]. Consequently, reducing CPU frequency allows us to lower CPU voltage, and in turn, decreases CPU power draw and energy consumption.

Commodity processors that actually supported DVFS did not appear in the market until early 2000, and even then, only in mobile computing platforms. This is because mobile computing platforms sought to reduce the energy usage of a processor so as to extend their battery life. It was not until 2003 that DVFS made its way into desktop processors, specifically the AMD Athlon64 processor. The main concern here was to reduce the heat stress and the noise level of a desktop computer. By late 2004, DVFS gained support in server-class processors such as the AMD Opteron and Intel Xeon EM64T processors because they dissipated significant heat and compromised the reliability of a computing system due to overheating. As a rule of thumb, Arrhenius' equation as applied to microelectronics notes that for every $10°C$ ($18°F$) increase in temperature, the failure rate of a system doubles. At present, all modern processors support DVFS.

The advanced configuration and power interface (ACPI) specification is also evolving to standardize the terms used to describe a DVFS-enabled processor. Specifically, when a processor is in the active state (the C0 state), it is in one of

TABLE 16.1   The Performance States of an AMD Athlon64 Processor

P-State	Frequency, GHz	Voltage, V
P0	2.0	1.5
P1	1.8	1.4
P2	1.6	1.3
P3	0.8	0.9

several performance states (the P-states). Although the P-states are implementation dependent, P0 always refers to the highest-performance state, and P1 to Pn refer to successively lower-performance states, up to an implementation-specific limit of n no greater than 16. So, the P0 state has the peak voltage and frequency, and the Pi state has a higher voltage and frequency than the Pj state for $i < j$. Table 16.1 gives one such example for the AMD Athlon64 3200+ processor. The frequency–voltage setting in each P-state is generally processor- and BIOS-specific.

To control a DVFS-enabled processor, commodity operating systems such as Linux provide an interface for the user or the software to use. For example, the Linux 2.6 kernel provides a DVFS interface called CPUFreq. This interface allows the user or software to request a desired P-state by writing the corresponding CPU frequency to a particular /sys file. Inside the kernel, a driver handles the actual P-state switches. Typically, the CPU manufacturer suggests a range of voltages to be used for each P-state through datasheet specification, and the system builder encodes the exact selection in BIOS. All this effort is to relieve a user from defining valid P-states by himself because not all frequency–voltage settings are operable.

16.2.2   DVFS Scheduling Algorithms

The use of DVFS-enabled processors on general-purpose computing systems (in contrast to real-time or embedded systems) was first proposed by Weiser et al. [9] who sought to reduce the energy consumption of a computer running interactive applications. In other words, Weiser et al. exploit system inactivity for energy-efficient computing by means of DVFS.

The scheduling algorithm proposed by Weiser et al. essentially calculates the CPU utilization ratio (i.e., the fraction of time that the CPU spends nonidle) in the previous time interval and uses it to predict the CPU utilization ratio of the next time interval. To determine which P-state to use, Weiser et al. interpret the CPU utilization ratio as the normalized workload. This interpretation has a nice property that there is a natural, one-to-one correspondence between the CPU utilization ratio and the desired normalized CPU frequency. Thus, if the CPU utilization ratio is 0.5 on a 2-GHz CPU, then setting the CPU frequency to 1 GHz is predicted to eliminate all CPU idle time (i.e., the CPU utilization ratio becomes 1).

While the CPU utilization ratio is easy to derive at runtime and does not require application-specific information, it does not provide enough information to accurately estimate the impact on a program's performance. As a result, DVFS algorithms based on CPU utilization can only provide loose control over DVFS-induced performance loss. This unwanted consequence has been observed by several studies including References 10–12. Thus, DVFS algorithms with application-specific information have been proposed in order to provide tighter control over performance loss.

For example, an application (or task) can be associated with a relative deadline, in terms of seconds, and a CPU work requirement, in terms of CPU cycles. In this setting, performance is typically formulated as a linear function of the CPU frequency (with an intercept of 0). This type of performance model predicts that the execution time doubles when the CPU frequency is halved. Unfortunately, this model overly exaggerates the impact that the CPU frequency has on the execution time. It is only in the worst case that the execution time doubles when the CPU frequency is halved; in general, the actual execution time is less than double. This phenomenon, called *sublinear performance scaling*, is a reflection of the memory wall.

There have been multiple DVFS algorithms proposed to exploit sublinear performance scaling in order to achieve higher energy efficiency. We refer to them as *memory-aware algorithms*. In this chapter, we target memory-aware, *interval-based* DVFS algorithms because they are generally easy to implement. A DVFS algorithm is considered interval-based if the algorithm reconsiders the use of the current P-state at the beginning of each fixed-length time interval, for example, 10 ms. The algorithm proposed by Weiser et al., for example, is an interval-based algorithm. Other types of DVFS algorithm also exist, including compiler-assisted, profile-based algorithms [13, 14]. However, these other types of algorithms are less transparent to end users, making them more difficult to apply to a wide range of applications.

16.2.3 Memory-Aware, Interval-Based Algorithms

A memory-aware, interval-based DVFS algorithm can be characterized by (i) the *metric* used to describe the computational intensity and (ii) the *formula* used to calculate the desired CPU frequency. The formula is often generated from an analytical model that relates the performance of a program to its computational intensity.

For example, Kotla et al. [15] used *instructions per cycle* (*IPC*) as their compute-intensive metric, that is, the higher the IPC, the higher the computational intensity. They proposed a performance model that breaks down the observed IPC into frequency-dependent and frequency-independent components. The model predicts the IPC at any CPU frequency given the two IPC components. The desired CPU frequency is selected based on the predicted IPCs of all possible frequencies against a performance requirement. In the algorithm, the performance-monitoring unit (PMU) is used to gather the necessary information to calculate the IPC components.

The PMU is used in the majority of memory-aware, interval-based DVFS scheduling algorithms. However, the implementation of a PMU-assisted DVFS algorithm is nontrivial. First, the PMU is notorious for its limited portability across different CPU types. For example, Choi et al. used the same intensity metric to design their DVFS algorithm. However, the sets of monitored events used to calculate the metric are different when the algorithm is implemented on two different types of Intel processor [16, 17]. Second, the correlation of event counts to performance is an indirect measure. In addition, the number of counters in the PMU is limited. As a result, the estimation errors of the metric are unavoidable. Hence, a PMU-assisted DVFS algorithm ought to minimize its dependence on the use of the PMU.

Another commonly used metric is *memory accesses per instruction* (*MPI*); the lower the MPI, the higher the computational intensity. For example, Freeh et al. used MPI in their DVFS algorithms [18–23]. They found out that the MPI is a better metric to use than the IPC because the metric value remains constant regardless of the CPU frequency changes. In contrast, the IPC varies greatly with the CPU frequency. They also found out that, while MPI is a good metric to measure the memory pressure, the metric alone is not sufficient to capture the I/O intensity. As a result, an additional metric was required in their algorithms to measure the intensity of the communication I/O.

In summary, two issues will need to be considered when designing a memory-aware, interval-based DVFS algorithm. First, the algorithm should use the PMU as little as possible. Second, the intensity metric should be as comprehensive as possible. In the next section, we present a metric that addresses the latter issue and a DVFS algorithm that addresses the former issue.

16.3 β-ADAPTATION: A NEW DVFS ALGORITHM

Here, we describe an interval-based DVFS algorithm that embraces the memory wall in order to address the power wall by exploiting sublinear performance scaling. In particular, the algorithm automatically detects memory-bound and I/O-bound program phases and exploits the sublinear performance scaling of these phases. Since the algorithm is based on β, a metric that measures the compute boundedness of an application, the algorithm is called β-adaptation.

16.3.1 The Compute-Boundedness Metric, β

The compute-boundedness metric used in β-adaptation was proposed by Hsu and Kremer [13]. This metric aims to quantify the compute boundedness of an application based on the application's performance sensitivity to CPU frequency changes. Because it focuses on *how* the performance is impacted and not *what* impacts the performance, the metric can include, implicitly, all non-CPU activities such as memory accesses and communication latency [21]. As a result, the metric works independently of whether the program is sequential or parallel since the metric is just a measure of how compute bound an application is, and so it does not matter whether the CPU is waiting for data from the memory system or from another node. In contrast, metrics such as the number of memory accesses per instruction (MPI) only concern memory pressure.

Specifically, the compute-boundedness metric that Hsu and Kremer proposed, denoted as β, is a value between 0 and 1 with 1 being totally compute bound:

$$\beta = \frac{T(f)/T(f_{\max}) - 1}{f_{\max}/f - 1} \qquad \text{for all } f < f_{\max}, \qquad (16.1)$$

where $T(f)$ is the execution time at the CPU frequency f and $f_{\max}$ is the peak CPU frequency. The metric essentially models the application's performance slowdown $T(f)/T(f_{\max}) - 1$ with respect to CPU slowdown $f_{\max}/f - 1$. By using the metric, Hsu and Kremer were able to state, for example, that the SPEC floating-point benchmark suite has a wider range of compute boundedness than the integer benchmark suite. Garg et al. [24] used the metric to characterize the workloads in a cloud environment.

An "implicit" assumption made by Hsu and Kremer is that β is *invariant* across all CPU frequencies. To see the significance of this, consider a totally memory-bound application whose performance can be modeled as $T(f) = c$, where c is a constant. If the compute-boundedness metric was chosen to be the ratio of $T(f)/T(f_{\max})$ to $f_{\max}/f$, that is, removing all "−1" terms in Equation 16.1, the metric value of a totally memory-bound application will become $f/f_{\max}$—a function of CPU frequency f. Adding the "−1" terms helps remove this variance; β of a totally memory-bound application becomes 0.

In β-adaptation, we make the same assumption that the compute-boundedness metric β is an application-specific constant.

16.3.2 The Frequency Calculating Formula, f^*

Ideally, if we know the value of β a priori, we can easily use Equation 16.1 to compute the desired CPU frequency f^* with respect to a given performance requirement δ (as a percentage), where

$$\frac{T(f^*)}{T(f_{\max})} - 1 \leq \delta. \qquad (16.2)$$

The performance requirement δ is defined as the normalized performance loss with respect to the execution time when the program is running at the peak CPU frequency (i.e., without the use of DVFS). The introduction of δ allows a user to specify desired energy-performance trade-offs. The larger the δ value, the larger the potential energy savings.

In β-adaptation, we calculate the desired CPU frequency f^* using the following formula:

$$f^* = \min\left\{f : \delta \geq \beta\left(\frac{f_{\max}}{f} - 1\right)\right\}, \qquad (16.3)$$

which simplifies to

$$f^* = \max\left(f_{\min}, \frac{f_{\max}}{1 + \delta/\beta}\right). \tag{16.4}$$

The formula is derived from Equations 16.1 and 16.2. Basically, we compute the lowest CPU frequency whose predicted performance slowdown $\beta\left(\frac{f_{\max}}{f} - 1\right)$ does not exceed the maximum possible performance slowdown δ. Note that we have made another assumption when deriving the formula; that is, running the program as slowly as possible to meet the deadline just in time will minimize the energy usage. This assumption is not valid for all δ values [21], but it is true for small δ values.

Unfortunately, we cannot assume that we know β a priori, as we desire that β-adaptation not require any application-specific information. While we could calculate the metric using at least two profile runs of the entire application at different frequencies before we make the real runs, we want to avoid doing this, particularly from an end user's perspective. Thus, the challenge for β-adaptation lies in the online estimation of β.

In the following section, we discuss how we address this challenge. The key is to identify one or more observable metrics that have the property of being invariant to CPU frequency changes.

16.3.3 The Online β Estimation

The β-adaptation algorithm assumes that the compute-boundedness metric β is an application-specific constant that needs to be estimated while the application is running. To estimate the value of β online, we have to identify one or more observable metrics that have the property of being invariant to CPU frequency changes. (Note that β is calculable but not observable.) The number of such metrics used in a DVFS algorithm determines the heavy or light use of the PMU.

In β-adaptation, we use the number of instructions as the observable metric that has the invariant property. Figure 16.3 provides an evidence for the validity of the above statement. The figure shows the progress of the number of instructions for running a synthetic benchmark, which has a mix of compute-bound and memory-bound phases, at different CPU frequencies. We can clearly see that the number of instructions increases at a steady rate. More importantly, the total number of instructions is invariant to CPU frequency changes. Thus, we chose the number of instructions as the observable metric to assist in the estimation of the β value online.

Assuming a fixed (unknown) number of instructions II, we can equate the performance slowdown with changes in workload processing rate, namely, the MIPS rate (i.e., millions of instructions per second):

$$\frac{T(f)}{T(f_{\max})} = \frac{II/T(f_{\max})}{II/T(f)} = \frac{\texttt{mips}(f_{\max})}{\texttt{mips}(f)}. \tag{16.5}$$

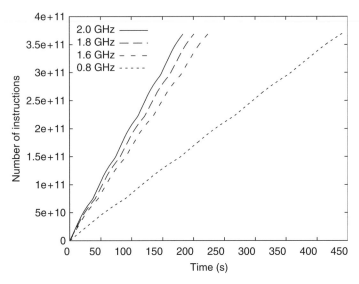

Figure 16.3 The workload distribution of the synthetic benchmark.

Combining it with Equation 16.1, we derive a new equation:

$$\frac{\texttt{mips}(f_{max})}{\texttt{mips}(f)} = \beta\left(\frac{f_{max}}{f} - 1\right) + 1, \tag{16.6}$$

where everything is observable except β.

To estimate β at runtime, we use a regression method over Equation 16.6 and leverage the fact that most DVFS-enabled microprocessors support a limited set of CPU frequencies. That is, given n CPU frequencies $\{f_1, \ldots, f_n\}$, we derive a particular β value that will minimize the least-squared error:

$$\min \sum_{i=1}^{n} \left| \frac{\texttt{mips}(f_{max})}{\texttt{mips}(f_i)} - \beta\left(\frac{f_{max}}{f_i} - 1\right) - 1 \right|^2. \tag{16.7}$$

By equating the first differential of Equation 16.7 to 0, we can derive β as a function of the MIPS rates and CPU frequencies as follows:

$$\beta = \frac{\sum_{i=1}^{n}\left(\frac{f_{max}}{f_i} - 1\right)\left(\frac{\texttt{mips}(f_{max})}{\texttt{mips}(f_i)} - 1\right)}{\sum_{i=1}^{n}\left(\frac{f_{max}}{f_i} - 1\right)^2}. \tag{16.8}$$

Now we know how to do online β estimation. We also know how to calculate the desired CPU frequency from a given β value, as described in the previous section. It is time for us to put them together. In the next section, we show how to combine the two techniques to implement the β-adaptation algorithm.

16.3.4   Putting It All Together

The β-adaptation algorithm is based on the use of two techniques: estimating the compute boundedness of an application, as exhibited by Equation 16.8, and calculating the desired CPU frequency, as captured by Equation 16.4. Figure 16.4 shows the details of the algorithm. In the figure, I stands for the interval length, for example, 1 second.

Specifically, the algorithm wakes up every I seconds. It then calculates the value of β using the most up-to-date MIPS rate, based on Equation 16.8. Once β is derived, the algorithm computes the CPU frequency f^* for the interval based on Equation 16.4. Since a DVFS-enabled processor only supports a limited set of frequencies, the computed frequency f^* may need to be emulated in some cases. This sequence of steps is repeated at the beginning of all subsequent time intervals until the program completes its execution.

The emulation of the computed frequency f^*, as detailed in step (4) of Figure 16.4, is a critical piece of the algorithm that greatly enhances the effectiveness of the β-adaptation algorithm, as we see later in this chapter. For

Hardware:
    n frequencies $\{f_1, \cdots, f_n\}$.
Parameters:
    I: the time-interval size (default 1 s).
    δ: slowdown constraint (default 5%).
Algorithm:
        (1) Initialize mips(f_i), $i = 1, \ldots, n$, by executing the
            program at f_i for I seconds.
    repeat
        (2) Compute coefficient β.

$$\beta = \frac{\sum_i \left(\frac{f_{\max}}{f_i} - 1\right)\left(\frac{\texttt{mips}(f_{\max})}{\texttt{mips}(f_i)} - 1\right)}{\sum_i \left(\frac{f_{\max}}{f_i} - 1\right)^2}$$

        (3) Compute the desired frequency f^*.

$$f^* = \max\left(f_{\min}, \frac{f_{\max}}{1 + \delta/\beta}\right)$$

        (4) Execute the current interval at f^*. (See
            Figure 16.5 for the emulation scheme.)
        (5) Update mips(f^*).
    until the program is completed.

Figure 16.4   The β-adaptation algorithm.

(4) Execute the current interval at f^*.
    (4a) Figure out f_j and f_{j+1}.

$$f_j \leq f^* < f_{j+1}$$

(4b) Compute the ratio r.

$$r = \frac{(1 + \delta/\beta)/f_{\text{max}} - 1/f_{j+1}}{1/f_j - 1/f_{j+1}}$$

    (4c) Run $r \cdot I$ seconds at frequency f_j.
    (4d) Run $(1 - r) \cdot I$ seconds at frequency f_{j+1}.

Figure 16.5   Step (4) of the β-adaptation algorithm.

example, to emulate a frequency of 1.9 GHz, the frequency emulation step can emulate the frequency by running at 1.8 GHz for $I/2$ seconds and at 2.0 GHz for the rest of the $I/2$ seconds. Details are shown in Figure 16.5, where the ratio r denotes the percentage of time to execute at frequency f_j.

Figure 16.6 shows the execution behavior of the β-adaptation algorithm, specifically f^*, on three synthetic workloads, each with different compute bound-edness. Each synthetic workload iterates between a compute-intensive phase and a memory-intensive phase. For the workload labeled by X:Y, it means that each

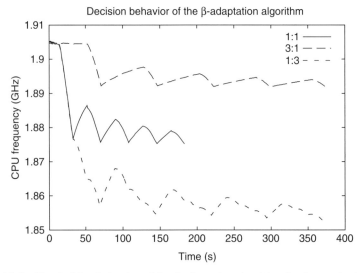

Figure 16.6   The decision behavior of the β-adaptation algorithm for the synthetic bench-mark.

compute-intensive phase takes X units of time to execute and each memory-intensive phase takes Y units of time to execute. More details on the synthetic workloads can be found in Section 16.4.2.

As shown in Figure 16.6, the β-adaptation algorithm quickly finds the proper value for f^* to be a little below 1.88 GHz and makes less and less fluctuations, as time goes by for the 1:1 workload. Similar behavior can be observed for the other two workloads. In a way, the effectiveness of the algorithm can also be attributed to the quick convergence of the values for β.

16.4 ALGORITHM EFFECTIVENESS

In this section, we present a series of analyses on the effectiveness of the β-adaptation algorithm. We start by comparing the experimental results of the β-adaptation algorithm with other DVFS algorithms in terms of physical measurements. We then present an in-depth discussion about two unique features of the algorithm—frequency emulation and the minimum dependence to the PMU—that lead to the effectiveness of the β-adaptation algorithm.

16.4.1 A Comparison to Other DVFS Algorithms

To evaluate the effectiveness of the β-adaptation algorithm, we compare its experimental results with four interval-based algorithms using the CPU utilization ratio or the IPC rate. Although we do not claim that the implemented DVFS algorithms represent a comprehensive comparison of all existing approaches, we feel that the range is wide enough to give us some hints about the effectiveness of β-adaptation. Following is a brief description of each algorithm that we implemented.

2step. This algorithm is based on the CPU utilization ratio and assumes dual CPU speeds in the processor. If the ratio is higher (or lower) than a predefined high (or low) threshold, the algorithm will set the CPU to the fastest (or slowest) speed. This algorithm is shown to be the most effective in an empirical study done by Grunwald et al. [11]. In our implementation, the two thresholds are 50% and 10%, respectively.

nqPID. This algorithm is also based on the CPU utilization ratio. It was proposed by Varma et al. as a refinement of *2step* [25]. Owing to its more complex mechanism for the prediction of the CPU utilization ratio borrowed from classical control theory, this algorithm significantly improved the control over performance loss that the *2step* algorithm lacks. The authors also found out that, unlike *2step*, the effectiveness of this algorithm is not critically dependent on the parameter values.

freq. This algorithm is based on the reclamation of the slack time between the actual processing time and the deadline [26, 27]. The algorithm keeps track of remaining CPU work in CPU cycles W_{left} and remaining time before the deadline in seconds T_{left}. The desired CPU frequency is then calculated as the work divided by the time, that is, $f^* = W_{\text{left}}/T_{\text{left}}$. This algorithm requires that the total amount of work be known a priori. In practice, the total work is often unpredictable [28] and not always a constant across frequencies [29].

mips. This algorithm is based on the IPC rate [30]. Given a target MIPS rate $\text{MIPS}_{\text{target}}$, the algorithm tracks the observed rate $\text{MIPS}_{\text{observed}}$ and adjusts the CPU frequency to $f^* = f_{\text{prev}} \cdot (\text{MIPS}_{\text{target}})/(\text{MIPS}_{\text{observed}})$, where f_{prev} is the frequency for the previous interval. In our experiments, each benchmark has its own target MIPS rate, which is derived by measuring the MIPS rate for the entire application and then dividing it by $(1 + \delta)$.

In order to acquire high fidelity experimental data, we set up our experiments to take physical measurements, as shown in Figure 16.7. The experimental results were collected through a Yokogawa WT210 digital power meter [31]. The power meter continuously sampled the instantaneous wattage at every 20 µs. The profiling and tested computer both ran the Linux operating system kernel. All the benchmarks were compiled by GNU compilers with optimization level -02. All the benchmarks were run to completion; each run took over a minute.

The hardware platform in our experiments was an HP NX9005 notebook computer. The choice of a notebook computer, instead of a desktop computer, was mainly due to our concern about measurement accuracy. Placing a shunt resistor in series with the desktop processor and its input power supply would induce large variations of current [32] and cause the power measurement to be imprecise. Given that the portion of system power consumption consumed by a processor in a notebook computer is generally much larger than the portion by a processor in a desktop computer, we feel that the measurement of a notebook computer provides an effective alternative.

The HP NX9005 computer includes an AMD Athlon XP-M 2200+ processor, 256-MB DDR SDRAM, 266-MHz front-side bus, a 30-GB hard disk, and a 15-in TFT LCD display. The processor has a total of 384-kB cache space. Because of the size of the cache, we use the SPEC CPU95 benchmarks in our tests instead of the more recent SPEC CPU2000 or CPU2006 benchmarks. Using the more recent SPEC CPU benchmarks would have magnified (and arguably, biased) the

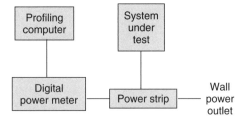

Figure 16.7   The experimental setup.

TABLE 16.2   The Effectiveness of Five Different DVFS Algorithms

Program	β	2step	nqPID	freq	mips	β-Adaptation
swim	0.02	1.00/1.00	1.04/0.70	1.00/0.96	1.00/1.00	1.04/0.61
tomcatv	0.24	1.00/1.00	1.03/0.69	1.00/0.97	1.03/0.83	1.00/0.85
su2cor	0.27	0.99/0.99	1.05/0.70	1.00/0.95	1.01/0.96	1.03/0.85
compress	0.37	1.02/1.02	1.13/0.75	1.02/0.97	1.05/0.92	1.01/0.95
mgrid	0.51	1.00/1.00	1.18/0.77	1.01/0.97	1.00/1.00	1.03/0.89
vortex	0.65	1.01/1.00	1.25/0.81	1.01/0.97	1.07/0.94	1.05/0.90
turb3d	0.79	1.00/1.00	1.29/0.83	1.03/0.97	1.01/1.00	1.05/0.94
go	1.00	1.00/1.00	1.37/0.88	1.02/0.99	0.99/0.99	1.06/0.96

Each table entry is in the format of *relative time/relative energy* with respect to the total execution time and system energy usage when running the application at the highest setting throughout the entire execution.

benefits of the algorithms because of the increased intensity of off-chip accesses due to larger data footprints. In any case, the SPEC CPU benchmarks exhibit a wide range of performance sensitivity to CPU frequency change, enabling us to capture the *average* effectiveness of the tested algorithms.

Table 16.2 presents the experimental results for the five interval-based DVFS algorithms. When a program is memory bound or I/O bound (β close to 0), there is substantial opportunity to reduce CPU energy consumption with negligible performance loss. In contrast, when a program is CPU bound, there is little opportunity to reduce CPU power and energy within a tight performance-loss bound of 5%. Moreover, none of these five DVFS algorithms could produce a DVFS schedule that had the exact performance degradation of 5%; the actual performance loss varied from one benchmark to another.

Among the five interval-based DVFS algorithms, the *β-adaptation* algorithm outperforms the others. In a sense, it verifies that our mechanism for computing CPU boundedness on the fly is of low overhead and that the algorithm is effective in providing tight control over performance loss due to DVFS as well as exploiting the sublinear performance slowdown for significantly more CPU power and energy savings. Algorithms *mips* and *nqPID* arguably rank second. Algorithm *mips* delivers better control over performance loss for all eight benchmarks that we tested, whereas algorithm *nqPID* performs better with respect to power and energy reduction but at the expense of more substantial performance loss. This is especially obvious for the CPU-bound benchmarks. Algorithms *freq* and *2step* clearly rank last in their effectiveness (or lack thereof).

So, what have we learned from this experiment? First, the number of instructions is a better metric for specifying the CPU work requirement than the number of CPU cycles. For the benchmarks we tested, we found that the number of instructions tends to remain constant across all settings. In contrast, the number of CPU cycles varies significantly depending on the executed DVFS schedule. For example, the swim benchmark, when running at the lowest setting, has only 60% of the CPU execution cycles running at the highest setting. Typically, algorithm *freq* uses the worst-case execution cycles, which in our case is the number of CPU cycles at the highest setting. This approach exaggerates the amount of the CPU work to be done and results in less effective energy reduction. This explains why algorithm *mips* performs better than algorithm *freq*.

Second, a large window size of past PMU reports is better than a small window size of past PMU reports. In the experiments, we found that the MIPS rate varies significantly from interval to interval, especially for CPU-intensive applications. However, the accumulated MIPS rate converges quickly. Thus, the use of the MIPS rate in a global manner seems to be more effective than the use of the rate in a local manner. This partially explains the effectiveness of algorithm *β-adaptation* compared to algorithm *mips*. One concern, however, for using a large window size is that the DVFS algorithm may be less responsive for programs that expose multiple execution phases of varying degrees of CPU boundedness.

Finally, we confirmed that CPU utilization by itself does not provide enough information about system timing requirements. As a result, the control over performance loss is unsatisfactory. This can be seen from the experimental results of algorithm *2step* and algorithm *nqPID*. Algorithm *2step* does not seem to perform any DVFS scheduling. This is because the CPU for the SPEC benchmarks is active almost all the time, that is, its CPU utilization is always full. In this case, there exists no optimal threshold values for *2step* to make it more effective. Algorithm *nqPID* refines algorithm *2step* by removing the threshold mechanism from the end user. While it is more effective than algorithm *2step* in terms of CPU power and energy reduction, the lack of enough information about deadlines makes it impossible to provide tight control over performance loss.

16.4.2 Frequency Emulation

A modern DVFS-enabled processor supports a limited set of discrete frequencies. As a consequence, the desired frequency, calculated by an interval-based DVFS algorithm, may not be supported directly. In the *β*-adaptation algorithm, we chose to emulate the frequency with its two neighboring supported frequencies. An alternative is to use a nearby supported frequency. In this section, we explore the importance of frequency emulation.

Consider a synthetic benchmark whose off-chip access pattern looks like Figure 16.8 with a sampling rate of 1 s. We designed the synthetic benchmark in such a way that the benchmark consists of two phases running interchangeably and iteratively. For Figure 16.8, the two phases follow each other, and each phase is iterated five times. The major difference between the two phases is that one phase contains a CPU-intensive workload while the other phase contains a memory-intensive workload. Many real applications exhibit this kind of off-chip access pattern, in particular, scientific codes that implement some type of iterative algorithm.

For the synthetic benchmark, we can enumerate all DVFS schedules in order to find the schedule that meets our needs. Assuming that each phase is allocated with one P-state from Table 16.1, we derive various performance and energy

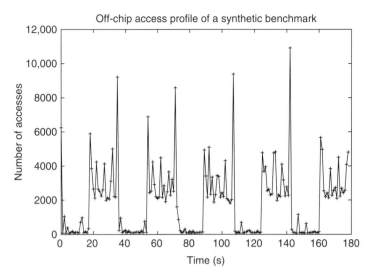

Figure 16.8   The off-chip access pattern of a synthetic benchmark.

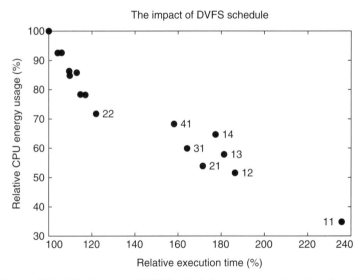

Figure 16.9   The impact of DVFS schedules on the synthetic benchmark.

impact from these schedules, as shown in Figure 16.9. Each point in the figure represents one distinct DVFS schedule. The XY mark next to a point indicates that the schedule associated with the point uses the Xth P-state to execute the CPU-intensive phase and uses the Yth P-state to execute the memory-intensive phase. Note that the higher the value of X or Y, the higher the CPU frequency.

Figure 16.9 provides several valuable information to us. First, running the synthetic benchmark at the slowest CPU speed (i.e., 0.8 GHz) for both phases, marked by point 11, hurts the benchmark performance significantly. Second, CPU energy reduction does not necessarily lead to system energy reduction. In fact, the DVFS schedule denoted by point 11 results in an increase in system energy consumption, although CPU energy usage is effectively reduced. Third, a DVFS schedule that reduces more CPU energy than the other schedule does not guarantee that the schedule will reduce more system energy consumption. We found out that naively running the CPU-intensive phase at the fastest CPU speed and the memory-intensive phase at the slowest speed (the DVFS schedule denoted by point 41) does not reduce more system energy consumption than running both phases at the fastest speed (the schedule denoted by 11). Finally, since all DVFS schedules involving the use of 0.8 GHz (from point 41 all the way to 11) sacrifice too much performance, that is, over 50%, it is undesirable to use the P3 state.

Figure 16.10 presents a zoomed view of the upper-left corner of Figure 16.9. From this zoomed graph, we acquire additional valuable information. In the previous paragraph, we argued against the use of the lowest CPU frequency. What about the second-lowest CPU frequency (i.e., 1.6 GHz)? From the figure, we see that the use or not use of this P-state depends on the degree of performance slowdown that a user would tolerate. If the performance slowdown is restricted within 8%, then the 1.6-GHz pair should not be used. Hence, a DVFS algorithm that assigns fixed P-states regardless of the performance requirement is not good.

Figure 16.10 shows an interesting (if not counterintuitive) case: the DVFS schedule denoted by point 34 finishes the program quicker than the schedule

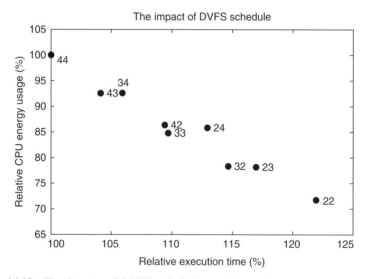

Figure 16.10 The impact of DVFS schedules on the synthetic benchmark—zoomed view.

denoted by 42. Intuitively, one would expect point 42 to locate on the left of point 34, meaning the preferred assignment of the CPU-intensive phases with a higher CPU frequency and the memory-intensive phases with a lower frequency. However, this is not always the case. These data points tell us that the induced execution time by a DVFS scheduling policy is quite complicated. For our example, it is the balance between different sensitivity levels of phases with respect to performance impact.

Hence, we have demonstrated that the intuition for setting the CPU frequency high for a CPU-intensive phase and low for a memory-intensive phase is inherently flawed. Furthermore, this pattern of setting the CPU-intensive phases to higher frequencies and memory-intensive phases to lower frequencies unnecessarily constrains the exploitation of DVFS for energy-efficient computing. For example, point 43 results in 4% performance slowdown while the next available scheduling policy following the above pattern is 42, which results in 9% performance slowdown. If the specified performance constraint is between 4% and 9%, then the pattern constraint only allows us to use scheduling policy 43 that underexploits the performance constraint and does not maximize the energy reduction.

Figure 16.11 shows the execution time and CPU energy consumption of running the synthetic benchmark at a single (possibly emulated) clock frequency from 2 GHz to 1.6 GHz at decrements of 0.25 GHz. As we can see from the figure, the use of a single CPU frequency to execute the synthetic benchmark provides various degrees of performance impact in a more predictable manner that is desired.

Finally, Figure 16.12 illustrates the effectiveness of the β-adaptation algorithm for the synthetic benchmark. The figure plots a set of five execution times and

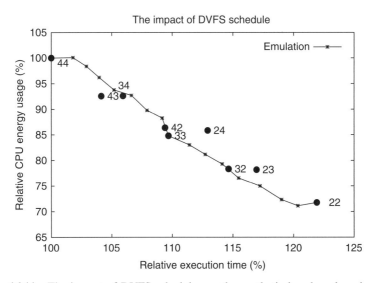

Figure 16.11   The impact of DVFS schedules on the synthetic benchmark—single frequency superimposed.

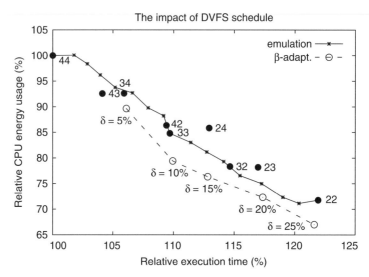

Figure 16.12   The energy savings delivered by the β-adaptation algorithm.

energy usage numbers for δ at 5%, 10%, 15%, 20%, and 25%, respectively. As we can see from the figure, the β-adaptation algorithm tightly regulates DVFS-induced performance slowdown, and in many cases, the actual performance slowdown is less than δ. More importantly, the algorithm performs better than the single-frequency scheme. Outperforming the single frequency indicates that the β-adaptation algorithm can emulate the desired single CPU frequency more precisely, which is also important.

In summary, through a series of experiments we found out that frequency emulation is critical to the effectiveness of the β-adaptation algorithm.

16.4.3   The Minimum Dependence to the PMU

As we mentioned earlier, many interval-based DVFS algorithms rely on the use of the PMU to compute their respective intensity metrics, thereby causing a portability problem across different hardware platforms. The β-adaptation algorithm only needs one event type, the number of instructions, and therefore minimizes the dependence on the PMU. In contrast, other similar algorithms such as [16, 17, 33–35] require two or more events to be monitored. In addition, they assume a specific performance behavior of the workload, whereas the β-adaptation algorithm does not. In this section, we explore these design issues in depth.

We start by contrasting the β-adaptation algorithm with Choi et al.'s algorithm [16, 17]. Choi et al. assume that the workload has the following execution-time model:

$$T(f) = w_{\text{on}} \cdot \frac{1}{f} + t_{\text{off}}, \tag{16.9}$$

where w_{on} and t_{off} are two metrics invariant to CPU frequency changes. In this model, the total execution time $T(f)$ at frequency f is decomposed into a frequency-dependent part and a frequency-independent part [36]. The frequency-dependent part models the time spent for the on-chip workload, in terms of CPU cycles w_{on}. The frequency-independent part models the time spent for off-chip accesses. The model may be inexact for out-of-order processors because on-chip execution may overlap with off-chip accesses [37, 38], but the error tends to be quite small in practice [16, 17].

The intensity metric that Choi et al. used in their algorithms, denoted as β_{CSP}, is the ratio of the frequency-independent part to the frequency-dependent part in Equation 16.9:

$$\beta_{CSP}(f) = f \cdot \frac{t_{off}}{w_{on}}. \qquad (16.10)$$

Basically, the metric β_{CSP} quantifies the memory boundedness. Its value lies in between 0 and ∞. The higher the β_{CSP}, the higher the memory boundedness. Since the β_{CSP} metric varies with CPU frequency changes, Choi et al.'s algorithm defines the metric as a vector of values, one for each CPU frequency. In contrast, the β-adaptation algorithm defines the metric as a single value because it is invariant to CPU frequency changes.

To compute β_{CSP}, Choi et al. applied the regression to the following equation:

$$\beta_{CSP}(f) = \frac{CPI(f)}{c_0} - 1 \quad \text{where} \quad CPI(f) = c_1 \cdot MPI + c_0 \qquad (16.11)$$

in order to estimate the value of c_0 and thus derive the β_{CSP} value [16]. This is done through observing two events, the number of instructions and the number of external memory accesses, and then calculating the number of CPU cycles per instruction $CPI(f)$ at frequency f and the number of memory accesses per instruction, MPI. Implicitly, they assume that MPI is invariant to CPU frequency changes.

In Reference 17, the equation changes as do the set of events monitored. The change is not due to the development of a better mechanism to compute β_{CSP}. Instead, it is because the new CPU type does not have PMU support for counting the number of memory accesses. As a result, three events are monitored instead of two.

Next, we contrast the β-adaptation algorithm with Ge et al.'s algorithm [33]. Both DVFS algorithms are based on the use of β. However, Ge et al.'s algorithm does not use regression to derive the β value. The algorithm estimates the on-chip computation time and off-chip access time directly. It assumes an execution-time model similar to Choi et al.'s algorithm:

$$T(f) = \sum_{i=cpu}^{L2} a_i \cdot \left(l_i \cdot \frac{f_{max}}{f} \right) + a_{mem} \cdot l_{mem}, \qquad (16.12)$$

where a_i's are the number of accesses to CPU, L1 cache, L2 cache, and the off-chip memory and l_i's are the average latency (at the peak CPU frequency) to these memory resources. On one hand, because of the model, the algorithm is able to compute the β directly without resorting to regression. On the other hand, four events need to be tracked to provide the values for a_i's. In addition, the values of l_i's are the averages of the execution times of some micro-benchmarks, which implicitly assume that the sampled execution times are drawn from the normal distribution. However, the assumption of the normal distribution may not hold in practice [39], affecting the accuracy of the execution-time model.

Huang and Feng's work [35] is similar to that of Ge et al. Their algorithm is also based on the use of β. By assuming an execution-time model, they were able to reformulate β as a function of the number of CPU stall cycles. As a result, the novelty of the algorithm is on how to estimate this number indirectly by means of the PMU. Huang and Feng proposed to derive this number from both on-chip measurement and off-chip measurement. The intention is to minimize effect of under- and over-estimation. To implement their algorithm, four events need to be monitored, some of which are very microarchtecture specific.

In summary, we compared the β-adaptation algorithm with other closely related algorithms to gain a deeper understanding of the design issues in a memory-aware DVFS algorithm. These other algorithms make stronger assumptions about the execution behavior, thereby resulting in greater dependence on the PMU. On one hand, the algorithm designed this way will be very effective on the hardware platform of the choice. On the other hand, the portability of the algorithm to other platforms is severely limited. The balance between effectiveness and portability becomes a design challenge in a memory-aware DVFS scheduling algorithm.

16.5   CONCLUSIONS AND FUTURE WORK

In this chapter, we demonstrated how we can embrace the memory wall to address the power wall for scientific computing. We proposed a software approach that provides the active-state power management of the CPU by means of DVFS and takes advantage of sublinear performance scaling in non-CPU activities. In detail, we presented a DVFS algorithm called the β-*adaptation algorithm*. This PMU-assisted, interval-based algorithm uses a compute-boundedness metric called β to capture the effect of sublinear performance scaling. By design, the algorithm minimizes its dependence on the PMU, which is essential for the portability of the algorithm. Through a series of physical measurements on real systems, the β-adaptation algorithm has proven to be effective. In particular, the algorithm provides tight control over DVFS-induced performance loss. We attribute part of the effectiveness to frequency emulation. Finally, the algorithm is simple to implement and transparent to the end users.

The β-adaptation algorithm can be improved in multiple ways. One particular direction is to use compiler hints as additional scheduling support. While this idea is not new [27, 40], the type of hint that the compiler should provide so that the overall DVFS algorithm is effective is still a research topic for general-purpose systems. To relieve the compiler from the difficulty of giving exact timing information off-line, we could have the compiler simply identify and distinguish execution phases of a program in terms of compute boundedness in an approximate manner. The β-adaptation algorithm can then be refined to compute the β value for each of these phases to further improve its effectiveness for memory-bound and I/O-bound programs.

ACKNOWLEDGMENTS

Part of the work was done while both authors were working for Los Alamos National Laboratory under the support of the US Department of Energy through contract W-7405-ENG-36.

REFERENCES

1. Manferdelli J, Govindaraju N, Crall C. Challenges and opportunities in many-core computing. Proc IEEE 2008;96:808–815.

2. Moore S. Multicore is bad news for supercomputers. IEEE Spectr 2008;45:11–15.

3. Wulf W, McKee S. Hitting the memory wall: implications of the obvious. SIGARCH Comput Arch News 1995;23(1):20–24.

4. Addressing Power and Thermal Challenges in the Datacenter, Intel Corporation, 2005 Jan, Intel Solution White Paper.

5. Mudge T. Special section on energy efficient computing. 2005; 54(6): 641–766.

6. Venkatachalam V, Franz M. Power reduction techniques for microprocessor systems. ACM Comput Surv 2005;37(3):195–237.

7. Nielsen L, Niessen C, Sparsø J, Berkel CV. Low-power operation using self-timed circuits and adaptive scaling of the supply voltage. IEEE Trans Very Large Scale Integr Syst 1994;2(4):391–397.

8. Mudge T. Power: a first class design constraint for future architectures. IEEE Comput 2001;34(4):52–58.

9. Weiser M, Welch B, Demers A, Shenker S. Scheduling for reduced CPU energy. In: Symposium on Operating Systems Design and Implementation; California, USA; 1994 Nov.

10. Pering T, Burd T, Brodersen R. The simulation and evaluation of dynamic voltage scaling algorithms. In: International Symposium on Low Power Electronics and Design; California, USA; 1998 Aug.

11. Grunwald D, Levis P, Farkas KI, Morrey CB III, Neufeld M. Policies for dynamic clock scheduling. In: Symposium on Operating System Design and Implementation; 2000 Oct. San Diego, California, USA;

12. Lorch J, Smith A. Operating system modifications for task-based speed and voltage scheduling. In: International Conference on Mobile Systems, Applications, and Services; California, USA; 2003 May.

13. Hsu C-H, Kremer U. The design, implementation, and evaluation of a compiler algorithm for CPU energy reduction. In: ACM SIGPLAN Conference on Programming Languages Design and Implementation; California, USA. 2003 Jun.

14. Hsu, C-H, Kremer U. Compiler-Directed Dynamic CPU Frequency and Voltage Scaling. In: Henkel J, Parameswaran S, editors. *Designing Embedded Processors: A Low Power Perspective*. Springer; Dordrecht, Netherlands; 2007.

15. Kotla R, Ghiasi S, Keller T, Rawson F. Scheduling processor voltage and frequency in server and cluster systems. In: Workshop on High-Performance, Power-Aware Computing; Colorado, USA; 2005 Apr.

16. Choi K, Soma R, Pedram M. Fine-grained dynamic voltage and frequency scaling for precise energy and performance trade-off based on the ration of off-chip access to on-chip computation time. In: Design Automation and Test in Europe; Paris, France. 2004 Feb.

17. Choi K, Soma R, Pedram M. Dynamic voltage and frequency scaling based on workload decomposition. In: International Symposium on Low Power Electronics and Design; California, USA; 2004 Aug.

18. Pan F, Freeh V, Smith D. Exploring the energy-time tradeoff in high-performance computing. In: Workshop on High-Performance, Power-Aware Computing; Colorado, USA; 2005 Apr.

19. Freeh V, Lowenthal D, Pan F, Kappiah N. Using multiple energy gears in MPI programs on a power-scalable cluster. In: ACM SIGPLAN Symposium on Principles and Practices of Parallel Programming; 2005 Jun.

20. Lim M, Freeh V, Lowenthal D. Adaptive, transparent frequency and voltage scaling of communication phases in MPI programs. In: International Conference for High Performance Computing, Networking, Storage and Analysis; Illinois, USA; 2006 Nov.

21. Freeh V, Pan F, Lowenthal D, Kappiah N, Springer R, Rountree B, Femal M. Analyzing the energy-time tradeoff in high-performance computing applications. IEEE Trans Parallel Distrib Syst 2007;18(6):835–848.

22. Freeh V, Kappiah N, Lowenthal D, Bletsch T. Just-in-time dynamic voltage scaling: exploiting inter-node slack to save energy in MPI programs. J Parallel Distrib Comput 2008;68(9):1175–1185.

23. Rountree B, Lowenthal D, de Supinski B, Schulz M, Freeh V, Bletsch T. Adagio: making DVS practical for complex HPC applications. In: International Conference on Supercomputing; Oregon, USA; 2009 Jun.

24. Garg S, Yeo C, Anandasivam A, Buyya R. Environment-conscious scheduling of HPC applications on distributed cloud-oriented data centers. J Parallel Distrib Comput 2011;71(6):732–749.

25. Varma A, Ganesh B, Sen M, Choudhary S, Srinivasan L, Jacob B. A control-theoretic approach to dynamic voltage scaling. In: International Conference on Compilers, Architectures, and Synthesis for Embedded Systems; California, USA; 2003 Oct.

26. AbouGhazaleh N, Mossé D, Childers B, Melhem R. Toward the placement of power management points in real time applications. In: Workshop on Compilers and Operating Systems for Low Power; California, USA; 2001 Sep.

27. Azevedo A, Issenin I, Cornea R, Gupta R, Dutt N, Veidenbaum A, Nicolau A. Profile-based dynamic voltage scheduling using program checkpoints in the COPPER framework. In: Design, Automation and Test in Europe Conference; Paris, France; 2002 Mar.

28. Lorch J, Smith A. Improving dynamic voltage algorithms with PACE. In: International Conference on Measurement and Modeling of Computer Systems; Massachusetts, USA; 2001 Jun.

29. Seth K, Anantaraman A, Mueller F, Rotenberg E. FAST: frequency-aware static timing analysis. In: International Real-Time Systems Symposium; Cancun, Mexico; 2003 Dec.

30. Childers B, Tang H, Melhem R. Adapting processor supply voltage to instruction-level parallelism. In: Kool Chips Workshop; California, USA; 2000 Dec.

31. Hirofumi N, Naoya N, Katsuya T. WT210/WT230 digital power meters. Yokogawa Technical Report 35; 2003.

32. Milenkovic A, Milenkovic M, Jovanov E, Hite D. An environment for runtime power monitoring of wireless sensor network platforms. In: IEEE Southeastern Symposium on System Theory; Alabama, USA; 2005 Mar.

33. Ge R, Feng X, Feng W, Cameron K. CPU MISER: a performance-directed, run-time system for power-aware clusters. In: International Conference on Parallel Processing; Xian, China; 2007 Sep.

34. Choi K, Soma R, Pedram M. Fine-grained dynamic voltage and frequency scaling for precise energy and performance trade-off based on the ratio of off-chip access to on-chip computation times. IEEE Trans Comput Aided Des 2005;24(1):18–28.

35. Huang S, Feng W. Energy-efficient cluster computing via accurate workload characterization. In: International Symposium on Cluster Computing and the Grid; Shanghai, China; 2009 May.

36. Hennessy J, Patterson D. Computer architecture: a quantitative approach. 3rd ed. San Mateo (CA): Morgan Kaufmann; 2002.

37. Hsu C-H, Kremer U, Hsiao M. Compiler-directed dynamic frequency and voltage scheduling. In: Workshop on Power-Aware Computer Systems; Massachusetts, USA; 2000 Nov.

38. Xie F, Martonosi M, Malik S. Compile time dynamic voltage scaling settings: Opportunities and limits. In: ACM SIGPLAN Conference on Programming Languages Design and Implementation; California, USA; 2003 Jun.

39. Settlemyer B, Hodson S, Kuehn J, Poole S. Confidence: analyzing performance with empirical probabilities. In: Workshop on Application/Architecture Co-design for Extreme-scale Computing; Crete, Greece; 2010 Sep.

40. AbouGhazaleh N, Mossé D, Childers B, Melhem R, Craven M. Collaborative operating system and compiler power management for real-time applications. In: IEEE Real-Time Embedded Technology and Applications Symposium; Washington DC, USA; 2003 May.

CHAPTER 17

MULTIPLE FREQUENCY SELECTION IN DVFS-ENABLED PROCESSORS TO MINIMIZE ENERGY CONSUMPTION

NIKZAD BABAII RIZVANDI, ALBERT Y. ZOMAYA, YOUNG CHOON LEE, ALI JAVADZADEH BOLOORI, and JAVID TAHERI

17.1 INTRODUCTION

Research on low power systems has received a great deal of attention in recent years since the sustainability of current technologies and practices has become a serious issue. A few example systems where lowering power usage is critical are listed below.

- *Wireless Sensors*. Several sensors extract data from the environment concurrently, transmit these data to a processing unit, and receive processed data accompanied by appropriate commands from the processing unit [1–4]. The sensors and their receiver/transmitter are generally powered by battery and/or solar cells.
- *Satellite Circuits*. Satellites typically involve massive number of complex circuits that must work in low power. These circuits are supplied by solar cells, the only available power supply in satellites.
- *Robots and Surveillance Devices*. These devices are heavily used in army, mine extraction, and difficult or unsafe environments for humans.
- *Cell Phones and Laptops*. These devices are powered by batteries that are expected to work for a long time.

In the meantime, stiff increases in energy price and the environmental impact of carbon dioxide emissions associated with energy generation and transportation

Energy-Efficient Distributed Computing Systems, First Edition.
Edited by Albert Y. Zomaya and Young Choon Lee.
© 2012 John Wiley & Sons, Inc. Published 2012 by John Wiley & Sons, Inc.

have forced the issue of reducing energy consumption to be extended to a broader range of system including high performance computing systems (HPCSs).

Various issues such as resource management in both software and hardware levels must be addressed to reduce energy consumption in HPCS. An important issue in hardware resource management is how to reduce power usage in processors. Recently, many hardware-based approaches have been proposed to efficiently reduce energy consumption, particularly for processors. Dynamic voltage–frequency scaling (DVFS) is perhaps the most appealing method incorporated into many recent processors. Energy savings with this method is based on the fact that the power consumption in CMOS circuits has direct relation with frequency and the square of voltage supply. In this case, the execution time and power consumption can be controlled by switching between processor's frequencies and voltages. Although this approach was initially designed for single-processor task scheduling [5], it has recently received much attention in multiprocessor systems as well [6, 7].

DVFS technique and task scheduling can be combined in two ways: (i) schedule generation and (ii) slack reclamation. In the schedule generation, tasks graph are (re)scheduled on DVFS-enabled processors in a global cost function including both energy saving and makespan to meet both energy and time constraints at the same time [8, 9]. In slack reclamation, which works as a postprocessing procedure on the output of scheduling algorithms, DVFS technique is used to minimize the energy consumption of tasks in a schedule generated by a separate scheduler. The existing methods based on DVFS technique, however, have two major shortcomings: (i) most of them focus on schedule generation and do not adequately take the slack reclamation approaches into account to save more energy and (ii) the existing slack reclamation methods use only one frequency for each task among all discrete set of processor's frequencies. Using one frequency usually results in uncovered slack time where processor and other devices only waste energy.

In this chapter, we focus on slack reclamation and propose a new slack reclamation technique, multiple frequency selection DVFS (MFS-DVFS). The key idea is to execute each task with a linear combination of more than one frequency such that this combination results in using the lowest energy by covering the whole slack time of the task. We have tested our algorithm with both random and real-world application task graphs and compared with the results in References 7 and 10. The experimental results show that our approach can achieve energy almost identical to the optimum energy saving.

17.2 ENERGY EFFICIENCY IN HPC SYSTEMS

Many electronic systems in our life such as satellite systems, cell phones, and game instruments use rechargeable batteries as their power supplies. Although the battery capacity has grown significantly in recent years (the battery capacity increases 5% per year), battery life is still the major drawback for most of the

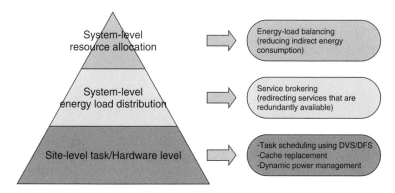

Figure 17.1   Energy consumption levels in HPCS.

electronic systems. In addition to power-aware battery-based systems, the issue of energy consumption has recently attracted a great amount of attention in HPCSs. Energy consumption issue in such systems can be classified into three groups: (i) system-level resource allocation, (ii) service-level energy load distribution, and (iii) task scheduling level (Fig. 17.1).

In the *system level*, the problem is how to distribute computational resources (e.g., CPU, network, memory, and I/O) between large-scale data storage and data processing centers (such as supercomputers and data centers). Fairly distributed resources among applications (or services) not only need to obtain individual adaptation among resources but also need to understand the interaction between individual resources when they work as a system. Therefore, the major chal- lenge here is to find both the relationship among system resources and their trade-off, which may cause an optimal balance between performance, QoS, and energy consumption [11]. Among the different technologies at system level for managing resources between workload, virtualization becomes a key technology in data centers. Virtualization allows the computational resources to be shared between different workload levels. Much of the incoming workload to data cen- ters is of medium size, often requiring a small fraction of the computational resources. The servers typically spend around 70% of their maximum power consumption even in low utilization. With virtualization, such a workload can run within a virtual machine (VM), causing significant savings in overall energy usage. The associated VMs may require fewer amounts of resources, and there- fore, they can be run on a single hardware unit. It is obvious that when less hardware is used, less energy is wasted for both operating and cooling of the servers.

At *service level*, energy reduction by load balancing, scheduling, and mapping workload is important. The main challenge is to utilize appropriate algorithms to both multiplex/demultiplex workload in order to save energy and make a trade-off between performance and service cost reduction because of energy savings. Also, to avoid hot spots in data centers due to high loaded nodes, services can be moved from nodes with high load and high temperature to nodes with smaller load and lower temperature. Generally, this movement of services should happen when the destination nodes can operate the services in an energy-efficient way [11].

At *site level data/task scheduling*, the focus of this chapter, the operating system (OS) and hardware configuration such as dynamic power management, microarchitecture techniques, and dynamic voltage scaling are used to decrease power. Here, the typical question could be

"What is the suitable OS/hardware configuration to process tasks in the shortest possible time and with minimum energy?"

17.3   EXPLOITATION OF DYNAMIC VOLTAGE–FREQUENCY SCALING

DVFS is a popular technique in computer architecture and is used to reduce the energy consumption of microprocessors or control the amount of the heat generated by circuits. This technique is commonly utilized in battery-based devices such as laptops and cell phones where decreasing the energy usage of battery is necessary. In addition, DVFS is used in high computing nodes not only to decrease the power of the nodes but also to save more energy to cool down the nodes' places. An approximation model shows that the dynamic power in CMOS circuits is a linear function of both switching frequency and square of the voltage, that is, CV^2f, where C is the effective switching capacity per clock cycle. Therefore, workload (or task) can save more energy when it is executed in lower voltage and frequency. In general, a computing node simultaneously executes several tasks with intertask relationships (e.g., precedence constraints). These intertask relationships typically incur slack time (idle time) between tasks where can be used by DVFS to reduce energy usage. Specifically, the slack time associated with a task is utilized to execute the task at a lower voltage–frequency; this in turn results in energy reduction.

There are two ways to combine scheduling and DVFS: (i) independent slack reclamation and (ii) integrated scheduling generation. The existing methods in literature based on these combinations have two major limitations: (i) most of them focus on integrating DVFS and scheduling (integrated schedule generation) and do not sufficiently consider the slack reclamation approaches to save more energy and (ii) the existing slack reclamation methods use only one frequency for each task among all discrete set of processor frequencies. Using one frequency usually results in uncovered slack time where processor and other devices only waste energy.

17.3.1   Independent Slack Reclamation

Independent slack reclamation works on the output of other scheduling algorithms as a postprocessing procedure by applying DVFS technique to minimize energy consumption of generated tasks by a scheduler. Kimura et al. [7] proposed an energy reduction algorithm for power-scalable clusters supporting DVFS. In a simplified version of this algorithm, the appropriate frequency is chosen among a set of processor frequencies for each task regarding its slack time. Another algorithm was proposed in Reference 10 to reclaim slack time for each task in a directed acyclic graph (DAG) by linear combination of the processor's highest and lowest frequencies. To the best of our knowledge, among the existing energy-aware algorithms in HPCSs, these two methods are the most similar approaches to our MFS-DVFS algorithm presented in this chapter. We address the simplified version of these two algorithms as reference DVFS (RDVFS) and maximum-minimum-frequency DVFS (MMF-DVFS) in the rest of this chapter and use them as benchmarks to evaluate the performance of our proposed algorithm.

17.3.2 Integrated Schedule Generation

In integrated schedule generation, task graphs are (re)scheduled on DVFS-enabled processors using a global cost function including both energy saving and makespan to meet both energy and time constraints at the same time [8, 9]. Therefore, the final schedule will be a trade-off between makespan and energy. Kappiah et al. [12] presented the just-in-time DVFS technique to fill slack time in MPI (message passing interface) programs. They utilized a system called *Jitter* to reduce the frequency on nodes with more slack times and fewer computations. Jitter aimed to make sure that the tasks came just in time without increasing overall execution time. The DVFS technique was applied in Reference 8 on processors that did not work in peak performance during execution of a parallel application. The best processor frequency of each task was selected by analyzing computation and communication power profiles collected before the execution. A method to reduce power consumption was presented in Reference 13 by adaptively activating and deactivating hardware resources and, in particular, memory for intensive HPC applications. Cache missing in accessing the main memory also plays an important role in adjusting and triggering processor slack times. Lee and Zomaya [9] presented a DVFS-based algorithm to minimize both completion time and energy consumption of precedence-constrained parallel jobs on HPCSs. This method tried to minimize a summation of two cost functions: completion time and energy. Consequently, the final result was a trade-off between the quality of scheduling and energy consumption. The concept of energy scalability in formal terms was introduced by Ding et al. [14]. In addition to studying the energy efficiency/isoefficiency concept, they extended an analytical model to investigate the trade-off between performance and energy saving in HPCS. Molnos and Goossens [15] classified the slack times in real-time applications into static, work, and shared lack groups for multiple dependent tasks on multiple DVFS-enabled processors. They proposed a dynamic dependency-aware task scheduling to adjust voltage/frequency of each processor regarding the tasks' real-time deadlines. A profile-based power-performance optimization method was presented in Reference 16 to also utilize DVFS in HPCS. Here, the execution of a program was divided into several regions. In trial steps, profile information of each region, including power and execution profiles was extracted and then utilized to find its best combination of the processors' voltages and frequencies. In Reference 17, an upper limit for system energy usage was selected externally. Subsequently, a combination of performance modeling and performance prediction was applied to reduce execution times with respect to their predefined energy usage upper limit. After creating models for both execution time and energy consumption, key parameters of models were estimated by executing a program for a small number of times and then regressing the estimated parameters. Here, for better estimation of parameters, the following steps were iterated until a proper schedule is achieved: (i) using models to predict each possible scheduling of tasks, (ii) executing the program a few times with the best predicted schedule, and (iii) updating estimated key parameters. Rountree et al. [18] proposed an energy-aware schedule generation algorithm for DVFS-enabled processors where a combination of all processor frequencies are used along with a linear programing method to perform the optimization.

17.4 PRELIMINARIES

In this section, the system, application, and energy models used in our study are described.

17.4.1 System and Application Models

In this work, we assume an HPCS composed of N homogeneous processors with individual memories. The switching time from one frequency to another is typically in microseconds (between 30 and 150 μs [19]), while the execution time of tasks is in milliseconds. Therefore, when compared with the tasks' execution time, the switching time can be ignored. We consider a set of M dependent tasks denoted as $A^{(1)}, A^{(2)}, \ldots, A^{(M)}$ represented by task graph or DAG. The kth task ($A^{(k)}$) has the following parameters (Fig. 17.2a): (i) $t_{OS}^{(k)}$ is the task execution time in the original scheduling without slack reclamation; (ii) $T^{(k)}$ is the whole time the processor assigns to this task and is a summation of the task's execution and slack times; (iii) $t_i^{(k)}$ represents the task execution time when it is executed in frequency f_i; (iv) $K^{(k)}$ is the number of tick cycles required for executing the task and can be calculated as $K^{(k)} = f_N t_{OS}^{(k)} = f_{RD}^{(k)} t_{RD}^{(k)}$, where f_N is the highest processor frequency; and (v) $f_{RD}^{(k)}$ and $t_{RD}^{(k)}$ are frequencies calculated from the RDVFS algorithm, explained in Section 17.5.2, and its associated time, respectively.

17.4.2 Energy Model

A typical DVFS-enabled processor can execute a task in a discrete set of frequencies ($f_1 < f_2 < \cdots > f_{N-1} < f_N$). For example, AMD Turion MT-34 can operate at six frequencies ranging from 800 to 1800 MHz [5]. The power consumption of a processor consists of two parts: (i) a dynamic part that is mainly

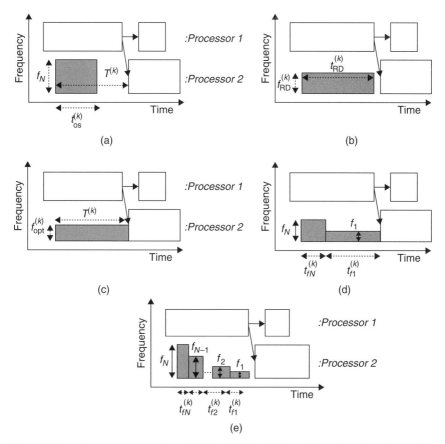

Figure 17.2 Time representation of MFS-DVFS and other algorithms: (a) the original scheduling, (b) the RDVFS algorithm, (c) the optimum continuous frequency, (d) the MMF-DVFS algorithm, and (e) our proposed method in this chapter (MFS-DVFS).

related to CMOS circuit switching energy and (ii) a static part that addresses the CMOS circuit leakage power [20]. In CPUs, the power consumption is formulated as [21]

$$\begin{cases} P_{\text{dynamic}} = C_{\text{eff}} f v^2 \\ P_{\text{leakage}} \propto v. \end{cases} \tag{17.1}$$

Here, C_{eff}, f, and v represent the effective capacitance and processor's frequency and voltage, respectively. Because the leakage power is always negligible when compared with the dynamic power [20], the overall energy consumption of the kth task ($A^{(k)}$) in DAG is calculated as

$$E^{(k)} = P_{\text{dynamic}} \, t_i^{(k)} + P_{\text{Idle}}(T^{(k)} - t_i^{(k)}). \tag{17.2}$$

CPU power consumption can be modeled as a convex function of frequency as $P_{\text{dynamic}} = \alpha f^3 + \gamma$ [21]. Therefore, the energy of kth task ($A^{(k)}$) in Equation 17.2 is changed to

$$E^{(k)} \approx (\alpha f^3 + \gamma)t_i^{(k)} + P_{\text{Idle}}(T^{(k)} - t_i^{(k)}). \qquad (17.3)$$

17.5   ENERGY-AWARE SCHEDULING VIA DVFS

In this section, we explain existing DVFS-based approaches to reduce energy consumption of processors by reclaiming the slack time for each task. Finally, we present our algorithm, MFS-DVFS, that uses a linear combination of frequencies to solve the stated problem.

17.5.1   Optimum Continuous Frequency

The optimal approach to remove slack time and as a result reduce energy consumption of a processor is to perform a task using a continuous frequency by the processor (Fig. 17.2c). Before moving further, proving the following theorems is necessary.

Theorem 17.1   *If f_1 and $f_2(> f_1)$ execute a task in t_1 and t_2, respectively, then, $E^{(k)}(f_1, t_1) < E^{(k)}(f_2, t_2)$.*

Proof:

$$E^{(k)}(f_2, t_2) - E^{(k)}(f_1, t_1) = (\alpha f_2^3 + \gamma)t_2 + P_{\text{Idle}}(T^{(k)} - t_2)$$
$$- (\alpha f_1^3 + \gamma)t_1 + P_{\text{Idle}}(T^{(k)} - t_1)$$
$$= \ldots$$
$$= (f_2 - f_1)[\alpha f_1 f_2(f_2 + f_1) - \gamma + P_{\text{Idle}}]$$
$$\geq 0$$

Generally, $P_{\text{Idle}} > \gamma$; therefore, Theorem 17.1 is proved.

Theorem 17.2   *If processor frequency is continuous (unrealistic assumption), the optimum energy for kth task is obtained when the task covers the whole task's slack time ($T^{(k)}$).*

Proof: The result in Theorem 17.1 shows that when a frequency covers the whole slack time, it gives the optimum power consumption. Note that this frequency may not exist unless the frequency set is continuous.

Refer to Theorem 17.2, for kth task $(A^{(k)})$, the optimum continuous frequency and its related energy are defined as $f^{(k)}_{\text{opt-cont}}$ and $E^{(k)}_{\text{opt-cont}}$ and are calculated as [10]

$$
\begin{cases}
f^{(k)}_{\text{opt-cont}} = f_N \dfrac{t^{(k)}_{\text{OS}}}{T^{(k)}} \\
E^{(k)}_{\text{opt-cont}} = [\alpha(f^{(k)}_{\text{opt-cont}})^3 + \gamma]T^{(k)}.
\end{cases}
\tag{17.4}
$$

In actual systems, however, frequencies must be chosen from a discrete set of frequencies. Also, finishing a task by its deadline may require choosing a frequency that is faster than the optimal frequency. Therefore, the *optimal discrete frequency* of kth task is the first frequency in the discrete set larger than $f^{(k)}_{\text{opt-cont}}$. This discrete frequency and its associated time are $f^{(k)}_{\text{RD}}$ and $t^{(k)}_{\text{RD}}$, respectively. The algorithm calculating this frequency is referred to as *RDVFS* for our comparison [7].

17.5.2 Reference Dynamic Voltage–Frequency Scaling (RDVFS)

RDVFS is a simplified version of the algorithm introduced by Kimura et al. [7] for power-scalable high performance clusters supporting DVFS. It reduces energy consumption of processors by selecting the smallest available processor frequency (f_{RDVFS}) capable of finishing a task in a given time frame (Fig. 17.2b). The details of RDVFS algorithm are shown in Figure 17.3.

RDVFS algorithm: slack reclamation by one frequency
Input: the scheduled tasks on a set of P processors
 1. **for** task $A^{(k)}$ scheduled on processor P_j
 2.   Compute the optimum continuous frequency ($f^{(k)}_{\text{opt-cont}}$) from Equation 17.4
 3.   Pick the closest higher frequency to $f^{(k)}_{\text{opt-cont}}$ in the cpu frequency set, e.g.

$$
\left.
\begin{array}{c}
[f_{\max}, \ldots, f_n, f_{n-1}, \ldots, f_{\min}] \\
f_{n-1} < f^{(k)}_{\text{opt-cont}} < f_n
\end{array}
\right\} \Rightarrow f^{(k)}_{\text{RDVFS}} = f_n
$$

 4. $t^{(k)}_{\text{RDVFS}} \leftarrow \dfrac{f^{(k)}_{\text{opt-cont}}}{f^{(k)}_{\text{RDVFS}}} T^{(k)}$

 5. $E_{\text{RDVFS}} \leftarrow f^{(k)}_{\text{RDVFS}} t^{(k)}_{\text{RDVFS}} + P_{\text{Idle}} \left(T^{(k)} - t^{(k)}_{\text{RDVFS}} \right)$

 6. **end for**
 7. **return** ($f^{(k)}_{\text{RDVFS}}$ and $t^{(k)}_{\text{RDVFS}}$ for all tasks)

Figure 17.3 RDVFS algorithm.

For each task assigned to a processor, f_{RDVFS}, which is the first frequency larger than optimal frequency ($f_{\text{opt-cont}}$) calculated from Equation 17.4, is likely to be the best discrete frequency candidate to execute the task within the given time frame and covering its related slack time. As mentioned before, a major limitation of RDVFS technique is the usage of only one frequency to execute the task.

17.5.3 Maximum-Minimum-Frequency for Dynamic Voltage–Frequency Scaling (MMF-DVFS)

The MMF-DVFS technique presented in Reference 10 is similar to RDVFS as both these approaches use DVFS to reduce energy consumption of scheduled dependent tasks in clusters. Unlike RDVFS algorithm which applies only one frequency to execute a task, MMF-DVFS uses a linear combination of maximum and minimum processor frequencies to achieve the optimal energy consumption regarding to slack time of the task, as shown in Figure 17.2d. Before explaining further details of MMF-DVFS, proving the following lemma is essential.

Lemma 17.1 If f_{DVFS} is the appropriate DVFS frequency obtained from RDVFS algorithm with task's energy consumption E_{DVFS}, then there is always a linear combination of the processor's minimum and maximum frequencies with energy consumption less than E_{DVFS}.

Proof: If f_N, f_1, and f_{DVFS} are the maximum, minimum, and appropriate DVFS processor frequencies extracted from DVFS algorithm, then the lemma indicates that the following nonequation always has nonzero values for t_{f_N} and t_{f_1} for kth task:

$$\begin{cases} E_{f_N} + E_{f_1} \leq E_{\text{DVFS}} \\ t_{f_N} + t_{f_1} \leq T. \end{cases} \tag{17.5}$$

According to Equation 17.3, $E_f \approx K f^3 t$. By combining this with Equation 17.5, we achieve the following equation:

$$\begin{cases} f^3{}_N {}^* t_{f_N} + f^3{}_1 {}^* t_{f_1} \leq f^3_{\text{DVFS}} {}^* (t_{f_N} + t_{f_1}) \\ t_{f_N} + t_{f_1} \leq T. \end{cases} \tag{17.6}$$

Assuming $t_{f_N} + t_{f_1} = T$, the Equation 17.6 converts to

$$0 \leq t_{f_N} \leq \frac{f_{\text{DVFS}} - f_1}{f_N - f_{\text{DVFS}}} {}^* t_{f_1},$$

indicating that there is always a valid positive t_{f_N} and t_{f_1}. The details of MMF-DVFS algorithm are shown in Figure 17.4.

MMF-DVFS algorithm: *linear combination of maximum and minimum*
   frequencies
Input: *the scheduled tasks on a set of P processors*
 1. **for** *task* $A^{(k)}$ *scheduled on processor* P_j
 2.   *Calculate amount of time for* $f_{\max}, f_{\min}$:

- $t_{f_N}^{(k)} \leftarrow \dfrac{f_{\mathrm{RDVFS}}^{(k)} t_{\mathrm{RDVFS}}^{(k)} - T^{(k)} f_1}{f_N - f_1}$

- $t_{f_1}^{(k)} \leftarrow \dfrac{T^{(k)} f_N - f_{\mathrm{RDVFS}}^{(k)} t_{\mathrm{RDVFS}}^{(k)}}{f_N - f_1}$

 3. $E(k)_{MMF\text{-}DVFS} \leftarrow f_N^3 t_N^{(k)} + f_1^3 t_1^{(k)}$

 4.   **end for**
 5. **return** *(the set of* $(t_N^{(k)}, t_1^{(k)})$ *for all tasks)*

Figure 17.4   MMF-DVFS algorithm.

The MMF-DVFS algorithm finds the appropriate time portions of the maximum and minimum frequencies to execute each scheduled task. It can be seen from Figure 17.7 that the MMF-DVFS algorithm works in the same way as RDVFS in the worst case.

In the next section, we present the MFS-DVFS algorithm, which uses a linear combination of a variety of processor frequencies instead of two to perform a predefined task (Fig. 17.2e). The new approach is more energy efficient compared to the other algorithms discussed earlier in this chapter; its energy saving is quite close to the case of using continuous optimum frequency.

17.5.4 Multiple Frequency Selection for Dynamic Voltage–Frequency Scaling (MFS-DVFS)

The RDVFS algorithm decreases task execution energy by choosing the best processor's speed with respect to the task's idle time [7]. As an example, a set of four tasks scheduled on two processors is shown in Figure 17.2a, where Figure 17.2b, c, and d shows the results of applying the RDVFS, optimum continuous frequency, and MMF-DVFS algorithms on the task, respectively. Figure 17.2e also shows the principle of MFS-DVFS algorithm, the proposed algorithm in this chapter. Initially, the task is executed for $t_N^{(k)}$ time units with the highest processor frequency, then its execution frequency is reduced to the second highest value and spends $t_{N-1}^{(k)}$ time units in this frequency. Then, the frequency decreases, and the task is executed in other frequencies until it is finished.

The key idea of MFS-DVFS is to execute tasks using a linear combination of available frequencies so that their slack times are fully filled/covered. MFS-DVFS can be defined as finding the best combination of available frequencies $(f_1 < \ldots < f_N)$ to perform a predefined task with K steps of computation within a predefined time T. Therefore, the minimization of power consumption of the kth task $(A^{(k)})$ in MFS-DVFS algorithm is formulated as an optimization problem as follows:

$$
\begin{cases}
\text{Min}: & E^{(k)} = \sum_{i=1}^{N} t_i^{(k)} (\alpha f_i^3 + \gamma) + P_{\text{Idle}} \left(T^{(k)} - \sum_{i=1}^{N} t_i^{(k)} \right) \\
\text{s.t.} & \\
& 1. \ \sum_{i=1}^{N} t_i^{(k)} f_i = K^{(k)} \\
& 2. \ \sum_{i=1}^{N} t_i^{(k)} \leq T^{(k)} \\
& 3. \ t_i^{(k)} \geq 0, \qquad \text{for} \quad i = 1, 2, \ldots, N.
\end{cases}
\tag{17.7}
$$

The optimization problem in Equation (17.7) represents the power consumption problem: how to choose $t_i^{(k)}$ so that the consumed energy of task $A^{(k)}$ is minimized. For executing the task, the processor has to use the same number of clock ticks in both RDVFS and MMF-DVFS algorithms as described by constraint 1 in Equation (17.7). Applying the two aforementioned theorems simplifies the optimization problem in Equation (17.7) to

$$
\begin{cases}
\text{Min}: & E^{(k)} = \sum_{i=1}^{N} t_i^{(k)} (\alpha f_i^3 + \gamma) \\
\text{s.t.} & \\
& 1. \ \sum_{i=1}^{N} t_i^{(k)} f_i = K^{(k)} \\
& 2. \ \sum_{i=1}^{N} t_i^{(k)} = T^{(k)} \\
& 3. \ t_i^{(k)} \geq 0, \qquad \text{for} \quad i = 1, 2, \ldots, N.
\end{cases}
\tag{17.8}
$$

To find the best possible values of $t_i^{(k)}$, this optimization algorithm must be applied to all tasks in the scheduling. There are cases that MFS-DVFS cannot improve the power consumption, for example, when a task reaches to f_1 (the lowest frequency) in the RDVFS algorithm or it has no idle time. Therefore, to improve the speed of MFS-DVFS algorithm, eligible tasks should be extracted before optimization

17.5.4.1 Task eligibility.
To simplify the formulation, let us consider four discrete values for frequencies (the real processors have normally four to five frequencies). In any case, the same procedure can be used for the higher number

of frequencies. The problem in Equation 17.7 becomes

$$
\begin{cases}
\text{Min}: & E^{(k)} = \sum_{i=1}^{4} t_i^{(k)} (\alpha f_i^3 + \gamma) \\[2mm]
\text{s.t.} & \\[1mm]
& 1.\ t_1^{(k)} f_1 + t_2^{(k)} f_2 + t_3^{(k)} f_3 + t_4^{(k)} f_4 = K^{(k)} \\[2mm]
& 2.\ t_1^{(k)} + t_2^{(k)} + t_3^{(k)} + t_4^{(k)} = T^{(k)} \\[2mm]
& 3.\ t_i^{(k)} \geq 0, \qquad \text{for} \quad i = 1, 2, \ldots, 4.
\end{cases}
$$

Merging constraints 2 and 3 results in

$$
\begin{cases}
t_1^{(k)} = \dfrac{T^{(k)} f_2 - K^{(k)}}{f_2 - f_1} - t_3^{(k)} \dfrac{f_2 - f_3}{f_2 - f_1} - t_4^{(k)} \dfrac{f_2 - f_4}{f_2 - f_1} \\[4mm]
t_2^{(k)} = \dfrac{K^{(k)} - T^{(k)} f_1}{f_2 - f_1} - t_3^{(k)} \dfrac{f_3 - f_1}{f_2 - f_1} - t_4^{(k)} \dfrac{f_4 - f_1}{f_2 - f_1}.
\end{cases}
$$

Therefore, the power consumption function changes to

$$
E^{(k)} = a_0^{(k)} + a_1^{(k)} t_3^{(k)} + a_2^{(k)} t_4^{(k)}, \tag{17.9}
$$

where

$$
\begin{aligned}
a_0^{(k)} &= (\alpha f_1^3 + \gamma) \dfrac{T^{(k)} f_2 - K^{(k)}}{f_2 - f_1} + (\alpha f_2^3 + \gamma) \dfrac{K^{(k)} - T^{(k)} f_1}{f_2 - f_1}, \\[3mm]
a_1^{(k)} &= (\alpha f_3^3 + \gamma) + (\alpha f_1^3 + \gamma) \dfrac{f_3 - f_2}{f_2 - f_1} - (\alpha f_2^3 + \gamma) \dfrac{f_3 - f_1}{f_2 - f_1}, \\[3mm]
a_2^{(k)} &= (\alpha f_4^3 + \gamma) + (\alpha f_1^3 + \gamma) \dfrac{f_4 - f_2}{f_2 - f_1} - (\alpha f_2^3 + \gamma) \dfrac{f_4 - f_1}{f_2 - f_1}.
\end{aligned} \tag{17.10}
$$

To guarantee achieving less energy consumption using MFS-DVFS algorithm, the following condition should be satisfied:

$$
a_0^{(k)} + a_1^{(k)} t_3^{(k)} + a_2^{(k)} t_4^{(k)} < E_{\text{RD}}^{(k)}.
$$

$a_0^{(k)} + a_1^{(k)} t_3^{(k)} + a_2^{(k)} t_4^{(k)}$ shows a three-dimensional surface, and the search region is where it satisfies the three following constraints: (i) $t_3^{(k)} \geq 0$, (ii) $t_4^{(k)} \geq 0$, and (iii) $E_{\text{RD}}^{(k)} > 0$. The first two constraints in Equation 17.11 are also considered by optimization in Equation 17.8. The only constraint that specifies the search region is constraint 3. If a task satisfies this constraint, then it can be concluded that there is a valid search region for this task where MFS-DVFS gives better result than RDVFS. Then linear programing explores this search region to find out the best suitable frequencies and their associated times. The details of MFS-DVFS algorithm are shown in Figure 17.5.

```
MFS-DVFS algorithm: linear combination of frequencies
Input: the scheduled tasks on a set of P processors
  1.  For task A^(k) scheduled on processor P_j
  2.      Apply RDVFS algorithm on this task
  3.      if E_RD^(k) > 0 for this task then
              - this task is eligible for MFS-DVFS
              - Solve optimization problem in Equation 17.6 by
                  linear programing
          else
              RDVFS is the optimal result
  4.      end if
  5.  end for
  6. return (the voltages and frequencies of optimal execution)
```

Figure 17.5   MFS-DVFS algorithm.

17.6 EXPERIMENTAL RESULTS

In this section, we present the results of energy consumption obtained from simulating our MFS-DVFS algorithm in comparison with RDVFS, MMF-DVFS, and optimum continuous frequency. In order to compare the algorithms, the following schedulers were used with a different number of processors: (i) list scheduling, (ii) list scheduling with longest processing time (LPT) first, and (iii) list scheduling with shortest processing time (SPT) first.

The simulations were carried out using the simulator we developed as a part of this study.

17.6.1 Simulation Settings

We use the voltage/frequency setting of two real processors in our simulations: Transmeta Crusoe [7] and Intel XScale [22]. Table 17.1 shows the voltage/frequency and the related power consumption of these processors following the convex models of each processor. These models use least-square curve fitting to fit a convex function $(\alpha f^3 + \gamma)$ on the frequency-power of two real processors, as shown in Figure 17.6.

We evaluate the performance of MFS-DVFS with two sets of task graphs: randomly generated and real-word parallel applications. The two real-world applications used in our experiments were LU decomposition and Gauss–Jordan method, with DAGs extracted from Reference 19. We applied a large number of variations in the number of processors and tasks for each application in our simulations. The random task graph set consisted of 1500 graphs with five graph sizes of 100, 200, 300, 400, and 500 nodes, together with three different schedulers on five sets of 2, 4, 8, 16, and 32 processors.

These task graphs have different number of tasks, task distributions, communication costs, and task dependencies. The execution cycle of these randomly

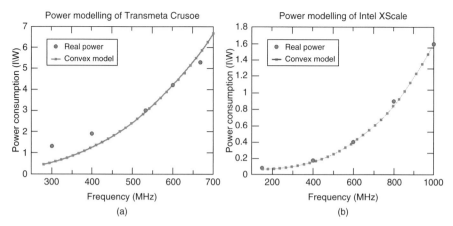

Figure 17.6 The least-square modeling of (a) Transmeta Crusoe, and (b) Intel XScale processors.

TABLE 17.1 **The Voltage/Frequency Setting of Two Real Processors in the Experiments with Their Power Consumption and Convex Models**

Level	Frequency (MHz)	Voltage (V)	Power (W)
	Transmeta Crusoe		
0	667	1.6	5.3
1	600	1.5	4.2
2	533	1.35	3.0
3	400	1.225	1.9
4	300	1.2	1.3
Convex model	$P = 1.94 \times 10^{-5} \left(\dfrac{f}{10^6} \right)^3 + 4.44$ mW		
	Intel XScale		
0	1000	1.8	1.6
1	800	1.6	0.9
2	600	1.3	0.4
3	400	1	0.17
4	150	0.75	0.08
Convex model	$P = 1.55 \times 10^{-6} \left(\dfrac{f}{10^6} \right)^3 + 60$ mW		

generated tasks varied from 5–10 million cycles from a uniform distribution. We used 150 real-world application task graphs based on LU decomposition algorithm in our experiments. For the real-wold application graph, the same number of task graphs, ranging from 100 to 500 tasks, with three schedulers and five sets of processors was investigated.

17.6.2 Results

The simulation results of normalized energy consumption for all DAGs (Figs. 17.7 and 17.8) are shown in Table 17.2. This table clearly denotes the superior performance of MFS-DVFS scheduling compared to the other approaches in all cases. Figure 17.8 shows the significance of all algorithms,

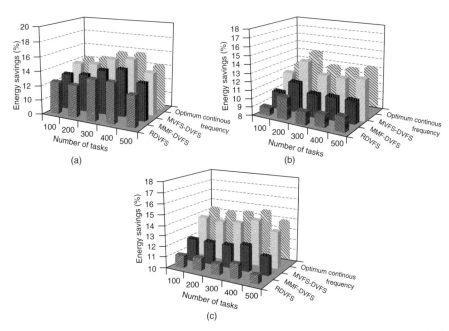

Figure 17.7 The normalized energy consumption on the number of tasks: (a) the typical list scheduler, (b) the list scheduler with longest processing time (LPT) first, and (c) the list scheduler with shortest processing time (SPT) first.

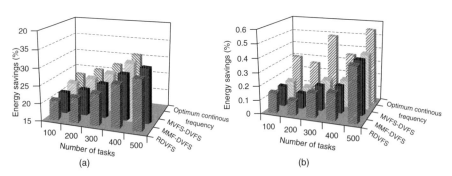

Figure 17.8 The normalized energy consumption of MFS-DVFS and other algorithms on the number of tasks for two real-world applications: (a) LU decomposition and (b) Gauss–Jordan method.

TABLE 17.2   The Energy Saving Percentage of MFS-DVFS and Other Algorithms on 1800 Random and Real Task Graphs

Experiment	Random Tasks, %	Gauss–Jordan Method, %	LU Decomposition, %
RDVFS	13.00	0.1	24.8
MMF-DVFS	13.50	0.11	25.5
MVFS-DVFS	14.40	0.11	27.0
Optimum continuous frequency	14.84	0.14	27.81

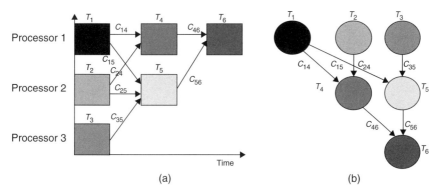

(a)   (b)

Figure 17.9   Gauss–Jordan task graph: (a) a sample scheduling of a three-level Gauss–Jordan task graph on three processors and (b) a Gauss–Jordan DAG for three levels. The communication costs (C_{ij}) are equal to 10 time units for all i and j.

including MFS-DVFS, in saving energy in LU decomposition, while these algorithms have less effect on performance in the case of Gauss–Jordan tasks. For a deeper examination of this behavior, a sample three-level Gauss–Jordan application job scheduling on three processors is shown in Figure 17.9. As explained earlier, since there is no idle time among the tasks in Gauss–Jordan graph applications, none of these algorithms can efficiently reduce energy consumption.

An interesting issue for further investigation is the relationship between energy consumption and the number of processors in our experiments. Increasing the number of processors expedites the processing time and consequently reduces the makespan; however, as a drawback, it also increases the system slack time. Figure 17.10 addresses this issue and illustrates the percentage of overall energy saving of the system on the number of processors for random and LU decomposition task graphs. The graphs in this figure reveal the fact that increasing the number of processors results in saving more energy.

The major limitation on most DVFS-based algorithms working with one frequency (such as the RDVFS algorithm) is that the frequency combinations are fixed. Those algorithms work better when the processor can run at any arbitrary

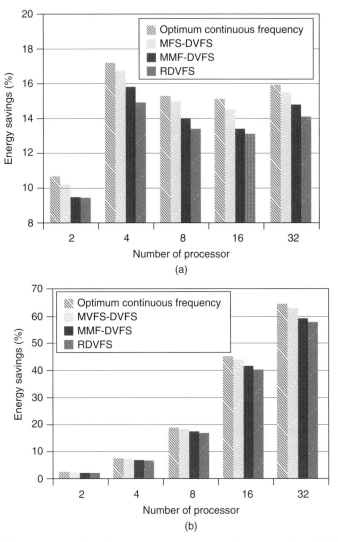

Figure 17.10 The comparison between the percentages of energy savings in MFS-DVFS with other algorithms on the number of processors: (a) 1500 randomly generated task graphs and (b) 300 LU decomposition task graphs.

set of frequencies. However, owing to technological constraints, the number of valid frequencies is limited so that these algorithms have to choose the most appropriate frequency among a set of frequencies defined by DVFS. According to the fixed number of tick cycles for a task (constraint 1 in Equation 17.8), the relation among $t_{\text{RD}}^{(k)}$, $f_{\text{RD}}^{(k)}$, f_N, and $t_{\text{OS}}^{(k)}$ for task $A^{(k)}$ is

$$t_{\text{RD}}^{(k)} = \frac{f_{\text{RD}}^{(k)}}{f_N} \, t_{\text{OS}}^{(k)}.$$

It is shown that although $t_{RD}^{(k)}$ is a continuous variable, it cannot accept all values; therefore, the slack time of tasks cannot be minimized. However, in MFS-DVFS algorithm, the relation between those variables is

$$f_{RD}^{(k)}t_{RD}^{(k)} = f_1 t_{1_{RD}}^{(k)} + f_2 t_{2_{RD}}^{(k)} + \cdots + f_N t_{N_{RD}}^{(k)},$$

which is one equation with more than one variable $\left(t_{1_{RD}}^{(k)}, \cdots, t_N^{(k)}\right)$ and might have many eligible results; thus, the appropriate values of these variables, with regard to the task conditions, can minimize the slack time and/or reduce energy consumption.

An overhead with MFS-DVFS and MMF-DVFS is the transition time of switching from one frequency to another. An almost true assumption is that the overhead of transition times is relatively much less than the execution times of tasks; therefore the transition times overhead can be neglected in the calculation. In our experiments, the tasks with T at least 20 times more than transition time is considered for the MFS-DVFS algorithm.

17.7 CONCLUSION

Since most traditional static task scheduling algorithms for HPCS do not consider power management, we addressed the energy issue with task scheduling and presented the MFS-DVFS algorithm. Our algorithm adopted the DVFS technique, a recent advance in processor design, to reduce energy consumption.

In this chapter, we studied the existing DVFS-based approaches to cover idle time, particularly, using a linear combination of more than one frequency to reduce energy consumption of processors. First, we noticed the energy model in DVS-enabled processors. Then, we formulated our algorithm (MFS-DVFS) as an optimization problem of all frequencies for each task and then solved it to find the suitable time portions. Simulation results of 1500 randomly generated task graphs and 300 real-world application task graphs showed the effectiveness of the MFS-DVFS algorithm compared with other algorithms.

ACKNOWLEDGMENT

The work reported in this chapter is in part supported by National ICT Australia (NICTA). Professor A. Y. Zomaya's work is supported by the Australian Research Council grant LP0884070.

REFERENCES

1. Kamyabpour N, Hoang DB. Modeling overall energy consumption in Wireless Sensor Networks. In: 11th International Conference on Parallel and Distributed Computing, Applications and Technologies (PDCAT-10); Perth, Australia; 2010 Dec 8–11.

2. Kamyabpour N, Hoang DB. A Task Based Sensor-Centeric Model for overall Energy Consumption, Computing Research Repository(CoRR), 2012.

3. Almiani K, Selvakennedy S, Viglas A. RMC: An Energy-Aware Cross-Layer Data-Gathering Protocol for Wireless Sensor Networks, presented at the 22nd International Conference on Advanced Information Networking and Applications (AINA), GinoWan, Okinawa, Japan, 2008.

4. Almiani K, Viglas A, Libman L. Energy-efficient data gathering with tour length-constrained mobile elements in wireless sensor networks, presented at The 35th Annual IEEE Conference on Local Computer Networks (LCN), Denver, Colorado, USA, 2010.

5. Zhuo J, Chakrabarti C. Energy-efficient dynamic task scheduling algorithms for DVS systems. ACM Trans Embed Comput Syst; 2008;7:1–25.

6. Ge R, Feng X, Cameron KW. Performance-constrained Distributed DVS Scheduling for scientific applications on power-aware clusters. In: Presented at the Proceedings of the 2005 ACM/IEEE Conference on Supercomputing; Washington, USA; 2005.

7. Kimura H, Sato M, Hotta Y, Boku T, Takahashi D. Empirical study on reducing energy of parallel programs using slack reclamation by DVFS in a power-scalable high performance cluster. In: IEEE International Conference on Cluster Computing; Barcelona, Spain; 2006. pp. 1–10.

8. Xiaojun R, Xiao Q, Ziliang Z, Bellam K, Nijim M. An energy-efficient scheduling algorithm using dynamic voltage scaling for parallel applications on clusters. In: Proceedings of 16th International Conference on Computer Communications and Networks, ICCCN 2007; Hawaii, USA; 2007. pp. 735–740.

9. Lee YC, Zomaya AY. Minimizing energy consumption for precedence-constrained applications using dynamic voltage scaling. In: Presented at the Proceedings of the 2009 9th IEEE/ACM International Symposium on Cluster Computing and the Grid (CCGrid); Shanghai, China; 2009.

10. Rizvandi NB, Taheri J, Zomaya AY, Lee YC. Linear combinations of DVFS-enabled processor frequencies to modify the energy-aware scheduling algorithms. In: Presented at the Proceedings of the 2010 10th IEEE/ACM International Symposium on Cluster, Cloud and Grid Computing (CCGrid); 2010 May 17–20; Melbourne, Australia.

11. Berl A, Gelenbe E, Girolamo M, Giuliani G, Meer H, Dang MQ, Pentikousis K. Energy-efficient cloud computing. Comput J 2009;53(7):1045–1051.

12. Kappiah N, Freeh VW, Lowenthal DK. Just in time dynamic voltage scaling: exploiting inter-node slack to save energy in MPI programs. In: Presented at the Proceedings of the 2005 ACM/IEEE conference on Supercomputing; Washington, USA; 2005.

13. Zhu Z, Zhang X. Look-Ahead Architecture Adaptation to Reduce Processor Power Consumption, *IEEE Micro*, vol. 25, pp. 10–19, 2005.

14. Ding Y, Malkowski K, Raghavan P, Kandemir M. Towards energy efficient scaling of scientific codes. In: IEEE International Symposium on Parallel and Distributed Processing, IPDPS 2008; Florida, USA; 2008. pp. 1–8.

15. Molnos A, Goossens K. Conservative dynamic energy management for real-time dataflow applications mapped on multiple processors. In: Presented at the 12th Euromicro Conference on Digital System Design, Architectures, Methods and Tools; Patras, Greece; 2009.

16. Hotta Y, Sato M, Kimura H, Matsuoka S, Boku T, Takahashi D. Profile-based optimization of power performance by using dynamic voltage scaling on a PC cluster. In: presented at the IEEE International Symposium on Parallel and Distributed Processing (IPDPS); Rhodes, Greece; 2006.

17. Springer R, Lowenthal DK, Rountree B, Freeh VW. Minimizing execution time in MPI programs on an energy-constrained, power-scalable cluster. In: Presented at the Proceedings of the 11th ACM SIGPLAN Symposium on Principles and Practice of Parallel Programming. New York; 2006.

18. Rountree B, Lowenthal DK, Funk Sh, Freeh VW, Supinski BR, Schulz M. Bounding energy consumption in large-scale MPI programs. In: Proceedings of the 2007 ACM/IEEE Conference on Supercomputing, SC '07; 2007, pp. 1–9.

19. Simunic T, Benini L, Acquaviva A, Glynn P, Micheli GD. Dynamic voltage scaling and power management for portable systems. In: Presented at the Proceedings of the 38th Annual Design Automation Conference; Las Vegas (NV); 2001.

20. Langen PD, Juurlink B. Trade-offs between voltage scaling and processor shutdown for low-energy embedded multiprocessors. In: Presented at the Embedded Computer Systems: Architectures, Modeling, and Simulation; Samos, Greece; 2007.

21. Chen J-J, Yang ChY, Kuo T.W, Shih Ch.Sh. Energy-efficient real-time task scheduling in multiprocessor DVS systems. In: Presented at the Proceedings of the 2007 Asia and South Pacific Design Automation Conference; 2007.

22. Xian C, Lu Y-H. Dynamic voltage scaling for multitasking real-time systems with uncertain execution time. In: Presented at the Proceedings of the 16th ACM Great Lakes symposium on VLSI. Philadelphia (PA); 2006.

CHAPTER 18

THE PARAMOUNTCY OF RECONFIGURABLE COMPUTING

REINER HARTENSTEIN

18.1 INTRODUCTION

In reconfigurable computing (RC), for example, by field-programmable gate array (FPGA), practically everything, which is running on traditional computing platforms, can be implemented. For instance, recently, the historical Cray 1 supercomputer has been reproduced as cycle-accurate and binary-compatible using a single Xilinx Spartan-3E 1600 development board running at 33 MHz (the original Cray ran at 80 MHz) [1]. RC [2, 3] is the paramount issue for continuing the progress of computing performance and for the survival of worldwide computing infrastructures. Section 18.2 stresses that worldwide, all our computer-based infrastructures are extremely important [4] for avoiding a massive crisis of the global and local economy. Section 18.3.1 warns of the future unaffordability of the electricity consumption of all the computers worldwide, visible and embedded, and briefs that low power circuit design [5–8] and other traditional "green computing" [9–11], although important and welcome, are by far not sufficient to guarantee affordability and not at all sufficient to support further progress for future applications of high performance computing (HPC). Thousands of books have been published about world economy, energy, CO_2, climate, survival on the globe, water, food, health, etc. Hundreds of them are about peak oil. I have listed just a few of them (12-89).

In contrast to the still dominant von Neumann (vN) machine, RC [90–92], the second RAM-based machine paradigm, introduced in Section 18.4, offers a drastic reduction of the electric energy budget and speedup factors by up to several orders of magnitude compared to using the vN paradigm, now beginning to lose its dominance [93, 94]. Sections 18.5.3 and 18.5.6 stress the urgency of moving RC from niche to mainstream and urge that we need a worldwide

Energy-Efficient Distributed Computing Systems, First Edition.
Edited by Albert Y. Zomaya and Young Choon Lee.
© 2012 John Wiley & Sons, Inc. Published 2012 by John Wiley & Sons, Inc.

mass movement of a larger format than that of the VLSI design revolution of around 1980, where only an urgently needed designer population has been missing [95–107]. This time a properly qualified programmer population is missing. But we need to push the envelope into two different directions. The VLSI design revolution has been the most effective project in the modern history of computing, but we need even more today. A dual-rail effort (Section 18.5.4) is needed for simultaneously developing the scene toward parallel programming for many-core architecture and for structural programming of RC, as well as heterogeneous systems including the cooperation of both paradigms.

Currently, the dominance of the basic computing paradigm is gradually wearing off (Section 18.4), with the growth of the area of RC applications bringing profound changes to the practice of scientific computing, cyber physical systems (CPS), and ubiquitous embedded systems, as well as new promises of disruptive new horizons for affordable very HPC. Owing to RC, the desktop personal supercomputer is also near [106]. To obtain the payoff from RC, we need a new understanding of computing and supercomputing, as well as of the use of accelerators (Section 18.5.7). For bridging the translational gap, the software/configware (SC) chasm, we need to think outside the box [4].

18.2 WHY COMPUTERS ARE IMPORTANT

Computers are very important to all of us. Computers are used by many millions of people around the world. Typical orders of magnitude in the computer application landscape are hundreds of applications, consisting of tens of thousands of programs, with millions of lines of code, having been developed by the expenditure of thousands of man-years investment volumes up to billions of dollars [4]. We must maintain these important infrastructures. Wiki "Answers pages" tell us why computers running this legacy software are indispensable in the world [108]. The computer is an electronic device used in almost every field even where it is most unexpected [109]. Now, we cannot imagine a world without computers. These days, computers are the tools for engineers and scientists and also they are used by many millions of people around the world.

The computer has become very important nowadays because it is accurate, is fast, and can accomplish many tasks easily. Otherwise, to complete many tasks manually much more time is required (Fig. 18.1). It can do very big calculations in just a fraction of a second. Moreover, it can store huge amount of data. We also get information on many different aspects using Internet on our computer. But there are more reasons why computers are important. Many more different kinds of local or even worldwide infrastructures will be controlled by networks of computers [109]. Here, computer crashes or software crashes may cause widespread disasters by domino effects [83–89]. In his novel, Hermann Maurer depicts the worldwide total chaos caused by a network crash in the year 2080, where millions of people die and the life of billions is threatened [84, 85]. A thrilling novel? Yes, but also a textbook about possible solutions.

Figure 18.1 Lufthansa reservation anno 1960. Reproduced with permission from [110].

Banks. Banks use computers to keep record of all transactions and other calculations. Computers provide speed, convenience, and security. Communication is another important aspect that has become very easy through Internet and e-mail. Computer communicates by telephone lines and wireless. Through e-mail, we can send messages to anybody in any part of the world in just a second, while if we write letter, it will reach in some days. So the Internet has made the Earth a global village and above all saves time. This would not be possible without computers. Internet helps to find information on every topic. It is the easiest and fastest way of research. Computer network makes the user capable of accessing remote programs and databases of the same or different organizations. Without computers we also would not have any automated teller machines (ATMs).

Business. Computers have now become an integral part of corporate life. They can do business transactions very easily and accurately and keep the record of all the profit and loss. Today, computers can be found in every store, supermarkets, restaurants, offices, etc., where special software is used in the computers to calculate the huge bills within seconds. One can buy and sell things online, bills and taxes can be paid online, and also the future of business can be predicted using artificial intelligence software. It also plays a very important role in the stock markets.

Business Information Systems. For the economy, business information systems are as essential as materials, energy, and traffic. Without business information systems, the economy would be extremely ineffective and inefficient. Business information systems are essential for globalization. Their significance for each enterprise include improving the productivity of the business processes (= rationalization), mastering complexity and volume, and making information available fast and everywhere, for any operations, for decisions, as well as strategically, for entrepreneurial planning on the creation of new business opportunities, that is, by e-business. If automobile manufacturers would not have PPC (product planning and control) systems, cars could not be manufactured in the desired wide variety. It would be like at the early times of Henry Ford, who said, "Cars can be delivered in any color, provided it is black."

Biological and Medical Science. Diagnostics of diseases can be performed and also treatments can be proposed with the help of computer. Many machines use computers that allow the doctor to view the different organs of our body, such as lungs, heart, kidneys. There is a special software that helps the doctor during the surgery.

Education. Today, the computer has become an important part of education because we are using computers in every field and without the knowledge of computer we cannot get a job and perform well in it. So computers can secure better job prospects. Knowledge about computer is must these days.

Media. Almost every type of editing and audiovisual compositions can be made using software especially made for this purpose. Some software can even make three-dimensional figures such as those used in cartoon films. Special effects for action and science fiction movies are also created on computer.

Travel and Ticketing. Computers do all the work of plane and train reservation. They show the data for vacant and reserved seats and also save the record for reservation. Let us imagine, Lufthansa would handle reservations like in 1960 (Fig. 18.1). Today, they could not handle their flight operations by this method.

Weather Predictions. Weather predictions by experts are made possible using supercomputers, which is another important application.

Sports. It is also used for umpiring decisions. Many times, the umpire has to go for the decision of a third umpire where the recording is seen again on computer and finally the umpire reaches to an accurate and a fair decision. Simulation software allows the sportsman to practice and improve his skills.

Car Safety. Here, the ultimate goal is a zero-fatality vehicle. Auto companies use computers for crash simulations to figure out how to build safer cars. GM, Ford, Honda, Mercedes-Benz, and other companies use this technology [111]. For computer simulations, such as one vehicle crashing into another, carmakers have the supercomputing power in-house. It has been publicly demonstrated that even a complex simulation of a full crash test with 1 million elements can take just 5 min to render using a cluster of Intel Xeon 5500 processors [111]. The latest HPC technology has enabled GM to move to an interactive design process for the entire vehicle and run a simulation with up to 4 million elements. American Honda has more than 3000 processors devoted to crash analysis [111]. Mercedes-Benz is now running approximately 5000 crash simulations for every new vehicle design. More sophisticated technology should help make much safer cars a reality in the not too distant future [111].

Other HPC Applications. HPC is pervasive enough so that it is used today not just by government and university researchers but also to design products ranging from cars and planes to golf clubs, microwave ovens, animated films, potato chips, diapers, and many other products.

CPS. CPS are computers or computer networks ready for real-time response, directly coupled to biological organisms or systems, to sensor networks, to organizations, or to technical networks. Figure 18.2 lists some CPS application examples.

Daily Life. Computers are used almost everywhere. Washing machines, microwave oven, and many other products use software. Moreover, we can store all the information about our important work, appointment schedules, and list of contacts. Computers play a very important role in our lives. We cannot imagine the world without computers. This technology is advancing at both industry and home. It is creating new mass markets by a variety of wireless smart portable devices [113]. It is necessary for everyone to have some basic computing knowledge. Otherwise, one cannot get a job, as computers have invaded almost all the fields.

Survival Risk of Mainframe Software. Tracing their roots back to IBM System/360 from the 1960s, mainframes became popular in banking, insurance, and other industries. Quite a number of companies still use older mainframes with 3270 terminal emulator and Disk Operating System (DOS) [114]. Representing cutting-edge technology when the oldest baby boomers were still teenagers, mainframe survival is in danger because of recruiting problems.

Risks of Domino Effects. The computer-based worldwide interconnectedness of all areas of life is highly risky. For instance, public power supply infrastructures are computer-controlled by intelligent networks, so that any local malfunction can trigger cross-border blackouts, causing widespread breakdowns: employees do not reach their workplace, subcontracted supply does not reach the assembly line, perishable goods do not reach their destination and/or cannot be cooled, etc. All our communication infrastructures

---

- Blackout-free electricity generation and distribution,
- Extreme-yield agriculture,
- Safe and rapid evacuation in response to natural or man-made disasters,
- Perpetual life assistants for busy, senior/disabled people,
- Location-independent acccss to world-class medicine,
- Near-zero automotive traffic fatalities, minimal injuries, and significantly reduced traffic congestion and delays,
- Reduce testing and integration time and costs of complex CPS systems (e.g., avionics) by 1–2 orders of magnitude,
- Energy-aware building and cities,
- Physical critical infrastructure that calls for preventive maintenance,
- Self-correcting cyber physical system for "one-off" applications,
- Disaster response: Large-scale emergency evacuation,
- Assistive devices.

Figure 18.2 Some grand challenge examples for CPS. Reproduced with permission from [112].

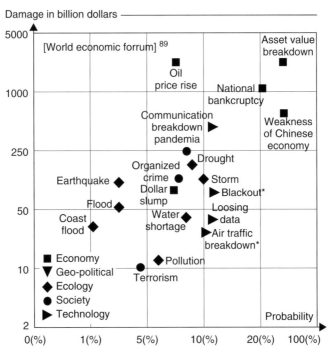

Figure 18.3   Global risks in economy. Reproduced with permission from [83]. *, other source.

are also highly vulnerable. For instance, blackouts have a lot of follow-up problems: phones and even cell phones do not work. Owing to the highly complex global interconnectedness, a minor bug may cause a huge disaster by chains of reactions. The World Economic Forum (WEF) has come to the conclusion [83] that by a wide variety of reasons, such risks have a very high probability (Fig. 18.3). Our computer-controlled economic and technical infrastructures have reached such an enormous complexity that we can hardly estimate all possible domino effects.

18.2.1   Computing for a Sustainable Environment

Computing for the future of the planet is more and more important for us because computing (computers, communications, applications) will make a major and crucial contribution to ensuring a sustainable future for the society and the planet. The "Power Down for the Planet" challenge is a national competition to fight global warming by pledging to reduce the amount of energy used by computers on campus and elsewhere. Also, computers are important because computing for a sustainable environment is essential for preserving our civilization and avoiding its collapse [12, 89].

The goal of green computing is simple [115]: reducing the use of harmful materials, maximizing energy efficiency, and promoting recyclability. Green computing [116] is the science of efficient and effective designing, manufacturing, usage, disposal, and recycling of computers and computer-related products (servers, networks, peripherals, etc.); it also includes creating technologies to help reduce harmful impact on the environment and to preserve natural resources. Wasting energy is costly and leads to a climate change from burning coal and oil.

With the major goal to minimize the carbon footprint of computing [117], "Green IT" consists of three parts: (i) designing products that are less polluting, less energy consuming, and easier to recycle; (ii) building more efficient data centers; and (iii) working on innovative projects that will enable, via IT contributions, the building of a more sustainable world. Green IT supports the smart measurement of the energy consumption of houses, public buildings, and other facilities, in order to be able to optimize the use of energy (smart meters) [118]. Green IT also supports education of the data center operators on enhanced energy optimization (green data centers [9–11]): use of telecommunication and teleconference to reduce travel requirements, installation of Web sites offering better information on carpooling or public transport possibilities to reduce traffic on our roads, and optimization of road traffic and transport logistics. Andy Hopper even sees four levels [119] at which innovation-driven developments in computing are effective:

1. Simulation and modeling are important tools that will help predict global warming and its effects. Much more powerful computing systems are required to make the predictions better, more accurate, and relevant.
2. The amount of infrastructure making up the digital world is continuing to grow rapidly and starting to consume significant energy resources.
3. Computing will play a key part in optimizing the use of resources in the physical world.
4. We are experiencing a shift to the digital world in our daily lives as witnessed by the wide-scale adoption of the World Wide Web.

Let me add a fifth level:

5. To help generate momentum and achieve these goals, it is important that a coordinated set of challenging international projects are investigated.

The WEF proposed to enable existing institutions to unleash public value by IT networking, catalyzing initiatives and unleashing human capital in the world [120]. Klaus Schwab said, "Our existing global institutions require extensive rewiring to confront contemporary challenges in an effective, inclusive and sustainable way." Organizations such as the UN, GATT, G8, and G20 are becoming increasingly inept at fixing what ails the world: goals of economic growth, climate protection, poverty eradication, conflict avoidance, human security, and promotion of shared values. The topics are the three *R*'s: *R*ethink, *R*edesign, and *R*ebuild [120].

The forum's "Global Redesign Initiative" report notes [121] "how the digital world has brought about cross-border integration by new technologies enabling virtual interaction have created a world that is much more complex and more bottom-up than top-down." The world has become economically, politically, and environmentally more interdependent, without a new set of international bureaucracies piled on the existing ones. It has been argued for a global system with graphic visualization tools to measure success, for a complete redesign the global legal system, for a global vaccine protocol, global intellectual property (IP) system, global risk management, etc. This means taking a Wikinomics approach—embracing more agile structures enabled by global networks for new kinds of collaboration such that there is no new set of international bureaucracies piled on the existing ones.

Governments need to launch a new paradigm to involve the citizens of the world through mass collaboration by a new medium of communications including tools such as digital brainstorms and town hall meetings: decision-making initiatives such as citizen juries and deliberative polling, execution tools such as policy wikis, and social networks within government and evaluation programs. This initiative demonstrates how important is it to reinvent computing and is the growth of IT and the Internet for broad engineering issues ensuring sustainability issues of the world such as smart energy production and distribution, intelligent water management, strengthening welfare, dealing with aging and young population, and mitigating risks [122].

18.3 PERFORMANCE PROGRESS STALLED

Disruptive architectural developments in industry stall further progress of IT with respect to energy inefficiency and performance improvements. Unaffordable operation cost by excessive power consumption is a massive future survival problem for existing cyber infrastructures, which we must not surrender. Because of the inevitable many-core architecture, contemporary computer systems are in an all-dominant programmability crisis. The progress of performance is massively stalled because of this "programming wall" caused by lacking scalability of parallelism and an ubiquitous programmer productivity gap [123–125]. Later, this chapter shows that reconfigurability is the silver bullet to obtain much better energy efficiency and performance by the upcoming heterogeneous methodology of HPRC (high performance reconfigurable computing). We also believe in the need for a massive campaign for migration of software to configware. Also, because of the multicore parallelism dilemma, we anyway need to reinvent programmer education [126]. The impact is a fascinating challenge to reach new horizons of research in computer science (CS). We need a new generation of talented innovative scientists and engineers to start the second history of computing. This chapter discusses its new world model.

18.3.1   Unaffordable Energy Consumption of Computing

The future of our worldwide total computing ecosystem is facing a mind-blowing and growing electricity consumption, together with a trend toward growing cost and shrinking availability of energy sources. Electricity consumption by the Internet alone causes more greenhouse gas emission than the worldwide air traffic. Will the Internet break [83–85, 127]? Consumer broadband connections in North America, Mexico, and Western Europe have reached 155 million by the end of 2007 and are predicted to reach 228 million by 2011. The Internet is being stressed more than ever with new technologies and larger e-mails, and the trend will accelerate. An explosion in services integrating video and software will intensify by the increasing popularity of games and the massive use of video on demand, high definition video, and pay-TV to the living room, as well as by newer services by mobile phone companies and multiple connected PCs [128] and devices using connections [127]. The Internet service providers should be able to assess how much more bandwidth will be required and how much headroom they have.

It has been predicted that by the year 2030, if current trends continue, worldwide electricity consumption by ICT infrastructures will grow by a factor of 30 [129], reaching much more than the current total electricity consumption of the entire world for everything, not just for computing. The trends are illustrated by an expanding wireless Internet and by a growing number of Internet users, as well as with tendencies toward more video on demand, high definition TV over the Internet, and shipping electronic books and efforts toward more cloud computing [130] and many other services. Other estimations claim that already now the greenhouse gas emission from power plants generating the electricity needed to run the Internet is higher than that of the total worldwide air traffic. There are more predictions [131, 132].

Already for today's petascale (10^{15} calculations/s) supercomputer systems with the annual power and cooling cost exceeding the acquisition cost of servers, the power consumption has become the leading design constraint [133]. Extrapolating from today's petascale systems to future exascale machines (10^{18} calculations/s, a processing capability close to that of the human brain [134]), the overall power consumption is estimated to be on the order of 10 GW [133, 134], twice the power budget of New York City with a population of 16 million (an earlier estimation for one system is 120 MW [135]). The electricity bill is a key issue for Google, Microsoft, Yahoo, and Amazon with their huge data farms at Columbia River [136] (Fig. 18.4). That is why Google recently submitted an application asking the Federal Energy Regulatory Commission for the authority to sell electricity [137] and has a patent for water-based data centers, using the ocean to provide cooling and power (using the motion of ocean surface waves to create electricity; Fig. 18.5) [138]. In the near future, the electricity bill of most facilities of Google will be substantially higher than the value of its equipment [139]. In 2005, Google's electricity bill was about US$50 million higher than

Figure 18.4 Google server farm at the Columbia River, © Melanie Conner/The New York Times/Redux/laif.

Figure 18.5   Pelamis Wave Power: electricity by the sea. Courtesy of Pelamis Wave Power [142].

the value of its equipment. Meanwhile, the cost of a data center is determined solely by the monthly power bill, not by the cost of hardware or maintenance [140]. Google's employee L. A. Barroso said [141], "The possibility of computer equipment power consumption spiraling out of control could have serious consequences for the overall affordability of computing."

Rapidly growing energy prices are predicted since the oil production has reached its peak by the year 2009 [143–145]. At present, 80% of the crude oil is coming from decline fields (Fig. 18.6). However, the demand is growing because of the developing standard of living in China, India, Brazil, Mexico, and newly industrializing countries. The World Energy Council estimates that the demand will double until the year 2050 [146]. We need at least "six more Saudi Arabias for the demand predicted already for 2030" (Fatih Birol, Chief Economist, IEA [147]). I believe that these predictions do not yet consider the rapidly growing electricity consumption of computers. So, maybe we will need 10 more Saudi Arabias. About 50% of the shrinking oil reserves are under water [148]. In consequence of the Gulf of Mexico oil spill, not all deepwater explorations will be allowed, insurance rates rise, and the crude oil prices will go further up (Fig. 18.7). Transitions from carbon fuels to renewables cannot completely fill the gap within at least two decades. This will cause a massive future survival problem for running cyber infrastructures, which we must not surrender because this is an important global economy issue. Or, should we dig more coal [149]? It makes sense, to measure computing performance not just by MIPS (million instructions per second), but by MIPS/watt or FLOPS/watt [150].

18.3.2   Crashing into the Programming Wall

For 40 years, semiconductor technology has followed Moore's law. Until about 2004, we obtained better performance by just waiting for the next-generation microprocessor with higher clock speed. Because of this free ride on Gordon Moore's law, the improvement of software performance has been the successful

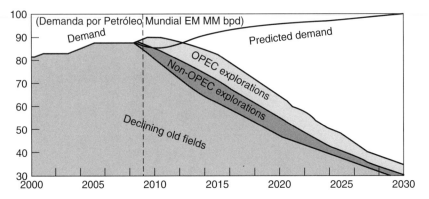

Figure 18.6   Beyond peak oil: declining future crude oil production [144, 145].

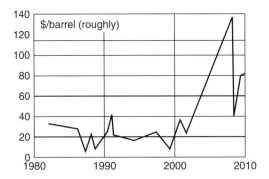

Figure 18.7   The end of cheap oil.

job of hardware designers. This development ended when the microprocessor industry changed strategy from a single CPU on a chip to many-core by increasing the number of on-chip processor cores instead of growing clock frequency. The "golden" CMOS era is gone [124]. Technology scaling does not deliver anymore significant performance speedup, and the increasing power density poses severe limitations. High performance is no more the job of hardware designers. We hit the "programming wall" since high performance now requires rare parallel programming skills [124, 151]. Great challenges for RC provide the answer [124, 125].

This "programming wall" [152] we know from supercomputing is not new. The dead supercomputer society list [153] demonstrates that almost all much earlier supercomputing projects and start-ups failed since parallel programming was required, which crashed into the parallel programming wall. This list is not even complete. More dead projects are listed elsewhere [154]. Even today, the vast majority of HPC or supercomputing applications was originally written for a single processor with direct access to main memory. But the first petascale supercomputers use more than 100,000 processor cores each, and distributed memory. Three real-world applications have broken the petaflop barrier (10^{15}

calculations/s) (Jaguar at ORNL) [152]. A slightly larger number has surpassed 100 teraflops (100×10^{12} calculations/s), mostly on IBM and Cray [152]. The scene hopes that dozens of applications are inherently parallel enough to be laboriously decomposed, sliced, and diced for mapping onto such highly parallel computers. But a large number of applications are only modestly scalable. More than 50% of the codes do not scale beyond eight cores, only about 6% can exploit more than 128 PE, still a tiny fraction of 100,000 or more available cores [152].

A very important issue is saving energy [155, 156]. But multicore processors tend to have tuned-down speeds. Down from 3 to 4 GHz (single-core), each core meanwhile runs at about half that speed. Some HPC or supercomputing sites report that some of their applications were running more slowly on their newest HPC system [152]. The x86-based Intel or AMD processors are dominant (in 2009), constituting almost 70% of the market. But multiplied collective peak performance comes without corresponding increases in network-on-chip (NoC) bandwidth, making it difficult to move data into and out of each core fast enough to keep the cores busy [152, 157]. We have to rethink Amdahl's law. Adding accelerators via a slow PCI bus adds to the problem. Both hardware and software advances are urgently needed.

We see that massive hardware parallelism from skyrocketing core counts is racing ahead of programming paradigms and programmer productivity. This parallel performance "wall" will reshape the nature of HPC code design and system usage [124]. The evolutionary path is not addressing the fundamental problems. A large number of HPC applications will need revolutionary changes to be fundamentally rethought and rewritten within the next 5–10 years by serious algorithm development. We have seen examples of mathematical models and algorithms that broke when pushed beyond. There are not enough people with the right kind of brainpower [158, 159]. Universities should produce more.

Semiconductor technology has followed Moore's aw throughout four decades. But continuing that pattern will require a breakthrough in energy-efficient design. With a very high probability, we will be forced to seek an entirely new paradigm [160]. This crisis and its key issues such as software scalability, memory, IO, storage bandwidth, and system resiliency stem from the fact that processing power is outpacing the capabilities of all the surrounding technologies.

In parallel computing, the realized real application performance is bad and getting worse [161]. Parallel computer programs are difficult to write: performance is affected by data dependencies, race conditions, synchronization, and parallel slowdown. The "parallel programming problem" has been addressed by HPC for more than 25 years with disappointing results. The more formal way based on languages did not really help [162], neither did more than hundreds of parallel programming languages (Table 18.1) nor the several hundred hardware description languages [163–166], which are also capable of expressing parallelism (Table 18.2). There are too many new prophets declaring another new route out of the wilderness of software development and maintenance since at least the invention of COBOL (Common Business Oriented Language) in 1959. Only a much too small number of specialized developers are halfway skilled

TABLE 18.1 Some Languages Designed for Parallelism[a]

A+	C*	Cthreads	FLASH	JavaSpace	Modula-3	Para++	Proteus	SUIF
ABCPL	C* m C	CUMULVS	TheFORCE	JIDL	Modula-P	Paradigm	PSDM	SuperPascal
ACE	C**	Curry	Fork	JoCaml	MultiLisp	Parafrase2	PSI	Synergy
ACT++	Cashmere	C Omega	Fortran-M	Join Java	Multipol	Paralation	PVM	TCGMSG
Active messages	CarlOS	DAGGER	Fotress	Joule	Munin	Parallaxis	QPC++	Threads.h++
ActorScript	CC++	DAPPLE	F-Script	Joyce	Nano-Threads	Parallel-C++	Quake	ThreadMarks
Ada	Chapel	Data Parallel C	FISh	Karma	NESL	ParLib++	Quark	Telegrphos
ADDAP	Charlotte	DC++	Fortran 90	Khoros	NetClasses++	ParLin	Quick	Titanium
Adl	Charm	DCE++	Fotress	KLimbo	Nexus	Parmacs	Threads	TRAPPER
Adsmith	Charm++	DDD	FX	KOAN-Fortran-S	Nial	Parti	R	UC
AFAPI	Chu	DICE	GA	LAM	Nimrod	pC	Rela	uC++
Afnix	ChucK	DIPC	GAMMA	Legion	NOW	pC++	SAC	Unified
Alef	Cid	distributed smalltalk	Glenda	Lilac	Objective-Linda	PCN	Sage++	Parallel C
Alice	Cilk	DOLIB	GLU	Limbo	Occam	PCP	SALSA	UNITY
ALWAN	Clojure	DOME	Go	Linda		PCU	SAM	V
	Cm-Fortran		GUARD				Scala	ViC*

AM	Co-array Fortran	DOSMOS	HAsL	LiPS	Octave	PDL	SCANDAL	VHDL
AMDC	Code	DRL	Haskell	Locust	Olenda	PEACE	SCHEDULE	Visifold
Amoeba	Concurrent	DSMthreads	HORUS	Lparx	Omega	PENNY	SciTL	V-NUS
Analytica	Concurrent Lua	E	HPC++	Lucid	OOF90	PET	SDDA	VPE
APL	Concurrent Pascal	Ease	Id	Maisie	OpenCL	PETSc	SHMEM	Win32
AppLeS	Converse	E	HPC++	Lucid	OOF90	PET	SDDA	VPE
ARIS	COOL	Eiffel	IMPACT	Mentat	Orca	Phosphorus	Sina	WinPar
Ateji PX	Corn	Eilean	ISETL-Linda	MetaChaos	Oz	Pict	SISAL	WWWinda
Aurora	CORRELA-TE	Emerald	ISIS	Midway	P++	POET	S-Lang	X10
Automap	CparPar	EPL	J	MilliPede	P3L	Polaris	SMI	XC
Axum	CPS	Erlang	JADA	Mirage	Pr-Linda	POOL-T	SONiC	XENOOPS
bb_threads	CRL	Excalibur	JADE	MOSIX	Pablo	POOMA	Split-C	XPC
Blaze	CSP	Express	Janus	MpC	PADE	POSYBL	SR	Zounds
BlockComm		Falcon	Java RMI	MpC++	PADRE	PRESTO	Stackless	ZPL
BSP		Filaments	javaPG	MPI	Panda	P-RIO	Sthreads	
C4		FM	JAVAR	Modula-2*	Papers	Prospero	Strands	

aReferences 157,167–169.

TABLE 18.2 Some Hardware Description Languages[a]

ABL	CoreFire	Impulse	Ruby
ABEL	CoWareC	Impulse C	SA-C
AccelChip	CUPL	JHDL	Scheme
AHDL	C2H	KARL	SML
AHPL	C2Verilog	Lava Haskell	SPARK
BDL	Dime-C	Lola	SpecC
Bluespec	DSS	MDL	Streams-C
BluespecLs	ELLA	Meta-HDL	SysGen
Brass	Erlang	Mitrion-C	Systems-C
Bach C	F#	MyHDL	System-Studio
BDL	Forge	NAPA-C	System TCS
CDL	HDCaml	Ocapi	Transmogrifier-C
CASH	Handel-C	OpenVera	LystemVerilog
Catapult-C	HardwareC	PALASM	Trident Compiler
Carte-C	Hardware Join Java	PAL	Verilog
CHiMPS	Hardw Verif Lan	Property Spec Lan	Verilog-AMS
Cocentric	Haskell	Ptolemy II	VHDL
Cones	HML	RC Toolbox	VHDL-AMS
Confluence	HVL	RHDL	Viva
ConvergenSC	Hydra	RTcode	

[a]References 163–166.

to write parallel code. Given this shortage of parallel programmers, we need to accept, however, that informal approaches are not working.

It has been proposed that to succeed with parallel programming in the multicore era, we must adopt a systematic approach obtained by an insight into how programmers think [170]. I do not agree. The thinking of programmers is far from being uniform. One expert predicts that shared memory computing will ultimately run out of steam. Another expert claims that distributed memory is good because it is efficient, scalable, and future-proof for increasingly distributed and nonuniform future hardware. A third one says that shared memory is good because it is compatible with existing sequential code and does not require retraining of developers. A fourth one means that if you extrapolate current trends, a decade from now we will be die-stacking cores and memory in NUMA (non-cache-coherent, nonuniform memory architecture) architecture with thousands of cores. A fifth one says that it is obvious that stream processing applications (e.g., DSP and graphics) generally do not need globally shared memory. I believe that programmers have to be taught how to think. They have to be taught how to "think parallel," find concurrent tasks in a program, synchronize for programming free from deadlock and race conditions, schedule tasks at the right granularity onto the processors of a parallel machine, and solve the data locality problem for correctly associating data with tasks. Too many sequential-only textual languages are around (Table 18.3), which are not helpful to support locality awareness that is urgently needed to understand parallelism and its bottlenecks.

TABLE 18.3 Some Programming Languages[a]

A+	Bertrand	Col	Emacs Lisp	Goo	Karel++	Mathematica	Nusa	Power-house	Seed7	Tom
A++	BETA	Cola	Emerald (PL)	GOTRAN	Kava	MATLAB	NXC	Power-Builder-4GL GUI	Self	TOM
A#.NET	Bigwig	ColdC	Englesi	GPSS	KEE	Maxima (see also Macsyma)	o:XML		Sense-Talk	Topspeed
A# (Axiom)	Bistro	Cold-Fusion	Epigram	Graph-Talk	Kiev		Oak	Power-Script	SETL	TPU
A-0 System	BitC	Cool	Erlang	GRASS	KIF	MaxScript	Oberon	PPL	Shakespeare	Trac
ABAP	BLISS	COMAL	Escapade	Green	Kite	Maya (MEL)	Object Lisp	Processing	Shift Script	T-SQL
ABC	Blitz Basic	Common Lisp (CL)	Escher	Groovy	Kogut	MDL	Object-LOGO	Prograph	SIMPLE	TTCN
ABC ALGOL	Blue		ESPOL	HAL/S	KRC	Mello-COMPLEX	Object Rexx	PROIV	SIMPOL	Turing
Abel	Bon	COMPASS	Esterel	Handel-C	KRYPTON	Mercury	Object Pascal	Prolog	Simscape	Turtle

TABLE 18.3 (Continued)

ABLE	Boo	Component-Pascal	Etoys	Harbour	ksh	Mesa	Objective-C	Visual Prolog	SIMSCRIPT	TUTOR
ABSET	Boomerang	COMIT	Euclid	IBM HAScript	KUKA	Mesham	Objective Caml	Promela	Simula	TXL
ABSYS	Bourne shell (including bash and ksh)	Converge	Euler	Haskell	L	Metafont	Objective-J	PROTEL	Simulink	Ubercode
Abundance		Coral 66	Euphoria	HaXe	L#.NET	MetaL	Obliq	Provide X	SISAL	Unicon
ACC	Corn	CMS EXEC	EXEC 2	High Level Assembly	L++.NET	Microcode	Obol	Pure	Slate	Uniface
Accent	BPEL	CorVision	F	HLSL	LabVIEW	Micro-Script	occam	Python	SLEEP	uniPaaS
ActForex	BUGSYS	Coq	F#	Hop	Ladder	MIIS	occam-p	Q	SLIP	UNITY
Action!	Build Professional	COWSEL	Factor	Hope	Lagoona	MillScript	Octave	Qi	SMALL	Unix shell
ActionScript	C	CPL	Falcon	Hugo	LANSA	MIMIC	OmniMark	QtSctipt	Smalltalk	Unlambda
Ace DASL	csh				Lasso	min	Onyx	QBASIC	SML	UnrealScript

ACT-III	C-	CSP	Fancy	Hume	LaTex	Mindscript	Opal	QuakeC	SNOBOL (SPIT-BOL)	USE
Ada	C++- ISO/IEC 14882	CSKA	Fantom	HyperTalk	Lava	Miranda	OpenEdge ABL	QPL	Snow	Vala
Adenine		Csound	Felix	I	Leadweaks	MIVA Script	OPL	R	Snowball	Genie
Afnix	C#- ISO/IEC 23270	Curl	Ferite	IBAL	Script	ML	OPS5	R++	SNUSP	VBA
Agda		Curry	FFP	IBM Basic assembly language	Leda	Moby	OptimJ	RAPID	SOAP	VBSript
Agena		Cyclone	FILETAB		Legoscript	Model 204	Oracle	Rapira	SOL	Verilog
Agora	C/AL	D	Fjölnir	IBM Informix-4GL	Limbo	Modula	Orc	Ratfiv	Span	VHDL
AIS	Cachè Object-Script	D#	FL		Limmor	Modula-2	ORCA/Modula-2	Ratfor	SPARK	Visual Basic
Balise		DASL	Flavors	IBM RPG	LINC	Modula-3	Orwell	RBScript	Spice	Visual Basic.NET
Aikido		DASL	Flex	ICI	Lingo	Mohol	Oxygene	rbx.Lua	SPIN	Visual C++
Alef	Caml	DataFlex	FLOW-MATIC		Linoleum	MOLSF	Oz	rc		Visual C++ Net
Alef++	Cat									

(*Continued*)

483

TABLE 18.3 *(Continued)*

ALF	Cayenne	Datalog	Fly	Icon	LIS	Mondrain	PARI/GP	REBOL	SP/k	Visual DataFlex
ALGOL 58	Cecil	DATA-TRIEVE	FOCAL	Id	LISA	MOO	Pascal-ISO 7185	Redcode	SPS	Visual DialogScript
ALGOL 60	Cel	dBase	FOCUS	IDL	Lisaac	Mortran		REFAL	Squeak	Visual FoxPro
ALGOL 68	Cesil	dc	FOIL	IMP	Lisp-ISO/IEC 13816	Moto	Pawn	Reia	Squirrel	Visual J++
Alice	CFML	DCL	FORMAC	Inform		Mouse	PCASTL	Revolution	SR	Visual Objects
Alma-0	Cg	Deesel (formerly G)	FormWare	Io	Lite C link title	MQL	PCF	rex	SSL	Vvvv
Ambi	Ch interpreter		@ Formula	Ioke	Lithe	MQ4	PEARL	REXX	Strand	WATFIV
Amiga E	(C/C++ interpreter)	Delphi	Forth	IPL	Little b	MQ5	Perl	Rlab	Stateflow	WATFOR
AMOS		Dialect	Fortran-ISO/IEC 1539	IPTSCRAE	Logix	MPD	PDL	ROOP	Subtext	WebQL
AMPLE	Chapel	DinkC		IronPython	Logo	MSIL	PHP	RPG	Suneido	Winbatch

AngelScript	CHAIN	Dialog Manager	Fortress	ISPF	Logtalk	CIL	Phrogram	RPL	SuperCollider	X++
Apex	Charity	DIBOL	FoxPro 2	ISWIM	LOTUS	MSL	Pico	RSL	SuperTalk	X10
APL	Chef	DL/I	FP	J	LPC	MSX BASIC	Pict	RTL/2	Swift	XBL
AppleScript	CHILL	DM	Franz Lisp	J#	LSE	MUMPS	Piet	Ruby	SYMPL	XC (e. XMOS)
Arc	CHIP-8	DotLisp	Frink	J++	LSL	Murphy Language	Pike	Rapid-BATCH	SyncCharts	XCODE
Arduino	chomski	Dylan	F-Script	JADE	Lua	Mythryl	PIKT	S	System-Verilog	xHarbour
ARexx	CHR	dylan.NET	Fuxi	JAGEX	Lucid	Napier88	PILOT	S2	T	XL
Argus	Chrome	Dynace	Gambas	Jako	Lush	NATURAL	Pizza	S3	TACL	XOTcl
ARLA	Chuck	DYNAMO	Game-Monkey Script	JAL	Lustre	NEAT chipset	PL-11	S-Lang	TACPOL	XPL
Asp	CICS	E	GML	Janus	LYaPAS	Neko	PL/0	S-PLUS	TADS	XPL0
Assembler	CIL	Ease	GAMS	JASS	Lynx	Nemerle	PL/B	SA-C	TAL	XQuaery
ari BASIC	Cilk	EASY	GAP	Java	M	NESL	PL/C	SAC	Tcl	XSLT
ATS	CL (Honeywell)	Easy PL/I	G-code	JavaScript	M2001	Net.Data	PL/I-ISO 6160	SAIL	Tea	XPath
AutoHotkey	CL (IBM)	Easycoder	GDL	JCL	M4	NetLogo	PL/M	SALSA	TELON-Mainframe	XML
AutoIt	Claire	EASYTRIEVE PLUS	Gibiane	JEAN	MAD	NewLISP	PL/P	SAM76		XMOS
Averest	Clarion			Join Java	MAD/I	NEWP	PL/SQL	SAS	Online IMS/	Y

(Continued)

485

TABLE 18.3 (*Continued*)

AWK	Clean	eC (Ecere c)	GJ	JOSS	Magik	Newton. Script	PL360	SASL	COBOL	Yorick
Axum	Clipper	ECMAScript	GLSL	Joule	Magma	NGL	PLANC	Sather	Generator	YAL
Ateji PX	CLIST	Ecol	GM	JOVIAL	MapBasic	Nial	Plankalkül	Sawzall	TECO	YQL
B	Clojure	eDeveloper	GML	Joy	Maple	Nice	PLEX	SBL	TELCOMP	YOIX
Bash	CLU	Edinburgh IMP	Go	JScript	MAPPER	Nickle	PLEXIL	Scala	gt-Telon	Z
BASIC	CMS-2	EGL	Go!	Jython	MARK-IV	Nomad2	Pliant	Scheme	TenCORE	Z notation
bc	COBOL-ISO/IEC 1989	Eiffel	GOAL	JSP	VISION BUILDER	Nosica	Plus	Scilab	TeX	Zeno
BCPL	Cobol-Script	Einstein	Gödel	JavaFX Script	Mary	NPL	POP-11	Scratch	TEX	Zomnon
BeanShell	Cobra	ELAN	Godiva	K		NQC	Poplog	Script.NET	TIE	ZOPL
Batch (Windows/DOS)		eastiC	GOM (Good Old Mad)	Kaleidoscope						
	MASM Microsoft	NSIS	PostScript	Sculptor 4GL	thinBasic	ZPL				
	CODE	Elf		Karel	Assembly x86	Nu	PortablE	Sed	Timber	ZZT-oop

[a]Reference 171.

Thousands of existing programming languages (only a subset is listed in Table 18.3) demonstrate the tradition that there is a wide variety of opinions and proposals around, pointing toward too many different directions to go. (There are even hundreds of esoteric languages [172, 173].) It is like seeking a needle in the haystack [151, 174]. It is also part of the vN syndrome [175]. For instance (no direction at all), with multicore systems becoming ubiquitous, there is some naive hope that "if you build it, they will come" [176] (good ideas or skilled programmers). Parallel programming has developed along informal, empirical lines. For instance, parallel global address space (PGAS) programming languages have existed for over a decade and could be far more productive than the message passing interface (MPI) still dominating HPC programming today. But only a few HPC users are ready to learn a new language that would also require rewriting HPC applications that could contain tens or hundreds of thousands of lines of code. Are we as humans multicore capable at all [177]? There is a school of thought telling us that humans are simply not built to comprehend multicore programming since our thought processes are inherently serial [177]. But this is not true. We are able to succeed in goal-oriented activities with respect to maps, schematics, networks, graphs, and all kinds games and sporting. Perhaps, a whole new programming paradigm is required that uses, for example, symbols, flowcharts, or other schematics [177].

What are the right models (or abstractions) to program for performance portability to all important parallel platforms? We should focus less on fashionable topics such as TM (transactional memory) and multithreading, which is considered harmful [178]. To be ready for discussions, also controversial discussions, we have to face several issues, such as migrating code from a uniprocessor to SMP (symmetric multiprocessor) models. We should be aware of several typical problems [179]: why going multicore could make applications run slower, what are the sources of race conditions, and what strategies to use for migrating a uniprocessor code to a multicore environment.

It is a disaster response that DARPA (Defense Advanced Research Projects Agency) selected Sandia Labs to launch the Ubiquitous High Performance Computing (UHPC) program [160] to design new supercomputer prototypes (completed by 2018?) to overcome current limiting factors, such as power consumption and architectural and programming complexity, by developing for scalability and entirely new computer architecture and programming models. The aim is to revolutionize the entire field of computing for fundamentally enabling a new model of computation by producing a highly dependable more energy-efficient computer that delivers 100–1000 times more performance and is easier to program than current systems. There are more such organizations; for example, the HPC Advisory Council (HPCAC) creates local Centers of Excellence worldwide for education, enhancing the HPC knowledge-base and exploring future solutions [180].

We cannot afford to relinquish RC. It may provide a method to effectively circumvent the programming wall. We will also urgently need this technology to cope with threatening unaffordable operation cost by excessive power consumption of the entirety of all vN computers worldwide. We need to migrate many application packages from software to configware. A sufficiently large programmer population qualified for reconfigurable platforms does not exist.

This is a challenge to reinvent computing for providing the qualifications needed not only for RC but also to cope with the many-core programming crisis. Intel's cancellation of the Tejas and Jayhawk processors indicated in May 2004 the end of frequency scaling's dominance to improve performance. "Multicore computers shift the burden of performance from hardware designers to software developers [181]." This crisis requires the migration of many software packages from monoprocessors to many-core platforms. A sufficiently large programmer population qualified for parallel programming does not exist. This results in a huge challenge of providing new educational approaches to create a dual-paradigm-savvy programmer population qualified for heterogeneous systems including both parallel software and configware. To deal efficiently with FPGAs, we also need robust and fast implementations of adequate configware compilers, for example, automated by formal techniques based on rewriting [182, 183]. But new compilers alone are not sufficient. Programmers should also be taught time to space mapping. One source said, "Intrinsic dimensionality rooted scaling laws to favor reconfigurable spatial computing over temporal computing" (N. N., Stone Ridge Technologies). It is highly important that the spatial character of RC introduces locality awareness into the mind of students learning programming.

Time to space mapping dates back to the early 1970s and even the late 1960s, years before the first hardware description languages came up [166, 184]. "The decision box (in the flow chart) turns into a demultiplexer. This is so simple! Why did it take 30 years to find out? [185]." Owing to notorious hardware/software gap, CS education was ignored for another 40 years, how simple this is. The impact is an encouraging challenge to reach new horizons of new CS research. We need new generations of talented innovative scientists and engineers to start the second history of computing. But this is less difficult than it looks like at first glance. "The biggest payoff will come from Putting Old Ideas into Practice (POIP) and teaching people how to apply them properly [186]."

18.4 THE TAIL IS WAGGING THE DOG (ACCELERATORS)

Invented by Ted Hoff in 1969, the introduction of the first microprocessor has been a revolution. The EE types in digital design have been well qualified using integrated circuits with gates and flip-flops inside to construct controllers. Just having been hired as employee No. 12 at Intel, Ted Hoff's idea to replace the wide variety of circuits by a GP (general purpose) circuit using principles known from mainframes was not welcomed. The crew with complete EE background thought this strange guy from Stanford with CS background is completely crazy. But Federico Faggin, who joined Intel about a year later, supported Ted's idea. In 1971, marketing of the 4004 microprocessor was started. Even to the customers of Intel, the idea of a programmable controller appeared strange. Replacing the soldering iron by a keyboard: is this not really crazy? To be able to sell this first

TABLE 18.4   Computer System Model of the Mainframe Era

Computer Machine Model of the Mainframe Era	Resources		Sequencer		
	Property	Program Source	Property	Programming Source	State Register
"CPU" instruction set processor	Hardwired	—	Programmable	Software (instruction stream)	Program counter

TABLE 18.5   The Postmainframe Machine

CPU/Accelerator Symbiosis	Resources		Sequencer		
	Property	Program Source	Property	Program Source	State Register
1. ASICs Hardwired accelerators	Hardwired	—	Hardwired	—	—
2. CPU Instruction set processor	Hardwired	—	Progra-mmable	Software (instruction stream)	Program counter

microprocessor, Intel was forced to give courses to about 100,000 people. But finally, Intel succeeded as we all know.

Using machine principles from the 1940s and after a dozen technology generations, the microprocessor meanwhile has become a Methusela, although some people still call it GP (Table 18.4). However, it cannot move forward without using crutches. Throughput requirements have grown faster than clock speed, so that the computer having this processor inside is even unable to drive its own display. This already happened in the 1990s or earlier. A growing variety of hardwired accelerators then came along with each PC, laptop, or other kinds computers, called *ASIC s* (*application-specific integrated circuits*). The tail is wagging the dog (Table 18.5). A variety of methods are available to provide massive speedup, including minimizing communication efforts and eliminating the need to store and communicate intermediate results, for example, by merging many simple operations into mega functions. ASIC accelerators not only provide speedups but also result in massive energy saving. A more recent example is an ASIC designed for the modern HD H.264 video encoding standard. Here, the 2.8-GHz Pentium 4 is 500 times worse in energy [187, 188]. Also a four processor Tensilica-based CMP is 500 times worse [187, 188].

18.4.1 Hardwired Accelerators

According to the state of the art in the 1990s, an accelerator typically was a non-vN accelerator (Table 18.5) [189]. But a good ROI (return on investment) with such ASICs used as accelerators was and is possible with a very high

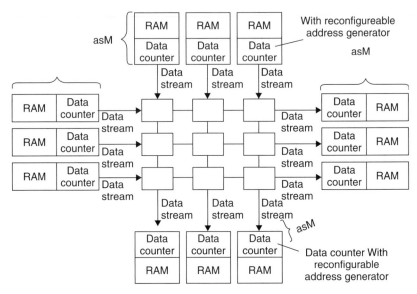

Figure 18.8   An example to illustrate data stream [191] machine principles.

production volume. Along with the continuing progress by Gordon Moore's law to shrinking feature sizes, the general expenses such as design cost, mask making, and preparing a production charge have been exploding. Meanwhile, the cost of a fab line has exceeded several billion US dollars (Fig. 18.8). Year by year, the ratio between ASIC design starts and FPGA design starts went backward [190] (Fig. 18.9).

For this reason, we now have to distinguish two kinds of such accelerators (rows 1 and 3 in Table 18.6): ASICs made from hardwired logic and configured onto FPGAs. These two kinds are distinguished by the binding time of their functionality: (i) before fabrication for fixed logic or hardwired logic devices (HWD) and (ii) after fabrication for (field-) programmable logic devices (PLDs). The term *field programmable* indicates that by reconfiguration the functionality can be changed also at the user's site by receiving new configuration code, from some memory or even over the Internet.

18.4.2   Programmable Accelerators

ASICs used as accelerators have massively lost market shares in favor of reconfigurable accelerators. Now, FPGA projects outnumber ASIC projects by >30 to 1 (Fig. 18.9) or even by 50 to 1 due to another estimation [192]. FPGAs [193] are structurally programmed from "configware" sources, which is fundamentally different from the instruction-stream-based "software" sources (Table 18.6). FPGAs come with a different operating system world organizing data streams and swapping configware for partially and dynamically reconfigurable platforms [194, 195]. FPGAs are supposed to be in 70% of all embedded systems [184].

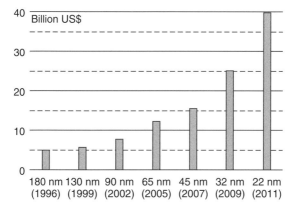

Figure 18.9 Fab line total cost (technology + R&D + revenue requirements). *Source:* International Business Strategies, Inc.

TABLE 18.6   Contemporary (Heterogeneous) Computer System Machine Model

Contemporary Computer System Machine Model	Resources		Sequencer		
	Property	Program Source	Property	Program Source	State Register
1. Hardwired accelerators	Hardwired (complex)	—	Hardwired	—	—
2. Instruction set processor	Hardwired (ALU)	—	Progra-mmable	Software (instruction stream)	Program counter
3. Reconfigurable accelerators	Programmable (complex)	Configware (configuration code)	Progra-mmable	Flowware (data streams)	Data counter(s)
4. Flowware-programmable accelerators like BEE[126]	Hardwired (complex)	—	Progra-mmable	Flowware (data streams)	Data counter(s)

Introduced in 1984, the fastest growing segment of the semiconductor industry for about two decades, and now a US$4-billion world market (almost 30% increase from last year; Peter Clarke from iSuppli estimates 43%), FPGAs are a well-proven technology that is rapidly heading for mainstream and also used in supercomputing by Cray, Silicon Graphics, and others [90, 196–198]. Estimations of the number of designers actively involved in FPGA design range from about 100,000 to over 500,000 engineers worldwide.

The partition between hardware and software can be moved throughout the design cycle. Low level hardware complexity is reduced or removed from design decisions. Many decisions can be removed from the early design process allowing a designer to focus on creating a product's unique functionality to serve a variety of marketing strategies [199]. Complex processor-based embedded systems can be created and changed easily. Here, a key issue is the high level product development approach implementing as much functionality as possible outside the hardware domain. The software and configware can be easily updated during and after the design process [199]: a powerful flexible way to define product functionality, allowing a product's competitive IP and the crucial user experience to be defined almost entirely in the reprogrammable domain [200]. Defining soft elements of the design can be updated at any time, even after the product has been deployed in the field. Systems on a Chip (SoC) can draw various benefits such as adaptability and efficient acceleration of computer-intensive tasks from the inclusion of dynamically reconfigurable platforms as a system component. Dynamic reconfiguration capabilities of current reconfigurable devices create an additional dimension in the temporal domain. During the design space exploration phase, overheads associated with reconfiguration and hardware/software interfacing need to be evaluated carefully in order to harvest the full potential of dynamic reconfiguration.

Using schematic or flowchart graphical design interfaces, IP blocks, software routines, and I/O systems can be quickly combined to explore and develop innovative product functionality without the need for low level engineering [199]. The pool of design data, also library parts, holds a single model of each block that incorporates all its elements. This model and IP cores can be simply dropped into the design, using a high level graphic-based capture system, regardless of their level of design abstraction. We can do much more than just programming the onboard FPGA [199]. By intelligent communication between hardware platform and the high level design software, the system could directly interact with all parts of the development board. Peripherals can then be swapped on the fly by automatically reconfiguring interface layers and configuration files. So the complete development system, including the physical hardware, acts as the one design environment. Hardware could conceivably become the final product in some circumstances.

The FPGA industry sprouted [201] (Table 18.7) from programmable read-only memory (PROM, invented in 1956), field-programmable read-only memory (FPROM), or one-time programmable nonvolatile memory (OTP NVM), and PLDs, where the setting of each bit is locked by a fuse or antifuse. Such PROMs

TABLE 18.7   Twin-Paradigm Fundamental Terminology

#	Source	Controlled by	Machine Paradigm	State Register Type	State Register Location
1	Software	Instruction streams	von Neumann	Program counter	In CPU
2	Configware	Configuration memory	Reconfigurable data paths	None	Hidden
3	Flowware	Reconfigurable address generator	Data stream machine	Data counter	In asM memory block

are used to store its program patterns permanently, programmable after fabrication, in contrast to ROM. Programmable more often than just once [201], first floating-gate UV erasable PLD came from General Electric in 1971. In 1973, National Semiconductor and in 1975, Signetics had introduced the mask-programmable PLA, and the so-called FPLAs (field-programmable logic arrays) came up in the early 1980s [201], also featuring very area-efficient layout similar as known from ePROM memory. Instead of just bits, coded forms of canonical Boolean expression patterns could be stored by PLAs or FPLAs.

Very high speedup could be obtained by matching hundreds of Boolean expressions within a single clock cycle instead of computing them sequentially. Together with a reconfigurable address generator [202], this brought a speedup of up to 15,000 [203–206] for a grid-based design rule checker in the early 1980s itself. Via the multiproject chip organization of the E.I.S. project, an FPLA (which was called *DPLA*) has been manufactured on a multiproject chip, with the capacity of 256 first FPGAs just appearing on the market (by Xilinx in 1984). In the early to mid-1980s, the multiuniversity E.I.S. project has been the German contribution to the Mead & Conway VLSI design revolution [95–105].

It is not only the particular acronyms FPLA and FPGA that are confusing (Table 18.8; Fig. 18.21). What is here the difference between "logic" and "gate"? "Logic" elements are very small with fixed interconnect: FPLAs have very dense layout such as memory. A "Gate" (CLB (configurable logic block)) needs more space. But FPGAs are more flexible by CLBs and routable wiring fabrics to interconnect CLBs (Fig. 18.10). In contrast to FPLAs, CLBs in FPGAs allow, for instance, to select 1 of the 16 logic functions (Fig. 18.11) from simple LUTs (lookup tables, Fig. 18.11).

TABLE 18.8   Confusing Terms: Not to be Used

Term	Once Introduced for
Dataflow	Indeterministic exotic machines
Firmware	Nested von Neumann machines
Microcode	
Microprogram	
Software or "soft"	No use other than for instruction streams

Figure 18.10   LUT example [207].

#	g_{00}	g_{01}	g_{10}	g_{11}	f (A,B)
0	0	0	0	0	0
1	0	0	0	1	A and B
2	0	0	1	0	B disables A
3	0	0	1	1	A
4	0	1	0	0	A disables B
5	0	1	0	1	B
6	0	1	1	0	A exor B
7	0	1	1	1	A or B
8	1	0	0	0	not (A or B)
9	1	0	0	1	A coin B
10	1	0	1	0	no (B)
11	1	0	1	1	B implies A
12	1	1	0	0	not (A)
13	1	1	0	1	A implies B
14	1	1	1	0	not (A and B)
15	1	1	1	1	1

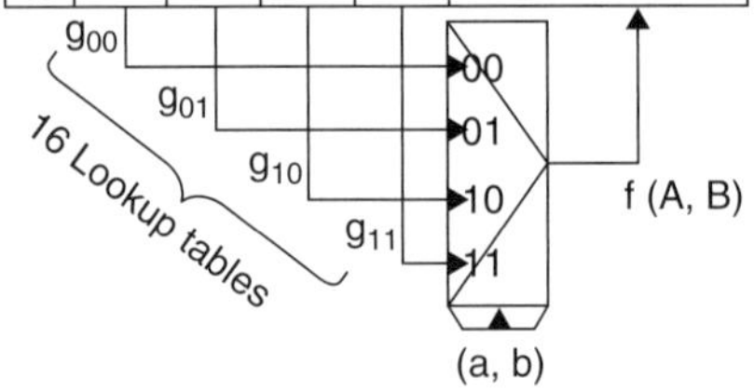

Figure 18.11 FPGA to ASIC design start ratio.

Beyond such fine-grained reconfigurability, the progress of Moore's law leads to higher abstraction levels with "coarse-grained reconfigurability" featuring also CFBs (configurable function blocks), which may be adders, multipliers, and/or many other functions [208–210]. The next step is mixed-grained "platform FPGAs," which also include one or several microprocessors, such as the PowerPC in earlier platform FPGAs from Xilinx (also see Section 18.5.3.3). However, the FPGA technology is worse than microprocessors: slower clock speed and massive reconfigurability overhead. Orders of magnitude higher performance with a worse technology: The Reconfigurable Computing Paradox (Section 18.5.2). Software engineering (SE) platforms are so massively inefficient, so Prof. C. V. Ramamoorthy from UC Berkeley has coined the term *The von Neumann Syndrome*.

18.5 RECONFIGURABLE COMPUTING

Reconfigurable computing prospects are on the rise [211]. However, FPGAs are the standard gear in high performance streaming appliances such as multimedia, medical imaging, routers, market data feeds, and military systems. The attractiveness of FPGAs is that they can be rapidly custom configured to run specific application workload efficiently. If a different workload needs to be run, the FPGA can be reconfigured accordingly. Switching the configurations takes just milliseconds. Accelerating real-life applications using FPGAs has really shown unprecedented levels of speed and savings in cost and energy for many applications [212]. But hardware acceleration, in general, has become the hot paradigm in computing, also with the top supercomputer systems in the world reaching the PetaFLOPS mark using hardware accelerators. Many high performance RC systems have been produced by top supercomputer manufacturers.

Again our common computer system model has changed [91] (Table 18.6, rows 1–3): accelerators have become programmable [213]. In contrast to an instruction set processor (CPU), which is programmed only by software, an RC platform needs two program sources (Table 18.6, row 3), namely, "configware" and "flowware," both not at all instruction stream based (configware is neither procedural nor imperative). Flowware has been derived from the data stream defined for systolic arrays [214, 215] already in the late 1970s. The term *flowware* makes sense to avoid confusion with a variety of data stream definitions. Flowware may also be used without configware for hardwired machines (Table 18.6, row 3), for example, BEE [92]. The term *flowware* avoids confusion rather than the term *dataflow* [216].

We now have to interface to each other two different programming paradigms: for programming the instruction set processors by traditional "software" and for programming the accelerators by configware, still ignored by SE. It is the dilemma of obsolete programmer qualifications. FPGAs require an unconventional programming model to configure the chip's logic elements and data paths before runtime. Some tools at least provide a halfway protection to the developer from hardware design issues or even explicit parallel programming, making the sorting out of CPU and FPGA code mappings the responsibility of the compiler and runtime system. We should characterize this niche and the progress of HPRC, as well as the associated challenges, and we should characterize the systemic productivity problem [123, 197]. We have to devise an orchestrated multilevel research agenda that is needed to move forward and identify the potential practical next steps for the community [212].

A growing trend is the use of FPGAs in embedded systems: ERC (embedded reconfigurable computing). FPGAs are supposed to be used in 70% of all embedded systems [217]. Originally, there has been a feeling that FPGAs are too slow, power-hungry, and expensive for many embedded applications, but this has changed. With low power and a wide range of small packages, particular FPGAs can be found in the latest handheld portable devices, including smartphones, eBooks, cameras, medical devices, industrial scanners, and military radios. Xilinx's first attempt at this was an FPGA with a processor inside. This time around, it is a processor with an FPGA grafted on. That is not just semantic hairsplitting: it is the big difference between these chips and the old ones. The new chips will boot up and run just like normal microprocessors, meaning no FPGA configuration is required at all [177]: FPGAs leap ahead. But embedded designers do not like FPGAs with CPUs inside [218]. FPGAs in this context have been very much seen as a hardware engineer's domain, with the softies allowed in to play at some late stage [219]. Xilinx preannounced a new family of devices "going beyond the FPGA," which they called *EPP* (extensible programming platform).

This EPP has a hardwired area with a top-end twin-core ARM Cortex-A9M processor unit and with a NEON multimedia processor, memory interfacing, peripherals, and a programmable fabric [219]. Instead of communicating across an FPGA, the two processors are connected by 2500 wires, providing much capacity for an AMBA-AXI bus and other communication protocols. Xilinx was stressing that this approach recognizes the increasingly dominant role of software in systems and is pushing EPPs as a way to first define the system in software and then carry out software and hardware design in parallel.

The totally changed concept of EPP makes these device more like heterogeneous SoC, allowing to have significant benefits for high performance applications such as wireless communication, automotive driver assistance, intelligent video surveillance. An EPP is an SoC with an embedded FPGA (eFPGA) that boots like a processor and acts as a processor [220]. Instead of a classical FPGA, an EPP is really a full-fledged processor. EPPs make the processor the center of the device with the programmable fabric as an extra. And this, argues Xilinx, now puts the software engineer first with the hardies following behind. In EPPs, the FPGA logic and the CPU will be programmable separately. The FPGA configuration will be handled by the processor(s) directly, not by a serial ROM. In other words, you have to tell the FPGA you want it configured. That is very un-FPGA-like [218] and not EPP-like. The approach of using both a processor and programmable fabric allows design to start at high level and the system to be implemented as software [219]. EPPs are a result of the new research topic NoC [221], which is a new paradigm for designing the on-chip hardware communication architecture based on a communication fabric, also including on-chip routers. NoC CAD tool flows also support mapping applications into NoC.

Apart from ERC, we have another RC scene: HPRC [196–198]). This is the combination of supercomputing and the use of reconfigurable platforms. Well known is the CHREC project [222] in the United States, which is heavily funded by the NSF. HPRC is a relatively new area, but has attracted a lot of interest in recent years, so that this entire new phrase has been coined to describe it [223]. HPRC uses FPGAs as accelerators for supercomputers [222]. HPC vendors such as Cray and SILICON Graphics are already supplying machines with ready-fitted FPGAs or have FPGAs in their product road maps. An example is the Cray XD1 incorporating Xilinx Virtex-II Pro FPGAs for application acceleration [224]. What are the benefits of using FPGAs in HPC? Also here, the first and most obvious answer is performance. HPC is renowned as that area of computing where current machine performance is never enough, leading us toward the dominance of heterogeneous systems. A problem yet to be solved is programmer productivity [196–198]. Programmers cannot work with hardware description languages like FPGA experts [124]. We have to bridge this gap. It is an educational challenge that programmers with this needed mix of skills are missing.

There is yet another embedded system scene, called *CPS* [112], where real-time behavior is a key issue. The major obstacle to use multicores for real-time applications is that we may not predict and provide any guarantee on real-time properties of embedded software on such platforms. Also, the way of handling the on-chip shared resources such as L2 cache may have a significant impact on the timing predictability. An interesting project proposes to use cache space isolation techniques to avoid cache contention for hard real-time tasks running on multicores with shared caches [225]. Dynamic reconfiguration capabilities of current reconfigurable devices can create an additional dimension in the temporal domain [183, 194, 226, 227]. During the design space exploration phase, overheads associated with reconfiguration and hardware/software interfacing need to be evaluated carefully in order to harvest the full potential of dynamic reconfiguration [228].

But there is also an area of concern. Both FPGA giants (Xilinx and Altera) are hitting 28 nm at the end of 2010. With reduced feature size of integrated circuits, transistors become less reliable. Transistors will be defective at manufacture time, also by process variations, and more of them will degrade and fail over the expected lifetime of a chip. Also an increasing number of soft errors will occur. The failure rate is growing. Causing major degradation, such failures are based on the physical mechanisms such as electromigration (EM), hot carrier degradation (HCD), and time-dependent dielectric breakdown (TDDB) [229]. Usually, manufacturers keep their failure rate statistics secret. However, with feature sizes of 20 nm and below the failure rate is a major problem (dark silicon [124]), so that fault tolerance methods should be applied [230]. Such fault tolerance techniques can be implemented on FPGAs by rerouting methods [231]. However, the fault detection required here is a nontrivial problem. The learning capabilities of artificial neural networks (ANNs) would be a welcome capability to organize such fault detection methods. ANNs could be seen as a future innovation for RC by enabling self-healing reconfigurable platforms based on self-learning [232–239]. But a very important component is still missing, requested by ANN pioneer Karl Steinbuch [232–235] already in 1960, which is capable of nondestructively storing the results of ANN learning processes: the memristor [240].

Having a joint development agreement with Hewlett-Packard, South Korea's Hynix Semiconductor Inc. is going to develop new materials and process integration technology to implement the memristor technology in its research and development laboratory. Being analog components, memristors are fundamentally distinguished from other nonvolatile computer memory (NVRAM) based on future technologies such as FeRAM or FRAM (ferroelectric RAM), MRAM (magnetoresistive RAM), PRAM (phase-change RAM), and RRAM or ReRAM (resistive RAM), which are digital. FRAM, MRAM, PRAM, and ReRAM are other next-generation NVRAM technologies with low power consumption because of their superior scaling characteristics and small cell size, having the potential to replace flash memory, DRAM, or even a hard drive. Maybe, even memristors could replace DRAMS and flash and hard disks, perhaps, as well as CDs and DVDs.

The small size of such memory elements would also be an important means to cope with the memory wall [241] because the total size of multicore on-chip memory capacity could be dramatically increased. Menta, founded in 2007 at Montpellier, France, and focusing on domain-specific eFPGAs, has announced to use MRAM instead of flash memory for configuration code to obtain architectural benefits for partial/dynamic reconfiguration as well as ease of fabrication with standard CMOS processes. Fujitsu just introduced an 8-bit microcontroller with embedded FRAM.

18.5.1   Speedup Factors by FPGAs

Energy efficiency of FPGAs is not new (Fig. 18.12). From CPU software to FPGA configware migrations, for a variety of application areas, speedup factors from almost 10 to up to more than 3 orders of magnitude have been published (Fig. 18.13) by a number of papers [242]. For example, most bioinformatics applications, image recognition (but not rendering), encryption/decryption, and FFT (fast Fourier transform)-based applications are ideally suited to FPGA silicon. More recently, for instance, a factor of 3000 has been obtained in 3D image processing for computer tomography. Biology showed speedup factors [243] up to 8723 (Smith–Waterman pattern matching, Table 18.9) [90, 244].; multimedia reports up to 6000 (real-time face detection). Cryptology reports for DES (Data Encryption Standard) breaking a speedup factor of 28514 (Table 18.9) [88]. Some of these speedup studies report energy-saving factors, like 3439 for the DES breaker example [90]. The same performance requires drastically less equipment. For instance, only one rack or half a rack and no air-conditioning, instead of a hangar full of racks. The energy-saving factors reported by these

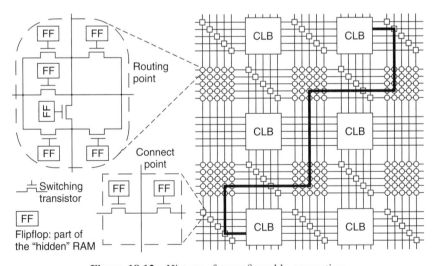

Figure 18.12   History of reconfigurable computing.

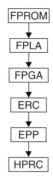

Figure 18.13   Better power efficiency by accelerators [245].

TABLE 18.9   Recent Speedup and Power-Save Data from Software to Configware Migration[a]

SGI Altix 4700 w. RC	Speedup	Save Factor		
100 RASC vs Beowulf Cluster	Factor	Power	Cost	Size
DNA and protein sequencing	8723	779	22	253
DES breaking	28,514	3439	96	1116

[a]References 90, 246.

studies tend to be roughly 10% of the speedup factor: the golden bullet for saving energy.

Dozens of papers [242] have been published on speedups obtained by migrating applications from software running on a CPU to configware for programming FPGAs [247]. Fig 18.13 shows a few speedup factors picked up from literature, reporting a factor of 7.6 in accelerating radiosity calculations [248], a factor of 10 for FFT, and a speedup factor of 35 in traffic simulations [249]. A speedup factor of 304 is reported for an R/T spectrum analyzer [250]. For digital signal processing and wireless communication, as well as image processing and multimedia, speedups were of 2 to almost 4 orders of magnitude [251, 252]. In the DSP area for MAC operations, a speedup factor of 100 has been reported compared to the fastest DSP on the market (2004) [253]. Already in 1997, comparde to the fastest DSP, a speedup between 7 and 46 has been obtained [254]. In multimedia, we find factors ranging from 60 to 90 in video rate stereovision [255], from 60 to 90 in real-time face detection [256], and of 457 for hyperspectral image compression [257]. In communication technology, we find a speedup of 750 for UAV radar electronics [258]. For acceleration of H.264 video encoding, a speedup factor of "only" 43.6 has been published [259]. For cryptography, speedups of 3>5 orders of magnitude have been obtained. For a commercially available Lanman/NTLM Key Recovery Server [260], a speedup of 50–70 is reported. Another cryptology application reports a factor of 1305. More recently, for DES breaking, a speedup by ×28514 has been reported [261] (Table 18.9).

For bioinformatics applications [182, 262], speedups have been obtained by 2–4 orders of magnitude. Compared to software implementations, sensational speedup factors have been reported for software to FPGA migrations. Speedups of up to 30 have been shown in protein identification [263] and of 133 [264] and up to 500,306 in genome analysis. The Smith–Waterman algorithm, used for protein and gene sequence alignment, is basically string matching that requires a lot of computational power [182]. Another study has demonstrated speedups of $100\times$ using Xilinx Virtex-4 hardware matched against a 2.2-GHz Opteron [265]. A speedup by 288 has been obtained with Smith–Waterman algorithm at the National Cancer Institute [266]. More recently, a speedup higher by more than an order of magnitude has also been obtained [267]. The CHREC project [222] reports running Smith–Waterman algorithm on a Novo-G supercomputer, a cluster of 24 Linux servers, each housing four Altera Stratix-III E260 FPGAs. According to this CHREC study, a four-FPGA node ran 2665 times faster than a single 2.4-GHz Opteron core [268].

Another Smith–Waterman DNA sequencing application that would take 2.5 years on one 2.2-GHz Opteron is reported to take only 6 weeks for 150 Opterons running in parallel. Using 150 FPGAs on NRL's Cray XD1 (speedup by 43) is reported to further reduce this time to 24 h, which means a total speedup of $7350\times$ over a single Opteron [269]. These are just a few examples from a wide range of publications [262–267, 270, 271], reporting substantial speedups by FPGAs. For the Smith–Waterman algorithm, the performance per dollar and per watt has been compared among FPGA, GPU (graphics processor), a cell processor, and a general purpose processor (GPP; Table 18.10) [220].

Software to configware migration and software to hardware migration depend on the same principles since both are time to structure mappings. The difference is binding time: before fabrication (hardware) or after fabrication time (configware). An example is the migration [3] of the well-known O(n2) running time bubble sort algorithm [273] fully based on memory-cycle-hungry CPU instruction streams, also for reading and storing the data. We map the inner loop into a bidirectional pipeline register array (Fig. 18.14) [3]. But this solution comes with

TABLE 18.10 Normalized Performance at Smith–Waterman Algorithm[a]

Platform	Performance per Dollar		Performance per Watt	
	Performance (MCUPS) per Dollar	Normalized Performance per Dollar	Performance (MCUPS) per Watt	Normalized Performance per Watt
FPGA	0.34	4.6	508	584
GPU	0.14	1.9	22	25
Cell BE	0.17	2.3	27	31
GPP	0.07	1.0	0.87	1

Abbreviation: MCUPS, mega cell updates per second.
[a]Reference 272.

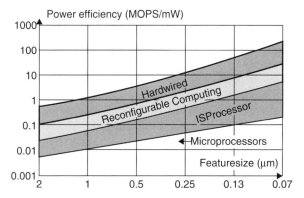

Figure 18.14 Speedup factors from software to configware migration.

access conflicts that are removed by splitting the operation into two phases. However, this solution wastes resources since at any time, only 50% of the conditional swap units are busy. For optimization, we change the algorithm into the shuffle sort algorithm [274, 275] having only half as many conditional swap units. For avoiding the break bubbling up, we move the contents of the k register pipeline up and down, each time by a single step. That is why we call it *shuffle sort*.

The algorithmic complexity turns from O(n2) to O(n). In a similar manner, other well-known algorithmic methods can be transformed to explore parallelism and locality, such as in dynamic programming as presented in Reference 182. Needing no CPU instructions brings additional massive speedup. Since software is usually stored outside CPU on-chip memory, the memory wall [241] and overhead phenomena typical to software cause performance by additional orders of magnitude worse than that of the migrated version.

18.5.2 The Reconfigurable Computing Paradox

Technologically, FPGAs are much less efficient than microprocessors [177, 276]. The clock speed is substantially lower. The routable reconfigurable wiring fabrics cause a massive wiring area overhead. There is also another massive overhead: reconfigurability overhead, where of the 200 transistors, maybe about 5 or less than 1 of them (Fig. 9 in Reference 276 serve the application, whereas the rest are used for reconfigurability (Fig. 18.10). Often, there is also routing congestion, so that not all CLBs can be used, causing further degradation of efficiency. Why does software to configware migration yield such massive improvements in speed and power consumption, although FPGAs are a much worse technology? It is the vN paradigm's fault.

Why does software to configware migration yield such massive improvements in speed and power consumption, although FPGAs are such a much worse technology? Measuring the gap between FPGAs and ASICs yields 30–40× area, 12–14× power, and 3–5× speed [277]. This means that for FPGAs, the product of area, time, and power is about 3 orders of magnitude higher than that for ASICs [124]. FPGAs have an enormous wiring overhead, and massive reconfigurability overhead (from a 100 transistors, maybe about 5 or less serve the application, whereas the rest provide the reconfigurability), and have a much slower clock speed than a CPU. Routing congestion may even further degrade FPGA efficiency. Because of a rapid increase in the number of on-chip devices, currently, in the range of billions of transistors, as well as the large number of metal layers, resources get "cheaper," and thus, the area cost of reconfigurable hardware is not anymore a limiting factor [124]. Owing to power limitations with future technologies, not all resources can be active at the same time. Such resources can then be used to offer reconfigurability and flexibility on a chip, also targeting fault tolerance. The consequence is that RC can fill, at least partially, the above gap.

RC has the potential to completely fill the above gap. Why? It is a paradigm issue: instruction streams versus data streams. To answer, it is the vN syndrome [175] that looks a bit unfair. It is the typical environment that is so inefficient so that the much better processor technology is left behind the leading edge by orders of magnitude. It is an SE issue that multiple levels of overhead lead to code sizes that hit the memory wall [241]. Nathan's law says that software is a gas that fills any available storage space (on-chip memory, extra semiconductor memory located outside the processor chip), as well as hard disks, and even the Internet. Here, the memory wall is a technology issue, not directly the paradigm's fault.

The question is why technologically much worse FPGAs are by orders of magnitude more efficient than vN-based microprocessors. It is a handicap of the vN paradigm, that computing by instruction streams is highly memory limited. It is handicap of the vN-type parallelism, that internode communication reduces computational efficiency. In RC, the magnitude of parallelism overcomes the clock frequency limitations. RC massively accelerates tasks by data streaming. RC minimizes memory size and memory bandwidth by data streams instead of instruction streams. Data stream computations across a long array (before storing results in memory) can achieve by orders of magnitude improved use of memory [247]. All this explains why RC performance and power consumption is by orders of magnitude more efficient than vN.

Let us also look into history. Prototyped in 1884, the Hollerith tabulator was the first electrical computer ready for mass production. Punchcard-driven it has been data-stream-driven RC. Since integrated circuits and transistors did not yet exist, the LUT was configured manually by banana plug wiring. About 60 years later, the vN-type ENIAC computer came up [278, 279], consuming electrical power of 200 kW and requiring a hangar full of equipment (see pictures in Reference 278, whereas the Hollerith machine had just the size of about two refrigerators (note: 60 years earlier). Just for computing a few ballistic tables, this gigantic difference of efficiency foreshadowed that vN becoming fashionable turned out to become the most dramatic misinvestment of many hundreds of billions of dollars. This disruptive about-turn to vN, the most disastrous decision in the history of computing, was the overture of all the problems of the

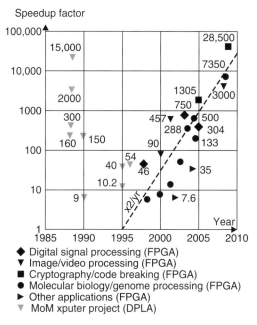

Figure 18.15 von Neumann principles.

vN syndrome, such as the never-ending software crisis approaching its fiftieth anniversary. "In an environment which has represented the absence of the need to think as the highest virtue this is a decided disadvantage" (Daniel Slotnick, 1967) [280].

Even today, based on modern microelectronics technology, already the principles of vN hardware are massively inefficient. Just about 5% of the hardware, the ALU, is doing the processing, whereas the other 95% hardware is overhead (Fig. 18.15) [187]. But orders of magnitude more inefficiency is caused by multiple overhead phenomena in the software required to follow this machine paradigm. The flood created by much more than a thousand programming languages having been developed (a subset listed in Table 18.3) seems to exhibit more a symptom of a lack of direction than of cleverness. Another symptom of chaos is replacing languages of high abstraction level, such as Pascal, by the assembler-like language C. The term software crisis is almost 50 years old. This term was coined by Prof. F. L. Bauer from TU Munich when, he was its general chair, he opened the first NATO Software Engineering Conference 1968 in Garmisch, Germany. Since then, literature, panels, and keynote addresses investigating the variety of overhead phenomena have been increasing [175, 176, 241].

The vN paradigm was criticized also by celebrities [281–284]. Peter Newman had appeared each month for 15 years on the critical "computers at risk" back pages of Communications of the ACM [285]. Nathan's law (by Nathan Myhrvold, a former CTO of Microsoft) said that software is a gas, which fills any available storage space: on-chip memory, extra semiconductor memory located outside the processor chip, as well as hard disks. It even fills the Internet. Niklaus Wirth's pre-many-core interpretation of Moore's law is "software is slowing faster than hardware is accelerating" [283]. Why, how often, and to what extent software fails is meanwhile its own subject era [281–287].

Why is vN paradigm so inefficient? It is not only the typical environment that is so inefficient, that the much better processor technology is left behind the leading edge by orders of magnitude. We can identify two different reasons: algorithmic complexity caused by the vN paradigm and architectural issues [287]. There is a number of attempts to explain at least particular symptoms of this syndrome (Fig. 18.10) [187, 188]. The most well-known architectural problem is the memory wall (Fig. 18.16) [284]. It is also an architecture-related SE issue that multiple levels of overhead lead to massive code sizes, which hit the memory wall [288]. The "memory wall" means that the time to access RAM outside the processor chip is currently slightly more than a factor of 1000, which is shorter than that to access on-chip memory [288]. This difference is growing by 50% every year.

The memory wall is really not fully the paradigm's fault. Smart cell phone architecture show embedded software approaches to cope with memory bandwidth problems. But instruction sequencing overhead is a consequence of the vN paradigm. After a full migration to static RC, an application uses zero instructions at runtime and is run by data streams only. But by migration, also the amount of data streams may be minimized by changing the algorithm. Here, an illustration example for reducing the algorithmic complexity is given by the migration

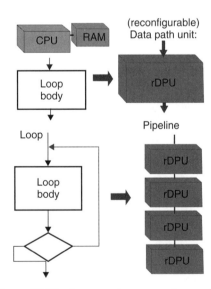

Figure 18.16 Loop to pipe conversion model.

of the well-known O(n2) complexity bubble sort algorithm away from vN. The algorithmic complexity turns from O(n2) into O(n)3. In a similar manner, other well-known algorithmic methods can be transformed to explore parallelism and locality, such as in dynamic programming as presented in Reference 227. The combination of these effects leads to massive speedup and massive saving of energy (Section 18.5.4).

Why does the migration from instruction streams to data streams lead to such massive speedup? How data are moved is also a key issue. CPUs usually move data between memory blocks and require instruction streams to carry it out (first row of Table 18.7). The movement of data is evoked by execution of instructions due to the vN paradigm. Also the execution of operations inside a CPU requires reading and decoding of instructions. On a reconfigurable platform, however, which can be modeled as a pipe network, data are moved directly from DPU to DPU. This means that operation execution inside a DPU (not having a program counter) is "transport triggered" (second row of Table 18.7). It is triggered via handshake by the arrival of the data item, not needing an instruction to call it. Not looking at dynamically reconfigurable systems (only for advanced courses [227]), we see that reconfigurable fabrics do not perform any instruction sequencing at runtime.

Of course, the data entering or leaving such an array (Fig. 18.8) have to be stored in memory. The data stream machine paradigm uses autosequencing memory (asM) blocks. Each asM has a reconfigurable address generator and data counter inside, so that no instruction streams are needed for address computation. All these data streams can be programmed via data-imperative languages [289], being a kind of sisters of classical imperative programming languages.

18.5.3 Saving Energy by Reconfigurable Computing

Recently, not only speedup but also energy-saving factors have been reported, roughly 1 order of magnitude lower than the speedup. Most recently, for DES breaking (a crypto application), 28,500 (speedup) versus 3439 (saving energy) and for DNA sequencing, 8723 (speedup) versus 779 (saving energy) (Table 18.9) [261]. This paper also reports factors for saving equipment cost (up to ×96) and reducing equipment size (up to 1116; Table 18.9). A hangar full of equipment is not needed when FPGAs are used in scientific computing. The pervasiveness of FPGAs is not limited to embedded systems, it is also spread over practically all areas of scientific computing, where high performance is required and access to a supercomputing center is not available or not affordable. The desktop supercomputer is near.

This chapter introduces the highly promising and important future roles of RC, emphasizes that it is a critical survival issue for computing-supported infrastructure worldwide, and stresses the urgency of moving RC from niche to mainstream. It urges acceptance of the massive challenge of reinventing computing, away from its currently obsolete CPU-processor-centric Aristotelian CS world model, over to a twin-paradigm Copernican model supporting energy-efficient heterogeneous systems by including the massive use of RC. This chapter also gives a flavor of the fundamentals of RC and the massive impact on the efficiency of computing it promises. Furthermore, the chapter outlines the educational barriers we have to surmount and the urgent need for major funding on a global scale to run a worldwide mass movement, of a dimension at least as far reaching as the Mead & Conway VLSI design revolution in the early 1980s [95–105]. The scenarios are similar: around 1980, an urgently needed designer population was missing. Now, a properly qualified programmer population is not available. This time the problem is more difficult, requiring a twin-paradigm approach for programming heterogeneous systems including both many-core processors and reconfigurable accelerators.

The idea of saving energy by RC is not new [245, 254]. It is the silver bullet to massively reduce the energy consumption of computing, by up to several orders of magnitude. RC is extremely important for the survival of the world economy. It has been reported more than a decade ago that for a given feature size, microprocessors using traditional compilers have been up to 500 times more power-hungry than a pure hardware mapping of an algorithm in silicon (Fig. 18.13) [245]. Speedup factors up to more than 4 orders of magnitude were reported from software to FPGA migrations (Fig. 18.13 [246, 248–252, 254–262, 290, 291]). The energy-saving factor is about 10% of the speedup factor, that is, still up to more than 3 orders of magnitude. A partial paradigm shift migrating only a part of the software into configware promises to save electricity by orders of magnitude.

18.5.3.1 Traditional green computing. Green computing (compare Section 18.2.1) uses conservative methods to save energy by more efficient modules, circuits, and components. For example, LED flat-panel displays need much less power than LCD-based plasma displays that need 150–500 W or more. Also much more power-efficient power supply modules are possible. The potential to save power is substantially less than an order of magnitude, maybe a factor of about 3 or 4. A special scene within green computing is low power circuit design, now also called low power system on-chip design (LPSoCD). Its most important conference series are about 30 years old: the PATMOS (oldest) and the ISLPED conference series [116]– [154, 156, 157, 160]–[160, 315] a brand new conference is the e-Energy [293, 316].

Several aspects are known for LPSoCD, such as leakage power, clock gating, active body bias (ABB), adaptive voltage scaling (AVS), dynamic voltage scaling (DVS), multiple supply voltages (MSVs), multithreshold CMOS (MTCMOS), power gating (PG), and power gating with retention (RPG) [140, 317]. However, the order of magnitude of the benefit to be expected from this subarea LPSoCD is rather low. By MSV, in using three Vdds, the power reduction ratio at best is about 0.4 [140]. LPSoCD is a matter of ASIC design, for example, of hardwired accelerator design. Only 3% of all design starts are ASIC designs (Fig. 18.9) with a trend leading further down. But in fact, low power design is also used for developing better power-efficient FPGAs to the benefit of RC. But we need a much higher potential of saving energy because "Energy cost may overtake IT equipment cost in the near future" [108]. "Green Computing has become an industrywide issue: incremental improvements are on track... But we may ultimately need revolutionary new solutions." [318] Let me correct this statement, "we will ultimately also need revolutionary solutions" (such as RC), since we need much higher efficiency [319].

18.5.3.2   The role of graphics processors. Accelerator use of general purpose graphics processing units (GPGPUs [304]) is a big fashion, so that there seems to be a perception that there is a battle between FPGAs and GPGPUs for GP HPC acceleration, with regard to speedup and power efficiency. However, the very busy hype on the accelerator use of GPGPU seems to be overexaggerated [306]. Depending on the class of algorithms, speedup factors just between ×1 and up to ×3 are reported, compared to "normal" x86-based many-core architecture use [305–307]. Since a compute-capable discrete GPU can draw much more than 200 W, other authors call this massive power draw a serious roadblock to the adoption, not only in embedded systems but also for data centers [308]. FPGAs from a new Xilinx 28-nm high performance, low power process developed by Xilinx and TSMC and optimized for high performance and low power are much better-off than GPUs (Table 18.10) [220].

NVIDIA hardware has the advantage of ECC memory support, local cache, asynchronous transfers, and a generally more sophisticated architecture geared for GP computing [311]. But AMD's offerings have the advantage of better performance per watt, at least for the 150-W FireStream 9350 product [311]. A recent paper on GPU-accelerated software packet router says, "We believe that the increased power consumption is tolerable, considering the performance improvement from GPUs." [309] But finally, it turns out that the GPU remains a specialized processor, so that we still need the traditional CPU after all. Intel is coming up with both on the same microchip [313].

NVIDIA needs Intel more than Intel needs the GPU designer [152]. The truth is that the NVIDIA Tesla boards use Intel Xeon chips to demonstrate the performance gains of a CPU/GPU combination. So the question is "why bother attacking the devil, if you have to dance with it?" [152] GPUs can be used for traditional graphics, advanced visualization, and floating point/vector processing. The rise of GPGPU computing will inexorably push graphics-flavored logic onto the CPU die [310] by the two big x86 chip vendors, AMD with their Fusion APU (accelerated processing unit) processors, maybe for early 2011 [311]. CPUs and GPUs will share the same silicon real estate. When manufactured below 32 nm, the earliest CPU-GPU server chips may come by 2012, or 2013. Maybe, GPGPUs as a kind of alternative many-core architecture are adding to the programming challenge [152]. NVIDIA's CUDA programming environment has become a premier software platform for GPGPU development, whereas AMD is sticking with the open standard OpenCL sometimes considered less capable and less mature [311]. But NVIDIA has the only conformant, publically available, production OpenCL GPU drivers. But in contrast to GPGPUs, socketed FPGAs can connect to an x86 CPU without host intervention, directly over the high performance native processor bus, like Intel's Front Side Bus (FSB), with PGA expansion modules by companies such as XtremeData, DRC Computer, and Nallatech and using compilers from tool makers such as Mitrionics, Celoxica, and Impulse Accelerated Technologies compiling C (or C-like) code into an FPGA logic. At the Intel Developer Forum in September 2010, Xilinx showcased the Intel® QuickPath Interconnect (Intel® QPI) technology for enabling the integration of FPGAs in HPC applications.

18.5.3.3 Wintel versus ARM. Most of the referenced CPU to FPGA migration speedup reporting papers (Section 18.5.1) have compared FPGAs with earlier Wintel processors, as well as with older types of FPGAs that are less power efficient. Are those data still useful? Are ARM processors more power efficient than x86? ARM processors are often powered by a small battery when being used extensively in consumer electronics, including PDAs, tablets, mobile phones, digital media and music players, handheld game consoles, calculators, and computer peripherals such as hard drives, printers, and routers. About 98% of the mobile phones sold in 2007 use at least one ARM processor. ARM licensed about 1.6 billion cores in 2005 [312]. In 2005, about 1 billion ARM cores went into mobile phones. Until January 2008, over 10 billion ARM cores have been built, and iSuppli predicts that 5 billion a year will ship in 2011. Cortex processors (ARMv7) now provide faster and more power-efficient options than all those previous-generation processors. Cortex-A targets applications processors, as needed by smartphones that previously used ARM9 or ARM11. Cortex-R targets real-time applications, and Cortex-M targets microcontrollers. "M" stands for an improved multiplier and a faster adder. In 2009, some manufacturers introduced netbooks based on ARM architecture CPUs in direct competition with netbooks based on Intel Atom. The new ARM Cortex seems to be more energy efficient than Intel Atom (but only in terms of GHz/W), but is only a simple 32-bit reduced instruction set computer (RISC), whereas Intel has a powerful 64-bit CISC architecture. The relative simplicity of ARM processors made them suitable for low power applications. This has made them dominant in the mobile and embedded electronics market as relatively low cost and small microprocessors and microcontrollers. How much will this affect the CPU to FPGA speedup and power-save comparison figures?

Current Intel x86 processors can deliver up to 3.6 GHz while consuming up to 130 W, or at the low end, 1.8 GHz at 40 W. The ARM line of chips has been reported to deliver 1 GHz at 700 mW [320] (down by ×50 in terms of GHz/W) and can reach up to 2 GHz while still consuming less than a watt (down by ×75 in terms of GHz/W). So the power savings seem to be substantial. But the situation is far from being that simple. Maybe more reasonable conclusions can be obtained by benchmarking, after ending the controversial discussion on which benchmark to use. However, benchmarks are not real life. But, we also have extremely power-efficient FPGAs (e.g., IGLOO [321]) that are also useful for battery-powered handheld devices. The evaluation of power-saving figures from software to configware migration is not as simple as it has been.

Intel started challenging ARM with its Atom processor by moving down-market and toward smartphones, and also by buying a unit of Infineon [322]. We see an emerging competition between ARM and x86 microprocessors [315]. Led by the Intel Atom, x86 chips are quickly migrating downward into embedded, low power environments, while ARM CPUs are beginning to flood upward into the more sophisticated and demanding market spaces currently dominated by x86 processors. Now, Intel is working on an x86-based ultramobile personal computer (UMPC) to "offer leading performance while reducing the footprint and power consumption" (Jon Jadersten), trying to invade ARM's traditional domain: low power handhelds. Intel has produced three "platforms" called *McCaslin, Menlow*, and *Moorestown*. Menlow consists of a Silverthorne 45-nm processor, a support chip called *Poulsbo* for controlling I/O and graphics, and a communications module that can be either Wi-Fi or WiMax capable. Moorestown combines the functionality of at least McCaslin and Menlow, reducing idle power consumption by an order of magnitude. Intel has also begun talks on mobile Internet devices (MIDs), a kind of more powerful iPhones. But this does not mean that FPGAs are not going to win. There are also indications that Apple plans to go FPGA [323]. Is Intel planning to buy an FPGA vendor? If not, I would not understand.

Microsoft is largely a x86 vendor, which means that most of these ARM implementations do not run a version of Windows, but run a version of Linux instead. Intel spends a lot of R&D for x86 on process and architecture. One example is the cost of verification with making over 1000 instructions work flawlessly, with predecoded logic, complex instruction caches, and many other techniques. Its versatility both in software and hardware made the x86 what it is. ARM versus x86 is basically an RISC versus a CISC debate. ARM has significant limitations and not yet the potential to replace x86 on the market. Does ARM not even reach the performance of 14-year-old Pentium? [324] What ARM brings to the table is very low power requirements for a given level of processor performance. ARM is fine when optimized for web browsing, writing, and watching video if you have the right video acceleration. For running something more, it will be too slow. To accelerate nonstandard codecs, it does not have enough instructions (such as extra multimedia ones) for playing such kind of video. Everything is getting compressed now for data saving. But ARM chips could hardly handle heavy compressed files such as WinRAR. Even the video subsystem of ARM Cortex-A8 is limited and memory is a slow 32-bit, DDR2 200 MHz. It needs faster RAM and more RAM. The double-precision floating-point throughput of ARM Cortex-A8 is also poor. In summary, FPGA superiority is not threatened.

I opine that with all the improvements ARM cores still have a weaker architecture than the first Intel Core (Banias) and Athlon (not 64) [324]. Where the ARM platform historically falls short is in multitasking, software breadth, and consistency between versions, especially the last one, where x86 remains relatively constant so that a piece of software can generally run on x86 products that are over a decade old. Each version of ARM generally requires a platform rewrite and this will make software offerings like application stores rather interesting to manage over the long term. Hardware virtualization, at least for the short term, will be difficult, because there is not a lot of extra performance overhead to run a virtual machine on ARM yet. The upcoming/next-generation Cortex-A class processor code-named "Eagle," for quad-core symmetric multiprocessing, intends to help redefine the smartphone landscape again. Will it be successful? So we do not yet need to declare our dramatic CPU to FPGA comparison figures (Section 18.5.1) for being obsolete.

Why does energy efficiency matter to ROI and the environment? Intel x86 chips have gained dominance in data centers. But because of the need to add so many more servers to meet our rising demand for computing, power considerations begin to determine the calculation. Cooling makes up nearly half the capital expenditure and almost two-thirds of the operation expense. However, for an Atom to ARM conversion, huge masses of software have to be rewritten, which means to port programs such as Windows. But even if the x86 domination ends, a transition to lower power server chips would take many years, if happening at all. FPGAs are still very far from being obsolete.

Meanwhile, much more power-efficient FPGAs are available. The exploding market for handheld smart devices creates pressure for low power. This has radically altered electronics design choices and decisions upstream. Expensive ASICs or custom ICs simply do not work in markets where cost is a factor, but the ability to hit tight market windows and adapt to changing technology standards is paramount. This paradigm shift requires FPGAs, which offer both low power capability and system design flexibility to meet time-to-market demands and changing user requirements and standards. For instance, GE Intelligent Platforms is developing a range of digital receiver, digital transceiver and FPGA processor products based on the Virtex-6 and 7 series FPGA families from Xilinx for applications such as software defined radio, signals intelligence, tactical communications, and radar [272], requiring more raw processing performance, greater capacity, higher speed I/O, and lower power consumption. An example is the power consumed by the FPGA of a converter design [299]. The comparison between low power FPGAs and low power CPUs is still massively in favor of the FPGAs as reported in Section 18.5.1. For instance, some authors reported a 103 mW FPGA [299]. With three new product families (Virtex-7, Kintex-7, Artix-7) fabricated by TSMC's 28-nm high-k metal gate (HKMG), high performance, low power (HPL) process technology, Xilinx has substantially improved power and performance, capacity, and price [300].

Being claimed to be the industry's lowest power and widest range of small packages, Actel's flash-based IGLOO FPGAs can be found in the latest handheld portable devices [321]. It has been designed for a wide array of handheld devices, including smartphones, eBooks, cameras, medical devices, industrial scanners, and military radios. Actel also offers a low power 15,000-gate IGLOO FPGA for 99 cents with a power consumption of only 5 μW, advertised as "more than 200x less static power than competitive FPGA offerings" [325]. Also Xilinx came up with much more power-efficient FPGAs. Our observation is that lower power consumption of current and future microprocessors stands against newer FPGAs also featuring much less power and much higher performance [9, 326].

The conclusion is that the role of migrations from software to RC as the silver bullet to massively save energy is not really affected, even in case that this bullet would be slightly slower (what has not yet been proved).

18.5.4   Reconfigurable Computing is the Silver Bullet

Since not offering improvements by orders of magnitude, traditional green computing (Section 18.5.3.1) is not threatening the paramount role of RC. The publication of speedups from software to configware migration started around 1995 (Fig. 18.13). Many of the published papers (Section 18.5.1) have compared FPGAs with earlier Wintel processors, as well as mostly with old types of FPGAs that are less power efficient. Although to publish saving energy by RC (Section 18.5.3) started a decade later, we may have a second look. But, we also have extremely power-efficient FPGAs (e.g., IGLOO [321]), which are also used for battery-powered handheld devices. The evaluation of power-saving figures from software to configware migration is not as simple as it has been.

Also, microprocessors are going low power (Section 18.5.4.1). Intel has begun talks on MIDs, a kind of more powerful iPhones. This does not mean that FPGAs are not going to win. There are indications that Apple plans to go FPGA [323]. I would understand if Intel is planning to buy an FPGA vendor. The upcoming/next-generation Cortex-A class processor "Eagle," intends to redefine the smartphone landscape again. However, we do not yet need to declare our dramatic CPU to FPGA comparison figures (Section 18.5.1) for being obsolete. Much more power-efficient FPGAs are also available. This has radically altered electronics design choices and decisions upstream. Expensive ASICs or custom ICs simply do not work in handheld smart devices markets where cost is a factor. The conclusion is that the role of migrations from software to RC as the silver bullet to massively save energy is not really affected, even when this bullet is slightly slower (what has not yet been proved). The very high energy consumption (Section 18.3.1) also urges us to revolutionize the fundamentals of programmer education. The conclusion is that also because of the programming wall (Section 18.3.2), we cannot avoid the need to reinvent computing. Since a lot of software has to be rewritten anyway for many-core (Section 18.5.6.1), a major migration campaign really makes sense (Section 18.5.6).

18.5.4.1   A new world model of computing. ASICs used as accelerators have massively lost market shares in favor of reconfigurable accelerators. Now, FPGA projects outnumber ASIC projects by 30 to 1 (Fig. 18.9 [327]), or even by 50 to 1 due to another estimation [192]. FPGAs are structurally programmed from "configware" sources, which are fundamentally different from the instruction-stream-based "software" sources (Table 18.6). FPGAs come with a different operating system world organizing data streams and swapping configware for partially and dynamically reconfigurable platform [195]. Introduced in 1984 and now a US$5-billion world market. Modern successors of FPGAs (Fig. 18.17) reach the market like EPPs. Also used for HPRC in supercomputing by Cray and Silicon Graphics, well-proven technology is rapidly heading mainstream.

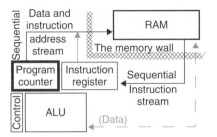

Figure 18.17   Interconnect fabrics example of a routable GA (gray line): example of one routed wire connecting two CLBs.

The traditional CPU-centric world model of the CS world is obsolete. It resembles the old Aristotelian geocentric world model. Its instruction-stream-based software-only tunnel view perspective hides structural and data stream aspects, thus massively threatening the progression of system performance, where we have to confront a dramatic capability gap. We need a generalized view, comparable to the Copernican world model not being geocentric. We need a model that also includes structures and data streams and supports time to space mapping, since scaling laws favor reconfigurable spatial computing over temporal computing. Exercising time to space mapping, also by programming data streams and by software to configware migration, provides important skills, for example, locality awareness, understanding and designing efficient many-core architecture and their memory organization being essential to cope with bottlenecks caused by bandwidth problems.

This new direction has not yet drawn the attention of the curriculum planner within the embedded systems scene. For CS, this is the opportunity of the century for heading toward new horizons and to preserve the affordability of its electricity consumption. This should be a wake-up call to CS curriculum development. Each of the many different application domains has only a limited view of computing and takes it more as a mere technique than as a science on its own. This fragmentation makes it very difficult to bridge the cultural and practical gaps since there are so many different actors and departments involved. We need the new CS world model to avoid the capability gap caused by that fragmentation. CS should take the full responsibility to merge RC with CS curricula for providing RC education from its roots. CS has the right perspective for a transdisciplinary unification in dealing with problems, which are shared across many different application domains. This new direction would also be helpful to reverse the current downtrend of CS enrollment.

Not only for the definition of the term "Reconfigurable Computing" (RC) it makes sense, to use a clear terminology—not only to improve education about how to reinvent computing. It is a sluttish use of terms if "soft" or "software" is used for everything, which is not hardware. The term *software* should be used only for instruction streams and their codes. However, we generalize the term *programming* (Fig. 18.18) such that procedural programming (in time domain)

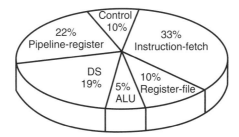

Figure 18.18   All but the ALU is overhead: x20 efficiency [187].

creates sequential code, like instruction streams (software) or data streams, which we call *flowware*, and "structural programming" (programming in space) creates "structural code," which we call *configware* since it can be used for the configuration of FPGAs or other reconfigurable platforms (Table 18.7).

This established terminology reveals (Table 18.8) that a software to configware migration means a paradigm shift, away from the traditional programmer's CPU-centric world model of computing, resembling the geocentric Aristotelian world model. To reinvent computing, we need a multiparadigm hetero system world model of computing science (Fig. 18.18), which models the coexistence of and the communication between (i) the traditional imperative software programming language mind-set with the CPUs running by software (instruction streams), (ii) the reconfigurable modules to be structurally programmed by configware, and (iii) an imperative data stream programming language mind-set with [289] data stream machines programmed by flowware for generating and accepting data streams (Table 18.7 also contains the data counter inside a reconfigurable address generator). We obtain an almost fully symmetric methodology: the only asymmetry is intraloop parallelism, possible for data streams, but not for instruction streams (Table 18.11). The semantic difference of these machine paradigms is the state register: the program counter (located with the ALU) for running the instruction streams in executing software, and the data counter(s) (located in memory block(s) [218, 274]) for running data streams in executing flowware.

Figure 18.18 illustrates this triple-paradigm "Copernican" world model replacing the vN-only-centric obsolete "Aristotelian" narrow tunnel view perspective of classical SE, which hides almost everything that is not instruction stream based. (The term *supersystolic* in Figure 18.8 stands for the generalization [172, 173, 191, 295–297] of the systolic array [214, 215]; nonlinear and nonuniform pipes are allowed, such as spiral, zigzag, and any excessively irregular shapes.) This generalized model will help us to come up with a new horizon of programmer education [328, 329] that masters overcoming the hardware/software chasm, having been a typical misconception of the ending first history of computing. The impact is a fascinating challenge to reach new horizons of research and development in CS. We need a new generation of talented innovative scientists and engineers to begin the second history of computing, not only for the survival of our important computer-based cyber infrastructure but also for developing and

TABLE 18.11   Software Languages versus Flowware Languages (Imperative Language Twins)[a]

#	Language Features	Software Languages	Flowware Languages
1	Sequencing managed by	Read next instruction, goto (instruction address), jump (to instruction address), instruction loop, and nesting, escapes instruction stream branching	Read next data item, goto (data address), jump (to data address), data loop, and nesting, escapes data stream branching
2	Parallelism	*No parallel loops*	*Yes, parallel loops* (by multiple data counters)
3	Data manipulation	Yes	*No* (hardwired or synthesis from configware language)
4	State register	Single *program counter* (in CPU)	One or more *data counter(s)* (in *asM* memory)
5	Instruction fetch	Memory cycle overhead	*No* memory cycle overhead
6	Address computation	Massive memory cycle overhead (depending on application)	Reconfigurable address generator(s) in asM: *no* memory cycle overhead

[a]Reference 278.

integrating exciting new innovative products for the transforming post-PC era global information and communication markets [289]. Masses of highly qualified new kinds of jobs must be created to meet the fascinating challenges of reinventing computing sciences, following the wide horizon of the new world model.

18.5.5   The Twin-Paradigm Approach to Tear Down the Wall

By going from hardwired accelerators to programmable (reconfigurable) accelerators, the traditional hardware/software chasm within CS education is turning into new horizons of SC interfacing. Mainstream academic SE education is crippling itself by ignoring that we now live in a twin-programming-paradigm world. Mainstream education also ignores the many-core programming crisis [330]. Why does SE still ignore this highly potent silver bullet candidate? Why? NIH effect? Not invented here?

Our contemporary model (Table 18.6, rows 1–3) now includes two procedural programming paradigms: software to schedule instruction streams and flowware to schedule data streams. This twin-paradigm model is a dichotomy and supports interlacing both machine paradigms. The ISP (CPU) model is the vN machine paradigm for sequencing by program counter. But flowware is based on sequencing by data counters. This counterpart and twin brother of the vN paradigm is the data stream machine paradigm.

Most primitives of a software language and a flowware language are mainly the same (Table 18.11). The only difference is the semantics: a software language deals with sequencing a program counter. A flowware language programs one or more data counters (generalized DMA, (direct memory access)) for sequencing data streams. This is the only asymmetry: just a single program counter (located in the CPU). But data stream machines may have several data counters running in parallel (located in asM data memory, generalized of DMA). Two exceptions make flowware languages more simple than software: (i) no data manipulation since being set up by reconfiguration via configware and (ii) parallelism inside loops, a data stream machine may have several data counters.

Since accelerators have become programmable, the traditional hardware/software chasm has become extremely intolerable. The supercomputing scene is on the way to learn that, via a vN strategy, the exascale computer will become unaffordable. We are forced to completely reinvent computing [331]. We need a generalization of SE by program engineering covering both time and space domains by including three paradigms: software, flowware [332], and configware [333] (Table 18.6; Fig. 18.19).

We need to rearrange undergraduate courses [334], following the advice of David Parnas [186]: "The biggest payoff will not come from new research but from putting old ideas into practice and teaching people how to apply them properly." Examples are two old simple rules of thumb: (i) loops turn into pipelines (the year 1979 and later [335]) and (ii) decision box turns into demultiplexer [336]. In the 1970s, when hardware description languages came up, a celebrity said "A decision box turns into a demultiplexer. This is so simple. Why did it take 30 years to find out?" [336]. It is the tunnel view perspective of SE. Also, the flowware paradigm is based on the data stream definition published in the late 1970s. We all need to extend our horizon to rediscover old stuff.

Programming education requires an interlacing twin-paradigm approach. Two dichotomies alleviate dual-rail teaching:

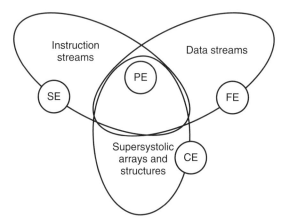

Figure 18.19 New CS world model. PE, program engineering; FE, flowware engineering; CE, configware engineering.

1. The machine paradigm dichotomy (vN versus data stream machine [49, 337, 338]).
2. The relativity dichotomy (time domain versus space domain, helps understand parallelization).

We are still affected by the "software crisis," although this term has been coined in 1968 [339]. Wikipedia says, "The software crisis was a term used in the early days of software engineering, before it was a well-established subject." [340] I disagree. In my opinion, SE is not yet a well-established subject. The software crisis has been and still is manifested by software that is difficult to maintain, very inefficient, of low quality, not meeting requirements, and by projects running overbudget and/or overtime, being unmanageable or canceled. Only about a decade ago, Niklaus Wirth's law says, "Software gets faster slower than hardware gets faster" [283] (apropos "slower faster": sometimes, should there not be even a comma between "slower" and "faster"?). It is widely agreed that here no "silver bullet" has yet been found. The software crisis is still far from being tamed. Dijkstra explained its causes [341] by the overall complexity made possible by growing processor performance, that is, by Moore's law. More recently, Microsoft's Nathan Myhrvold even argues that Nathan's law is driving Moore's law by the demand software creates, like a gas that fills its container. Let me even go further: this gas is not only filling growing memory microchips (Moore's law) but also growing disc space by Kryder's law [342], leaving Moore's law behind at a snail's pace. This gas is also filling the Internet with its communication bandwidth capacity for growing numbers of surfers and of e-mails growing in size; video on demand, Internet radio and TV, voice over IP; and growing numbers of smart mobile phones and Blackberries and what else is using it and its server farms [136] and cloud computing space [130] (whose law is this?).

The software crisis has become worse by the parallel programming wall now having become more dramatic by the many-core dilemma beginning around 2004. Now, the programming model is different. Software reuse and task partitioning have become more difficult [343]. We encounter multiple challenges [331], such as shared resource contentions, how to implement timing behavior [331] and to control timing precision and safety requirements [344], as well as to achieve simultaneously both low power and high performance. It is questionable whether a larger number of slower processors are more efficient. We need to construct new timing models describing all possible timed traces of bus and memory requests [345]. We have to cope with a wide classification variety of hardware architecture [346]: multithreading, homogeneous versus heterogeneous [347], message passing, shared memory, UMA (uniform memory architecture) or NUMA, SMP versus AMP (asymmetric multiprocessor), etc. The impact of very high energy consumption by all computers worldwide offers a higher success potential than most other energy and climate policy issues. Future unaffordability of our total

TABLE 18.12 Similar Scenario: SE Revolution versus Mead & Conway VLSI Design Revolution[a]

#	Scene	Problem	Interactions	Claims	Solution
1	M & C revolution	VLSI designer population missing	Semiconductor technology vs computer science	Technology claimed *it is* their job (but could not follow Moore's law)	Separating: create VLSI design education scene
2	Proposed SE revolution	Innovative programmer population missing	SE vs RC	SE claims, it is *not* their job	Merging: include RC into SE education

[a]References 95–105.

computer operating cost is looming. The further predominance of the vN programming paradigm is intolerable. We urgently need to motivate opinion leaders in SE and curriculum recommendation task forces.

18.5.6 A Mass Movement Needed as Soon as Possible

The scenario resembles the VLSI design revolution, the most effective project in the history of modern CS (row 1, Table 18.12). Originally, the semiconductor technology experts claimed that they master circuit design with the left hand. The Moore curve approaching 1000 transistors per chip turned this into a design crisis with a missing qualified designer population. VLSI design education has been founded as a separate discipline outside technology, supported by a new textbook, especially written for people without technology background [101]. Within 3 years, these courses have been introduced by more than a hundred universities worldwide.

We now have a similar scenario (row 2, Table 18.12). Is this not a strong motivation for the SE scene? No, not yet. In contrast to the VLSI revolution, the SE community claims that RC is not their job, and the solution is merging instead of separating (last 2 columns of Table 18.12). We again need such innovative education efforts: professors back to school. We need a worldwide mass movement qualifying most programmers for twin-paradigm programming, ready for a worldwide changeover of many applications, what will create a lot of jobs for at least a decade. But in contrast to the VLSI design revolution, we have to merge two so far separate disciplines: software-based CPU programming methodology with flowware and configware-based RC. New horizons in saving massive amounts of energy and very HPC will be opened up by this generalization of SE.

Until today, masses of IBM 360 compatible software packages are still running. Since most of the programmers (the baby boom generation) who wrote that stuff are retired, a bunch of universities is starting courses on "mainframe programming" for their (hopefully) successors. We see the massive inertial effects of legacy software. What are the consequences of planning major software to configware migration campaigns to save energy by reducing the energy consumption of all our IT infrastructure? We will need much effort in selecting the candidates for migration.

18.5.6.1 Legacy software from the mainframe age. This section discusses why massive software to configware migration makes sense. What are the reasons why a migration from microprocessors to FPGAs makes sense, although FPGAs seem to be massively less effective from a technological point of view. The explanation for this paradox is the unbelievable inefficiency of software based on the vN paradigm.

Origins of legacy software may reach back by almost half a century, like that of mainframe software. IBM and CA Technologies (Islandia, NY, USA, maker of mainframe software) are hard-pressed to replace the aging corps of baby boomers who support their still-indispensable mainframe business [114] (SW still compatible with IBM 360 mainframes). IBM commands 85% of the mainframe market with some 10,000 mainframes used by 4000–5000 customers around the globe [114]. Some companies still employ an older mainframe with a screen known as a 3270 terminal emulator, which evokes the decades-old DOS, that predated Microsoft (MSFT) Windows [111]. The roots of modern mainframes can be traced back to the introduction of IBM System/360 in the mid-1960s, when the oldest baby boomers were still teenagers. With their ability to reliably process millions of instructions per second, mainframes became popular in banking, insurance, and other industries that required high power computing. For that era's CS students, the mainframe represented cutting-edge technology.

For IBM, mainframes are a high margin business, generating additional software and service revenues. Margins for mainframes are about 70%, compared with 46% for the company's margins as a whole [114]. The resulting worker shortage poses a threat to IBM. If unresolved, the lack of engineers adept at designing, programming, and repairing mainframes could curb demand for one of IBM's most profitable products by alternatives including Hewlett-Packard (HPQ) or Dell (DELL) servers to run networks, Web operations, and a growing range of the computing tasks once entrusted to mainframes.

Teaching such mainframe skills is out of vogue at many universities. Many engineers capable of tinkering with the refrigerator-sized machines are nearing retirement. "This inescapable demographics will be trouble for the platform" [114]. So IBM has created a curriculum designed to encourage the teaching of mainframe skills and distributed it to institutions of higher learning in 61 countries and began distributing its System z Academic Initiative to 24 colleges and universities in 2003. The number swelled to 700 this year and is expected to reach 1000 institutions by the end of 2011 [114]. Aside from training new mainframe workers, CA Technologies aims to keep existing mainframe experts in place longer. It offers flexible work schedules such as 3-day-work weeks. The company will even consider letting seasoned engineers take summers off. CA Technologies hires about 40–50 people a year and also encourages retiring workers to mentor younger ones.

18.5.7   How to Reinvent Computing

The key issue is the CS education dilemma. To save massive amounts of energy, we need a worldwide changeover of many applications, from vN machines to FPGAs. This may take more than a decade and will also create a lot of jobs. However, FPGAs are still a niche technology since we have yet to train and qualify a sufficiently large population of programmers for FPGA programming. Advanced training of such programmers needs support everywhere, at regional, national, and global levels. This section emphasizes that RC is a critical survival issue for computing-supported infrastructure worldwide and stresses the urgency of moving RC from niche to mainstream. It urges acceptance of the massive challenge of reinventing computing, away from its currently obsolete CPU-processor-centric Aristotelian CS world model to a twin-paradigm Copernican model. A massive software to configware migration campaign is needed. This warrants clever planning to optimize the effort to obtain the expected results, and which software packets should be migrated first should be known. All this requires massive R&D and education efforts, taking many years. Lobbying for the massive funding should be started immediately. We should address politicians at all levels: community level, state level, national level, and the EU level.

To explain all this to politicians is very difficult. Since politicians always watch the sentiment of their voter population, we efficiently have to teach the public, which is a challenge. Without a strong tailwind from the media, lobbying seems to be almost without success. All this has to be completed as soon as possible, as long as we can still afford such a campaign. To succeed with such a challenging educational campaign, the foundation of a consortium is needed for running an at least Europe-wide project.

Before going to reinvent computing, let us have a look at the current scenario. The rate of ASIC-to-FPGA conversions continues to escalate. But methodology and tool flow questions impact the bottom line. Successful switching from ASICs to FPGAs depends very much on the tools, practices, and processes chosen for the FPGA development work. With high quality tools and complete, well-integrated solutions of vendor-independent ESL, IP reuse, verification, synthesis, and PCB flow, designers need not learn a new tool set for every FPGA vendor's products and a company does not lose its freedom of FPGA vendor choice. This frees to pragmatically select the device that best fits the project needs, without concern for prior tool usage. For PCB development, it is necessary to carefully consider whether the process is predictable and well integrated, is consistent from project to project, and offers the flexibility to move to another FPGA vendor.

The remarkable phenomenon of Electronics IP providers exists not only for ASICs but also for configware onto FPGAs. First IP providers have been founded in the 1990s, and some of them have been acquired by others: Altium, Ansoft, ANSYS, ARM, Artisan, Cadence, CEVA, Logic Vision, Magma, Mentor Graphics, MIPS, Monolithic, Mosys, Nassda, Sinplicity, Synopsys, Parthus, Rambus, Verisity, VirageLogic, and Total. MIPS was founded in 1984 but turned to the IP business later on and since 1998 was officially called "MIPS Technologies." The

IP ecosystem is also for FPGAs that are still RTL (register transfer language)-dominated because most FPGA vendors use RTL flow, so porting the design to another FPGA is not extremely complicated like it is in microprocessors where legacy code plays a high role for market dominance. The inherently parallel RTL application is mapped automatically parallelized by CAD tools; however, it is not necessarily free of bugs such as issues of nanosecond real-time response times or data throughput requirements. The required visibility is not provided by traditional debug/trace tools. So it is not always easier to port IPs both for ASICs and FPGAs, as both use RTL. All this is still one of the major difficulties for many-core solutions. Merging both worlds is really a challenge.

FPGAs are also used everywhere for high performance in scientific computing, where this is really a new computing culture and not at all a variety of hardware design. Instead of H/S codesign we have here SC codesign, which is really a computing issue. This major new direction of developments in science will determine how academic computing will look in 2015 or even earlier. The instruction-stream-based mind-set will loose its monopoly-like dominance and the CPU will quit its central role to be more of an auxiliary clerk and also for software compatibility issues.

An introduction to RC (91, 212, 213, 218, 219, 221–244, 247–271, 273–289, 246, 290, 291, 299–303) should regard the background to be expected from the reader. This chapter mainly addresses a bit IT-savvy people in the public and its mass media, as well as "software engineers." Here an introduction is difficult since in both communities, people typically know nothing or almost nothing about RC. To move RC from its niche market into mainstream, massive funding is needed for R&D and to reinvent programming education. To yield the attention of media and the politicians, we need a highly effective campaign by mass media.

Up to 32 cores per chip have already been preannounced. Already six, eight, or more CPUs mostly connect to each other instead of getting work done [340]. Transitioning from single core to multicore can certainly be a difficult design challenge. What issues are encountered when moving from single core to multicore? Before multicore, programmers had it easy. The same old software runs on the new chips much faster, just by a free ride on Moore's curve. However, software designed for single core may run slower on a multicore machine. Computer games and some telecommunications and compression/decompression applications are relatively easy to parallelize.

But complex applications that involve a great deal of data are not easy to parallelize. Often the algorithm has to be changed and the application has to be recoded. Parallel applications require highly sophisticated debugging tools to cope with new kinds of bugs introduced by the parallelism. To take advantage of the additional cores, most applications have to be rewritten, unfortunately also introducing new types of bugs [340]. Programmers are not trained to think toward parallel processing. For the required style of parallel programming, a sufficiently large qualified programmer population is far from existing.

The following list outlines the educational barriers we have to surmount and the urgent need for major funding on a global scale to run a worldwide mass movement, of a dimension as far reaching as the Mead & Conway style of microelectronics revolution in the early 1980s.

1. A mass migration from software to configware for the benefits of saving massive amounts of energy, much higher performance, and gaining high flexibility.

2. From time to time, only a smaller part of legacy software can be migrated. For optimization, we need to develop a migration priority list to identify the most promising candidates.

3. In the future, we also will have to decide whether to also use neurocomputing [4, 228, 239, 348, 349]. To overcome the limits derived by the increasing complexity and the associated workload to maintain such complex infrastructure, one possibility is to adopt self-adaptive and autonomic computing systems. A self-adaptive and autonomic computing system is a system able to configure, heal, optimize, and protect itself without the need for human intervention.

4. Another obstacle is that a qualified programmer population needed for such a mass movement campaign is missing and should be available at least throughout the beginning of this decade.

Programmers have to be prepared for the migration of their software. In any case, the result will mostly be hetero systems, where programmers with an instruction-stream-based sequential-only mind-set are not qualified. Educating, or reeducating, programmers is mandatory. Or even to keep one's head above water. And as quick as possible, we have to reinvent courses at academia and all other kinds of schools and have to upgrade our highly obsolete curriculum plans and recommendations. We have to take care of a massive programmer productivity decline for the following four reasons:

1. To cope with the many-core crisis where more parallel programming qualifications are a must.

2. To resolve the extreme shortage of programmers qualified for RC.

3. To program hetero systems (like modern FPGAs featuring all the following three: reconfigurable fabrics, hardwired blocks, and CPUs), requiring twin-paradigm programming skills.

4. To determine if the upcoming memristor technology [131] the area of neurocomputing (4, 221, 224, 228, 239–245, 247–271, 273–279, 281–289, 246, 290, 291, 301–324, 350, 325, 326, 340, 348, 349, 351) could lead us in the future to hetero systems requiring triple-paradigm skills.

In consequence, we need innovative undergraduate programming courses [352] that also teach a sense of locality. Such a sense of locality needed for classical parallel programming is already coming along in RC, with time to space mapping required to structurally map an application to the data stream side of the twin-paradigm approach. This means that teaching the structural programming of RC also exercises the sense of locality needed for traditional parallel programming. The extension of the nonsequential part of education should be optimized not to scare away undergraduate students. Twin-paradigm laboratory courses should be MathWorks supported and model based, mainly at the abstraction level of pipe networks.

vN scales up cost, performance, power, cooling, and reliability concerns [280]. Bill Dally summarizes [353], performance = parallelism/efficiency = locality, high performance requires parallelism of operations given by RC platforms. Efficiency is possible by optimum locality of data and program code since the movement of data and instruction streams is the reason of bottlenecks by resource contention and bandwidth limitations. These locality problems are the reason that programming embedded systems and supercomputers have become a very complex and difficult area of research and development. In heterocomputing systems, RC is a very important accelerator of locality and parallelism.

That is why RC should urgently become mainstream. Several reasons have prevented RC from truly becoming mainstream [354]. The execution model is inherently different from the traditional sequential paradigm, where we can reason about state transition sequences much better than in a hardware or a concurrent execution model. As a consequence, the development and validation of tools is substantially a traditional hardware mind-set. For software developers, it is always this mythical chip that got added by the hardware designer onto the board. The problem we have to solve is how to teach programming FPGAs to programmers? What new models, languages, and tools?

The key issue is programmer productivity. It is a handicap of vN-oriented textual programming languages that layers of abstraction hide critical sources and limit efficient programming for parallel execution by lacking locality awareness. We need to reinvent the tool flow for programming both many-core and RC. Better tools are also urgently needed since acceleration by RC also requires more programming effort because an in-depth application study is required. Tools are still limited and above all fairly bridled. This means programmers must master the details of not only software development but also hardware design. Such a set of skills is also not taught as part of major electrical engineering courses severely constraining the pool of engineering with the "right" mind-set for programming RC to a selected few. Moreover, the recent evolution of FPGAs and to some extent coarse-grain RC architecture make programmer and performance portability a little less difficult at best.

We need to model and program real-time and embedded applications [346]. What model and language should we use for hetero systems development? The language inflation does not motivate to invent a new language (Tables 18.1–18.3). We should investigate primitives and models available in existing languages with programming of multicore and the efforts on the way to address them. Currently, popular in the many-core side are also open solutions such as OpenMP [355] and several tools from Intel to help programmers exploit its multicore processors. Since also exploiting locality of reference, the partitioned global address space (PGAS), a parallel programming model, seems to be attractive for solving twin-paradigm problems. The PGAS model is the basis of Unified Parallel C, Co-array Fortran, Titanium, Fortress, Chapel, and X10. A candidate could be the programming language X10 developed by IBM, which is designed for parallel programming using the partitioned global address space (PGAS) model [356]. X10, also exploiting locality of reference, uses the concept of parent and child relationships for activities and supports user-defined primitive structure types, globally distributed arrays, and structured and unstructured parallelism. We definitely should look at SPEAR (221, 224, 230–245, 247–271, 273–289, 246, 290, 291, 301–324, 350, 325, 326, 329–345, 347–349, 351, 352, 354, 357–364), a tool set developed for hetero systems within the framework of the MOR-PHEUS project [226] funded by the European Union. What about UML? We should investigate whether UML offers interesting features [346]. What can we learn from OpenCL and other languages [365]? What about functional languages (Table 18.13) or dataflow languages (Table 18.14)?

Lowering the barrier of access of RC to the average programmers is one of the objectives of the REFLECT project [213] by retaining the "traditional" imperative programming mind-set in a high level language (HLL) environment such as MATLAB [366] and relying on the concepts of aspects to provide a clean mechanism (at source code level) for the advanced user to provide key

TABLE 18.13   Some Functional Languages[a]

Alice	Curl	J	Mathematica	Opal	Scala
APL	Curry	Joy	Miranda	OPS5	Scheme
CAL	Dylan	Kite	ML	Poplog	Spreadsheets
Charity[a]	Erlang	Lisp	Standard ML	Q	Tea
Clean[a]	F#	Little b	Mythryl	R	
Clojure	Haskell[a]	Logo	Nemerle	REFAL	
Common Lisp	Hop	Lush	Ocam	Russell	

[a] Purely functional.

TABLE 18.14   Some Dataflow Languages[a]

AviSynth	G	Max/Msp	Prograph	SISAL	vvvv
BMDFM	JMax	Microsoft	Pure Data	SPACE-	VHDL
Clojure	LabVIEW	Monk	Quartz Composer	AREVAs	Verilog
DUP	LAU	MoPL		Tersus	XEE
Fastflow	Lily	VPL	Show and Tell	VBIS	X10
Hartmann pipelines	Lucid	OpenWire	Simulink	VEE	VBIS
	Lustre	OZ	SAC	VisSim	

[a] Reference 350.

information for a compilation and synthesis tool to do a good job in mapping the computation to hardware. The approach should be by no means fully automatic [354]. Instead, we have the programmer involved but controlling the high level aspects of the mapping while the tools take care of the low level, error-prone steps. We may learn a lot from all this.

There has been no lack of effort in this area. But the silver bullet has not yet been completed. But we see it coming up from the highly promising new horizon: a model-based twin-paradigm methodology to master hetero of all three: single core, multicore, and reconfigurable computing. Let me propose the acronym RC2RC (reconfigurable computing to reinvent computing), or R2R. We need to rewrite textbooks for R2R (RT4R2R), and all our friends should become reinvent computing evangelists (RCEs) (or R2R evangelists (R2RE)). A qualified programmer population for hetero systems does not exist. We should kick off a worldwide mass movement by learning from the Mead & Conway VLSI design revolution, which started around 1980, since a designer population did not exist [95, 105].

Within an increasingly complex value chain (Fig. 18.20), we are hit by the impact of vertical disintegration (Fig. 18.21). Currently, we see here at IP core level the challenging battle between FPGAs and MPSoC-like platforms which results in a battle between software programming and RTL programming (RTL programming using hardware languages such as VHDL or Verilog) [124]. We must extend the "traditional" imperative programming mind-set (for software) by a twin-paradigm imperative mind also including an imperative data stream programming methodology (for "flowware"; for terminology, see Table 18.11) [289]. We obtain an almost fully symmetric methodology: the only asymmetry is intraloop parallelism, possible for data streams but not for instruction streams (Table 18.11). The semantic difference of these machine paradigms is the state register: the program counter (located with the ALU) for running the instruction streams in executing software, and data counter(s) (located in memory block(s) [204, 274]) for running data streams in executing flowware. Using schematic or flowchart graphical design interfaces, IP blocks, software routines, and I/O systems can be quickly combined to explore and develop innovative product functionality without the need for low level engineering (Section 18.4.2) [199].

We can do more than just programming the onboard FPGA [199]. By intelligent communication between hardware platform and the high level design software, the system could directly interact with all parts of the development board. Peripherals can then be swapped on the fly by automatically reconfiguring interface layers and configuration files. So the complete development system, including the physical hardware, acts as the one design environment. Hardware could conceivably become the final product.

Recently, the drag-and-drop LabVIEW graphical programming environment [367, 368] came up as an FPGA development environment [369]. Unlike textual hardware description languages, it is inherently parallel. LabVIEW 2010 has some interesting features for FPGA specialists including extended IP input, fast cycle-accurate simulation, new compilation options, and a new route to system

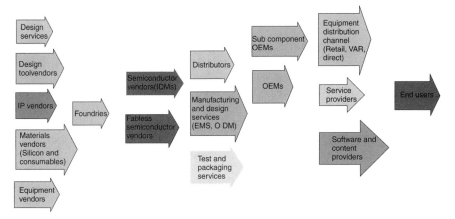

Figure 18.20   Complexity of the value chain. IP, intellectual property; IDM, integrated device manufacturer; EMS, electronics manufacturing service; ODM, original design manufacturer; OEM, original equipment manufacturer; VAR, value-added reseller. *Source:* Manfred Glesner; Gartner.

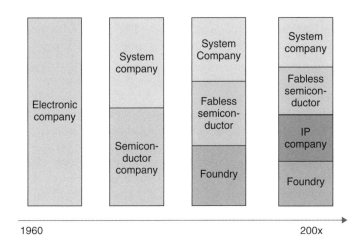

Figure 18.21   Vertical disintegration. *Source:* Manfred Glesner.

integration [369]. This environment now provides much closer coupling with the Xilinx Core Generator tool for loading code into FPGAs mounted in a range of boards [369]. It is possible to return to the LabVIEW screen to create the system surrounding the FPGA, adding IO and other peripherals. The features of this product are good examples to provide ideas for what we need for parallel programming both, many-core and RC platforms and hetero systems of both. We need a well-designed graphic user interface showing the architecture of the NoC and beyond providing the visualization of locality to identify critical locations with possible bottlenecks by shared resource contention and bandwidth limitations.

The sequential-only oriented Turing-only world has perished. We need to recognize that we are now living in the world of hetero computing. Getting familiar with LabVIEW may give us some inspirations about the direction to go. Also the call for papers of the 4th Workshop on Programmability Issues for Heterogeneous Multicores (MULTIPROG-2011) is very helpful by listing what we really need in this world to solve the programmability crisis [370]. For discovering and understanding parallelism, performance, bottlenecks, dependency problems, and debugging, we need understandability tools, discovery tools, locality awareness tools, and benchmarking tools.

Usually, it is very difficult to understand the code generated by compiler optimizations and other compiler techniques. We urgently need visualization of locality. Maybe, other understandability tools could also be helpful here. We urgently need a much better understanding of memory system architecture, NoC architecture, and, entire many-core SoC architecture and their routes of code and data. We need more knowledge about what architectural support do we need for compilers and programming models. Textual language extensions tend to be not very helpful, since being sequential-only-based, textual descriptions are typically very difficult for understanding parallelism. I opine that model-driven understandability tools based on real-time graphics should be the way to go. Inspirations from LabVIEW and Simulink [366] and their user interfaces may be useful.

18.6   CONCLUSIONS

This chapter has emphasized that RC is a critical survival issue for computing-supported infrastructure worldwide and has stressed the urgency of moving RC from niche to mainstream. It is a critical issue for two reasons. One problem is the trouble with multicore: chipmakers are designing microprocessors that most programmers cannot program [167]. RC is a key part of the solution to cope with the parallel programming wall. The other problem is the dramatically high energy consumption by vN computing, caused by the vN syndrome. A mass migration of applications from software to configware for running RC platforms is needed. For both problems, the qualified programmer population does not exist. Although providing some remarks about the multicore dilemma and proposals for its solution, this chapter mainly covered the side of RC. But we cannot completely separate these problem areas from each other, since the same programmer population has to be retrained to be qualified for programming hetero systems including both paradigms: parallel data streams coming with reconfigurable platforms and parallel instruction streams.

FPGAs have a relatively low technology maturity and small user base compared to software. This will change. Large parts of FPGA solution development is spent on learning specific FPGA board APIs and debugging in hardware FPGAs Achilles' heel is in their long development time, since relatively low level HDLs such as VHDL or Verilog are still dominant. Other directions of development try to work with C language sources, such as Stone Ridge Technologies with its FPGA board and the development kit with the Impulse C tool set from Impulse Accelerated Technologies. A product review [371] reports that software developers write HLL algorithms that rapidly compile to optimized RTL runtime language targeting Stone Ridge's RDX-11 FPGA board and development kit. They report that for designs with significant nonsequential logic, the speed improvements can be $10–100\times$ and that compared to hand-coded RTL, the design entry takes only two-thirds the time and the iterations, one-eighth the time. We have to check this and need to reinvent major parts of this area.

We urgently need a worldwide mass movement of R&D and education to be more massively funded and supported than the Mead & Conway VLSI design revolution in the early 1980s, which so far has been the most effective project in the history of modern computing science [95–99]. This chapter urges to accept the massive challenge of reinventing computing, away from its currently obsolete CPU-processor-centric Aristotelian CS world model, to a twin-paradigm Copernican model. A massive software to configware migration campaign is needed. First this requires clever planning to optimize all its aspects. We also need to develop plans deciding which software packets need to be migrated and which of them should be migrated first. All this requires many years, probably a decade of massive R&D and education efforts. We cannot afford to hesitate. Lobbying for the massive funding should be started right now. We should address politicians at all levels: community level, state level, national level, and the EU level. To explain all this to politicians is very difficult. Since politicians always watch the sentiment of their voter population, we efficiently have to teach the public, which is a dramatic challenge. How do we effectively reach as many as possible people by the media? Scientific studies point toward embedding into amusing or entertaining stories, presentation inside docusoaps, soap operas, reality shows, or infotainment formats [372]. Without the support by a strong tailwind from the media, lobbying does not seem to have any chance. All this has to be completed as soon as possible and as soon as we can still afford such massive activities. To succeed with such a challenging educational campaign, the foundation of a powerful consortium to be funded at all levels is needed for running an at least Europe-wide project.

LIST OF ABBREVIATIONS

ALU	Arithmetic/Logic Unit
AMP	Asymmetric Multiprocessor
ASIC	Application-Specific Integrated Circuit
ASIP	Application-Specific Instruction Set Processor
asM	Autosequencing Memory
ASMP	Asymmetric Multiprocessor

CABAC	Context-Adaptive Binary Arithmetic Coding
ccNUMA	Cache Coherent NUMA
CE	Computer Engineering
CS	Computer Science
CHREC	NSF Center for High Performance Reconfigurable Computing
CLB	Configurable Logic Block
CMP	Chip Multiprocessor
CoMA	Cache Only Memory Access
CPU	Central Processing Unit
DEPS	Dynamic Energy/Performance Scaling
DNA	Deoxyribonucleic Acid
DPA	Data Path Array
DPU	Data Path Unit
DSM	Distributed Shared Memory
DSP	Digital Signal Processing
DVFS	Dynamic Voltage/Frequency Scaling
EDA	Electronics Design Automation
eASIC	partly FPGAstyle ASIC
ePLA	e-Programmable LA
EPP	Extensible Programmable Platform
ePROM	e-programmable PROM
ERC	Electrical Rules Checker
ESL	Electronic System-Level Design
EU	European Union
FDMP	Function-Distributed MP
FIR	Finite Impulse Response
FME	Flash Media Encoder
FP	Field Programmable
FPGA	Field-Programmable GA
FPL	Field-Programmable Logic
FPLA	Field-Programmable PLA
FPU	Floating Point Unit
FRAM	Ferroelectric RAM
GA	(routable) Gate Array
HPC	High Performance Computing
HPRC	High Performance RC
HWD	Hardwired Device
ICT	Information and Communication Technology
IEA	International Energy Agency
IME	Integer Motion Estimation
IP	Intellectual Property
IT	Information Technology
LA	(compact) Logic Array
LCMP	Loosely Coupled MP
LUT	Lookup Table
MA	Memory Architecture
MAC	Multiply/Accumulate Unit
MIPS	Million Instructions per Second
MoPL	Map-Oriented PL

MP	Multiprocessor
MRAM	Magnetoresistive RAM
NoRMA	No Remote Memory Access
NUMA	Nonuniform MA
PC	Personal Computer
PL	Programming Language
PLA	Programmable LA
PLD	Programmable Logic Device
PROM	Programmable ROM
PU	Processing Unit
r	reconfigurable or FP
RAM	Random Access Memory
RC	Reconfigurable Computing
rDPA	Reconfigurable DPA
rDPU	Reconfigurable DPU
rE	reconfigurable Element
ROI	Return on Investment
ROM	Read-Only Memory
RTL	Register Transfer Language
R&D	Research and Development
SCTP	Stream Control Transmission Protocol
SE	Software Engineering
SMP	Symmetric Multiprocessor
STM	Software Transactional Memory
TDP	Thermal Design Power
TM	Transactional Memory
UMA	Uniform MA
VLSI	Very Large-Scale Integrated
vN	von Neumann
WCET	Worst-Case Execution Time

REFERENCES

1. Maxfield C. Reproducing a Cray 1 supercomputer in a single FPGA, EE Times; 2010 Sep 3. Available at http://www.eetimes.com/design/programmable-logic/4207359/Reproduce-Cray-1-supercomputer-in-a-single-FPGA.

2. Bobda Ch. *Introduction to Reconfigurable Computing-Architectures, Algorithms, Applications*; Springer; 2007.

3. Cardoso J, Huebner M, editors. *Reconfigurable Computing*. New York: Springer-Verlag; 2010.

4. Hartenstein R. The grand challenge to reinvent computing. In: XXX Congress of the SBC; 2010 July 20–23; Belo Horizonte, MG, Brazil. Available at http://www.inf.pucminas.br/sbc2010/anais/pdf/semish/st03_02.pdf.

5. Jammy R (keynote). Emerging low power technologies: CMOS or beyond CMOS?. In: 2010 International Symposium on Low Power Electronics and Design (ISLPED); 2010 Aug 18–20; Austin (TX).

6. Dadgour H, Banerjee K. A New paradigm in the design of energy-efficient digital circuits using laterally-actuated double-gate NEMS. In: 2010 International Symposium on Low Power Electronics and Design (ISLPED); 2010 Aug 18–20; Austin (TX).

7. Niu Dimin, et al.. Low-power dual-element memristor-based memory design. In: 2010 International Symposium on Low Power Electronics and Design (ISLPED); 2010 Aug 18–20; Austin (TX).

8. Amerasekera A (keynote). Ultra low power electronics in the next decade. In: 2010 International Symposium on Low Power Electronics and Design (ISLPED); 2010 Aug 18–20; Austin (TX).

9. LeCompte C. Green Data Centers; 2010 March 11, GigaOM (BusinessWeek).

10. Kharif O. Green Data Centers Blossom; 2007 May 30, Business Week.

11. Lin FLY, He L, Cong J. Low-power FPGA using pre-defined dual-Vdd/dual-Vt fabrics. In: 2004 ACM/SIGDA 12th International Symposium on FPGAs; 2004; Monterey (CA).

12. Nussbaum B. The world after oil; 1984 June 29; Touchstone.

13. Hartmann Th, Kretzschmar G. *Unser Ausgebrannter Planet: Von der Weisheit der Erde und der Torheit der Moderne*. Riemann Verlag; 2000.

14. Leggett J. *Carbon War: Global Warming and the End of the Oil Era*. Routledge; 2001.

15. Donaldson S. *Giant Earthquake Will Drain World's Oil Supplies Like a Flushing Toilet*. Weekly World News; 2002.

16. Campbell CJ. *The Coming Oil Crisis*. Multi-Science Publishing Co. Ltd.; 2004.

17. Heinberg R. *Powerdown: Options and Actions for a Post-Carbon World*. New Society; 2004.

18. Ruppert MC, Fitts CA. *Crossing the Rubicon: The Decline of the American Empire at the End of the Age of Oil*. New Society Publishers; 2004.

19. Goodstein D. *Out of Gas: The End of the Age Of Oil*. W.W. Norton & Company; 2005.

20. Smil V. *Energy at the Crossroads: Global Perspectives and Uncertainties*. The MIT Press; 2005.

21. Roberts P. *The End of Oil: On the Edge of a Perilous New World*. Mariner Books; 2005.

22. Marbach E, des Ölgipfels J. *Ein Peak-Oil-roman*. Verlag Solare Zukunft; 2005.

23. Heinberg R. *The Party's Over: Oil, War and the Fate of Industrial Societies*. New Society; 2005.

24. Blanchard RD. *The Future of Global Oil Production: Facts, Figures, Trends And Projections, by Region*. McFarland & Company; 2005.

25. Kunstler JH. *The Long Emergency: Surviving the End of Oil, Climate Change, and Other Converging Catastrophes of the Twenty-First Century*. Grove Press; 2006.

26. Gründinger W. *Die Energiefalle: Ein Rückblick auf das Erdölzeitalter*. Beck; 2006.

27. Cordesman AH, Al-Rodhan KR. *The Global Oil Market: Risks and Uncertainties*. Center for Strategic & International Studies; 2006.

28. Shah S. *Crude: The Story of Oil*. Seven Stories Press; 2006.

29. Maugeri L. *The Age of Oil: The Mythology, History, and Future of the World's Most Controversial Resource*. Praeger; 2006.

30. Noreng O. *Crude Power: Politics and the Oil Market*. I. B. Tauris; 2006.

31. Simmons MR. *Twilight in the Desert: The Coming Saudi Oil Shock and the World Economy*. John Wiley and Sons; 2006.

32. Deffeyes KS. *Beyond Oil: The View from Hubbert's Peak*. Hill and Wang; 2006.

33. Pfeiffer DA. *Eating Fossil Fuels: Oil, Food and the Coming Crisis in Agriculture*. New Society; 2006.

34. Mabro R. *Oil in the Twenty-First Century: Issues, Challenges, and Opportunities*. Oxford University Press; 2006.

35. Simmons MR. *Wenn der Wüste das öl ausgeht: Der kommende ölschock in Saudi-Arabien-Chancen und Risiken*. FinanzBuch Verlag; 2006.

36. Campbell CJ, Liesenborghs F, Schindler J, Zittel W, Roth H. *ölwechsel!: Das Ende des Erdölzeitalters und die Weichenstellung für die Zukunft*. DTV; 2007.

37. Leeb S, Strathy G. *The Coming Economic Collapse: How You Can Thrive When Oil Costs $200 a Barrel*. Business Plus; 2007.

38. Merrill KR. *The Oil Crisis of 1973–1974*. Bedford/St. Martin's; 2007.

39. Tertzakian P. *A Thousand Barrels a Second: The Coming Oil Break Point and the Challenges Facing an Energy Dependent World*. McGraw-Hill; 2007.

40. Adams W, Al-Awadi AS, McCormack R, Gelpke B. *A Crude Awakening-The Oil Crash*, DVD. DOCURAMA; 2007.

41. Heinberg R. *Peak Everything: Waking Up to the Century of Declines*. New Society; 2007.

42. Maugeri L. *The Age of Oil: What They Don't Want You to Know About the World's Most Controversial Resource*. The Lyons Press; 2007.

43. Strahan David. *The Last Oil Shock*. John Murray; 2007.

44. Moroney J, Simmons M. *Power Struggle: World Energy in the Twenty-First Century*. Praeger; 2008.

45. Petermann J. *Sichere Energie im 21. Jahrhundert*. Hoffmann und Campe; 2008.

46. Raggam A, Faißner K. *Zukunft ohne öl: Lösungen für Verkehr, Wärme und Strom*. Stocker; 2008.

47. Marbach E. *Peakoil Reloaded*. Marbach, Eva Verlag; 2008.

48. Mills RM. *The Myth of the Oil Crisis: Overcoming the Challenges of Depletion, Geopolitics, and Global Warming*. Praeger; 2008.

49. Greer JM. *The Long Descent: A User's Guide to the End of the Industrial Age*. New Society; 2008.

50. Gruss P. *Die Zukunft der Energie: Die Antwort der Wissenschaft. Ein Report der Max-Planck-Gesellschaft*. C.H. Beck; 2008.

51. Heinberg R, Bayer M, Hickisch B. *öl-Ende: "The Party's Over"-Die Zukunft der industrialisierten Welt ohne öl*. Riemann Verlag; 2008.

52. Müller-Kraenner S. *Energy Security*. Earthscan Publications Ltd.; 2008.

53. Victor DG, Jaffe AM, Hayes MH. *Natural Gas and Geopolitics: From 1970 to 2040*. Cambridge University Press; 2008.

54. Eschbach A. *Ausgebrannt: Thriller*. Bastei Verlag; 2008.

55. Seifert T, Werner K. *Schwarzbuch öl*. Ullstein; 2008.

56. Clarke D. *The Battle for Barrels: Peak Oil Myths & World Oil Futures*. Profile Books; 2009.

57. Kelly C. *Take Peak Oil Seriously-It'll be Here Much Sooner Than You Think*. Toronto Star; 2009.

58. Bryce R. *Gusher of Lies: Dangerous Delusions of "Energy Independence"*. Public Affairs; 2009.

59. Rawles JW. *Patriots: A Novel of Survival in the Coming Collapse*. Ulysses Press; 2009.

60. Hartmann T, Rees W, Wood JJ. *Crude Impact*, DVD. DOCURAMA; 2009.

61. Zittel W, Rubin J. *Schindler: Geht uns das Erdöl aus?: Wissen was stimmt*. Herder V; 2009.

62. Rubin J. *Why Your World Is About to Get a Whole Lot Smaller*. Random House; 2009.

63. Tertzakian P, Hollihan K. *The End of Energy Obesity: Breaking Today's Energy Addiction for a Prosperous and Secure Tomorrow*. John Wiley and Sons; 2009.

64. Heinberg R. *Blackout-Coal, Climate and the Last Energy Crisis*. New Society; 2009.

65. Zillmer H-J. *Der Energie-Irrtum: Warum Erdgas und Erdöl unerschöpflich sind*. Herbig; 2009.

66. Steiner Ch. *$20 Per Gallon: How the Inevitable Rise in the Price of Gasoline Will Change Our Lives for the Better*. Grand Central Publishing; 2010.

67. Maass P. *Crude World: The Violent Twilight of Oil*. Knopf; 2009.

68. Shiva V. *Leben ohne Erdöl: Eine Wirtschaft von unten gegen die Krise von oben*. Rotpunktverlag, Zürich; 2009.

69. Rawles JW. *How to Survive the End of the World as We Know It: Tactics, Techniques, and Technologies for Uncertain Times*. Plume; 2009.

70. Greer JM. *The Ecotechnic Future: Envisioning a Post-Peak World*. New Society Publishers; 2009.

71. Schindler J, Held M, Würdemann G. *Postfossile Mobilität: Wegweiser für die Zeit nach dem Peak Oil*. Vas-Verlag für Akademische Schriften; 2009.

72. Ruppert MC, Campbell C. *Confronting Collapse: The Crisis of Energy and Money in a Post Peak Oil World*. Chelsea Green Publishing; 2009.

73. Pascual C, Elkind J. *Energy Security: Economics, Politics, Strategies, and Implications*. Brookings Institution Press; 2009.

74. Friedman G. *The Next 100 Years: A Forecast for the 21st Century*. Anchor; 2010.

75. Maugeri L. *Beyond the Age of Oil: The Myths, Realities, and Future of Fossil Fuels and Their Alternatives*. Praeger; 2010.

76. Stiglitz J. *Freefall*. Penguin; 2010.

77. Miegel M. *Exit: Wohlstand ohne Wachstum*. Propyläen; 2010.

78. Rubin J, Petersen K. *Warum die Welt immer kleiner wird: öl und das Ende der Globalisierung*. Hanser; 2010.

79. Rubin J. *Why Your World is About to Get a Whole Lot Smaller: Oil and the End of Globalisation*. Virgin Books; 2010.

80. Lewis M. *The Big Short*. Penguin; 2010.

81. Lewis M. *The Big Short: Inside the Doomsday Machine*. W.W. Norton & Co; 2010.

82. Bryce R. *Power Hungry: The Myths of "Green" Energy and the Real Fuels of the Future*. Public Affairs; 2010.

83. Ginsburgh H, et al. *Angst vor dem Dominoeffekt*. Wirtschaftswoche; 2010.

84. Maurer H. *Das Paranetz-Zusammenbruch des Internet*, Roman. Freya Verlag; 2004.

85. Maurer H. *The Paranet*, novel. Freya Verlag; 2004.

86. Roubini N, Mihm S, Neubauer J, Pyka P. *Das Ende der Weltwirtschaft und ihre Zukunft: Crisis Economics*. Campus Verlag; 2010.

87. Ruppert M. *Collapse*, DVD. MPI HOME VIDEO; 2010.

88. Bower T. *Oil: Money, Politics, and Power in the 21st Century*. Grand Central; 2010.

89. Rhodes R. *The Coming Oil Storm: The Imminent End of Oil . . . and Its Strategic Global Role in End-Times Prophecy*. Harvest House Publishers; 2010.

90. El-Ghazawi T, et al. The promise of high-performance reconfigurable computing. IEEE Comput 2008; 41(2): 69–76. Available at http://ite.gmu.edu/~kgaj/publications/journals/GWU_GMU_UIUC_USC_Computer_2008.pdf.

91. Bobda C. *Introduction to Reconfigurable Computing: Architectures*. Springer-Verlag; 2007.

92. Chang C, et al. *The Biggascale Emulation Engine (Bee)*, summer retreat. UC Berkeley; 2001.

93. Hartenstein R. Morphware and configware. In: Zomaya A, editor. *Handbook of Nature-Inspired and Innovative Computing*. Springer; 2005, Chapter 11.

94. Hartenstein R. Basics of reconfigurable computing. In: Henkel J, Parameswaran S, editors. *Embedded Computing-A Low Power Perspective*. Springer-Verlag; 2007, Chapter 20.

95. Wallich P. *Profile: Lynn Conway—Completing the Circuit*. Scientific American Magazine; 2000.

96. Conway L. The MPC adventures: experiences with the generation of VLSI design and implementation methodologies; microprocessing and microprogramming. Euromicro J 1982; 10(4): 209–228. Available at http://ai.eecs.umich.edu/people/conway/VLSI/MPCAdv/MPCAdv.pdf.

97. National Research Council. *Funding a Revolution*. National Academies Press; 1999.

98. Kilbane NN. The book that changed everything. Electronic Design News; 2009 Feb 11.

99. Kilbane D. Lynn Conway-A trailblazer on professional, personal levels. In: El. Design; 2003 Oct.

100. Available at http://partners.academic.ru/dic.nsf/dewiki/362215.

101. Mead C, Conway L. *Introduction to VLSI Systems*. Addison-Wesley; 1980.

102. Conway L. *The MIT '78 VLSI System Design Course*. Xerox PARC; 1979.

103. Hon R, Sequin C. *A Guide to LSI Implementation*. Xerox PARC; 1978.

104. Conway L, Bell A, Newell M. MPC79: A Large-Scale Demonstration of a New Way to Create Systems in Silicon, LAMBDA, the Magazine of VLSI Design. 2nd Quarter 1980.

105. Available at http://lexikon.freenet.de/Mikrochip-Entwurfs-Revolution.

106. Hartenstein R. *Configware für Supercomputing: Aufbruch zum Personal Supercomputer*. Praxis der Informationsverarbeitung und Kommunikation (PIK); 2005.

107. Hartenstein R (invited paper). Reconfigurable Computing: Paradigmen-Wechsel erschüttern die Fundamente der Informatik; Prof. Glesners 60th birthday workshop; 2003 Aug 29; Darmstadt, Germany. Available at http://xputers.informatik.uni-kl.de/staff/hartenstein/lot/HartensteinGlesner60.pdf.

108. Available at http://wiki.answers.com/QWhy_are_computers_important_in_the_world.

109. Teich J. Invasive computing-basic concepts and foreseen benefits. In: ARTIST Summer School Europe; 2010 Sept 5–10; Autrans, France.

110. Denert E. *Erfahrungen und Einsichten eines Software-Unternehmers*. TU Kaiserslautern; 2004.

111. Cowhey NN. *HPC Technology Makes Car Safety Job 1*. HPCwire; 2010. Available at http://www.hpcwire.com/news/HPC-Technology-Makes-Car-Safety-Job-1-100088164.html.

112. Lee EA. Cyber-physical systems-are computing foundations adequate? In: Position Paper for NSF Workshop On Cyber-Physical Systems; 2006 Oct 16–17; Austin (TX).

113. Cowhey PF, Aronson JD. *Transforming Global Information and Communication Markets*. MIT Press; 2009.

114. King R. *Big Tech Problem as Mainframes Outlast Workforce*. Bloomberg Business Week; 2010.

115. Scudder R. Definitions in green computing. 2010 Jan 29, BRIGHT HUB. Available at http://www.brighthub.com/environment/green-computing/articles/62742.aspx.

116. Immitzer M. Information and Communication Technologies Enable More Energy-Efficient Societies, e-Energy 2010 April 13–15; Passau, Germany.

117. Marwedel Peter, Engel Michael. Plea for a holistic analysis of the relationship between information technology and carbon-dioxide emissions. ARCS; 2010 Feb 22–25; Hannover, Germany. Available at http://ls12-www.cs.tu-dortmund.de/publications/papers/arcs-10-marwedel.pdf.

118. Scudder R. Top rated energy efficient computer monitors. 2010 Mar 7, BRIGHT HUB. Available at http://www.brighthub.com/environment/green-computing/reviews/65304.aspx#ixzz0vzotrQYK.

119. Hopper Andy. Computing for the future of the planet. Trans R Soc A 2008; 366(1881): 3685–369. Available at http://www.cl.cam.ac.uk/research/dtg/~ah12/CFP%20paper.pdf.

120. N. N. Davos, rethink, redesign and rebuild; 2010 Jan 27. Channel 4 News. Available at http://www.channel4.com/news/articles/business_money/davos+rethink+redesign+and+rebuild/3517427.

121. Don Tapscott: The Dubai Summit on Redesigning Global Cooperation and Problem Solving; 2009 Nov 26; The Huffington Post. Available at http://www.huffingtonpost.com/don-tapscott/the-dubai-summit-on-redes_b_371730.html.

122. Micheli GD. Nano-systems: Devices, Circuits, Architectures and Applications. In: ARTIST Summer School Europe; 2010 Autrans, France.

123. Brunelli C, Campi F, Picard D, Garzia F, Nurmi J. Reconfigurable hardware: the holy grail of matching performance with programming productivity. In: 18th International Conference on Field Programmable Logic and Applications (FPL 2008); 2008 Sept 8–10; Heidelberg, Germany.

124. Ahmed SZ, Sassatelli G, Torres L, Rougé L. Survey of new trends in Industry for Programmable hardware: FPGAs, MPPAs, MPSoCs, Structured ASICs, eFPGAs and new wave of innovation in FPGAs. In: 20th International Conference on Field Programmable Logic and Applications (FPL 2010); 2010 Aug 31- Sep 2; Milano, Italy. Available at http://www.lirmm.fr/~ahmed/files/FPL10/Zahid_FPL10_SurveyPaper.pdf, Available at http://conferenze.dei.polimi.it/FPL2010/presentations/W1_B_1.pdf.

125. Ahmed SZ, Eydoux J, Rougé L, Cuelle J-B, Sassatelli G, Torres L. Exploration of power reduction and performance enhancement in LEON3 processor with ESL reprogrammable eFPGAin processor pipeline & as a co-processor. In: The Design, Automation, and Test in Europe (DATE) Conference; 2009 April 20–24; Nice, France. Available at http://www.date-conference.com/proceedings/PAPERS/2009/DATE09/PDFFILES/03.3_4.PDF, Available at http://www.lirmm.fr/~ahmed/files/DATE09/DATE09_SZA_03.3_4_slides.pdf.

126. Charette RN. Why software fails, IEEE Spectrum; 2005 Sep.

127. Garlick J. Will the internet break? *ISP Economics Assessment to 2012*. Screen Digest; 2008.

128. Somavat P, Jadhav S, Namboodiri V. Accounting for the energy consumption of personal computing including portable devices, e-Energy; 2010 April 13–15; Passau, Germany.

129. Fettweis G. ICT energy consumption-trends and challenges. In: WPMC'08; 2008 Sep 8–11; Lapland, Finland. Available at http://www.vodafone-chair.com/publications/2008/Fettweis_G_WPMC_08.pdf.

130. Ross P. Cloud Computing's Killer App: Gaming, IEEE Spectrum; 2009 Mar.

131. Estrin D, et al. Internet predictions. IEEE Internet Comput 2010; 14(1): 12–42. DOI: 10.1109/MIC.2010.12.

132. Boeing N. Wie bändigt man ein Energiemonster? 2007 Oct 26, Heise Technology Review. Available at http://www.heise.de/tr/artikel/Wie-baendigt-man-ein-Energiemonster-280483.html.

133. Feng W-C. On the second coming of green destiny? In: International Conference on Energy-Aware HPC; 2010 Sep 16–17, 2010; Hamburg, Germany. Available at http://ena-hpc.org/index.html.

134. Pawlowski SS. Exascale science—the next frontier in high performance computing. In: 24th International Conference on Supercomputing; 2010 June 1–4; Tsukuba, Japan.

135. Kogge P, editor. *ExaScale Computing Study: Technology Challenges in Achieving Exascale Systems*. 2008. Available at http://www.cse.nd.edu/Reports/2008/TR-2008-13.pdf.

136. Katz R. Tech Titans Building Boom-Google, Microsoft, and other Internet giants race to build the mega data centers that will power cloud computing, IEEE Spectrum; 2009 Feb. Available at http://www.spectrum.ieee.org/feb09/7327.

137. Nuez R. Google is Going into the Electricity Business. The Huffington Post; 2010 June 6. Available at http://www.huffingtonpost.com/ramon-nuez/google-is-going-into-the_b_417035.html.

138. Available at http://en.wikipedia.org/wiki/Pelamis_Wave_Energy_Converter.

139. Zomaya A, et al. Interweaving heterogeneous metaheuristics using harmony search. In: International Parallel & Distributed Processing Symposium; 2009 May 23–29; Rome, Italy.

140. Rabaey J. *Low Power Design Essentials*. Springer Verlag; 2009.

141. Barroso LA. The Price of Performance; 2005 Oct 18, ACMqueue. Available at http://queue.acm.org/detail.cfm?id=1095420.

142. Pelamis Wave Power Ltd. Edinburgh, Scotland. Available at http://www.pelamiswave.com, Available at http://www.pelamiswave.com/image-library.

143. Blendinger W. Post peak—abstieg vom peak oil. In: ASPO Annual Conference; 2010 Mai 18; Berlin.

144. Aleklett K. Post peak—the future of the oil-production. In: ASPO Annual Conference; 2010 Mai 18; Berlin.

145. Gabrielli de Azevedo JS. Petrobras e o Novo Marco Regulatório. S ao Paulo; 2009 Dec 1.

146. Hajek S. Dynamik unterschätzt, Wirtschaftswoche 34, 2010 Aug 8.

147. Birol F. Leave oil before it leaves us, THE INDEPENDENT (UK); 2008 March 2. Available at http://www.youtube.com/watch?v = m377Is4tGF0.

148. Ginsburg H. Unterm Wasser liegt die Zukunft, Wirtschaftswoche 23; 2010 June 7.

149. Mills MP. *The Bottomless Well: The Twilight of Fuel, the Virtue of Waste, and Why We Will Never Run Out of Energy*. Basic Books; 2006.

150. Bekas C, Curioni A. A new energy aware performance metric. In: International Conference on Energy-Aware HPC; 2010 Sep 16–17; Hamburg, Germany. Available at http://ena-hpc.org/index.html.

151. Hartenstein R (keynote). Directions of programming research: seeking a needle in the haystack? In: BGME 2010, 1st Brazilian-German Workshop on Micro and Nano Electronics; 2010 Oct 6–8; Porto Alegre, RS, Brazil177

152. Conway S. Multicore Processing: Breaking through the Programming Wall-Big challenges lie on the software side in efficiently corralling hardware's runaway parallelism, 2010 Aug 10, Scientific Computing.

153. Kissell KevinD: The Dead Supercomputer Society; http://www.paralogos.com/DeadSuper/.

154. Ames KR, Brenner A, editors. *Frontiers of Supercomputing II: A National Reassessment*. University of California Press; 1994.

155. Albers S. Energy-efficient algorithms. Commun ACM 2010.

156. Saxe E. Power-efficient Software. Commun ACM 2010.

157. Irwin MJ. Shared caches in multicores: the good, the bad, and the ugly/. In: 37th ISCA; 2010 June 19–23; Saint Malo, France.

158. Guzdial M, Robertson J. Too much programming too soon? Commun ACM 2010.

159. Guzdial M. How we teach introductory computer science is wrong. Available at http://cacm.acm.org/blogs/blog-cacm/45725.

160. Izydorczyk J, Izydorczyk M. Microprocessor scaling: what limits will hold? Computer 2010; 43(8): 20–26.

161. Ben-Ari NN, Sandia National Labs. DARPA selects Sandia National Laboratories to design new supercomputer prototype, 2010 Aug 18; PHYSORG.com. Available at http://www.physorg.com/wire-news/43576779/darpa-selects-sandia-national-laboratories-to-design-new-superco.html.

162. Ben-Ari M. Objects never? Well, Hardly Ever! Commun ACM 2010; 53(9).

163. Ohtsuki T, Ruehli Albert, Hartenstein Reiner. *Circuit Analysis, Simulation, and Design*. Elsevier; 1987.

164. Hartenstein R, editor. *Hardware Description Languages*. Elsevier; 1986.

165. Breuer M, Hartenstein R, editors. *Computer Hardware Description Languages and their Applications*. Elsevier; 1981.

166. Hartenstein R. *Fundamentals of Structured Hardware Design*. Elsevier; 1977.

167. Patterson D. The trouble with multicore, IEEE Spectrum, 2010 July.

168. Available at http://en.wikipedia.org/wiki/Parallel_computing.

169. Available at http://en.wikipedia.org/wiki/List_of_concurrent_and_parallel_programming_languages.

170. Selwood D. Showing off in San Jose. Embedded Technol J 2010.

171. Available at http://en.wikipedia.org/wiki/List_of_programming_languages.

172. Available at http://esolangs.org/wiki/Language_list.

173. Available at http://esolangs.org/wiki/Joke_language_list.

174. Dally B (keynote). Moving the needle: effective computer architecture research in academy and industry. In: 37th ISCA; 2010 June 19–23; Saint Malo, France.

175. Hartenstein R (invited paper). The von Neumann Syndrome. In: Stamatis Vassiliadis Memorial Symposium, The Future of Computing; 2007 Sep 28; Delft, NL. Available at http://helios.informatik.uni-kl.de/staff/hartenstein/Hartenstein-Delft-Sep2007.pdf.

176. Mattson T, Wrinn M. Parallel Programming: Can we PLEASE get it right this time? DAC 2008; 2008 June 8–13; Anaheim (CA).

177. Turley J. Whither embedded part deux. Embedded Technol J 2010. Available at http://www.techfocusmedia.net/embeddedtechnologyjournal/feature_articles/20100525-esc2/.

178. Udell J. Loose coupling and data integrity. Jon's Radio: Jon Udell's Radio Blog 2002 Aug 6. Available at http://radio.weblogs.com/0100887/2002/06/19.html.

179. Anderson M. *Understanding Multi-Core in Embedded Systems*. Falls Church (VA): The PTR Group; 2010.

180. Hartenstein NN, HPC Advisory Council. *HPC Advisory Council Forms Worldwide Centers of Excellence*. HPCwire; 2010.

181. Larus J. Spending Moore's dividend. Commun ACM 2009.

182. Jacobi R, Ayala-Rincón M, Carvalho L, Llanos C, Hartenstein R. Reconfigurable systems for sequence alignment and for general dynamic programming. Genet Mol Res 2005; 4(3): 543–552.

183. Ayala M, Llanos C, Jacobi R, Hartenstein R. Prototyping time and space efficient computations of algebraic operations over dynamically reconfigurable systems modeled by rewriting-logic; ACM TODAES 2006; 11(2).

184. Hartenstein R. The history of KARL and ABL. In: Mermet J, editor. *Fundamentals and Standards in Hardware Description Languages*. Kluwer; 1993. Available at http://xputers.informatik.uni-kl.de/staff/hartenstein/karlHistory.html.

185. Parnas NN. (I forgot the celebrity's name). Computer Magazine; 1970 or 1971.

186. DL (keynote): Teaching for change. In: 10th Conference on Software Engineering Education and Training (CSEET); 1997 April 13–16; Virginia Beach (VA).

187. Hameed R, et al. Understanding sources of inefficiency in general-purpose chips. In: 37th ISCA; 2010 June 19–23; Saint Malo, France.

188. Chen TC, et al. Analysis and architecture design of an HDTV720p 30 frames/s H.264/AVC encoder. IEEE Trans Circ Syst Video Technol 2006; 16(6): 673–688.

189. Hartenstein R (invited paper). The microprocessor is no more general purpose: why future reconfigurable platforms will win. In: Proceedings International Conference on Innovative Systems in Silicon, ISIS'97; 1997 Oct 8–10; Austin (TX); 1997.

190. Tredennick N (keynote). Computing in transition, 2007 Nov 11; SC Reno (NV).

191. Kress R. KressArray: what is the achievement? Generalization of the Systolic Array. Available at http://xputers.informatik.uni-kl.de/staff/hartenstein/lot/GeneralizedSystolicArray.pdf.

192. Morris K: Kicking a dead horse-FPGAs going the distance against ASIC. FPGA Struct ASIC J 2009 Available at http://www.fpgajournal.com.

193. Conner N. *FPGAs for Dummies-FPGAs Keep You Moving in a Fast-changing World*. Wiley; 2008.

194. Paulsson K, Hübner M, Becker J. *Exploitation of Dynamic and Partial Hardware Reconfiguration for On-line Power/Performance Optimization*. FPL; 2008.

195. Becker J, Hübner M (invited talk). *Run-time Reconfigurabilility and other Future Trends*. Ouro Preto, Brazil: SBCCI; 2006.

196. El-Araby E, et al.. Exploiting partial runtime reconfiguration for high-performance reconfigurable computing. ACM Trans Reconfig Technol Syst (TRETS) 2009; 1(4).

197. El-Araby E, et al. Productivity of high-level languages on reconfigurable computers: An HPC perspective. In: ICFPT 2007 International Conference on Field-Programmable Technology; 2007 Dec; Japan.

198. El-Araby E, et al. Comparative analysis of high level programming for reconfigurable computers: methodology and empirical study. In: III Southern Conference on Programmable Logic (SPL2007); 2007 Feb; Mar Del Plata, Argentina.

199. Evans R. *Treat Programmable Hardware Design as a High Level System Task*. EE Times; 2010. Available at http://www.eetimes.com/design/programmable-logic/4008929/Treat-programmable-hardware-design-as-a-high-level-system-task.

200. Siegel S. Applying open standards to FPGA IP. In: 11th Annual Workshop on High Performance Embedded Computing: MIT Lincoln Laboratory; 2007 Sept 18–20; Lexington (MA), USA238.

201. Sharma AK. *Programmable Logic Handbook: PLDs, CPLDs, and FPGAs*. McGraw-Hill; 1998.

202. Herz M, et al. Memory organisation for stream-based reconfigurable computing. In: IEEE ICECS 2002; Sep 15–18; Dubrovnik, Croatia. Available at http://www.michael-herz.de/publications/AddressGenerators3.pdf.

203. Available at http://xputer.de/fqa.html#anchor81257.

204. Hartenstein R, Hirschbiel A, Weber M. A novel paradigm of parallel computation and its use to implement simple high performance hardware. In: InfoJapan'90; 1990; Tokyo, Japan.

205. Hartenstein R, et al. (invited reprint243). *A Novel Paradigm of Parallel Computation and its Use to Implement Simple High Performance Hardware*, Future Generation Computer Systems No 7 .North-Holland Publ. Co.; 1991/92. pp. 181–198.

206. Weber M, et al. Automatic synthesis of cheap hardware accelerators for signal processing and image preprocessing. In: 12. DAGM-Symposium Mustererkennung; 1990; Oberkochen-Aalen, Germany.

207. Hartenstein R. Wozu noch Mikrochips? *Einführung in Methoden der Technischen Informatik*. Bruchsal/Chicago: IT Press Verlag; 1964.

208. Hartenstein Reiner (invited embedded tutorial). Coarse grain reconfigurable architectures. In: Asia and South Pacific Design Automation Conference; 2001 Jan 30-Feb 2; Yokohama, Japan.

209. Hartenstein R (embedded tutorial). A decade of reconfigurable computing: a visionary retrospective. In: Design Automation and Test in Europe (DATE); 2001 Mar; Munich, Germany. Available at http://hartenstein.de/date01hartenstein.pdf.

210. Nageldinger U. Design-space exploration for coarse grained reconfigurable architectures [PhD dissertation]. Germany: TU Kaiserslautern; 2000. Available at http://xputers.informatik.uni-kl.de/papers/publications/NageldingerDiss.html.

211. Feldman M. *Reconfigurable Computing Prospects on the Rise*. HPCwire; 2008. Available at http://www.hpcwire.com/features/Reconfigurable-Computing-Prospects-on-the-Rise_35498449.html.

212. El-Ghazawi T (keynote). Computing with FPGAs: where does it stand and what is next? In: FPGAworld'2010; 2010 Sept 6; Copenhagen, Denmark.

213. Hartenstein R, Herz M, Hoffmann T, Nageldinger U. Exploiting contemporary techniques in reconfigurable accelerators. In: Proceedings FPL'98; 1998 Aug 31–Sep 3; Tallinn, Estonia. Available at http://www.michael-herz.de/publications/paper100.pdf.

214. Kung SY. *VLSI Array Processors*. Prentice-Hall, Inc.; 1988.

215. Petkov N. *Systolic Parallel Processing*. North Holland Publishing Co.; 1992.

216. Gajski D, et al. *A Second Opinion on Data-flow Machines and Languages*. IEEE Computer; 1982.

217. Isaacs Dan. *De-Mystifying FPGAs for Software Engineers*. Boston (MA): ESC; 2010.

218. Turley J. How many times does CPU go into FPGA? Embedded Technol J 2010.

219. Selwood D. EPP-A platform to bridge a gap? Embedded Technol J 2010.

220. Lysaght P (keynote). The programmable logic perspective. In: FPL-2010; 2010 Sep; Milano, Italy.

221. Shen J-S, Hsiung P-A, editors. *Dynamic Reconfigurable Network-On-Chip Design: Innovations for Computational Processing and Communication*. Information Science Publishers; 2010.

222. Available at http://www.chrec.org/.

223. Baxter R, et al. *High-Performance Reconfigurable Computing—the View from Edinburgh*. Edinburgh: AHS; 2007.

224. Storaasli OO, Strenski D. Exceeding 100X Speedup/FPGA-Cray XD1 timing analysis yields further gains. In: Proceedings Cray Users Group; 2009. Available at http://www.nccs.gov/wp-content/uploads/2010/01/Storaasli-paper.pdf.

225. Yi W (keynote). Cache-aware scheduling and analysis for multicores. In: CSE '09 International Conference on Computational Science and Engineering; 2009 Aug 29–31; Vancouver, BC, Canada.

226. Voros N, Nikolaos R, Rosti A, Hübner M, editors. *Dynamic System Reconfiguration in Heterogeneous Platforms-The MORPHEUS Approach*. Springer Verlag; 2009.

227. Hübner M, Goehringer D, Noguera J, Becker J. Fast dynamic and partial reconfiguration Data Path with low Hardware overhead on Xilinx FPGAs. In: Proceedings RAW 2010 Apr; Atlanta, USA.

228. Santambrogio MD (keynote). From reconfigurable architectures to self-adaptive autonomic systems. In: CSE '09 International Conference on Computational Science and Engineering; 2009 Aug 29–31; Vancouver, BC, Canada.

229. Borkar S. Designing reliable systems from unreliable components: the challenges of transistor variability and degradation. IEEE Micro 2005; 25(6): 10–16.

230. Sourdis I, Gaydadjev G. HiPEAC: upcoming challenges in reconfigurable computing. In: Cardoso JMP, Hübner M, editors. *Reconfigurable Computing*. Springer-Verlag; 2011.

231. Kastensmidt FL, Carro L, Reis R. *Fault-Tolerance Techniques for SRAM-Based FPGAs*. Springer US; 2009.

232. Hartenstein R. Volume 25, *Steinbuch: Neue Deutsche Biographie (NDB)*. Berlin: Duncker & Humblot; 2010.

233. Widrow B, Hartenstein R, Hecht-Nielson R. 1917 Karl Steinbuch 2005-Eulogy. In: IEEE Computational Intelligence Society Newsletter; 2005.

234. Steinbuch K. Die Lernmatrix. Kybernetik 1961; 1: 36–45.

235. Steinbuch K, Piske U. Learning matrices and their applications. IEEE Trans Electron Comput 1963; 12: 846–862.

236. Rojas R. *Neural Networks*. Springer Verlag; 1996.

237. Hecht-Nielson R. *Neurocomputing*. Addison-Wesley; 1990.

238. Mead CA. *Analog VLSI and Neural Systems*. Addison-Wesley; 1989.

239. Braga ALS, Llanos CH, Ayala-Rincón M, Becker J, Hübner M, Göhringer D, Obie J, Hartenstein R. Evaluating performance, power consumption and resource utilization of hardware/software artificial neural networks. In: BGME 2010, 1st Brazilian-German Workshop on Micro and Nano Electronics; 2010 Oct 6–8; Porto Alegre, RS, Brazil.

240. Williams RS. How we found the missing memristor, IEEE Spectrum; 2008 Dec.

241. McKee S. Reflections on the memory wall. In: 1st Conference on Computing Frontiers; 2004; Ischia, Italy.

242. Hartenstein R. Why we need reconfigurable computing education. *1st International Workshop on Reconfigurable Computing Education (RC education 2006)*. Germany: KIT Karlsruhe Institute of Technology; 2006. Available at http://helios.informatik.uni-kl.de/RCeducation06/RCe-i1.pdf.

243. Lienhart G. Beschleunigung hydrodynamischer N-Körper-simulationen mit rekon-figurierbaren rechensystemen. In: Joint 33rd Speedup & 19th PARS Workshop; 2003 Mar 19–21; Basel, Switzerland.

244. Schäfer BC, et al. Implementation of the discrete element method using reconfig-urable computing (FPGAs). In: 15th ASCE Engineering Mechanics Conference; 2002 June 2–5; New York, NY284.

245. Claasen T. High speed: not the only way to exploit the intrinsic computational power of silicon. In: ISSCC-1999; 1999 Feb. pp. 22–25.

246. Available at http://www.picocomputing.com/press/KeyRecoveryServer.pdf.

247. Available at http://ce.et.tudelft.nl/cecoll/slides/09/0925_Flynn.pdf.

248. Gaffar AA, Luk W. *Accelerating Radiosity Calculations*. FCCM; 2002.

249. Gokhale M, et al. Acceleration of traffic simulation on reconfigurable hardware. In: 2004 MAPLD International Conference; 2004 Sep 8–10; Washington (DC).

250. Hammes J, Poznanovic D. Application development on the SRC Computers, Inc. systems. In: RSSI Reconfigurable Systems Summer Institute; 2005 July 11–13; Urbana-Champaign (IL).

251. Chitalwala E. Starbridge solutions to supercomputing problems. In: RSSI Reconfig-urable Systems Summer Institute; 2005 July 11–13; Urbana-Champaign (IL).

252. Haynes SD, Cheung PYK, Luk W, Stone J. SONIC-A plug-in architecture for video processing, FPL 99.

253. Roelandts W (keynote). *FPGAs and the Era of Field Programmability*. Antwerp, Belgium: FPL; 2004.

254. Rabaey J. *Reconfigurable Processing: The Solution to Low-Power Programmable DSP*. ICASSP; 1997.

255. Darabiha A. Video-Rate Stereo Vision on Reconfigurable Hardware [M. thesis]. University of Toronto; 2003.

256. McCready R. Real-time face detection on a configurable hardware platform [M. thesis]. University of Toronto

257. Fry T, Hauck S. *Hyperspectral Image Compression on Reconfigurable Platforms*. IFCCM; 2002.

258. Buxa P, Caliga D. Reconfigurable processing design suits UAV radar Apps. COTS J 2005: 296.

259. Colenbrander RR, et al. Co-design and implementation of the H.264/AVC motion estimation algorithm using Co-simulation. In: Proceedings 11th EUROMICRO Conf. on Digital System Design Architectures, Methods and Tools (DSD 2008); 2008 Sep 3–5; Parma, Italy. pp. 210–215.

260. Dittrich F. World's Fastest Lanman/NTLM Key Recovery Server Shipped, Picocom-puting; 2006.

261. Gaj K, El-Ghazawi T. *Cryptographic Applications*. Urbana-Champaign (IL): RSSI Reconfigurable Systems Summer Institute; 2005. USA301.

262. Gu Y, et al. *FPGA Acceleration of Molecular Dynamics Computations*. FCCM; 2004.

263. Alex A, Rose J, et al. *Hardware Accelerated Novel Protein Identification*. FPL; 2004.

264. Nallatech NN. press release; 2005.

265. Feldman M. *In Fermi's Wake, a Place for FPGAs?* HPCwire; 2009.

266. Storaasli NN (Starbridge). *Smith-Waterman Pattern Matching*. National Cancer Institute; 2004.

267. Strenski OO, Strenski D. *Experiences on 64 and 150 FPGA Systems*. Urbana-Champaign (IL): Reconfig- *urable* Systems Summer Institute; 2008.

268. Feldman M. *The FPGA crowd reacts*. HPCwire; 2009.

269. Kuulusa M. *DSP Processor Based Wireless System Design*. Tampere University of Technology, Publ. No. 296313.

270. Available at http://www.bu.edu/caadlab/FCCM05.pdf.

271. Singpiel H, Jacobi C. *Exploring the Benefits of FPGA Processor Technology for Genome Analysis at Acconovis*. Heidelberg, Germany: ISC; 2003; 2003. Available at http://www.hoise.com/vmw/03/articles/vmw/LV-PL-06-03-9.html.

272. Available at http://www.scientificcomputing.com/articles-HPC-Multicore-Processing-Breaking-through-the-Programming-Wall-081010.aspx.

273. Knuth D. The art of computer programming. Volume 3, *Sorting and Searching*. Addison-Wesley; 1973.

274. Hartenstein R, Hirschbiel A, Weber M. MOM-map-oriented machine-a partly custom-designed architecture compared to standard hardware. In: Proceedings IEEE CompEuro; 1989 May; Hamburg, Germany.

275. Duhl M. *Incremental Development and Description of a Shuffle Sort Array Circuit in hyperKARL from the Algorithm Representation of the Bubble Sort Algorithm*. Projektarbeit, Informatik, Univ Kaiserslautern; 1988.

276. Hartenstein R. Implications of Makimoto's Wave. Available at http://hartenstein.de/ImplicationsMakimotosWave2.pdf.

277. Kuon I, Tessier R, Rose J. FPGA architecture: survey and challenges. Found Trends Electron Des Automat 2008; 2(2): 135–253.

278. Available at http://en.wikipedia.org/wiki/ENIAC.

279. Weik MH. The ENIAC Story; 1961 Jan-Feb issue of ORDNANCE (Journal American Ordnance Association). Available at http://ftp.arl.mil/~mike/comphist/eniac-story.html.

280. Flynn M. Accelerating computations using data parallelism, CE TU Delft colloquium; 2009 Sept. 270.

281. J. Can programming be liberated from the von Neumann style? Commun ACM 1978; 21(8): 613–641.

282. Dijkstra E. The GOTO considered harmful. Commun ACM 1968; 11(3): 147–148.

283. Wirth N. A plea for lean software. IEEE Comput 1995; 28(2): 64–68.

284. Arvind, et al. *A critique of Multiprocessing the von Neumann Style*. ISCA; 1983.

285. Neumann PG. 216x "Inside Risks", (18 years in ack cover, each issue of C_ACM), 1985–2003.

286. Backus NN, Chaos 1995, The Standish Group. Available at http://www.projectsmart.co.uk/docs/chaos-report.pdf.

287. Hartenstein R, Koch G. The universal Bus considered harmful. In: EUROMICRO Workshop on the Microarchitecture of Computer Systems; 1975 June 23–25; Nice, France.

288. Hennessy JL, Patterson DA. *Computer Architecture: a Quantitative Approach*. Morgan-Kaufman; 1990.

289. Becker J, et al. Data-procedural Languages for FPL-based Machines, FPL'94, 1994 Sep 7–10; Prague.

290. Available at http://www.srccomp.com/ReconfigurableProcessing_UAVs_COTS-Journal_Oct05.pdf.

291. Available at http://www.ncsa.uiuc.edu/Conferences/RSSI/presentations.html.

292. Nowka K (keynote). Technology variability and uncertainty implications for power efficient VLSI systems. In: 2010 International Symposium Low Power Electronics & Design (ISLPED); 2010 Aug 18–20; Austin (TX).

293. Da Costa G, et al. Multi-facet approach to reduce energy consumption in clouds and grids: the GREEN-NET framework, e-Energy 2010 Apr 13–15; Passau, Germany.

294. Abstract at: http://hartenstein.de/Reiners-keynote-Porto-Alegre.pdf.

295. Available at http://en.wikipedia.org/wiki/Esoteric_programming_languages.

296. Hartenstein R, Kress R. A datapath synthesis system for the reconfigurable datapath architecture. In: Asia and South Pacific Design Automation Conference, ASP-DAC'95; 1995 Aug/Sept; Makuhari, Chiba, Japan. 1995

297. Kress R. A fast reconfigurable ALU for xputers [PhD dissertation]. Kaiserslautern University of Technology; 1996. Available as a booklet only.

298. Available at http://www.ocpip.org/uploads/documents/HPEC07_Mercury_ssiegel_poster_v1.pdf.

299. M SRG, Reddy PC. Design and FPGA implementation of high speed, low power digital up converter for power line communication systems. Eur J Sci Res 2009; 25(2). Available at http://www.eurojournals.com/ejsr_25_2_07.pdf.

300. Baxter NN (XILINX). Xilinx redefines power, performance, and design productivity with three new 28nm FPGA families. FPGA and Program Logic J. Available at http://www.techfocusmedia.net/fpgajournal/ondemand/2010062501-xilinx/.

301. LO LC. Memristor—the missing circuit element. IEEE Trans Circ Theory 1971; 18: 507–519.

302. Available at http://www.civil.columbia.edu/em2002/proceedings/papers/126.pdf.

303. Available at http://edu.cs.tut.fi/kuulusa296.pdf.

304. Available at http://gpgpu.org/.

305. Lee VW, et al. Debunking the 100X GPU vs. CPU myth. In: 37th ISCA; 2010 June 19–23; Saint-Malo, France.

306. Vaduc R, et al. On the limits of GPU acceleration. In: USENIX Workshop Hot-Par'2010; 2010 June 14–15; Berkeley (CA).

307. Bordawekar R, Bundhugula U, Rao R. Believe it or Not! Multicore CPUs can Match GPUs for FLOP-intensive Applications! IBM Research Report; 2010 April 23; Yorktown Heights (NY).

308. Scogland T, Lin H, Wu-chun Feng: a first look at integrated GPUs for green high-performance computing. In: International Conference on Energy-Aware HPC; 2010 Sept 16–17; Hamburg, Germany. Available at http://ena-hpc.org/index.html.

309. Han S, Jang K, Park KS, Moon S. PacketShader: a GPU-accelerated software router. In: SIGCOMM'10; 2010 Aug 30–Sep 3; New Delhi, India.

310. Feldman M. *A GPU on Every Chip*. HPCwire; 2010. Available at http://www. hpcwire.com/blogs/A-GPU-on-Every-Chip-101104834.html.

311. Latif L. AMD turns up the heat on Nvidia's GPGPUs; 2010 Aug 17; The Inquirer.

312. Available at http://www.theinquirer.net/inquirer/feature/1727688/amd-heat-nvidias-gpgpus.

313. King I. Intel to make processor with built-in graphics, Challenging AMD; 2010 Sep 9; Bloomberg.

314. Available at http://www.bloomberg.com/news/2010-09-08/intel-to-show-off-new-chip-with-graphics-tackle-amd-challenge.html?cmpid=yhoo.

315. Rabaey J (keynote). Going beyond turing: energy-efficiency in the Post-Moore Era. In: 2010 International Symposium on Low Power Electronics and Design (ISLPED); 2010 Aug 18–20; Austin (TX).

316. Chiaraviglio L, Matta I. GreenCoop: Cooperative green routing with energy-efficient servers, e-Energy; 2010 Apr 13–15; Passau, Germany.

317. Freeman C. Power Reduction for FPGA using Multiple Vdd/Vth; 2006 Apr 3. Available at http://deimos.eos.uoguelph.ca/sareibi/TEACHING_dr/ENG6530_RCS_html_dr/outline_W2010/docs/LECTURE_dr/TOPIC15_dr/2006_dr/Cecille_topic_presentation_april3.pdf.

318. Simon H (invited presentation). Leibniz-Rechenzentrum, TU Munich; 2009; Garching, Germany.

319. Simon H. The greening of HPC-will power consumption become the limiting factor for future growth in HPC. HPC User Forum; 2008 Oct 13–14, Stuttgart, Germany.

320. Higginbotham S. Watch out intel. Marvell to Make ARM-based Server Chips; 2010 May 11, GigaOM (Busness Week).

321. Holland C. *GE Seek Early Adopters for FPGA Boards*. EE Times; 2010. Available at http://www.eetimes.com/electronics-news/4205834/GE-seek-early-adopters-for-FPGA-boards.

322. Leske N, Randewich N. Intel buys infineon unit and expands wireless offer; 2010 Aug 30, Reuters. Available at http://www.reuters.com/article/idUSTRE67Q3J820100830.

323. Krazit T. *iPhone 3.0 Code Hints at Future Apple Hardware*. CNET News; 2009. Available at http://news.cnet.com/8301-13579_3-10200292-37.html.

324. Smith V. The coming war: ARM versus x86. Van's Hardw J 1020; 271. Available at http://vanshardware.com/2010/04/the-coming-war-arm-versus-x86/.

325. Available at http://www.fpgaworld.com/modules.php?name=News&file=article&sid=297.

326. Tuan T, Rahman A, Das S, Trimberger S, Kao S. A 90-nm Low-Power FPGA for Battery-Powered Applications. In: IEEE Transactions CAD-26; 2007 Feb.

327. Gartner, 2009.

328. Cardoso JMP. New challenges in computer science education. In: 10th Annual SIGCSE Conference on Innovation and Technology in Computer Science Education; 2005 June 27–29; Monte de Caparica, Portugal.

329. Salewski F, Wilking D, Kowalewski S. Diverse hardware platforms in embedded systems lab courses: a way to teach the differences. In: The first Workshop on Embedded Systems Education-WESE 2005; 2005 Sep 22; Jersey City (NJ).

330. Bhattacharyya S, et al. OpenDF, a dataflow toolset for reconfigurable hardware and multicore systems. In: Swedish Workshop on Multicore Computing (MCC-08); 2008 Nov 27–28; Ronneby, Sweden.

331. Smith B (keynote). Reinventing computing. In: LACSI Symposium; 2006 Santa Fe (NM). Available at http://www.cct.lsu.edu/~estrabd/LACSI2006/Smith.pdf.

332. Available at http://flowware.net/.

333. Available at http://configware.org.

334. Surhone LM, Tennoe MT, Henssonow F, editors. *Von Neumann Syndrome*. Betascript Publishing; 2011.

335. Bondalapati K, Prasanna VK. Mapping loops onto reconfigurable architectures. In: 8th International Workshop on Field-Programmable Logic and Applications; 1998 Sep; Tallinn, Estonia.

336. Bell C, et al. The description and use of Register-Transfer Modules (RTM's). In: IEEE Trans-C21/5; 1972 May.

337. Available at http://anti-machine.org.

338. Available at http://data-streams.org.

339. Bauer FL. (coined,, software crisis'). In: 1st NATO Software Engrg Conference; 1968, Garmisch, Germany.

340. Moore S. Multicore is bad news for supercomputers. In: IEEE Spectrum; 2008 Nov.

341. Dijkstra E (Turing award lecture). The humble programmer. Commun ACM 1972; 15(10): 859–866.

342. Walter C. *Kryder's Law*. Scientific American Magazine; 2005. Available at http://www.sciam.com/article.cfm?id = kryders-law.

343. Yi W. Towards real-time applications on multicore plartforms: the timing problem and possible solutions, ARTIST Summer School Europe; 2010, Autrans, France.

344. Ernst R. Formal performance analysis and optimization of safety-related embedded systems, ARTIST Summer School Europe; 2010 Sept 5–10; Autrans, France.

345. Takada H. Challenges of hard real-time operating systems, ARTIST Summer School Europe; 2010 Sept 5–10; Autrans, France.

346. Faugere M, et al. MARTE: also an UML profile for modeling AADL applications. In: 12th IEEE International Conf. on Engrg Complex Computer Systems (ICECCS 2007); Auckland, New Zealand.

347. Hartenstein R. Warum Computer neu erfunden werden müssen. Available at http://hartenstein.de/ComputerNeuErfinden.pdf. discussion contribution at the conference, Neu, gut, besser? Innovation als Thema in den Medien. Available at

http://hartenstein.de/innovation/. 2. und 3. 2012 Feb, Tutzing, Germany, Greer JM. *The Long Descent: A User's Guide to the End of the Industrial Age*. New Society; 2008.

348. Porter R. Evolution on FPGAs for feature extraction [PhD thesis]. Australia: Queensland Un. of Technology Brisbane; 2001.

349. Rajapakse JC, Omondi AR, editors. *FPGA Implementations of Neural Networks*. Springer; 2006.

350. Available at http://en.wikipedia.org/wiki/Dataflow_programming#Languages.

351. Available at http://www.pooka.lanl.gov/content/pooka/green/Publications_files/imageFPGA.pdf.

352. Hartenstein R (keynote). Reconfigurable computing: boosting software education for the Multicore Era. In: Proceedings SPL 2010 Porto Galinhas Beach; 2010 24–26; Brazil, March.

353. Janneck J. *Dataflow Programming*. Autrans, France: ARTIST Summer School Europe; 2010.

354. Cardoso JMP, Hübner M, editors. *Reconfigurable Computing*. Springer-Verlag; 2011.

355. Available at fttp://www.openmp.org.

356. Available at http://x10.codehaus.org/.

357. Grasset A, Taylor R, Stephen G, Knäblein J, Schneider A. Specification tools for spacial design, in Data-procedural Languages for FPL-based Machines, FPL'94, 1994 Sep 7–10; Prague.

358. Available at http://web.apb-tutzing.de/apb/cms/index.php?id = 3121.

359. Morris K. Who are you people? . . .and What do you want? FPGA and Struct ASIC J 1398. Available at http://www.fpgajournal.com/articles_2008/20080715_survey.htm.

360. Available at http://en.wikipedia.org/wiki/Software_crisis.

361. modified version of a list from Wikipedia

362. Baruah S. Scheduling issues in mixed-criticality systems, ARTIST Summer School Europe; 2010 Sept 5–10; Autrans, France.

363. Benini L. Programming heterogeneous many-core platforms in nanometer technology, ARTIST Summer School Europe; 2010 Sept 5–10; Autrans, France.

364. Lícko NN. Developing parallel programs—A discussion of popular models, 2010 Sep, Oracle White paper. Available at http://www.oracle.com/technetwork/server-storage/solarisstudio/documentation/oss-parallel-programs-170709.pdf.

365. Lícko M, Schier J, Tichý M, Kühl M. MATLAB/Simulink based methodology for rapid-FPGA-prototyping. In: 13th International Conference on Field Programmable Logic and Applications (FPL 2003); 2003 Sept 1–3; Lisbon, Portugal.

366. Johnson GW, Jennings R. *LabVIEW Graphical Programming*. McGraw-Hill; 2006.

367. Essick J. *Hands on Introduction to LabVIEW for Scientist and Engineers*. Oxford Univ Press; 2008.

368. Selwood D. Drag-and-drop vs. HDL? FPGA Program Logic J.

369. 4th Workshop on Programmability Issues for Heterogeneous Multicores (MULTIPROG-2011); 2011 Jan 23; Heraklion, Crete, Greece. Available at http://multiprog.ac.upc.edu/.

370. Maxfield C. *C-to-FPGA Integration Gives Prototyping 10X Boost*. EE Times; 2010. Available at http://www.eetimes.com/electronics-products/electronic-product-reviews/fpga-pld-products/4207362/C-to-FPGA-integration-gives-prototyping-10X-boost-.

371. Michelsen G, Godemann J (Herausgeber). *Handbuch der Nachhaltigkeits-kommunikation: Grundlagen und Praxis*. Oekom Verlag; 2005.

372. Available at http://en.wikipedia.org/wiki/List_of_programming_languages_by_category#Functional_languages.

CHAPTER 19

WORKLOAD CLUSTERING FOR INCREASING ENERGY SAVINGS ON EMBEDDED MPSoCs

OZCAN OZTURK, MAHMUT KANDEMIR, and SRI HARI KRISHNA NARAYANAN

19.1   INTRODUCTION

We can roughly divide the efforts on energy savings in embedded multiprocessor system-on-a-chip (MPSoC) architecture into two categories. In the first category are the studies that employ processor voltage/frequency scaling. The basic idea is to scale down voltage/frequency of a processor if its current workload is less than the workload of other processors. In comparison, the studies in the second category shut down unused processors (i.e., put them into low power states along with their private memory components) during the execution of the current computation. Both these techniques, that is, voltage scaling and processor shutdown, can be applied at the software level (e.g., directed by an optimizing compiler) or hardware level (e.g., based on a past history-based workload/idleness detection algorithm). It is also conceivable to combine these two techniques under a unified optimizer.

Each of these techniques has its advantages and drawbacks. For example, a processor shutdown-based scheme may not be applicable if there is no unused processor (note that this does not mean that the workload of all the processors in the MPSoC are similar). Similarly, the effectiveness of a voltage-scaling-based scheme is limited by the number of voltage/frequency levels supported by the underlying hardware. In general, exploiting processor/memory shutdown saves more energy when it is applicable (as it reduces leakage energy significantly) or when we have only a couple of voltage/frequency levels to use. If this is not the case, then voltage scaling can be effective (and in some cases, it is the

Energy-Efficient Distributed Computing Systems, First Edition.
Edited by Albert Y. Zomaya and Young Choon Lee.
© 2012 John Wiley & Sons, Inc. Published 2012 by John Wiley & Sons, Inc.

only choice). On the basis of this discussion, one can expect a unified scheme to be successful. However, we want to reiterate that if there is no unused (idle) processor in the current workload assignment, such a unified scheme simply reduces to a voltage-scaling-based approach.

Our goal in this chapter is to explore a workload (job) clustering scheme that combines voltage scaling with processor shutdown.[1] The uniqueness of the proposed unified approach is that it maximizes the opportunities for processor shutdown by carefully assigning workload to processors. It achieves this by clustering the original workload of processors in as few processors as possible. In this chapter, we discuss the technical details of this approach to energy saving in embedded MPSoCs. The proposed approach is based on ILP (integer linear programing); that is, it determines the optimal workload clustering across the processors by formulating the problem using ILP and solving it using a linear solver. In order to check whether this approach brings any energy benefits over pure voltage scaling, pure processor shutdown, or a simple unified scheme, we implemented four different approaches within our linear solver and tested them using a set of eight array/loop-intensive embedded applications. Our simulation-based analysis reveals that the proposed ILP-based approach (i) is very effective in reducing the energy consumptions of the applications tested and (ii) generates much better energy savings than all the alternate schemes tested (including one that combines voltage/frequency scaling and processor shutdown).

19.2   EMBEDDED MPSoC ARCHITECTURE, EXECUTION MODEL, AND RELATED WORK

The chip multiprocessor we consider in this work is a shared-memory architecture, that is, the entire address space is accessible by all processors. Each processor has a private L1 cache, and the shared memory is assumed to be off-chip. Optionally, we may include a (shared) L2 cache as well. Note that several architecture from academia and industry fit in with this description [1–4]. We keep the subsequent discussion simple using a shared bus as the interconnect (although one could use fancier/higher bandwidth interconnects as well). We also use the MESI protocol (the choice is orthogonal to the focus of this chapter) to keep the caches coherent across the CPUs. We assume that voltage level and frequency of each processor in this architecture can be set independent of the others and also that processors can be placed into low power modes independently. This chapter focuses on a single-issue, five-stage (instruction fetch (IF), instruction decode/operand fetch (ID), execution (EXE), memory access (MEM), and write-back (WB) stages) pipelined datapath for each on-chip processor.

Our application execution model in this embedded MPSoC can be summarized as follows. We focus on array-based embedded applications that are constructed from loop nests. Typically, each loop nest in such an application is small but

---

[1]In this chapter, we use the terms *processor showdown* and *low power mode* interchangeably.

executes a large number of iterations and accesses/manipulates large data sets (typically multidimensional arrays of signals). We employ a loop-nest-based application parallelization strategy. More specifically, each loop nest is parallelized independent of the others. In this context, parallelizing a loop nest means distributing its iterations across processors and allowing processors to execute their portions parallelly. For example, a loop with 1000 iterations can be parallelized across 10 processors by allocating 100 iterations to each processor.

There are many proposals for power management of a processor capable of dynamic voltage scaling. Most of them are at the operating system level and are either task based [5] or interval based [6]. While some proposals aim at reducing energy without compromising performance, a recent study by Grunwald et al [7] observed noticeable performance loss for some interval-based algorithms using actual measurements. Most of the existing compiler-based studies, such as Reference 8, target single-processor architecture. In comparison, our work targets at a chip multiprocessor-based environment and combines voltage scaling and processor shutdown. Wu et al. [9] present and analyze a voltage/frequency scaling scheme, but they do not consider processor shutdown. Kadayif et al. [10] employs processor a shutdown-based mechanism but does not consider voltage/frequency scaling. In our experimental evaluation, we compare our approach to pure voltage/frequency scaling and also to pure processor shutdown.

19.3   OUR APPROACH

19.3.1   Overview

Figure 19.1 compares four different alternate schemes that save energy in an embedded MPSoC architecture. It is assumed, for illustrative purposes, that the architecture has six processors. Figure 19.1a shows the workloads of the processors (i.e., the jobs assigned to them) in a given loop nest. These are assumed to be the loads either estimated by the compiler or calculated through profiling and are for a single nest. Figure 19.1b and 19.1c show the scenarios with approaches based on pure voltage/frequency scaling and pure processor shutdown, respectively. In (b), four out of our six processors take advantage of voltage scaling (note that P_5 is not used in the computation at all). In (c), on the other hand, we can place only one processor (P_5) in the low power mode. A combination of these two approaches is depicted in Figure 19.1d. Basically, this version combines the benefits of voltage/frequency scaling and processor shutdown. Finally, the result that can be obtained by the ILP approach proposed in this chapter is illustrated in Figure 19.1e. Note that what our approach essentially does is to cluster the total amount of computational load in as fewer processors as possible so that the number of unused processors is maximized. In this particular case, the original load of three processors (P_2, P_3, and P_4) is combined and assigned to processor P_2. As a result, processors P_3 and P_4 can be also placed in the low power mode (along with their private memory components) to maximize energy savings, in addition to P_5. The next section gives the technical details

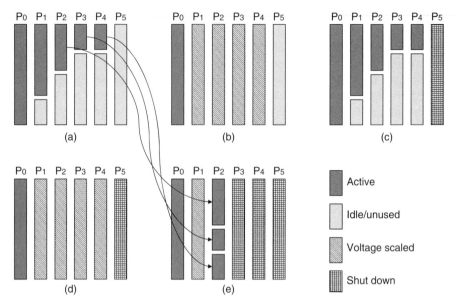

Figure 19.1 Comparison of different energy-saving approaches for a six-processor architecture. Arrows indicate how the workloads (jobs) are clustered by our approach.

of this approach. When there are opportunities, our approach can also use voltage/frequency scaling for the clustered jobs. It is important to point out that the benefits from our approach can be expected to be even more significant when the number of voltage/frequency levels is small. In such a case, an approach based on pure voltage/frequency scaling cannot stretch the execution time of a processor to fill the available slack completely.

However, we first need to clarify two important issues. Someone may ask at this point "why has the application (corresponding to the scenario in Figure 19.1a) not been parallelized at the first place as shown in Figure 19.1e?" There are several reasons for this. First, most current code parallelizers do not consider any energy optimizations. Therefore, there is really little reason for calculating the workload of individual processors and thus little opportunity for workload clustering. Second, the conventional parallelizing compilers try to use as many processors as possible for executing a given computation unless there exists a compelling reason to do otherwise (e.g., the excessive synchronization costs). Third, in many cases, trying to cluster computation in very few processors can have an impact on execution cycles. Since most parallelizing compilers do not predict or quantify this impact, they do not attempt such clustering, being on the conservative side.

The second issue is that it is possible that the scenario depicted in Figure 19.1e has poor data locality as compared to scenarios in Figure 19.1b, 19.1c, and 19.1d. This is because conventional code parallelizers generally try to achieve good data locality by ensuring that each processor mostly uses the same set of data elements as much as possible (i.e., high data reuse). As a result, the scenario in Figure 19.1e can lead to an increase in data cache misses, which in turn increases overall energy consumption. This overhead should also be factored in our clustering approach to ensure a fair comparison.

The main contribution of the ILP approach proposed in this chapter is to obtain, for each loop nest in an application, the result shown in Figure 19.1e, given the initial scenario (workload assignment) shown in Figure 19.1a, and thus reduce energy consumption.

19.3.2   Technical Details and Problem Formulation

This section elaborates on the ILP model used to represent the problem. In our problem, there exist a set of jobs (workloads) that have to be executed on a set of available processors in the embedded MPSoC such that the total energy spent by the system is minimal and the execution of the jobs is completed within a specified time limit, T_{max}.[2] The processors can run different jobs at different voltage and frequency levels, which affects energy consumption. The energy expended by each processor is the sum of the dynamic energy as well as the leakage energy expended while running. The rest of this section describes the ILP model in detail.

19.3.2.1   System and job model.   We assume that the jobs are members of the set J consisting of J_{max} elements and the processors belong to the set P in which there are P_{max} elements. The processors can run at V_{num} discrete set of voltage/frequency levels (as supported by the architecture). It is assumed that only one job can run on a processor at anytime and that once a job starts running on a processor, it runs uninterrupted to completion. However, a processor can be assigned to run more than one job, as a result of workload clustering. The duration for which the job occupies the processor is dependent on the supply voltage/frequency as well as the frequency at which the processor is running that particular job. The time (latency) each job takes up at different voltage levels is specified in the array Job_Length(j, v). Similarly, the dynamic energy spent by each job at different voltage levels varies and is captured by Job_Dynamic(j, v).[3] Total_Energy is the sum of the energies spent by all jobs on all processors due to their running as well as the leakage energy consumed by the processors. This is the metric whose value we want to minimize.

---

[2]In this chapter, we do not assume a specific code (loop nest) parallelization strategy. Rather, we assume that each loop nest is parallelized using one of the known techniques. For each loop nest, T_{max} is determined by the processor with the largest workload. This is to ensure that our workload clustering does not have a negative impact on execution times.

[3]Here, j represents a job (workload) and v represents a voltage (frequency) level. In our implementation, the entries ofJob_Length(j, v) and Job_Dynamic(j, v) are filled using profiling. All energy estimations are performed using Wattch [11] under the 70-nm process technology. The increase in data cache misses as a result of clustering is captured during our profiling.

TABLE 19.1   Notation Used in Our Model

Notation	Explanation
Job_Dynamic(j, v)	Dynamic energy for running job (workload) j at voltage v
Job_Length(j, v)	Time taken to run job j at voltage v
$X(p, j, v)$	Value is 1 if job j runs on processor p at voltage v
J	Set of jobs
P	Set of processors
T_max	Time deadline before which all jobs must finish
J_max	Total number of jobs to be executed
P_max	Total number of processors available
V_num	Total number of voltage (and frequency) levels available
Total_Energy	Total energy consumption of the system (to be minimized)
Leakage_Value	Leakage energy spent by a processor if it is not shut down

19.3.2.2 *Mathematical programing model.* The constraints specified below give the mathematical representation of our model. We use 0-1 ILP. This ILP formulation is executed for each loop nest separately. Table 19.1 gives the notation used in our formulation.

Job Assignment Constraints. The 0-1 variable $X(p, j, v)$ determines whether processor p runs job j at voltage/frequency level v. One job runs completely on one processor, and all jobs are scheduled to run only once. This is specified as follows:

$$\forall \, p \in P \quad \forall j \in J \quad \forall v \in V \quad X(p, j, v) \in \{0|1\}, \tag{19.1}$$

$$\forall \, j \in J \sum_{p=0}^{P_{max}-1} \sum_{v=0}^{V_{num}-1} X(p, j, v) = 1. \tag{19.2}$$

Constraint 19.1 expresses the term $X(j, p, v)$ as a binary variable; a processor either runs the job or it does not. Constraint 19.2 states that each job can be run only on one processor and that all jobs are assigned to some processors (i.e., no job is left unassigned). Notice that we want to determine the value of $X(p, j, v)$ for all p, j, and v.

Deadline Constraints. Jobs are assigned to processors as long as they can meet the time deadline that is specified. Constraint 19.3 expresses this:

$$\forall p \in P \sum_{j=0}^{J_{max}-1} \sum_{v=0}^{V_{num}-1} X(p, j, v) * \text{Job\_Length}(j, v) \leq T_{max}. \tag{19.3}$$

Note that T_{max} is determined, for each loop nest, by the longest (largest) workload.

Clustering and Processor Shutdown Constraints. Multiple jobs are run on the same processor not only if the number of jobs, J_{max}, exceeds the number of processor, P_{max}, but also if such an arrangement reduces the overall energy spent by the system. In case a processor is not assigned any job, because of clustering of jobs, because $J_{\text{max}} < P_{\text{max}}$, or because of both these reasons, then it is shut down. Such a processor does not consume any dynamic energy, as it has no jobs running on it and it does not consume any leakage energy since it is shut down (except for some small amount of leakage in memory components). Constraint 19.4 is introduced to capture processor shutdown:

$$\forall p \in P, \forall j \in J, \forall v \in V \quad \text{Busy}(p) \geq X(p, j, v). \quad (19.4)$$

For a particular processor p, $\text{Busy}(p)$ is necessarily 1 if any of the values in $X(p, j, v)$ is 1. Through this constraint, the value of $\text{Busy}(p)$ is not explicitly expressed if all values in $X(p, j, v)$ are 0. However, a value of 1 in $\text{Busy}(p)$ adds leakage to the overall energy. As the objective of the ILP-based model is to reduce energy, $\text{Busy}(p)$ will be assigned to be 0 if all values in $X(p, j, v)$ are 0.[4]

Leakage and Dynamic Energy Calculation. The following expressions capture the leakage energy and dynamic energy spent by the system as the sum of the leakage and dynamic energies, respectively, spent by each processor. The total amount of dynamic energy spent by a processor is the sum of the dynamic energies spent for each job that is run on that processor. This is captured by expression 19.5:

$$\text{D\_Energy} = \sum_{p=0}^{P_{\text{max}}-1} \sum_{j=0}^{J_{\text{max}}-1} \sum_{v=0}^{V_{\text{num}}-1} X(p, j, v) * \text{Job\_Energy}(j, v). \quad (19.5)$$

Expression (19.6) calculates the leakage energy spent. As mentioned earlier, if $\text{Busy}(p)$ is 1, then leakage is spent by processor p.

$$\text{L\_Energy} = \text{Leakage\_Value} * \sum_{p=0}^{P_{\text{max}}-1} * \text{Busy}(p). \quad (19.6)$$

Objective Function. The objective function, which is the total energy spent by the system, is the sum of the leakage and dynamic energies. This is the objective function that our approach tries to minimize:

$$\text{TotaL\_Energy} = \text{D\_Energy} + \text{L\_Energy}. \quad (19.7)$$

The constraints and expressions mentioned in this section are sufficient to express our problem within ILP. We next look at the additional constraints that can be used in order to handle two special cases.

---

[4]To preserve data in memory components, a shutdown processor consumes some leakage [12]. Our experiments are performed based on this principle. However, in our presentation of the ILP formulation, we assume no leakage consumption in the shutdown state for ease of presentation.

Additional Constraints. If two or more jobs run on the same processor, the order in which they are executed may be important and this can be found out by the following constraints. The term $\text{Seq}(p, j_1, j_2)$ is defined as being 1 if j_1 and j_2 both run on processor p and j_1 precedes j_2 in execution. Constraint 19.8 specifies $\text{Seq}(p, j_1, j_2)$ as being binary, and constraint 19.9 specifies that two jobs cannot both precede each other:

$$\forall p \in P, \forall j_1 \in J, \forall j_2 \in J \,|\, j_1 \neq j_2$$

$$\text{Seq}(p, j_1, j_2) \in \{0|1\}, \tag{19.8}$$

$$\forall p \in P, \forall j_1 \in J, \forall j_2 \in J \,|\, j_1 \neq j_2 \,\text{Seq}(p, j_1, j_2) +$$

$$\text{Seq}(p, j_2, j_1) \leq . \tag{19.9}$$

Constraint 19.10 links $X(j, p, v)$ and $\text{Seq}(p, j_1, j_2)$ by stating that two processors need be sequenced only if they are executed on the same processor:

$$\forall\, p \in P, \forall j_1 \in J, \forall j_2 \in J \,|\, j_1 \neq j_2 \,\text{Seq}(p, j_1, j_2) \geq$$

$$[1 - \text{Seq}(p, j_2, j_1)] * \left(\sum_{v1=0}^{V_{\text{num}}-1} X(j_1, p, v1) \right.$$

$$\left. + \sum_{v2=0}^{V_{\text{num}}-1} X(j_2, p, v2) - 1 \right). \tag{19.10}$$

Finally, constraint 19.11 states the transitive nature of sequenced jobs. That is, if job j_1 precedes j_2 and j_2 precedes j_3 then job j_1 necessarily precedes job j_3.

$$\forall p \in P, \forall j_1 \in J, \forall j_2 \in J \forall j_3 \in J \,|\, j_1 \neq j_2 \neq j_3,$$

$$\text{Seq}(p, j_1, j_3) \geq \text{Seq}(p, j_1, j_2) + \text{Seq}(p, j_2, j_3) - 1. \tag{19.11}$$

Voltage/Frequency Scaling without Clustering. To model classical voltage/frequency scaling within our ILP formulation, an input value $\text{Assign}(j, p)$ should specify the processor on which each job runs. Furthermore, by connecting this value to that of $X(j, p, v)$, all jobs are forced to run on the assigned processors alone. This connection can be captured by the following constraint:

$$\forall p \in P, \forall j \in J \sum_{v=0}^{V_{\text{num}}-1} X(p, j, v) = \text{Assign}(p, j). \tag{19.12}$$

Clustering without Voltage/Frequency Scaling. To model job clustering without voltage and frequency scaling, we need to constrain the choice of available voltage frequency levels to either each processor individually or all processors. In the case of constraining the voltage levels of all processors to one value, constraint 19.13 can be used to ensure that no jobs are assigned voltage levels other than the one specified.

$$\forall p \in P, \forall j \in J, \forall v \in V - \{v'\} \quad X(p, j, v) = 0. \qquad (19.13)$$

To constrain each individual processor to an independent voltage level, constraint 19.14 can be used:

$$\forall p \in P, \forall j \in J, \forall v \in V - \{v'_p\} \quad X(p, j, v) = 0. \qquad (19.14)$$

Here, v' and v'_p are the universal and individual (for processor p) voltage levels, respectively. These constraints simply limit the voltage levels to be used. In this case, the decision to cluster jobs together on a processor is made by our solver and depends on whether it results in a lowered overall energy consumption.

19.3.2.3 Example. This section presents an example and demonstrates how the ILP method and the heuristic method operate in practice. Table 19.2 shows the constant parameters for the system. There are four jobs (workloads) to be run on four processors. Each job can be run at five different voltage/frequency levels, and the deadline for the completion of the jobs is 6 time units. These values are selected for illustrative purpose only.

Array Job_Dynamic(j, v) provides the dynamic energy spent in running each job at different voltage/frequency levels and is assumed to be obtained (through profiling) as follows:

$$\text{Job\_Dynamic} = \begin{pmatrix} 1 & 2 & 3 & 4 & 5 \\ 2 & 4 & 6 & 8 & 10 \\ 2 & 3 & 5 & 6 & 8 \\ 3 & 6 & 9 & 12 & 15 \end{pmatrix}.$$

TABLE 19.2 Constant Parameters Used in the Example

Constant	Value
T_{max}	6 time units
J_{max}	4
P_{max}	4
V_{num}	5
Leakage_Value	5 energy units

Array Job_Length(j, v) provides the execution time (latency) of each job at different voltage/frequency levels and is assumed to be as follows:

$$
\text{Job\_Length} = \begin{pmatrix}
6 & 5 & 4 & 3 & 2 \\
12 & 10 & 8 & 6 & 4 \\
9 & 7 & 3 & 2 & 1 \\
24 & 15 & 12 & 9 & 6
\end{pmatrix}.
$$

$X(p, j, v)$ values returned by our ILP solver are presented in Table 19.3. From this table, it can be gathered that there are two jobs executed on processor 0, one job each is executed on processors 2 and 3, and no job is executed on processor 1. All jobs finish on or before the specified deadline. The total dynamic energy spent is 32 units, which is calculated as follows:

$$
\begin{aligned}
\text{D\_Energy} = {}& X(0, 0, 3) * \text{Job\_Dynamic}(0, 3) + X(0, 2, 2) * \text{Job\_Dynamic}(2, 2) \\
& + X(0, 1, 3) * \text{Job\_Dynamic}(1, 3) + X(0, 3, 4) * \text{Job\_Dynamic}(3, 4) \\
= {}& 1 * 4 + 1 * 5 + 1 * 8 + 1 * 15 = 32.
\end{aligned}
$$

Since three processors are used, 15 energy units are spent as leakage. This calculation can be given by

$$
\text{L\_Energy} = 3 * \text{Leakage\_Value} = 3 * 5 = 15.
$$

As a result, the total energy spent is the sum of the dynamic and leakage energies spent by all processors. Therefore, we have

$$
\text{Total\_Energy} = \text{D\_Energy} + \text{L\_Energy} = 32 + 15 = 47.
$$

Our heuristic approach, on the other hand, proceeds as follows. In the primary phase, all jobs are assigned greedily to a processor in which they can complete within the time limit, T_{max} (6 units). Job 0 is assigned to processor 0 at voltage level 4. Thus, it occupies 2 units of time on processor 0. Job 1 requires 4 time units to finish its execution. Hence, it is assigned to processor 0 since processor 0 has 4 time units free. Now, processor 0 is completely assigned, whereas processors

TABLE 19.3 $X(p, j, v)$ Values Determined by the ILP Approach

$X(p, j, v)$	Interpretation
$X(0, 0, 3)$	Processor 0 runs job 0 at voltage level 3
$X(0, 2, 2)$	Processor 0 runs job 2 at voltage level 2
$X(2, 3, 4)$	Processor 2 runs job 3 at voltage level 4
$X(3, 1, 3)$	Processor 3 runs job 1 at voltage level 3

1, 2, and 3 are free. Job 2 takes 1 time unit to run and is assigned to processor 1. Job 3 takes 6 time units to execute. As processors 0 and 1 do not require 6 units of available execution time, job 3 is assigned to processor 2. This completes the first phase of the heuristic algorithm.

In the second phase, each processor is examined in turn and one job is chosen from each processor with a slack for voltage/frequency scaling. Processor 0 has no available free time, so no job on it can be scaled. Processor 1 has only job 2 running on it. This job can be scaled from level 4 to level 2. This increases its execution time by 2 units but reduces its energy consumption from 8 to 5 units. Processor 2 has no slack, and hence, job 3, which is running on it, cannot be scaled. $X(p, j, v)$ values returned by our heuristic approach are shown in Table 19.4. The dynamic energy spent with this heuristic approach is calculated as follows:

$$
\begin{aligned}
\text{D\_Energy} =\ & X(0, 0, 4) * \text{Job\_Dynamic}(0, 4) \\
& + X(0, 1, 4) * \text{Job\_Dynamic}(1, 4) + X(0, 2, 2) * \text{Job\_Dynamic}(2, 2) \\
& + X(0, 3, 4) * \text{Job\_Dynamic}(3, 4) \\
=\ & 1 * 5 + 1 * 10 + 1 * 5 + 1 * 15 = 35.
\end{aligned}
$$

As three processors are used, 15 energy units are spent as leakage. This calculation is shown below.

$$
\text{L\_Energy} = 3 * \text{Leakage\_Value} = 3 * 5 = 15.
$$

As before, the total energy spent is the sum of the dynamic and leakage energies spent. This can be computed as follows:

$$
\text{Total\_Energy} = \text{D\_Energy} + \text{L\_Energy} = 35 + 15 = 50.
$$

In this example, the ILP method saves 3 energy units over the heuristic method. This example also demonstrates that the ILP approach can be used as an upper bound to test the quality of the solutions returned by heuristics.

TABLE 19.4 $X(p, j, v)$ Values Determined by the Heuristic Approach

$X(p, j, v)$	Interpretation	Scaled
$X(0, 0, 4)$	Processor 0 runs job 0 at voltage level 4	No
$X(0, 1, 4)$	Processor 0 runs job 1 at voltage level 4	No
$X(1, 2, 2)$	Processor 1 runs job 2 at voltage level 2	Yes
$X(2, 3, 4)$	Processor 2 runs job 3 at voltage level 4	No

19.4   EXPERIMENTAL EVALUATION

We present only energy results in this section. The reason is that none of the techniques evaluated increases original execution cycles (i.e., we do not exceed T_{max} in any loop nest). Specifically, for each loop nest, the processor with the largest workload sets the limit for voltage/frequency scaling and processor shutdown. The ILP solver used in our experiments is lp_solve [13]. We observed that the ILP solution times with the application codes in our experimental suite varied between 56.7 s and 13.2 min. Considering the large energy savings, these solution times are within tolerable limits.

All the experimental results are obtained using the SIMICS simulation platform [14]. Specifically, we embedded in the SIMICS platform timing and energy models that help us simulate the behavior of the following four schemes: VS (pure voltage/frequency scaling-based approach), SD (pure processor shutdown-based approach), VS+SD (a unified approach that combines VS and SD), and CLUSTERING (the ILP-based approach proposed in this chapter). The default simulation parameters used in our experiments are listed in Table 19.5. In the last three schemes, when a processor is unused in the current loop nest, it is shut down and its L1 instruction and data caches are placed in the low power mode. The specific low power mode used in this chapter is from Reference 12.

TABLE 19.5   The Default Simulation Parameters

Simulation Parameter	Value
Processor speed	400 MHz
Number of processors	8
Lowest/highest voltage levels	0.8 V/1.4 V
Number of voltage levels	4
Instruction cache	8 KB
	Two-way associative
	32-B blocks
Data cache	8 KB
	Two-way associative
	32-B blocks
Memory	32 MB (banked)
Off-chip memory access latency	100 cycles
Bus arbitration delay	5 cycles
Replacement policy	Strict LRU
Cache dynamic energy consumption	0.6 nJ
Memory dynamic energy consumption	1.17 nJ
Leakage energy consumption for 32 B	
Normal operation	4.49 pJ
Shutdown state	0.92 pJ
Resynchronization time for shutdown state	30 ms
Resynchronization time for voltage scaling	5 ms

We used eight array/loop-intensive applications for evaluating the four approaches mentioned earlier: 3D, DFE, LU, SPLAT, MGRID, WAVE5, SPARSE, and XSEL. 3D is an image-based modeling application that simplifies the task of building 3D models and scenes. DFE is a digital image filtering and enhancement code. LU is an LU decomposition program. SPLAT is a volume rendering application that is used in multiresolution volume visualization through hierarchical wavelet splitting. MGRID and WAVE5 are C versions of two Spec95FP applications. SPARSE is an image processing code that performs sparse matrix operations, and finally, XSEL is an image rendering code. These C programs are written in such a fashion that they can operate on inputs of different sizes. We first ran these applications through our simulator without any voltage scaling or processor shutdown. This version of an application is referred to as the base version or the base execution in the remainder of this chapter. The energy consumptions (which include energies spent in processors, caches, interconnects, and off-chip memory) under the base execution are 272.1, 388.3, 197.9, 208.4, 571.0, 466.2, 292.2, and 401.5 mJ for 3D, DFE, LU, SPLAT, MGRID, WAVE5, SPARSE, and XSEL, respectively. The energy results presented in this section are given as normalized values with respect to this base execution.

To calculate the dynamic energy consumptions for caches and memory, we used the Cacti tool [15]. We approximated the leakage energy consumption by assuming that the leakage energy per cycle for 4-KB Static Random Access Memory (SRAM) is equal to the dynamic energy consumed per access to a 32-B data from the same SRAM. Note that this assumption tries to capture the anticipated importance of leakage energy in the future, as leakage becomes the dominant part of energy consumption for 0.10-? (and below) technologies for the typical internal junction temperatures in a chip. In the shutdown state, a processor and its caches consume only a small percentage of their original (per cycle) leakage energy. However, when a processor and its data and instruction caches in the shutdown state are needed, they need to be reactivated (resynchronized). This resynchronization costs extra execution cycles as well as extra energy consumption as noted in Reference 12, and all these costs are captured in our simulations and included in all our results.

Our first set of results, the normalized energy consumptions with the different schemes, are presented in Figure 19.2. Each group of bars in this graph correspond to an application, and the last group of bars gives the average results across all eight applications. The energy savings achieved by the VS scheme is not very large (6.55% on average). There are two main reasons for this. The first one is the inherent characteristics of some applications. More specifically, when there are no long idle periods, VS is not applicable. The second reason is the limited number of voltage/frequency levels used in the default configuration (Table 19.5). In comparison, the SD scheme behaves in a different manner. While it is not applicable in some cases (e.g., in applications DFE, MGRID, SPARSE, and XSEL), the energy savings it brings is significant in cases where it is applicable. VS + SD simply combines the benefits of the VS and SD schemes, reducing to VS when SD is not applicable. The average energy savings (across

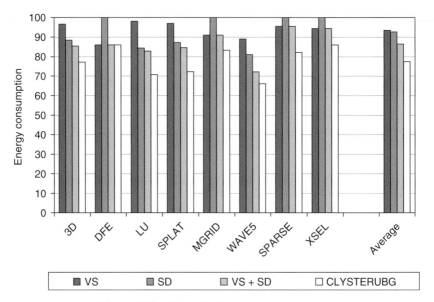

Figure 19.2 Normalized energy consumptions.

all eight applications) achieved by SD and VS + SD are 7.36% and 13.52%, respectively. The highest energy savings is obtained by our ILP-based approach, which is 22.65% on average. These results clearly show the potential benefits of our ILP-based workload clustering approach.

To better illustrate where our energy benefits are coming from, we give in Figure 19.3 the percentage of time each processor spends in the active and idle states for procedure mx3-raw.c, one of the 13 subprograms in application MGRID. We see from this graph that our ILP-based approach is able to increase the number of idle processors. We observed similar trends with most of the other procedures in our applications. These results explain the energy benefits observed in Figure 19.2.

Our second set of results, given in Figure 19.4, looks at the behavior of our approach and VS + SD when the number of available voltage/frequency levels is varied. Each point on the *x*-axis corresponds to a different number of voltage/frequency levels and INF means an infinite number of levels (i.e., mimicking a continuous voltage/frequency scaling scenario). All other simulation parameters are as shown in Table 19.5. One can make three observations from these results. First, both the approaches take advantage of increased number of voltage/frequency levels. This in a sense should be expected because more voltage/frequency levels means finer granular management of idle periods. Second, for all the voltage/frequency levels tried, our approach generates better results than the VS + SD scheme. This is a direct impact of workload clustering. Third, the gap between the case where we have eight voltage/frequency levels and continuous scaling (INF) is not great, meaning that we may not need to go beyond eight levels at all.

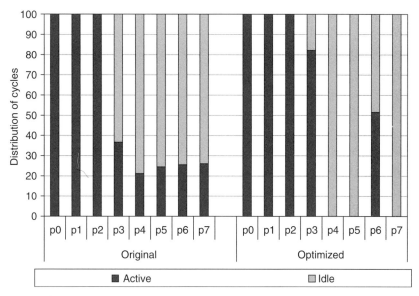

Figure 19.3   The active and idle periods of processors in the mx3-raw.c routine from MGRID.

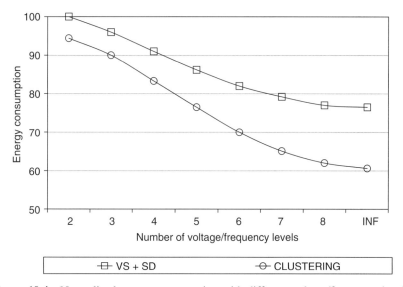

Figure 19.4   Normalized energy consumption with different voltage/frequency levels.

Our last set of results investigates the influence of the number of processors on our energy savings. They are given in Figure 19.5. As before, the remaining simulation parameters are set to their default values given in Table 19.5. Our first observation is that the VS scheme does not scale very well. The main reason for

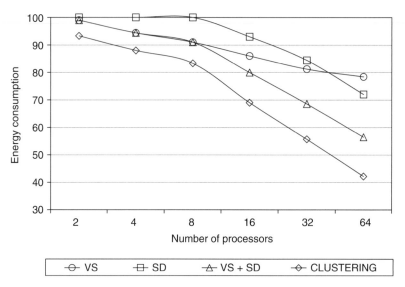

Figure 19.5   Normalized energy consumptions with different processor counts.

this is the limited number of available voltage/frequency levels in our default configuration. In contrast, the SD version generates really good results as we increase the number of processors. This is due to the fact that the loop parallelizer is not able to take advantage of the increased number of processors, and consequently, many processors remain idle, thereby increasing the opportunities for SD. As expected, the VS + SD version combines the benefits of VS and SD. The highest savings is observed with our clustering-based approach since it is able to take advantage of additional processors by putting them in the low power mode (if the loop parallelizer is not able to utilize them).

19.5   CONCLUSIONS

This chapter proposes a workload clustering scheme for embedded MPSoCs that combines voltage scaling with processor shutdown. The uniqueness of the proposed unified approach is that it maximizes the use of processor shutdown by clustering workloads (jobs) in as few processors as possible. We tested this approach along with three alternate schemes using a simulation-based platform and eight embedded applications. Our experiments show that this clustering approach is very effective in reducing energy consumption and generates better results than the three alternative schemes evaluated. Our results also show that the savings brought by this approach increases as the number of voltage/frequency levels or the number of processors is increased.

REFERENCES

1. Barroso LA, Gharachorloo K, McNamara R, Nowatzyk A, Qadeer S, Sano B, Smith S, Stets R, Verghese B. Piranha: a scalable architecture based on single-chip multiprocessing. In: Proceedings of ISCA'2000; Vancouver BC, Canada.

2. Olukotun K, Nayfeh BA, Hammond L, Wilson K, Chang K. The case for a single chip multiprocessor. In: Proceedings of ASPLOS'1996; Cambridge, Massachusetts.

3. Sudharsanan S. MAJC-5200: A High Performance Microprocessor for Multimedia Computing, Parallel and Distributed Image Processing, Video Processing, and Multimedia (PDIVM) Workshop, Cancun, Mexico, 2000.

4. Edahiro M, Matsushita S, Yamashina M, Nishi N. A Single-Chip Multiprocessor for Smart Terminals, IEEE Micro, volume 20, pp 12–20, 2000.

5. Shin Y, Choi K, Sakurai T. Power optimization of real-time embedded systems on variable speed processors. In: Proceedings of the International Conference on Computer-Aided Design; California, USA; 2000 Nov.

6. Govil K, Chan E, Wasserman H. Comparing algorithms for dynamic speed-setting of a low-power CPU. In: Proceedings of the 1st ACM International Conference on Mobile Computing and Networking; California, USA; 1995 Nov.

7. Grunwald D, Levis P, Farkas K, Morrey C III, Neufeld M. Policies for dynamic clock scheduling. In: Proceedings OSDI'2000; California, USA.

8. Saputra H, Kandemir M, Vijaykrishan N, Irwin M, Hu J, Kremer U. Energy-conscious compilation based on voltage scaling. In: Proceedings of ACM SIGPLAN Joint Conference LCTES'02 and SCOPES'02; 2002 Jun; Berlin, Germany.

9. Wu Q, Juang P, Martonosi M, Clark DW. Formal on-line methods for voltage/frequency control in multiple clock domain microprocessors. In: Proceedings of ASPLOS'2004; Massachusetts, USA.

10. Kadayif I, Kandemir M, Sezer U. An integer linear programming based approach for parallelizing applications in on-chip multiprocessors. In: Proceedings of DAC'2002; New Orleans, Louisiana.

11. Brooks D, Tiwari V, Martonosi M. Wattch: a framework for architectural-level power analysis and optimizations In: Proceedings of ISCA; 2000; Canada.

12. Flautner K, Kim N, Martin S, Blaauw D, Mudge T. Drowsy caches: simple techniques for reducing leakage power. In: Proceedings of ISCA; 2002.

13. Notebaert P. lp _solve. Available at ftp://ftp.es.ele.tue.nl/pub/lp_solve/; 2012.

14. Tian T. Improving the Embedded Intel Architecture Design Process with Simics, Intel White Paper, November 2011. http://download.intel.com/design/intarch/papers/326341.pdf.

15. Wilton S, Jouppi N. Cacti: an enhanced cache access and cycle time model. IEEE J Solid State Circ 1996;31(5):677–688.

CHAPTER 20

ENERGY-EFFICIENT INTERNET INFRASTRUCTURE

WEIRONG JIANG and VIKTOR K. PRASANNA

20.1 INTRODUCTION

Internet is built as a packet switching network. The kernel function of Internet infrastructure, including routers and switches, is to forward the packets that are received from one subnet to another subnet. The packet forwarding is accomplished by using the header information extracted from a packet to look up the forwarding table maintained in the routers/switches. Owing to rapid growth of network traffic, packet forwarding has long been a performance bottleneck in Internet infrastructure.

Figure 20.1 shows the block diagram of a modern Internet router. A router contains two main architectural components: a routing engine and a packet forwarding engine. The routing engine on the control plane processes routing protocols, receives inputs from network administrators, and produces the forwarding table. The packet forwarding engine on the data plane receives packets, matches the header information of the packet against the forwarding table to identify the corresponding action, and applies the action for the packet. The routing and forwarding engines perform their tasks independently, although they constantly communicate through high throughput links [1].

The core function of network routers is IP lookup, where the destination IP address of each packet is matched against the entries in the routing table. Each routing entry consists of a prefix and its corresponding next-hop interface. Table 20.1 shows a sample routing table where we assume 8-bit IP addresses. A prefix in the routing table represents a subset of IP addresses that share the same prefix, and the prefix length is denoted by the number following the slash. The nature of IP lookup is longest prefix matching (LPM) [2]. In other words, an

Energy-Efficient Distributed Computing Systems, First Edition.
Edited by Albert Y. Zomaya and Young Choon Lee.
© 2012 John Wiley & Sons, Inc. Published 2012 by John Wiley & Sons, Inc.

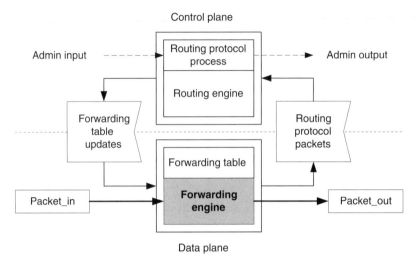

Figure 20.1 Block diagram of the router system architecture.

TABLE 20.1 Example IP Lookup Table

Prefix/Length	Next-Hop Interface
00000000/1	P1
01000000/3	P4
10000000/2	P2
11000000/3	P6
11000000/2	P5

IP address may match multiple prefixes, but only the longest matching prefix is used to retrieve the next-hop information. For example, a packet with destination IP address 11010010 will match the prefixes 110* and 11* in Table 20.1. But 110* becomes the longest matching prefix. Therefore, that packet is forwarded to the corresponding next-hop interface, P6.

20.1.1 Performance Challenges

As the Internet becomes even more pervasive, performance of the network infrastructure that supports this universal connectivity becomes critical with respect to throughput and power. Traditionally, performance has been achieved by increasing the maximum network throughput to handle bursty traffic.

The harsh truth about the power–throughput relationship of today's network infrastructures is that power efficiency is often sacrificed in order to obtain higher throughput through brute-force expansion. A single high-end core router that switches 640 Gbps full-duplex network traffic can consume over 10 kW of power [3, 4], whereas a high-end service gateway capable of 10–45 Gbps routing and

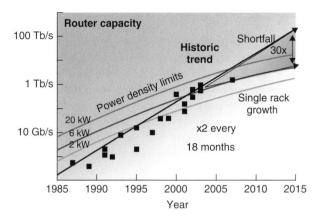

Figure 20.2   Router capacity limited by power. Reproduced with permission from [7].

firewall throughput can take 1–5 kW of power [5, 6]. Both the large amount of total energy and the high power density cause serious problems for the industry and the environment through the operation and maintenance of these network equipments.

- The historical trend (Fig. 20.2) shows that the capacity of backbone routers had doubled every 18 months until 5 years ago. At present, terabit routers with 10–15 kW are at the limit due to the power density. As a result, a 30-fold shortfall in capacity will be seen by 2015 as compared to the historical trend for single rack routers [7].
- The high power density imposes a strenuous burden on the cooling of the network equipment. According to [8], a hardware component that consumes 50–100 W/ft^2 can require 1.3× to 2.3× more power for its cooling. In other words, every wattage that is saved from the critical operation of the network equipment reduces up to 3.3 W of total power dissipation.
- The high power and cooling also implies high monetary investments and energy costs. This fact is especially true for network infrastructures where the equipment (nodes) often need to be placed strategically near the center of metropolitan areas. At 500 W/ft^2, it will cost $5000/ft^2, or $250 million in total, to equip a 50,000 ft^2 facility as a data center [9].

Some recent investigations [7, 10] show that power dissipation has become the major limiting factor for next-generation routers and predict that expensive liquid cooling may be needed in future routers. Packet forwarding has been a major performance bottleneck for network infrastructure [11]. Power/energy consumption by forwarding engines has become an increasingly critical concern [12, 13]. Recent analysis by researchers from Bell labs [7] reveals that almost two-thirds of power dissipation inside a core router is due to IP forwarding engines.

20.1.2 Existing Packet Forwarding Approaches

20.1.2.1 Software approaches. The nature of IP lookup is LPM. The most common data structure in algorithmic solutions for performing LPM is some form of trie [2]. A trie is a binary tree, where a prefix is represented by a node. The value of the prefix corresponds to the path from the root of the tree to the node representing the prefix. The branching decisions are made based on the consecutive bits in the prefix. If only 1 bit is used to make branching decision at a time, then a trie is called a unibit trie. The prefix set in Figure 20.3a corresponds to the unibit trie in Figure 20.3b. For example, the prefix "010*" corresponds to the path that starts at the root and ends in node P3: first a left turn (0), then a right turn (1), and finally, a turn to the left (0). Each trie node contains two fields: the represented prefix and the pointer to the child nodes. By using the optimization called *leaf-pushing* [14], each node needs only one field: either the pointer to the next-hop address or the pointer to the child nodes. Figure 20.3c shows the leaf-pushed unibit trie that is derived from Figure 20.3b.

Given a leaf-pushed unibit trie, IP lookup is performed by traversing the trie according to the bits in the IP address. When a leaf is reached, the prefix associated with the leaf is the longest matched prefix for that IP address. The corresponding next-hop information of that prefix is then retrieved. The time to look up a unibit trie is equal to the prefix length. The use of multiple bits in one scan can increase the search speed. Such a trie is called a multibit trie. The

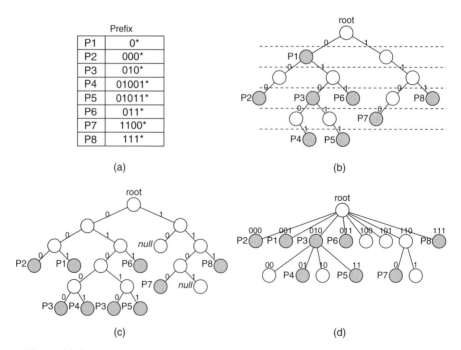

Figure 20.3 (a) Prefix set, (b) unibit trie, (c) leaf-pushed trie, and (d) multibit trie.

number of bits scanned at a time is called the *stride*. Figure 20.3d shows the multibit trie for the prefix entries in Figure 20.3a. The root node uses a stride of 3, while the node that contains P3 uses a stride of 2. Multibit tries that use a larger stride usually result in a much larger memory requirement, while some optimization schemes have been proposed for memory compression [11, 15].

The well-known tree bitmap algorithm [11] uses a pair of bit maps for each node in a multibit trie. One bit map represents the children that are actually present, and the other represents the next-hop information that is associated with the given node. Children of a node are stored in consecutive memory locations, which allows each node to use just a single child pointer. Similarly, another single pointer is used to reference the next-hop information that is associated with a node. This representation allows every node in the multibit trie to occupy a small amount of memory.

20.1.2.2 Hardware approaches. With the advances in optical networking technology, link rates in Internet infrastructure are being pushed from OC-768 (40 Gbps) to even higher rates [16]. Such high rates demand that IP lookup in routers must be performed in hardware. For instance, 40 Gbps links require a throughput of 8 ns per lookup for a minimum size (40 bytes) packet. Such throughput is impossible using existing software-based solutions [2, 17]. Most hardware-based solutions for high speed IP lookup fall into two main categories: TCAM (ternary content addressable memory)-based and DRAM/SRAM (dynamic random access memory/static random access memory)-based solutions. Although TCAM-based engines can retrieve IP lookup results in just one clock cycle, their throughput is limited by the relatively low speed of TCAMs. They are expensive and offer little flexibility for adapting to new addressing and routing protocols [18]. As shown in Table 20.2, SRAM outperforms TCAM with respect to speed, density, and power consumption. However, traditional SRAM-based solutions, most of which can be regarded as some form of tree traversal, need multiple clock cycles to complete a lookup. For example, trie [2], a treelike data structure representing a collection of prefixes, is widely used in SRAM-based solutions. It needs multiple memory accesses to search a trie to find the longest matched prefix for an IP packet.

20.2 SRAM-BASED PIPELINED IP LOOKUP ARCHITECTURES: ALTERNATIVE TO TCAMs

Several researchers have explored pipelining in order to significantly improve the throughput of SRAM-based IP lookup engines. Taking trie-based solutions

TABLE 20.2   Comparison of TCAM and SRAM Technologies

	TCAM (18 Mb chip)	SRAM (18 Mb chip)
Maximum clock rate (MHz)	250 [19]	450 [20, 21]
Cell size (# of transistors per bit) [22]	16	6
Power consumption (W)	12~15 [23]	≈0.1 [24]

as an example, a simple pipelining approach is to map each trie level onto a pipeline stage with its own memory and processing logic. One IP lookup can be performed every clock cycle. However, this approach results in unbalanced trie node distribution over the pipeline stages. Memory imbalancing has been identified as a dominant issue for pipelined architectures [25, 26]. In an unbalanced pipeline, the "fattest" stage, which stores the largest number of trie nodes, becomes a bottleneck. It adversely affects the overall performance of the pipeline for the following reasons: First, it needs more time to access the larger local memory. This leads to reduction in the global clock rate. Second, a fat stage results in many updates, due to the proportional relationship between the number of updates and the number of trie nodes stored in that stage. Particularly during the update process caused by intensive route insertion, the fattest stage can also result in memory overflow. Furthermore, since it is unclear at hardware design time which stage will be the fattest, memory with the maximum size must be allocated for each stage. This results in memory wastage.

Basu and Narlikar [26] and Kim and Sahni [27] both reduce the memory imbalance by using variable strides to minimize the largest trie level. However, even with their schemes, the size of the memory of different stages can have a large variation. As an improvement on [27], Lu and Sahni [28] propose a tree-packing heuristic to further balance the memory, but it does not solve the fundamental problem of how to retrieve one node's descendants that are not allocated in the following stage. Furthermore, a variable stride multibit trie is difficult for hardware implementation especially if incremental updating is needed [26].

Baboescu et al. [29] propose a ring pipeline architecture for trie-based IP lookup. The memory stages are configured in a circular, multipoint access pipeline, so that lookups can be initiated at any stage. The trie is split into many small subtries of equal size. These subtries are then mapped to different stages to create a balanced pipeline. Some subtries have to wrap around if their roots are mapped to the last several stages. Although all IP packets enter the pipeline from the first stage, their lookup processes may be activated at different stages. Hence, all the IP lookup packets must traverse the pipeline twice to complete the trie traversal. The throughput is thus 0.5 lookups per clock cycle. Kumar et al. [30] extended the circular pipeline with a new architecture called the Circular, Adaptive and Monotonic Pipeline (CAMP). It has multiple entrance and exit points, so that the throughput can be increased at the cost of output disorder and delay variation. It uses several *request queues* to manage access conflicts between the new request and the one from the preceding stage. Its worst-case throughput is less than 1 lookups per clock cycle while maintaining balanced memory across pipeline stages.

Owing to the nonlinear structure, neither the ring pipeline nor the CAMP can under worst cases maintain a throughput of one lookup per clock cycle. Also, neither of them properly supports the *write bubble* proposed in Reference 26 for the incremental route update. Jiang et al. [31, 32] propose a fine-grained node-to-stage mapping scheme for linear pipeline architectures. It is based on the heuristic that allows any two nodes on the same level of a trie to be mapped

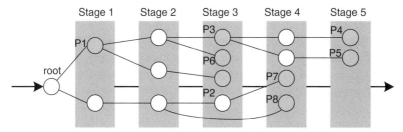

Figure 20.4 Mapping the unibit trie (shown in Figure 20.3b) onto the linear pipeline [31, 32].

onto different stages of a pipeline. Balanced memory distribution across pipeline stages is achieved while a high throughput of one packet per clock cycle is sustained. The linear pipeline architecture supports incremental route updates without disrupting the ongoing IP lookup operations. Figure 20.4 shows the mapping result for the unibit trie in Figure 20.3b using the fine-grained mapping scheme. To allow two nodes on the same trie level to be mapped to different stages, each node stored in the local memory of a pipeline stage has two fields. One is the memory address of its child node in the pipeline stage where the child node is stored. The other is the distance to the pipeline stage where the child node is stored. When a packet is passed through the pipeline, the distance value is decremented by 1 when it goes through a stage. When the distance value becomes 0, the child node's address is used to access the memory in that stage.

20.3 DATA STRUCTURE OPTIMIZATION FOR POWER EFFICIENCY

Although SRAM-based pipeline architectures have been proposed as a promising alternative to power-hungry TCAMs for IP lookup engines in next-generation routers [32, 33], they may still suffer from high power/ energy consumption, due to the large number of memory accesses for each IP lookup [34]. The overall power consumption for each IP lookup in SRAM-based engines can be expressed as in Equation 20.1:

$$\text{Power}_{\text{overall}} = \sum_{i=1}^{H} [P_m(S_i, \cdots) + P_l(i)]. \tag{20.1}$$

Here, H denotes the number of memory accesses, $P_m(.)$ the function of the power dissipation of a memory access (which usually has a positive correlation with the memory size), S_i the size of the ith memory that is being accessed, and $P_l(i)$ the power consumption of the logic that is associated with the ith memory access. Since the logic dissipates much less power than the memories in the memory-dominant architectures [30, 35], the main focus of our work is on reducing the power consumption of the memory accesses. Note that the power consumption of a single memory is affected by many other factors, such as the fabrication technology and sub-bank organization, which are beyond the scope of our work.

Since the energy consumption for each memory access is the product of the power consumption and the memory access time, the energy consumption per IP lookup is identical to its power consumption times the clock period. In this chapter, *power* if not specified, refers to the power/energy consumption per IP lookup.

20.3.1 Problem Formulation

Little work has been done on data structure optimization for power-efficient SRAM-based IP lookup engines. In this section, we focus on fixed-stride multibit tries where all nodes at the same level have the same stride. Fixed-stride multibit tries are attractive for hardware implementation due to their ease for route update [11].

We use the following notations. Let W denote the maximum prefix length. $W = 32$ for IPv4. Let $S = \{s_0, s_1, \cdots, s_{k-1}\}$ denote the sequence of strides for building a k-level multibit trie. Let $|S|$ denote the number of strides in S ($|S| = k$). $\sum_0^{k-1} s_i = W$. Considering the hardware implementation for tree-bitmap-coded multibit tries, we cap the length of strides at $s_i < B_s, i = 0, 1, \cdots, k - 1$, where B_s is a predefined parameter, called the *stride bound*.

20.3.1.1 Non-pipelined and pipelined engines.

An SRAM-based non-pipelined IP lookup engine stores the entire trie in a single memory. Any IP lookup may need to access the memory multiple times. Hence, the worst-case power consumption of a SRAM-based non-pipelined IP lookup engine can be modeled by Equation 20.2, where $\text{Power}_{\text{memory}}$ and $\text{Power}_{\text{logic}}$ denote the power consumption of the memory and the logic, respectively:

$$\text{Power} = (\text{Power}_{\text{memory}} + \text{Power}_{\text{logic}}) \cdot k. \tag{20.2}$$

The logic dissipates much less power than the memories in the memory-intensive architectures [30, 36, 37]. For example, [37] shows that the memory dissipates almost an order of magnitude higher power than the logic in field-programmable gate array (FPGA) implementation of a pipelined IP lookup engine. Thus, we do not consider the power consumption of the logic. The optimal stride problem can be formulated as

$$\min_{k=1,2,\cdots,W} \min_{S(k)} P_m(M(S(k))) \cdot k, \tag{20.3}$$

where $M(S)$ denotes the memory requirement of the multibit trie built using S. $P_m(M)$ is the power function of the SRAM of size M.

For a SRAM-based pipelined IP lookup engine, its worst-case power consumption can be modeled by Equation 20.4, where H denotes the pipeline depth, that is, the number of pipeline stages. $\text{Power}_{\text{memory}}(i)$ and $\text{Power}_{\text{logic}}(i)$ denote the power consumption of the memory and the logic in the ith stage, respectively:

$$\text{Power} = \sum_{i=1}^{H} \left[\text{Power}_{\text{memory}}(i) + \text{Power}_{\text{logic}}(i) \right]. \qquad (20.4)$$

Similar to the non-pipelined engine, we omit the power consumption of the logic. Also, assuming that the memory distribution across the pipeline stage is balanced, the optimal stride problem can be formulated as

$$\min_{S} \left\{ \left[P_m \left(\frac{M(S)}{H} \right) \right] \cdot \max \left(|S|, H \right) \right\}, \qquad (20.5)$$

where $M(S)$ denotes the memory requirement of the multibit trie built using S. $P_m(M)$ is the power function of the SRAM of the size M. The number of memory accesses is determined by the $|S|$ and H. When $H < |S|$, multiple clock cycles are needed to access a stage. To achieve high throughput, we let $H \geq |S|$.

Since $|S| = k \leq W$, we can rewrite Equation 20.5 to be

$$\min_{k=1,2,\cdots,W} \min_{S(k)} \left[P_m \left(\frac{M(S(k))}{H} \right) \right] \cdot H. \qquad (20.6)$$

To solve Equations 20.3 and 20.6, we can first fix k and find the optimal $S(k)$ so that the power consumption is minimized for the given k. Then, we compare the power consumption for different k's to obtain the overall optimal S.

20.3.1.2 *Power function of SRAM.*

Before we solve the above optimization problem, we need to figure out the power function of the SRAM with respect to its size M: $P_m(M)$. There is some published work on comprehensive power models of SRAM [38–40]. But these detailed "white box" models do not show the direct relationship between the power consumption and the memory size. We use CACTI tool [40] to evaluate both the dynamic and the static power consumption of SRAMs of different sizes and then obtain the function parameters through curve fitting ("black box" modeling).

According to [38, 39], when the word width is constant, both the high-level dynamic and static power consumption of SRAMs can be approximately represented in the form of

$$P(M) = A \cdot M^B, \qquad (20.7)$$

where M is the memory size and A and B are the parameters whose values are different for dynamic and static power.

We vary the SRAM size from 256 bytes to 8 Mbytes while keeping the word width to be 8 bytes and obtain their power consumption using CACTI tool [40]. After curve fitting, we obtain $A_{\text{dynamic}} = 2.07 \times 10^{-4}$, $B_{\text{dynamic}} = 0.50$,

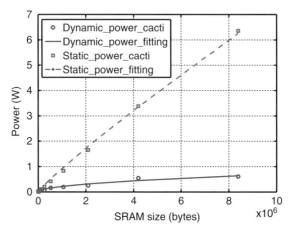

Figure 20.5   Power versus SRAM size.

$A_{\text{static}} = 1.57 \times 10^{-6}$, and $B_{\text{static}} = 0.95$. The results from both CACTI and curve fitting are shown in Figure 20.5.

Hence, $P_m(M) = A_{\text{dynamic}} M^{B_{\text{dynamic}}} + A_{\text{static}} M^{B_{\text{static}}} \approx 10^{-6}(207M^{0.5} + 1.6M)$. Then, Equations 20.3 and 20.6 become Equations 20.8 and 20.9, respectively:

$$\min_{k=1,2,\cdots,W} \min_{S(k)} (207M(S(k))^{0.5} + 1.6M(S(k))) \cdot k, \tag{20.8}$$

$$\min_{k=1,2,\ldots,W} \min_{S(k)} (207M(S(k))^{0.5} H^{0.5} + 1.6M(S(k))). \tag{20.9}$$

For a given k, when $M(S(k))$ is minimized, the power consumption is also minimized. Thus, the above problems can be reduced to finding the optimal stride so that the memory requirements are minimized.

20.3.2   Special Case: Uniform Stride

In the original tree bitmap paper [11], the authors suggest using the same stride for all the nodes except for the root node. We call such a special fixed-stride multibit trie a *multibit trie with uniform stride*. The stride used by the root, s_0, is called the initial stride. Given k, we can find the optimal S by exhaustive search over different initial strides. In each iteration, $s_i = \left\lceil \frac{W-s_0}{k-1} \right\rceil, i = 1, 2, \ldots, k-1$.

20.3.3   Dynamic Programming

Srinivasan and Varghese [14] have developed a dynamic-programming-based solution to minimize the memory requirement of a k-level multibit trie. Sahni and Kim [41] made further improvement to reduce the complexity of the algorithms. However, those algorithms focused on the naive implementation of multibit tries, without considering the tree bitmap coding technique [11], for compressing the memory requirement of multibit tries.

Similar to [14] and [41], we use the following notations:

- O denotes the unibit trie for the given set of prefixes.
- $nNode(i)$ denotes the number of nodes at the ith level of O.
- $nPrefix(i,j)$ denotes the total number of prefixes contained between the ith and the jth levels of O.
- $T(j, r), r \le j + 1$, denotes the cost (the memory requirement) of the best way to cover levels 0 through j of O using exactly r expansion levels.

The dynamic programming recurrence for T is

$$T(j, r) = \min_{m=\max(r-2, j-B_s)}^{j-1} \{T(m, r-1) +$$

$$nNode(m+1) \cdot 2^{B_s} \cdot 2/32 + \qquad (20.10)$$

$$nNode(j+1) + nPrefix(m+1, j)\},$$

$$T(j, 1) = 2^{j+1}. \qquad (20.11)$$

Note that all the strides except the initial one are capped by the stride bound (B_s). In hardware implementation, the length of the bitmaps is determined by B_s. Algorithm FixedStride(W,k), as shown in Figure 20.6, computes $T(W-1, k)$, which is the minimum memory requirement to build a k-level tree-bitmap-coded multibit trie. The complexity of algorithm FixedStride(W,k) is $O(k \cdot W \cdot B_s)$. After obtaining $T(W-1, k)$, we can follow the track of the corresponding $M(*, *)$ to find the optimal S in $O(k)$ time.

20.3.4 Performance Evaluation

We used 17 real-life backbone routing tables from the Routing Information Service (RIS) [42]. Their characteristics are shown in Table 20.3. Note that the routing tables rrc08 and rrc09 are much smaller than others, since the collection of these two data sets ended on September 2004 and February 2004, respectively [42].

We conducted the experiments for both non-pipelined and pipelined architectures. We evaluated the impacts of different architecture parameters on the power-optimal design of the data structure. The architecture parameters include the stride type, the stride bound, and the pipeline depth. For fixed-stride tree-bitmap-coded multibit tries, two stride types are considered. The first uses uniform strides, as described in Section 20.3.2. The second uses optimal strides, whose value is capped by B_s, as discussed in Section 20.3.3.

```
Input: O
Output: T(W − 1, k), S(k)
  1: // Compute T(W − 1, k)
  2: for j = 0 to W − 1 do
  3:     T(j, 1) = 2^{j+1}
  4: end for
  5: for r = 2 to k do
  6:    for j = r − 1 to W − 1 do
  7:       minCost = MaxValue
  8:       for m = max (r − 2, j − B_s) to j − 1 do
  9:          cost = T(m, r − 1) + nNode(m + 1) · 2_s^B · 2 + nNode(j + 1) +
                    nPrefix(m + 1, j)
 10:          if cost < minCost then
 11:             T(j, r) = minCost
 12:             M(j, r) = m
 13:          end if
 14:       end for
 15:    end for
 16: end for
 17: // Compute S(k) = {s_i}, i = 0, 1, ⋯ , k − 1
 18: m = W − 1
 19: for r = k to 1 do
 20:    s_{r−1} = m − M(m, r)
 21:    m = M(m, r)
 22: end for
```

Figure 20.6   Algorithm: FixedStride(W,k).

20.3.4.1 Results for non-pipelined architecture. First, we set $B_s = 4$ and examined the results for the non-pipelined architecture using uniform and optimal strides. The results are shown in Figure 20.7. In both cases, the power was minimized when $k = 5$ and $S = 16, 4, 4, 4, 4$.

Then we varied the stride bound (B_s). Figure 20.8 shows the results by using two different stride bounds: $B_s = 2$ and $B_s = 6$ for the architecture that uses optimal stride. For $B_s = 2$, the power was minimized when $k = 9$ and $S = 16, 2, 2, 2, 2, 2, 2, 2, 2$. For $B_s = 6$, the minimal power was achieved when $k = 4$ and $S = 17, 5, 5, 5$.

20.3.4.2 Results for pipelined architecture. Figure 20.9 shows the power consumption of the pipelined architecture using the two stride types. The pipeline depth (h) was set to be equal to k. The stride bound B_s was 4. Both cases achieved the optimal power performance when $k = 6$ and $S = 13, 4, 4, 4, 4, 3$.

Figure 20.10 shows the results by using different stride bounds for the optimal stride. We set $h = k$. For $B_s = 2$, the power was minimized when $k = 9$ and $S = 16, 2, 2, 2, 2, 2, 2, 2, 2$. For $B_s = 6$, the minimal power was achieved when $k = 5$ and $S = 16, 4, 4, 4, 4$.

**TABLE 20.3   Representative Routing Tables
(Snapshot on April 4, 2009)**

Routing Table	Number of Prefixes	Number of Prefixes w/Length < 16
rrc00	300365	2366(0.79%)
rrc01	282852	2349(0.83%)
rrc02	272504	2135(0.78%)
rrc03	285149	2354(0.83%)
rrc04	294231	2381(0.81%)
rrc05	284283	2379(0.84%)
rrc06	283835	2337(0.82%)
rrc07	280786	2347(0.84%)
rrc08	83556	495(0.59%)
rrc09	132786	991(0.75%)
rrc10	283573	2347(0.83%)
rrc11	282761	2350(0.83%)
rrc12	284469	2350(0.83%)
rrc13	289849	2355(0.81%)
rrc14	278750	2302(0.83%)
rrc15	299211	2372(0.79%)
rrc16	288218	2356(0.82%)

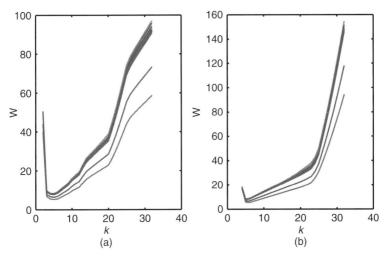

Figure 20.7   Power results of the non-pipelined architecture using (a) the uniform stride
and (b) the optimal stride ($B_s = 4$).

We also conducted experiments using different pipeline depths. Both cases
achieved the minimal power consumption when $k = 6$ and $S = 13, 4, 4, 4, 4, 3$.
These are the same as the results for $h = k$ (Fig. 20.9b). This means that the
pipeline depth has little impact on determining the optimal strides for pipelined
architectures.

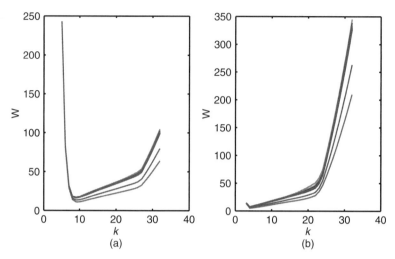

Figure 20.8 Power results of the non-pipelined architecture using (a) optimal stride $B_s = 2$ and (b) optimal stride $B_s = 6$.

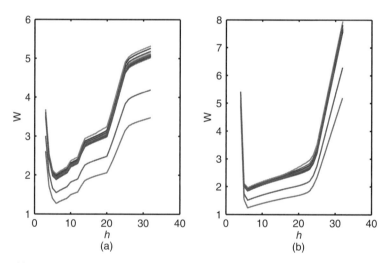

Figure 20.9 Power results of the pipelined architecture using (a) the uniform stride and (b) the optimal stride ($B_s = 4$).

20.4 ARCHITECTURAL OPTIMIZATION TO REDUCE DYNAMIC POWER DISSIPATION

This section exploits several characteristics of Internet traffic and of the pipeline architecture, to reduce the dynamic power consumption of SRAM-based IP forwarding engines. First, as observed in Reference 43, Internet traffic contains a

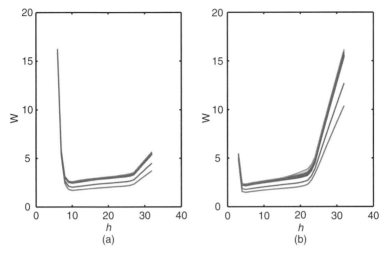

Figure 20.10   Power results of the pipelined architecture using (a) $B_s = 2$ and (b) $B_s = 6$.

large amount of locality, where most packets belong to few flows. By caching the recently forwarded IP addresses, the number of memory accesses can be reduced so that power consumption is lowered. Unlike previous caching schemes, most of which need an external cache to be attached to the main forwarding engine, we integrate the caching function into the pipeline architecture itself. As a result, we do away with complicated cache replacement hardware and eliminate the power consumption of the "hot" cache [44]. Second, since the traffic rate varies from time to time, we freeze the logic when no packet is input. We propose a local clocking scheme in which each stage is driven by an independent clock and is activated only under certain conditions. The local clocking scheme can also improve the caching performance. Third, we note that different packets may access different stages of the pipeline, which leads to a varying access frequency onto different stages. Thus we propose a fine-grained memory enabling scheme to make the memory in a stage sleep when the incoming packet is not accessing it. Our simulation results show that the proposed schemes can reduce the power consumption by up to 15-fold. We prototype our design on a commercial FPGA device and show that the logic usage is low while the backbone throughput requirement (40 Gbps) is met.

20.4.1 Analysis and Motivation

We obtained four backbone Internet traffic traces from the Cooperative Association for Internet Data Analysis (CAIDA) [45]. The trace information is shown in Table 20.4, in which the numbers in the parenthesis are the ratio of the number of unique destination IP addresses to the total number of packets in each trace.

TABLE 20.4 Real-Life IP Header Traces

Trace	Date	Number of packets	Number of unique IPs
equinix-chicago-A	20090219	460448	31923(6.93%)
equinix-chicago-B	20090219	2811616	182119 (6.48%)
equinix-sanjose-A	20080717	3473762	233643 (6.73%)
equinix-sanjose-B	20080717	2200188	115358 (5.24%)

20.4.1.1 Traffic locality. According to Table 20.4, regardless of the length of the packet trace, the number of unique destination IP addresses is always much smaller than that of the packets. These results coincide with those of previous work on Internet traffic characterization [46]. Owing to TCP burst, some destination IP addresses can be connected very frequently in a short time span. Hence, caching has been used effectively in exploiting such traffic locality to either improve the IP forwarding speed [46] or help balance the load among multiple forwarding engines [43]. This chapter uses the caching scheme to reduce the number of memory accesses so that the power consumption can be lowered.

20.4.1.2 Traffic rate variation. We analyze the traffic rate in terms of the number of packets at different times. The results for the four traces are shown in Figure 20.11, in which the X-axis indicates the time intervals and the Y-axis the

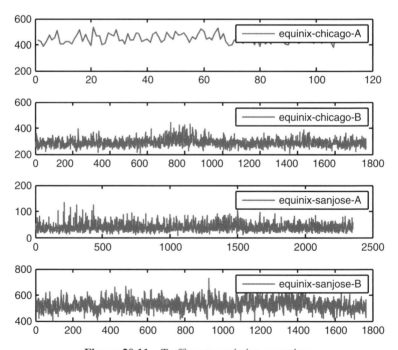

Figure 20.11 Traffic rate variation over time.

number of packets within each time interval. As observed in other papers [47], the traffic rate varies from time to time. Although the router capacity is designed for the maximum traffic rate, power consumption of the IP forwarding engine can be reduced by exploiting such traffic rate variation in real life.

20.4.1.3 Access frequency on different stages. The unique feature of the SRAM-based pipelined IP forwarding engine is that different stages contain different sets of trie nodes. Given various input traffic, the access frequency to different stages can vary significantly. For example, we used a backbone routing table from the RIS [42] to generate a trie, mapped the trie onto a 25-stage pipeline, and measured the total number of memory accesses on each stage for the four input traffic traces. The results are shown in Figure 20.12, in which the access frequency of each stage is calculated by dividing the number of memory accesses on each stage by that on the first stage. The first stage is always accessed by all packets, while the last few stages are seldom accessed. According to this observation, we should disable the memory access in some stages when the packet is not accessing the memory in that stage.

20.4.2 Architecture-Specific Techniques

We propose a caching-enabled SRAM-based pipeline architecture for power-efficient IP forwarding, as shown in Figure 20.13. Let H denote the pipeline

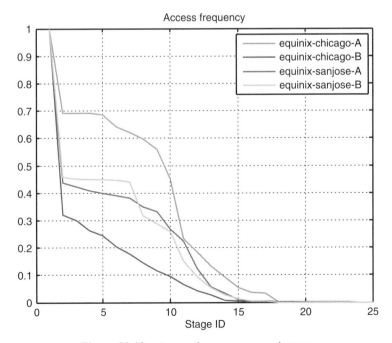

Figure 20.12 Access frequency on each stage.

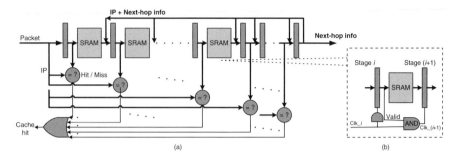

Figure 20.13 Pipeline with (a) inherent caching and (b) local clocking.

depth, that is, the number of stages in the pipeline. These H stages store the mapped trie nodes. Every time the architecture receives a packet, the incoming packet compares its destination IP address with the packets that are already in the pipeline. It will be considered as a "cache hit" if there is a match, even though the packet has not retrieved the next-hop information yet. To preserve the packet order, the packet that is having a cache hit still goes through the pipeline. However, no memory access is needed for this packet, so that the power consumption for this packet is reduced.

20.4.2.1 Inherent caching. Most existing caching schemes need to add an external cache to the forwarding engine. However, the cache itself can be power intensive [44] and also needs extra logic to support cache replacement. The relatively long pipeline delay can also result in low cache hit rates in traditional caching schemes [43]. Our architecture implements the caching function without appending extra caches. As shown in Figure 20.13a, the pipeline itself acts as a fully associative cache, where the existing packets in all the stages are matched with the arriving packet. If the arriving packet (denoted as Pkt_{new}) matches a previous packet (denoted as Pkt_{exist}) that is already existing in the pipeline, Pkt_{new} has a cache hit even though Pkt_{exist} has not retrieved its next-hop information. Then Pkt_{new} will go through the pipeline with the cache hit signal set to "1." On the other hand, Pkt_{new} does not obtain the next-hop information until Pkt_{exist} exits the pipeline.

As shown in Figure 20.13a, the packet exiting the pipeline will forward its IP address and its retrieved next-hop information to all the previous stages. The packets in the previous stages compare with the forwarded IP address. The packet matching the forwarded IP address will take the forwarded next-hop information as its own and carry the retrieved next-hop information along when traversing the rest of the pipeline.

20.4.2.2 Local clocking. Most of the existing pipelined IP lookup engines are driven by a global clock. The logic in a stage is active even when there is no packet to be processed. This results in unnecessary power consumption. Furthermore, since the pipeline keeps forwarding the packets from one stage to the next stage at the highest clock frequency, the pipeline will contain few packets if the traffic rate is low. Since the pipeline is built as a cache that is dynamic and sensitive to input traffic, few packets in the pipeline indicates a small number of cached entries, which results in a low cache hit rate.

To address this issue, we propose a local clocking scheme in which each stage is driven by an individual clock. Only the following constraint must be met to prevent any packet loss:

Constraint 1: If the clock of the previous stage is active and there is a packet in the current stage, the clock of the current stage must be active.

Hence, we design the local clocking as shown in Figure 20.13b where "Clk" represents the clock signal. The clock of a stage will not be active until the stage contains a valid packet and its preceding stage is forwarding some data to the current stage. To prevent clock skew, some delay logic is added in the data path of the clock signal of the previous stage. In a real implementation, we do not use the AND gate, which may result in glitches. Instead, we use clock buffer primitives provided by Xilinx design tools [48].

20.4.2.3   *Fine-grained memory enabling.* As discussed earlier, the access frequency to different stages within the pipeline varies. Current pipelined IP forwarding engines keep all memories active for all the packets, which results in unnecessary power consumption. Our fine-grained memory enabling scheme is achieved by gating the clock signal with the read enable signal for the memory in each stage. The read enable signal becomes active only when the packet goes to access the memory in the current stage. In other words, the read enable signal will remain inactive in any of the following four cases: no packet is arriving, the distance value of the arriving packet is larger than 0, the packet has already retrieved its next-hop information, or the cache hit signal carried by the packet is set to "1."

20.4.3   Performance Evaluation

We prototyped our design (denoted "Proposed") and the baseline pipeline (denoted "Baseline") that did not integrate the proposed schemes, respectively, on FPGA using Xilinx ISE 10.1 development tools. The target device was Xilinx Virtex-5 XC5VFX200T with -2 speed grade. Table 20.5 shows the post place and route results where "Both" denotes both designs[1]. Although our design used more logic resource than the baseline, the design consumed still a small amount of the overall on-chip logic resources. Both designs achieved a clock frequency of 125 MHz while using the same amount of BlockRAMs. Such a clock frequency results in a throughput of 40 Gbps for minimum size (40 bytes) packets, which meets the current backbone network rate.

The dynamic power consumption of a pipelined IP lookup engine can be modeled as Equation (20.12), where p denotes the packet to be looked up,

---

[1]Owing to the limitation of the size of on-chip memory, both designs supported 70K prefixes, which is one-fourth of the current largest backbone routing table. However, our architecture can be extended by using external SRAMs.

TABLE 20.5   Resource Utilization

	Design	Used	Available	Utilization
Number of slices	Baseline	569	30,720	1.85%
	Proposed	748	30,720	2.43%
Number of bonded IOBs	Both	73	960	7%
Number of block RAMs	Both	295	456	64%

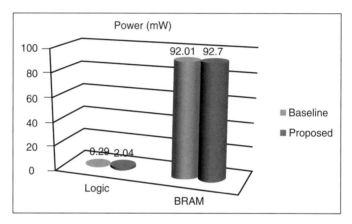

Figure 20.14   Profiling of dynamic power consumption in a pipelined IP lookup engine.

H the pipeline depth, $N(p)$ the number of packets, and $\text{Power}_{\text{memory}}(i, p)$ and $\text{Power}_{\text{logic}}(i, p)$ denote the power consumption of the memory and of the logic in the ith stage by p, respectively:

$$\text{Power} = \frac{\sum_p \sum_{i=1}^{H} [\text{Power}_{\text{memory}}(i, p) + \text{Power}_{\text{logic}}(i, p)]}{N(p)}. \qquad (20.12)$$

We profiled the power consumption of the memory and of the logic based on our FPGA implementation results. Using the XPower Analyzer tool provided by Xilinx, we obtained the power consumption for the baseline and our design, as shown in Figure 20.14. As we expected, the power consumption by memory dominated the overall power dissipation of the pipelined IP lookup engine.

Based on the profile data of the power consumption in the architecture, we developed a cycle-accurate simulator for our pipelined IP lookup engine. We conducted the experiments using the four real-life backbone traffic traces given in Table 20.4 and evaluated the overall power consumption.

First, we examined the impact of the fine-grained memory enabling scheme. We disabled both inherent caching and local clocking and then ran the simulation under two different conditions: (i) without fine-grained memory enabling (denoted as "wo/FME") and (ii) with fine-grained memory enabling (denoted as "w/FME"). Figure 20.15 compares the results, where the results of (ii) are set to

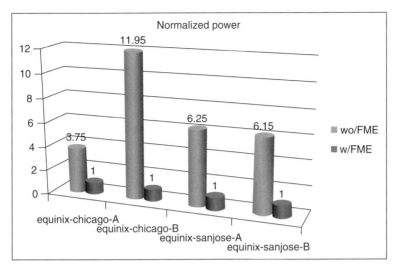

Figure 20.15   Power reduction with fine-grained memory enabling.

be the baseline and the results of (i) are divided by those of (ii). According to Figure 20.15, fine-grained memory enabling can achieve up to 12-fold reduction in power consumption.

Second, we evaluated the impact of the inherent caching and local clocking schemes. We enabled the fine-grained memory enabling scheme and then ran the simulation under three different conditions: (i) without either inherent caching or local clocking (denoted as "Baseline"), (ii) with inherent caching but without local clocking (denoted as "Cache only"), and (iii) with both schemes (denoted as "Cache + LC"). The results are shown in Figure 20.16 where the results without

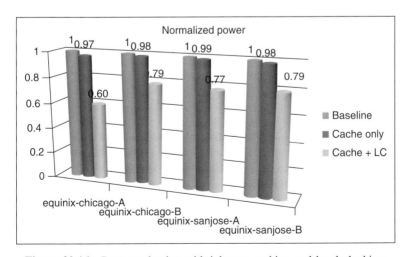

Figure 20.16   Power reduction with inherent caching and local clocking.

both schemes are set as the baseline. Without local clocking, the reduction in power consumption using caching was very little, because of the low cache hit rate (e.g., 1.65% for equinix-chicago-B). Local clocking improved the cache hit rate (e.g., the cache hit rate for equinix-chicago-B increased to 45.9%), which resulted in higher reduction in power consumption.

Overall, when all the three proposed schemes were enabled, the architecture achieved 6.3-, 15.2-, 8.1-, and 7.8-fold reduction in power consumption, for the four traffic traces, respectively.

20.5 RELATED WORK

Reducing the power consumption of network routers has been a topic of significant interest [10, 13, 49]. Most of the existing work focuses on system- and network-level optimizations.

Chabarek et al. [10] enumerate the power demands of two widely used Cisco routers. The authors further use mixed integer optimization techniques to determine the optimal configuration at each router in their sample network for a given traffic matrix. Nedevschi et al. [49] assume that the underlying hardware in network equipment supports sleeping and dynamic voltages and frequency scaling. The authors propose to shape the traffic into small bursts at edge routers to facilitate sleeping and rate adaptation.

Power-efficient IP lookup engines have been studied from various aspects. However, to the best of our knowledge, little work has been done on pipelined SRAM-based IP lookup engines. Some TCAM-based solutions [23, 34] propose various schemes to partition a routing table into several blocks and perform IP lookup on one of the blocks. Similar ideas can be applied for SRAM-based multipipeline architectures [50]. Those partitioning-based solutions for power-efficient SRAM-based IP lookup engines do not consider either the underlying data structure or the traffic characteristics and are orthogonal to the solutions proposed in this chapter.

Kaxiras and Keramidas [51] propose an SRAM-based approach called *IPStash for power-efficient IP lookup*. IPStash replaces the full associativity of TCAMs with set associative SRAMs to reduce power consumption. However, the set associativity depends on the routing table size and thus may not be scalable. For large routing tables, the set associativity is still large, which results in low clock rate and high power consumption.

Traffic rate variation has been exploited in some recent papers for reducing power consumption in multicore-processor-based IP lookup engines. In Reference 52, clock gating is used to turn off the clock of unneeded processing engines of multicore network processors to save dynamic power when there is a low traffic workload. In Reference 53, a more aggressive approach of turning off these processing engines is used to reduce both dynamic and static power consumption. Dynamic frequency and voltage scaling are used in References 47 and 54, respectively, to reduce the power consumption of the processing engines. However, those schemes still consume large power in the worst case when the traffic rate is consistently high. Some of those schemes require large buffers to store the input packets so that they can determine or predict the traffic rate. But the large packet buffers result in high power consumption. Also, these schemes do not consider the latency for the state transition, which can result in packet loss in case of bursty traffic.

20.6 SUMMARY

Power (energy) consumption has emerged as a new challenge in the design of packet forwarding engines for next-generation Internet infrastructure. Although TCAMs are widely used for high speed packet forwarding, they suffer from high power consumption. We propose mapping state-of-the-art algorithmic solutions onto parallel architectures that are based on low-power memory such as SRAM.

We exploited data structure optimization to reduce the power consumption. We formulated the problems by revisiting the conventional time–space trade-off in multibit tries. To minimize the worst-case power consumption for a given architecture, a dynamic programming framework was developed to determine the optimal strides for constructing tree bitmap coded multibit tries. Simulation using real-life backbone routing tables showed that careful design of the data structure, with awareness of the underlying architecture, could achieve dramatic reduction in power consumption. Different architectures could result in different optimal data structures with respect to power efficiency.

We proposed several novel architecture-specific techniques to reduce the dynamic power dissipation in SRAM-based pipelined IP lookup engines. First, the pipeline was built as an inherent cache that exploited effectively the traffic locality with minimum overhead. Second, a local clocking scheme was proposed to exploit the traffic rate variation and to improve the caching performance. Third, a fine-grained memory enabling scheme was used to eliminate unnecessary memory accesses for the input packets. Simulation using real-life traffic traces showed that our solution achieved up to 15-fold reduction in dynamic power dissipation.

ACKNOWLEDGMENT

This work is supported by the United States National Science Foundation under grant No. CCF-1116781.

REFERENCES

1. Juniper Networks T1600 Core Router. Available at http://www.juniper.net.
2. Ruiz-Sanchez MA, Biersack EW, Dabbous W. Survey and taxonomy of IP address lookup algorithms. IEEE Netw 2001;15(2):8–23.

3. Cisco CSR-1 Carrier Routing System. Available at www.cisco.com/web/go/crs.

4. Juniper Networks T-series Routing Platforms. Available at http://www.juniper.net/products/tseries/100051.pdf.

5. Cisco ASR 1000 Series Aggregation Services Routers. Available at http://www.cisco.com/en/US/prod/collateral/routers/ps9343/data_sheet_c78-447652.pdf.

6. Juniper Networks SRX 5000 Services Gateways. Available at http://www.juniper.net/products/srx/dsheet/100254.pdf.

7. Lyons AM, Neilson DT, Salamon TR. Energy efficient strategies for high density telecom applications. In: Princeton University, Supelec, Ecole Centrale Paris and Alcatel-Lucent Bell Labs Workshop on Information, Energy and Environment; SUPELEC, France; 2008 June.

8. Sawyer R. Calculating Total Power Requirements for Data Centers. White Paper #3. American Power Conversion; 2004. Available at http://www.apcmedia.com/salestools/VAVR-5TDTEF_R0_EN.pdf).

9. Anthes Gary. Data Centers Get A Makeover; 2004 Nov. Available at http://www.computerworld.com/printthis/2004/0,4814,97021,00.html.

10. Chabarek J, Sommers J, Barford P, Estan C, Tsiang D, Wright S. Power awareness in network design and routing. In: Proceedings of INFOCOM; Phoenix, USA; 2008. pp. 457–465.

11. Eatherton W, Varghese G, Dittia Z. Tree bitmap: hardware/software IP lookups with incremental updates. SIGCOMM Comput Commun Rev 2004;34(2):97–122.

12. Taylor DE. Survey and taxonomy of packet classification techniques. ACM Comput Surv 2005;37(3):238–275.

13. Gupta M, Singh S. Greening of the Internet. In: Proceedings of SIGCOMM; Karlsruhe, Germany; 2003. pp. 19–26.

14. Srinivasan V, Varghese G. Fast address lookups using controlled prefix expansion. ACM Trans Comput Syst 1999;17:1–40.

15. Song H, Turner J, Lockwood J. Shape shifting trie for faster IP router lookup. In: Proceedings of ICNP; Boston, USA; 2005. pp. 358–367.

16. Brad Reed. Verizon moving to 100 Gbps network in '09. Available at http://www.networkworld.com/news/2008/031008-verizon-100gpbs-network.html.

17. Gupta P, McKeown N. Algorithms for packet classification. IEEE Netw 2001;15(2):24–32.

18. Taylor DE, Lockwood JW, Sproull TS, Turner JS, Parlour DB. Scalable IP lookup for programmable routers. In: Proceedings of INFOCOM, Volume 2; New York, USA; 2002. pp. 562–571.

19. IDT Network Search Engines. Available at http://www.idt.com/?catid = 58522.

20. Cypress Sync SRAMs. Available at http://www.cypress.com.

21. SAMSUNG High Speed SRAMs. Available at http://www.samsung.com.

22. Akhbarizadeh MJ, Nourani M, Vijayasarathi DS, Balsara T. A non-redundant ternary CAM circuit for network search engines. IEEE Trans VLSI Syst 2006;14(3):268–278.

23. Zheng K, Hu C, Lu H, Liu B. A TCAM-based distributed parallel IP lookup scheme and performance analysis. IEEE/ACM Trans Netw 2006;14(4):863–875.

24. CACTI 5.3. Available at http://quid.hpl.hp.com:9081/cacti/.

25. Gupta P, Lin S, McKeown N. Routing lookups in hardware at memory access speeds. In: Proceedings of INFOCOM; San Francisco, USA; 1998. pp. 1240–1247.

26. Basu A, Narlikar G. Fast incremental updates for pipelined forwarding engines. In: Proceedings of INFOCOM; San Francisco, USA; 2003. 64–74.

27. Kim KS, Sahni S. Efficient construction of pipelined multibit-trie router-tables. IEEE Trans Comput 2007;56(1):32–43.

28. Lu W, Sahni S. Packet forwarding using pipelined multibit tries. In: Proceedings of ISCC; Cagliari, Italy; 2006.

29. Baboescu F, Tullsen DM, Rosu G, Singh S. A tree based router search engine architecture with single port memories. In: Proceedings of ISCA; Madison, USA; 2005. pp. 123–133.

30. Kumar S, Becchi M, Crowley P, Turner J. CAMP: fast and efficient IP lookup architecture. In: Proceedings of ANCS; San Jose, USA; 2006. pp. 51–60.

31. Jiang W, Prasanna VK. A memory-balanced linear pipeline architecture for trie-based IP lookup. In: Proceedings of Hot Interconnects (HotI '07); Stanford, USA; 2007. pp. 83–90.

32. Jiang W, Wang Q, Prasanna VK. Beyond TCAMs: An SRAM-based parallel multi-pipeline architecture for terabit IP lookup. In: Proceedings of INFOCOM; Phoenix, USA; 2008. pp. 1786–1794.

33. Carli LD, Pan Y, Kumar A, Estan C, Sankaralingam K. Flexible lookup modules for rapid deployment of new protocols in high-speed routers. In: Proceedings of SIGCOMM; Barcelona, Spain; 2009.

34. Zane F, Narlikar GJ, Basu A. CoolCAMs: Power-efficient TCAMs for forwarding engines. In: Proceedings of INFOCOM; San Franciso, USA; 2003.

35. Peng L, Lu W, Duan L. Power efficient IP lookup with supernode caching. In: Proceedings of Globecom; Washington, USA; 2007.

36. Hasan J, Vijaykumar TN. Dynamic pipelining: making IP-lookup truly scalable. In: Proceedings of SIGCOMM; Philadelphia, USA; 2005. pp. 205–216.

37. Jiang W, Prasanna VK. Reducing dynamic power dissipation in pipelined forwarding engines. In: Proceedings of ICCD; Lake Tahoe, USA; 2009.

38. Do MQ, Drazdziulis M, Larsson-Edefors P, Bengtsson L. Parameterizable architecture-level SRAM power model using circuit-simulation backend for leakage calibration. In: Proceedings of ISQED; San Jose, USA; 2006. pp. 557–563.

39. Liang X, Turgay K, Brooks D. Architectural power models for SRAM and CAM structures based on hybrid analytical/empirical techniques. In: Proceedings of ICCAD; San Jose, USA; 2007. pp. 824–830.

40. Thoziyoor S, Ahn JH, Monchiero M, Brockman JB, Jouppi NP. A comprehensive memory modeling tool and its application to the design and analysis of future memory hierarchies. In: Proceedings of ISCA; Beijing, China; 2008. pp. 51–62.

41. Sahni S, Kim KS. Efficient construction of multibit tries for IP lookup. IEEE/ACM Trans Netw 2003;11(4):650–662.

42. RIS Raw Data. Available at http://data.ris.ripe.net.

43. Jiang W, Prasanna VK. Parallel IP using multiple SRAM-based pipelines. In: Proceedings of IPDPS; Miami, USA; 2008.

44. Zhang C. A low power highly associative cache for embedded systems. In: Proceedings of ICCD; San Jose, USA; 2006.

45. Walsworth C, Aben E, Claffy KC, Andersen D. The caida anonymized 2009 internet traces. Available at http://www.caida.org/data/passive/passive_2009_dataset.xml. 2009.

46. Liu H. Routing prefix caching in network processor design. In: Proceedings of ICCCN; Phoenix, USA; 2001. pp. 18–23.

47. Kennedy A, Wang X, Liu Z, Liu B. Low power architecture for high speed packet classification. In: Proceedings of ANCS; San Jose, USA; 2008. pp. 131–140.

48. Xilinx Virtex-5 FPGAs. Available at http://www.xilinx.com/products/virtex5/.

49. Nedevschi S, Popa L, Iannaccone G, Ratnasamy S, Wetherall D. Reducing network energy consumption via sleeping and rate-adaptation. In: NSDI; San Francisco, USA; 2008. pp. 323–336.

50. Jiang W, Prasanna VK. Towards green routers: Depth-bounded multi-pipeline architecture for power-efficient IP lookup. In: Proceedings of IPCCC; Austin, USA; 2008. pp. 185–192.

51. Kaxiras S, Keramidas G. IPStash: a set-associative memory approach for efficient IP-lookup. In: INFOCOM; Miami, USA; 2005. pp. 992–1001.

52. Luo Y, Yu J, Yang J, Bhuyan LN. Conserving network processor power consumption by exploiting traffic variability. ACM Trans Archit Code Optim 2007;4(1).

53. Kokku R, Shevade UB, Shah NS, Dahlin M, Vin HM. Energy-efficient packet processing; 2004. Available at http://www.cs.utexas.edu/users/rkoku/RESEARCH/energy-tech.pdf.

54. Mandviwalla M, Tzeng N-F. Energy-efficient scheme for multiprocessor-based router linecards. In: Proceedings of SAINT; Phoenix, USA; 2006.

CHAPTER 21

DEMAND RESPONSE IN THE SMART GRID: A DISTRIBUTED COMPUTING PERSPECTIVE

CHEN WANG and MARTIN DE GROOT

21.1 INTRODUCTION

The advance in information technologies in the recent years provides new opportunities for the modernization of traditional power grids. The term *Smart Grid* is often used to name the effort of integrating the Internet with power delivery infrastructure and enabling a variety of services on the integrated networks. The driving force behind the Smart Grid comes from various directions, mainly including reducing greenhouse gas emissions (environmental factor), enhancing reliability and energy independence (political factor, especially in the United States), and improving electric grid efficiency (economic factor). The goal of the move is to transform the business model of the entire electrical power industry [1].

The Demand Response and Smart Grid Coalition (DRSG) defines *Smart Grid* as follows [2]:

"The Smart Grid is the concept of having all supply and demand resources dynamically managed via a combination of data, communications and controls, whereby the operation of the grid for reasons of economics, security, reliability, emissions, etc., can be optimized in real time."

The National Institute of Standards and Technology (NIST) in the United States gives a conceptual model for the Smart Grid as shown in Figure 21.1 [3]. Traditional power grids deliver electricity from points of generation to consumers along the dashed lines. Between the two ends are the power transmission

Energy-Efficient Distributed Computing Systems, First Edition.
Edited by Albert Y. Zomaya and Young Choon Lee.
© 2012 John Wiley & Sons, Inc. Published 2012 by John Wiley & Sons, Inc.

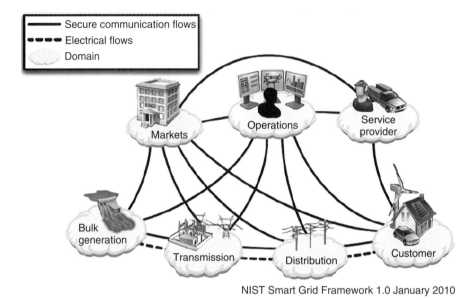

NIST Smart Grid Framework 1.0 January 2010

Figure 21.1 NIST Smart Grid conceptual model.

systems and power distribution systems. The former deliver electricity from power generators to the distribution substations, while the latter deliver electricity from distribution stations to consumers. Information flows shown in solid lines effectively form a new grid on top of the traditional power grid. The flow of information can create a new electricity market that enables value-added services to be established for the good of power generators, distributors, and consumers.

Demand response (DR) is an application area with growing importance in existing power grids. It is a prime example of a value-added service that can benefit greatly from Smart Grid technologies.

"Demand Response is a tariff or program established to motivate changes in electric use by end-use customers in response to changes in the price of electricity over time, or to give incentive payments designed to induce lower electricity use at times of high market prices or when grid reliability is jeopardized." [4]

In the electricity market, DR can benefit both suppliers and consumers. It may improve the reliability of power transmission and distribution networks by offering methods to reduce electricity demand during peak time. On the other hand, it helps consumers to cut energy cost by encouraging changes that may result in reduced energy use when the electricity network is stressed. Traditional DR is often implemented through a manual process and targets large energy consumers. Typically, a producer or power grid operator offers a few predefined DR programs to consumers who are willing to participate. These programs are designed to reduce energy use by shutting down devices of participating consumers. A consumer may sign up to participate in a DR program and agree on a contract with the producer or operator. The consumer often receives payment by reducing its energy use when asked to do so (via predefined DR events) according to the contract. The manual process often requires staff to first receive e-mails, phone calls, or pager signals and then requires them to act on DR events to execute their DR strategies [5].

DR can be automated with the support of Smart Grid technologies. With an infrastructure that can meter consumption and pass the metering data and control information over IP networks in real time, it is possible to exploit more complex and effective DR strategies. First, the existing DR processes and protocols can be implemented using computer systems. A lot of work has been done in this area in recent years. Second, the information flow in the emerging Smart Grid links various related parties in the electricity market to form a distributed computing system, and these parties can collaborate with each other to deliver interesting DR schemes. In this chapter, we review techniques and protocols to implement existing DR programs. We particularly focus on characteristics of the Smart-Grid-based distributed system that can potentially produce effective DR schemes.

The remainder of the chapter is organized as follows: Section 21.2 reviews the existing DR practices and the Smart Grid technologies that have impact on the future of DR, Section 21.3 discusses automating DR in a distributed system context and shows how the distributed algorithms can be applied to this new field, and Section 21.4 summarizes the chapter.

21.2 DEMAND RESPONSE

There is an increasing amount of academic work on DR in recent years. Caves et al. [6] point out that the disconnection between retail consumption decisions and wholesale cost is a problem in the current electricity market. They further indicate that a very modest amount of DR would easily reduce the price spikes significantly. Kirschen [7] also shows that enhancing the ability of the demand side to respond to price signals can benefit not only end users but also the whole electricity market. However, due to concerns over the cost of installing necessary equipment and managing a manual DR process, the number of end users participating in DR programs is small. Kirschen [7] suggests end users could take advantage of a new type of contract with retailers to broaden participation in the market. In this section, we first review the existing practice in detail and then discuss automated DR technologies that can be used to implement DR strategies.

21.2.1 Existing Demand Response Programs

We use the DR programs of the New York Independent System Operator (NYISO) as an example to describe how DR works in existing power grids. The NYISO is a company with a mission to manage the efficient flow of power, as well as administrating and monitoring the wholesale electricity markets in

New York. There are other operators around the world with similar responsibility, for example, the New England ISO (http://www.iso-ne.com), the California ISO (http://www.caiso.com) in the United States, and the AEMO (http://www.aemo.com.au) in Australia.

In New York, peak hourly electricity demand can be 80% higher than the average hourly demand [8]. This large variation in demand is a great challenge to the reliability of the power grid in this region. NYISO offers the following three types of DR programs to pay consumers for curtailing their energy use during the high demand period of the power grid. Each of the three programs requires the participants to be able to provide a minimal reduction amount when needed.

- *Day-Ahead Demand Response Program (DADRP).* The DADRP allows consumers to bid load reduction in the wholesale electricity market. A generator offers payment for a certain amount of load reduction on a day-ahead basis. The participants of this program submit bids that include the hours they are willing to reduce electricity use in the next day, the amount of reduction, and the required compensation from the market. A load reduction bid from a participant is accepted if it is less expensive than the offer of the generator. Once the bid is accepted, the market operator notifies the participant of the scheduled load reduction. During the period of scheduled reduction, the consumption of the participant is metered. The difference between the metered load and a baseline calculated from normal energy use by this participant during the corresponding period is the basis for calculating the actual payment to the participant. If the participant fails to meet the amount of the scheduled load reduction, it will be charged at the higher of the day-ahead price or the spot market price for the shortfall.

- *Emergency Demand Response Program (EDRP).* Unlike DADRP, the EDRP is a voluntary program. In EDRP, when electricity supply could be jeopardized, participants of this program are expected, but not obliged to reduce their consumption or transfer load for a given period. The program provider usually gives notice 1 day before an expected emergency event and is able to confirm that participants are needed 2 h before the event. Similar to DADRP, the difference between the metered load and a baseline calculated based on the normal energy use of a participant during the time frame of the event is used to calculate the payment to the participant. In contrast to DADRP, there is no penalty for zero reduction as a participant is not obliged to reduce load during the event.

- *Special Case Resource Program (ICAP).* The ICAP allows a participant to have a relatively long-term contract with the program provider. The participant receives payment for an agreement to provide load reduction capacity during times when electricity supply could be jeopardized. Participants are notified and confirmed in advance of any anticipated need for curtailment of the capacity specified in their contracts. The metered load of the consumer during the event is compared with the reduction capacity promised. If the promised capacity is not delivered, the long-term contractual payment is reduced. The contracted load reduction capacity can be sold in the whole-sale capacity market, and the actual payment to a participant is determined by the price in the market.

These DR programs are mainly designed to improve reliability of the power grid. Among the three programs, the DADRP leaves more room for consumers to optimize their own economic benefit through the bidding process in comparison with the EDRP and ICAP.

In addition to the above-mentioned programs, NYISO has a Demand-Side Ancillary Service Program (DSASP). This program is to establish an instanta-neous and continuous two-way communication channel to enable remote mea-surement of electricity consumption. The metering data is transmitted every 6 s to NYISO and incorporated to system operations.

On the generator and market operator side, the Security Constrained Unit Commitment (SCUC) program [9–11] is a widely used method for making DR schedules. The objective of SCUC is to find a unit time schedule, for example, an hourly schedule, for generation, reserve, and price sensitive load in order to satisfy generation and reserve requirements, transmission constraints, and other operational constraints without compromising the reliability of the power grid. The reserve capacity used in SCUC can come from DR participants. Therefore, the output of SCUC contains DR schedules, which will be dispatched via various DR programs offered by market operators.

These programs are effective in reducing peak electricity use. The NYISO data show that the peak load on August 2, 2006, was reduced by 1000 MW through a combination of the three DR programs [8]. DR is now considered an essential component of a properly functioning electricity market.

These programs, particularly EDRP and ICAP, are not invoked frequently to fulfill the potential of DR. One reason is that in the existing electricity market a big share of electricity is sold through forward contracts or the day-ahead market. There are also inadequate communication channels between generators and consumers to exchange supply and demand changes in a timely manner. Another reason is that many small consumers cannot directly participate in these programs due to their inability to receive and act on requests to control loads in a timely manner to meet the minimum response requirements.

Smart Grid technologies may potentially fill the capacity gap and become the game changer to fulfill the potential of DR. In the following, we discuss efforts to establish additional links between generators and consumers that can be used to implement more effective DR schemes under the context of the Smart Grid.

21.2.2 Demand Response Supported by the Smart Grid

The Smart Grid offers new opportunities for improving traditional DR programs. *Energy Storage* and *Advanced Metering Infrastructure* (AMI) are two important technologies that can potentially automate DR programs and seamlessly inte-grate them as part of daily activity in electricity markets. In particular, these technologies can extend DR out to small consumers, such as small businesses and residential users, to help them achieve cost savings while simultaneously improving the reliability of power grids.

Energy storage plays an increasingly important role in the electricity market. It has various forms, for example, energy storage devices (ES), power-electronics-connected distributed energy resources (DERs), hybrid generation-storage systems (ES-DER), and plug-in electric vehicles (PEVs). The deployment of energy storage will give consumers and generators the flexibility needed to deal with demand and price spikes in the market. One can imagine that energy storage plays a role similar to a content delivery network that caches high demand Web sites and shares the load across multiple servers.

AMI is a set of hardware, software, and communication technologies that enable measurement, collection, and analysis of energy use. AMI also makes it possible for a remote service to interact with consumers regarding their energy use. "Smart metering" [12] and domestic energy management devices [13] are two examples of technologies that are available for consumers to collect their energy consumption data in real time. As an initial step toward the Smart Grid, these technologies can draw consumers' attention to their energy consumption and raise their awareness of any patterns or cost implications. Raising awareness of consumers is an important part of reducing their energy use during peak demand. A report [14] shows that 5–15% energy saving can be achieved if the metering data also includes clearly understood reference points for improving billing. With the help of on-line energy monitoring tools such as Google PowerMeter [15, 16], consumers can easily track the energy use of smart meter-connected appliances over time. The metering data can be then used by consumers to manage their budget, predict future energy use, and identify changes that can be made to save energy and cut cost. As an example, Google PowerMeter also provides consumers the capability of forming a community to work together on energy-saving strategies. The number of utilities and devices that work with such Web services is steadily increasing.

Furthermore, a large amount of work on "smart house" technologies [17] and *home energy management* (HEM) [18] will enrich functionality of this kind of Web services. Energy management consultancy and delegation can be provided in the form of Web services as well, and a cost-effective service-oriented platform can be formed for small-energy consumers to better manage their energy use. Potentially, these technologies will allow a trusted party to remotely manage the energy use of consumers by aggregating their DR capacity and executing DR strategies using the combined capacity based on a range of service agreements. In Reference 19, we treated efficient energy management as a service and gave a three-tier architecture to enable this service to automate energy management for small businesses and residential consumers. The consumers can define access control policies for an energy service provider (ESP) to execute agreed DR programs on their behalf.

The diversity of smart metering technologies and service models built on the metering data may create interoperability issues. For the purpose of amplifying the benefit of DR to the large scale, there is a need to standardize DR-related data representation and data exchange protocols. The *Open Automated Demand Response Communication Specification*, or *OpenADR* [20], is an example of such a DR standardization effort. The development of OpenADR started in 2002 following the California electricity crisis. Work was carried out by the Demand Response Research Center (DRRC), which is managed by the Lawrence Berkeley National Laboratory. OpenADR is now a standard of the OASIS (Organization for the Advancement of Structured Information Standards). OpenADR defines the data model of DR signals exchanged between a utility (or an independent system operator such as NYISO) and consumers. The DR programs running inside the control systems on the consumer side can act upon the arrival of these signals without human intervention. At the core of OpenADR is the abstraction of the DR event delivery infrastructure called *Demand Response Automation Server* (*DRAS*). DRAS defines the following interfaces:

- *Utility and ISO Operator Interface*. It is the interface for a utility or an ISO to set up a DR program, which includes configuring a predefined DR program and dynamic pricing in the DRAS as well as adding DR clients of this utility or ISO. A DR program defines DR event launching endpoints. It also maps the program to events and client feedback signals.
- *DRAS Client Interface*. It is the interface that defines how a DR event is passed to the automated control system in the facility of a consumer participating in the DR program. It also defines an interface for the client to report back to the DRAS how the facility responds to the event.
- *Participant Operator Interface*. It is the management interface for DR participants to configure the way they are involved in the DR program. A participant can be either a facility manager or an aggregator. An aggregator is a party that manages a set of facilities and provides a single interface for the utility or ISO of these facilities.

The setup and execution process of a simple DR program includes the following steps:

1. A utility or ISO sets up the DR program in its internal information system and then configures the program in the DRAS. The configuration includes signing up facility managers to allow them to access the DRAS as clients.
2. The facility manager configures the DRAS client side and its Energy Management and Control System (EMCS) to enable shedding or shifting load according to possible DR events.
3. When a condition is satisfied, the information system inside a utility or ISO initiates a DR event. A notifier submits the event to the DRAS. The event contains information such as the program type, event time, geographic location of the event, and customer list.
4. The DRAS sends the event to all DRAS clients in the program, and the latter in turn send instructions to their internal EMCS to shed or shift load.

5. The DRAS client of a facility sends back the load status to the DRAS to notify the utility or ISO of its response to the DR event.

6. The utility or ISO measures the actual usage in the facility and settles payment with the facility.

These steps may vary for different DR programs; for example, in a DR program that allows demand bidding, a facility manager needs to set up bidding information in its DRAS client and add a step to receive the bidding result from the DRAS.

In general, OpenADR attempts to automate traditional DR programs by defining a set of protocols that connect information systems running inside utilities and EMCSs running in the consumer sites. OpenADR can be seen as a transitional standard, as it is targeted at using Smart Grid technologies to transform existing DR programs. Once the supply side and the demand side in the electricity market are linked more closely through the growing use of information technologies, there are more opportunities to exploit than just transforming existing practices. In fact, the Smart Grid paradigm is gradually turning DR into a computing problem in a distributed system. We discuss this scenario in the next section.

21.3 DEMAND RESPONSE AS A DISTRIBUTED SYSTEM

As the use of information technologies rapidly grows in the electrical power industry, people start to realize that many tasks in this domain can be leveraged to run as Web services. Some even argue that applications such as DR may even take advantage of cloud computing to augment the capacity of utilities [21]. As mentioned in the previous section, existing DR programs are designed by utilities or ISOs. These programs are not activated often partially because the demand side does not have sufficient information to cooperate with the supply side or to make DR decisions in their own interests. This situation may change when consumers understand their own consumption better and have access to price signals along with other market information. It is possible that consumers themselves can initiate DR purely for their own benefit. Independent rational adjustment of energy use patterns on the consumer side can also make the whole market better off. In this section, we discuss how the DR can be improved in a well-connected distributed computing system.

21.3.1 An Overlay Network for Demand Response

Parties involved in DR can be seen as an overlay network on top of the power grid. As shown in Figure 21.2, the suppliers and consumers are linked through a two-level network:

- Links on the top level connect distributed generators, distributed storage, ISOs, market operators, large energy consumers, and ESPs. The information

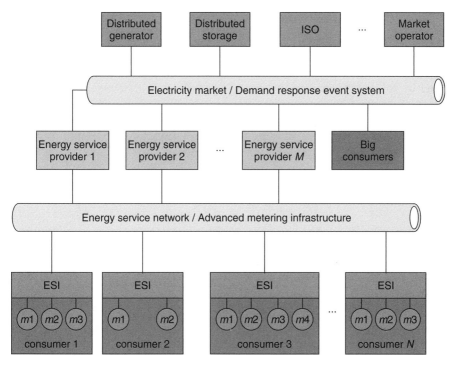

Figure 21.2   The energy service network. ESI, energy surface interface.

exchanged between these players includes dynamic pricing information and DR events. This scenario is similar to the present electricity market practice as captured by OpenADR except that a generic ESP replaces the aggregator role.

• Links on the bottom level connect ESPs and small or medium consumers. The information exchanged between them includes metering data, remote management instructions, and feedback, as well as other service-specific data. An ESP plays the aggregator's role for small or medium consumers as in the current DR practice. It also plays the delegator's role to manage energy use for its customers. Moreover, it provides metering data storage, analysis, and electricity use prediction services.

The overlay network mainly supports two DR use cases. In the first case, a player on the top level requests DR for the purpose of power grid reliability. We call this scenario *event-driven DR*. In the second case, an ESP balances the load of its consumers to avoid demand spikes for the purpose of cutting cost for its customers. We call this scenario *cost-driven DR*.

21.3.2 Event Driven Demand Response

Event-driven DR is initiated by the parties on the supply side. A party on the top level of Figure 21.2 is concerned about the reliability of the power grid or its power generation facility, which can be damaged by demand spikes and load variability. Demand spikes and load variability can be significantly higher when charging facilities are widely deployed for PHEVs (plug-in hybrid electric vehicles) or PEVs [21]. Therefore, party the would like to pay for a certain amount of load shed from its consumers in exchange for the stability of power generation or transmission. Willingness can be represented as a DR event in the following format:

$$(requester, load, price, \{participant\}),$$

in which *requester* is the party that initiates DR activity, *load* is the minimal amount of electricity use the party requests its consumers to shed, *price* is the unit price the party would like to pay for the load reduction, and *{participant}* is a set of consumers or ESPs who can shed consumption or aggregate a set of small consumers for load shedding in order to help the requester achieve reliability. The base price for load shedding is calculated according to the network reliability analysis from the supplier's perspective. The event is then propagated to the targeted participants in the list. Once receiving the event, big consumers often perform curtailment according to prenegotiated contracts. An ESP also contracts with the requester. The contract is reached based on the aggregated load shed capability at a given time frame from the consumers who subscribe to the ESP. On receiving the event, the service provider optimizes load shedding among these consumers.

The method for optimizing the schedule of load curtailment among a set of participants is similar on both the supplier and the ESP level. They differ on the constraints. We use a simple example of scheduling load reduction on the ESP level to illustrate this. Table 21.1 shows the baseline energy use of three consumers C_1, C_2, and C_3 at time t. We assume that these consumers subscribe to the same ESP and are flexible about load shedding as long as the unit price is acceptable. The price may differ between consumers and so can the amount of load shed. The price function of a consumer is agreed with its ESP during the contract negotiating process.

Suppose that the ESP receives a DR event requesting load shedding of 35 MW for time t at an average unit price no more than \$300. The task of the provider is

TABLE 21.1 Consumer Energy Use

Consumer	Baseline Energy Use (MW)
C_1	20
C_2	30
C_3	35

to schedule the load shed among C_1, C_2, and C_3 at a minimal cost. The minimal cost reflects the overall willingness of all consumers to reduce their load. The cost can be calculated as below:

$$\text{minimize} \quad \sum_C f_C(l_C) \cdot l_C,$$
$$\text{subject to} \quad \sum_C l_C \geq L,$$
$$\sum_C f_C \leq P,$$

where f_C is the price function of load shed for consumer C, l_C is the amount of load shed from C, and L is the total load shed requested in the incoming DR event. We assume the unit price for the load shed is a function of the amount of curtailment delivered by C, which can be modeled by quadratic equations [22]. We assume the following cost functions for C_1, C_2, and C_3 in this simple example:

$$f_{C_1}(l) = 2l^2 + (1 - 0.6)l,$$
$$f_{C_2}(l) = l^2 + 2(1 - 0.8)l,$$
$$f_{C_3}(l) = 3l^2 + (1 - 0.3)l.$$

The cost functions are illustrated in Figure 21.3.

By solving this nonlinear optimization problem, we get the optimal schedule for load shed as shown in Table 21.2. It produces the minimized overall cost for the DR activity at $8411.352.

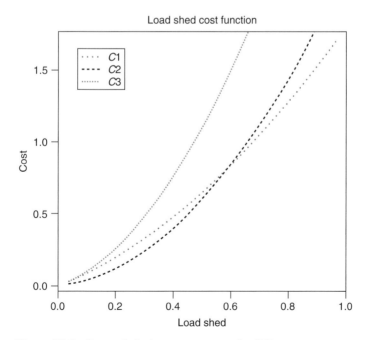

Figure 21.3   Demand shed versus payment for different consumers.

TABLE 21.2   The Optimal Load Shed

Consumer	Load Shed (MW)	Unit Price
C_1	15.221	243.848
C_2	10.916	240.517
C_3	8.863	241.857

As shown in the example, event-driven DR consists of the following components:

- computer-processable contract that describes the cost function;
- price and other constraints of a consumer;
- protocol for reaching such a contract and a DR event system;
- market mechanism to set the price and schedule the curtailment.

21.3.3   Cost Driven Demand Response

With the increase in the deployment of smart meters, consumers, particularly, small consumers, will be increasingly aware of the price of the electricity they purchase. The awareness will further make pricing an important means to trigger change in consumers' demand. It is likely that dynamic and market-based electricity pricing will become the norm in future retail contracts. In such a price-driven market, demand can be adjusted to respond to certain market and power grid conditions without the need for a party to explicitly create DR events to stimulate demand changes. It is in each consumer's interest to respond to price signals and reduce energy cost. Dynamic price information also gives consumers visibility of the overall market demand and power grid conditions. They can therefore make local adjustments to respond to the price change. In this scenario, the chance that a DR program as described in Section 21.2 is activated will be further reduced. An operator will reduce its responsibility to monitoring consumption through smart metering infrastructure and to regulating the market. In this section, we discuss the mechanisms for cost-driven DR.

We consider that the pricing of electricity over a given time interval is based on the supply and demand ratio. We denote the size of the minimal time interval as s. By dividing a given time frame into a sequence of contiguous time intervals denoted by $T =< t_1, t_2, \ldots, t_n >$, we have a vector of prices, denoted by $< p_1, p_2, \ldots, p_n >$, for these intervals. The electricity price in each interval is determined by the overall demand and the electricity generation capacity during this interval, which can be represented as [23]

$$p_i = \alpha \left(\frac{D_i}{\mathrm{CAP}_i} \right)^{c-1}, 1 \leq i \leq n, \qquad (21.1)$$

in which D_i is the total demand, CAP_i is the generation capacity of the market during time interval t_i, and α and c are two free variables.

We assume that the pricing of a group of consumers can be isolated to those consumers outside the group. This can be achieved through subscribing to the same ESP who is able to purchase a certain amount of electricity ahead for time frame T in the upper layer market and cover the purchase cost through resale in the retail market. The retail price, therefore, reflects the supply and demand among the group of subscribers. The ESP can adjust supply using energy storage and local generation capacity it controls. With this setting, it is possible for consumers to form groups through ESPs for managing and optimizing their energy use.

Each consumer may exhibit a range of patterns in electricity use. The energy consumption profile of a set of consumers $U = \{u_1, u_2, \ldots, u_l\}$ can be represented using the following matrix $\mathcal{M}$:

$$\mathcal{M} = \{(u_i, \{(p_j, \{(t_k, r_k)\}_{k=1}^n)\}_{j=1}^m)\}_{i=1}^l, \tag{21.2}$$

where p_j is the electricity use pattern of a consumer u_i, m is the maximum number of different patterns of a consumer, and r_k is the energy consumption rate during time interval t_k.

Let us consider that a consumer has a dominant electricity use pattern, which is used by the consumer most often according to the historical data collected through metering. Other patterns the same consumer exhibits occasionally can be derived from the dominant pattern via one of the following two methods.

- *Demand Shift*. The time intervals of consumption in the dominant pattern are shifted and gaps with zero consumption can be inserted between these intervals.
- *Demand Reduction*. The consumption rate in a time interval is reduced, but the reduced consumption may stretch to other time intervals. This applies to users who have access to local generation or energy storage with limited capacity or to the use of appliances such as air conditioners that can preheat or precool rooms and work on reduced capacity during peak hours.

Table 21.3 shows an example of $\mathcal{M}$, in which each row represents different energy consumption patterns during $T = < t_1, t_2, t_3, t_4 >$.

Under the pricing model given in Equation 21.1, the overall cost is minimal when the load normalized by the capacity of an interval is evenly distributed among the given sequence of time intervals [19]. Finding an optimal solution for distributing the load is an NP-hard problem, as it requires computing the cost of all the combinations of different user consumption patterns. In the following, we describe an approximation algorithm for this problem.

TABLE 21.3   Sample Electricity Consumption Profiles

Consumer	Use Pattern	t_1	t_2	t_3	t_4
u_1	1	1 kW	—	—	—
	2	—	1 kW	—	—
	3	—	—	1 kW	—
	4	—	—	—	1 kW
u_2	1	—	2 kW	—	—
	2	—	—	2 kW	—
	3	—	—	—	2 kW
	4	1 kW	1 kW	—	—
	5	2 kW	—	—	—
u_3	1	1 kW	1 kW	—	—
	2	—	1 kW	1 kW	—
	3	—	—	1 kW	1 kW

Algorithm 21.1: The Scheduling Algorithm

Input: User energy consumption profile $\mathcal{M}$,
           capacity in given time intervals: $\text{CAP} = \{c_i\}|_{i=t_0}^{t_{n-1}}$
Output: A schedule $\mathcal{S}$ for the energy consumption of the
            user set

```
{
    L = {l_i}|_{i=t_0}^{t_{n-1}} is a demand vector with initial value 0;
    normalize the consumption rates with C (r'_i = r_i/c_i);
    M' <- the normalized consumption profile;
    sort patterns in M' in ascending order with comparator
      PatternComp;
    for each pattern p
    {
      if p.u has not been scheduled
      {
        schedule the demand vector of p, denoted by p.r
          to minimize Max_{i∈T}(l_i + p.r_i);
        for each time interval i ∈ T
          l_i += p.r_i;
        mark p.u as scheduled and add p to S;
      }
    }
    return S;
}

int PatternComp(p1, p2)
/* returns -1 if p1 < p2; 1 if p1 > p2; 0 if p1 = p2 */
{
    m_{p1} = MAX_T(p1.r_k);
    m_{p2} = MAX_T(p2.r_k);
```

```
if m_p1 > m_p2
   return 1;
if m_p1 < m_p2
   return -1;
/* if equal, compare the overlap degrees with other
   patterns */
```

$$T1 = \{t_k | p1.r_k > 0\};$$

$$T2 = \{t_k | p2.r_k > 0\};$$

$$f_{p1} = \frac{\sum_{p \in M, p.u \neq p1.u} \sum_{T1} p.r_k}{|T1|};$$

$$f_{p2} = \frac{\sum_{p \in M, p.u \neq p2.u} \sum_{T2} p.r_k}{|T2|};$$

```
/* the pattern with higher overlapped consumption rate
   is bigger */
if f_p1 > f_p2
   return 1;
if f_p1 < f_p2
   return -1;
return 0;
}
```

The algorithm gives priority to the patterns with small peak consumption rates in an attempt to keep the overall peak load low. It also attempts to schedule demands to different time intervals to avoid a demand spike in some "congested" time intervals. This is achieved by a scoring function in *PatternComp*. When two patterns have the same peak consumption rate, the demand of the pattern that overlaps other patterns to a greater extent scores higher.

As an example, the overall consumption of consumers with profiles given in Table 21.3 is shown in Figure 21.4(a). We assume the dominant pattern of a consumer is the first row in the consumer's pattern list, that is, p_1 in the profile table. Algorithm 21.1 produces a schedule as shown in Figure 21.4(b). Pattern 4 of $u1$, denoted by $p_{u1,4}$, is scheduled first because it has the smallest overlapping consumption (3 kW) compared to $p_{u1,1}$ (4 kW), $p_{u1,2}$ (5 kW), and $p_{u1,3}$(4 kW). Similarly, $p_{u2,4}$ is scheduled because it has the smallest overlapping consumption (2.5 kW) compared to $p_{u3,1}$ (4 kW), $p_{u3,2}$ (3.5 kW), and $p_{u3,3}$ (3 kW). We can see that the peak demand during T is reduced from 3 kW in time interval t_2 to 2 kW in time interval t_4 after scheduling. The overall cost saving can be significant depending on the parameter settings of Equation 21.1; for example, when the capacity is 4 kW in a time interval, $\alpha = 3.0$, and $c = 5.0$, the initial overall cost is 3.22, while the overall cost after scheduling is only 0.41.

From the example, we can see that the potential cost saving is a strong incentive for consumers to participate in DR activities. The coordination of consumption patterns may result in a lower price. Unlike event-driven DR,

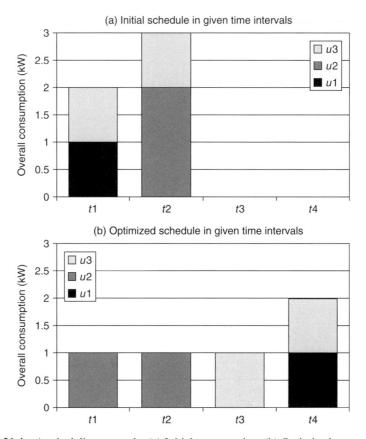

Figure 21.4   A scheduling example. (a) Initial consumption. (b) Optimized consumption.

the marginal benefit of a certain load distribution on T is estimated from the consumer's perspective, not triggered by DR events generated by a market operator. However, as one may notice, the algorithm assumes that each consumption pattern has the same benefit for the consumer and a consumer is not sensitive to the difference in consumption patterns. It is apparently not the case under many circumstances because shifting the time of energy use and shedding load may cause inconvenience or other loss for a consumer. When each pattern has different benefit for each consumer, a mechanism is needed to redistribute the overall cost saving achieved through the DR activities. Consumers who are willing to adopt patterns that have lower benefit to them should be compensated by the mechanism. In another words, a *redistribution mechanism* should encourage consumers to make changes for the social benefit.

In order to do so, there needs to be a method to measure the cost of pattern change. This can be done through the negotiation between consumers and ESPs in a manner similar to the DR contract negotiation in the event-driven DR scenario. Potentially, this requires a market for participants to trade their DR capacities. A simpler way to measure the cost of pattern change is to measure the distance between two patterns and use the distance to calculate the value of the pattern change. We consider a consumer's dominant pattern brings the consumer the maximum benefit from energy use during T. The farther another pattern of the consumer is from the dominant pattern in distance, the bigger benefit loss the pattern change may cause to the consumer. As a result, a larger portion of the social benefit should be paid back to the consumer. How to measure the distance of two patterns remains an open problem. Wang and de Groot [24] give a method that treats patterns as time series and uses dynamic time warping (DTW) as a metric to compare two patterns.

In general, cost-driven DR enables consumers to optimize their energy use simply by coordinating consumption patterns. With the potential wide adoption of energy storage and local generation devices, this model is promising to maximize the benefit of DR.

21.3.4 A Decentralized Demand Response Framework

Recently, electricity markets have started to move to open DR programs for a broad range of consumers through proxies. For example, to increase participation, the California Independent System Operator (CAISO) allows DR aggregators, or curtailment service providers, to bid DR on behalf of retail consumers directly in the ISO energy markets [25]. The move promises a flexible DR framework in the future. From the perspective of the link structure of the electricity infrastructure, the existing topology of power grids reveals certain small-world property as shown in Reference 26. This property matches many link patterns in decentralized information systems such as the Web, which indicates that there is an opportunity to exploit a decentralized model to organize DR systems with good scalability. As the electricity market gradually lowers its barriers and opens to more and more consumers, it is likely that the future DR framework will become decentralized. The role of aggregating proxies is also likely to be virtualized through well-designed computing algorithms and communication protocols. Consumers may even form a fully decentralized system to implement DR for their own benefit.

The scenario is shown in Figure 21.5, in which all parties in the DR market are linked through an energy service network that delivers DR events. An energy service network can be seen as an overlay network on top of the Internet. The overlay can be organized in a structured [27], an unstructured [28], or a hybrid [29] manner. The network has a standard access interface for participating parties to identify themselves as well as to send and receive data. Each party has a DR membership engine. The membership engine is used by a user node to look up other user nodes to work together for delivering DR. The engine also facilitates the coordination of a group of users by passing events related to their DR activities. With the membership engine, a virtual coordinator can be created via customized membership protocols. Each party also has a DR processing engine. A DR processing engine determines how to process an event from the underlying energy service network. A user may specify rules to customize its response to

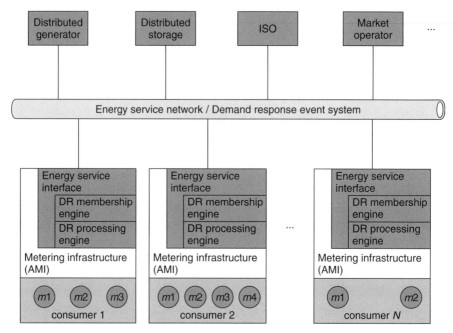

Figure 21.5   The decentralized energy service network.

DR events. This framework removes the upstream layer and establishes direct connection between suppliers and consumers. The decentralized DR framework can handle an increasing number of DR participants and create new types of DR programs via the self-organized coordination among consumers. This framework also provides underlying mechanisms for consumers to efficiently manage their consumption to deliver both event-driven and cost-driven DRs.

21.3.5   Accountability of Coordination Decision Making

As electricity is a product with special importance in people's daily life, it is essential to ensure that the flexibility introduced by the Smart Grid does not affect the reliability of power grids or cause damage to users. To achieve this, the coordination protocols of automated DR should be carefully designed so that decisions carried out by the systems should be made accountable. A natural step toward solving this problem is to extend DR contracts to cover accountability and to deploy auditing services inside DR systems. These services are responsible for monitoring a subnet and detecting anomalies according to a set of agreed contracts.

We use a simple example to explain this point. Nowadays, some smart meters enable a service provider to remotely switch on or off the circuits connected to the meters. An ESP is, therefore, capable of managing the energy use for a consumer remotely. If a consumer signs a contract and delegates the energy management to the service provider, the consumer may benefit from reduced energy bills while the ESP may have the flexibility to produce better schedules. However, currently there is no mechanism to justify the decisions the service provider makes on behalf of its users. Ensuring security alone cannot address this problem. There is a need for supporting accountability in such a market.

We discussed in [30] how to use an external party to maintain a state machine for a service consumer and a service provider to make their interactions accountable according to a contract. Under the DR context, an external party can play a role in collecting market information and sampling anonymized meter readings and then validating the control commands sent from a service provider or coordinator based on this data. In the example mentioned above, a consumer node keeps a log recording its interactions with the corresponding service provider. A minimal set of information can be extracted from the log and transmitted to an auditing service. By aggregating such information from a set of consumers linked to the service provider or coordinator, the auditing service will be able to detect anomalies when problems occur. With such a special type of services, the market can be enhanced with the ability to hold a party responsible for its actions. Furthermore, complex monitoring and auditing mechanisms can be developed to detect the danger of catastrophic failure in the whole Smart Grid.

21.4 SUMMARY

In this chapter, we reviewed existing DR practices and the impact of Smart Grid technologies on DR. We classified automated DR into two categories: one is mainly driven by DR events and the other by cost reduction. Event-driven DR is initiated by suppliers or market operators, while the cost-driven approach is predominantly initiated by consumers. We discussed the framework that supports the two approaches. In both cases, distributed computing principles play an important role. We argued that the whole DR system may evolve into a decentralized one to allow consumers to gain more control over their consumption. We also briefly discussed how to support accountability in a flexible DR framework. With a market with appropriate policies to guide the energy use behaviors of rational consumers, it is possible that the self-organized DR will gradually dominate the market and supplier-driven DR will be required only occasionally.

REFERENCES

1. Litos Strategic Communication. Smart Grid: An Introduction. U.S. Department of Energy; 2008. Available at http://www.oe.energy.gov/DocumentsandMedia/DOE_SG_Book_Single_Pages(1).pdf, accessed in 2011.
2. Demand Response and Smart Grid Coalition. Accelerating the use of demand response and smart grid technologies is an essential part of the solution to America's Energy, Economic and Environmental Problems. DRSG; 2008. Available at http://www.drsgcoalition.org/policy/DRSG_Policy_Recommendations_to_Accelerate_DR_and_Smart_Grid-2008-11-24.pdf, accessed in 2011.

3. Office of the National Coordinator for Smart Grid Interoperability. NIST Framework and Roadmap for Smart Grid Interoperability Standards, Release 1.0. NIST Special Publication 1108. 2010. Available at http://www.nist.gov/ public_affairs/releases/upload/smartgrid_interoperability_final.pdf, accessed in 2011.

4. U.S Department of Energy. Benefits of demand response in electricity markets and recommendations for achieving them. [online]. 2006. Available at http://energy.gov/ sites/prod/files/oeprod/DocumentsandMedia/DOE_Benefits_of_Demand_Response_ in_Electricity_Markets_and_Recommendations_for_Achieving_Them_Report_to_ Congress.pdf, accessed in 2012.

5. Piette MA, Watson DS, Motegi N, Kiliccote S, Xu P. *Automated Critical Peak Pricing Field Tests: Program Descriptioin and Results*. Berkeley (CA): Lawrence Berkeley National Laboratory. LBNL-59351; 2006. Available at http://drrc.lbl.gov/system/files/59351.pdf.

6. Caves D, Eakin K, Faruqui A. Mitigating price spikes in wholesale markets through market-based pricing in retail markets. Electr J 2000;13(3):13–23.

7. Kirschen DS. Demand-side view of electricity markets. IEEE Trans Power Syst 2003;18(2):520–527.

8. Lynch MS. Opening Remarks & Presentation. NYISO Symposium: The Future is Now: Energy Efficiency, Demand Response and Advanced Metering; New York, USA; June 2007. Available at http://www.nyiso.com/public/webdocs/products/ demand_response/general_info/nyiso_symposium06272007_final.pdf, accessed in 2011.

9. Guy JD. Security constrained unit commitment. IEEE Trans Power Apparatus Syst 1971;PAS-90(3):1385–1390.

10. Cohen AI, Brandwahjn V, Chang S-K. Security constrained unit commitment for open markets; 1999. pp. 39–44.

11. Parvania M, Fotuhi-Firuzabad M. Demand response scheduling by stochastic SCUC. IEEE Trans Smart Grids 2010;1(1):89–98.

12. Marvin S, Chappells H, Guy S. Pathways of smart metering development: shaping environmental innovation. Comput Environ Urban Syst 1999;23(2):109–126.

13. James G, Cohen D, Dodier R, Platt G, Palmer D. A deployed multi-agent framework for distributed energy applications. In: *AAMAS '06: Proceedings of the 5th International Joint Conference on Autonomous Agents and Multiagent Systems*. New York: ACM; 2006. pp. 676–678.

14. Darby S. *The Effectiveness of Feedback on Energy Consumption. A Review for Defra of the Literature on Metering, Billing and Direct Displays*. Environmental Change Institute, University of Oxford; 2006. Available at http://www.eci.ox.ac.uk/ research/energy/downloads/smart-metering-report.pdf, accessed in 2011.

15. Wald M, Helft M. Google taking a step into power metering. New York Times. 2009. Available at http://www.nytimes.com/2009/02/10/technology/companies/10grid.html, accessed in 2010.

16. Google Inc. Google powermeter; 2010. Available at http://www.google.com/ powermeter/about/index.html, accessed in 2010.

17. Helal S, Mann W, El-Zabadani H, King J, Kaddoura Y, Jansen E. The gator tech smart house: a programmable pervasive space. IEEE Comput 2005;38(3):50–60.

18. Cisco Inc. Bringing the Smart Grid Into the Home: the Value of Home Energy Management for Utilities. CISCO White Paper; 2010. Available at http://poweronltd.ca/wp-content/uploads/2011/03/Bringing-the-Smart-Grid-into-the-Home.pdf, accessed in 2012.

19. Wang C, de Groot M, Marendy P. A service-oriented system for optimizing residential energy use. In: IEEE International Conference on Web Services, ICWS 2009, Los Angeles, CA, USA, 6–10 July 2009, pp. 735–742.

20. Piette MA, Ghatikar G, Kiliccote S, Koch E, Hennage D, Palensky P, McParland C. Open automated demand response communications specification (version 1.0). California Energy Commission, PIER Program. CEC-500-2009-063 and LBNL-1779E; 2009. Available at http://openadr.lbl.gov/pdf/cec-500-2009-063.pdf, accessed in 2012.

21. Ipakchi A, Albuyeh F. Grid of the future. IEEE Power Energy Mag 2009;7(2):52–62.

22. Fahrioglu M, Alvarado FL. Using utility information to calibrate customer demand management behavior models. IEEE Trans Power Syst 2001;16(2):317–322.

23. Bessembinder H, Lemmon ML. Equilibrium pricing and optimal hedging in electricity forward markets. J Finance 2002;LVII(3):1347–1382.

24. Wang C, de Groot M. Managing end-user preferences in the smart grid. In e-Energy; 2010. pp. 105–114.

25. California ISO. Draft Final Proposal for the Design of Proxy Demand Resource (PDR). California Independent System Operator Corporation; 2009. Available at http://www.caiso.com/241d/241da56c5950.pdf, accessed in 2011.

26. Wang Z, Scaglione A, Thomas RJ. Generating statistically correct random topologies for testing smart grid communication and control networks. IEEE Trans Smart Grids 2010;1(1):28–39.

27. Balakrishnan H, Kaashoek MF, Karger DR, Morris R, Stoica I. Looking up data in p2p systems. Commun ACM 2003;46(2):43–48.

28. Clarke I, Sandberg O, Wiley B, Hong TW. Freenet: A distributed anonymous information storage and retrieval system. In: Federrath H, editor. Volume 2009, *Designing Privacy Enhancing Technologies*, *Lecture Notes in Computer Science*. Berlin, Heidelberg: Springer-Verlag; 2001. pp. 46–66. 10.1007/3-540-44702-4_4.

29. Qiu D, Srikant R. Modeling and performance analysis of bittorrent-like peer-to-peer networks. In: SIGCOMM '04: Proceedings of the 2004 Conference on Applications, Technologies, Architectures, and Protocols for Computer Communications. New York: ACM; 2004. pp. 367–378.

30. Wang C, Nepal S, Chen S, Zic J. Cooperative data management services based on accountable contract. In Cooperative Information Systems (CoopIS) 2008 International Conference; 2008. Monterrey, Mexico. pp. 301–318.

CHAPTER 22

RESOURCE MANAGEMENT FOR DISTRIBUTED MOBILE COMPUTING

JONG-KOOK KIM

22.1 INTRODUCTION

A distributed mobile computing (DMC) environment can be a combination of an ad hoc mobile network and a cellular network with a heterogeneous mixture of mobile devices. As an ad hoc network has the flexibility of dynamically reorganizing the network and allowing peer-to-peer communication, a distributed computing environment that focuses on ad hoc mobile network is an area of research that is interesting and will be needed as more mobile devices are being utilized by many users. A DMC environment can be viewed as a heterogeneous computing (HC) environment consisting of mobile battery-powered computing devices that communicate using wireless connections, where HC is the coordinated use of various resources with different capabilities to satisfy the requirements of varying task/application mixtures. An ad hoc network environment enables users to communicate and share computational load and results with other users in the system in a peer-to-peer fashion to coordinate efforts to complete tasks or accomplish a mission (an example is shown in Figure 22.1). Examples of applications of DMC may include wildfire fighting, disaster management, military situations [1], and personal mobile clouds.

When the devices are wireless and mobile, the limited battery capacity becomes a constraint and power or energy management becomes a critical issue to prolong the overall system's longevity and to complete more tasks or applications. The battery capacity can also be heterogeneous for homogeneous devices because of battery lifetime, usage, and/or recharging. The heterogeneity of the resources and tasks in this DMC system can be exploited to maximize the performance or the cost-effectiveness of the system [2–5]. An important

Energy-Efficient Distributed Computing Systems, First Edition.
Edited by Albert Y. Zomaya and Young Choon Lee.
© 2012 John Wiley & Sons, Inc. Published 2012 by John Wiley & Sons, Inc.

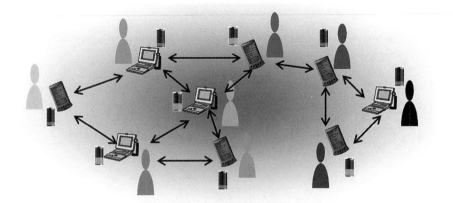

Figure 22.1 An example of the DMC environment illustrating different devices and battery states.

research problem is how to manage resources to prolong the system longevity and to complete as many tasks as possible. The function of resource management can be divided into the allocation of tasks onto machines and the ordering of task execution in a machine. The combination of both activities is called *mapping* or *resource allocation*. Usually, a resource management system (RMS) takes care of allocating resources of a certain system. The power management and mobility aspects further complicate the resource management problem.

There are two different types of mapping. Static mapping is performed when tasks are mapped in an off-line planning phase, for example, planning the schedule for a set of production jobs. Dynamic mapping is performed when the tasks are mapped in an on-line fashion, for example, when tasks arrive at unpredictable intervals and are mapped as they arrive (the workload is not known a priori). In both cases, the mapping problem has been shown, in general, to be NP-complete [6–8]. Thus, the development of heuristic techniques to find near-optimal solutions for the problem is an active research area [2, 3, 9–18].

In this research, the *dynamic mapping* of tasks onto devices is studied because the DMC system has many dynamic changes; that is, new tasks are requested without prior knowledge and devices are mobile so information about the system is time-varying in a manner that is not known a priori. Therefore, a method for dynamically mapping tasks onto the "best" device is needed. For the efficient use of the available overall system energy, it may be best for certain tasks to be executed on a remote, rather than the local, device. The reasons are (i) limited energy remaining on the local device, (ii) a remote device can execute the task using less energy, and (iii) a remote device can complete the task by its deadline. As described in Reference 15, dynamic mapping heuristics can be grouped into two categories, immediate and batch mode. Each time a mapping is performed, immediate mode heuristics only consider the new task for mapping, whereas batch mode may consider the new task and tasks awaiting execution, thus having more information about the task mixture before mapping. Both types of heuristics are considered in this work.

The power management for the computation is accomplished using dynamic voltage scaling (DVS) [19]. DVS is based on exploiting the relationship between the CPU supply voltage of a device and the power usage (e.g., ARM7D [20] and Crusoe [21]). The relationship between power and energy is that energy consumed is power multiplied by the amount of time power is used. The relationship between power and voltage is a strictly increasing convex function and is frequently represented by a polynomial of at least second degree [22]. Most processors that support DVS use discrete levels. The DVS technique allows the reduction of a CPU's energy usage (through CPU voltage (clock frequency) reduction) at the expense of increasing the task execution time. The DVS mechanism in this research will be managed by the system administrator or the resource manager and is transparent to the user. For the environment in Section 22.3, where mobility and a multihop environment is considered, the power management for the communication of data is accomplished by using the variable-range transmission power control (VTPC) [23] technique. Using this method, the communication power can be decreased or increased according to the distance between the source device and destination device.

In the ad hoc DMC environment modeled, the devices are wireless and can communicate with each other (e.g., peer-to-peer communication). An example scenario can be a wildfire-fighting situation in a remote forest area, where the firefighters are equipped with mobile devices that will form an ad hoc network. For the environment in Section 22.2.2, devices are assumed to be close enough to allow a single-hop ad hoc network, whereas the environment in Section 22.3 is a generalized version where multihop communications are considered. Using a device, a user can request a program (task) to be executed, receive data, and send data. A device performing computation may receive input data from other devices or external sources. The resulting output will be sent back to the task requester.

The motivation and challenges of a DMC environment include (i) dynamically mapping tasks onto wireless devices while managing power using DVS and VTPC, (ii) considering the mobility of devices, (iii) prolonging the system longevity while completing as many tasks as possible, and (iv) designing an energy-aware protocol to assist efficient overall system-level energy consumption.

The next section presents a single-hop energy-constrained environment without mobility being considered. Section 22.3 generalizes this environment to a multihop environment. In Section 22.4, future work for the DMC environment is discussed.

22.2 SINGLE-HOP ENERGY-CONSTRAINED ENVIRONMENT

22.2.1 System Model

The research in this section is based on our work in Reference 24. In the environment for this portion of our research, the devices are wireless with varying limited battery capacity (energy) and can communicate with each other (e.g., peer-to-peer communication). The devices in this research are assumed to be close enough to allow a single-hop ad hoc network. The batteries for these devices are assumed to be recharged after a certain amount of time. For example, in the firefighting scenario it is typical for firefighters to have a scheduled break for food and rest after a shift so that they can recharge their batteries at that time. The effect of mobility of the devices in this environment is negligible such that all the devices can communicate directly to each other (i.e., the devices are maintaining a single-hop network). The single-hop ad hoc grid environment is controlled by an RMS to maximize the goal stated toward the end of the next paragraph. The users are allowed one battery for the operation of a given device for an interval of time. The devices use DVS for power management. The number and value of the discrete voltage levels may vary among the devices.

The users send task requests to the RMS. Once a task request is received, the RMS assigns a device and sends a task execution command (Fig. 22.2). If input data is required, the data is communicated directly to the executing device from the source. A source could be other wireless devices or outside sources (e.g., a weather station). The result of the task execution (e.g., a wind direction estimate) is sent back to the task requester device, if the task was not executed on that device (task requester device). Tasks have different priority levels (i.e., high, medium, or low) and a deadline. It is assumed that the system is oversubscribed, and therefore, there is not enough total energy and/or time to complete all tasks by their individual deadlines. The primary goal of this research is to complete as many high priority tasks by their deadlines as possible during a given interval of time (i.e., 8 h). The secondary performance goal is to maximize the sum of the weighted priorities of medium- and low-priority tasks completed by their deadlines during that interval of time. This sum builds on the flexible integrated system capability (FISC) measure in Reference 25. The important objective of an RMS is to complete as many tasks as possible while taking the system-level energy into consideration. The reason for the primary goal is because, in

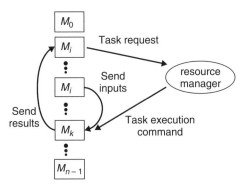

Figure 22.2 An example of a single-hop ad hoc grid heterogeneous computing environment.

this environment, high-priority-level tasks are considered to be infinitely more important than medium- and low-priority tasks and need to be completed. For the secondary goal, it is still beneficial to complete as many tasks as possible, but because tasks have different priorities (value), the goal considers this difference.

In terms of designing resource management heuristics that will generate robust resource allocations [26], the three robustness questions from Reference 27 need to be considered for this environment. The first question is what behavior of the system makes it robust? Here, we say the system is operating in a robust way if it can execute all the high priority tasks. The second question is what uncertainty is the system robust against? In this study, it is the uncertainty of which and when tasks of different priorities will arrive. The third question is quantitatively, how robust is the system? If we strictly enforce the robustness requirement of completing all the high priority tasks, then the robustness metric that can be used to compare two different resource allocations that complete all the high priority tasks is the value of the medium- and low-priority tasks it can complete in addition to the high priority tasks. If neither resource allocation can complete all the high priority tasks or meet the strict requirement, the one that completes a greater percentage of the high priority tasks is better. Alternatively, in the situation where the system is so oversubscribed that none of the heuristics used can complete all the high priority tasks, the robust requirement can be relaxed so that a given prespecified percentage (<100) of the high priority tasks can be completed.

The communication of inputs and results is assumed to be done directly from device to device (i.e., a single-hop ad hoc network) using the IEEE 802.11b standard (a popular wireless standard). In this research, only one device receives or sends data at any instant in time. This scheme is desirable when a certain quality of service must be met for the tasks. If other communications are allowed while a task is still communicating, then the communication time for that task is no longer guaranteed, which complicates the quantification of the communication time. A time-division-multiplexed communication scheme may be considered in future work.

In this environment, it is assumed that the types of devices that may connect to the system are known. In addition, there is a predetermined set of tasks that a user can request. However, it is not known a priori exactly which tasks will be requested and when they will be requested. In an example military scenario, there are predetermined types of wireless devices allowed to connect to the military system. In this environment, there is a set of tasks that may be requested for execution (e.g., target determination and troop deployment decisions). A requested task is executed on an assigned device and the information is sent back to the task requester. Because it is assumed that all the devices and the tasks are known, the task execution times on those devices are assumed to be known to the RMS. The estimated execution times of each task on each machine is assumed to be known based on user-supplied information, experiential data, experiments, task profiling and analytical benchmarking, or other techniques [4, 28–31]. Determination of the execution times is a separate research problem, and the assumption of such information is a common practice in mapping research [29, 30, 32–33].

It is assumed that all devices are equipped with all programs required and only input data is needed to execute a task and send back results. Thus, the time to communicate a task request to the RMS and to send a task execution command to a device is assumed to be negligible. We make the simplifying assumption that the RMS is located on a dedicated machine that has unlimited power and that the devices are within transmission range of the RMS (the relaxation of these assumptions may be considered in future work).

22.2.2 Related Work

There has been much research on power-constrained (power-aware) resource management in uniprocessors [34–37]. The research in Reference 34 presents (i) a static scheduling solution of periodic tasks on a processor assuming the worst-case scenario, (ii) a dynamic reclaiming algorithm for tasks that complete before their worst-case scenario, and (iii) an adaptive speed adjustment mechanism to anticipate the probable early completion of future task executions. A power min-imizing approach for variable-voltage systems is developed in Reference 35, where tasks are periodic and independent. The method described in Reference 36 assumes a dynamic preemptive environment where periodic independent tasks arrive and leave a system. In Reference 37, a formal analysis of the minimum energy scheduling problem is provided for a single processor and a model that assumes a task with an arrival time and deadline. The difference between these studies and our research is that our energy-constrained ad hoc grid environment considers multiple heterogeneous devices and nonperiodic independent tasks with priorities and deadlines that need input and/or output communicated. The fact that our environment has heterogeneous multiple devices adds new issues to the resource allocation problem.

Some research projects have explored a multiprocessor environment with static resource management [38–41]. In Reference 38, a genetic algorithm is used to synthesize distributed heterogeneous embedded systems. Using a static schedule derived from a list scheduling scheme, the study in Reference 39 does static and dynamic power management. The work in Reference 40 describes a linear programing method that statically schedules periodic tasks on heterogeneous pro-cessing elements. The research in Reference 41 assumes homogeneous processors and frame-based tasks. In static mapping, information of all tasks is known and the execution time of the heuristic itself is not a constraint. The difference is that our research explores a dynamic environment where the arrival time of a task is not known before its arrival and the task mapping time must be fast.

The research in Reference 42 statically schedules periodic tasks onto homo-geneous processing elements first using the tool in Reference 38 and then slots are created in this static schedule to accommodate aperiodic tasks with hard deadlines. They assume that the minimum interval between two hard aperiodic tasks is larger than the lowest common multiple period of all periodic tasks.

Then an on-line scheduler modifies the system to minimize the response times for aperiodic tasks with soft deadlines. The static schedule is unchanged, and the soft aperiodic tasks are run when there is unused time. In our research, all the devices are heterogeneous and all tasks are aperiodic with hard deadlines. Because all tasks are aperiodic, slots are not created among task periods, that is, the RMS approaches are quite different. Furthermore, our research considers the case where not all tasks with hard deadlines can complete and does not assume a minimum interval between the arrivals of two tasks.

The research in Reference 43 tries to send tasks to another device to be computed. It uses a distributed economic-based subcontracting protocol to determine which device to use, and its goal is to find a device that can execute tasks to save energy. A cost is associated with devices that are willing to execute a task for other devices. The device that wants to move one of its tasks to another device bargains with those willing devices. The underlying model of our work differs in that the environment in our research assumes that all devices are capable of DVS and tasks have deadlines and priorities.

References 44 and 45 study static RMSs for minimizing energy consumption for a heterogeneous ad hoc grid. The differences are that in our research, the heuristics operate dynamically, each device supports DVS, tasks have priorities, and it is assumed that not all tasks are completed before their hard deadlines.

22.2.3 Heuristic Descriptions

22.2.3.1 Mapping event. A dynamic mapping approach is designed to assign resources to new tasks faster than the anticipated average arrival rate of the tasks. Therefore, the heuristics that are developed have a limit on the time each computation of a new mapping can take. A mapping event occurs when a new task arrives. For immediate mode heuristics, at any mapping event, only the new task is considered for mapping onto devices. For batch mode heuristics, at any mapping event, the new task and the tasks in the device queues still awaiting execution are considered together for device assignment, that is, previously mapped but unexecuted tasks can be *remapped*. The exception is that the first task in each machine's wait queue (this task is not the task that is currently executing) is not considered for remapping. The reason for this is to reduce the chance of a device becoming idle if during a mapping event the currently executing task finishes. While it is still possible that a device may become idle, it is highly unlikely for the assumptions in this research (mean execution times of tasks and mean execution times of mapping events described in Sections 22.2.4 and 22.2.5, respectively). These tasks that are considered for remapping are called *mappable tasks*. If a task arrives while a mapping event is in progress, the current mapping event is not disturbed. When the current mapping event is completed, the next mapping event starts and includes any tasks that have arrived.

22.2.3.2 Scheduling communications. The following are the same for all heuristic approaches. All communications are scheduled as early as possible. If there are previous communications scheduled, then current ones are inserted in the gaps between the ones already scheduled if it is possible to fit the entire communication within the gap, or else they are put at the end of the communication scheduling queue. Communications from different sources can be scheduled in different gaps.

22.2.3.3 Opportunistic load balancing and minimum energy greedy heuristics.
The immediate mode opportunistic load balancing (OLB) heuristic is a common method for scheduling tasks. At a mapping event, among the devices that can execute the new task without violating its deadline and have enough energy to complete the task, the heuristic selects the device that will be ready (i.e., executes all the tasks already in its queue) first to map the new task. This is a simplistic method that ignores the relationship between the needs of the task to be assigned and the capability of the devices in the ad hoc grid. At a mapping event, the immediate mode minimum energy greedy (MEG) heuristic selects the device that can complete the task by its deadline and execute the task using a minimum amount of energy. This is a scheme that ignores other tasks that are already in the system. For both heuristics, if no device can complete the task by its deadline, the task is deleted from the system. The *energy consumed status* and *the device availability status (system status)* are updated at every mapping event.

22.2.3.4 ME-MC heuristic.
The immediate mode minimum energy minimum completion (ME-MC) time heuristic is based on the general concept of the switching algorithm (SA) in Reference 15. The basic idea behind this heuristic is to first try to map tasks onto their "best" machine according to some metric. But when the load on the system becomes unbalanced, the strategy is changed to balance the load. When the load is balanced then the scheme is changed back to the "best" machine method. For this method, a load balance ratio is used to determine whether the system is load balanced.

In this study, two different load balance ratios are calculated. One is for the high priority tasks and the other is for the medium- and low-priority tasks. The reason for the two different load balance ratios is that when high priority tasks arrive they are inserted behind the last high priority task and in front of all medium- and low-priority tasks or at the front of a device's wait queue. The *primary load balance ratio* is the ratio of the earliest device availability time over all the devices in the suite to the latest device availability time. For this ratio, the device availability times are determined using the last high priority task in each queue. If there are no high priority tasks in a device queue, then the device available time is the completion time of the task that is running if it is the only task on the device. If there are other tasks on the device, then the device available time is the completion time of the first waiting task. The *secondary load balance ratio* is same as the primary load balance ratio except that it is calculated with all tasks. For both the load balance ratios, a common high threshold and low threshold are established by experimentation (high threshold > low threshold).

Initially, the system maps new tasks onto the minimum energy consumption device using the slowest speed level. If the task that arrived is a high priority task and there are no devices that can complete the high priority task by its deadline, then the speed level of the devices is increased starting from device 0 using the method described below to test if there are devices that can complete the high priority task with a speed level increase. When increasing a device's speed level, the total number of speed levels of a device is taken into consideration. For example, assume a device 1 that has 16 speed levels and a device 2 that has 4 speed levels. If device 1 increased its speed levels at least four times, only then device 2 is considered for speed level increase. Only the speed level for the device finally selected for mapping is increased. Once the speed level of a device is increased to a faster level, the device will not try to execute tasks at a lower speed level later. All tasks mapped earlier will be completed faster than when the speed level was lower (before the speed level is increased), thus guaranteeing that tasks mapped earlier are completed by their deadline. At any mapping event, the speed level is increased at most two times. This is to avoid increasing the speed level to accommodate the current task while not leaving enough energy for future use.

The SA heuristic can be summarized by the following procedure. The total energy consumed is equal to the total CPU energy used plus the energy used for communication (details of CPU and communication energy are discussed in Section 22.2.4).

(1) Determine the priority level of the new task.
(2) Calculate the primary (or secondary) load balance ratio.
(3) If the primary (or secondary) load balance ratio is greater than the high threshold, then the current method is to use the minimum *energy consumption* device to map the new task.

   If the primary (or secondary) load balance ratio is less than the low threshold, then the current method is to use the minimum *completion* time (MCT) device to map the new task.

   If low threshold is less than or equal to primary (or secondary) load balance ratio that is less than or equal to high threshold, then the current method is the one used at the previous mapping event to map the new task.
(4) If the task is a medium- or low-priority task, assuming that it will be mapped at the end of a device queue, determine all devices that can complete the task by its deadline.

   if the task cannot be completed on any device, it is deleted from the system

   else, select a device using the current method, map the task to this device, and schedule all communications using the method in Section 22.2.3.2.
(5) Initialize "iteration" to the number of speed level changes on the device where the speed level was changed the most.

   If the task is a high priority task, assuming that it will be mapped (inserted) after the last high priority task in a device queue, determine all devices that can complete the task by its deadline.

do until a device is selected for mapping or iteration is increased twice.

if the task cannot be completed before its deadline on any device, increase the speed level (*note that when trying to increase a device's speed level, the total number of speed levels of a device is taken into consideration*).

for each device, increase one speed level if the (maximum number of speed levels over all devices)/(total number of levels on the device) ≤ iteration and test if the device can complete the task.

iteration = iteration + 1 else, select a device using the current method and map the task to this device.

if the task cannot be completed on any device, return all device's speed level to the level before this task arrived and drop the task, or else return all unselected devices' speed levels to the level before this task arrived.

(6) Check all devices as follows. If there is enough energy on a device to continually execute at the highest speed level and transmit data for the rest of the remaining time (until the end of the 8-h period), then the speed level for that device is increased to the highest speed level.

(7) Update the system status.

22.2.3.5 *ME-ME heuristic.* The batch mode minimum energy minimum energy (ME-ME) heuristic is based on the general concept of the Min-Min (greedy) idea in Reference 8. The Min-Min type heuristic performed very well in previous studies of different environments [11, 15]. The basic idea of a Min-Min type heuristic is to find the "best" device for all tasks that are considered and then among these task/device pairs to select the "best" pair to map first. To determine which device or which task/device pair is the best, a fitness value is used. The *fitness value* of a task on a given device for this study is (i) the energy consumed for high priority tasks and (ii) the energy consumed multiplied by the weighted priority divided by the execution time of the task for medium- and low-priority tasks. The energy consumed is equal to the energy used by the CPU plus the energy used for communication. This method also starts the simulation using the slowest speed level of devices to map tasks.

The ME-ME procedure starts at a mapping event, and it is assumed that none of the mappable tasks are mapped, that is, they are not in any device queue.

(1) First, all high priority tasks and then the rest of the tasks are considered.

(2) All high priority tasks in the mappable task list are checked to see if they can be completed by their deadline.

(3) If there are some tasks that cannot be completed on any device then the speed level is increased or the task is dropped using the method detailed in step 5 of Section 22.2.3.4.

(4) For each high priority task in the mappable task list, find the device that gives the task its minimum fitness value (the first "ME") among the devices

that can complete the task by its deadline using the current speed level and ignoring other tasks in the mappable task list.

(5) Among all the task/device pairs found from above, find the pair that gives the minimum fitness value (the second "ME"), map the task to the device, and remove the task from the mappable task list. Input or results communication is scheduled using the method in Section 22.2.3.2.

(6) Update the system status.

(7) Carry out steps 2–6 until all high priority tasks are mapped, and then do the same for medium- and low-priority tasks but the speed level should not be increased.

(8) Check all devices as follows. If there is enough energy on a device to continually execute at the highest speed level and transmit data for the rest of the remaining time (until the end of the 8-h period), then the speed level for that device is increased to the highest level.

(9) Update the system status.

22.2.3.6 *CRME heuristic.* The batch mode contention-resolved minimum energy (CRME) heuristic is based on the general concept of the Sufferage idea in Reference 15. The CRME heuristic applies the same fitness value calculation used in the ME-ME heuristic (Section 22.2.3.5) but when deciding which task to map, the task that "suffers" most, if not mapped to its "first choice machine," is selected.

The CRME procedure starts at a mapping event. When the mapping event begins, it is assumed that none of the mappable tasks are mapped, that is, they are not in any device queue.

(1) All high priority tasks are considered first, then the other tasks are considered.

(2) All high priority tasks in the mappable task list are checked if they can be completed by their deadline.

(3) If there are some tasks that cannot be completed on any device then the speed level is increased or the task is dropped using the method detailed within step 5 of Section 22.2.3.4.

(4) For each task in the mappable task list, find the device that gives the task its minimum fitness value among the devices that can complete the task by its deadline using the current speed level, ignoring other tasks in the task list.

(5) If there is contention among any of the high priority tasks (i.e., two or more high priority tasks have the same minimum fitness value device), select the task that will suffer the most (the task with the largest difference of fitness value between the best and the second best devices) to map onto the device selected. Or else, map all the high priority tasks.
All communications are scheduled using the method in Section 22.2.3.2.

(6) Remove the above-mapped task(s) from the mappable task list.

(7) Update the device availability and energy consumed status.

(8) Repeat steps 2–7 until all high priority tasks are mapped, and do the same for the medium- or low-priority tasks but the speed level should not be increased.

(9) Check all devices as follows. If there is enough energy on a device to continually execute at the highest speed level and transmit data for the rest of the remaining time (until the end of the 8-h period), then the speed level for that device is increased to the highest speed level.

(10) Update the system status.

22.2.3.7 Originator and random.

The immediate mode *originator* heuristic executes the task on the device that originated the task. This heuristic is run to compare to the performance of heuristics that utilizes other devices in the system. The immediate mode *random* heuristic maps the new task on a randomly selected device when the new task arrives. This heuristic is run to compare to the performance of the guided heuristics. The following is for both heuristics. The method in Section 22.2.3.2 is used for communication scheduling. If the selected device cannot complete the task by its deadline or there is not enough energy to complete the task, the task is deleted from the system. The energy consumed status is updated at every mapping event.

22.2.3.8 Upper bound.

Two upper bound (UB) methods are presented in this section. Each time the environment is simulated, the overall UB is determined by selecting the tighter bound of the two methods.

The first UB (UB1) uses the arrival time of tasks, priority of tasks, the deadline of the tasks, and the time interval between the arrivals of tasks based on the UB in Reference 14. The bound ignores the communication and the energy consumed. The tasks that have arrived before or at the mapping event are called *selectable tasks*. At any mapping event, only the selectable tasks are considered for the calculation of the UB. Let $ETC(i, j)$ be the estimated time to complete (ETC) of task i on device j, and let Q_i be equal to the priority weighting of task i divided by the minimum $ETC(i, j)$ over all machines. The scheme starts by initializing all the tasks' remaining ETC values, $rETC(i, j)$, to the minimum $ETC(i, j)$ over all devices. The UB1 follows the procedure described below.

(1) At a mapping event, determine the *total aggregate computation time* (*TACT*) until the next task arrives. That is, TACT is equal to the time interval between arrival times of the new task and the next task multiplied by the number of machines.

(2) Selectable tasks with $rETC(i, j) > 0$ are put in a task list.

(3) Sort high priority tasks in the task list using minimum ETC values. Then the medium- and low-priority tasks are sorted together based on Q_i.

(4) If there are high priority tasks in the task list, select the high priority task a that has the minimum ETC value else, select the medium- or low-priority task a with the highest Q_a from the task list.

(5) If TACT $<$ rETC(a, j)

if the selected task is high priority,

subtract TACT from rETC(a, j)

if the selected task is medium or low priority

add ($Q_a \times$ TACT) to the secondary metric

subtract TACT from rETC(a, j)

done (i.e., TACT $= 0$)

if TACT $\geq$ rETC(i, j)

if the selected task is high priority

add one to the primary metric (i.e., the number of high priority tasks completed)

subtract rETC(a, j) from TACT (this becomes the new TACT), rETC$(a, j) = 0$

if the selected task is medium or low priority

add ($Q_a \times$ TACT) to the secondary metric (i.e., the sum of the weighted priorities of medium- and low-priority tasks)

subtract rETC(a, j) from TACT (this becomes the new TACT), rETC$(a, j) = 0$

(6) Repeat steps 4 and 5 until TACT is equal to 0 or there are no selectable tasks with rETC$(a, j) > 0$.

(7) Repeat steps 1–6 until the end of the simulation.

The second UB (UB2) uses the energy consumed information of tasks. The total energy available is the sum of all devices' maximum energy available. The energy consumed is the energy used by the CPU plus the energy used for communication. The UB2 starts by determining the minimum energy consumed over all devices for each task. Then the high priority tasks are ordered in the task list using minimum energy consumed, and then the medium- and low-priority tasks are ordered using the minimum energy consumed divided by the weighted priority. Using this order, the number of tasks completed is computed by adding the energy consumed by the tasks until the sum exceeds the total energy available. While two methods were attempted, UB1 was always tighter than UB2 for the cases considered here. This is despite the fact that, in general, UB1 is an unreachable loose bound for this environment.

The UB calculation explicitly considers all the high priority tasks first for completion and then if the system has resources left they are used for the medium- and low-priority tasks. Recall that the primary goal of this research is to complete as many high priority tasks as possible. Therefore, the UB for the medium- and low-priority tasks completed is shown (in the results) only when a heuristic can achieve the UB on the high priority task. Only then it is valid to compare the medium- and low-priority tasks completed against the UB calculated.

22.2.4 Simulation Model

A total of 10 types of wireless computing devices and 50 task types are used in the simulated system. Because the devices and the tasks are known, the ETC each of the tasks on each of these different devices is known. In each simulation of a system, eight devices are picked with equal probability. The arrival of tasks is simulated by mean intertask arrival times using a Poisson distribution. Three scenarios with mean intertask arrival times of 10, 8, and 6 s are considered. The mean intertask arrival times are given to loosely generate more and more tasks for the system to handle. At the beginning, the system can handle most of the tasks, and later, where there are a lot of tasks, the system could only complete a percentage of the tasks. The system is simulated for 480 min (i.e., 8-h work time), with eight bursty periods of 10 minutes that do not overlap with each other. The bursty periods have faster arrival rates (mean is twice as fast as the rate of the normal period).

A 10×50 ETC matrix of the 50 types of tasks on 10 types of devices taking heterogeneity into consideration is generated using the gamma distribution method described in Reference 46, with a COV of 0.9 for task heterogeneity and 0.6 for device heterogeneity. Two means, 60 and 600 s, are used for the ETC matrix. The mean execution time is chosen to represent applications such as downloading files (such as maps or weather reports) and generating strategies. When a task is determined to arrive, 1 of the 50 task types is selected with equal probability. A *trial* is defined as one such simulation of the HC system (one 10×50 ET matrix). For each of the six scenarios (three mean intertask arrival time multiplied by two mean execution times), 50 trials are run for all heuristics.

Each task is assigned a priority level of high, medium, or low, with equal likelihood. The levels of medium and low are given a weighting of four and one, respectively. The weighting is to calculate the performance of the value of medium- and low-priority tasks completed by their deadlines (secondary goal) if the number of high priority tasks completed by their deadlines (primary goal) is comparable for some heuristics.

For each device, the maximum battery capacity, the maximum CPU energy consumption rate, and the number of discrete levels for DVS are given. The discrete levels for DVS correspond to the speed at which the CPU is run and are defined as *speed levels*. The environment assumes the IEEE 802.11b standard for wireless communication. It is assumed that the data communication and the task computation or execution can be done simultaneously. On the basis of the two types of wireless devices (a laptop and a handheld device), the energy consumption rates are determined. These two devices can be selected with equal probability. The maximum CPU energy consumption rates are determined using a uniform distribution with a range of 0.1–0.3 for laptops or 0.01–0.03 for handheld devices. The reason for the two ranges is that the CPU energy consumption rate of a laptop is about 10 times higher than that of a handheld device (based on sample devices from the Dell Web site). On the basis of the sample communication adapters (e.g., Linksys) for the two types of devices, the transmission energy consumption rate is 0.6 (about three times the CPU energy consumption rate of a laptop) or 0.2 (about one-third of the transmission energy consumption rate of a laptop) for the laptops or the handheld devices, respectively. The reception energy consumption rate and the idle (communication) energy consumption rate are assumed to be 65% and 25% of the transmission power consumption rate, respectively. For the simulation study, the maximum battery capacity (energy) of device j, $BC(j)$, is set to the maximum CPU energy consumption rate plus the transmission energy consumption rate, multiplied by the maximum operation time. The maximum operation time is determined using a uniform distribution with a range of 1–2 h. This means that if the CPU is used at the maximum speed level and the device is always transmitting then the battery capacity is only enough to operate the device for 1–2 h.

To simplify DVS, this research assumes that each voltage level of a processor corresponds to a clock cycle speed level for the processor. Each device can have 2, 4, 8, or 16 discrete speed levels with equal probability. After the number of levels is decided, the relative speed of each level is determined. The lowest speed level of a device is assumed to be one-third of the maximum speed level (e.g., if the maximum speed level is 1.2 GHz, the lowest speed level will be 400 MHz). We make the simplifying assumption that task execution time varies linearly with the discrete speed level. It is assumed that the voltage switching is done dynamically and that the overhead associated with the switching is negligible (20–150 µs). The power consumption as a function of speed (voltage) levels is assumed to be a quadratic function. For the example with four speed levels assume that the maximum energy consumption rate is $\alpha = 0.16$. Using a simple equation, maximum energy consumption rate $= \alpha \times$ (relative speed of a speed level to the maximum speed level)^2, where α is 0.16. The relative speed of the slowest speed level is 1/3 of the maximum speed level, next will be 5/9 and 7/9 of the maximum speed level (linear). Using these fractions, the energy consumption rates for each speed level are calculated. In this example, the energy consumption rates would be $0.16 \times 1/9, 0.16 \times 25/81, 0.16 \times 49/81$, and 0.16 from the slowest speed level to the fastest (maximum) speed level. When the CPU of the device is idle, the CPU energy consumption rate is assumed to be 1/12 of the maximum energy consumption rate.

The eight devices are assumed to transmit and receive at the speed of 1 Mbps. When tasks need to communicate input or output, it is assumed that only one communication is allowed at a time. If multiple tasks need input data at a moment in time, only one task at a time may receive its input data (no broadcasting, only point-to-point transfer). For simulation purposes, the size of the input data was calculated using 10 kB as the mean and a COV of 0.7, with the maximum size being 1 MB. The size of the result (output) was calculated using 10 kB as the mean and a COV of 0.7, with the maximum size being 10 MB. A task may receive input from all other devices and from one outside source (e.g., a weather station for forecast reports). The maximum total number of inputs a task may need would be eight. The average number of input sources was 2.5 (the number of input sources was calculated using a normal distribution with mean 2.5 and a minimum of zero and maximum of eight sources).

In a real system, the hard deadline of a task may be set by the user that requested the task, the task designer, or the system operator/administrator. This research assumes that when the task arrives, the deadline of the task is given. For our simulation studies, the deadline of task i was equal to the sum of its arrival time, the overall mean execution time of all tasks, two times the median execution time of task i on all devices, the expected communication time (input and result), and the expected communication wait time (= the mean number of input receptions (2.5) multiplied by 7 and by the mean input communication time plus 7 multiplied by the mean result communication time).

22.2.5 Results

The simulation results for the different mean execution times and mean intertask arrival times are shown. For the random, originator, and OLB heuristics, two different DVS usages were studied. One is to use the fastest speed level for the high priority tasks while using the slowest speed level for the medium- and low-priority tasks. Thus, the speed level used of any given device depends on the task priority. The other is to use the median speed level for all tasks. The median speed level of a device would be the (total number of levels of a device)/2. Therefore, if there are 16 discrete speed levels for a device starting from level 1 being the slowest, then the median speed level would be level 8. Preliminary tests show that the performance of heuristics using the first method is better than that using the second method. The first method is used for all figures.

Figure 22.3 shows the performance of the heuristics when the mean task execution is 60 s. The 95% confidence interval of the performance is shown in the figure. Because the confidence intervals of ME-ME and CRME heuristics overlap, these two heuristics are considered to perform comparably. The ME-MC heuristic was a close third. The average running times, in seconds per mapping event, of random, originator, OLB, MEG, ME-MC, ME-ME, and CRME are 0.00001, 0.00001, 0.00004, 0.00005, 0.0015, 0.28, and 0.34, respectively.

Figure 22.4a shows the performance while increasing the mean task arrival rates (decreasing mean intertask arrival times). As the mean task arrival rates increase, the number of tasks in the system also increases and the percentage of high priority tasks completed decreases. The average number of tasks per trial was 3373, 4185, and 5688 for mean intertask arrival times of 10, 8, and 6 s, respectively. This average includes tasks with a mean execution time of 600 s.

Figure 22.5 shows the results when the mean task execution time is increased to 600 s. Overall, the performance degraded. Because of the longer mean execution time, the tasks are more likely to be dropped. The 95% confidence interval of the performance is shown in the figure. Because the confidence intervals of ME-ME and CRME heuristics overlap, these two heuristics are considered to perform

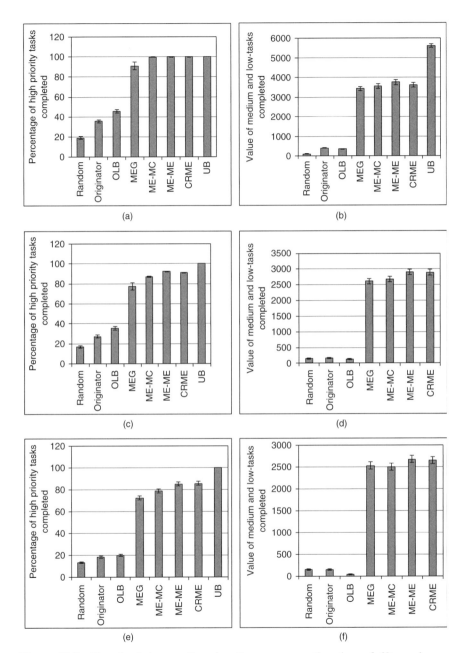

Figure 22.3   The simulation results using the mean execution time of 60 s and mean intertask arrival of 10 s for (a) and (b), 8 s for (c) and (d), and 6 s for (e) and (f). (a), (c), and (e) show the percentage of high priority tasks completed. (b), (d), and (f) show the value of medium- and low-priority tasks completed.

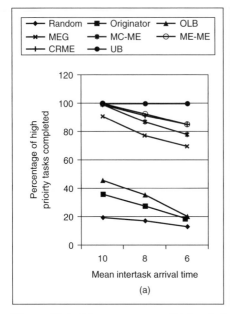
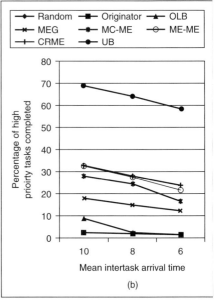

Figure 22.4   The percentage of high priority tasks completed is shown. The mean execution time of (a) 60 s and (b) 600 s and mean intertask arrival times of 10, 8, and 6 s are used. The results for random and originator are colocated in (b).

comparably. Figure 22.4b shows the performance while increasing the mean task arrival rates (decreasing mean intertask arrival times). Similar to Figure 22.4a, when the mean task arrival rates increase, the number of tasks in the system increases and the percentage of high priority tasks completed decreases.

As it gets more difficult to complete high priority tasks (as there are more tasks in the system due to increased task arrival rate or as the mean task execution times are increased), the batch mode heuristics ME-ME and CRME perform better than the rest of the heuristics (Fig. 22.5). While remapping, the batch mode heuristics (ME-ME and CRME) consider all mappable tasks in the system and the order in which the tasks are mapped can be different from the previous mapping event. Therefore, the tasks can be assigned to another machine that is better suited or they can be rescheduled. The ME-MC only considers the new task that arrived, and once the task is mapped, it is neither moved to another device nor rescheduled. Also, MC-ME can only increase the speed level for one device per mapping event.

The ME-MC, ME-ME, and CRME heuristics explicitly consider the high priority tasks first (in the batch for ME-ME and CRME heuristics) to complete. The rest of the heuristics run the high priority tasks using the fastest speed level, giving the high priority tasks a higher chance of completing. Table 22.1 compares the heuristics described in this research.

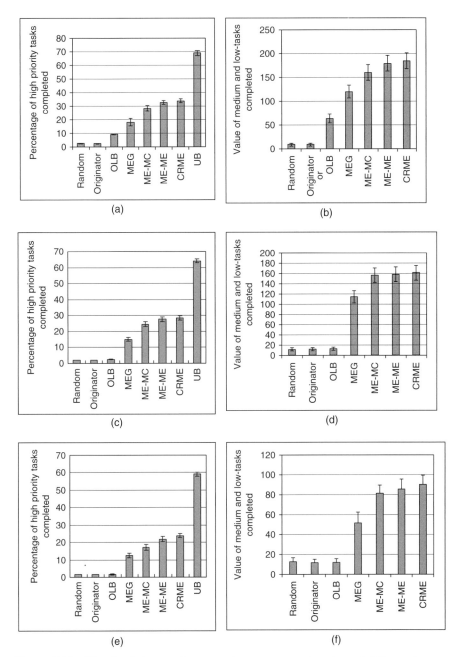

Figure 22.5 The simulation results using the mean execution time of 600 s and mean intertask arrival of 10 s for (a) and (b), 8 s for (c) and (d), and 6 s for (e) and (f). (a), (c), and (e) show the percentage of high priority tasks completed. (b), (d), and (f) show the value of medium- and low-priority tasks completed.

TABLE 22.1 Summary of the Heuristic Methods Used in this Research

Name	Mode	Key Idea	TC	Perf.	Best
Random	I	Random	1	Bad	
Originator	I	Task requester completes own tasks	1	Bad	
OLB	I	Locate the first available device	$O(M)$	Not good	
MEG	I	Locate the device that uses the minimum energy	$O(M)$	Okay	
ME-MC	I	Switch between two methods to locate the suitable device	$O(M)$	Good	When there is a tighter constrain on time
ME-ME	B	Two-phase greedy	$O(N^2)$	Good	As more tasks are in the system
CRME	B	Determine the task that will suffer most if not given the preference	$O(N^2)$	Good	As more tasks are in the system

TC, time complexity.
The mode, key idea, TC, overall performance (Perf.), and when a method performs the best are briefly described. I and B for the mode column are the immediate mode and batch mode, respectively. M and N for the TC calculation is the number of machines and number of tasks, respectively.

22.2.6 Summary

An ad hoc grid HC environment was modeled and simulated. Seven dynamic heuristics were designed, developed, and evaluated using the HC environment. The environment includes randomly arriving tasks with priorities and a deadline, as well as devices with limited battery capacity that use DVS for power management. In this scenario, a resource manager needs to exploit the heterogeneity of the tasks and resources while managing energy. The primary goal of this study was to complete as many high priority tasks as possible, under the constraint of available system energy, during a given interval of time. The secondary goal was to complete as many medium- and low-priority tasks as possible to maximize the sum of the weighted priorities of medium- and low-priority tasks completed by their deadlines with the same constraints as the primary goal. A mathematical UB was derived.

The batch mode ME-ME and contention-resolved minimum energy heuristics were the best and they performed comparably. However, they required significantly more time than the immediate mode heuristics. In cases where the mean task execution times are short, the immediate mode ME-MC time heuristic may be preferable because it is very fast and can perform nearly comparably to the two best heuristics in some scenarios.

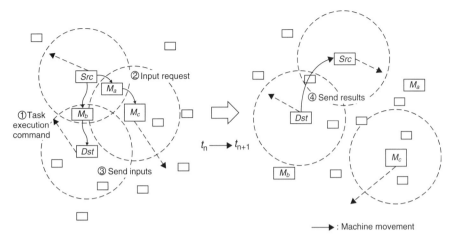

Figure 22.6   An example of a multihop distributed mobile computing environment.

22.3   MULTIHOP DISTRIBUTED MOBILE COMPUTING ENVIRONMENT

22.3.1   The Multihop System Model

The environment considered in this section is a multihop DMC system, where the devices are mobile and communicate with each other by wireless means. The difference between this section and the previous section is that as devices are mobile, the communication between devices can disconnect and a new path or device may be needed for communication and/or computation. For this environment, the DVS [19] method is used for computation power management and the VTPC [23] technique is used for communication power/energy management. The number and value of discrete voltage levels can be different for all devices, but the number and value of VTPC power levels for all devices are the same. The DVS and VTPC mechanisms in this research may be managed by the system administrator or the resource manager and are transparent to the user. All devices have their own RMS for distributed resource management. It is assumed that the RMS knows all the devices' information and the tasks' execution times on the devices that it can connect. The estimated execution times of each task on each device is assumed to be known based on user-supplied information, experiential data, task profiling, and analytical benchmarking, or other techniques [28, 31]. Devices have different mobility capability and battery capacity. It is assumed that the batteries for these devices may be recharged after a certain amount of time. Using a device, a user can request a program (task) to be executed, receive data, and send data. A device executing a task may receive input data from other devices. The output result after completing a given task will be sent back to the task requester, as shown in Figure 22.6.

All tasks have a deadline, the arrival of tasks is unknown, that is, when and where the task is requested is not known a priori, execution times of tasks are assumed to be known only when the task is requested, and execution times of tasks can be different and have affinity to different machines. The detailed operation procedure of the DMC is as follows:

1. Tasks are requested by various users (i.e., source or src) from their own devices.
2. The RMS on the task requester device decides on a destination device that can complete the task while considering some or all combinations of the energy consumption, task deadline, expected task completion time (includes wait time, communication time, and processing time), and execution times of tasks. The task execution command plus relevant data is sent to the destination device (① in Figure 22.6).
3. If the requested task needs input information from another device (i.e. input device), an input request is sent to that device (② in Figure 22.6). Inputs are sent to the destination device, and the task starts when all inputs arrive (③ in Figure 22.6).
4. After the task execution is completed ($t_n \rightarrow t_n + 1$ in Figure 22.6), the destination device sends back the results to the source device (④ in Figure 22.6).

The goal of this DMC system is to complete as many tasks as possible by their deadline. A mapping event occurs when a new task is requested to be executed in the DMC system. The role of the RMS would be to assign the tasks that are requested to maximize the goal. Therefore, for this example DMC system, simple and fast heuristics are designed and/or enhanced from previous researches to analyze which methods may be best for certain scenarios.

22.3.2 Energy-Aware Routing Protocol

22.3.2.1 *Overview.* In order to intelligently utilize the heterogeneous DMC system considered, a routing protocol that takes energy into consideration is needed because of the energy constraint on the system. A power-aware routing scheme has been demonstrated [47] using the distance to the destination, and the consumed energy of a node was considered separately in the route selection. Geographical and energy-aware routing, proposed in Reference 48, consider both the distance to the destination and the consumed energy of a node. The protocol that considers the remaining energy (RE) of the node and transmission power was proposed in Reference 49. In Reference 50, a protocol is studied that considers the data transmission power of source node and data reception/transmission power of the intermediate routing node. For the example DMC system described here, two energy-aware protocols are introduced that are modified from the destination-sequenced distance vector (DSDV) method that will provide a better routing of data for an energy-aware DMC environment. The reason for using and the advantage of the DSDV protocol is that DSDV makes routing tables through periodic routing update, and therefore, the path information between two devices is already available as soon as there is a task request. In the DMC environment described, the routing information must be known before the decision to execute task on a device is made because when a decision is being made, the energy consumption of the device (i.e., processing energy and communication energy) must be taken into consideration as well. The estimated communication energy consumption will be determined by the route that will be taken between nodes. Unlike the existing researches, our protocol makes a routing table that includes the current state and estimated future states of the intermediate device(s). The energy-aware protocol is an extended and enhanced version of the DSDV protocol and is described in detail in Sections 22.3.2.3 and 22.3.2.4. Several simple heuristics that allocate tasks onto resources are used to compare the performance of the two protocols against the original DSDV protocol. The performance goal will be the same as in Section 22.3.1, which is to complete as many tasks as possible before their deadline.

22.3.2.2 DSDV. As described in Reference 51, the DSDV [52] protocol is a proactive routing algorithm based on the idea of the classical Bellman–Ford routing algorithm with certain improvements. Each node maintains the routing table with all possible destinations within the network, and the number of required hops to reach the destination is also maintained in the table. For table consistency, the routing information is propagated to update the routing table periodically.

22.3.2.3 DSDV remaining energy. The main idea for the DSDV remaining energy (DSDV-RE) is that when it updates the routing table, among the same shortest distance routes from a source to a destination, it chooses the path with the intermediate nodes with more RE than others (Fig. 22.7); that is, if the DSDV update results in the same number of hops (metric) for a certain route then the path with the intermediate node(s) that has more RE is chosen for the data transmission. In this research, we constrain the algorithm to consider paths with less than three hops, but this restriction can be extended without the loss of generality.

22.3.2.4 DSDV-energy consumption per remaining energy. The main idea of the DSDV-energy consumption per remaining energy (DSDV-CR) is that when the protocol updates the routing table, among the same shortest distance routes from a source to a destination, if there is a path with an idle intermediate node, it chooses that path (Fig. 22.8a and b). If there is no path where the intermediate node(s) is idle, that is, all possible intermediate nodes are executing other tasks, the path with the total minimum energy consumption per remaining energy (CR) is selected for data communication (Fig. 22.8c). CR is the total energy consumption (ET), which is the energy that will be consumed to complete all tasks allocated for the device divided by the current RE.

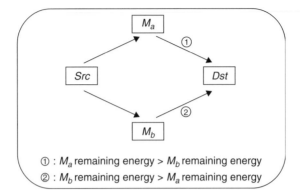

Figure 22.7   An example of how DSDV-RE will choose routes is shown.

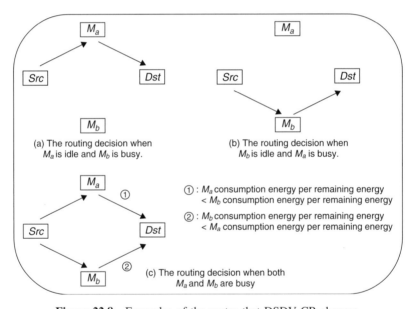

Figure 22.8   Examples of the routes that DSDV-CR chooses.

22.3.3 Heuristic Description

22.3.3.1 *Random.* In the random heuristic, a task is assigned to a randomly selected device among the selectable devices. The DVS level for a task on a device is the highest level that can complete the task by its deadline. The random heuristic is used as a baseline to compare other heuristics.

22.3.3.2 *Estimated minimum total energy (EMTE).* The estimated minimum total energy (EMTE) heuristic assigns the requested task on the device that consumes the minimum estimated total energy (i.e., communication and computation energy) to try to extend the lifetime of the overall system while completing as many tasks as possible. The estimated total energy consumption is derived from the estimated coordinates of the devices using the current speed and direction of the selectable devices for communication and the estimated execution time of the task for computation. The DVS level for a task on a device is the lowest level that can complete the task by its deadline. The procedure is as follows:

1. At a mapping event, the estimated total energy consumption (i.e., the communication energy plus the computation energy) of all selectable devices is calculated. The communication energy is calculated using the estimated distance between the two devices, and computation energy is obtained using the lowest DVS level to complete by the task's deadline.
2. The task will be allocated to the device that can complete the task by its deadline while using the minimum total energy.

22.3.3.3 K-percent-speed (KPS) and k-percent-energy (KPE). The
K-percent-speed (KPS) and K-percent-energy (KPE) heuristics are extended from the K-percent best heuristic [15]. When the number of selectable devices is M and m is the number of K-percent devices among M, the KPS heuristic selects the minimum total energy device (communication and computation energy) from the m minimum execution time (MET) devices. But the KPE heuristic chooses the MET device among the m minimum total energy consumption devices. In this chapter, the value of K is selected as 0.5 empirically and the DVS level for a task on a device is the lowest level that can complete the task by its deadline. The procedure is as follows:

1. When a mapping event occurs, the total execution time (for KPS) or the estimated total energy consumption (for KPE) is determined for all selectable devices and m minimum total execution time or total energy consumption devices are determined.
2. Then, among the m number of devices, the requested task is assigned to the device that has the minimum energy consumption (for KPS) or the MET (for KPE).

22.3.3.4 Energy ratio and distance (ERD). The energy ratio and distance
(ERD) heuristic uses energy ratio and distance to assign the requested task onto a device. The energy ratio is the estimated total energy usage divided by the RE on a device. The estimated total energy is calculated using the method described in Section 22.3.3.2. Then, the ratio is multiplied by the distance (in meters). The intuition behind this method is that the device that is nearest and has a low energy ratio will be picked for execution of the task using less energy and extending the lifetime of the system. The procedure is as follows:

1. At a mapping event, the energy ratio multiplied by the current distance (V) from the source to the destination device is calculated for all selectable devices.
2. The device with the minimum V is selected to execute the task.

22.3.3.5 *ETC and distance (ETCD).* The estimated time to complete and distance (ETCD) heuristic is similar to the ERD method. However, the ETCD heuristic uses the ETC data instead of estimated total energy consumption. The ETCD heuristic regards a task's ETC as directly related to the computation energy and distance as the communication energy. The DVS level for a task on a device is always the highest level. The procedure is as follows:

1. At a mapping event, the ETC multiplied by the distance (W) for all selectable devices is calculated.
2. The device with the minimum W is selected to execute the task.

22.3.3.6 *Minimum execution time (MET).* The MET heuristic executes the task on the device that has the minimum ETC [15]. The advantage of this method is that a task is sent to the fastest device for the task. In the MET heuristic, communication among devices (communication energy) is not considered. The highest DVS level is used for all devices.

22.3.3.7 *Minimum completion time (MCT) and minimum completion time with DVS (MCT-DVS).* The MCT heuristic assigns the task to the device that has the MCT [15]. Unlike the MET heuristic, the MCT considers both computation time and communication time. The communication time is the time to send the task to the destination device plus the time to receive the results. The DVS level used for a task on a device is the highest level for MCT and the lowest DVS level that can complete the task by its deadline for the MCT-DVS method. The procedure is as follows:

1. For all selectable devices, the total time to complete on the device using the highest DVS level for the MCT heuristic and the lowest possible DVS level for the MCT-DVS heuristic are calculated.
2. The device that has the MCT is chosen to execute the task.

22.3.3.8 *Switching algorithm (SA).* The SA heuristic is used in Reference 15 and it is redesigned for this environment. As described in Reference 15, the MET heuristic can potentially create load imbalance across devices by assigning many more tasks to some devices than to others, whereas the MCT heuristic tries to balance the load by assigning tasks for earliest completion time. The SA heuristic uses the MCT and MET heuristics in a cyclic fashion depending on the load distribution across the devices. The purpose is to have a heuristic with the desirable properties of both the MCT and the MET methods. The procedure is as follows:

1. Let the maximum (latest) ready time over all selectable devices be r_{max} and the minimum (earliest) ready time be r_{min}.
2. Then, the load balance index (LBI) across the devices is given by LBI $=$ r_{min}/r_{max}. The parameter LBI can have any value in the interval [0, 1]. If LBI is 1.0, then the load is evenly balanced across the devices. If LBI is 0, then at least one device has not yet been assigned a task. Threshold values, Th, for the ratio LBI is chosen to be 0.6 empirically.
3. The SA heuristic begins mapping tasks using the MCT heuristic and also when the value of LBI is smaller than Th. If the value of LBI is bigger than Th, the SA uses the MET method to map the task.

22.3.4 Simulation Model

This research introduces and evaluates the heuristic methods to efficiently schedule tasks, allocate resources for tasks, and save energy for future use for the underlying environment. To evaluate the heuristics for this research, the energy-aware DMC simulator [24] called *EArDruM* is used, which is based on the network simulator 2 (NS-2) [53].

For the simulation, six types of wireless devices are used (Table 22.2) and each device has three different number of voltage levels of 2, 4, and 8. Therefore, there will be 18 different types of devices that may be introduced in the DMC system. The maximum battery capacity (energy) of each device is set to the maximum CPU energy consumption level plus the maximum transmission energy consumption level, multiplied by the maximum operation time. The maximum operation time is determined using a gamma distribution with a mean of 2 h. This means that if the CPU and wireless module use the maximum (highest) level, then the battery capacity is only enough to operate the device for 2 h on average. The mobility of the devices is random in the sense that the direction, duration, and speed are randomly determined using a uniform distribution (from NS-2). To determine whether the device can send the results back to the task requester, a simple method of estimated time multiplied by the current speed and the current direction is used to estimate the position of the destination device.

TABLE 22.2 **Parameter Setting in the Simulations**

Simulation Parameter	Value
Network area	1500×1500 m
Maximum transmission range	500 m
Data/header packet size	1000/40 B
Simulation time	28,800 s
Data rate	1 Mbps
Maximum speed of device	6 m/s
Traffic model	application/FTP
Ad hoc routing protocol	DSDV

To simplify DVS, this research assumes that each voltage level of a processor corresponds to a clock cycle speed level for the processor and that the task execution time varies proportional to the speed level. Each device can have 2, 4, or 8 discrete speed levels with equal probability. The active power shown in Reference 54 is used for the maximum power used for the highest speed level for each device type. After the number of levels is decided for all tasks, the relative speed of each level is determined. The lowest speed level of a device is assumed to be one-third of the maximum speed level (e.g., if the maximum speed level is 624 MHz, then the lowest speed level will be 208 MHz). The rest of the levels are determined dividing the gap between the maximum and lowest speed level equally according to the number of levels in each device (linearly). The power usage at each of the levels for all devices is determined using the simplified relationship of power being proportional to the square of voltage, the number of levels, and the voltage and active power in Reference 54. It is assumed that the voltage switching is done dynamically and that the overhead associated with the switching is negligible (20–150 μs).

In each simulation of a system, 20, 30, 40, and 50 devices (nodes) among the 18 types are picked with equal probability. The arrival (request) of tasks is simulated by using a Poisson distribution with a mean intertask arrival time of 6 s.

For all tasks, the ETC values of the 18 types of devices taking heterogeneity into consideration is randomly generated using the gamma distribution method described in Reference 46. The mean execution time of 200 s is used for the ETC matrix. The mean execution time is chosen to represent applications such as processing data (such as maps or weather reports) and generating strategies. The size of the task and output (result to the source) data was calculated using 100 kB as the mean and a COV of 0.7 using gamma distribution. The size of the input and the other communication data was calculated using 10 kB as the mean and a COV of 0.7 using gamma distribution.

This research assumes that when the task is requested for or arrives into the system, the deadline of the task is given. For the simulation studies, the deadline of task i was equal to the sum of its arrival time, the overall mean execution time of all tasks, the median execution time of task i on all devices, and the expected communication time of sending the task and receiving the result, multiplied by a constant to allow for the waiting of other tasks in the system that are already being executed or queued for execution.

The IEEE 802.11b standard is applied for wireless communication and communication power consumption value is based on the specification in References 57 and 58. On the basis of the two-ray ground reflection model [53] in NS-2, whenever communication occurs, the transmission power and the discrete transmission power level are determined according to the transmission range (for 10, 50, 100, 150, 200, 250, 350, and 500 m) using VTPC.

A trial is defined as one such simulation of the system. For each of the eight scenarios (one mean intertask arrival time × two mean execution times × four different number of devices), 30 trials are run for 28,800 s (i.e., 8 h) for each heuristic. More details are shown in Table 22.2.

22.3.5 Results

22.3.5.1 *Distributed resource management.* The experimental evaluation of the 10 heuristics is performed in this research. The 6 of the 10 heuristics (random, EMTE, KPS, KPE, ERD, MCT-DVS) apply DVS, and the rest of them (ETCD, MET, MCT, SA) do not use the DVS technique. The graphs in the Figure 22.9 show the percentage of tasks completed that is averaged from 30 trials.

Figure 22.9a shows the performance of the heuristics when the mean task arrival time is 6 s and the mean task execution time is 200 s. The results show that the heuristics that do not use the energy information and that the DVS technique tends to perform better than the heuristics that do use the technique. However, the percentage of dead devices for heuristics shown in Figure 22.9b indicates that the percentage for heuristics using the DVS technique is lower than the percentage for the heuristics that do not. This allows us to speculate that although the heuristics that use the DVS do not perform well in our simulation,

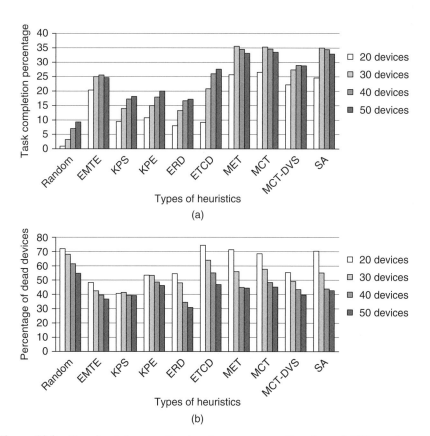

Figure 22.9 The simulation result using the mean execution time of 200 s and mean intertask arrival of 6 s for (a) and (b).

if the simulation time is extended, the system will be alive longer, thus having a chance to do better in terms of completing more tasks by their deadline.

When the system is scarce, that is, the number of participating devices is small, the probability of the destination device moving out of range, thus failing to send back the results, becomes greater. Therefore, the distance between devices can become an important factor when trying to send the requested task and receive the results. When there are 20 devices in the system, the ETCD heuristic performs the best because it explicitly uses the distance in the decision process. The MET and MCT heuristics did well overall, this is because although they do not explicitly use distance, both heuristics use the time information and the highest DVS level to complete tasks as quickly as possible before the intended destination device goes out of range. As the SA method uses MET and MCT, SA performs comparably to both MET and MCT. The MCT-DVS method that uses the lowest DVS level to complete a given task before the deadline does poorly than the original MCT method. This may be because in some cases, the DVS level chosen and the device's mobility cause the task to fail.

22.3.5.2 Energy-aware protocol. The multihop DMC environment is tested using the two energy-aware routing methods, and the performance is compared against the original DSDV method. Four simple heuristics are used for the comparison: the random, EMTE, KPS, and KPE methods. The mean intertask arrival time is 6 s (using a gamma distribution) for all the results obtained in this chapter. Figures 22.10 and 22.11 show the percentage of tasks completed using the mean task execution time of 100 and 200 s (using a gamma distribution), respectively. The number of devices in the system is increased from 20 to 50 to 100, and the results are shown. Each scenario was simulated for 30 runs, and the average is shown in the figures. The random method was always the worst in all the scenarios. The energy-considered heuristics (ME, KPS, and KPE) are better than the random method, but their performances are comparable among themselves. The DSDV, DSDV-RE, and DSDV-CR protocols show similar performance for 20 and 50 nodes in Figure 22.10. However, when there are 100 nodes in the system, there is a difference in the percentage of tasks completed. Both DSDV-RE and DSDV-CR perform better than DSDV, and in Figure 22.10d, the performance of DSDV-CR is increased by 37% of the performance of DSDV. Similarly, in Figure 22.11, all the protocols perform similarly for 20-node and 50-node systems. However, as shown in Figure 22.11d, the performance of DSDV-CR is increased by 33% of the performance of DSDV. This implies that the RE information plus the estimated future energy usage is a valuable information that can be used to enhance the original routing protocol.

22.3.6 Summary

In Section 22.3.1, a distributed resource management scheme, for example, DMC environment, was modeled and simulated. The devices in the system are heterogeneous in the sense that they have different computation speed, battery capacity,

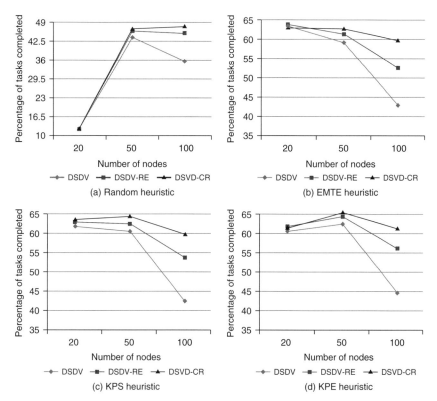

Figure 22.10 Percentage of tasks completed for intertask arrival time of 6 s and mean task execution time of 100 s for varying number of nodes in the system.

DVS levels, and mobility. The tasks are heterogeneous, arrive randomly, and have deadlines. A total of 10 dynamic heuristics were designed and evaluated for the system. As the resource management is decentralized, all devices have a decision-making module for intelligent resource allocation. The main goal of this research is to complete as many tasks as possible, under the constraint of available system energy and during a given interval of time. There are many challenges that a resource manager faces in this environment and one of them is the mobility of devices compared to Section 22.2. In all scenarios, the MET and MCT methods perform the best. In the example of DMC environment, it may be best when a task is assigned to the device that can complete the task as soon as possible. One of the reasons could be that as devices move, they can be disconnected from each other resulting in the failure to complete a given task (i.e., cannot send the results back to the task requester). When a task is completed as fast as possible, the penalty incurred because of the devices' mobility may be minimized. However, as the two methods always use the highest DVS level, they use more energy than the methods that consider lower DVS levels. This means that the system has a higher probability of lasting longer if there is no constraint

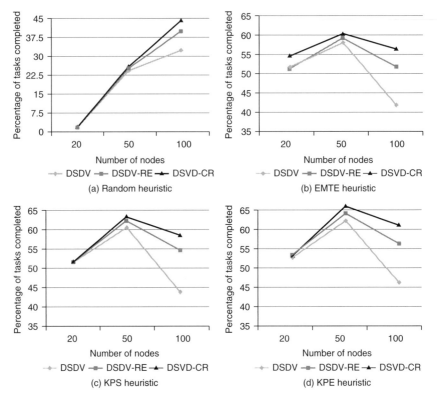

Figure 22.11   Percentage of tasks completed for intertask arrival time of 6 s and mean task execution time of 200 s for varying number of nodes in the system.

on the simulation time and thus may complete more tasks while the system that uses MET and MCT may run out of overall energy at an earlier time.

In Section 22.3.2, an attempt to increase the performance of the overall DMC system is made by enhancing one of the widely used routing protocol that is also one of the default protocols in NS-2. The original DSDV protocol was compared with an enhanced energy-aware routing protocol. As it is important for the DMC system to save energy because there is a constraint on energy for all mobile devices, it is imperative that the routing protocol also provides assistance in the efficient use of the system-wide energy. The routing protocol introduced in this chapter uses explicit energy information such as RE of nodes and energy consumption per remaining energy (CR) of nodes to determine the route for nodes such that the DMC system can use the information to make an intelligent decision on where and when the task is sent and executed. The performance of the protocol that uses the CR information is shown to increase the performance of a resource allocation method by 30–38% than the original DSDV protocol.

22.4   FUTURE WORK

There can be many possible directions for future research based on this study. With asynchronous battery recharging as opposed to the synchronous recharging model described in this chapter (which assumes all team members begin a mission together), the problem of completing tasks while efficiently using the system energy will be the same, but the complexity of the heuristics will increase and the metric will need to be adapted for individual dynamic changes of available battery energy. Another aspect of future work would be to include the option of decreasing the speed of a processor at a later time for the research in Section 22.2. In addition, we can consider relaxing the assumption that the RMS is executed on a device with unlimited energy.

Other challenges for DMC include (i) comparison and evaluation of distributed resource management and centralized resource management and different environments, (ii) enhanced decision-making methods for such different environments, (iii) use of different underlying topology that was used for the routing protocol, (iv) analysis and enhancement of other protocols that can be used in the DMC environment, (v) an improved method of estimating the mobility or the position of the devices, and (vi) applying or adapting the DMC environment model to other similar systems such as mobile cloud computing or personal mobile cloud computing.

ACKNOWLEDGMENT

This research was supported in part by the National Research Foundation of Korea, grant No. 2009–0076378. Parts of Chapter 22.2 has first appeared in the IEEE Transactions of Parallel and Distributed Systems and Parts of Chapter 22.3 has first appeared in the Proceedings of the International Conference on Parallel and Distributed Processing Techniques and Applications (PDPTA'10: July, USA), Editor: Hamid R. Arabnia, ISBN#:1-60132-158-9.

REFERENCES

1. Marinescu D, Marinescu G, Ji Y, Boloni L, Siegel HJ. Ad hoc grids: communication and computing in a power constrained environment. Workshop on Energy-Efficient Wireless Communications and Networks 2003 (EWCN 2003), 22nd International Performance, Computing, and Communications Conf. (IPCCC); 2003 Apr. pp. 113–122.

2. Braun TD, Siegel HJ, Maciejewski AA. Heterogeneous computing: goals, methods, and open problems. 2001 International Conference on High Performance Computing (HiPC 2001); Lecture Notes in Computer Science ISSN: 0302-9743; Hyderabad; 2001 Dec., pp. 307–318.

3. Eshaghian MM, editor. Heterogeneous computing. Norwood (MA): Artech House; 1996.

4. Freund RF, Siegel HJ. Heterogeneous processing. IEEE Comput 1993;26(6):13–17.

5. Maheswaran M, Braun TD, Siegel HJ. Heterogeneous distributed computing. Webster JG, editor. Volume 8, Encyclopedia of electrical and electronics engineering New York (NY): John Wiley; 1999. pp. 679–690.

6. Coffman EG, Jr., editor. Computer and job-shop scheduling theory. New York (NY): John Wiley & Sons; 1976.

7. Fernandez-Baca D. Allocating modules to processors in a distributed system. IEEE Trans Software Eng 1989;SE-15(11):1427–1436.

8. Ibarra OH, Kim CE. Heuristic algorithms for scheduling independent tasks on non-identical processors. J ACM 1977;24(2):280–289.

9. Barada H, Sait SM, Baig N. Task matching and scheduling in heterogeneous systems using simulated evolution. 10th IEEE Heterogeneous Computing Workshop (HCW 2001), in the Proceedings of 15th Intertational Parallel and Distributed Processing Symposium (IPDPS 2001); Apr 15; 2001. Paper HCW.

10. Banicescu I, Velusamy V. Performance of scheduling scientific applications with adaptive weighted factoring. 10th IEEE Heterogeneous Computing Workshop (HCW 2001), in the Proceedings of 15th International Parallel and Distributed Processing Symposium (IPDPS 2001); Apr 06; 2001. Paper HCW.

11. Braun TD, Siegel HJ, Beck N, Boloni L, Freund RF, Hensgen D, Maheswaran M, Reuther AI, Robertson JP, Theys MD, Yao Bin. A comparison of eleven static heuristics for mapping a class of independent tasks onto heterogeneous distributed computing systems. J Parallel Distrib Comput 2001;61(6):810–837.

12. Foster I, Kesselman C, editors. The grid: blueprint for a new computing infrastructure. San Fransisco (CA): Morgan Kaufmann; 1999.

13. Freund RF, Gherrity M, Ambrosius S, Campbell M, Halderman M, Hensgen D, Keith E, Kidd T, Kussow M, Lima JD, Mirabile F, Moore L, Rust B, Siegel HJ. Scheduling resources in multiuser, heterogeneous, computing environments with SmartNet. 7th IEEE Heterogeneous Computing Workshop (HCW 1998); 1998 Mar. pp. 184–199.

14. Kim J-K, Shivle S, Siegel HJ, Maciejewski AA, Braun TD, Schneider M, Tideman S, Chitta R, Dilmaghani RB, Joshi R, Kaul A, Sharma A, Sripada S, Vangari P, Yellampalli SS. Dynamically mapping tasks with priorities and multiple deadlines in a heterogeneous environment. J Parallel Distrib Comput 2007;67(2):154–169.

15. Maheswaran M, Ali S, Siegel HJ, Hensgen D, Freund RF. Dynamic mapping of a class of independent tasks onto heterogeneous computing systems. J Parallel Distrib Comput 1999;59(2):107–121.

16. Michalewicz Z, Fogel DB. How to solve it: modern heuristics. New York (NY): Springer-Verlag; 2000.

17. Wu M-Y, Shu W, Zhang H. Segmented min-min: a static mapping algorithm for meta-tasks on heterogeneous computing systems. 9th IEEE Heterogeneous Computing Workshop (HCW 2000); Washington, USA; 2000 May. pp. 375–385.

18. Yarmolenko V, Duato J, Panda DK, Sadayappan P. Characterization and enhancement of dynamic mapping heuristics for heterogeneous systems. Int'l Workshop on Parallel Processing; 2000 Aug. pp. 437–444.

19. Weiser M, Welch B, Demers A, Shenker S. Scheduling for reduced CPU energy. USENIX Symposium on Operating Systems Design and Implementation; California, USA; 1994 Nov. pp. 13–23.

20. ARM processor. Available at http://www.arm.com. Accessed 2009 July.

21. Crusoe/Efficeon Processor. Available at http://www.transmeta.com. Accessed 2009 July.

22. Hong I, Qu G, Potkonjak M, Srivastava M. Synthesis techniques for low-power hard real-time systems on variable voltage processors. 19th IEEE Real-Time Systems Symposium (RTSS '98); Madrid, Spain 1998 Dec. pp. 95–105.

23. Gomez J, Campbell AT. A case for Variable-range transmission power control in wireless ad hoc networks. IEEE Transactions on Mobile Computing; Vol. 6; No. 1; Jan. 2007; pp. 87–99.

24. Kim JS. Energy-aware distributed mobile computing for real-time single-hop ad hoc mobile environments [Master's thesis]. Korea University; 2010. p. 60.

25. Kim J-K, Hensgen DA, Kidd T, Siegel HJ, John DSt, Irvine C, Levin T, Porter NW, Prasanna VK, Freund RF. A flexible multi-dimensional QoS performance measure framework for distributed heterogeneous systems. Cluster Comput 2006;9(3):281–296. Special Issue on Cluster Computing in Science and Engineering.

26. Ali S, Maciejewski AA, Siegel HJ, Kim J-K. Measuring the robustness of a resource allocation. IEEE Trans Parallel Distrib Syst 2004;15(7):630–641.

27. Ali S, Maciejewski AA, Siegel HJ. Perspectives on robust resource allocation for heterogeneous parallel systems. In: Rajasekaran Sanguthevar; Reif John, editors. Handbook of parallel computing: models, algorithms, and applications. Boca Raton (FL): Chapman & Hall/CRC Press; 2008. pp. 41–1—41– 30;

28. Ali S, Braun TD, Siegel HJ, Maciejewski AA, Beck N, Boloni L, Maheswaran M, Reuther AI, Robertson JP, Theys MD, Yao B, Characterizing resource allocation heuristics for heterogeneous computing systems. In: Hurson AR, editor. Advances in computers volume 63. Parallel, distributed, and pervasive computing. Amsterdam (The Netherlands): Elsevier; 2005. pp. 91–128.

29. Ghafoor A, Yang J. A distributed heterogeneous supercomputing management system. IEEE Comput 1993;26(6):78–86.

30. Khokhar A, Prasanna VK, Shaaban ME, Wang C. Heterogeneous computing: challenges and opportunities. IEEE Comput 1993;26(6):18–27.

31. Yang J, Ahmad I, Ghafoor A. Estimation of execution times on heterogeneous supercomputer architectures. International Conference on Parallel Processing; New York, USA; 1993 Aug. pp. I–219–I–226.

32. Kafil M, Ahmad I. Optimal task assignment in heterogeneous distributed computing systems. IEEE Concurrency 1998;6(3):42–51.

33. Xu D, Nahrstedt K, Wichadakul D. QoS and contention-aware multi-resource reservation,'. Cluster Comput 2001;4(2):95–107.

34. Aydin H, Melhem R, Mosse D, Mejia-Alvarez P. Power-aware scheduling for periodic real-time tasks. IEEE Trans Comput 2004;53(5):584–600.

35. Hong I, Kirovski D, Qu G, Potkonjak M, Srivastava MB. Power optimization of variable-voltage core-based systems. IEEE Trans Comput-Aided Des Integr Circ Syst 1999;18(12):1702–1714.

36. Mejia-Alvarez P, Levner E, Mosse D. Power-optimized scheduling server for real-time tasks. IEEE Real-Time and Embedded Technology and Applications Symposium; Washington, USA; 2002 Sep. pp. 239–250.

37. Yao F, Demers A, Shenker S. A scheduling model for reduced CPU energy. 36th Annual Symposium on Foundations of Computer Science; 1995. pp. 374–382.

38. Dick RP, Jha NK. MOCSYN: multiobjective core-based single-chip system synthesis. Design Automation & Test in Europe Conference; 1999 Mar. pp. 263–270.

39. Mishra R, Rastogi N, Dakai Z, Mosse D, Melhem R. Energy aware scheduling for distributed real-time systems. International Parallel and Distributed Processing Symposium 2003 (IPDPS 2003); 2003 Apr.

40. Yu Y, Prasanna VK. Energy-balanced task allocation for collaborative processing in wireless sensor networks. ACM/Kluwer J Mobile Netw Appl (MONET) 2005;10(1):115–131. Special Issue on Algorithmic Solutions for Wireless, Mobile, Ad Hoc and Sensor Networks.

41. Zhu D, Melhem R, Childers BR. Scheduling with dynamic voltage/speed adjustment using slack reclamation in multiprocessor real-time systems. IEEE Trans Parallel Distrib Syst 2003;14(7):686–700.

42. Luo J, Jha NK. Power-conscious joint scheduling of periodic task graphs and aperiodic tasks in distributed real-time embedded systems. International Conference on Computer-Aided Design; New Jersey, USA; 2000 Nov. pp. 357–364.

43. Shang L, Dick RP, Jha NK. DESP: a distributed economics-based subcontracting protocol for computation distribution in power-aware mobile ad hoc networks. IEEE Trans Mobile Comput; 3 (1): 33–45.

44. Shivle S, Castain R, Siegel HJ, Maciejewski AA, Banka T, Chindam K, Dussinger S, Pichumani P, Satyasekaran P, Saylor W, Sendek D, Sousa J, Sridharan J, Sugavanam P, Velazco J. Static allocation of resources to communicating subtasks in a heterogeneous ad hoc grid environment. J Parallel Distrib Comput 2006;66(4):600–611. Special Issue on Algorithms for Wireless and Ad-hoc Networks.

45. Shivle S, Siegel HJ, Maciejewski AA, Banka T, Chindam K, Dussinger S, Pichumani P, Satyasekaran P, Saylor W, Sendek D, Sousa J, Sridharan J, Sugavanam P, Velazco J. Mapping subtasks with multiple versions on an ad hoc grid. Parallel Comput 2005;31(7):671–690. Special Issue on Heterogeneous Computing.

46. Ali S, Siegel HJ, Maheswaran M, Hensgen D, Ali S. Representing task and machine heterogeneities for heterogeneous computing systems. Tamkang J Sci Eng 2000;3(3):195–207. Special 50th Anniversary Issue.

47. Stojmenovic I Lin X. Power aware localized routing in wireless networks. IEEE Trans Parallel Distrib Syst 2001;12(11):1122–1133.

48. Yu Y, Govindan R, Estrin D. Geographical and energy aware routing: a recursive data dissemination protocol for wireless sensor networks. UCLA Computer Science Department technical report; May 2001. UCLA/CSD-TR-01-0023.

49. Tarique M, Tepe KE, Naserian M. Energy saving dynamic source routing for ad hoc wireless networks. Modeling and Optimization in Mobile, Ad Hoc, and Wireless Networks; 2005 Apr. pp. 305–310.

50. Ito S, Yoshigoe K. Consumed-energy-type-aware routing for wireless sensor networks. Wireless Telecommunications Symposium; 2007 Apr. pp. 1–6.

51. Mahdipour E, Rahmani AM, Aminian E. Performance evaluation of destination sequenced distance vector (DSDV) routing protocol. International Conference on Future Networks; 2009 Mar. pp. 186–190.

52. Perkins CE, Bhagwat P. Highly dynamic destination-sequenced distance-vector routing (DSDV) for mobile computers. Proceedings of the SIGCOMM' 94 Conference on Communications Architectures, Protocols and Applications; New York, USA; 1994 Aug. pp. 234–244.

53. Fall K, Varadhan K. The ns manual. Available at http://www.isi.edu/nsnam/ns/. Accessed 2010 Jan.

54. Intel PXA270 Processor Datasheet. Available at http://www.phytec.com/pdf/datasheets/PXA270_DS.pdf. 2009.

55. NokiaMobile Phones. Nokia C110/C111 wireless LAN card,' User guide. Available at http://nds1.nokia.com/phones/files/guides/C110-C111_usersguide_en.pdf.   Accessed 2009 July.

56. Communications Socket. Low Power Wireless LAN Card,' Datasheet. Available at http://www.quad.de/Datashe/Socket_WLAN.pdf. Accessed 2009 July.

57. Kim J-K, Siegel HJ, Maciejewski AA, Eigenmann R. Dynamic resource management in energy constrained heterogeneous computing systems using voltage scaling. IEEE Trans Parallel Distrib Syst 2008;19(11):1445–1457.

CHAPTER 23

AN ENERGY-AWARE FRAMEWORK FOR MOBILE DATA MINING

CARMELA COMITO, DOMENICO TALIA, and PAOLO TRUNFIO

23.1 INTRODUCTION

An increasing number of cell-phone and PDA-based data-intensive applications have been recently developed. Examples include cell-phone-based systems for body health monitoring, vehicle monitoring, and wireless security systems. Monitoring data in small embedded devices for smart appliances and onboard monitoring using nanoscale devices are examples of such applications that we may see in the near future. Support for advanced data analysis and mining is necessary for such applications.

Data mining in such mobile/embedded devices faces various challenges because of several reasons such as (i) low bandwidth networks, (ii) relatively small storage space, (iii) limited availability of battery power, (iv) slower processors, and (v) small displays to visualize the results. We need to design algorithms and systems that can perform data analysis by optimally utilizing the limited resources.

A key aspect to be addressed to enable effective and reliable data mining over mobile devices is ensuring energy efficiency, as most mobile devices are battery power operated and lack a constant source of power. Most commercially available mobile computing devices such as PDA's and mobile phones have battery power, which would last for only a few hours. Therefore, the next generation of data mining applications for such embedded and mobile devices must be designed to minimize the energy consumption. Software power utilization and minimization have been studied in various contexts [1–5], but to the best of our knowledge, only very few studies have been devoted to energy requirements for data mining algorithms [6].

Energy-Efficient Distributed Computing Systems, First Edition.
Edited by Albert Y. Zomaya and Young Choon Lee.
© 2012 John Wiley & Sons, Inc. Published 2012 by John Wiley & Sons, Inc.

This chapter proposes a general architecture for pervasive data mining over mobile devices focusing on energy efficiency. In the proposed architecture, a mobile device can play the role of data producer, data analyzer, client of remote data miners, or a combination of these. As such, we envision an architecture in which there are several distributed mobile devices and stationary servers where the mobile devices can run some steps of the data mining task, or some lightweight data mining algorithms.

We characterize the energy consumption in the system by introducing a new energy model paying particular attention to the energy communication costs.

Moreover, to efficiently manage resources and allow mobile-to-mobile collaborations, we clustered the network organizing the devices into local groups. The main design principles of our clustering scheme are to allow self-configuration and adaptation of the network and prolong its lifetime by distributing energy consumption among clusters. In such a way, mobile devices cooperate in a peer-to-peer style to perform a data mining process, tackling the problem of energy capacity and processing power limitations. Whenever a resource-limited computing device (client) in such a cooperative environment has a set of tasks (or subtasks) to be executed (which may have dependencies and communication requirements among themselves), it uses all available resources in nearby computing devices (servers).

The remainder of the chapter is organized as follows. Section 23.2 presents the overall architecture of the proposed framework. The software components inside each mobile device are described in Section 23.3. Section 23.4 details the energy characterization and the proposed cost model. The introduced energy-efficient clustering scheme is illustrated in Section 23.5. Finally, Section 23.6 concludes the chapter.

23.2 SYSTEM ARCHITECTURE

The system presented here is designed to enable *mobile-to-mobile data mining* (M2M DM) applications having energy efficiency as the primary goal. In the following, we present the overall architecture of the system.

A typical M2M-DM scenario includes *stationary nodes* (e.g., computer servers) and *mobile devices* (e.g., mobile phones, PDAs). Stationary nodes can act as server nodes for executing the data mining tasks submitted by mobile clients. On the other hand, the possibility of performing data mining over a mobile device may include several application scenarios in which a mobile device can play the role of data producer, data analyzer, client of remote data miners, sever, or a combination of these. More specifically, we can envision five basic scenarios for mobile data mining.

1. The mobile device is used as a terminal for ubiquitous access to a remote server that provides some data mining services. In this scenario, the server analyzes data stored in a local or a distributed database and delivers the results of the data mining task to the mobile device for its visualization.

2. Data generated in a mobile context are gathered through a mobile device and sent in a stream to one or more remote server(s) to be stored in a local database. Data can be periodically analyzed using specific data mining algorithms and the results used for making decisions about a given purpose.

3. Mobile devices are used to perform local data mining analysis. Owing to the limited computing power and memory/storage space of today's mobile devices, it is not possible to perform heavyweight data mining tasks on such devices. However, some steps of a data mining task (e.g., data selection and preprocessing) or very simple mining tasks on small data sets can be executed on mobile devices.

4. The mobile device acts as a data mining server for other mobile clients. As stated earlier, data analysis provided by a mobile device may include either lightweight data mining algorithms or some steps of the whole process.

5. A mobile device acts as a gateway for other mobile devices. In this case, even if the mobile gateway itself does not provide processing, it plays the fundamental role of linking poorly connected devices to a remote processing node.

The system architecture, depicted in Figure 23.1, has been designed to allow on-demand collaborations among mobile nodes. Examples of mobile-to-mobile collaborations regard several areas such as disaster relief, construction management, and health care. In order to promote and easy collaborations when two or more mobile users, who are members of the same organization or simply collaborate, meet each other, we let them group into *clusters* referred to as *mobile groups*. Consequently, the M2M-DM architecture includes some stationary nodes and a number of mobile groups.

Cluster formation is an important issue to be addressed. Clusters may be formed based on many criteria such as communication range, number and type of mobile devices, and their geographical location. In particular, we group the mobile devices on the basis of their transmission range. More precisely, when two or more coworkers standing within a given area meet, their mobile devices will discover each other and create an ad hoc network in order to form a cluster. Each cluster has a node referred to as the *cluster head*, which acts as the coordinator for the cluster, manages the other nodes within the cluster, and interacts with the other local groups in the network.

Figure 23.1 shows the interactions among the different components of the architecture. Stationary nodes are connected through the Internet and can interact with the other nodes (including the mobile ones) to execute a data mining task. Mobile nodes within a group interact through ad hoc connections (e.g., Wi-Fi, Bluetooth) that we refer to as *M2M connections*, represented by dotted arrows in Figure 23.1. Interactions among mobile groups (*cluster-to-cluster connections*) take place through ad hoc connections among the cluster heads of the groups and are represented by dotted–dashed arrows. Mobile groups are connected to stationary nodes through their cluster head (*mobile-to-stationary connections*) by exploiting an Internet connection (e.g., Wi-Fi, WiMAX). All types of interactions

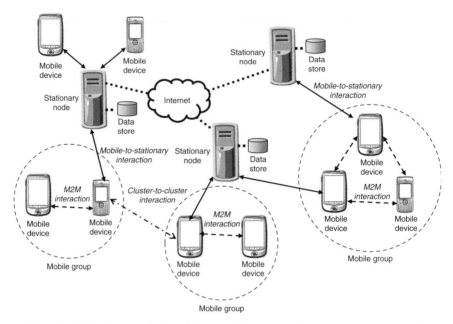

Figure 23.1   The M2M-DM architecture. The arrows denote remote service calls.

take place either to ask for a data mining request or to cooperate in order to collaboratively execute a data mining task.

In the M2M-DM architecture, both stationary and mobile nodes provide a specialized set of services, as detailed below. Stationary nodes provide three groups of functionalities:

- *Knowledge discovery* helps to execute or support the different steps of the knowledge discovery process (preprocessing, data mining, visualization, etc.).
- *Data management* allows to store and retrieve data (e.g., data generated by either mobile devices or third-party data providers).
- *Coordination* allows mobile devices to organize themselves into groups and manage computations cooperatively (e.g., registration services, discovery services).

Mobile devices provide the following groups of functionalities:

- *M2M knowledge discovery* helps to execute knowledge discovery tasks that can be executed on limited resources, such as preprocessing, visualization, or lightweight data mining processes.
- *M2M resource management* allows to monitor the local resources (e.g., memory, CPU load, battery status) to establish whether the device is able to execute a data mining task.

- *M2M coordination* enables mobile devices to organize themselves into local groups on a temporary basis for on-purpose knowledge discovery applications.
- *M2M interaction* allows interactions among nodes inside or outside the group. The interactions with nodes external to the group are realized through the cluster head that acts as a gateway toward the outside of the group.

23.3 MOBILE DEVICE COMPONENTS

Mobile nodes include a set of software components that cooperatively perform the functionalities introduced in the previous section. As shown in Figure 23.2, each node includes four software components: *resource information service (RIS)*, *M2M coordination service (MCS)*, *energy-aware scheduler (EAS)*, and *knowledge discovery service (KDS)*.

The RIS is responsible for collecting information about all the resources inside a mobile node and the context in which an application is running in order to adapt its execution. To this aim, the RIS is composed of two modules implementing the above-cited features:

- *Resource Monitoring Module*. It informs the system about the mobile device resources' measurement, such as the available memory, CPU utilization,

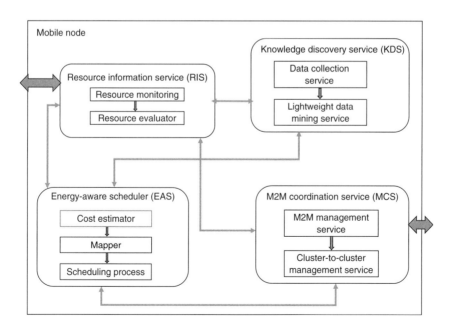

Figure 23.2   Software components inside each mobile device.

battery consumption, battery level, remaining time to fill memory, and network connectivity performance.

- *Resource Evaluator Module*. This module acts as a resource measurement receiver from both local and environmental resources. It then takes some actions on the basis of the received measures, that is, choosing the most suitable configuration for the data mining task. Moreover, the module is responsible for starting the data mining task with the appropriate parameters.

The MCS is responsible for coordination among mobile devices and includes two modules:

- *Mobile-to-Mobile Management Module*. It includes mechanisms aiming at the coordination of the nodes within a group, such as cluster formation and maintenance, joining of a new node to a group, cluster-head election, and cooperative data mining task execution.
- *Cluster-to-Cluster Management Module*. It provides mechanisms allowing mobile devices to organize themselves into clusters, such as cluster-to-cluster interactions to the end of a data mining task allocation, and coordination to collaboratively execute a data mining task.

The EAS is the component responsible for task assignment among local groups. It implements a scheduling strategy aimed at prolonging network lifetime by distributing energy consumption among local groups. In such an approach, whenever a resource-limited computing device (client) has a set of tasks to be executed, it uses the energy resources in nearby computing devices (servers) and an efficient task assignment is found in such a way that the total consumed energy is minimized. The scheduler interacts with the RIS through its resource monitoring and resource evaluator modules. Moreover, the scheduler is also tightly related to the KDS component, as it is actually the scheduler that activates the data mining process. The EAS includes three modules:

- *Cost Estimator Module*. This module exploits information about availability, performance, and cost of resources collected by the RIS component. It deals with the actual calculation of the estimation functions on the basis of the perceived status of resources with respect to time, energy, and load constraints.
- *Mapper Module*. This module schedules the tasks. It embeds a scheduling algorithm, and a matchmaker that takes into account resource characteristics incorporates interdependencies among resource groups or types, and computational and I/O cost evaluations to map the available resource units to newly scheduled tasks according to a prespecified mapping objective function.
- *Scheduling Process Module*. This module guides the scheduling activity. It receives jobs, requests the corresponding schedules to the mapper, and orders the execution of scheduled tasks.

The KDS is responsible for the execution of the knowledge discovery task over a mobile device. It includes two modules:

- *Data Collection Module*. This module provides access or stores mechanisms for data to be processed or generated as a result of a data mining process. Typically, only a limited amount of data can be stored on a mobile device. Therefore, this module manages the interaction with a stationary node that will act as a storage node or as a source for data.
- *Lightweight Data Mining Module*. It is responsible for managing the execution of a data mining task on the mobile device, where it is possible. If the mobile resources are not (or no more) sufficient to carry out the whole computation, this module can delegate the process to another node(s). As an example, this may happen when the resource measures indicate that the device cannot achieve the required accuracy according to the incoming data rate. In such a case, the node sends a request to a data mining server (either stationary or mobile) to continue the current process with the specified accuracy.

23.4 ENERGY MODEL

Mobile nodes are battery powered [7], which makes energy a critical concern. Thus, the main aim of a mobile ad hoc network (MANET) is to conservatively consume the energy to increase the lifetime of the network. One of the possible approaches to effectively manage a MANET is to cluster the network to distribute the load evenly throughout the whole network and to schedule the jobs among the cluster.

The power consumed by mobile devices during the execution of an application is defined as the rate at which energy is consumed. Although the terms *power* and *energy* are sometimes used interchangeably in the literature, we are concerned usually with energy efficiency, as batteries have a finite supply of energy. The *instantaneous power* consumed by a process can be defined as

$$P(t) = V(t) \times I(t), \tag{23.1}$$

where $V(t)$ is the supply voltage, $I(t)$ is the current, and t stands for the time index. On the other hand, energy consumption over an interval $t_1 - t_2$ is defined as

$$E = \int_{t_1}^{t_2} P(t)dt, \tag{23.2}$$

Therefore, a technique that reduces power consumption will save energy only if it does not increase the execution time by a factor that exceeds the gains from the power reduction.

Energy consumption of mobile devices depends on the computation and the communication loads. We define E_i as the rate of energy consumption of node i

in the time interval δt, which is the sum of all energy consumption for communication, ET_i, and computation, EC_i, of all the assigned tasks to node i within the time interval δt:

$$E_i = EC_i + ET_i. \tag{23.3}$$

Our approach is to estimate the energy consumption for computation and to analytically evaluate the energy consumed for communication. This issue is the main aim of this section.

As our study focuses on energy-efficient execution of data mining applications in a mobile context, the computation load mainly concerns execution of data mining tasks. We aim to identify the energy consumption characteristics of some commonly used statistical and data mining tasks running onboard a mobile device. Thus, we characterize a data mining algorithm in terms of the energy consumed over a specific mobile device and for a given data set. In doing that, we also consider the results in Reference 6, where the performance of specific data mining algorithms from the energy consumption perspective is experimentally quantified.

Some definitions are introduced to support the proposed energy model.

Definition 23.1 If we denote the residual energy available at node i at time t as $RE_i(t)$, the residual life of node i at time t, $RL_i(t)$, is defined as follows:

$$RL_i(t) = RE_i(t)/E_i. \tag{23.4}$$

Definition 23.2 The transmission range of node i, denoted as TR_i, transmitting with power level P_i, is the maximum distance from node i where connectivity with another node exists.

Definition 23.3 The reachability power is the transmission power level at which a destination node j is reachable from a source node i and is denoted as RP_{ij}. Obviously, the transmission power level of a node i has to be greater or equal to the power necessary to reach a given destination node j, that is, $P_i \geq RP_{ij}$.

According to Reference 8, we assume a commonly used wireless propagation model where the received signal power attenuates proportionally to $TR^{-\alpha}$, where TR is the transmission range and α is the loss constant, typically between 2 and 4 depending on the wireless medium. On the basis of this model, we can introduce the definition of a wireless link. A wireless link exists between two mobile devices if the transmitting node transmits with sufficiently high power such that the signal-to-interference-plus-noise ratio (SINR) at the receiving node is greater than a given threshold value δ. The threshold value δ is chosen to achieve a desired bit error rate for the given modulation scheme and data rate. The power required to support a wireless link at a given data rate between node i and node j is given by the following equation:

$$RP_{ij} \simeq r_{ij}^{\alpha}, \tag{23.5}$$

where r_{ij} is the distance between nodes i and j, with $r_{ij} \leq TR_i$. Thus, node i can reach node j if and only if node i transmits at a power P_i greater than or equal to r_{ij}^{α}, $P_i \geq r_{ij}^{\alpha}$.

On the basis of the above formula, we can introduce the definitions of wireless link and node neighbors as follows.

Definition 23.4 A wireless link exists between the two nodes i and j if the transmitting node i transmits with a power greater or equal to r_{ij}^{α}, $P_i \geq r_{ij}^{\alpha}$. In other words, a link among every pair of nodes (i, j) exists if the distance among them is lower than the transmission range of the transmitting node i, $r_{ij} \leq TR_i$.

Definition 23.5 The neighbors of a node i are the nodes falling in its transmission range TR_i. As such, a wireless link can be established between the node i and each of its neighbors. The number of active wireless links of a node i is the denoted as the *degree* of node i.

From the above definitions, it is evident that the connectivity of the network depends on the transmission range of nodes.

In particular, each connection link has a cost that is proportional to the power necessary to sustain the communication as expressed in Equation 23.5. However, the energy consumed by a node for communication also depends on the state of the node. Considering the network interface of a mobile device, this can be in four states: (i) transmit mode; (ii) receive mode; (iii) idle mode, this is the default mode for ad hoc network and in such a state a node can transmit or receive; and (iv) sleep mode, which is characterized by really low power consumption. In this state, the interface can neither transmit nor receive until it is woken up and it changes state. Energy consumption does not always reflect active communication in the network. Experimental results reveal that the energy consumption of mobile devices in an idle state is only slightly smaller than that in a transmitting or receiving state as evidenced from the study in Reference 9. This because in MANETs nodes must always be ready to receive traffic from neighbors due to the absence of base station nodes. Thus, a network interface operating in ad hoc mode can not be in a sleep mode, but it has to continuously listen to the wireless channel, thus consuming a constant idle energy power. Therefore, every node *overhears* every packet transmission occurring in its transmission range, thus consuming energy uselessly. Hence, the idle energy consumption is referred to as *overhearing*.

Overhearing heavily affects the energy consumption of the mobile device. In particular, owing to overhearing, a new cost in the computation of per-packet energy consumption is introduced and it is the cost for discarding overheard packets. Therefore, to model the energy consumed for communication, the costs to send, receive, and discard a packet must be included. Consequently, the energy consumed by a node i for communication can be defined by the following equation:

$$ET_i = E_{send_i} + E_{receive_i} + E_{discard_i}. \qquad (23.6)$$

The overall cost of a packet transmission is the sum of the costs due to the sending of the node and its reception. Potential receivers of a packet are the destination node(s) and the nodes overhearing the packet. A packet may be sent as broadcast or point-to-point traffic. The former is received by all hosts within the transmission range of the sender; the latter is discarded by nondestination hosts. It is important to note that the costs of receiving and discarding are multiplied by the number of hosts that receive or discard the traffic.

The cost, $E_{send_{ij}}$, for a node i to send a point-to-point packet to a node j is modeled as a linear function as described by the following equation:

$$E_{send_{ij}} = RP_{ij} * (T_{latency} + MSG_{size}/BW_{ij}), \qquad (23.7)$$

where $T_{latency}$ is the network latency time, MSG_{size} is the size of the message exchanged among nodes i and j, and BW_{ij} is the bandwidth connecting the two nodes. Thus, in the equation, both cost items are a function of the power level necessary to sustain a link between the source and the destination node. Note that in the point-to-point transmission, referring to the IEEE 802.11 network interface, it is necessary to take into account the MAC protocol interactions. The transmitting node sends a request-to-send (RTS) control message to identify the destination node that in turn replies with a clear-to-send (CTS) message. The transmitting node, after having received the CTS message, sends the data and awaits an ACK from the destination. These control messages introduce a small further overhead compared to the broadcast transmission.

The cost for such messages is same and it is represented by Equation 23.7, except for the message size.

Furthermore, the MAC protocol control messages favor the overhearing, as detailed in the following section (Eq. 23.14).

In case broadcast transmission is used to send the packet, it requires a power level necessary to reach the most faraway node (denoted as j_{max}) among the ones within the sender transmission range, and the Equation 23.7 changes as

$$E_{broad_i} = RP_{ij_{max}} * (T_{latency} + MSG_{size}/BW_{ij_{max}}). \qquad (23.8)$$

The aggregate energy cost of node i for sending packets (communicating whether data or just synchronization messages) is the sum of the costs on all communication links having i (let us say k_1) as transmitting node for point-to-point transmissions or the broadcast cost otherwise. That is

$$E_{send_i} = \begin{cases} \sum_{j=1}^{k_1} E_{send_{ij}} & \text{if point-to-point} \\ E_{broad_i} & \text{otherwise} \end{cases} \qquad (23.9)$$

According to Reference 9, in general, the cost for a node i to receive a packet can be described by the following equation:

$$E_{r_i} = E_{r_v} * MSG_{size} + E_{r_f}. \qquad (23.10)$$

In the above equation, there is a fixed reception cost component associated with device state changes and channel acquisition overhead and an incremental component that is proportional to the size of the packet. The incremental cost of receiving data once the data channel is acquired is expected to be the same for both broadcast and point-to-point traffic. The fixed cost in the point-to-point transmission other than the channel access cost also includes the costs associated with the above-described MAC control messages. Consequently, Equation 23.10 is rewritten as two different equations depending on whether the point-to-point or broadcast transmission is used:

$$E_{r_{pp_i}} = E_{r_v} * \text{MSG}_{size} + E_{r_{pp_f}}, \tag{23.11}$$

$$E_{r_{broad_i}} = E_{r_v} * \text{MSG}_{size} + E_{r_{broad_f}}. \tag{23.12}$$

The aggregate energy cost of a node i for receiving, $E_{receive_i}$, is the sum of all the costs on all communication links (let us say k) having i as the receiving node. If n_{pp} are the contemporary point-to-point active receiving links of node i and n_{broad} are the contemporary broadcast active receiving links of node i, the overall receiving cost of node i is defined through the following equation:

$$E_{receive_i} = n_{pp} * E_{r_{pp_i}} + n_{broad} * E_{r_{broad_i}}. \tag{23.13}$$

As said before, a network interface overhears all traffic sent and received by nearby nodes. Thus, it is important to consider the energy consumed during the processing of point-to-point traffic due to the discarding of the packets by the nonrecipients of those packets. Nondestination nodes within the transmission range of either the transmitting or receiving nodes overhear the traffic. In particular, nodes within the range of the transmitting node but not in the range of the destination overhear only the sender packets. Conversely, nodes within the range of the destination but not in that of the sender overhear only the packets sent by the destination node. Referring to the IEEE 802.11 MAC protocol, this means that nodes in the range of the sender overhear both the RTS message and the actual data packet, whereas nodes in range of the destination overhear the CTS and ACK messages. The cost of discarding is comparable to that of receiving, and thus, it can be expressed through Equation 23.10 with proper coefficients:

$$E_{d_i} = E_{d_v} * \text{MSG}_{size} + E_{d_f}. \tag{23.14}$$

Thus, if the number of contemporary discardings is n_{disc}, the overall cost for discarding of a node i is

$$E_{discard_i} = n_{disc} * E_{d_i}. \tag{23.15}$$

23.5 CLUSTERING SCHEME

In a wireless MANET, which changes its topology dynamically, efficient resource allocation, energy management, and routing can be achieved through adaptive *clustering* of the mobile nodes.

In a clustering scheme, the mobile nodes are divided into virtual groups. Generally, devices geographically adjacent are allocated into the same cluster. Under a cluster structure, mobile nodes may be assigned a different function, such as *cluster head* or *cluster member*. A cluster head normally serves as a local coordinator for its cluster, performing intracluster transmission arrangement, data forwarding, and so on.

A cluster member is usually called an *ordinary node*, which is a non-cluster-head node without any intercluster links.

Clustering in the M2M architecture allows to achieve scalability. However, constructing and maintaining a cluster structure introduces a significant overhead to the network management costs. Thus, the clustering cost represents a key issue to validate the effectiveness and scalability enhancement of the clustering structure. The main items contributing to these costs are due to:

- forming and maintaining the clustering structure in a highly dynamic environment;
- reconfiguration cost to keep the network connected due to nodes mobility;
- energy drain.

In a dynamic network, explicit message exchanges among mobile nodes are necessary. To maintain the clustering structure, when the network topology changes, the clustering-related information exchange increases, consuming considerable bandwidth and mobile nodes energy. Owing to the dynamic nature of the mobile nodes, cluster head affiliation and reaffiliations impact the stability of the network, and hence, reconfigurations of clusters are necessary. This is an important issue since frequent cluster head changes seriously affect the performance of clustering scheme. Consequently, the choice of cluster heads is of crucial importance. Choosing cluster heads is an NP-hard problem [10]. Existing solutions to this problem are based on greedy heuristic approaches, without retaining the stability of the network topology [10].

In some clustering schemes, the cluster structure has to be completely rebuilt over the whole network when some local events take place, for example, the movement or death of a mobile node, resulting in some cluster-head reelections (reclustering) [11]. This is called the *ripple effect* of reclustering: the reelection of one cluster head may affect the structure of many clusters and cause the cluster-head reelection over the network. Thus, the ripple effect of reclustering may greatly affect the performance of the clustering scheme. Furthermore, most schemes assume that mobile nodes are static when cluster formation is in progress because a mobile node can decide to become a cluster head only after it exchanges some specific information with its neighbors and assures that it holds some specific attribute in its neighborhood. With a frozen period of motion, each mobile node can obtain accurate information from neighboring nodes, and the initial cluster structure can be formed with some specific characteristics. However, this assumption may not be applicable in an actual scenario, where mobile nodes may move all the time.

Hence, the required explicit control message exchange, the ripple effect of reclustering, and the stationary assumption for cluster formation are the main costs of a cluster-based MANET.

In the literature, there are several approaches to cluster MANETs. The clustering schemes can be classified according to different criteria. For example, depending on whether a cluster head is required, clustering protocols can be classified as cluster-head-based clustering [12–20] and non-cluster-head-based clustering [21, 22]. Or, on the basis of the hop distance between node pairs in a cluster, clustering schemes can be divided into one-hop clustering and multihop clustering. Aside from such physical parameters, clustering schemes can also be differentiated based on some criterion related to the clustering design principles. According to this criterion, the proposed clustering schemes for MANETs can be grouped into six categories. (i) Dominating set (DS)-based clustering [12, 23] tries to find a DS for a MANET so that the number of mobile nodes that participate in route search or routing table maintenance can be reduced. (ii) Low maintenance clustering schemes [13, 22] aim at providing stable cluster architecture for upper-layer protocols with little cluster maintenance cost. By limiting reclustering situations or minimizing explicit control messages for clustering, the cluster structure can be maintained well without excessive consumption of network resources for cluster maintenance. (iii) Mobility-aware clustering [14, 15, 21] takes the mobility behavior of mobile nodes into consideration. This is because the mobile nodes' movement is the main cause of changes to the network topology. By grouping mobile nodes with similar speed into the same cluster, the intracluster links can be greatly tightened and the cluster structure can be correspondingly stabilized in the face of moving mobile nodes. (iv) Energy-efficient clustering [16–18] manages to use the battery energy of mobile nodes more wisely in a MANET. By eliminating unnecessary energy consumption of mobile nodes or by balancing energy consumption among different mobile nodes, the network lifetime can be remarkably prolonged. (v) Load-balancing clustering schemes [16–19] attempt to limit the number of mobile nodes in each cluster to a specified range so that clusters are of similar size. Thus, the network loads can be more evenly distributed in each cluster. (vi) Combined-metrics-based clustering [20] usually considers multiple metrics, such as node degree, cluster size, mobility speed, and battery energy, in cluster configuration, especially in cluster-head decisions. With the consideration of more parameters, cluster heads can be more properly chosen without giving bias to mobile nodes with specific attributes. Also, the weighting factor for each parameter can be adaptively adjusted in response to different application scenarios.

In the next section, we present our clustering approach. The main design principles of our clustering scheme are to allow self-configuration and adaptation of the network and prolong its lifetime by distributing energy consumption among clusters. More precisely, we cluster the network with three primary goals in mind:

- prolonging network lifetime by distributing energy consumption among local groups;
- minimizing the total transmission power aggregated over all nodes involved in the computation;
- using adaptive network topology to reduce energy consumption.

23.5.1   Clustering the M2M Architecture

Architecture for wireless systems should be able to dynamically adapt itself with the changing network configurations. For MANETs, since the position of each node changes over time, the clustering protocol must be able to dynamically update its links in order to maintain strong connectivity. A network protocol that achieves this is said to be self-reconfiguring. A major focus of this chapter is the design of a self-reconfiguring network protocol that consumes the least amount of energy possible.

Accordingly, our clustering scheme is based on a fully distributed cluster formation algorithm where nodes make autonomous decisions, and no global communication is needed to set up the clusters but only local decisions are made autonomously by each node. This means that the proposed M2M architecture is self-organized into mobile clusters. More precisely, the clustering formation scheme we propose makes it possible that when mobile devices meet, that is, they are within the same transmission range, they can form a mobile group. The self-organization nature of the clustering scheme adopted distributes the responsibility among the different mobile nodes. In such a way, there is no node in charge of the overall organization; each individual node interacts directly with the other one in its transmission range in a peer-to-peer fashion.

In the design of the clustering scheme, we made the following assumptions: (i) the number of mobile nodes in the network changes as nodes change dynamically their position, (ii) a given node can belong to only one cluster at a given time, and (iii) there are no fixed cluster-head nodes in the cluster formation process.

As said before, choosing cluster heads optimally is an NP-hard problem [10]. As this topic is not the focus of our work, we just make a discussion on how such an issue could be handled. The number of cluster heads depends on many factors such as the number of nodes in network, their physical location, the transmission power, and the energy level. Each cluster head will cover an area that is determined by its transmission range. However, the size of each local group is restricted by the ability of the current cluster head of the group to manage the nodes in the group. Thus, the total number of nodes per unit area should be restricted so that the cluster head in that area can manage all the nodes. If a certain zone becomes densely populated because of migration of nodes from other zones, then the cluster head might not be able to handle all the traffic generated by the nodes. In our approach, we aim to elect the minimum number of cluster heads that can support all the nodes in the system, satisfying constraints relative to the number of nodes a cluster head can manage. In other words, we limit the degree of the cluster heads to be lower of a given threshold that can be determined on the basis of the energy and processing capacity of the node.

It is evident that choosing cluster heads is a key operation in clustering formation and evolution processes. Any node in the network can become a cluster head if it has the necessary functionality, such as processing and transmission power. However, a node to be considered a candidate for cluster head also has to satisfy constraints relative to energy and location of nodes. Thus, the clustering formation algorithm proposed takes into account both location and energy metrics as described in the following section.

Clusters are formed by grouping nodes within the same transmission range because correlation is strongest among data signals from nodes located close to each other. Furthermore, the battery power can be efficiently used within a certain transmission range: a node will consume less power to communicate with closer-distance nodes. On the basis of this design assumption, the transmission power level of a node is an important parameter to take into account in the choice of cluster heads. Another important parameter is the number of neighbors of a node, that is, its degree. The higher the number of neighbors of a node, the greater the likelihood of being elected cluster head. However, owing to processing and power restrictions, each node is able to efficiently manage a number of neighbors bound by its current load.

In a dynamic network, node mobility plays a key role in terms of energy depletion due to clustering formation and maintenance. Thus, the clustering structure should be maintained as much stable as possible avoiding frequent cluster head changes that would require reaffiliation of nodes and cluster-head reelection. Therefore, a node with lower mobility has a higher chance of being a cluster head. According to Reference 20, we estimate node mobility by taking the average of the distances covered by it in the last t period of times. In particular, we take the average of last t distances covered by the node. This gives a prediction of node mobility characteristics. Thus, we introduce the mobility parameter M as described by the following equation:

$$M_i(t) = 1/t \sum_{j=1}^{t} \sqrt{(x_j - x_{j-1})^2 + (y_j - y_{j-1})^2}, \qquad (23.16)$$

where the values (x_j, y_j) and (x_{j-1}, y_{j-1}) are the coordinates of node i at time j and $j - 1$.

As the main objective of our work is to maximally extend the life of all the nodes in the network, we aim to balance the load proportional to the available energy of each node.

In our approach, load balancing depends on the number of neighbors a cluster head can nominally efficiently handle, but rather, this value is determined by the current load of the node. As such, each topological and scheduling decision is made by balancing the intra- and intercluster energy loads. In particular, to balance the energy load over all the nodes in the network, each time a new task is submitted to be executed, it will be scheduled in such a way that the total consumed energy is minimized. We do not give any details about and insights into the energy-aware scheduling in MANETs, as such a topic is not the focus of this work. We just want to highlight here that in order to obtain an energy-efficient management of the network, it is not possible to, aside from specific scheduling solutions and algorithms, address the energy issue in a cooperative mobile environment such as the M2M architecture. In such an approach, whenever a resource-limited computing device has a task to be executed, it uses the energy resources in nearby computing devices with the overall aim to maximally extend network lifetime.

According to the above discussion, we introduce a combined weighted metric that takes into account the following node parameters: degree (DG), mobility (M), residual life (RL), and transmission power (P). Depending on specific applications, any or all of these parameters can be used in the metric to elect the cluster heads. Thus, to establish whether a node i can be elected a cluster head, the *cluster-head selection function* (*CHS*), $CHS_i(t)$, is defined. Such a function is described by the following equation:

$$CHS_i(t) = \alpha RL_i(t) + \beta M_i(t) + \gamma P_i(t) + \delta DG_i(t), \tag{23.17}$$

where α, β, γ, and δ are the weights corresponding to the above-cited performance parameters.

Using the proposed weighted approach, in the following we describe the clustering formation process. This process can be divided in two phases: (i) network setup and (ii) network evolution.

As said before, our objective is to let nodes within the same transmission range to organize into local groups. Beacons could be used to determine the presence of neighbor nodes. During the initial cluster set up, a node with higher value of the *CHS* function among its one-hop neighbors is elected as the cluster head and its one-hop not-already-affiliated neighbors become the members of the just formed cluster. These nodes are then excluded while selecting the next higher weighted nodes. In case of equality in the node weights, the node with higher energy level is preferred as the cluster head. This process is repeated till all the nodes are assigned with their role as either a head or a member of the cluster.

The network evolution process can be outlined as follows. A mobile node i that has to join the network should establish whether it can join an already existing cluster or it has to create a new one. To this aim, the node i sends an *announcement* message to check the presence of any nodes within its transmission range. Two things could happen:

- The node does not receive a reply. In such a case, it will form a new group and will elect itself the cluster head of the group.
- The node receives one or more replies. If node i has more than a group within its transmission range, it will receive more responses. In such a case,

the node will join the group that will allow to extend the network lifetime as well as achieve load balancing. This means that it will join the local group that maximizes the life of the whole network:

$$Max \sum_{j=1}^{N} \alpha_j \mathrm{RL}_{LG_j}(t), \qquad (23.18)$$

where RL_{LG_j} denotes the residual life of local group LG_j and N is the number of groups in the network. In particular, the residual life of each local group is described by the following equation:

$$\mathrm{RL}_{\mathrm{LG}_i} = \sum_{j=1}^{N_{\mathrm{LG}_i}} \alpha_j \mathrm{RL}_j(t), \qquad (23.19)$$

where N_{LG_j} is the number of nodes within the local group LG_j, RL_i is the residual life of node i in the group, and the generic parameter α_j takes into account the importance of the node i in the local group.

To balance the load among the clusters, the degree of the cluster heads is also evaluated during the joining phase. In particular, in the choice of the group to join, the node i will choose, among the ones with the lower residual life, the group having the cluster head with the minimum degree.

The clustering evolution phase may require cluster-head reelections. This may happen because of different reasons. The main difference in the cluster-head reelection process is whether a reaffiliation is needed. It is often the case that cluster-head reelection affects only nodes within a cluster without causing any reaffiliations but only changing the cluster-head role from a node to another of the same cluster. In some other cases, reaffiliations are necessary. More precisely, the cluster-head reelection process takes place if one of the following events occur:

- *Cluster-head node location changes as nodes move.* When a mobile device i that is already in the network is moving out of the range of the group to which it belongs, it becomes thus unreachable to the other nodes in the group. In such a case, a reaffilitation is needed—the node i can join another cluster following the cluster formation algorithm described above.
- *To expand the life of a group.* Periodically, it could be necessary to perform a rotation of the cluster-head role in the group in such a way to expand the group lifetime. This reduces the number of reaffiliations, thus lowering the cluster maintenance cost. Particularly, a periodic check over the current cluster head could be performed (i) to evenly distribute the load among the nodes within a cluster, (ii) to avoid decrease in the cluster-head life under a given threshold, and (iii) because at a certain point, another node in the cluster has a value of the *CHS* function better than that of the cluster head.

- *Cluster head drains out of battery power*. In such a case, reaffiliation is also necessary when none of the other nodes in the cluster is able to act as cluster head. Thus, a reorganization of the nodes in the cluster is necessary.
- *A new node joins the system*. Also in such a case one or more reaffiliations may be necessary.

In the case where no reaffilitaion is needed, the overhead introduced by the reelection process is clearly low compared to the reaffiliation case.

23.6 CONCLUSION

The development of software frameworks for running data mining tasks on cooperating mobile devices will allow to exploit such devices for novel data analysis applications. Handling the energy efficiency issue is a significant contribution for making mobile devices effective platforms for supporting complex applications in nomadic scenarios.

The architecture presented in this chapter is a first step toward the implementation of a framework for energy-efficient mobile-to-mobile data mining. We are currently working in four main directions:

1. defining a formal energy model for a mobile data mining scenario;
2. defining an energy-aware adaptive distributed clustering scheme based on a combined weighted metric, wherein a node with lower mobility and greater residual life is assigned higher weight so that cluster stability can be improved;
3. defining a scheduling strategy that takes into account the energy requirements of algorithms and the energy capability of the devices;
4. implementing a prototype of the system, starting from the implementation of the software components devoted to cluster formation, energy measurements, and scheduling.

REFERENCES

1. Barr K, Asanovic K. Energy aware lossless data compression. USENIX/ACM International Conference Mobile Systems, Applications, and Services; San Francisco, USA; 2003. pp. 231–244.
2. Li Z, Wang C, Xu R. Computation offloading to save energy on handheld devices: a partition scheme. ACM International Conference Compilers, Architecture, and Synthesis for Embedded Systems; Atlanta, USA; 2001. pp. 238–246.
3. Rudenko A, Reiher P, Popek GJ, Kuenning GH. Saving portable computer battery power through remote process execution. SIGMOBILE Mobile Comput Commun Rev 1998;2(1):19–26.
4. Flinn J, Satyanarayanan M. Energy-aware adaptation for mobile applications. Symposium on Operating Systems Principles; 1999. pp. 48–63.

5. Gurun S, Krintz C. Addressing the energy crisis in mobile computing with developing power aware software. UCSB, Computer Science Department, Technical Report; 2003.

6. Bhargava R, Kargupta H, Powers M. Energy consumption in data analysis for on-board and distributed applications. ICML'03 workshop on Machine Learning Technologies for Autonomous Space Applications; Washington, DC USA; 2003.

7. Fife LD, Gruenwald L. Research issues for data communication in mobile Ad-Hoc network database systems. ACM SIGMOD RECORD 2003;32(2):42–47.

8. Rappaport TS. *Wireless Communications: Principles and Practices*. 2nd ed. Prentice Hall; New Jersey, USA; 2002.

9. Feeney LM. An energy-consumption model for performance analysis of routing protocols for mobile ad hoc networks. Mobile Netw Appl J 2001;6(3):239–250.

10. Basagni S, Chlamtac I, Farago A. A generalized clustering algorithm for peer-to-peer networks. Workshop on Algorithmic Aspects of Communication, satellite workshop of ICALP 97; Bologna, Italy; 1997.

11. Lin CHR, Gerla M. A distributed architecture for multimedia in dynamic wireless networks. IEEE GLOBECOM; Singapore; 1995. pp. 1468–1472.

12. Chen Y-ZP, Liestman AL. Approximating minimum size weakly-connected dominating sets for clustering mobile ad hoc networks. 3rd ACM International Symposium Mobile Ad Hoc Networking and Computing; 2002. pp. 165–172.

13. Yu JY, Chong PHJ. 3hBAC (3-hop between Adjacent Clusterheads): a novel non-overlapping clustering algorithm for mobile ad hoc networks. IEEE Pacrim 03, 2003; Volme 1; Singapore; 2003. pp. 318–21.

14. Basu P, Khan N, Little TDC. A mobility based metric for clustering in mobile ad hoc networks. IEEE ICDCSW'01; 2001. pp. 413–418.

15. McDonald AB, Znati TF. Design and performance of a distributed dynamic clustering algorithm for Ad-Hoc networks. 34th Annual Simulation Symposium; Boston, USA; 2001. pp. 27–35.

16. Amis AD, Prakash R. Load-balancing clusters in wireless ad hoc networks. 3rd IEEE ASSET'00; 2000. pp. 25–32.

17. Wu J, et al. On calculating power-aware connected dominating sets for efficient routing in ad hoc wireless networks. J Commun Netw 2002;4(1):59–70.

18. Ryu J-H, Song S, Cho D-H. New clustering schemes for energy conservation in two-tiered mobile Ad-Hoc networks. IEEE ICC'01, Volume 3. 2001. pp. 862–66.

19. Ohta T, Inoue S, Kakuda Y. An adaptive multihop clustering scheme for highly mobile ad hoc networks. The 6th International Symposium on Autonomous Decentralized Systems (ISADS'03); 2003. pp. 293–300.

20. Chatterjee M, Das S, Turgut D. WCA: a weighted clustering algorithm for mobile ad hoc networks. Cluster Comput J 2002;5(2):193–204.

21. McDonald AB, Znati TF. A mobility-based framework for adaptive clustering in wireless ad hoc networks. IEEE JSAC 1999;17:1466–1487.

22. Lin CR, Gerla M. Adaptive clustering for mobile wireless networks. IEEE JSAC 1997;15:1265–1275.

23. Das B, Bharghavan V. Routing in ad hoc networks using minimum connected dominating sets. IEEE ICC 97; Urbana, USA. 1997; pp. 376–380.

CHAPTER 24

ENERGY AWARENESS AND EFFICIENCY IN WIRELESS SENSOR NETWORKS: FROM PHYSICAL DEVICES TO THE COMMUNICATION LINK

FLÁVIA C. DELICATO and PAULO F. PIRES

24.1 INTRODUCTION

Wireless sensor networks (WSNs) represent a new domain of distributed computing that has attracted great research interest over the last years. A WSN is composed of a large number of tiny battery-operated devices equipped with one or more sensing units, processor, memory, and wireless radio. The main goal of WSNs is to collect data about physical phenomena and deliver them to user applications through one or more exit points called *sink nodes*. Sink nodes are powerful devices, often a personal computer, that are in charge of gathering all the sensor-collected data, further processing them, and making them available to external networks such as the Internet. Sensor nodes act in a collaborative way to accomplish sensing tasks providing data with scale and both spatial and temporal resolutions very difficult (or even impossible) to achieve using other monitoring techniques. The WSN capability of extracting environmental information from a large geographic area, sometimes in inhospitable and/or remote places, in a timely and accurate manner, has the potential to bring about a radical change in the way we interact with the environment. Therefore, WSNs currently represent the most promising technology to fully connect the physical realm with the digital world.

There is a wide range of applications that can benefit from the use of WSNs, such as structural monitoring [1]; habitat [2], wildlife [3], and environmental monitoring [4]; machine condition monitoring [5]; surveillance systems [6]; medical monitoring [7]; and location tracking [8]. To enable the practical usage of

Energy-Efficient Distributed Computing Systems, First Edition.
Edited by Albert Y. Zomaya and Young Choon Lee.
© 2012 John Wiley & Sons, Inc. Published 2012 by John Wiley & Sons, Inc.

WSNs, there are currently several state-of-the-art sensor node platforms available on the market, for instance, Intel Telos [9], Sun SPOT [10], and the Mica family [11], which target different application requirements. Research on WSNs has progressed dramatically in the past decade. The hardware, particularly the radio technology, is quickly improving, leading to cheaper, faster, smaller, and longer-lasting nodes [12]. Although cost and size considerations imply that the resources available to individual nodes are severely limited, recent advances in technology lead us to believe that limited processor and memory are temporary constraints in WSNs that tend to disappear with fast developing fabrication techniques [13]. The energy constraint, on the other hand, remains as a critical issue that needs to be tackled so that WSNs can be widely used.

WSN nodes are endowed with limited power supply, usually provided by a nonrechargeable battery. A key feature of such networks is their capacity to operate unattended for large periods of time; this is a critical requirement in many application domains, such as habitat monitoring, in which the target area needs to be kept undisturbed to allow the proper data acquisition. Considering that WSNs often have hundreds or thousands of sensors and that they should work unattended, once the node battery is depleted, battery or node replacement is nondesirable or even unfeasible. One possible way to minimize this drawback is using strategies for harvesting energy from the environment [14]. However, the energy obtained from natural sources is often unreliable and unstable along the time. Therefore, it is crucial that WSNs are aware of their own energy and cleverly handle its consumption in order to maximize their operational lifetime. To extend the WSN lifetime, the energy efficiency needs to be tackled in a holistic approach, encompassing all levels of the whole network, from individual components of the sensor node hardware to energy-efficient protocols that govern the network operation.

The lifetime of a WSN can be measured by the time elapsed before all (or a significant portion of) nodes have been drained out of their battery power or the network no longer meets the requirements of connectivity, coverage, or any other application-specific parameter of quality, which directly affects the network usefulness.

Current techniques for improving energy efficiency include conventional low power hardware designs [15, 16], which focus on the energy consumption in circuit and architecture level of the single node [17], and energy-efficient strategies and protocols [18–20], which act in the network-wide level, in different layers of the WSN stack, such as routing, scheduling, and medium access control (MAC). At the node level, since a large amount of energy is consumed by node components (CPU, radio, etc.) even if they are idle, power management schemes can be used to switch-off node components that are not temporarily needed. Moreover, techniques of dynamic reconfiguration such as dynamic modulation scaling (DMS) (used to reconfigure modulation schemes in communication), dynamic voltage scaling (DVS) (used to reconfigure voltages and operating frequency of processors), and adaptive sampling rate (used to change the sampling rate of sensors) enable reconfiguration of the sensor network hardware at runtime to adapt to external dynamics, providing a novel approach to design energy-efficient WSNs [21].

In this chapter, we present a comprehensive survey on several aspects of energy awareness and efficiency in WSNs. Our goal is not to give an in-depth explanation on existent techniques and solutions but instead to provide a broad "map" compiling and organizing all the knowledge developed in this field over the last years. Such survey is organized using a knowledge representation tool called *Concept Maps* [22]. Such representation is widely used as a learning tool. However, its use as a tool for capturing the knowledge of experts is growing at a fast rate [23]. Since the research in the field of energy-aware WSNs has already created a large body of knowledge that is not fully organized yet, we believe that the construction of concept maps can be very useful not only to organize the already consolidated knowledge but also to promote the creative thinking on such knowledge bringing about new categorizations, relationships, and/or propositions.

A concept map is a top-down diagram showing the relationships between concepts, including cross-connections among concepts, and their instances. Concepts are usually enclosed in circles or boxes, and relationships between concepts are indicated by a connecting line linking two concepts. Words on the connecting lines, referred to as *linking words* or *linking phrases*, specify the relationship between the two concepts. According to Novak and Cañas [23], concepts are defined as a *"perceived regularity in events or objects, or records of events or objects, designated by a label."* Propositions are statements about some object or event in the universe, either naturally occurring or constructed. Propositions contain two or more concepts connected using linking words or phrases to form a meaningful statement.

One characteristic of concept maps is that the concepts are represented in a hierarchical fashion with the most inclusive, most general concepts at the top of the map and the more specific, less general concepts arranged hierarchically below. The hierarchical structure for a particular domain of knowledge also depends on the context in which that knowledge is being applied or considered. Therefore, it is advisable to build concept maps with reference to some particular question we seek to answer, which is often called a *focus question*. The concept map may pertain to some situation or event that we are trying to understand through the organization of knowledge in the form of a concept map, thus providing the context for the concept map. In this chapter, the central question is *"How to wisely manage energy in a WSN in order to extend its lifetime?"* The hierarchical organization of concept maps fits well with the way energy awareness is tackled in WSNs since the existent strategies spread over different levels (from the entire network to individual node components) and can be suitably described in a top-down fashion. Another important characteristic of concept maps is the inclusion of cross-links. These are relationships or links between concepts in different segments or domains of the concept map, or between concepts in different maps. Cross-links help to see how a concept in one domain of knowledge represented on the map is related to a concept in another domain shown on the map.

In the creation of new knowledge, cross-links often represent creative leaps on the part of the knowledge producer.

The use of a hierarchical structure and the presence of cross-links are features of concept maps that are important in the facilitation of creative thinking. A final feature that may be added to concept maps consists in specific examples of events or objects that help to clarify the meaning of a given concept.

In the next sections, we start by describing the network and node models we are assuming in this survey. Then, using concept maps as a guide and an organizational scheme, we depict the main current strategies and approaches for enabling energy awareness and management in a WSN, organized in three different levels: (i) the level of individual nodes, (ii) the level representing the communicating neighboring nodes, and (iii) the level of the entire network. In the following, we discuss current solutions for the first two levels. Solutions for the third level are addressed in Chapter 11 of this book.

24.2 WSN AND POWER DISSIPATION MODELS

Before describing the concept maps and their constituent concepts created to represent the strategies to promote energy awareness and efficiency in WSNs, we first need to present the generic network and node architecture we are assuming in this survey, as well as the sources of power dissipation related to each component of a WSN node. This section encompasses such issues.

24.2.1 Network and Node Architecture

To keep a unique notation along the chapter, we illustrate the network and node architecture considered in this work by using a concept map as well (Fig. 24.1). Regarding the WSN components, we assume a network composed of one or more sink nodes (sometimes referred to as *base station*) and a (possibly huge) number of sensor nodes deployed over a large geographic area (called *sensing field* or *target area*). Data are collected from the sensing field and transferred from sensor nodes to the sink through a multihop communication protocol. The sink node is a powerful (not constrained) device, often a personal computer, which acts as an interface between the WSN and client applications, frequently through external networks such as the Internet.

Regarding individual sensor nodes, we consider that each sensor is composed of software and hardware components. Sensor hardware has four main components: (i) a sensing subsystem including one or more sensors (with associated analog-to-digital converters (ADCs)) for data acquisition, (ii) a processing subsystem including a microcontroller and memory for local data processing, (iii) a communication subsystem for wireless data communication, and (iv) a power supply subsystem.

The *sensing subsystem* is responsible for monitoring the environment and is composed of a sensing device and an ADC. The sensing device produces

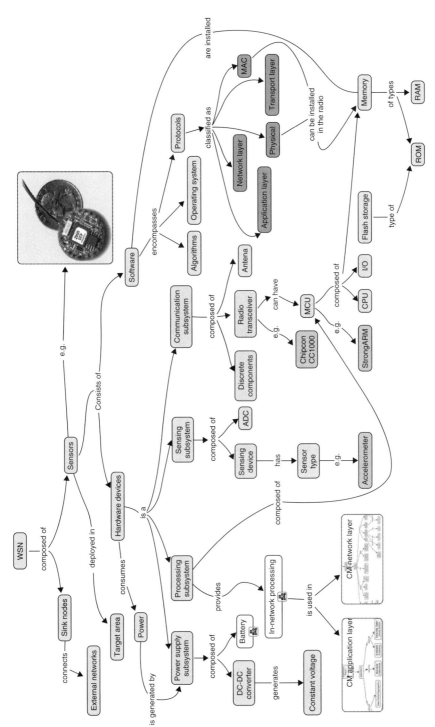

Figure 24.1 WSN model concept map.

677

a measurable response, codified as a continual analog signal, to a change in the physical phenomenon being monitored, translating such changes to electrical signals. The continual analog signal sensed by the sensors is digitized by the ADC and sent to controllers for further processing. There is a diversity of sensors that measure environmental parameters such as pressure, movement, temperature, light intensity, sound, magnetic fields, acceleration, and image. Such sensors can be classified into the passive and active. Passive sensors sense the physical environment without emitting energy (or radiation) into the environment, but they only detect the energy that is naturally available, for example, temperature sensors. Active sensors, on the other hand, actively probe the environment by emitting some kind of energy (microwave, sound, light, etc.) in order to detect the changes that occur on the transmitted energy; for example, in sonar sensors, a speaker (piezoelectric transducer) is used to emit a short burst of sound (ping) that is reflected by objects in front of the device and returned to the detector, another piezoelectric transducer. That means it emits and detects energy at the same time.

The *processing subsystem* provides in-network processing capacity to the sensors and is composed of a microcontroller unit (MCU). The sensor's capability of performing in-network processing is used by algorithms and protocols from different layers in the WSN stack. In the concept map showed in Figure 24.1, we can see a cross-link in the concept representing the in-network processing. Such cross-link denotes the relationship between this concept in the domain of the WSN components and this same concept representing the usage of such feature, for instance, by concepts from the application and the network layers. The concept maps representing these layers are included in Chapter 11, since they are issues from the network-wide level.

The sensor MCU is a small computer on a single integrated circuit containing a processor core, storage medium (both ROM and RAM memories), ADCs, and programmable input/output peripherals. The MCU is responsible for controlling sensors, data and program storage, and executing communication protocols and signal processing algorithms on the gathered sensor data. The tight integration and low power consumption of MCUs makes them ideal for use in embedded systems such as WSN sensor nodes. Examples of MCUs are Intel StrongARM microprocessor, Cypress M8C, JENNIC JN5148, and Atmel AVR [24].

The *communication subsystem* is responsible for delivering data or control messages to neighboring nodes and is typically composed of a radio transceiver, an antenna, and a set of discrete components used to configure its features, such as the signal intensity and sensibility. Transceivers provide the functionality of both transmitter and receiver combined into a single device. In general, the radio transceiver can operate according to four different operational modes: receiving, transmitting, idle, and sleeping [25]. Current generation transceivers have a built-in microprocessor that performs communication-specific operations. Examples of radio transceivers are the RF Monolithics TR1000 [26], the Chipcon CC1000 [27], and the Semtech SX1211 [28].

The *power supply subsystem* is composed of the battery and the DC-DC converter (Fig. 24.2). The battery supplies power to the whole sensor node and hence plays a vital role in determining the sensor node lifetime. Batteries are the most commonly used energy storage medium in WSNs. There are several prominent types of commonly available battery technologies: alkaline, lithium, nickel metal hydride, and, more recently, the lithium iron disulfide (Li/FeS_2) batteries, which offer the advantages of extended operating temperatures, capacity, and shelf life [29]. In order to avoid issues associated with varying battery voltages, the power supply subsystems rely on the DC-DC converter, which take as input varying input voltages and produce a stable, constant output voltage. Standard regulators require the input voltage be greater than the desired output voltage. Boost converters can output voltages that are higher than the input voltage [29]. There are two factors that affect battery life that are widely exploited in many energy-saving techniques for WSNs. The first factor that affects battery lifetime is the rated capacity factor [30]. Every battery has a rated current capacity specified by the manufacturer. Drawing higher current than the rated value leads to a significant reduction in battery life. Depending on the battery type, the minimum required current consumption of sensor nodes often exceeds the rated current capacity, leading to suboptimal battery lifetime. The second factor that affects battery lifetime is the relaxation factor. The effect of high discharge rates can be minimized through battery relaxation, that is, the cutoff or significant reduction of the discharge of the battery current. This phenomenon enables the battery to recover a portion of its lost capacity. Battery lifetime can be significantly increased if the system is operated such that the current drawn from the battery is frequently reduced to very low values or is completely shut off [31].

Software components encompass the sensor operating system (OS), protocols from the different layers of the WSN stack (application, transport, network, MAC, and physical), and algorithms. All the software components are installed in the MCU memory of the processing subsystem. The protocols from the MAC and physical layers can be alternatively installed in the MCU memory of the radio component.

24.2.2 Sources of Power Dissipation in WSNs

The first step in designing energy-aware and energy-efficient WSNs involves analyzing the power dissipation characteristics of a sensor node. Systematic power analysis of a sensor node is crucial to identify potential energy bottlenecks in the system, which can then be the target of strategies for managing the energy consumption. Of course, the actual energy consumption depends on the specific node hardware. For instance, in Reference 30, it is shown that the power characteristics of a mote-class node are quite different from those of a stargate node. However, the following remarks generally hold [30].

- The communication subsystem has much higher energy consumption than the processing subsystem. It has been shown that transmitting 1 B may

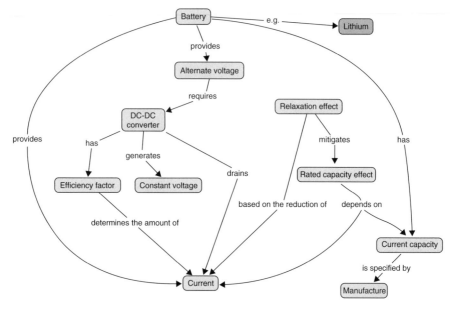

Figure 24.2   WSN battery model concept map.

consume as much as executing a few thousand instructions [32]. Therefore, communication should be traded for computation whenever it is possible.

- The radio energy consumption is of the same order in the reception, transmission, and idle states, while the power consumption drops of at least one order of magnitude in the sleep state. Therefore, the radio should be put to sleep (or turned off) whenever it is possible.
- Depending on the specific application, the sensing subsystem might be another significant source of energy consumption, even greater than the communication subsystem [33].

On the basis of the node architecture presented in Section 24.2.1, and considering the above overall statements about the behavior of energy WSN consumption, now we can describe the sources of power dissipation in each node component. We can divide the power consumption in WSNs into three domains: radio communication, sensing, and data processing (Fig. 24.3).

The communication subsystem is the primary energy consumer from all these three domains. Modern transceivers used in WSNs [29] consume between 15 and 300 mW of power when sending and receiving. There are several factors that affect the power consumption characteristics of a radio transceiver, including the radio duty cycle, modulation scheme, data sending rate (bit rate), and transmission distance. The transmission distance dictates the required transmission power. The farther a signal must travel, more energy has to be used. The relationship between power output and distance traveled is a polynomial with an

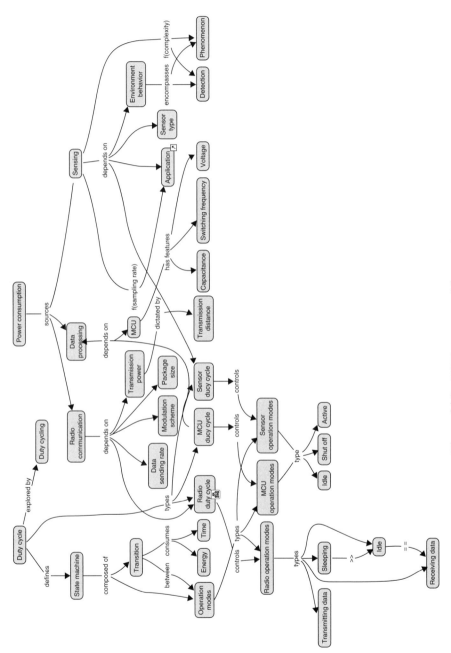

Figure 24.3 WSN energy model concept map.

exponent of between 3 and 4 [34]. The radio operational duty cycle (see more on this subject in Section 24.3.1.1) defines the period of time the radio is active and transmitting or receiving data. An important observation is that transceivers consume approximately the same amount of energy when in receiving or idle mode and that the energy spent in the receiving mode can be of the same order of that in transmitting mode for low power short distance transmissions. The actual power emitted out of the antenna only accounts for a small fraction of the transceiver's energy consumption. A significant fraction goes to internal operation. Because of this, the overall costs of radio communication can easily be dominated by the receiver power consumption. Therefore, it is better to completely shut down the transceiver rather than leave it in the idle mode when it is not transmitting or receiving data. Before and after a transmission/reception, time and energy must be spent to configure and power up the transceiver. So, it is important to amortize the start-up power over more transmitted bits to reduce the power cost per bit of transmissions. One way to decrease the operational duty cycle of the transceiver is by sending multiple bits per symbol. This can be achieved by modulation schemes such as the M-ary modulation [35]. Using M-ary modulation, however, will increase the circuit complexity and power consumption of the radio. In addition, when M-ary modulation is used, the efficiency of the power amplifier is also reduced. This implies that more power will be needed to obtain reasonable levels of transmit output power. A discussion on the use of different modulation schemes for purposes of energy savings is presented in Section 24.3.1.3.

There are several sources of power consumption in the sensing subsystem, including (i) signal sampling and conversion of physical signals to electrical ones, (ii) signal conditioning, and (iii) analog to digital conversion [30]. Another factor that influences the energy consumption is the type of sensor. In general, passive sensors consume negligible power relative to other WSN subsystems. However, active sensors can consume a significant amount of power. Analyzing the power consumption of a sensor, one important factor is how quickly a sensor can be activated, sampled, and deactivated [29]. In most cases, sensors are capable of producing thousands of samples per second. However, the application often requires only a few samples per minute. Therefore, the data sampling rate needs to be tuned so that application requirements are met while energy is not wasted. Besides satisfying the application sampling rate, it is also essential that the sensor is able to enter and exit a low power state quickly. The power consumption of a sensor is equally dependent on the amount of time it takes to read the sensor as it is to the current consumption. For example, if a sensor takes 100 ms to turn on and generate a reading and it consumes just 1 mA at 3 V, it will cost 300 μJ per sample. This is the same amount of energy as a sensor that consumes 1000 mA of current at 3 V but takes just $100\mu s$ to turn on and sample [29]. Moreover, the energy spent with sensing is affected by the complexity of the monitored phenomenon and of the detection process, both being related to the behavior of the environment. Finally, similarly to the radio, the sensing subsystem can also exploit duty cycle mechanisms so that it can remain active only when is necessary to sample data and then soon switching to a power save mode, thus saving energy.

The power consumption of microcontrollers varies greatly according to their processing capabilities. Therefore, the choice of a microcontroller should be dictated by the application requirements to achieve a close match between the performance level offered by the processor and the one demanded by the application. Another significant energy-related feature of microcontrollers is the sleep mode power consumption. The CPU is a major contributor to the power consumption of sensors' idle mode. During idle periods, the CPU will stop execution and enter in a low power sleep state [29], making use of duty cycle mechanisms. The processor only needs to maintain its memory and maintain time synchronization so it can properly wake-up when necessary. Moreover, the power consumption levels of the various modes, the transition costs, and the amount of time spent by the MCU in each mode all have a significant bearing on the total energy consumption (battery lifetime) of the sensor node.

24.3 STRATEGIES FOR ENERGY OPTIMIZATION

In order to effectively reduce the overall power consumption in a WSN and to prolong its lifetime, several strategies need to be used, often simultaneously, at different levels of the network architecture. Akyildiz et al. [18] described the WSN protocol stack as being composed of five protocol layers, consisting of the traditional OSI-ISO protocol stack, and three *management planes*: power, mobility, and task management. The management planes are orthogonal to the protocol layers, and in our survey, we particularly address the *power management plane* that is in charge of managing how the available power is used by the network nodes. This component, included in the concept map in Figure 24.4 as the concept *power management and awareness*, defines a set of policies to guide the behavior of the whole network aiming at minimizing the energy consumption at different levels. Such policies have to consider the generic requirements of any network, such as guaranteeing the connectivity, as well as requirements of the different target applications, and exploiting their specific features. For instance, in event-driven applications, the WSN can be set to spend most of the time in a power-saving mode until the occurrence of an event of interest.

The power-saving policies in a WSN act at different levels: (i) the level of individual node, called *intranode* in our map; (ii) the level representing the communication link between neighboring (often one-hop distant) nodes, called *internode*; and (iii) the level of the entire network, that we called *network wide*. It is important to mention that the intra- and internode levels have a trade-off relation that should be exploited for the purpose of energy saving. Since the communication is the most energy-costly operation in WSNs, it is frequently better to perform as much in-network processing as possible in the sensor data (e.g., by applying some data aggregation operation within the node) in order to decrease the number of transmitted messages, thus trading transmission for processing energy.

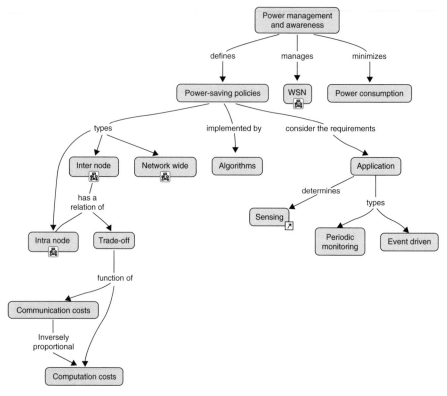

Figure 24.4   Concept map representing the power management in WSN.

The next sections explain in detail the policies belonging to the first two levels. The network-wide level is addressed in Chapter 11.

24.3.1   Intranode Level

Recent advances in the design of ultralow power processors and circuits have enabled the development of ultralow power processors for WSNs [36]. The design of optimized low power processors can contribute to the energy saving in a WSN since it is the core of the system. However, the energy efficiency achieved by the use of techniques for designing low power systems based on fixed hardware platforms is limited, and more significant gains can be obtained by combining such hardware techniques with dynamic power management policies. In this sense, intranode policies for power management are the first step toward an energy-aware and energy-efficient WSN. Such policies encompass hardware and software optimization techniques that exploit the knowledge and behavior of individual sensor nodes.

Most intranode policies are implemented in the node OS, although some of them are implemented at the MAC layer or as algorithms on top of such a layer. We identified four main different enabling techniques to implement the policies at the intranode level (Fig. 24.5): (i) duty cycling, (ii) adaptive sensing, (iii) DVS, and (iv) OS task scheduling. They are described in details in the following sections.

24.3.1.1 *Duty cycling.* The term *duty cycle* is defined as the fraction of time a node is active during its lifetime (Fig. 24.5). One commonly used power management policy is based on turning off hardware components when they are not needed and waking them up whenever necessary, establishing a small duty cycle for the nodes based on events occurring in the monitored environment. Thus, techniques based on duty cycling rely on the fact that active nodes do not need to maintain their radios, processor, and sensing devices continuously on. Whenever there is no interesting activity in the WSN, the nodes can switch off their sensing and processor and put their radio in a low power sleep mode, thus alternating between sleep and wake-up periods. Although the duty cycling technique operates at the level of the individual node, it is exploited by strategies and protocols for energy saving at both the internode and the network-wide levels. Such feature is highlighted in the concept maps by the presence of cross-links, relating the duty cycling concept in the map that represents the intranode policies to this same concept in the maps representing the internode and the data link policies (Chapter 11).

There are several useful operation modes for a WSN node, depending on the number of the states of each individual node component, that is, microprocessor,

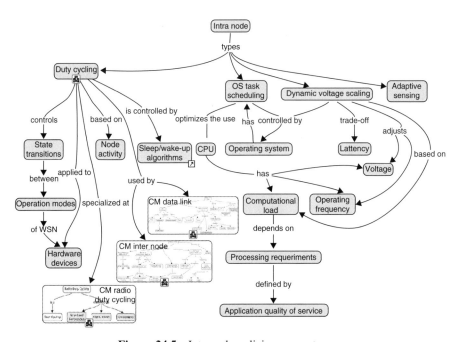

Figure 24.5 Intranode policies concept map.

memory, sensing subsystem, and radio transceiver. Different states are characterized by different amounts of power consumption, and state transitions have a nonnegligible power and time overhead. Policies defining a duty cycling scheme actuate by changing such states, and they can be separately defined for each individual component of the sensor node. From the basic sensor node architecture considered in this chapter, there are three subsystems that can be put into different low power states: the sensing, the communication (radio), and the processing subsystem. However, there are combinations of component states that produce nonuseful operation modes for the sensor node. For instance, it does not make sense to activate the sensing device while keeping the processor turned off, since the environmental data needs to be processed after collected. On the other hand, the sensing subsystem can be put to sleep while the processor is in an active state to perform data fusion operations over data received from neighboring nodes.

Besides considering only operation modes that are useful, there are other concerns to be addressed to define duty cycling policies. First, since it is hard to predict when an event of interest will occur in the future, it is a challenging issue to schedule the activation and deactivation of components so that they are active exactly when they are requested and inactive in the remaining time. Moreover, since the time for start-up components is nonnegligible, operation in a power-saving mode is energy efficient only if the time spent in that mode is greater than a given threshold. It is also important to consider the state of computation when turning components on/off to save energy. The state of the computation represents the state of the application and its restrictions in a given instant of time, which can have a direct influence on decisions taken by a power manager. The start-up delay should also be considered regarding the data accuracy required by the application, since if a sensor takes too long to wake up, such QoS parameter could not be met. Finally, it is also important to consider the state of the neighboring nodes in terms of their radio operation because if a node wakes up to send a message and there is no neighbor to receive it, this could generate a packet lost, thus resulting in energy waste.

Therefore, the core issue in duty-cycling-based policies is deciding the state transition policy of nodes [37], taking into account the current execution states and application requirements. Although duty cycle techniques can be defined without relying on network-wide aspects such as topology or connectivity, since sensor nodes perform collaborative tasks, they need to coordinate their sleep/wake-up periods. Thus, a sleep/wake-up scheduling algorithm is an integral part of any duty cycling policy. It is typically a distributed algorithm (thus we included it in both our intra- and internode maps) that controls which and when sensor node components transition from active to sleep and then back. It allows neighboring nodes to be active at the same time, thus enabling the exchange of packets even when nodes operate with a low duty cycle. The need for taking into account information from different levels in a WSN system (application, radio subsystem, and the node hardware) denotes the cross-layer [38] characteristic of duty cycle policies. Therefore, if further aspects from the network level are considered along with intra- and internode levels, in a cross-layer and integrated approach, more significant gains in energy savings can be achieved.

To enable duty cycle of hardware components, the OS needs to provide a set of primitives to power on and off the sensors [39]. The companion sleep/wake-up scheduling algorithm can be implemented within the MAC protocol or as a protocol on top of the MAC layer. The latter approach allows optimizing functions of medium access based on the specific sleep/wake-up pattern used. On the other hand, independent sleep/wake-up algorithms allow higher flexibility, as they can be tailored to the application requirements and, in principle, be used with any MAC protocol.

In most WSNs, wireless communication is the major source of energy consumption during system operation, thus significant savings can be achieved by an efficient policy of duty cycling applied to the radio subsystem. However, the assumption that data acquisition consumes significantly less energy than data transmission does not hold in several practical applications of WSNs where the power consumption of the sensing activity may be comparable or even greater than that of the radio [33]. So, recent research efforts have being focusing on proposals to optimize the operation of sensing devices as well. The following sections detail approaches for power management based on duty cycling of the radio and the sensing device.

Duty cycling and sleep/wake-up algorithms for the radio subsystem. The most effective policy for energy saving is putting the radio transceiver in the (low power) sleep mode whenever communication is not required [39]. Ideally, the radio should be switched off as soon as there is no data to send/receive and then switched on as soon as a new data packet becomes ready. In this way nodes alternate between active and sleep periods depending on the current network activity. So, sleep/wake-up algorithms for the radio subsystem need to be concerned with the generation of sensing data by the own node as well as with incoming packets generated by neighboring nodes.

As discussed, sleep/wake-up algorithms can be implemented integrated on the MAC protocol or as independent protocols on top of this layer (i.e., at the network or the application layer). We discuss energy-efficient MAC protocols in Chapter 11, so in this section, we focus on independent sleep/wake-up algorithms for the radio subsystem. Such algorithms can be further subdivided into three main categories [40]: on-demand, scheduled rendezvous, and asynchronous schemes (Fig. 24.6).

On-demand algorithms use the most intuitive approach to power management based on sleep/wake-up. The basic idea is that a node should wake up only when another node wants to communicate with it. This approach can significantly minimize energy consumption, being particularly suitable for event-driven WSN applications with a very low duty cycle (e.g., fire detection, surveillance of machine failures). In such scenarios, sensor nodes remain most of the time in a monitoring state, only passively sensing the environment, until the detection of an event of interest that then triggers the nodes' transition to a data transmission state. From the three considered categories, on-demand algorithms can potentially achieve the maximum energy saving, since nodes keep active only for the minimum time required for communication while ensuring a low latency as the target node wakes up immediately when it detects a waiting message.

The main problem associated with on-demand algorithms is how to inform the sleeping node that a node needs to communicate with it. The implementation of such schemes typically requires two different channels: a data channel and a wake-up channel. Although it would be possible to use a single radio with two different channels, existent proposals [41, 42] rely on two different radios in order to prevent deferring the transmission of signal on the wake-up channel if a packet transmission is in progress on the other channel, thus reducing the wake-up latency [39]. So, the on-demand approach has the practical drawback of the additional cost for the second radio. Another drawback is the possible mismatch between the coverage of the two radios.

An alternative solution is the use of a *scheduled rendezvous approach*. The basic idea behind such schemes is that each node should wake up at the same time as its neighbors. Typically, nodes wake up periodically according to a wake-up schedule and remain active for a short time interval to communicate with their neighbors. After this time, they go to sleep until the next rendezvous time. The main advantage of such schemes is that when a node is awake it is guaranteed that all its neighbors are awake as well. This allows sending broadcast messages to all neighbors [40]. As a drawback, scheduled rendezvous schemes require that nodes are synchronized in order to wake up at the same time. Clock synchronization in WSN has been the focus of extensive research. The reader can refer to References 43 and 44 for detailed surveys on time synchronization techniques. In the following, we assume that nodes are synchronized using some existent synchronization protocol.

Proposals of scheduled rendezvous protocols differ in the way nodes sleep and wake up during their lifetime. The simplest way is using a fully synchronized pattern [45], in which all nodes in the network wake up at the same time according to a periodic pattern. Owing to its simplicity, this scheme is used in several practical implementations including TinyDB [46] and TASK [47]. Although simple, this scheme allows a low duty cycle provided that the active time is significantly smaller than the wake-up period. A further improvement can be achieved by allowing nodes to switch off their radio when no activity is detected for at least

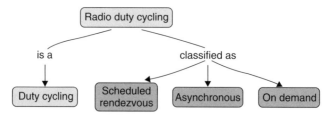

Figure 24.6 Concept map representing the radio duty cycling taxonomy.

a time-out value [48]. The main drawback of fully synchronized approaches is that all nodes become active at the same time after a long sleep period and thus try to transmit simultaneously (generally, these schemes assume that an underlying contention-based MAC protocol is used for data transfer), generating a high number of collisions. In addition, such a scheme is not very flexible since the size of wake-up and active periods is fixed and does not adapt to variations in the traffic pattern and/or network topology.

Some sleep/wake-up schemes take advantage of the internal network organization (controlled by routing protocols) by specifying active times of different nodes according to their position in the routing tree. Although the routing tree can suffer frequent changes, both for purposes of load balance and because of the presence of faulty nodes, under the assumption that nodes are static, it remains stable for a reasonable amount of time [49] so that sleep/wake-up algorithms can exploit its features. In the staggered wake-up pattern [45], nodes located at different levels of the data-gathering tree wake up at different times. The active parts of different levels of the tree are arranged in such way that the fraction of active period a node uses to receive packets from its children is adjacent to the fraction it uses to send packets to its parent, thus minimizing the energy dissipation while transitioning from sleep to active mode [39]. The staggered wake-up pattern is also called the *backward staggered pattern* [45], as it optimizes packet latency in the backward direction, that is, from leaf nodes to the root. Such direction is the common pattern of data flow in WSNs, where data is generated by multiple sources (sensor nodes) and sent to typically one sink node. The (backward) staggered scheme was first proposed in the framework of TinyDB [46] and TAG [50].

According to Anastasi et al. [39], in comparison with the fully synchronized approach, the staggered scheme has several advantages. First, since nodes at different levels of the data-routing tree wake up at different times, at a given time, only a (small) subset of nodes in the network will be active. Thus, the number of collisions is potentially lower. For the same reason, the active period of each node can be significantly shortened with respect to the fully synchronized scheme, thus resulting in higher energy savings. On the other hand, the staggered scheme has some drawbacks in common with the fully synchronized scheme. One of them is that such a scheme has limited flexibility due to the fixed duration of the active and wake-up periods. The active period is often the same for all nodes in the network, and ideally, it should be as low as possible not only for energy saving but also for minimizing the latency experienced by packets to reach the root node. In addition, since nodes located at different levels of the data-gathering tree manage different amounts of data, active periods should be sized on an individual basis. Finally, even assuming static nodes, topology changes and variations in the traffic patterns are still possible. The active period of nodes should thus adapt dynamically to such variations.

Motivated by the aforementioned drawbacks of adopting a fixed duration for wake-up periods, an adaptive and low latency staggered scheme is proposed in References 50 and 51. By setting the length of the active period to the minimum value consistently with the current network activity, this adaptive scheme not only minimizes the energy consumption but also provides lower average packet latency in comparison to a fixed staggered scheme. In addition, by allowing different lengths of the active period for nodes belonging to the same level, but associated with different parents, it also reduces the number of collisions. Additional approaches for scheduled rendezvous sleep/wake-up algorithms can be found in Reference 39.

The third type of sleep/wake-up algorithms is the *asynchronous algorithms*. These algorithms allow each node to wake up independent of the others by guaranteeing that neighbors always have overlapped active periods within a specified number of cycles. This goal is achieved by properties implied in the sleep/wake-up scheme, thus no explicit information exchange is needed among nodes. Asynchronous wake-up schemes have been explored in the context of ad hoc networks [52, 53] and several existent approaches can be successfully used in WSNs.

As a final remark, while power-saving policies based on radio duty cycling can provide significant energy gains, it is important to consider that sensor nodes communicate using short data packets. The shorter the packets, the higher the dominance of start-up energy [18]. Hence, such policies need to be carefully used to get the maximum lifetime of a sensor node. In fact, if, for instance, the radio is blindly turned off during each idling slot, over a period of time, we might end up expending more energy than if the radio had been left on.

Duty cycling of sensing devices. Duty cycling technique applied to the sensing device consists of waking up the sensorial system only for the time needed to acquire a new set of samples and powering it off immediately after. This strategy allows energy savings provided that the dynamics of the phenomenon to be monitored are time invariant and known in advance [33]. Such hypotheses hold mainly for periodical monitoring applications. For periodic sensing applications, the (fixed) sampling rate is computed a priori, based on partial available information about the process to be monitored and assuming that the process dynamics are stationary. In this case, all the sensors in the WSN can be configured to wake up according to the defined sensing intervals, acquire the data with the defined rate, and then go to sleep until the next interval. For event-driven applications, in which the monitored phenomenon has an unpredictable behavior, the duty cycle technique still can be used, but in a very application-specific way and coordinated with a topology control scheme (see more in Chapter 11). In this case, some nodes can be configured to be in a sleep mode for a given time interval, provided the WSN assures a degree of sensing coverage enough to enable the detection of an event of interest. There are event-driven applications with less astringent time requirements; for instance, in an application for flooding detection, a delay of 2 min in detecting a potential flooding is not critical. Other applications, as for instance intrusion detection, are time critical, and any delay in the event detection cannot be tolerated. So, besides the coverage degree, the specific time requirements of the application need to be considered when defining a policy for duty cycle in event-driven scenarios.

To enable duty cycle of sensing devices, the OS needs to provide a set of primitives to power on and off the sensors. Such primitives would be used by the power management policies. Moreover, several aspects must be considered to ensure an effective handling of the duty cycle policy, failing which might result in invalid acquired data and/or energy dissipation larger than that associated with the always-on mode.

Each sensor is characterized by a set of functional characteristics, for example, wake-up latency and break-even cycle, that affect the energy management of the sensor. The wake-up latency is the time required by the sensor to generate a correct value once activated. Clearly, if the sensor reading is performed before the wake-up latency has elapsed, the acquired data is not valid. The break-even cycle is defined as the rate at which the power consumption of a node with a power management policy is equal to that of not-power-managed node. Such value is in inverse proportion to the power consumption overhead introduced by the non-ideal on/off sensor transition and represents the highest sampling rate for which applying a power management is worth. Moreover, the break-even cycle is not fixed since the energy consumed by the sensor during normal operations and in on–off transitions depends on the supply voltage, which changes over time [54]. Therefore, in order to achieve an effective sensor-specific energy management, the OS drivers should be designed by using, at least, information about wake-up latency and break-even cycle [54].

24.3.1.2 Adaptive sensing.

As aforementioned, in periodic monitoring applications, the sensor sampling rate can be predefined according to a previous overall knowledge of the behavior of the monitored phenomenon. As a consequence, and to assure the accuracy required by the application, such rate is often larger than necessary (oversampling), resulting in energy wasting. A better approach would be to adopt an adaptive sensing strategy in which sensors would sample the environment using a rate dynamically adapted, according to the actual and current dynamics of the monitored phenomenon. By reducing the number of samples generated by the sensors, an efficient sensing strategy also reduces the amount of data to be processed and possibly transmitted by sensors, thus generating further energy savings. Adaptive sensing and sensor duty cycling are complementary approaches that can be used in combination to reduce the energy consumed by a sensor. The concept map in Figure 24.7 shows a taxonomy for current adaptive sensing strategies proposed in Reference 33.

Hierarchical sensing assumes that multiple sensing devices are installed on sensor nodes, each presenting its own accuracy and power dissipation and observing the same event. In most cases, simple and energy-efficient sensors are used to provide coarser readings or trigger an event. Advanced, more complex sensors give more accurate readings of the physical property at the cost of greater energy consumption. The idea behind hierarchical sensing techniques is to dynamically select which of the available sensors must be activated by trading off accuracy for energy conservation [33]. An example of hierarchical sensing applied to fire emergency management is presented in Reference 55. In this example, the WSN field is equipped with static sensors that monitor the environment. When the static nodes detect an anomaly in a given area, for instance, the occurrence of high temperatures, they inform such event to the base station. As a consequence, the base station sends a mobile sensor unit, equipped with more sophisticated sensors, to investigate the event. After collecting the necessary data, the mobile sensor unit returns to the base station and reports the acquired data.

A different hierarchical sensing approach for object detection is presented in Reference 56. Sensors are equipped with CMOS (complementary metal-oxide semiconductor) camera modules that are configured to provide low resolution images to reduce energy consumption. If potential targets are detected by image processing, the cameras are reconfigured to a fine-grained, high quality mode and object detection is performed by images collected by the reconfigured cameras. After this process, the cameras are configured back to the power-saving low resolution operation.

Adaptive sampling strategies dynamically adapt the sampling rate based on spatial and/or temporal correlations between the sensed data. Spatial correlation tries to reduce the energy-sensing consumption exploring the fact that measurements taken by sensor nodes that are spatially close to each other do not differ significantly. On the other hand, temporal correlations are based on the idea that if the monitored phenomenon evolves slowly with time so that subsequent samples do not differ very much, it is possible to reduce the sampling rate without any loss of relevant information. Both correlations can be combined to further reduce the number of samples to be acquired. Examples of spatial correlation are described in References 57 and 58. Dai-Hua and Wei-Hsin [58] explored spatial correlation to reduce the number of nodes used to send data to the sink. A spatial Correlation-Based Collaborative MAC (CC-MAC) protocol is proposed to regulate access and prevent redundant transmissions from close sensors. An iterative node selection algorithm, which runs at the sink node, computes a correlation radius based on the maximum distortion tolerable by the application. This information is then broadcasted to sensor nodes during the network setup. During the operational phase, the CC-MAC protocol prevents the transmission of redundant information by selecting a single node within an area determined by the correlation radius to transmit its data to the sink. Examples of temporal correlation are described in References 59 and 60. The approach described

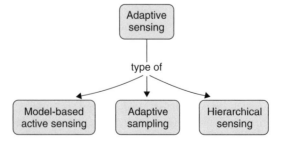

Figure 24.7 Concept map representing the strategies for adaptive sensing.

in Reference 60 dynamically adjusts the sampling rate collectively. Sensors are allowed to autonomously adjust the sampling rate depending on the (estimated) data stream characteristics, provided such sampling rate is within a specified range. If the desired modification in the sampling rate is more than that allowed by the range, a new sampling interval is requested from the sink. The estimation of the future values of a stream is computed using a Kalman filter based on the previously gathered data. Large prediction errors denote unexpected behavior of the streaming data or an interesting event. The sampling interval is adjusted based on the prediction error. At the sink node, new sampling intervals are allocated to the requesting sensors based on the available bandwidth, network contention, and streaming source priority [60]. Since the computational load is high, the algorithm is executed at the base station and the new estimated sampling rates are sent to each sensor node. It is important to note that when using adaptive sampling, data losses introduced by the sensor network cannot be tolerated, and 100% reliability is required in the communication from sensor nodes to the sink. This can be achieved by using retransmissions of missed data, forward error correction (FEC), and multipath routing techniques. All these techniques increase the percentage of data correctly delivered to the sink at the cost of additional energy consumed by the radio [33].

Model-based active sensing uses forecasting models to build an abstraction of the sensed phenomenon. The forecasting model is built with an initial set of sampled data. Then, the model is used to predict the data instead of performing a continuous sampling in the field. Therefore, the energy dissipated for data sensing and transmission is saved. To verify the accuracy of the model, actual data needs to be sensed from time to time. Whenever the requested data accuracy is not satisfied, the model is updated to meet the new dynamics of the observed phenomenon. The effectiveness of this approach is bound by both the accuracy of the model and the nature of the observed phenomenon. Examples of model-based active sensing are presented in References 60–62. The approach described in Reference 62 uses a limited-window linear regression model to forecast samples. Whenever the predicted value falls outside the confidence interval, the sampling frequency is increased up to a predefined maximum value while the model is updated. If the prediction lies within the confidence interval, the sampling frequency is decreased by a given factor, unless a minimum predefined frequency is reached. The proposal described in Reference 62 also encompasses a routing protocol that makes decisions integrating both sensing and communication tasks in order to save further energy. According to the protocol, sensors that are not forwarding data can perform additional sampling, and routes in which data is sampled with lower frequency are preferred to routes in which nodes spend more energy for sampling.

24.3.1.3 *Dynamic voltage scale (DVS).* While shutdown techniques can save energy by turning off idle components, additional savings can be achieved by optimizing the sensor node performance in the active state [63, 64]. DVS is a technique that enables intelligent trade-offs between energy consumption and

operational fidelity [65]. The DVS technique aims at adjusting the voltage and the operating frequency of the node CPU based on its computational load and taking into account the instantaneous processing requirements defined by the quality of service requested by the application. Most microprocessor-based systems have a time-varying computational load, and hence, peak system performance is not always required. DVS exploits this fact by dynamically adapting the processor's supply voltage and operating frequency to just meet the instantaneous processing requirement, thus trading off unutilized performance for energy savings. DVS-based power management, when applicable, has been shown to have significantly higher energy efficiency compared to shutdown-based power management because of the convex nature of the energy–speed curve [66].

The utilization of DVS technique requires consideration of time constraints because the changes in operating frequency interfered with the computation time given a fixed computation workload [21]. Hence, a scheduling algorithm is usually accompanied with DVS technique to guarantee the time constraint, especially in real-time applications. Researchers have worked on scheduling algorithms for using DVS in different applications. In References 67 and 68, real-time scheduling of computation tasks for a sensor node was proposed to reduce energy consumption in computing stochastic computational tasks. In Reference 5, DVS was used to achieve an energy-efficient WSN for dynamic system monitoring of large-scale and capital-intensive machines. Several modern processors such as Intel StrongARM and Intel PXA271 (used in the Imote2 sensor node) support scaling of voltage and frequency to provide energy efficiency to the system.

24.3.1.4 OS task scheduling. The OS is ideally suitable to implement power management policies, since it has global knowledge of the performance and fidelity requirements of all the applications, and can directly control the underlying hardware resources, fine tuning the available performance-energy controls. At the core of the OS is a task scheduler, which is responsible for scheduling a given set of tasks to run on the system while ensuring that timing constraints are satisfied. System lifetime can be considerably increased by incorporating energy awareness into the task scheduling process [69, 70].

The energy-aware real-time scheduling algorithm proposed in Reference 69 exploits two observations about the operating scenario of wireless systems to provide an adaptive power versus fidelity trade-off. The first observation is that these systems are inherently designed to operate resiliently in the presence of varying fidelity in the form of data losses and errors over wireless links. This ability to adapt to changing fidelity is used to trade-off against energy. Second, these systems exhibit significant correlated variations in computation and communication processing load because of the underlying time-varying physical phenomena. This observation is exploited to proactively manage energy resources by predicting processing requirements. The voltage is set according to predicted computation requirements of individual task instances, and adaptive feedback control is used to keep the system fidelity (e.g., timing violations) within the application specifications.

24.3.2 Internode Level

The internode level policies actuate on the communication link between neighboring nodes, and they are based on three main techniques (Fig. 24.8): (i) adapting the transmission power of radios, (ii) DMS, and (iii) optimizations at the link layer. Besides these techniques, sleep/wake-up algorithms, which are a companion of duty cycle polices and were already explained in Section 24.3.1.1 are also included in this level.

24.3.2.1 Transmission power control. In a wireless channel, the electromagnetic wave propagation can be modeled as a power law function that depends on the distance between the transmitter and receiver. Independent of which propagation model is used (e.g., free space model, two-ray ground, shadowing [71]), the received power decreases with the distance. Considering that a primary requirement of all networks is to have connectivity among the participating nodes, the level of connectivity in wireless networks depends on the transmission power of the nodes. If the transmit power is too small, the network might be disconnected (i.e., there may be multiple disconnected clusters of nodes instead of a single overall connected network). However, as we mentioned in Section 24.2.2, the energy spent in radio transmissions is proportional to the distance (and the transmission power). Therefore, transmitting at excessively high power is inefficient in terms of energy. Moreover, it is inefficient because of the mutual interference in the shared radio channel [72]. Thus, it is intuitively clear that the optimal transmit power is the minimum power sufficient to guarantee network connectivity [73–75].

To provide system designers with the ability to dynamically control the transmission power, the radio hardware of most sensor platforms provides a register to specify the transmission power level at runtime. For instance, the CC2420 radio in Crossbow MicaZ motes provides 32 transmission levels

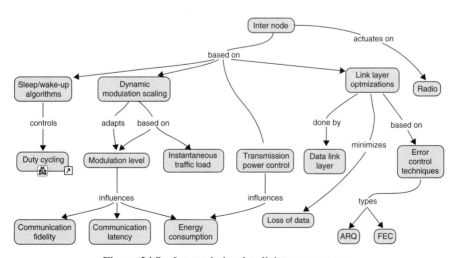

Figure 24.8 Internode level policies concept map.

ranging from -25 to 0 dBm output, while the SensiumTMplatform supports 8 levels ranging from -23 to -7 dBm output. So, it is feasible and desirable to specify the minimum transmission power level that achieves both the required connectivity and communication reliability while saving power and increasing the system lifetime [76]. Power control refers to techniques that adapt the transmission power level to optimize a single wireless transmission. Algorithms for transmission power control (known as *TPC*) have been proposed to make the communication between transmitter and receiver at the needed minimum power, prolonging the network lifetime. The research in this area is not new since this issue was extensively addressed in the context of wireless networks (mobile and ad hoc). Recent works have investigated this issue in the specific context of WSNs.

Several solutions for TPC in multihop wireless networks use a single transmission power for the whole network [77], thus not fully exploiting the capacity of setting the transmission power provided by the radio hardware to reduce energy consumption. Other works assume that each node chooses a single transmission power for all its neighbors [78], while others assume that nodes use different transmission powers for different neighbors [79]. However, in spite of being a more complex solution, to achieve the maximum possible power savings, the ideal solution is to adjust the transmission power of a node on a link-by-link basis. Indeed, Gomez and Campbell [80] analyzed the benefits of TPC in wireless multihop networks and showed that per-link range adjustments outperform global range transmission adjustments by 50% in terms of power savings. These results indicate that such approach is the most suitable for WSNs.

Lin et al. [76] proposed ATPC, an adaptive TPC algorithm for WSNs. ATPC achieves good values for the average energy consumption in transmission when compared with other approaches. The algorithm is based on dynamically adjusting the transmission power through on-demand feedback packets. Such packets report information about the current quality of the link and are used to build a model for each neighbor of a given node. ATPC tunes the transmission power according to changes in the quality of monitored links. One drawback of this proposal is its high memory consumption. Another proposal that considers a per-link TPC is presented in Reference 81, where two TPC protocols for WSNs are proposed, which can be embedded into any existing MAC protocol. The first one (called *Hybrid*) calculates the ideal transmission power using a closed control loop that iterates over the available transmission powers in order to maintain a target link quality. The second one (called *AEWMA*) determines the ideal transmission power based on the reception power, transmission power, and average noise. Experimental evaluation showed that the proposed algorithms were able to decrease the energy consumption by up to 57% in comparison with B-MAC the standard MAC protocol of the Mica 2 platform, thus illustrating in terms of energy the improvements such TPC techniques can achieve.

24.3.2.2 Dynamic modulation scaling.
As we have seen in Section 24.3.2.1, the radio technology used in the wireless link between sensor

nodes plays an important role in the energy management of WSNs. At this level, DMS is another emerging hardware technique that has been used in a similar way as DVS to reduce energy consumption, in this case, trading energy with transmission delay and communication fidelity. DMS technique consists of dynamically adapting the modulation level of the radio to match the instantaneous traffic load, as part of the radio power management. The concept of changing modulation level on the fly to save the communication energy was first proposed by Schurgers et al. in 2001 [82].

Multilevel (M-ary) modulation is the key aspect of DMS [83]. In an M-ary modulation, M is the number of levels or symbols used for modulation purpose such that $M = 2^b$, where b indicates the number of bits per symbol and is known as the *constellation size*. For transmitting a data packet of size S, the total transmission time is determined by the used symbol rate RS and the modulation level. The symbol rate RS specifies the number of symbols transmitted per unit time, while the modulation level denotes the number of bits that defines a symbol, thus the multiplication of RS and b gives the actual data rate used to compute the transmission time. As the constellation size b increases, power consumed by hardware as well as output power increases. So, for a particular transmission system, the value of b should be optimized for each specific symbol rate. The energy consumption in data transmission is proportional to the transmission data rate. Increasing the constellation size b increases the energy consumed for transmission; however, more number of bits is transmitted per symbol, thus increasing the data rate and as a consequence resulting in fast transmission and reduced delay. This is the trade-off that algorithms for DMS need to manage.

Significant research has been done on scheduling algorithms for DMS to provide significant energy savings while meeting the required time constraints. Several works have analyzed DMS along with other techniques for energy efficiency at the MAC or the network levels [63, 84, 85]. Yu e al. [63] provided algorithmic solutions to the problem of scheduling packet transmission for data gathering in WSNs by exploring modulation scaling. In Reference 85, a control scheme was proposed using modulation scaling to minimize energy consumption while ensuring application requirements. Yeh [21] investigated reconfiguration techniques that enable the WSN hardware to adapt its energy consumption to external dynamics through the integrated use of DVS, DMS, and additional techniques at the network-wide level. Since DVS and DMS techniques trade energy savings against the computation and communication time, respectively, the author claims that when only limited time is available for the sensor node, it becomes critical to allocate the time resource for minimizing the total energy consumption. Therefore, a time allocation mechanism, called *dynamic time allocation* (DTA), was also developed in order to determine the optimal share of computation time and transmission time subject to the time constraint. The use of DVS, DMS, and DTA, along with an efficient scheme for node activation, achieved an energy reduction of up to 50%, thus demonstrating the potential of such techniques to prolong the WSN lifetime.

24.3.2.3 Link layer optimizations. Strategies for achieving energy efficiency at the level of the data link layer encompass both the solutions that address the network as a whole and the solutions that act in a link-by-link base. The first type is classified in the network-wide category according to our concept map. Such strategies include solutions for managing the network logic topology, by selectively activating subsets of nodes while putting others to sleep, and efficient algorithms for the MAC sublayer; they are described in Chapter 11. However, in this section, we briefly discuss some strategies that actuate at the level of the link layer but are more concerned with the communicating link between neighboring nodes, instead of considering the whole network. In this sense, mechanisms for data reliability, including techniques for error detection and correction, can be exploited for purposes of energy savings. Even when not explicitly aiming at increasing the WSN energy efficiency, link layer techniques play an indirect role in reducing energy consumption. The use of a good error control scheme minimizes the number of times a packet is retransmitted, thus reducing the power consumed at both the transmitter and the receiver.

Energy-efficient error control. Several WSN applications, for instance, medical, surveillance, and target tracking applications, require data to be transmitted with high reliability. There are several challenges involved in achieving reliability on WSNs. First of all, wireless communication channels are typically characterized by high error rates. Channels in WSNs are often unreliable, with high probability of introducing bursts of errors, and are susceptible to further problems such as the hidden terminal problems and dynamic changes in connectivity. Moreover, the wireless channel is nonstationary, and the channel bit error rate (BER) varies over time.

A second challenge concerns the fact that a same WSN can be used (sometime simultaneously) for several applications, demanding different types of sensor data and with different QoS requirements. The last challenge is the fact that sensor node resources are severely restricted. WSN nodes have limited power source, computational power, and memory space, and thus, the algorithm to achieve reliability should not be computationally or storage intensive [86].

To deal with the typically high error rate and to increase the apparent quality of a wireless communication channel, the two commonly used techniques in the data link layer are automatic repeat request (ARQ) and FEC. FEC uses error correcting codes to combat bit errors by adding redundant bits to information packets before they are transmitted [87]. This redundancy is used by the receiver to detect and correct errors. On the other hand, ARQ provides only error detection capability and makes no attempt to correct any erroneous packets received, instead it is requested that the packets received in error be retransmitted.

FEC and ARQ are two basic categories of error control techniques. The advantages of ARQ are its relative simplicity, reasonable throughput levels, and no overhead in a nonerror scenario. Its main disadvantages are the retransmitting costs in terms of huge delays and energy whenever an error occurs. Considering the high probability of errors in WSNs and also the fact that packet transmission is one of the most energy-costly operations performed by a sensor node, retransmitting packets has to be done as few times as possible. The main advantage of FEC is that since there are no retransmissions, there are no time delays in the message flows (or only a bound small delay, considering the encoding and decoding operations) [86]. A disadvantage is that the postdecoding error rate rapidly increases with increasing channel error rate. In order to obtain high system reliability, several error patterns must be corrected, thus requiring a powerful code, making the codec hard to implement and imposing a high transmission overhead. When the error correcting code is not strong enough to correct the error and recover the data, packets can get lost. In order to overcome their individual drawbacks, the combination of these two basic classes of error control schemes, called *hybrid ARQ schemes*, has been developed [87].

ARQ, FEC, and other mechanisms to detect and correct errors in the data link layer are typically static. Moreover, most reliability protocols use a single loss recovery algorithm for all nodes and applications in the network [88]. Although such a static and uniform approach for dealing with errors is very straightforward, it has several drawbacks, mainly when applied in wireless network environments. For instance, in a static FEC scheme, in order to guarantee a given QoS requirement, the worst case needs to be considered for the characteristics of a channel. As a consequence, FEC techniques are associated with unnecessary overhead that reduces throughput when the error rate in the channel is above the worst case. According to Ahn et al. [89], the deterministic selection of the appropriate FEC code size degrades the performance by mismatching the FEC strength to the underlying channel BER. When the channel BER widely varies, which is the case in WSNs, the amount of FEC codes should be dynamically adapted for further performance improvement.

Regarding the uniformity treatment, nodes and applications in a WSN may have diversified features, constraints, and requirements, thus a more flexible approach to deal with errors is needed to optimize the energy efficiency.

Therefore, in the context of energy-efficient WSNs, techniques for error detection and correction must be adaptive to the changing conditions of the wireless medium as well as to the different requirements of applications and characteristics of individual nodes. Moreover, mechanisms such as FEC and ARQ have inherent overheads (due to either retransmissions or the increase in the packet size), so they need to be carefully used in order to really achieve gains in energy saving. Trade-offs should be exploited whenever possible. In the case of FEC, for instance, the so-called coding gain can be traded off to improve the BER at a given transmission energy or to increase energy efficiency for a given BER.

Ahn et al. [89] initially analyzed the traffic behavior in the WSN wireless channel and arrived at some important conclusions about the error rates. The performed measurements showed that average BER per second (ABERPS) or average BER per minute (ABERPM) fluctuate continually from 0 to 10^{-3}, even though ABERPS changes more abruptly than ABERPM. The traffic analysis also indicates that the ABERPM at a given time differs from the next ABERPM only by 30% in maximum. According to the authors, these two observations imply that once a dynamic FEC algorithm dynamically chooses the appropriate FEC code size, matching to the slowly varying channel status, it can significantly improve the performance over these wireless channels. So they proposed the adaptive FEC code control (AFECCC) algorithm that adjusts the FEC code size based on the channel status. The proposed algorithm uses the arrival of acknowledgment packets as an indicator of the channel state. Using such indicator, the algorithm selects from different, predefined, discrete number of FEC levels. The stay time on each level before dropping to the lower one is dynamically decided in proportion to its previous success rate. The more frequently AFECCC adopts a level, the longer it stays at this level. They performed experiments modeling the wireless channels by a two-state Markov chain and using packet traces collected from real sensor networks. The results of the performed simulations confirmed that the proposed algorithm performs better (in terms of throughput) than any static FEC algorithms and two dynamic hybrid ARQ/FEC algorithms: the link adaptation incremental redundancy (LA-IR) II and the retrace recursive LA-IR (described in Reference 90). On the basis of the total transmission overhead over the entire BER range, the authors believe that AFECCC is more energy efficient than the static FEC and LA-IR algorithms, even though it executes around some tens of instructions per packet. However, they did not directly measure the energy consumption in their experiments.

The work by Agarwal et al. [86] directly addresses the energy efficiency in the proposed approach for error control in WSNs. Moreover, the different types of sensing data handled by such networks were taken into account. An adaptive and universal codec (encoder/decoder) was presented, which can process the information on various kinds of sensed data. Also, adaptive coding schemes that involve different codes are used to take advantage of the variations in the wireless channel conditions. The proposed FEC scheme is called *Adaptive Universal FEC* (AuFEC) and it is based on the Reed–Solomon codec. The authors adopt a hardware/software codesign methodology to efficiently implement the codec. The results of the implementation of the proposed system on *wireless motes* showed that up to 56% of power savings could be achieved with less than 4% overhead of the running system costs. Therefore, their proposal effectively contributes to increasing the energy efficiency in a WSN.

Meer et al. [91] present a solution for error control in WSN that adopts a very interesting and holistic approach. Indeed, such solution could fit better in the classification of network-wide solutions (Chapter 11), but we retain it here since its goal is the same as the other works presented in this section. The proposed scheme is classified as an adaptive error control (AEC), since they use different hybrid ARQ schemes, based on a set of variables gathered from the environment. In their proposal, they exploit several intrinsic and specific features of WSNs to make energy-efficient decisions about the error control technique to be used. More specifically, they adopt a data-centric approach and consider three features of WSN to assign each packet a value that denotes its importance in the networks. Such features are the multihop data routing, the in-network data aggregation, and the data redundancy, typical of WSNs. By adopting a data-centric approach, each node can decide for itself which error control scheme to apply, based on the content of a data packet (and its assignee "value"). Meer et al. [91] described a way of determining the importance of a packet (a scheme called *packet importance valuation* (PIV)) and also a way to decide when to apply which error control scheme. Regarding the value assigned to each packet, the first parameter to consider is that when using a multihop routing, a packet gets more important if it has traversed more nodes (hops) in its path toward the sink node. Therefore, it should receive different error control treatment along the path. The amount of energy spent in error control should compensate for the amount of energy wasted if the packet gets lost. Regarding data aggregation, the importance value of a packet carrying data that already suffered aggregation should be increased in detriment of packets containing individual (raw) data. Finally, regarding the data redundancy (a feature that they addressed as the *N-out-of-K Principle*), the authors claim that since several neighboring sensors often monitor a common phenomenon, the lost of some packets will not compromise the final reliability of data delivered to the application. According to the authors, it is intuitive that a packet containing information that N other sensors are also measuring and reporting is less important than a packet from a sensor with only $N/2$ other sensors measuring the same variable. Therefore, the importance of a packet should be increased when there are fewer other sensors available measuring the same environmental variables. Using the proposed approach, nodes can apply a severe error control scheme to packets that contain important information, that is, packets that have aggregated data, packets that already traversed a number of nodes, which means that a certain amount of energy was already invested, while packets that contain less vital information will have a simpler form of error control. They performed a set of experiments, in different conditions, and the results showed that for scenarios with high error rate (22.5%), which are most frequent in WSNs, the proposal performed much better than using only an ARQ scheme. Where the only-ARQ setting consumed about 17000 energy units in the single bit error situation, the PIV consumed around 7000 energy units, which is less than half the energy used for only-ARQ. The conclusion of their work is that only-ARQ has a very high reliability but consumes a lot of energy, whereas not using error control does not use a lot of energy but cannot guarantee a reasonable high level of reliability. The solutions provided by the use of PIV are somewhere halfway. They guarantee a more reasonable level of reliability while consuming less energy than only-ARQ.

24.4   FINAL REMARKS

The importance of managing energy in a clever way is the most crucial issue in the WSNs domain. In this chapter, we presented and discussed several of the current techniques for managing the energy efficiency and awareness in such environment. It was not our goal to exhaust the theme since the range of possible solutions is huge and encompasses distinct layers of software as well as components of hardware, involving knowledge from different expertise. New solutions are arising and existent ones are being enhanced every moment. So, we hope to have achieved the main purpose of organizing the various approaches in a didactic way, thus providing an initial road map to understand the field and perform further investigations.

ACKNOWLEDGMENTS

This work is partially supported by the National Council for Scientific and Technological Development and by CAPES through processes 201090/2009-0 and 477229/2009-3 for Flávia C. Delicato and 480359/2009-1 and 4073-09-06 for Paulo F. Pires.

REFERENCES

1. Xu N, Rangwala S, Chintalapudi KK, Ganesan D, Broad A, Govindan R, Estrin D. A wireless sensor network for structural monitoring. In: Proceedings of the ACM SenSys; 2004 Nov; Baltimore (MD).

2. Mainwaring A, Culler D, Polastre J, Szewczyk R, Anderson J. Wireless sensor networks for habitat monitoring. In: Proceedings of the 1st ACM International Workshop on Wireless Sensor Networks and Applications; 2002 Sept; Atlanta (GA). pp. 88–97.

3. Liu T, Sadler CM, Zhang P, Martonosi M. Implementing software on resource-constrained mobile sensors: experiences with Impala and ZebraNet. In: Proceedings of the International Conference on Mobile Systems, Applications, and Services; 2004; Boston (MA).

4. Werner-Allen G, Lorincz K, Johnson J, Lees J, Welsh M. Fidelity and yield in a volcano monitoring sensor network. In: Proceedings of the 7th Symposium on Operating Systems Design and Implementation; 2006 Nov 06–08; Seattle (WA). pp. 381–396.

5. Gao R, Fan Z. Architectural design of a sensory-node-controller for optimized energy utilization in sensor networks. IEEE Trans Instrum Meas 2006; 55(2): 415–428.

6. Arora A, Dutta P, Bapat S, Kulathumani V, Zhang H, Naik V, Mittal V, Cao H, Demirbas M, Gouda M, Choi Y, Herman T, Kulkarni S, Arumugam U, Nesterenko M, Vora A, Miyashita M. A line in the sand: a wireless sensor network for target detection, classification, and tracking. Comput Netw 2004; 46: 605–634.

7. Shnayder V. Chen B, Lorincz K, Thaddeus RF, Jones F, Welsh M. Sensor networks for medical care. In Proceedings of the 3rd international conference on Embedded networked sensor systems. New York: SenSys '05. ACM; 2005. pp. 314–314.

8. Chen M-X, Hu C-C, Weng W-Y. Dynamic object tracking tree in wireless sensor network. EURASIP J Wireless Commun Netw 2010, Volume 2010, Article ID 386319, pp. 1–8.

9. Polastre J, Szewczyk R, Culler D. Telos: enabling ultra-low power wireless research. In: Proceedings of the 4th International Symposium of Information Processing in Sensor Networks; 2005; Los Angeles (CA). pp. 370–375.

10. SUN SPOT web site. Available at http://www.sunspotworld.com/. Accessed 2010 Oct 10.

11. Hill J, Culler D. Mica: a wireless platform for deeply embedded networks. IEEE Micro 2002; 22(6): 12–24.

12. Lin C, Xiong N, Park JH, Kim T. Dynamic power management in new architecture of wireless sensor networks. Int J Commun Syst 2009; 22(6): 671–693.

13. He T, Krishnamurthy S, Stankovic JA, et al. Energy-efficient surveillance system using wireless sensor networks. In: Proceedings of the 2nd International Conference on Mobile Systems, Applications, and Services (MobiSys); 2004 June 06–09; Boston (MA).

14. Rahimi M, Shah H, Sukhatme GS, Heideman J, Estrin D. Studying the feasibility of energy harvesting in a mobile sensor network. In: Proceedings of the IEEE International Conference on Robotics and Automation; 2003; Taipei, Taiwan.

15. Hill J, Horton M, Kling R, Krishnamurthy L. The platforms enabling wireless sensor network. Commun ACM 2004; 47(6): 41–46.

16. Hill J, Szewczyk R, Woo A, Hollar S, Culler D, Pister K. System architecture directions for networked sensors. In: Proceedings of the 9th International Conference on Architectural Support for Programming Languages and Operating Systems; 2000 Nov 12–15; Cambridge (MA).

17. Wentzloff DD, Calhoun BH, Min R, Wang A, Ickes N, Chandrakasan AP. Design considerations for next generation wireless power-aware microsensor nodes. In: Proceedings of the 17th International Conference on VLSI Design (VLSID$04); 2004; Mumbai, India. pp. 361–367.

18. Akyildiz I, Su W, Sankarasubramaniam Y, Cayiric E. A survey on sensor networks. IEEE Commun Mag 2002; 40(8): 102–114.

19. Al-Karaki J, Kamal A. Routing techniques in wireless sensor networks: A survey. IEEE Wireless Commun 2004; 11(6): 6–28.

20. Demirkol I, Ersoy C, Alagoz F. MAC protocols for wireless sensor networks: A survey. IEEE Commun Mag 2006; 44(4): 115–121.

21. Yeh C-T. Dynamic reconfiguration techniques for wireless sensor networks [Masters theses]. University of Massachusetts; 2008. Available at http://scholarworks. umass.edu/theses/119, Last access in May 2012.

22. Novak JD, Musonda D. A twelve-year longitudinal study of science concept learning. Am Educ Res J 1991; 28(1): 117–153.

23. Novak JD, Cañas AJ. The theory underlying concept maps and how to construct and use them. Technical Report IHMC CmapTools 2006-01 Rev 01–2008. Florida Institute for Human and Machine Cognition; 2008. Available at: http://cmap.ihmc.us/ Publications/ResearchPapers/TheoryUnderlyingConceptMaps.pdf.

24. Wireless Sensor Network (WSN) Wiki. Microcontrollers. Available at http://wsn. oversigma.com. Accessed 2010 Oct 15.

25. Akyildiz I, Su W, Sankarasubramaniam Y, Cayirci E. Wireless sensor networks: a survey. Comput Netw 2002; 38(4): 393–422.

26. RFM. TR1000 hybrid transceiver. Available at: http://www.rfm.com/products/ data/tr1000.pdf. Accessed 2010 Oct 15.

27. Texas Instruments. RF/IF and ZigBee solutions. Available at http://www.ti.com/lprf. Accessed 2010 Oct.

28. SEMTECH. SX1211. Available at http://www.semtech.com/wireless-rf/rf-transceivers/sx1211. Accessed 2010 Oct 15.

29. Hill JL. System Architecture for Wireless Sensor Networks [dissertation]. Berkley (MI): University of California; 2003.

30. Raghunathan V, Schurghers C, Park S, Srivastava M. Energy-aware wireless microsensor networks. IEEE Signal Process Mag 2002; 19(2): 40–50.

31. Chiasserini CF, Rao RR. Pulsed battery discharge in communication devices. In: Proceedings of the 5th Annual ACM/IEEE International Conference on Mobile Computing and Networking; 1999 Aug 15–19; Seattle (WA). New York: MobiCom '99. ACM; 1999. pp. 88–95. DOI: http://doi.acm.org/10.1145/313451.313488.

32. Pottie G, Kaiser W. Wireless integrated network sensors. Commun ACM 2000; 43(5): 51–58.

33. Alippi C, Anastasi G, Di Francesco M, Roveri M. Energy management in sensor networks with energy-hungry sensors. IEEE Instrum Meas Mag 2009; 12(2): 16–23.

34. McLarnon B. VHF/UHF/Microwave radio propagation: a primer for digital experimenters. Available at: http://www.tapr.org/ve3jf.dcc97.html. Accessed 2010 Oct 15.

35. Shih E, Cho S, Ickes N, Min R, Sinha A, Wang A, Chandrakasan A. Physical layer driven protocol and algorithm design for energy-efficient wireless sensor networks. In: Proceedings of the 7th Annual International Conference on Mobile Computing and Networking; 2001; Rome, Italy.

36. Kelly C, Ekanayake VN, Manohar R. SNAP: A sensor-network asynchronous processor. In: Proceedings of the 9th IEEE Symposium on Asynchronous Circuits and Systems; 2003; Vancouver, BC, Canada. pp. 132–140.

37. Benini L, DeMicheli G. *Dynamic Power Management: Design Techniques & CAD Tools*. Norwell (MA): Kluwer Academic Publishers; 1997.

38. Song L. Cross layer design in wireless sensor networks [PhD thesis]. Department of Electrical and Computer Engineering, University of Toronto; 2006.

39. Anastasi G, Conti M, Di Francesco M, Passarella A. Energy conservation in wireless sensor networks: A survey. Ad Hoc Netw 2009; 7(3): 537–568.

40. Armstrong T. Wake-up based power management in Multi-hop wireless networks. Available at http://www.eecg.toronto.edu/$~$trevor/Wakeup/index.html. Accessed 2010 Oct 2.

41. Schurgers C, Tsiatsis V, Srivastava MB. STEM: topology management for energy efficient sensor networks. In: Proceedings of the IEEE Aerospace Conference; 2002 Mar 10–15; Big Sky, Montana.

42. Schurgers C, Tsiatsis V, Ganeriwal S, Srivastava MB. Optimizing sensor networks in the energy-latency-density design space. IEEE Trans Mobile Comput 2002; 1(1): 70–80.

43. Faizulkhakov YR. Time synchronization methods for wireless sensor networks: A survey. Program Comput Softw 2007; 33(4): 214–226, Plenum Press.

44. Sivrikaya F, Yener B. Time synchronization in sensor networks: A survey. IEEE Netw 2004; 18(4): 45–50.

45. Keshavarzian A, Lee H, Venkatraman L. Wakeup scheduling in wireless sensor networks. In: Proceedings of the 7th ACM International Symposium on Mobile Ad Hoc Networking and Computing (MobiHoc); 2006 May; Florence (Italy). pp. 322–333.

46. Madden S, Franklin M, Hellerstein J, Hong W. TinyDB: an acquisitional query processing system for sensor networks. ACM Trans Database Syst 2005; 30(1): 122–173.

47. Buonadonna P, Gay D, Hellerstein J, Hong W, Madden S. TASK: sensor network in a box. In: Proceedings of the European Workshop on Sensor Networks (EWSN); 2005 Jan 31-Feb 2; Istanbul, Turkey.

48. Dam TV, Langendoen K. An adaptive energy-efficient MAC protocol for wireless sensor networks. In: The 1st ACM Conference on Embedded Networked Sensor Systems (Sensys'03); 2003 Nov; Los Angeles (CA).

49. Lu G, Krishnamachari B, Raghavendra CS. An adaptive energy-efficient and low-latency Mac for data gathering in wireless sensor networks. In: Proceedings of 18th International Parallel and Distributed Processing Symposium; 2004 April; Santa Fe (NM). pp. 224, 26–30.

50. Madden S, Franklin M, Hellerstein J, Hong W. TAG: a tiny AGgregation service for Ad-Hoc sensor networks. In: Proceedings of the Annual Symposium on Operating Systems Design and Implementation (OSDI); 2002; Boston (MA).

51. Anastasi G, Conti M, Di Francesco M, Passarella A. An adaptive and low-latency power management protocol for wireless sensor networks. In: Proceedings of the 4th ACM International Workshop on Mobility Management and Wireless Access (MobiWac); 2006 Oct 2; Torremolinos, Spain.

52. Tseng Y, Hsu C, Hsieh T. Power saving protocols for IEEE 802.11 Ad Hoc networks. In: Proceedings of the IEEE Infocom; 2002 June; New York.

53. Zheng R, Hou J, Sha L. Asynchronous wakeup for Ad Hoc networks. In: Proceedings of the ACM MobiHoc; 2003 June 1–3; Annapolis (MD). pp 35–45.

54. Kim N, Choi S, Cha H. Automated sensor-specific power management for wireless sensor networks. In: Proceedings of the IEEE Conference on Mobile Ad Hoc and Sensor Systems (MASS); 2008 Sept 29 - Oct 2; Atlanta (GA).

55. Baggio A. Wireless sensor networks in precision agriculture. In: Proceedings of the ACM Workshop on Real-World Wireless Sensor Networks (REALWSN); 2005 June; Stockholm, Sweden.

56. Hartung C, Han R, Seielstad C, Holbrook S. FireWxNet: a multitiered portable wireless system for monitoring weather conditions in wildland fire environments. In: Proceedings of the International Conference on Mobile Systems, Applications and Services; 2006; Uppsala, Sweden. pp. 28–41.

57. Mielke AM, Brennan SM, Smith MC, Torney DC, Maccabe AB, Karlin M. JF. Independent sensor networks. IEEE Mag Instrum Meas 2005; 8(2): 33–37.

58. Dai-Hua W, Wei-Hsin L. Wireless transmission for health monitoring of large structures. IEEE Trans Instrum Meas 2006; 55(3): 972–981.

59. Bertocco M, Gamba G, Sona A, Vitturi S. Experimental characterization of wireless sensor networks for industrial applications. IEEE Trans Instrum Meas 2008; 57(8): 1537–1546.

60. Antifakos S, Michahelles F, Schiele B. Proactive instructions for furniture assembly. In: Proceedings of the Ubicomp; 2002 Sept; Gothenburg, Sweden.

61. Ottman GK, Hofmann HF, et al. Adaptive piezoelectric energy harvesting circuit for wireless remote power supply. IEEE Trans Power Electron 2002; 17(5): 669–776.

62. Anthony J. Energy Harvesting Projects. In: Collections of articles on IEEE Pervasive Computing; 2005 Jan–Mar. pp. 69–71.

63. Yu Y, Krishnamachari B, Prasanna VK. Energy-latency tradeoffs for data gathering in wireless sensor networks. In: Proceedings of the 23rd Conference of the IEEE Communications Society (INFOCOM); 2004; Hong Kong.

64. Sinhua A, Chandrakasan A. Dynamic power management in wireless sensor network. IEEE Des Test Comput 2001; 18(2): 62–74.

65. Pering TA, Burd TD, Brodersen RW. The simulation and evaluation of dynamic voltage scaling algorithms. In: Proceedings of the International Symposium on Low Power Electronics and Design (ISLPED); California, USA; 1998. pp. 76–81.

66. Cassandras C, Zhuang S. Optimal dynamic voltage scaling for wireless sensor nodes with real-time constraints. In: Proceedings of the International Symposium on Intelligent Systems in Design and Manufacturing; 2005; Boston (MA).

67. Pillai P, Shin KG. Real-time dynamic voltage scaling for low-power embedded operating systems. In: Proceedings of the ACM Symposium on Operating Systems Principles; 2001; Alberta, Canada.

68. Raghunathan V, Spanos P, Srivastava M. Adaptive power-fidelity in energy aware wireless embedded systems. In: Proceedings of the IEEE Real Time Systems Symposium; 2001; London.

69. Yao F, Demers A, Shenker S. A scheduling model for reduced CPU energy. In: Proceedings of the Annual Symposium on Foundations of Computer Science; Milwaukee, USA; 1995. pp. 374–382.

70. Rappaport TS. *Wireless Communications, Principles and Practice*. Prentice Hall; Upper Saddle River, NJ, US; 1996.

71. Panichpapiboon S, Ferrari G, Tonguz OK. Optimal transmit power in wireless sensor networks. IEEE Trans Mobile Comput 2006; 5(10): 1432–1447.

72. Narayanaswamy S, Kawadia V, Sreenivas RS, Kumar PR. Power control in Ad-Hoc networks: theory, architecture, algorithm and implementation of the COMPOW protocol. In: Proceedings of the European Wireless 2002 Next Generation Wireless Networks: Technologies, Protocols, Services, and Applications; 2002 Feb; Florence, Italy. pp. 156–162.

73. Agarwal S, Katz R, Krishnamurthy SV, Dao SK. Distributed power control in Ad-Hoc wireless networks. In: Proceedings of the IEEE International Symposium on Personal, Indoor, and Mobile Radio Communications (PIMRC); 2001 Sept; London, Volume 2. pp. F59–F66.

74. Ramanathan R, Rosales-Hain R. Topology control of multihop wireless networks using transmit power adjustment. In: Proceedings of the IEEE Conference on Computer Communications (INFOCOM); 2000 March; Tel Aviv, Israel, Volume 2. pp. 404–413.

75. Lin S, Zhang J, Zhou G, Gu L, Stankovic JA, He T. ATPC: adaptive transmission power control for wireless sensor networks. In: Proceedings of the 4th International Conference on Embedded Networked Sensor Systems; 2006; Boulder (CO). pp. 223–236.

76. Santi P, Blough DM. The critical transmitting range for connectivity in sparse wireless Ad Hoc networks. IEEE Trans Mobile Comput 2003; 2: 25–39.

77. Kubisch M, Karl H, Wolisz A, Zhong LC, Rabaey J. Distributed algorithms for transmission power control in wireless sensor networks. In: Proceedings of the IEEE Wireless Communications and Networking Conference (WCNC); 2003 Mar; New Orleans (LA).

78. Xue F, Kumar PR. The number of neighbors needed for connectivity of wireless networks. Wireless Netw 2004; 10: 169–181.

79. Gomez J, Campbell AT. A case for variable-range transmission power control in wireless multihop networks. In: Proceedings of the IEEE INFOCOM; 2004 Mar 07–11; Hong Kong, Volume 2. pp. 1425–1436.

80. Correia LH, Macedo DF, dos Santos AL, et al. Transmission power control techniques for wireless sensor networks. Comput Netw 2007; 51(17): 4765–4779.

81. Schurgers C, Aberthorne O, Srivastava M. Modulation scaling for energy aware communications. In: Proceedings of the 2001 International Symposium on Low Power Electronics and Design; 2001 Aug; Huntington Beach (CA). pp. 96–99.

82. Joshi G, Jardosh S, Ranjan P. Bounds on dynamic modulation scaling for wireless sensor networks. In: Proceedings of the 3rd International Conference on Wireless Communication and Sensor Networks (WCSN '07); 2007 Dec 13–15; Allahabad, India. pp. 13–16.

83. Yao Y, Giannakis G. Energy-efficient scheduling for wireless sensor networks. IEEE Trans Commun 2005; 53(8): 1333–1342.

84. Yang Z, Yuan Y, He J, Chen W. Adaptive modulation scaling scheme for wireless sensor networks. IEICE Trans Commun 2005; E88-B(3): 882–889.

85. Agarwal R, Popovici E, O'Flynn B. Adaptive wireless sensor networks: a system design approach to adaptive reliability. In: Proceedings of the 2nd International Conference on Wireless Communication and Sensor Networks (WCSN '06); 2006 Dec 17–19; Allahabad, India. pp. 216–225.

86. Liu H, Ma H, et al. Error control schemes for networks: an overview. Mobile Netw Appl 1997; 2: 167–182.

87. Wang C, Sohraby K, Li B, Daneshmand M. A survey of transport protocols for wireless sensor networks. IEEE Netw 2006; 20(3): 34–40.

88. Ahn J-S, Hong S-W, Heidemann J. An adaptive FEC code control algorithm for mobile wireless sensor networks. J Commun Netw 2005; 7(4): 489–499.

89. Levisianou A, Assimakopoulos C, Pavlidou F-N, Polydoros A. A recursive IR protocol for multicarrier communications. In: Proceedings of the 6-th International OFDM-Workshop; 2001 Sept; Hamburg, Czech Republic. pp. 22–1–22–4.

90. Meer J, Nijdam M, Bijl M. Adaptive error control in a wireless sensor network using packet importance valuation. In: Hardware/Software Co-design; 2003; Enschede, The Netherlands.

91. Zhao L, Zhang W-H, Xu C-N, Xu Y-J, Li X-W. Energy-aware system design for wireless sensor network. Acta Automat Sin Elsevier 2002; 32(6): 892–899.

CHAPTER 25

NETWORK-WIDE STRATEGIES FOR ENERGY EFFICIENCY IN WIRELESS SENSOR NETWORKS

FLÁVIA C. DELICATO and PAULO F. PIRES

25.1 INTRODUCTION

Wireless sensor networks (WSNs) are distributed systems composed of hundreds to thousands of low cost, battery-powered, and reduced-size devices, endowed with processing, sensing, and wireless communication capabilities. One major reason for the increasing interest in WSNs in the past few years is their potential pervading in application areas for which traditional networks are unsuitable. Instead of a deployment scenario in which few powerful sensing devices are linked by either wired connections or single-hop wireless connections, WSN nodes consist of multiple microsensors able of communicating and self-organizing in order to compose a wireless ad hoc network for meeting application demands. The topic of WSNs can be considered as one of the truly multidisciplinary research efforts, bringing together researchers from a wide range of fields: from chemists who develop the sensors to engineers focusing on wireless platforms and hardware components to computer scientists who develop the software services to biologists, oceanographers, and physicians (to name a few) involved in the myriad of applications that can benefit from using such networks.

However, several challenges remain to be overcome before WSNs can be widely employed and can reach their full potential. One major challenge is the highly limited energy capacity of the sensor nodes. Such a severe constraint requires the adoption of strategies for energy awareness and efficiency throughout the whole network, from the design of individual components of the node hardware to the entire protocol stack, including the application layer.

Energy-Efficient Distributed Computing Systems, First Edition.
Edited by Albert Y. Zomaya and Young Choon Lee.
© 2012 John Wiley & Sons, Inc. Published 2012 by John Wiley & Sons, Inc.

As we mentioned in Chapter 1, to effectively reduce the overall power consumption in a WSN and to extend its lifetime, several strategies need to be employed, often simultaneously, at different levels of the network architecture. Therefore, power-saving policies in a WSN act at different levels: (i) the level of individual node, called *intranode*; (ii) the level representing the communication link between neighboring (often one-hop distant) nodes, called *internode*; and (iii) the level of the entire network, which we called *network wide*. In Chapter 1, we addressed the solutions for energy efficiency from the standpoint of individual nodes and communicating neighboring nodes. In this chapter, we present a comprehensive survey on the third level, the network-wide aspects of energy management in WSNs. Policies for energy efficiency at such level (Fig. 25.1) exploit the knowledge on the WSN behavior as a whole in order to achieve more significant energy savings than only considering individual or neighboring nodes. These policies are implemented as software programs that actuate at the different protocol layers of the WSN stack. Therefore, in this chapter, we describe solutions in the following layers of the WSN stack: (i) data link, (ii) network, (iii) transport, and (iv) application layers. Solutions belonging to the physical layer basically operate on individual nodes, for instance, addressing modulation scaling and power control. Therefore, they were discussed in Chapter 1.

Energy-aware software solutions include the development of energy-efficient communication protocols and also exploit cross-layer [1] interactions involving different layers of the protocol stack. The cross-layer behavior is present in several solutions discussed in this survey that encompass more than a single protocol layer, often crossing through nonadjacent layers. In the context of the cross-layer paradigm, a crucial issue in WSNs is the participation of the application layer to guide decisions of all the other layers. Several works, such as References 2 and 3, highlighted the close relationship between application requirements and the WSN performance and demonstrated that application-specific optimizations may increase the WSN overall performance, mainly with regard to the energy consumption.

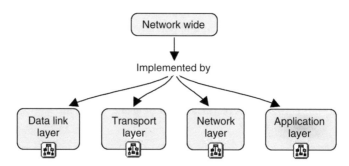

Figure 25.1   Concept map representing network-wide energy optimization policy.

Regarding the WSN components, in our survey, we assume a network composed of one or more sink nodes (sometimes referred to as *base station*) and a (possibly huge) number of sensor nodes deployed over a large geographic area (called *sensing field* or *target area*). Data are collected from the sensing field and transferred from sensor nodes to the sink nodes through a multihop communication protocol. Regarding individual sensor nodes, we consider that each sensor is composed of software and hardware components. Sensor hardware has four main components: (i) a sensing subsystem including one or more sensors (with associated analog-to-digital converters) for data acquisition, (ii) a processing subsystem including a microcontroller and memory for local data processing, (iii) a communication subsystem for wireless data communication, and (iv) a power supply subsystem.

In the same way as presented in Chapter 1, this survey is also organized using a knowledge representation tool called *Concept Maps* [4]. A concept map is a top-down diagram showing the relationships between concepts, including cross-connections among concepts, and their instances. The concepts in such maps are represented hierarchically with the most inclusive, most general concepts at the top of the map and the more specific, less general concepts arranged below. In this chapter, the same central question addressed in Chapter 1 is being posed: "How to wisely manage energy in a WSN in order to extend its lifetime?" However, in this chapter, we discuss the answers to such questions from the standpoint of the entire WSN.

25.2 DATA LINK LAYER

The data link layer is responsible, among other things, for the multiplexing of data streams, medium access, and error control, ensuring reliable point-to-point and point-to-multipoint connections in a communication network [5]. Power management in this layer can be achieved through the use of protocols for topology control and through energy-efficient MAC protocols (Fig. 25.2).

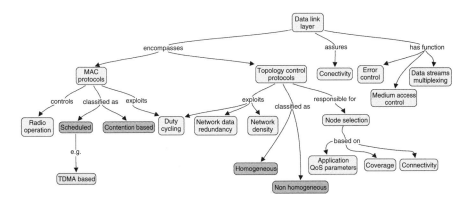

Figure 25.2 Concept map representing data link layer energy-saving policies.

25.2.1 Topology Control Protocols

An important design feature of WSNs that can be useful for extending network lifetime is their typical high density of nodes. On one hand, this feature increases robustness against node failures and decreases energy costs by favoring multiple hop communications. On the other hand, this very same characteristic leads [6] to a large redundancy in sensor-collected data. Topology control protocols exploit the latter aspect by dynamically selecting a reduced set of sensors to remain active in the execution of a sensing task, thus adapting the network logical topology based on the application requirements. Besides the turning off of redundant nodes, the network topology is also affected by changes in the transmission power of nodes. Since it is, in general, more energy efficient to transmit packets over several short hops than a single long hop, dynamically reducing transmission power can provide overall energy savings. Therefore, there are protocols for topology control that exploit this feature. For instance, in Reference 7, a cooperative, lightweight, and fully distributed approach is proposed to adaptively tune the transmission power of sensors in order to match local connectivity constraints.

Topology control and duty cycling (Chapter 20) are complementary techniques that implement duty cycling with different granularity: while topology control protocols save energy by activating a subset of nodes from the entire WSN to remain active, duty cycling policies achieve further gains by minimizing the operational time of active nodes.

Several criteria, including QoS parameters specific to the target application, can be used to decide which nodes and when to activate [8]. However, in spite of the adopted criteria, any solution for topology control needs to guarantee at least the WSN connectivity and preferably the sensing coverage as well. Since the goal of a WSN is to monitor some geographic area, it has to maintain a full sensing coverage respecting a certain spatial precision, even when it operates in power-save mode. Besides, a successful node selection scheme must also provide satisfactory connectivity so that active nodes can report collected data to the application (through the sink node).

In the past years, several researchers have been investigating the problem of topology control in WSNs, most of them with the aim of achieving high levels of energy efficiency. Detailed surveys on topology control in wireless ad hoc network and WSN are available in References 9–11. In the following, we review some of the main proposals for topology control in WSNs.

Existent topology control protocols can be classified according to different parameters. One of the classifications reported in the literature is based on constraints over the range assignment [10]. According to such criterion of classification, protocols for topology control can be homogeneous or nonhomogeneous [11]. *Homogeneous* approaches assume a common transmission power level for all the nodes in the WSN, and the main goal is often to find the minimum power level, the so-called critical transmitting range (CTR), such that the resulting network graph has specific properties in terms of connectivity. The computation of CTR considers the statistics of node distribution and mobility and is based on the use of either graph theory [12] or probabilistic approaches [13]. *Nonhomogeneous* approaches assume that nodes are able to choose different transmitting ranges provided they do not exceed the maximum range.

Another parameter that can be used for purposes of classification is the network property that the protocols aim to assure. The majority of works considered coverage and/or connectivity guarantees as the unique requirement. For instance, in References 14 and 15, techniques of linear programming are used to select the minimum set of active nodes able to maintain the complete sensing coverage of the network. Other protocols, such as SPAN [16], GAF (geographical adaptive fidelity) [17], and AFECA (adaptive fidelity energy-conserving algorithm) [18], guarantee network connectivity, but they do not address sensing coverage. SPAN [16] guarantees the connectivity requirement in WSNs by adaptively electing a suitable number of "coordinators" of all nodes in the network. Coordinators stay awake continuously and perform multihop routing, while the remainder nodes stay in sleeping mode, periodically checking if they need to wake up and become a coordinator. Both GAF and AFECA protocols address the requirement of routing fidelity along with the network connectivity.

ASCENT (*a*daptive *s*elf-*c*onfiguring *s*ensor *n*etworks *t*opology) [19] and OTC (optimized topology control) [20] guarantee network connectivity by additionally promoting load balance among nodes in a WSN. In ASCENT, a node decides whether to join the active network topology or continue to sleep based on information about neighbor density and packet loss that are measured locally by the node. A node may reduce its duty cycle if it detects high data losses due to collisions. ASCENT has the potential for significant reduction of packet loss rate, thus increasing energy savings. Moreover, it encompasses a load balance policy that allows nodes to switch state from time to time in order to ensure all nodes share the task of providing global connectivity equally, thus distributing the energy load. OTC is a novel topology control algorithm that increases network lifetime while maintaining connectivity, guaranteeing multihop reachability from any source to any destination, and providing a reasonable throughput. In order to ensure connectivity, OTC uses the two-hop neighborhood information to sequentially select a subset of nodes to be active among all nodes in the neighborhood. Moreover, to ensure fairness and an even distribution of the energy consumption, the role of active nodes is periodically rotated.

In Reference 19, a solution is provided to meet both coverage and connectivity requirements. However, none of the aforementioned protocols seek for a balance between the quality of data generated for the application and the energy consumption of the network. The works described in References 22 and 23 tackled the problem of maximizing the lifetime of a WSN while guaranteeing a minimum level of quality at the application level. In those works, the problems of node selection and data routing are jointly addressed and solved as a problem of generalized maximum flow. Those works presented both an optimal and a heuristic solution with a totally centralized approach, based on global information.

Delicato et al. [24] proposed a different approach in which the selection of nodes to be active aims to extend the network lifetime while meeting application-specific QoS requirements. They formalized the problem of node selection as a knapsack problem and adopted a greedy heuristic for solving it. The proposed solution tries to maximize residual energy and relevance from the application point of view of the active nodes while assuring both connectivity and sensing coverage. Moreover, different from approaches based on computational intensive techniques of linear programming, which are restricted to run off-line, such approach is light enough to be executed on-line and inside the network.

As a final remark, it is important to mention that topology control was traditionally used in wireless networks as a technique to reduce radio interference. By minimizing interference in WSNs, data corruption and the consequent need for retransmissions can be minimized, thus achieving further energy savings [10].

25.2.2 Energy-Efficient MAC Protocols

Medium access control (MAC) protocols specify how nodes share the communication channel and directly controls the activities of radio units. Since the radio is the most power-consuming component of a typical WSN node, an energy-efficient MAC protocol can significantly contribute to extend the overall network lifetime [25]. Energy-efficient MAC protocols should consider a set of reasons that make sensor battery to drain quickly [26–27] thus wasting energy. The main relevant sources of energy waste at the MAC level are listed in the following.

- *Packet Collisions*. They are the major source of energy waste. When two packets are transmitted at the same time and collide, they become corrupted and must be discarded, requiring their retransmission thus increasing the energy consumption.
- *Overhearing*. It denotes the reception of packets by nodes that are not their destination. Overhearing unnecessary traffic can be a dominant factor of energy waste, especially in heavy traffic load environments and dense networks.
- *Idle Listening*. Since a node does not know when the data traffic is generated from other nodes, its transceiver continuously remains in the receiving mode even when there is no data traffic. This feature is commonly named as *idle listening*. It is thus desirable to completely shut down the radio rather than only put it in the idle mode. However, *frequent switching* between modes, especially switching from sleep to active mode, leads to more energy being spent than when leaving the radio transceiver unit in idle mode because of nonnegligible consumption of the radio start-up.
- *Control Packet Overhead*. Sending, receiving, and listening for control packets consume energy. Since control packets do not directly convey useful application data, they reduce the effective network throughput. Energy-efficient MAC protocols should minimize the number of control packets required in data transmission.

- *Overemitting*. This is caused by the transmission of a message when the destination node is in sleep mode or not ready to receive. This results in energy waste and needs to be avoided to improve energy efficiency.
- *Traffic Fluctuations*. WSNs usually generate traffic that fluctuates in place and time, resulting in peak loads that may generate network congestion that consequently increases the probability of collisions. Therefore, time and energy are wasted on waiting in the random back-off procedure.
- *Packet Size*. Choosing the appropriate *packet size* is also an important issue from the energy point of view. As the packet size gets smaller, the transition energy becomes dominant to the energy consumed during receiving and transmitting of packets.

Therefore, energy-efficient MAC protocols save energy by controlling the radio in order to avoid or minimize idle listening, collisions/retransmissions, unwanted overhearing, and overemitting. As previously discussed, the most common and effective way to conserve energy is to turn the sensor node radio transceiver and processor units into a low power sleep state when these resources are not needed. Since WSN MAC protocols are in control of the radio operation, they can be used in combination with duty cycling techniques to achieve significant energy gains. Indeed, most of WSN MAC protocols implement a low duty cycle scheme for power management.

MAC protocols have been extensively studied in wireless networks in general and more recently in WSNs. Most WSN MAC protocols have similarities in their effort to reduce energy consumption. According to the mechanism adopted for collision avoidance (CA), MAC protocols can be broadly divided into two groups: *scheduled* and *contention based* [29]. *Scheduled* MAC protocols avoid interference among communications by scheduling nodes onto different subchannels that are divided by time, frequency, or orthogonal codes. Since these subchannels do not interfere with each other, MAC protocols in this group are largely collision free. Organizing sensor nodes according to a common schedule provides the capability to reduce message retransmission, idle listening, and overhearing, thus achieving high energy efficiency. One commonly used scheduled protocol is based on the TDMA technique [30].

Rather than divide the channel into subchannels and preallocate transmissions, in MAC protocols based on *contention* nodes compete for a shared channel, resulting in probabilistic coordination. A contention mechanism is used to decide which node is allowed to access the channel at any moment. Contention-based protocols have several advantages compared to scheduled protocols. First, since the channel is allocated on an on-demand basis, such protocols scale better and accommodate easily to changes in the network topology. Second, they do not require strict time synchronization like, for instance, TDMA-based protocols. Third, they, in general, have a lower delay and potentially higher throughput at lower traffic loads, which is often the case in WSNs. However, they have a serious drawback for use in WSNs: they are potentially very inefficient in energy, suffering from all the sources of energy waste discussed in the beginning of this section. Traditional contention-based MAC protocols require all nodes to continuously listen to the channel due to unpredictable packet transmission by its neighboring nodes, hence introducing the problem of idle listening. Collisions can occur during the contention period. Therefore, in order to be adopted in WSNs, such class of protocol should make extensive use of low duty cycle to conserve energy and employ additional CA or collision detection methods to deal with the possibilities of collision. Classical examples of contention-based MAC protocols include ALOHA [31] and carrier sense multiple access (CSMA) [32].

25.2.2.1 Scheduled MAC protocols in WSNs. Although there are other techniques adopted by scheduled MAC protocols, we focus on TDMA since it is the most popular in WSNs. In TDMA-based MAC protocols [33–38], time is divided into (periodic) frames and each frame consists of a number of slots. Every node is assigned to one or more time slots per frame, according to a scheduling algorithm, and uses such slots for transmitting/receiving packets to/from other nodes. Scheduled protocols such as TDMA are potentially attractive for WSNs because of their energy efficiency, including other advantages. First, since slots are preallocated to individual nodes, such protocols are collision free; there is no energy wasted on collisions due to channel contention. Second, TDMA naturally supports low duty cycle operation. A node only needs to turn on its radio during the slot that it is assigned to transmit or receive. Finally, overhearing can be easily avoided by turning off the radio during the slots of other nodes. However, the advantages arising from the scheduling-based approaches come at the cost of building and maintaining the schedule and requiring fine-grained time synchronization among nodes to align slot boundaries. Moreover, since only one sensor node is allowed to use a time slot, any unused time generates a waste of resource. In addition, TDMA-based MAC protocols have limited scalability and are not flexible to changes in the network, which are two disadvantages that limit their use in WSNs since such networks are typically dynamic and composed of a large number of nodes.

In EMAC protocols [37], besides the time being divided into *time slots*, each time slot is further divided in three sections: the *communication request* (CR), the *traffic control* (TC), and the *data* sections. A node can assign only one slot to itself and is said to control this slot. In the CR section, other nodes can issue requests to the node that is controlling the current time slot. Communication in this section is not guaranteed collision free. Nodes that do not have a request for the current slot owner will keep their transceiver in a low power state during the entire CR section. The controller of a time slot will always transmit a TC message in the time slot. When a time slot is not controlled by any node, all nodes will remain in sleep state during that slot. The time slot controller also indicates in its TC message what communication will take place in the data section. If a node is neither addressed in the TC section nor its request was approved, then it can remain in a power-save mode during the entire data section. After the TC section, the actual data transfer takes place.

Another example of TDMA-based protocol is LMAC (lightweight medium access control) [38], which was conceived based on the ideas of EMAC but with further improvements, achieving higher energy efficiency. Unlike traditional TDMA-based systems, the time slots in LMAC are not divided among the network nodes by a central manager. Instead, a distributed algorithm is used. The main goal of the protocol is to minimize the number of transceiver switches, to make the sleep interval for sensor nodes adaptive to the amount of data traffic, and to limit the complexity of implementation. It employs the same approach of EMAC in which a node is only allowed to transmit a single message per frame. During its time slot, a node will always transmit a message that consists of two parts: control message and a data unit. The control message has a fixed size and is used for several purposes, such as to maintain synchronization between the nodes. If a node is addressed in a control message, it will listen to the data unit, which might not fill the entire remainder of the time slot. Both transmitter and receiver(s) turn off their transceivers after the message transfer has completed. A short time-out interval ensures that nodes do not waste energy for idle listening in time slots that are not controlled by any node.

25.2.2.2 *Contention-based MAC protocols.*

In spite of the aforementioned problems, contention-based protocols are the most popular class of MAC protocols for WSNs [26, 39]. To improve the energy consumption of these protocols, duty cycling is performed by tightly integrating channel access functionalities with a sleep/wake-up scheme. These protocols are based on the CSMA technique, whose central idea is listening to the medium to detect if it is busy before transmitting. However, in multihop wireless networks, CSMA alone is not suitable due to the hidden terminal problem [40]. CSMA/CA, adopted by the wireless LAN standard [41], uses a RTS-CTS handshake to reduce the costs of collisions generated by the hidden terminal problem. On the basis of CSMA/CA, Karn [42] proposed MACA (multiple access with collision avoidance), which added a duration field in both RTS and CTS packets indicating the amount of data to be transmitted, so that other nodes know how long they should back off. Some protocols for wireless networks based on CSMA/CA can be used in WSNs [43, 44], whereas others were specifically designed to WSNs, for instance, S-MAC (sensor MAC) [26] protocol that executes a variant of MACA. Other protocols use different techniques, always focusing on avoiding the problems of collision, overhearing, and idle listening, while keeping nodes in a low duty cycle.

A well-known WSN MAC protocol that makes use of carrier sense and RTS-CTS is S-MAC [26]. It adopts a periodic sleep/listen schedule based on locally managed node synchronization. Every node can establish its own schedule or follow the schedule of a neighbor through a random distributed algorithm. Neighboring nodes using the same schedule form a *virtual cluster*. If two neighboring nodes reside in two different virtual clusters, they wake up at listen periods of both clusters, acting as a bridge. The channel access time is divided into two parts. In the listen period, nodes exchange *sync* and RTS/CTS packets for CA. In the remaining period, the actual data transfer is performed. The sender and the destination nodes are kept awake to communicate to each other. Nodes not involved with the communication process can sleep until the next listen period. To avoid high latencies, S-MAC uses an adaptive listening scheme. A node overhearing its neighbor's transmissions wakes up at the end of the transmission for a short period of time. If the node is the next hop of the transmitter, the neighbor can send the packet to it without waiting for the next schedule.

One very popular contention-based MAC protocol is B-MAC (Berkeley MAC) [39], which is deployed along with the TinyOS operating system [45]. To achieve a low duty cycle, B-MAC uses an asynchronous sleep/wake scheme based on periodic listening called *low power listening* (LPL). Nodes periodically wake up to check the channel for activity. After waking up, nodes remain active for a wake-up time in order to properly detect eventual ongoing transmissions. While the wake-up time is fixed, the check interval can be specified by the application. One drawback of B-MAC is that it does not include a mechanism to avoid or minimize the hidden terminal problem.

Besides scheduled and contention-based protocols, we can identify a class of *hybrid* MAC protocols [46]. Hybrid protocols adapt the protocol behavior to the level of contention in the network. They behave as a contention-based protocol when the level of contention is low and switch to a TDMA scheme when the level of contention is high. The greatest advantage of hybrid MAC protocols comes from their easy and fast adaptability to traffic conditions, which can save a large amount of energy, but this advantage comes at the cost of the protocol complexity, which limits its range of applications.

As we discussed, most of the overheads that produce the sources of energy waste are incurred by MAC protocols based on contention techniques. In scheduled protocols such as TDMA, problems such as overhearing and collision do not occur, since each node knows a priori exactly in which slots it should transmit and receive. However, these advantages come at the cost of increasing the complexity of the protocol, which leads to reduced flexibility to handle traffic fluctuations and changes in the network topology, besides resulting in a larger control packet overhead. We could also observe that the main source of energy gains for MAC protocols is adopting duty cycle techniques. TDMA-based protocols are especially useful for power conservation since a node can sleep between its assigned time slots, waking up in time to receive and transmit messages. However, as it is often the case, there is a trade-off to be handled: MAC protocols that give nodes high duty cycle can respond to traffic and network changes more quickly but consume energy at a higher rate. On the other hand, a lower duty cycle MAC protocol can save energy, but low activity levels put a limit on the protocol's complexity, the potential network capacity, and the message latency. Periodic sleep may result in high latency, especially for multihop routing algorithms, since all immediate nodes have their own sleep schedules. The latency caused by periodic sleeping is called *sleep delay* [26]. Adaptive listening technique can be used to improve the sleep delay and thus the overall latency. In such technique, the node that overhears its neighbor's transmissions wakes up for a short time at the end of the transmission. Hence, if the node is the next-hop node, its neighbor could pass data immediately.

25.3   NETWORK LAYER

The policies for achieving energy awareness and efficiency at the network layer (Fig. 25.3) are basically implemented as routing protocols, either as part of the routing algorithm itself or as constraints to be used in the routing strategies.

The main task of a WSN is to forward the sensed data gathered by sensor nodes to one or more sink nodes. One simplistic approach to accomplish this task is the direct data transmission. In this case, each node directly sends its sensing data to the sink. However, if the sink is far from the sensing area (a common situation in WSNs), the nodes will prematurely die because of the excessive energy consumption for delivering data over such large distances. Therefore, a preferable approach is to forward data from source nodes to the sink through multiple, intermediary nodes, using a multihop communication paradigm. In this context, the goal of routing protocols is to select a path to deliver data from sources (sensor nodes) to destination (one or more sink nodes). Ad hoc routing techniques already proposed in the literature do not usually fit the specific requirements of WSNs. Among the specific features of WSNs that distinguish them from other networks, the following affect the design of routing protocols.

1. Sensor nodes are very resource constrained; however, all the nodes in a WSN have both communication and computation capacities, thus each node can act as a router and at the same time perform some kind of processing in the data before forwarding them; such in-network processing is one way of achieving energy efficiency.

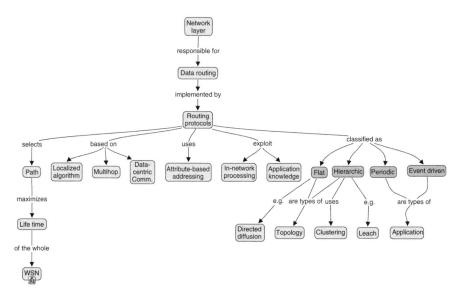

Figure 25.3   Concept map for network layer policies.

2. Considering the typically high number of nodes in a WSN, it is not feasible to adopt a scheme of global addressing such as the classical Internet Protocol (IP) address. Instead, sensor nodes are commonly identified only by a local address. Several early works [47] have suggested the use of data-centric, attribute-based schemes for addressing WSNs, instead of traditional address-centric schemes such as IP. In the data-centric approach, nodes are addressed by attributes, such as their geographical location or the type of data they provide, or by their interest in some type of sensing data. Routing protocols should exploit such features by building routing paths from nodes identified as sources (nodes that provide a given type of data) toward nodes identified as sinks (nodes that are interested in a certain type of data).

3. The typical pattern of data traffic in WSNs is many to one since data generated from several sensors distributed over multiple regions flow to only one (or a small number of) sink node.

4. Sensor-generated data are characterized by a high level of redundancy since the network is often dense and different neighbor sensors are prone to monitor the same physical phenomena. Such redundancy can be exploited by in-network processing, trading communication for computation in order to save energy.

From these features, we can see that there is a need for routing protocols, tailored to the WSN environment, that take into account all of its idiosyncrasies. There are different policies that can be adopted by routing protocols for purposes of energy savings. Some policies exploit characteristics of the WSNs, such as the in-networking processing, high density of nodes, and many-to-one communication pattern, to improve the energy efficiency in the strategies for data forwarding, while others explicitly use information about node's current energy to make routing decisions. In the latter policies, the routing itself is energy aware, denoting the cases of WSN routing protocols that aim at selecting a path that minimize the overall energy consumption and thus extend the network lifetime. To allow an increase in the WSN lifetime, such protocols need to take into account additional parameters beyond the hop count commonly used in conventional networks. Moreover, they have to consider the even distribution of traffic throughout the network in order to avoid overloading the sensors in a given path. The many-to-one communication paradigm is preferably used to accommodate the typical traffic pattern in WSNs, and such paradigm often results in nonuniform energy drainage in the network. Overloading a set of sensors located in the more frequently used path can cause their premature death, thus producing a fragmentation in the WSN and preventing the delivery of sensor-generated data to the sink.

Several routing protocols have been specifically designed for WSNs with focus on energy efficiency. Most such protocols are based on localized algorithms [48] and on the multihop, data-centric communication [49, 50], besides exploiting some application-specific knowledge in the data forwarding process. Localized algorithm is a special kind of distributed algorithm in which nodes participating in a distributed processing interact only with nodes localized in a restricted neighborhood, while the system as a whole meets a global goal. Localized algorithms are potentially attractive because they reduce redundancy and save energy, as well as only a subset of nodes in the network is invoked for a specific task. Moreover, since the energy spent in transmission is proportional to the distance, neighboring interactions are intrinsically energy efficient.

One feature exploited by WSN routing protocols for purposes of energy efficiency is the in-network capability of nodes, which allows to trade communication with processing. In this sense, routing trees generated by routing protocols are also used as aggregation trees, providing points in which data collected by nodes positioned as leaves in the tree are gathered and submitted to some fusion process so that only the resulting processed data is forwarded to upper levels in the tree (and can be further processed). Therefore, information related to the data fusion process, such as the aggregation degree and the aggregation delay, should be take into account by the routing protocols. Data fusion is an important strategy for energy efficiency in WSNs, and it is detailed more in Section 25.5.2.

There are several classifications for WSN routing protocols, each one emphasizing a different aspect of their behavior. Regarding the logical topology of the network, which directly influences the strategy adopted for data forwarding, routing protocols can be classified as flat or hierarchical (clustered), besides those that are based on direct transmission. As we previously mentioned, data transmission directly from source to sink nodes is very energy inefficient, mainly in large WSNs. Therefore, the multihop approach is the most suitable for WSNs. Since the required transmission power increases as the square of the distance between source and destination, multiple short message transmission hops require less power than one long hop. Flat and hierarchical protocols adopt a multihop approach and therefore are more energy efficient. Section 25.3.1 describes examples of flat and hierarchical WSN routing protocols.

Finally, the characteristics of the application running on the top of the network should be taken into account by energy-efficient routing protocols. WSN applications can be divided in two main classes according to the periodicity of data communication: event driven and periodical monitoring. In event-driven WSN applications, data is sent whenever an event of interest occurs. In periodical monitoring applications, all nodes in a target area send their generated data to the sink at each predefined time interval. In order to increase energy saving, routing protocols are usually implemented to support one single class of application. In periodical monitoring networks, routes are periodically reconstructed, while in event-driven networks routes are built on-demand, whenever an event occurs, since the cost of constant updates is prohibitive in this scenario. Examples of WSN routing protocols suitable for event-driven applications are SPIN [51], TTDD [51], and directed diffusion [47, 53, 54], while a typical example of protocol suitable to periodical applications is LEACH (low energy adaptive clustering hierarchy) [55–57].

To illustrate one of the event-driven protocols, the work presented in Reference 54 recently proposed routing protocol for flat networks, with a focus on prolonging the WSN lifetime. This protocol uses the metrics *received signal strength* and the *available energy* to identify an energy-efficient path that minimizes packet collisions and increases the network lifetime. Therefore, it is one example of an energy-aware protocol since the information of current node energy drives the decisions on route formation. A node is selected to forward the data based on its residual energy level and signal strength. Ideally, the greater the energy in the node and the farther the node from the previous one, it is more likely to be selected as the next hop. The nodes that are not selected to forward data are put in a sleep state in order to conserve energy. The results of the simulations reported in Reference 54 showed that the protocol performs well in terms of both network lifetime and packet delivery ratio.

25.3.1 Flat and Hierarchical Protocols

In flat protocols, all sensor nodes of the network are considered "equal" in terms of routing. When a node has data to send, it must find a route, which consists of multiple hops (intermediate nodes), to the sink. A drawback of these protocols is that, normally, the probability of participating in the process of data transmission is higher for the nodes around the sink than for nodes far away from it. Therefore, nodes close to the sink tend to have their energy depleted faster, thus preventing the delivery of data to the application. Therefore, such approach can limit the global operational lifetime of the network.

Directed diffusion [47, 53] was one of the first protocols specifically designed for WSNs. It adopts a flat topology, a data-centric approach and exploits the in-network capability of WSN nodes to save energy. In directed diffusion, individual nodes reduce the sampled waveform generated by a target into a relatively coarse-grained "event" description. Such description contains a set of attributes. Applications that request data send out interests through some sink in the network. These interests are also represented as a set of attributes. If the attributes of source-node-generated data match these interests, a gradient is set up within the network and data will be pulled toward the sinks. Intermediate nodes are capable of caching and modifying data, thus reducing redundancy and saving energy. Directed diffusion is a protocol more suitable for event-driven applications. It also provides a more energy-efficient variation called *geographic and energy-aware routing protocol* [58], which helps to define a closed geographic region for propagating interests that improves performance by avoiding the interest messages to flood the entire network. Other examples of flat protocols are EAR (energy-aware routing) [59] and rumor routing [60].

For large-scale networks and for achieving higher energy efficiency related to data transmission, a technique that can be adopted by routing protocols is the clustering of the network, generating a hierarchical logical topology. Routing protocols that adopt a cluster-based approach divide the whole set of nodes (according to some criterion, often the geographical proximity) into partitions controlled by an elected leader node, often called *cluster head* (*CH*). Therefore, nodes in such type of networks play different hierarchical roles: each node is either a cluster member (low level in the hierarchy) or a CH. The highest level in the hierarchy is played by the sink node. Such approaches make use of some algorithm for cluster formation and require the coordination among nodes within a cluster. After gathering data sent by all its cluster members, the CH can perform some processing in such data (e.g., a fusion) and send it to the sink node. The communication inside the cluster is often accomplished by adopting a TDMA schedule. Since the distance among cluster members and the respective CHs is, in general, smaller than the distance between these sensors and the sink, sensors in a cluster save transmission energy. In order to not overload the CH, a periodic rotation of the leader among the sensors in a cluster is often adopted.

Clustering can also be beneficial for purposes of energy saving because it favors data fusion procedures. Cluster members can collaborate about recent data measurements and determine how much information should be transmitted to the user application. By averaging data values collected within the cluster, the algorithm can trade data resolution for transmission power. Also for energy saving, in areas where there are a redundant number of sensors, a clustering algorithm can be used to select which nodes better represent data samples for the region and which ones can be put in a power-save mode.

One of the first hierarchical, cluster-based protocols for WSN was LEACH [55–57]. LEACH is a self-organizing, adaptive protocol that uses randomization to distribute the energy load evenly among all the sensors in the network. In this protocol, the process of cluster formation is distributed among sensors. Any sensor may become a leader with probability X. The CH generates a TDMA schedule and transmits it in broadcast for all sensors in the cluster. After some time, each sensor enters again in the phase of cluster formation, and this cycle is repeated until the complete exhaustion of the energy source of all sensors in the WSN. Since LEACH algorithm randomly rotates the high energy role of CH, its functions are shared equally among the various sensors and battery power is expended equally among them. In addition, LEACH performs local data fusion to compress the amount of data sent from the clusters to the base station, further reducing energy dissipation and enhancing system lifetime. LEACH is a protocol suitable for periodical applications that assume the network always has data to send.

In LEACH, the CH selection is probabilistic, depending only on the number of times a node has been CH, and the residual energy of nodes is not considered in the cluster formation process. This adoption of probability for becoming a CH is based on the assumption that all nodes start with an equal amount of energy and that all nodes have data to send during each frame. Therefore, in spite of being energy efficient, LEACH in its original version is not considered an energy-aware protocol. Heinzelman et al. [57] proposed some changes in the original LEACH algorithm, and in this new version, the node with the higher energy should have the larger probability to become the CH. The authors argue that if instead of being homogeneous in energy, the nodes have different amounts of energy (or an event-driven application is used instead of periodical monitoring), those nodes with more energy should be CHs more often than the nodes with less energy, in order to ensure that all nodes die at approximately the same time. This can be achieved by setting the probability of becoming a CH as a function of a node's energy level relative to the aggregate energy remaining in the network, rather than as a function of the number of times the node has been CH, as in the original LEACH algorithm. In such approach, each node must have an estimate of the total energy of all nodes in the network to compute the probability of it becoming a CH. As a result, each node will not be able to make a decision to become a CH if only its local information is known. Therefore, this protocol is not based on a localized algorithm, and as a drawback, its scalability can be poor.

Other hierarchical protocols also make explicit use of the information of node energy in the decisions involved in cluster formation and CH election. For instance, CODA (congestion detection and avoidance) [61] is an example of energy-aware cluster-based protocol that is aimed at addressing the unbalance of energy depletion caused by different distances from the sink by dividing the whole network into a few groups based on the node's distance to the sink node and the routing strategy. Each group has its own number of clusters and member nodes, and the number of clusters is differentiated in terms of the distance to the sink; the farther the distance, the more clusters are formed. CODA achieved better performance in terms of network lifetime and dissipated energy than those protocols that apply the same probability for the number of clusters to the whole network, such as LEACH. However, the CODA algorithm relies on global information of node position and therefore does not scale well. Younis and Fahmy [62] proposed HEED, a hybrid, energy-efficient, distributed clustering algorithm that periodically selects the CH from a cluster according to both the node residual energy and a secondary parameter, such as node proximity to its neighbors or node density. HEED is a localized algorithm, so it incurs low message overhead, and it achieves fairly uniform CH distribution across the network. Its main drawback is that it requires multiple broadcasting for cluster formation and thus consumes energy in this phase.

Chan and Perrig [63] proposed an unequal clustering size model for network organization, which can lead to more uniform energy dissipation among CH nodes, thus increasing network lifetime. Ye et al. [64] presented EECS (energy-efficient clustering scheme), a clustering algorithm that achieves an even CH distribution with no iteration and introduces a weighted function for the ordinary node (non-CH) to make a decision about the best cluster to join to. In EECS, CHs are the nodes with more residual energy and selected in a distributed manner through localized radio communication.

However, the approach of considering the absolute value of node residual energy as the major criterion to elect a CH can lead to an unbalance in the overall energy consumption, and thus, at a long term, such solutions may perform poor for the goal of prolonging the network lifetime. According to Liu et al. [65], such approaches do not help balancing the energy load for the proper nodes, especially in circumstances of highly energy heterogeneous nodes, and in these cases, such behavior may cause the problem of quickly exhausting some nodes.

In order to solve such drawback, the authors presented a novel distributed and energy-efficient hierarchical clustering scheme, called *EAP* (*extensible authentication protocol*). In EAP, a node with a high ratio of residual energy to the average residual energy of all the neighbor nodes in its cluster range will have a large probability to become the CH. This can better handle heterogeneous energy circumstances than existing clustering algorithms, which elect the CH only based on a node's own residual energy. According to the results of the performed evaluations, EAP significantly outperforms LEACH and HEED in terms of both network lifetime and the amount of data gathered.

Other examples of hierarchical protocols are TEEN [66], APTEEN [67], HPAR [68], ICA [69], and STALK [70].

25.4 TRANSPORT LAYER

The transport layer helps to maintain the flow in WSNs and to guarantee end-to-end reliability and QoS. It provides mechanisms (i) to mitigate congestion that arises from the variance of injected traffic within the network, (ii) to recover packet loss due to congestion and queue overflow, (iii) to provide fairness in bandwidth allocation, and (iv) to order delivery of packets, in case packets are fragmented at the transmitter end [71, 72]. De facto transport control protocols of wired networks such as TCP (transport control protocol) [73] and UDP (user datagram protocol) [74] are not suitable to WSNs due to the unique characteristics of such environment [72]. One main reason is that in WSNs several new factors can result in congestion, such as the typical convergent nature of upstream traffic and the limited wireless bandwidth. The upstream traffic is the primary traffic direction in WSN and denotes a many-to-one type of communication from the sensor nodes to the sink. The control messages occasionally sent by sink nodes generate traffic in the opposite direction, named *downstream traffic*, for the purposes of query and control. Another reason why transport protocols for wired networks are not suitable for WSN is that wireless channel introduces packet loss due to the typically high bit error rate, which not only affects reliability of data but also wastes energy. As a consequence, transport protocols specifically tailored for WSNs are required, and the two major problems that such protocols need to cope with are congestion and packet loss [75]. Both problems have a direct impact on the overall energy efficiency of a WSN. Since the requirements of fairness and packet ordering, as well as of responsibility of transport protocols, are not directly related to energy, they are not addressed in this chapter.

Typically, WSN transport layer protocols mitigate congestion using three mechanisms (Fig. 25.4): congestion detection, congestion notification, and transmission rate adjustment [76]. Congestion can be detected by monitoring queue length [77, 78], packet service time [79], or the ratio of packet service time over packet interarrival time at intermediate nodes [80]. In the case of WSNs that use a CSMA-based MAC protocol, channel loading can also be measured and used as an indication of congestion [78]. The congestion occurrence must be propagated from the congested node to the upstream sensor nodes (closer to the

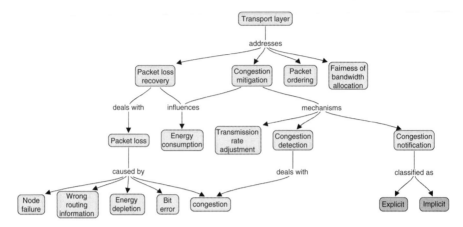

Figure 25.4   Concept map for transport layer policies.

sink) or the source nodes that contribute to congestion. Existent WSN transport protocols propagate such information using two approaches: explicit congestion notification and implicit congestion notification. The former uses special control messages to notify the involved sensor nodes of congestion, such as the suppression messages adopted in Reference 78. The latter approach piggybacks congestion information in ordinary data packets. By receiving or overhearing such packets, sensor nodes can access the piggybacked information. To mitigate congestion, a sensor node can adjust its transmission rate on receiving the congestion information. Depending on the available information, simple schemes such as additive increase multiplicative decrease (AIMD) [78, 81] or more elaborated ones such as those described in References 79 and 80 can be used to accurately adjust the transmission rate.

Regarding the packet loss, there are several factors that contribute for it in WSNs. Among the main reasons, in wireless environments, congestion, bit error, node failure, wrong or outdated routing information, and energy depletion can cause packet loss, leading to loss of reliability and energy inefficiency. Packet loss can be mitigated by increasing the data-sending rate of source nodes or introducing retransmission-based loss recovery. However, the former approach is not energy efficient compared to the latter. The loss recovery method is more active and energy efficient to address WSN reliability [76]. WSN transport layer protocols commonly address loss recovery by two different approaches: end to end and hop by hop. In the end-to-end approach, the end points (destination or source nodes) are responsible for loss detection and notification [71]. To enforce end-to-end loss recovery, a sender node generally uses a closed-loop feedback scheme where it waits for the reply message from the destination end point. On the other hand, hop-by-hop loss recovery uses an open-loop nonfeedback process. Each approach has its own advantages and limitations. End-to-end reliability approaches are simple and robust, but they produce more in-network traffic. On the other hand, hop-by-hop approaches quickly suppress the spots of congestion with fewer number of in-network control packets, thus saving considerable amount of sensor energy. However, the drawback is that hop-by-hop loss recovery cannot assure message delivery in the presence of frequent network topology changes because of node relocation, addition, and failures. Since less ongoing packets can result in saved energy, the trade-off between end-to-end and hop-by-hop approaches is an important design factor that influences WSN lifetime.

In the past years, several works were published describing new transport protocols tailored to WSNs. The surveys presented in References 76 and 82 contain a comprehensive list and analysis of current WSN transport protocols. Next, we briefly describe transport protocols specifically designed with focus on energy efficiency.

ESRT (event-to-sink reliable transport) [81, 83] aims at providing reliability and congestion control in an energy-efficient way. The notion of reliability is defined with respect to the number of data packets originated by any event that are reliably received at the sink node. The sink node runs the ESRT algorithm to decide whether the event is being reliably detected or not. To do this, the sink node tracks the event reporting frequency (f) of the successfully received packets originated by a particular event within a time interval and matches it with the required reliability metric. ESRT tries to operate on the optimum point where any event is reliably reported to the sink without causing congestion to the network. ESRT assumes that the sink node has a high power radio and can reach all the sensor nodes in a single broadcast message. The sink broadcasts the newly calculated value of f to the whole sensor network. On receiving the event reporting frequency, each sensor node calculates its event reporting duration and checks the buffer level at the end of each reporting interval to guess any possible congestion. Whenever a sensor node faces congestion, it sets a congestion enabled bit of the event report packet. When these packets arrive at the sink node, it gets an overall view of the congestion level of the network. ESRT conserves energy by controlling the value of f.

SenTCP [84] is an energy-efficient congestion control protocol intended for upstream traffic flow. SenTCP measures the degree of congestion in every intermediate sensor node using the values of (i) average local packet-servicing time, (ii) local packet interarrival time, and (iii) the buffer occupancy. SenTCP uses a hop-by-hop congestion control in which each intermediate sensor issues a feedback signal to its neighbors, in the event of congestion, which carries the local congestion degree and the buffer occupancy ratio. The feedback signal is used for the neighboring sensor nodes to adjust their local data-sending rate. The hop-by-hop feedback control regulates congestion quickly and reduces packet dropping, which in turn conserves energy and increases the throughput. SenTCP always uses the shortest path to forward data. Therefore, this protocol minimizes the average node energy consumption. However, the overall network lifetime can be compromised since the nodes on the shortest path will be used until their power is exhausted [85].

Different from SenTCP, in Reference 86 is presented a framework that mitigates congestion by creating alternative paths to avoid the congested paths instead of reducing the data-sending rate. The creation of alternative paths involves several nodes that are not in the initial shortest path from sources to the sink. The use of these nodes leads to a balanced energy consumption, avoiding the power depletion of nodes on the shortest path, thus prolonging WSN lifetime [86, 87].

Priority-based congestion control protocol (PCCP) [80] is a hop-by-hop upstream congestion control protocol for WSNs. PCCP provides a different throughput to each sensor node in a multihop WSN by attaching a weighted fairness value to each node. PCCP offers a different degree of priority indexes such that a sensor node with a higher priority index and also sensor nodes that inject more traffic receive more bandwidth. PCCP further defines the priority index for both self-generating traffic and transit traffic. PCCP infers the degree of congestion through packet interarrival time and packet service time and then imposes hop-by-hop congestion control depending on the measured congestion degree and the priority index. PCCP uses implicit congestion notification to avoid transmission of additional control messages and therefore helps improve the energy efficiency. Congestion information is piggybacked in the header of data packets. PCCP allows the application layer to dynamically override the priority index of any sensor node(s) of any particular region, whenever it is needed.

Asymmetric reliable transport (ART) [88] provides bidirectional end-to-end reliability and upstream congestion control in WSNs. ART uses an energy-aware algorithm that selects a subset of sensor nodes called *essential nodes* (*E-nodes*), which can cover the whole area to be sensed in an energy-efficient way. ART forms a subnetwork consisting of those E-nodes, and only those E-nodes take part in reliable data transfer to the upstream and downstream nodes. The algorithm takes into account the remaining battery power in the sensors so that sensors running low on battery have a smaller chance of being essential. This gives flexibility for balancing the available energy in the network among all sensors, thus providing a longer network lifetime. ART has three important features [71]: (i) non-E-nodes do not face end-to-end communication overhead, (ii) ART uses a distributed energy-aware congestion control, and (iii) less number of nodes takes part in loss recovery. ART provides a reliability guarantee in both downstream and upstream flows. For reliable query propagation (downstream flow), it adopts two measures. The first measure is connectionless and reactive where the sink node simply sends the query fragments without worrying about any loss. It is the responsibility of the receiving E-nodes to detect a query fragment loss by taking a look at the sequence order; then, as a recovery measure, it sends back an NACK (negative acknowledgment) to the sink node. The second measure resembles connection-oriented communication where the sink node proactively handles the loss detection using the time-out mechanism. A time-out event without getting any ACK (positive acknowledgment) for a particular query fragment makes the sink resend the fragment. End-to-end event reliability is assumed to be achieved if the first message containing the event information, which is sent by the E-nodes, is reliably received by the sink. For event reliability—used in applications that require only successful event detection, but not successful transmission of all packets [81]—E-nodes are responsible for detecting the event-message loss and recovering it. Each E-node enables a control bit to notify the sink that this message portrays the first event message, which enforces the sink to reply back with an ACK.

Rosberg et al. [89] proposed a hybrid system that combines a modified version of the ESRT protocol [81, 83] with the implicit and explicit automatic repeat request (ieARQ) protocol [89]. This hybrid system adaptively switches between ESRT and ieARQ to achieve energy efficiency under a statistical reliability constraint. The ESRT protocol starts at the source sensor node where data is sampled. After H_{sw} hops, the algorithm proceeds with ieARQ. H_{sw} is a dynamic hop threshold that depends on the path length and link error rate. The ieARQ adapts the maximum number of retransmissions in each hop based on the channel error estimations in order to reach a predetermined statistical reliability threshold. Rosberg et al. 90 defined statistical reliability with level β as a QoS level where during every predetermined time window, a predetermined amount of random sensed data is delivered to the sink node from every source, each with a probability of at least β. Therefore, reliability is actually determined by the required quality of the aggregated sensed data delivered to the sink, rather than the reliability of individual data sample. Thus, the proposed hybrid algorithm allows WSN users to control the balance between energy efficiency and data reliability.

25.5 APPLICATION LAYER

This layer encompasses algorithms that require internode collaboration and exploit intranode level policies for energy management, thus often presenting a cross-layer behavior. We identify two different types of algorithms in this layer (Fig. 25.5): algorithms for task allocation and algorithms of data fusion and/or aggregation. Both types exploit the in-network processing capability of sensor nodes. Task allocation, also known as *task scheduling algorithms*, aims at partitioning the application in smaller tasks and allocating them to different sensor nodes, trying to parallelize their execution in an energy-efficient way (minimizing the communication cost). Data fusion and aggregation algorithms exploit the inherent redundancy in the sensor-generated data in order to minimize data transmissions, thus trading computation for communication costs.

25.5.1 Task Scheduling

WSNs can be considered as application-oriented networks, in the sense that in order to operate properly and to achieve their maximum usefulness, such networks need to be optimized to the specific goals of the target application. Application requirements are often described as high level missions such as "detect fires,"

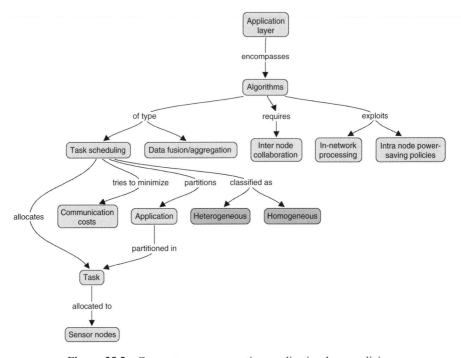

Figure 25.5   Concept map representing application layer policies.

"monitor temperature in a given area," and "report the presence of an intruder," [91]. Such high level descriptions need to be translated to low level tasks to be executed by sensor nodes. This translation and the distribution of the required work over the network nodes should be preferably transparent to the application that is built on top of the WSN. In this section, we address power management techniques used in the context of distributing application tasks over the WSN.

Most WSN applications require distributed signal and collaborative data processing. Therefore, techniques for performing energy-aware distributed processing have attracted interest of recent investigations. Such techniques exploit the WSN capacity of performing in-network processing and focus on the problem of distributing the processing in an energy-efficient way. To enable collaborative in-network processing, the following problems must be solved:

- assigning tasks to sensors;
- determining the execution sequence of tasks;
- scheduling communication between sensors.

In the field of high performance computing, the first problem is referred to as *task mapping* and the second one as *task scheduling* [92]. In this context, the problem of task scheduling and mapping in WSN assumes that an application can be divided into a number of interdependent tasks and deals with the distribution of such tasks to the WSN nodes. Different allocation of these tasks on the network nodes consumes different amounts of energy. Therefore, the main general goal of a task scheduler in this environment is to find a scheduling (or allocation) that maximizes the network lifetime, with additional constraints related to the application requirements (e.g., time). Since energy consumption in WSNs is mainly related to wireless communication, most of the works on task scheduling for WSNs propose algorithms to allocate tasks so that communication cost is minimized. One major difference from conventional scheduling algorithms is that such works focus on meeting hard time deadlines. Instead, in WSN, the main constraint is not time, but energy, so existent solutions consider that time requirement is of least importance, preceded by energy consumption, battery awareness, availability, and other application-specific parameters.

Several works have been investigating this topic in the past years, assuming different characteristics for the network (as multihop/single hop, homogeneous/heterogeneous) as well as using different approaches to represent the structure of the WSN application and to formulate the scheduling problem. The most commonly used approach to model WSN applications consists of considering a application as a set of communicating tasks and representing them as a directed acyclic graph (DAG) [93]. Therefore, the problem of task scheduling is reduced to a graph problem and solutions from this context are sought. In this section, we review some works in this area classified by their assumption regarding the heterogeneity of the WSN nodes.

Examples of works that consider a WSN composed of homogeneous nodes are References 92, 94–96. In EcoMapS, Tian et al. [92] modeled tasks and their dependencies as a DAG and considered a cluster-based network topology where each cluster has a star topology, with the CH in the middle. The CH is responsible for assigning the tasks in each cluster, as well as for mediating communication. The proposed algorithm is based on the list scheduling technique [97], in which tasks are ordered in a list so that each task is set after its predecessors and the most critical path is put first. Then the minimum schedule length subject to energy constraints is sought.

Yu and Prasanna [94] also represented the application as a DAG and proposed an energy-balanced task allocation. They consider a single-hop cluster of sensor nodes connected through multiple wireless channels and enabled with dynamic voltage scaling (DVS). Therefore, in their work the task allocation problem consists, besides assigning tasks to sensors and scheduling computation and communication activities, of assigning the most suitable voltage settings for executing each task. They consider an epoch-based scenario [98], where an instance of the application is executed during the beginning of each epoch and must be completed before the end of the epoch. Their general goal is to find an allocation so that the lifetime of the cluster is maximized. The proposed algorithm aims at minimizing the maximal energy dissipation among all sensor nodes during each epoch, subject to the latency, exclusive access, and task placement constraints. Two important differentials of such work are (i) the idea of energy-balanced task allocation, so their algorithm takes into account the fact that the remaining energy can vary among sensor nodes and (ii) the fact that they consider the time and energy costs of both the computation and communication activities (most works consider only the communication cost). An integer linear programming (ILP) formulation of the problem is initially presented, and then, since the time complexity of the ILP formulation is large, a polynomial time three-phase heuristic is also proposed.

Tian et al. [95] proposed a localized and cross-layer task mapping and scheduling solution (called *RT-MapS*) for DVS-enabled WSNs. They assumed deadline-constrained applications executed in a single-hop cluster of a homogeneous WSN. In order to better represent the broadcast feature of wireless communication, they proposed to extend DAG representation of applications as a hypergraph, thus adopting a novel high level application model, referred to as *Hyper-DAG*. The design objective of RT-MapS is to minimize energy consumption subject to application deadline constraints. In RT-MapS, communication and computation are jointly scheduled in two phases: (i) task mapping and scheduling and (ii) DVS phase. In the first phase, two low complexity task mapping and scheduling algorithms, CNPT [99] and Min-Min algorithm [100], are implemented and extended in order to incorporate their proposed communication scheduling algorithm. The DVS technique is implemented in the DVS phase to further reduce energy consumptions.

Tian and Ekici [96] extended the proposal presented in Reference 95 for multihop WSNs. They proposed an application-independent solution, called *multihop task mapping and scheduling* (*MTMS*), to provide the in-network computation capacity required by real-time applications in WSNs. Applications are represented as Hyper-DAG, and the proposed algorithm MTMS aims to guarantee application deadlines with minimum energy consumption. MTMS not only maps and schedules computation tasks to sensors in parallel in order to accelerate execution but also addresses communication scheduling among sensors to exchange intermediate results in a multihop cluster of nodes. Besides, to further optimize energy consumption, the authors also presented an algorithm for DVS. Similar to RT-MapS, MTMS consists of two phases: a task mapping and scheduling phase and a DVS phase. In the first phase, computation tasks are assigned to sensors, their execution sequence is decided, and communications between sensors are scheduled based on the communication dependency constraints. For the first phase, the authors proposed the algorithm called *task schedule search engine* (*TSSE*), an extension of the Min-Min algorithm [100]. The goal of the TSSE algorithm is to minimize energy consumption subject to deadline constraints. The original Min-Min algorithm is designed for traditional parallel processing without considering wireless communication scheduling. To solve this problem, the authors developed a new multihop communication scheduling algorithm based on the proposed Hyper-DAG representation of tasks and multihop channel model. The communication scheduling algorithm is then used by the TSSE algorithm during task scheduling to meet the communication dependency constraints. Schedules generated by the modified Min-Min algorithm are further optimized with the DVS algorithm.

Examples of proposals that consider heterogeneous WSNs are References 91, 101, and 102, all of them making use of DAG to represent the WSN application. Park and Srivastava [102] presented an energy-efficient task assignment and migration framework for WSNs. In their proposal, the task assignment problem is addressed as an optimization problem. Therefore, a cost function is proposed encompassing energy consumption, latency, and additional constraints, and the goal is to minimize such cost function. The simulated annealing method [103] is used to solve the task transformation and assignment problem.

Voinescu et al. [91] proposed a scheduling algorithm for single-hop, heterogeneous WSNs, with a focus on maximizing network lifetime while satisfying some allocation constraints such as energy constraint, compatibility of tasks to a given node or topology, and the purpose of the network. They considered that the task to be scheduled is the smallest indivisible part of an application and can be classified into sensing tasks, actuating tasks, computation tasks, etc. The proposed scheduler uses some basic information for each task: its importance, an affinity to a certain type of node (a smoke-sensing task can only be assigned to wireless nodes that have a smoke sensor), a frequency with which to run (if the task is repeatable), and dependencies. The scheduler chooses which assignment is best for purposes of energy consumption. The authors model the tasks and their dependencies as a DAG where the edges represent data dependencies, and with assigned costs being the maximal number of bits transmitted between the tasks. Therefore, the scheduling problem is reduced to a known graph problem, called the *min k-cut problem*, for which a polynomial algorithm has been found in 1988 [104].

25.5.2 Data Aggregation and Data Fusion in WSNs

Data aggregation in WSNs (Fig. 25.6) consists of combining data generated by different sensor nodes with the purposes of augmenting the perception on the monitored phenomenon, eliminating spurious data, and decreasing the amount of redundant transmissions, thus saving energy [105]. Great redundancy is commonly present in WSNs due to the high density of nodes and the fact that they are often monitoring a common phenomenon, therefore producing data strongly correlated. On one hand, minimizing such redundancy using techniques for data aggregation is a very effective way to reduce energy consumption [53, 106]. On the other hand, individual readings of sensors may be inaccurate and of low significance for the client application. Inaccuracies of sensor measurements can be generated by different sources, such as strong variations or interferences in the monitored environment and intrinsic imprecision on sensor calibrations. Moreover, the sensing capability of an individual sensor is restricted to a limited spatial region called as the *sensing range*. In order to produce useful information and meet the requirement of sensing coverage of each application, data from several sensors need to be used. In this context, the combination of data arising from different sources to provide suitable temporal and spatial coverage to the application is an important task in WSNs. Data aggregation techniques can be used as

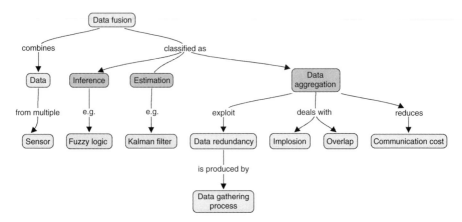

Figure 25.6 Concept map representing data fusion and data aggregation in WSN.

an effective way to accomplish such task, processing data from multiple sensors in order to filter noise measurements and thus providing more accurate interpretation of data generated by a large number of sensors. Therefore, in WSNs, data can be aggregated with two goals: improve the accuracy and save energy.

There are different definitions for data aggregation. According to Cohen et al. [107], "data aggregation comprises the collection of raw data from pervasive data sources, the flexible, programmable composition of the raw data into less voluminous refined data, and the timely delivery of the refined data to data consumers." In the context of WSNs, such a term is often used as a synonym for data fusion [108, 109]. In spite of being possible to consider both terms as synonyms, often data fusion encompasses more sophisticated techniques to combine data from multiple sources, with the main goal of improving the accuracy of the generated data. Indeed, although several techniques of data fusion are used to save energy, some methods applied to fuse data can be quite complex, and the required processing may consume more energy than the simple forwarding of raw data. On the other hand, data aggregation always aims at reducing the amount of data to be transmitted. As van Renesse [109] defines, "aggregation is the ability to summarize," which means that the amount of data is reduced, thus saving energy. In this sense, data aggregation can be considered as a subset of data fusion techniques that exploit the in-networking capacity of WSN nodes to filter out redundancies and save transmission energy. The idea is to take advantage of the node computation capacity and perform the desired fusion algorithm while data is routed toward the sink node. Krishnamachari et al. [110] argued that the adoption of data aggregation shifts the focus from address-centric approaches of establishing routes between pairs of nodes to a data-centric approach of finding routes from multiple sources to a destination that allows and promotes the in-network consolidation of data. One of the first works to exploit the in-network data aggregation was directed diffusion protocol [47, 53]. In such a protocol, nodes coordinate to establish data-centric gradients for data forwarding and to perform distributed sensing of an environmental phenomenon. Significant energy saving is achieved when intermediate nodes in the routes provided by the gradients aggregate responses to queries issued by applications.

Since our subject in this chapter is on strategies for energy efficiency, we focus mainly on data aggregation techniques (Section 25.5.2.2). Nevertheless, in Section 25.5.2.1, we briefly discuss some uses of data fusion to achieve energy savings in WSNs.

25.5.2.1 Approaches of data fusion for energy efficiency. Like data aggregation, there are different definitions for data fusion as well. According to Hall and Llinas [111], it can be defined as "a process dealing with the automatic detection, association, correlation, estimation, and combination of data and information from multiple sources." Data fusion techniques use the observations of events from multiple sensors as the input and integrate the information in order to achieve increased accuracies and new inferences that could not be achieved using a single source of data [111]. In WSNs, data fusion can be used for improving data accuracy and saving energy.

As we previously mentioned, data aggregation can be classified as a type of data fusion technique. Such classification takes into account the purpose or goal with which the technique is applied. Other classifications for data fusion techniques exist, considering different criteria such as the data abstraction level, type of data, parameters, and mathematical foundation [112]. Within the criterion based on the purpose, besides data aggregation, other purposes for which data fusion is commonly used are inference and estimation. Both techniques can be used to achieve energy efficiency in WSNs.

Inference methods are applied in the context of using data fusion for decision-making processes. A decision is taken based on the knowledge of the perceived situation. Decision-making paradigms include Bayesian decision making, Dempster–Shafer inference, fuzzy logic, and semantic information fusion. Fuzzy logic has been successfully applied in different ways with the aim of optimizing the energy consumption in WSNs. Several works use fuzzy logic for decisions related to the routing strategy. For instance, Gupta et al. [113] applied fuzzy reasoning to select the best CHs in a clustered WSN, taking into account the node density, energy level, and node centrality with respect to the whole cluster. Also, for the purpose of energy-efficient routing, Srinivasan et al. [114] proposed the use of a fuzzy controller at each node that, at the time of route discovery, makes a decision to send back or continue processing the data packets based on (i) the interests (query) received, (ii) the type of data being sensed, and (iii) an estimate of the node battery power level.

Semantic information fusion is essentially an in-network inference process in which raw sensor data is processed so that nodes exchange only the resulting semantic interpretations [112]. The semantic abstraction allows a WSN to optimize its resource utilization when collecting, storing, and processing data. Semantic information fusion usually comprises two phases: knowledge base construction and pattern matching (inference). The first phase (usually off-line) aggregates the most appropriate knowledge abstractions into semantic information, which is then used in the second phase (on-line), a pattern matching phase, for fusing relevant attributes and providing a semantic interpretation of sensor data [115–117].

Estimation methods were inherited from control theory and use the laws of probability to compute a process state vector from a measurement vector or a sequence of measurement vectors [118]. Examples of estimation methods are maximum likelihood, least squares, and Kalman filters. In WSNs, estimation methods can be used to save energy instead of always transmitting the whole data stream from source nodes to the sink node. A prediction scheme can be used in both the sources and sink, and only when the estimated value differs from the actual value by more than a predefined error, data needs to be transmitted to the sink. The work described in Reference 119 adopts a dual prediction scheme based on least-squares filters to achieve this goal. Using the proposed least mean square (LMS) adaptive algorithm on a publicly available, real-world (office environment) temperature data set, the authors achieved up to 92% reduction in communication while maintaining a minimal accuracy of $0.5°C$. In Reference 120, a dual Kalman filter approach was proposed with the same goal: both source and sink nodes predict the sensed value so that the source node sends data only when it knows the sink prediction is incorrect.

25.5.2.2 Data aggregation strategies.
Kulik et al. [51] defined data aggregation as a technique used to overcome two problems: *implosion* and *overlap*. In the former, data sensed by one node is duplicated in the network due to the data routing strategy (e.g., flooding). The *overlap* problem happens when two different nodes disseminate the same data. This might occur whenever the network density is high, and therefore, the sensor nodes are redundant, meaning that they sense the same property in the same place. In both cases, the redundancy generated for different reasons might have its negative impact (e.g., waste of energy and bandwidth) reduced using data aggregation techniques.

Data aggregation can be a simple operation of duplicate suppression or it can encompass more sophisticated operations. Duplicate suppression is the straightest approach that consists of, whenever multiple sources send the same data, intermediate nodes and will forward only one of them [56]. Such simple approach eliminates redundancy by discarding duplicate data. The use of maximum or minimum function is also possible. However, the most common techniques of data aggregation are the summarization functions, commonly used by query languages (e.g., SQL) to retrieve summarized data in database systems. Madden et al. [121] discussed the implementation of five basic aggregation operations, that is, count, min, max, sum, and average, based on the TinyOS platform and demonstrated that such generic approach for aggregation leads to significant energy savings. Such database approach for data aggregation was successfully adopted in several works. Madden et al. [122] proposed TinyDB, a distributed query processor that offers simple extensions to SQL to control data acquisition and allows the user to specify temporal and event-based aggregates in WSNs. TinyDB includes a mechanism for user-defined, SQL-like aggregates and a metadata management system that supports optimizations over them. TinyDB has many of the features of a traditional query processor (e.g., the ability to select, join, project, and aggregate data), but it also incorporates a number of other features designed to minimize power consumption via *acquisitional* techniques. According to the authors, these techniques can provide orders of magnitude improvements in power consumption and increased accuracy of query results over nonacquisitional systems that do not actively control when and where data is collected.

Madden et al. [98] argued that since aggregation is so central to WSN applications, it must be provided as a core service by the system software. Instead of a set of extensible APIs (application programming interfaces) programmed in low level languages such as C, the authors believe that an aggregation service, consisting of a generic, easily invoked high level programming abstraction, should be provided by sensor platforms. Such approach enables users of WSNs, who often are not network experts, to focus on their application logic, unburdening them of dealing with specificities of the underlying embedded OS and hardware. To achieve their goal, they developed Tiny AGgregation (TAG), a generic aggregation service for networks of TinyOS motes. TAG provides a simple, declarative interface for data collection and aggregation, inspired by selection and aggregation facilities in database query languages. Besides, TAG distributes and executes aggregation queries in the WSN in a time- and power-efficient way. They adopted an SQL-style query syntax but extended the five basic aggregation functions to incorporate more complex operations.

Another aggregation function that can be identified in WSNs is packaging [2]. Packaging groups several observations in one single packet, with the goal of avoiding the overhead of the MAC protocol when sending several packets.

Data aggregation can also include complex techniques based on mathematical and statistical methods, which allow combining data with different meanings. However, these methods are more often part of the broader range of data fusion techniques (Section 25.5.2.1).

The use of data aggregation in WSNs and its impact on energy consumption have been the subject of extensive investigation. Several works already demonstrated its overall benefits, while others discussed the challenges, such as the establishment of efficient aggregation trees and the involved trade-offs (as latency and data accuracy). Regarding the overall advantages, Kulik et al. [51] proposed the SPIN protocol that performs traffic reduction for information dissemination by using metadata negotiations between sensors in order to avoid redundant and/or unnecessary data propagation through the network. Krishnamachari and colleagues [110] described the impact of source-destination placement on the energy costs and the delay associated with data aggregation. They also investigated the complexity of optimal data aggregation. Intanagonwiwat et al. [123] evaluated the impact (latency and robustness) of a greedy aggregation algorithm in high density networks. The proposed greedy aggregation approach improves path sharing and achieves significant energy savings when the network has high node densities, in comparison with the opportunistic approach.

Depending on the network organization, in-network data aggregation may occur in different ways, according to the logical topology and routing strategy. In hierarchical networks, usually a two-hop communication takes place. One hop for the cluster members to reach the CH, and another hop for CHs to reach the sink node. In this type of communication, data aggregation is performed by CHs that send the results to the sink. An example of hierarchical solutions for WSNs where CHs perform data aggregation is LEACH [55, 113, 124–127].

In flat networks, data aggregation should be executed by every node that takes part in the routing process. Some proposals assume performing the aggregation in an opportunistic way by intermediate nodes along the multihop path from sources to sink nodes, while others consider building an aggregation tree. Examples of multihop communication with in-network aggregation include Pegasis [128] and the directed diffusion family of algorithms [47, 49, 53]. In Pegasis [128], sensors form chains so that each node transmits and receives from a nearby neighbor. Gathered data moves from node to node, gets aggregated, and is eventually transmitted to the sink. Nodes take turns to transmit so that the average energy spent by each node is reduced. Another example is Reference 129, where the authors addressed the problem of finding an efficient schedule that specifies the way in which data should be collected and aggregated from all source nodes and transmitted to the sink. Given the location of the sensors and the sink, they provided a near-optimal maximum lifetime data aggregation (MLDA) algorithm to find a data gathering schedule that maximizes the time until the first sensor has its energy depleted. The proposed algorithm significantly outperforms existing data gathering protocols in terms of system lifetime.

However, most existent proposals are based on the build of an aggregation tree. Since there is a strong dependence between the aggregation tree and the routing tree, several approaches integrate aggregation functions as part of the routing protocol or strategies. Other works assume the building of trees explicitly for purposes of aggregation, independent of the underlying data routing. In both cases, the building of an optimal aggregation tree is a critical issue in the aggregation process. Such tree needs to be built using as few nodes and resources as possible to guarantee the aggregation and (in some cases) delivery of data generated by source nodes. Finding an optimal routing tree, connecting sources to sinks, is shown to be an NP-complete problem very similar to the Steiner tree [50]. Several heuristics have been proposed for this problem. Krishnamachari et al. [110] provided theoretical results regarding the NP-completeness related to the formation of an optimal aggregation tree. They evaluated three heuristics for this purpose: the centered-at-nearest-source (CNS) tree, the shortest-path tree (SPT), and the greedy incremental tree (GIT). In the CNS tree, each source sends its data directly to the source closest to the sink; in the SPT, each source sends its data to the sink along the shortest path between both nodes; and in the GIT, the routing tree starts with the shortest path between the sink and the nearest source, and at each step after that, the source closest to the current tree is included in the tree. SPT is the most popular scheme because of its low complexity and short delay. However, the achieved energy savings with SPT significantly varies with the change in the network topology. Krishnamachari et al. [110] showed that the GIT heuristic is the best of the three. However, its distributed version, described in Reference 130, requires a lot of communication and memory usage because every node needs to know its shortest paths to the other nodes in the network. Motivated by that inefficient energy cost, Nakamura et al. [131] proposed the InFRA heuristic, which finds the shortest paths that maximize data aggregation, and has an O(1)-approximation ratio. Ding et al. [132] proposed a tree-based routing algorithm based on nodes' residual energy, so that nodes with more energy are likely to perform data aggregation and routing. Once the tree is built, leaf nodes are turned off to save energy.

Besides proposals for data aggregation based on flat and hierarchical network topologies, there are works that assume a hybrid approach, in which there are multiple hops connecting source nodes to their CH and/or multiple hops connecting CHs to the sink node(s). In such a scenario, both flat and hierarchical in-network aggregation can be combined. The aforementioned strategy proposed by Nakamura et al. [131] illustrates a routing algorithm for hybrid networks performing in-network data aggregation.

Besides the network topology, there are other important parameters, as well as trade-offs, to be considered in data aggregation strategies. One important factor is the degree of spatial correlation of data monitored by nodes in close proximity. The higher the degree, the better the benefits that can be achieved by data aggregations. Alhtough most works assume that neighboring nodes always report similar data, there are cases in which such assumption does not hold. Rocha et al. [133] discussed the issue of neighboring nodes that are not semantically correlated and the need for building clusters based on the semantical similarity of nodes in order to achieve a more efficient data aggregation and thus save energy.

Two other important parameters to be considered are the aggregation degree and the aggregation delay. The former denotes the ratio between the number of received messages and the number of forwarded messages, in a given node performing aggregation. Aggregation delay is the delay generated by the time interval an aggregator node needs to wait for data messages to be aggregated before transmitting the resultant aggregated data packet. Higher values for aggregation degree and aggregation delay imply an overall higher aggregation (a larger number of messages being aggregated), thus increasing the energy savings. However, there is an important trade-off to be managed here. High values for aggregation degree can compromise the data accuracy, while high values of aggregation delay can compromise the latency. For applications that require original and accurate measurements, the summarization provided by data aggregation operations may represent an accuracy loss [106]. In fact, although many applications might be interested only in summarized data, we cannot always assert whether or not the summarized data is more accurate than the original data set [112]. Therefore, aggregation degree and delay parameters need to be carefully tuned taking into account both the requirements of energy efficiency and the application QoS, finding a balance between these two conflicting goals. Two important works tackling this issue are Reference 106, where the authors have discussed the trade-off between energy consumption and accuracy when aggregation functions are used to summarize data from a WSN, and Reference 134, where the authors have discussed the trade-offs between energy consumption and transmission delay in the presence of data aggregation. Another work [135] analyzed the trade-offs among communication delay, energy consumption, and data accuracy of the partial data aggregation technique and discussed the obtained results.

Another very interesting work is Reference 136, in which the authors explicitly took into account the cost of processing data aggregation and evaluated the trade-off between reducing the energy consumption and preserving information integrity in the aggregation process. According to the authors, although most aggregation strategies discussed in the literature do not consider the cost of processing, there are occasions when the aggregation process is more costly than the direct forward of data without employing aggregation. The greater the number of packets aggregated, the better the benefit of using aggregation with respect to not using it. Aggregation, however, cannot be increased indefinitely without the loss of important information. Motivated by this finding, they developed and analyzed an energy consumption model, performed an entropy estimation for this model, and identified a set of conditions under which aggregation can be less costly than nonaggregation. They claim that the provided results can be used by network designers to further investigate the conditions when aggregation can increase the system performance and to design WSN protocols that are capable of increasing both the network lifetime and the fidelity of the generated data.

25.6   FINAL REMARKS

In this chapter, we discussed strategies for energy management in WSNs that deal with the whole network, exploiting the specificities of each layer while addressing their relationships and dependencies.

It is important to mention that for reasons of lack of space, we did not explicitly describe solutions for cross-layer design in WSNs, an approach that directly addresses the issue of energy saving. Cross-layer design may be defined as "the breaking of OSI hierarchical layers in communication networks" [1] or "protocol design by the violation of reference layered communication architecture is cross-layer design with respect to the particular layered architecture" [137]. The breaking of OSI hierarchical layers or the violation of reference architecture includes merging of layers, creating new interfaces, or providing additional interdependencies between any two layers [138]. Therefore, the central idea of a cross-layer design in WSNs is, instead of following a strictly layered design, in which protocols in one layer only directly interact whit the subjacent ones, to allow the control and exchange of information over two or more layers in order to achieve significant improvements in the energy performance by exploiting the interactions between these various layers. For resource-constrained systems such as WSNs, optimization across all layers provides huge improvements in the energy efficiency, thus it is important to exploit such feature in the design of protocols and frameworks for WSNs. Cross-layer issues mainly focus on two aspects: (i) the protocol design and (ii) the framework design along with implementation-related issues. For further information on the former aspect, the reader can refer to Reference 139, in which the authors have presented a comprehensive review of the state of art of cross-layer protocols. For the latter aspect, the readers can refer to Reference 140, in which the current proposals for cross-layer frameworks are described and analyzed.

ACKNOWLEDGMENTS

This work is partially supported by the National Council for Scientific and Technological Development and by CAPES, through processes 201090/2009-0 and 477229/2009-3 for Flávia C. Delicato and 480359/2009-1 and 4073-09-06 for Paulo F. Pires.

REFERENCES

1. Song L. Cross layer design in Wireless Sensor Networks [PhD thesis]. Department of Electrical and Computer Engineering, University of Toronto; 2006.
2. He T, Blum BM, Stankovic JA, Abdelzaher T. AIDA: Adaptive application independent data AGgregation in wireless sensor network. ACM Trans Embed Comput Syst Special issue on Dynamically Adaptable Embedded Systems 2004;3(2):426–457.; vol. no. pp.
3. Tilak S, Abu-Ghazaleh NB, Heinzelman W. A taxonomy of wireless microsensor network models. ACM SIGMOBILE Mobile Comput Commun Rev 2002;6(2):28–36.
4. Novak JD, Cañas AJ. The theory underlying concept maps and how to construct them. Technical Report IHMC CmapTools 2006-01. Florida Institute for Human and Machine Cognition; 2006.
5. Akyildiz I, Su Weilian, Sankarasubramaniam Y, Cayirci E. A survey on sensor networks. IEEE Commun Mag 2002;40(8):102–114.
6. Xu Y, Bien S, Mori Y, Heidemann J, and Estrin D. Topology control protocols to conserve energy in wireless Ad Hoc networks. CENS Technical Report UCLA, Number 6. Los Angeles (CA); 2003.
7. Costa P, Cesana M, Brambilla S, Casartelli L. A cooperative approach for topology control in Wireless Sensor Networks. Pervasive Mobile Comput 2009;5(5):526–541.
8. Anastasi G, Conti M, Di Francesco M, Passarella A. Energy conservation in Wireless Sensor Networks: A survey. Ad Hoc Netw 2009;7(3):537–568.
9. Karl H, Willig A. Topology control. In: Karl H, Willig A, editors. *Protocols and Architectures for Wireless Sensor Networks*. 1st ed.John Wiley and Sons; 2005. Chapter 10.

10. Gupta V, Pandey R. Data fusion and topology control in Wireless Sensor Networks. WSEAS Trans Signal Proc 2008;4(4):150–172.

11. Santi P. Topology control in wireless Ad Hoc and sensor networks. ACM Comput Surv 2005;37(2):164–194.

12. Penrose M. A strong law for the largest nearest-neighbour link between random points. J Lond Math Soc 1999;60:951–960.

13. Yi C, Wan P. Asymptotic critical transmission ranges for connectivity in wireless ad hoc networks with Bernoulli nodes. In: Proceedings of IEEE Wireless Communication and Networking Conference (WCNC); 2005; New Orleans (LA). pp. 2219–2224.

14. Meguerdichian S, Potkonjak M. Low power 0/1 coverage and scheduling techniques in sensor networks. UCLA Technical Reports 030001; 2003 Jan.

15. Chakrabarty K, Iyengar SS,, Qi H, Cho E. Grid coverage for surveillance and target location in distributed sensor networks. IEEE Trans Comput 2002;51(12):1448–1453.

16. Chen B, Jamieson K, Balakrishnan H, Morris R. Span: an energy-efficient coordination algorithm for topology maintenance in Ad Hoc wireless networks. ACM Wireless Netw 2002;8(5):481–494.

17. Xu Y, Heidemann J, Estrin D. Adaptive energy-conserving routing for multihop Ad Hoc networks. Research Report 527. USC/Information Sciences Institute; 2000 Oct. http://www.isi.edu/~johnh/PAPERS/Xu00a.html

18. Xu Y, Heidemann J, Estrin D. Geography-informed energy conservation for Ad-Hoc routing. In: Proceedings of the 7th Annual ACM/IEEE International Conference on Mobile Computing and Networking; California, USA; 2001. pp. 70–84.

19. Cerpa A, Estrin D. ASCENT: adaptive self-configuring sEnsor networks topologies. IEEE Trans Mobile Comput 2004;3(3):272–285.

20. Ababneh N, Selvakennedy S. OTC: an optimized topology control algorithm for Wireless Sensor Networks. In: Proceedings of the 8th International Conference on Parallel and Distributed Computing, Applications and Technologies (PDCAT); 2007 Dec 3–6; Adelaide, Australia.

21. Wang X, Xing G, Zhang Y, Lu C, Pless R, and Gill C Integrated coverage and connectivity configuration in Wireless Sensor Networks. In: Proceedings of the ACM SenSys03; 2003 Nov; Los Angeles (CA).

22. Perillo M, Heinzelman W. Sensor management policies to provide application QoS. Elsevier AdHoc Netw J 2003;1:235–246.

23. Perillo M, Heinzelman W. Optimal sensor management under energy and reliability constraints. In: Proceedings of the IEEE Wireless Communications and Networking Conference; 2003 March; New Orleans (LA).

24. Delicato F, Protti F, Pirmez L, de Rezende JF. An efficient heuristic for selecting active nodes in Wireless Sensor Networks. Comput Netw 2006;50(18):3701–3720.

25. Yahya B, Ben-Othman J. Towards a classification of energy aware MAC protocols for Wireless Sensor Networks. Wireless Commun Mobile Comput 2009;9(12):1572–1607.

26. Ye W, Heidemann J, Estrin D. Medium access control with coordinated adaptive sleeping for Wireless Sensor Networks. IEEE/ACM Trans Netw 2004;12(3):493–506.

27. Jones C, Sivalingam K, Agrawal P, Chen JC. A survey of energy efficient network protocols. Wireless Netw 2001;7:343–358.

28. Lettieri P, Srivastava B. Advances in wireless terminals (I). IEEE Personal Commun 1999;6(1):6–19.

29. Ye W, Heidemann J. Medium access control in Wireless Sensor Networks. In: Raghavendra C, Sivalingam K, Znati T, editors. *Wireless Sensor Networks*. Kluwer Academic Publishers; Norwell, MA, USA, 73–91;2004; Chapter 4.

30. Rappaport T. *Wireless Communications: Principles & Practice*. New Jersey: Prentice-Hall, Inc.; 1996.

31. Abramson N. Development of the ALOHANET. IEEE Trans Inf Theory 1985;31(2):119–123.

32. Kleinrock L, Tobagi F. Packet switching in radio channels: Part I - carrier sense multiple access modes and their throughput delay characteristics. IEEE Trans Commun 1975;23(12):1400–1416.

33. Arisha K, Youssef M, Younis M. Energy-aware TDMA-based MAC for sensor networks. In: Proceedings of the IEEE Workshop on Integrated Management of Power Aware Communications, Computing and Networking (IMPACCT 2002); 2002 May; New York.

34. Haartsen J. The bluetooth radio system. IEEE Personal Commun 2000;7(1):28–36.

35. Li J, Lazarou GA. Bit-map-assisted energy-efficient MAC scheme for Wireless Sensor Networks. In: Proceedings of the International Symposium on Information Processing in Sensor Networks (IPSN); 2004 April; Berkeley (CA). pp. 56–60.

36. Rajendran V, Obracza K, Garcia-Luna Aceves JJ. Energy-efficient, collision-free medium access control for Wireless Sensor Networks. In: Proceedings of the ACM SenSys; 2003 Nov; Los Angeles (CA).

37. Dulman S, Hoesel L, Nieberg T, Havinga P. Collaborative communication protocols for Wireless Sensor Networks. In: Proceedings of the European Research on Middleware and Architectures for Complex and Embedded Systems Workshop; 2003 April; Italy.

38. van Hoesel L, Havinga P. A lightweight medium access protocol (LMAC) for Wireless Sensor Networks. In: Proceedings of the 1st International Workshop on Networked Sensing Systems (INSS 2004); 2004 June; Tokyo, Japan.

39. Polastre J, Hill J, Culler D. Versatile low power media access for sensor networks. In: Proceedings of the Second ACM Conference on Embedded Networked Sensor Systems (SenSys); 2004 Nov 3–5; Baltimore (MD).

40. Tobagi F, Kleinrock L. Packet switching in radio channels: Part II - the hidden terminal problem in carrier sense multiple access and the busy-tone solution. IEEE Trans Commun 1975;23(12):1417–1433.

41. LAN MAN Standards Committee of the IEEE Computer Society. *Wireless LAN Medium Access Control (MAC) and Physical Layer (PHY) Specification*. New York: IEEE, IEEE Std 802.11–1999 edition; 1999.

42. Karn P. MACA: A new channel access method for packet radio. In: Proceedings of the 9th ARRL Computer Networking Conference; 1990 Sept; Ontario, Canada. pp. 134–140.

43. IEEE 802.15.4, Part 15.4: Wireless Medium Access Control (MAC) and Physical Layer (PHY) Specifications for Low-Rate Wireless Personal Area Networks (LR-WPANs),2003 May.

44. Mirza D, Owrang M, Schurgers C. Energy-efficient wakeup scheduling for maximizing lifetime of IEEE 802.15.4 networks. In: Proceedings of the International Conference on Wireless Internet (WICON); 2005 July; Budapest, Hungary. pp. 130–137.

45. Hill J, Szewczyk R, Woo A, Hollar S, Culler D, Pister K. System Architecture Directions for Networked Sensors. In: Proceedings of the 9th International Conference on Architectural Support for Programming Languages and Operating Systems (ASPLOS); 2000 Nov 12–15; Cambridge (MA).

46. Rhee I, Warrier A, Aia M, Min J. Z-MAC: a Hybrid MAC for Wireless Sensor Networks. In: Proceedings of the ACM SenSys; 2005 Nov; San Diego (CA).

47. Intanagonwiwat C, Govindan R, Estrin D. Directed diffusion: a scalable and robust communication paradigm for sensor networks. In: Proceedings of the 6th Annual International Conference on Mobile Computing and Networking (MobiCOM '00); 2000 Aug; Boston (MA). pp. 56–67.

48. Qi H, Kuruganti PT, Xu Y. The development of localized algorithms in Wireless Sensor Networks invited paper. Sensors 2002;2:286–293.

49. Heidemann J, Silva F, Intanagonwiwat C, Govindan R, Estrin D, Ganesan D. Building efficient Wireless Sensor Networks with low-level naming. In: Proceedings of the 18th ACM Symposium on Operating Systems Principles; 2001 Oct 21–24; Banff, Alberta, Canada. pp. 146–159.

50. Krishnamachari B, Estrin D, Wicker S. Modeling data-centric routing in Wireless Sensor Networks. In: Proceedings of the 21st Annual Joint Conference of the IEEE Computer and Communications Societies; 2002 June 23–27; New York.

51. Kulik J, Heinzelman W, Balakrishnan H. Negotiation-based protocols for disseminating information in Wireless Sensor Networks. Wireless Netw 2002;8:169–185.

52. Ye F, Luo H, Cheng J, Lu S, Zhang L. Two-tier data dissemination model for large-scale wireless sensors networks. In: Proceedings of the ACM/IEEE International Conference on Mobile Computing and Networking (MobiCom 2002); 2002 Sept; Atlanta (GA).

53. Intanagonwiwat C, Govindan R, Estrin D, et al. Directed diffusion for wireless sensor networking. ACM/IEEE Trans Netw 2002;11(1):2–16.

54. Vidhyapriya R, Vanathi PT. Energy aware routing for Wireless Sensor Networks. In: Proceedings of the International Conference on Signal Processing, Communications and Networking (ICSCN); 2007 Feb 22–24. pp. 545–550.

55. Heinzelman W. Application-specific protocol architectures for wireless networks [PhD dissertation]. Cambridge (MA): Massachusetts Institute of Technology; 2000.

56. Heinzelman W, Chandrakasan A, Balakrishnan H. Energy efficient communication protocol for wireless microsensor networks. In: Proceedings of the 33rd Hawaii Int. Conf. System Sciences (HICSS); 2000 Jan; Maui (HI). pp. 8020–8029.

57. Heinzelman WB, Chandrakasan AP, Balakrishnan H. An application-specific protocol architecture for wireless microsensor networks. IEEE Trans Wireless Commun 2002;1(4):660–670.

58. Yu Y, Govindan R, Estrin D. Geographical and energy aware routing: a recursive data dissemination protocol for Wireless Sensor Networks. UCLA Computer Science Department Technical Report UCLA/CSD-TR-01-0023. 2001.May

59. Shah RC, Rabaey JM. Energy aware routing for low energy Ad Hoc sensor network. In: Proceedings of the IEEE Wireless Communications and Networking conference (WCNC); Florida, USA; 2002 Mar, Volume 1. pp. 17–21.

60. Braginsky D, Estrin D. Rumor routing algorithm for sensor networks. In: Proceedings of the First ACM International Workshop on Wireless Sensor Networks and Applications (WSNA 2002); 2002 Sept; USA.

61. Lee SH, Yoo JJ, Chung TC. Distance-based energy efficient clustering for Wireless Sensor Networks. In: Proceedings of the 29th Annual IEEE International Conference on Local Computer Networks (LCN); 2004; Tampa (FL).

62. Younis O, Fahmy S. HEED: A hybrid, energy-efficient, distributed clustering approach for Ad Hoc sensor networks. IEEE Trans Mobile Comput 2004;3:366–379.

63. Chan H, Perrig A. ACE: an emergent algorithm for highly uniform cluster formation. In: Proceedings of the 1st European Workshop on Sensor Networks (EWSN); 2004 Jan 19–21; Berlin, Germany.

64. Ye M, Li CF, Chen G, Wu J. EECS: an energy efficient clustering scheme in Wireless Sensor Networks. Int J Ad Hoc Sens Netw 2007;3:99–119.

65. Liu M, Cao J, Chen G, Wang X. An energy-aware routing protocol in Wireless Sensor Networks. Sensors 2009;9(1):445–462.

66. Manjeshwar A, Agrawal D. TEEN: A routing protocol for enhanced efficiency in Wireless Sensor Networks. In: Proceedings of the 15th International Parallel and Distributed Processing Symposium; 2001 April; San Francisco (CA). pp. 2009–2015.

67. Manjeshwar A, Agrawal DP. APTEEN: A Hybrid Protocol for Efficient Routing and Comprehensive Information Retrieval in Wireless Sensor Networks. In: Proceedings of the 2nd Workshop on Parallel and Distributed Computing Issues in Wireless Networks and Mobile Computing; 2002 April 15–19; Ft. Lauderdale (FL).

68. Li Q, Aslam J, Rus D. Hierarchical power-aware routing in sensor networks. In: Proceedings of the DIMACS Workshop on Pervasive Networking; 2001 May 21; Rutgers University, New Jersey.

69. Maia EHB, Loureiro AAF, Câmara D. ICA: inter cluster routing algorithm for Wireless Sensor Networks. In: Proceedings of the Brazilian Symposium on Computer Networks; 2004 May; Gramado, RS, Brazil.

70. Demirbas M, Arora A, Nolte T, Lynch NA. Brief announcement: STALK: a self-stabilizing hierarchical tracking service for sensor networks. In: Proceedings of the PODC; 2004 July; St. John's, Newfoundland, Canada.

71. Rahman A, Saddik E, Gueaieb W. Wireless sensor network transport layer: state of the art. Sensors: Advancement In Modeling, Design Issues, Fabrication And Practical Applications 2008;21:221–245.

72. Jones J, Atiquzzaman M. Transport protocols for Wireless Sensor Networks: state-of-the-art and future directions. Int J Distrib Sens Netw 2007;3(1):119–133.

73. Postel J. Transmission control protocol. STD 7, RFC 793, University of South California, Technical Report. Information Sciences Institute; 1981. pp. RFC–793.

74. Postel J. User datagram protocol. STD 6, RFC 768, University of South California, Technical Report. Information Sciences Institute; 1980. p RFC–768.

75. Pereira PR, Grilo A, Rocha F, Nunes M, Casaca A, Chaudet C, Almstrm P, Johansson M. End-to-end reliability in Wireless Sensor Networks: survey and research challenges. In: Proceedings of the EuroFGI Workshop on IP QoS and Traffic Control; 2007 Dec, Lisbon, Portugal.

76. Wang C, Daneshmand M, Li B, Sohraby K. A survey of transport protocols for Wireless Sensor Networks. IEEE Netw 2006;20(3):34–40.

77. Hull B, Jamieson K, Balakrishnan H. Mitigating congestion in Wireless Sensor Networks. In: Proceedings of the ACM Sensys '04; 2004 Nov 3–5; Baltimore (MD).

78. Wan C-Y, Eisenman SB, Campbell AT. CODA: congestion detection and avoidance in sensor networks. In: Proceedings of the ACM Sensys '03; 2003 Nov; Los Angeles (CA).

79. Ee C-T, Bajcsy R. Congestion control and fairness for many-to-one routing in sensor networks. In: Proceedings of the ACM Sensys '04; 2004 Nov Baltimore (MD).

80. Wang C, Sohraby K, Lawrence V, Li B Hu Y. Priority-based congestion control in Wireless Sensor Networks. In: Proceedings of the IEEE international Conference on Sensor Networks, Ubiquitous, and Trustworthy Computing; 2006 June 5–7; Taichung, Taiwan.

81. Sankarasubramaniam Y, Akan OB, Akyildiz IF. ESRT: event-to-sink reliable transport in Wireless Sensor Networks. In: Proceedings of the 4th ACM International Symposium on Mobile Ad Hoc Networking and Computing (MobiHoc '03); 2003 June 1–3; Annapolis (MD). pp. 177–188.

82. Wang C, Sohraby K, Hu Y, Li B, Tang W. Issues of transport control protocols for Wireless Sensor Networks. In: Proceedings of the International Conference on Communications, Circuits and Systems (ICCCAS); 2005 March; Hong-Kong, China.

83. Akan O, Akyildiz I. Event-to-sink reliable transport in Wireless Sensor Networks. IEEE/ACM Trans Netw 2005;13(5):1003–1016.

84. Wang C, Sohraby K, Li B. SenTCP: A hop-by-hop congestion control protocol for Wireless Sensor Networks. In: Proceedings of the IEEE INFOCOM; 2005; Miami (FL).

85. Sergiou C, Vassiliou V. Alternative path creation vs data rate reduction for congestion mitigation in Wireless Sensor Networks. In: Proceedings of the 9th ACM/IEEE International Conference on Information Processing in Sensor Networks; 2010 April 12–16; Stockholm, Sweden, IPSN '10. New York: ACM; 2010. 394–395. DOI: http://doi.acm.org/10.1145/1791212.1791271.

86. Sergiou C, Vassiliou V, Pitsillides A. Reliable data transmission in event-based sensor networks during overload situation. In: Proceedings of the 3rd International Conference on Wireless Internet; 2007 Oct 22–24; Austin (TX).

87. Vassiliou V, Sergiou C. Performance study of node placement for congestion control in Wireless Sensor Networks. In: Proceedings of the 3rd International Conference on New Technologies, Mobility and Security; 2009 Dec 20–23; Cairo, Egypt. pp. 173–180.

88. Tezcan N, Wang W. ART: an asymmetric and reliable transport mechanism for Wireless Sensor Networks. Int J Sens Netw 2007;2(3–4):188–200.

89. Rosberg Z, Liu RP, Dong A, Dinh LT, Jha S. ARQ with implicit and explicit ACKs in sensor networks. In: Proceedings of the IEEE Globecom; 2008; New Orleans (LA).

90. Rosberg Z, LiuRosberg RP, Dinh TL, Dong YF, Jha S. Statistical reliability for energy efficient data transport in Wireless Sensor Networks. Wireless Netw 2010;16(7):1913–1927.

91. Voinescu A, Tudose DS, Tapus N. Task scheduling in Wireless Sensor Networks. In: Proceedings of the 2010 6th International Conference on Networking and Services; 2010 March 7–13; Cancun, Mexico.

92. Tian Y, Ekici E, Ozguner F. Energy-constrained task mapping and scheduling in Wireless Sensor Networks. In: Proceedings of the IEEE International Conference on Mobile Ad-Hoc and Sensor Systems Conference; 2005 Nov; Washington (DC).

93. Tian Y, Gu Y, Ekici E, Ozguner F. Dynamic critical-path task mapping and scheduling for collaborative in-network processing in multi-hop Wireless Sensor Networks. In: Proceedings of the International Conference on Parallel Processing Workshops; Columbus, USA. 2006.

94. Yu Y, Prasanna VK. Energy-balanced task allocation for collaborative processing in Wireless Sensor Networks. ACM/Kluwer J Mobile Netw Appl 2005;10(1–2):115–131.

95. Tian Y, Jarupan B, Ekici E, Ozguner F. Real-time task mapping and scheduling for collaborative in-network processing in DVS-enabled Wireless Sensor Networks. In: Proceedings of the IEEE International Parallel and Distributed Processing SYMPOSIUM (IPDPS '06); Rhodes Island, Greece; 2006 April. pp. 1–10.

96. Tian Y, Ekici E. Cross-layer collaborative in-network processing in multihop Wireless Sensor Networks. IEEE Trans Mobile Comput 2007;6(3):297–310.

97. Gibbons PB, Muchnick SS. Efficient instruction scheduling for a pipelined architecture. SIGPLAN Not 2004;39(4):167–174.

98. Madden S, Franklin M, Hellerstein J, Hong W. TAG: a Tiny AGgregation service for Ad-Hoc sensor networks. In: Proceedings of the Annual Symposium on Operating Systems Design and Implementation (OSDI); 2002; Boston (MA).

99. Hagras T, Janecek J. A high performance, low complexity algorithm for compile-time job scheduling in homogeneous computing environments. In: Proceedings of the International Conference on Parallel Processing Workshops; 2003 Oct; Kaohsiung, Taiwan. pp. 149–155.

100. Braun TD, Siegel HJ, Beck N, et al. A comparison of eleven static heuristics for mapping a class of independent tasks onto heterogeneous distributed computing systems. J Parallel Distrib Comput 2001;61(6):810–837.

101. Goh LK, Veeravalli B. An energy-balanced task scheduling heuristic for heterogeneous Wireless Sensor Networks. In: Proceedings of the 15th International Conference on High Performance Computing; 2008 Dec 17–20; Bangalore, India. pp. 257–268.

102. Park H, Srivastava MB. Energy-efficient task assignment framework for Wireless Sensor Networks. (TR-UCLA-NESL-200309-03) Technical Report. UC Los Angeles (CA): Center for Embedded Network Sensing. Available at http://escholarship.org/uc/item/9q5244gn. Accessed 2010 Oct 5.

103. Devadas SA, Newton AR. Algorithms for hardware allocation in data path synthesis. IEEE Trans Comput Aided Des Integr Circ Syst 1989;8(7):768–781.

104. Goldschmidt O, Hochbaum D. Polynomial algorithm for the k-cut problem. In: Proceedings of the 29th Annual Symposium on Foundations of Computer Science; California, USA; 1988 Oct. pp. 444–451.

105. Krishnamachari B, Estrin D, Wicker S. The impact of data Aggregation in Wireless Sensor Networks. In: Proceedings of the International Workshop of Distributed Event Based Systems (DEBS); 2002; Vienna, Austria. pp. 575–578.

106. Boulis A, Ganeriwal S, Srivastava M. AGgregation in sensor networks: an energy-accuracy tadeoff. In: Proceedings of the 1st IEEE International Workshop on Sensor Network Protocols and Applications (SNPA); 2003; Ankorage (AL).

107. Cohen NH, Purakayastha A, Turek J, Wong L, Yeh D. Challenges in flexible AGgregation of pervasive data. IBM Research Report RC 21942 (98646). Yorktown Heights (NY): IBM Research Division; 2001.

108. Kalpakis K, Dasgupta K, Namjoshi P. Efficient algorithms for maximum lifetime data gathering and AGgregation in Wireless Sensor Networks. Comput Netw 2003;42(6):697–716.

109. van Renesse R. The importance of aggregation. In: Schiper A, Shvartsman AA, Weatherspoon H, Zhao BY, editors. Volume 2584, *Future Directions in Distributed Computing: Research and Position Papers, Lecture Notes in Computer Science*. Springer-Verlag, Berlin Heidelberg 2003. pp. 87–92.

110. Krishnamachari B, Estrin D, Wicker S. Impact of data AGgregation in Wireless Sensor Networks. In: Proceedings of the International workshop of Distributed Event Based Systems (DEBS); 2002 July; Vienna, Austria. pp. 575–578.

111. Hall DL, Llinas J. An introduction to multisensor data fusion. IEEE 1997;85(1):6–23.

112. Nakamura EF, Loureiro AA, Frery AC. Information fusion for Wireless Sensor Networks: methods, models, and classifications. ACM Comput Surv 2007;39(3).

113. Gupta I, Riordan D, Sampalli S. Cluster-head election using fuzzy logic for Wireless Sensor Networks. In: Proceedings of the 3rd Annual Communication Networks and Services Research Conference (CNSR'05); 2005; Halifax, Canada. pp. 255–260.

114. Srinivasan T, Chandrasekar R, Kumar VV. A fuzzy, energy efficient scheme for data centric multipath routing in Wireless Sensor Networks. In: Proceedings of the IFIP International Conference on Wireless and Optical Communications Networks; 2006; Bangalore, India.

115. Friedlander DS, Phoha S. Semantic information fusion for coordinated signal processing in mobile sensor networks. Int J High Perf Comput Appl 2002;16(3):235–241.

116. Friedlander DS. Semantic information extraction. In: Iyengar SS, Brooks RR, editors. *Distributed Sensor Networks*. Boca Raton (FL): CRC Press; 2005. pp. 409–417, Chapter 21.

117. Whitehouse K, Liu J, Zhao F. Semantic streams: a framework for composable inference over sensor data. In: Proceedings of the 3rd European Workshop on Wireless Sensor Networks (EWSN'06); 2006 Feb 13–15; Zurich, Switzerland. pp. 5–20.

118. Bracio BR, Horn W, MÖller DPF. Sensor fusion in biomedical systems. In: Proceedings of the 19th Annual International Conference of the IEEE Engineering in Medicine and Biology Society; 1997; Chicago (IL), Volume 3. pp. 1387–1390.

119. Santini S, Romer K. An adaptive strategy for quality-based data reduction in Wireless Sensor Networks. In: Proceedings of the 3rd International Conference on Networked Sensing Systems (INSS'06); 2006; Chicago (IL). pp. 29–36.

120. Jain A, Chang EY, Wang YF. Adaptive stream resource management using Kalman filters. In: Proceedings of the 2004 ACM SIGMOD International Conference on Management of Data (SIGMOD'04); 2004; Paris, France. pp. 11–22.

121. Madden S, Szewczyk R, Franklin MJ, Culler D. Supporting aggregate queries over Ad-Hoc Wireless Sensor Networks. In: Proceedings of 4th IEEE Workshop on Mobile Computing and Systems Applications; 2002; New York.

122. Madden S, Franklin MJ, Hellerstein JM, Hong W. TinyDB: an acquisitional query processing system for sensor networks. ACM Trans Database Syst 2005;30(1):122–173.

123. Intanagonwiwat C, Estrin D, Govindan R, Heidemann J. Impact of network density on data AGgregation in Wireless Sensor Networks. In: Proceedings of the 22nd IEEE International Conf. Distributed Computing Systems (ICDCS'02); 2002; Vienna, Austria. pp. 457–458.

124. Halgamuge MN, Guru SM, Jennings A. Energy efficient cluster formation in Wireless Sensor Networks. In: Proceedings of the 10th International Conference on Telecommunications (ICT'03); 2003; Papeete, French Polynesia, Volume 2. pp. 1571–1576.

125. Kochhal M, Schwiebert L, Gupta S. Role-based hierarchical self organization for wireless ad hoc sensor networks. In: Proceedings of the 2nd ACM International Conference on Wireless Sensor Networks and Applications (WSNA'03); 2003; San Diego (CA). pp. 98–107.

126. Mhatre V, Rosenberg C. Homogeneous vs heterogeneous clustered sensor networks: a comparative study. In: Proceedings of the 2004 IEEE International Conference on Communications (ICC'04); 2004; Paris, France, Volume 6. pp. 3646–3651.

127. Hoang AT, Motani M. Collaborative broadcasting and compression in cluster-based Wireless Sensor Networks. In: Proceedings of the 2nd European Workshop on Wireless Sensor Networks (EWSN'05); 2005; Istanbul, Turkey. pp. 197–206.

128. Lindsey S, Raghavendra CS. PEGASIS: power efficient gathering in sensor information systems. In: Proceedings of the IEEE Aerospace Conference; Big Sky, Montana, USA; 2002.

129. Kalpakis K, Dasgupta K, Namjoshi P. Maximum lifetime data gathering and AGgregation in Wireless Sensor Networks. In: Proceedings of the IEEE International Conference on Networking; 2002; Atlanta (GA).

130. Bauer F, Varma A. Distributed algorithms for multicast path setup in data networks. Trans Netw 1996;4(2):181–191.

131. Nakamura EF, De Oliveira HA, Pontello LF, Loureiro AA. On demand role assignment for event-detection in sensor networks. In: Proceedings of the 11th IEEE International Symposium on Computers and Communication (ISCC'06); 2006; Cagliari, Italy. pp. 941–947.

132. Ding M, Cheng X, Xue G. AGgregation tree construction in sensor networks. In: Proceedings of the 58th IEEE Vehicular Technology Conference (VTC-Fall); 2003; Orlando (FL). pp. 2168–2172.

133. Rocha AR, Santos IL, Pirmez L, Delicato FC, Gomes DG; de Souza JN. Semantic clustering in Wireless Sensor Networks. In: Proceedings of the IFIP Advances in Information and Communication Technology; 2010; Brisbane, Australia, Volume 327/2010. pp. 3–14.

134. Yu Y, Krishnamachari B, Prasanna V. Energy-latency tradeoffs for data gathering in Wireless Sensor networks. In: Proceedings of the IEEE INFOCOM; vol. 1, March 2004, pp. 244–255.

135. Li W, Bandai M, Watanabe T. Tradeoffs among delay, energy and accuracy of partial data AGgregation in Wireless Sensor Networks. In: Proceedings of the 24th IEEE International Conference on Advanced Information Networking and Applications; 2010 April 20–23; Perth, Australia. pp. 917–924.

136. Galluccio L, Palazzo S, Campbell AT. Modeling and designing efficient data AGgregation in Wireless Sensor Networks under entropy and energy bounds. Int J Wireless Infor Netw 2009;16(3):75–183.

137. Srivastava V, Motani M. Cross-layer design: a survey and the road ahead. IEEE Commun Mag 2005;43(12):112–119.

138. Madani SA. Cross layer design for low power Wireless Sensor Networks [PhD dissertation]; Vienna University of Technology, Austria; 2008.

139. Melodia T, Vuran MC, Pompili D. The state of the art in cross-layer design for Wireless Sensor Networks. In: Proceedings of EuroNGI Workshops on Wireless and Mobility; 2006 July; Como, Italy.

140. Zhao N, Sun L. Research on cross-layer frameworks design in Wireless Sensor Networks. In: Proceedings of the 3rd International Conference on Wireless and Mobile Communications (ICWMC); 2007 March 4–9; Guadeloupe, French Caribbean.

CHAPTER 26

ENERGY MANAGEMENT IN HETEROGENEOUS WIRELESS HEALTH CARE NETWORKS

NIMA NIKZAD, PRITI AGHERA, PIERO ZAPPI, and TAJANA S. ROSING

26.1 INTRODUCTION

In recent years, there has been a significant and growing interest in wireless health monitoring systems. Today's mobile phones are putting considerable processing power in the pockets and purses of people everywhere. Combined with ever-shrinking and affordable sensors that can communicate with mobile phones, the vision of large-scale sensor networks that keep people informed about their personal health and their environment is becoming a reality. This data can be rapidly communicated and shared with a patient's doctor to allow the monitoring of health conditions without requiring the user to be directly observed by a medical professional.

Most such systems are made up of a collection of body-worn sensors; sensors in the environment; a device, such as a mobile phone, that aggregates the data from these sensors; and a back-end server (BE) where the data can be stored for future study and observation by the user or a trained professional. Given the mobile and wireless nature of the sensors and the local aggregator (LA), it is no surprise that battery life is a major concern for such systems. The collection, filtering, processing, location tagging, and reporting of this health data can put significant strain on the battery life of a user's mobile phone and sensors.

A typical wireless health monitoring system collects a variety of readings from sensors on or around a user's body. While some of the data that is collected, such as heart rate and blood pressure information, may be relevant only to the collecting user, some data may be relevant to other nearby people. An example of

Energy-Efficient Distributed Computing Systems, First Edition.
Edited by Albert Y. Zomaya and Young Choon Lee.
© 2012 John Wiley & Sons, Inc. Published 2012 by John Wiley & Sons, Inc.

such data may be air quality or humidity information, which is collected from the surrounding environment and does not contain any personal information about the collecting user. Two nearby users may sense, filter, process, and forward the same exact environmental health information. However, if the BE that collects these readings knows where the measurements were taken and what users are in the vicinity, an opportunity exists to reduce the number of redundant sensor readings from that environment.

Regardless of whether a system is monitoring personal or environmental health information, it will be responsible for collecting sensor readings, performing data fusion and feature extraction to identify events of interest, and forwarding this information over a wireless network to a BE for long-term storage and future study. Given the heterogeneous nature of a wireless health monitoring system, different components of the system offer vastly different processing and communication capabilities. While some tasks such as the collection of readings from the environment must occur on sensors, tasks such as feature extraction, depending on the computational requirements of the processing, could be done on the sensor node, at the LA that collects readings from multiple sensors, or could be handled by the BE before the data is stored. When tasks in a wireless health system are handled, they can have a drastic effect on the energy consumption and lifetime of a system.

Two methods of improving the energy efficiency of a wireless health monitoring system are explored in this work. First, location information is utilized to identify users that are expected to collect redundant environmental sensor readings. The BE generates predictions for what a user would report based on what its neighbors report, and based on the amount of available battery life for each user and each of other users near it, the rate at which any individual user collects sensor readings can be drastically reduced, resulting in significant energy savings. Second, when a health monitoring system collects and processes sensor data, the choice of where it does processing in the system has a drastic effect on the computational and communication energy costs of the entire system. Given a task graph of all jobs to be completed in such a system, tasks can be dynamically and efficiently distributed among sensors, the LA, and the BE to minimize energy consumption and improve system lifetime. Significant power savings can be obtained in a wireless health monitoring system by controlling the rate at which data is collected in a system and controlling where that data is processed.

The rest of the chapter is organized as follows. The system model, describing the different components that make up a wireless health monitoring system, including a method of describing the hierarchy and flow of tasks in a health monitoring system, is introduced first. The following section presents a method of minimizing redundant environmental sensor readings to save energy by utilizing location information, followed by a way of dynamically assigning those tasks in a system to minimize energy consumption and extend battery life. Results and analysis of the introduced approaches are presented in the results section, which is followed by a conclusion.

26.2 SYSTEM MODEL

The typical wireless health monitoring system (Fig. 26.1) has three main components: sensors, a LA, and a BE. One or more sensors carried by a user along with one LA (such as a cellular phone) form a body area network (BAN). The function of these sensors is to monitor a user's health and to detect specific events on the user's body or in the surrounding environment (e.g., low blood pressure, carbon monoxide exposure, heart rate). Sensors may be built directly into the LA or may communicate with it wirelessly, forwarding raw or processed sensor readings. The LA collects data from the sensors in the BAN and may process it further before sending to a centralized BE. Wireless communication between sensors and the LA is often handled over a Bluetooth or ZigBee connection, while communication between the LA and BE is handled over WLAN and WWAN. The BE may do additional processing on the data it receives before storing it in a database to be used for tracking a user's health history or to do further analysis in the future. In a heterogeneous architecture such as this, devices differ widely in their processing and communication abilities, as well as in their available energy budget. While sensors and the LA are battery powered in such a system, limiting their processing power and the amount of data they can reasonably report, the BE is assumed to have no energy or processing constraints.

The BE consists of a sophisticated infrastructure that offers storage capabilities for user data as well as redundancy to deal with any failures in the infrastructure. It maintains a complete history of sensor readings and event detections for each participating user. In addition to providing valuable information to users regarding their health, this data can be shared with a user's doctor to help monitor effects of a treatment or to diagnose a condition. Data collected about a user's environment is also valuable to other users in the area, providing a way of predicting the conditions a user was exposed to when they lack the proper sensors to monitor the environment directly.

26.2.1 Health Monitoring Task Model

Tasks of a wireless health care system can be modeled as a directed acyclic graph (DAG) $G = (T, C)$, where node set T represents the set of n sensing/processing

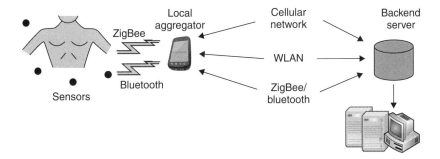

Figure 26.1 Wireless health care system architecture.

tasks, $T : i = 1, 2, \ldots n$ and C is the set of edges that represent communication tasks between nodes, $C : i = 1, 2, \ldots n$. $C_{ij} \in C$ represents a precedence relation between tasks $T_i, T_j \in T$, and the data produced by task T_i should be communicated to T_j before T_j can start its processing. The weights W_{ij} on edge $C_{ij} \in C$ represent the amount of data that needs to be transmitted from task T_i to T_j. Tasks that do not have any predecessors are called *source tasks*, and tasks that do not have successors are called *sink tasks*.

In such a system, body-worn sensors are represented as source tasks, generating the data used in the rest of the system. Sink tasks represent logging of the processed data on the BE. Given a DAG representing the tasks and flow of data in a wireless health care system, the goal is to minimize the total energy consumed by each battery in the system until the system dies and increase system battery life, defined as the shortest battery life of all devices in the system.

The tasks of the DAG are further characterized by the set of variables and constants provided in Table 26.1. These variables together define communication and computation energy cost of task i on resource r. For example, E_{Rir} defines energy consumed by task i to receive its input data on resource r in terms of resource r's receive power P_{Rr}, its average receive data rate μ_{Rr}, and time to receive task i's input data from its predecessor task j given by $\left(\frac{w_{ji}}{\mu_{Rr}} \right)$. The

TABLE 26.1   Variables and Constants

E_{Br}	Battery capacity of resource r
P_{Rr}	Power consumed by the receiver of resource r
P_{Tr}	Power consumed by the transmitter of resource r
P_{Er}	Power consumed in the execution of a task by resource r
t_{ir}	Execution time of task i on resource r
w_{ij}	Weight of the edge from task i to task j
b_{ir}	$b_{ir} \in \{0, 1\} s.t. b_{ir} = 1$ if task i is assigned to resource r
μ_{Rr}	Average data rate of the receiver on resource r
μ_{Tr}	Average data rate of the transmitter on resource r
pred_{ij}	$\text{pred}_{ij} \in \{0, 1\} s.t. \text{pred}_{ij} = 1$ if task j is a predecessor of task i
suc_{ij}	$\text{suc}_{ij} \in \{0, 1\} s.t. \text{suc}_{ij} = 1$ if task j is a successor of task i
E_{Rir}	Energy consumed by a resource r to receive input data for task i $$= \sum_{j=1}^{n} \{\text{pred}_{ij} * (1 - b_{jr}) * P_{Rr} * (w_{ji}/\mu_{Rr})\}$$
E_{Tir}	Energy consumed by a resource r to transmit input data for task i $$= \sum_{j=1}^{n} \{\text{suc}_{ij} * (1 - b_{jr}) * P_{Tr} * (w_{ij}/\mu_{Tr})\}$$
E_r	Total energy consumed by a resource r $$= \sum_{j=1}^{n} \{b_{ir}(E_{Rir} + P_{Er} * t_{ir} + E_{Tir})\}$$
s_i	Start time of task i
τ_i	End time of task i
d_i	Deadline of task i

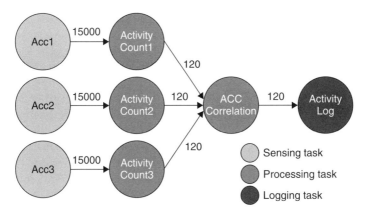

Figure 26.2 Example task graph.

receiving energy cost of a task is nonzero only when the task's predecessor is bound to a different resource than the resource the current task is bound to. The total energy E_r consumed by a resource r, is the sum of computation energy of all tasks assigned on r, energy to receive input of these assigned tasks, and transmission energy to transmit the output of these tasks to its successor on other resources.

A sample task graph for activity detection is presented in Figure 26.2. Three accelerometers (Acc1, Acc2, and Acc3) are placed on a user's hand, waist, and leg to determine whether the user is sitting, walking, or running. These three sensing tasks represent source tasks in the graph. The successors of these sensing tasks (Activity-Count1, 2, 3) are responsible for feature extraction from the accelerometer data. ACC-Correlation is responsible for identifying a user's state based on the three predecessor tasks' outputs, while Activity-Log is a sink task bound to the BE that is responsible for the logging of changes in a user's state. Each of the tasks in a task graph has a start time s_i, an end time τ_i and a deadline d_i associated with it. To maintain the task precedence, the start time of a successor should be greater than the end time of its predecessor. Thus, in this task graph $s_{\text{Activity Count1}} > \tau_{\text{ACC1}}$.

The defined system and task models are an important part of the next two sections, especially in Section 26.4.2, where a mincut of the task graph is used to find efficient partitions of the tasks between the system components. In the collaborative sensing approach, presented next, the focus is primarily on the BE and LA components, which are responsible for identifying nearby, redundant readings and controlling the rate of environmental sensing.

26.3 COLLABORATIVE DISTRIBUTED ENVIRONMENTAL SENSING

In a wireless health monitoring system, some of the data collected by a user node, such as their heart rate, is relevant only to that individual. That data must be collected by each user node and is never shared with other users. However, environmental data collected in a health monitoring system is relevant not only to the individual who senses and reports the information but also to any other users in the area. Examples of such data may be temperature, humidity, and air quality readings. The sensing, filtering, location tagging, and reporting of this environmental data can be extremely expensive from an energy perspective, a major problem in any battery-powered mobile system. While having multiple nearby users contribute sensor readings for the same environmental conditions may be valuable for ensuring the accuracy and quality of the data, these redundant sensor readings put significant strain on the system battery life. As the BE receives this data from user nodes in the environment, it may identify users that are near one another and providing similar data. The BE may utilize this information to create predictions for environmental sensor readings in an area, thus the rate at which any individual user node must sense this data can be significantly reduced proportional to its remaining battery life and the battery life of neighboring user nodes.

However, maintaining and communicating to user nodes a detailed sensing schedule that would ensure that one user in an area is reporting data for any given time period is prohibitively expensive because highly mobile users do not have the same neighbors for long. Instead, it is desirable to duty cycle sensors at a rate derived from current conditions and the number and state of nodes in close proximity of a user. A simple rate would be significantly easier to communicate to a user and would only be updated when conditions had changed enough and may be tuned to control the trade-off between energy consumption and accuracy in the system (Fig. 26.3).

Our approach consists of two main steps. The first is to identify users located near one another in the environment and to group them together based on their location information, as users located near one another are likely to provide the same or similar sensor readings about their environment. Second, after the groups of users have been identified, the sensing rate for each user is calculated. This

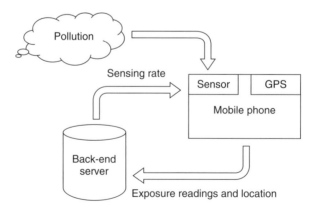

Figure 26.3   An overview of the steps of the embedded software algorithm.

rate is based on the mobility of the user, its the distance from other users, and the amount of energy available at the user node relative to neighboring users. The calculated sensing rate for each user significantly reduces the number of redundant environmental sensor readings and is updated as conditions change.

26.3.1 Node Neighborhood and Localization Rate

Identifying users in the environment that are located near one another is critical for collaborative environmental sensing to be successful. To make this possible, each user node provides occasional updates on their position to the BE, utilizing localization techniques made available by sensors either worn on the body or built into the LA, such as GPS. This localization of the user is an expensive process for a BAN, so the rate at which these updates are made and reported to the BE should be minimized without sacrificing too much in accuracy. The set of users considered near a particular user is considered that user's *neighborhood* (Fig. 26.4).

Each time a user node i provides its latest position, the server updates its map of user locations and recomputes the reporting user node's neighborhood of nodes, N_i. Each node is the center of its own neighborhood. All other user nodes within range R of node i are considered to be in the same general area and provide correlated environmental sensor readings. This neighborhood information is strictly maintained on the BE, ensuring that no user node is aware of the number of other users around them or their identities. In addition to these benefits in privacy, this frees the mobile devices in the network from maintaining a large table of other user locations and computing their nearest neighbors, which is a concern on the BE.

The rate at which nodes provide updates on their position, l_{rate}, is based on the mobility of the user. If a user node is found to be highly mobile, its localization rate may be increased to ensure its set of neighboring nodes is accurate, while a user that is found to move very little or not at all may reduce its localization rate,

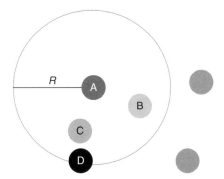

Figure 26.4 An example of a possible node neighborhood, centered around node A. Nodes B, C, and D are considered members of node A's neighborhood, as they fall within the distance R of the node.

significantly reducing the number of expensive GPS readings that must be taken. By utilizing sensors such as accelerometers, location updates may be disabled completely until significant movement is detected; however, for the remainder of this work, we assume that such information is not available and make use of time-out-based location updates.

$$l_{\text{rate}} = \begin{cases} \dfrac{\Delta l}{\hat{l}} & (\Delta l \geq \hat{l}) \\ \dfrac{\Delta l + \hat{l}}{2\hat{l}} & (\Delta l < \hat{l}), \end{cases} \tag{26.1}$$

where Δl is the amount of change in position between the most recent and previous localization measurements and $\hat{l}$ is the distance between localization attempts as required by the application and environmental condition being monitored. Given a user node's current position and velocity (based on the last two location updates), a prediction for how long it would take a user to travel $\hat{l}$ can be computed and used to schedule the next localization attempt. If the environmental condition being tracked is known to change slowly and gradually, a large $\hat{l}$ value may be used. If the condition changes suddenly and often or if the system would simply require more data from a region, a smaller value of $\hat{l}$ may be used. In this work, we assume that $\hat{l}$ is equal to the radius of the neighborhood, R, such that a user provides an updated location when it is predicted to leave its own neighborhood.

26.3.2   Energy Ratio and Sensing Rate

Once a user node's set of neighboring nodes has been computed, the environmental sensing duty cycle rate, s_{rate}, may be computed for each of its sensors. Each time a user node i reports its latest positional information to the BE, it also reports its residual energy e_i. A user node's residual energy e_i is used along with the total energy of all nodes in N_i, designated as E_i, to compute its individual s_{rate}.

$$E_i = \sum_{j \in N_i} e_j \cdot f(d_j), \tag{26.2}$$

$$s_{\text{rate}} = \frac{e_i}{E_i}, \tag{26.3}$$

where d_j is the distance between node i and a node j found in N_i and $f(d_j)$ is a correlation function of the distance between the two nodes. The effect of this function is to scale the amount of energy a node in N_i contributes to E_i based on how far it is from node i. This function will be dependent on the type of environmental condition being tracked and how close user nodes would have to be to provide similar readings. Some possible functions are

$$f(d) = \begin{cases} 1 - \dfrac{d}{R} \text{ (Linear)} \\ e^{-\frac{d^2}{R^2}} \text{ (Gaussian)} \\ c \text{ (Constant)}. \end{cases} \qquad (26.4)$$

The goal is to give greater weight to nodes that are closer to the center of the neighborhood, as they are likely more correlated than further nodes. How correlated these nodes should be is dependent on the environmental condition being tracked and the requirements of the application.

26.3.3   Duty Cycling and Prediction

Environmental sensor readings and localization data is usually provided by a user node on a regular period, t_B. When a node receives an updated sensing or localization rate from the BE, a new period is calculated on the user node:

$$t_S = \frac{t_B}{s_{rate}}, \qquad (26.5)$$

$$t_L = \frac{t_B}{l_{rate}}, \qquad (26.6)$$

where t_S is the new sensing period and t_L is the new localization period.

These periods are then used to control the rate of sensing and how often localization updates are made. Each environmental sensor carried by a user or built into a user's phone has its own t_S, so that sensors that are popular in an area may be duty cycled to reduce power consumption, while underrepresented sensors continue to report readings at their normal or slightly reduced rate. Likewise, a large enough t_L allows the GPS on an LA to be duty cycled. This duty cycling of the GPS provides especially significant power savings, as localization attempts are extremely expensive. Some GPS devices require being powered for a minimum amount of time after a reading (usually about 30 s) and also require enough time to acquire a signal from the GPS satellites (usually about 10 s). When t_L is greater than this combined time, duty cycling of the GPS module is possible. In general, duty cycling the sensing and localization of a health monitoring system reduces the amount of processing that must be done in the system and the total amount of data to be forwarded over the wireless channel to the LA and BE.

Each time a user node i provides an environmental sensor reading to the BE, the reported data is used to create predictions for each user node in N_i. The same correlation function $f(d_j)$ used to weight energy contributions can also be used to determine how much weight to give to a neighboring user node's sensor reading in another node's prediction calculation. For each period t_B where a sensor reading is not provided by a user node, the weighted average of neighboring nodes during that period may be used as a prediction to fill in the gap in sensor reading history.

By utilizing these predictions, a user is able to maintain a complete history of environmental data while significantly reducing the number of required sensor readings. While the above approach is useful for reducing the number of readings a system may have to make, a great deal of data must still be collected and processed in the system. Given that some tasks must be completed, an opportunity exists to exploit the heterogeneity of the system and distribute processing tasks among the different components of the system to minimize power consumption and extend battery life. The next section describes how a health task graph can be utilized to assign the sensing and processing tasks within a system to minimize processing and communication power consumption.

26.4 TASK ASSIGNMENT IN A BODY AREA NETWORK

Wireless health care systems, such as the one described above, are hierarchical and heterogeneous in nature, with components having different energy and processing capabilities. Such a system is responsible for multiple tasks, such as the sensing and processing the health information and communicating it to the BE. Some of these tasks, such as feature extraction from the sensor data, may be completed on the sensor node, LA, or BE. By dynamically adjusting where these tasks are completed in the system, it is possible to minimize energy consumption and improve system battery life.

It is possible to derive an optimal task assignment with the use of integer linear programing (ILP)-based solutions, which is described in the next section. Given the computationally expensive nature of ILPs, two dynamic graph-based partitioning algorithms are presented in Section 26.4.2, which are computationally efficient and are able to adapt in real time to changing system conditions.

26.4.1 Optimal Task Assignment

With the use of ILP, it is possible to compute the optimal task assignment for two main objectives (i) *ILPGreen*—minimizing system energy consumption and (ii) *ILPLife*—maximizing system lifetime. These static solutions act as a baseline to compare against to measure the performance of the dynamic solutions that are presented in the following section.

ILPGreen computes the most efficient task allocation that minimizes the total energy consumption of the system, as shown in Table 26.2. The structure of the task graph used for computing the ILP solution is similar to the DAG described before, but it includes explicit communication tasks between two dependent sensing and processing tasks to simplify the ILP formulation. An example of such a graph transformation is shown in Figure 26.5.

ILPGreen assigns tasks with the aim of reducing total energy consumption without considering the battery capacity of each system component and the rate

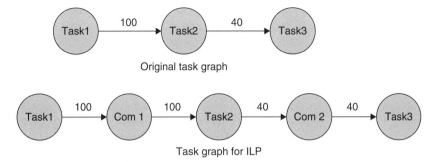

Figure 26.5 Task graph transformation for ILP.

TABLE 26.2   ILP Objective and Constraints

$ILP\,$Green: $= \min\left(\sum_{r=1}^{m-1} E_r\right)$	Minimize system energy
$ILP\,$Life: $= \min_i\left\{\max_r \frac{E_{r,i}}{\text{Bat}_r}\right\}$ where $r = 1, 2, \ldots m - 1$	Maximize system life
(a) $\forall i, \sum_{r=1}^{m} b_{i,r} = 1$	Total allocation constraint: Each task is assigned to one and only one resource
(b) $E_r \leq \text{Bat}_{E_r}$	Battery capacity constraint
(c) $(b_{jm} + b_{jm-1}) = 1$ if $(b_{im} = 1 \wedge \text{pred}_{ij} = 1)$	Resource allocation constraint 1: Predecessor tasks of a task mapped to the back end are mapped to either the back end or the local aggregator
(d) $(b_{jm-1}) + \sum_{k=1}^{m-2} b_{jk}) = 1$ if $(b_{im-1} = 1 \wedge \text{pred}_{ij} = 1)$	Resource allocation constraint 2: Predecessor tasks of a task mapped to the local aggregator are mapped to either the local aggregator or a sensor
(e) $b_{jk} = 1$ where $k = 1, 2, \ldots m - 2$ if $(b_{ik} = 1 \wedge \text{pred}_{ij} = 1)$	Resource allocation constraint 3: Predecessor tasks of a task mapped to a sensor are mapped to the sensor
(f) $s_i \geq \max(0, \tau_j)\forall j$, where $\text{pred}_{ij} = 1$	Start time constraint: The starting time for tasks must be greater than the finishing time of all its predecessor tasks
(g) $\tau_i = s_i + \sum_{r=1}^{m}\{b_{ir} * (t_{ir} + \sum_{j=1}^{n} \text{pred}_{ij} * (1 - b_{jr}) + \text{suc}_{ij} * (1 - b_{jr}))\}$	Finishing time constraint: The finishing time of a task is the start time plus the time it takes to receive, execute, and send the data for the task

at which the battery is depleted. It is possible that the task assignment generated by *ILPGreen* may assign tasks to resources with critically low battery levels, resulting in a shorter system lifetime. Therefore, it may be desirable to instead have the entire system function as long as possible.

ILPLife is an alternative solution with the goal of maximizing the system lifetime using a min-max formulation on the rate of energy drain relative to the available battery capacity at each component in the system. *ILPLife* has the same constraints and variables as *ILPGreen* but computes a solution aimed at maximizing system life, as shown in Table 26.2. The approach of maximizing the battery lifetime is based on the desire to balance the energy consumption of all resources such that each resource consumes approximately the same percentage of its remaining energy. The resource with the highest ratio between consumption rate and remaining energy will deplete its energy source first.

A complete formulation of *ILPGreen* and *ILPLife*, with goals and constraints, is presented in Table 26.2. Among the resources r, resource m denotes the BE and resource $m-1$ denotes the LA. Solutions are found by each ILP for b_{ir}, the mapping of tasks i to resources r. E_r represents the total energy consumed by a resource after tasks have been assigned to it. For *ILPGreen*, the goal is to minimize the sum of energy consumed by all resources other than the BE. The goal for *ILPLife* is to minimize the maximum percentage of energy consumed among mobile resources. In Table 26.2, E_r/E_{Br} represents the percentage of energy consumed by a resource.

An open-source ILP solver called $lp-solve$ [1] was used to obtain the optimal task assignment for each task set. An issue with computing the optimal solution with an ILP is that as the number of tasks in the task set increases, execution time of $lp-solve$ increases exponentially. An ideal system should be able to adapt the task assignment to changing conditions during runtime, such as changes in the wireless channel due to a user mobility, changes in terrain, changes in task execution time, and the addition of tasks due to event-based monitoring. Such changes may have drastic effects on the communication and computation costs in the system. An ideal location to compute the task assignment for the system would be on the LA, as it is in a centralized location in the system and could react more quickly to changing conditions than the BE could. However, running an ILP-based solution on a mobile device is not efficient, as the ILP computation took over 100 s for a set of 20 tasks when run on a desktop computer. To address this issue, more efficient and dynamic solutions were developed to better suit the needs of a wireless health monitoring system.

26.4.2 Dynamic Task Assignment

Two fast, dynamic, and energy-efficient task assignment algorithms were developed for use in a wireless health system. *DynAGreen* (Dynamic task Assignment for a Greener solution) was developed with the objective of minimizing the total energy consumption of the system. This was later extended into *DynAGreenLife* to balance both system energy consumption and system lifetime. These algorithms are designed to run periodically on the LA, monitoring changes in the communication channel, system workload, and remaining battery life to compute the best task assignment for the desired objective.

26.4.2.1 *DynAGreen algorithm.* The DynAGreen algorithm is designed to minimize the energy consumption of a wireless health care monitoring system. Stone's method [2] has been adopted to find an assignment of tasks to the system components. A hierarchical flow graph partitioning technique is used to partition tasks between different components. Figure 26.6 provides an outline of the *DynAGreen* algorithm.

The hierarchical partitioning is applied in two steps. First, a flow graph is constructed from the set of tasks and is partitioned between an infinite energy BE and a supernode BAN, consisting of the set of sensors and LA. Weights on the edges of the graph represent communication and computation costs, and partitioning is completed using a maxflow-mincut algorithm. The minimum weight cutset represents a split of tasks between the BE and BAN that minimizes energy consumption. The maxflow-mincut algorithm proposed in Reference 3 was implemented to compute this split of tasks. The following are the details of each step of the algorithm.

1. Computation energy cost parameters $(E_{\mathrm{CPU}a}, E_{\mathrm{CPU}i})$ and communication energy cost parameters $(E_{tx}, E_{\mathrm{idle}}, E_{rx})$ for all resources are initialized/updated. Here, $E_{\mathrm{CPU}a}(r)$ and $E_{\mathrm{CPU}i}(r)$ represent energy consumed

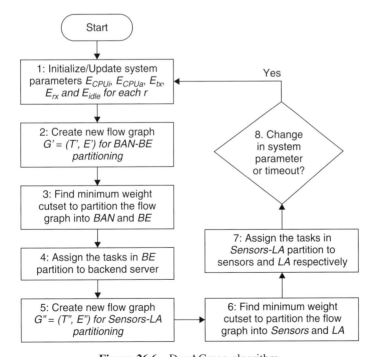

Figure 26.6 DynAGreen algorithm.

by a CPU in active and idle states, respectively, and E_{tx}, E_{idle}, and E_{rx} represent energy consumed by the radio during the transmit, receive, and idle states, respectively. In the first run of the algorithm, they are initialized with default values, and in subsequent runs, they are updated based on the radio interface monitoring.

2. Tasks are partitioned between BAN and BE such that total computation energy cost of performing tasks in the BAN partition and communication energy cost of sending output of those tasks to BE are minimized. To achieve this objective, we transform the given task graph into a flow graph, with communication and computation energy cost as flow values, BAN as a source node and BE as a sink node such that the minimum weight cutset represents the total computation and communication energy cost for the partition. Following is a formal description of this transformation:

   - A flow graph $G' = (T', E')$ from given task graph $G = (T, E)$ is created by adding BAN and LA nodes to T and adding E_{BAN} and E_{BE} edge sets to E. Formally, $T' = T \cup \{BAN,BE\}$ and $E' = E \cup E_{BAN} \cup E_{BE}$. BAN node collectively represents sensors and LA. E_{BAN} and E_{BE} are added to represent computation energy cost of the tasks on BE and BAN, respectively, while edges in E represent communication energy cost.

   - E_{BAN} is a set of edges from BAN to the each node t in T. The weight of the edge (BAN, t) is equal to the computational cost of task t on BE and is defined by $w(BAN, t)$ in Table 26.3. The rationale behind this weight assignment is if a mincut includes edge (BAN, t) then it means that t is in the BE partition and the computational cost of performing this task on BE is added to the weight of the cutset. We consider BE to have unlimited energy source, and hence, the computation energy cost of performing a task on BE is set to 0 in Table 26.3. If a task t is bound to a sensor or the LA node, the minimum weight cutset should not include the edge (BAN, t). This is achieved by setting the weight of the edge (BAN, t) to ∞ as per Table 26.3.

   - E_{BE} is a set of edges from each node t in T to BE with weight of edge (t, BE) equal to the computational cost of task t on LA as defined by $w(t, BE)$ in Table 26.3, where $E_{CPU}(t, LA)$ is the computation energy cost of running task t on LA. This weight assignment has similar rationale

TABLE 26.3   Weights of Edges in BAN-BE Partition

Edge	Value	Condition
$w(BAN, t)$	0	If task t is not bound to sensor or LA
	∞	If task t is bound to sensor or LA
$w(t, BE)$	$E_{CPU}(t, LA)$	If task t is not bound
	0	If task t is bound to sensor or LA
	∞	If task t is bound to BE
$w_{wan}(t_p, t_s)$	$E_{radio}(t_p, LA)$	Where radio = LA's WAN radio

to the (BAN, t) weight assignment. If a mincut includes edge (t, BE) then it means that t is in BAN partition and computation cost of performing this task on BAN is added to the weight of the cutset. Note that in Table 26.3, LA parameters are used to calculate computation energy cost as BAN is represented by the LA during this stage of the algorithm. We enforce this edge to be part of the minimum weight cutset by setting its weight to 0 as per Table 26.3 if the task is bound to a sensor or LA. Similarly we enforce that this edge is not part of minimum weight cutset by setting its weight to ∞ if the task is bound to BE.

- Edge (t_p, t_s) in E represents the intertask communication link between the predecessor task t_p and its successor task t_s. The weight of edge (t_p, t_s) is equal to the communication cost of sending t_p's output from LA to BE and is defined by $w_{\text{wan}}(t_p, t_s)$ in Table 26.3, where $E_{\text{radio}}(t_p, \text{LA})$ is the communication energy consumed by task t_p on resource LA. Note that system parameters of the LA are used to compute communication energy cost of BAN.

3. The minimum weight cutset is found to partition the constructed flow graph into BAN and BE partitions. In Reference 2, Stone proves that such a minimum weight cutset provides an optimal task assignment for a two-processor system. By using their findings, it can be said that the resulting BAN-BE task partition minimizes the energy cost.

4. Since the minimum energy cost partition between the BAN and BE has been computed, tasks in the BE partition are assigned to BE, while tasks in the BAN partition need to be assigned on to *sensors* and the LA in subsequent steps of the algorithm. $T_{\text{BAN}} \subseteq T$ is defined as a set of tasks in the BAN partition and $E_{\text{BAN}} \subseteq E$ as a set of edges among tasks in T_{BAN}.

5. All the sensors are collectively represented by a single source node, *Sensors*, and the LA is represented by a single sink node, LA, in the *Sensors-LA* flow graph. As per our system model, all tasks are traced back to one or more sensing tasks by following their predecessor chain. These sensing tasks are preassigned to sensors or the LA. A processing task that receives its input from more than one sensor cannot be assigned to a sensor, as the system model does not allow sensors to communicate with each other directly. Such a task has to be assigned on to the LA or BE. By assigning appropriate weights on the edges in a flow graph, it can be ensured that such tasks cannot be in the *sensors* partition. This also implies that if a task is in the *sensors* partition, it should receive its input from only one sensor and we can find that sensor by tracking the given task's predecessors. So this way, even though the Sensors node in the flow graph represents multiple sensors, after finding mincut, we can assign tasks in Sensors partition to the appropriate sensor. Similar to BAN-BE partitioning, we partition tasks between Sensors and LA such that the total computation and communication energy cost of the system is minimum. To achieve this objective, the Sensors-LA flow graph is created from the remaining tasks, with communication and computation energy cost as flow values such that

the minimum weight cutset represents the total of computation and communication energy cost for the partition. The following is a formal description of this transformation:

- A new flow graph G'' is created for the Sensors-LA partition using all tasks in the BAN partition and then adding Sensors, LA and a set of proxy tasks. For all the tasks in T_{BAN} whose successors are assigned on BE, new task nodes are created, which are bound to LA and act as transmission tasks to BE and are represented by set T_{proxy}. These proxy tasks are added to represent the communication energy cost of forwarding output of a predecessor task from a sensor to the LA so that it can be forwarded further to BE. Edges of this new graph consist of the following edge sets: E_{BAN} representing communication energy cost, E_{LA} representing the computation cost of LA, E_{Sensors} representing the computation energy cost of sensors, and E_{proxy} representing the proxy task assignment on the LA. Formally, this new flow graph is defined as $G'' = (T'', E'')$, where $T'' = (T_{\mathrm{BAN}} \cup T_{\mathrm{proxy}} \cup \{\mathrm{Sensors,LA}\})$ and $E'' = (E_{\mathrm{BAN}} \cup E_{\mathrm{Sensors}} \cup E_{\mathrm{LA}} \cup E_{\mathrm{proxy}})$.

- E_{Sensors} is the set of edges from the Sensors node to each node t in $T_{\mathrm{BAN}} \cup T_{\mathrm{proxy}}$, with its weight equal to the computational cost of running task t on LA and it is defined by $w(\mathrm{Sensors}, t)$ in Table 26.4. The rationale behind this weight assignment is that if a mincut includes edge $(\mathrm{Sensors}, t)$ then it suggests that t is in the LA partition and computation cost of performing this task on LA is added to the weight of the cutset. If a task t is bound to a sensor, it must be ensured that the minimum weight cutset does not include edge $(\mathrm{Sensors}, t)$. This objective is achieved by setting the weight of the edge $(\mathrm{Sensors}, t)$ to ∞ as per Table 26.4. Similarly, if a task t is bound to LA, inclusion of this edge is guaranteed in the minimum weight cutset by setting $w(\mathrm{Sensors}, t)$ to 0.

- E_{LA} is the set of edges from each node t in $T_{\mathrm{BAN}} \cup T_{\mathrm{proxy}}$ to LA with its weight equal to the computational cost of running task t on Sensors and is defined by $w(t, \mathrm{LA})$ in Table 26.4, where $E_{\mathrm{CPU}}(t, \mathrm{Sensor})$ is the computation energy cost of running task t on a sensor. As noted earlier, if a task receives its input from multiple sensors, it can only be assigned on

TABLE 26.4 Weights of Edges in Sensor-LA Partition

Edge	Value	Condition
$w(\mathrm{Sensors}, t)$	$E_{\mathrm{CPU}}(t, \mathrm{LA})$	If task t is not bound
	0	If task t is bound to LA
	∞	If task t is bound to a sensor
$w(t, \mathrm{LA})$	$E_{\mathrm{CPU}}(t, \mathrm{Sensor})$	If task t is not bound
	0	If task t is bound to a sensor
	∞	If task t is bound to LA
$w_{\mathrm{BAN}}(t_{\mathrm{p}}, t_{\mathrm{s}})$	$E_{\mathrm{radio}}(t_{\mathrm{p}}, \mathrm{Sensor})$	Where radio = source sensor's radio

LA and hence is considered bounded on LA. Any task t bounded to LA has $w(t, \text{LA})$ set to ∞ to ensure that this edge does not become part of minimum weight cutset. If a task t is bound to a sensor, the $w(t, \text{LA})$ is set to 0, ensuring that edge (t, LA) is part of the minimum weight cutset. For a task t that is not bound to a sensor or the LA, we find the sensor generating its input (by traversing through the task's predecessors chain to find the root task and its associated sensor) and we use that sensor's CPU parameters for setting computation energy cost of the edge.

- E_{proxy} is the set of edges (t_p, t_s) where $t_p \in T_{\text{BAN}}$ and $t_s \in T_{\text{proxy}}$, and E_{BAN} is the set of edges (t_p, t_s) where $t_p, t_s \in T_{\text{BAN}}$. The weight for edge $(t_p, t_s) \in E_{\text{BAN}} \cup E_{\text{proxy}}$ is the communication cost of transmitting t_p's output from its source Sensors to LA and is given by $w_{\text{BAN}}(t_p, t_s)$ in Table 26.4, where $E_{\text{radio}}(t_p, \text{Sensor})$ is the communication energy consumed by task t_p on resource Sensor.

6. We find the minimum weight cutset to partition the constructed flow graph into Sensors and LA partition. This Sensors-LA task partition results in a task assignment that has minimum energy cost.

7. Tasks in the Sensor partition are assigned to respective sensors, and tasks in the LA partition are assigned to LA. Even though Sensors node in flow graph represents multiple sensors, after finding mincut, tasks can be assigned in the Sensors partition to the appropriate sensor.

8. To detect the changes in system characteristics, communication cost parameters such as the transmission power and time spent in various states (receive, transmit, idle, sleep) by the radio on each resource are measured and updated. This measurement is done over LCM (least common multiple) of the period of all tasks in the task graph. One should go back to step 1 when a significant change (30%) in communication cost parameters is detected.

To provide an example of the described algorithm in action, the task set initially introduced in Figure 26.2 is processed to find an assignment of its tasks to minimize energy consumption. The first step is to calculate the BAN-BE partition, as shown in Figure 26.7. Notice that two new nodes, BAN and BE, are added to the original graph. All edges from the BAN to tasks have a computational cost of running tasks on the BE as their weight, defined in Table 26.3. The computational cost of running the task on the BE is considered to be 0, as battery life is not affected by the computation. If a task must be bound to a particular sensor, the weight of its edge from BAN is ∞, ensuring it is not a part of the mincut.

The weights of edges between tasks represent the communication costs of having the two tasks running on different components in the system. The LA's wide area network radio energy parameters are used for communication cost calculations, as a trade-off is being found between computing a given task on BAN and or forwarding the data to be processed on the BE. The given mincut in Figure 26.7 provides a split of tasks between the BAN and BE that minimizes

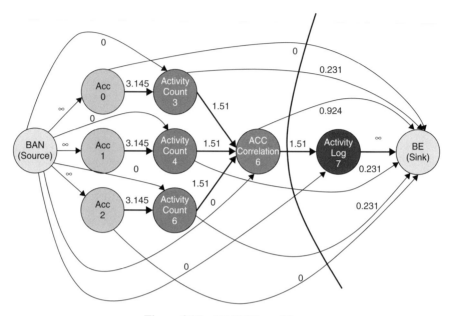

Figure 26.7 BAN-BE partition.

the energy consumption. The next step is then to determine the split of tasks between sensors and the LA.

The second step is to calculate the Sensors-LA partition, as shown in Figure 26.8. As before, new nodes are introduced into the graph, this time a Sensor node and an LA node. In this example graph, *ACC Correlation Proxy* was also added because its successor is assigned on the BE. This is to factor in the cost of transmitting its predecessor's output to LA in case its predecessor is assigned to a sensor. Since the system model does not allow for intersensor communication, tasks with multiple sources of input may not be assigned to a sensor device and must hence be assigned to the LA. An example of such a task in the graph shown would be *ACC Correlation*. This constraint also requires that any tasks in a chain in the Sensors part of the cut must be assigned to the same sensor node, as part of the chain may not be completed on a different sensor.

26.4.2.2 DynAGreenLife algorithm. The *DynAGreenLife* algorithm is designed to optimize for both system energy consumption and lifetime. It is a variation of the *DynAGreen* algorithm and differs primarily in how it handles the Sensors-LA partitioning. In BAN-BE partitioning, the BAN is always prioritized, and therefore, the differential battery charges of sensors and the LA do not make any difference on the partitioning process. However, for the Sensors-LA partition, *DynAGreenLife* considers the available battery life of the sensors and the LA in addition to the computational and communication costs to determine the weights used in the flow graph. When a sensor's battery level is relatively low compared to its LA, the weight of the edges from that sensor to tasks is increased. This in

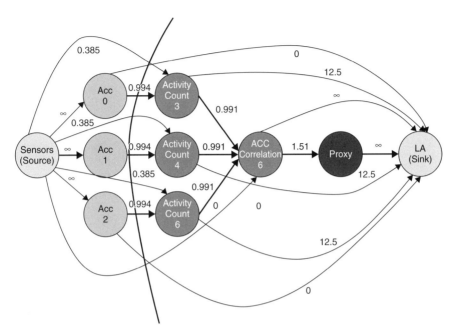

Figure 26.8   Sensor-LA partition.

turn increases the likelihood of the cutset assigning the tasks to the LA, even if it may be more efficient to process the task on the sensor node. In cases such as this, where a component may have significantly less battery life than other components in the system, making changes to the task assignment that increases the total energy consumption of the system may improve system lifetime by delaying the time until the first device failure. This change in the algorithm results in a balance between system energy and system life optimization.

The actual *DynAGreenLife* algorithm follows the same steps as *DynAGreen*, as described earlier, except for step 5. While energy cost calculations and partitioning of tasks between the BAN and the BE are handled the same as before, the graph used for Sensor-LA partitioning is created with different weights. These edge weights are computed by first calculating the weights for *DynAGreen* and multiplying those weights by a factor that is dependent on the relative battery charge of the sensor and the LA. Equations 26.7–26.9 define weights of edges in the flow graph, utilizing definitions of weights in Table 26.4:

$$w'(\text{Sensors}, t) = w(\text{Sensors}, t) * \frac{E_{\text{bat}}(s) + E_{\text{bat}}(\text{LA})}{E_{\text{bat}}(\text{LA})}, \quad (26.7)$$

$$w'(t, \text{LA}) = w(t, \text{LA}) * \frac{E_{\text{bat}}(s) + E_{\text{bat}}(\text{LA})}{E_{\text{bat}}(s)}, \quad (26.8)$$

$$w'_{\text{BAN}}(t_{\text{p}}, t_{\text{s}}) = w_{\text{BAN}}(t_{\text{p}}, t_{\text{s}}) * \frac{E_{\text{bat}}(s) + E_{\text{bat}}(\text{LA})}{E_{\text{bat}}(\text{LA})}. \tag{26.9}$$

When using the same task set in Figure 26.2 as used in the previous example, *DynAGreen* and *DynAGreenLife* generate the same BAN-BE flow graph and partition. The two algorithms differ in their output, however, when computing the Sensors-LA partitioning, as seen in Figure 26.9. In the given example, the LA has critical battery levels and multiplies a factor $\frac{E_{\text{bat}}(s)+E_{\text{bat}}(\text{LA})}{E_{\text{bat}}(\text{LA})}$ to the weight of the edges from Sensors to task nodes, as well as the edges between tasks, while the edges from tasks to LA are multiplied by $\frac{E_{\text{bat}}(s)+E_{\text{bat}}(\text{LA})}{E_{\text{bat}}(s)}$. As $\frac{E_{\text{bat}}(s)+E_{\text{bat}}(\text{LA})}{E_{\text{bat}}(\text{LA})} > \frac{E_{\text{bat}}(s)+E_{\text{bat}}(\text{LA})}{E_{\text{bat}}(s)}$, it is likely that the partition created by the mincut will place more tasks on the sensor nodes.

As evidenced by Figure 26.10, the execution time of *DynAGreenLife* is very similar to that of *DynAGreen*, suggesting that both approaches are computationally efficient and suitable for dynamic task assignments. The computational time of the ILP-based solution (on the order of seconds) is significantly higher than that of the dynamic algorithms (order of milliseconds). ILPGreen's execution time increases exponentially with the number of tasks in the task graph. Because of this low computational overhead compared to ILPGreen, the *DynAGreen* and *DynAGreenLife* approaches enable frequent execution to address dynamically changing system parameters and can be computed on a mobile LA.

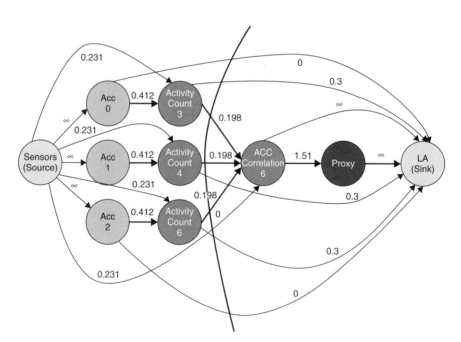

Figure 26.9   Sensor-LA partition.

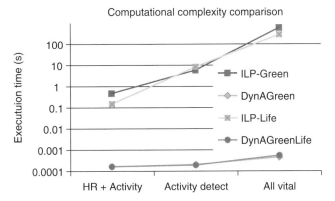

Figure 26.10 Runtimes for a variety of task sets using each of the developed ILP and dynamic solutions.

26.5 RESULTS

Each of the above algorithms for both collaborative sensing and dynamic task assignment were implemented in the QualNet network simulator and run under a variety of scenarios and settings. In the section below, the experimental setup and results for each set of experiments are discussed.

26.5.1 Collaborative Sensing

The neighborhood and duty cycling approaches detailed earlier were implemented within the QualNet network simulator. Simulations were run with varying neighborhood sizes of $R = [25 \text{ m}, 50 \text{ m}, 75 \text{ m}, 100 \text{ m}, 150 \text{ m}, 200 \text{ m}]$, as well as for different correlation functions. The three functions provided in Equation 26.4 were implemented and used. Furthermore, a simple model that would represent a standard sensing and reporting model where readings are taken at regular intervals has been implemented as a baseline. A total of 1000 nodes were randomly distributed over a 1-km×1-km free space area and they then followed a random walk around the region at speeds up to 2 m/s to simulate walking. Each node connected to the same BE that maintained client information and reported back updated sensing and localization rates. Measurements were taken to see the effects of increasing the neighborhood range on the total amount of data being reported to the BE as well as the amount of error introduced by estimating sensor values based on the readings of one's neighborhood.

For use in the simulations, a model was created to generate possible distributions of pollution data in a region as an example of the type of environmental data that may be tracked. The model approximates values of measured carbon monoxide levels throughout San Diego county on a moderate quality day, where measurements between 0 and 10 ppm are expected. The EPA standard for safe outdoor carbon monoxide exposure is 9 ppm [4].

The gas sensor node is modeled after the MiCS-5121 metal oxide semiconductor carbon monoxide gas sensor from e2v [5]. Sensors such as this make use of a heating element inside them, which can have a significant impact on power consumption. For the experiments, power consumption was estimated to be 90 mW during a 20-s heating period and 10 mW during a 10-s sampling period when the heating element is turned off. This also implies that sensor readings cannot be taken more often than once every 30 s.

A GPS module takes several seconds, approximated to be 10 s here, to acquire a signal and determine its location and continues to power itself for some set time, usually 30 s, after the reading. The power consumption during these active periods was measured by Kjaergaard et al. [6] to be approximately 324 mW. When the GPS and gas sensor modules are both shut off, there is a baseline power consumption of 62 mW.

A detailed report of mobile phone network throughput and power consumption is given by Diaz Zayas and Gomez [7]. From their results, we model the power consumption of the radio while idle to be 420 mW and during active periods to be 1300 mW, with a download rate of 25.29 kbps and an upload rate of 0.69 kbps on a UMTS network. Each update of either gas sensor readings or of the latest location and energy information from a mobile node is 128 B, requiring approximately 0.1855 s to send. Updates from the server are of the same size and complete in approximately 0.005 s.

The baseline to which the results of the simulations are compared to is based on an environmental monitoring system with no energy management or duty cycling policies implemented. The system collects a gas sensor and GPS reading every 30 s (the period of the gas sensor) and transmits it to the BE. In this baseline system, each sensor node has an average power consumption of 0.838 W during simulations.

26.5.1.1 *Results.*

The correlation functions presented in Equation 26.4 were implemented to relate user contributions, and we measured the impact of parameter R on the power consumption of the system and the amount of error introduced into predictions. Figure 26.11 compares the performance of these three functions. The error is presented as the percentage difference between a user's stored exposure history, made up of measurements and predictions, and the actual levels a user was exposed during the simulation. As the neighborhood size increases, nodes send fewer localization and exposure updates and include further and further away samples in their prediction calculations. The constant model, which puts equal weight on all nodes in a neighborhood regardless of distance, offers slightly better power consumption than the other models as it takes fewer exposure readings. However, this comes at a significant cost in terms of error, especially at larger neighborhood sizes. Such a model would only be useful when the exposure levels are expected to be the same throughout the region, for example, in the case of pollutants such as ozone. Correlation functions based on a linear or Gaussian approach provide similar power savings and significantly reduce the amount of error in the predictions. Eventually, the power savings converge at

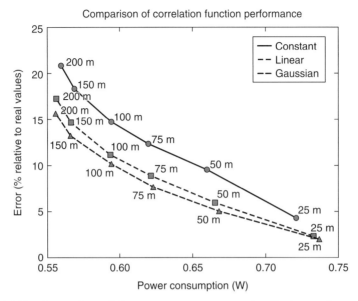

Figure 26.11 Comparison of the error versus energy trade-off when nodes are mobile for the three implemented correlation functions.

larger neighborhood sizes, as the system approaches the minimum threshold for localization updates and the average number of sensor readings by any individual node begins to approach zero. The power savings when using large neighborhood sizes are arguably not worth the additional error introduced into predictions and could have even higher error rates if users begin moving rapidly in between long localization attempts.

There is a clear trade-off between the amount of power consumed and the amount of error in the system, with diminishing power savings at higher neighborhood sizes (Fig. 26.12). During runtime, a node could dynamically change its neighborhood size to provide better accuracy when battery levels are the highest and to grow its neighborhood size as battery levels begin to reach critical levels to minimize the applications impact on the remaining battery life.

Figures 26.13 and 26.14 compare the performance of the system in cases where the nodes remain stationary and are moving at walking pace randomly around the region. Our simulations showed average exposure errors ranging from 0.06% (stationary nodes, 25 m neighborhood size) to 15.6% (mobile, 200 m). Much of the variance found in the error measurements, as seen in Figure 26.13, can be explained by users falling in the same neighborhood spatially but being on the border between regions of high and low pollution levels. The mobile cases have even great variance in their error, as the neighborhood created for a node at its last localization update is no longer accurate because users move around between updates. This suggests that while the average prediction values are accurate and have small error over a large time frame, individual points

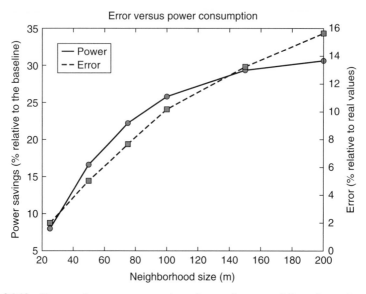

Figure 26.12   Error and power consumption when nodes are mobile and correlated using the Gaussian model.

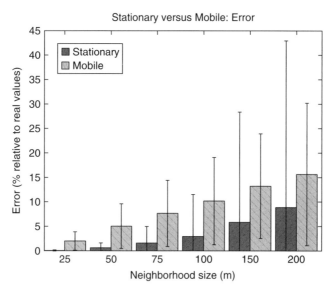

Figure 26.13   Error when using the Gaussian correlation function in deployments of stationary and mobile nodes for a variety of neighborhood sizes.

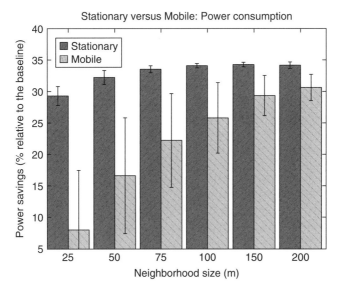

Figure 26.14 Power consumption, relative to the baseline, when using the Gaussian correlation function in deployments of stationary and mobile nodes for a variety of neighborhood sizes.

may offer large errors, and intelligent filtering and postprocessing methods should be implemented on the back end to minimize the impact of these readings.

Figure 26.14 shows that the stationary case also presents the best in power savings, showing reductions in power consumption between 32.5% and 37.1% when using the Gaussian correlation function, as it rapidly reduces the number of expensive localization attempts as the system recognizes that the user has not been mobile in between attempts. With larger neighborhood sizes, the mobile case begins to approach these savings as well, with reductions in power consumption between 12.1% and 33.6%. Consumption can be further reduced through the use of the constant and linear correlation functions, but at the expense of additional error. These power savings could also be increased by exploring the use of additional sensors, such as accelerometers on a user's mobile phone, to detect movement and trigger location updates only when necessary, as suggested in other works such as Reference 8.

If the baseline algorithm is changed such that readings are taken every 60 s instead of the original 30-s rate, the GPS and gas sensors can occasionally be turned off, dropping the baseline power consumption down to 0.668 W. The range of savings from our algorithm with the Gaussian correlation function drops to between 8.4% and 21.1% in the mobile scenario, as the baseline is closer to the minimum power consumption limit of the system. While longer duty cycles may improve power consumption, it comes at the expense of fewer samples and location updates, which can drive up error rates for highly mobile users.

Our approach is most effective in applications requiring frequent updates and becomes less effective in cases where sensor readings are collected from users relatively rarely, such as once an hour.

26.5.2 Dynamic Task Assignment

In this section, the dynamic task assignment techniques are evaluated in terms of their effect on both the system battery life and energy consumption. Results for different wireless health care system task sets are presented, and the performance of the *DynAGreen* and *DynAGreenLife* algorithms are compared with the static solution generated by *ILPGreen* and *ILPLife* under various conditions. The abilities of the algorithms to adapt to changing system conditions are also demonstrated. It is shown that the *DynAGreenLife* algorithm balances both system life and system energy effectively, significantly outperforming the static ILP solutions when faced with changing conditions.

Three main task graphs were used for the experiments, which are described in Table 26.5. Each task has an arrival rate, number of instructions to be executed, and number of output bytes. There is also a deadline associated with each task, which is assumed to be equal to the period of the task for simplicity. Tasks in Table 26.6 mainly represent tasks in preventive health care systems such as PALMS [9]. QualNet provides accurate wireless channel models, a variety of wireless protocols along with their energy models, battery models, and mobility model. A simple model was added for computational energy consumption, and it used CPU current loads provided in the MicaZ and Intel XScale processor specifications. The complete list of parameters used in these simulations are provided in Table 26.5.

Sensor nodes are modeled as *MicaZ* nodes with *ZigBee(802.15.4)* radios. The LA is modeled as a *UMTS-UE* (User Equipment, i.e., Handset) with an additional ZigBee radio interface and CPU speed of 400 MHz. QualNet provides an energy model for the MicaZ node and specified a constant transmit power of 3 dBm. For UMTS, a generic energy model was configured and specified—10 dBm as the minimum transmit power and 30 dBm as maximum transmit power. The UMTS

TABLE 26.5 Experimental Workload

Task Graph	No. of sensors	No. of tasks	Application
HR + Activity	2	6	ECG sensor detects heart rate per minute. While accelerometer keeps track of activity.
Activity detect	3	8	Detects a person's activity using three accelerometers.
All vital	5	20	Logs all vital signs such as heart rate, blood pressure, and activity in addition to location.

TABLE 26.6   Simulator Parameters

Components	Characteristics	Value
ZigBee radio	Propagation channel frequency	905 MHz
	Propagation pathloss model	Two-ray
	PHY 802.15.4-TX Power	3.0 dBm
UMTS radio	Propagation channel frequency	2.4 GHz
	Propagation pathloss model	Two-ray
	PHY UMTS MAX TX Power	30.0 dBm
	PHY UMTS MIN TX Power	−10.0 dBm
	Power amplifier inefficiency factor	6.5
	Transmit power consumption	100.0 mW
	Receive power consumption	130.0 mW
	Idle power consumption	120.0 mW
	Sleep power consumption	0.0 mW
	Supply voltage	3.0 V
Sensor CPU	Active current	50 mA
	Frequency	8 MHz
	Voltage	3.0 V
LA CPU	Active current	308.33 mA
	Frequency	400 MHz
	Voltage	3.0 V

protocol uses a dynamic power control algorithm and sets the radio transmit power depending on channel condition. A 2.4-GHz carrier frequency was used for UMTS and 905-MHz carrier frequency for ZigBee.

The handset is connected to the BE via the UMTS network and with sensors via the ZigBee radio. Tasks assigned to the resources send data to the next resource over UDP if any of its successor tasks are not assigned on the same resource. Logic for periodic task execution, data transmissions, radio link parameter measurement and reporting, task assignment control messaging, and execution of the dynamic algorithms at the application layer was implemented. An ILP was created for each task graph, and an open-source ILP solver called *lp-solve* [1] was used to get the optimal task assignments for each of them.

26.5.2.1   *Performance in static conditions.* In the initial set of experiments, it was assumed that static system parameters such as the arrival rate of tasks, computational complexity, and wireless channel conditions remain constant. Battery energy was set to 100 mA h for sensors and 300 mA h for cell phones to reduce experiment runtime. The respective system lifetimes achieved by each task assignment generated by the ILPs and dynamic algorithms were noted and compared against the state-of-the-art strategy of streaming all data to the BE for processing (All-On-BE).

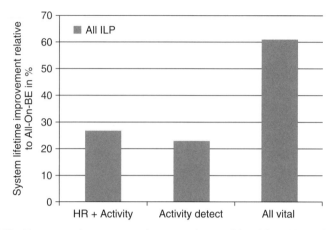

Figure 26.15 Percentage improvement in system battery life achieved in static conditions compared to All-On-BE.

In static conditions, each ILP came up with the same task assignment for our given task graphs. In Figure 26.15, the percentage improvement in system battery life is shown, based on the task assignments as determined by both ILPs with respect to All-On-BE strategy. For the all-vital task graph, which has a higher number of processing tasks, both of the ILPs perform approximately 60% better than All-On-BE. On average, the ILP solutions improve system battery life by 37%. These results show that task assignment can significantly impact the system lifetime. Dynamic algorithms were also executed and it was observed that the proposed dynamic algorithms performed within 0.001% of the ILP solutions, returning results very close to the optimal solution.

Experiments also measured the average energy consumed by each of the task assignments in the above set of experiments. Figure 26.16 shows the percentage energy savings achieved by each ILP and dynamic solution compared to the All-On-BE strategy. All dynamic algorithms gained up to 42% energy savings, which is similar to that gained by the optimal assignment given by *ILPGreen* and *ILPLife*.

The *ILPs*, *DynAGreen*, and *DynAGreenLife* algorithms, each of which have different objectives, perform similarly. One key reason for this is that it is assumed that sensors and cell phones are fully charged at the start of the experiment. In general, this is not always true, as sensors and cell phones have different battery consumption rates. Unlike a sensor battery, which often has a single function, a cell phone battery is consumed rapidly as it performs other tasks in addition to health monitoring tasks. In addition, cell phones are charged more often compared to sensors.

Consider a situation where the cell phone has critically low battery while the sensors are almost fully charged. If an algorithm such as *ILPGreen* or *DynA-Green* is used, the actual energy level of these components is not taken into consideration, as it purely optimizes for minimizing energy consumption in the

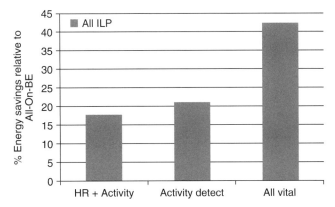

Figure 26.16 Percentage reduction in energy consumption achieved in static conditions compared to All-On-BE.

system. It will merely focus on ensuring that the distribution of tasks among the various components (sensors, cell phone, back end) is such that the total energy is minimized regardless of the remaining battery charge of the different devices.

Figure 26.17 shows the battery life improvement as obtained by the ILPs and the DynA family of algorithms compared to a typical All-On-BE strategy. It is evident from these experiments that task assignment techniques make a huge difference of up to 140% in battery life compared to following a simplistic approach of performing all processing on BE as shown in Figure 26.17. The results also show that *ILPLife* and *DynAGreenLife* achieve a higher system life than *ILPGreen* and *DynAGreen*. This is because the task partitions in *ILPGreen* and *DynAGreen* are purely focused on a green partitioning of the tasks without taking any consideration of the available battery charge of the system devices.

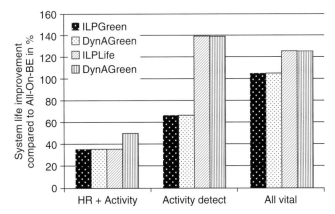

Figure 26.17 Percentage improvement in system battery life achieved compared to All-On-BE when run in static conditions.

It can also be observed that *ILPLife* has a lower system life compared to *DynA-GreenLife*. This is due to the fact that *DynAGreenLife* periodically performs task repartitioning so that the task allocation changes to better optimize for system life. Although the goal is to attempt a graceful reduction in energy consumption proportionately across devices to increase system life, task allocation to devices is discrete in nature with tasks having different fixed values resulting in allocation and hence an energy reduction that is not exactly proportionate across devices relative to their battery levels. Depending on the tasks assigned, some nodes may deplete their energy more than desired. Hence, a periodic repartitioning is necessary. However, due to the cost of executing an ILP, only a static initial allocation based on the ILP is utilized. Thus, the DynA algorithms have a better chance at producing a longer system life because of their lower cost of execution and periodic task repartitioning.

When it comes to system battery life, *DynAGreenLife* outperforms *DynAGreen* by up to 43%. On the other hand, *DynAGreen* is a "greener" solution as it outperforms *DynAGreenLife* in terms of total energy consumption.

26.5.2.2   *Dynamic adaptability.* In the following set of experiments, changes to various runtime characteristics were simulated and used to demonstrate the capability of *DynAGreenLife* to change the task assignments on the fly to optimize system life (Fig. 26.18) and system energy (Fig. 26.19) with varying system characteristics. In all the following sections, it is assumed that the battery level is at 300 mA for each sensor and that the cell phone has critically low battery level of 100 mA. Improvements in system energy are shown using the dynamic task assignment given by *DynAGreenLife* with respect to the static assignment obtained by *ILPGreen* during initial setup. This emphasizes the fact that dynamic task assignment is necessary for an energy-efficient solution in wireless health

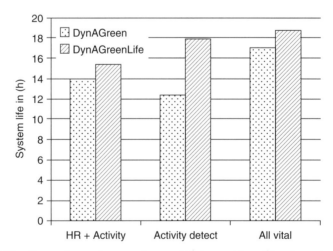

Figure 26.18   Comparison of system battery lifetime achieved by dynamic algorithms when run in static conditions.

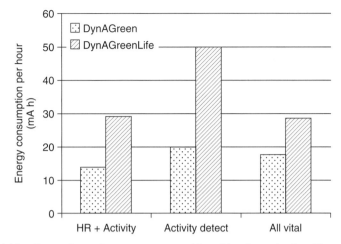

Figure 26.19 Comparison of system energy achieved by dynamic algorithms when run in static conditions.

care systems. The low execution time (milliseconds) for the proposed dynamic algorithm makes it a viable technique for dynamic adaptation.

To detect the changes in system characteristics, various radio link parameters are measured such as transmit power and time spent in various states (receive, transmit, idle, sleep) by radio on each resource (Table 26.7). This measurement is done over a period in which tasks execution is repeated. The LCM of the period of all tasks is used for this. This window gives a reproducible workload on each resource so that comparison of the various costs over different windows is fair. For the experimental task sets, this window period is around 1 min. Filtering is used to smooth out an unusual spike in measurement. The dynamic algorithm is run to recompute task assignment only if the change in system parameters is more than 30% compared to the last run of algorithm. This threshold can be changed for different system implementation. Such a threshold helps reduce the frequency of algorithm execution and also avoids oscillations in assignment. This threshold was selected empirically for the simulation environment, and it is envisioned that designers of a particular system would set these parameters based

TABLE 26.7 Percentage Improvement in System Life in Case of Change in Wireless Channel Conditions

		Percentage of System Life Improvement Achieved by *DynAGreenLife* Relative to		
Algorithm	Task Graph	*ILP*-Green	*ILP*-Life-Far	*ILP*-Life-Near
DynAGreenLife	HR + Activity, %	23.79	23.79	68.68
	Activity detection, %	24.88	−6.53	37.47
	All vital, %	22.14	22.14	4.28

on observed task assignment oscillations and control the frequency of algorithm execution.

To demonstrate the dynamic adaptability of *DynAGreenLife*, an urban scenario with random mobility, multiple base stations, and large terrain area was simulated in experiments. In this scenario, the dynamic algorithms adapt quickly to changing system parameters and this results in better performance compared to the statically computed optimal solution obtained using ILPs.

The experimental scenario was expanded to include a larger terrain with multiple base stations and random mobility of the user to demonstrate that the algorithms can handle real-life urban situations and perform better than the ILP-based solutions. Near the edge of the cell, handoffs may occur from one base station to another. At the edge, the link conditions are typically unfavorable regardless of the base station that the device may be communicating with along with the handoffs. After a handoff, if the user is closer to the center of the new base station that it is communicating with, different task assignments may be chosen depending on the communication costs and the associated energy efficiency. To study the impact of such varying link conditions, experiments with random mobility with multiple serving base stations were simulated.

For the experimental study, a 4900-m×4900-m terrain with four base stations (node B) was used in the QualNet simulator, as shown in Figure 26.20. During the simulation, the user moves randomly in this terrain in any direction with one of the three speed ranges determined by us to simulate user moving in a car, in a bike, and by walking. The user pauses for a predefined duration (15 or 45 min). This experiment is used to demonstrate how quickly the *DynAGreenLife* algorithm can adapt to changes in link conditions and also whether it makes sense to recompute the assignment when conditions are changing rapidly.

For this set of experiment, only the *DynAGreenLife* algorithm is considered, as it balances both system life and system energy and should be used as a practical solution to energy-efficient task assignment problem. Table 26.8 compares the

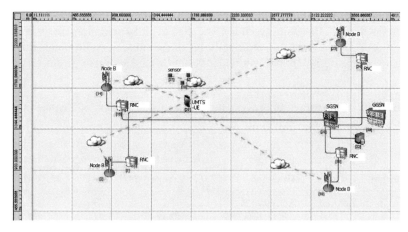

Figure 26.20   Simulation terrain.

TABLE 26.8   Percentage Improvement in System Life of *DynAGreenLife* in Case of Random Mobility in the Urban Scenario

Task Graph: HR + Activity

		Percentage of Improvement in Life Relative to		
Speed	Pause Duration, min	*ILP*-Far	*ILP*-Near	All-On-BE
Car	15	24.17	3.15	47.19
Car	45	5.90	3.39	18.68
Bike	15	15.87	6.17	26.84
Bike	45	8.36	8.36	18.70
Walk	15	9.58	3.62	19.67
Walk	45	23.42	5.78	47.46

Task Graph: Activity Detection

		Percentage of Improvement in Life Relative to		
Speed	Pause Duration, min	*ILP*-Far	*ILP*-Near	All-On-BE
Car	15	67.81	17.23	67.81
Car	45	47.88	6.84	47.88
Bike	15	34.53	9.71	34.53
Bike	45	87.98	5.7	87.98
Walk	15	43.15	6.12	43.15
Walk	45	32.51	12.09	32.51

Task Graph: All Vital

		Percentage of Improvement in Life Relative to		
Speed	Pause Duration, min	*ILP*-Far	*ILP*-Near	All-On-BE
Car	15	21.36	2.3	70.07
Car	45	12.06	3.9	42.34
Bike	15	22.44	2.45	45.93
Bike	45	8.64	3.48	42.8
Walk	15	14.18	8.28	46.73
Walk	45	34.88	7.36	56.59

system life given by the *DynAGreenLife* algorithm to *ILPLife*-Far, *ILPLife*-Near, and All-On-BE. *ILPLife*-Far is the assignment obtained by *ILPLife* using higher communication cost assuming the user is away from the base station, and *ILPLife*-Near is the assignment computed by *ILPLife* assuming the user is closer to the base station. Improvements due to the dynamic adaptability of the algorithm depends on how different the system parameters are from the initial condition used for ILP solution. These two variations are used to cover ILP solution with best and worst communication cost between cell phone and base station.

As explained earlier, link condition is monitored every 1 min (which is the LCM of all task periods) and *DynAGreenLife* is run when the change in communication cost is 30% more than the last run of the algorithm. It is observed that while a person is moving in a car, it is possible to achieve up to 68% improvement in system life and 25% on an average compared to *ILPLife*-Far and up to 18% improvement compared to *ILP*-Near. Similarly, in case of a person who is on a bike or walking, higher improvements are observed compared to *ILPLife*-Far. A user location trace for these experiments indicates that the user remains closer to the base station most of the time, and hence, improvements over *ILPLife*-Near are not as significant as the improvement over *ILPLife*-Far.

Looking at the results in Table 26.8, one would suggest a simple heuristic technique is to switch between the task assignments provided by *ILPLife*-Near and *ILPLife*-Far depending on a user's proximity to a base station. Such a solution, labeled as ILP-Flipflop in Figure 26.21 would not handle other additional changes in the system, such as changes in workload, addition of new tasks in the task set, and channel conditions between worst and best. To demonstrate this, experiments were run with the same random mobility described in the previous section but with an additional change in execution time of processing tasks every hour. Changes in execution time represent a practical scenario in which a processing task might be asked to produce better quality result by doing more processing. Figure 26.21 shows the result of such experiments for all three task sets.

It is observed that in this scenario, the *DynAGreenLife* algorithm is up to 30% and on an average 21% better than the *ILP-Flipflop* technique described above. It is also observed that the improvements are even more evident when the user is mobile.

26.6 CONCLUSION

Two complimentary methods of improving the energy efficiency of a wireless health monitoring system were explored in this work. First, location information

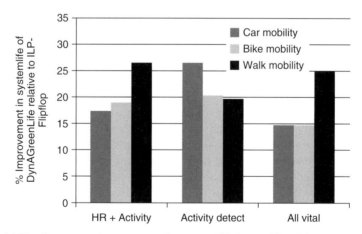

Figure 26.21 Percentage improvement in system lifetime achieved by *DynAGreenLife* relative to ILP-Flipflop in presence of multiple changing conditions.

was utilized to identify users that are expected to collect redundant environmental sensor readings. The BE-generated predictions for what a user would report based on what its neighbors reported, and based on the amount of available battery life for each user and each of other user near it, the rate at which any individual user collects sensor readings was drastically reduced. By reducing the number of localization attempts, sensor readings, and reports to the BE we are able to reduce power consumption up to 37.1% at an average error between 0.06% and 15.6% when using a Gaussian function to determine the expected correlation between neighboring users.

Second, when a health monitoring system collects and processes sensor data, the choice of where it does processing in the system has a drastic effect on the computational and communication energy costs of the entire system. Given a task graph of all jobs to be completed in such a system, tasks were dynamically and efficiently distributed among sensors, the LA, and the BE to minimize energy consumption and improve system lifetime. Compared to the all-on-back-end strategy, the presented algorithms achieved 1.4 times longer system lifetimes. In the case where system conditions changed during use, the presented dynamic solutions outperformed their ILP counterparts by up to 88%.

Using these two complimentary approaches, significant power savings can be obtained in a wireless health monitoring system, significantly increasing the battery and system life.

REFERENCES

1. Lp-solve. Available at http://lpsolve.sourceforge.net/5.5/.
2. Stone HS. Multiprocessor scheduling with the aid of network flow algorithms. IEEE Trans Softw Eng 1977;SE-3(1):85–93.
3. Boykov Y, Kolmogorov V. An experimental comparison of min-cut/max- flow algorithms for energy minimization in vision. IEEE Trans Pattern Anal Mach Intell 2004;26(9):1124–1137.
4. United States Environmental Protection Agency: Indoor Air Quality. 2010. Available at http://www.epa.gov/iaq/co.html.
5. e2v gas sensor technology: Metal Oxide Semiconductor. Available at http://www.e2v. com/products-and-services/sensors/gas-sensors/our-gas-sensor-%technology/metal-oxide-semiconductors/.
6. Kjaergaard MB, Langdal J, Godsk T, Toftkjaer T. Entracked: energy-efficient robust position tracking for mobile devices. In: MobiSys '09: Proceedings of the 7th International Conference on Mobile Systems, Applications, and Services. ACM: New York; 2009. pp. 221–234.
7. Diaz Zayas A, Gomez PM. A testbed for energy profile characterization of IP services in smartphones over live networks. Mobile Netw Appl 2010;15:330–343. 10.1007/s11036-010-0228-8.
8. Paek J, Kim J, Govindan R. Energy-efficient rate-adaptive gps-based positioning for smartphones. In: MobiSys '10: Proceedings of the 8th International Conference on Mobile Systems, Applications, and Services. ACM: New York; 2010. pp. 299–314.
9. CWPHS projects. Available at http://cwphs.calit2.net/index.php?option=com%_content&view=article&id=68&Ite%mid=79.

INDEX

Energy-Efficient Distributed Computing Systems, First Edition.
Edited by Albert Y. Zomaya and Young Choon Lee.
© 2012 John Wiley & Sons, Inc. Published 2012 by John Wiley & Sons, Inc.

WILEY SERIES ON PARALLEL AND DISTRIBUTED COMPUTING
Series Editor: Albert Y. Zomaya

Parallel and Distributed Simulation Systems / Richard Fujimoto

Mobile Processing in Distributed and Open Environments / Peter Sapaty

Introduction to Parallel Algorithms / C. Xavier and S. S. Iyengar

Solutions to Parallel and Distributed Computing Problems: Lessons from Biological Sciences / Albert Y. Zomaya, Fikret Ercal, and Stephan Olariu (*Editors*)

Parallel and Distributed Computing: A Survey of Models, Paradigms, and Approaches / Claudia Leopold

Fundamentals of Distributed Object Systems: A CORBA Perspective / Zahir Tari and Omran Bukhres

Pipelined Processor Farms: Structured Design for Embedded Parallel Systems / Martin Fleury and Andrew Downton

Handbook of Wireless Networks and Mobile Computing / Ivan Stojmenović *(Editor)*

Internet-Based Workflow Management: Toward a Semantic Web / Dan C. Marinescu

Parallel Computing on Heterogeneous Networks / Alexey L. Lastovetsky

Performance Evaluation and Characteization of Parallel and Distributed Computing Tools / Salim Hariri and Manish Parashar

Distributed Computing: Fundamentals, Simulations and Advanced Topics, *Second Edition* / Hagit Attiya and Jennifer Welch

Smart Environments: Technology, Protocols, and Applications / Diane Cook and Sajal Das

Fundamentals of Computer Organization and Architecture / Mostafa Abd-El-Barr and Hesham El-Rewini

Advanced Computer Architecture and Parallel Processing / Hesham El-Rewini and Mostafa Abd-El-Barr

UPC: Distributed Shared Memory Programming / Tarek El-Ghazawi, William Carlson, Thomas Sterling, and Katherine Yelick

Handbook of Sensor Networks: Algorithms and Architectures / Ivan Stojmenović *(Editor)*

Parallel Metaheuristics: A New Class of Algorithms / Enrique Alba (*Editor*)

Design and Analysis of Distributed Algorithms / Nicola Santoro

Task Scheduling for Parallel Systems / Oliver Sinnen

Computing for Numerical Methods Using Visual C++ / Shaharuddin Salleh, Albert Y. Zomaya, and Sakhinah A. Bakar

Architecture-Independent Programming for Wireless Sensor Networks / Amol B. Bakshi and Viktor K. Prasanna

High-Performance Parallel Database Processing and Grid Databases / David Taniar, Clement Leung, Wenny Rahayu, and Sushant Goel

Algorithms and Protocols for Wireless and Mobile Ad Hoc Networks / Azzedine Boukerche (*Editor*)

Algorithms and Protocols for Wireless Sensor Networks / Azzedine Boukerche (*Editor*)

Optimization Techniques for Solving Complex Problems / Enrique Alba, Christian Blum, Pedro Isasi, Coromoto León, and Juan Antonio Gómez (*Editors*)

Emerging Wireless LANs, Wireless PANs, and Wireless MANs: IEEE 802.11, IEEE 802.15, IEEE 802.16 Wireless Standard Family / Yang Xiao and Yi Pan (*Editors*)

High-Performance Heterogeneous Computing / Alexey L. Lastovetsky and Jack Dongarra

Mobile Intelligence / Laurence T. Yang, Augustinus Borgy Waluyo, Jianhua Ma, Ling Tan, and Bala Srinivasan (*Editors*)

Advanced Computational Infrastructures for Parallel and Distributed Adaptive Applicatons / Manish Parashar and Xiaolin Li (*Editors*)

Market-Oriented Grid and Utility Computing / Rajkumar Buyya and Kris Bubendorfer (*Editors*)

Cloud Computing Principles and Paradigms / Rajkumar Buyya, James Broberg, and Andrzej Goscinski

Energy-Efficient Distributed Computing Systems / Albert Y. Zomaya and Young Choon Lee (*Editors*)